R. Gupta's®

POPULAR MASTER GUIDE

BHU-CHS

BANARAS HINDU UNIVERSITY-CENTRAL HINDU SCHOOL

School Entrance Test (SET)

9th Class

- All Topics Covered as per Latest Exam Pattern
- Chapterwise Theory Notes with Latest Solved Papers

by

RPH Editorial Board

2027 EDITION

RAMESH PUBLISHING HOUSE, NEW DELHI

Published by
O.P. Gupta *for* Ramesh Publishing House

Admin. Office
12-H, New Daryaganj Road, Opp. Officers' Mess,
New Delhi-110002 ✆ 23275224, 23245124

E-mail: info@rameshpublishinghouse.com
For Online Shopping: www.rameshpublishinghouse.com

Showroom
• Balaji Market, Nai Sarak, Delhi-110006 ✆ 23282525 📱 9354373464
• 4457, Nai Sarak, Delhi-110006

Book Code: R-2907

ISBN: 978-93-5477-831-5

Price: ₹ 540

Printed at: Deepak Offset, Delhi

CONTENTS

❑❑❑

Method of Selection & Entrance Test Syllabus For Class IXth

- The Question Paper will be up to class VIII standard comprising 100 MCQs of subjects—English, Hindi, Mathematics, Social Science and Science.
- On the basis of the marks obtained in the Entrance Test a Merit List will be drawn for admission in each class and a candidate will be given a seat in the concerned class strictly on the basis of the merit. In case of a tie the Banaras Hindu University Guidelines will be followed.
- A Question Booklet containing the questions and a separate Answer Sheet shall be provided to the candidate at the beginning of the Test.
- Each question shall be followed by four alternative answers. The candidate is required to identify the one which he/she feels to be the correct answer and record the answer by darkening the **appropriate oval** in the answer sheet with **Blue/Black Ball Point pen only**.
- The answer will be treated incorrect if more than one oval is darkened or an oval is darkened improperly. Any other method of marking such as tick mark, cross mark, use of dot, line mark and half-filled oval or marks outside the oval shall not be evaluated.
- If any question is not attempted and the candidate leaves all the ovals against that question as blank, such an answer will be awarded **zero** mark.

❑❑❑

Previous Years' Paper

BHU–CENTRAL HINDU SCHOOL

School Entrance Test (SET), Class 9th, 2025

(Exam held on 11-05-2025)

1. Number of boys and girls in a class are in ratio 7 : 5. The number of boys is 8 more than the number of girls. The total class strength is:

1. 50
2. 38
3. 52
4. 48

2. By selling a radio for ₹ 950, a man loses 5%. What per cent shall he gain by selling it for ₹ 1040?

1. 5%
2. 4%
3. 6%
4. 8%

3. A works twice as fast as B. If both of them can together finish a piece of work in 12 days, then B alone can do it in:

1. 36 days
2. 24 days
3. 18 days
4. 20 days

4. The ratio between the radius of the base and the height of a cylinder is 2 : 3. Find the total surface area of the cylinder, if its volume is 1617 cm^3.

1. 770 cm^2
2. 780 cm^2
3. 800 cm^2
4. 880 cm^2

5. If the area of equilateral triangle is $4\sqrt{3}\ cm^2$, then each side of the equilateral triangle is:

1. $\frac{4}{\sqrt{3}}$ cm
2. 4 cm
3. $\frac{2}{\sqrt{3}}$ cm
4. 2 cm

6. If the algebraic expression $7\sqrt{2}x^2 - 10x - 4\sqrt{2}$ has two factors, then the factors are:

1. $(4 - 7\sqrt{2}x)^2$
2. $(7\sqrt{2}x - \sqrt{3})(x - \sqrt{2})$
3. $(x + \sqrt{2})(7\sqrt{2} - 4)$
4. $(x - \sqrt{2})(7\sqrt{2}x + 4)$

7. If $x + \frac{1}{x} = 4$, then the value of $x^4 + \frac{1}{x^4}$ is:

1. 196
2. 194
3. 198
4. 192

8. The simplified value of $\left(\frac{1}{27}\right)^{\frac{2}{3}}$ is:

1. $\frac{1}{9}$
2. $-\frac{1}{9}$
3. 9
4. 27

9. The compound interest on ₹ 4000 at 10% per annum for 2 years is:

1. ₹ 480
2. ₹ 800
3. ₹ 900
4. ₹ 840

10. How many diagonals are there in a polygon having 12 sides?

1. 60
2. 54
3. 30
4. 27

11. Which of the following is ***not*** a constituent of petroleum?

1. Paraffin wax
2. Petrol
3. Lubricating oil
4. Coke

12. Exhaustible natural resources are:

1. Unlimited in quantity
2. Not dependent on nature
3. Limited in quantity
4. Not exhausted by human

13. Which of the following statements is ***not*** true for organic manure?

1. It enhances water holding capacity of soil.
2. It has a balance of all plant nutrients.
3. It provides humus to soil.
4. It improves texture of soil.

1. 4	**2.** 2	**3.** 1	**4.** 1	**5.** 2	**6.** 4	**7.** 2
8. 3	**9.** 4	**10.** 2	**11.** 4	**12.** 3	**13.** 2	

14. The disease caused by a protozoan and spread by an insect is:

1. Dengue 2. Malaria
3. Polio 4. Measles

15. The two micro-organisms which live in symbiotic association in lichens are:

1. Fungus and protozoa 2. Bacteria and protozoa
3. Alga and bacteria 4. Alga and fungus

16. Choose the correct statement about the inflammable substances:

1. Low ignition temperature and can not catch fire easily.
2. High ignition temperature and can catch fire easily.
3. Low ignition temperature and can catch fire easily.
4. High ignition temperature and can not catch fire easily.

17. Which among the following is considered as the cleanest fuel?

1. Wood 2. Petrol
3. Kerosene 4. Hydrogen gas

18. Magnesium ribbon on burning in air produces:

1. Magnesium oxide, water and light
2. Magnesium oxide and heat
3. Magnesium oxide, heat and light
4. Magnesium oxide, water and heat

19. The place meant for conservation of biodiversity in their natural habitat is:

(*i*) zoological garden (*ii*) botanical garden
(*iii*) wildlife sanctuary (*iv*) national park

1. (*i*) and (*ii*) 2. (*ii*) and (*iii*)
3. (*iii*) and (*iv*) 4. (*i*) and (*iv*)

20. Reproduction by budding takes place in:

1. hydra 2. amoeba
3. paramecium 4. snakes

21. In the list of animals given below, hen is the odd one out. Select the reason for this:

Human being, cow, dog, hen

1. It undergoes internal fertilization.
2. It is oviparous.
3. It is viviparous.
4. It undergoes external fertilization.

22. AIDS can spread from an infected person to another person through:

1. Sharing food 2. Blood transfusion
3. Sharing comb 4. Mosquito bite

23. The belief that the mother is completely responsible for the sex of the child is wrong, because the child:

1. Gets sex chromosome only from the mother
2. Develops in the body of the mother
3. Gets one sex chromosome from the mother and the other from the father
4. Gets sex chromosome only from the father

24. Growing different crops alternately on the same land is technically called:

1. Crop alternation 2. Crop rotation
3. Crop revolution 4. Crop change

25. Two objects repel each other. This repulsion could be due to:

1. Frictional force only
2. Electrostatic force only
3. Magnetic force only
4. Either a magnetic or an electrostatic force

26. Figure shows a container filled with water. Which of the following statements is ***correct*** about pressure of water?

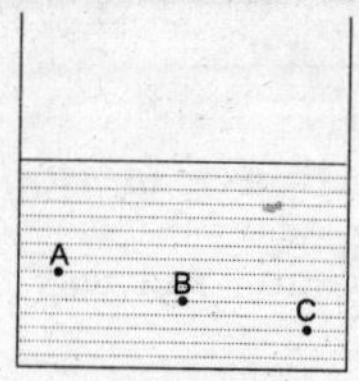

1. Pressure at A > Pressure at B > Pressure at C
2. Pressure at A = Pressure at B = Pressure at C
3. Pressure at A < Pressure at B > Pressure at C
4. Pressure at A < Pressure at B < Pressure at C

27. A toy car released with the same initial speed will travel farthest on:

1. Muddy surface 2. Polished marble surface
3. Cemented surface 4. Bricks surface

28. The loudness of sound depends on:

1. It's amplitude 2. It's frequency
3. It's time period 4. It's speed

29. Which of the following statement is ***incorrect***?

1. Sound is produced by vibrations
2. Sound requires a medium for propagation
3. Light and sound both require a medium for propagation
4. The speed of sound is lesser than the speed of light

30. Boojho's uncle has set up an electroplating factory near his village. He should dispose off the waste of the factory:

1. In the nearby river
2. In the nearby pond
3. In the nearby corn field
4. According to the disposal guidelines of the local authority

14. 2	**15.** 4	**16.** 3	**17.** 4	**18.** 3	**19.** 3	**20.** 1	**21.** 2	**22.** 2
23. 3	**24.** 1, 2	**25.** 4	**26.** 4	**27.** 2	**28.** 1	**29.** 3	**30.** 4	

31. Who was James Mill?
1. A Scottish economist and political Philospher
2. A linguist appointed as junior judge at the Supreme Court
3. President of the Board of control of the Company
4. Scottish Missionary

32. What was the system under which peasants were forced to grow indigo on their land?
1. Permanent settlement
2. Mahalwari settlement
3. Ryotwari settlement
4. Nij and Ryoti system

33. Which of the following is *correctly* matched?
1. 1855 – Santhal Rebel
2. 1940 – Bastar Rebel
3. 1920 – Kols Rebel
4. 1948 – Warli Rebel

34. Who decided that Bahadur Shah Zafar would be the last Mughal King?
1. Lord Dalhousie 2. Thomas Munro
3. Lord Ripon 4. Lord Canning

35. The English Education Act was introduced in which year?
1. 1835 2. 1854
3. 1864 4. 1913

36. 'Oru jati, oru matam, oru daivam manushyanu' famous statement was given by:
1. Shri Narayan Guru 2. Ghasidas
3. Haridas Thakur 4. Jyotirao Phule

37. What was the main feature of 'Government of India Act 1935'?
1. Complete Independence
2. Abolition of British Rule
3. Establishment of Indian Republic
4. Provincial Autonomy

38. Who was founder of 'Khudai Khidmatgar'?
1. Mahatma Gandhi
2. Muhammad Ali Jinnah
3. Khan Abdul Ghaffar Khan
4. Syed Ahmad Khan

39. Which of these is a non-renewable resource?
1. Natural Gas 2. Solar Energy
3. Wind Energy 4. Tidal Energy

40. What is Sustainable development?
1. Overuse of resources
2. Development without conservation
3. Meeting present needs without harming future generations
4. Ignoring environmental concerns

41. Which soil is best suited for growing cotton?
1. Desert Soil 2. Red Soil
3. Sandy Soil 4. Black Soil

42. Viticulture is related with cultivation of ______.
1. Silkworms 2. Vegetable, flowers
3. Grapes 4. Breeding of fish

43. Which of the following is a small-scale industry?
1. Cement Industry 2. Handicaraft Industry
3. Petroleum refinery 4. Automobile industry

44. Which industry is called the "Sunrise Industry"?
1. Information Technology
2. Textile Industry
3. Coal Industry
4. Cement Industry

45. Which of the following is an example of country that has experienced a loss of population number due to emigration?
1. United States of America
2. Australia
3. India
4. Sudan

46. Which Fundamental Right was removed by 44th Amendment?
1. Right to Property 2. Right to Education
3. Right to Equality 4. Right to Freedom

47. Which part of the Constitution deals with Fundamental Rights?
1. Part I 2. Part II
3. Part III 4. Part IV

48. Which European country banned students from wearing religious symbols in public schools?
1. Germany 2. France
3. U.K. 4. Spain

49. Who presides over the Rajya Sabha?
1. President 2. Prime Minister
3. Vice-President 4. Chief Minister

50. The 'Right to Education Act' provides free education for children of which of the following age group?
1. 0-6 years 2. 6-14 years
3. 14-18 years 4. 18-25 years

31. 1	**32.** 4	**33.** 1	**34.** 4	**35.** 1	**36.** 1	**37.** 4	**38.** 3	**39.** 1	**40.** 3
41. 4	**42.** 3	**43.** 2	**44.** 1	**45.** 4	**46.** 1	**47.** 3	**48.** 2	**49.** 3	**50.** 2

Directions (Qs. No. 51 to 53): *Each question has a sentence with three part labelled (1), (2) and (3). Read each sentence to find out whether there is any error in any labelled part and indicate your response. If you find no error, your response should be indicated as (4):*

51. (1) He said to him,/ (2) "Athletics are/ (3) my favourite sport'./ (4) No error

52. (1) My boss/ (2) prefers tea/ (3) than coffee./ (4) No error

53. (1) He does not/ (2) have any idea/ (3) about the meeting./ (4) No error

Directions (Qs. No. 54 to 56): *Select the word which is nearest in the meaning to the underlined word:*

54. His ardent support for the cause made him a well-known figure in the community.

1. Mild 2. Passionate
3. Indifferent 4. Weak

55. The serene lake was the perfect spot for spending a peaceful afternoon.

1. Noisy 2. Chaotic
3. Calm 4. Polluted

56. She had incessant need to check her phone, even during meetings.

1. Rare 2. Constant
3. Temporary 4. Unimportant

Directions (Qs. No. 57 & 58): *Select the word which is opposite in the meaning to the underlined word:*

57. His attitude was arrogant, which made it difficult to work with him.

1. Humble 2. Proud
3. Confident 4. Rude

58. The professor's explanation was obscure, and left the students confused.

1. Clear 2. Confusing
3. Complicated 4. Vague

Directions (Qs. No. 59 to 61): *Fill in the blanks with appropriate articles (a, an, the):*

59. I have ____ cat and ____ dog.

1. a, the 2. an, a
3. the, a 4. a, a

60. ____ Earth revolves around ____ Sun.

1. An, the 2. The, a
3. The, the 4. A, the

61. She has _____ unique way of solving problems that makes her stand out.

1. a 2. an
3. the 4. no article

Directions (Qs. No. 62 to 64): *Fill in the blanks with appropriate forms of the words given in brackets:*

62. The team performed ____ (exception) in the finals, winning the championship.

1. exception 2. exceptionally
3. exceptional 4. except

63. The professor _____ (impress) the students with the detailed and engaging lecture that he delivered.

1. impresses 2. impressing
3. impressed 4. impressively

64. Her argument was so _____ (convince) that even her opponents agreed with her point of view.

1. convincing 2. convinced
3. convincingly 4. convince

Directions (Qs. No. 65 & 66): *In these questions, a particular relationship is given. A similar relationship has to be identified from among the given alternatives:*

65. Miser : Wealth :: Glutoon : ?

1. Food 2. Pleasure
3. Energy 4. Greed

66. Benevolent : Kind :: Malevolent : ?

1. Angry 2. Good
3. Evil 4. Generous

Directions (Qs. No. 67 to 70): *Choose the appropriate option after reading the following conversation:*

Teacher : Good morning, Sarah, Did you complete your homework?

Student : Yes, I did, Ma'am. Here it is.

Teacher : Great! Let me check it. What part did you find difficult?

Student : I struggled with the last question about fractions.

Teacher : No worries, we'll go gover that in class.

The teacher greeted Sarah and asked her if she __(67)__ her homework. Sarah replied that she __ (68)__ it and handed it over. The teacher aksed Sarah which part she __(69)__ difficult. Sarah explained that she __(70)__ with the last question about fractions.

67. 1. had completed 2. complete
3. is completing 4. completes

51. 2	**52.** 3	**53.** 4	**54.** 2	**55.** 3	**56.** 2	**57.** 1	**58.** 1	**59.** 4
60. 3	**61.** 1	**62.** 2	**63.** 3	**64.** 1	**65.** 1	**66.** 3	**67.** 1	

68. 1. did   2. had done
3. has done   4. does

69. 1. had found   2. finds
3. find   4. finding

70. 1. struggle   2. has struggled
3. is struggling   4. struggles

71. शुद्ध वर्तनी वाला शब्द है:
1. उज्ज्वल   2. उज्जवल
3. ऊज्ज्वल   4. ऊज्जवल

72. 'सूरसागर' के रचनाकार हैं:
1. तुलसीदास   2. सूरदास
3. कबीर   4. जायसी

73. 'गंगाजल' में समास है:
1. कर्म तत्पुरुष   2. करण तत्पुरुष
3. संबंध तत्पुरुष   4. अधिकरण तत्पुरुष

74. 'पानी की कहानी' के लेखक हैं:
1. रामचन्द्र शुक्ल   2. निर्मल वर्मा
3. डॉ. नगेन्द्र   4. रामचन्द्र तिवारी

75. 'अवधी' किस क्षेत्र के आस-पास बोली जाती है?
1. प्रयागराज   2. मेरठ
3. दिल्ली   4. मथुरा

76. 'बैठक' में प्रत्यय है:
1. बै   2. ठक
3. क   4. बैठ

77. 'करुण रस' का स्थायी भाव है:
1. शोक   2. उत्साह
3. भय   4. निर्वेद

78. यह लड़का हमारे विद्यालय का है– वाक्य में 'यह' क्या है?
1. संबंधवाचक सर्वनाम   2. निजवाचक सर्वनाम
3. परिमाणवाचक विशेषण   4. सार्वनामिक विशेषण

79. शुद्ध वर्तनी वाला शब्द है:
1. संन्यासी   2. सन्यासी
3. सन्नयासी   4. सनयासी

80. 'विनय पत्रिका' के रचनाकार हैं:
1. तुलसीदास   2. सूरदास
3. कबीर   4. जायसी

81. 'वनवास' में समास है:
1. कर्म तत्पुरुष   2. करण तत्पुरुष
3. संबंध तत्पुरुष   4. अधिकरण तत्पुरुष

82. 'टोपी उछालना' मुहावरे का अर्थ है:
1. बेइज्जती करना   2. सत्ता पलटना
3. सम्मान करना   4. मुसीबत मोल लेना

83. 'पुनर्मुद्रण' में उपसर्ग है:
1. पुन   2. मुद्रण
3. पुनः   4. द्रण

84. 'ब्रज' किस क्षेत्र के आस-पास बोली जाती है?
1. प्रयागराज   2. मेरठ
3. गाजीपुर   4. मथुरा

85. बादल का पर्यायवाची **नहीं** है:
1. मेघ   2. जलधर
3. नीरद   4. जलधि

86. 'शान्त रस' का स्थायी भाव है:
1. शोक   2. उत्साह
3. भय   4. निर्वेद

87. 'करण कारक' का उदाहरण है:
1. स्नेहा कलम से लिखती है
2. रेलगाड़ी प्लेटफार्म से जा चुकी है
3. सवार घोड़े से गिरा
4. वृक्ष से पत्ता गिरा

88. 'मनोहर' का सही संधि-विच्छेद है:
1. मानो + हर   2. मन + हर
3. मनः + हर   4. म + नोहर

89. 'क्षणिक' का विलोम शब्द है:
1. सूक्ष्म   2. कालातीत
3. शाश्वत   4. अंत

90. कारण के भेद होते हैं:
1. तीन   2. आठ
3. पाँच   4. दो

91. The value of $\dfrac{3^{-5}\times 10^{-5}\times 125}{5^{-7}\times 6^{-5}}$ is:
1. 5^{-5} 2. 5^{3}
3. 3^{-5} 4. 5^{5}

68. 2	69. 1	70. 2	71. 1	72. 2	73. 3	74. 4	75. 1	76. 3	77. 1	78. 4	79. 1
80. 1	81. 4	82. 1	83. 3	84. 4	85. 4	86. 4	87. 1	88. 3	89. 3	90. 2	91. 4

92. For the given equation: $\frac{3x-2}{4} - \frac{2x+3}{3} = \frac{2}{3} - x$, the value of 'x' is:

1. $x = 2$ 2. $x = -2$
3. $x = 3$ 4. $x = 4$

93. The measures of two adjacent angles of a parallelogram are in the ratio 3 : 2. The largest angle is:

1. 75° 2. 120°
3. 108° 4. 60°

94. After 20% discount Arun brought a shirt in ₹ 1600. What is its marked price?

1. ₹ 2000 2. ₹ 1800
3. ₹ 2200 4. ₹ 2400

95. The sum of first 21 odd numbers is:

1. 440 2. 441
3. 430 4. 442

96. If the surface area of a cube is 600 cm^2, then the length of its one side is:

1. 10 cm 2. 20 cm
3. 100 cm 4. $10\sqrt{6}$ cm

97. If $(2^{3x-1} + 10) \div 7 = 6$, then the value of 'x' is:

1. $x = 3$ 2. $x = 2$
3. $x = -3$ 4. $x = -1$

98. If $\frac{3}{5}$ of a number exceeds its $\frac{2}{7}$ by 44, then the number is:

1. 70 2. 280
3. 140 4. 160

99. What least number must be added to 15370 to make it a perfect square?

1. 6 2. 4
3. 5 4. 9

100. The ages of A and B are in ratio 5 : 7. Four years from now the ratio of their ages will be 3 : 4. The present age of B is:

1. 28 years 2. 30 years
3. 40 years 4. 32 years

EXPLANATORY ANSWERS

1. Boys : Girls = 7 : 5

Let, Boys = $7x$, Girls = $5x$

Difference = $7x - 5x = 2x$

$2x = 8$

$x = 4$

Total strength = $7x + 5x = 12x$

$= 12 \times 4 = 48.$

2. Loss = 5%

Selling Price (SP_1) = 950

Cost Price (CP) = 950 ÷ (95/100)

= 950 × (100/95) = 1000

New Selling Price (SP_2) = 1040

Gain = 1040 − 1000 = 40

Gain % = $\left(\frac{40}{1000}\right) \times 100 = 4\%$.

3. Let, B's 1-day work = x

Then A's 1-day work = $2x$

(A + B)'s 1-day work = $3x$

Given, time = 12 days

So, $3x = \frac{1}{12}$

$x = \frac{1}{36}$

Time taken by B alone

$= 1 \div \left(\frac{1}{36}\right) = 36$ days

4. Radius : Height = 2 : 3

Let, radius = $2k$, height = $3k$

Volume = $\pi r^2 h$

$= \pi(2k)^2(3k) = 12\pi k^3$

$12\pi k^3 = 1617$

Using $\pi = \frac{22}{7}$

$k^3 = 1617 \div \left(\frac{264}{7}\right)$

$k^3 = \frac{343}{8}$

$k = \frac{7}{2}$

Radius $r = 2k = 7$ cm

Height $h = 3k = \frac{21}{2}$ cm

Total Surface Area = $2\pi r(r + h)$

$= 2\pi \times 7 \times \left(7 + \frac{21}{2}\right)$

92. 1	**93.** 3	**94.** 1	**95.** 2	**96.** 1	**97.** 2	**98.** 3	**99.** 1	**100.** 1

$$= 14\pi \times \frac{35}{2} = 245\pi$$

$$= 245 \times \frac{22}{7} = 770 \text{ cm}^2.$$

5. $A = \frac{\sqrt{3}}{4}a^2, A = 4\sqrt{3}$

$$\frac{\sqrt{3}}{4}a^2 = 4\sqrt{3}$$

$$\frac{a^2}{4} = 4$$

$$a^2 = 16$$

$$a = 4 \text{ cm}.$$

6. Check by multiplication:

$$(x-\sqrt{2})(7\sqrt{2}x+4) = x(7\sqrt{2}x+4)-\sqrt{2}(7\sqrt{2}x+4)$$

$$= 7\sqrt{2}x^2+4x-7(\sqrt{2}\cdot\sqrt{2})x-4\sqrt{2}$$

$$= 7\sqrt{2}x^2+4x-14x-4\sqrt{2}$$

$$= 7\sqrt{2}x^2-10x-4\sqrt{2}$$

This matches the given expression exactly.

7. Given:

$$x+\frac{1}{x} = 4$$

Square:

$$\left(x+\frac{1}{x}\right)^2 = x^2+\frac{1}{x^2}+2 = 16$$

$$x^2+\frac{1}{x^2} = 14$$

Square again:

$$\left(x^2+\frac{1}{x^2}\right)^2 = x^4+\frac{1}{x^4}+2$$

$$14^2 = x^4+\frac{1}{x^4}+2$$

$$196 = x^4+\frac{1}{x^4}+2$$

$$x^4+\frac{1}{x^4} = 194.$$

8. $\left(\frac{1}{27}\right)^{-\frac{2}{3}} = \left[\left(\frac{1}{27}\right)^{\frac{1}{3}}\right]^{-2} = \left(\frac{1}{3}\right)^{-2} = \frac{1}{\left(\frac{1}{3}\right)^2} = 3^2 = 9.$

9. Principal = 4000, Rate = 10% per annum,

Time = 2 years

$$A = P\left(1+\frac{R}{100}\right)^T$$

$$A = 4000\left(1+\frac{10}{100}\right)^2$$

$$A = 4000(1.1)^2$$

$$A = 4000 \times 1.21 = 4840$$

Compound Interest = A − P = 4840 − 4000 = 840.

10. Number of sides $n = 12$

$$\text{Number of diagonals} = \frac{n(n-3)}{2}$$

$$= \frac{12(12-3)}{2}$$

$$= \frac{12 \times 9}{2} = 54.$$

11. Petroleum gives products such as petrol, lubricating oil, paraffin wax, diesel, etc. Coke is obtained from coal, not from petroleum, so it is not a constituent of petroleum.

12. Exhaustible natural resources are those resources which exist in limited amounts in nature and can be completely used up by human activities if not conserved properly.

13. Organic manure improves soil structure, increases water-holding capacity, adds humus, and improves soil texture. However, it does not contain a balanced proportion of all essential plant nutrients; nutrients are present in small and variable amounts depending on the source. Hence, this statement is not true for organic manure.

14. Malaria is caused by a protozoan parasite (Plasmodium) and is transmitted by the bite of an infected female Anopheles mosquito, which is an insect vector. The other diseases listed are caused by viruses, not protozoa.

15. Lichens are formed by a symbiotic association between an alga and a fungus. The alga prepares food by photosynthesis, while the fungus provides shelter, protection, and absorbs water and minerals.

16. Inflammable substances are those substances which ignite very easily. This property is due to their low ignition temperature, meaning they require very little heat to start burning. Because of this low ignition temperature, they catch fire easily. Hence, the statement that correctly describes inflammable substances is option 3.

17. Hydrogen gas is considered the cleanest fuel because on burning it produces only water vapour as the product. It does not release smoke, carbon dioxide, ash, or harmful gases that cause air pollution. Wood, petrol, and kerosene all release pollutants during combustion. Therefore, hydrogen gas is the cleanest fuel among the given options.

18. When magnesium ribbon burns in air, it reacts with oxygen to form magnesium oxide. This reaction is highly exothermic and produces a bright white light along with heat. No water is formed in this reaction. Thus, the correct products are magnesium oxide, heat, and light.

19. Conservation of biodiversity in its natural habitat is known as *in situ* conservation. Wildlife sanctuaries and national parks protect plants and animals in the environments where they naturally live. Zoological gardens and botanical gardens are ex situ conservation methods. Hence, the correct answer is wildlife sanctuary and national park.

20. Budding is a form of asexual reproduction in which a new organism develops as an outgrowth (bud) from the parent body. Hydra reproduces by budding. Amoeba reproduces by binary fission, Paramecium by transverse binary fission, and snakes reproduce sexually. Therefore, reproduction by budding takes place in hydra.

21. Human being, cow, and dog are viviparous animals, meaning they give birth to young ones directly. Hen, on the other hand, is oviparous, which means it lays eggs. Although all four animals undergo internal fertilization, hen differs from the other three specifically in the mode of reproduction. Therefore, hen is the odd one out because it is oviparous, making option 2 the correct reason.

22. AIDS is caused by the HIV virus, which spreads through direct contact with infected body fluids such as blood, semen, vaginal fluids, and breast milk. Transfusion of infected blood can directly transmit the virus. Sharing food, combs, or mosquito bites does not transmit HIV.

23. In humans, the mother always contributes an X chromosome, while the father contributes either an X or a Y chromosome. The combination determines the sex of the child. Hence, the belief that only the mother is responsible is wrong because both parents contribute equally to the sex determination.

24. Crop rotation is the agricultural practice of growing different crops alternately on the same field in successive seasons. This method helps maintain soil fertility, reduces pest buildup, and improves crop yield. The other terms are not scientifically accepted agricultural practices.

25. Repulsion between two objects can occur if both objects have like electric charges, causing electrostatic repulsion, or like magnetic poles, causing magnetic repulsion. Friction does not cause repulsion. Therefore, the repulsion could be due to either magnetic or electrostatic force.

26. In a liquid at rest, pressure increases with depth because $P = P_0 + \rho g h$. If A is at the least depth, B deeper, and C deepest (as shown in such standard container diagrams), then $h_A < h_B < h_C \Rightarrow P_A < P_B < P_C$.

27. For the same initial speed, the car travels farthest where friction is minimum. Polished marble offers the least friction among the given surfaces, so the retarding force is smallest and distance covered is maximum.

28. Loudness depends on the amplitude of vibration of the sound wave. Greater amplitude means more energy carried by the wave and hence a louder sound; frequency mainly affects pitch.

29. Sound needs a material medium, but light can travel through vacuum. So the statement that both require a medium is incorrect, while the others are correct.

30. Electroplating waste contains harmful chemicals and heavy metal salts. It must be treated and disposed of only as per authorised local pollution-control/disposal rules, not into rivers, ponds, or fields.

31. James Mill was a Scottish historian, economist, and political philosopher. He is well known for writing A History of British India, in which he critically described Indian society and culture from a colonial perspective. Hence, option 1 is correct.

32. Under the indigo cultivation system, peasants were forced to grow indigo either on the landlord's own land (Nij cultivation) or on the peasants' land (Ryoti system). This coercive system led to severe exploitation of peasants. Therefore, option 4 is correct.

33. The Santhal Rebellion took place in 1855–56 against British authority and moneylenders in present-day Jharkhand and West Bengal. The other pairs are historically incorrect, making option 1 the correct match.

34. Lord Canning, the Governor-General during the Revolt of 1857, decided that Bahadur Shah Zafar would be the last Mughal emperor. After the revolt, the Mughal dynasty was abolished and Bahadur Shah Zafar was exiled. Hence, option 4 is correct.

35. The English Education Act was introduced in 1835, based on Macaulay's Minute, to promote English education and Western learning in India. Therefore, option 1 is the correct answer.

36. The famous statement "*Oru jati, oru matam, oru daivam manushyanu*" meaning "One caste, one religion, one God for humankind" was given by Shri Narayan Guru. He was a great social reformer from Kerala who worked against caste discrimination and promoted social equality and human unity.

37. The main feature of the Government of India Act, 1935 was the introduction of provincial autonomy. Under this Act, provinces were given autonomy to administer themselves, and elected Indian ministers were made responsible to provincial legislatures, though the British still retained overall control.

38. *Khudai Khidmatgar* was founded by Khan Abdul Ghaffar Khan, also known as the Frontier Gandhi. It was a non-violent movement in the North-West Frontier Province that worked for social reform and supported India's freedom struggle through peaceful means.

39. Natural gas is a non-renewable resource because it is formed over millions of years and once exhausted cannot be replenished within a human lifetime. Solar, wind, and tidal energy are renewable sources as they are continuously available in nature.

40. Sustainable development means using resources in such a way that present needs are fulfilled without compromising the ability of future generations to meet their own needs. It emphasizes balanced development along with environmental conservation and responsible resource use.

41. Cotton requires soil that can retain moisture and is rich in lime and potash. Black soil, also known as regur soil, has high moisture-retention capacity and is therefore best suited for cotton cultivation.

42. Viticulture is the branch of agriculture that deals specifically with the cultivation of grapes. It includes grape production, harvesting, and processing, especially for table grapes and wine-making.

43. Small-scale industries operate with low capital investment and use simple tools and skilled manual labour. The handicraft industry fits this description, unlike cement, petroleum, or automobile industries which are large-scale.

44. Information Technology is called the "Sunrise Industry" because it has grown rapidly in recent decades, created large-scale employment, and has high future growth potential compared to traditional industries.

45. Sudan is an example of a country that has experienced a decline in population growth due to emigration, as many people have migrated abroad because of economic difficulties and internal conflicts.

46. The 44th Constitutional Amendment Act, 1978 removed the Right to Property from the list of Fundamental Rights. It was shifted to Article 300A as a legal right, meaning it is no longer a Fundamental Right but still protected by law.

47. Fundamental Rights are contained in Part III of the Indian Constitution, covering Articles 12 to 35. These rights ensure equality, freedom, protection against exploitation, religious freedom, cultural rights, and constitutional remedies.

48. France banned students from wearing conspicuous religious symbols, such as hijabs, crosses, and turbans, in public schools to uphold the principle of secularism (laïcité). Therefore, France is the correct answer.

49. The Vice-President of India is the ex-officio Chairman of the Rajya Sabha and presides over its proceedings. The President does not preside over the Rajya Sabha sessions.

50. The Right to Education Act, 2009 guarantees free and compulsory education for all children in the age group of 6 to 14 years, making education a Fundamental Right under Article 21A of the Constitution.

51. The noun *athletics* refers to a field of sport and is treated as a singular noun in standard usage. Therefore, it should be "Athletics is my favourite sport." The error lies in part (2).

52. The verb *prefer* is followed by to, not *than*. The correct construction is "prefers tea to coffee." Hence, the error is in part (3).

53. The sentence "He does not have any idea about the meeting" is grammatically correct. There is no error in any of the labelled parts.

54. The word *ardent* means showing strong enthusiasm or intense feeling. *Passionate* is the closest in meaning, while the other options convey the opposite or unrelated meanings.

55. *Serene* means peaceful, quiet, and untroubled. Among the options, *calm* best matches this meaning. The other options suggest disturbance or pollution.

56. *Incessant* means continuing without interruption. *Constant* accurately conveys this idea, whereas the other options imply infrequency, short duration, or lack of importance.

57. The word *arrogant* means having an exaggerated sense of one's own importance or abilities. Its opposite is *humble*, which means modest and not proud. The other options either support arrogance or are unrelated, so option 1 is correct.

58. *Obscure* means unclear or difficult to understand. The opposite meaning is *clear*, which signifies something that is easy to understand and well explained. Hence, option 1 is correct.

59. The sentence refers to two non-specific animals mentioned for the first time. Therefore, the correct articles are indefinite articles before both nouns: "I have a cat and a dog."

60. *Earth* and *Sun* are unique celestial bodies. When referring to such unique objects, the definite article the is used. Hence, the correct sentence is "The Earth revolves around the Sun."

61. The word *unique* begins with a consonant sound (/ju:/), not a vowel sound. Therefore, the correct article is *a*, not an. The sentence correctly reads "She has a unique way of solving problems that makes her stand out."

62. The verb "performed" needs an adverb to describe how the team performed. "Exceptionally" is the adverb form of *exception* and correctly fits: "performed exceptionally in the finals."

63. The sentence is in past tense because it refers to a completed action ("delivered" is past). So the correct verb form is "impressed": "The professor impressed the students..."

64. The blank describes the noun "argument", so an adjective is required. "Convincing" means persuasive and fits correctly: "Her argument was so convincing..."

65. A miser is strongly associated with wealth (he hoards wealth). Similarly, a glutton is strongly associated with food (he overeats). Hence, Glutton : Food.

66. Benevolent means kind or well-meaning. Malevolent means wishing harm or being ill-intentioned, i.e., evil. Therefore, the similar relationship is Malevolent : Evil.

67. The reporting verb is in the past tense ("asked"), so the reported action that happened before that must be in the past perfect tense. Therefore, "asked her if she had completed her homework" is grammatically correct.

68. Sarah's reply is reported after the teacher's question, and the action of completing homework was already finished before she handed it over. Hence, the past perfect tense "had done" is required.

69. The teacher's question refers to Sarah's experience before the conversation was reported. To maintain correct sequence of tenses in indirect speech, "which part she had found difficult" is the correct form.

70. The sentence explains Sarah's difficulty, which has relevance up to the present context of the conversation. Therefore, the present perfect tense "has struggled" correctly conveys an action whose effect is still felt.

71. यह शब्द सही वर्तनी में उज्ज्वल लिखा जाता है। इसमें 'ज्ज्' का संयुक्त व्यंजन तथा 'वल' का प्रयोग शुद्ध है। अन्य विकल्पों में या तो अनावश्यक मात्रा का प्रयोग है या संयुक्त व्यंजन की त्रुटि है।

72. 'सूरसागर' के रचनाकार भक्तिकाल के प्रसिद्ध कवि सूरदास हैं। यह कृष्ण-भक्ति पर आधारित एक महत्वपूर्ण काव्य ग्रंथ है।

73. गंगाजल = गंगा का जल। यहाँ 'का' संबंध सूचक कारक है, इसलिए इसमें संबंध तत्पुरुष समास होता है।

74. 'पानी की कहानी' के लेखक रामचंद्र तिवारी हैं। इस पाठ में लेखक ने ओस की एक बूँद को माध्यम बनाकर जल के चक्र का अत्यंत रोचक, वैज्ञानिक और भावपूर्ण वर्णन किया है। बूँद अपनी आत्मकथा के रूप में यह बताती है कि उसका निर्माण हाइड्रोजन और ऑक्सीजन की रासायनिक क्रिया से हुआ, वह वाष्पीकरण, संघनन और वर्षा जैसी विभिन्न अवस्थाओं से होकर कैसे यात्रा करती है, और किस प्रकार जल जीवन के लिए अनिवार्य है। यह रचना विज्ञान और साहित्य का सुंदर समन्वय प्रस्तुत करती है।

75. अवधी भाषा मुख्यतः अवध क्षेत्र में बोली जाती है, जिसमें प्रयागराज और उसके आस-पास का क्षेत्र शामिल है। मेरठ, दिल्ली और मथुरा ब्रज व खड़ी बोली क्षेत्र में आते हैं।

76. शब्द बैठक का निर्माण बैठ + क से हुआ है। यहाँ मूल शब्द बैठ है और इसमें क प्रत्यय जुड़ा है, जिससे संज्ञा बनती है। अतः सही उत्तर विकल्प 3 है।

77. करुण रस का स्थायी भाव शोक होता है। करुण रस में दुख, पीड़ा और करुणा की अनुभूति होती है, जिसका मूल भाव शोक ही है। इसलिए विकल्प 1 सही है।

78. वाक्य "यह लड़का हमारे विद्यालय का है" में *यह* शब्द *लड़का* संज्ञा की विशेषता बता रहा है और स्वयं संज्ञा के साथ प्रयुक्त है। इसलिए यह सार्वनामिक विशेषण है, न कि सर्वनाम। अतः सही उत्तर विकल्प 4 है।

79. संन्यासी शब्द की यही शुद्ध वर्तनी है। इसमें सम् + न्यास से बना शब्द है, इसलिए 'संन्यासी' का प्रयोग सही है। अन्य विकल्पों में वर्ण-विन्यास की त्रुटि है।

80. 'विनय पत्रिका' के रचनाकार गोस्वामी तुलसीदास हैं। यह भक्तिकाल की एक प्रमुख कृति है, जिसमें ईश्वर के प्रति विनय और भक्ति की भावनाएँ व्यक्त की गई हैं।

81. वनवास = वन में वास। यहाँ 'में' स्थान (अधिकरण) का बोध कराता है, इसलिए इसमें अधिकरण तत्पुरुष समास होता है।

82. 'टोपी उछालना' मुहावरे का सही अर्थ किसी की बेइज्जती करना या सार्वजनिक रूप से अपमान करना होता है। हिंदी भाषा और संस्कृति में *टोपी* को मान-सम्मान और प्रतिष्ठा का प्रतीक माना गया है। इसलिए किसी की टोपी उछालना उसकी इज़्ज़त को ठेस पहुँचाने, उसे नीचा दिखाने या लज्जित करने का भाव प्रकट करता है। उदाहरण के रूप में– "भरी सभा में किसी की टोपी उछालना शिष्टाचार के विरुद्ध है।"

83. पुनर्मुद्रण = पुनः + मुद्रण। यहाँ 'पुनः' का अर्थ है 'फिर से', जो मूल शब्द *मुद्रण* से पहले जुड़कर नया शब्द बनाता है, अतः यही उपसर्ग है।

84. ब्रज भाषा मुख्य रूप से मथुरा और उसके आस-पास के क्षेत्र में बोली जाती है। यह कृष्ण-लीला और ब्रज साहित्य से विशेष रूप से जुड़ी हुई है।

85. बादल के पर्यायवाची मेघ, जलधर, नीरद हैं, जबकि जलधि का अर्थ समुद्र होता है। इसलिए जलधि बादल का पर्यायवाची नहीं है।

86. शान्त रस का स्थायी भाव निर्वेद (वैराग्य, उदासीनता, सांसारिक आसक्ति से विरक्ति) होता है। शान्त रस में मन की पूर्ण शांति और तटस्थ भाव की अनुभूति होती है, जिसका आधार निर्वेद ही है।

87. करण कारक उस साधन को दर्शाता है जिसके द्वारा कोई कार्य किया जाता है। इस वाक्य में *कलम* लिखने का साधन है और 'से' विभक्ति चिह्न लगा है, इसलिए यह करण कारक का सही उदाहरण है।

88. मनोहर शब्द का सही संधि-विच्छेद मनः + हर है। यहाँ विसर्ग संधि के कारण मनः का ':' बदलकर 'ो' हो गया है और शब्द मनोहर बना है।

89. क्षणिक का अर्थ है अल्पकालिक या थोड़े समय के लिए रहने वाला। इसका विलोम शाश्वत है, जिसका अर्थ है सदा रहने वाला या स्थायी।

90. हिंदी व्याकरण में कारक के आठ भेद माने जाते हैं–कर्ता, कर्म, करण, संप्रदान, अपादान, अधिकरण, संबंध और संबोधन। इसलिए सही उत्तर विकल्प 2 है।

91. $\dfrac{3^{-5} \times 10^{-5} \times 125}{5^{-7} \times 6^{-5}}$

$$10^{-5} = (2 \times 5)^{-5} = 2^{-5}5^{-5},$$
$$125 = 5^3,\ 6^{-5} = (2 \times 3)^{-5}$$
$$= 2^{-5}3^{-5}$$

$$= \frac{3^{-5} \times 2^{-5} \times 5^{-5} \times 5^3}{5^{-7} \times 2^{-5} \times 3^{-5}}$$

Cancel 2^{-5} and 3^{-5} from numerator and denominator:

$$= \frac{5^{-2}}{5^{-7}} = 5^{-2+7} = 5^5.$$

92. $\dfrac{3x-2}{4} - \dfrac{2x+3}{3} = \dfrac{2}{3} - x$

LCM of 4 and 3 = 12

$$\frac{3(3x-2)-4(2x+3)}{12} = \frac{2}{3} - x$$
$$\frac{9x-6-8x-12}{12} = \frac{2}{3} - x$$
$$\frac{x-18}{12} = \frac{2}{3} - x$$

Multiply both sides by 12:

$$x - 18 = 8 - 12x$$
$$13x = 26$$
$$x = 2.$$

93. In a parallelogram, adjacent angles are supplementary. Let the two adjacent angles be $3x$ and $2x$.

$$3x + 2x = 180°$$
$$5x = 180°$$
$$x = 36°$$

Thus, the angles are:

$$3x = 3 \times 36° = 108°$$
$$2x = 2 \times 36° = 72°$$

Hence, the largest angle is 108°.

94. Discount = 20%

So, the paid price is 80% of the marked price.

$$80\% \text{ of MP} = 1600$$
$$\text{MP} = \frac{1600 \times 100}{80}$$
$$\text{MP} = 2000$$

Therefore, the marked price is ₹ 2000.

95. The sum of the first n odd numbers is given by: n^2

Here, n 21.

$$\text{Sum} = 21^2 = 441$$

So, the sum of the first 21 odd numbers is 441.

96. Surface area of a cube = $6a^2$

Given: $6a^2 = 600$

$$a^2 = \frac{600}{6} = 100$$
$$a = 10 \text{ cm}.$$

97.
$$\frac{2^{3x-1}+10}{7} = 6$$
$$2^{(3x-1)} + 10 = 42$$
$$2^{(3x-1)} = 32 = 2^5$$
$$3x - 1 = 5$$
$$3x = 6$$
$$x = 2.$$

98. Let the number be x.
$$\frac{3}{5}x - \frac{2}{7}x = 44$$
LCM of 5 and 7 = 35
$$\frac{21x - 10x}{35} = 44$$
$$\frac{11x}{35} = 44$$
$$11x = 1540$$
$$x = 140$$
Thus, the required number is 140.

99. We check the nearest perfect squares around 15370.
$$124^2 = 15376$$
$$15376 - 15370 = 6$$
So, the least number to be added to 15370 to make it a perfect square is 6.

100. Let the present ages of A and B be $5x$ and $7x$ respectively.

Four years from now:
$$\frac{5x+4}{7x+4} = \frac{3}{4}$$
Cross-multiplying:
$$4(5x + 4) = 3(7x + 4)$$
$$20x + 16 = 21x + 12$$
$$21x - 20x = 16 - 12$$
$$x = 4$$
Present age of B:
$$7x = 7 \times 4 = 28 \text{ years}$$
Hence, the present age of B is 28 years.

Previous Years' Paper

BHU–CENTRAL HINDU SCHOOL

School Entrance Test (SET), Class 9th, 2024

(Exam held on 29-04-2024)

1. Which of the following is called "Black Gold"?

1. Coke
2. Coal Tar
3. Petroleum
4. Coal Gas

2. Large scale storage of grains is done in:

1. Granaries
2. Silos
3. Both 1 & 2
4. Gunny bags

3. Name the scientist who discovered the process of conversion of sugar into alcohol:

1. Alexander Flemming
2. Rudolf Virchow
3. Louis Pasteur
4. Edward Jenner

4. Those species of plants and animals which are found exclusively in a particular area are called:

1. Exotic species
2. Endemic species
3. Endangered species
4. Invasive species

5. The production of male hormone, testosterone and female hormone, estrogen is under the control of which endocrine gland?

1. Testis, Ovary
2. Adrenal Gland
3. Pituitary Gland
4. Thyroid Gland

6. Pressure exerted by water at the bottom of the container depends on:

1. Volume of the water in container
2. Height of the column of container
3. Surface area of the container
4. Both 1 and 2 above

7. The frictional force exerted by fluids is called:

1. Rolling Friction
2. Contact Force
3. Sliding Friction
4. Drag

8. Ultrasound equipments tracking many medical problems works at frequencies:

1. 20 to 20,000 Hz
2. 2000 Hz
3. More than 20,000 Hz
4. Less than 20 Hz

9. Which of the following part of eye senses colour?

1. Cornea
2. Iris
3. Cones
4. Retina

10. In the experiment, if electrodes are immersed in water and current is passed, bubbles of Oxygen & Hydrogen are produced. Oxygen bubbles are formed on:

1. Positive Terminal
2. Negative Terminal
3. In water
4. On the wall of container

11. Anthrax disease is caused by:

1. *Bacillus thuringiensis*
2. *Bacillus anthracis*
3. *Bacillus subtilis*
4. *Bacillus megaterium*

12. Tin cans, used for storing food, are made by electroplating:

1. Iron onto Tin
2. Tin onto copper
3. Tin onto Iron
4. Aluminium onto Tin

13. Petrol engine releases which of the following gas?

1. Sulphur dioxide
2. Carbon dioxide
3. Oxides of nitrogen
4. Carbon monoxide

14. The calorific value of a fuel is expressed as:

1. KJ/Kg
2. J/g
3. J/Kg
4. KJ/g

15. The head of the safety match box contains the mixture of:

1. Antimony trisulphide & potassium manganate
2. Antimony trisulphide & potassium chlorate
3. Antimony trisulphide & potassium florate
4. Red phosphorus & Antimony trisulphide

1. 3	**2.** 3	**3.** 3	**4.** 2	**5.** 3	**6.** 2	**7.** 4	**8.** 3
9. 3	**10.** 1	**11.** 2	**12.** 3	**13.** 4	**14.** 1	**15.** 2	

16. Frictional force on an object in a fluid does ***not*** depends on:

1. Speed with respect to fluid
2. Shape of the object
3. Mass of the object
4. Nature of the fluid

17. In different zones of candle flame, the colour of outer zone of complete combustion, middle zone of partial combustion & innermost zone of unburnt wax are:

1. Yellow, Blue, Black 2. Black, Yellow, Blue
3. Blue, Yellow, Black 4. Blue, Black, Yellow

18. Match the following micro-organism with their plant diseases:

Plant Disease	**Micro-Organism**
A. Citrus Canker	(*i*) Virus
B. Rust of Wheat	(*ii*) Bacteria
C. Yellow Vein Mosaic of Bhindi	(*iii*) Fungus

1. A-(*iii*), B-(*ii*), C-(*i*)
2. A-(*i*), B-(*ii*), C-(*iii*)
3. A-(*ii*), B-(*iii*), C-(*i*)
4. A-(*iii*), B-(*i*), C-(*ii*)

19. During dry weather, while combing hair, sometimes we experience hair flying apart. The force responsible for this is:

1. Force of gravity 2. Electrostatic force
3. Force of friction 4. Magnetic force

20. If an object oscillates 5 times in one second, what would be its frequency?

1. 0.05 Hz 2. 0.5 Hz
3. 5 Hz 4. 20 Hz

21. 'रंग लाना' मुहावरे का अर्थ है:

1. असर जमाना 2. प्रभाव उत्पन्न करना
3. परिवर्तन लाना 4. किसी चीज को रंगना

22. शुद्ध वर्तनी वाला शब्द है:

1. गरुण 2. गरूड़
3. गरुड़ 4. गरूण

23. श्रीरामचरितमानस के रचनाकार हैं:

1. वाल्मीकि 2. तुलसीदास
3. वेदव्यास 4. चक्रवर्ती राजगोपालाचारी

24. 'देशभक्ति' में समास है:

1. अपादान तत्पुरुष 2. करण तत्पुरुष
3. कर्म तत्पुरुष 4. सम्प्रदान तत्पुरुष

25. 'मगही' किस क्षेत्र के आस-पास बोली जाती है?

1. लखनऊ 2. पटना
3. कुरुक्षेत्र 4. दिल्ली

26. 'आशातीत' का क्या अर्थ है?

1. आशा से अधिक 2. आशा से कम
3. आशा का न होना 4. निराशा

27. 'उत्साह' किस रस का स्थायी भाव है?

1. वीर रस 2. शान्त रस
3. शृंगार रस 4. भयानक रस

28. वह मेरा घर है।– इस वाक्य में 'मेरा' है:

1. संज्ञा 2. सर्वनाम
3. सार्वनामिक विशेष्य 4. सार्वनामिक विशेषण

29. वह बहुत सुन्दर स्थान है।– वाक्य में 'बहुत' है:

1. विशेषण 2. प्रविशेषण
3. गुणवाचक विशेषण 4. निपात

30. जब तुम आओगे, तब मैं जाऊँगा।– अर्थ के आधार पर वाक्य भेद है:

1. विधिवाचक वाक्य 2. संकेतवाचक वाक्य
3. आज्ञावाचक वाक्य 4. संदेहवाचक वाक्य

31. 'जो बहुत बोलता है' के लिए एक शब्द होगा:

1. वाचाल 2. अतिवादी
3. वक्ता 4. प्रतिवादी

32. किस समूह में सभी पर्यायवाची शब्द **नहीं** हैं?

1. अरविन्द, सरोज, पद्म, अबुज
2. दिनकर, सूर्य, भास्कर, रवि
3. नदी, सरिता, तटिनी, विटप
4. नेत्र, चक्षु, नयन, आँख

33. उ, ऊ और प-वर्ग के वर्णों का उच्चारण-स्थान है:

1. कंठ 2. ओठ
3. तालु 4. मूर्द्धा

34. 'भीषण' किस विशेष्य के लिए सबसे उचित विशेषण होगा?

1. मधुर 2. तिक्त
3. प्रेम 4. युद्ध

35. सही क्रम में इन चिह्नों (!), (।), (,), (;) के नाम हैं:

1. अर्द्धविराम, पूर्णविराम, अल्पविराम, विस्मयादिबोधक
2. पूर्णविराम, अल्पविराम, अर्द्धविराम, विस्मयादिबोधक
3. अल्पविराम, पूर्णविराम, विस्मयादिबोधक, अर्द्धविराम
4. विस्मयादिबोधक, पूर्णविराम, अल्पविराम, अर्द्धविराम

16. 3	**17.** 3	**18.** 3	**19.** 2	**20.** 3	**21.** 2	**22.** 3	**23.** 2	**24.** 4	**25.** 2
26. 1	**27.** 1	**28.** 2	**29.** 2	**30.** 2	**31.** 1	**32.** 3	**33.** 2	**34.** 4	**35.** 4

36. 'सप्तर्षि' में कौन-सा समास है?

1. बहुव्रीहि समास
2. द्वंद्व समास
3. द्विगु समास
4. तत्पुरुष समास

37. 'आंधी आयी और समूचा वातावरण धूलि-धूसरित हो गया।' वाक्य में समुच्चयबोधक अव्यय है:

1. आयी
2. समूचा
3. और
4. धूलि-धूसरित

38. अति + अधिक की सही संधि होगी:

1. अत्याधिक
2. अतिअधिक
3. अत्यंत्याधिक
4. अत्यधिक

39. इनमें से हिन्दी के कहानी लेखक के रूप में कौन प्रसिद्ध हैं?

1. सुमित्रानंदन पंत
2. रामधारी सिंह 'दिनकर'
3. मैथिलीशरण गुप्त
4. प्रेमचंद

40. सच्चाई से बड़ी कोई शक्ति नहीं है। वाक्य में 'सच्चाई' है:

1. गुणवाचक संज्ञा
2. भाववाचक संज्ञा
3. व्यक्तिवाचक संज्ञा
4. द्रव्यवाचक संज्ञा

41. Find the correctly spelt:

1. Assessory
2. Accessry
3. Acessory
4. Accessory

Directions (Qs. No. 42 to 45): *Each question has a sentence with three parts labelled (1), (2) and (3). Read each sentence to find out whether there is any error in any labelled part and indicate your response. If you find no error, your response should be indicated as (4):*

42. (1) Every boy and every girl/ (2) were given a packet/ (3) of sweets./ (4) No error

43. (1) Neither of the/ (2) two men was/ (3) very strong./ (4) No error

44. (1) Our happiness or our sorrow/ (2) is largely due/ (3) to our own actions./ (4) No error

45. (1) He found an one rupee/ (2) coin yesterday in the backyard/ (3) of his house./ (4) No error

Directions (Qs. No. 46 to 48): *Select the word of phrase which is nearest in the meaning to the underlined word or phrase:*

46. This is what makes the city so alluring.

1. Attractive
2. Scary
3. Polluted
4. Daunting

47. It's a very profound statement for a lad of 21, but he's right.

1. Beautiful
2. Careless
3. Meaningless
4. Sincere

48. The expressed their disquiet about the terms of the contract.

1. Interest
2. Greed
3. Anxiety
4. Happiness

Directions (Qs. No. 49 & 50): *Select the word or phrase which is opposite in the meaning to the underlined word or phrase:*

49. I was surprised by the meek submission of the rebels.

1. Humble
2. Devotee
3. Kind
4. Overbearing

50. Sometimes, forgiveness helps turn your antagonists into allies.

1. Enemy
2. Relative
3. Supporter
4. Foster

Directions (Qs. No. 51 to 55): *Fill in the blanks with appropriate words given below:*

51. Both _____ boys are intelligent.

1. A
2. The
3. An
4. No article

52. _____ Mankind should love Nature.

1. A
2. The
3. An
4. No article

53. We met _____ European girl in Rishikesh.

1. The
2. An
3. A
4. No article

54. They began about a quarter past _____ one o'clock in the morning.

1. A
2. The
3. An
4. No article

55. She is good _____ playing the piano.

1. At
2. In
3. With
4. By

Directions (Qs. No. 56 to 60): *Choose the appropriate option after reading the following conversation:*

Sunny : Where are you going?
Rekha : I am going to collect my report card of class VII.
Sunny : Did you not collect it?
Rekha : I could not collect it because I was sick.

36. 3	**37.** 3	**38.** 4	**39.** 4	**40.** 2	**41.** 4	**42.** 2	**43.** 4	**44.** 4	**45.** 1
46. 1	**47.** 4	**48.** 3	**49.** 4	**50.** 3	**51.** 2	**52.** 4	**53.** 3	**54.** 4	**55.** 1

Sunny asked Rekha where __(56)__ going. Rekha replied that __(57)__ going to collect her report card of class VII. Sunny again asked if __(58)__ not collected it. Rekha replied in affirmative that __(59)__ not collect it because __(60)__ sick.

56. 1. He was 2. She was 3. He is 4. She is

57. 1. She was 2. He was 3. Was he 4. Was she

58. 1. He had 2. Had she 3. She had 4. She did

59. 1. She can 2. She could 3. Could she 4. He could

60. 1. He was 2. She was 3. Was she 4. Was he

61. By what number should $\frac{-33}{16}$ be divided to get $\frac{-11}{4}$?

1. $\frac{2}{3}$ 2. $\frac{3}{2}$ 3. $\frac{3}{4}$ 4. $\frac{4}{11}$

62. Find m, if $\frac{8}{729} \times \left(\frac{4}{18}\right)^{-6} = \left(\frac{2}{9}\right)^{2m-1}$

1. 0 2. –1 3. 1 4. 2

63. The product of two numbers is 1296. If one number is 16 times the other, then the numbers are:

1. (9, 144) 2. (12, 108) 3. (24, 54) 4. (18, 72)

64. If $\left(x + \frac{1}{x}\right) = 12$, then the value of $x - \frac{1}{x}$ is:

1. $\pm\sqrt{121}$ 2. $\pm\sqrt{144}$ 3. $\pm\sqrt{140}$ 4. $\pm\sqrt{169}$

65. If $4x^2 + y^2 = 40$ and $xy = 6$, then the value of $2x + y$ is:

1. 0 2. ±8 3. ±6 4. $\pm\sqrt{42}$

66. Two numbers are such that the ratio between them is 3 : 5. If each is increased by 10, the ratio between the new numbers so formed is 5 : 7, then the original numbers are:

1. 9, 15 2. 12, 20 3. 15, 25 4. 18, 30

67. If 52 men can do a piece of work in 35 days, in how many days 28 men will do it?

1. 25 days 2. 16 days 3. 45 days 4. 65 days

68. 15 boys earn ₹ 900 in 6 days, how much will 20 boys earn in 7 days?

1. ₹ 1,400 2. ₹ 1,500 3. ₹ 1,600 4. ₹ 1,450

69. A water tank can be filled by a tap in 4 hours and emptied by an outlet pipe in 5 hours. How long will it take to fill the water tank if both the tap and the pipe are opened together?

1. 10 hours 2. 12 hours 3. 20 hours 4. 25 hours

70. What will be the per cent of pure gold in 20 carat gold, if 24 carat gold is hundred per cent gold?

1. $80\frac{2}{3}\%$ 2. $81\frac{1}{3}\%$ 3. 82% 4. $83\frac{1}{3}\%$

71. If m is 5% of n and n is 24% of p. If $m = 480$, then the value of p is:

1. 40,000 2. 44,000 3. 36,000 4. 32,000

72. In the given figure ABCD is a parallelogram and angle bisector of ∠A and ∠B meet at O. The value of ∠AOB is:

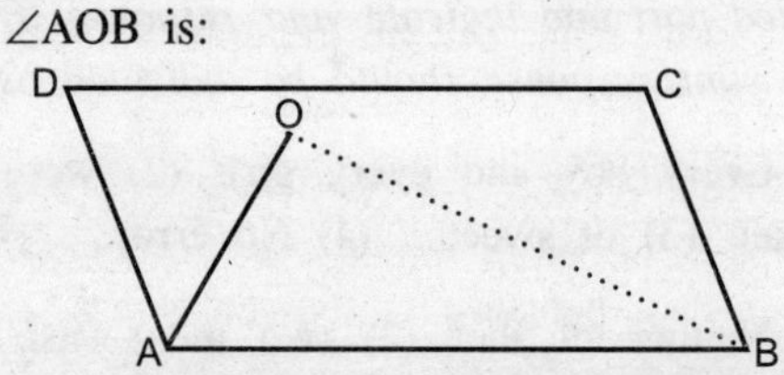

1. Less than 90° 2. More than 90° 3. Equal to 90° 4. None of these

73. One of the diagonals of a rhombus is equal to one of its side, then the angles of the rhombus is:

1. 100°, 80°, 100°, 80°
2. 90°, 90°, 90°, 90°
3. 110°, 70°, 110°, 70°
4. 120°, 60°, 120°, 60°

74. Three cubes of sides 3 cm, 4 cm and 5 cm are melted and a new cube is formed. The side of new cube is:

1. 9 cm 2. 8 cm 3. 17 cm 4. 6 cm

56. 2	**57.** 1	**58.** 3	**59.** 2	**60.** 2	**61.** 3	**62.** 2	**63.** 1	**64.** 3	**65.** 2
66. 3	**67.** 4	**68.** 1	**69.** 3	**70.** 4	**71.** 1	**72.** 3	**73.** 4	**74.** 4	

75. The sum of the radius of the base and height of a solid cylinder is 37 m. If the total surface area of the solid cylinder is 1628 m^2, then the circumference of its base is:

1. 34 m 2. 44 m
3. 47 m 4. 54 m

76. If $(x^2 + y^2) = 74$ and $xy = 35$, then the value of $x^3 + y^3$ is:

1. 560 2. 496
3. 486 4. 468

77. How many sides does a regular polygon have if the measure of an exterior angle is 24°?

1. 15 2. 14
3. 13 4. 12

78. The value of, $\frac{4^{-1/2} \times 2^{1/2} \times 3^{-4}}{8 \times 8^{-1/2} \times 6^{-3}}$ is:

1. $\frac{1}{2}$ 2. $\frac{1}{3}$
3. $\frac{2}{3}$ 4. $\frac{2\sqrt{2}}{3}$

79. Wheel of a cycle with diameter 56 cm complete 100 revolution to reach the destination. The total distance covered by the cycle is:

1. 175 m 2. 176 m
3. 177 m 4. 277 m

80. There is a profit of 12% on selling a watch for ₹ 2,800. What will be the cost price of the watch?

1. ₹ 2,000 2. ₹ 2,200
3. ₹ 2,500 4. ₹ 2,700

81. Which ministry under the government of India launched the app- 'G20 India'?

1. Ministry of Culture
2. Ministry of Tourism
3. Ministry of Education
4. Ministry of External Affairs

82. When and where was the battle between Nawab Siraj-ud-daulah and Robert Clive fought?

1. Buxar - 1764 2. Plassey - 1757
3. Buxar - 1756 4. Plassey - 1857

83. Which of the following is ***incorrectly*** matched?

1. Mysore - Haider Ali
2. Jhansi - Rani Laxmi Bai
3. Jodhpur - Shivaji
4. Punjab - Maharaja Ranjit Singh

84. Jon Fosse won the Nobel Prize in which of the following fields in 2023?

1. Chemistry 2. Literature
3. Peace 4. Physics

85. Where did Gautama Buddha teach his first sermon after attaining enlightenment?

1. Bodh Gaya 2. Lumbini
3. Sarnath 4. Sankhissa

86. When was the kingdom of Jhansi annexed by the British authorities under doctrine of lapse?

1. 1856-57 2. 1853-54
3. 1859-60 4. 1850-51

87. The process of covering the bare ground between plants with a layer of organic matter like straw to retain moisture is called:

1. Mulching 2. Rock dam
3. Contour barriers 4. Intercropping

88. Which of the following was the first iron and steel plant in the country before 1947?

1. Tata Iron and Steel Company Limited
2. Jharia Coal Fields
3. Rourkela Steel Plant
4. Salem Steel Plant

89. Which of the following is also known as the 'Golden Fibre'?

1. Cotton 2. Maize
3. Jute 4. Millets

90. Who of the following was recently appointed the governor of Odisha?

1. Raghubar Das 2. Naveen Patnaik
3. Dinesh Tripathi 4. Manisha Sharma

91. The book that keeps the record of all the endangered animals and plants in India is called:

1. Black Book 2. Extinction log
3. Red Data Book 4. Green Data Book

92. What was the name and species of the first mammal to be cloned?

1. Alex, Goat 2. Dolly, Sheep
3. Sophia, Humanoid 4. Aaron, Turtle

93. What is the farming duration for Rabi crops?

1. June to August 2. June to September
3. January to June 4. October to March

75. 2	**76.** 4	**77.** 1	**78.** 3	**79.** 2	**80.** 3	**81.** 4	**82.** 2	**83.** 3	**84.** 2
85. 3	**86.** 2	**87.** 1	**88.** 1	**89.** 3	**90.** 1	**91.** 3	**92.** 2	**93.** 4	

94. Which of the following is classified as a modern irrigation method?

1. Moat 2. Chain pump
3. Drip system 4. Johad system

95. Which of the following is *correctly* matched?

1. Swami Dayanand Saraswati – Brahma Samaj
2. Ram Mohan Roy – Arya Samaj
3. Swami Vivekanand – Ramkrishna Mission
4. Annie Besant – Deccan Education Society

96. Abhinav Bindra is associated with which sport?

1. Shooting 2. Wrestling
3. Lawn Tennis 4. Football

97. When did the British Parliament transfer the powers of the East India Company to the British Crown?

1. 1857 2. 1860
3. 1862 4. 1858

98. The scale used to measure the magnitude of power of an earthquake is called:

1. Fleming's scale
2. Barometer
3. Richter scale
4. Electroscope

99. Which of the following is *not* a constituent of Petroleum?

1. CNG 2. LPG
3. Kerosene 4. Paraffin Wax

100. Which of the following laws in pre-independence India gave British government the ability to arrest people and keep them in prisons without a trial?

1. Subsidiary Alliance – 1765
2. Vernacular Press Act – 1878
3. Doctrine of Lapse – 1859
4. Rowlatt Act – 1919

EXPLANATORY ANSWERS

1. Petroleum is commonly called "Black Gold" because it is dark in colour and extremely valuable as a major source of energy and many useful products (petrol, diesel, kerosene, plastics, lubricants, etc.).

2. Large-scale storage of grains is done in granaries and silos because both are established systems meant for bulk storage over long periods. Granaries are large storage buildings or warehouses where grains are stored, often in gunny bags, and they provide protection from moisture, pests, and spoilage. Silos are tall cylindrical structures made of concrete or metal, specifically designed for storing grains in bulk and preventing damage from insects, rodents, and humidity. Gunny bags alone are not considered a large-scale storage structure; they are used within granaries. Hence, both granaries and silos together correctly represent large-scale grain storage.

3. Louis Pasteur discovered that yeast carries out fermentation, converting sugar into alcohol (and carbon dioxide), and established the scientific understanding of this biological process.

4. Species (plants or animals) found only in a particular specific area and nowhere else naturally are called endemic species (for example, many island species are endemic to that island).

5. The pituitary gland controls the production of testosterone and estrogen indirectly by releasing gonadotropic hormones (FSH and LH), which regulate the functioning of testes and ovaries, thereby controlling sex hormone production.

6. Pressure at the bottom of a liquid depends on the height (depth) of the liquid column and the liquid's density, not on total volume or container shape/area. Mathematically,

$$P = \rho g h$$

So, as h increases, bottom pressure increases.

7. The frictional force exerted by fluids (liquids or gases) on an object moving through them is called drag. It opposes the motion of the object and depends on factors such as speed, shape of the object, and nature of the fluid.

8. Ultrasound equipment works at frequencies above 20,000 Hz, which is beyond the audible range of human hearing. These high-frequency sound waves are used in medical imaging because they can penetrate body tissues and reflect back to form images.

9. Cones are specialized photoreceptor cells in the retina that are responsible for colour vision and sharp detailed vision, especially in bright light. They respond to different wavelengths corresponding to different colours.

10. In the electrolysis of water, oxygen gas is produced at the positive terminal (anode), while hydrogen gas is produced at the negative terminal (cathode). This occurs because oxidation (loss of electrons) takes place at the anode, leading to oxygen formation.

94. 3 **95.** 3 **96.** 1 **97.** 4 **98.** 3 **99.** 1 **100.** 4

11. Anthrax is an infectious disease caused by the bacterium Bacillus anthracis, which forms spores and mainly affects cattle and other grazing animals, but can also infect humans through contact with infected animals or animal products.

12. Tin cans used for storing food are made by electroplating tin onto iron. Tin is less reactive and non-toxic, so coating iron with tin prevents corrosion and protects food from contamination.

13. A petrol engine releases carbon monoxide due to incomplete combustion of petrol. This gas is colourless, odourless, and highly poisonous, making it one of the most dangerous vehicular pollutants.

14. The calorific value of a fuel is expressed in kilojoules per kilogram (kJ/kg). It represents the amount of heat energy produced when one kilogram of fuel is completely burned.

15. The head of a safety match contains a mixture of antimony trisulphide and potassium chlorate, which helps in initiating combustion when the match is struck against the rough surface of the matchbox.

16. The frictional force (drag) experienced by an object moving in a fluid depends on its speed relative to the fluid, the shape of the object, and the nature (viscosity, density) of the fluid. It does not depend directly on the mass of the object, so mass is not a determining factor for fluid friction.

17. In a candle flame, the outer zone undergoes complete combustion and appears blue due to high temperature, the middle luminous zone shows yellow colour due to partial combustion and glowing soot particles, and the innermost zone contains unburnt wax vapours and appears dark or black.

18. Citrus canker is caused by bacteria, rust of wheat is caused by a fungus, and yellow vein mosaic of bhindi is caused by a virus.

Hence, the correct matching is A–(*ii*), B–(*iii*), C–(*i*).

19. During dry weather, rubbing a comb through hair transfers electric charges. Hair strands acquire the same type of charge and repel each other due to electrostatic force, causing them to fly apart.

20. Frequency is defined as the number of oscillations completed in one second. If an object makes 5 oscillations in 1 second, then

$$\text{Frequency} = \frac{\text{Number of oscillations}}{\text{Time}}$$

$$= \frac{5}{1} = 5 \text{ Hz}$$

Therefore, the correct frequency is 5 Hz.

21. 'रंग लाना' मुहावरे का अर्थ किसी प्रयास, कार्य या योजना का सफल होना अथवा उसका अपेक्षित प्रभाव उत्पन्न करना होता है, जैसे—कड़ी मेहनत अंततः रंग लाई।

22. 'गरुड़' भगवान विष्णु का वाहन माने जाने वाले पक्षी का सही और शुद्ध वर्तनी वाला शब्द है। अन्य विकल्पों में मात्रा अथवा वर्ण-विन्यास की त्रुटि है।

23. 'श्रीरामचरितमानस' की रचना गोस्वामी तुलसीदास ने अवधी भाषा में की थी। यह ग्रंथ रामकथा का भक्तिपूर्ण और लोकभाषा में रचित काव्यात्मक रूप है।

24. 'देशभक्ति' शब्द का समास-विग्रह 'देश के लिए भक्ति' होता है। तत्पुरुष समास में उत्तर पद (भक्ति) प्रधान होता है और विग्रह में प्रयुक्त कारक-चिह्न लुप्त हो जाता है। यहाँ 'के लिए' का संबंध सम्प्रदान कारक से है, इसलिए 'देशभक्ति' में सम्प्रदान तत्पुरुष समास होता है।

25. 'मगही' भाषा मुख्य रूप से बिहार के पटना और उसके आस-पास के क्षेत्रों में बोली जाती है। यह पूर्वी भारत की प्रमुख लोकभाषाओं में से एक है।

26. 'आशातीत' शब्द का अर्थ है आशा से बढ़कर या अपेक्षा से अधिक। इसका प्रयोग तब होता है जब परिणाम या घटना अनुमान से कहीं अधिक हो।

27. 'उत्साह' वीर रस का स्थायी भाव है। वीर रस में साहस, पराक्रम और दृढ़ संकल्प की भावना प्रकट होती है, जिसका मूल भाव उत्साह होता है।

28. वाक्य "वह मेरा घर है" में 'मेरा' शब्द उत्तम पुरुषवाचक सर्वनाम का संबंधवाचक (निजवाचक) रूप है। यह मूलतः 'मैं' सर्वनाम का विकारी रूप है और स्वामित्व का बोध कराता है। यहाँ 'मेरा' को स्वतंत्र रूप से भी प्रयोग किया जा सकता है, जैसे—"वह घर मेरा है", जहाँ यह स्पष्ट रूप से सर्वनाम ही रहता है। अतः इस वाक्य में 'मेरा' को सर्वनाम के रूप में ही वर्गीकृत करना व्याकरण की दृष्टि से सही है।

29. वाक्य "वह बहुत सुन्दर स्थान है" में 'बहुत' शब्द सुन्दर विशेषण की मात्रा बताता है। विशेषण की विशेषता बताने वाले शब्द को प्रविशेषण कहते हैं।

30. वाक्य "जब तुम आओगे, तब मैं जाऊँगा" में एक कार्य का होना दूसरे कार्य पर निर्भर है। इस प्रकार के वाक्य संकेतवाचक वाक्य कहलाते हैं, क्योंकि इनमें शर्त या संकेत का भाव होता है।

31. 'जो बहुत बोलता है' व्यक्ति के लिए वाचाल शब्द प्रयोग किया जाता है। इसका अर्थ अधिक बोलने वाला या बातूनी व्यक्ति होता है।

32. इस समूह में सभी शब्द पर्यायवाची नहीं हैं क्योंकि नदी, सरिता, तटिनी नदी के पर्याय हैं, जबकि विटप का अर्थ वृक्ष होता है। इसलिए यह समूह सही नहीं है।

33. उ, ऊ स्वर तथा प-वर्ग (प, फ, ब, भ, म) के वर्णों का उच्चारण ओठ (ओष्ठ्य) से होता है। अतः इनका उच्चारण-स्थान ओठ है।

34. 'भीषण' शब्द अत्यधिक उग्र, भयानक या तीव्र अर्थ देता है। इसका सबसे उपयुक्त प्रयोग युद्ध के लिए होता है, जैसे–भीषण युद्ध।

35. दिए गए चिह्नों (!), (।), (,), (;) के नाम क्रमशः विस्मयादिबोधक, पूर्णविराम, अल्पविराम और अर्द्धविराम होते हैं।

36. 'सप्तर्षि' शब्द का विग्रह सात ऋषि होता है। जहाँ संख्या (सप्त = सात) पूर्वपद होती है और समस्त पद किसी समूह का बोध कराता है, वहाँ द्विगु समास होता है।

37. वाक्य "आंधी आयी और समूचा वातावरण धूलि-धूसरित हो गया।" में 'और' शब्द दो वाक्यांशों को जोड़ रहा है, इसलिए यह समुच्चयबोधक अव्यय है।

38. 'अति' + 'अधिक' की संधि में इ + अ = य हो जाता है, जिससे सही संधि रूप अत्यधिक बनता है। अन्य विकल्प संधि-नियमों के अनुसार सही नहीं हैं।

39. प्रेमचंद हिन्दी साहित्य के सबसे प्रसिद्ध कहानीकार माने जाते हैं। उन्होंने सामाजिक यथार्थ पर आधारित अनेक प्रसिद्ध कहानियाँ और उपन्यास लिखे, जैसे–'कफन', 'पूस की रात', 'गोदान' आदि।

40. वाक्य "सच्चाई से बड़ी कोई शक्ति नहीं है।" में 'सच्चाई' किसी गुण या भाव का बोध कराती है जिसे न देखा जा सकता है और न छुआ जा सकता है, इसलिए यह भाववाचक संज्ञा है।

41. Accessory is the correctly spelt word. The other options contain spelling errors such as missing or misplaced letters.

42. In the sentence "Every boy and every girl were given a packet of sweets," the subject 'Every boy and every girl' is grammatically singular in sense. Therefore, the verb should be 'was given', not 'were given'. Hence, the error lies in part (2).

43. In the sentence "Neither of the two men was very strong," the subject 'Neither' is singular and correctly takes the singular verb 'was'. The sentence is grammatically correct.

44. In "Our happiness or our sorrow is largely due to our own actions," the verb agrees with the nearer subject 'our sorrow', which is singular. Hence, the use of 'is' is correct.

45. The phrase 'an one rupee' is incorrect. Since 'one' begins with a consonant sound (/w/), the correct article is 'a', not 'an'. Therefore, the error is in part (1).

46. The word 'alluring' means highly attractive or tempting. Hence, Attractive is the nearest meaning.

47. The word 'profound' means deep, serious, and showing thoughtful insight. In the given sentence, "It's a very profound statement for a lad of 21, but he's right," the emphasis is on the depth, seriousness, and genuineness of thought expressed in the statement. Among the given options, 'sincere' best conveys this sense of earnestness and depth of feeling or thought in context. Hence, option 4 correctly matches the meaning intended in the sentence.

48. Disquiet' means uneasiness, worry, or anxiety. Thus, Anxiety is the closest meaning.

49. The opposite of 'meek' (submissive, gentle) is overbearing (domineering, arrogant). Hence, option 4 is correct.

50. The word 'antagonists' means opponents or enemies. The question asks for the opposite meaning. A supporter is someone who stands with, helps, or backs another person, which is the direct opposite of an antagonist. Hence, Supporter is the correct antonym in this context.

51. The definite article 'the' is used with 'both' when referring to two specific persons or things already known or identified. Hence, "Both the boys are intelligent" is grammatically correct.

52. 'Mankind' is used in a general sense to denote the whole human race. When used in this universal sense, no article is required. Therefore, "Mankind should love Nature" is correct.

53. Although 'European' begins with a vowel letter, it starts with a consonant sound /ju:/ ("yoo"). Therefore, the correct article is 'a', making the sentence "We met a European girl in Rishikesh."

54. When time expressions like 'one o'clock' are used with phrases such as "past," "to," or "quarter," no article is used before the number. Hence, "about a quarter past one o'clock" is correct.

55. The adjective 'good' is followed by the preposition 'at' to indicate skill or proficiency in an activity. Therefore, "She is good at playing the piano" is grammatically correct.

56. In indirect speech, the present continuous tense "Where are you going?" changes to past continuous. Since the subject is Rekha, the correct form is "she was going."

57. The sentence "I am going to collect my report card..." changes into reported speech as "she was going to collect her report card", with tense shifted to past.

58. The original direct question is "Did you not collect it?", which is in the simple past tense. When such a question is changed into indirect (reported) speech, the simple past tense correctly changes into the past perfect tense. In reported yes/no questions, the structure used is if/whether + subject + verb (not inversion). Therefore, the correct construction is "Sunny again asked if she had not collected it." Hence, option 3. She had is grammatically and structurally correct.

59. The sentence "I could not collect it..." remains 'could' in indirect speech because it already expresses past ability. Therefore, "she could not collect it" is correct.

60. The reason clause "because I was sick" changes to "because she was sick", with the subject changed to third person and tense remaining past.

61. We are given

$$\frac{-33}{16} \div x = \frac{-11}{4}$$

Dividing by a number is the same as multiplying by its reciprocal:

$$\frac{-33}{16} = \frac{-11}{4} \times x$$

$$x = \frac{-33}{16} \div \frac{-11}{4} = \frac{-33}{16} \times \frac{4}{-11}$$

$$x = \frac{33 \times 4}{16 \times 11} = \frac{132}{176} = \frac{3}{4}.$$

62. Given the equation

$$\frac{8}{729} \times \left(\frac{4}{18}\right)^{-6} = \left(\frac{2}{9}\right)^{2m-1}$$

First, standardise all terms to the same base:

$$8 = 2^3,\ 729 = 9^3,\ \frac{4}{18} = \frac{2}{9}$$

So, $$\frac{8}{729} = \left(\frac{2}{9}\right)^3$$

Substituting:

$$\left(\frac{2}{3}\right)^3 \times \left(\frac{2}{9}\right)^{-6} = \left(\frac{2}{9}\right)^{2m-1}$$

Using the law of exponents (same base ⇒ add powers):

$$\left(\frac{2}{9}\right)^{3+(-6)} = \left(\frac{2}{9}\right)^{2m-1}$$

$$\left(\frac{2}{9}\right)^{-3} = \left(\frac{2}{9}\right)^{2m-1}$$

Equating exponents:

$$-3 = 2m - 1$$
$$-2 = 2m$$
$$m = -1$$

Hence, the correct option is 2: –1.

63. Let the smaller number be x. Then the larger number is $16x$.

$$x \times 16x = 1296$$
$$16x^2 = 1296 \Rightarrow x^2 = 81$$
$$\Rightarrow \quad x = 9.$$

Thus the numbers are 9 and $16 \times 9 = 144$.

64. Given, $$x + \frac{1}{x} = 12$$

Square both sides:

$$\left(x + \frac{1}{x}\right)^2 = 12^2$$

$$x^2 + \frac{1}{x^2} + 2 = 144$$

So, $$x^2 + \frac{1}{x^2} = 144 - 2 = 142$$

Now, $$\left(x - \frac{1}{x}\right)^2 = x^2 + \frac{1}{x^2} - 2$$
$$= 142 - 2 = 140$$

Therefore, $$x - \frac{1}{x} = \pm\sqrt{140}$$

Hence, the correct option is 3: $\pm\sqrt{140}$.

65. Given, $4x^2 + y^2 = 40,\ xy = 6$

Consider:

$$(2x + y)^2 = 4x^2 + y^2 + 4xy$$
$$= 40 + 4(6)$$
$$= 40 + 24 = 64$$
$$2x + y = \pm\sqrt{64} = \pm 8.$$

66. Let the original numbers be $3x$ and $5x$. After increasing each by 10, the ratio becomes 5 : 7.

$$\frac{3x+10}{5x+10} = \frac{5}{7}$$

$$7(3x + 10) = 5(5x + 10)$$
$$21x + 70 = 25x + 50$$
$$70 - 50 = 25x - 21x$$
$$20 = 4x \Rightarrow x = 5$$

So the numbers are $3x = 15$ and $5x = 25$.

67. Work = Men × Days (constant)

$$52 \times 35 = 28 \times D$$

$$D = \frac{52 \times 35}{28}$$

$$D = \frac{13 \times 35}{7}$$

$$D = 13 \times 5 = 65.$$

68. Earning depend directly on the number of boys and the number of days.

First, find the earning per boy per day:

$$\text{Earning per boy per day} = \frac{900}{15 \times 6} = \frac{900}{90} = 10$$

Now, for 20 boys working for 7 days:

$$\text{Total earning} = 20 \times 7 \times 10 = 1400.$$

Hence, the correct answer is ₹ 1,400.

69. Rate of filling by tap $= \frac{1}{4}$ tank per hour.

Rate of emptying by outlet pipe $= \frac{1}{5}$ tank per hour.

Net rate when both are opened together:

$$\frac{1}{4} - \frac{1}{5} = \frac{5-4}{20} = \frac{1}{20}$$

Time required to fill the tank:

$$\frac{1}{\frac{1}{20}} = 20 \text{ hours}$$

Therefore, the correct answer is 20 hours.

70. 24 carat gold is 100% pure.

Purity of 20 carat gold:

$$\frac{20}{24} \times 100 = \frac{5}{6} \times 100 = 83\frac{1}{3}\%$$

Hence, the correct option is 4.

71. Given:

$$m = 5\% \text{ of } n, n = 24\% \text{ of } p, \text{m} = 480$$

From the first relation:

$$0.05n = 480 \Rightarrow n = \frac{480}{0.05} = 9600$$

From the second relation:

$$0.24p = 9600 \Rightarrow p = \frac{9600}{0.24} = 40000$$

Therefore, the correct option is 1: 40,000.

72. in parallelogram ABCD,

$$\angle A + \angle B = 180°$$

The angle bisector of $\angle A$ makes $\frac{\angle A}{2}$ and that of $\angle B$ makes $\frac{\angle B}{2}$.

The angle between the two bisectors is:

$$\frac{\angle A}{2} + \frac{\angle B}{2} = \frac{180°}{2} = 90°$$

Hence, $\angle AOB = 90°$

So, the correct option is 3.

73. Let the side of the rhombus be s and one interior angle θ. In a rhombus, a diagonal is

$$d = 2s\cos\left(\frac{\theta}{2}\right) \text{(one diagonal)}$$

$$d' = 2s\sin\left(\frac{\theta}{2}\right) \text{(other diagonal)}$$

Given: one diagonal equals a side, so either

$$2s\cos\left(\frac{\theta}{2}\right) = s \text{ or } 2s\sin\left(\frac{\theta}{2}\right) = s$$

$$2\cos\left(\frac{\theta}{2}\right) = 1 \Rightarrow \cos\left(\frac{\theta}{2}\right) = \frac{1}{2}$$

$$\Rightarrow \frac{\theta}{2} = 60° \Rightarrow \theta = 120°$$

or

$$2\sin\left(\frac{\theta}{2}\right) = 1 \Rightarrow \sin\left(\frac{\theta}{2}\right) = \frac{1}{2}$$

$$\frac{\theta}{2} = 30° \Rightarrow \theta = 60°$$

Thus angles are 60° and 120°. Hence option 4.

74. Volume is conserved on melting.

$$V_{new} = 3^3 + 4^3 + 5^3$$

$$= 27 + 64 + 125$$

$$= 216 \text{ cm}^3$$

If side of new cube is a, then

$$a^3 = 216$$

$$\Rightarrow a = \sqrt[3]{216} = 6 \text{ cm}.$$

75. Given $r + h = 37$. Total surface area of a solid cylinder:

$$\text{TSA} = 2\pi r(r + h)$$

So, $2\pi r(37) = 1628$

Using $\pi = \frac{22}{7}$:

$$2 \times \frac{22}{7} \times r \times 37 = 1628$$

$$\frac{44 \times 37}{7} r = 1628$$

$$\frac{1628}{7} r = 1628 \Rightarrow r = 7$$

Circumference of base:

$$2\pi r = 2 \times \frac{22}{7} \times 7 = 44 \text{ m}.$$

76. $x^2 + y^2 = 74,\ xy = 35$

$$(x + y)^2 = x^2 + y^2 + 2xy$$
$$= 74 + 2(35)$$
$$= 74 + 70 = 144$$
$$x + y = \sqrt{144} = 12$$

(also –12 is possible)

Using $(x + y)^3 = x^3 + y^3 + 3xy(x + y)$

$$12^3 = x^3 + y^3 + 3(35)(12)$$
$$1728 = x^3 + y^3 + 1260$$
$$x^3 + y^3 = 1728 - 1260 = 468$$

Hence, the value is 468, so the matching option is 4.

77. For a regular polygon,

$$\text{Exterior angle} = \frac{360°}{n}$$

Given exterior angle = 24°:

$$24 = \frac{360}{n} \Rightarrow n = \frac{360}{24} = 15.$$

78. Given, $\dfrac{4^{-\frac{1}{2}} \times 2^{\frac{1}{2}} \times 3^{-4}}{8 \times 8^{-\frac{1}{2}} \times 6^{-3}}$

Write all terms with prime bases:

$$4^{-\frac{1}{2}} = (2^2)^{-\frac{1}{2}} = 2^{-1},\ 8 = 2^3,$$
$$8^{-\frac{1}{2}} = (2^3)^{-\frac{1}{2}} = 2^{-\frac{3}{2}}$$
$$6^{-3} = (2 \times 3)^{-3} = 2^{-3} \times 3^{-3}$$

Substitute:

$$\frac{2^{-1} \times 2^{\frac{1}{2}} \times 3^{-4}}{2^3 \times 2^{-\frac{3}{2}} \times 2^{-3} \times 3^{-3}}$$

Simplify numerator:

$$2^{-1+\frac{1}{2}} \times 3^{-4} = 2^{-\frac{1}{2}} \times 3^{-4}$$

Simplify denominator:

$$2^{3-\frac{3}{2}-3} \times 3^{-3} = 2^{-\frac{3}{2}} \times 3^{-3}$$

Now divide:

$$\frac{2^{-\frac{1}{2}} \times 3^{-4}}{2^{-\frac{3}{2}} \times 3^{-3}} = 2^{-\frac{1}{2}-\left(-\frac{3}{2}\right)} \times 3^{-4-(-3)}$$
$$= 2^1 \times 3^{-1} = \frac{2}{3}$$

Hence, the correct option is 3:

79. Circumference $= \pi d = \pi \times 56$ cm $= 56\pi$ cm

Distance in 100 revolutions

$$= 100 \times 56\pi = 5600\pi \text{ cm}$$
$$5600\pi \text{ cm} = 56\pi \text{ m}$$
$$56\pi = 56 \times \frac{22}{7}$$
$$= 8 \times 22 = 176 \text{ m.}$$

80. Profit $= 12\% \Rightarrow$ SP = 112% of CP

$$\text{CP} = \text{SP} \times \frac{100}{112} = 2800 \times \frac{100}{112}$$
$$\text{CP} = 2800 \times \frac{25}{28}$$
$$= 100 \times 25 = 2500.$$

81. The 'G20 India' app was launched under India's G20 Presidency framework by the Ministry of External Affairs, which led many official G20 communication and outreach initiatives.

82. The battle between Nawab Siraj-ud-Daulah and Robert Clive was fought at Plassey in 1757.

83. This pair is incorrectly matched because Shivaji was associated with the Maratha power in western India, not with Jodhpur (a Rajput state).

84. Jon Fosse was awarded the Nobel Prize in Literature (2023) for his innovative plays and prose that give voice to the unsayable and explore human existence with deep literary expression.

85. After attaining enlightenment at Bodh Gaya, Gautama Buddha delivered his first sermon at Sarnath, known as the Dharmachakra Pravartanasutra* (Turning of the Wheel of Dharma).

86. The kingdom of Jhansi was annexed by the British in 1853–54 under Lord Dalhousie's Doctrine of Lapse after the death of Raja Gangadhar Rao.

87. The process of covering bare soil with organic matter like straw, leaves, or grass to conserve moisture and improve soil fertility is called mulching.

88. TISCO (established in 1907 at Jamshedpur) was the first iron and steel plant in India before independence.

89. Jute is known as the Golden Fibre because of its natural golden sheen and high economic value, especially in eastern India.

90. Raghubar Das was recently appointed as the Governor of Odisha.

91. The Red Data Book maintains records of endangered species of plants and animals, documenting those facing the risk of extinction in India.

92. Dolly was the first mammal successfully cloned from an adult somatic cell, and she was a sheep.

93. Rabi crops are sown in winter (October–November) and harvested in spring (March–April), hence their farming duration is October to March.

94. The drip irrigation system is a modern method that supplies water directly to plant roots, conserving water and improving efficiency.

95. Swami Vivekanand founded the Ramakrishna Mission to promote spiritual and social service based on the teachings of Sri Ramakrishna.

96. Abhinav Bindra is an Indian shooter and the first Indian to win an individual Olympic gold medal (Beijing 2008).

97. In 1858, through the Government of India Act, the British Parliament transferred power from the East India Company to the British Crown.

98. The Richter scale is used to measure the magnitude (power) of earthquakes.

99. CNG (Compressed Natural Gas) is not a constituent of petroleum; it is derived mainly from natural gas, whereas LPG, kerosene, and paraffin wax are petroleum products.

100. The Rowlatt Act empowered the British government to arrest and detain people without trial, severely curtailing civil liberties in pre-independence India.

ENGLISH

1

Verb Patterns

The *Pattern* of a verb shows the various forms it assumes, either by inflection or by combination with parts of other verbs, in order to mark voice, tense, number, person and mood.

The following are the principal parts of a verb in the English language:

(*a*) The Present Tense

(*b*) The Past Tense

(*c*) The Past Participle

The verbs are of two kinds. They are:

(*a*) Strong Verbs

(*b*) Weak Verbs

Verbs that form their past tense and past participle by a change of the inside vowel in the present are called *strong verbs. e.g.,*

Present Tense	*Past Tense*	*Past Participle*
Come	Came	Come
Do	Did	Done
Fall	Fell	Fallen
Write	Wrote	Written
Speak	Spoke	Spoken

Verbs that form their past tense and past participle by adding *-ed, -d* or *-t* to the present, with or without change of the inside vowel are called *weak verbs. e.g.,*

Present Tense	*Past Tense*	*Past Participle*
Believe	Believed	Believed
Burn	Burnt	Burnt
Talk	Talked	Talked
Sleep	Slept	Slept
Walk	Walked	Walked

The following is a list of *strong verbs* and *weak verbs*:

Present Tense	*Past Tense*	*Past Participle*
Abet	Abetted	Abetted
Abide	Abode	Abode
Am/Be	Was	Been
Are	Were	Been
Aver	Averred	Averred
Abhor	Abhorred	Abhorred
Arise	Arose	Arisen
Awake	Awoke	Awoken
Beat	Beat	Beaten
Befall	Befell	Befallen
Bandy	Bandied	Bandied
Bed	Bedded	Bedded
Behold	Beheld	Beheld
Believe	Believed	Believed
Beseech	Besought	Besought
Behave	Behaved	Behaved
Bethink	Bethought	Bethought
Bind	Bound	Bound
Bleed	Bled	Bled
Bless	Blessed	Blessed
Win	Won	Won
Withstand	Withstood	Withstood
Work	Worked	Worked
Welcome	Welcomed	Welcomed
Will	Would	—
Write	Wrote	Written
Wake	Woke	Woken
Wear	Wore	Worn
Withdraw	Withdrew	Withdrawn
Withhold	Withheld	Withheld
Wed	Wedded	Wedded
Whip	Whipped	Whipped
Worry	Worried	Worried
Wrong	Wronged	Wronged
Yell	Yelled	Yelled
Yield	Yielded	Yielded
Zigzag	Zigzagged	Zigzagged

Each of the following verbs has exactly the same form in present tense, past tense and past participle:

Present Tense	*Past Tense*	*Past Participle*	*Present Tense*	*Past Tense*	*Past Participle*
Beset	Beset	Beset	Outbid	Outbid	Outbid
Bet	Bet	Bet	Put	Put	Put
Bid	Bid	Bid	Quit	Quit	Quit
Burst	Burst	Burst	Read	Read	Read
Broadcast	Broadcast	Broadcast	Recast	Recast	Recast
Cast	Cast	Cast	Reset	Reset	Reset
Cost	Cost	Cost	Rid	Rid	Rid
Cut	Cut	Cut	Set	Set	Set
Forecast	Forecast	Forecast	Shed	Shed	Shed
Hit	Hit	Hit	Slit	Slit	Slit
Hurt	Hurt	Hurt	Split	Split	Split
Knit	Knit	Knit	Spread	Spread	Spread
Let	Let	Let	Thrust	Thrust	Thrust
Miscast	Miscast	Miscast	Underbid	Underbid	Underbid
			Upset	Upset	Upset

Note 1: The past tense and the past participle of *bid*, when used in the sense of *order* or *tell*, are *bade* and *bidden* respectively.

2: The past tense as well as the participle of *Knit,* when used in the sense of *make (a garment, etc) by forming wool, silk etc, yarn into connecting loops; make a plain stitch, is knitted.*

AGREEMENT OF SUBJECTS AND VERBS

It is very important that the verb in a sentence should obey the subject, otherwise the sentence will be considered wrong. The rules are:

1. When the Subject is a Singular Noun it takes a singular verb, *e.g.,*

(*i*) Mohit **makes** a noise in the class.

(*ii*) The child is **crying** for a cake.

2. When two singular nouns are joined with 'and' and they refer to two different persons, the plural verb should be used, *e.g.,*

(*i*) The novelist and the poet **were** honoured by the government.

(*ii*) The black and the white dogs **bark** at the strangers.

☛ Article 'the' is used with both the subjects.

If article is used only once, singular verb should be used.

(*i*) The painter and singer **is** going abroad.

(*ii*) The white and black dog **has** a bushy tail.

3. When the subjects together give a single idea, singular verb is used.

(*i*) Slow and steady **wins** the race.

(*ii*) Rice and curry **is** my favourite dish.

4. A collective noun takes a singular verb when it acts as a whole, but it takes a plural verb when the individual, of which it is composed are considered separately.

(*i*) The committee **was** unanimous on imposing the new law.

(*ii*) The committee **have** given their separate opinions in the matter.

5. When the subjects are joined by neither . . . nor, either . . . or, and 'or', the verb should obey the last subject.

(*i*) Rakesh or his friends **have** been selected for the match.

(*ii*) His friends or Rakesh **has** been selected for the match.

(*iii*) Neither Rohit nor his brothers **are** going abroad.

(*iv*) Neither his brothers nor Rohit **is** going abroad.

(*v*) Either Sohan or his sisters **were** dancing at the function.

(*vi*) Either his sisters or Sohan **was** dancing at the function.

6. Either, neither, either of, neither of, take singular verb.

(*i*) Either boy **was** honest.

(*ii*) Neither girl **was** allowed to leave the premises.

(*iii*) Either of the boys **was** ready to help the old man.

(*iv*) Neither of the girls **was** asked to join the extra classes.

7. Some nouns are always used as plurals so, they take plural verbs.

(*i*) Where **are** your glasses?

(*ii*) His pants are attractive.

(*iii*) Cattle **are** grazing in the field.

(*iv*) Whose scissors **are** these?

8. Some nouns are always used as singulars, so, they take singular verbs.
   (*i*) What **is** the latest news?
   (*ii*) The furniture in the house **is** of a poor quality.
   (*iii*) Mumps **is** not a fatal disease.
   (*iv*) Physics **is** a tough subject.

9. Nouns formed by alongwith, as well as, together with, accompanied by, etc., take verb according to the first subject.
   (*i*) I, as well as you, **am** to blame.
   (*ii*) You, as well as I, **are** going to see a movie.
   (*iii*) John, accompanied by his parents, **is** going to visit the Taj.
   (*iv*) His parents, accompanied by John, **are** going to visit the Taj.
   (*v*) His brothers, together with Vivek, **are** ready to whitewash the fence.

10. To indicate something hypothetical or not factually true, plural verb 'were' with *as if* is used.
   (*i*) He talks as if he **were** a king.
   (*ii*) She dresses herself as if she **were** a princess.

MULTIPLE CHOICE QUESTIONS

Directions: *In the following questions choose the correct options to fill in the blanks.*

1. The bus with all its passengers .... lost.
   A. were B. was
   C. are D. would

2. You as well as I .... responsible for this work.
   A. am B. are
   C. was D. is

3. Raghava like all his companions .... a spoiled child.
   A. are B. were
   C. is D. will be

4. Pen and ink .... required for me.
   A. are B. were
   C. is D. has required

5. Every girl and every boy .... attended the seminar.
   A. have B. has
   C. is D. are

6. Not only she but all her sisters ...... been married.
   A. has B. have
   C. is D. are

7. There .... nothing but miseries in life.
   A. is B. are
   C. were D. will be

8. Neither prose nor poem .... given.
   A. were B. was
   C. has D. have

9. Either he or I .... wrong.
   A. is B. are
   C. am D. were

10. Either Sulekha or Rekha .... coming here.
   A. are B. is
   C. were D. have

11. .... the child or his parents to blame?
   A. Is B. Are
   C. Were D. Has

12. You and I .... neighbours.
   A. am B. are
   C. was D. has

13. The house with all its belongings ..... sold away.
   A. were B. are
   C. was D. must

14. Either water or juice .... required.
   A. is B. are
   C. were D. has

15. There were not as many tables as .... required.
   A. was B. were
   C. is D. are

16. They each .... a book.
   A. have B. are
   C. has D. is

17. He and I .... close friends.
   A. is B. am
   C. was D. are

18. She as well as I .... guilty.
   A. is B. are
   C. am D. must be

19. Rohan .... not read more on this chapter.
   A. needs B. has been need
   C. need D. had been need

20. He came .... to his aunt.
   A. run B. running
   C. to run D. in run

21. She dislikes .... meat.
   A. eat to B. to eat
   C. eating D. to eating

22. He likes ....
   A. sing to B. singing
   C. to sing D. to singing

23. We are ready .... the match.
A. play to B. to playing
C. playing D. to play

24. .... is injurious to health.
A. Smoking B. To smoke
C. To smoking D. Smoke to

25. He loves .... raw vegetables.
A. eaten B. eating
C. to eating D. eat to

26. He seemed .... finished his homework.
A. have to B. to have
C. having D. to having

27. Either Arpan or his friends .... asked to pay a visit to the university.
A. has been B. have been
C. has D. have

28. Where .... your spectacles?
A. is B. are
C. were D. have

29. Measles .... not a fatal disease.
A. is B. are
C. has D. have

30. He walks as if he .... a prince.
A. was B. were
C. have been D. has been

31. The captain alongwith his team mates .... reached the ground.
A. have B. has
C. is D. are

32. The jury ..... given its opinion.
A. has B. have
C. is D. are

33. Slow and steady .... the race.
A. win B. wins
C. has wins D. have win

34. The poet and the novelist .... invited by the PM.
A. is B. are
C. has D. have

35. Mathematics .... a tough subject.
A. is B. are
C. has D. have

36. Either girl .... in a sad mood.
A. was B. were
C. has D. have

37. They will .... performed on the stage.
A. had B. has
C. have D. be

38. Ravi is .... to railway station.
A. went B. going
C. goes D. to

39. We will .... playing this match at Green Park Stadium.
A. be B. being
C. have D. has

40. He will .... a glass of water.
A. drank B. drink
C. drunk D. drinks

ANSWERS

1	2	3	4	5	6	7	8	9	10
B	B	C	C	B	B	A	B	C	B
11	**12**	**13**	**14**	**15**	**16**	**17**	**18**	**19**	**20**
A	B	C	A	B	A	D	A	C	B
21	**22**	**23**	**24**	**25**	**26**	**27**	**28**	**29**	**30**
C	B	D	A	B	B	B	B	A	B
31	**32**	**33**	**34**	**35**	**36**	**37**	**38**	**39**	**40**
B	A	B	B	A	A	C	B	A	B

★★★

2

Sequence of Tenses

1. Tense indicates a point in time or period of time in the past, present, or future tense.

2. Tense is related to the form of verb. The verb may consist of a single word, or a main verb and one or more auxiliary words. There are normally three forms of the verb, say, V_1, V_2, V_3 and for convenience a fourth form V_4 as 'verb + ing' may be assumed.

Forms of Verb

V_1	V_2	V_3	V_4
Write	Wrote	Written	Writing
Read	Read	Read	Reading
Go	Went	Gone	Going
...	...	...	...

A Comparative Chart Regarding Tenses and Verbs

Simple Present	Simple Past	Simple Future
V_1	V_2	shall/will + V_1
Present Continuous	**Past Continuous**	**Future Continuous**
is/am/are + V_4	was/were + V_4	shall/will + be + V_4
Present Perfect	**Past Perfect**	**Future Perfect**
has/have + V_3	had + V_3	shall/will + have + V_3
Present Perfect Cont.	**Past Perfect Cont.**	**Future Perfect Cont.**
has/have + been + V_4	had + been + V_4	shall/will + have been + V_4

Tenses, their application and examples:

SIMPLE PRESENT

A. A present state of affairs.	A. My sister lives in Kashmir.
B. A general fact.	B. The sun rises in the east.
C. Habitual actions.	C. I listen to the radio in the mornings.
D. Future time-tables.	D. My flight leaves at 10:00.

PRESENT CONTINUOUS

A. A specific action that is occurring.	A. Arvind is watching TV (right now).
B. A general activity that takes place.	B. These days, I'm taking it easy.
C. Future arrangements.	C. I'm inviting Hari to the party on Friday.

SIMPLE PAST

A. An action that began and ended at a particular time in the past.	A. The mail came early this morning.
B. An action that occurred over a period of time but was completed in the past.	B. Dad worked in advertising in the past.
C. An activity that took place regularly in the past.	C. We jogged every morning before class.

PAST CONTINUOUS

	Usage		Examples
A.	Interrupted Actions.	A.	I was sewing when the telephone rang.
B.	A continuous state over a period of time but was completed in the past.	B.	She was looking very ill, I was meeting lots of people at that time.
C.	Events planned in the past.	C.	Neetu was leaving for Jammu but had to make a last minute change
D.	Expressing a future intent.	D.	Jyoti is going to bring her sister tonight.
E.	Predicting an event.	E.	You are going to pass the test, don't worry.

SIMPLE FUTURE

	Usage		Examples
A.	Making a future decision.	A.	I will call you after lunch.
B.	Predicting a future event.	B.	You will pass the test, don't worry.
C.	Indicating willingness to do something.	C.	If I don't feel better soon, I will go to the doctor.

FUTURE CONTINUOUS

	Usage		Examples
A.	An action that will be going at a particular time in the future.	A.	At noon tomorrow, I will be taking the children to their piano lessons.
B.	Future actions which have already been decided.	B.	I will be wearing my black dress to the dinner.

PRESENT PERFECT

	Usage		Examples
A.	An action that happened at an unspecified time.	A.	She has never climbed a mountain. I'm sorry, I have forgotten your Name.
B.	An action that has recently occurred.	B.	He has just gone to sleep.
C.	An action that began in the past and continues up to the present (often used with "for" or "since").	C.	Jack has lived in Shri Nagar all his life. I have been here since Monday. He has known her for two weeks.
D.	An action that happened repeatedly before now.	D.	We have flown across the Pacific four times. I've failed my driver's test twice.

PRESENT PERFECT CONTINUOUS

	Usage		Examples
A.	An action that began in the past and has just recently ended.	A.	Have you been ringing the Bell?
B.	An action that began in the past and continues in the present.	B.	Lokesh has been studying for two hours.
C.	An action repeated over a period of time in the past and continuing in present.	C.	Suresh has been playing since he was fifteen.

PAST PERFECT

	Usage		Examples
A.	An action that occurred before another past action.	A.	Tarun had left hours beforewe got there.
B.	An action that was expected to occur in the past.	B.	I had hoped to know about the job before now.

PAST PERFECT CONTINUOUS

	Usage		Examples
A.	An action that occurred before another past action.	A.	His eyes hurt because he had been reading for eight hours.
B.	An action that was expected to occur in the past.	B.	I had been expecting a change in his attitude.

FUTURE PERFECT

	Usage		Examples
A.	An action that will be completed before a particular time in the future.	A.	By next July, my parents will have been married for fifty years.

FUTURE PERFECT CONTINUOUS

	Usage		Examples
A.	Emphasizing the length of time that has occurred before a specific time in the future.	A.	By May, my father will have been working at the same job for thirty years.

MULTIPLE CHOICE QUESTIONS

Directions: *Find the correct word(s) that completes the sentence according to tenses.*

1. The manner in which bombs ...... in five trains within a short span of time suggests that it is a part of a conspiracy.
A. explode B. exploding
C. exploded D. has been exploding

2. What ..... the postage for an airletter?
A. are B. am
C. is D. be

3. I don't really know how to ..... the problem.
A. tackle B. tackling
C. do tackle D. did tackle

4. ...... a two-inch margin on each page for the teacher's remarks.
A. Leave B. Has left
C. Leaves D. Left

5. We ..... such a wonderful time at the party last night.
A. has B. have
C. had D. are having

6. Due to a failure of some traffic lights, traffic ...... very slowly.
A. move B. is moving
C. has moved D. had moved

7. ...... the earlier train will give us the chance to do some shopping.
A. Catch B. To catch
C. Having caught D. Catching

8. 'Please' and 'Thank you' are the little courtesies by which we ...... the machine of life oiled and running smoothly.
A. keep B. keeps
C. keeping D. were keeping

9. The French ..... reputed to have a very good sense of humour.
A. is B. was
C. are D. will be

10. Life ...... to death as pleasure is to pain.
A. is B. was
C. are D. will be

11. Do you know ..... ?
A. where she comes from
B. where does she come from
C. where from she comes
D. from where does she come

12. Few works of reference ..... so valuable as the Encyclopaedia Britannica.
A. is B. was
C. are D. will be

13. The paths of glory ..... but to the grave.
A. leads B. lead
C. leading D. have lead

14. ..... at three o'clock, I heard the rumble of thunder.
A. Walk B. Walks
C. Walking D. Walked

15. The thief ..... all the money.
A. made up B. made off with
C. made do with D. made good

16. Pakistan lost a crucial wicket just when they ..... to be doing so well, and that led to their eventual defeat.
A. seem B. seems
C. have seemed D. seemed

17. In high school many of us never realised the importance that grammar would ..... in later life.
A. plays B. played
C. play D. have played

18. I was ...... at his colossal lack of knowledge about the Continent of Africa.
A. astounded B. astounding
C. have astounded D. had astounded

19. The veracity of the Minister's statement cannot be ...... by people who have no access to official records.
A. verify B. verifies
C. verified D. have verified

20. You haven't had your lunch yet, ... you?
A. are B. aren't
C. have D. haven't

21. A woman came in with a baby who, she said, ... a safety pin.
A. was just swallowing B. swallowed
C. had just swallowed D. just swallowed

22. The telephone ..... several times before I answered it.
A. was ringing B. has rung
C. had rung D. would ring

23. An employment advertisement should ..... the number of vacancies.
A. specifies B. specify
C. be specifying D. have specified

24. A crescendo of metallic thuds arose from the market, where the iron-smiths were ..... the pieces of metals.
A. hammers B. to hammer
C. hammering D. having hammered

25. Ambition is one of those passions which are never ..... .
A. satisfy B. satisfies
C. satisfying D. satisfied

26. Like any other country India ...... its fair share of superstitions.
A. has B. have
C. had D. having

27. The miser ..... avidly at the pile of gold coins in front of him.
A. gaze B. gazes
C. gazed D. has gazed

28. The pilot ..... about the storm before he took off.
A. has been warned B. have been warned
C. had been warned D. was warned

29. On account of the dearth of grass on the arid plains the cattle became ..... .
A. amaciated B. amaciating
C. amaciate D. amaciates

30. I ..... a herd of cows in the field.
A. sees B. saw
C. seeing D. has seen

31. Besides other provisions, that shopkeeper ..... in cosmetics too.
A. deals B. deal
C. dealing D. has deal

32. That rule ..... applicable to everyone.
A. be B. were
C. is D. are

33. I ...... revenge on you.
A. take B. taking
C. shall take D. takes

34. The ruling party .... its own house in order.
A. put B. shall have to put
C. will have to put D. have to put

35. To all intents and purposes, the manager ..... the master of the firm.
A. be B. is
C. are D. were

36. He ...... to prison for his crime.
A. sent B. send
C. has sent D. was sent

37. Restoration of old paintings .... a job for the experts.
A. is B. are
C. has D. have

38. Once he ..... the agreement, he won't be able to back out.
A. sign B. signing
C. has signed D. had signed

39. She ..... a brief appearance at the end of the party.
A. put on B. put in
C. put across D. put up

40. The battalion operating from the mountain was able to ..... three enemy divisions.
A. tie up B. tie down
C. tie on D. tie with

ANSWERS

1	2	3	4	5	6	7	8	9	10
C	C	A	A	C	B	D	A	C	A
11	**12**	**13**	**14**	**15**	**16**	**17**	**18**	**19**	**20**
A	C	B	C	B	D	C	A	C	C
21	**22**	**23**	**24**	**25**	**26**	**27**	**28**	**29**	**30**
C	C	B	C	D	A	C	C	A	B
31	**32**	**33**	**34**	**35**	**36**	**37**	**38**	**39**	**40**
A	C	C	C	B	D	A	C	B	B

★ ★ ★

3

Articles and Determiners

ARTICLES

The family of the articles has only three members. They are : A, An and The. However, they fall under two groups :

(*a*) Definite Article

(*b*) Indefinite Article

'The' is known as definite article whereas 'a' and 'an' are known as indefinite articles.

Use of the Definite Article 'The'

'The' is used before:

1. The superlative degree, *e.g.*,
   He is the ablest man of the town.
   (ablest is a superlative degree)
2. The name of states, countries etc. having a descriptive name, *e.g.*,
   (*i*) The J & K is a small state. (J & K is a descriptive name)
   (*ii*) He lives in the U.S.A. (U.S.A. is a descriptive name)
   (But 'the Delhi' and 'the America' are wrong because neither Delhi nor America is a descriptive name)
3. The names of the scriptures, *e.g.*,
   The Gita is a holy book. (Gita is a scripture)
4. Name of newspapers, *e.g.*,
   The Tribune is published from Chandigarh.
5. Name of rivers, canals, seas, oceans, bays, gulfs, groups of islands etc., *e.g.*,
   (*i*) The Ganga is a holy river.
   (*ii*) The Indian Ocean is the deepest ocean.
   (*iii*) The Persian Gulf is a narrow gulf.
6. The name of famous buildings, *e.g.*,
   The Taj is one of the best buildings in India.
7. The names of nationals, sects and communities, *e.g.*,
   (*i*) The English defeated the Germans in the World War.
   (*ii*) The rich should help the poor.
   (*iii*) The Hindus believe in the caste system.
8. Proper nouns used as common nouns, *e.g.*,
   (*i*) Kalidas is the Shakespeare of India.
   (*ii*) Delhi is the London of India.
9. Famous historical events, *e.g.*,
   The Industrial Revolution changed the face of England.
10. The directions and the celestial bodies, *e.g.*,
    The sun rises in the east.
11. Titles, *e.g.*,
    Akbar, the Great was loved by his subjects.

Do not use 'the':

1. Before languages :
   The English is an international language. (Incorrect)
   English is an international language. (Correct)
2. Before the names of games, *e.g.*,
   The hockey is a popular game. (Incorrect)
   Hockey is a popular game. (Correct)

Use of the Indefinite Articles 'A' and 'An'

'A' is used before:

1. All singular common nouns beginning with a consonant, *e.g.*,
   (*i*) A boy sings a song.
   (*ii*) A black and a white cow were grazing in the field.
2. If a word begins with a vowel but gives the sound of a consonant, 'a' should be used before it, *e.g.*,
   (*i*) He was helped in his work by a European.
   (*ii*) He is a one-eyed man.
   (*iii*) It is a useful work.

'An' is used as follows:

1. All singular common nouns beginning with a vowel (*i.e.*, a, e, i, o, u), *e.g.*,
   (*i*) He is an artist.
   (*ii*) He is an old man.
   (*iii*) I intend to buy an umbrella.
2. If a word starts with a consonant but gives the sound of a vowel, 'an' should be used before it, *e.g.*,
   (*i*) Brutus is an honourable man.
   (*ii*) He is an honour to his profession.
   (*iii*) He is an L.L.B.
   (*iv*) He is an M.A.
   (*v*) You will reach there in an hour.

DETERMINERS

Determiners are actually Adjectives. They are always followed by nouns.

Determiners are of the following kinds:

1. Demonstrative Determiners
e.g., this, that, these, those

2. Possessive Determiners
e.g., my, our, your, his, her, its, their

3. Quantitative Determiners
e.g., some, any, much, enough, sufficient, whole, a little the little, little, all, both

4. Numerical Determiners
e.g., a few, some, few, the few, any, several, many, no, etc
One, two, three ... (Cardinals)
First, second, third ... (Ordinals)

5. Distributive Determiners
e.g., either, neither

MULTIPLE CHOICE QUESTIONS

Directions (Q. No. 1-20): *Fill in the blanks with suitable articles. If no article is required, choose option 'D'.*

1. Please give me .... orange.
A. a B. an
C. the D. No article

2. ...... boyhood of Rahul was full of happy events.
A. A B. An
C. The D. No article

3. I daily read .... Indian Express.
A. a B. an
C. the D. No article

4. My brother bought .... new car yesterday.
A. a B. an
C. the D. No article

5. Many valuable herbs are found on ..... Himalayas.
A. a B. an
C. the D. No article

6. .... Ganga is a sacred river.
A. A B. An
C. The D. No article

7. .... Mahabharata is the longest epic.
A. A B. An
C. The D. No article

8. ...... rich should help the poor.
A. A B. An
C. The D. No article

9. .... more you sing, the happier we feel.
A. A B. An
C. The D. No article

10. The countries which lie near ...... equator keep high temperature.
A. a B. an
C. the D. No article

11. My friend plays ...... violin perfectly well.
A. a B. an
C. the D. No article

12. My uncle is ..... MA.
A. a B. an
C. the D. No article

13. I shall board ...... Flying Mail.
A. a B. an
C. the D. No article

14. John is ...... Newton of our class.
A. a B. an
C. the D. No article

15. Rohit daily eats ...... egg.
A. a B. an
C. the D. No article

16. I have ...... white and a black cow.
A. a B. an
C. the D. No article

17. What ...... beautiful bird it is!
A. a B. an
C. the D. No article

18. She is ...... best player of tennis in our school.
A. a B. an
C. the D. No article

19. ......Yamuna passes through Delhi.
A. A
B. An
C. The
D. No article

20. ...... Nile is the longest river.
A. A
B. An
C. The
D. No article

Directions (Q. No. 21-40): *In the following questions choose the correct options to fill in the blanks.*

21. .... dogs were barking at the strangers.
A. Some
B. Any
C. Much
D. Less

22. The girl bought her father .... juice.
A. few
B. some
C. any
D. many

23. You should take .... honey everyday.
A. any
B. many
C. a little
D. a few

24. .... boy was punished by the teacher.
A. Either
B. All
C. Any
D. Many

25. .... girl was asked to join the army.
A. None
B. Neither
C. All
D. Any

26. .... water in the jug has been drunk by Mohan.
A. The little
B. The few
C. A few
D. Few

27. I shall play .... piano at the party.
A. some
B. any
C. the
D. few

28. .... labourers were found dead in the mine.
A. Any
B. Fewer
C. Many
D. Less

29. Could I borrow .... umbrella?
A. our
B. your
C. yours
D. my

30. My brother is standing in the .... row.
A. any
B. many
C. some
D. first

31. Give me .... rice.
A. some
B. few
C. a few
D. any

32. .... sheep grazing on the slope of the hill had gone away.
A. Any
B. The few
C. This
D. Much

33. Have you got .... magazines to read?
A. all
B. much
C. some
D. little

34. I have .... money that I want to invest in shares.
A. any
B. much
C. less
D. some

35. There is .... owl on the branch of the tree.
A. a
B. the
C. an
D. some

36. My brother is .... MBA.
A. a
B. an
C. the
D. any

37. Have you got .... cheese?
A. some
B. many
C. a few
D. few

38. No, I have not got .... cheese.
A. many
B. few
C. any
D. some

39. There is only .... milk left in the bottle.
A. enough
B. few
C. much
D. a little

40. There is .... hope of his recovery.
A. any
B. little
C. many
D. few

ANSWERS

1	2	3	4	5	6	7	8	9	10
B	C	C	A	C	C	C	C	C	C
11	12	13	14	15	16	17	18	19	20
C	B	C	C	B	A	A	C	C	C
21	22	23	24	25	26	27	28	29	30
A	B	C	A	B	A	C	C	B	D
31	32	33	34	35	36	37	38	39	40
A	B	C	D	C	B	A	C	D	B

★ ★ ★

4

Prepositions

A *Preposition* is a word which is placed before a noun or a pronoun to show its relation to some other word in the sentence.

(*i*) I saw a goat *in* the field.

(*ii*) I am fond *of* hot coffee.

In sentence (*i*), the word *in* shows the relation between two things—*goat* and *field*.

In sentence (*ii*), the word *of* shows the relation between the attribute expressed by the adjective *fond* and *tea*.

The words *in* and *of* are here used as prepositions.

Use of Important Prepositions

1. Among, Between

'**Among**' is used for more than two persons or things; '**Between**' is used only for two.

Examples:

(*i*) Distribute these sweets *among* the poor students of the class.

(*ii*) Distribute these books *between* Ram and Shyam.

2. Among, In

'**Among**' is used before collective plural nouns. '**In**' is used before collective singular nouns.

Examples:

(*i*) I found him standing *among* the crowd.

(*ii*) I saw him in the crowd.

3. Beside, Besides

'**Beside**' means 'by the side of'; '**Besides**' means 'in addition to'.

Examples:

(*i*) The daughter was sitting *beside* her mother.

(*ii*) *Besides* his relatives, he invited his friends also.

4. In, Within

'**In**' means at the expiry of a period of time in future, '**Within**' means before the expiry of a period of time in any tense.

Examples:

(*i*) She will return *in* a week.

(*ii*) I shall finish my work *within* a weak.

5. On, Upon

'**On**' is used for things at rest; '**Upon**' is used for things in motion.

Examples:

(*i*) He is sitting *on* the floor.

(*ii*) The dog sprang *upon* the table.

6. By, With

'**By**' denotes the agent or doer; '**With**' denotes the instrument with which anything is done.

Examples:

(*i*) The bird was killed *by* the hunter with an arrow.

(*ii*) He beat the dog *with* a stick.

(*iii*) I shall reach here *by* five o'clock.

7. After, In

'**After**' means at the end of a period of time in the past; '**In**' means at the end of a period of time in future.

Examples:

(*i*) I shall return your book *in* a week.

(*ii*) He returned the book *after* a week.

8. For, From, Since

'**For**' is used before a noun denoting a period of time with all the tenses. '**From**' is used before a noun or phrase denoting a point of time, it is used in all the tenses. '**Since**' is used before a noun or phrase denoting some point of time and is always preceded by a verb in the perfect continuous tense or third form of a verb.

Examples:

(*i*) We have been playing cards *for* two hours.

(*ii*) She stayed with her uncle *from* the 15th of March to the 15th of May.

(*iii*) I have been reading this book *since* morning.

9. Above, Over

'**Above**' means 'higher from'; **Over** is used in the following four senses:

(*i*) In the sense of 'above', *e.g.*,

At noon, the sun is *over* our heads.

(*ii*) In the sense of 'beyond', *e.g.*,

I cannot get *over* my disappointment.

(*iii*) In the sense of 'Superiority', *e.g.*,
God *over* all blesses for ever more.

(*iv*) In the sense of 'Conclusion', *e.g.*,
It is all *over* with me.

10. At, Towards

'**At**' denotes the idea of aim; '**Towards**' denotes the idea of destination.

Examples:

(*i*) He threw the stone *at* the cat.

(*ii*) He went *towards* the house.

11. At, In, On

(*i*) '**At**' is used with small towns and villages.

Examples :

(*a*) He was born *at* Sonepat.

(*b*) He lives *at* village Bangra.

(*ii*) '**At**' is used before a noun denoting a definite point of time.

Example:

He called on me *at* 9 p.m. yesterday.

(*iii*) '**In**' is used with the names of big cities, provinces and countries.

Examples:

(*a*) His father lives *in* England.

(*b*) His younger brother lives *in* Lucknow.

(*iv*) '**In**' is used before the names of months and years.

Example:

His elder sister was born *in* 1972 *in* the month of May.

(*v*) '**On**' is used with dates and names of days.

Examples :

(*a*) I joined college *on* the 26th April.

(*b*) He will leave for Kolkata *on* Wednesday next.

Important Information

1. '**In**' is also used in the following phrases :
In the morning; In the evening, In winter, In summer.
2. '**In**' also denotes a place inside anything, *e.g.*,
He travelled *in* a crowded bus.
3. '**At**' is used in the following phrases :
At home, *At* the station, *At* work, *At* play.

12. Below, Beneath

'**Below**' means 'of lower level in position, dignity and expectation' etc. '**Beneath**' means 'under'.

Examples:

(*i*) It is *below* my dignity to talk to her.

(*ii*) They rested *beneath* the shade of a tree.

13. In, Into, To

'**In**' expresses Rest or Motion inside anything. '**Into**' expresses Motion towards the inside of anything or change from one medium to another. '**To**' denotes motion from one place to another.

Examples:

(*i*) The boys are *in* the room.

(*ii*) Translate this passage from English *into* Hindi.

(*iii*) Every morning he goes *to* the temple.

14. Till, By, Of, Off

'**Till**' means upto or not earlier than.

'**By**' means not later than.

'**Of**' shows cause, source, separation, quality, contents, possession, apposition, point of reference, space in time etc.

'**Off**' shows separation at a near distance, and detached condition.

Consider the following examples:

(*i*) I shall work *till* 5 a.m.

(*ii*) Asha died *of* cancer.

(*iii*) The nib *of* the pen is made *of* gold.

(*iv*) He presented me a bottle *of* perfume.

(*v*) Our principal is a man *of* principles.

(*vi*) He lived in the house *of* his friend.

(*vii*) *By* this time tomorrow, I'll have finished my job.

(*viii*) My house is *off* the road.

(*ix*) The book fell *off* the table.

MULTIPLE CHOICE QUESTIONS

Directions: *Tick the correct preposition for the blank in each of the following sentences.*

1. He applied ...... the manager.
A. for B. to
C. with D. by

2. Trust ...... God and do the right.
A. in B. for
C. to D. with

3. She is worthy ...... a prize.
A. with B. for
C. to D. of

4. Mr. Gomes has no taste ...... music.
A. of B. for
C. with D. to

5. You are hard ...... hearing.
A. at B. of
C. with D. for

6. He is sure ...... his success.
A. for B. with
C. on D. of

7. Preeti was warned ...... the danger ahead.
A. for B. at
C. of D. about

8. I am thankful ...... you for a good advice.
A. for B. with
C. to D. of

9. Deepak would not surrender .... the police.
A. with B. to
C. for D. on

10. The small plant in your lawn is very sensitive .... touch.
A. on B. with
C. to D. about

11. Divya was sure to succeed ..... the examination.
A. for B. in
C. to D. with

12. Geeta was jealous ...... Ravina's beauty.
A. to B. with
C. for D. of

13. He was ignorant ..... what was happening there.
A. for B. of
C. to D. with

14. Your pen is inferior ...... mine.
A. than B. with
C. from D. to

15. Reenu is no match ...... Meenu.
A. to B. for
C. with D. upon

16. It is necessary ...... you to apply for this job.
A. on B. with
C. for D. to

17. Be loyal ...... your country.
A. for B. to
C. on D. with

18. Mukesh is junior ...... me.
A. than B. to
C. from D. of

19. Deepika was innocent ...... the crime.
A. of B. with
C. from D. to

20. I am desirous.... joining the Indian cricket team.
A. for B. of
C. to D. on

21. Pradeep is not eligible ...... the post.
A. to B. on
C. upon D. for

22. Does she believe ...... God?
A. to B. for
C. in D. over

23. Mr. Posh was charged..... the murder of his aunt.
A. for B. with
C. on D. to

24. Tagore is famous (or popular) ...... Indians.
A. for B. with
C. to D. towards

25. Kalidasa is famous ...... his drama the *Shakuntalam*.
A. for B. with
C. on D. about

26. He applied ...... the post of a teacher.
A. to B. on
C. for D. at

27. I differ ...... you in this matter.
A. from B. with
C. for D. above

28. My pen differs ...... yours.
A. with B. from
C. for D. upon

29. The air escaped out ...... the balloon.
A. from B. of
C. to D. under

30. I am confident ...... success.
A. of B. to
C. from D. about

ANSWERS

1	2	3	4	5	6	7	8	9	10
B	A	D	B	B	D	D	D	B	D
11	**12**	**13**	**14**	**15**	**16**	**17**	**18**	**19**	**20**
B	D	B	D	B	D	B	B	A	B
21	**22**	**23**	**24**	**25**	**26**	**27**	**28**	**29**	**30**
D	C	B	B	A	C	B	B	A	A

★★★

5

Synonyms & Antonyms

SYNONYMS

Ardent	eager, avid
Arduous	difficult, troublesome, tough
Aspire	hope, wish
Astonish	amaze, confound
Authentic	genuine, actual
Awesome	astonishing, amazing, fearful
Ban	bar, debar
Bare	denuded exposed
Bear	carry, bring
Beautiful	attractive, charming
Becoming	attractive, graceful
Benchmark	model, example
Benevolent	bountiful, benign
Bewitch	attract, captivate
Boisterous	noisy, clamorous
Bonny	handsome, attractive, healthy
Brave	bold, courageous
Break	crack, separate
Brief	laconic, curt
Bright	shining, flashing
Brisk	active, lively
Broad	generous, capacious
Build	assemble, construct
Busy	brisk, active
Cajole	coax, dupe
Call	announce, shout
Calm	peaceful, mild
Candid	fair, frank
Capacious	spacious, roomy
Care	anxiety, concern
Catchy	attractive, captivating
Charming	attractive, appealing
Chief	main, key
Clean	pure, spotless

Clever	apt, intelligent
Clumsy	bungling, awkward
Colossal	giant, enormous
Compact	dense, condensed
Conspicuous	clear, apparent
Cordial	agreeable, cheerful
Credulous	trustful, unsuspicious
Cruel	atrocious, barbarous
Dangerous	alarming, hazardous
Dazzling	glorious, radiant
Deceive	cheat, betray
Deep	profound, bottomless
Delicate	fragile, weak, tender
Delight	ecstasy, happiness
Deny	disprove, rebuf
Eager	ardent, avid
Effective	active, capable
Elegant	beautiful, artistic
Emerge	arise, appear
Encouraging	cheerful, promising
Enormous	colossal, gigantic
Faded	dim, dull
Fair	clean, honest
Fascinating	attractive, bewitching
Foolish	imprudent, senseless
Frank	candid, ingenuous
Garrulous	chattering, gossiping
Generous	liberal, benevolent
Genuine	bonafide, authentic
Gloomy	dark, sad
Glorious	magnificent, excellent
Great	colossal, enormous
Haughty	assuming, arrogant
Hefty	big, robust

Humane	benign, gentle
Humble	modest, meek
Idle	lazy, inactive
Illogical	faulty, incorrect
Immense	enormous, colossal
Impudent	bold, brazen
Indolent	lazy, sluggish
Intelligent	clever, bright
Keen	ardent, avid
Kind	benevolent, benign
Laconic	brief, curt
Leading	dominating, chief
Lively	agile, active
Lucid	evident, clear
Magnificent	excellent, glorious

Morose	gloomy, sad
Neglect	disdain, ignore
Obedient	submissive, amenable
Obscure	cloudy, vague
Obstinate	stubborn, firm
Opulent	lavish, affluent
Overnight	fault, mistake
Peaceful	harmonious, friendly
Polite	humble, civil
Prolific	teeming, bountiful
Radiant	bright, glorious
Rejoicing	delight, cheer
Sad	gloomy, depressed
Select	choose, opt
Silence	calm, peace

ANTONYMS

Abhor	Admire, love, adore
Adore	hate, abhor
Alert	listless, careless
Annex	remove, unfasten
Apex	bottom, nadir
Ban	allow, permit
Beautiful	awful, ugly
Benign	stern, harsh
Boisterous	quiet, peaceful
Brief	lengthy, extensive
Calm	stir, agitate
Careful	careless, unconcerned
Clear	cloudy, vague
Clever	clumsy, boring
Colossal	diminutive, small
Compatible	incompatible, inapt
Courageous	cowardly, timid
Damaging	useful, advantageous
Dangerous	safe, harmless
Deceit	honesty, candour
Delicate	harsh, indelicate
Deny	admit, accept
Dim	bright, clear
Eager	impassive, lazy
Efficient	inefficient, inept
Emerge	enter, fall
Encourage	deter, depress
Engaging	repulsive, unattractive
Fair	unfair, prejudiced
Fake	genuine, bonafide
Fascinating	unattractive, disgusting

Ferocious	mild, gentle
Gallant	cowardly, fearful
Gentle	aggressive, harsh
Gigantic	tiny, puny
Glorious	dull, dim
Handy	clumsy, inept
Happy	unhappy, gloomy
Hard	soft, flexible
Honest	dishonest, unfair
Huge	minute, puny
Idle	active, busy
Illogical	logical, coherent
Incorrect	correct, accurate
Indecent	decent, modest
Innocent	cunning, dishonest
Kind	unkind, cruel
Lazy	active, diligent
Like	unlike, diverse
Lovable	hateful, abhorrent
Major	minor, unimportant
Meek	arrogant, stubborn
Merry	sad, gloomy
Morose	happy, delightful
Nadir	apex, Zenith
Nonsense	sense, wisdom
Object	admire, accept
Obscure	clear, vivid
Overbearing	humble, modest
Peaceful	agitated, disturbed
Playful	gloomy, morose
Polite	impolite, ill-mannered

Proficient	incompetent, unskilled
Promising	unpromising, discouraging
Realistic	unrealistic, fanciful
Refined	unrefined, boorish
Reject	accept, select
Robust	feeble, frail
Secure	insecure, unsafe
Sensible	senseless, stupid
Sluggish	energetic, brisk
Tempting	untempting, unattractive
Tepid	zealous, eager
Timid	arrogant, bold
True	untrue, false
Ungainly	elegant, attractive
Unmannerly	mannerly, polite
Valid	invalid, illegal
Verbose	curt, brief
Violent	calm, quiet

MULTIPLE CHOICE QUESTIONS

Directions (Qs. No. 1 to 40): *In the following questions, each word is followed by four options A, B, C & D. Select the option which best expresses the meaning of the given word.*

1. ABSURD
A. Foolish B. Simple
C. Courageous D. Silly

2. ABANDON
A. Lose B. Profit
C. Vacate D. Foil

3. CAJOLE
A. Pause B. Lenient
C. Blast D. Lure

4. COMBAT
A. Fight B. Conflict
C. Shoot D. Quarrel

5. LAMENT
A. Condone B. Console
C. Complain D. Contribution

6. DEBACLE
A. Disgrace B. Defeat
C. Collapse D. Decline

7. SHIVER
A. Fear B. Tremble
C. Shake D. Ache

8. TORTURE
A. Terror B. Harassment
C. Torment D. Tranquility

9. LAUDABLE
A. Lovable B. Commendable
C. Profitable D. Oblivious

10. FIXED
A. Sterile B. Static
C. Stubborn D. Parennial

11. QUEER
A. Unfamiliar B. Cute
C. Curious D. Strange

12. SUFFICIENT
A. Fit B. Proper
C. Adequate D. Vast

13. GLOSS
A. Brightness B. Soothing
C. Rubbing D. Miracle

14. LONGING
A. Prune B. Apathy
C. Curtail D. Craving

15. JEER
A. Applaud B. Magnanimity
C. Avoid D. Scoff

16. ZENITH
A. Minimum B. Nadir
C. Plant D. Peak

17. GARB
A. Distort B. Dress
C. Trivial D. Rage

18. ABHOR
A. Rude B. Reconcile
C. Crave D. Detest

19. YIELD
A. Shun B. Incisive
C. Retain D. Surrender

20. YOKE
A. Twist B. Release
C. Link D. Extra

21. VENT
A. End B. Strode
C. Opening D. Cure

22. INDICT
A. Allege B. Condemn
C. Warn D. Accuse

23. VENUE
A. Agenda B. Time
C. Distance D. Place

24. FAKE
A. Loyal B. Original
C. Trustworthy D. Imitation

25. PONDER
A. Pollution B. Evaluation
C. Anticipation D. Think

26. BRIEF
A. Limited B. Small
C. Little D. Short

27. GARRULITY
A. Credulity B. Senility
C. Loquaciousness D. Speciousness

28. FURORE
A. Excitement B. Worry
C. Flux D. Anteroom

29. NEUTRAL
A. Unbiased B. Non-aligned
C. Undecided D. Indifferent

30. LAMENT
A. Complain B. Comment
C. Condone D. Console

31. ADVERSITY
A. Failure B. Helplessness
C. Misfortune D. Crisis

32. TURN UP
A. Land up B. Show up
C. Crop up D. Come up

33. DEIFY
A. Flatter B. Challenge
C. Worship D. Face

34. ERROR
A. Misadventure B. Misgiving
C. Ambiguity D. Blunder

35. SHALLOW
A. Artificial B. Superficial
C. Foolish D. Worthless

36. MASSACRE
A. Murder B. Stab
C. Assassinate D. Slaughter

37. COMBAT
A. Conflict B. Quarrel
C. Feud D. Fight

38. VORACIOUS
A. Wild B. Hungry
C. Angry D. Quick

39. IMPROMPTU
A. Offhand B. Unimportant
C. Unreal D. Effective

40. RABBLE
A. Mob B. Noise
C. Roar D. Rubbish

Directions (Qs. Nos. 41 to 75): *In the following questions, each word is followed by four options A, B, C and D. Select the option which looks like the antonym of the given word.*

41. TRAGIC
A. Dramatic B. Strong
C. Gentle D. Comic

42. ORAL
A. Verbal B. Sane
C. Minor D. Written

43. ADMIRE
A. Hate B. Unlike
C. Dislike D. Enough

44. VIOLENT
A. Gentle B. Savage
C. Haughty D. Decline

45. ADVERSITY
A. Windfall B. Inprosperity
C. Prosperity D. Slave

46. GENUINE
A. Spurious B. Obscure
C. Countless D. Apathetic

47. GRUDGE
A. Essence B. Guile
C. Goodwill D. Ill-will

48. STIFF
A. Soft B. Courteous
C. Lively D. Flexible

49. VANITY
A. Conceit B. Pride
C. Ostentious D. Humility

50. FRONT
A. Upper B. Unusual
C. Back D. Rear

51. TANGIBLE
A. Solid B. Actual
C. Concrete D. Ethereal

52. ATTRACT
A. Lured B. Longing
C. Repel D. Disguise

53. COMFORT
A. Discomfort B. Discontent
C. Uncomfort D. Miscomfort

54. WELCOME
A. Repel B. Accept
C. Resist D. Fight

55. TACTFUL
A. Naive B. Loose
C. Strict D. Uncivilized

56. DUTIFUL
A. Harmful B. Watchful
C. Forgetful D. Remiss

57. RIGID
A. Flux B. Adoptable
C. Yielding D. Adaptable

58. RARE
A. Petty B. Poor
C. Small D. Common

59. ZEAL
A. Despair B. Calmness
C. Passiveness D. Indifference

60. FAMILIAR
A. Dangerous B. Strange
C. Friendly D. Unpleasant

61. AMUSED
A. Abused B. Astonished
C. Saddened D. Jolted

62. SHRINK
A. Spoil B. Expand
C. Stretch D. Contract

63. GENUINE
A. Fraudulent B. Direct
C. Candid D. Forthright

64. VIOLENT
A. Tame B. Harmless
C. Humble D. Gentle

65. PATCHY
A. Clear B. Simple
C. Attractive D. Uniform

66. STRINGENT
A. General B. Vehement
C. Lenient D. Magnanimous

67. FLIMSY
A. Frail B. Filthy
C. Firm D. Flippant

68. BUSY
A. Occupied B. Engrossed
C. Relaxed D. Engaged

69. ADAPTABLE
A. Adoptable B. Flexible
C. Yielding D. Rigid

70. LOVE
A. Villainy B. Hatred
C. Compulsion D. Force

71. BALANCE
A. Disbalance B. Misbalance
C. Debalance D. Imbalance

72. RELINQUISH
A. Abdicate B. Renounce
C. Possess D. Deny

73. MOUNTAIN
A. Plain B. Plateau
C. Precipice D. Valley

74. FICKLE
A. Courageous B. Sincere
C. Steadfast D. Humble

75. PERENNIAL
A. Frequent B. Regular
C. Lasting D. Rare

ANSWERS

1	**2**	**3**	**4**	**5**	**6**	**7**	**8**	**9**	**10**
D	C	D	A	C	C	B	C	B	B
11	**12**	**13**	**14**	**15**	**16**	**17**	**18**	**19**	**20**
D	C	A	D	D	D	B	D	D	C
21	**22**	**23**	**24**	**25**	**26**	**27**	**28**	**29**	**30**
C	C	D	D	D	D	C	A	A	A
31	**32**	**33**	**34**	**35**	**36**	**37**	**38**	**39**	**40**
C	B	C	D	B	D	D	B	A	A
41	**42**	**43**	**44**	**45**	**46**	**47**	**48**	**49**	**50**
D	D	C	A	C	A	C	D	D	D
51	**52**	**53**	**54**	**55**	**56**	**57**	**58**	**59**	**60**
D	C	A	C	A	D	D	D	D	B
61	**62**	**63**	**64**	**65**	**66**	**67**	**68**	**69**	**70**
C	C	A	D	D	C	C	C	D	B
71	**72**	**73**	**74**	**75**					
D	C	D	C	D					

★ ★ ★

6

Comprehension Passages

Directions: *Read the following passages and answer the questions given below each.*

PASSAGE-1

There is no general agreement about how the planets were formed. The most widely accepted theory is that about 5000 millions years ago swirling clouds of matter began to condense. Through the action of centrifugal force, the heavier molecules were concentrated near the centre of the eddies and the lighter, gaseous material was thrown out towards the periphery. Such is the theory. What is known is that nine satellites began orbiting round the sun. These are the planets.

The planet on which man lives is the third closest to the sun, with the third shortest orbit. It also has something none of the others has—an atmosphere that can support life in all the manifold forms that exist on our planet. There may be satellites circling other stars in other parts of the universe that have the right ingredients for some sort of life to evolve, but the earth is the only one in the solar system.

1. According to the passage, the planets are
A. nothing but condensed clouds
B. a collection of gaseous material
C. a collection of condensed swirling material
D. a collection of centrifugal forces

2. The theory of the formation of the planets
A. is generally agreed upon by everyone
B. is a debatable one
C. covers a very wide area
D. is fairly well-known

3. A planet is a 'heavenly body' which moves round
A. the sun
B. a star
C. a satellite of the solar system
D. the universe

4. One essential difference between the earth and the other planets is that
A. the atmosphere of the earth makes possible the presence of life on it
B. the earth draws the heavier molecules into its centre through the action of centrifugal force
C. only the earth is on the periphery of the solar system
D. the earth has the capacity to come into closer contact with the sun

5. The writer claims that the life-supporting atmosphere
A. is there on other planets in the solar system
B. may be there on the other satellites in the universe
C. may evolve on other satellite circling other stars in the universe
D. cannot evolve anywhere outside the earth

PASSAGE-2

Through the break between the trees, she looked into one of the lighted windows above the shop. She could see the cartons of biscuits neatly piled near the far wall. Against her conscious wishes Cissy's saliva glands started pumping the fluid into her mouth. She felt her heart beating strongly from the top of her throat into the back of her mouth. There is nobody, she thought. I can dash in and take a box and dash out again. I know it is a sin but the Lord will not punish us if we are so hungry.

1. The whole passage is a description of
A. Cissy's courage for stealing
B. Cissy's plans before stealing
C. Cissy's temptation before stealing
D. Cissy's greed for stealing

2. How do you know that Cissy felt guilty?
A. She knew what she was doing was morally wrong
B. She felt her heart pounding inside her chest
C. She was saying her prayers before she went to steal
D. She knew that she was about to do something selfish

3. Why did her heart beat strongly?
A. She thought nobody was watching her
B. She was thinking of stealing the biscuits
C. She was eager to taste the biscuits
D. She was ill and was running temperature

4. How was Cissy able to see the cartons of biscuits?
   A. She had very good eyesight
   B. She was able to smell the biscuits
   C. She saw another child eating biscuits
   D. She was aided by a light in the room

5. What was Cissy's reaction when she saw the biscuit cartons?
   A. She wanted to eat all the biscuits
   B. She felt like vomiting
   C. Her mouth started watering
   D. She thought of all the toffees she had eaten

PASSAGE-3

A certain Ameer was on a voyage in his ship when a great storm arose. One of the slaves on board, who had never been to sea, began to wail and cry out in fear. This went on for sometime and no one could silence him. In anger the Ameer asked, 'Is there no one here who can silence this wretched coward?'

A philosopher, who happened to be a passenger, said, 'I think I can quiet this man, Sir, if you give me full permission to do as I please with him.'

'Go ahead,' said the Ameer, 'you have my permission'.

1. What kind of prose is used in this extract?
   A. Informative   B. Argumentative
   C. Lyrical   D. Narrative

2. The verb 'to wail' means
   A. to smile   B. to call
   C. to weep   D. to speak

3. The word 'voyage' means
   A. travelling by sea
   B. walking on foot
   C. riding a horse
   D. swimming in sea

4. The slave was afraid because
   A. the Ameer was about to beat him
   B. there was a storm in the sea
   C. he was about to be thrown into the sea
   D. the journey was not coming to an end

5. The philosopher volunteered to
   A. throw off the slave
   B. persuade the slave
   C. silence the slave
   D. kill the slave

PASSAGE-4

We stand poised precariously and challengingly on the razor's edge of destiny. We are now at the mercy of atom bombs and the like which would destroy us completely if we fail to control them wisely. And wisdom in this crisis means sensitiveness to the basic values of life; it means a vivid realisation that we are literally living in one world where we must either swim together or sink together. We cannot afford to tamper with man's single-minded loyalty to peace and international understanding. Anyone who does it is a traitor not only to man's past and present, but also to his future, because he is mortgaging the destiny of unborn generations.

1. Form the tone and style of the passage it appears that the writer is
   A. unware of the global power situation
   B. a humanist with a clear foresight
   C. a prose writer with a fascination for images and metaphors
   D. a traitor who wishes to mortgage the destiny of future generations

2. The phrase "razor's edge of destiny" stands for
   A. an enigma that cuts through the pattern of life like the edge of a razor
   B. a critical situation that foreordains the future
   C. a sharp line of division that marks the alternative courses of action in the future
   D. destiny having sharp edges

3. According to the writer "wisdom" in the present crisis means
   A. responsibility to the "unborn generations"
   B. awareness that we stand poised precariously on the razor's edge of destiny
   C. awareness of the basic values of life
   D. determination to ban nuclear weapons

4. The author is so concerned about the threat of nuclear weapons because he feels that
   A. his country is threatened by a nuclear power
   B. a nuclear war will destroy human civilisation
   C. all countries are interlinked and one cannot escape the consequences of what happens to another country
   D. the world is on the brink of disaster

5. The best way to escape complete annihilation is an atomic war is
   A. to ban nuclear weapons
   B. to turn to religion
   C. to work for international understanding and harmony
   D. to invent more powerful weapons

PASSAGE-5

The editorial policy of a popular daily is controlled by two chief factors. The first is the interest of the advertisers from whom it gets the money which enables it to keep up its large circulation. No widely circulated newspaper dare support a public policy, howsoever much in the national interest, that might conflict with the vested interests of its advertisers. On the other hand, any product that refuses to pay the advertising rates of a powerful national organ will be denounced, smashed and driven off the market. You are not allowed to use any product that dissociates itself from the advertising ring. All this is understandable, since big circulation spells bankruptcy if the paper has to depend on its sales for its revenue.

1. According to this passage, one of the chief factors that controls the editorial policy of a newspaper is
A. the interest of the nation
B. the interest of the reader
C. the interest of the advertisers
D. its cost of production

2. Big circulation spells bankruptcy if the paper depends on its sale for its revenue because
A. to retain its big circulation, it will have to be sold far below the cost of its production
B. the advertisers will not be there to support its cost production
C. the advertisers would drive it out of circulation
D. it will not be able to pursue the policy that would be in the interest of the nation

3. A widely circulated newspaper cannot support a public policy
A. if it is not in the national interest
B. even if it is in the national interest
C. if it supports the interest of the advertiser
D. unless it supports the interest of the advertiser

4. If a producer refuses to pay high rates of advertisement in a widely circulated newspaper
A. the circulation of the newspaper will decrease
B. the rival producers/advertisers will come forward with advertisements against that producer
C. the newspaper will see to it that the product of that producer is driven off the market
D. the newspaper will cut its number of pages to reduce its cost of production

5. The expression *"vested interests of its advertisers"* means
A. selfish motives of the advertisers
B. concerns securely possessed by the advertisers
C. something from which the advertisers get interest
D. something by which the advertisers interests are enhanced

PASSAGE-6

It was very hot. Suddenly at about 3 o'clock in the afternoon, there fell such an abundance of rain that 150 men of the grand guard, in order not to be submerged, were obliged to leave a large depression in which they were hidden. Much to their amazement there began to fall on the ground all about a considerable number of toads, the size of hazelnuts, which began to jump about in every direction. M. Gayet (the soldier who provided this information), who could not believe that these myriad reptiles fell with the rain, stretched out his handkerchief at the height of a man, his comrades holding the corners; they caught a considerable number of toads, most of which had the posterior part elongated into a tail, that is to say, in the tadpole state. During this rain storm, which lasted about half an hour, the men of the grand guard felt very distinctly on their hats and on their clothing the blows struck by falling toads. As a final proof of the reality of this phenomenon, M. Gayet reports that after the storm the three-cornered hats of the men of the guard held in their folds some of the reptiles.

1. A suitable title for this passage would be
A. A Mystery
B. A Rain of Toads
C. Long Time Ago
D. M. Gayet's Report

2. What proof does M. Gayet give to prove that what happened was real?
A. Toads were found in the depression
B. Soldiers felt the toads striking blows as they fell
C. 150 men of the grand guard swore it rained toads
D. Toads, were found in the guards' hats after the rain stopped

3. From where could this account have been taken?
A. A novel
B. A weather report
C. A newspaper
D. A pamphlet

4. The soldiers left their hiding places because they
A. were scared of toads
B. were ordered to
C. were getting wet
D. might have drowned there

5. M. Gayet and his friends caught the toads in
A. a handkerchief
B. their hats
C. their clothing
D. the depression

PASSAGE-7

Workers who repeat the same operation day after day can take no pleasure or pride in their work. Their chief pleasure in life is outside the factory. Their work is dull, and they spend their time with one eye on the clock. It is realised that modern work is often dull, and in some factories wireless set or a gramophone is turned on to provide music for the workers. The title of a common programme given by the British Broadcasting Corporation is "Music while you work". The provision of entertainment while the factory wheels are turning does not cause the work-people to neglect their duty; on the contrary, it increases output. In spite of various attempts to brighten the lives of workers, however, the average man in a factory is rather to be pitied than envied. The dullness of his life is one of the drawbacks of mass production.

1. The workers pass their time in the factory looking at the clock because
A. their work is dreary and uninteresting
B. their pleasure lies outside the factory
C. they wish to deceive the management
D. they want to get their salary without working

2. Some modern factories play radio or gramophone music for workers to
A. distract them from their work
B. reduce the dull nature of their work
C. make them forget the clock
D. cheer them up while working

3. Labourers doing only one type of work throughout their service
A. become experts in that type of work
B. are proud of their ability to do one type of work
C. do not like their work
D. take a lot of interest in their work

4. The modern system of mass production is responsible for
A. the dismal condition of labourers
B. the dullness of the life of the workers
C. the comfortable life of the labourers
D. the miserable condition of the labourers

5. Providing entertainment facilities to the workers when the factory work is going on may cause
A. the labourers to neglect their work
B. rise in the production quantity
C. the labourers to forget the monotony of work
D. a great fall in the output

PASSAGE-8

S.N. Bose is the only physicist whose name is linked with Einstein in all the textbooks of Physics. This is because he hit on a brilliant method whose value Einstein immediately recognised and proclaimed to the scientific world with all the prestige of his great name. In retrospect, it is now clear that even Einstein could not foresee the full power and application range of Bose's idea. Bose's work, along with its subsequent development by Fermi, provides the basis for dividing all the elementary particles of nuclear Physics into two categories—the *bosons* (after Bose) and the *fermions* after Fermi.

1. What Einstein really did for Bose was that
A. he allowed his name to be linked with S.N. Bose in all the textbooks of Physics
B. he fully recognised and proclaimed to the scientific world the importance of Bose's discovery
C. he eventually recognised and proclaimed to the scientific world the importance of Bose's discovery
D. he immediately, though not fully, recognised and proclaimed to the scientific world the importance of Bose's discovery

2. Bose and Fermi worked in the same field; Fermi's work
A. came before that of Bose
B. was published after that of Bose
C. came at the same time as that of Bose
D. led directly to Bose's discovery

3. The main contribution of S.N. Bose was that, he
A. alone divided the elementary particles into two new categories
B. in collaboration with Fermi, divided the elementary particles into two new categories
C. evolved a theory which was further developed by Fermi, and their research led to the division of the elementary particles into two new categories
D. discovered nuclear energy

4. The correct definition of 'Nuclear Physics' is that it is a branch of Physics that
A. involves the study of nuclear weapons
B. studies the application of nuclear energy
C. deals with atoms, their nuclear structure and behaviour
D. studies the nucleus or central part of all particles

5. Einstein endorsed the research done by Bose because he knew
A. it was an original work
B. it would bring about revolutionary changes in Nuclear Physics
C. it would have a powerful impact on other scientists
D. Bose was a dedicated scientist

PASSAGE-9

We are tempted to assume that technological progress is real progress and that material success is the criterion of civilisation. If the Eastern people become fascinated by machines and techniques and use them, as Western nations do, to build huge industrial organisations and large military establishments, they will get involved in power politics and drift into the danger of death. Scientific and technological civilisation brings great opportunities and great rewards but also great risks and temptations. Science and technology are neither good nor bad. They are not to be tabooed but tamed and assigned their proper place. They become dangerous only if they become idols.

1. According to the author, people think that real progress lies in
   A. material success and technological growth
   B. worshipping idols and having faith in them
   C. having large industries and political power
   D. taking risks and facing temptations
2. From the passage one gathers that the Eastern people must
   A. appreciate scientific achievements
   B. build huge industrial organisations
   C. avoid being controlled by machines and techniques of industrial production
   D. be fascinated by machines
3. According to the author, science and technology should be
   A. tabooed and eliminated from life
   B. used in a controlled and careful manner
   C. encouraged and liberally used
   D. made compulsory in education
4. According to the author, science and technology will bring benefits to
   A. only Western nations
   B. only Eastern countries
   C. nobody
   D. all, if tamed properly
5. According to the author, science and technology are
   A. totally harmless
   B. extremely dangerous
   C. to be treated as idols
   D. are useful, if they are not worshipped blindly

PASSAGE-10

The awareness of equal corruption will be a better emotional basis for the so-called multi-racial Commonwealth, of which much is made than its professed principle—the pursuit of common aims in world politics, aims which are so rarefied that a large volume of artificial political oxygen is needed to keep that body-politic breathing. After all, it cannot be denied that even the United States and the Russia are pursuing common aims in world affairs, such as peace, disarmament, democracy, technological progress, as well as freedom as understood by each. But that is not preventing them from doing things which might lead to the destruction or near destruction of mankind. Thus, common aims would seem to be very undependable as guarantees for goodwill and cooperation among nations. On the contrary, a frank admission of being equal sinners would at least encourage charity and discourage moral arrogance. That would be a better foundation for integration for international and multi-racial cooperation.

1. The Superpowers may claim to have the same laudable objectives, but
   A. do not work earnestly to achieve them
   B. undo each other's efforts
   C. still act against the interests of mankind
   D. do not see them in the right perspective
2. The Commonwealth is characterised by
   A. the failure of the constituents to
   B. the racial nature of its membership work for the same goals
   C. uniform lack of moral standards
   D. constant redefining of objectives
3. The thrust of the author's argument is that
   A. the Commonwealth has outlived its utility
   B. membership of the Commonwealth be restricted to the superpowers
   C. members are equally responsible for the present state of world politics
   D. international peace and cooperation are unattainable
4. International cooperation can come about, if
   A. nations become aware of their own failings and discard pride
   B. charitable organizations are encouraged
   C. different races are treated on the basis of equality
   D. nations guilty of immoral actions are exposed
5. Common goals are desirable, but these
   A. do not ensure international co-operation
   B. lead to unnecessary tensions
   C. encourage rivalry between superpowers
   D. lead to destruction of mankind

PASSAGE-11

There was a marked difference of quality between the personages who haunted the near bridge of brick and the personages who haunted the far one of stone. Those of lowest character preferred the former, adjoining the town; they did not mind the glare of the public eye. They had been of no account during their successes; and though they might feel dispirited, they had no sense of shame in their ruin. Instead of sighing at their adversaries they spat, and instead of saying the iron had entered into their souls they said they were down on their luck. The miserables, who would pause on the remoter bridge were of a politer stamp—persons who did not know how to get rid of the weary time. The eyes of this species were mostly directed over the parapet upon the running water below. While one on the downward bridge did not mind who saw him so and kept his back to the parapet to survey the passer-by, one on this never faced the road, never turned his head at coming footsteps, but, sensitive to his own condition, watched the current whenever a stranger approached, as if some strange fish interested him, though every finned thing had been poached out of the river years before.

1. People belonging to the lower strata, in their moments of distress
A. remembered their days of glory
B. dressed shabbily to earn sympathy
C. visited the brick-made bridge
D. felt ashamed of their failures

2. The two bridges were known
A. for their similar design
B. for being equi-distant from town
C. for being haunted places
D. for attracting dejected people to them

3. In this passage, the author is trying to
A. explain the differences between the construction of two bridges
B. describe the way different sections of people like to dress
C. explain the variety of ways in which strangers can be treated
D. describe how people of different classes behaved when unhappy

4. The attitude of the lowly and genteel towards strangers was
A. virtually the same
B. entirely different
C. completely indifferent
D. virulently hostile

5. The bridge of stone was frequented by
A. all the sections of society
B. those fond of fishing
C. the sophisticated but luckless
D. None of these

PASSAGE-12

When talking to a reporter early in the season, a coach tends to talk down the abilities of his new man. He does not want his team to become known as a favourite because, if the team loses, he will be criticised for not making the most of his material. Even when he knows he has a great team, a coach avoids favourable publicity. He realises that over-confidence, injuries, an error on the field or the better luck of his opponent may wreck any season.

1. When talking to a reporter, a coach usually
A. praises his team
B. highlights the qualities of the new members of the team
C. does not acquaint him with the full potentialities of the new players
D. derides his rival teams

2. If a favourite team loses the game, its fans
A. feel let down
B. accuse its members of lack of commitment
C. blame the coach for not providing necessary training
D. want to coach to be fired

3. If his team is elevated to the position of a favourite, it may
A. become over-confident
B. feel obliged to win the game
C. have enthusiastic fans in the field
D. easily intimidate its rivals

4. In spite of everything being favourite, a team may lose the game if its opponents
A. are smarter
B. have just as good material
C. are favoured by chance and circumstances
D. are more relaxed than it is

5. In spite of good players, a team may lose the game if
A. there is no coordination among its members
B. a few players get injured in the field
C. its morale is not high
D. it cannot understand the strategies of its opponents

PASSAGE-13

Though it may be inessential to the imagination, travelling is necessary for an understanding of men. Only with long experience and the opening of his wares on many a beach where his language is not spoken, will the merchant come to know the worth of what he carries and what is parochial and what is universal in his choice. Such delicate goods as justice, love and honour, courtesy and indeed all the things we care for, are valid everywhere but they are variously moulded and often differently handled and sometimes nearly unrecognisable if you meet them in a foreign land and the art of learning fundamental common values is perhaps the greatest gain of travelling to those who wish to live at ease among their fellows.

1. Travelling helps those who
A. wish to make money
B. want to learn foreign languages
C. wish to learn fundamental common values
D. want to resolve differences amongst people

2. When we meet other people while we travel, we learn to differentiate between
A. friends and foes
B. local and universal values
C. imagination and understanding
D. communities and nationalities

3. The things we care for are available in foreign lands in
A. some form or the other
B. unrecognisable forms
C. plenty
D. easily recognisable forms

4. The author terms justice, love, honour and courtesy as delicate goods because they are
A. fragile B. perishable
C. desirable D. important

5. According to the passage, travelling leads to
A. selling our wares to the others
B. establishing our superiority over foreigners
C. exploiting foreign lands
D. understanding human nature

PASSAGE-14

The first word-book to embody the ideals of the age was Nathaniel Bailey's *Universal Etymological Dictionary of the English Language,* originally published in 1721 and then, in a beautiful volume with illustrations by Flaxman, in 1731. This edition was the basis of Samuel Johnson's *Dictionary* of 1755; through Johnson, it influenced all subsequent lexicographical practice. The position of dictionary pioneer, commonly granted to Johnson or to Noah Webster, belongs in reality to one of the few geniuses lexicography ever produced: Nathaniel Bailey. Johnson extended Bailey's technique and also revised Bailey's crude etymologies on the basis of Francis Junius' book. Most Englishmen used the word *dictionary* as a mere synonym for Johnson's *Dictionary.* Being regarded as the ideal word-book, it continued in common use until 1990.

1. Nathaniel Bailey's *Dictionary* had
A. no influence on later dictionaries
B. a direct influence on later dictionaries
C. an indirect influence on later dictionaries
D. an influence on Francis Junius' *dictionary* only

2. Johnson's Dictionary was
A. an improvement upon Bailey's *Dictionary*
B. a simplified version of Bailey's *Dictionary*
C. nothing but a copy of Bailey's *Dictionary*
D. fundamentally different from Bailey's *Dictionary*

3. The publication of Johnson's dictionary was separated from the Flaxman edition of Bailey's dictionary by
A. 24 years B. 10 years
C. 125 years D. 34 years

4. In the 19th century most Englishmen used the word "dictionary" as a synonym for Johnson's *Dictionary* probably because
A. it was the oldest English dictionary
B. it was the only English dictionary published till then
C. it was more convenient for them to use this shortened form
D. it was the ideal and most commonly used dictionary

5. According to the author, the real pioneer of lexicography was
A. Noah Webster B. Samuel Johnson
C. Flaxman D. Nathaniel Bailey

PASSAGE-15

We stumbled slowly along in the darkness, with the black loom of the craggy hills around us, and the yellow speck of light burning steadily in front. There is nothing so deceptive as the distance of a light upon the pitch-dark night and sometimes the glimmer seemed to be far away upon the horizon and sometimes it might have been within a few yards from us. But at last we could see whence it came and then we knew that we were very close.

1. The passage as a whole indicates that the mission of the author and his companion was
A. to investigate the nature of the countryside
B. to detect the movements of suspicious characters
C. to study supernatural phenomena
D. to trace the light to its place of origin

2. The word "stumbled" in the first line suggests that the narrator and his friend
A. had very poor sight
B. were walking on an uneven road
C. had their attention fixed on the distant light
D. were trying to keep their movements secret

3. The last sentence suggests that when they discovered the source of the light,
A. they were surprised by its closeness
B. they were greatly relieved
C. they were very pleased
D. they were utterly disappointed

4. The author and his friend were walking
A. across a dark, bushy stretch
B. along a lonely, winding road
C. across a lonely, hilly countryside
D. along an ill-lit and ill-maintained forest road

5. For the narrator and his friend, the effect of the dim light was
A. to create confusion with regard to distance
B. to brighten an otherwise hopeless situation
C. to indicate divine intervention
D. to lessen the difficulty of their mission

PASSAGE-16

We started pitching the highest camp that has ever been made. Everything took five times as long as it would have taken in a place where there was enough air to breathe; but at last we got the, tent up and when we crawled in, it was not too bad. There was only a light wind, and inside it was not too cold for us to take off our gloves. At night most climbers take off their boots; but I prefer to keep them on. Hillary, on the other hand, took his off and laid them next to his sleeping bag.

1. The narrator of the story is
   A. an airline pilot B. a mountaineer
   C. a traveller D. a tourist
2. In this passage, 'we' refers to
   A. the author and his friends
   B. the author and his friend
   C. the author and his wife
   D. None of the above
3. They crawled into the tent because
   A. they must have been too tired to work
   B. the entrance to the tent must have been low
   C. they had heavy loads on their back
   D. they wanted to hide from enemies
4. They took a long time to finish the work because
   A. they were very tired
   B. it was very cold
   C. there was not enough air to breathe
   D. it was very dark
5. When they crawled into the tent
   A. they took off their gloves because it was not very cold
   B. they could not take off their gloves because it was very cold
   C. they took off their gloves though it was very cold
   D. they did not take off their gloves though it was not cold

PASSAGE-17

All sources of energy upon which industry depends are wasted when they are employed, and industry is expending them at a continually increasing rate. Already coal has been largely replaced by oil and oil is being used up so fast that the East and the West alike consider it to be necessary for their prosperity. And what is true of oil is equally true of other natural resources. Everyday, in fact, many miles of forests are turned into newspapers, but there is no known process by which newspapers can be turned into forests. You will say that this need not worry us, since newspapers will be replaced by radio, but radio requires electricity, electricity requires power and power requires raw materials.

1. The central contention of the passage is that
   A. industries should be closed down, since they expend all sources of energy
   B. newspapers should not be allowed to destroy forests
   C. an all-out effort is necessary for the preservation of natural resources that ultimately supply power
   D. power should be generated in abundance
2. The 'and' in the first sentence has the force of
   A. as well as B. besides
   C. still D. though
3. The statement 'many miles of forests are turned into newspapers' means
   A. many miles of forests have become as dry as newspapers
   B. devastation of vast areas of forests is a newsworthy item
   C. a good part of forests has been felled and converted into newsprint
   D. large numbers of trees in forests are converted into raw materials to supply power for the machines that print newspapers
4. According to this passage, oil has become necessary for the prosperity of a nation because
   A. it is cheaper than coal
   B. it is more useful than coal
   C. the East and the West think so
   D. it is now the chief source of energy
5. According to this passage, the most indispensable item for an industrialised society is
   A. the radio
   B. raw materials
   C. power
   D. electricity

PASSAGE-18

Democratic societies from the earliest times have expected their governments to protect the weak against the strong. No "era of good feeling" can justify discharging the police force or giving up the idea of public control over concentrated private wealth. On the other hand, it is obvious that a spirit of self-denial and moderation on the part of those who hold economic power will greatly soften the demand for absolute equality. Men are more interested in freedom and security than in an equal distribution of wealth. The extent to which Government must interfere with business, therefore, is not exactly measured by the extent to which economic power is concentrated into a few hands. The required degree of government interference depends mainly on whether economic powers are oppressively used, and on the necessity of keeping economic factors in a 'tolerable state of balance.'

But with the necessity of meeting all these dangers and threats to liberty, the powers of government are unavoidably increased, whichever political party may be in office. The growth of government is a necessary result of the growth of technology and of the problems that go with the use of machines and science. Since the government in our nation, as well as in all civilised nations, must take on more powers to meet its problems, there is no way to preserve freedom except by making democracy more powerful.

1. 'Era of good feeling' in second sentence can mean
   A. time of prosperity
   B. time of adversity
   C. time without government
   D. time of police atrocities
2. 'Tolerable state of balance' in the last sentence of the first paragraph may mean
   A. a reasonable amount of government interference
   B. an adequate level of police force
   C. a reasonable check on economic power
   D. a reasonable level of economic equality
3. A spirit of moderation on the part of the economically sound people would make the less-privileged
   A. unhappy with their lot
   B. clamourless for absolute equality
   C. unhappy the rich people
   D. more interested in freedom and security
4. The advent of science and technology has
   A. increased the chances of economic inequality
   B. increased the freedom of people
   C. increased the powers of the government
   D. increased the tyranny of the political parties
5. The growth of government is necessitated
   A. to curb the accumulation of wealth in a few hands
   B. to deploy the police force wisely
   C. to monitor science and technology
   D. to make the rich and the poor happy

PASSAGE-19

Youth today do not realise that one is modern only when his thoughts and actions bring out something new, which can set an example to the rest of the world. Imitating only the Western outlook in life-style, leaving aside their values, is not what modernism is. Should we consider a youth modern if he opts for a dozen girlfriends and then pretends to be ignorant when dowry in marriage is concerned?

The family also plays a vital role in shaping one's life. If the urban population in India is divided into two broad divisions, the elite and the middle class, we will find that youths belonging to both these classes suffer from severe frustrations. The parents in the higher society are so busy with their work that their children are left neglected. Loneliness, tensions arising out of parent's unhappy relations and family feuds result in psychiatric depression in the youth.

The case is similar in the middle class families, though with a difference. Lack of attention at home ruins them. The situation is not so grave with the girls as they generally prefer to stay at home, whatever its conditions be. But young men, desperate to find some refuge; quite often come in contact with drugs, alcohol and other illegal activities. Neither are they happy with the society nor is the society happy with them.

1. The passage is concerned with
   A. the urban youth
   B. the elite class youth
   C. the middle class youth
   D. the modern girls
2. Youths in the elite class families are
   A. lonely and depressed
   B. prone to drug-addiction
   C. desperate for revenge
   D. angry and defiant
3. Being truly modern means
   A. imitating the West
   B. opting for a dozen girl-friend
   C. accepting dowry in marriage
   D. doing something exemplary
4. The situation in case of the girls is
   A. desperate B. menacing
   C. not so serious D. gloomy
5. Young men seek refuge in
   A. dozen girl-friends
   B. modernism
   C. drugs, alcohol, etc.
   D. dowry in marriage

PASSAGE-20

In the evening we decided to pitch camp as the weather was not encouraging. The wind was high and gathering storm clouds predicted a wild wet night. Moreover, we had arrived at a spot which looked promising for a camp. A level expanse in the lee of a high hill afforded some shelter from the wind; fresh water was near at hand in a stream which flowed across the plain; a copse of trees provided adequate supplies of fuel; and the dry grasses which abounded on the hillside would enhance the comfort of our beds.

Each member of the party was allotted a task. Some erected the tents; others prepared a scanty meal; yet others attended to the needs of the ponies that were now exhausted after a very strenuous day. As the angry sun sank, the bustle of activity was hushed into silence and each man settled down to sleep.

1. As the weather was not encouraging we decided to
   A. set up the camp
   B. pack up the camp
   C. extend the camp
   D. shift the camp

2. The camp site looked encouraging because
A. it was sheltered by some trees
B. the dry grass would provide fuel
C. we had been promised that spot
D. it was level and sheltered

3. The day had been very
A. exciting B. tiring
C. boring D. comfortable

4. The task given to some members was to
A. pitch the tents B. prepare a hot meal
C. walk the ponies D. allot the tasks

5. This passage is about the selection of
A. a suitable home
B. a suitable place for animals
C. a suitable place to camp
D. a suitable route for trekking

ANSWERS

PASSAGE-1

1	2	3	4	5
A	C	A	A	C

PASSAGE-2

1	2	3	4	5
C	A	B	D	C

PASSAGE-3

1	2	3	4	5
D	C	A	B	C

PASSAGE-4

1	2	3	4	5
B	C	C	B	C

PASSAGE-5

1	2	3	4	5
C	B	D	C	B

PASSAGE-6

1	2	3	4	5
B	D	B	D	A

PASSAGE-7

1	2	3	4	5
A	D	C	B	B

PASSAGE-8

1	2	3	4	5
D	B	C	C	B

PASSAGE-9

1	2	3	4	5
A	C	B	D	D

PASSAGE-10

1	2	3	4	5
C	C	C	A	A

PASSAGE-11

1	2	3	4	5
C	D	D	B	C

PASSAGE-12

1	2	3	4	5
C	C	A	C	D

PASSAGE-13

1	2	3	4	5
C	C	B	D	D

PASSAGE-14

1	2	3	4	5
B	A	A	D	D

PASSAGE-15

1	2	3	4	5
D	B	A	C	A

PASSAGE-16

1	2	3	4	5
B	B	B	C	A

PASSAGE-17

1	2	3	4	5
C	C	C	C	B

PASSAGE-18

1	2	3	4	5
A	A	B	C	D

PASSAGE-19

1	2	3	4	5
A	A	D	C	C

PASSAGE-20

1	2	3	4	5
A	D	B	A	C

★★★

7

Phrases and Clauses

PHRASES

The Phrase

A group of words which does not have a finite verb and does not make a complete sense on its own, is known as a Phrase, *e.g.*,

(*i*) We'll play hockey **in the evening**.

(*ii*) **It being a hot day**, we decided not to go out for a picnic.

(*iii*) She ran away **to escape punishment**.

The three kinds of phrases are:

I. Noun Phrases: The phrase which does the function of a Noun is called a Noun Phrase.

(*i*) He likes **oranges**. (Noun)

(*ii*) He likes **to eat oranges**. (Noun Phrase)

The word 'oranges' is a noun and it can be replaced with the phrase 'to eat oranges'. In other words the said phrase acts like a noun therefore, it is a noun phrase.

II. Adverb Phrases: A phrase which does the function of an Adverb is called an Adverb Phrase. Most of the Adverb Phrases refer to the manner, place, time, *e.g.*,

1. (*i*) She knocked at/on the door **gently**. (Adverb of Manner)

   (*ii*) She knocked the door **in a gentle way**. (Adverb Phrase showing Manner)

2. (*i*) I found a coin **here**. (Adverb of Place)

   (*ii*) I found a coin **on this spot.** (Adverb Phrase referring to Place)

3. (*i*) You shall do it **now**. (Adverb of Time)

   (*ii*) You shall do it **at the very moment**. (Adverb Phrase referring to Time)

III. Adjective Phrases: A phrase which does the function of an Adjective is called an Adjective Phrase. Most often an Adjective can be replaced with an adjective phrase.

1. (*i*) Tagore was **a famous man**. (Adjective)

   (*ii*) Tagore was **a man of fame** (Adjective Phrase)

2. (*i*) She is **a cunning lady**. (Adjective)

   (*ii*) She is **a lady full of cunningness**. (Adjective Phrase)

3. (*i*) It is **a round stone**. (Adjective)

   (*ii*) It is **a stone of round shape**. (Adjective Phrase)

CLAUSES

The Clause

A group of words which has a subject and a finite verb but which still does not convey the full sense is known as a clause. Broadly speaking there are three kinds of clauses.

1. The Principal Clause.
2. The Coordinate Clause.
3. The Subordinate Clause.

When we just talk of a clause, we mean most often a subordinate clause which is also known as a dependent clause. A subordinate clause together with a principal clause conveys the full sense. *e.g.*,

(*i*) I know that he likes mangoes best.

(*ii*) Although he was well prepared he could not make an impressive speech.

(*iii*) The boy who scored a century is my classmate.

The three kinds of subordinate clauses are:

I. Adjective Clause: A clause which acts as an adjective is known as Adjectives clause. Most often it can replace an adjective or adjective phrase *e.g.*,

1. Mrs Sharma has a **black** purse. (Adjective)
2. Mrs Sharma has a purse of **black colour.** (Adjective Phrase)
3. Mrs Sharma has a purse **which is black in colour**. (Adjective clause)

Relative Pronouns which make Adjective clauses

• who • whose • whom • which • that
• as • what • whatsoever

Relative Adverbs which make Adjective clauses

• when • why • how • whenever
• where • wherever

Adjective clauses which are made by Relative Pronouns

1. This is the cat **that has sharp claws.**
2. Gopal is the boy **who lives at outskirts of our town.**
3. Jack **whom we met at the toy shop** is a good singer.
4. The boy **whose father is a doctor** was not allowed to go inside the operation theatre.
5. The chef **who prepared meal for us** belongs to France.
6. He is such a boy **as I like.**
7. **What I am looking for** is a post in the army.

Adjective clauses which are made by Relative Adverbs

1. I do not know the place **where she saw a snake.**
2. You may go to the place **wherever you like.**
3. I do not know the time **when the storm started.**
4. I do not know the reason **why he resigned his job.**

II. Adverb Clause: An Adverb clause is the clause which does the function of an Adverb. Most often it replaces an Adverb or an Adverb Phrase. It may modify a verb, an adjective or another adverb, *e.g.*,

1. Amar is taller **than you** (are).
2. **As soon as the boy saw the snake**, he cried loudly.
3. **If you work hard**, you'll get good marks.

III. Noun Clauses: The clause which does the function of a Noun is known as a Noun clause. The noun clause can act in the following ways:

1. As the Subject to a Verb:
   - **Why you are crying** we fail to understand.
   - **Where he will go,** nobody cares.
   - **How he earned money** is known to all.
   - **When he will wake up** is not sure.

2. As Object to a Participle:
   - **Knowing that his father will not rebuke him,** he starts disturbing his sister.
   - **Finding that the necklace lying on the ground** was of gold, he picked it up.
   - **Saying that he did not know French** he started singing English songs.
   - They started playing in the ground **thinking that nobody will object to it.**

3. As Object to an Infinitive:
   - I would like to know **whether you are going to the USA or Russia.**
   - He wants to say **whether his brother will come back or not.**
   - She wants to inform **why she did not attend the meeting.**

4. As Object to a Preposition:
   - He stuck to **what he believed.**
   - Listen to **what she says.**
   - She objected to **what you said.**

5. As Object to a Verb:
   - I do not understand **why he behaves like this.**

6. As Complement to a Verb:
   - His fear is **that he will be asked about the murder.**
   - It seems **that he would catch the train.**

7. Case in Apposition to a Noun or a Pronoun:
   - The fact **that he is honest is known to all.**
   - The reason **why he failed in the examination is not far to seek.**

MULTIPLE CHOICE QUESTIONS

Directions (Q.No. 1-5): *Rewrite each of the following sentences, replacing the adjectives in italics with adjective phrases of the same meaning:*

1. It was a *spacious* room.
A. It was a room of much space.
B. It was a room of long length.
C. It was a room of more width.
D. It was a room of great height.

2. They spent a *sleepless* night.
A. They spent a night with less sleep.
B. They spent a night without much sleep.
C. They spent a night without sleep.
D. They spent a night unsleep.

3. She is a *professional* singer.
A. She is a singer professional.
B. She follows/has the profession of singing.

C. She is a professor of singing.
D. She is a professional of singing.

4. That was a *cowardly* act.
A. That was a coward act.
B. That was a cowardice act.
C. That was an act of coward.
D. That was an act of cowardice.

5. That was a *courageous* act.
A. That was a courage action.
B. That was an act of courage.
C. That was an action of courage.
D. That was an encouraging act.

Directions (Q.No. 6-10): *Rewrite each of the following sentences, replacing the adjective phrases in italics with adjectives of the same meaning:*

6. He is a man *with a bad temper.*
A. He is a bad-tempered man.
B. He is a low-tempered man.
C. He is a high-tempered man.
D. He is a sharp-tempered man.

7. An elephant *with a white skin* is considered sacred by some people.
A. An elephant with a fair skin is considered sacred by some people.
B. An elephant with a fair complexion is considered sacred by some people.
C. A white elephant is considered sacred by some people.
D. A sacred elephant is considered white by some people.

8. His diary contained many pages *with no writing on them.*
A. His diary contained many white pages.
B. His diary contained many unwritten pages.
C. His diary contained many dry pages.
D. His diary contained many wet pages.

9. Everyone will admit that you are a man *of sense.*
A. Everyone will admit that you are a sense man.
B. Everyone will admit that you are a sensuous man.
C. Everyone will admit that you are a man-sensible.
D. Everyone will admit that you are a sensible man.

10. Gandhiji was a leader of *great fame.*
A. Gandhiji was a great famous leader.
B. Gandhiji was a famous leader.
C. Gandhiji was a famous great leader.
D. Gandhiji was a great leader of fame.

Directions (Q.No. 11-15): *Rewrite each of the following sentences, replacing the adverb in italics with an adverb phrase of the same meaning:*

11. Pitch the tent just *here.*
A. Pitch the tent just there.
B. Pitch the tent just at this place.
C. Pitch the tent just anywhere.
D. Pitch the tent just now.

12. Don't talk *impudently.*
A. Don't talk in an impudent way/manner.
B. Don't talk in impudent.
C. Don't talk impudence.
D. Don't talk impudicity.

13. I answered the question *promptly.*
A. I answered the question prompt.
B. I answered the question promptness.
C. I answered the question prompitude.
D. I answered the question with promptness or in a prompt way/manner.

14. They were hurrying *homeward.*
A. They were hurrying towards the home.
B. They were hurrying forward the home.
C. They were hurrying ahead the home.
D. They were hurrying into the home.

15. He thanked me *profoundly.*
A. He thanked me profundity.
B. He thanked me profound way.
C. He thanked me with profundity or in a profound way.
D. He thanked me profoundness.

Directions (Q.No. 16-20): *Rewrite each of the following sentences, replacing the adverb phrase in italics with an adverb of the same meaning:*

16. The boy went near the tiger *without any fear.*
A. The boy went near the tiger fearlessly.
B. The boy went near the tiger fearless.
C. The boy went near the tiger fearlessness.
D. The boy went near the tiger fearsome.

17. He answered my question *with great reservation.*
A. He answered my question reserved.
B. He answered my question reservedness.
C. He answered my question reservedly.
D. He answered my question reservoir.

18. I hope he will come *at a very early date.*
A. I hope he will come earlier.
B. I hope he will come soon.
C. I hope he will come earliest.
D. I hope he will come fast.

19. You will succeed *in the long run.*
A. You will succeed soon.
B. You will succeed running long.
C. You will succeed running longer.
D. You will succeed finally.

20. The chief guest arrived *at that moment.*
A. The chief guest arrived late.
B. The chief guest arrived then.
C. The chief guest arrived earlier.
D. The chief guest arrived momentarily.

Directions (Q.No. 21-30): *Complete each of the following sentences by adding an adjective clause:*

21. Jack is the boy ....
A. who won the first prize.
B. whom won the first prize.
C. which won the first prize.
D. this won the first prize.

22. The bird .... was a parrot.
A. who was green in colour
B. which was green in colour
C. whom was green in colour
D. it was green in colour

23. The thing .... was a knife.
A. who you saw on the road
B. whom you saw on the road
C. which you saw on the road
D. it you saw on the road

24. I do not exactly know the place .... this coin.
A. where he found this coin
B. there he found the coin
C. here he found the coin
D. that he found the coin

25. I do not know the time ....
A. then he left for the bus stop.
B. now he left for the bus stop.
C. when he left for the bus stop.
D. since he left for the bus stop.

26. Do you know the reason ....
A. because he does not help you.
B. since he does not help you.
C. as he does not help you.
D. why he does not help you.

27. The man .... was an army officer.
A. whose was tall and strong
B. who was tall and strong
C. whom was tall and strong
D. which was tall and strong

28. He .... was caught by the police.
A. it was a thief
B. this was a thief
C. that was a thief
D. who was a thief

29. That object .... is actually a purse.
A. which looks like a book
B. that looks like a book
C. who looks like a book
D. what looks like a book

30. You may go to the place ....
A. what you want.
B. whom you want.
C. where you want.
D. whose you want.

Directions (Q.No. 31-40): *Complete each of the following sentences by adding a noun clause:*

31. I do not know ....
A. who broke the windowpane.
B. which broke the windowpane.
C. whom broke the windowpane.
D. why broke the windowpane.

32. I am not sure ....
A. if he will come to see you or not.
B. about he will come to see you or not.
C. whether he will come to see you or not.
D. that he will come to see you or not.

33. Saying .... he began to sing.
A. which he was a good singer
B. that he was a good singer
C. this he was a good singer
D. it he was a good singer

34. Listen to ....
A. it she says.
B. this she says.
C. which she says.
D. what she says.

35. Please allow him to say ....
A. what he wants.
B. which he wants.
C. that he wants.
D. this he wants.

36. He guessed ....
A. it he could not climb up the hill.
B. this he could not climb up the hill.
C. that he could not climb up the hill.
D. which he could not climb up the hill.

37. Knowing .... he decided to go to England.
A. that he had no relatives in India
B. it he had no relatives in India
C. this he had no relatives in India
D. which he had no relatives in India

38. I wanted to know ....
A. what she would deliver her maiden speech.
B. who she would deliver her maiden speech.
C. which she would deliver her maiden speech.
D. when she would deliver her maiden speech.

39. He asserted ....
A. it he was honest.
B. this he was honest.
C. that he was honest.
D. which he was honest.

40. I cannot say ....
A. what she looks like.
B. why she looks like.
C. when she looks like.
D. where she looks like.

Directions (Q.No. 41-50): *Complete each of the following sentences by adding an adverb clause using the conjunction given in brackets:*

41. Stay here (until) ....
A. until he come back.
B. until I come back.
C. until you come back.
D. until she come back.

42. (As soon as) .... we'll go to see a movie.
A. As soon as she've finished
B. As soon as he've finished
C. As soon as I've finished
D. As soon as mother've finished

43. My brother is reading a novel (while) ....
A. while my sister is colouring the pictures.
B. while my sister was colouring the pictures.
C. while my sister has been colouring the pictures.
D. while my sister have been colouring the pictures.

44. Do (as) ....
A. as you instruct.
B. as you were instruct.
C. as you have been instruct.
D. as you are instructed.

45. He sits (as if) ....
A. as if he were a king.
B. as if he was a king.
C. as if he is a king.
D. as if he will be a king.

46. (As soon as) .... he began to smile.
A. As soon as the boy found his lost coin
B. As soon as the boy find his lost coin
C. As soon as the boy will find his lost coin
D. As soon as the boy founded his lost coin

47. He is thinner (than) ....
A. than himself.
B. than you.
C. than hisself.
D. than yourself.

48. I can lend you a hundred rupee note (provided that) ....
A. provided that you returns it to me by the end of this month.
B. provided that you returned it to me by the end of this month.
C. provided that you will return it to me by the end of this month.
D. provided that you return it to me by the end of this month.

49. (Since) .... we should postpone our tour to India.
A. Since we can't catch the flight now,
B. Since we shouldn't catch the flight now,
C. Since we couldn't catch the flight now,
D. Since we wouldn't catch the flight now,

50. (As long as) .... you need not worry about anything.
A. As long as I were here,
B. As long as I am here,
C. As long as I was here,
D. As long as I have been here,

ANSWERS

1	2	3	4	5	6	7	8	9	10
A	C	B	D	B	A	C	B	D	B
11	**12**	**13**	**14**	**15**	**16**	**17**	**18**	**19**	**20**
B	A	D	A	C	A	C	B	D	B
21	**22**	**23**	**24**	**25**	**26**	**27**	**28**	**29**	**30**
A	B	C	A	C	D	B	D	A	C
31	**32**	**33**	**34**	**35**	**36**	**37**	**38**	**39**	**40**
A	C	B	D	A	C	A	D	C	A
41	**42**	**43**	**44**	**45**	**46**	**47**	**48**	**49**	**50**
B	C	A	D	A	A	B	D	A	B

★★★

8

Active and Passive Voice

A sentence in active voice focuses on the person or thing doing the action.
A sentence in passive voice focuses on the person or thing affected by the action. e.g.,
The idol was built. (Active voice)
Someone built the idol. (Passive voice)

Transformation of voice

- *Voice and Tense are closely associated with each other.*
- *Tense remains the same while transforming the voice.*

MULTIPLE CHOICE QUESTIONS

Directions (Qs. 1 to 30): *In each of the following questions, a sentence is given in Active Voice. Below it are given four alternatives suggesting the Passive Voice form of the given sentence. Choose the correct alternative.*

1. They will have helped you.
A. You will have helped by them.
B. You will have been helped by them.
C. You will be helped by them.
D. You will be helped by them.

2. Open the door.
A. Door may be opened.
B. Let the door be open.
C. Let the door be opened.
D. Door be opened.

3. I am reading a book.
A. A book is read by me.
B. A book is being read by me.
C. A book has been read by me.
D. A book is been read by me.

4. Why did your brother write such a letter?
A. Why your brother wrote such a letter?
B. Why was by brother written such a letter?
C. Why was such a letter written by your brother?
D. Why was written such a letter by your brother?

5. Did you run a great risk?
A. Was a great risk run by you?
B. Was run a great risk by you?
C. Was by you run a great risk?
D. Had you run a great risk?

6. Was he knocking at the door?
A. Was the door being knocked at by him?
B. Was the door being knocked by him?
C. Was the door knocked by him?
D. Was the door knocking at him?

7. What was Rani doing?
A. What was done by Rani?
B. What was Rani being done?
C. What was being done by Rani?
D. What was being doing Rani?

8. Why were you wasting your Time?
A. Why was your time being wasted?
B. Why was your time being wasted by you?
C. Why was your time wasted by you?
D. Why was your time wasted?

9. She has laid out a small garden.
A. A small garden has been laid by her.
B. A small garden has laid out her.
C. A small garden being laid by her.
D. A small garden has been laid out by her.

10. She had already solved all the sums.
A. All the sums had already been solved by her.
B. All the sums have already been solved by her.
C. All the sums have been solved by her.
D. All the sums are solved by her.

11. He will have posted the letter.
A. The letter has been posted by him.
B. The letter will be posted by him.
C. The letter will have been posted by him.
D. The letter is posted by him.

12. They will have sold all the books by 4 P.M.
A. All the books will be sold by 4 P.M.
B. All the books will have been sold by 4 P.M.
C. All the books were being sold by 4 P.M.
D. All the books must be sold by 4 P.M.

13. Do you speak English?
A. Is English spoken by you?
B. Does English spoken by you?
C. Is English being spoken by you?
D. Does English being spoken by you?

14. Had they seen me before?
A. Had myself been seen by them before?
B. Had me being seen by them before?
C. Had I been seen by them before?
D. Had I being seen by them before?

15. May I take this pen?
A. May this pen will be taken by me?
B. May this pen shall be taken by me?
C. May this pen should be taken by me?
D. May this pen be taken by me?

16. Can we send it by air?
A. Can this be sent by air?
B. Can it be sent by air?
C. Can it go by air?
D. Can it be send by air?

17. Who wrote this book?
A. By whom was this book written?
B. By whom is this book written?
C. By whom was this book being written?
D. By whom is this book being written?

18. What did you buy?
A. What is bought by you?
B. What is being bought by you?
C. What was bought by you?
D. What was being bought by you?

19. Whom do you want?
A. Who is wanted by you?
B. Who is being wanted by you?
C. You are wanted by whom?
D. You are being wanted by whom?

20. When will you raise this question?
A. When this question will be raised by you?
B. When will this question be raised by you?
C. When this question is being raised by you?
D. When is this question being raised by you?

21. Who did this?
A. This was done by whom?
B. By whom was this done?
C. Who has done this?
D. By whom this was done?

22. One should keep one's promises.
A. Promises should be kept.
B. One's promises should be kept by one.
C. Promises must be kept.
D. One's promises one should keep.

23. Give the order.
A. Order given.
B. Order be given.
C. Let the order be given.
D. Order may be given by you.

24. You will have to do it.
A. It will be done by you.
B. It will have to be done by you.
C. It has to be done by you.
D. It would have to be done by you.

25. Keep to the left.
A. You are ordered to keep to the left.
B. You ought to keep to the left.
C. You are advised to keep to the left.
D. You must keep to the left.

26. They will arrange a party.
A. A party will have to be arranged by them.
B. A party they will have to arrange.
C. A party will be arranged by them.
D. A party by them will be arranged.

27. Someone has picked my pocket.
A. My pocket is picked.
B. My pocket has picked.
C. My pocket has been picked.
D. My pocket was picked.

28. He kept me waiting.
A. I kept waiting for him.
B. I kept waiting by him.
C. I was waiting for him.
D. I was kept waiting by him.

29. Why do you tell a lie?
A. Why is a lie told by you?
B. Why is told a lie by you?
C. Why is told by you a lie?
D. Why has a lie been told by you?

30. I have written a letter.
A. A letter is written by me.
B. A letter has been written by me.
C. A letter was written by me.
D. A letter had been written by me.

Directions (Qs. 31 to 35): *In the following questions, a sentence has been given in Active/Passive Voice. Out of the four alternatives suggested, select the one that Best Expresses the same sentence in Passive/Active Voice.*

31. Circumstances will oblige me to go.
A. I will oblige the circumstances and go.
B. I shall be obliged to go by the circumstances.
C. Under the circumstances, I should go.
D. I shall be obliged by the circumstances to go.

32. We waste much time on trifles.
A. Much time was wasted on trifles.
B. Much time will be wasted on trifles.
C. Much time is wasted by us on trifles.
D. Much time is wasted on trifles.

33. Mohan gave the beggar an old shirt.
A. An old shirt was given to Mohan by the beggar.
B. An old shirt was given to the beggar by Mohan.
C. The beggar is given an old shirt by Mohan.
D. An old shirt is given to the beggar by Mohan.

34. They have made him a king.
A. A king has been made by him.
B. He was made a king by them.
C. They have been made king by him.
D. He has been made a king by them.

35. Who taught you English?
A. By whom English was taught to you?
B. By whom you were taught English?
C. By whom was English taught to you?
D. By whom are you taught English?

Directions (Qs. 36 to 45): *In each of the following questions, a sentence is given in Passive Voice. Below it are given four alternatives suggesting the Active Voice form of the given sentence. Choose the correct alternative.*

36. He was made a king.
A. He became a king.
B. They made him a king.
C. They had made him a king.
D. He has been made a king.

37. Good news is expected by us.
A. We are expecting good news.
B. We have been expecting good news.
C. We had expected good news.
D. We expect good news.

38. The child must be looked after.
A. The child you must look after.
B. You must look after the child.
C. You must look the child after.
D. You may look after the child.

39. What is wanted by you?
A. What you want?
B. What did you want?
C. What do you want?
D. What you do want?

40. Your father is known to me.
A. I am known to your father.
B. I know your father.
C. I have known your father.
D. I knew your father.

41. She may be told the story by you.
A. The story may be told by you to her.
B. You may tell the story to her.
C. You may tell her the story.
D. You may tell to her the story.

42. Duty ought to be done.
A. Let duty be done.
B. One ought to do one's duty.
C. One should do his duty.
D. Do your duty.

43. Is English spoken by you?
A. Did you speak English?
B. Do you speak English?
C. Have you spoken English?
D. Do you know how to speak English?

44. Gold coins are contained in this box.
A. This box contains gold coins.
B. This box has contained gold coins.
C. This box is containing gold coins.
D. This box has gold coins.

45. Character is revealed by manners.
A. Manners revealed character.
B. Manners reveal character.
C. Manners have revealed character.
D. Manners do reveal character.

ANSWERS

1	2	3	4	5	6	7	8	9	10
B	C	B	C	A	A	C	B	D	A
11	**12**	**13**	**14**	**15**	**16**	**17**	**18**	**19**	**20**
C	B	A	C	D	B	A	C	A	B
21	**22**	**23**	**24**	**25**	**26**	**27**	**28**	**29**	**30**
B	A	C	B	C	C	C	D	A	B
31	**32**	**33**	**34**	**35**	**36**	**37**	**38**	**39**	**40**
D	C	B	D	C	B	D	B	C	B
41	**42**	**43**	**44**	**45**					
C	B	B	A	B					

★ ★ ★

9

Direct and Indirect Narration

The words spoken by a speaker are known to be in Direct Speech.

The words spoken by somebody and expressed by someone else with some modification are known as Indirect Speech. e.g.,

(a) Rohit says to me, "You do not understand me." *(Direct Speech)*

(b) Rohit tells me that I do not understand him. *(Indirect Speech)*

MULTIPLE CHOICE QUESTIONS

Directions (Qs. 1 to 13): *Select the correct indirect speech for the following sentences:*

1. I said to him, "I shall help you."
A. I told him that I can help him.
B. I told him that I would help him.
C. I told him that I will help him.
D. I told him that I shall be helping him.

2. My Teacher said to me, "The earth revolves round the sun."
A. My teacher told me that the earth revolves round the sun.
B. My teacher told me that the earth revolve round the sun.
C. My teacher told me that the earth had been revolving round the sun.
D. My teacher told me that the earth has been revolving round the sun.

3. I said to my friend, "My father daily goes for a walk."
A. I told my friend that my father daily goes for a walk.
B. I told my friend that my father daily went for a walk.
C. I told my friend that my father has to go for a walk.
D. I told my friend that my father had gone for a walk.

4. He said to me, "May God bless you!"
A. He requested that God can bless me.
B. He prayed that God can bless me.
C. He prayed that God might bless me.
D. He prayed that God will bless me.

5. The patient said, "Thank you, doctor."
A. The patient thanked the doctor.
B. The patient requested the doctor with thanks.
C. The patient told the doctor thanks.
D. The patient suggested the doctor thanks.

6. Satish said, "No, I shall not talk to him."
A. Satish told that he should not talk to him.
B. Satish suggested that he would not have talked to him.
C. Satish exclaimed with sorrow that he would not talk with him.
D. Satish refused to talk to him.

7. The child said, "What a lovely place!"
A. The child exclaimed with sorrow that it was a lovely place.
B. The child thought that the place was lovely.
C. The child exclaimed with joy that the place was very lovely.
D. The child suggested that the place was lovely.

8. He said, "What a fool I have been!"

A. He told himself with sorrow that he was a fool.
B. He confessed with regret that he had been a great fool.
C. He said himself a fool.
D. He suggested that he could be a fool.

9. He said, "Alas! I am ruined."

A. He told me that he had been ruined.
B. He exclaimed with joy that he had been ruined.
C. He exclaimed with sorrow that he was ruined.
D. He told me that he should not be ruined.

10. The accused said, "I am not guilty."

A. The accused exclaimed with sorrow that I am not guilty.
B. The accused exclaimed with joy that he was not guilty.
C. The accused stated that he was not guilty.
D. The accused told me that he has not been guilty.

11. My teacher said, "The earth is round".

A. My teacher said that the earth was round.
B. My teacher says that the earth is round.
C. My teacher said that the earth is round.
D. My teacher ordered that the earth is round.

12. He said, "What a place it is!"

A. He said that it was a very fine place.
B. He said that is a very fine place.
C. He said that the place is fine.
D. He exclaimed with joy/surprise that it was a very fine place.

13. Ria said, "Shall I thread the needle?"

A. Ria asked if she should thread the needle.
B. Ria asked if she shall thread the needle.
C. Ria ordered if she should thread the needle.
D. Ria says that if she would thread the needle.

Directions (Qs. 14 to 33): *Pick out the correct alternative that completes the incomplete sentence which is changed into indirect narration.*

14. She said to me, "I shall see you as soon as I get time."

She told me:

A. that she will see me as soon as she will get time.
B. that she would see me as soon as she would get time.
C. she would see me whenever she got time.
D. that she would see me whenever she gets time.

15. My secretary said to me, "Your plane will leave if you do not go at once."

My secretary told me that:

A. her plane would leave if she did not go at that time.
B. her plane would leave if I do not go at once.
C. my plane would leave if I did not go at that very time.
D. my plane will leave if I did not go at that time.

16. My mother said to me, "Don't quarrel among yourselves".

My mother:

A. forbade me to quarrel among ourselves.
B. asked me not to quarrel among ourselves.
C. asked me that not to quarrel among ourselves.
D. asked me to quarrel not among ourselves.

17. Her father said to her mother, "Excuse the daughter."

Her father:

A. requested her mother to excuse the daughter.
B. asked her mother to excuse the daughter.
C. asked her mother to have excused the daughter.
D. asked her mother to have been excused.

18. He said to his friend, "Wait here till father comes."

He requested his friend:

A. to wait here till father had come.
B. that to wait there till his friend came.
C. to wait there till father came.
D. to wait here until his friend came.

19. She said to her maid, "Run and catch the thief."

She ordered her maid:

A. ran and catch the thief.
B. that to run and to catch the thief.
C. ran and caught the thief.
D. to run and catch the thief.

20. Anita said to Sunita, "What are you doing?"

Anita asked Sunita:

A. what she will be doing.
B. that what she is doing.
C. that what she was doing.
D. what she was doing.

21. She said to me, "Are you meeting me today?"

She enquired of me:

A. whether I am meeting her that day.
B. whether I was meeting her today.
C. whether I was meeting her that day.
D. I was meeting her that day.

22. Nitish said to me, "When did you buy this pen?"

Nitish asked me:

A. when I was to buy that pen.
B. when I would buy that pen.
C. when I had bought that pen.
D. when I was buying that pen.

23. She said to me, "Are you going to market?"

She enquired of me:

A. I am going to market.
B. I was going to market.
C. if I was going to market.
D. if I had been going to the market.

24. Damini said, "Why did not you change your clothes?"

Damini asked me:

A. why I had not changed my clothes.
B. why I did not change my clothes.
C. why I would not change my clothes.
D. why I have not been changing my clothes.

25. Umesh said to me, "Have you read that novel?"

Umesh asked me:

A. if he was reading that novel.
B. if he had read that novel.
C. if I had read that novel.
D. if I was reading that novel.

26. She said to me, "I shall forgive you."

She told me:

A. that she will forgive me.
B. that she was going to forgive me.
C. that she will not forgive me.
D. that she would forgive me.

27. I said to her, "It was very hot last night."

I told her:

A. that it had been very hot the previous night.
B. that it was very hot the previous night.
C. that it has been very hot the last night.
D. that it had been very hot this night.

28. She said to me, "I thank you for the help you have given."

She:

A. told me that she thanked me for the help I had given.
B. thanked me for the help I have given.
C. thanked to me for the help I have given.
D. thanked me for the help I had given.

29. Mohini said to me, "Trust in God."

Mohini advised me:

A. that I should trust in God.
B. should trust in God.
C. trusted in God.
D. to trust in God.

30. I said to him, "Let us go to school."

I told him:

A. we would go to school.
B. we shall go to school.
C. that we would go to school.
D. that we should go to school.

31. Rajni said, "May God bless you?"

Rajni:

A. exclaimed with wish that God might bless me.
B. expressed a wish that God might bless me.
C. asked God to bless me.
D. shouted with joy to bless me.

32. My mother said to me, "Do not have so many friends."

My mother forbade me:

A. to have so many friends.
B. not to have so many friends.
C. to have been so many friends.
D. to possess so many friends.

33. Ram said, "Pay attention to me."

Ram asked:

A. pay attention to him.
B. paid attention to him.
C. having paid attention to him.
D. to pay attention to him.

Directions (Qs. 34 to 50): *In questions below, the sentences have been given in Direct/Indirect Speech. Out of the four alternatives suggested select the one which best expresses the given sentence in Indirect/Direct Speech.*

34. She said that her brother was getting married.

A. She said, "Her brother is getting married."
B. She told, "My brother is getting married."
C. She said, "My brother is getting married."
D. She said, "My brother was married."

35. "Please don't go away", she said.

A. She said to please her and not go away.
B. She told me to go away.
C. She begged me not to go away.
D. She begged that I not go away.

36. "If you don't keep quiet I shall shoot you", he said to her in a calm voice.

A. He warned her to shoot if she didn't keep quiet calmly.
B. He said calmly that I shall shoot you if you don't be quiet.
C. He warned her calmly that he would shoot her if she didn't keep quiet.
D. Calmly he warned her that be quiet or else he will have to shoot her.

37. I told him that he was not working hard.

A. I said to him, "You are not working hard."
B. I told him, "You are not working hard."
C. I said, "You are not working hard."
D. I said to him, "He is not working hard."

38. She said that she would finish the work the next day.
A. She said, "I will finish the work the next day."
B. She said, "I will finish the work tomorrow."
C. She said, "You will finish the work tomorrow."
D. She said, "I finished the work."

39. She said to him, "Why don't you go today?"
A. She asked him why he did not go that day.
B. She said to him that why he don't go today.
C. She asked him not to go today.
D. She asked him why he did not go today.

40. "Are you alone, my son?" asked a soft voice close behind me.
A. A soft voice asked that what I was doing there alone.
B. A soft voice said to me are you alone son.
C. A soft voice from my back asked if I was alone.
D. A soft voice close behind me asked if I was alone.

41. My cousin said, "My room-mate had snored throughout the night."
A. My cousin said that her room-mate snored throughout the night.
B. My cousin told me that her room-mate snored throughout the night.
C. My cousin complained to me that her room-mate is snoring throughout the night.
D. My cousin felt that her room-mate may be snoring throughout the night.

42. He asked Rama if he needed his help then.
A. He said to Rama, "Do you need my help?"
B. He told Rama, "Tell me if you need help."
C. He asked Rama, "Do I need your help?"
D. He said to Rama, "Do you need my help now?"

43. Nita ordered her servant to bring her a cup of tea.
A. Nita told her servant, "Bring a cup of tea."
B. Nita said, "Bring me a cup of tea."
C. Nita said to her servant, "Bring me a cup of tea."
D. Nita said to her servant, "Bring her that cup of tea."

44. He exclaimed with joy that India had won the Sahara Cup.
A. He said, "India has won the Sahara Cup."
B. He said, "India won the Sahara Cup."
C. He said, "How! India will win the Sahara Cup."
D. He said, "Hurrah! India has won the Sahara Cup."

45. The boy said, "Who dare call you a thief?"
A. The boy enquired who dared call him a thief.
B. The boy asked who called him a thief.
C. The boy told that who dared call him a thief.
D. The boy wondered who dared call a thief.

ANSWERS

1	2	3	4	5	6	7	8	9	10
B	A	A	C	A	D	C	B	C	C
11	**12**	**13**	**14**	**15**	**16**	**17**	**18**	**19**	**20**
C	D	A	B	C	A	B	C	D	D
21	**22**	**23**	**24**	**25**	**26**	**27**	**28**	**29**	**30**
C	C	C	A	C	D	A	A	A	D
31	**32**	**33**	**34**	**35**	**36**	**37**	**38**	**39**	**40**
B	A	D	C	C	C	A	B	A	D
41	**42**	**43**	**44**	**45**					
A	D	C	B	A					

★ ★ ★

10

One Word Substitution

There are many single words in English language which can be perfectly used for a number of words. These words help in expressing ideas in a short and correct manner for the right occasion. Such words not only increase the vocabulary but also enable you to economise in the use of words to a great extent.

Multiple Word Expression	*Substitution*
One who always looks towards the bright side of things	*Optimist*
One who always looks towards the dark side of things	*Pessimist*
The time when one develops from a child into an adult	*Adolescence*
The process of growing more plants in order to form a forest	*Afforestation*
The science which deals with farming	*Agriculture*
From some other country or place etc.	*Alien*
A term, etc. giving more than one meaning	*Ambiguous*
A vehicle which is used to carry sick persons	*Ambulance*
An animal which can live both in water and on land	*Amphibian*
A lawless situation when there is no government	*Anarchy*
Belonging to the history of thousands of years old	*Ancient*
Something happening once a year	*Annual*
A very old object but still valuable	*Antique*
Words of opposite meanings	*Antonyms*
Words of similar meanings	*Synonyms*
Signatures of a famous person	*Autograph*
A government led by one person with absolute authority	*Autocracy*
A written work of one's own life history	*Autobiography*
A person who has never been married	*Bachelor*
A person usually having no hair on his head	*Bald*
A place where one can deposit money and get interest	*Bank*
A person who cuts our hair	*Barber*
A building/group of buildings where soldiers live	*Barracks*
A person who makes buns and biscuits	*Baker*
A person who lives by asking people for food and money without doing any useful job	*Beggar*
The crime of having married to two persons at the same time	*Bigamy*
The branch of science which deals with the study of plants	*Botany*
Able to speak two languages	*Bilingual*
Able to speak more than two languages	*Polyglot*
The branch of science which deals with the living organisms	*Biology*
A powerful snow storm	*Blizzard*
A great successful book or movie	*Blockbuster*
A short news on the radio or TV	*Bulletin*

Multiple Word Expression	*Substitution*
A system in which the most important works are organised by the government officials	*Bureaucracy*
A person who has no vision in his eyes	*Blind*
A page or a series of pages on which the information of days, weeks, months, etc. is given	*Calendar*
A person who eats human flesh	*Cannibal*
A complete list of items often arranged alphabetically	*Catalogue*
A sudden disaster	*Catastrophe*
A period of 100 years	*Century*
A branch of science which deals with chemicals	*Chemistry*
A printed leaf usually issued by banks that we sign to carry certain financial deal	*Cheque*
A person who makes or mends shoes	*Cobbler*
A group of people who has been chosen by others to make decisions on their own	*Committee*
A building in which nuns live	*Convent*
An animal which feeds on other animals	*Carnivorous*
A person who does criticism	*Critic*
A person who cannot hear	*Deaf*
A condition in which one loses a lot of water from one's body because of vomiting, etc.	*Dehydration*
A system of government in which the people cast their votes to elect their leaders	*Democracy*
The study of skin problems	*Dermatology*
A large stretch of land covered with sand	*Desert*
The art of managing relationships between countries	*Diplomacy*
A piece of information about the words in a book form	*Dictionary*
A piece of information about the telephone numbers of the people in a book form	*Directory*
A person in charge of a newspaper, magazine etc.	*Editor*
A person who thinks he is better than others	*Egoist*
To leave your country and settle in some other country	*Emigrate*
A book or series of books giving almost all knowledge about an area or some persons, etc.	*Encyclopaedia*
Study of insects	*Entomology*
Time when day and night are of the same duration	*Equinox*
To sell things out of the country	*Export*
To purchase things from some other country	*Import*
A plant or animal no longer in existence	*Extinct*
A situation when there is a shortage of food for a long period of time	*Famine*
An amount of money that we pay for some action or services	*Fee*
Something related to women	*Feminine*
An animal strong and aggressive	*Ferocious*
A piece of land where plants grow easily from the soil that is favourable to them	*Fertile*
A work of literature having some imaginary events	*Fiction*
A large amount of water covering certain area	*Flood*
A person who sells flowers	*Florist*
A religious ceremony for burying or cremating a dead person	*Funeral*
A substance which kills fungus	*Fungicide*
A person studying or having studied the diseases and the related things of female reproductory system	*Gynaecologist*
The murder of the people of the same group, race or country	*Genocide*
A substance which kills germs	*Germicide*
A situation in which many people die because of fire during war	*Holocaust*
The act of killing a person deliberately	*Homicide*
A word having the pronunciation as the other one does but differing in meaning	*Homophone*
A word having the same spelling as the other one does but it is pronounced in some other way	*Homonym*
A person who is attracted towards the person of the same sex	*Homosexual*
Go across and parallel to the ground	*Horizontal*

Multiple Word Expression	*Substitution*
A substance which kills the insects	*Insecticide*
That cannot be corrected	*Incorrigible*
That cannot be defeated	*Invincible*
That cannot be eaten	*Inedible*
That cannot be seen	*Invisible*
A place in a school or college where books are kept for the benefit of students, teachers etc.	*Library*
A place in a school or college where scientific experiments are performed	*Laboratory*
An official who is a judge in the lowest court	*Magistrate*
A piece of music or a book before it is printed	*Manuscript*
Something related to men	*Masculine*
One who believes in the existence of God	*Theist*
One who does not believe in the existence of good	*Atheist*
That can be believed	*Credible*
That cannot be believed	*Incredible*
That which dissolves in a solvent	*Soluble*
That which does not dissolve in a solvent	*Insoluble*
Handwriting that can be read	*Legible*
Handwriting that cannot be read	*Illegible*
A person who does jobs beneficial to mankind	*Philanthropist*
A person who goes on foot	*Pedestrian*
A person who fights for his own country	*Patriot*
An act of killing oneself	*Suicide*
A woman whose husband is dead	*Widow*
A man whose wife is dead	*Widower*
A person who eats both vegetarian and non-vegetarian food	*Omnivorous*
Something which is present everywhere at the same time	*Omnipresent*
One who knows everything	*Omniscient*
A child who does not have parents	*Orphan*
An award, etc. given after the death of the recipient	*Posthumous*
The place where animals are kept for amusement and for the knowledge of the public	*Zoo*
The science which deals with the study of animals	*Zoology*

MULTIPLE CHOICE QUESTIONS

Directions: *In questions given below, out of the four alternatives, choose the one which can be substituted for the given words/sentences.*

1. Something that relates to everyone in the world
A. General B. Common
C. Usual D. Universal

2. An expression of mild disapproval
A. Warning B. Denigration
C. Impertinence D. Reproof

3. One who is not easily pleased by anything
A. Maiden B. Medieval
C. Precarious D. Fastidious

4. Murder of a king
A. Infanticide B. Matricide
C. Genocide D. Regicide

5. A remedy for all diseases
A. Stoic B. Marvel
C. Panacea D. Recompense

6. A dramatic performance
A. Mask B. Mosque
C. Masque D. Mascot

7. Study of birds
A. Orology B. Optology
C. Ophthalmology D. Ornithology

8. Ready to believe
A. Credulous B. Credible
C. Creditable D. Incredible

9. Incapable of being seen through
A. Ductile B. Opaque
C. Obsolete D. Potable

10. One who eats everything
A. Omnivorous B. Omniscient
C. Irresistible D. Insolvent

11. A place where bees are kept is called
A. An apiary B. A mole
C. A hive D. A sanctuary

12. One who cannot be corrected
A. Incurable B. Incorrigible
C. Hardened D. Invulnerable

13. One who is in charge of a museum
A. Curator B. Supervisor
C. Caretaker D. Warden

14. Continuing fight between parties, families, clans, etc.
A. Enmity B. Feud
C. Quarrel D. Skirmish

15. A voice loud enough to be heard
A. Audible B. Applaudable
C. Laudable D. Oral

16. A paper written by hand
A. Handicraft B. Manuscript
C. Handiwork D. Thesis

17. Habitually silent or talking little
A. Servile B. Unequivocal
C. Taciturn D. Synoptic

18. To slap with a flat object
A. Chop B. Hew
C. Gnaw D. Swat

19. A person who speaks many languages
A. Linguist B. Monolingual
C. Polyglot D. Bilingual

20. A light sailing-boat built specially for racing
A. Canoe B. Yacht
C. Frigate D. Dinghy

21. A fixed orbit in space in relation to earth
A. Geological B. Geo-synchronous
C. Geo-centric D. Geo-stationary

22. A style in which a writer makes a display of his knowledge
A. Pedantic B. Verbose
C. Pompous D. Ornate

23. A religious discourse
A. Preach B. Stanza
C. Sanctorum D. Sermon

24. A place that provides refuge
A. Asylum B. Sanatorium
C. Shelter D. Orphanage

25. Detailed plan of a journey
A. Travelogue B. Travelkit
C. Schedule D. Itinerary

26. A person who insists on something
A. Disciplinarian B. Stickler
C. Instantaneous D. Boaster

27. A drawing on transparent paper
A. Red print B. Blue print
C. Negative D. Transparency

28. One who believes that all things and events in life are predeter-mined is a
A. Fatalist B. Puritan
C. Egoist D. Tyrant

29. A school boy who cuts classes frequently is a
A. Defeatist B. Sycophant
C. Truant D. Martinet

30. The act of violating the sanctity of the church is
A. Blasphemy B. Heresy
C. Sacrilege D. Desecration

31. A place where monks live as a secluded community
A. Cathedral B. Diocese
C. Convent D. Monastery

32. One who is fond of fighting
A. Bellicose B. Aggressive
C. Belligerent D. Militant

33. Tending to move away from the centre or axis
A. Centrifugal B. Centripetal
C. Axiomatic D. Awry

34. Words inscribed on tomb
A. Epitome B. Epistle
C. Epilogue D. Epitaph

35. Leave or remove from a place considered dangerous
A. Evade B. Evacuate
C. Avoid D. Exterminate

36. Original inhabitants of a country
A. Aborge B. Aborger
C. Aborgory D. Aborigins

37. Government by the officials
A. Theocracy B. Plutocracy
C. Bureaucracy D. Democracy

38. Incapable of being exhausted
A. Inexhaustible B. Unexhaustible
C. Exhaustable D. Non-tired

39. A person of good understanding, knowledge and reasoning power
A. Expert B. Intellectual
C. Snob D. Literate

40. One absorbed in his own thoughts and feelings rather than in things outside
A. Scholar B. Recluse
C. Introvert D. Intellectual

41. One who is indifferent to pains and pleasure of life
A. stoic B. metaphysical
C. pessimist D. sceptic

42. List of names of persons showing duties to be performed by each in turn
A. notice B. bulletin
C. roster D. agenda

43. Long angry speech of criticism or accusation
A. track record B. tirade
C. taut D. outburst

44. One who is in favour of never drinking alcoholic drinks
A. idealist B. uxorious
C. teetotaller D. unalcoholic

45. Trying to win favour by flattery and charm
A. smarmy B. shrewish
C. toady D. loquacious

46. A decision on which one cannot go back
A. incorrigible B. irrevocable
C. rigid D. invulnerable

47. The science that studies the varieties of human race
A. phrenology B. physiology
C. sociology D. ethnology

48. A person who hates women
A. philogynist B. philatelist
C. misogamist D. misogynist

49. A group of people in a particular grade in an organisation
A. colleague B. staff
C. echelon D. commission

50. Honourably discharged from service
A. emeritus B. latitudinarian
C. infallible D. meritorious

51. One who does not believe in the existence of God
A. atheist B. altruist
C. agnostic D. flippant

52. The large money paid for an early retirement
A. goldmine B. golden handshake
C. gratuity D. lion's share

53. A hater of learning and knowledge
A. misologist B. misogynist
C. philologist D. philanthropist

54. One who lives and acts for the welfare of others
A. misanthrope B. credulous
C. altruist D. gregarious

55. Mental weariness for want of occupation
A. desperate B. depression
C. fatigue D. ennui

56. That which makes it difficult to recognise the presence in real of somebody or something
A. cover B. mask
C. make-up D. camouflage

57. To bear a hand in one's new business
A. partnership B. interfere
C. assist D. join

58. One who renounces the world and practices self-discipline in order to attain salvation
A. devotee B. ascetic
C. theist D. parsimonious

59. A place where gambling is practiced
A. hotel B. motel
C. casino D. stadium

60. A sad song is a
A. dirge B. elegy
C. ditty D. knell

ANSWERS

1	2	3	4	5	6	7	8	9	10
D	D	D	D	C	C	D	A	B	A
11	**12**	**13**	**14**	**15**	**16**	**17**	**18**	**19**	**20**
A	B	A	B	A	B	C	D	A	B
21	**22**	**23**	**24**	**25**	**26**	**27**	**28**	**29**	**30**
D	A	D	A	D	B	D	A	C	C
31	**32**	**33**	**34**	**35**	**36**	**37**	**38**	**39**	**40**
D	A	A	D	B	B	C	A	B	C
41	**42**	**43**	**44**	**45**	**46**	**47**	**48**	**49**	**50**
A	C	B	C	A	B	D	D	C	A
51	**52**	**53**	**54**	**55**	**56**	**57**	**58**	**59**	**60**
A	B	A	C	D	D	C	B	C	A

★★★

हिन्दी

(क) भाषिक अनुप्रयोग और व्याकरणिक कुशलताएँ

1

वर्ण विचार

वर्ण

वर्ण वह मूल ध्वनि है जिसका खण्ड नहीं किया जा सकता है। जैसे—अ, आ, क्, ख्, ग्, च्, ट् आदि।

वर्ण को लिखने के लिए जिन चिह्नों का प्रयोग किया जाता है, उसे अक्षर कहते हैं। अक्षर का अर्थ है, जिसका क्षर न हो अर्थात् जो नष्ट न हो।

वर्णमाला : वर्णों के समूह को वर्णमाला कहते हैं। अंग्रेजी में इसे ही Alphabet कहते हैं। हिन्दी वर्णमाला को दो भागों में विभक्त किया जा सकता है—(*i*) स्वर (*ii*) व्यंजन

स्वर (Vowel)

स्वर उन मूल ध्वनियों या वर्णों को कहा जाता है जिनका उच्चारण बिना किसी अवरोध के होता है। वस्तुतः इनका उच्चारण अबाध एवं स्वतंत्रतापूर्वक होता है। हिन्दी के भाषा-वैज्ञानिकों ने स्वर वर्णों की संख्या ग्यारह निर्धारित की है। स्वर निम्नलिखित हैं :—अ, आ, इ, ई, उ, ऊ, ए, ऐ, ओ, औ, ऋ।

विद्वानों का एक वर्ग 'ऋ' को अब हिन्दी वर्णमाला के अन्तर्गत नहीं रखता है। क्योंकि इसका प्रयोग मात्र तत्सम शब्दों में ही होता है। वास्तव में 'ऋ' के प्रयोग की अपनी सीमाएँ हैं।

स्वरों का वर्गीकरण : सामान्यतः स्वरों का वर्गीकरण चार आधारों पर किया जाता है—

(*i*) उच्चारण काल
(*ii*) उत्पत्ति
(*iii*) जाति
(*iv*) उच्चारण स्थान।

उच्चारण-काल का आधार : उच्चारण-काल का आधार स्वर के उच्चारण में लगे हुए समय से है। कुछ स्वर ऐसे हैं जिनके उच्चारण में कम समय लगता है और कुछ ऐसे हैं जिनके उच्चारण में अधिक। उच्चारण में लगे समय का मापन मात्रा से किया जाता है। उच्चारण के काल-मान को मात्रा कहते हैं। उच्चारण-काल के आधार पर स्वरों के दो भेद किये जाते हैं :

(क) ह्रस्व स्वर (Short Vowel)
(ख) दीर्घ स्वर (Long Vowel)

(क) **ह्रस्व स्वर** : जिनके उच्चारण में समय कम लगता है उन स्वरों को ह्रस्व स्वर कहते हैं। जैसे—अ, इ, उ, ए, ऋ।

(ख) **दीर्घ स्वर** : जिनके उच्चारण में अधिक समय लगता है, उन्हें दीर्घ स्वर कहते हैं। जैसे—आ, ई, ऊ, ऐ, औ।

उत्पत्ति का आधार : उत्पत्ति को आधार मानकर भी स्वरों का वर्गीकरण दो रूपों में किया गया है—(i) मूल स्वर (ii) संधि स्वर

(*i*) **मूल स्वर** : मूल स्वर उन स्वरों को कहते हैं जिनकी उत्पत्ति में दूसरे स्वरों की आवश्यकता नहीं होती है। जैसे—अ, इ, उ, ऋ।

(*ii*) **संधि स्वर** : संधि स्वर उन स्वरों को कहते हैं जिनकी उत्पत्ति मूल स्वरों के योग से होती है। संधि स्वर के भी दो भेद हैं—(अ) दीर्घ संधि स्वर (ब) संयुक्त संधि स्वर

(अ) **दीर्घ संधि स्वर** : किसी एक मूल स्वर में उसी मूल स्वर के योग से बने स्वर को दीर्घ संधि कहते हैं। जैसे : आ, ई, ऊ।

(ब) **संयुक्त संधि स्वर** : दो भिन्न स्वरों के मेल से निर्मित स्वर संयुक्त संधि स्वर कहे जाते हैं। जैसे—अ + इ = ए, अ + उ = ओ, आ + ए = ऐ, आ + ओ = औ। इस प्रकार—ए, ऐ, ओ, औ—संयुक्त संधि स्वर हैं।

जाति का आधार : जाति के आधार पर स्वरों को निम्नलिखित वर्गों में विभक्त किया गया है—

(*i*) सवर्ण स्वर (*ii*) असवर्ण स्वर

(*i*) **सवर्ण स्वर** : सवर्ण स्वर वे हैं जिनका उच्चारण समान स्थान तथा प्रयत्न से होता है। इन्हें सजातीय स्वर भी कहते हैं। जैसे : अ, आ, इ, ई, उ, ऊ।

(*ii*) **असवर्ण स्वर** : असवर्ण स्वर वे हैं जिनका उच्चारण अलग-अलग स्थानों तथा असमान प्रयत्नों से होता है। इसे विजातीय स्वर भी कहते हैं। जैसे : अ + इ = ए, आ + ए = ऐ, अ + उ = ओ, अ + ओ = औ।

उच्चारण-स्थान का आधार

स्वरों के उच्चारण में जिह्वा तथा ओष्ठ की विशेष भूमिका है। अतएव इनको आधार मानकर स्वरों के अनेक भेद किये गये हैं।

जिह्वा के भागों के आधार पर

स्वरों के उच्चारण में कभी जिह्वा का अग्रभाग काम करता है तो कभी पश्चभाग और कभी मध्यभाग। अतः इस दृष्टि से स्वरों के निम्नलिखित भेद हो सकते हैं:

(*i*) **अग्रस्वर :** ये वे स्वर हैं जिनके उच्चारण में जिह्वा का अग्रभाग कार्य करता है। जैसे—इ, ई, ए, ऐ।

(*ii*) **मध्य स्वर :** यह स्वर जिह्वा के मध्य भाग से उच्चरित होता है। जैसे—अ।

(*iii*) **पश्च स्वर :** पश्च स्वर वे स्वर हैं जिनका उच्चारण जिह्वा के पश्चभाग से होता है। जैसे—आ, उ, ऊ, ओ, औ।

जिह्वा की ऊँचाई के आधार पर : तालु और जिह्वा के मध्य की ऊँचाई के अनुसार स्वरों के निम्नलिखित चार भेद हैं :-

(*i*) **संवृत :** संवृत स्वरों के उच्चारण में जिह्वा तालु से नीचे सटी रहती है। जैसे—इ, ई, उ, ऊ।

(*ii*) **अर्द्ध संवृत :** अर्द्ध संवृत स्वरों के उच्चारण करते समय जिह्वा अपेक्षाकृत कम सटी रहती है। जैसे—ए, ओ।

(*iii*) **विवृत :** विवृत स्वर के उच्चारण में जिह्वा ऊपर उठी रहती है। जैसे :—आ।

(*iv*) **अर्द्ध विवृत :** अर्द्ध विवृत स्वर के उच्चारण में जिह्वा विवृत की अपेक्षा कुछ समय ऊपर जाती है। जैसे—ऐ, औ।

ओष्ठ की स्थिति के आधार पर

इसके अनुसार स्वरों के तीन भेद किये गए हैं :

(*i*) **वर्तुल :** वर्तुल स्वर वे हैं जिनके उच्चारण में ओष्ठ की स्थिति गोलाकार हो जाती है। जैसे—उ, ऊ।

(*ii*) **अर्द्ध वर्तुल :** इन स्वरों के उच्चारण में ओष्ठ वर्तुल स्वरों की अपेक्षा कुछ कम गोल होते हैं। जैसे—ओ, औ।

(*iii*) **अवर्तुल :** ऐसे स्वर जिनके उच्चारण में ओष्ठ फैले रहते हैं, अवर्तुल कहे जाते हैं। जैसे—इ, ई, ए, ऐ, अ, आ।

व्यंजन (Consonant)

व्यंजन : वे ध्वनियाँ जिनके उच्चारण में बाहर निकलती हुई वायु मुख विवर में किसी न किसी स्थान पर बाधित होती है, व्यंजन कहलाती हैं। व्यंजन ध्वनि का उच्चारण स्वतंत्र रूप से नहीं होता है। अर्थात् इनके उच्चारण में स्वर की सहायता की आवश्यकता पड़ती है। जैसे—क, च, ट, त, प, आदि। हिन्दी में व्यंजन ध्वनियों की संख्या 33 है।

व्यंजन की परिभाषा दूसरे प्रकार से भी दी जा सकती है। जिन वर्णों का उच्चारण किसी दूसरे वर्ण की सहायता से (स्वर की सहायता से) होता है या स्वरों की सहायता के बिना नहीं हो सकता—उन्हें व्यंजन वर्ण कहते हैं। 'अ' के बिना व्यंजन का उच्चारण संभव नहीं है। उदाहरण—क् + अ = क, ग् + अ = ग आदि।

व्यंजनों को निम्नलिखित वर्गों में रखा जाता है:

क वर्ग	क ख ग घ ङ
च वर्ग	च छ ज झ ञ
ट वर्ग	ट ठ ड ढ ण
त वर्ग	त थ द ध न
प वर्ग	प फ ब भ म
अन्तस्थ	य र ल व
उष्म	श ष स ह
संयुक्त व्यंजन	क्ष त्र ज्ञ
द्विगुण व्यंजन	ड़ ढ़
अनुस्वार	(ं)
विसर्ग	(:)

हिन्दी व्यंजन ध्वनियों का उच्चारण निम्नलिखित आधार पर किया जाता है—

(*i*) उच्चारण स्थान के आधार पर

(*ii*) उच्चारण प्रयत्न के आधार पर

उच्चारण स्थान के आधार पर

ध्वनि का उच्चारण मुख के जिस स्थान विशेष से होता है उसको उस ध्वनि विशेष का उच्चारण स्थान कहा जाता है। उच्चारण स्थान को दृष्टि में रखकर व्यंजन के निम्नलिखित भेद किये गये हैं :

(क) कंठ्य (ख) तालव्य (ग) मूर्धन्य (घ) दन्त्य (ङ) ओष्ठ्य (च) दन्तोष्ठ्य (छ) नासिक्य (ज) कण्ठ तालव्य (झ) कण्ठोष्ठ्य

(क) कंठ्य : कंठ से उच्चरित ध्वनियों को कंठ्य ध्वनियाँ कहते हैं। जैसे—क, ख, ग, घ, ङ। अ, आ, और विसर्ग भी।

(ख) तालव्य : तालु से उच्चारण की जाने वाली ध्वनियाँ तालव्य ध्वनियाँ कही जाती हैं। जैसे—च, छ, ज, झ, ञ, श, य। इ, ई भी।

(ग) मूर्धन्य : मूर्धा का स्थान कठोर तालु और कोमल तालु के मध्य है। जैसे : ट, ठ, ड, ढ, ण।

(घ) दन्त्य : दन्त्य ध्वनियाँ वे हैं जिनके उच्चारण में जिह्वा ऊपर की दन्तावली का स्पर्श करती है। जैसे—त, थ, द, ध, न, ल, स।

(ङ) ओष्ठ्य : वे ध्वनियाँ जिनका उच्चारण दोनों ओष्ठों के सम्पर्क में आने से होता है ओष्ठ्य कहलाती हैं। जैसे—प, फ, ब, भ, म। उ, ऊ भी।

(च) दन्तोष्ठ्य : दन्तोष्ठ्य वे ध्वनियाँ हैं जिनका उच्चारण ऊपर की दन्तावली और अधरोष्ठ के सम्पर्क से होता है।

(छ) नासिक्य : जिन ध्वनियों के उच्चारण में नासिका की सहायता लेनी पड़ती है उन्हें नासिक्य या आनुनासिक ध्वनियाँ कहते हैं। जैसे—ङ, ञ, ण, न, य।

(ज) कण्ठ तालव्य : जिन ध्वनियों के उच्चारण में तालु और कण्ठ दोनों को सहयोग करना पड़ता है, उन्हें कण्ठ तालव्य ध्वनियाँ कहते हैं। जैसे—ए, ऐ।

(झ) कण्ठोष्ठ्य : वे ध्वनियाँ कण्ठोष्ठ्य हैं जिनका उच्चारण कण्ठ और ओष्ठ्य के मिले-जुले प्रयत्न से होता है। जैसे—ओ, औ।

उच्चारण प्रयत्न के आधार पर

व्यंजन ध्वनियों के उच्चारण-काल में उनमें स्पष्टता लाने के लिए जो क्रिया करनी पड़ती है उसे 'प्रयत्न' कहते हैं।

उच्चारण-प्रयत्न की दृष्टि से हिन्दी के व्यंजनों का वर्गीकरण निम्नलिखित है–

(क) **स्पर्श :** इन व्यंजनों के उच्चारण के समय वागेन्द्रिय विभिन्न उच्चारण अवयवों को संस्पर्शित करती है। वस्तुतः इनके उच्चारण-काल में वायु बाहर निकलते समय अवरुद्ध होती है। तदन्तर वायु वेग से बाहर निकलती है और उसी समय व्यंजन ध्वनि का निर्माण करती है। इस प्रक्रिया से उत्पन्न व्यंजन को स्पर्श व्यंजन कहते हैं। क वर्ग, च वर्ग, ट वर्ग, तथा प वर्ग की व्यंजन ध्वनियाँ स्पर्श हैं।

(ख) **उष्म :** कुछ ध्वनियों के उच्चारण के समय वायु पूर्ण रूप से अवरुद्ध नहीं होती वरन् आंशिक रूप में अवरुद्ध होती है। इस समय वायु मुख-विवर से संकीर्ण मार्ग से बाहर निकलती है जिससे उसका संघर्षण होता है। इस संघर्षण की क्रिया से उत्पन्न ध्वनि को उष्म कहते हैं। श, ष, स, ह उष्म व्यंजन ध्वनियाँ हैं।

(ग) **पार्श्विक :** पार्श्विक ध्वनि के उच्चारण में जिह्वा का अगला हिस्सा मसूड़े को स्पर्श करता है और वायु जिह्वा के दाहिने तथा बायें पार्श्व से बाहर निकल जाती है। केवल 'ल' ध्वनि पार्श्विक है।

(घ) **लुण्ठित :** लुण्ठित ध्वनि वह है जिसके उच्चारण में जिह्वा का अग्रांश दन्त मूल को छूता है और छूते समय उसमें कम्पन उत्पन्न होता है। केवल 'र' लुण्ठित व्यंजन ध्वनि है।

(ङ) **उत्क्षिप्त :** इन ध्वनियों को उच्चारित करते समय जिह्वा का निचला हिस्सा कठोर तालु को ताड़ित करता है अर्थात् उसमें ठोकर मारता है और तेजी से सामान्य स्थिति में लौट आता है। ड़, ढ़ उत्क्षिप्त ध्वनियाँ हैं।

(च) **अल्पप्राण :** जिन वर्णों के उच्चारण में अल्पप्राण अर्थात् कम वायु की आवश्यकता पड़ती है, उन्हें अल्पप्राण कहते हैं। प्रत्येक वर्ण की प्रथम, तृतीय, पंचम ध्वनियाँ अल्पप्राण होती हैं। जैसे–क, ग, ङ, च, ज, ञ, ट, ड, ण, त, द, न, प, ब, म तथा य, र, ल, व अल्पप्राण हैं।

(छ) **महाप्राण :** महाप्राण ध्वनियाँ वे हैं जिनके उच्चारण में अधिक वायु की जरूरत होती है। इन ध्वनियों के उच्चारण में हकार की ध्वनि सुनाई देती पड़ती है। प्रत्येक वर्ग के द्वितीय, और चतुर्थ व्यंजन महाप्राण हैं। जैसे–ख, घ, छ, झ, ठ, ढ़, थ, ध, फ, भ, तथा श, ष, ह।

(ज) **घोष व्यंजन :** घोष व्यंजन वे हैं जिनके उच्चारण में स्वर यंत्रों में प्रकम्पन होते हैं। इन्हें नाद ध्वनियाँ भी कहते हैं। प्रत्येक वर्ग का तीसरा, चौथा और पाँचवा व्यंजन घोष या नाद वर्ण है। जैसे–ग, घ, ङ, ज, झ, ञ, द, ध, न, ब, भ, म।

(झ) **अघोष व्यंजन :** अघोष व्यंजन के उच्चरित होने में स्वर यंत्रों में कम्पन नहीं होता है। प्रत्येक वर्ग का प्रथम और द्वितीय वर्ण अघोष होता है। जैसे–क, ख, च, छ, त, थ, प, फ।

(ञ) **अन्तस्थ वर्ण :** य और व को अंतस्थ माना जाता है।

नवागत ध्वनियाँ

हिन्दी में कुछ विदेशी ध्वनियों का आगम हुआ है। ये ध्वनियाँ मूलतः अरबी-फारसी की हैं जो उर्दू के माध्यम से हिन्दी में पहुँची हैं। इन ध्वनियों को हिन्दी ने आत्मसात् कर लिया है। जैसे–क़, ख़, ग़, ज़, फ़।

अनुस्वार और विसर्ग

अनुस्वार और विसर्ग भी व्यंजन वर्ण हैं। अनुस्वार के लिए एक बिन्दु तथा विसर्ग के लिए दो बिन्दुओं का प्रयोग किया जाता है। अनुस्वार का प्रयोग स्वर/व्यंजन के ऊपर तथा विसर्ग का स्वर/व्यंजन के बाद किया जाता है। जैसे–अं, अः, पं, तः।

वर्तनी विवेक

अशुद्ध	शुद्ध	अशुद्ध	शुद्ध
आर्दश	आदर्श	अत्योक्ति	अत्युक्ति
आसीस	आशीष	अद्यपि	यद्यपि
आवश्यक्ता	आवश्यकता	तथापी	तथापि
आल्हाद	आह्लाद	असाढ़	आषाढ़
आशिर्वाद	आशीर्वाद	अध्यात्मिक	आध्यात्मिक
आमिश	आमिष	ऐतिहासज्ञ	इतिहासज्ञ
आधीन	अधीन	इतिहासिक	ऐतिहासिक
अधीनस्त	अधीनस्थ	संसारिक	सांसारिक
गृहस्त	गृहस्थ	समाजिक	सामाजिक
आरोग्यता	आरोग्य	अभीष्ठ	अभीष्ट
निरोग	नीरोग	इक्षा	इच्छा
अंधेर	अँधेरा	अस्थान	स्थान
आंख	आँख	अतिथी	अतिथि

अशुद्ध	शुद्ध	अशुद्ध	शुद्ध
अर्थात	अर्थात्	समीती	समिति
भगवान	भगवान्	इकठ्ठा	इकट्ठा
श्रीमान	श्रीमान्	इक्षुक	इच्छुक
श्रीमति	श्रीमती	स्वक्ष	स्वच्छ
अवकास	अवकाश	महत्व	महत्त्व
अर्ध	अर्द्ध	उद्येश	उद्देश्य
अहिल्या	अहल्या	उज्वल	उज्ज्वल
द्रोपती	द्रौपदी	उंगली	उँगली
द्वारिका	द्वारका	उलटा	उल्टा
इसाई	ईसाई	चिन्ह	चिह्न
ईर्षा	ईर्ष्या	एश्वर्य	ऐश्वर्य
आनाथ	अनाथ	उपलक्ष	उपलक्ष्य
असहनीय	असह्य	उलंघन	उल्लंघन

अशुद्ध	शुद्ध	अशुद्ध	शुद्ध	अशुद्ध	शुद्ध	अशुद्ध	शुद्ध
अपरान्ह	अपराह्न	उँषा	उषा	श्रृजन	सृजन	वनिक	वणिक्
पूर्वान्ह	पूर्वाह्न	अहसास	एहसास	द्वैवार्षिक	द्विवार्षिक	विधिवत	विधिवत्
मध्यान्ह	मध्याह्न	कवियित्रि	कवयित्री	द्रविभूत	द्रवीभूत	विरहणी	विरहिणी
स्वास्थ	स्वास्थ्य	कौशिल्या	कौशल्या	पृष्ट	पृष्ठ	वैमनस्यता	वैमनस्य
कार्यकर्म	कार्यक्रम	धूआं	धुआँ	पत्नि	पत्नी	विद्यार्थि	विद्यार्थी
कार्रवाही	कार्यवाही	नारायन	नारायण	निछावर	न्यौछावर	वापिस	वापस
कार्यबाई	कार्रवाई	रामायन	रामायण	निरपराधी	निरपराध	वक्तागण	वक्तृगण
केन्द्रीयकरण	केन्द्रीकरण	अर्चणा	अर्चना	भागिरथी	भागीरथी	श्राप	शाप
औद्योगीकरण	उद्योगीकरण	नबाब	नवाब	मिश्रदेश	मिस्रदेश	शुद्धीकरण	शुद्धिकरण
गूंगा	गूँगा	जबाब	जवाब	महाराजा	महाराज	शक्ती	शक्ति
कैलाश	कैलास	नुपुर	नूपुर	मृन्मय	मृण्मय	शाहस	साहस
कनिष्ट	कनिष्ठ	नैपुण्यता	नैपुण्य, निपुणता	मूर्छा	मूर्च्छा	विभूती	विभूति
कौतुहल	कौतूहल	निर्गुणी	निर्गुण	मूहुर्त	मुहूर्त	श्रीयुत्	श्रीयुत
कोमलांगिनी	कोमलांगी	निछावर	न्यौछावर	यथेष्ठ	यथेष्ट	श्री युक्त	श्री युत
गरदन	गर्दन	निरिह	निरीह	मुंह	मुँह	संग्रहीत	संगृहीत
गरिष्ट	गरिष्ठ	परिशिष्ठ	परिशिष्ट	महानतम	महत्तम	श्रेष्ट	श्रेष्ठ
गर्द्धव	गर्दभ	प्राप्ती	प्राप्ति	मंत्रीवर	मंत्रिवर	सदृश्य	सदृश
चर्मोत्कर्ष	चरमोत्कर्ष	पूज्यनीय	पूज्य, पूजनीय	मंत्रीमण्डल	मंत्रिमण्डल	सप्ताहिक	साप्ताहिक
चांद	चाँद	प्रमाणिक	प्रामाणिक	यशलाभ	यशोलाभ	विहंगिनी	विहंगी
चक्षूरोग	चक्षुरोग	प्रदर्शिनी	प्रदर्शनी	राजागण	राजगण	स्थायीत्व	स्थायित्व
चारदीवारी	चहारदीवारी	प्रज्ज्वलित	प्रज्वलित	लिपी	लिपि	समुद्रिक	सामुद्रिक
ज्योत्सना	ज्योत्स्ना	प्रसंशा	प्रशंसा	रूग्न	रुग्ण	स्वामी भक्ति	स्वामिभक्ति
जगत	जगत्	परिस्थिती	परिस्थिति	ललायित	लालायित	हितैशी	हितैषी
ज्येष्ट	ज्येष्ठ	पौरुषत्व	पौरुष, पुरुषत्व	रूपया	रुपया	सैना	सेना
जगबन्धु	जगद्बन्धु	पाठार	पठार	मैथली	मैथिली	सेनिक	सैनिक
तिलांजली	तिलांजलि	पक्षीगण	पक्षिगण	महान	महान्	पृथवी	पृथ्वी
तत्कालिक	तात्कालिक	बाल्मिकी	वाल्मीकि	याज्ञवल्क	याज्ञवल्य	दयालू	दयालु
तत्व	तत्त्व	ब्रम्ह	ब्रह्म	रुक्मणी	रुक्मिणी	इन्दू	इन्दु
तलाब	तालाब	बृज	ब्रज	धूली	धूलि	हिन्दु	हिन्दू
त्रिवार्षिक	त्रैवार्षिक	बृजभाषा	ब्रजभाषा	अंजली	अंजलि	गुरू	गुरु
तरुछाया	तरुच्छाया	बांस	बाँस	शशी भूषण	शशिभूषण	रितु	ऋतु
त्रितीय	तृतीय	बारात	बरात	जागरन	जागरण	व्यंग	व्यंग्य
तदोपरान्त	तदुपरान्त	बंगला	बँगला	अन्तरराष्ट्रीय	अन्तर्राष्ट्रीय	बधू	वधू
द्वन्द	द्वन्द्व	बुद्धिवान	बुद्धिमान	सन्यासी	संन्यासी	बृहस्पति	वृहस्पति
दूकान	दुकान	भष्म	भस्म	बन्दना	वन्दना	बुद्धवार	बुधवार
दाइत्व	दायित्व	भीस्म	भीष्म	परिनाम	परिणाम	तृया	त्रिया
दिवारात्रि	दिवारात्र	भाग्यमान	भाग्यवान	लक्षमण	लक्ष्मण	स्त्रीयाँ	स्त्रियाँ
धोका	धोखा	पाठान	पठान	नदीयाँ	नदियाँ	महीलाएँ	महिलाएँ
पुरष्कार	पुरस्कार	विकाश	विकास	भूगोलिक	भौगोलिक	ऐतिहासिक	ऐतिहासिक
श्रृंगार	शृंगार	व्यवहारिक	व्यावहारिक	ऐनक	ऐनक	जै	जय
श्रृष्टि	सृष्टि	बीणा	वीणा	पाठान	पठान	प्रतिक्षा	प्रतीक्षा
सूचि	सूची	बिमार	बीमार	छिपकिली	छिपकली	गीतांजली	गीतांजलि
संसारिक	सांसारिक	संपत्ती	संपत्ति	एंपायर	अंपायर	अगामी	आगामी
बजाए	बजाय	शिखिर	शिखर	महाबलि	महाबली	सूनसान	सुनसान

वस्तुनिष्ठ प्रश्नोत्तर

1. व्याकरण–
   A. भाषा की लिपि निर्धारित करता है
   B. भाषा को सुबोध बनाता है
   C. भाषा का रूप निर्धारित करता है
   D. भाषा के वर्णों का अध्ययन करता है

2. वर्ण–
   A. स्वर हैं B. व्यंजन हैं
   C. ध्वनियाँ हैं D. उच्चारण हैं

3. हिन्दी में कितने वर्ण हैं?
   A. 56 B. 26
   C. 44 D. 36

4. स्वर/स्वरों–
   A. मूल ध्वनियाँ हैं
   B. को किसी अन्य ध्वनि की सहायता के बिना उच्चरित किया जा सकता है
   C. की संख्या 11 है
   D. उपरोक्त सभी

5. जिन स्वरों के उच्चारण में 'अ' के उच्चारण के बराबर समय लगता है, उन्हें क्या कहते हैं?
   A. दीर्घ स्वर B. ह्रस्व स्वर
   C. प्लुत स्वर D. पूर्ण स्वर

6. क् + ष =
   A. श B. क्ष
   C. ष D. उपर्युक्त में से कोई नहीं

7. व्यंजन तीन प्रकार के होते हैं–(*i*) स्पर्श, (*ii*) अन्तस्थ और (*iii*)....
   A. ऊष्म B. कन्ठ्य
   C. दन्तोष्ठ D. नासिका

8. त, थ, द, ध, का उच्चारण–
   A. दाँतों के साथ जिह्वा के मेल से होता है
   B. कंठ और ओठों के मेल से होता है
   C. केवल ओठों से होता है
   D. जीभ के प्रयोग के बिना होता है

9. एक या एक से अधिक वर्णों के संयोग से बनी ध्वनियों को क्या कहते हैं?
   A. स्वर B. व्यंजन
   C. शब्द D. रूढ़ि

10. 'पाठशाला' शब्द किस वर्ग का है?
   A. यौगिक
   B. रूढ़ि
   C. योगरूढ़ि
   D. उपर्युक्त में से कोई नहीं

निर्देश (प्रश्न संख्या 11 से 25 तक): *इन प्रश्नों में स्वर या मात्रा की दृष्टि से शब्द को अशुद्ध रूप में लिया गया है। नीचे दिए गए चार विकल्पों में से शुद्ध रूप चुनिए।*

11. A. निलिप्त B. निर्लप्त
   C. निर्लिप्त D. निर्लीप्त

12. A. इच्छादुम B. इच्छाद्रम
   C. इच्छाद्रुम D. इच्छादम

13. A. द्विरूक्ति B. दिरुक्ति
   C. द्विरक्ती D. द्विरुकती

14. A. विसमृति B. विसमरती
   C. विस्मती D. विस्मृति

15. A. जगतापाण B. जगतप्राण
   C. जगत्प्राण D. जगत्पाण

16. A. आर्शीवाद B. आशिर्वाद
   C. आशीर्वाद D. आर्शिवाद

17. A. सास्टांग B. साष्टांग
   C. सस्टांग D. शाष्टांग

18. A. परिस्थती B. परीस्थिति
   C. परिस्थिति D. परिस्थिती

19. A. पृक्रति B. प्रकृती
   C. प्रिकृति D. प्रकृति

20. A. वाँक्षनीय B. वाँछनीय
   C. वाँछनिय D. वान्छनीय

21. A. स्वर्गिय B. र्स्वगीय
   C. स्वर्गीय D. स्वर्गीअ

22. A. विस्वास B. विश्वास
   C. वीश्वास D. विष्वास

23. A. प्रज्वलित B. प्रज्जलित
   C. प्रज्जवलित D. प्रजलित

24. A. कौशल्या B. कोशल्या
   C. कौसल्या D. कोसल्या

25. A. पूज्यनीय B. पूजनीय
   C. पुजनीय D. पूजनिय

निर्देश (प्रश्न संख्या 26 से 40 तक): *नीचे दिए गए वाक्यों में गहरे काले शब्दों की वर्तनी के लिए चार-चार विकल्प दिए गए हैं। इनमें से एक विकल्प में शब्द की वर्तनी शुद्ध है। उस विकल्प को चुनिए–*

26. चारों ओर **उजज्वल** चाँदनी फैली थी
   A. उज्वल B. उज्ज्वल
   C. उज्जवल D. उजज्वल

27. हमें नियमों का **उलंल्वन** नहीं करना चाहिए
A. उल्लंघन B. उलंल्वन
C. उलंघन D. ऊल्लंघन

28. हम **जान्तंत्रिक** पद्धति में विश्वास करतें हैं
A. जानतांत्रिक B. जनतांत्रिक
C. जनतांत्रीक D. जनतंत्रिक

29. इस पुस्तक के अन्त में दो **परिशिष्ठ** दिए गए हैं
A. परिशिष्ठ B. प्ररिशिष्ट
C. परिशिष्ट D. प्रशिष्ट

30. आपके दर्शन कर मैं स्वयं को **कृत्यकृत्य** अनुभव करता हूँ
A. कृत्यकृत B. कृत्यक्रत्य
C. कृत्कृत्य D. कृतकृत्य

31. यदि आप **विद्वेशपूर्ण** अफवाहें फैलाते हैं तो आपके साथी भी यही करने लगेंगे
A. विद्धेषपूर्ण B. विद्वेशपूर्ण
C. वीद्वेशपूर्ण D. विद्वेषपूर्ण

32. अपने **तात्कालीक** कर्त्तव्य के अतिरिक्त अन्य किसी भी बात पर विचार न कीजिए
A. तत्कालिक B. तात्कालिक
C. तातकालिक D. तात्कालीक

33. आइए पढ़-लिखकर स्वयं को **लाभान्वीत** करें
A. लाभान्वित B. लाभानिवित
C. लाभान्वीत D. लाभन्वित

34. कानपुर एक महत्वपूर्ण **व्यावसाइक** केन्द्र है
A. व्यावसायक B. व्यावसाइक
C. व्यावसाईक D. व्यावसायिक

35. प्रगति मैदान **प्रदर्शिनी** के लिए उपयुक्त स्थान है
A. पृदर्शनी B. प्रदर्शनी
C. प्रदर्शिनी D. प्रियदर्शिनी

36. अपने पूर्वजों के **पदचिन्हों** पर चलना हमारा कर्त्तव्य है
A. पादचिह्नों B. पदचिह्नों
C. पदचिह्नों D. पदचिण्हों

37. कल **साँयकाल** का मौसम बड़ा ही सुहावना था
A. सायंकाल B. सायकाल
C. साँयकाल D. सायमकाल

38. विक्रमी **संवत** ईसवी सन् से 57 वर्ष आगे रहता है
A. संवत् B. संबत
C. सम्वत D. समवत्

39. **युधिस्टिर** सबसे बड़े पाण्डव थे
A. युधिस्थिर B. युधिस्टिर
C. युधिष्ठिर D. युधष्ठिर

40. प्रधानमंत्री ने **मंत्रिमण्डल** के बैठक की अध्यक्षता की
A. मन्त्रिमन्डल B. मन्त्रिमण्डल
C. मन्त्रीमण्डल D. मंत्रीमण्डल

41. क्ष, त्र, ज्ञ वर्ण है :
A. संयुक्त व्यंजन B. उष्म व्यंजन
C. स्पर्श व्यंजन D. अंतःस्थ व्यंजन

42. फ, ब किस प्रकार के वर्ण हैं?
A. दंतोष्ठ्य B. मूर्धन्य
C. तालव्य D. ओष्ठ्य

43. ध्वनि किसकी लघुत्तम इकाई है?
A. शब्द B. भाषा
C. वाक्य D. अक्षर

44. बिना अवरोध के उच्चारित होने वाले वर्ण कहलाते हैं :
A. घोष B. स्पर्श
C. स्वर D. व्यंजन

45. इनमें से कौन स्पर्श व्यंजन है?
A. क–वर्ग B. च–वर्ग
C. त–वर्ग D. ये सभी

उत्तरमाला

1	2	3	4	5	6	7	8	9	10
C	C	C	D	B	B	A	A	C	A
11	**12**	**13**	**14**	**15**	**16**	**17**	**18**	**19**	**20**
C	C	A	D	C	C	B	C	D	A
21	**22**	**23**	**24**	**25**	**26**	**27**	**28**	**29**	**30**
C	B	C	A	B	B	A	B	C	D
31	**32**	**33**	**34**	**35**	**36**	**37**	**38**	**39**	**40**
D	B	A	D	B	B	A	A	C	B
41	**42**	**43**	**44**	**45**					
A	D	B	C	D					

★ ★ ★

2

शब्दभेद (स्रोत/उत्पत्ति)

शब्द

ध्वनियों के मेल से बने सार्थक वर्ण समुदाय को 'शब्द' कहते हैं। दूसरे शब्दों में—एक अक्षर या एक से अधिक अक्षरों का समूह, जिसका कुछ अर्थ होता है, शब्द कहा जाता है।

जैसे—पुष्प, पहाड़, लड़का, मैं, तुम आदि।

शब्दों का वर्गीकरण

साधारणतः शब्दों का वर्गीकरण चार आधारों पर किया जाता है। ये आधार निम्नलिखित हैं :

(1) व्युत्पत्ति के आधार पर
(2) उत्पत्ति के आधार पर
(3) अर्थ के आधार पर
(4) विकार के आधार पर

व्युत्पत्ति के आधार पर

व्युत्पत्ति के आधार पर शब्दों के तीन भेद होते हैं :-

(क) रूढ़ (ख) यौगिक (ग) योगरूढ़

(क) रूढ़ : रूढ़ वे शब्द हैं जिनका खण्ड नहीं हो सकता। यदि इन शब्दों को खण्डित कर दिया जाता है तो उनके खण्डों का कोई अर्थ नहीं होता। जैसे—नाक, कान, घर, जल, फल, शीला, सीता, राम, हल, रात आदि।

(ख) यौगिक : वे शब्द जिनका निर्माण अन्य शब्दों के या प्रत्ययों के जोड़ से होता है, यौगिक कहे जाते हैं। जैसे—पाठशाला, दहीवाली, नाकवाला, शक्तिवान, पानीवाला आदि।

(ग) योगरूढ़ : योगरूढ़ शब्द दूसरे शब्दों के योग से निर्मित होते हैं। खण्ड करने पर इनके प्रत्येक खण्ड या योग का अपना अर्थ होता है। परन्तु जब दोनों खण्डों को एक कर दिया जाता है तो उस शब्द का अपना एक विशेष अर्थ होता है। इस प्रकार, योगरूढ़ वे शब्द हैं जो दूसरे शब्दों के योग से बनते हैं और प्रत्येक योग का अपना अर्थ होता है तथापि उनका एक विशेष अर्थ होता है।

उदाहरणतः जलज में जल का अर्थ है पानी और 'ज' का अर्थ है—जन्म लेने वाला। इस प्रकार दोनों का अर्थ हुआ जल में जन्म लेने वाला। परन्तु यह शब्द जल में उत्पन्न होने वाले सेवार आदि अन्य पदार्थों के लिए व्यवहृत नहीं होता है, वरन् कमल के लिए रूढ़ हो गया है और उससे मात्र कमल का बोध होता है। इसी प्रकार जलद, कुशल, पीताम्बर, लम्बोदर आदि शब्द हैं।

उत्पत्ति के आधार पर

उत्पत्ति के अनुसार शब्दों का वर्गीकरण निम्नलिखित है : (क) तत्सम (ख) तद्भव (ग) देशज (घ) विदेशज

(क) तत्सम : तत्सम मूलतः संस्कृत के शब्द हैं। संस्कृत के इन शब्दों के प्रयोग हिन्दी में ज्यों-के-त्यों होते हैं। जैसेः—कवि, घृत, अग्नि, रवि, माता, भ्राता, पिता, अमृत, महान् आदि।

(ख) तद्भव : तद्भव वे शब्द हैं जिनका विकास संस्कृत के शब्दों से हुआ है। तद्भव का अर्थ है—'तत्' (तस्य) = उसके अर्थात् 'संस्कृत से' और 'भव' अर्थात् उत्पन्न। जैसे—घृतः = घी, अग्नि = आग, कर्म = काम, दाध = दही, अमृत = अमरित, कार्य = कारज, दुग्ध = दूध, जन्म = जनम, धर्म = धरम आदि।

(ग) देशज : देशज का अर्थ है—देश में उत्पन्न। हिन्दी भाषा के वे शब्द जो भारत की विभिन्न बोलियों एवं भाषाओं से आए हैं, देशज कहे जाते हैं। जैसे—कटोरी, थाली, पेट, पैर, पेड़, लोटा, डोरी आदि।

(घ) विदेशज : हिन्दी भाषा के वे शब्द जिनका आगम विदेशी भाषाओं से हुआ है, विदेशज शब्द कहे जाते हैं। जैसे—चाक़ू, मोटर, ट्रेन, स्टेशन, आदमी, अमीर, फालतू, किताब, तारीख़, तकिया, गवाह, देहात, जहर, बाल्टी, चेहरा, लगाम, क़ालीन, कैंची, बेग़म, तम्बाकू, बहादुर, प्रेस, पार्टी, स्टेशन, गजट, डायरी, रेडियो, नम्बर, नोटिस आदि।

अर्थ के आधार पर

अर्थ के अनुसार शब्दों के दो भेद हैं :

(क) सार्थक (ख) निरर्थक

(क) सार्थक : सार्थक शब्द वे हैं, जिनका कुछ अर्थ होता है। जैसे—घर, घोड़ा, कमल, कलम, पुस्तक आदि। ये सभी शब्द सार्थक हैं, क्योंकि इन शब्दों के कहने से किसी परिचित पदार्थ का बिम्ब बनता है। जैसे—पुस्तक कहने से पढ़ने के काम में आने वाली किताब का बोध होता है। इस प्रकार ऊपर सभी शब्द सार्थक हैं।

(ख) **निरर्थक :** निरर्थक शब्द वे हैं जिनका कुछ भी अर्थ नहीं होता है। जैसे—अल्ल, बल्ल, गर्र, फर्र, मलक, नीपा, धदू आदि।

विकार के आधार पर

विकार के अनुसार सार्थक शब्दों के दो भेद किए गए हैं : (क) विकारी (ख) अविकारी

(क) विकारी शब्द

विकारी शब्द वे शब्द हैं, जिनके रूप में विकार या परिवर्तन होता है। यह विकार लिंग, वचन और कारक में होता है। जैसे—घोड़ा।

लिंग के कारण परिवर्तन	घोड़ा से घोड़ी।
वचन के कारण परिवर्तन	घोड़ा से घोड़े, घोड़ों।
कारक के कारण परिवर्तन	घोड़ा से घोड़ों ने, घोड़े से आदि।

विकारी शब्दों के भेद

विकारी शब्दों के चार भेद हैं : *(i)* संज्ञा *(ii)* सर्वनाम *(iii)* विशेषण *(iv)* क्रिया

(i) **संज्ञा :** संज्ञा का अर्थ है नाम। किसी वस्तु, व्यक्ति, स्थान आदि के नाम को संज्ञा कहते हैं। जैसे—घर, पटना, कलम, बुढ़ापा आदि।

(ii) **सर्वनाम :** सर्वनाम उन शब्दों को कहते हैं जिनका प्रयोग संज्ञा के स्थान पर होता है। जैसे—वह, मैं, तुम, उस, आप, वे आदि।

(iii) **विशेषण :** संज्ञा अथवा सर्वनाम की विशेषता प्रकट करने वाले शब्द को विशेषण कहते हैं। जैसे—सुन्दर, मोटा, लाल, काला, दुबला आदि।

(iv) **क्रिया :** क्रिया उन शब्दों को कहते हैं जिनसे किसी काम का होना या करना प्रकट हो, जैसे—खाना, रोना, हँसना, लिखना आदि।

(ख) अविकारी शब्द

वे शब्द जिनके रूप में विकार अथवा परिवर्तन नहीं होता है, अविकारी शब्द कहलाते हैं, अर्थात लिंग, वचन और कारक की दृष्टि से कोई परिवर्तन या विकार नहीं होता है। अविकारी शब्द 'अव्यय' भी कहलाते हैं।

अविकारी शब्दों के चार भेद हैं—

(i) क्रिया विशेषण *(ii)* समुच्चय बोधक *(iii)* सम्बन्ध बोधक *(iv)* विस्मयादि बोधक

(i) **क्रिया विशेषण :** क्रिया की विशेषता प्रकट करने वाले शब्द क्रिया विशेषण कहलाते हैं। जैसे—धीरे-धीरे, जल्दी-जल्दी आदि।

(ii) **समुच्चय बोधक :** समुच्चय बोधक शब्द वे हैं जो दो शब्दों, वाक्यों या वाक्यांशों को परस्पर जोड़ते हैं। जैसे—परन्तु, किन्तु, तथा और आदि।

(iii) **सम्बन्ध बोधक :** सम्बन्ध बोधक वे अव्यय हैं जो एक शब्द का दूसरे शब्द से सम्बन्ध स्थापित करते हैं। जैसे—ऊपर, नीचे, समीप, पास, निकट आदि।

(iv) **विस्मयादि बोधक :** विस्मय, हर्ष, शोक, घृणा, आदि भावों को प्रकट करने के लिए जिन शब्दों का प्रयोग किया जाता है, उन्हें विस्मयादि बोधक अव्यय कहते हैं। जैसे—हाय! छिः! अरे! हे! आदि।

प्रमुख विदेशी शब्द

अंग्रेजी भाषा के शब्द

अफसर, अपील, अस्पताल, ऑर्डर, ऑर्डरली, इंच, इंजन, इन्जीनियर, इन्सपेक्टर, एजेन्ट, एजेन्सी, कप्तान, कम्पनी, कमिश्नर, कमीशन, कैम्प, कोर्ट, क्वार्टर, क्रिकेट, केबिन, गार्ड, गजट, गवर्नर, गारंटी, जेलर, जेल, डॉक्टर, डायरी, डेयरी, डिप्टी, डिस्ट्रिक्ट, ट्यूशन, टीचर, पेन, पेंसिल, पॉकेट, नोटिस, नर्स, नम्बर, पार्टी, पार्सल, प्लेट, पाउडर, मीटिंग, मिनिस्टर, मोनीटर, मेनेजमेंट, मार्केट, म्युनिस्पेलटी, पार्लियामेंट, क्वालिटी, कॉलेज, कस्टमर, टिकट, चेन, चैलेंज, टेलीविजन, रेडियो, कम्प्यूटर, मीडिया, मेम्बर, ट्राफिक, ट्रेन, प्लेटफार्म, ड्रेस, ड्रामा, कार्बन, हेलिकॉप्टर, कॉर्पोरेशन आदि।

अरबी भाषा के शब्द

अमीर, अजीब, अजब, अहमियत, आखिर, आदमी, अक्ल, असर, आदत, इनाम, इज्जत, इमारत, इलाज, ईनाम, औरत, औलाद, कसूर, कदम, कर्ज, किस्त, किस्मत, कसम, कीमत, कसरत, कुर्सी, किताब, खबर, खत्म, खराब, गरीब, जवाब, तकदीर, तारीख, तकिया, तमाशा, तरक्की, दिमाग, दवा, दावा, दावत, दावात, दफ्तर, दुकान, दौलत, नतीजा, नशा, नकद, नकल, नहर, फकीर, फैसला, बहस, मुहावरा, माल, मालूम, मल्लाह, मवाद, मौसम, मुसाफिर, लिफाफा, लायक, वकील, शराब, हिम्मत, हैजा, कैद, हक, हुक्म, हाल, हवालात, हाकिम आदि।

तुर्की भाषा के शब्द

उर्दू, कालीन, कैंची, कुली, कुर्की, चेचक, चमचा, चुगली, चकमक, तमगा, तलाश, तोप, बहादुर, बेगम, लफंगा, लाश, सुराग, कुर्ता, खच्चर, दारोगा, बारूद आदि।

पुर्तगाली भाषा के शब्द

अलकतरा, अनन्नास, आया, आलपीन, आलमारी, इंसान, इस्तिरी, कमीज, किरानी, कमरा, काजू, गमला, गोदाम, गोभी, चाभी, तम्बाकू, तौलिया, नीलाम, पादरी, पिस्तौल, फीता, मेज, लबादा, साया आदि।

फारसी भाषा के शब्द

आराम, आमदनी, अफसोस, आतिशबाजी, आवारा, आफत, आवाज, आईना, उम्मीद, कबूतर, कमीना, कुश्ती, किशमिश, कमरबन्द, किनारा, खाल, खुद, खामोश, खरगोश, खुश, खुराक, खूब, गल्ला, गवाह, गिरफ्तार, गरम, गुलाब, चाबुक, चिराग, चश्मा, चर्खा, चूंकि, चेहरा, जहर, जिन्दगी, जादू, जान, जुर्माना, जोश, तमाशा, तेज, तीर, ताक, ताजा, दीवार, देहात, दुकान, दरबान, दंगल, दिल, दवा, नाव, पलंग, पैदावार, पलक, पुल, पारा, पेशा, बहरा, बीमार, मुफ्त, मोर्चा, मुर्गा, मरहम, याद, यार, रंग, रात, लेकिन, शादी, शोर, सितारा, सरदार, सरकार, सूद, सौदागर आदि।

तत्सम-तद्भव शब्द

तत्सम	तद्भव	तत्सम	तद्भव	तत्सम	तद्भव	तत्सम	तद्भव
आम्र	आम	अग्नि	आग	दंश	डंक	धान्य	धान
उष्ट्र	ऊँट	वत्स	बच्चा	नव्य	नया	मुक्ता	मोती
नव	नौ	मध्य	में	पौत्र	पोता	मित्र	मीत
शलाका	सलाई	गृह	घर	दूर्वा	दूब	मृत्यु	मौत
पुष्प	फूल	मयूर	मोर	दृष्टि	दीठि	रिक्त	रीता
नारिकेल	नारियल	हरिद्रा	हल्दी	धरित्री	धरती	रक्षिका	राखी
कर्पूर	कपूर	घृत	घी	स्थाल	थाली	पंक्ति	पाँत
सक्तु	सत्तू	हस्त	हाथ	प्रस्तर	पत्थर	पाद	पाँव
चतुर्दश	चौदह	क्षीर	खीर	ग्रन्थि	गाँठ	ज्येष्ठ	जेठ
घोटक	घोड़ा	दुग्ध	दूध	क्षुद्र	छोटा	यम	जम
चंचु	चोंच	मेघ	मेह	द्यूत	जुआ	त्वरित	तुरत
शत	सौ	कार्य	काज	तादृश	तैसा	स्थल	थल
क्षेत्र	खेत	कर्ण	कान	रात्रि	रात	नृत्य	नाच
हस्ति	हाथी	दन्त	दाँत	वारिद	बादल	नासिका	नाक
तिक्त	तीता	वधू	बहू	विद्युत	बिजली	पूप	पूआ
कर्म	काम	स्वर्णकार	सोनार	वंशी	बाँसुरी	ध्वनि	धुन
चत्वारि	चार	अक्षि	आँख	भद्र	भला	गर्दभ	गदहा
पर्यंक	पलंग	कच्छप	कछुआ	भ्रातृ	भाई	निर्झर	झरना
अग्रणी	अगाड़ी	उपवास	उपास	भिक्षा	भीख	दण्ड	डण्डा
अक्षर	आखर	उच्च	ऊँचा	भ्रू	भौंह	तृण	तिनका
अट्टालिका	अटारी	कोटि	करोड़	भक्त	भगत	निर्वाह	निबाह
अगणित	अनगिनत	चित्रक	चीता	वंश	बाँस	ताम्र	ताम्बा
आमसक	आँवला	चतुष्पाद	चौपाया	लवण	नोन	योद्धा	जोधा
आलस्य	आलस	चतुर्वेदी	चौबे	यज्ञोपवीत	जनेऊ	युवक	जवान
कपाट	किवाड़	चैत्र	चैत	निमंत्रण	न्योता	शर्करा	शक्कर
कुम्भकार	कुम्हार	चतुर्थ	चौथा	श्वसुर	ससुर	शून्य	सूना
चन्द्रिका	चाँदनी	क्षुर	छुरा	शृंगार	सिंगार	श्रावण	सावन
कोकिल	कोयल	छिद्र	छेद	सर्व	सब	उल्लास	हुलास
कंकण	कंगन	कुपुत्र	कपूत	हरित	हरा	सूर्य	सूरज
कुष्ठ	कोढ़	चणक	चना	शृंगाल	सियार	शिंशपा	शीशम
काक	कौआ	चर्मकार	चमार	स्रोत	सोत	भ्रमर	भौंरा
कार्तिक	कातिक	घट	घड़ा	स्वर्ण	सोना	महिषी	भैंस
आश्चर्य	अचरज	चक्रवाक	चकवा	स्वामी	साईं	श्मशान	मसान
आदित्यवार	इतवार	तीक्ष्ण	तीखा	शृंग	सींग	मत्स्य	मछली
दधि	दही	पुस्तिका	पोथी	संध्या	सांझ	मस्तक	माथा
घृणा	घिन	पाषाण	पाहन	श्वाँस	साँस	मशक	मच्छर
गृहणी	घरनी	मिष्ट	मीठा	स्वजन	साजन	शूचि	सूई
ग्राहक	गाहक	पृष्ठ	पीठ	शिक्षा	सीख	शूकर	सूअर
ग्राम	गाँव	पूर्ण	पूरा	सूत्र	सूत	सर्प	साँप
गंभीर	गहरा	प्रतिच्छाया	परछाई	शय्या	सेज	हट्ट	हाट
गर्त	गड्ढ़ा	पश्चाताप	पछतावा	हरिण	हिरन	ओष्ठ	होंठ
युक्ति	जुगत	पर्पट	पापड़	हीरक	हीरा	शाक	साग
जंघा	जाँघ	पार्श्व	पास	श्रेणी	सीढ़ी	स्वप्न	सपना

वस्तुनिष्ठ प्रश्नोत्तर

1. उत्पत्ति की दृष्टि से शब्दों के कितने भेद हैं?
A. चार B. छह
C. आठ D. दस

2. तद्भव शब्द के कितने भेद बताए गए हैं?
A. दो B. चार
C. आठ D. दस

3. हिन्दी में 'अल्ला' किस विदेशी शब्द का रूपांतर है?
A. तुर्की B. फारसी
C. अरबी D. उपर्युक्त में से कोई नहीं

4. रचना/बनावट के अनुसार शब्दों के कितने भेद हैं?
A. एक B. दो
C. तीन D. चार

5. 'पीला-पान' निम्न में से किस प्रकार का शब्द है?
A. रूढ़ B. यौगिक
C. योगरूढ़ D. इनमें से कोई नहीं

6. निम्न में से कौन-सा शब्द योगरूढ़ है?
A. लम्बोदर B. पंकज
C. चक्रपाणि D. इनमें से सभी

7. 'आलपीन' किस विदेशी शब्द का हिन्दी रूप है?
A. पुर्तगाली B. तुर्की
C. अंग्रेजी D. इनमें से कोई नहीं

8. निम्न में से कौन-सा शब्द असंगत है?
A. अफसोस B. आतिशबाजी
C. आमदनी D. किताब

9. निम्न में से कौन योगरूढ़ है?
A. आग-बबूला B. दूध-वाला
C. छल-छंद D. पंकज

10. निम्न में से कौन संस्कृत का तत्सम रूप नहीं है?
A. गोमल B. घोटक
C. हरिद्रा D. आग

11. निम्न शब्दों में से कौन-सा मूल शब्द है?
A. नाक B. कान
C. मुंह D. इनमें से सभी

12. 'अपील' निम्न में से किसका तत्सम रूप है?
A. पुर्तगाली B. अंग्रेजी
C. अरबी D. फारसी

13. 'अधिकरण' शब्द रूप में कौन-सा शब्द रूप असंगत है?
A. अ B. करण
C. अधि D. इनमें से सभी

14. 'लालिमा' शब्द में कौन-सा प्रत्यय है?
A. इमा B. एमा
C. ईमा D. इनमें से कोई नहीं

15. 'इत' प्रत्यय से निर्मित शब्दों में कौन असंगत है?
A. पंचाइत B. संगीत
C. गोराइत D. रंगत

16. 'आई' प्रत्यय से बने शब्दों में कौन सही है?
A. चतुराई B. भलाई
C. बुराई D. इनमें से सभी

17. 'निपटारा' शब्द में कौन-सा प्रत्यय है?
A. आरा B. अरा
C. रा D. इनमें से कोई नहीं

18. 'पौरूषेय' में कौन-सा प्रत्यय है?
A. एय B. ए
C. ऐ D. इनमें से कोई नहीं

19. 'शौकीन' शब्द रूप से मूल शब्द को अलग कर प्रत्यय बताएं?
A. ईन B. कीन
C. ई D. इनमें से कोई नहीं

20. 'बांसुरी' शब्द रूप में कौन-सा प्रत्यय है?
A. सुरी B. री
C. बाँ D. इनमें से कोई नहीं

21. 'उमस' शब्द रूप से मूल शब्द और प्रत्यय को अलग कर मूल शब्द को लिखें?
A. मस B. उम
C. स D. इनमें से सभी

22. 'जमींदार' शब्द रूप में से प्रत्यय को अलग कर प्रत्यय को लिखें?
A. दार B. र
C. मींदा D. इनमें से कोई नहीं

23. नीचे दिए गए शब्दों में से कौन तत्सम रूप है?
A. गोबर B. घोड़ा
C. शत D. खीर

24. 'तम्बाकू' निम्न में से किस विदेशी शब्द का हिन्दी रूप है?
A. अरबी B. फारसी
C. पुर्तगाली D. अंग्रेजी

25. 'चक्रपाणि' निम्न में से किस तरह का शब्द है?
A. रूढ़ B. यौगिक
C. योगरूढ़ D. इनमें से कोई नहीं

26. 'लालटेन' निम्न में से किस विदेशी शब्द का तद्भव रूप है?
A. पुर्तगाली B. अंग्रेजी
C. अरबी D. तुर्की

27. दिए गए रूढ़ शब्दों में से कौन-सा असंगत है?
A. नाक B. कान
C. पीला D. पंकज

28. 'अधि' उपसर्ग से बने शब्दों में से कौन-सा असंगत है?
A. अधिपति B. अधिकार
C. अधिपाठक D. अत्यधिक

29. 'निपटारा' शब्द में कौन-सा प्रत्यय लगा है?
A. टारा B. आरा
C. पिटारा D. इनमें से कोई नहीं

30. 'आना' प्रत्यय से निर्मित शब्द-रूपों में से कौन-सा असंगत है?
A. मिलाना B. उठाना
C. सिरहाना D. इनमें से कोई नहीं

31. 'सुहावना' शब्द-रूप में से प्रत्यय को छांटिए?
A. हावना B. आवना
C. अवना D. वना

32. 'आहट' प्रत्यय से निर्मित शब्द रूपों में से कौन-सा असंगत है?
A. गड़गड़ाहट B. गुर्राहठ
C. चिकनाहट D. कड़वाहट

33. निम्न में से कौन-सा देशज प्रत्यय का उदाहरण है?
A. आहट B. इयल
C. ओड़ा D. उपरोक्त में सभी

34. 'प्यास' शब्द-रूप में कौन-सा प्रत्यय लगा है?
A. आश B. आष
C. आस D. इनमें से सभी

35. 'न' प्रत्यय से निर्मित शब्द रूपों में से कौन-सा असंगत है?
A. चलन B. कथन
C. पतन D. इनमें से कोई नहीं

36. 'धुंधला' शब्द-रूप में से प्रत्यय को अलग करें?
A. ल B. अला
C. ला D. आला

37. 'लालसा' शब्द-रूप में से प्रत्यय को अलग छांटिए?
A. स B. सा
C. आसा D. लसा

38. 'पीहर' शब्द-रूप में से प्रत्यय से मूल शब्द को छांटिए?
A. पीह B. हर
C. पहर D. इनमें से कोई नहीं

39. 'मेहनताना' मूल शब्द से प्रत्यय को अलग करें?
A. आना B. मेहनत
C. ताना D. इनमें से कोई नहीं

40. निम्न में से कौन-सा शब्द यौगिक का उदाहरण नहीं है?
A. विद्यालय B. हिमालय
C. आग-बबूला D. झट

41. 'जलज' निम्न में से किस तरह का शब्द है?
A. रूढ़ B. यौगिक
C. योगरूढ़ D. उपरोक्त में से सभी

42. 'चाबी' निम्न में से किस विदेशी शब्द का हिन्दी रूप है?
A. अंग्रेजी B. पुर्तगाली
C. अरबी D. फारसी

43. 'कुली' किस विदेशी भाषा का शब्द है?
A. तुर्की B. अरबी
C. पुर्तगाली D. अंग्रेजी

44. निम्न में से कौन-सा विदेशी उपसर्ग का उदाहरण है?
A. हर B. कम
C. बद D. इनमें से सभी

45. निम्न में से किस शब्द में अंग्रेजी उपसर्ग हैं?
A. हैड ऑफिस
B. सब-इंस्पेक्टर
C. को-ऑपरेटिव
D. उपरोक्त सभी में

उत्तरमाला

1	2	3	4	5	6	7	8	9	10
A	A	C	C	B	A	A	D	D	D
11	**12**	**13**	**14**	**15**	**16**	**17**	**18**	**19**	**20**
D	B	C	A	D	D	A	A	A	B
21	**22**	**23**	**24**	**25**	**26**	**27**	**28**	**29**	**30**
B	B	C	C	C	B	D	D	B	D
31	**32**	**33**	**34**	**35**	**36**	**37**	**38**	**39**	**40**
B	B	D	C	D	C	B	B	A	D
41	**42**	**43**	**44**	**45**					
C	B	A	D	D					

★ ★ ★

3

पर्याय/विलोम

पर्यायवाची शब्द

किसी शब्द के समान अर्थ के लिए जिन शब्दों को प्रयोग में लाया जाता है उन्हें पर्यायवाची शब्द कहा जाता है। आशय यह है कि पर्याय का अभिप्राय 'बदले में आने वाला' से लिया गया है। पर्यायवाची शब्द को 'प्रतिशब्द' भी कहते हैं। हिन्दी के कुछ पर्यायवाची शब्द निम्नांकित हैं—

अग्नि — पावक, आग, दहन, हुताशन, ज्वलन, कृशानु।

अमृत — सुधा, अमिय, पीयूष, मधु, जीवनोदक।

अधम — नीच, दुष्ट, पामर, खल, दुर्जन।

अन्न — अनाज, राशि, धान्य, दाना।

नदी — सरिता, नद, पयश्विनी, आपगा, तरंगिणी।

नरक — यमपुर, यमलोक, यमालय, कृतान्तगेह।

पवित्र — निर्मल, विमल, पावन, शुद्ध, विशुद्ध।

पर्वत — नग, पहाड़, भूधर, गिरि, तुंग, अद्रि।

पण्डित — सुधी, विद्वान, मनीषी, प्रबुद्ध, कोविद।

पेड़ — पादप, वृक्ष, तरू, विटप, द्रुय, गाछ।

पुत्र — सुत, बेटा, तनय, आत्मज, लड़का, तनुज।

पुत्री — सुता, बेटी, तनया, आत्मजा, लड़की, तनुजा।

पृथ्वी — भू, धरा, वसुधा, वसुन्धरा, अवनि, मही।

भूपति — नृप, नरेश, राजा, नरपति, भूपाल।

हवा — वायु, समीर, पवन, अनिल, समीरण।

सरस्वती — वीणापाणि, शारदा, माहश्वेता, पद्मासना, वाणी, भारती।

साँप — सर्प, अहि, नाग, विषधर, भुजंग, व्याल, पन्नग।

समुद्र — सागर, उदधि, पयोधि, नदीस, सिन्धु, रत्नाकर, जलधि।

दुःख — पीड़ा, कष्ट, व्यथा, वेदना, यातना, खेद, सन्ताप।

विष्णु — वज्रपाणि, विश्वम्भर, माधव, दामोदर, लक्ष्मीपति, गोविन्द, नारायण।

तालाब — सरोवर, सर, जलाशय, पोखर, पुष्कर, पद्माकर, ताल, तड़ाग।

बाण — तीर, शर, नाराच, विशिख, शिलीमुख।

वाटिका — बाग, उपवन, बगीचा, उद्यान, आराम।

समूह — समुदाय, वृन्द, दज, झुण्ड, मण्डली, टोली, जत्था।

फूल — पुष्प, पुहुप, प्रसून, सुमन, कुसुम, सारंग।

ब्रह्मा — विधि, स्वयंभू, चतुरानन, प्रजापति, विधाता, पितामह।

भौंरा — मधुप, भ्रमर, भृंग, मधुकर, षट्पद, भँवरा।

शिव — महेश्वर, शंकर, चन्द्रशेखर, नीलकण्ठ, त्रिलोचन, शंभु, पशुपति, महादेव, त्रिनेत्र।

मुनि — संन्यासी, अवधूत, साधु, सन्त, योगी, वैरागी।

यमुना — कालिन्दी, तरणि-तनुजा, सूर्य-सुता, जमुना, रवि-तनया।

बादल — मेघ, घन, घटा, अम्बुद, नीरद, पयोधर, जलधर, वारिद, जलद।

बिजली — विद्युत, क्षणदा, चपला, चंचला, दामिनी, क्षणप्रभा, तड़ित, सौदामिनी।

इच्छा — वांछा, अभिलाषा, कामना, स्पृहा, मनोरथ।

आम — रसाल, आम्र, अमृतफल, सहकार।

गाय — गौ, धेनु, सुरभि, गौरी, दोग्धी, सौरमेयी।

चन्द्रमा — चाँद, शशि, रजनीश, राकेश, राकापति, सुधाकर, मयंक, चन्द्र।

दूध — गोरस, दुग्ध, पय, क्षीर।

देवता — सुर, अमर, देव, निर्जर, विबुध।

धन — अर्थ, द्रव्य, वित्त, सम्पदा, सम्पत्ति, दौलत, विभूति।

पक्षी — खग, विहग, विहंग, परिन्दा, पखेरू, चिड़िया, द्विज, अण्डज।

गणेश — गणपति, गजानन, विनायक, एकदंत, लम्बोदर, मोदकप्रिय।

गदहा — खर, गर्दभ, रासभ, वैशाखनन्दन, धूसर, वेशर।

गंगा — भागीरथी, जाह्नवी, त्रिपथगा, मंदाकिनी, देवापमा, देवनदी, सुरसरि।

कुबेर — यक्षराज, धनपति, किन्नरेश, धनराज, धनद, यक्षपति।

किरण — रश्मि, अंशु, कर, मरीचि, मयूख, गो, प्रभा, अर्चि।

किनारा — कूल, तट, कगार, तीर, छोर।

इन्द्र — सुरपति, देवेन्द्र, देवराज, मधवा, पुरन्दर, वासव, शचीपति, बिड़ौजा।

ईश्वर	–	परमात्मा, प्रभु, ईश, ब्रह्मा, भगवान्, जगदीश, परमपिता।
आँख	–	लोचन, दृग, नेत्र, नयन, चक्षु, दृष्टि, अक्षि।
घोड़ा	–	अश्व, घोटक, वाजि, हय, तुरंग, सैन्धव, हरी।
आकाश	–	गगन, अम्बर, व्योम, नभ, आसमान, अनन्त।
राक्षस	–	दैत्य, दनुज, दानव, यातुधान, निशाचर, रजनीचर।
कपड़ा	–	वस्त्र, पट, अम्बर, वसन, चीर, परिधान।
कामदेव	–	मदन, मन्मथ, अनंग, पुष्पधन्वा, पंचशर।
चतुर	–	निपुण, दक्ष, कुशल, चालाक, होशियार, विज्ञ, नागर।
अनुपम	–	अनूठा, अद्वितीय, अद्भुत, अपूर्व, अनूप, विलक्षण।
अहंकार	–	घमण्ड, दर्प, अभिमान, दंभ।
मछली	–	मीन, मत्स्य, झख, शफरी, नस-जीवन।
माता	–	माँ, जननी, अम्बा, अम्मा।
पत्थर	–	पाहन, पाथर, पाषाण, अश्म, उपस, प्रस्तर।
नाव	–	नौका, पतंग, बेड़ा, जलयान, डोंगी, तरी, तरणी।
रात	–	निशा, रजनी, विभावरी, रात्रि, यामिनी, रैन, शर्वरी, राका।
पत्नी	–	वधू, भार्या, दारा, कलय, प्राणप्रिय, अर्द्धांगिनी।
सोना	–	कंचन, कनक, हेम, सुवर्ण, कसधौत, हाटक, हिरण्य।
हाथी	–	गज, द्विप, करी, कुंजर, द्विरद, नाग।
हाथ	–	कर, हस्त, पाणि।
स्त्री	–	महिला, नारी, कान्ता, कामिनी, वनिता, रमणी।
सूर्य	–	दिनकर, दिवाकर, भास्कर, मार्तण्ड, दिनेश, दिनमान, अंशुमाली, भानु, रवि।
सिंह	–	शेर, मृगराज, शार्दूल, मृगेन्द्र, केशरी, व्याघ्र, वनराज, पंचानन, पंचमुख।
सुन्दर	–	सलिल, रुचिर, चारु, मनोहर, रमणीय, कमनीय, अभिराम।
सेवक	–	भृत्य, नौकर, अनुचर, चाकर, किंकर, दास, परिचारक।

विपरीतार्थक शब्द

विपरीतार्थक शब्द वे हैं जो दिए गए किसी शब्द का विलोम या उल्टा अर्थ बताते हैं।

शब्द	विपरीतार्थक शब्द	शब्द	विपरीतार्थक शब्द
उत्तम	अधम	आभ्यंतर	बाध्य
अन्तर्मुखी	बहिर्मुखी	आस्तिक	नास्तिक
सुगम	अगम	आर्द्र	शुष्क
सुलभ	दुर्लभ	आत्मा	परमात्मा
सुबोध	दुर्बोध	आयात	निर्यात
सरस	नीरस	आसक्त	अनासक्त
अन्तर्द्वन्द्व	बहिर्द्वन्द्व	अन्धकार	प्रकाश
अल्पायु	दीर्घायु	अथ	इति
अग्रज	अनुज	अवनि	अम्बर
आगमन	प्रस्थान	अधिक	न्यून
आदि	अन्त	अज्ञ	विज्ञ
अनुलोम	प्रतिलोम	अतिवृष्टि	अनावृष्टि
अति	अल्प	अँधेरा	उजाला
अमर	मर्त्य	अनुकूल	प्रतिकूल
अमावस्या	पूर्णिमा	अनिवार्य	वैकल्पिक
अनुरक्ति	विरक्ति	अल्पमत	बहुमत
आकाश	पाताल	अनुगामी	अग्रगामी
आगामी	गत/विगत	अपव्ययी	मितव्ययी
आदर	निरादर	अपमान	सम्मान
आय	व्यय	अपना	पराया
आशा	निराशा	अनुराग	विराग

शब्द	विपरीतार्थक शब्द	शब्द	विपरीतार्थक शब्द
आविर्भाव	तिरोभाव	अपेक्षा	उपेक्षा
अन्तर्धान	तिरोधान	अल्पसंख्यक	बहुसंख्यक
आकर्षण	विकर्षण	अमृत	विष
उत्कर्ष	अपकर्ष	अरुचि	सुरुचि
उत्थान	पतन	अभिशाप	वरदान
उन्नत	अवनत	आवृत्त	अनावृत्त
उन्नति	अवनति	इहलोक	परलोक
जय	पराजय	कटु	मधु
इच्छा	अनिच्छा	कठोर	कोमल
इष्ट	अनिष्ट	कपट	निष्कपट
उपकार	अपकार	कनिष्ठ	ज्येष्ठ
उत्साह	निरुत्साह	कर्मण्य	अकर्मण्य
उर्वर	उरुसर	कीर्ति	अपकीर्ति
उऋण	ऋणी	वक्र	सरल
उग्र	शान्त	सुन्दर	कुरूप
शान्त	अशान्त	क्रय	विक्रय
उतार	चढ़ाव	खरीद	फरोख्त
उच्च	निम्न	कृत्रिम	प्राकृतिक
उदय	अस्त	कृतज्ञ	कृतघ्न
उँच	नीच	कृष्ण	शुक्ल
उद्याचल	अस्ताचल	खण्डन	मण्डन

शब्द	विपरीतार्थक शब्द	शब्द	विपरीतार्थक शब्द
उदार	कृपण	गणतन्त्र	राजतन्त्र
उत्कृष्ट	निकृष्ट	गरल	सुधा
उत्तीर्ण	अनुत्तीर्ण	स्वर्ग	नरक
उपयुक्त	अनुपयुक्त	गुण	दोष
उपसर्ग	प्रत्यय	गुप्त	प्रकट
उपयोग	अनुपयोग	गुरु	लघु
सदुपयोग	दुरूपयोग	विपन्न	सम्पन्न
उधार	नकद	राजा	रंक
हर्ष	विषाद	अमीर	गरीब
एक	अनेक	धनी	निर्धन
एड़ी	चोटी	दुर्बल	सबल
एकत्र	विकीर्ण	घर	बाहर
ग्राह्य	त्याज्य	चर	अचर
गृहस्थ	संन्यासी	चिरन्तन	नश्वर
आद्य	अन्त्य	चोर/असाधु	साधु
आम	खास	छूत	अछूत
ऐश्वर्य	अनैश्वर्य	जागरण	निद्रा
ऐतिहासिक	अनैतिहासिक	जंगम	स्थावर
करुण	निष्ठुर	जीवित	मृत
झूठ	सच	जंगली	पालतू
मिथ्या	सत्य	प्राचीन	नवीन/अर्वाचीन
ताप	शीत	प्रत्यक्ष	परोक्ष
तीव्र	मन्द	प्रवृत्ति	निवृत्ति
तुच्छ	महान्	प्रशंसा	निन्दा
तुकान्त	अतुकान्त	प्रसिद्ध	अप्रसिद्ध
दक्षिण	उत्तर	प्रेम	घृणा
पूरब	पश्चिम	पूर्णता	अपूर्णता
प्रलय	सृष्टि	पूर्ण	अपूर्ण
दुर्जन	सज्जन	बन्धन	मोक्ष/मुक्ति
स्वच्छ	अस्वच्छ	पूर्ववर्ती	परवर्ती
संश्लिष्ट	विश्लेषित	सफल	असफल/निष्फल
स्वामी	सेवक	पुरातन	नूतन
देशज	विदेशज	पुराना	नया
देव	दानव	बर्बर/असभ्य	सभ्य
देवता	राक्षस	अन्तरंग	बहिरंग
धर्म	अधर्म	बलवान	बलहीन
धैर्य	अधैर्य	भद्र	अभद्र
नश्वर	शाश्वत	भेद	अभेद
नगर	ग्राम	लघुता	गुरुता

शब्द	विपरीतार्थक शब्द	शब्द	विपरीतार्थक शब्द
नागरिक	ग्रामीण	लिप्त	निर्लिप्त
नाम	अनाम	लोभी	निर्लोभी
नाथ	अनाथ	लौकिक	अलौकिक
निरर्थक	सार्थक	विमुख	सम्मुख
निरामिष	सामिष	विधवा	सधवा
निर्लज्ज	सलज्ज	विशिष्ट	साधारण
नैसर्गिक	कृत्रिम	विस्तृत	संक्षिप्त
परमार्थ	स्वार्थ	विधि	निषेध
पक्ष	विपक्ष	विवेक	अविवेक
पराजय	जय/विजय	वीर	कायर
पण्डित	मूर्ख	वृद्धि	ह्रास
परतन्त्र	स्वतन्त्र	व्यावहारिक	अव्यावहारिक
आजाद	गुलाम	आसक्ति	अनासक्ति
पाप	पुण्य	वैतनिक	अवैतनिक
पुरस्कार	तिरस्कार	सदाचारी	दुराचारी
प्रधान	गौण	समास	व्यास
सम	विषम	सदय	निर्दय
सक्रिय	निष्क्रिय	समष्टि	व्यष्टि
सगुण	निर्गुण	सम्मुख	विमुख
सहयोगी	प्रतियोगी	समूल	निर्मूल
सखा/मित्र	शत्रु	सार्थक	निरर्थक
सशंक	निस्संक	सात्विक	तामसिक
सापेक्ष	निरपेक्ष	साकार	निराकार
साक्षर	निरक्षर	सुपात्र	कुपात्र
सुगन्ध	दुर्गन्ध	सुपथ	कुपथ
सुशील	दुःशील	सुमति	कुमति
सुकर्म	कुकर्म	स्तुत्य	निंद्य
स्थूल	सूक्ष्म	क्षम्य	अक्षम्य
मूर्त	अमूर्त	श्री गणेश	इति श्री
सुर	असुर	श्लील	अश्लील
सुकाल	अकाल	शोषक	पोषक
सुदूर	सन्निकट	शासक	शासित
सुसंगति	कुसंगति	स्तुति	निन्दा
सौभाग्य	दुर्भाग्य	शिक्षित	अशिक्षित
सम्पन्न	विपन्न	श्वेत	श्याम
संकल्प	विकल्प	श्रव्य	दृश्य
सन्धि	विच्छेद	हास	रुदन
सन्तोष	असन्तोष	हित	अहित
संघटन	विघटन	हिंसा	अहिंसा

वस्तुनिष्ठ प्रश्नोत्तर

निर्देश (प्रश्न संख्या 1 से 15 तक): *नीचे एक शब्द दिया गया है। दिए गए चार विकल्पों में से पर्यायवाची शब्द ज्ञात करना है।*

1. अनन्त
A. विष्णु B. अतिशय
C. असंख्य D. आकाश

2. आडम्बर
A. ढोंग B. तम्बू
C. दर्प D. आवाज

3. कपाल
A. अदृष्ट B. खप्पर
C. भाग्य D. माथा

4. छंद
A. आवरण B. पद
C. बंधन D. आचरण

5. ऐश्वर्य
A. बड़ाई B. विलास
C. सुख D. सम्पदा

6. खर
A. रावण B. कुंठित
C. गधा D. मूर्ख

7. पक्षी
A. नीरज B. नभ
C. विहग D. सरसिज

8. कमल
A. कुसुम B. पुष्प
C. प्रसून D. पुंडरीक

9. चतुरानन
A. ब्रह्मा B. इन्द्र
C. विष्णु D. देवता

10. जल
A. घटा B. नीर
C. दिनकर D. सुधाकर

11. अमृत
A. सुधा B. कौमुदी
C. मन्मथ D. सुधाकर

12. इच्छा
A. अमिय B. हर्ष
C. आकांक्षा D. रश्मि

13. उद्यान
A. धाम B. कुसुमाकर
C. आलय D. वाटिका

14. अन्त्य
A. समाप्त B. अन्तिम
C. नीच D. कुलीन

15. घर
A. सदन B. उपवन
C. पंचशर D. हुताशन

निर्देश (प्रश्न संख्या 16 से 25 तक): *निम्नलिखित वाक्यों में गहरे काले शब्दों के लिए पर्यायवाची जोड़ों का चयन कीजिए।*

16. **मछली** का चित्र किसने बनाया है?
A. मीन–मत्स्य B. सफरी–धात्री
C. जलनिगग्नि–मकर D. भामा–मत्स्य

17. **नारी** स्वभावतः कोमल होती है
A. त्रिया–भामिनी B. कामिनी–दामिनी
C. रमणी–कालिन्दी D. कान्ता–निशा

18. सूर्य का **प्रकाश** सम्पूर्ण धरा को आलोकित करता है
A. दिनकर–ज्योति B. छवि–प्रभाकर
C. ज्योति–दीप्ति D. प्रस्तर–अचला

19. कितना सुन्दर **घर** है?
A. शान्ति–निकेतन B. गृह–वाटिका
C. पंकज–भवन D. धाम–आलय

20. समुद्र मंथन में निकले **अमृत** के लिए देव–दानव में युद्ध शुरू हो गया
A. सुधा–मधु B. सोम–मंगल
C. रसाल–पियूष D. दृग–सुरभोग

21. **तालाब** का जल सूख गया है
A. झील–सरोवर B. तड़ाग–खड़ग
C. ताल–अवयव D. जलाशय–सरिता

22. कितना सुन्दर **पुष्प** है
A. सुमन–भ्रमर B. सुता–सुमन
C. सुमन–कुसुम D. उर्पी–प्रसून

23. **आसमान** में तारे हैं
A. व्योम–गगन B. अम्बर–लोचन
C. भवन–सैन्धव D. अम्बु–अम्बर

24. सुगन्धित **पवन** बह रही है
A. समीर–अनिल B. मारुत–अनल
C. वात–शैल D. वायु–प्रवाह

25. **घोड़ा** सड़क पर अड़कर भड़क गया
A. हय–मुकुल B. तुरंग–घोटक
C. वाजि–अम्बुज D. गदह–तुरंग

निर्देश (प्रश्न संख्या 26 से 30 तक): *निम्नलिखित विकल्पों में से कौन-सा दिए गए शब्द का सही पर्यायवाची नहीं है?*

26. देवता
A. सुर B. असुर
C. अमर D. निर्जर

27. तारा
A. अम्बु B. तारक
C. नक्षत्र D. नखत

28. बेटा
A. पुत्र B. सुत
C. आत्मज D. अग्रज

29. मनुष्य
A. नर B. महीपाल
C. मनुज D. मानव

30. गणेश
A. गणपति B. गौरीसुत
C. मतंग D. गजानन

निर्देश (प्रश्न संख्या 31 से 45 तक): *नीचे दिए गए शब्दों के विलोम के लिए चार-चार विकल्प दिए गए हैं। उनमें से उचित विकल्प का चयन कीजिए।*

31. कृपण
A. अधम B. दानी
C. कृतघ्न D. कनिष्ठ

32. क्षणिक
A. शाश्वत B. संक्षेप
C. विरह D. क्षुद्र

33. स्वदेश
A. गाँव B. नगर
C. परदेश D. स्वर्ग

34. स्तुति
A. सेवक B. निवेदन
C. प्रार्थना D. निन्दा

35. सर्दी
A. गर्मी B. धूप
C. उष्ण D. शीतल

36. शान्त
A. लघु B. चंचल
C. डरपोक D. बहादुर

37. भीगा
A. सूखा B. नरम
C. उष्ण D. गरम

38. कुसुम
A. वज्र B. नारी
C. खिन्न D. ठंडा

39. तम
A. सम B. कृश
C. नम D. प्रकाश

40. नख
A. शिख B. अनित्य
C. श्याम D. निन्दा

41. भौतिक
A. पाश्चात्य B. दैविक
C. दैहिक D. आध्यात्मिक

42. अवनि
A. आकाश B. अम्बर
C. गगन D. आसमान

43. कर्कशा
A. कोमल B. निर्मल
C. विह्वल D. व्याकुल

44. अवनत
A. बढ़ना B. उत्कर्ष
C. ऊँचा D. उन्नत

45. अति
A. न्यून B. कम
C. अल्प D. नगण्य

उत्तरमाला

1	2	3	4	5	6	7	8	9	10
C	A	D	B	D	C	C	D	A	B
11	**12**	**13**	**14**	**15**	**16**	**17**	**18**	**19**	**20**
A	C	D	C	A	A	A	C	D	A
21	**22**	**23**	**24**	**25**	**26**	**27**	**28**	**29**	**30**
A	C	A	A	B	B	A	D	B	C
31	**32**	**33**	**34**	**35**	**36**	**37**	**38**	**39**	**40**
B	A	C	D	A	B	A	A	D	A
41	**42**	**43**	**44**	**45**					
D	B	A	D	C					

★ ★ ★

4

शब्द विवेक (शब्द प्रयोग में सूक्ष्म अंतर)

युग्म शब्द को श्रुतिसम भिन्नार्थक या समोच्चरित शब्द भी कहा जाता है। इस प्रकार के दो शब्दों में मामूली-सा अन्तर होता है। वह अन्तर मात्रागत या वर्णगत होता है। फलतः ऐसे शब्द सुनने में एक समान तो लगते हैं लेकिन अर्थ भिन्न-भिन्न होते हैं। हिन्दी में ऐसे शब्दों की संख्या अत्यधिक है। नीचे वैसे प्रमुख शब्द युग्मों को अर्थ सहित प्रस्तुत किया जा रहा है–

1. अंश = भाग/हिस्सा
   अंस = कन्धा
2. अपेक्षा = आवश्यकता/उम्मीद
   उपेक्षा = अवहेलना
3. अभिराम = सुन्दर
   अविराम = लगातार
4. अनल = आग
   अनिल = हवा
5. अवलम्ब = आश्रय/सहारा
   अविलम्ब = शीघ्र
6. अन्त = समाप्त/खत्म
   अन्त्य = अन्तिम
7. अभिहित = कथित
   अविहित = अनुचित
8. अम्बुज = कमल
   अम्बुद = बादल
9. अलि = भ्रमर
   अली = सखी
10. उपकार = भलाई
    अपकार = बुराई
11. अजिक = ललाट
    अलीक = झूठ
12. अभिनय = स्वांग
    अविनय = उद्दण्डता
13. अतल = तलहीन
    अतुल = जिसकी तुलना न हो सके
14. अकथ = जो कहा नहीं जाय
    अथक = बिना थके हुए।
15. अन्न = अनाज
    अन्य = दूसरा
16. आदि = आरम्भ/शुरू
    आदी = अभ्यस्त, अदरक
17. अभय = निर्भय
    उभय = दोनों
18. अर्जन = संग्रह
    अर्चन = पूजा
19. अमित = अत्यधिक
    अमीत = शत्रु
20. अणु = सूक्ष्म कण
    अनु = पीछे
21. अशक्त = असमर्थ
    असक्त = विरक्त
22. अब्ज = कमल
    अब्द = बादल
23. अवधि = समय
    अवधी = अवध की भाषा
24. अभ्यास = अनुशीलन
    अभ्याश = पड़ोस
25. आभरण = आभूषण
    आमरण = मरण तक
26. आकर = खान
    आकार = आकृति
27. आयत = चतुर्भुज
    आयात = बाहर से लाना
28. आर्त = दुःखी
    आर्द्र = गीला
29. आवास = वास स्थान
    आभास = झलक
30. आवृत्त = घिरा हुआ
    आवृत्ति = दुहराना
31. इत्र = सुगन्धित पदार्थ
    इतर = दूसरा
32. स्त्री = महिला
    इस्त्री = कपड़े पर कलप करना
33. अरि = दुश्मन
    अरी = स्त्री के लिए सम्बोधन

34. उद्यत = तैयार, तत्पर
उद्धत = उद्दण्ड

35. ॠतु = मौसम
ॠत = सत्य

36. कश = चाबुक
कष = कसौटी

37. कुल = वंश
कूल = किनारा

38. कलि = कलियुग
कली = अधखिला फूल

39. कपिश = मटमैला
कपीश = बन्दरों का राजा

40. कर्म = कार्य
क्रम = सिलसिला

41. कंगाल = दरिद्र
कंकाल = ठठरी (मानव की)

42. कटिबद्ध = तैयार
कटिबन्ध = कमर बन्द

43. करोड़ = सौ लाख की संख्या
क्रोड़ = गोद

44. कृत = किया हुआ
क्रीत = खरीदा हुआ

45. कृपण = कंजूस
कृपाण = कटार

46. कृषाण = किसान
कृशानु = आम

47. क्रान्ति = उलटफेर, आन्दोलन
कांति = चमक

48. कुट = किला
कूट = पहाड़ की चोटी

49. कुजन = दुर्जन
कूजन = पक्षियों का कलरव

50. केशर = सिंह की गर्दन के बाल
केसर = कुमकुम

51. कोष = खजाना
कोश = शब्द-संग्रह
कोस = दो मील दूरी

52. खाद = उर्वरक
खाद्य = खाने की सामग्री

53. खोया = भूल गया
खोआ = दूध से निर्मित खाद्य पदार्थ

54. गिरि = पर्वत
गिरी = बीज/गूदा

55. चषक = प्याला
चसक = आदत

56. चरण = पैर
चारण = भाट

57. चिर = पुराना
चीर = वस्त्र

58. चिता = शव जलाने के लिए लकड़ियों की शय्या
चीता = एक हिंसक पशु

59. गृह = घर
ग्रह = नक्षत्र

60. करण = इन्द्रियाँ, करण कारक
कर्ण = कान

61. कुच = स्तर
कूच = प्रस्थान

62. कौर = ग्रास
कोर = किनारा

63. चतुष्पद = चौपाया
चतुष्पथ = चौराहा

64. चक्रवात = बवंडर
चक्रवाक = चकवा पक्षी

65. छत्र = छाता
छात्र = विद्यार्थी

66. क्षति = हानि
क्षिति = पृथ्वी

67. जलज = कमल
जलद = बादल

68. नीरज = कमल
नीरद = बादल

69. जघन्य = गर्हित
जघन = जाँच

70. जगत् = संसार
जगत = कुएँ का चबूतरा

71. जामन = दूध जमाने के लिए प्रयुक्त पदार्थ
जामुन = एक फल

72. जेठ = वर्ष का एक महीना
ज्येष्ठ = बड़ा (उम्र में)

73. टुक = थोड़ा
टूक = टुकड़ा

74. टोटा = घाटा
टोंटा = बन्दूक का कारतूस

75. तरणि = सूर्य
तरणी = नाव

76. दाई = धामी, नौकरानी
दायी = जवाबदेह

77. दारु = लकड़ी
दारू = शराब

78. दिवा = दिन
दीया = दीपक
79. दिन = दिवस
दीन = गरीब
80. द्विप = हाथी
द्वीप = टापू
81. दुर्ग = गढ़
दुर्गा = एक देवी
82. दमन = दबाना
दामन = आँचल
83. तक्र = मट्ठा
तर्क = बहस
84. द्रव्य = धन
द्रव = तरल पदार्थ
85. देव = देवता
दैव = भाग्य
86. नहर = कृत्रिम नदी
नाहर = सिंह
87. नग = पहाड़
नाग = सर्प
88. नगर = शहर
नागर = चतुर व्यक्ति
89. नाश = ध्वंस
नास = सुंघनी
90. नारी = स्त्री
नाड़ी = नब्ज
91. निसान = झण्डा
निशान = चिह्न, प्रतीक
92. निर्जर = देवता
निर्झर = झरना
93. निहित = छिपा हुआ
निहत = मरा हुआ
94. नियत = निश्चित
नीयत = इरादा
नियति = भाग्य
95. नमित = नत
निमित्त = कारण
96. नीर = जल
नीड़ = घोंसला
97. निर्माण = बनाना
निर्वाण = मोक्ष
98. नकल = अनुकरण
नकुल = नेवला, पाण्डवों में एक
99. निधन = मृत्यु
निर्धन = गरीब
100. नित = प्रतिदिन
नीत = लाया हुआ
101. नीम = एक पेड़
नींव = आधार
102. नेत्र = आँख
नेतृ = नेता
103. पुरुष = मर्द
परुष = कठोर
104. परिधान = वस्त्र
प्रधान = मुख्य
105. पवन = हवा
पावन = पवित्र
106. पाहन = पत्थर
पाहुन = अतिथि
107. परवाह = चिन्ता
प्रवाह = बहाव
108. प्रहर = समय
प्रहार = चोट
109. परिताप = दुःख
प्रताप = पराक्रम
110. पथ = मार्ग
पथ्य = रोगी का भोजन
111. पट्ट = तख्ता
पट = वस्त्र
112. प्रमाण = सबूत
प्रणाम = नमस्कार
113. परिणाम = फल
परिमाण = मात्रा
114. प्रणय = प्रेम
परिणय = विवाह
115. परदेश = दूसरा देश
प्रदेश = प्रान्त, राज्य
116. परीक्षा = इम्तहान
परिक्षा = कीचड़
117. प्रदीप = दीपक
प्रतीप = उल्टा
118. पानी = जल
पाणि = हाथ
119. पास = निकट
पाश = बन्धन
120. पिक = कोयल
पीक = पान का थूक
121. प्रेषित = भेजा हुआ
प्रोषित = प्रवासी
122. फन = कला
फण = साँप का फण

123. बलि = बलिदान
बली = वीर
124. बहन = भगिनी
वहन = ढोना
125. बहु = बहुत
बहू = पुत्रवधू
126. बार = दफा
वार = दिन
127. वाण = तीर
बान = आदत
128. बात = वचन
वात = हवा
129. भवन = घर
भुवन = संसार
130. भट = योद्धा
भट्ट = पण्डित
131. भाल = ललाट
भार = वजन
132. मल = गन्दगी
मल्ल = पहलवान
133. मणि = रत्न
मणी = सर्प
134. मद = अहंकार
मद्य = शराब
135. मनुज = मनुष्य
मनोज = कामदेव
136. मांस = गोश्त
मास = महीना
137. मात्र = केवल
मातृ = माता
138. मेध = यज्ञ
मेघ = बादल
139. मेदा = पेट
मैदा = बारीक आटा
140. रत = तल्लीन
रक्त = खून
141. रेचक = दस्तावर
रोचक = रुचिकर
142. लक्ष = लाख
लक्ष्य = उद्देश्य
143. लवण = नमक
लवन = खेत की फसल की कटाई
144. वस्तु = चीज
वास्तु = इमारत, भवन
145. अकुल = बिना कुल के
आकुल = व्याकुल
146. वरद = वर देने वाला
विरद = यश
147. वरण = चुनना
वरन् = बल्कि
148. वाद = विचार/सिद्धान्त
वाद्य = बाजा
149. वदन = मुख
बदन = शरीर
150. विस्मृत = भूला हुआ
विस्मित = आश्चर्य में पड़ा हुआ
151. विपिन = जंगल
विपन्न = दुःखी, निर्धन
152. वित्त = धन
वृत्त = गोलाकार
153. विष = जहर
विस = कमल का डण्ठल
बीस = उन्नीस से एक अधिक संख्या
154. सम = समान
शय = संचय
155. सहर = सबेरा
शहर = नगर
156. शव = लाश
शब = रात
157. सिता = चीनी
सीता = जानकी
158. शस्त्र = हथियार
शास्त्र = ग्रन्थ
159. सर = तालाब
शर = बाण
160. सुर = देवता
सूर = अंधा
शूर = वीर
161. सुत = बेटा
सूत = सारथी, धागा
162. सप्त = सात
शप्त = शाप ग्रस्त
163. शंकर = शिव
संकर = दोगला
164. सर्ग = काव्य का अध्याय
स्वर्ग = कल्पित लोक
165. स्वपच = स्वयंवाकी
श्वपच = चाण्डाल
166. सत्व = सार
स्वत्व = अधिकार

167. समिति = सभा
सम्मति = सलाह

168. शय्या = बिछावन
सज्जा = सजावट

169. संग = साथ
संघ = समिति, संगठन

170. शाला = घर
साला = पत्नी का भाई

171. सबल = ताकतवर
शवल = चितकबरा

172. सर्व = सभी
शर्व = शंकर

173. सुगन्ध = खुशबू
सौगन्ध = कसम

174. शुक्ति = सीप
सूक्ति = अच्छी उक्ति

175. शीशा = काँच
सीसा = एक धातु

176. सती = पतिव्रता नारी
शती = शताब्दी

177. श्वेत = सफेद
श्वेद = पसीना

178. शुक = सुग्गा
शूक = जौ

179. शिखर = चोटी (पर्वत की)
शेखर = सिर

180. शक्ल = चेहरा
सकल = सम्पूर्ण

181. हरि = विष्णु
हरी = हरे रंग की

182. सुमन = फूल
सुअन = पुत्र

183. संदेह = शक
सदेह = सशरीर

184. स्व = अपना
श्व = आने वाला दिन

185. शुचि = पवित्र
सूची = विषय क्रम

186. सुधि = स्मरण
सुधी = समझदार, विद्वान्

187. हल = जोतने का यंत्र
हल् = शुद्ध व्यंजन

188. भंगि = लहर
भंगी = मेहतर

189. दूत = संवाददाता
द्यूत = जुआ का खेल

190. देश = राज्य
द्वेष = शत्रुता

191. तरंग = लहर
तुरंग = घोड़ा

192. चालक = ड्राइवर
चालाक = चतुर

193. लोम = रोवाँ
लोभ = लालच

194. बिना = रहित, अभाव
वीणा = एक वाद्य यंत्र

195. प्रसाद = कृपा
प्रासाद = महल

196. भित्ति = दीवार
भीति = डर

197. मूल = जड़
मूल्य = दाम

198. अक्ष = धुरी
यक्ष = एक देव योनि

199. अश्व = घोड़ा
अश्म = पत्थर

200. आसन = बैठने की वस्तु
अशन = भोजन

201. अह = दिन
अहि = साँप

202. अणि = सूई की नोक
अनी = फौज

203. दारा = पत्नी
द्वार = दरवाजा

204. पृथा = कुन्ती
प्रथा = रीति

205. श्रवण = कान
स्रवन = बहना

206. श्याम = श्री कृष्ण
स्याम = एक देश

207. वृन्द = समूह
वृन्त = डण्ठल

208. मित = थोड़ा
मित्र = दोस्त

209. दुरति = पाप
दुरत = छिपा

210. चार = चार की संख्या
चारु = सुन्दर

वस्तुनिष्ठ प्रश्नोत्तर

निर्देश (प्रश्न संख्या 1 से 40 तक): *अधोलिखित प्रश्नों में दिए गए शब्द युग्मों के सही अर्थभेद का विकल्प चयन कीजिए।*

1. अंश - अंस ....
A. भाग - संख्या B. भाग - कंधा
C. कंधा - भाग D. संख्या - कंधा

2. अंत्य - अंत
A. अंतिम - समाप्त होना B. समाप्त होना - अंत्यज
C. अनंतिम - समाप्त D. समाप्त - अनंतिम

3. अनल - अनिल ....
A. जल - वायु B. वायु - जल
C. अग्नि - वायु D. वायु - धूप

4. अंगना, अँगना ....
A. लक्ष्मी - दरवाजा B. आँगन - द्वार
C. स्त्री - आँगन D. आँगन - लक्ष्मी

5. अन्न - अन्य ....
A. गेहूँ - चावल B. अनाज - दूसरा
C. धान - कोई D. धान - कण

6. आसन - असन ....
A. बैठने की वस्तु - भोजन B. गद्दी - मिठाई
C. फूल - फल D. गद्दी - कुर्सी

7. उपेक्षा - अपेक्षा ....
A. अपमान - सम्मान B. निरादर - आवश्यकता
C. आवश्यकता - अपमान D. अपमान - तिरस्कार

8. असक्त - अशक्त ....
A. बली - निर्बल B. निर्बल - आसक्त
C. विरक्त - शक्तिहीन D. योगी - बीमार

9. आगम - अगम ....
A. पुराण - समुद्र B. शास्त्र - अथाह
C. महाकाव्य - फुटकर काव्य D. वेद पुराण - अज्ञात

10. उभय - अभय ....
A. सब - निर्भीक B. निर्भीक - सब
C. दोनों - निर्भय D. सभी - साहसी

11. अकथ - अथक ....
A. अवर्णनीय - बिना थके, लगातार
B. अद्वितीय - उत्साह का भाव
C. अलौकिक - बहादुरीपूर्वक
D. इनमें से कोई नहीं

12. अरी!, अरि ....
A. हे माई, भयानक
B. किसी नारी को संबोधन - शत्रु
C. प्रिय को संबोधन - अमित्र
D. प्रिय को उलाहना - भयंकर व्यक्ति

13. यक्ष - अक्ष ....
A. यायावर - घुमंतू B. किन्नर देवजाति - धुरी
C. पार्वत्य - मौलिक D. गंधर्व - चक्कर

14. आदी - आदि ....
A. साग - पुराना B. अदरक - आरंभ, वगैरह
C. भूमिज - क्षितिज D. कोई नहीं

15. इतर - इत्र ....
A. दूसरा - तेल B. सुगंधि - रस
C. दूसरा - सुगंध D. सुगंध - खुशबू

16. ऋतु - ऋत ....
A. मौसम - सत्य B. जलवायु - जगत्
C. जलवायु - ईश्वर D. जगत - ईश्वर

17. कृती - कृति ....
A. रचयिता - पुस्तक B. निपुण - कर्मकर्ता - रचना
C. बहादुर - सुलेख D. चतुर - कहानी

18. क्रीत - कृत ....
A. बाजार - वस्तु B. वस्तु - खरीद
C. खरीदा हुआ - किया हुआ D. पाया हुआ - बेचा हुआ

19. कर्ण - कारण ....
A. श्रवण - क्रिया
B. कान - तृतीया विभक्ति करण कारक
C. शरीर का अंग - व्याकरण का अंग
D. भाषा का अंग - शरीर का अंग

20. कपिश - कपीश ....
A. कडुआ - जानवर
B. मलिन, मटमैला - हनुमान, सुग्रीव
C. गंदा - वीर
D. मैला - शक्तिशाली

21. कर्कट - करकट ....
A. कठोर - गंदा B. केकड़ा - कूड़ा
C. जीव - गंदगी D. जलचर - भूमिस्थ

22. कपि - कपी ....
A. बंदर - घिरनी B. जीव - रहट
C. फलभक्षी - जल प्रदायी D. कोई नहीं

23. क्षात्र - छात्र ....
A. क्षत्रिय संबंधी - विद्यार्थी
B. योद्धा - शिक्षार्थी
C. युद्ध में जाने वाला - विद्यालय जाने वाला
D. विजेता - सुशिक्षित

24. चीता - चिता ....
A. शेर - श्मशान
B. मृत्यु - चिंता
C. श्मशान - मृत्यु
D. एक जानवर - शवदाह हेतु लकड़ी का ढेर

25. चारु - चार ....
A. सुंदर - आदमी B. गिनती - खूबसूरत
C. सुंदर - चार (गिनती का) D. अलौकिक - असंख्य

26. जगत् - जगत ....
A. दुनिया - मैदान B. संसार - कुएँ का चबूतरा
C. विस्तार - संकोच D. चबूतरा - विश्व

27. टूक - टुक ....
A. लकड़ी - आवाज B. स्पष्ट - ठक, ठक
C. टुकड़ा - थोड़ा D. एक हिस्सा - आधा हिस्सा

28. तरि - तरी ....
A. नाव - तलछट, गीलापन B. नदी - तलहटी
C. किनारा - कीचड़ D. तालाब - सड़ा कीचड़

29. तर्क - तक्र ....
A. बहस - रस B. वाद विवाद - पेय
C. बहस, विवाद - मट्ठा D. बातचीत - गोरस

30. दात - दाँत ....
A. दाता - एक अंग B. दाता - एक दाँत
C. दान - मुँह के दाँत D. पुण्य - याचक

31. दाई - दायी ....
A. दासी, (पालिका) - दाता, जवाबदेह
B. नौकरानी - अधिकारी
C. सेवक - दानी
D. सहायिका - नौकरानी

32. दैव - देव ....
A. सत्कर्य - देवता B. देवता - धर्मात्मा
C. मान - सुर D. भाग्य - देवता

33. दारू - दारु ....
A. तरल - ठोस B. पेय - जलाऊ
C. शराब - लकड़ी D. मूल्यवान् - सूखा काठ

34. दीवा - दिवा ....
A. अँधेरा - उजाला B. दीपक - दिन
C. प्रकाश - अंधकार D. ज्योति - प्रकाश

35. नाई - नाईं ....
A. बाल बनाने वाला - तरल, भाँति
B. व्यवसायी - समान
C. प्रजा - दाता
D. श्रमजीवी - तरह-तरह से

36. चीर - चिर ....
A. घोठी - पुरानी B. साड़ी - प्राचीन
C. पहनावा - बीता समय D. कोई ठीक नहीं

37. निर्जर - निर्झर ....
A. न जलने वाला - प्रवाह
B. देवता - झरना
C. मानव - नदी
D. नदी - सड़क

38. नंदी - नांदी ....
A. देव - वाचाल
B. देवगो - सिफारिश
C. शिव का बैल - मंगलाचरण
D. कोई ठीक नहीं

39. प्रसाद - प्रासाद
A. भोग, (कृपा) - महल B. पकवान - देवालय
C. देवालय - अनुकंपा D. कोई भी सही नहीं

40. परिक्षा - परीक्षा ....
A. जल - खोज B. कीचड़ - इम्तहान
C. तलछट - आविष्कार D. परिणाम - असहाय

उत्तरमाला

1	2	3	4	5	6	7	8	9	10
B	A	C	C	B	A	B	C	B	C
11	**12**	**13**	**14**	**15**	**16**	**17**	**18**	**19**	**20**
A	B	B	B	C	A	B	C	B	B
21	**22**	**23**	**24**	**25**	**26**	**27**	**28**	**29**	**30**
B	A	A	D	C	B	C	A	C	C
31	**32**	**33**	**34**	**35**	**36**	**37**	**38**	**39**	**40**
A	D	C	B	A	B	B	C	A	B

★★★

5

पद परिचय एवं पद भेद की पहचान

संज्ञा (Noun)

किसी व्यक्ति, वस्तु, स्थान, व्यापार तथा भाव आदि के नाम को संज्ञा कहते हैं। जैसे—हिमालय, गंगा, कोलकाता, वेद, आकाश, सुख, दुःख, खेती आदि। संज्ञा एक विकारी शब्द है।

संज्ञा के भेद

संज्ञा का वर्गीकरण जीवन्तता, गणना, व्युत्पत्ति, एवं अर्थ के आधार पर किया गया है। लेकिन जीवन्तता, गणना, व्युत्पत्ति का आधार मानकर किया गया वर्गीकरण विशेष महत्त्वपूर्ण नहीं है। अर्थ के आधार पर किया गया वर्गीकरण ही परम्परागत है। अधिकांशतः विद्वानों ने संज्ञा के पाँच भेद माने हैं :

(i) व्यक्तिवाचक संज्ञा *(ii)* जातिवाचक संज्ञा *(iii)* द्रव्यवाचक संज्ञा *(iv)* समूहवाचक संज्ञा *(v)* भाववाचक संज्ञा।

(i) **व्यक्तिवाचक संज्ञा :** किसी विशेष व्यक्ति या स्थान का नाम बोध कराने वाली संज्ञा को व्यक्तिवाचक संज्ञा कहते हैं। जैसे—शीला, राकेश, कानपुर, इलाहाबाद, भारत, यमुना आदि। व्यक्तिवाचक संज्ञा के अन्तर्गत निम्नलिखित नामों का समावेश होता है :-

व्यक्तियों के नाम—रमेश, शीला, ज्ञानप्रकाश, बिहारी, कालिदास।
दिशाओं के नाम—पूर्व, पश्चिम, उत्तर, दक्षिण।
नदियों के नाम—यमुना, महानन्दा, गंगा, सिन्धु, गोमती आदि।
गाँवों के नाम—कल्याणपुर, रामपुर, लालगँज आदि।
देशों के नाम—भारत, रूस, चीन, जापान आदि।
वस्तुओं के नाम—रामायण (ग्रंथ), महाभारत (ग्रंथ), टाइटन (घड़ी), फिलिप्स (रेडियो), ओनीडा (टेलीविजन) आदि।
समुद्रों के नाम—प्रशान्त महासागर, भूमध्य सागर, हिन्द महासागर, आदि।

इसी प्रकार त्योहारों एवं उत्सवों के नाम, पुस्तकों एवं समाचार-पत्रों के नाम, चौराहों तथा सड़कों के नाम, पर्वतों के नाम, राज्यों के नाम, ग्रह तथा नक्षत्रों के नाम, भाषाओं के नाम, वस्तुओं आदि के नाम भी व्यक्तिवाचक संज्ञा में समाविष्ट होते हैं।

(ii) **जातिवाचक संज्ञा :** जिस संज्ञा से एक ही प्रकार की वस्तुओं या प्राणी की पूरी जाति का बोध होता है, उसे जातिवाचक संज्ञा कहते हैं। जैसे—घोड़ा, गाय, बाघ, स्त्री, लड़का, पुस्तक, सड़क, विद्यालय आदि।

जातिवाचक संज्ञा के अन्तर्गत आगत शब्दों को अधोलिखित कोटियों में बाँटा जा सकता है—

जानवरों के नाम—बैल, ऊँट, भैंस, शेर, हिरण आदि।
स्थानों के नाम—मैदान, पाठशाला, औषधालय आदि।
वस्तुओं के नाम—घड़ी, आलमारी, पंखा, किताब, आदि।
सम्बन्धियों के नाम—चाचा, मामा, मौसी, भाई आदि।
व्यवसायों एवं पदों के नाम—लोहार, कुम्हार, मोची, अध्यापक, धोबी आदि।
प्राकृतिक तत्त्वों के नाम—वर्षा, गर्मी, भूकम्प, तूफान आदि।

(iii) **द्रव्यवाचक संज्ञा :** द्रव्यवाचक संज्ञा से धातु या किसी द्रव्य का बोध होता है, जिसे तौला या नापा जा सकता है तथा जिससे अन्य वस्तुओं का निर्माण होता है। जैसे—सोना, चाँदी, ताँबा, लोहा, पीतल, दूध, पानी, तेजाब, तेल, पारा, घी आदि।

(iv) **समूहवाचक संज्ञा :** समूहवाचक संज्ञा को समुदायवाचक संज्ञा भी कहते हैं। वस्तुतः जिस संज्ञा से पदार्थ या प्राणियों के समूह का बोध होता है, उसे समूहवाचक संज्ञा कहते हैं। जैसे—सेना, सभा, कक्षा, मेला, दल, गुच्छा, कुञ्ज, भीड़ आदि।

(v) **भाववाचक संज्ञा :** भाववाचक संज्ञा वह संज्ञा है, जिससे किसी वस्तु या प्राणी के स्वभाव, गुण, धर्म, व्यापार एवं दशा का बोध होता है। जैसे—वीरता, चतुराई, मिठास, बुढ़ापा, बचपन, चाल, खेल, दौड़ आदि।

भाववाचक संज्ञा का निर्माण

भाववाचक संज्ञाओं का निर्माण तद्धित और कृदन्त प्रत्ययों को विभिन्न शब्द भेदों में लगाकर किया जाता है। उदाहरणार्थ—

जातिवाचक संज्ञा से

जातिवाचक संज्ञा	भाववाचक संज्ञा	जातिवाचक संज्ञा	भाववाचक संज्ञा
पशु	पशुता	स्त्री	स्त्रीत्व
मनुष्य	मनुष्यता	विद्वान्	विद्वता
पंडित	पांडित्य/पंडिताई	शत्रु	शत्रुता
लड़का	लड़कपन	बूढ़ा	बुढ़ापा
दास	दासत्व	बंधु	बंधुत्व
ग्राम	ग्रामीण	शहर	शहरी

देहात	देहाती	मित्र	मित्रता
भ्राता	भ्रातृत्व	साधु	साधुता
देह	दैहिक	माता	मातृत्व
जाति	जातीयता	घर	घरेलू
समाज	सामाजिकता	मूर्ख	मूर्खता

विशेषण से–

विशेषण	भाववाचक संज्ञा	विशेषण	भाववाचक संज्ञा
सुन्दर	सुन्दरता	कठोर	कठोरता
कुरूप	कुरूपता	मधुर	मधुरता
गर्म	गर्मी	उष्ण	उष्णता
ठंडा	ठंडक	छोटा	छुटपन/छोटापन
सर्द	सर्दी	लम्बा	लम्बाई
चौड़ा	चौड़ाई	ऊँचा	ऊँचाई
काला	कालापन	मीठा	मिठास
लाल	लाली	चतुर	चतुराई
नीला	नीलापन	बड़ा	बड़ाई/बड़प्पन
कड़वा	कड़वाहट/कड़वापन	पवित्र	पवित्रता
मैला	मैल	शीतल	शीतलता
गंदा	गंदगी	मलिन	मलिनता
लघु	लघुता	गुरु	गुरुता
खुरदरा	खुरदरापन	लचीला	लचीलापन
धूर्त	धूर्तता	ठोस	ठोसपन
ईमानदार	ईमानदारी	दक्ष	दक्षता
कर्मठ	कर्मठता	पटु	पटुता
निपुण	निपुणता	भिन्न	भिन्नता
शिष्ट	शिष्टता	एक	एकता
वीर	वीरता	नीच	नीचता
उच्च	उच्चता	क्लिष्ट	क्लिष्टता
कायर	कायरता	सभ्य	सभ्यता
नपुंसक	नपुंसकता	शांत	शांति
उज्ज्वल	उज्ज्वलता	नम्र	नम्रता
क्षुद्र	क्षुद्रता	लोभी	लोभ
लालची	लालच	क्रोधी	क्रोध
डरावना	डर	भयावह	भय
आश्चर्य जनक	आश्चर्य	संक्षिप्त	संक्षिप्तता
दीर्घ	दीर्घता		

क्रिया से–

क्रिया	भाववाचक संज्ञा	क्रिया	भाववाचक संज्ञा
चढ़ना	चढ़ाई/चढ़ाव	विकसित होना	विकास
पढ़ना	पढ़ाई	विचारना	विचार
लड़ना	लड़ाई	निकलना	निकास
उठना	उठाव	सजाना	सजावट
बहना	बहाव	लिखना	लिखावट
खींचना	खिंचाव	दौड़ना	दौड़
लूटना	लूट	सिसकना	सिसकी
घुलना	घोल	झाड़ना	झाड़
बोलना	बोल	फूँकना	फूँक
कूदना	कूद	घबराना	घबराहट
झुकना	झुकाव	बनाना	बनावट
तनना	तनाव	मिलाना	मिलावट

लिंग (Gender)

'व्याकरण' में लिंग, पुरुष एवं स्त्री जाति के लिए प्रयुक्त चिह्न को कहा जाता है। इसे परिभाषित करते हुए कहा जा सकता है–"लिंग उसे कहते हैं जिससे संज्ञा के स्त्री या पुरुष होने का बोध हो।" दूसरे शब्दों में–"जिस चिह्न से व्यक्ति या वस्तु की स्त्री या पुरुष जाति का ज्ञान हो, उसे लिंग कहते हैं।"

लिंग-भेद

हिन्दी में लिंग के दो भेद मान्य हैं–*(i)* पुल्लिंग *(ii)* स्त्रीलिंग

(i) **पुल्लिंग (Masculine Gender) :** 'पुल्लिंग' संज्ञा के उस रूप को कहा जाता है, जिससे उसके पुरुष होने का बोध होता है। जैसे–राजेश, मुकेश, प्रमोद, सूर्य, चाँद, बैल, घोड़ा इत्यादि।

(ii) **स्त्रीलिंग (Feminine Gender) :** स्त्रीलिंग से आशय संज्ञा के उस रूप से है जिससे उसके स्त्री होने का पता चले। जैसे–राधा, शीला, घोड़ी, बकरी, तितली, मैना, कोयल, मुर्गी आदि।

लिंग-निर्णय के नियम

पुल्लिंग शब्दों के पहचान के लिए नियम :

1. हिन्दी में वे तत्सम शब्द जो अकारान्त हैं, साधारणतः पुल्लिंग होते हैं।
   जैसे–ग्रंथ, हल, फल, जल, सूर्य, अध्यक्ष आदि।
   अपवाद–पुस्तक।
2. प्राणियों में मनुष्य, बड़े पशु आदि में नर पुल्लिंग होते हैं और नारी स्त्रीलिंग होती हैं।
   जैसे–आदमी, बैल, घोड़ा, बकरा, कुत्ता, गधा, हाथी आदि। क्योंकि ये सभी नर बोधक शब्द हैं।
3. कुछ प्राणियों के लिंग-निर्णय का आधार व्यवहार है। व्यवहार के आधार पर लिंग-निर्णय विशेषतः कीड़ों, छोटे पक्षियों या जिनमें नर-मादा का अन्तर कठिन है–का होता है।
   जैसे–बन्दर, तीतर, बटेर, चीता आदि पुल्लिंग हैं जबकि मछली, मैना, गौरैया, कोयल स्त्रीलिंग हैं।

4. अप्राणिवाचक संज्ञाओं का लिंग-निर्णय रूप के आधार पर होता है। पुल्लिंग शब्दों के उदाहरण के तौर पर निम्नलिखित शब्द दिये जाते हैं-
   (क) द्रव पदर्थों (liquid) के नाम–दही, पानी, शर्बत, घी, तेल, सिरका इत्यादि।
   (ख) धातुओं के नाम–लोहा, ताम्बा, सोना, पीतल, जस्ता आदि। **अपवाद**–चाँदी।
   (ग) ग्रहों के नाम–मंगल, बुध, शुक्र, शनि, आदि। **अपवाद**–पृथ्वी।
   (घ) वनस्पतियों के नाम–सागौन, अशोक, महुवा, पीपल, आम, ताड़, बाँस आदि। **अपवाद**–नीम, जामुन, आदि।
   (ङ) अनाजों के नाम–चना, उड़द, जौ, गेहूँ, चावल, धान, मटर, आदि। **अपवाद**–अरहर, मक्का, ज्वार, मूँग, आदि।
   (च) रत्नों के नाम–हीरा, मोती, माणिक, नीलम, मूँग, जवाहर आदि। **अपवाद**–मणि
   (छ) दिनों के नाम–सोम, मंगल, रवि, गुरु आदि।
   (ज) पहाड़ों के नाम–विन्ध्याचल, हिमालय, हिन्दुकुश आदि।
   (झ) जल और स्थल भागों के नाम–नगर, द्वीप, देश, समुद्र, घर, आकाश, पाताल आदि। **अपवाद**–नदी, झील, घाटी आदि।
   (ञ) भाव वाचक संज्ञाएँ–जिनके अन्त में ना, वा, पा, आव, पन, आ होते हैं प्रायः पुल्लिंग होते हैं। जैसे :–घेरा, डेरा, बसेरा, बुढ़ापा, बड़प्पन, बहाव, चढ़ाव आदि।
   (ट) हिन्दी के वे संज्ञाएँ जिनके अन्त में आकार होता है पुल्लिंग होती हैं। परन्तु इसमें संस्कृत के तत्सम शब्द शामिल नहीं होंगे और न हिन्दी के 'इया' प्रत्यय को लगाकर बने हुए शब्द ही।
   जैसे–रुपचा, छाता, आटा, पैसा, पहिया, कपड़ा, चमड़ा आदि।
   (ठ) कृदन्त संज्ञाएँ–जिनके अन्त में 'आन' होता है। जैसे–नहान, उठान, मिलान आदि।

स्त्रीलिंग शब्दों की पहचान

1. हिन्दी में जिन संज्ञाओं के अन्त में आ, इ, उ, हो, वे स्त्रीलिंग मानी जाती हैं। हिन्दी की ये संज्ञाएँ संस्कृत से हिन्दी में आयी हैं।
   उदाहरण :
   आ वन्दना, प्रार्थना, कविता, दया, क्षमा, कृपा, रेखा आदि।
   इ सिद्धि, मति, गति, रीति, नीति, विधि, निधि आदि।
   उ मृत्यु, रेणु, धेनु, आदि।

2. ऐसी भाव वाचक संज्ञाएँ जिनके अन्त में ट, वट, आई, ता, हट, हो स्त्रीलिंग होती हैं।
   उदाहरण :
   ट खाट, बाट, हाट आदि।
   वट मिलावट, लिखावट, सजावट आदि।
   आई लड़ाई, मिठाई, भलाई, चढ़ाई आदि।
   ता लघुता, प्रभुता, ममता, क्षमता आदि।
   हट अकुलाहट, घबड़ाहट, आहट आदि।
3. हिन्दी की उन संज्ञाओं को स्त्रीलिंग माना जाता है जिनके अन्त में ई, इया, ऊ, ख, त, स, हो। जैसे-
   ई नदी, चिट्ठी, टोपी, धोती, रोटी, चलनी आदि।
   अपवाद–घी, दही, जी, मोती, पानी, यही।
   इया खटिया, डिबिया, मचिया, पुड़िया, बुढ़िया, आदि।
   ऊ लू, बालू, झाड़ू, गेरू, दारू आदि।
   ख राख, भूख, कोख, साख, आँख, ईख, रेख आदि।
   अपवाद–रूख।
   त बात, रात, लात, छत आदि।
   स मिठास, रास (लगाम), ओस, प्यास, साँस, आदि।
   अपवाद–निकास, निवास।
4. कृदन्त की अकारान्त संज्ञाएँ भी स्त्रीलिंग होती हैं।
   जैसे–लूट, दौड़, चमक, पुकार, छाप, मार, समझ आदि।
   अपवाद–मेल, बिगार, नाच, खेल।
5. अनुस्वारांत संज्ञाएँ भी स्त्रीलिंग होती हैं।
   जैसे–खड़ाऊँ, चूँ आदि।
6. नदियों के नाम स्त्रीलिंग होते हैं।
   जैसे–गंगा, यमुना, गोमती, कृष्णा, बेतवा आदि।
   अपवाद–ब्रहमपुत्र, सोन, सिन्धु।
7. नक्षत्रों के नाम स्त्रीलिंग होते हैं।
   जैसे–अश्विनी, रोहिणी, अनुराधा, कृत्तिका आदि।
8. तिथियों के नाम स्त्रीलिंग होते हैं।
   जैसे–प्रतिपदा, दूज, तीज, चौथ, अष्टमी, नवमी आदि।
9. किराने के पदार्थों के नाम स्त्रीलिंग होते हैं।
   जैसे–इलायची, सुपारी, लौंग, दालचीनी आदि। **अपवाद**–जीरा, नमक, कपूर, केसर आदि।
10. भोजनों के नाम स्त्रीलिंग होते हैं।
   जैसे–खीर, दाल, खिचड़ी, कढ़ी, पकौड़ी, पूड़ी, कचौड़ी, आदि।
   अपवाद–भात, रायता, दूध, पराठा, हलुआ आदि।

वचन (Number)

वचन का शाब्दिक अर्थ है–बोली। परन्तु हिन्दी में व्याकरण की दृष्टि में वचन का अर्थ संख्या से लिया जाता है। इसलिए वचन को परिभाषित करते हुए कहा जा सकता है–संज्ञा, सर्वनाम, विशेषण और क्रिया के जिस रूप से संख्या का बोध होता है, उसे वचन कहते हैं।

वचन के भेद

हिन्दी में वचन के दो भेद माने गए हैं–(1) एकवचन (2) बहुवचन

(1) एकवचन (Singular Number) : जैसा कि नाम से स्पष्ट है, एकवचन विकारी शब्द का वह रूप है जिससे एक ही व्यक्ति

या वस्तु का बोध होता है। उदाहरण—घोड़ा दौड़ता है। गाय चरती है। इन वाक्यों में 'घोड़ा' और 'गाय' से एक जानवर का बोध होता है। अतः ये एकवचन हैं।

(2) बहुवचन (Plural Number) : बहुवचन वह विकारी शब्द है जिससे एक से अधिक वस्तुओं, व्यक्तियों आदि का बोध होता है। जैसे—घोड़े चरते हैं। गायें दौड़ती हैं। 'घोड़े' और 'गायें' कहने से एक से अधिक जानवरों का बोध होता है। अतः ये बहुवचन हैं।

वचन के रूपान्तर : यद्यपि वचन के कारण संज्ञा, सर्वनाम, विशेषण और क्रिया के रूप में परिवर्तन होता है तथापि सर्वनाम, विशेषण और क्रिया के रूप मूलतः इनसे जुड़ी संख्या पर ही आधारित होते हैं। अतएव एकवचन में संज्ञा शब्दों के रूपान्तर की ही प्रमुखता है।

वचन के अधीन संज्ञा के रूप दो तरह से परिवर्तित होते हैं—

(1) विभक्ति रहित

(2) विभक्ति सहित

विभक्ति रहित संज्ञाओं के बहुवचन बनाने के नियम

विभक्ति रहित संज्ञाओं का बहुवचन साधारणतः निम्नलिखित नियमों के अन्तर्गत बनाया जाता है-

1. पुल्लिंग संज्ञा के आकारान्त को एकारान्त कर बहुवचन बनाया जाता है। यथा-

एकवचन	**बहुवचन**	**एकवचन**	**बहुवचन**
घोड़ा	घोड़े	गधा	गधे
लड़का	लड़के		

अपवाद—मामा, नाना, बाबा, पिता, योद्धा, आत्मा, देवता, जामाता आदि। इन शब्दों के रूप दोनों वचनों में समान होते हैं।

2. पुल्लिग आकारान्त शब्दों के अतिरिक्त अन्य मात्राओं से अन्त होने वाले शब्दों के रूप दोनों वचनों में एक समान रहते हैं। जैसे—

एकवचन	**बहुवचन**	**एकवचन**	**बहुवचन**
एक बालक	चार बालक	एक डाकू	चार डाकू
एक भाई	चार भाई	एक जौ	चार जौ

3. आकारान्त स्त्रीलिंग शब्दों के अन्त में 'एँ' जोड़ने से बहुवचन बनता है। जैसे—

एकवचन	**बहुवचन**	**एकवचन**	**बहुवचन**
शाखा	शाखाएँ	लता	लताएँ
माता	माताएँ	महिला	महिलाएँ

4. अकारान्त स्त्रीलिंग संज्ञा के बहुवचन शब्द में आगत अंतिम अ को यें कर देने से बनता है। जैसे—

एकवचन	**बहुवचन**	**एकवचन**	**बहुवचन**
गाय	गायें	रात	रातें
बात	बातें	आँख	आँखें
याद	यादें		

5. दीर्घ या ह्रस्व इकारान्त संज्ञाओं को ह्रस्व इकारान्त कर उनके अन्त में याँ जोड़ देने से बहुवचन बनता है। जैसे—

एकवचन	**बहुवचन**	**एकवचन**	**बहुवचन**
नारी	नारियाँ	पहेली	पहेलियाँ
लड़की	लड़कियाँ	सहेली	सहेलियाँ
नीति	नीतियाँ	नदी	नदियाँ
घड़ी	घड़ियाँ	छड़ी,	छड़ियाँ
धोती	धोतियाँ	साड़ी	साड़ियाँ

6. जिन स्त्रीलिंग शब्दों के अन्त में 'या' आता है, 'या' पर चन्द्रबिन्दु लगाकर बहुवचन बनाया जाता है जैसे—

एकवचन	**बहुवचन**	**एकवचन**	**बहुवचन**
बुढ़िया	बुढ़ियाँ	चिड़िया	चिड़ियाँ
गुड़िया	गुड़ियाँ	डिबिया	डिबियाँ
दुनिया	दुनियाँ		

7. ह्रस्व या दीर्घ ऊकारान्त स्त्रीलिंग संज्ञाओं को ह्रस्व उकारान्त बनाकर अन्त में 'एँ' लगाने से बहुवचन का निर्माण होता है। जैसे-

एकवचन	**बहुवचन**	**एकवचन**	**बहुवचन**
धेनु	धेनुएँ	वस्तु	वस्तुएँ
बहू	बहुएँ	ऋतु	ऋतुएँ

8. कुछ शब्द समष्टि मूलक होते हैं। जैसे—गण, कुल, वृन्द, समूह, वर्ग, लोग, जन, मण्डल, दल, ग्राम, मण्डली आदि। ये शब्द विशेषतः वहाँ जोड़े जाते हैं, जहाँ दोनों वचनों में पुल्लिंग अथवा स्त्रीलिंग में एक ही रूप होते हैं।

उदाहरण :

एकवचन	**बहुवचन**	**एकवचन**	**बहुवचन**
पाठक	पाठकगण	आप	आप लोग
तुम	तुम लोग	छात्र	छात्रगण
विद्यार्थी	विद्यार्थीगण		

विभक्ति सहित संज्ञाओं के बहुवचन बनाने के नियम

सविभक्ति संज्ञाओं के बहुवचन बनाने के सामान्य नियम निम्नलिखित हैं—

1. संस्कृत शब्दों को छोड़कर हिन्दी के अकारान्त, आकारान्त तथा एकारान्त संज्ञाओं के अन्तिम अ, आ, ए के बदले बहुवचन बनाने में इसे 'ओ' कर दिया जाता है। जैसे-

एकवचन	**बहुवचन**
नर	नरों (का)
चीता	चीतों (द्वारा)
चोर	चोरों (ने)
घोड़ा	घोड़ों (को)

विभक्ति चिह्नों के साथ प्रयोग :

(क) नरों की कहानी।

(ख) चीतों का भय।

(ग) चोरों की पकड़।

(घ) घोड़ों की हिनहिनाहट।

2. संस्कृत आकारान्त संज्ञाओं तथा हिन्दी एवं संस्कृत की सम्पूर्ण अकारान्त, उकारान्त, ऊकारान्त तथा आकारान्त संज्ञाओं को बहुवचन बनाने के लिए अन्त में 'ओं' जोड़ना पड़ता है। ऊकारान्त में 'ओं' सम्पृक्त करने के पूर्व उसे उकारान्त करना पड़ता है। जैसे–

एकवचन	बहुवचन	विभक्ति चिह्नों के साथ प्रयोग
कला	कलाओं	कलाओं का प्रदर्शन
घर	घरों	घरों में जाओ
वधू	वधुओं	वधुओं का सम्मेलन

3. समस्त इकारान्त और ईकारान्त संज्ञाओं का बहुवचन बनाने के लिए अन्त में 'यों' जोड़ना पड़ता है। ईकारान्त संज्ञाओं में 'यों' जोड़ने के पूर्व ई का इ कर दिया जाता है। जैसे–

एकवचन	बहुवचन	विभक्ति चिह्नों के साथ प्रयोग
नारी	नारियों	नारियों की स्थिति
नदी	नदियों	नदियों का प्रवाह
कवि	कवियों	कवियों की वाणी
कपि	कपियों	कपियों का समूह

कारक (Case)

संज्ञा या सर्वनाम के उस रूप को कारक कहते हैं जिससे उसका सम्बन्ध वाक्य के अन्य शब्दों विशेषतः क्रिया के साथ प्रकट होता है। वास्तव में, विभक्ति चिह्नों से युक्त संज्ञा या सर्वनाम शब्द ही वाक्य में अन्य शब्दों से सम्बन्ध प्रकट करते हैं।

ने, को, से, द्वारा–आदि विभक्ति चिह्न हैं। कारक का एक उदाहरण इस प्रकार है–'मोहन ने बाग में डण्डे से आम तोड़ा।' इस वाक्य में मोहन ने, डण्डे से, और आम संज्ञाओं के रूपान्तरण हैं। जिस तत्त्व के द्वारा इन रूपान्तरित संज्ञाओं का सम्बन्ध तोड़ा, क्रिया से स्पष्ट होता है, वही कारक है।

कारक-चिह्न

हिन्दी में कारक के आठ भेद माने जाते हैं :

	कारक	विभक्ति या कारक चिह्न
1.	कर्त्ता	ने
2.	कर्म	को
3.	करण	से, द्वारा
4.	सम्प्रदान	को, के लिए
5.	अपादान	से
6.	सम्बन्ध	का, के, की, रा, रे, री, ना, ने, नी
7.	अधिकरण	में, पर
8.	सम्बोधन	हे, हो, अरे, अजी, अहो आदि।

कारक-चिह्न/विभक्ति/परसर्ग

हिन्दी में कारक का ज्ञान कराने के लिए संज्ञा या सर्वनाम के साथ जो प्रत्यय लगाये जाते हैं, उन्हें ही व्याकरण में विभक्ति कहते हैं। हिन्दी में चूँकि विभक्ति चिह्न पद से अलग प्रयुक्त होते हैं इसलिए इन्हें 'परसर्ग' भी कहा जाता है। परसर्ग का शब्दिक अर्थ है–पीछे जुड़ना। कारक चिह्न सदैव संज्ञा या सर्वनाम के पीछे जुड़ते हैं।

(i) **कर्त्ता कारक :** कर्त्ता का अभिप्राय है, करने वाला। वाक्य में जो क्रिया सम्पन्न करता है, उसे कर्त्ता कहा जाता है। जैसे–राम पढ़ता है। सुरेश पत्र लिखता है। इन वाक्यों में राम और सुरेश कर्त्ता कारक हैं क्योंकि ये ही क्रिया को सम्पादित करने वाले हैं।

(ii) **कर्म कारक :** कर्त्ता द्वारा सम्पादित क्रिया का फल जिस पर पड़ता है, उसे 'कर्म' कहते हैं। जैसे–शीला ने राजेश को पढ़ाया। इस वाक्य में कर्त्ता है–शीला, क्रिया है–पढ़ाना। पढ़ाना क्रिया का फल राजेश पर स्पष्ट पड़ रहा है। इसलिए यहाँ राजेश कर्म कारक की स्थिति में है।

(iii) **करण कारक :** वाक्य में करण कारक उस शब्द को कहते हैं जो क्रिया को पूर्ण करने में साधन के रूप में कर्ता का सहायक होकर आता है। जैसे–मैं कलम से लिखता हूँ। इस वाक्य में 'कलम से' करण कारक है क्योंकि लेखन-क्रिया में कलम साधन है।

(iv) **सम्प्रदान कारक :** कर्त्ता क्रिया की सिद्धि जिसके लिए करता है अथवा जिसको कुछ देता है, उसे प्रकट करने वाले शब्द रूप को सम्प्रदान कारक कहते हैं। जैसे–श्याम मीरा के लिए खिलौने लाया। राकेश शीला के लिए रोता है। इन वाक्यों में लाना और रोना क्रियाएँ क्रमशः मीरा और शीला के लिए सम्पादित की जा रही हैं। इसलिए मीरा और शीला के लिए शब्द रूप सम्प्रदान कारक है।

(v) **अपादान कारक :** वाक्य में अलगाव सूचित करने वाला शब्द अपादान कारक कहलाता है। जैसे–शारदा नहर गंगा नदी से निकली है। पेड़ से पत्ते गिरते हैं। इन वाक्यों में निकलना और गिरना क्रियाओं के अलग होने का भाव क्रमशः गंगा नदी और पेड़ से स्पष्ट हो रहा है। अतएव इन दोनों शब्दों की स्थिति अपादान कारक में है।

(vi) **सम्बन्ध कारक :** संज्ञा, सर्वनाम का वह रूप जिससे वाक्य में आगत अन्य शब्द के साथ जुड़ाव या सम्बन्ध का बोध हो सम्बन्ध कारक कहलाता है। सम्बन्ध कारक का सम्बन्ध क्रिया के साथ प्रत्यक्ष नहीं होता है। जैसे–शीला की पुस्तक। रमेश का घोड़ा। मेरी कलम।

इन वाक्यों में शीला की, रमेश का, मेरी–क्रमशः पुस्तक, घोड़ा, कलम से लगाव स्पष्ट करते हैं। अतः ये सम्बन्ध कारक हैं।

(vii) **अधिकरण कारक :** संज्ञा या सर्वनाम के उस रूप को अधिकरण कारक कहते हैं जिससे वाक्य में क्रिया के आधार का बोध

होता है। जैसे—गाय बाग में चरती है। विद्यालय में 400 विद्यार्थी हैं। इन वाक्यों में 'बाग में' और 'विद्यालय में' अधिकरण कारक हैं। क्योंकि वे क्रमशः गाय के चरने के लिए तथा विद्यार्थियों के लिए आधार का काम करते हैं।

(viii) **सम्बोधन कारक :** वाक्य में वक्ता श्रोता का ध्यान अपनी ओर खींचने के लिए अथवा उसे सचेत करने के लिए संज्ञा के जिस रूप को प्रयुक्त करता है उसे सम्बोधन कारक कहते हैं। जैसे—अरे राकेश, तुमने यह क्या हाल कर रखा है। इस वाक्य में 'अरे राकेश' सम्बोधन कारक है, क्योंकि इस पद द्वारा ध्यानाकृष्ट किया गया है। सम्बोधन कारक का सम्बन्ध क्रिया के साथ नहीं होता है। इसका प्रयोग बिना चिह्न के भी हो सकता है। जैसे गुरुदेव, क्षमा करें। यहाँ गुरुदेव सम्बोधन कारक है।

सर्वनाम (Pronoun)

सर्वनाम दो शब्दों से मिलकर बना है—सर्व + नाम। सर्व का अर्थ है 'सब' और 'नाम' का अर्थ 'संज्ञा' है। जिन विकारी शब्दों का प्रयोग संज्ञा के बदले में होता है, उन्हें सर्वनाम कहते हैं। जैसे—तुम, मैं, आप, यह, वह, जो, सो, कोई, कुछ, कौन, क्या इत्यादि।

सर्वनाम का प्रयोग कर वाक्य को संज्ञा के पुनरुक्ति दोष से बचाया जाता है। सर्वनाम की सर्वोपरि विशेषता यह है कि उससे उसी संज्ञा का बोध होता है जिससे उसका पूर्वापर सम्बन्ध होता है। किन्तु संज्ञा से केवल उसी का बोध होता है, जिसका वह नाम है। उदाहरण के लिए 'घोड़ा' कहने से मात्र घोड़ा का ही बोध होता है, पुस्तक, गाय आदि का ज्ञान नहीं होता। लेकिन 'वह' कहने से पूर्वापर सम्बन्ध के अनुरूप ही संज्ञा का पता चलता है।

सर्वनाम के भेद

सर्वनाम के सात भेद माने गये हैं :

(1) पुरुषवाचक सर्वनाम
(2) निजवाचक सर्वनाम
(3) निश्चयवाचक सर्वनाम
(4) अनिश्चयवाचक सर्वनाम
(5) सम्बन्धवाचक सर्वनाम
(6) प्रश्नवाचक सर्वनाम
(7) साकल्पवाचक सर्वनाम

(1) **पुरुषवाचक सर्वनाम**—जो सर्वनाम—बोलने वाले, सुनने वाले और जिसके विषय में कुछ कहा जाए—का बोध कराते हैं, उन्हें पुरुषवाचक सर्वनाम कहते हैं।
जैसे—मैं, तुम, वह आदि।
पुरुषवाचक सर्वनाम तीन प्रकार के होते हैं :
(क) उत्तम पुरुष (ख) मध्यम पुरुष (ग) अन्य पुरुष

(क) उत्तम पुरुष—उत्तम पुरुष में वक्ता या लेखक आते हैं। जैसे—मैं, हम।

(ख) मध्यम पुरुष—मध्यम पुरुष में—तू, तुम, आप, आते हैं। जिससे कोई बात बोली या कही जाती है उसे मध्यम पुरुष कहते हैं।

(ग) अन्य पुरुष—जिसके विषय में कुछ कहा, लिखा या सुना जाए—वह अन्य पुरुष कहलाता है। जैसे—वह, वे।

(2) **निजवाचक सर्वनाम**—जो सर्वनाम स्वयं या निज का बोध कराने वाले हैं उन्हें निजवाचक सर्वनाम कहते हैं। जैसे—मैं आप चला जाऊँगा। तुम आप वहाँ चले जाना। मैं अपने को सुधार लूँगा। यहाँ 'आप' निजवाचक सर्वनाम है।

निजवाचक सर्वनाम 'आप' एक ही तरह दोनों वचनों में आता है और तीनों पुरुषों में इसका प्रयोग किया जा सकता है।

(क) निजवाचक सर्वनाम 'आप' का प्रयोग किसी संज्ञा, सर्वनाम के निश्चय के लिए होता है। जैसे—मैं आप आया हूँ।
(ख) निजवाचक 'आप' का प्रयोग दूसरे व्यक्ति के निराकरण के लिए होता है। जैसे—उन्होंने मुझे रहने को कहा और आप चलते बने।
(ग) सर्वसाधारण के अर्थ में भी आप का प्रयोग होता है। जैसे—आप भला तो जग भला।
(घ) निश्चय के अर्थ में कभी-कभी 'आप' के साथ 'ही' जोड़ा जाता है। जैसे—मैं आप ही चला आया था।

निजवाचक आप और पुरुषवाचक आप में अन्तर

पुरुषवाचक आप मध्यम पुरुष में आदर सूचक के रूप में प्रयुक्त होता है। इसका रूप तू के स्थान पर होता है। जैसे—आप कब आयेंगे? आप कहाँ जा रहे हैं?

निजवाचक 'आप' शब्द स्वयं या खुद के लिए होता है। जैसे—वह अपने आप आ जायेगा। मैं आप ही बुरा हूँ।

(3) **निश्चयवाचक सर्वनाम**—जिस सर्वनाम से किसी निश्चित व्यक्ति या वस्तु का बोध होता है, उसे निश्चयवाचक सर्वनाम कहते हैं। जैसे—यह, वह आदि। यह का बहुवचन 'ये' और 'वह' का बहुवचन 'वे' है।

(4) **अनिश्चयवाचक सर्वनाम**—जिस सर्वनाम से किसी निश्चित व्यक्ति, वस्तु या स्थान का बोध न हो, उसे अनिश्चयवाचक सर्वनाम कहते हैं।
जैसे—कोई, कुछ आदि।
उदाहरण : कोई आ रहा है। कुछ भी लेते आना।
साधारणतः 'कोई' अनिश्चित व्यक्ति के लिए आता है और 'कुछ' अनिश्चित वस्तु के लिए।

(5) **सम्बन्धवाचक सर्वनाम**—जिस सर्वनाम से संज्ञा या अन्य सर्वनाम के साथ सम्बन्ध जाना जाता है, उसे सम्बन्धवाचक सर्वनाम कहते हैं। जैसे—जो आयेगा सो जायेगा। जिसकी लाठी उसकी भैंस। यहाँ 'जिस' और 'उस' सम्बन्ध वाचक सर्वनाम हैं। वर्तमान हिन्दी में 'सो', 'तिस', 'तिन' शब्दों के स्थान पर 'यह' और 'उन' का प्रयोग भी शुद्ध माना जाता है।

(6) **प्रश्नवाचक सर्वनाम**–जिस सर्वनाम शब्द से प्रश्न का बोध हो, उसे प्रश्नवाचक सर्वनाम कहते हैं। जैसे–क्या, कौन आदि।

उदाहरण :

तुम्हारा नाम क्या है?

आप क्या चाहते हैं?

कौन आ रहा है?

'कौन' शब्द व्यक्ति के विषय में तथा 'क्या' शब्द वस्तु के विषय में प्रश्न के निमित्त प्रयोग में लाया जाता है।

(7) **साकल्पवाचक सर्वनाम**–इस सर्वनाम में साकल्य या समूह का बोध होता है। जैसे–सब, कुल, सकल आदि। इसे समूह बोधक भी कहते हैं।

सर्वनाम की विशेषताएँ

(1) सर्वनाम का लिंग के अनुसार रूपात्मक परिवर्तन नहीं होता है। मैं, तुम, यह, वह इत्यादि सर्वनाम पुरुष और स्त्री दोनों के लिए प्रयोग में लाये जाते हैं।

(2) सर्वनाम के कारकीय रूपों में सम्बन्ध कारक नहीं होता है।

(3) सर्वनाम के कारकीय रूपों में सम्बन्ध कारक का केवल 'का' रूप लिंग से प्रभावित होता है।

जैसे–उसकी पुत्री। उसका पुत्र।

मेरी पुत्री। मेरा पुत्र।

सर्वनाम का लिंग

लिंग की दृष्टि से सर्वनाम में किसी प्रकार का परिवर्तन उपस्थित नहीं होता। उसका रूप सदैव एक-सा विद्यमान रहता है। वाक्य में उनका प्रयोग चाहे पुल्लिंग के लिए हो या स्त्रीलिंग के लिए। मैं, तुम, हम, वह, वे आदि सर्वनामों का प्रयोग दोनों लिंगों में एक जैसा होता है।

जैसे– मैं खेलता हूँ। लड़का कहेगा।

मैं खेलती हूँ। लड़की कहेगी।

लड़का और लड़की पुल्लिंग स्त्रीलिंग संज्ञाओं के स्थान पर प्रयुक्त 'मैं' सर्वनाम के रूप में किसी प्रकार का परिवर्तन नहीं हुआ।

सर्वनाम का वचन

सर्वनाम का प्रयोग दोनों वचनों में संज्ञा की तरह ही होता है। जैसे–

एकवचन	**बहुवचन**
वह	वे
यह	ये
मैं	हम

विशेषण (Adjective)

संज्ञा या सर्वनाम शब्दों की विशेषता बताने वाले शब्दों को विशेषण कहते हैं। जैसे–लाल पैण्ट, पाँच आम, मोटा लड़का, अच्छी लड़की आदि। ऊपर के उदाहरणों में लाल, पाँच, मोटा, अच्छी आदि विशेषण हैं।

विशेषण के भेद

विशेषण के निम्नलिखित भेद हैं–

(1) सार्वनामिक विशेषण
(2) संख्यावाचक विशेषण
(3) गुणवाचक विशेषण
(4) परिमाणवाचक विशेषण
(5) व्यक्तिवाचक विशेषण
(6) प्रविशेषण

(1) **सार्वनामिक विशेषण**–ऐसे सर्वनाम शब्द जो विशेषण के रूप में प्रयुक्त किये जाते हैं, वे सार्वनामिक विशेषण कहे जाते हैं। क्या, कोई, कुछ, यह, वह, कौन, जो, सो, जैसा, कैसा, इतना, उतना आदि सार्वनामिक विशेषण के उदाहरण हैं। वस्तुतः ऐसे शब्द सर्वनाम और विशेषण दोनों ही का कार्य करते हैं। जब क्रिया के पूर्व उन शब्दों का प्रयोग होता है तब वे सर्वनाम होते हैं और जब उनका प्रयोग किसी संज्ञा के साथ होता है तब उन्हें विशेषण कहा जाता है। जैसे–

सर्वनाम	**विशेषण**
वह पढ़ रहा है।	वह लड़का पढ़ रहा है।
यह देखो।	यह घोड़ा देखो।

सार्वनामिक विशेषण के दो भेद हैं–

(क) मूल सार्वनामिक विशेषण
(ख) यौगिक सार्वनामिक विशेषण

(क) **मूल सार्वनामिक विशेषण**–मूल सार्वनामिक विशेषण वे हैं जिनमें वचन एवं कारक के कारण किसी प्रकार का परिवर्तन उपस्थित नहीं होता। जैसे–यह, वह, कौन, जो, सो, कोई कुछ, क्या आदि।

(ख) **यौगिक सार्वनामिक विशेषण**–ये मूल सर्वनाम में प्रत्यय लगाकर बनाये जाते हैं तथा इनका रूप कारक एवं वचन के अनुसार बदलता रहता है। जैसे–कैसा, कैसी, ऐसा, ऐसे, ऐसी, जैसा, जैसे, जैसी। इसी प्रकार वैसा, तैसा, इतना, उतना, जितना, कितना आदि।

(2) **संख्यावाचक विशेषण**–संख्यावाचक विशेषण के द्वारा संज्ञा या सर्वनाम की संख्या का ज्ञान होता है। संज्ञा-सर्वनाम की संख्यात्मक विशेषता स्पष्ट करने के कारण ही इसे संख्यावाचक विशेषण कहा जाता है। जैसे–दस घोड़े, चालीस गायें, कुछ आदमी, सब अध्यापक। यहाँ दस, चालीस, कुछ, सब–संख्यावाचक विशेषण हैं। क्योंकि इनसे संख्या की संख्यात्मक स्थिति का आभास मिलता है।

संख्यावाचक विशेषण के दो प्रकार हैं–

(क) निश्चित संख्यावाचक
(ख) अनिश्चित संख्यावाचक

(क) **निश्चित संख्यावाचक विशेषण**–निश्चित संख्या का बोध कराने वाले विशेषण को निश्चित संख्यावाचक विशेषण कहते हैं। जैसे–आठ लड़कियाँ, तीस रुपये।

(ख) **अनिश्चित संख्यावाचक विशेषण**–संज्ञा या सर्वनाम की निश्चित संख्या का बोध न कराने वाले विशेषण को अनिश्चित संख्यावाचक विशेषण कहा जाता है। जैसे–कुछ मकान, सब घोड़े।

(3) **गुणवाचक विशेषण**–जिस शब्द से संज्ञा या सर्वनाम का गुण स्पष्ट होता है, उसे गुणवाचक विशेषण कहते हैं। गुण के अन्तर्गत संज्ञा या सर्वनाम के रूप, रंग, स्थान, स्वभाव आदि स्थितियों का स्पष्टीकरण होता है। गुण से आशय अच्छे और बुरे दोनों से है। जैसे–सुन्दर पुरुष, गरीब किसान, दुष्ट आदमी, काला घोड़ा, मोटी स्त्री, सूखा खेत, शान्त अध्यापक।

(4) **परिमाणवाचक विशेषण**–जिन शब्दों के द्वारा परिमाण अर्थात् माप, तौल इत्यादि का बोध होता है, उन्हें परिमाणवाचक विशेषण कहते हैं। जैसे–बहुत पानी, थोड़ा दूध, कुछ अनाज, सब तेल। इसके दो भेद हैं–(क) निश्चित परिमाणवाचक (ख) अनिश्चित परिमाणवाचक।

(क) **निश्चित परिमाणवाचक**–जिससे परिमाण की निश्चित स्थिति का पता चलता है, उसे निश्चित परिमाणवाचक विशेषण कहते हैं। जैसे–दो किलो दूध, चार गज कपड़ा।

(ख) **अनिश्चित परिमाणवाचक**–जिससे निश्चित परिमाण का बोध नहीं होता है, उसे अनिश्चित परिमाणवाचक विशेषण कहते हैं।
जैसे–कुछ अनाज, सब तेल।

(5) **व्यक्तिवाचक विशेषण**–व्यक्तिवाचक संज्ञा से निर्मित विशेषणों को व्यक्तिवाचक विशेषण कहते हैं।
जैसे–कानपुर-कानपुरी, बनारस-बनारसी, पटना-पटनियाँ, कलकत्ता-कलकतिया आदि।

(6) **प्रविशेषण**–विशेषण की एक नयी कोटि भी बनायी गयी है। इसका नाम प्रविशेषण है। प्रविशेषण वे शब्द हैं जो विशेषण की विशेषता बताते हैं।
जैसे–शीला अति सुन्दर है।
राणा प्रताप बड़े साहसी थे।
राजेश अत्यन्त मेधावी छात्र है।

विशेषण का पद परिचय

विशेषण के पद-परिचय में लिंग, वचन, विशेषण, विशेषण का भेद, विशेष्य और कारक बताए जाते हैं।

जैसे–मानव श्रेष्ठतम कृति है।

श्रेष्ठतम–विशेषण, गुणवाचक विशेषण, पुल्लिंग, एकवचन, विशेष्यकृति, उत्तमावस्था, विशेष्य विशेषण।

क्रिया (Verb)

क्रिया–वाक्य में जिस शब्द से किसी काम का होना या करना ज्ञात होता है, उसे क्रिया कहते हैं। जैसे–लिखना, पढ़ना, खाना, खेलना, दौड़ना, रोना, आना, जाना आदि।

क्रिया विकारी शब्द है जिसके रूप, लिंग, वचन और पुरुष के अनुसार बदलते हैं।

धातु

क्रिया जिस मूल शब्द से बनती है, उसे धातु कहते हैं। क्रिया का निर्माण 'धातु' में 'ना' जोड़ने से होता है। क्रिया से 'ना' हटा देने पर जो शेष बचता है, वही धातु कहलाता है। जैसे–लिख, खा, आ, जा, पढ़ आदि धातु हैं।

धातु के भेद–धातु मुख्यतः दो प्रकार के होते हैं–

(1) मूल धातु
(2) यौगिक धातु

(1) **मूल धातु**–मूल धातु किसी पर आधारित न होकर स्वतंत्र होता है। जैसे–पढ़, लिख, खा, देख इत्यादि।

(2) **यौगिक धातु**–यौगिक धातु का निर्माण प्रत्येक के जुड़ाव से होता है। यौगिक धातु का निर्माण मुख्यतः तीन प्रकार से होता है–

(*i*) धातु में जब प्रत्यय का योग किया जाता है तब अकर्मक से सकर्मक और प्रेरणार्थक धातु की रचना होती है।

(*ii*) धातु के साथ धातु को संपृक्त करने से संयुक्त धातु की रचना होती है।

(*iii*) संज्ञा या विशेषण से नाम धातु का निर्माण होता है।

प्रेरणार्थक क्रिया–(धातु)–जिससे यह ज्ञात होता हो कि कर्त्ता स्वयं नहीं कर रहा है बल्कि कार्य करने के लिए किसी अन्य को प्रेरित कर रहा है, वह प्रेरणार्थक क्रिया कहलाती है।

जैसे–**पढ़ना** = पढ़ाना/पढ़वाना।
चलना = चलाना/चलवाना।

यौगिक क्रिया–(धातु)–दो या दो से अधिक धातुओं के मेल से जिस क्रिया का निर्माण होता है, उसे यौगिक क्रिया कहते हैं। जैसे–गिर पड़ना, मार देना, रख देना इत्यादि।

नाम धातु–जिस धातु की रचना संज्ञा या विशेषण से होती है, उसे नाम धातु कहते हैं। जैसे–हाथ से हथियाना, लात से लतियाना इत्यादि।

क्रिया के भेद

साधारणतः क्रिया के भेद दो आधारों पर किये जाते हैं–

(*i*) रूप के आधार पर (*ii*) अर्थ के अनुसार

रूप के अनुसार क्रिया के भेद

रूप के अनुसार क्रिया के दो भेद हैं–

(क) सकर्मक क्रिया (ख) अकर्मक क्रिया

(क) **सकर्मक क्रिया**—जिस क्रिया के साथ कर्म के प्रयोग की अपेक्षा होती है, अथवा जो क्रिया कर्म के साथ आती है, उसे सकर्मक क्रिया कहते हैं। सकर्मक क्रिया को सम्पादित करने वाला यद्यपि कर्त्ता ही होता है, किन्तु उसके कार्य का फल कर्म पर पड़ता है। जैसे—राम रोटी खाता है। इस वाक्य में प्रयुक्त क्रिया खाता है—सकर्मक है, क्योंकि उसका एक कर्म है। रोटी खाने वाला राम है लेकिन उसकी क्रिया खाना का फल रोटी पर पड़ता है। वह जाता है। यहाँ जाना क्रिया सकर्मक है। इस वाक्य में यद्यपि कर्म का प्रयोग नहीं हुआ है लेकिन कर्म के प्रयोग की आवश्यकता है। 'जाता है' के पहले घर, गाँव, स्कूल, मंदिर या किसी विशेष स्थान का बोधक शब्द रखा जा सकता है।

(ख) **अकर्मक क्रिया**—जिस क्रिया का प्रयोग बिना कर्म के होता है अर्थात् जिस क्रिया के साथ कर्म का प्रयोग न हो, वह अकर्मक क्रिया कहलाती है। अकर्मक क्रिया के कर्त्ता का फल कर्त्ता पर ही पड़ता है। जैसे—वह रोता है। यहाँ प्रयुक्त 'रोना' क्रिया अकर्मक है। क्योंकि इस वाक्य में न तो कोई कर्म है और न उसके प्रयोग की आवश्कता ही महसूस होती है। रोना क्रिया का फल कर्त्ता 'वह' पर ही पड़ रहा है।

अर्थ के अनुसार क्रिया के भेद

(क) समापिका क्रिया
(ख) असमापिका क्रिया

(क) **समापिका क्रिया**—समापिका क्रिया वह क्रिया है जिससे पूर्णता का भाव प्रकट होता है। दूसरे शब्दों में कहा जा सकता है—"वह क्रिया जो संदेह या आकांक्षा को समाप्त कर देती है, समापिका क्रिया है।" जैसे—रमेश मैदान में खेलता है। इस वाक्य में 'खेलता है' समापिका क्रिया है क्योंकि इसके बाद रमेश क्या करता है, इस तरह का संदेह नहीं रह जाता।

(ख) **असमापिका क्रिया**—असमापिका क्रिया वह है जिससे अपूर्णता का भाव जाना जाता है। इस क्रिया से सन्देह या आकांक्षा का समापन नहीं होता और आगे जानने की जरूरत महसूस होती है। जैसे—'राम ने आते ही...।' यदि इस वाक्य को यहीं छोड़ दिया जाए तो आकांक्षा होगी कि 'क्या किया'? इस आकांक्षा की समाप्ति तभी होगी जब आगे वाक्य जोड़ दिया जाए—'बच्चों को प्यार किया।' अब पूरा वाक्य हुआ। राम ने आते ही बच्चों को प्यार किया। इस प्रकार आते ही, आते हुए, आकर इत्यादि असमापिका क्रियाएँ हैं।

काल (Tense)

काल क्रिया के उस रूपान्तरण को कहते हैं जिससे कार्य-व्यापार का समय और उसके पूर्ण अथवा अपूर्ण अवस्था का बोध हो।

जैसे— राम खाता है।
राम जायेगा।
मोहन ने खाया।

काल के भेद

क्रिया के मुख्यतः तीन काल हैं—(1) वर्तमान काल (2) भूतकाल (3) भविष्यत् काल

(1) वर्तमान काल

'वर्तमान काल' में क्रिया से कार्य होने का बोध होता है अर्थात् इसमें क्रिया के व्यापार की निरन्तरता का स्पष्टीकरण होता है। जैसे—'वह पढ़ता है।' —इस वाक्य में पढ़ने की क्रिया हो रही है।

वर्तमान काल के भेद

(क) सामान्य वर्तमान
(ख) अपूर्ण वर्तमान/तात्कालिक वर्तमान
(ग) पूर्ण वर्तमान
(घ) संभाव्य वर्तमान

(क) **सामान्य वर्तमान**—सामान्य वर्तमान उसे कहते हैं जिसमें क्रिया का वर्तमान काल में होना जाना जाता है।

जैसे— मोहन जाता है।
राम पढ़ता है।
गीता देखती है।

(ख) **अपूर्ण वर्तमान**—इसका दूसरा नाम तात्कालिक वर्तमान भी है। अपूर्ण वर्तमान में इस बात का बोध होता है कि क्रिया वर्तमान काल में जारी है। जैसे—मैं पत्र लिख रहा हूँ। सुरेश गाना गा रहा है।

(ग) **पूर्ण वर्तमान**—इस काल से यह ज्ञात होता है कि क्रिया वर्तमान काल में सम्पन्न हो चुकी है। जैसे—राम गया है। रमेश ने रोटी खायी है।

(घ) **संभाव्य वर्तमान**—इस काल में कार्य के पूर्ण होने की संभावना रहती है। जैसे—राम खाया हो। वह सोया हो।

(2) भूतकाल

भूतकाल का अर्थ है—बीता हुआ समय अर्थात् क्रिया के जिस रूपान्तरण से कार्य के समापन का बोध हो, उसे भूतकाल की क्रिया कहते हैं। जैसे—राम खा चुका था। वह सोया था। सीता ने गाया।

भूतकाल के भेद

भूतकाल के छः भेद हैं—

(क) सामान्य भूत — (घ) अपूर्ण भूत
(ख) आसन्न भूत — (ङ) संदिग्ध भूत
(ग) पूर्ण भूत — (च) हेतु हेतु मद् भूत

(क) **सामान्य भूत**—इस काल की क्रिया से यह ज्ञात होता है कि कार्य स्वाभाविक रीति से हुआ अर्थात् क्रिया के विशेष समय का बोध नहीं होता। जैसे—राम ने पत्र लिखा। मोहन गया।

(ख) आसन्न भूत–इस बात के द्वारा यह ज्ञात होता है कि क्रिया की समाप्ति निकट भूत में तत्काल हुई। जैसे–राम पत्र लिख चुका है। वह अभी आया था।

(ग) पूर्ण भूत–पूर्ण भूत की क्रिया से यह स्पष्ट पता चलता है कि क्रिया की समाप्ति सुदूर भूत में ही हो चुकी है अर्थात् क्रिया के सम्पादित होने के समय का स्पष्ट ज्ञान होता है।

जैसे–राम ने रावण को मारा था। आशा ने गीत गाया था।

(घ) अपूर्ण भूत–इस काल की क्रिया से यह ज्ञात होता है कि भूतकाल में कार्य निरन्तर जारी था।

जैसे–रमेश पुस्तक पढ़ रहा था। सुरेश खाना खा रहा था।

(ङ) संदिग्ध भूत–संदिग्ध भूत में इस बात का सन्देह बना रहता है कि कार्य समाप्त हुआ या नहीं। जैसे–तुमने लिखा होगा। उसने चुराया होगा।

(च) हेतु हेतु मद् भूत–इस काल में यह पता चलता है कि यद्यपि क्रिया का समापन भूतकाल में होना था। परन्तु किसी कारणवश नहीं हो सका।

दूसरे शब्दों में हम कह सकते हैं कि इस काल में कार्य के होने की शर्त लगी रहती है अर्थात् एक क्रिया की सिद्धि में दूसरी क्रिया शर्त बनकर प्रयुक्त होती है।

जैसे– यदि तुम पढ़ते तो परीक्षा पास करते।
यदि वर्षा होती तो पैदावार अच्छी होती।

(3) भविष्यत् काल

वह क्रिया जो भविष्य में होनी है, उसे भविष्यत् काल की क्रिया कहा जाता है।

जैसे– वह खाएगा।
वह नौकरी करेगा।
रमेश व्यापार करेगा।

भविष्यत् काल के भेद

(क) सामान्य भविष्यत् (ख) हेतु हेतु मद् भविष्यत्
(ग) सम्भाव्य भविष्यत्

(क) सामान्य भविष्यत्–इस काल की क्रिया से यह पता चलता है कि कार्य स्वाभाविक रीति से भविष्य में पूरा होगा।

जैसे–मैं लिखूँगा। वह गाँव जायेगा।

(ख) हेतु हेतु मद् भविष्यत्–इस काल की क्रिया से यह प्रकट होता है कि भविष्य में एक क्रिया का होना दूसरी क्रिया पर निर्भर करता है।

जैसे– अध्यापक आएं तो पढ़ाएं।
विद्यार्थी पढ़े तो परीक्षा उर्त्तीण करे।

(ग) संभाव्य भविष्यत्–इस काल की क्रिया से भविष्यत् काल में कार्य के होने की संभावना का बोध होता है।

जैसे– सम्भव है, वह पत्र लिखे।
सम्भवतः वह कल आए।

अव्यय (Indeclinable)

'अव्यय' ऐसे शब्द या शब्दांश को कहते हैं जिसके रूप में लिंग, वचन, कारक इत्यादि के कारण कोई विचार (परिवर्तन) उत्पन्न नहीं होता। जैसे–जब, तब, यहाँ, वहाँ, कब, क्यों, वाह, आह, ठीक, अरे, और, तथा, एवं, किन्तु, परन्तु, बल्कि, इसलिए, अतः, अतएव, चूँकि, अर्थात्, इत्यादि।

अव्यय के भेद

अव्यय के चार भेद हैं–

(1) क्रिया विशेषण (Adverb)
(2) सम्बन्ध बोधक (Preposition)
(3) समुच्चय बोधक (Conjunction)
(4) विस्मयादि बोधक (Interjection)

क्रिया-विशेषण

'क्रिया-विशेषण' ऐसे अविकारी शब्दों को कहा जाता है जो क्रिया-विशेषण या दूसरे क्रिया-विशेषण की विशेषता बतलाते हैं। दूसरे शब्दों में–क्रिया के अर्थ में विशेषता उत्पन्न करने वाले शब्दों को क्रिया विशेषण कहते हैं।

जैसे– तुम तेज दौड़ते हो।
राम वहाँ जा रहा है।

उपर्युक्त वाक्यों में 'तेज' और 'वहाँ' विशेषता बताने वाले शब्द हैं। कभी-कभी क्रिया-विशेषण, विशेषण या दूसरे क्रिया-विशेषण शब्दों की विशेषता बतलाते हैं।

जैसे– वह बहुत अच्छा लड़का है।
तुम बहुत जल्दी आए।

क्रिया-विशेषण के भेद

क्रिया-विशेषण का विभाजन निम्नलिखित तीन आधारों पर होता है–

(*i*) प्रयोग के आधार पर (*ii*) रूप के आधार पर
(*iii*) अर्थ के आधार पर

(*i*) क्रिया-विशेषण के भेद (प्रयोग के आधार पर)

प्रयोग के अनुसार क्रिया-विशेषण के तीन भेद हैं :–

(क) साधारण क्रिया-विशेषण (ख) संयोजक क्रिया-विशेषण
(ग) अनुबद्ध क्रिया-विशेषण

(क) साधारण क्रिया-विशेषण–वाक्य में स्वतंत्र रूप से प्रयोग किये जाने वाले क्रिया-विशेषण शब्द साधारण क्रिया-विशेषण कहलाते हैं।

जैसे–रमेश, जल्दी जाओ।
अरे, ठग कहाँ गया।
हाय! अब वह क्या करेगा।

(ख) संयोजक क्रिया-विशेषण–जो क्रिया विशेषण दो उपवाक्यों को जोड़ने के लिए प्रयुक्त होते हैं, उन्हें संयोजक क्रिया-विशेषण कहते हैं।

जैसे–जब अध्यापक आयेंगे, तब बच्चे पढ़ेंगे।
जहाँ अभी कानपुर शहर है, वहाँ किसी समय जंगल था।

(ग) अनुबद्ध क्रिया-विशेषण—अनुबद्ध क्रिया विशेषण वे हैं जिनका प्रयोग वाक्य में अवधारण (निश्चय) के लिए किसी भी शब्द-भेद के साथ होता है।

जैसे—मैं उसका पता मात्र जानता हूँ।
यह तो किसी ने चालाकी की है।
शीला मुझे जानती तक नहीं।

—ही, भर, केवल, मात्र, भी आदि अवधारण के लिए आते हैं, अतः ये अनुबद्ध क्रिया-विशेषण हैं।

***(ii)* क्रिया-विशेषण के भेद (रूप के आधार पर)**

रूप के अनुसार क्रिया-विशेषण को तीन भागों में वर्गीकृत किया गया है—

(क) मूल क्रिया-विशेषण
(ख) यौगिक क्रिया-विशेषण
(ग) स्थानीय क्रिया-विशेषण

(क) मूल क्रिया-विशेषण—मूल क्रिया-विशेषण ऐसे क्रिया-विशेषण हैं जो किसी शब्द के मेल से नहीं बनते हैं।

जैसे—नीचे, नजदीक, दूर, ऊपर, अभी, फिर, पुनः आदि।

(ख) यौगिक क्रिया-विशेषण—यौगिक क्रिया-विशेषण दूसरे शब्दों के मेल से बनते हैं। दूसरे शब्दों के योग से निर्मित होने के कारण इन्हें यौगिक क्रिया-विशेषण कहते हैं।

जैसे—साल भर, रात भर, प्रति वर्ष, हर दिन, हृदय से आदि। यौगिक क्रिया-विशेषण का निर्माण संज्ञा, सर्वनाम, विशेषण, धातु और अव्यय के मेल से होता है।

यौगिक क्रिया-विशेषण का निर्माण—यौगिक क्रिया-विशेषण साधारणतः निम्नलिखित शब्दों के मेल से बनते हैं :

संज्ञा द्विरुक्ति से—साल-साल, घर-घर, वन-वन, बीच-बीच, हाथों-हाथ।

दो संज्ञाओं के मेल से—हाथ-पाँव, घर-बाहर, एड़ी-चोटी, नख-शिख, सुबह-शाम।

विशेषणों की द्विरुक्ति से—साफ-साफ, ठीक-ठीक, थोड़ा-थोड़ा।

संज्ञा और विशेषणों के मेल से—हर-घड़ी, एक-साथ, एक-बार।

क्रिया-विशेषणो की द्विरुक्ति से—धीरे-धीरे, बैठे-बैठे, पहले-पहले, कभी-कभी।

दो क्रिया-विशेषणों के मेल से—नीचे-ऊपर, दूर-पास, आजकल, आस-पास, जब-तब।

अनुकरण वाचक शब्दों की द्विरुक्ति—धड़ाधड़, फटाफट, खटाखट, टनाटन, भनाभन।

अव्ययों के मेल से—यथाशक्ति, यथाक्रम, अनुक्रम, प्रतिदिन, अजन्म, भरपेट।

पूर्वकालिक कृदन्त और विशेषण के मेल से—विशेषकर, एक-एक कर, मुख्यकर।

(ग) स्थानीय क्रिया-विशेषण—ऐसे दूसरे शब्द, जो बिना परिवर्तन के किसी विशेष स्थान पर क्रिया-विशेषण के स्थान पर प्रयुक्त होते हैं स्थानीय क्रिया-विशेषण कहलाते हैं।

जैसे—वह अपना सिर पढ़ेगा।

***(iii)* क्रिया-विशेषण के भेद (अर्थ के आधार पर)**

अर्थ के अनुसार क्रिया-विशेषण के निम्नलिखित भेद हैं—

(क) परिमाणवाचक क्रिया-विशेषण—जिन शब्दों के द्वारा परिमाण का बोध होता है, उन्हें परिमाणवाचक क्रिया विशेषण कहते हैं। ये निम्नलिखित प्रकार से वर्गीकृत हो सकते हैं।

वे परिमाणवाचक क्रिया विशेषण जो कम मात्रा काबोध कराते हैं।

(i) अधिकता बोधक—बहुत, भारी, खूब, अत्यन्त, अतिशय, बड़ा।
(ii) न्यूनता बोधक —कम, अल्प, अत्यल्प, कुछ, जरा, किंचित्।
(iii) पर्याप्ति बोधक—केवल, बराबर, बस, काफी, यथेष्ठ।
(iv) तुलना-वाचक—अधिक, कम, जितना, उतना, कितना, बढ़कर।
(v) श्रेणी-वाचक—क्रम-क्रम से, बारी-बारी से, यथा-क्रम, थोड़ा-थोड़ा, तिल-तिल आदि।

(ख) रीतिवाचक क्रिया-विशेषण—इनकी संख्या बहुत अधिक है। नीचे मुख्य रीतिवाचक क्रिया-विशेषण दिये जाते हैं।

(क) प्रकार – यथा, तथा, ऐसे, कैसे, जैसे, सहज, अनायास, साक्षात्, हौले, पैदल।
(ख) निश्चय – सचमुच, सही, निस्सन्देह, अवश्य, वस्तुतः इत्यादि।
(ग) स्वीकार – हाँ, जी, ठीक, सच।
(घ) अनिश्चय – शायद, कदाचित, यथासंभव।
(ङ) कारण – किसलिए, क्यों, काहे को।
(च) निषेध – न, नहीं, मत।
(छ) अवधारण – भी, ही, मात्र, भर, तक, तो, सा।

(ग) स्थान वाचक क्रिया-विशेषण—इसके द्वारा स्थान का ज्ञान होता है। इसके दो भेद हैं :—

(1) स्थितिवाचक—यहाँ, वहाँ, ऊपर, नीचे, पीछे, बाहर, भीतर, पास, सर्वत्र इत्यादि।
(2) दिशावाचक—इधर, उधर, किधर, दाएँ, बाएँ, इस तरफ, उस तरफ आदि।

(घ) कालवाचक क्रिया-विशेषण—इसके द्वारा समय का ज्ञान होता है। इसका वर्गीकरण तीन भागों में किया गया है :—

समय वाचक—आज, कल, परसों, नरसों, तरसों, जब, तब, सबेरे, शाम, तुरन्त इत्यादि।

अवधि वाचक—आजकल, नित्य, सदा, लगातार, दिनभर, कब का।

पौनः पुन्य वाचक—प्रतिदिन, एक, दूसरे, तीसरे, बार-बार, बहुधा इत्यादि।

(ड़) गुणवाचक क्रिया-विशेषण—जिन शब्दों से क्रिया का गुण प्रकट होता है, उनको गुण वाचक क्रिया-विशेषण कहते हैं। जैसे—वह तेज भागता है।

सम्बन्ध-बोधक

सम्बन्ध-बोधक वे अविकारी शब्द हैं जो संज्ञा या सर्वनाम के अनन्तर प्रयुक्त होकर वाक्य में आगत अन्य शब्दों के साथ उसका सम्बन्ध प्रकट

करते हैं। जैसे—परिश्रम के बिना सफलता नहीं मिलती। उसने कक्षा पाँच तक पढ़ा। इन वाक्यों में 'बिना' और 'तक' शब्द सम्बन्ध-बोधक हैं।

सम्बन्ध-बोधक के भेद—सम्बन्ध-बोधक अव्यय का वर्गीकरण प्रयोग, अर्थ और व्युत्पत्ति के आधार पर अधोलिखित रूप में किया गया है—

प्रयोग के अनुसार भेद—प्रयोग के अनुसार सम्बन्ध-बोधक के दो भेद हैं—(*i*) सम्बद्ध, (*ii*) अनुबद्ध

(*i*) **सम्बद्ध-सम्बन्ध-बोधक**—सम्बद्ध सम्बन्ध-बोधक अव्यय का प्रयोग वाक्य में संज्ञा की विभक्तियों के बाद होता है।
जैसे—परिश्रम के बिना, पूजा से पहले, घर के बाहर, घोड़े के ऊपर।

(*ii*) **अनुबद्ध सम्बन्ध-बोधक**—अनुबद्ध सम्बन्ध-बोधक अव्यय वाक्य में संज्ञा के विकृत रूप के अनन्तर प्रयुक्त होता है।
जैसे—मित्रों सहित, कटोरे भर, पाँचवी तक, सैनिकों समेत।

अर्थ के अनुसार सम्बन्ध-बोधक के भेद

(*i*) काल-वाचक—आगे, पीछे, पूर्व, पश्चात्, लगभग, बाद, उपरान्त आदि।
(*ii*) स्थान-वाचक—आगे, पीछे, नीचे, तले, सामने, पास, निकट, भीतर, यहाँ, वहाँ, बीच, बाहर, दूर।
(*iii*) दिशा-वाचक—प्रति, ओर, तरफ, पार, आरपार, आसपास।
(*iv*) साधन-वाचक—जरिये, द्वारा, मारफत, हाथे, सहारे, बल करके।
(*v*) हेतु-वाचक—लिए, वास्ते, सीमित, खातिर, कारण, हेतु, मारे।
(*vi*) विषय-वाचक—बाबत, बनिस्बत, विषय, भरोसे इत्यादि।
(*vii*) व्यतिरेक-वाचक—सिवाय, अलावा, बिना, अतिरिक्त, रहित, बगैर।
(*viii*) विरोध-वाचक—समान, तरह, तुल्य, अनुसार, अनुरूप, भाँति, नाई, सरीखा, खिलाफ, प्रतिकूल, विपरीत, उल्टे।
(*ix*) विनिमय-वाचक—बदले, पलटे, एवज, जगह।
(*x*) सहचर-वाचक—संग, समेत, साथ, वश, स्वाधीन, सहित, अधीन।
(*xi*) संग्रह-वाचक—तक, भर, मात्र, पर्यंत।
(*xii*) तुलना-वाचक—अपेक्षा, बनिस्बत, आगे, सामने।

व्युत्पत्ति के अनुसार सम्बन्ध-बोधक के भेद

व्युत्पत्ति के अनुसार सम्बन्ध-बोधक के निम्नलिखित भेद हैं—
(*i*) मूल सम्बन्ध-बोधक
(*ii*) यौगिक सम्बन्ध-बोधक

(*i*) **मूल सम्बन्ध-बोधक**—हिन्दी में मूल सम्बन्ध-बोधक अव्यय वे हैं जो दूसरे शब्दों के योग से नहीं बनते हैं।
जैसे—बिना, पर्यंत, नाईं, पूर्वक, समेत इत्यादि।

(*ii*) **यौगिक सम्बन्ध-बोधक**—यौगिक सम्बन्ध-बोधक वे हैं जो दूसरे शब्दों के योग से बनते हैं।
जैसे—उपेक्षा, मारफत, भीतर, दरम्यान।

यौगिक सम्बन्ध-बोधक का निर्माण—इसका निर्माण अधोलिखित शब्दों से होता है :—

संज्ञा से—पलटे, मारफत, लेखे, बदले, विषय, पालते, नाच आदि।
विशेषण से—समान, तुल्य, उल्टा, ऐसा, जैसा, योग्य, सरीखा आदि।
क्रिया-विशेषण से—ऊपर, भीतर, यहाँ, बाहर, पास, पीछे, इत्यादि।
क्रिया से—करके, लिए, मारे, जाने।

समुच्चय बोधक

जो अव्यय दो या दो से अधिक शब्दों, वाक्यांशों अथवा वाक्यों को जोड़ता या अलग करता है, उसे 'समुच्चय बोधक' अव्यय कहते हैं। जैसे—"राम और लक्ष्मण वन गए।" यहाँ 'और' अव्यय दो वाक्यों 'राम वन गए', 'लक्ष्मण वन गए' को जोड़ता है। इस वाक्य में और समुच्चय बोधक है।

समुच्चय बोधक अव्यय के भेद

समुच्चय बोधक अव्यय के दो प्रमुख भेद हैं—(*i*) समानाधिकरण समुच्चय बोधक, (*ii*) व्यधिकरण समुच्चय बोधक

(*i*) **समानाधिकरण समुच्चय बोधक**—समानाधिकरण समुच्चय बोधक उन अव्ययों को कहते हैं जो दो मुख्य वाक्यों या समान स्थिति वाले पदों अथवा वाक्य खण्डों को जोड़ते हैं। इनके चार उपभेद निम्नलिखित हैं—
संयोजक—और, तथा एवं, अब और व।
विभाजक—या, वा, अथवा, किंबा, कि, न कि, नहीं तो, न न, चाहे....चाहे।
विरोध दर्शन—बल्कि, मगर, परन्तु, किन्तु, तेकिन, पर, वरन्।
परिमाण दर्शक—इसलिए, अतः, अतएव, सो।

(*ii*) **व्यधिकरण समुच्चय बोधक**—व्यधिकरण समुच्चय बोधक अव्यय उसे कहते हैं जिसका प्रयोग प्रधान वाक्य या उसके समानाधिकरण वाक्य खण्डों को जोड़ने के लिए होता है। इनके भी चार भेद हैं—
कारक वाचक—क्योंकि, चूँकि, कि, कारण, इसलिए, जो कि।
उद्‌देश्य वाचक—कि, जो, इसलिए, ताकि।
संकेत वाचक—जो....तो, यदि....तो, चाहे, परन्तु, यद्यपि, तो... भी, अगर, कि।
स्वरूप वाचक—कि, जो, अर्थात्, याने, मानो।

विस्मयादि बोधक अव्यय

'विस्मयादि बोधक अव्यय' वे पद हैं जिनका प्रयोग वक्ता के शोक, हर्ष आदि मनोभावों की अभिव्यक्ति के लिए होता है। किन्तु उनका सम्बन्ध वाक्य या उसके किसी विशेष पद से नहीं होता है।

जैसे—हाय! अब वह नहीं रहा। इस वाक्य में हाय विस्मयादि बोधक अव्यय है। इसका सम्बन्ध न तो वाक्य से है और न किसी पद से।

विस्मयादि बोधक अव्यय के भेद

विस्मयादि बोधक अव्ययों का वर्गीकरण अधोलिखित रूप में किया गया है—

(*i*) हर्ष बोधक —आहा! वाह-वाह! धन्य-धन्य! शाबाश! जय-जय! कैसा मनोरम दृश्य!
(*ii*) शोक बोधक —आह! ऊह! हा-हा! दइया रे! राम-राम! बाप रे! आदि।
(*iii*) आश्चर्य बोधक —वाह! हैं! ऐ! ओहो! क्या! वाह वा!
(*iv*) अनुमोदन बोधक—ठीक! वाह! शाबाश! हाँ-हाँ! अच्छा!
(*v*) तिरस्कार बोधक—छिः! हट! अरे! धिक्! दुर्! चुप!
(*vi*) स्वीकार बोधक—हाँ! जी हाँ! अच्छा! जी! ठीक! बहुत अच्छा!
(*vii*) सम्बोधन बोधक—अरे! रे! लो! हे! अहो! अजी! जी! अरी!

वस्तुनिष्ठ प्रश्नोत्तर

1. कौन-से शब्द अविकारी होते हैं?
A. सर्वनाम B. देशज
C. क्रिया-विशेषण D. यौगिक

2. निम्नलिखित वाक्यों में से किस वाक्य में अकर्मक क्रिया है?
A. राम आम खाता है B. उसने कमीज पहनी
C. पुष्पा रोती है D. मैंने उसे पुस्तक दी

3. संज्ञा के स्थान पर प्रयुक्त होने वाले शब्द को क्या कहते हैं?
A. सर्वनाम B. सार्थक
C. अविकारी D. अव्यय

4. मुख्यतः काल कितने हैं?
A. पाँच B. चार
C. तीन D. दो

5. 'वह पढ़ रहा है'–यह कौन-सा काल है?
A. भूतकाल B. भविष्यत् काल
C. वर्तमान काल D. अपूर्ण काल

6. मूल क्रिया के अतिरिक्त वाक्य में जितनी भी क्रियाएँ आती हैं, उन्हें क्या कहते हैं?
A. अकर्मक क्रिया B. सहायक क्रिया
C. गौण क्रिया D. रंजक क्रिया

7. 'इधर-उधर कहीं मत जाना' में 'इधर-उधर' व्याकरण की दृष्टि से क्या है?
A. क्रिया-विशेषण B. विशेषण
C. सर्वनाम D. क्रिया

8. निम्नलिखित शब्दों में से कौन-सा शब्द अविकारी है?
A. घोड़ा B. आजकल
C. संकेत D. नदी

9. निम्नलिखित शब्दों में से कौन-सा शब्द स्त्रीलिंग है?
A. दही B. मधु
C. मोती D. धातु

10. 'कक्षा' कौन-सी संज्ञा है?
A. जातिवाचक B. भाववाचक
C. समुदायवाचक D. व्यक्तिवाचक

11. हिन्दी में कितने 'कारक' होते हैं?
A. दस B. आठ
C. पाँच D. तीन

12. विशेषण उन शब्दों को कहते हैं, जो–
A. संज्ञा के स्थान पर इस्तेमाल किए जाएं
B. संज्ञा की विशेषता प्रकट करें
C. क्रिया की विशेषता प्रकट करें
D. अपने आप में पूर्ण हों

13. नीचे कुछ शब्दों के पुल्लिंग और स्त्रीलिंग के जोड़े दिए हुए हैं। कौन-सा जोड़ा गलत है?
A. शूद्र-शूद्रा B. ग्वाला-ग्वालिन
C. कबूतर-कबूतरी D. बाल-बाली

14. सतीश ने आम खाये। इसमें 'आम' शब्द–
A. एकवचन है B. बहुवचन है
C. दोनों है D. दोनों में से कोई नहीं है

15. 'दया' भाववाचक संज्ञा है। इससे विशेषण बनेगा–
A. दयालु B. दीनता
C. दयात्व D. दयता

16. 'पढ़ना' से भाववाचक संज्ञा क्या बनेगी?
A. पाठ B. पठनीय
C. पढ़ाई D. पाठक

17. निम्नलिखित में से कौन-सा शब्द विशेषण है?
A. पशुता B. यौवन
C. चातुर्य D. दुष्ट

18. गली में 'तीसरा' मकान श्याम का है। यहाँ 'तीसरा' व्याकरण की दृष्टि से क्या है?
A. बहुवचन B. विशेषण
C. संज्ञा D. अव्यय

19. 'ने' किस कारक की विभक्ति है?
A. करण B. कर्म
C. कर्ता D. सम्प्रदान

20. 'यश' व्याकरण की दृष्टि से क्या है?
A. विशेषण B. संज्ञा
C. क्रिया D. क्रिया-विशेषण

21. 'श्रीमान' का स्त्रीलिंग है–
A. पत्नी B. श्रीमती
C. देवी D. महोदया

22. निम्न में से कौन-सा शब्द तद्भव है?
A. अग्नि B. हाथ
C. रात्रि D. कर्ण

23. निम्न वाक्यों में से किस वाक्य में क्रिया कर्मवाच्य है?
A. राम के पिता अध्यापक हैं
B. वे सब काश्मीर जायेंगे
C. उत्सव में राष्ट्रीय गीत गाया गया
D. बच्चे पार्क में खेल रहे हैं

24. 'उसे' का बहुवचन है–
A. उसको B. उससे
C. उन्हें D. उसका

25. 'हमें' का एकवचन है–
A. हम B. हमको
C. मुझे D. मुझसे

26. निम्न में से कौन-सा शब्द तत्सम नहीं है?
A. दुग्ध B. चूर्ण
C. क्षेत्र D. माता

27. निम्न में से कौन-सा शब्द अविकारी नहीं है?
A. आज B. कल
C. ऊपर D. घोड़ा

28. 'मीठा' विशेषण है। इससे भाववाचक संज्ञा बनेगी–
A. मीठात्व B. मीठापन
C. मिठास D. मिठाई

29. 'राधा तेज दौड़ती है'। इसमें तेज शब्द क्या है?
A. क्रिया B. क्रिया-विशेषण
C. विशेषण D. उपरोक्त में से कोई भी नहीं

30. जो शब्द संज्ञा के बदले प्रयुक्त होता है, उसे कहते हैं–
A. सर्वनाम B. क्रिया
C. विशेषण D. क्रिया-विशेषण

31. निम्न में से कौन-सा शब्द सर्वनाम है?
A. मेरी B. उन्होंने
C. हमारे D. उपरोक्त तीनों

32. निम्न में से भाववाचक संज्ञा है–
A. मोहन B. खिलाड़ी
C. बचपन D. मैदान

33. निम्न में से कौन-सा शब्द विशेषण है?
A. रोग B. घोड़ा
C. गाँव D. शोक

34. निम्न में से कौन-सी अकर्मक क्रिया है?
A. चुराना B. माँगना
C. लेना D. हँसना

35. निम्न में से कौन-सी सकर्मक क्रिया है?
A. सोना B. हँसना
C. रोना D. देखना

36. पंडित की भाववाचक संज्ञा है–
A. पंडित्व B. पंडिताइन
C. पंडिताऊ D. पांडित्य

37. 'विद्वान्' का स्त्रीलिंग है–
A. विद्वानी B. विद्यावती
C. विदुषी D. विदुषिनी

38. निम्नलिखित में से कौन-सा शब्द भाववाचक संज्ञा नहीं है?
A. बन्धुत्व B. प्रभुता
C. मानवता D. कुशल

39. 'दैनिक' क्या है?
A. संज्ञा B. सर्वनाम
C. क्रिया D. विशेषण

40. 'श्रद्धा' का विशेषण क्या बनता है?
A. श्रद्धास्पद B. श्रद्धेय
C. श्रद्धालु D. उपर्युक्त में से कोई भी नहीं

41. उपसर्ग का प्रयोग होता है, शब्द के–
A. मध्य में B. आदि में
C. अन्त में D. आदि और अंत दोनों में

42. सर्वनाम का प्रयोग किसके बदले किया जाता है?
A. क्रिया-विशेषण B. क्रिया
C. विशेषण D. संज्ञा

43. व्याकरण की दृष्टि से 'प्रेम' शब्द क्या है?
A. भाववाचक संज्ञा B. विशेषण
C. अव्यय D. क्रिया

44. 'मैंने' कौन-सा कारक है?
A. कर्ता B. कर्म
C. करण D. सम्प्रदान

45. 'सेवक' का स्त्रीलिंग है–
A. सेवका B. सेवकाइन
C. सेवकी D. सेविका

उत्तरमाला

1	2	3	4	5	6	7	8	9	10
C	C	A	C	C	B	A	B	D	C
11	**12**	**13**	**14**	**15**	**16**	**17**	**18**	**19**	**20**
B	B	D	B	A	C	D	B	C	B
21	**22**	**23**	**24**	**25**	**26**	**27**	**28**	**29**	**30**
B	B	C	C	C	D	D	C	B	A
31	**32**	**33**	**34**	**35**	**36**	**37**	**38**	**39**	**40**
D	C	D	D	D	D	C	D	D	C
41	**42**	**43**	**44**	**45**					
B	D	A	A	D					

★ ★ ★

6

अशुद्ध वाक्य को शुद्ध करना

	अशुद्ध वाक्य		शुद्ध वाक्य
1.	कई रेलवे कर्मचारियों की गिरफ्तारी हुई।	–	रेलवे के कई कर्मचारियों की गिरफ्तारी हुई।
2.	वह दण्ड देने योग्य है।	–	वह दण्डित होने योग्य है/वह दण्ड पाने योग्य है।
3.	सौ रुपए सधन्यवाद प्राप्त हुए।	–	सौ रुपए प्राप्त हुए। धन्यवाद!
4.	महाविद्यालय की ओर से प्रधानमंत्री को अभिनन्दन पत्र प्रदान किया गया।	–	महाविद्यालय की ओर से प्रधानमंत्री को अभिनन्दन पत्र अर्पित किया गया।
5.	कुत्ता दरवान की तरह दुम हिलाता हुआ दरवाजे पर खड़ा रहता था।	–	कुत्ता दुम हिलाता हुआ दरवान की तरह दरवाजे पर खड़ा रहता था।
6.	इन बातों के बावजूद भी वह नहीं समझ सका।	–	इन बातों के बावजूद वह नहीं समझ सका।
7.	ये बातें केवल दिखावा भर थीं।	–	ये बातें केवल दिखावा थीं/ये बातें दिखावा भर थीं।
8.	दक्षिण का अधिकांश भाग पठार है।	–	दक्षिण का अधिक भाग पठार है।
9.	मेरी निगाह मेरे मित्र की ओर थी।	–	मेरी निगाह मित्र की ओर थी।
10.	प्रधानाध्यापक लड़के चुनेंगे।	–	प्रधानाध्यापक लड़कों को चुनेंगे।
11.	मैंने लिख चुका था।	–	मैं लिख चुका था।
12.	मैंने इस गाड़ी से जाना है।	–	मुझे इस गाड़ी से जाना है।
13.	कर्ण बहुत बड़े दायक थे।	–	कर्ण बहुत बड़े दाता थे।
14.	इसका कोई अर्थ नहीं होता।	–	इसका कुछ अर्थ नहीं होता।
15.	आओ, तुम भी कोई काम कर लो।	–	आओ, तुम भी कुछ काम कर लो।
16.	श्री कृष्ण के अनेकों नाम हैं।	–	श्री कृष्ण के अनेक नाम हैं।
17.	उसकी गर्दन शर्म से नीचे थी।	–	उसकी गर्दन शर्म से नीची थी।
18.	मैं आपकी श्रद्धा करता हूँ।	–	मैं आप पर श्रद्धा रखता हूँ।
19.	सरकार शान्ति-व्यवस्था के लिए पुलिस पर निर्भर करती है।	–	सरकार शान्ति-व्यवस्था के लिए पुलिस पर निर्भर रहती है।
20.	मैं अपने गुरु के उँपर बहुत श्रद्धा रखता हूँ।	–	मैं अपने गुरु पर बहुत श्रद्धा रखता हूँ।
21.	कृष्ण और सुभद्रा भाई-बहन थीं।	–	कृष्ण और सुभद्रा भाई-बहन थे।
22.	राम और श्याम विद्यालय जा रहा है।	–	राम और श्याम विद्यालय जा रहे हैं।
23.	राम और सीता वन को जा रही थीं।	–	राम और सीता वन को जा रहे थे।
24.	शायद वे जरूर जाएँगे।	–	शायद वे जाएँगे/वे जरूर जाएँगे।
25.	मेरी स्त्री बीमार है।	–	मेरी पत्नी बीमार है।
26.	शरीफ पुरुष किसी को तंग नहीं करते।	–	शरीफ लोग किसी को तंग नहीं करते/सज्जन पुरुष किसी को तंग नहीं करते।
27.	इस समस्या का कोई उपाय नहीं है।	–	इस समस्या का कोई समाधान नहीं है।
28.	हो सकता है वह अवश्य पास हो जाए।	–	हो सकता है वह पास हो जाए।
29.	किसी और दूसरे आदमी को भेज दीजिए।	–	किसी और को भेज दीजिए/किसी दूसरे को भेज दीजिए।
30.	यह दवा बहुत तत्काल असर दिखाती है।	–	यह दवा तत्काल असर दिखाती है।
31.	यहाँ तरुण नवयुवकों की शिक्षा का प्रबन्ध है।	–	यहाँ नवयुवकों की शिक्षा का प्रबन्ध है।
32.	प्रत्येक दिन स्नान करना चाहिए।	–	प्रतिदिन स्नान करना चाहिए।

	अशुद्ध वाक्य		शुद्ध वाक्य
33.	सैनिकों ने खूँखार अस्त्र-शस्त्रों से हमला किया।	—	सैनिकों ने विनाशकारी अस्त्र-शस्त्रों से हमला किया।
34.	हैजे आदि से हजारों लोग मर गए।	—	हैजा आदि से हजारों लोग मर गए।
35.	पूज्यनीय पिताजी को प्रणाम।	—	पूज्य पिताजी/पूजनीय पिताजी को प्रणाम।
36.	उसकी सौन्दर्यता पर सब मुग्ध थे।	—	उसके सौन्दर्य पर सब मुग्ध थे। या, उसकी सुन्दरता पर सब मुग्ध थे।
37.	अत्याधिक कार्य स्वास्थ को बिगाड़ देता है।	—	अत्यधिक कार्य स्वास्थ्य को बिगाड़ देता है।
38.	भिखारी ने राजा को आशीर्वाद प्रदान किया।	—	भिखारी ने राजा को आशीर्वाद दिया।
39.	प्राणीमात्र पर दया करो।	—	प्राणिमात्र पर दया करो।
40.	झगड़े का श्री गणेश तब हुआ जब जुलूस पर किसी ने पत्थर फेंक दिया।	—	झगड़े का आरम्भ तब हुआ जब जुलूस पर किसी ने पत्थर फेंक दिया।
41.	मेरा पतलून मैला है।	—	मेरी पतलून मैली है।
42.	उसकी दादी अभी जिन्दी है।	—	उसकी दादी अभी जिन्दा है।
43.	राम ने बाजार जाना है।	—	राम को बाजार जाना है।
44.	आज की ताजी खबर पढ़िए।	—	आज की ताजा खबर पढ़िए।
45.	हमने उनकी योजनाओं को दुम दबाकर स्वीकार कर लिया।	—	हमने उनकी योजनाओं को विवश होकर स्वीकार कर लिया।
46.	वह विद्वान महिला थीं।	—	वह विदुषी थीं।
47.	इसका उत्तरदाइत्व आपके उँपर है।	—	इसका उत्तरदायित्व आप पर है।
48.	उनकी मृत्यु से नगर की अपूर्व क्षति हुई।	—	उनकी मृत्यु से अपूरणीय क्षति हुई।
49.	साहित्य और जीवन का घोर सम्बन्ध है।	—	साहित्य और जीवन का घनिष्ठ सम्बन्ध है।
50.	ईश्वर उसकी मृत आत्मा को शान्ति दें।	—	ईश्वर उसकी आत्मा को शान्ति दें।
51.	आप खाना खाने आ जाओ।	—	आप खाना खाने आ जाएँ।
52.	आप कहोगे।	—	आप कहेंगे।
53.	अगर मैं गलती करूँ तो आप मुझे दुरुस्त कर दें।	—	अगर मैं गलती करूँ तो आप मुझे सुधार दें।
54.	काँग्रेस ने भारत की अच्छाई के अनेक कार्य किए।	—	काँग्रेस ने भारत की भलाई के लिए अनेक कार्य किए।
55.	उसका पैर गरम आग पर पड़ गया।	—	उसका पैर आग पर पड़ गया।
56.	शब्द केवल संकेत मात्र होते हैं।	—	शब्द केवल संकेत होते हैं। या, शब्द संकेत मात्र होते हैं।
57.	उसकी दृष्टि चित्र में गड़ी थी।	—	उसकी दृष्टि चित्र पर गड़ी थी।
58.	वे लगन के साथ देश की सेवा कर रहे हैं।	—	वे लगनपूर्वक देश की सेवा कर रहे हैं।
59.	फिर, कुछ देर से उसने कहा।	—	फिर, कुछ देर बाद उसने कहा।
60.	केवल कहने मात्र से कुछ नहीं होता।	—	केवल कहने से कुछ नहीं होता।
61.	चाहे जैसे भी हो, तुम वहाँ जाओ।	—	चाहे जैसे हो, तुम वहाँ जाओ।
62.	सभी प्रकार की चीज मौजूद थी।	—	सभी प्रकार की चीजें मौजूद थीं।
63.	आपके एक-एक शब्द तुले हुए होते हैं।	—	आपके एक-एक शब्द नपे-तुले होते हैं।
64.	आपकी राय से यह काम जरूरी है।	—	आपकी राय में यह काम जरूरी है।
65.	आपकी पुस्तक धन्यवाद सहित लौटाता हूँ।	—	आपकी पुस्तक धन्यवादपूर्वक लौटाता हूँ।
66.	हमारे बाप-दादाओं ने कभी ऐसा नहीं किया।	—	हमारे बाप-दादा ने कभी ऐसा नहीं किया।
67.	सबों ने यही राय दी।	—	सबने यही राय दी।
68.	संज्ञा की प्रशंसा करने वाले शब्द विशेषण होते हैं।	—	संज्ञा की विशेषता बताने वाले शब्द विशेषण होते हैं।
69.	मुझे प्रायः समस्त काम अपने हाथों करना पड़ता है।	—	मुझे प्रायः सम्पूर्ण काम अपने हाथों करना पड़ता है।
70.	सूरदास के उँपर डॉ॰ हजारी प्रसाद द्विवेदी ने एक उत्तम ग्रंथ लिखा है।	—	सूरदास के सम्बन्ध में डॉ॰ हजारी प्रसाद द्विवेदी ने एक उत्तम ग्रंथ लिखा है।
71.	अधिकांश धन व्यर्थ गया।	—	धन का अधिकांश व्यर्थ गया।
72.	राम का भविष्य शंकर के उँपर निर्भर है।	—	राम का भविष्य शंकर पर निर्भर है।
73.	इन दोनों में केवल यही अन्तर है।	—	इन दोनों में यही अन्तर है।
74.	उसे एक चिट्ठी लिखना होगा।	—	उसे एक चिट्ठी लिखनी होगी।

	अशुद्ध वाक्य		शुद्ध वाक्य
75.	यह बात हृदय से सम्भव है वे न मानें।	–	सम्भव है यह बात वे हृदय से नहीं मानें।
76.	आज उपशिक्षा मंत्री जी नगर में पधार रहे हैं।	–	आज शिक्षा उपमंत्री जी नगर में पधार रहे हैं।
77.	अधिकांश उर्दू के कवि शृंगारी कविता लिखते हैं।	–	उर्दू के अधिकतर कवि शृंगारी कविता लिखते हैं।
78.	उसकी आवाज कान में सुनाई पड़ी।	–	उसकी आवाज सुनाई पड़ी/उसकी आवाज कान में पड़ी।
79.	वह कहते हैं।	–	वे कहते हैं।
80.	थोड़ी देर बाद वे वापस लौट आए।	–	थोड़ी देर बाद वे लौट आये। या, थोड़ी देर बाद वे वापस आए।
81.	उन्हें मृत्युदण्ड की सजा मिली।	–	उन्हें मृत्युदण्ड मिला।
82.	उसी आदमी को, जो आपके पास जायेगा, यह पुस्तक दे दिजिए।	–	उसी आदमी को, जो आपके पास जाएगा, यह पुस्तक दे दीजिए।
83.	मेरा विश्वास मेरी आँखों पर भी नहीं है।	–	मेरा विश्वास अपनी आँखों पर भी नहीं है।
84.	वह अनेक प्रकार के बहाने बनाने लगा।	–	वह अनेक बहाने बनाने लगा।
85.	आप अपनी ताकत के बल पर यह काम करना चाहते हैं।	–	आप अपने बल पर यह काम करना चाहते हैं। या, आप अपनी ताकत पर यह काम करना चाहते हैं।
86.	मैं आज प्रातःकाल के समय वहाँ गया था।	–	मैं आज प्रातःकाल वहाँ गया था।
87.	कृपया यह बताने का अनुग्रह करें।	–	कृपया यह बतलावें। या, यह बतलाने की कृपा करें। या, यह बतलाने का अनुग्रह करें।
88.	सारे देशभर में यह बात फैल गई।	–	सारे देश में यह बात फैल गई/या, देशभर में यह बात फैल गई।
89.	वह इस बात की व्यवस्था का कोई प्रबन्ध नहीं कर सकता।	–	वह इस बात की व्यवस्था नहीं कर सकता/या, वह इस बात का प्रबन्ध नहीं कर सकता।
90.	देश की रक्षा का भार तुम्हारे उँपर है।	–	देश की रक्षा का भार तुम पर है।
91.	दंगे में दस मनुष्य मरे और पन्द्रह आदमी घायल हुए।	–	दंगे में दस आदमी मरे और पन्द्रह घायल हुए।
92.	कुछ पशु खेती के काम में आने के सिवा वे धर्म की दृष्टि से भी पूज्य हैं।	–	कुछ पशु खेती के काम में आने के अतिरिक्त धर्म की दृष्टि से भी पूज्य हैं।
93.	वह खाने-पीने के व्यंजन बना रही थी।	–	वह व्यंजन बना रही थी।
94.	प्रायः ऐसे अवसर आते हैं जिसमें लोगों को कभी-कभी अपना मत बदलना पड़ता है।	–	प्रायः ऐसे अवसर आते हैं जिनमें लोगों को अपना मत बदलना पड़ता है।
95.	आगरा के निकट दो रेलगाड़ियाँ लड़ गईं।	–	आगरा के निकट दो रेलगाड़ियों की टक्कर हो गई।
96.	वृक्ष में फल लगे हैं।	–	वृक्ष पर फल लगे हैं।
97.	उसने उधर देखा और बोला।	–	उसने उधर देखा और कहा।
98.	वहाँ पूड़ियाँ और झरने का पानी पीकर हमलोग आगे बढ़े।	–	वहाँ पूड़ियाँ खाकर और झरने का पानी पीकर हमलोग आगे बढ़े।
99.	मैं यह काम किया चाहता हूँ।	–	मैं यह काम करना चाहता हूँ।
100.	मेरे को ऐसा मत कहो।	–	मुझको ऐसा मत कहो।
101.	वे कोई स्कूल नहीं खोले थे।	–	उन्होंने कोई स्कूल नहीं खोला था।
102.	पंजाब के मुसलमान वहाँ प्रवेश किए थे।	–	पंजाब के मुसलमानों ने वहाँ प्रवेश किया था।
103.	लड़ाई के द्वारा लोगों ने खूब धन कमाया।	–	लड़ाई के समय लोगों ने खूब धन कमाया।
104.	यह बीमारी देश में लड़ाई के द्वारा फैली थी।	–	देश में यह बीमारी लड़ाई के कारण फैली थी।
105.	उन्होंने सरलता के साथ उत्तर दिया।	–	उन्होंने सरलतापूर्वक उत्तर दिया।
106.	उनके विरुद्ध मुकदमा चलाया गया।	–	उन पर मुकदमा चलाया गया।
107.	पूर्व इसके कि कोई हँसे, हम हँस पड़े।	–	किसी के हँसने के पहले हम स्वयं हँस पड़े।
108.	परीक्षा की प्रणाली बदलना चाहिए।	–	परीक्षा की प्रणाली बदलनी चाहिए।
109.	मैं तुम्हारे साथ नहाकर चलूँगा।	–	मैं नहाकर तुम्हारे साथ चलूँगा।
110.	शुद्ध गाय का दूध सेवन करो।	–	गाय का शुद्ध दूध सेवन करो।
111.	इतने वेतन से केवल दाल-रोटी हो जाती है।	–	इतने वेतन से केवल दाल-रोटी ही मिल पाती है।

	अशुद्ध वाक्य		शुद्ध वाक्य
112.	प्रेमचन्द जी ने पर्याप्त मात्रा में कहानी और उपन्यास लिखे।	–	प्रेमचन्द जी ने पर्याप्त संख्या में कहानी और उपन्यास लिखे।
113.	अनेकों बार समझाने पर भी वह नहीं समझा।	–	अनेक बार समझाने पर भी वह नहीं समझा।
114.	वह आगामी वर्ष हरिद्वार गया था।	–	वह गत् वर्ष हरिद्वार गया था।
115.	वह धर्मशालें में गया है।	–	वह धर्मशाला में गया है।
116.	मित्रों! उसकी भाग्य फूट गई।	–	मित्रों! उसका भाग्य फूट गया।
117.	हमें अपने माता-पिता का आदर करना चाहिए।	–	हमें माता-पिता का आदर करना चाहिए।
118.	उन्हें व्यर्थ रुपए देने से कोई लाभ नहीं है।	–	उन्हें रुपए देने से कोई लाभ नहीं/ अथवा, उन्हें रुपए देना व्यर्थ है।
119.	शास्त्रीजी की मृत्यु से हमें बड़ा खेद हुआ।	–	शास्त्री जी के निधन से हमें बहुत दुःख हुआ।
120.	शोक है कि आपने मेरे पत्रों का उत्तर नहीं दिया।	–	दुःख है कि आपने मेरे पत्रों के उत्तर नहीं दिए।
121.	एक-एक करके सभी चले गए।	–	एक-एक कर सभी चले गए।
122.	यह ग्रंथ दोहा और चौपाइयों में लिखा गया है।	–	यह ग्रंथ दोहे और चौपाइयों में लिखा गया है।
123.	मैं माता का दर्शन करने गया था।	–	मैं माता के दर्शन करने गया था।
124.	यही वे कारण हैं जिनके कारण देश में अशान्ति बढ़ रही है।	–	यही वे कारण हैं जिनसे देश में अशान्ति बढ़ रही है।
125.	ऐसी एकाध बातें और देखने में आती हैं।	–	ऐसी एकाध बात और देखने में आती है।
126.	प्रत्येक छोटी-मोटी विशेषताओं को देखना चाहिए।	–	प्रत्येक छोटी-मोटी विशेषता को देखना चाहिए।
127.	उन्होंने हाथ जोड़ा।	–	उन्होंने हाथ जोड़े।
128.	हम तो शादी में अवश्य ही जाएँगे।	–	हम शादी में अवश्य जाएँगे।
129.	तुम्हारा सब काम गलत होता है।	–	तुम्हारे सब काम गलत होते हैं।
130.	वह तो केवल आप ही पर निर्भर है।	–	वह तो केवल आप पर निर्भर है।
131.	उनकी आँखों की दृष्टि शून्य आकाश की ओर थी।	–	उनकी दृष्टि शून्य आकाश की ओर थी। या, उनकी आँखें शून्य आकाश की ओर थीं।
132.	वे सब काल-चक्र के पहिए के नीचे दब गए।	–	वे सब काल-चक्र में डूब गए।
133.	लड़का मिठाई लेकर भागता घर आया।	–	लड़का मिठाई लेकर दौड़ता हुआ घर आया।
134.	उसके अंग-अंग में सौन्दर्यता भरी थी।	–	उसके अंग-अंग में सौन्दर्य था।
135.	दो दिन की बदली के पीछे आज सूर्य निकला है।	–	दो दिन की बदली के बाद आज सूर्य निकला है।
135.	कोयला जलकर राख हो गई।	–	कोयला जलकर राख हो गया।
136.	सारा राज्य उसके लिए एक थाती थी।	–	सारा राज्य उसके लिए एक थाती था।
137.	मैं अपनी बात का स्पष्टीकरण करने के लिए तैयार हूँ।	–	मैं अपनी बात के स्पष्टीकरण के लिए तैयार हूँ।
138.	यह चित्र, गाँधी जी जब यहाँ पधारे थे। उस समय लिया गया था।	–	यह चित्र उस समय लिया गया था, जब गाँधी जी यहाँ पधारे थे।
139.	शत्रु उस पर टूट गए।	–	शत्रु उस पर टूट पड़े।
140.	लोग रविवार के दिन छुट्टी मनाते हैं।	–	लोग रविवार को छुट्टी मनाते हैं।
141.	उनकी एक आँख कानी थी।	–	वे काने थे।
142.	भीष्म पितामह आजन्म ब्रह्मचारी रहे।	–	भीष्म पितामह आजीवन ब्रह्मचारी रहे।
143.	वह अपनी विद्या समाप्त करके ही कुछ काम करेगा।	–	वह अपनी शिक्षा समाप्त करके ही कुछ काम करेगा।
144.	चावल का चिन्तनीय अभाव है।	–	चावल का अभाव चिंतनीय है।
145.	वह व्यक्ति ही क्या, जो कभी दुःख नहीं उठाया।	–	वह व्यक्ति ही क्या, जिसने कभी दुःख नहीं उठाया।
146.	यहाँ सर्वोत्कृष्ट ज्वर की चिकित्सा होती है।	–	यहाँ ज्वर की सर्वोत्कृष्ट चिकित्सा होती है।
147.	घड़ा और लोटा में पानी है।	–	घड़े और लोटे में पानी है।
148.	नौकर से कहो कि मेरा सामान तैयार रखो।	–	नौकर से कहो कि मेरा सामान तैयार रखे।
149.	गाँधी का देश सदैव आभारी रहेगा।	–	देश गाँधी का सदैव आभारी रहेगा।
150.	मैंने यह बात उनके द्वारा सुनी थी।	–	मैंने यह बात उनसे सुनी थी।

वस्तुनिष्ठ प्रश्नोत्तर

निर्देश (प्रश्न संख्या 1 से 4 तक): *निम्नलिखित अशुद्ध वाक्यों के शुद्ध रूप का नीचे दिए विकल्पों में से चयन कीजिए।*

1. मैं तेरे को बता दूँगा
A. मैं बता तुझको दूँगा
B. मैं तुम्हें बता दूँगा
C. मैं तुझको बता दूँगा
D. सभी वाक्य सही हैं

2. पेड़ों पर कोयल बोल रही थी
A. पेड़ पर कोयलें बोल रही थीं
B. पेड़ पर कोयल बोल रही थी
C. पेड़ों पर कोयल थी
D. सभी वाक्य सही हैं

3. मुझे भारी दुःख हुआ
A. मुझे बहुत दुःख हुआ
B. मुझे दुःखी हुआ
C. मुझे ज्यादा दुःख हुआ
D. सभी वाक्य सही हैं

4. वह पूर्णतया उत्तीर्ण हो गया
A. वह एकदम उत्तीर्ण हो गया
B. वह उत्तीर्ण हो गया
C. वह एकदम पास हो गया
D. सभी वाक्य सही हैं

निर्देश (प्रश्न संख्या 5 से 31 तक): *निम्नलिखित में शुद्ध वाक्य का चयन कीजिए।*

5. A. एक गीतों की पुस्तक ला दो
B. गीतों की एक पुस्तक ला दो
C. पुस्तक एक गीतों की ला दो
D. पुस्तक गीतों की एक ला दो

6. A. बन्दर को काटकर चाकू से फल खिला दो
B. चाकू से बन्दर को काटकर फल खिला दो
C. चाकू से फल काटकर बन्दर को खिला दो
D. फल काटकर चाकू से बन्दर को खिला दो

7. A. बाघ और बकरी एक घाट पर पानी पीती हैं
B. बाघ और बकरी एक घाट पर पानी पीते हैं
C. बाघ और बकरी पानी पीते हैं एक घाट पर
D. बाघ और बकरी पीते हैं पानी एक घाट पर

8. A. मैं गाने की कसरत कर रहा हूँ
B. मैं गाने का अभ्यास कर रहा हूँ
C. मैं गाने का शौक कर रहा हूँ
D. मैं गाने का व्यायाम कर रहा हूँ

9. A. उसकी अवस्था चालीस वर्ष की है
B. उसकी आयु चालीस वर्ष की है
C. उसका बात मत करो
D. आपका पत्र सधन्यवाद मिला

10. A. मैं जाते-जाते रुक गया
B. मैं जा रहा था पर रुक गया
C. मैं जा रहा था और रुक गया
D. अचानक जाते-जाते रुक गया

11. A. उसे जाने दो, रोको मत
B. रोको मत, उसे जाने दो
C. मत रोको, उसे जाने दो
D. उसे जाने ही दो, रोको नहीं

12. A. रात दस बजे गाड़ी आएगी
B. दस बजे रात में गाड़ी आएगी
C. रात में दस बजे गाड़ी आएगी
D. गाड़ी रात में दस बजे आएगी

13. A. रामचन्द्रजी को दशरथ ने चौदह वर्ष का वनवास दिया
B. दशरथ ने राम को चौदह वर्षों के लिए वनवास दिया
C. चौदह वर्षों का वनवास दशरथ ने राम को दिया
D. दशरथ ने राम को चौदह वर्षों का वनवास दिया

14. A. सम्भवतः कल तक वर्षा हो जाएगी
B. सम्भवतः कल तक अवश्य वर्षा हो जाएगी
C. कल तक निश्चित रूप से वर्षा होने की संभावना है
D. सम्भावना है कि कल तक निश्चय ही वर्षा होगी

15. A. हिन्दी के विकास के मुख्य तीन काल हैं, केवल
B. हिन्दी के विकास के तीन ही मुख्य काल हैं
C. तीन मुख्य काल हिन्दी के विकास के हैं
D. हिन्दी के विकास के तीन काल मुख्य हैं

16. छात्र द्वारा अवकाश के प्रार्थना-पत्र के अन्त में लिखा जाना चाहिए
A. आपका शिष्य
B. आपका आज्ञाकारी शिष्य
C. आपका छात्र
D. आपका स्नेही

17. A. जो जैसा कभी बोता है वैसा काटता है
B. वह जैसा कभी बोएगा है वैसा काटेगा
C. जो जैसा बोएगा वैसा ही काटेगा
D. जिसने जब जैसा बोया उसने तब वैसा काटा

18. A. मेरे को घर जाना चाहिए
B. मैंने घर जाना चाहिए
C. मुझे घर जाना चाहिए
D. मुझको घर को जाना चाहिए

19. 'मुझे केवल दस रुपए मात्र मिले' वाक्य अशुद्ध है, क्योंकि
A. वाक्य में **मुझे** नहीं होना चाहिए
B. वाक्य में **मिले** अन्त में नहीं होना चाहिए
C. वाक्य में **रुपए** मात्र से पूर्व नहीं होना चाहिए
D. वाक्य में **केवल** नहीं होना चाहिए

20. A. हमारे यहाँ तरुण नवयुवकों को काम सिखाया जाता है
B. पंडित जी की मृत्यु का हमें खेद है
C. यही नहीं, बल्कि वे वहाँ से चले भी आए
D. मुझसे यह काम सम्भव नहीं हो सकता

21. A. वहाँ भारी-भरकम भीड़ जमा थी
B. जो धन का भूखा है, वह साधु नहीं है
C. मुझे इस अधिवेशन का समाचार नहीं मिला था
D. मेरी कविता मुद्रित हो रही है

22. सही वाक्य का चयन कीजिए
A. देश सदा महात्मा गांधी का ऋणी रहेगा
B. महात्मा गांधी का देश सदा ऋणी रहेगा
C. महात्मा गांधी का सदा देश ऋणी रहेगा
D. देश महात्मा गांधी का सदा ऋणी रहेगा

23. A. परिवर्तन का यह अर्थ नहीं कि कदापि अतीत की सर्वथा उपेक्षा की जाए
B. परिवर्तन का अर्थ यह कदापि नहीं कि अतीत की सर्वथा उपेक्षा की जाए
C. परिवर्तन का अर्थ यह कदापि नहीं कि अतीत की सर्वथा अपेक्षा की जाए
D. परिवर्तन का यह अर्थ कदापि नहीं कि अतीत की सर्वथा उपेक्षा की जाए

24. A. जानते हैं किसी को कि इस बात को सताया न जाए
B. जानते हैं इस बात को किसी को सताया न जाए
C. इस बात को जानते हैं किसी को कि सताया नहीं जाए
D. इस बात को जानते हैं कि किसी को सताया न जाए

25. A. सीटी की आवाज जिधर से आ रही थी मैं उधर ही दौड़ पड़ा
B. बस सीटी की आवाज जिधर से आ रही थी मैं उधर ही दौड़ पड़ा
C. सीटी की आवाज जिधर से आ रही थी बस उधर ही मैं दौड़ पड़ा
D. जिधर से सीटी की आवाज आ रही थी मैं उधर ही दौड़ पड़ा

26. A. अधिकारियों ने कागजात का निरीक्षण किया
B. अधिकारियों ने कागजात का परीक्षण किया
C. अधिकारियों ने कागजात की जाँच की
D. अधिकारियों ने कागजात का अन्वेषण किया

27. A. भारत में अनेकों जातियाँ हैं
B. भारत में अनेक जातियाँ हैं
C. भारत में अनेकों जाति हैं
D. भारत में अनेक जाति हैं

28. A. वह दण्ड देने योग्य है
B. वह दण्ड के योग्य है
C. वह दण्ड लेने योग्य है
D. वह दण्ड पाने योग्य है

29. A. फल बच्चे को काटकर खिलाओ
B. बच्चे को काटकर फल खिलाओ
C. बच्चे को फल काटकर खिलाओ
D. काटकर फल बच्चे को खिलाओ

30. A. उसे अनुत्तीर्ण होने की आशा है
B. उसे अनुत्तीर्ण होने की आशंका है
C. उसे अनुत्तीर्ण होने का शक है
D. उसे अनुत्तीर्ण होने का संशय है

31. A. कल पाठ पढ़कर आइए
B. पाठ पढ़कर कल आइए
C. पाठ पढ़कर आइए कल
D. कल पाठ पढ़कर आइए

निर्देश (प्रश्न संख्या 32 से 46 तक): *निम्नलिखित अशुद्ध वाक्य के लिए चार-चार विकल्प दिए गए हैं। सही विकल्प चुनिए।*

32. जो मिठाइयाँ पसन्द हों आप खा लो
A. जो मिठाई पसन्द हों आप खा लो
B. जो मिठाई पसन्द हो तुम खा लो
C. जो मिठाइयाँ पसन्द हों तुम खा लो
D. जो मिठाइयाँ पसन्द हों उन्हें आप खाइए

33. हम बचपन में वहाँ जाता रहा
A. हम बचपन में वहाँ जाएंगे
B. हम बचपन में वहाँ जाते रहे हैं
C. मैं बचपन में वहाँ जाता रहा
D. मैं बचपन में वहाँ जाऊँगा

34. प्रत्येक व्यक्ति कविता नहीं कर सकते
A. प्रत्येक व्यक्ति कविता कर सकते हैं
B. प्रत्येक व्यक्ति कविता नहीं कर सकते हैं
C. प्रत्येक व्यक्ति कविता नहीं कर सकता
D. हर व्यक्ति कविता कर सकते हैं

35. हेम नरेश को पुस्तक दिया
A. हेम नरेश की पुस्तक दी
B. हेम ने नरेश को पुस्तक दी
C. हेम नरेश का पुस्तक देगा
D. हेम ने नरेश का पुस्तक दिया

36. मन्त्री ड्राइवर को कार चलवाता है
A. मन्त्री ड्राइवर से कार चलवाता है
B. मन्त्री ड्राइवर की कार चलवाता है
C. मन्त्री ड्राइवर के लिए कार चलवाता है
D. मन्त्री ड्राइवर पर कार चलवाता है

37. A. जीवन और साहित्य का घोर सम्बन्ध है
B. जीवन और साहित्य का निकट सम्बन्ध है
C. जीवन और साहित्य का घनिष्ठ सम्बन्ध है
D. जीवन और साहित्य का गहरा सम्बन्ध है

38. A. सूर्य पश्चिम को अस्त होता है
B. मुझे विद्यालय जाना है
C. मैं तो आप के ऊपर निर्भर हूँ
D. लड़ाई में लोगों ने खूब कमाया

39. A. यह अध्यापक बहुत श्रेष्ठ पढ़ाता है
B. आज गोपाल उसके अपने काम से शहर गया
C. यह गाय बहुत प्यासी है
D. मानव ईश्वर की सबसे उत्कृष्टतम कृति है

40. A. रमेश के अन्दर बहुत विद्वता है
B. रमा विदुषी महिला है
C. सभी श्रेणियों के लोग वहाँ उपस्थित थे
D. धन्यवाद देता हूँ मैं उन्हें

41. A. आवश्यकता आविष्कार की जननी है
B. आविष्कार की जननी आवश्यकता है
C. आविष्कार आवश्यकता की जननी है
D. जननी है आविष्कार की आवश्यकता

42. A. मैं आपसे कुछ नहीं कह सकता हूँ
B. कुछ नहीं कह सकता हूँ मैं आपसे
C. आपसे मैं कुछ नहीं कह सकता हूँ
D. आपको मैं कुछ नहीं कह सकता हूँ

43. A. गंगा का उद्गम स्थल गंगोत्री में है
B. गंगा का उद्गम स्थल गंगोत्री पर है
C. गंगा का उद्गम स्थल गंगोत्री से है
D. गंगा का उद्गम स्थल गंगोत्री है

44. A. मुझे आज की बैठक का समाचार नहीं था
B. मैंने अभी लखनऊ जाना है
C. पाप को डरो, पानी से नहीं
D. एक कप चाय मुझे भी देना

45. A. विष्णु के अनेकों नाम हैं
B. कन्या पराया धन होती है
C. वह पढ़ता-पढ़ता सो गया
D. मैं रोज गाने की कसरत करता हूँ

46. A. आज हमारी सौभाग्यवती कन्या का विवाह है
B. उसने गीत की दो-चार लड़ियाँ ही सुनाई
C. देखो, कहीं उसकी नींद न खुल जाए
D. यह कार्य आप पर निर्भर करता है

निर्देश (प्रश्न संख्या 47 से 50 तक): *निम्नलिखित प्रश्नों के दिए गए वाक्यों के काले भाग में कुछ न कुछ त्रुटि है। उसके शुद्ध रूप को नीचे के विकल्प से ज्ञात कीजिए। यदि काले भाग में कोई गलती न हो तो अपने उत्तर के रूप में (D) अर्थात् कोई सुधार आवश्यक नहीं है, को इंगित कीजिए।*

47. समाज एवं देश के बहुमुखी विकास के लिए तन, मन, धन से प्रयत्न करना होगा **केवल मात्र कागजी योजनाओं** से कोई लाभ नहीं होगा
A. केवल सिर्फ कागजी योजनाओं
B. सिर्फ मात्र कागजी योजनाओं
C. मात्र कागजी योजनाओं
D. कोई सुधार आवश्यक नहीं है

48. बढ़ती महंगाई के कारण **देशी घी खरीदने** की सार्थकता लोगों में नहीं रह गई
A. देशी घी खरीद सकने
B. देशी घी खरीद करने
C. देशी सामान खरीद सकने
D. कोई सुधार आवश्यक नहीं है

49. बैठक कक्ष **केवल महिलाओं के उपयोग के लिए है**
A. केवल महिलाओं द्वारा इसका उपयोग होना चाहिए
B. केवल महिलाओं के उपयोग में लाना चाहिए
C. इसका उपयोग केवल महिलाओं द्वारा हो
D. कोई सुधार आवश्यक नहीं है

50. सभी घायल **भर्ती किए गए तथा ध्यान रखा गया**
A. अन्दर दाखिल हुए और ध्यान दिया गया
B. दाखिल हुए और ध्यान दिया गया
C. भर्ती किए गए और ध्यान रखा गया
D. कोई सुधार आवश्यक नहीं

उत्तरमाला

1	2	3	4	5	6	7	8	9	10
C	B	A	B	B	C	B	B	A	A
11	**12**	**13**	**14**	**15**	**16**	**17**	**18**	**19**	**20**
B	A	D	A	A	B	C	C	D	D
21	**22**	**23**	**24**	**25**	**26**	**27**	**28**	**29**	**30**
D	A	D	D	D	C	B	B	D	B
31	**32**	**33**	**34**	**35**	**36**	**37**	**38**	**39**	**40**
B	D	C	C	B	A	C	B	C	B
41	**42**	**43**	**44**	**45**	**46**	**47**	**48**	**49**	**50**
A	A	D	D	B	C	C	D	D	D

★ ★ ★

7

वाक्य रचनान्तरण (सरल/संयुक्त/मिश्र)

वाक्य

वाक्य सार्थक शब्दों का वह समूह है जिससे बोलने अथवा लिखने वाले का तात्पर्य पूरी तरह स्पष्ट हो जाता है। जैसे : वह निर्धन लेकिन परिश्रमी बालक है। रीता गीत गाती है।

उपवाक्य

जब किसी एक भाव को स्पष्ट करने के लिए किसी एक वाक्य के अंश-रूप में दो या दो से अधिक वाक्यों का उपयोग किया जाता है, तब उन अंश या खण्ड वाक्यों में प्रत्येक को उपवाक्य कहा जाता है।

जैसे– 'मैं जानता हूँ कि वे मेरे मित्र हैं।'

इस वाक्य में 'मैं जानता हूँ' तथा 'वे मेरे मित्र हैं' दोनों ही उपवाक्य या खण्डवाक्य कहलाएँगे।

उपवाक्य के भेद

उपवाक्य के दो भेद हैं :

1. प्रधान उपवाक्य, 2. आश्रित उपवाक्य

1. **प्रधान उपवाक्य**–जो उपवाक्य पूरे वाक्य से पृथक होकर भी अपना स्वतन्त्र एवं पूर्ण अर्थ रखता है उसे प्रधान उपवाक्य कहते हैं। जैसे–'मैं जानता हूँ कि वे मेरे मित्र हैं।' इस वाक्य में 'मैं जानता हूँ'–प्रधान उपवाक्य है।
2. **आश्रित उपवाक्य**–जो उपवाक्य प्रधान उपवाक्य के बिना अपना अर्थ स्पष्ट नहीं कर सकता वह 'आश्रित उपवाक्य' कहलाता है। आश्रित उपवाक्य अर्थ के लिए वस्तुतः प्रधान उपवाक्य पर आश्रित रहता है।
   जैसे–'मैं जानता हूँ कि वे मेरे मित्र हैं'–में 'वे मेरे मित्र हैं' –आश्रित उपवाक्य है।

आश्रित उपवाक्य के भेद

1. संज्ञा उपवाक्य
2. विशेषण उपवाक्य
3. क्रिया उपवाक्य

1. **संज्ञा उपवाक्य**–जो आश्रित उपवाक्य संज्ञा का दायित्व निर्वाह करता है उसे 'संज्ञा उपवाक्य' कहते हैं।
   जैसे–'मैं नहीं जानता कि वे कब लौटेंगे।'–इस वाक्य का उपवाक्य 'वे कब लौटेंगे' 'जानता' क्रिया के कर्म के रूप में कार्य कर रहा है इसलिए संज्ञा उपवाक्य है।
2. **विशेषण उपवाक्य**–जो आश्रित उपवाक्य विशेषण का कार्य करता है, उसे विशेषण उपवाक्य कहते हैं।
   जैसे–वह लड़का **जो कल यहाँ आया था** बीमार है।
   वह अपने नौकर को **जिसने चोरी की है** पीट रहा है।
   वह अपने नौकर को उस छड़ी से पीट रहा है **जिसे उसने कल ही खरीदी है**। इनमें प्रत्येक रेखांकित उपवाक्य विशेषण का कार्य कर रहा है।
   विशेषण उपवाक्य मुख्यतः जो, जिसको, जिससे, जिसके लिए, जिसका, जिसमें आदि से प्रारम्भ होता है।
3. **क्रिया उपवाक्य**–जो उपवाक्य क्रिया विशेषण का कार्य करे उसे क्रिया विशेषण उपवाक्य कहते हैं।
   जैसे–**जब पानी बरसता है** तब मेढक बोलता है।
   जहाँ वह मन्दिर बना हुआ है वहाँ एक दिन यज्ञ हुआ था।
   इन वाक्यों में प्रत्येक रेखांकित उपवाक्य क्रिया विशेषण उपवाक्य हैं। क्यों ये उपवाक्य क्रिया विशेषण का कार्य करते हैं। क्रिया विशेषण उपवाक्य का आरम्भ विशेषतः निम्नलिखित शब्दों से होता है– जब, ज्योंही, जब-जब, जहाँ-कहाँ, जिधर, जैसे, मानो, ज्यों-ज्यों, जैसे-जैसे, जहाँ तक, चूँकि, ताकि, शायद, तथापि आदि।

वाक्य के भेद

वाक्यों के भेद सामान्यतः दो आधारों पर किए जाते हैं–

(क) रचना के आधार पर

(ख) अर्थ के आधार पर

रचना के आधार पर

रचना के आधार पर वाक्य के तीन भेद होते हैं–1. सरल वाक्य 2. मिश्र वाक्य 3. संयुक्त वाक्य

1. **सरल वाक्य**–जिस वाक्य में एक ही उपवाक्य होता है, उसे सरल वाक्य कहते हैं। इसमें केवल एक कर्त्ता और एक क्रिया होती है।
   जैसे– राम ने रावण का वध किया।
   बच्चे खेल रहे हैं।
   वह मेरा मित्र है।
1. **मिश्र वाक्य**–जिस वाक्य में एक प्रधान उपवाक्य तथा एक या अधिक आश्रित उपवाक्य हो उसे मिश्र वाक्य कहते हैं।

जैसे–तुम वहाँ आ सकते हो जहाँ मैं रहता हूँ।
मैं उस व्यक्ति को जानता हूँ जो तुम्हारा मित्र है।
हमसे वह पुस्तक खो गई है जो तुमने हमें दी थी।

3. **संयुक्त वाक्य**–जिस वाक्य में दो या दो से अधिक प्रधान उपवाक्य हों और वे परस्पर किसी अव्यय द्वारा जुड़े हों तो वह संयुक्त वाक्य कहलाता है।
जैसे–मैं आया और वह चल दिया।
उसने परिश्रम किया किन्तु असफल रहा।
संयुक्त वाक्य में सरल तथा मिश्र दोनों प्रकार के वाक्य प्रविष्ट हो सकते हैं। प्रधान उपवाक्यों को जोड़ने वाले शब्द प्रायः निम्नलिखित होते हैं।
यथा–और, तथा, एवं, व, वा, या, अथवा, परन्तु, पर, किन्तु, बल्कि, इसलिए, सो, अतः आदि।

अर्थ के आधार पर

अर्थ के आधार पर वाक्य के मुख्यतः आठ भेद होते हैं:–

1. **विधि वाचक वाक्य**–जिस वाक्य से किसी बात के होने का बोध हो उसे विधि वाचक वाक्य कहते हैं।
जैसे–अच्छे लोग सदा मधुर भाषण करते हैं।
2. **निषेध वाचक वाक्य**–जिस वाक्य से आज्ञा, अनुरोध, आदेश आदि का भाव प्रकट हो, उसे आज्ञा वाचक वाक्य कहते हैं।
जैसे–परिश्रम कभी व्यर्थ नहीं जाता।
3. **आज्ञा वाचक वाक्य**–जिस वाक्य से आज्ञा, अनुरोध, आदेश आदि का भाव प्रकट हो, उसे आज्ञा वाचक वाक्य कहते हैं।
जैसे–कभी चोरी न करो।
यहाँ आइये।
4. **प्रश्न वाचक वाक्य**–जिस वाक्य से किसी प्रकार के प्रश्न का बोध हो उसे प्रश्न वाचक वाक्य कहते हैं।
जैसे– तुम क्या चाहते हो?
5. **विस्मयादि बोधक वाक्य**–जिस वाक्य से हर्ष, शोक, विस्मय आदि का बोध हो उसे विस्मयादि बोधक वाक्य कहते हैं।
जैसे– अहा! कितना सुन्दर फल है।
6. **इच्छा वाचक वाक्य**–जिस वाक्य से इच्छा या आशंका का बोध हो उसे इच्छा वाचक वाक्य कहते हैं।
जैसे– भगवान, आपको दीर्घायु करें।
7. **संदेह वाचक वाक्य**–जिस वाक्य से किसी प्रकार के संदेह का बोध हो उसे संदेह वाचक वाक्य कहते हैं। जैसे–वे लोग आ रहे होंगे। वह शायद बीमार है।
8. **संकेत वाचक वाक्य**–जिस वाक्य से किसी शर्त या संकेत का बोध हो उसे संकेत वाचक वाक्य कहते हैं।
जैसे–यदि वह पढ़ता तो निश्चय ही उत्तीर्ण होता।

वाक्य-विस्तार

किसी भी वाक्य के मुख्य रूप से दो अंग होते हैं–

(1) उद्देश्य
(2) विधेय।

उद्देश्य

वाक्य में जिस वस्तु या व्यक्ति के बारे में कुछ कहा जाता है उसे उद्देश्य कहते हैं। वाक्य की समाविका क्रिया का कर्त्ता ही उद्देश्य होता है।

जैसे– सीता पुस्तक पढ़ती है।
मेरी माताजी इन दिनों बीमार हैं।
मैं उन्हें जानता हूँ।

इन वाक्यों में सीता, माताजी, मैं–उद्देश्य अथवा कर्त्ता शब्द हैं। उद्देश्य का अपना विस्तार भी होता है। संज्ञा, सर्वनाम, विशेषण, क्रिया विशेषण, क्रियार्थक संज्ञा, वाक्यांश आदि सभी उद्देश्य का रूप ले सकते हैं।

जैसे–

1. संज्ञा–गाय रँभाती है।
2. सर्वनाम–वे घर जाते हैं।
3. विशेषण–मेहनती छात्र सफलता पाते हैं।
4. क्रिया–धीरे-धीरे चलो।
5. क्रियार्थक संज्ञा–टहलना स्वास्थ्यप्रद होता है।
6. वाक्यांश–दूसरे की निन्दा अच्छी नहीं होती।

उद्देश्य का विस्तार–उद्देश्य की विशेषता वाले शब्दों को उद्देश्य का विस्तार कहते हैं।

जैसे–दुष्ट जनों की संगति अच्छी नहीं होती है। विस्तार शब्दों के भिन्न-भिन्न रूप होते हैं।

जैसे–

1. विशेषण–दुष्टजन त्याज्य हैं।
2. सम्बन्ध कारक–मेरी पुस्तक खो गई है।
3. क्रिया द्योतक–सोता हुआ व्यक्ति जाग उठा।
4. प्रश्न बोधक–क्या चाहते हो?
5. वाक्यांश–निरन्तर परिश्रम करने वाला छात्र सुखी होता है।
6. संबोधनात्मक–हे भाई! तुम कौन हो?

विधेय

उद्देश्य के सम्बन्ध में जो कुछ कहा जाता है उसे विधेय कहते हैं। जैसे–राम-श्याम खेल रहे हैं। विधेय 'साधारण और जटिल' दो प्रकार के होते हैं। विधेय के साथ यदि पूरक शब्द आता है तब विधेय 'जटिल' कहलाता है। संज्ञा, विशेषण, सम्बन्ध वाचक तथा क्रिया विशेषण प्रायः पूरक शब्दों के रूप में आते हैं।

1. संज्ञा–मेरे मित्र अध्यापक हैं।
2. विशेषण–वह छात्र मेधावी है।
3. सम्बन्ध वाचक–यह पुस्तक तो आपकी है।
4. क्रिया विशेषण–तुम कहाँ खो गए थे।

विधेय का विस्तार–विधेय के सम्बन्ध में जो कुछ कहा या लिखा जाए उसे विधेय का विस्तार कहते हैं। जैसे–घोड़ा धीरे-धीरे दौड़ रहा है। वह घर लौटते ही गिर पड़ा।

विधेय का विस्तार निम्नलिखित रूपों में होता है–

कर्म	–	बच्चा सेब खाता है।
विशेषण	–	आभा विदुषी है।
क्रिया विशेषण	–	घोड़ा धीरे-धीरे दौड़ रहा है।
सम्बन्ध सूचक	–	पुत्र के साथ माँ चली गई।
क्रिया द्योतक	–	मोटर पों-पों करती चली गई।

पूर्वकालिक क्रिया	–	वह उठकर दौड़ पड़ा।
पद वाक्यांश	–	बाजार से लौटने के बाद वह सो गया।
करण कारक	–	उसने मुझे बेंत से मारा।
सम्प्रदान कारक	–	गरीबों के लिए उसने दान दिया।
अपादान कारक	–	वृक्ष से पत्ते गिरते हैं।
अधिकरण कारक	–	वह पिता पर आश्रित है।

मिश्र वाक्य से सरल वाक्य में रूपान्तरण

मिश्र वाक्य		सरल वाक्य
1. सीता ने कहा कि मैं घर जाऊंगी।	–	1. सीता ने घर जाने के लिए कहा।
2. 'संशय की एक रात' खंडकाव्य है, वैसे ही 'प्रवाद पर्व भी खंडकाव्य है।	–	2. 'संशय की एक रात' की भांति 'प्रवाद पर्व भी खंडकाव्य है।
3. जब बारिश होती है, तब फूल लिखते हैं।	–	3. बारिश होने पर फूल खिलते हैं।
4. जो लोग अध्ययन करते हैं, वे अच्छा लिख पाते हैं।	–	4. अध्ययन करने वाले लोग अच्छा लिख पाते हैं।
5. जितना सुख हमें घर में मिलता है, उतना और जगह नहीं।	–	5. घर जितना सुख हमें और जगह नहीं मिलता।

सरल वाक्य से मिश्र वाक्य में रूपान्तरण

सरल वाक्य		मिश्र वाक्य
1. परिश्रमी को सफलता मिलती है।	–	1. जो परिश्रमी होता है, उसे सफलता मिलती है।
2. गंभीर संवेदनाओं के कवि का सम्मान सभी करते हैं।	–	2. जिनके पास गंभीर संवेदनाएं होती हैं, ऐसे कवि का सम्मान सभी करते हैं।
3. हमारे परिवार ने अपने सम्मानित कवि के नाम पर पुस्तकालय बनवाया।	–	3. हमारे परिवार ने एक पुस्तकालय बनवाया, जो हमारे सम्मानित कवि के नाम पर है।

संयुक्त वाक्य से सरल वाक्य में रूपान्तरण

संयुक्त वाक्य		सरल वाक्य
1. वे अब दिखाई नहीं देते, क्योंकि बाजार जाते हैं।	–	1. वे बाजार जाने के कारण अब दिखाई नहीं देते।
2. तुम इतनी उछल-कूद मचा रहे हो, लेकिन यह व्यर्थ है।	–	2. तुम व्यर्थ ही इतनी उछल-कूद मचा रहे हो।
3. वह न केवल पढ़ता, अपितु पढ़ाता भी है।	–	3. वह पढ़ने के साथ-साथ पढ़ाता भी है।
4. वह दिनभर पढ़ता है और रात में सोता है।	–	4. वह दिनभर पढ़कर रात में सोता है।
5. बारिश हो रही थी इसलिए छुट्टी भी मिली।	–	5. बारिश होने पर ही छुट्टी मिली।
6. वह बहुत भागा, परंतु असफल रहा।	–	6. बहुत भागने पर भी वह असफल रहा।

मिश्र वाक्य से संयुक्त वाक्य में रूपान्तरण

मिश्र वाक्य		संयुक्त वाक्य
1. मैंने जो पुस्तक लिखी थी, वह छप गई।	–	1. मैंने पुस्तक लिखी थी और वह छप गई।
2. हालांकि मुझे लिखना था, फिर भी नहीं लिख पाया।	–	2. मुझे लिखना था किंतु नहीं लिख पाया।
3. जब दुर्घटना की खबर सुनी, तब मन दुखी हो गया।	–	3. दुर्घटना की खबर सुनी और मन दुखी हो गया।
4. जब भी मैं विकास के घर गया, मेरा आदर सत्कार हुआ।	–	4. विकास के घर मेरा आदर भी हुआ और सत्कार भी।

संयुक्त वाक्य से मिश्र वाक्य में रूपान्तरण

संयुक्त वाक्य		मिश्र वाक्य
1. वे मेधावी छात्रा हैं, इसलिए उन्हें सफलता अवश्य मिलेगी।	–	1. वे मेधावी छात्रा हैं, उन्हें सफलता अवश्य मिलेगी।
2. वहाँ सब तरफ हरियाली है और वहीं वह नदी है।	–	2. जहाँ सब तरफ हरियाली है, वहीं वह नदी है।
3. विशाल ने एक मोबाइल खरीदा है और वह नया है।	–	3. विशाल ने जो मोबाइल खरीदा है, वह नया है
4. शिक्षक ने सबको गृहकार्य करने को कहा एवं स्वयं करने को कहा।	–	4. शिक्षक ने कहा कि सबको गृहकार्य स्वयं करना है।

वस्तुनिष्ठ प्रश्नोत्तर

1. आज बहुत पानी गिरा।—यह कैसा वाक्य है?
A. साधारण वाक्य B. मिश्र वाक्य
C. संयुक्त वाक्य D. उपवाक्य

2. 'उससे अब अकेले नहीं रहा जाता है'। यह कैसा वाक्य है?
A. कर्तृवाक्य B. कर्मवाच्य
C. भाववाच्य D. इनमें से कोई नहीं

3. 'वहाँ जाओ'। यह कैसा वाक्य है?
A. निषेधवाचक B. प्रश्नवाचक
C. आज्ञावाचक D. अनुरोधवाचक

4. 'उसने कहा कि मैं घर जाऊँगा'। यह कैसा वाक्य है?
A. सरल वाक्य B. संयुक्त वाक्य
C. मिश्र वाक्य D. प्रश्नवाचक वाक्य

5. 'तुम यह काम मत करो।' यह कैसा वाक्य है?
A. आज्ञावाचक B. निषेधवाचक
C. प्रश्नवाचक D. विस्मयवाचक

6. 'हो सकता है राम का काम बन जाय।' यह कैसा वाक्य है?
A. निषेधवाचक B. प्रश्नवाचक
C. संदेहवाचक D. आज्ञावाचक

7. 'अरे! उसने तो कमाल कर दिया।' यह कैसा वाक्य है?
A. प्रश्नवाचक B. निषेधवाचक
C. विस्मयवाचक D. इच्छावाचक

8. 'राम क्रिकेट खेलता है पर अच्छा नहीं।' यह कैसा वाक्य है?
A. सरल वाक्य B. संयुक्त वाक्य
C. मिश्र वाक्य D. इनमें से कोई नहीं

9. 'ज्यों ही मैंने दरवाजा खोला कि वह आ गया।' यह कैसा वाक्य है?
A. सरल वाक्य B. संयुक्त वाक्य
C. मिश्र वाक्य D. इनमें से कोई नहीं

10. 'वह आए तो काम बन सकता है।' यह कैसा वाक्य है?
A. इच्छाबोधक B. संदेहसूचक
C. संकेतार्थक D. विधानार्थक

11. तुम विद्यालय के लिए यह कर दो या रमेश को बोल दो।
A. संयुक्त वाक्य B. मिश्र वाक्य
C. सरल वाक्य D. इनमें से कोई नहीं

12. मजदूर मेहनत करता है, किंतु उसके लाभ से वंचित रहता है।
A. सरल वाक्य B. मिश्र वाक्य
C. संयुक्त वाक्य D. इनमें से कोई नहीं

13. प्रत्येक धर्म सिखाता है कि आपस में भाई-चारे से रहो।
A. मिश्र वाक्य B. संयुक्त वाक्य
C. सरल वाक्य D. इनमें से कोई नहीं

14. मुझे विश्वास है कि आप अवश्य आएँगे।
A. मिश्र वाक्य B. संयुक्त वाक्य
C. सरल वाक्य D. इनमें से कोई नहीं

15. अल्प ज्ञानी व्यक्ति बुद्धिमान की कद्र करना क्या जाने।
A. सरल वाक्य B. संयुक्त वाक्य
C. मिश्र वाक्य D. इनमें से कोई नहीं

16. नीति कहती है कि तुम गलत के साथ गलत मत करो।
A. सरल वाक्य B. संयुक्त वाक्य
C. मिश्र वाक्य D. इनमें से कोई नहीं

17. दुष्ट व्यक्ति की मित्रता स्थायी नहीं होती।
A. सरल वाक्य B. संयुक्त वाक्य
C. मिश्र वाक्य D. इनमें से कोई नहीं

18. अमर के रहते विद्यालय के किसी छात्र को सर्वश्रेष्ठ खिलाड़ी की पदवी नहीं मिल सकती।
A. मिश्र वाक्य B. संयुक्त वाक्य
C. सरल वाक्य D. इनमें से कोई नहीं

19. मैंने किरायेदार नहीं रखे, मुसीबत मोल ले ली।
A. सरल वाक्य B. मिश्र वाक्य
C. संयुक्त वाक्य D. इनमें से कोई नहीं

20. समय पर पश्चाताप करना ही बुद्धिमानी की बात है।
A. सरल वाक्य B. मिश्र वाक्य
C. संयुक्त वाक्य D. इनमें से कोई नहीं

21. रचना की दृष्टि से वाक्य के कितने भेद होते हैं?
A. तीन B. पाँच
C. छह D. आठ

22. सरल वाक्य में कितने कर्ता और कितनी क्रिया होती है?
A. एक कर्ता, एक क्रिया
B. एक कर्ता, एक क्रिया, एक सहायक क्रिया
C. दो क्रिया एक कर्ता
D. दो कर्ता दो क्रिया

23. अधोलिखित में से वाक्य के (रचना के आधार पर) भेद कौन-से हैं?
A. सरल वाक्य B. मिश्र वाक्य
C. संयुक्त वाक्य D. उपर्युक्त तीनों

24. **धूप निकली है** में कितने उद्देश्य और कितने विधेय हैं?
A. एक उद्देश्य एक विधेय B. एक उद्देश्य दो विधेय
C. उपर्युक्त दोनों D. कोई नहीं

25. सरल वाक्य में कितने उद्देश्य और कितने विधेय होते हैं?
A. एक उद्देश्य एक विधेय B. दो उद्देश्य एक विधेय
C. दो विधेय दो उद्देश्य D. उपर्युक्त में से कोई ठीक नहीं

26. मिश्र वाक्य में कितनी समापिका क्रियाएँ होती हैं?
A. दो B. एक या एक से अधिक
C. कोई D. कोई ठीक नहीं

27. वह कौन ऐसा भारतीय है जो गाँधीजी को नहीं जानता। कौन-सा वाक्य है?
A. सरल वाक्य B. मिश्र वाक्य
C. संयुक्त वाक्य D. कोई नहीं

28. मिश्र वाक्य में कितने वाक्य होते हैं?
A. एक मुख्य वाक्य एक उपवाक्य
B. दो मुख्य वाक्य
C. दो उपवाक्य
D. कोई ठीक नहीं

29. मुख्य वाक्य और उपवाक्य में किसकी संगति होती है?
A. भाव की B. ध्वनि की
C. अर्थ की D. किसी की नहीं

30. जहाँ साधारण और मिश्र वाक्यों का मेल संयोजक अव्ययों द्वारा होता है, उसे कहते हैं–
A. सरल वाक्य B. मिश्र वाक्य
C. संयुक्त वाक्य D. विधि वाक्य

31. संयुक्त वाक्य में कैसे वाक्य अव्ययों द्वारा संयुक्त किए जाते हैं?
A. सरल वाक्य B. मिश्र वाक्य
C. उपर्युक्त दोनों D. कोई ठीक नहीं

32. मैं नहा चुका तब वह साबुन ताया। कौन-सा वाक्य है?
A. विधिवाचक, सरल वाक्य
B. विधिवाचक, मिश्र वाक्य
C. विधिवाचक, संयुक्त वाक्य
D. कोई नहीं

33. तुम नहाओ और तुम्हारे बाद सभी नहायें। कौन-सा वाक्य है?
A. आज्ञावाचक सरल वाक्य
B. आज्ञावाचक मिश्र वाक्य
C. आज्ञावाचक संयुक्त वाक्य
D. कोई नहीं

34. राम घर पहुँच गया होगा। कैसा वाक्य है?
A. विधि वाक्य B. विस्मयवाचक वाक्य
C. संदेहवाचक वाक्य D. संकेतवाचक वाक्य

35. वह परीक्षा में उत्तीर्ण हो। कैसा वाक्य है?
A. विधिवाचक वाक्य B. इच्छावाचक वाक्य
C. संकेतवाचक वाक्य D. संदेहवाचक वाक्य

36. तुम न बचाते तो वह डूब जाता। कैसा वाक्य है?
A. संकेतवाचक वाक्य B. इच्छावाचक वाक्य
C. संदेहवाचक वाक्य D. विस्मयवाचक वाक्य

37. संकेतवाचक वाक्य निर्भर रहता दूसरे वाक्य की–
A. संभावना पर B. धारणा पर
C. अवधारणा पर D. इच्छा पर

38. जिस वाक्य में किसी बात के होने का बोध हो उसे कहते हैं–
A. आज्ञावाचक वाक्य B. संदेहवाचक वाक्य
C. इच्छावाचक वाक्य D. विधिवाचक वाक्य

39. जिस वाक्य में दुख एवं सुख का बोध हो उसे कहते हैं–
A. संकेतवाचक वाक्य B. संदेहवाचक वाक्य
C. विस्मयवाचक वाक्य D. विधिवाचक वाक्य

40. अहा! तुम्हारे आने से सभी प्रसन्न हैं। वाक्य में कौन-सा भाव है?
A. संदेह का B. विस्मय का
C. इच्छा का D. संकेत का

उत्तरमाला

1	2	3	4	5	6	7	8	9	10
A	C	C	C	B	C	C	B	C	C
11	**12**	**13**	**14**	**15**	**16**	**17**	**18**	**19**	**20**
A	C	A	A	A	C	A	C	C	A
21	**22**	**23**	**24**	**25**	**26**	**27**	**28**	**29**	**30**
A	A	D	A	A	B	B	A	C	C
31	**32**	**33**	**34**	**35**	**36**	**37**	**38**	**39**	**40**
C	B	C	C	B	A	A	A	C	B

★ ★ ★

8

मुहावरा

मुहावरा का शाब्दिक अर्थ 'अभ्यास' है। किन्तु उस वाक्यांश अथवा शब्द समूह को मुहावरा कहते हैं जो अपने साधारण अर्थ को त्याग कर एक विशेष अर्थ प्रकट करने लगता है। मुहावरों के प्रयोग से भाषा का सौंदर्य एवं उसकी शीलता बढ़ जाती है।

नीचे कुछ मुहावरे, उसका अर्थ तथा वाक्यों में प्रयोग दिया जा रहा है–

- **अंग-अंग ढीला होना**—*बहुत थक जाना*
  अपनी बहिन की शादी में काम करते-करते मेरा ***अंग-अंग ढीला*** हो गया।
- **अंगारे उगलना**—*क्रोध में अति कठोर शब्द कहना*
  जब औरंगजेब के दरबार में शिवाजी ने अपना अपमान होते देखा तो वे ***अंगारे उगलने*** लगे।
- **अँगूठा दिखाना**—*इनकार करना*
  स्वार्थी मित्र संकट के समय सहायता माँगे जाने पर ***अँगूठा दिखाकर*** चले जाते हैं।
- **अंधे की लकड़ी होना**—*एकमात्र सहारा*
  अब तो बेटा तुम ही हमारे लिए ***अन्धे की लकड़ी*** के समान हो।
- **अँधेरे घर का उजाला होना**—*इकलौता बेटा*
  रामू मेरे छोटे भाई की एकमात्र संतान है। वही उसके ***अँधेरे घर का उजाला*** है।
- **अक्ल के पीछे लाठी लिए फिरना**—*हमेशा उल्टा काम करना*
  हमारा एक साथी तो हर समय ***अक्ल के पीछे लाठी लिए फिरता*** है।
- **अक्ल पर पत्थर पड़ना**—*बुद्धि नष्ट हो जाना*
  तुम्हारी तो ***अक्ल पर पत्थर पड़*** गए हैं जो तुम मेरी बात समझते ही नहीं।
- **अपना उल्लू सीधा करना**—*स्वार्थ सिद्ध करना*
  वह ***अपना उल्लू सीधा करके*** चलता बना।
- **अपना-सा मुँह लेकर रह जाना**—*लज्जित होना*
  हम वहाँ बड़ी उम्मीद लेकर गए थे, किन्तु उसने ऐसी निराशापूर्ण बात कही जिससे हमें ***अपना-सा मुँह लेकर रह जाना*** पड़ा।
- **अपनी खिचड़ी आप पकाना**—*सबसे अलग रहना*
  कुछ लोग ऐसे स्वभाव के होते हैं कि वे किसी से मिलना ही नहीं चाहते; ***अपनी खिचड़ी आप ही पकाते*** हैं।
- **अपने मुँह मियाँ मिट्ठू बनना**—*अपनी प्रशंसा स्वयं करना*
  अपने मुँह मियाँ मिट्ठू बनने से क्या होता है, दूसरे लोग तुम्हारी प्रशंसा करें तब बात है।
- **अपने पैरों पर खड़े होना**—*आत्मनिर्भर होना*
  जब तक तुम इस योग्य न हो जाओ कि ***अपने पैरों पर खड़े हो*** सको तब तक तुम्हें विवाह के बारे में सोचना भी नहीं चाहिए।
- **आँख की किरकिरी होना**—*अप्रिय होना*
  राम व्यर्थ में ही मुझे अपनी ***आँख की किरकिरी*** समझता है।
- **आँख चुराना**—*सामने आने से घबराना*
  जब से उसने मेरा पेन लिया है, तब से वह ***आँखें चुराता*** फिरता है।
- **आँखें नीली-पीली करना**—*क्रोध में आना*
  मैंने ऐसा कोई गलत काम नहीं किया है; आप व्यर्थ में ***आँखें नीली-पीली न करें***।
- **आँखें फेर लेना**—*उपेक्षा करना*
  स्वार्थी मित्र संकट के समय में ***आँखें फेर लेते*** हैं।
- **आँखों का तारा होना**—*अत्यन्त प्रिय*
  कृष्ण अपने माँ-बाप की ***आँखों का तारा*** है।
- **आँखों का पानी ढल जाना**—*बेशर्म हो जाना*
  उसके माँ-बाप उसे बहुतेरा समझाते-बुझाते हैं, किन्तु उसकी ***आँखों का तो पानी ढल*** गया है। उस पर किसी बात का असर होता ही नहीं।
- **आँखों में धूल झोंकना**—*धोखा देना*
  जो लोग दूसरों की ***आँखों में धूल झोंकने*** की कोशिश करते हैं, वे वस्तुतः अपने को ही धोखा देते हैं।
- **आकाश-पाताल एक करना**—*बहुत अधिक परिश्रम करना*
  राम ने नौकरी प्राप्त करने के लिए ***आकाश-पाताल एक कर*** दिया।
- **आग पर घी डालना**—*क्रोध को बढ़ाना*
  तुम्हारा टोकना तो ***आग पर घी डालने*** जैसा था।
- **आटे-दाल का भाव मालूम होना**—*जीवन में कष्टों का अनुभव करना*
  अब तक तो तुम अकेले थे, कुछ पता ही नहीं चला; अब तुम्हें ***आटे-दाल का भाव मालूम होगा***।
- **आम के आम और गुठलियों के दाम**—*दोहरा लाभ*
  मूँगफली के व्यापार में ***आम के आम और गुठलियों के दाम*** मिलते हैं; क्योंकि उसकी गिरी से तेल निकाल कर खली बिक जाती है और मूँगफली का छिलका भी बिक जाता है।
- **आस्तीन का साँप**—*विश्वासघाती*
  उस पर कभी विश्वास मत करो, वह ***आस्तीन का साँप*** है।
- **ईंट से ईंट बजाना**—*नष्ट-भ्रष्ट कर देना*
  शिवाजी ने मुगल साम्राज्य की ***ईंट से ईंट बजा*** दी।

- **ईद का चाँद होना**—*बहुत कम दिखाई पड़ना*
तुम तो ***ईद के चाँद हो गए*** हो; कभो इधर आते ही नहीं।
- **उड़ती चिड़िया पहचानना**—*मन की बात ताड़ लेना*
मुझसे क्यों छिपाते हो, ***मैं उड़ती चिड़िया पहचान*** लेता हूँ।
- **उल्लू सीधा करना**—*काम निकालना*
अधिकांश लोग ***उल्लू सीधा*** होते ही बात नहीं करते।
- **ऊँट के मुँह में जीरा**—*आवश्यकता से बहुत कम देना*
एक रोटी से उसका क्या बनेगा, यह तो उसके लिए ***ऊँट के मुँह में जीरा*** की तरह है।
- **एक अनार सौ बीमार**—*किसी चीज की माँग आपूर्ति से अधिक होना*
यह वस्तु मैं किस-किस को दूँ, इसके माँगने वाले इतने अधिक हैं कि यह ***एक अनार सौ बीमार*** वाली बात हो रही है।
- **एक तीर से दो शिकार करना**—*एक साथ दो मतलब पूरे करना*
तुम्हारे ऐसा कहने से ***एक तीर से दो शिकार*** होंगे, सबके सामने उसकी पोल खुल जाएगी और तुम्हारा काम भी बन जाएगा।
- **एक थैली के चट्टे-बट्टे होना**—*एक ही स्वभाव के*
तुम सब ***एक ही थैली के चट्टे-बट्टे हो***, कोई किसी से कम नहीं।
- **एक हाथ से ताली न बजना**—*किसी काम के लिए एक ही व्यक्ति उत्तरदायी नहीं होता*
एक हाथ से ताली नहीं बजती, तुमने भी अवश्य कुछ-न-कुछ ऐसी बात जरूर की होगी, जिसका यह परिणाम निकला।
- **ओखली में सिर देना**—*जानते हुए किसी कष्ट में पड़ना*
अब तो ***ओखली में सिर दे ही दिया*** है, इस काम को पूरा करना ही है।
- **कच्ची गोलियाँ खेलना**—*अनुभव की कमी होना*
मैंने कोई ***कच्ची गोलियाँ नहीं खेली*** हैं, जो मैं तुम्हारी बातों में आ जाऊँ।
- **कटे पर नमक छिड़कना**—*दुःखी को और दुःखी करना*
तुम यह बात कहकर ***कटे पर नमक छिड़कना*** चाहते हो।
- **कठपुतली की तरह नाचना**—*किसी के कहने के अनुसार कार्य करते रहना*
पता नहीं उसने महेश पर कैसा जादू किया है कि वह उसके सामने ***कठपुतली की तरह नाचता*** रहता है।
- **कब्र के मुर्दे उखाड़ना**—*पुरानी बातों की याद दिलाना*
जो बात हो गई सो हो गई; ***कब्र के मुर्दे उखाड़ने*** से क्या लाभ।
- **कलई खुलना**—*सच्ची बात प्रकट हो जाना*
तुम कब तक अपने फेल होने की बात को छिपाओगे, एक न एक दिन तो ***कलई खुलेगी*** ही।
- **कलेजा दो टूक होना**—*बहुत दुःखी होना*
तुमने आज जैसी बातें कही हैं, उनसे मेरा ***कलेजा दो टूक हो*** गया है।
- **कलेजे पर साँप लोटना**—*डाह से जलना*
मेरी तरक्की देखकर उसके ***कलेजे पर साँप लोट*** गया।
- **काँटे बिछाना**—*रुकावटें पैदा करना*
जो दूसरे के मार्ग में ***काँटे बिछाता*** है, वह स्वयं ही उसमें उलझता है।
- **काटो तो खून नहीं**—*डर से पीला पड़ जाना*
चोरी करते पकड़े जाने पर उसकी दशा ऐसी हो गई कि ***काटो तो खून नहीं***।
- **काठ का उल्लू**—*मूर्ख*
वह पढ़ा-लिखा तो बहुत है, किन्तु सांसारिक मामलों में ***काठ का उल्लू*** है।
- **कान का कच्चा**—*बिना जाँच किये प्रत्येक बात पर विश्वास कर लेना*
जो व्यक्ति ***कान के कच्चे*** होते हैं वे मित्र बनाने योग्य नहीं होते।
- **कान पर जूँ न रेंगना**—*तनिक भी ध्यान न देना*
मैंने उसे बार-बार समझाया कि पढ़ाई-लिखाई की ओर ध्यान दो, परन्तु उसके ***कान पर जूँ तक न रेंगी***।
- **कान में तेल डालना**—*किसी की बात न सुनना*
कृष्णा के नौकरी कर लेने पर सबने उसकी टीका-टिप्पणी की, किन्तु वह ***कान में तेल डाले*** रही।
- **किताब का कीड़ा होना**—*दिन-रात पढ़ते रहना*
रवीन्द्र किसी बात से मतलब नहीं रखता, वह तो ***किताब का कीड़ा*** है।
- **किस खेत की मूली**—*अत्यन्त तुच्छ*
तुम हो ***किस खेत की मूली***, मैं तुम जैसों की बिल्कुल परवाह नहीं करता।
- **कोल्हू का बैल बनना**—*दिन-रात काम में लगे रहना*
तुम तो हर समय ***कोल्हू के बैल ही बने*** रहते हो, तभी तो तुम्हारा स्वास्थ्य ठीक नहीं रहता।
- **कौड़ी-कौड़ी को मोहताज होना**—*पास में एक पैसा न होना*
जबसे उसकी नौकरी छूटी है, तबसे वह ***कौड़ी-कौड़ी को मोहताज*** हो गया है।
- **खटाई में पड़ना**—*उलझ जाना*
तुम्हारी तरक्की का मामला ***खटाई में पड़*** गया है।
- **खाने दौड़ना**—*झल्ला उठना*
मैंने कुछ कहा भी है कि आप ***खाने दौड़*** रहे हैं।
- **खून-पसीना एक करना**—*अत्यधिक परिश्रम करना*
तुम्हारे इस मामले में तो कृष्ण ने ***खून-पसीना एक कर*** दिया।
- **गंगाजली उठाना**—*हाथ में गंगाजल लेकर सौगन्ध खाना*
मैं ***गंगाजली उठाकर*** कहता हूँ कि मैं बिल्कुल निर्दोष हूँ।
- **गज-भर की छाती होना**—*उत्साह से भर जाना*
अपनी पुत्री के परीक्षा में प्रथम आने से उसकी ***गज-भर की छाती हो*** गई।
- **गहरा हाथ मारना**—*बहुत माल प्राप्त करना*
जगदीश ने अपने पुत्र के विवाह में ***गहरा हाथ मारा*** है।
- **गाँठ का पूरा**—*धनी व्यक्ति*
वह ऊपर से कैसा ही प्रतीत हो, किन्तु है ***गाँठ का पूरा।***
- **गागर में सागर भरना**—*थोड़े शब्दों में बहुत-कुछ कह देना*
वह बहुत कम बोलता है किन्तु जब भी बोलता है तो उसकी बातों में ***गागर में सागर भरा*** होता है।
- **गाजर-मूली समझना**—*बहुत तुच्छ समझना*
शिवाजी मुगल सैनिकों को ***गाजर-मूली की तरह समझते*** थे।
- **गाढ़े पसीने की कमाई**—*मेहनत से कमाया हुआ धन*
यह मेरे ***गाढ़े पसीने की कमाई*** है, मैं नहीं चाहता कि इसे व्यर्थ में पानी की तरह बहाया जाए।

- **गिरगिट की तरह रंग बदलना**—*कभी कुछ कहना और कभी कुछ*
  आजकल विधान सभाओं के अनेक सदस्य ***गिरगिट की तरह रंग बदलते*** दिखाई देते रहते हैं।
- **गुड़ गोबर करना**—*बना काम बिगाड़ देना*
  तुमने ये शब्द कहकर सारा ***गुड़ गोबर कर*** दिया।
- **गोबर गणेश**—*मूर्ख*
  तुम बिल्कुल ***गोबर गणेश*** हो, अपने हित की बात ही नहीं समझते।
- **घड़ों पानी पड़ना**—*अति लज्जित होना*
  चुगली करने की बात खुल जाने पर उस पर ***घड़ों पानी पड़*** गया।
- **घर का दिया बुझ जाना**—*इकलौते पुत्र की मृत्यु होना*
  दीपक उसका इकलौता पुत्र था, उसके मर जाने से उसके ***घर का दिया ही बुझ*** गया।
- **घाट-घाट का पानी पीना**—*जगह-जगह से अनुभव प्राप्त करना*
  मुसीबत के दिनों में उसे ***घाट-घाट का पानी पीना*** पड़ा है।
- **घाव पर नमक छिड़कना**—*दु:खी को (कठोर शब्दों से) और दु:खी करना*
  तुम्हारे ये शब्द ***घाव पर नमक छिड़कने*** का काम कर रहे हैं।
- **घास काटना**—*किसी काम को लापरवाही से करना*
  घास मत काटो, जरा धीरे-धीरे अच्छी तरह पढ़ो।
- **घी के दीये जलाना**—*खूब खुशियाँ मनाना*
  जिस दिन मेरे भाई की नौकरी लग जायेगी उस दिन मैं ***घी के दीये जलाऊँगा***।
- **घुटने टेक देना**—*हार मान लेना*
  सैल्युकस ने चन्द्रगुप्त मौर्य के आगे ***घुटने टेक दिये***।
- **घोड़े बेचकर सोना**—*निश्चिन्त होकर सोना*
  बहिन का विवाह करने के पश्चात् वह ऐसे सो गया मानो ***घोड़े बेचकर सोया*** हो।
- **चलता पुर्जा**—*चालाक व्यक्ति*
  चन्द्र बड़ा ही ***चलता पुर्जा*** है, उससे बचकर रहना।
- **चाँदी का जूता मारना**—*रुपये के बल पर दबाना*
  वह तो ***चाँदी का जूता मारती*** है और सबसे अपना काम करा लेती है।
- **चाँदी होना**—*अत्यधिक लाभ होना*
  आजकल महँगाई के जमाने में व्यापारियों की ***चाँदी*** है।
- **चादर देखकर पाँव फैलाना**—*अपनी शक्ति के अनुसार कार्य करना*
  बुद्धिमानी इसी में है कि ***चादर देखकर पाँव फैलाये*** जायें अन्यथा जीवन में बड़ी कठिनाई का सामना करना पड़ता है।
- **चार चाँद लगना**—*शोभा बढ़ना*
  वह सुन्दर तो है ही, पर इस साड़ी को पहनने पर उसकी सुन्दरता में ***चार चाँद लग*** जाते हैं।
- **चार दिन की चाँदनी**—*थोड़े दिनों का सुख*
  तुम इतना घमण्ड क्यों करते हो, यह सुख तो ***चार दिन की चाँदनी*** है, कभी दु:ख के दिन भी आ सकते हैं।
- **चिकना घड़ा होना**—*किसी बात का असर न पड़ना*
  वह तो बिल्कुल ***चिकना घड़ा हो*** गया है, उस पर कहे-सुने का असर पड़ता ही नहीं।
- **चिराग लेकर ढूँढना**—*बहुत छानबीन करना*
  तुम यदि ***चिराग लेकर भी ढूँढो,*** तब भी तुम्हें ऐसा सज्जन नहीं मिलेगा।
- **चुल्लू भर पानी में डूब मरना**—*मुँह दिखाने योग्य न रहना*
  तीसरी बार भी परीक्षा में फेल होने पर उसे ***चुल्लू भर पानी में डूब मरना*** चाहिए।
- **चूना लगाना**—*धोखा देना*
  कितनी ही सावधानी से काम लो, किन्तु कभी-कभी दुकानदार ***चूना लगा*** ही देते हैं।
- **चोली-दामन का साथ होना**—*अटूट सम्बन्ध होना*
  भारत और नेपाल का ***चोली दामन का साथ*** है।
- **छक्के छूटना**—*हिम्मत हार जाना*
  भारतीयों की वीरता देखकर पाकिस्तानी सैनिकों के ***छक्के छूट*** गए।
- **छठी का दूध याद आना**—*घोर कष्ट में पड़ना*
  मैं तुम्हें ऐसी मार लगाऊँगा कि ***छठी का दूध याद आ*** जायेगा।
- **छप्पर फाड़कर देना**—*बिना परिश्रम किए धन मिलना*
  भगवान् जब देता है तो ***छप्पर फाड़कर देता*** है।
- **छाती पर मूँग दलना**—*हमेशा दु:ख देना*
  तू इस तरह ***छाती पर मूँग ही दलता*** रहेगा या कहीं जाकर कुछ काम खोजने की कोशिश भी करेगा?
- **जरा-सा मुँह निकल आना**—*दुर्बल हो जाना*
  उस पर इन दिनों इतना काम पड़ा है कि उसका ***जरा-सा मुँह निकल आया*** है।
- **जली-कटी कहना**—*कठोर बातें कहना*
  वह हमेशा ***जली-कटी कहता*** रहता है, पता नहीं वह क्या चाहता है।
- **जहर का घूँट पीकर रह जाना**—*अपमान को चुपचाप सहन कर लेना*
  यद्यपि उसने सबके सामने मेरा अपमान किया किन्तु फिर भी मैं आपका ख्याल करके ***जहर का घूँट पीकर रह*** गया।
- **जहर की पुड़िया**—*उपद्रवी व्यक्ति*
  वह सीधी नहीं है, ***जहर की पुड़िया*** है।
- **झंडा गाड़ना**—*अधिकार करना*
  शिवाजी ने तोरण के किले को जीतकर उस पर अपना ***झंडा गाड़*** दिया।
- **टोपी उछालना**—*अपमानित करना*
  महेश ने सबके सामने मेरी ***टोपी उछाली,*** यह उसने ठीक नहीं किया।
- **ठोकना-बजाना**—*अच्छी तरह परखना*
  जिस तरह तुम हरेक वस्तु परख कर खरीदते हो उसी तरह मित्र भी ***ठोक-बजाकर*** बनाना चाहिए।
- **डंके की चोट पर**—*खुल्लमखुल्ला स्पष्ट शब्दों में कहना*
  मैं ***डंके की चोट पर*** कहता हूँ कि किसी भी हालत में उसका साथ नहीं छोड़ूँगा।
- **डूबते को तिनके का सहारा**—*असहाय को थोड़ी सहायता भी काफी काम कर जाती है*
  तुम्हारी थोड़ी सहायता ही ***डूबते को तिनके का सहारा*** के समान सिद्ध हुई।

- **डेढ़ चावल की खिचड़ी पकाना**—*सबसे अलग रहकर कार्य करना*
कुछ लोग ऐसे होते हैं जो ***डेढ़ चावल की खिचड़ी पकाना*** चाहते हैं, परन्तु समाज ऐसे लोगों का सम्मान नहीं करता।
- **ढेर हो जाना**—*मर जाना*
उसने डाकू पर लाठी का एक ही प्रहार किया कि वह ***ढेर हो*** गया।
- **तलवार के घाट उतारना**—*तलवार से मारना*
हल्दीघाटी के मैदान में राजपूतों ने असंख्य मुगल सैनिकों को ***तलवार के घाट उतार*** दिया।
- **तारे गिनना**—*रात-भर जागना*
मैं उसकी स्मृति में रात-भर ***तारे गिनता*** रहा, एक पल को भी नींद नहीं आई।
- **तिल का ताड़ बनाना**—*छोटी-सी बात को बहुत बढ़ाना*
बहुत लोगों को ***तिल का ताड़ बनाने*** में बड़ा आनन्द आता है।
- **तिलों में तेल न होना**—*कोई आशा न होना*
तुम किससे पार्टी (दावत) माँग रहे हो; इन ***तिलों में तेल नहीं*** है।
- **तेली का बैल होना**—*रात-दिन काम में लगा रहना*
तुम तो हमेशा ***तेली के बैल*** के समान काम में लगे रहते हो।
- **थाली का बैंगन होना**—*स्वार्थवश कभी किसी का साथ देना और कभी किसी का*
तुम तो बिल्कुल ***थाली के बैंगन हो***, तुम्हारा कोई भरोसा नहीं।
- **दाँत काटी रोटी**—*गहरी मित्रता*
जोशी और कैलाश में ***दाँत काटी रोटी*** थी किन्तु पता नहीं क्यों आजकल वे एक-दूसरे से दूर-दूर रहते हैं।
- **दाँत खट्टे करना**—*हरा देना*
शिवाजी ने औरंगजेब की सेना के ***दाँत खट्टे कर*** दिए।
- **दाल में काला होना**—*किसी बात की शंका होना*
वह बार-बार इधर आता है, अवश्य कुछ ***दाल में काला*** है।
- **दिन दूनी रात चौगुनी**—*बहुत तेज गति से*
स्वतन्त्रता मिलने के उपरान्त भारत ने ***दिन दूनी रात चौगुनी*** उन्नति की है।
- **दूध का दूध पानी का पानी**—*सच्चा न्याय*
राजा विक्रमादित्य अत्यन्त पेचीदे मामलों में भी ***दूध का दूध पानी का पानी*** कर देते थे।
- **दो नावों में पैर रखना**—*दोनों पक्षों का समर्थन करना*
जो लोग ***दो नावों पर पैर रखते*** हैं, वे किसी के भले नहीं बन पाते।
- **धूप में बाल सफेद न करना**—*बहुत अनुभवी होना*
मेरे ***बाल धूप में सफेद नहीं*** हुए हैं, मैं सबकुछ जानता हूँ।
- **नाक पर मक्खी न बैठने देना**—*किसी को कुछ कहने का अवसर न देना*
वह बहुत ही सिद्धान्तवादी है, ***नाक पर मक्खी भी नहीं बैठने*** देता।
- **पाँचों उँगलियाँ घी में होना**—*बहुत लाभ होना*
आजकल व्यापारियों की ***पाँचों उँगलियाँ घी*** में हैं।
- **पाँव उखड़ जाना**—*हारकर भागना*
राणा सांगा की विशाल सेना को देखकर बाबर की सेना के ***पाँव उखड़*** गए।
- **पापड़ बेलना**—*मुसीबत झेलना (परिश्रम करना)*
मैंने अपनी जिन्दगी में बड़े ***पापड़ बेले*** हैं, तब कहीं जाकर यह दिन देखने को मिला है।
- **पेट का हल्का होना**—*किसी बात को छिपा न सकना*
जो मनुष्य ***पेट के हल्के होते*** हैं, वे सबके बुरे बन जाते हैं।
- **पौ बारह होना**—*लाभ ही लाभ होना*
आजकल व्यापारियों की ***पौ बारह*** है।
- **बाल की खाल निकालना**—*सूक्ष्म विवेचन करना*
तर्क करने वाले प्रत्येक बात में ***बाल की खाल निकालते*** हैं।
- **बाल बाँका न होना**—*तनिक भी हानि न होना*
आग में प्रहलाद का तो ***बाल भी बाँका न हुआ*** किन्तु उसकी बुआ होलिका जलकर भस्म हो गई।
- **मुँह में पानी भर आना**—*लालच आना*
लोमड़ी ने जब अंगूर लटकते हुए देखे तो उसके ***मुँह में पानी भर आया***।
- **मुट्ठी गरम करना**—*रिश्वत देना*
तुम्हें इस काम के लिए अधिकारियों की ***मुट्ठी गरम करनी*** पड़ेगी।
- **रंग में भंग पड़ना**—*मजा किरकिरा होना*
उत्सव के समय यकायक पानी बरसने से ***रंग में भंग पड़*** गया।
- **लकीर का फकीर होना**—*पुरानी रीति पर चलना*
तुम तो बिल्कुल ***लकीर के फकीर हो,*** किसी बात को तर्क की कसौटी पर कसना ही नहीं चाहते।
- **सफेद झूठ बोलना**—*सरासर झूठ बोलना*
तुम ***सफेद झूठ बोलते*** हो; ऐसा कभी नहीं हो सकता।
- **सिर पर कफन बाँधना**—*मरने के लिए तैयार होना*
भारत को स्वतन्त्र कराने के लिए अनेक वीरों ने ***सिर पर कफन बाँध*** लिया था।
- **सिर पर भूत सवार होना**—*किसी धुन पर अड़े होना*
जब शान्ति के ***सिर पर भूत सवार होता*** है, तो फिर उसे कोई नहीं समझा सकता।
- **सूर्य को दीपक दिखाना**—*महान् व्यक्ति का परिचय देने की कोशिश करना*
स्वामी विवेकानन्द के सम्बन्ध में कुछ कहना ***सूर्य को दीपक दिखाना*** ही है।
- **हाथ धोकर पीछे पड़ना**—*बुरी तरह सताना*
वह तो ***हाथ धोकर मेरे पीछे पड़*** गया है, मैं कितना ही अच्छा काम करूँ, वह कोई-न-कोई गलती निकाल ही देता है।
- **हाथ-पाँव फूल जाना**—*बहुत घबरा जाना*
दंगाइयों के अचानक घर में घुस जाने पर मेरे ***हाथ-पाँव फूल*** गए।
- **हाथों के तोते उड़ जाना**—*सुध-बुध खोना*
दुकान खोलते ही जब सेठ जी ने देखा कि तिजोरी खुली पड़ी है, तो उनके ***हाथ के तोते उड़*** गए।

वस्तुनिष्ठ प्रश्नोत्तर

निर्देश : *नीचे प्रत्येक प्रश्न में एक मुहावरा दिया गया है और उसके नीचे A, B, C, D विकल्प के सामने उसका (मुहावरे का) अर्थ दिया गया है। चारों अर्थों में से जो अर्थ आपको सर्वाधिक उपयुक्त लगे, उस पर सही का निशान लगाइये।*

1. आँख नीली-पीली करना
A. उत्सुकता से देखना B. सावधान हो जाना
C. बहुत क्रुद्ध होना D. हैरानी प्रकट करना

2. आन की आन में
A. एकदम B. अपमान करते हुए
C. इज्जत देना D. अपने आप

3. एक की चार लगाना
A. गप्प मारना B. अपनी बात ऊपर रखना
C. अनेक बहाने बनाना D. झूठी शिकायत करना

4. कसर निकालना
A. कमी पूरी करना B. उदारता दिखाना
C. बदला लेना D. चैन से न बैठने देना

5. खटपट होना
A. झगड़ा होना B. शोर होना
C. आवाज होना D. शान्ति भंग होना

6. अन्धे की लकड़ी
A. सबसे बड़ा सहारा
B. एक मात्र आशा
C. आशा की किरण
D. असहाय व्यक्ति का एकमात्र सहारा

7. अक्ल पर पत्थर पड़ना
A. अक्ल का उपयोग न करना B. बुद्धि काम न देना
C. बुद्धि नष्ट हो जाना D. मंद बुद्धि होना

8. अपना उल्लू सीधा करना
A. अपना काम निकालना
B. अपने को विपत्ति से मुक्त करना
C. अपना काम पूरा होने पर मुँह फेर लेना
D. दूसरे को उल्लू बनाकर अपना हित साधना

9. अपना-सा मुँह लेकर रह जाना
A. पराजित होना B. लज्जित होना
C. निराश होना D. हिम्मत पस्त होना

10. अपने मुँह मियाँ मिट्ठू बनना
A. डींग मारना B. रोब जमाना
C. स्वयं अपनी प्रशंसा करना D. अपने माल की तारीफ करना

11. आँख चुराना
A. आँखें न मिलाना B. शरमाना
C. सामने न आना D. डराना

12. आँखें फेर लेना
A. बेमुरव्वत
B. शिष्टाचार न बरतना
C. मिलना-जुलना बंद कर देना
D. उपेक्षा करना

13. आँधी के आम
A. सस्ती वस्तु
B. खराब वस्तु
C. बिना परिश्रम के प्राप्त वस्तु
D. मुफ्त मिली वस्तु

14. आग उगलना
A. मारने को दौड़ना B. खरी-खोटी सुनाना
C. बहुत क्रोध दिखाना D. क्रोध से पागल होना

15. आस्तीन का साँप
A. छिपा रुस्तम B. गुदड़ी का लाल
C. समय पर साथ न देना D. विश्वासघाती

16. ईद का चाँद होना
A. बहुत कम दिखाई देना B. बहुत प्रिय होना
C. बहुत सुन्दर होना D. बहुत लाड़ला होना

17. एक थैली के चट्टे-बट्टे
A. एक ही गुट के B. एक जैसी प्रकृति के
C. एक ही जाति-धर्म के D. एक से एक बढ़ कर

18. कागजी घोड़े दौड़ाना
A. मंसूबे बाँधना B. लिखा-पढ़ी करना
C. कागज काला करना D. व्यर्थ का काम करना

19. कान का कच्चा
A. दूसरों की बात न सुनने वाला
B. एक कान से सुनना दूसरे से निकाल देना
C. बिल्कुल बर्दाश्त न करना
D. दूसरों की बातों पर सहज विश्वास करना

20. गच्चा खाना
A. धोखे में ठगा जाना B. पराजित होना
C. हार मानना D. आरोप में फँस जाना

21. कोल्हू का बैल
A. दिन-रात काम करते रहना
B. बड़ी मेहनत व ईमानदारी से काम करना
C. एक ही काम करने लायक होना
D. एक ही काम करते-करते ऊब जाना

22. खरी-खोटी सुनाना
A. गाली देना B. भला-बुरा कहना
C. खबरदार करना D. बड़े-छोटे का लिहाज न करना

23. गंगा नहाना
A. पुण्य कमाना
B. किसी बड़े काम को पूरा करके राहत महसूस करना
C. भविष्य में अच्छा काम करने का संकल्प लेना
D. स्वास्थ्य-लाभ करना

24. गाल बजाना
A. स्वाद ले-लेकर खाना B. डींग मारना
C. प्रसन्न होना D. अशिष्ट व्यवहार करना

25. घास काटना
A. छोटा-मोटा काम करना
B. व्यर्थ समय गँवाना
C. ऐसा काम करना, जिसमें परिश्रम के अनुसार लाभ न हो
D. किसी काम को बेपरवाही से करना

26. घुटने टेकना
A. प्रणाम करना B. पराजय स्वीकार करना
C. गुलामी स्वीकार करना D. हिम्मत हारना

27. चूना लगाना
A. चापलूसी करके अपना काम निकालना
B. धोखा देना
C. कठोर बात कहना
D. सफाई करना

28. जहर का घूँट पीकर रह जाना
A. पराधीन होना
B. बड़ा अपमान सहकर भी चुप रहना
C. क्रोध दबा जाना
D. स्वयं मुसीबत मोल लेना

29. गले मढ़ना
A. पीछे पड़ना B. आगा-पीछा न सोचना
C. मुसीबत मोल लेना D. जबरदस्ती दे देना

30. टोपी उछालना
A. अपमान करना B. अत्यधिक खुशी व्यक्त करना
C. अच्छी तरह परखना D. इज्जत करना

31. डंके की चोट पर कहना
A. अपमानित करना B. खुल्लमखुल्ला कहना
C. कोई लिहाज न करना D. भला-बुरा सब कह डालना

32. तारे गिनना
A. व्यर्थ का काम करना
B. असम्भव काम की कोशिश करना
C. रात-भर जागना
D. सोने की भरसक कोशिश करना

33. दाँत काटी रोटी
A. जूठा भोजन
B. गहरी दोस्ती
C. चारों तरफ से संकटों से घिरा
D. रूखा-सूखा भोजन

34. दाल में काला होना
A. मजा न आना
B. किसी बात का संदेह होना
C. किसी संकट की शुरुआत
D. संकट की घड़ी में नई मुसीबत आ जाना

35. नौ-दो ग्यारह होना
A. लेन-देन पूरा होना B. भाग जाना
C. पूरा ध्यान रखना D. सौदेबाजी करना

36. पहाड़ टूट पड़ना
A. बहुत नुकसान होना B. भारी मुसीबत आ जाना
C. असम्भव बात होना D. उथल-पुथल होना

37. पाँचों उँगलियाँ घी में होना
A. रोज बढ़िया भोजन मिलना B. गुलछर्रे उड़ाना
C. अत्यधिक लाभ होना D. चैन से दिन गुजरना

38. पेट का हल्का होना
A. अपच होना
B. क्रोधी होना
C. किसी बात को गुप्त न रख पाना
D. जल्दी ही घबरा जाना

39. पेट में दाढ़ी होना
A. बहुत लालची होना
B. धूर्त होना
C. बहुत मोटा होना
D. छोटी आयु में ही बहुत चतुर-चालाक होना

40. बट्टा लगना
A. कीमत घट जाना B. कलंक लगना
C. घाटा होना D. पोल खुल जाना

41. बहती गंगा में हाथ धोना
A. आसानी से काम पूरा कर लेना
B. दूसरों को मौके का लाभ उठाते देखकर खुद भी मौके का लाभ उठा लेना
C. सबकी हाँ में हाँ मिलाना
D. मौका हाथ से न जाने देना

42. बातों में आना
A. झूठ पर विश्वास करना
B. बात को पी जाना
C. भेद प्रकट कर देना
D. किसी की बातों पर विश्वास कर लेना

43. भंडा फूटना
A. बेइज्जती होना B. भेद खुल जाना
C. बँटवारा होना D. मन की भड़ास निकालना

44. भूत सवार होना
A. पागल होना
B. किसी के वश में होना
C. किसी बात/काम के पीछे पड़ जाना
D. जी-तोड़ मेहनत करना

45. मक्खियाँ मारना
A. गंदे काम करना
B. खाली बैठे रहना
C. समय व्यतीत करने हेतु कुछ-न-कुछ करते रहना
D. आनन्द करना

46. माथा ठनकना
A. क्रोध आना B. याद आना
C. सन्देह होना D. उपाय सूझना

47. मुँह में पानी भर आना
A. लालच आना B. खाने की इच्छा होना
C. हड़पने का उपाय सोचना D. प्रसन्न हो जाना

48. रफूचक्कर हो जाना
A. बचकर भाग जाना B. मैदान छोड़कर भाग जाना
C. छिप जाना D. सरपट भागना

49. लट्टू होना
A. लोट-पोट होना B. मुग्ध होना
C. प्रभावित होना D. आगे-पीछे चक्कर लगाना

50. शेखी बघारना
A. बड़ी-बड़ी बातें करना B. बढ़ा-चढ़ाकर आत्मप्रशंसा करना
C. घमंड करना D. कोरी बातें करना

51. सब्ज़ बाग दिखाना
A. खुश करना B. सांत्वना देना
C. झूठी आशा बँधाना D. सफेद झूठ बोलना

52. साँप का बच्चा
A. जहरीला B. दुश्मन
C. स्वभाव से दुष्ट D. तेज गति से भागने वाला

53. सितारा गर्दिश में होना
A. घाटा होना B. बुरे दिन होना
C. पराजित होना D. पतन होना

54. सिर धुनना
A. पछताना B. लज्जित होना
C. तंग करना D. शोक मनाना

55. हवा बाँधना
A. सबको दबाकर रखना B. धाक जमाना
C. खुशामद करना D. साँस रोकना

56. हाथ तंग होना
A. कंजूस होना B. किफायत करना
C. रुपये पैसे की कमी होना D. कंगाल हो जाना

57. शह देना
A. दुलराना B. डराना
C. उकसाना D. धमकाना

58. सिर खाना
A. परेशान करना B. रट लगाना
C. शोर करना D. शरारत करना

59. सीधा करना
A. पीटना B. आदत सुधारना
C. अकड़ दूर करना D. रास्ते पर लाना

60. सौ बात सुनाना
A. लम्बी बात करना B. भला-बुरा कहना
C. मीन-मेख निकालना D. जिद करना

उत्तरमाला

1	2	3	4	5	6	7	8	9	10
C	A	D	C	A	D	C	A	B	C
11	**12**	**13**	**14**	**15**	**16**	**17**	**18**	**19**	**20**
C	D	C	C	D	A	B	B	D	A
21	**22**	**23**	**24**	**25**	**26**	**27**	**28**	**29**	**30**
A	B	B	B	D	B	B	B	D	A
31	**32**	**33**	**34**	**35**	**36**	**37**	**38**	**39**	**40**
B	C	B	B	B	B	C	C	D	B
41	**42**	**43**	**44**	**45**	**46**	**47**	**48**	**49**	**50**
B	D	B	C	B	C	A	A	B	B
51	**52**	**53**	**54**	**55**	**56**	**57**	**58**	**59**	**60**
C	C	B	A	B	C	C	A	C	B

★★★

9

लोकोक्ति

लोकोक्ति पूर्ण वाक्य हुआ करती है। यह किसी घटना विशेष का निष्कर्ष होती है। यह एक ओर वास्तविकता का संकेत देती है तो दूसरी ओर तीखी आलोचना या व्यंग्य प्रस्तुत करती है। कथन को प्रभावशाली बनाने में लोकोक्तियाँ बहुत महत्व रखती हैं। नीचे कुछ वाक्य प्रयोग सहित लोकोक्तियाँ दी जा रही हैं–

- **अपनी करनी पार उतरनी**– *अपना कार्य ही फलदायक होता है।*
  जीवन में दूसरों का सहारा ढूँढने से क्या होता है, अपनी करनी पार उतरनी।
- **अंधेर नगरी चौपट राजा**– *अन्याय का बोलबाला।*
  अयोग्य अधिकारी होने पर सभी कामों में धांधली चलती है, ठीक ही कहा गया है–अंधेर नगरी चौपट राजा।
- **हाथ पतला होना**– *दयनीय दशा होना।*
  व्यापार में घाटा हो गया इसलिए आजकल उसका हाथ पतला है।
- **अपनी-अपनी ढपली, अपना-अपना राग**– *मनमानी।*
  संगठन के अभाव में लोग अपनी-अपनी ढपली, अपना-अपना राग अलापते हैं।
- **लाल गुदड़ी में नहीं छिपते**– *होनहार का व्यक्तित्व छिपा नहीं रह सकता।*
  राजीव अपने जीवन में संघर्ष कर रहा है। असाधारण प्रतिभा के बावजूद उसे मंजिल नहीं मिल रही, लेकिन उसके साथी भरोसा दिलाते हैं–लाल गुदड़ी में भी नहीं छिपते।
- **खेल खिलाड़ी का, पैसा मदारी का**– *मेहनत किसी की, लाभ दूसरे का।*
  पूँजीवादी व्यवस्था की सबसे बड़ी बुराई यही है कि खेल खिलाड़ी का, पैसा मदारी का।
- **कंगाली में आटा गीला**– *एक मुसीबत पर दूसरी मुसीबत आ पड़ना।*
  विजय की नौकरी छूट गई, ऊपर से घर में नल खराब हो गया। इस पर विजय की पत्नी कहने लगी–कंगाली में आटा गीला।
- **गोदी में बैठकर दाढ़ी नोंचे**– *भला करने वाले के साथ दुष्टता करना।*
  समय ऐसा आ गया है कि लोग गोदी में बैठकर दाढ़ी नोंचने लगते हैं।
- **चोर को कहें चोरी कर और साह से कहें जागते रहो**– *दो पक्षों को लड़ाने वाला।*
  संजीव ने पड़ोसी से कहकर रामपाल के यहाँ छापा डलवा दिया और फिर रामलाल को बता दिया कि छापा किसने डलवाया है। उसकी हरकत पर लोग कह उठे चोर को कहें चोरी कर और साह से कहें जागते रहो।
- **दादा कहने से बनिया गुड़ देता है**– *मधुर वाणी से काम बन जाता है।*
  आजकल समय ऐसा आ गया है जब दादा कहने से ही बनिया गुड़ देता है।
- **दीवार के भी कान होते हैं**– *रहस्य की बात गुपचुप करनी चाहिए।*
  अजय, विजय को विनय की चोरी की दास्तान सुनाने लगा तो विजय ने अजय से कहा–धीरे बोलो, दीवार के भी कान होते हैं।
- **न रहेगा बाँस न बजेगी बाँसुरी**– *मूल कारण को रफा-दफा करे तो झगड़ा-फसाद ही न हो।*
  अध्यापक ने विद्यार्थी से कहा, तुम आलस्य त्याग दो इससे तुम्हें सफलता एवं उत्तम स्वास्थ्य प्राप्त होगा क्योंकि न रहेगा बाँस न बजेगी बाँसुरी।
- **तबेले की बला बंदर के सिर**– *अपराध करे कोई, पकड़ा जाये कोई और।*
  पुलिस वालों की तबेले की बला बंदर के सिर रखने की आदत हो गई है।
- **रानी रूठेगी तो अपना सुहाग लेगी**– *रूठने से अपना ही नुकसान होता है।*
  पुत्र के विवाह में दामाद के न आने से दुखी शर्मा जी को कहना पड़ा, 'रानी रूठेगी तो अपना सुहाग लेगी।'
- **अपना रख पराया चख**– *अपनी नहीं दूसरों की चीज का इस्तेमाल करना।*
  संजय बहुत चालाक है, वह अपना रख पराया चख की नीति पर चलता है।
- **आए थे हरि भजन को ओटन लगे कपास**– *उच्च लक्ष्य लेकर चलना पर कोई घटिया काम करने लगना।*
  पार्टी के कार्यकर्ता जागृति अभियान पर निकले लेकिन रास्ते में शराब और जुए में मस्त हो गए तो नेताजी को कहना पड़ा–आए थे हरि भजन को ओटन लगे कपास।
- **खग जाने खग ही की भाषा**– *एक साथ काम करने वाले एक-दूसरे के भाव-इशारे समझ जाते हैं।*
  दलाल के इशारे दूसरा दलाल समझ जाता है और किसान देखता रह जाता है, सच है–खग जाने खग ही की भाषा।
- **कोयला होय न ऊजला सौ मन साबुन धोय**– *दुष्ट व्यक्ति की प्रकृति में कोई परिवर्तन नहीं होता उसे चाहे कितनी ही सीख दी जाए।*
  मास्टर जी ने गाँव के विकास को हर प्रकार से समझाया कि वह बुरी आदतें छोड़ दें लेकिन वह नहीं माना। हारकर मास्टर जी को मानना पड़ा कोयला होय न ऊजला सौ मन साबुन धोय।

- **चमड़ी जाय पर दमड़ी न जाय**–*बहुत कंजूसी।*
सेठ लालाराम स्टेशन से पैदल घर सामान उठाकर आ गए तो बीबी बोली सेठ जी आप भी चमड़ी जाय पर दमड़ी न जाय कहावत में विश्वास रखते हैं।
- **गागर में सागर भरना**–*संक्षेप में विस्तृत बात कह देना।*
बिहारी ने अपने दोहों में गागर में सागर भर दिया है।
- **गुड़ खाए गुलगुलों से परहेज**–*बनावटी त्याग।*
स्वामीजी प्याज नहीं खाते, परन्तु प्याज की बनी पकौड़ियाँ खा लेते हैं, ऐसे ही लोगों के लिए कहा गया है–गुड़ खाए गुलगुलों से परहेज।
- **मार के आगे भूत भागे**–*मार से सब डरते हैं।*
पुलिस ने उसे मारा तो उसने अपराध कबूल लिया। सच है, मार के आगे भूत भागता है।
- **होनहार बिरवान के होत चीकने पात**–*होनहार बालक के लक्षण आरम्भ से ही दिखाई देने लगते हैं।*
विकास के कार्यकलाप देखकर सभी यही कहते हैं–होनहार बिरवान के होत चीकने पात।
- **चौबे गये छब्बे बनने दुब्बे बनकर आये**–*लाभ के बदले हानि हो जाना।*
प्रेस में प्रश्न-पत्र छापने वाले शर्मा जी ने मॉडल पेपर निकालकर प्रकाशक बनने का प्रयास किया जिसमें घाटा हो गया और उनकी दशा पर लोग कहने लगे, चौबे गये छब्बे बनने दुब्बे बनकर आये।
- **हाथ मलना**–*कुछ प्राप्त न होना।*
विनय को इनाम मिला और मैं हाथ मलता रह गया।
- **अब पछताए होत क्या जब चिड़ियाँ चुग गईं खेत**–*नुकसान हो जाने के बाद पछताना बेकार।*
परीक्षा के दिनों में अरविन्द ने पढ़ाई नहीं की, फेल तो होना ही था, जब वह रोने लगा तो पिता ने कहा–अब पछताए होत क्या जब चिड़ियाँ चुग गईं खेत।
- **आम के आम गुठलियों के दाम**–*दोहरा लाभ।*
राजेश गन्ने का रस बेचता है और छीलन गौशाला वाले खरीदकर ले जाते हैं। इस प्रकार उसके तो आम के आम गुठलियों के दाम हैं।
- **उल्टा चोर कोतवाल को डांटे**–*दोषी होने पर धौंस जमाना।*
राजेश से कक्षा में देर से आने के लिए मॉनीटर ने कारण पूछा तो राजेश ने कहा, 'तुम्हें मतलब'? तुम क्या अध्यापक हो, जाओ अपना काम करो। उसका जवाब सुनकर एक लड़का कह उठा, उल्टा चोर कोतवाल को डाँटे।
- **अपना ही पैसा खोटा तो परखने वाले का क्या दोष**–*अपनी ही चीज खराब हो तो दूसरे को दोष देना उचित नहीं।*
अजय ने पड़ोसी की लड़की छेड़ दी। इस पर उसकी माँ अजय के घर आकर उसे बुरा भला कहने लगी, इस पर उसके पिताजी बोले अपना ही पैसा खोटा हो तो परखने वाले का क्या दोष।
- **न अंधे को न्यौता देते न दो जने आते**–*न यह काम करते न बवाल खड़ा होता।*
संजीव ने एक विधवा से विवाह किया, जिसके दो बच्चे थे। फिर जब अपने दो बच्चे हो गए तो गुजारा कठिन हो गया, इस पर मित्र ने समझाया न अंधे को न्यौता देते न दो जने आते।
- **चोरी का माल मोरी में**–*गलत ढंग से अर्जित धन गलत ढंग से ही खर्च होता है।*
मनोहर ने रिश्वत लेकर खूब धन कमाया, लेकिन बच्चे की बीमारी में सब खर्च हो गया, इस प्रकार चोरी का माल मोरी में चला गया।
- **घर की मुर्गी दाल बराबर**–*घर की वस्तु का आदर नहीं होता।*
व्यक्ति कितना ही महान् हो, घर में उसका मूल्यांकन उतना नहीं हो सकता है, क्योंकि घर की मुर्गी दाल बराबर होती है।
- **कहीं की ईंट कहीं का रोड़ा, भानुमती ने कुनबा जोड़ा**–*इधर-उधर की सामग्री एकत्र करके कोई रचना करना।*
राजग गठबंधन की सरकार कहीं की ईंट कहीं का रोड़ा, भानुमती ने कुनबा जोड़ा वाली सरकार थी।
- **काठ की हाण्डी बार-बार नहीं चढ़ती**–*अन्याय बार-बार नहीं चलता।*
जितेन्द्र बिना टिकट यात्रा के अपराध में पकड़ा ही गया, ठीक ही कहा गया है कि काठ की हाण्डी बार-बार नहीं चढ़ती।
- **काला अक्षर भैंस बराबर**–*निरक्षर व्यक्ति के लिए पुस्तकें व्यर्थ हैं।*
हमें कागज क्यों दिखाते हो, हमारे लिए काला अक्षर भैंस बराबर।
- **खरबूजे को देखकर खरबूजा रंग बदलता है**–*जब कोई व्यक्ति अपने साथी के अनुसार आचरण करने लगता है तब यह कहावत कही जाती है।*
राहुल द्रविड़ को शानदार बल्लेबाजी करते देख लक्ष्मण ने भी शानदार बल्लेबाजी करके भारत को ऑस्ट्रेलिया के विरुद्ध मैच जिता दिया, तब ऑस्ट्रेलिया के खिलाड़ियों को कहना पड़ा–खरबूजे को देखकर खरबूजा रंग बदलता है।
- **खुदा गंजे को नाखून नहीं देता**–*अयोग्य को अधिकार नहीं मिलता।*
अकर्मण्य व्यक्ति को अधिकार नहीं मिल पाते हैं, क्योंकि खुदा गंजे को नाखून नहीं देता।
- **इस हाथ दे उस हाथ ले**–*कर्म का फल शीघ्र मिलता है।*
दूसरों का सम्मान करने से स्वयं को सम्मान मिलता है। ठीक ही है–इस हाथ दे उस हाथ ले।
- **आधी छोड़ सारी को धावै, आधी मिलै न पूरी पावै**–*अधिक लोभ करने से हानि ही होती है।*
भाजपा ने समयपूर्व चुनाव करा दिये कहीं हार न जाये, सच भी है आधी छोड़ सारी को धावै, आधी मिलै न पूरी पावै।
- **ईश्वर की माया, कहीं धूप कहीं छाया**–*संसार में कहीं दुख है कहीं सुख है।*
किसी घर दूध घी की बहार है और किसी घर सूखी रोटी भी नहीं है, ठीक ही कहा गया है–ईश्वर की माया कहीं धूप कहीं छाया।
- **उल्टे बाँस बरेली को**–*विपरीत कार्य करना।*
शीला फिरोजाबाद गयी तो चूड़ियाँ ले गई तब रीना बोली–दीदी तुमने तो उल्टे बाँस बरेली वाली कहावत चरितार्थ कर दी, फिरोजाबाद तो चूड़ियों का शहर है।
- **आज का बनिया कल का सेठ**–*काम करते रहने से आदमी बड़ा हो ही जाता है।*
अजय ने सुनील से कहा निराश मत हो मित्र, मेहनत से कार्य करते रहो एक दिन इसी फर्म में तरक्की पा जाओगे। कहावत भी है आज का बनिया कल का सेठ।

- **एक सड़ी मछली सारे तालाब को गन्दा कर देती है**–*अच्छे समाज को एक बुरा व्यक्ति कलंकित कर देता है।*
  मुहल्ले में एक धंधा करने वाली के बस जाने से पूरा मुहल्ला बदनाम हो गया। सच है एक सड़ी मछली सारे तालाब को गन्दा कर देती है।
- **एक तो करेला फिर नीम चढ़ा**–*दोहरा कटुत्व।*
  सुधा एक तो पढ़ने में कमजोर है और दूसरे शिक्षकों के प्रति उसका व्यवहार ठीक नहीं है, ऐसे लोगों के लिए कहा गया है–एक तो करेला फिर नीम चढ़ा।
- **एक पंथ दो काज**–*एक उपाय से दो कार्यों का होना।*
  रामू हिन्दी विषय में एम.ए. की तैयारी कर रहा था। उसने साहित्यरत्न का भी फार्म भर दिया, इस प्रकार उसके एक पंथ दो काज हो गए।
- **ऊँची दुकान फीका पकवान**–*केवल बाहरी दिखावा।*
  हमने अन्नपूर्णा होटल का नाम बहुत सुना था, लेकिन जब हमने वहाँ खाना खाया तो न अच्छा खाना था न सफाई। सोचकर रह गये ऊँची दुकान फीका पकवान।
- **आप मियाँ जी माँगते द्वार खड़े दरवेश**–*अति दरिद्र के यहाँ भिक्षा माँगने वालों का आना।*
  विजय कर्ज के बोझ से दबा था, फिर भी उसकी पत्नी साधुओं को प्रतिदिन खिलाती थी। यह देखकर लेनदार ने कहा आप मियाँ जी माँगते द्वार खड़े दरवेश।
- **अपना हाथ जगन्नाथ**–*स्वयं किया हुआ कार्य फलदायी होता है।*
  घर का कार्य नौकरों से कराने की अपेक्षा स्वयं करना अच्छा है। अपना हाथ जगन्नाथ।
- **घी का लड्डू टेढ़ा भला**–*काम की वस्तु कम अच्छी रहने पर भी ठीक रहती है।*
  राज का व्यवहार अजीबो-गरीब है लेकिन वह बहुत योग्य है। अतः नियोक्ता उसे घी का लड्डू टेढ़ा भला अनुसार सहन करते हैं।
- **आटे के साथ घुन भी पिसता है**–*दोषी व्यक्ति का साथी निर्दोष भी मारा जाता है।*
  सोनू ने चोरी नहीं की लेकिन वह मोनू का साथी तो है, अतः पुलिस उसे भी पकड़कर ले गई। इसे कहते हैं आटे के साथ घुन भी पिसता है।
- **अंधे के हाथ बटेर**–*अनायास कोई वस्तु मिल जाना।*
  मंजू की शादी गुड्डू से हो गई तो दोनों को जानने वाला कह उठा अंधे के हाथ बटेर लग गई।
- **कहाँ राजा भोज कहाँ गंगू तेली**–*छोटे आदमी की बड़े आदमी से क्या तुलना।*
  मदर टेरेसा की सिस्टर निर्मला से तुलना क्या चीज है? कहाँ राजा भोज कहाँ गंगू तेली।
- **खिसयानी बिल्ली खम्भा नोचे**–*शर्म के मारे क्रोध करने लगना।*
  विजय चोरी करते पकड़ा गया तो माता-पिता को कोसने लगा कि मुझे अच्छी सीख क्यों नहीं दी। सही है खिसयानी बिल्ली खम्भा नोचे।
- **थोथा चना बाजे घना**–*कम ज्ञान या गुण रखने वाला बातें बढ़-चढ़कर करता है।*
  जब कोई गुणहीन व्यक्ति अपनी प्रशंसा करने लगता है तब यह कहावत चरितार्थ होती है।
- **आँख के अंधे नाम नैनसुख**–*नाम बड़ा और गुण उसके विपरीत।*
  माता-पिता ने बालक का नाम धनीराम रखा. लेकिन बड़ा होकर धनीराम को दो जून की रोटी जुटानी भारी पड़ रही है, अतः किसी ने सही कहा है–आँख के अंधे नाम नैन सुख।
- **धोबी का कुत्ता घर का न घाट का**–*निकम्मा व्यक्ति।*
  नीरज ने नौकरी छोड़ दी और व्यापार में भी असफल रहा तो माता-पिता ने कहा–धोबी का कुत्ता घर का न घाट का।
- **दूर के ढोल सुहावने**–*दूर की वस्तु अच्छी लगना।*
  सुनील को चीन का बना कपड़ा अधिक पसन्द है, जबकि भारत का बना कपड़ा काफी अच्छा होता है, ठीक ही कहा गया है–दूर के ढोल सुहावने।
- **मान न मान मैं तेरा मेहमान**–*जबरदस्ती का मेहमान।*
  सुरेश ने राजेश को पार्टी में आने का न्यौता नहीं दिया लेकिन वह फिर भी आ धमका तो इस पर लोग कहने लगे मान न मान मैं तेरा मेहमान।
- **अंधे की लकड़ी**–*बेसहारे का सहारा।*
  विनय अपने बूढ़े बाप का इकलौता पुत्र था, अचानक कल उसका देहान्त हो गया तो रामलाल ने कहा–अंधे की तो लकड़ी ही टूट गई।
- **भागते भूत की लँगोटी भली**–*जिस व्यक्ति से कुछ भी मिलने की आशा न हो, उससे यदि थोड़ा भी मिल जाता है, तब यह कहावत प्रयुक्त होती है।*
  अजय ने विकास को 500 रुपये उधार दिए थे, बड़ी मुश्किल से 100 रुपये विकास ने वापस दिये तो अजय ने सोचा भागते भूत की लँगोटी ही भली।
- **मन चंगा तो कठौती में गंगा**–*यदि मन शुद्ध है तो तीर्थाटन की आवश्यकता नहीं है।*
  मनुष्य मन से पवित्र है तो सभी तीर्थ उसके पास हैं अतः भक्त रविदास ने कहा है–मन चंगा तो कठौती में गंगा।
- **मुल्ला की दौड़ मस्जिद तक**–*सीमित क्षेत्र तक पहुँच।*
  पवन अधिक-से अधिक ग्राम प्रधान के पास जाएगा, मुल्ला की दौड़ मस्जिद तक।
- **यह मुँह और मसूर की दाल**–*जब कोई व्यक्ति अपनी योग्यता से अधिक पाने की अभिलाषा करता है तब यह कहावत चरितार्थ होती है।*
  बी.ए. में तृतीय श्रेणी में पास हुआ विवेक पी.सी.एस. की बात करने लगा तो अजय ने उससे कहा–यह मुँह और मसूर की दाल।
- **क्या काबुल में गधे नहीं होते**–*अच्छे स्थान पर बुरे लोग भी होते हैं।*
  दफ्तर में सचिन का मोबाइल चोरी हो गया–जब उसने कहा कि किसी बाहरी आदमी ने चोरी की है तो अजय ने कहा–क्या काबुल में गधे नहीं होते।

वस्तुनिष्ठ प्रश्नोत्तर

निर्देश (प्रश्न संख्या 1 से 10 तक): *नीचे प्रत्येक प्रश्न में एक लोकोक्ति दी गई है और उसके नीचे A, B, C, D विकल्प के सामने उसका (लोकोक्ति का) अर्थ दिया गया है। चारों अर्थों में से जो अर्थ आपको सर्वाधिक उपयुक्त लगे, उस पर सही का निशान लगाइये।*

1. काठ की हाँडी बार-बार नहीं चढ़ती
A. किसी भी व्यक्ति को बार-बार धोखा नहीं दिया जा सकता
B. धोखा देने की एक ही तरकीब बार-बार सफल नहीं होती
C. धोखा देने की सब तरकीबें हर बार सफल नहीं होतीं
D. ठगने वाला हर बार अपनी तरकीब बदलता रहता है

2. खिसियानी बिल्ली खंभा नोचे
A. निराश व्यक्ति किसी-न-किसी वस्तु का सहारा ढूँढता है
B. किसी काम में सफल न होने पर अपना क्रोध अन्य किसी पर अकारण प्रकट करना
C. असफल व्यक्ति ऊटपटाँग काम करने लगता है
D. असफलता का दोष किसी अन्य व्यक्ति के सिर मढ़ना

3. खोदा पहाड़ निकली चुहिया
A. साधारण कार्य के लिए असाधारण प्रयत्न करना
B. असाधारण प्रयत्न के बाद अति छोटी सफलता मिलना
C. ऐसा फल निकलना, जिसकी अपेक्षा न हो
D. परिणाम, प्रयत्न के बिल्कुल विपरीत हो

4. घर की मुर्गी दाल बराबर
A. घर में विद्यमान चीज खूब जमकर (इफरात) इस्तेमाल होती है
B. घर का खाना सबसे बढ़िया होता है चाहे मुर्गी हो या दाल हो
C. घर में उपलब्ध वस्तु को अधिक महत्व नहीं दिया जाता
D. घर में पली मुर्गी को दाल भी खिलाई जाती है

5. चोर की दाढ़ी में तिनका
A. चोर सदैव सशंकित रहता है
B. चोर को लगता है कि सब उसके बारे में जानते हैं
C. पापी को अपने पाप का भय बना रहता है
D. चोर चोरी करते समय अपना कुछ-न-कुछ सबूत जरूर छोड़ जाता है

6. जिसकी लाठी उसकी भैंस
A. जबरदस्त सबसे अपनी बात मनवा लेता है
B. जबरदस्त को जो वस्तु पसन्द आ जाती है, वह उसे लेकर ही दम लेता है
C. जबरदस्त किसी की परवाह नहीं करता
D. जबरदस्त की लाठी में बल होता है

7. दूध का दूध–पानी का पानी
A. निष्पक्ष न्याय
B. जैसे को तैसा
C. अन्यायी को दण्ड
D. ऐसा न्याय, जिससे दोनों पक्ष संतुष्ट हों

8. नौ नकद न तेरह उधार
A. नकद के नौ और उधार के तेरह बराबर होते हैं
B. नकद के नौ अच्छे, उधार के तेरह नहीं अच्छे
C. अधिक लाभ के लोभ में उधार देना हानिकारक होता है
D. उधार की दुकान अधिक दिन नहीं चल पाती

9. बन्दर क्या जाने अदरक का स्वाद
A. गँवार व्यक्ति को गुणों की पहचान नहीं होती
B. गँवार व्यक्ति के गुण छिपे ही रहते हैं
C. गँवार व्यक्ति गुण-दोष पहचानने की कोशिश नहीं करता
D. गँवार व्यक्ति को कोई उत्तम वस्तु मिल जाये तो भी वह उसकी कद्र नहीं करता

10. साँप मरे न लाठी टूटे
A. असम्भव कार्य
B. दोनों प्रकार के लाभ मिलना
C. काम भी हो जाये और नुकसान (हानि) भी न उठानी पड़े
D. बिना नुकसान उठाये कोई बड़ा काम नहीं होता

निर्देश (प्रश्न संख्या 11 से 15 तक): *निम्नलिखित वाक्यांशों के लिए उपयुक्त लोकोक्तियाँ बताइए।*

11. अल्प समय के लिए अधिकार हाथ में आने पर मनमानी करना
A. सौ दिन चोर का एक दिन साहूकार का
B. बंदर की आशनाई घर में आग लगाई
C. अंधे को अंधेरे में बहुत दूर की सूझी
D. एक दिन का बादशाह बनना और चमड़े का सिक्का चलाना

12. सत्ता सम्पन्न व्यक्ति मदांध हो ही जाते हैं
A. प्रभुता पाय काह मद नाहीं
B. फटे में पाँव दफ्तर में नाव
C. आँख न दीदा काढ़े कसीदा
D. ऊँट मक्का की ओर भागता है

13. हराम की कमाई व्यर्थ जाती है
A. आदमी जानै बसे, सोना जाने कसै
B. आप मियाँजी माँगते दूर खड़े दरवेश
C. चोरी का माल मोरी में
D. अन्धी पीसे कुत्ते खाएं

14. विपदा सब पर आती है
A. चाँद को भी ग्रहण लगता है
B. इब्तदाए इश्क है रोता है क्या, आगे आगे देखिए होता है क्या
C. एक तवे की रोटी, क्या छोटी क्या मोटी
D. आसमान से गिरा, खजूर में अटका

15. केवल दिखावे से नाम नहीं मिलता

A. जोग जुगत व जानी, कपड़े रंग भये बिरागी

B. खेत खाए गदहा, मारा जाए जुलहा

C. आप मरे बिना स्वर्ग नहीं मिलता

D. कहने से कुम्हार गधे पर नहीं चढ़ता

निर्देश (प्रश्न संख्या 16 से 20 तक): *प्रत्येक प्रश्न में दी गई गहरे काली छपी लोकोक्तियों के अर्थ के लिए सही विकल्प का चयन कीजिए।*

16. रीता की पड़ोसी उसे रोज **जली-भुनी** सुनाती है

A. किसी वस्तु का जलाना

B. भला-बुरा कहना

C. कड़वी बात करना

D. सब कुछ कहना

17. घर से निकलने के बाद राजेश को **आटे-दाल का भाव मालूम हो गया**

A. आटे-दाल के लिए लाइन में खड़े होना

B. आटे-दाल का भाव ज्ञात करना

C. आटा-दाल खरीदना

D. वास्तविकता का ज्ञान होना

18. नीतू के लिए **काला अक्षर भैंस बराबर** है

A. अल्प ज्ञान रखना

B. अक्षरों का काला होना

C. अक्षर व भैंस का बराबर होना

D. बिल्कुल निरक्षर होना

19. रेखा को जरा भी चिन्ता नहीं थी, क्योंकि उसका तो यह हाल है कि **सावन सूखे न भादो हरे**

A. नुकसान न होना

B. अत्यधिक लाभ प्राप्त होना

C. हमेशा एक-सी दशा में रहना

D. कपटपूर्ण व्यवहार

20. मोहन बेकार में अदालत के चक्कर लगा रहा है, जबकि उसे **लेना एक न देना दो**

A. किसी से कोई मतलब न होना

B. गुप्त बात भी छिपी नहीं रह सकती

C. सार रहित

D. एक लेकर दो देना

निर्देश (प्रश्न संख्या 21 से 30 तक): निम्नलिखित लोकोक्तियों को उचित शब्दों से पूर्ण करें।

21. होनहार .... के होत चीकने पात

A. पुरुष B. बिरवान

C. जवान D. पंडित

22. ऊँची दुकान .... पकवान

A. अच्छे B. पूरे

C. फीके D. मीठे

23. एक पन्थ दो ....

A. काम B. काज

C. पाठ D. राह

24. दिन-दूना .... चौगुना

A. माह B. रात

C. चार D. काम

25. सब .... बाईस पसेरी

A. आम B. नाम

C. पान D. धान

26. घर आया .... भी नहीं निकाला जाता

A. मेहमान B. कुत्ता

C. रिश्तेदार D. ब्राह्मण

27. धोये जो सौ बार तौ .... होये ना सेत

A. कपड़ा B. आदमी

C. काजर D. गन्दा

28. ज्यों-ज्यों भीजे .... त्यों-त्यों भारी होय

A. कामरी B. कमली

C. उधारी D. कर्जा

29. सौ सुनार की एक .... की

A. कुम्हार B. मल्लाह

C. इस्पात D. लोहार

30. करम के बलिया पकाई .... हो गया दलिया

A. भात B. रोटी

C. खीर D. मेवा

उत्तरमाला

1	2	3	4	5	6	7	8	9	10
B	B	B	C	B	A	A	C	A	C
11	**12**	**13**	**14**	**15**	**16**	**17**	**18**	**19**	**20**
D	A	C	A	A	B	D	D	C	A
21	**22**	**23**	**24**	**25**	**26**	**27**	**28**	**29**	**30**
B	C	B	B	D	B	C	A	D	C

★★★

(ख) अपठित बोधात्मक प्रश्न

अभ्यास 1

प्रेममार्गी शाखा के प्रमुख कवि मलिक मोहम्मद जायसी संसार से इतने विरक्त नहीं थे। वे लोक तथा परलोक दोनों की साधना चाहते थे। उन्होंने अपने 'पद्मावत' में मसनवी परम्परा के अनुकूल शेरशाह की वंदना की है। उन्होंने लौकिक प्रेमगाथाओं के रूपक द्वारा परमार्थिक प्रेम की साधना की है। पद्मावती की प्रेम-कथा जो पृथ्वीराज रासो में वीर रस के आश्रित गौण थी, वह जायसी की 'पद्मावत' में मुख्यता प्राप्त कर लेती है। पद्मावत में कथा भी है और रूपक के द्वारा अलौकिक तत्त्वों की व्यंजना भी है। यद्यपि जायसी मुसलमान थे तथापि वे भारतीय संस्कृति से पूर्णतया परिचित थे। थोड़े बहुत हेर-फेर के साथ उनके काव्य में भारतीय अन्तर-कथाओं और धार्मिक परम्पराओं का उल्लेख हुआ है। उसमें रासो की अपेक्षा अन्विति अधिक है और आरंभ से लेकर अन्त तक शैली और भाषा की एकरसता है। पद्मावत प्रबंधकाव्य का एक अच्छा उदाहरण कहा जा सकता है।

—काव्य के रूप, डॉ. गुलाब राय

1. मलिक मोहम्मद जायसी थे :
   A. अवधी भाषा के प्रथम कवि
   B. सूफी सन्त कवि
   C. शेरशाह सूरी के सभासद्
   D. जायस के नागरिक

2. जायसी के सर्वोत्कृष्ट ग्रंथ का नाम है :
   A. आखिरी कलाम
   B. अखरा बट
   C. पद्मावत
   D. मधुमालती

3. उक्त गद्य खण्ड का उपयुक्त शीर्षक हो सकता है :
   A. पद्मावत का कथानक
   B. पद्मावत परिचय
   C. जायसी और उनका पद्मावत
   D. कविवर जायसी

4. पद्मावत महाकाव्य की भाषा है :
   A. ब्रजभाषा
   B. भोजपुरी
   C. खड़ी बोली
   D. अवधी

5. अवधी भाषा के सर्वाधिक लोकप्रिय महाकाव्य का नाम है :
   A. रामचरितमानस B. पद्मावत
   C. मधुमालती D. मृगावती

अभ्यास 2

सामान्य दुष्टों की वन्दना में या तो भय रहता है, या व्यंग्य। परन्तु जहाँ हम हानि होने के पहले ही हानि के कारण की वन्दना करने लगते हैं, वहाँ हमारी वन्दना के मूल में भय नहीं बल्कि उसकी स्थायी दशा की आशंका है। इस वंदना में दुष्टों को थपकी देकर सुलाने की चाल है जिसमें विघ्न-बाधाओं से जान बच सके। आशंका से उत्पन्न यह नम्रता गोस्वामी जी को आश्रय से आलंबन बना देती है। जब स्फुट अंशों के संचारीभावों तथा अनुभवों को छोड़कर वंदना के पीछे निहित भावना की दृष्टि से देखते हैं तो यह आश्रय से संक्रमित आलंबन का उदाहरण बन जाता है। सन्तों, देवताओं तथा राम की वन्दना पर्याप्त नहीं इसलिए दुष्टों की भी वन्दना की जाती है। इससे दुष्टों के महत्त्व की मायिक सृष्टि होती है और वह उन्हें और भी उपहास्य बना देती है।

—हास्य के सिद्धान्त तथा मानस में हास्य
प्रो. जगदीश पाण्डेय

1. दुष्ट वन्दना के पीछे कवि का उद्देश्य है :
   A. दुष्टों को लज्जित करना
   B. दुष्टों को थपकी देकर सुलाना
   C. दुष्टों से अपना बचाव करना
   D. दुष्टों का सहयोग प्राप्त करना

2. रामचरितमानस एक भक्ति काव्य है। इसमें दुष्ट वंदना का रहस्य है :
   A. तुलसी की व्यापक दृष्टि
   B. तुलसी का सभी को राममय देखना
   C. तुलसी की उदारता
   D. तुलसी का शील-सौजन्य

3. उपरोक्त अवतरण का उपयुक्त शीर्षक हो सकता है :
   A. तुलसी की दुष्ट वंदना
   B. तुलसी की उदारता
   C. तुलसी का मानवीय दृष्टिकोण
   D. उपर्युक्त तीनों

4. देवताओं, महापुरुषों, सज्जनों के साथ दुष्टों की वंदना इसलिए सार्थक कही जाएगी कि महाकवि तुलसी :
   A. संत कवि थे
   B. उदार चेता थे
   C. हित-अनहित और अपने-पराये की भावना से ऊपर उठ चुके थे
   D. निर्वैरता चाहते थे

5. जीवन में हास्य का महत्त्व इसलिए है कि वह जीवन को :
   A. प्रेरणा देता है B. आनन्दित करता है
   C. आगे बढ़ाता है D. सरस बनाता है

अभ्यास 3

इन्द्र यह सुनकर स्वयं महर्षि दधीचि के आश्रम में गए और उन्हें मजबूरी कह सुनायी। ऋषि जग-कल्याण के लिए सहर्ष अपना शरीर त्यागने के लिए तैयार हो गए। उनकी हड्डियों से त्वष्ठा ने वज्र बनाया। इस वज्र को हाथ में लेकर इन्द्र दुगुने उत्साह से वृत्रासुर के सम्मुख गए। उनके मेघरूपी रथ के गर्जन से एक बार वृत्रासुर का कलेजा काँप गया। उनके साथ चलते हुए मरुत जोर-जोर से उनकी जयजयकार कर रहे थे। इन्द्र ने सबसे पहले अपने वज्र से वृत्रासुर की माया को काट दिया। फिर भी वह दैत्य बड़ा शक्तिशाली था। अपनी माया से विछिन्न होकर भी वह बहुत देर तक इन्द्र से जूझता रहा। लेकिन अन्त में इन्द्र ने वज्र के प्रहार से वृत्रासुर का सिर काट दिया। वृत्रासुर के मरते ही रुका हुआ जल बह निकला, नदी-नाले फिर से भर उठे और देखते-ही-देखते खेत लहलहा उठे।

1. महर्षि दधीचि एक ऐसे ऋषि थे जिन्होंने :
A. देवताओं की रक्षा के लिए अपने शरीर का त्याग किया था
B. योग बल से अपने शरीर को त्याग कर वृत्रासुर के वध हेतु वज्र बनाने के लिए इन्द्र को अपनी अस्थियाँ सुलभ करा दी थीं
C. वृत्रासुर के वध में इन्द्र की सहायता की थी
D. वृत्रासुर का वध किया था

2. हमें इस अवतरण से यह प्रेरणा मिलती है कि परोपकार के लिए आवश्यकता पड़ने पर :
A. अपने शरीर भी दे देना चाहिए
B. अपना सर्वस्व दे देना चाहिए
C. अपनी अस्थियाँ दे देनी चाहिए
D. अपनी सम्पत्ति दे देनी चाहिए

3. इस गद्यांश का उपयुक्त शीर्षक हो सकता है :
A. दधीचि का आत्मदान B. दधीचि का सर्वस्व दान
C. वृत्रासुर वध D. इन्द्र का कोप

4. निम्नलिखित में से सही कथन पर निशान लगाइए :
A. वृत्रासुर इन्द्र का प्रतिद्वन्द्वी था
B. वृत्रासुर एक आततायी राक्षस था
C. वृत्रासुर एक महाप्रतापी राक्षस था, जिसने जलावरोध कर रखा था
D. वृत्रासुर उपर्युक्त में से कोई नहीं था

इस उद्धरण में प्रयुक्त निम्नलिखित शब्दों के सही अर्थों पर निशान लगाइए :

5. महर्षि
A. मुनि B. ऋषि जो ब्राह्मण न हो
C. ऋषि जो ब्राह्मण हो D. ऋषियों का एक पद विशेष

6. जगकल्याण :
A. संसार का हित
B. संसार की भलाई
C. संसार को सुख देना
D. संसार के लिए आनन्द की व्यवस्था करना

7. वज्र :
A. एक प्रकार का बाजा
B. एक प्रकार का शस्त्र
C. एक प्रकार का आघात
D. पत्थर गिरना या बिजली गिरना

अभ्यास 4

महाकवि सूरदास का 'सूर-सागर' भागवत के आधार पर लिखा हुआ ग्रंथ है। इसीलिए महाकवि 'सूर' ने भी ब्रह्म का यही स्वरूप ग्रहण किया और भगवान श्रीकृष्ण को अपनी उपासना का केन्द्र मानकर वैष्णव सम्प्रदाय के सिद्धान्तों का ही प्रतिपादन किया है। वास्तव में वैदिक ऋचाओं में वर्णित सिद्धान्त ही वैदिक धर्म के प्रकाण्ड आचार्यों द्वारा प्रचारित हुए हैं। काल और स्थिति के अनुसार धार्मिक सिद्धान्तों में भी परिवर्तन होना आवश्यक है। सर्वप्रथम दृष्टि से भगवान कृष्ण ने इन वैदिक सिद्धान्तों में कुछ परिवर्तन कर सूरकालीन वैष्णव धर्म का शिलान्यास किया। अत: भगवान कृष्ण को ही वैष्णव धर्म का प्रथम आचार्य कहना अनुचित न होगा। धार्मिक और ऐतिहासिक अनुसंधानों के अनुसार वेदों और संहिताओं की रचना भिन्न-भिन्न काल में हुई है। उदाहरणार्थ—यजुर्वेद संहिता में केशी नामक राक्षस का कृष्ण द्वारा वध किए जाने का उल्लेख है। इससे प्रमाणित होता है कि यह संहिता कृष्ण जन्म के बाद लिखी गई है।

—सूरदर्शन, डॉ. कृष्ण लाल 'हंस'

1. उक्त गद्यांश का सारांश एक पंक्ति में इस प्रकार हो सकता है :
A. श्रीमद्भागवत ग्रंथ सूर-सागर की रचना का आधार है
B. श्रीमद्भागवत नहीं अपितु ब्रह्म वैवर्त्त पुराण सूर-सागर का आधार है
C. महाभारत ग्रंथ सूर-सागर का आधार है
D. वैदिक ऋचाएँ सूर-सागर का आधार हैं

2. हिन्दी साहित्य में भक्ति तथा रीति काल को सम्मिलित करके तीन उत्तम कवि माने गए हैं, जिनमें प्रथम स्थान :
A. सूरदास का है B. तुलसीदास का है
C. केशवदास का है D. देव का है

3. महाकवि सूरदास भक्तिकाल में सगुण भक्ति की :
A. कृष्ण भक्ति शाखा के कवि थे
B. राम कृष्ण दोनों की भक्ति शाखा के कवि थे
C. स्मार्त्त कवि थे
D. उपर्युक्त किसी शाखा के कवि नहीं थे

4. इस गद्यांश का उपयुक्त शीर्षक हो सकता है :
A. सूर-सागर का प्रणयन
B. वैष्णव धर्म के प्रथम आचार्य श्रीकृष्ण
C. परब्रह्म श्रीकृष्ण
D. वैष्णव धर्म का शिलान्यास

5. सूर-सागर की कथा श्रीमद्भागवत के :
A. दशम स्कंध से ली गई है
B. एकादश स्कंध से ली गई है
C. नवम स्कंध से ली गई है
D. उपर्युक्त किसी स्कंध से नहीं ली गई है

अभ्यास 5

''पर्वतीय पथ और पत्थरों की चोट से टूटे नाखून और चुटीली उँगलियों के बीच में ढाल बनी मूँज की चप्पल मानो मनुष्य को पशु बनाकर खुर न देने वाले परमात्मा का उपहास कर रही हो। पाँव से दो बालिश्त ऊँचा और ऊनी-सूती पैबन्दों से बना हुआ पाजामा मनुष्य की लज्जाशीलता की विडम्बना जैसा लगता था। किसी से कभी मिले हुए पुराने कोट में, नीचे के मटमैले स्तर की झाँकी देती हुई, ऊपरी तह तार-तार फटकर झालरदार हो उठी थी और सब अपने पहनने वाले को एक झबरे जन्तु की भूमिका में उपस्थित करती थी। अस्पष्ट रंग और अनिश्चित रूप वाली दोपलिया टोपी के छेद से रूखे बाल जहाँ-तहाँ झाँककर मैले पानी और उसके बीच-बीच में झाँकते हुए सेवार की स्मृति करा देते थे।'' **—स्मृति की रेखाएँ, महादेवी वर्मा**

1. श्रीमती महादेवी वर्मा द्वारा किया गया उक्त रेखांकन 'स्मृति की रेखाएँ' नामक पुस्तक से है। यह रेखांकन :
   A. एक निर्धन व्यक्ति का है
   B. एक पहाड़ी नागरिक का है
   C. एक पहाड़ी मजदूर का है
   D. उपरोक्त में से किसी का नहीं है
2. उपर्युक्त गद्यांश का सार्थक शीर्षक हो सकता है :
   A. एक विपन्न कुली
   B. एक पर्वतीय श्रमिक
   C. निर्धनता एक अभिशाप
   D. करुणा की मूर्ति
3. महादेवी वर्मा की शैली की समीक्षा-मात्र एक पंक्ति में कर पाना असंभव है। फिर भी, कहा जा सकता है कि उनकी काव्य-शैली की तरह उनकी गद्य शैली भी :
   A. भावना प्रधान है B. चित्रांकन प्रधान है
   C. कल्पना प्रधान है D. मनोरम है
4. महादेवी वर्मा विरचित अनेक काव्यग्रंथ, निबन्ध तथा रेखाचित्र हैं। कुछ एक के नाम हैं :
   A. दीपशिखा, यामा
   B. अतीत के चलचित्र, स्मृति की रेखाएँ
   C. नीरजा, नीहार
   D. उपरोक्त सभी
5. इस गद्य कृति के अतिरिक्त महादेवी वर्मा द्वारा रचित प्रमुखतम गद्य कृति का नाम है :
   A. अतीत के चलचित्र B. मेरा परिवार
   C. पथ के साथी D. शृंखला की कड़ियाँ

अभ्यास 6

''आरोग्य रक्षा के नियम माँ-बाप को न मालूम रहने के कारण उनके बाल-बच्चों को भोग भुगतने पड़ते हैं। उनकी जो दुर्गति होती है, उन पर जो आफतें आती हैं उनका ठौर-ठिकाना नहीं। हजारों बच्चे तो माँ-बाप की असावधानी और मूर्खता के कारण पैदा होते ही मर जाते हैं। जो बचते हैं उनमें लाखों अशक्त, निर्बल और जन्म-रोगी होते हैं और करोड़ों ऐसे नीरोग और सबल नहीं होते जैसे होने चाहिए। अब इन सबको आप जोड़ डालिए तो आपको मालूम हो जाएगा कि माँ-बाप की नादानी के कारण सन्तति को कितनी हानि उठानी पड़ती है; कितना दुःख सहना पड़ता है।''

—शिक्षा, आचार्य महावीर प्रसाद द्विवेदी

1. इस गद्य खण्ड का उपयुक्त शीर्षक हो सकता है :
   A. स्वास्थ्य रक्षा
   B. माता-पिता और उनके बच्चों का स्वास्थ्य
   C. नीरोग रहने के उपाय
   D. स्वस्थ कैसे रहें?
2. आचार्य पं. महावीर प्रसाद द्विवेदी अपने समय के :
   A. श्रेष्ठ विद्वान् थे
   B. शीर्षस्थ समालोचक थे
   C. हिन्दी भाषा के प्रबल पक्षधर और आचार्य थे
   D. श्रेष्ठ आयुर्वेदाचार्य थे
3. हिन्दी के निबन्ध साहित्य के विकास में आचार्य द्विवेदी का स्थान :
   A. शीर्षस्थ था B. समालोचक जैसा था
   C. प्रवर्तक जैसा था D. उन्नायक जैसा था
4. आचार्य पं. महावीर प्रसाद द्विवेदी निम्नलिखित में से किस/किन पत्रिका/पत्रिकाओं के सम्पादक थे?
   A. साहित्य संदेश B. सरस्वती
   C. विशाल भारत D. उपर्युक्त तीनों
5. सन्तति का अर्थ होता है :
   A. पत्नी तथा पुत्र B. आत्मीय जन
   C. सम्बन्धी लोग D. औलाद (बाल-बच्चे)

अभ्यास 7

''अन्तिम क्षण थे, सर्वदा के लिए वियोग हो रहा था। देखती आँखों शाहजहाँ का सर्वस्व लूट रहा था और वह भारत सम्राट हताश हाथ-पर-हाथ धरे बेबस बैठा था और अपनी किस्मत को रो रहा था। सिंहासनारूढ़ हुए कोई तीन वर्ष भी नहीं बीते थे कि उसकी प्रियतमा इस लोक से विदा लेने की तैयारी कर रही थी। शाहजहाँ की सभी आशाओं पर, उसकी सारी उमंगों पर पाला पड़ रहा था।...''

''हाय अन्त हो गया, सर्वस्व लुट गया! प्रेमी, जीवन-यात्रा का एकमात्र साथी सर्वदा के लिए छोड़कर चल बसा। भारत सम्राट शाहजहाँ की प्रेयसी, साम्राज्ञी मुमताज महल सदा के लिए इस लोक से विदा हो गई। शाहजहाँ भारत का सम्राट था, जहान का शाह था, किन्तु वह भी अपनी प्रेयसी को जाने से रोक न सका।'' **—ताज, महाराज कुमार रघुबीर सिंह**

1. इस गद्यांश में अभिव्यक्ति के लिए प्रयुक्त शैली को हम क्या कहेंगे?
   A. विचार प्रधान शैली B. व्यास शैली
   C. भाव प्रवण शैली D. कल्पना प्रधान शैली
2. इस गद्यांश में व्यक्त विचार यह दर्शाते हैं कि कोई व्यक्ति कितना ही साधन-सम्पन्न, सक्षम तथा सबल क्यों न हो, किन्तु वह महाबली काल के समक्ष :
   A. एक भुनगा-सा होता है

B. अति तुच्छ होता है
C. किंकर्तव्यविमूढ़ हो जाता है
D. चुप हो जाता है

3. उक्त गद्यांश का सर्वाधिक उपयुक्त शीर्षक हो सकता है :
A. महाबली काल B. मुमताज की मृत्यु
C. शाहजहाँ की बेबसी D. प्रेयसी वियोग

4. उक्त गद्यांश में लेखक को शाहजहाँ की मन:स्थिति को चित्रित करने में :
A. बहुत कम सफलता मिली है
B. अत्यधिक सफलता मिली है
C. किंचित् सफलता मिली है
D. प्रशंसनीय सफलता मिली है

5. वियोग से तात्पर्य है:
A. वैमनस्य B. विलाप
C. मेल-मिलाप D. बिछुड़ना

अभ्यास 8

आचार्य शुक्ल जी के गंभीर निबंध 'चिंतामणि' में संग्रहीत हैं। उनमें दो प्रकार के निबंध हैं, एक तो भावों के विश्लेषण से सम्बन्ध रखने वाले निबंध जो भाव-विषयक होते हुए भी आवश्यक नहीं हैं वरन् उच्चकोटि के विचारात्मक हैं, दूसरे साहित्यिक जिनमें कुछ सैद्धांतिक आलोचना से संबंध रखते हैं, जैसे—'साधारणीकरण और व्यक्ति वैचित्र्यवाद' और कुछ व्यावहारिक आलोचनाओं के हैं, जैसे 'भारतेन्दु हरिश्चन्द्र'। आचार्य शुक्ल जी के मनोवैज्ञानिक निबंधों की भी अन्विति उनकी आलोचनाओं से की जा सकती है, वे भारतीय रस सिद्धान्त पर अवलम्बित हैं और उनका सम्बन्ध जीवन सागर के निजी अवगाहन से है। इन निबंधों के भावों का विश्लेषण पर्याप्त मात्रा में हुआ है किन्तु जीवन से चुने हुए उपयुक्त उदाहरणों के कारण यह विश्लेषण दुरूह नहीं होने पाया है। 'लज्जा और ग्लानि' का आधार भारत की आत्मग्लानि है, 'लोभ और प्रीति' का अन्तर समझ लेने पर जायसी के 'रत्नसेन' के प्रेम की आलोचना भली प्रकार समझी जा सकती है।

—काव्य के रूप, डॉ. गुलाब राय

1. उक्त गद्यांश का सम्यक् अनुशीलन करने से पता चलता है कि लेखक ने :
A. शुक्ल जी को समझने में काफी प्रयास किया था
B. शुक्ल जी के साहित्य का सम्यक् अध्ययन किया था
C. शुक्ल जी से दिशाबोध ग्रहण किया था
D. शुक्ल जी को समीप से देखा था

2. डॉ. गुलाब राय की शैली थी :
A. कथा शैली B. भावना प्रवण शैली
C. विवेचना प्रधान शैली D. विश्लेषणात्मक शैली

3. डॉ. गुलाब राय ने आचार्य शुक्ल की शैलियों का जो वर्गीकरण किया है वह :
A. अत्यन्त वैज्ञानिक है B. शोधपूर्ण है
C. सर्वांगीण है D. यथातथ्य है

4. उक्त गद्यांश के लिए उचित शीर्षक होगा :
A. आचार्य शुक्ल की निबंध-शैली
B. शुक्ल जी की निबंध-कला
C. निबंध कला और शुक्ल जी
D. हिन्दी के श्रेष्ठ निबंधकार शुक्ल जी

5. अन्विति का अर्थ है :
A. अनुरक्ति B. तालमेल
C. आलोचना D. अर्चना

अभ्यास 9

चीन में न तो वर्ण व्यवस्था थी न जाति-पाँति का भेदभाव। परम्परा के अनुसार सम्मान के मुख्य पात्र क्रमश: विद्वान्, राज्य पदाधिकारी, योद्धा और अध्यापक थे। साधारण लोगों में नौ श्रेणियाँ थीं। अन्न उत्पन्न करने वाले, माली, लकड़हारे, पशु-पक्षी पालने वाले, बुनकर, नौकर-चाकर, कारीगर, व्यापारी और फुटकर काम करने वाले। कुलीनों तथा साधारण लोगों में अथवा श्रेणियों और व्यवसायों में ऊँच-नीच का भेद कायम था। पर यह विभेद नगण्य-सा था। अपनी योग्यता के अनुसार मनुष्य का स्थान घटता-बढ़ता था। लोग आपस में विवाह आदि बिना किसी बाधा के करते थे। चीनियों में विद्वान् और सेनापति विशेष आदर के पात्र समझे जाते थे। हिजड़े, भाँड, गुलाम, हरकारे, वेश्याएँ नीचे के स्तर के लोग थे। चीन में गुलामों की दशा उतनी खराब नहीं थी जितनी रोम तथा यूरोप के देशों के मध्य युग में थी। गुलामों से घरेलू काम कराये जाते थे। उनकी विशेष जाति नहीं थी। उन्हें यद्यपि खरीदा-बेचा जा सकता था तथापि उनसे न तो नीच काम कराए जाते थे और न उन्हें सताया जाता था।

—विश्व इतिहास, डॉ. रामप्रसाद त्रिपाठी

1. उक्त उद्धरण के अध्ययन से पता चलता है कि मध्यकालीन चीन में :
A. जाति प्रथा प्रचलित थी
B. सामाजिक जीवन काफी समुन्नत था
C. सामाजिक जीवन वैभवपूर्ण था
D. वर्ण-व्यवस्था से रहित था

2. उक्त उद्धरण का उपयुक्त शीर्षक हो सकता है :
A. मध्यकालीन चीन का सामाजिक जीवन
B. मध्यकालीन चीन में सामाजिक व्यवस्था
C. चीनी समाज में विविधता
D. चीनी समाज में गिरावट

3. उक्त गद्य खण्ड का सारांश एक पंक्ति में इस प्रकार व्यक्त किया जा सकता है :
A. अन्य तत्कालीन समाजों की तुलना में मध्यकाल में चीन का सामाजिक जीवन समुन्नत था
B. चीन का मध्यकालीन समाज विकास के शिखर पर था
C. चीन मध्यकालीन राज्यों में अग्रणी था
D. मध्यकालीन चीन का सामाजिक जीवन विकासोन्मुख था

4. चीन के सामाजिक इतिहास का अनुशीलन करने से पता चलता है कि चीन में :
A. सामाजिक भेदभाव अवश्य था भले ही वहाँ वर्ण-व्यवस्था नहीं थी

B. समाज के सभी सदस्य एक-सा जीवन नहीं जीते थे
C. चीनी समाज गुलामों को उत्पीड़ित करता था
D. मध्यकालीन चीन में नागरिक सुविधाओं का अभाव था

5. चीन में विशेष आदर के पात्र समझे जाते थे :
A. हिजड़े और भाँड B. विद्वान् और वेश्याएँ
C. विद्वान् और सेनापति D. कारीगर और व्यापारी

अभ्यास 10

''मनुष्य जब नई-नई सच्चाइयों को देखता है तब वह अपना नैतिक कर्त्तव्य समझता है कि उनके अनुसार व्यवहार करे परन्तु ऐसे मौकों पर धर्म उसके रास्ते में रुकावट बनकर खड़ा होता रहा है। जब गैलीलियो ने इस बात का पता लगाया कि सूर्य पृथ्वी के इर्द-गिर्द नहीं घूमता, पृथ्वी सूर्य के गिर्द घूमती है, तो उसने अपना नैतिक कर्त्तव्य समझा कि सच्चाई को जाहिर करे। उसने जब इस सत्य को प्रकट किया तो धर्म के ठेकेदारों ने उसे जेल में डाल दिया, और उसे तब छोड़ा जब उसने कह दिया कि उसका विचार गलत था। संसार का इतिहास इस बात का साक्षी था कि धर्म सत्य को दबाता रहा है। रूढ़िवाद ने बुद्धिवाद का विरोध किया। इस दृष्टि से धर्म और विज्ञान की लड़ाई एक तरह से धर्म और नीति की लड़ाई है।''

—समाजशास्त्र के मूल तत्त्व, सत्यव्रत सिद्धान्तालंकार

1. ''धर्म और विज्ञान की लड़ाई, धर्म और नीति की लड़ाई है।'' इस कथन का आशय है :
A. धर्म ने सत्य को स्वीकार नहीं किया
B. धर्म और नीति ने मिलकर सत्य को दबाया
C. धर्म और नीति ने सत्य को स्वीकार नहीं किया
D. रूढ़िवाद ने बुद्धिवाद को नकारा

2. उक्त गद्यांश का आशय है :
A. धर्म और सत्य का सनातन संघर्ष
B. ज्ञान के रास्ते में धर्म बाधक
C. धर्म और नीति द्वारा विज्ञान की अवहेलना
D. विज्ञान द्वारा धर्म और नैतिकता का पर्दाफाश

3. इस गद्यांश का उपयुक्त शीर्षक हो सकता है :
A. धर्म और विज्ञान
B. धर्म और नैतिकता पर विज्ञान का प्रभाव
C. विज्ञान की लड़ाई
D. नैतिकता

4. समाजशास्त्र का अध्ययन आवश्यक है :
A. जीवन की सफलता के लिए
B. सामाजिक पुनर्निर्माण के लिए
C. सामाजिक सुव्यंवस्था के लिए
D. उपर्युक्त किसी के लिए नहीं

5. 'जाहिर' से अभिप्राय है :
A. प्रकाशित B. धूमिल
C. स्थापित D. उजागरीप्रकट

उत्तरमाला

अभ्यास-1

1	2	3	4	5
B	C	C	D	A

अभ्यास-2

1	2	3	4	5
B	B	A	B	D

अभ्यास-3

1	2	3	4	5	6	7
B	B	C	C	C	A	B

अभ्यास-4

1	2	3	4	5
A	B	A	B	A

अभ्यास-5

1	2	3	4	5
C	B	A	D	A

अभ्यास-6

1	2	3	4	5
B	C	C	B	D

अभ्यास-7

1	2	3	4	5
C	C	C	D	D

अभ्यास-8

1	2	3	4	5
B	C	D	A	B

अभ्यास-9

1	2	3	4	5
D	B	A	A	C

अभ्यास-10

1	2	3	4	5
D	B	A	B	D

★★★

MATHS

1

Rational Numbers

Rational Numbers

A rational number is defined as a rational number of the form $\frac{p}{q}$, where p and q are integers and $q \neq 0$.

The set of rational numbers encloses the set of integers and fractions. The rules given above for addition, subtraction, multiplication and division also apply on rational numbers.

Rational numbers that are not integral will have decimal values. These values can be of two types:

(a) Terminating (or Finite) Decimal Fractions:

For example : $\frac{17}{4} = 4.25$, $\frac{21}{5} = 4.2$ and so forth

(b) Non-terminating Decimal Fractions: Amongst non-terminating decimal fractions there are two types of decimal values:

(i) **Non-terminating Periodic Fractions:** These are non-terminating decimal fractions of the type $x.a_1a_2a_3...a_n\ a_1a_2a_3...a_n\ a_1a_2a_3...a_n$ written as $x.\overline{a_1 a_2 a_3...a_n}$

For example : $\frac{1}{3} = 0.3333 \ldots = 0.\overline{3}$

$\frac{16}{3} = 5.333 \ldots = 5.\overline{3}$ and so on.

(c) Non-terminating Non-periodic Fractions: These are the form $x.\ b_1b_2b_3...b_n\ c_1c_2c_3...\ c_n$

For example : 5.2731687143...

Pure Recurring Decimal : A decimal in which all the digits after the decimal point are repeated. For Example : $0.\overline{6}$, $0.\overline{16}$, ...$0.\overline{123}$.

Mixed Recurring Decimal : A decimal in which at least one of the digits after the decimal points is not repeated and then same digit and digits are repeated.

For example : $2.1\overline{6}$, $0.3\overline{5}$, $0.78\overline{5}$

Conversion of Pure Recurring of the form $\frac{p}{q}$:

Example 1: (i) $0.\overline{3}$, (ii) $0.\overline{35}$, (iii) $0.\overline{585}$

(i) Let $x = 0.\overline{3}$ Then,

$x = 0.3333...$ ...(i)

$10x = 3.3333...$ ...(ii)

On subtracting (i) from (ii), we get

$9x = 3$

$x = \frac{3}{9} = \frac{1}{3}$

$\Rightarrow 0.\overline{3} = \frac{1}{3}$ i.e., $0.333... = \frac{1}{3}$

(ii) Let $x = 0.\overline{35}$ Then,

$x = 0.353535...$ ...(i)

$100x = 35.3535...$ ...(ii)

On subtracting (i) from (ii), we get

$99x = 35$

$x = \frac{35}{99}$

$\therefore 0.\overline{35} = \frac{35}{99}$

(iii) Let $x = 0.\overline{585}$, Then

$x = 0.585\ 585\ 585$ ...(i)

$1000x = 585.585\ 585...$ ...(ii)

On subtracting (i) from (ii)

$999x = 585$

$x = \frac{585}{999}$

$\therefore\ 0.\overline{585} = \frac{585}{999}$.

Shortcut : Write down the bar digit in numerator of a fraction and write down the same number of digit 9 in denominator of the fraction. For example:

$0.\overline{3} = \frac{3}{9}$, $0.\overline{35} = \frac{35}{99}$, $0.\overline{585} = \frac{585}{999}$,

$2.\overline{3} = 2 + 0.\overline{3} = 2 + \frac{3}{9} = 2 + \frac{1}{3} = 2\frac{1}{3} = \frac{7}{3}$

$15.\overline{32} = 15 + 0.\overline{32} = 15 + \frac{32}{99} = 15\frac{32}{99}$

Conversion of Mixed Recurring Fraction into $\frac{p}{q}$ form :

$0.235\ 35\ 35 \ldots = 0.2\overline{35}$

Let $x = 0.2\overline{35}$

Then, $10x = 2.\overline{35}$

$10x = 2 + 0.\overline{35}$

$10x = 2 + \frac{35}{99}$

$10x = \frac{2 \times 99 + 35}{99} = \frac{198 + 35}{99}$

$10x = \frac{233}{99} \Rightarrow x = \frac{233}{990}$

(*ii*) $15.7\overline{12}$

Let $x = 15.7\overline{12}$

Then, $10x = 157.\overline{12}$

$10x = 157 + 0.\overline{12}$

$10x = 157 + \frac{12}{99}$

$10x = 157 + \frac{4}{33}$

$10x = \frac{157 \times 33 + 4}{33}$

$10x = \frac{5185}{33}$

$x = \frac{5185}{330}$

Irrational Numbers: A number is an irrational number, if it has a non-terminating and non-repeating decimal representation *i.e.*, irrational number can not be written in the form of $\frac{p}{q}$, where p and q are both integers and $q \neq 0$.

For example : $\sqrt{2}, \sqrt{3}$.

If a and b are two positive rational numbers such that ab is not a perfect square of a rational number then, $\sqrt{ab}$ is an irrational number lying between a and b. Also if a, b are rational numbers, then $\frac{a+b}{2}$ is a rational number between them.

Example 1 : Insert a rational and an irrational number between 2 and 3.

Sol. A rational Number between 2 and 3

$= \frac{2+3}{2} = 2.5$

An irrational Number between 2 and 3

$= \sqrt{2 \times 3} = \sqrt{6}$

Some useful results on Rational/Irrational Number

(*i*) $\sqrt{n}$ is rational number if n is a perfect square. For example, $\sqrt{4}, \sqrt{9}, \sqrt{16}$

(*ii*) Negative of an irrational number is an irrational number.

(*iii*) The sum of a rational number and an irrational number is an irrational number.

(*iv*) The product of a non-zero rational number and an irrational number is an irrational number.

(*v*) The sum, difference, product and quotient of two irrational number need not be an irrational number.

(*vi*) π is an irrational number.

(*vii*) Decimal expansion of a rational number is either terminating or non-terminating (recurring).

(*viii*) Decimal expansion of an irrational number is non-terminating non-recurring.

(*ix*) A real number is either rational or irrational number.

Comparison of Fraction

1. If the denominator of the fractions are same, the largest is one whose numerator is the largest.

   Example : Which is the largest fraction among $\frac{3}{8}, \frac{7}{8}$ and $\frac{5}{8}$?

   Solution: $\frac{7}{8}$

2. If the numerators of the fractions are same, the largest is one whose denominator is the smallest.

   Example : Which is the largest fraction among $\frac{5}{2}, \frac{5}{7}$ and $\frac{5}{9}$?

   Solution : $\frac{5}{2}$

3. If neither the numerators nor denominators of the fraction are same then they are converted into equivalent fractions of the same, denominator by taking the L.C.M. of the denominators of the given fractions. Then the fractions are compared according to (1).

   Example : Which is the largest fraction among $\frac{1}{2}, \frac{2}{3}, \frac{4}{5}$ and $\frac{5}{8}$.

   Solution : LCM of 2, 3, 5 and 8 = 120

   Then, $\frac{1}{2} = \frac{1 \times 60}{2 \times 60} = \frac{60}{120}$

   $\frac{2}{3} = \frac{2 \times 40}{3 \times 40} = \frac{80}{120}$

$$\frac{4}{5}=\frac{4\times 24}{5\times 24}=\frac{96}{120}$$

$$\frac{5}{8}=\frac{5\times 15}{8\times 15}=\frac{75}{120}$$

Largest fraction = $\frac{96}{120}$, that is $\frac{4}{5}$

4. Two fractions can also be compared by cross multiplication method.

Example : Which is greater $\frac{6}{13}$ or $\frac{5}{7}$?

Solution: Step 1 : Cross multiplying the two given fractions

$$\frac{6}{13} \times \frac{5}{7}$$

We get 6 × 7 = 42 and 13 × 5 = 65

Step 2 : Since 65 is greater than 42 and in 65, the numerator of $\frac{5}{7}$ is included.

$\therefore$ $\frac{5}{7}$ is greater than $\frac{6}{13}$.

5. If the difference of the numerator and denominator of each of the given fractions be same, then the fraction of the largest numerator is the largest.

Example : Which one of the following fractions is the largest $\frac{2}{3}, \frac{3}{4}, \frac{5}{6}$ and $\frac{9}{10}$?

Solution : Since in each of the given fractions the difference between the numerator and denominator is same and the largest numerator is 9. Therefore, the largest fraction is $\frac{9}{10}$.

Multiple Choice Questions

1. The decimal form of an irrational number is neither .... nor ....

A. terminating, repeating
B. terminating, non-repeating
C. non-terminating, non-repeating
D. non-terminating, repeating

2. π is a/an :

A. rational number
B. irrational number
C. neither rational nor irrational number
D. None of these

3. The decimal representation of a rational number is either .... or ....

A. terminating, recurring
B. non-terminating, non-recurring
C. terminating, non-terminating, recurring
D. None of these

4. Which one of the following statements is true?

A. The sum of two irrational numbers is always an irrational number.
B. The sum of two irrational numbers is always a rational number.
C. The sum of two irrational numbers may be a rational number or an irrational number.
D. The sum of two irrational numbers is always an integer.

5. Which of the following is a correct statement?

A. Sum of two irrational numbers is always irrational.
B. Sum of a rational and irrational number is always an irrational number.
C. Square of an irrational number is always a rational number.
D. Sum of two rational numbers can never be an integer.

6. Which of the following statements is true?

A. Product of two irrational numbers is always irrational.
B. Product of a rational and an irrational number is always irrational.
C. Sum of two irrational numbers can never be irrational.
D. Sum of an integer and a rational number can never be an integer.

7. Which of the following is irrational?

A. $\sqrt{\frac{4}{9}}$ B. $\frac{4}{5}$
C. $\sqrt{7}$ D. $\sqrt{81}$

8. Which of the following is irrational?

A. 0.14
B. $0.14\overline{16}$
C. $0.\overline{1416}$
D. 0.1014001400014

9. Which of the following is rational?

A. $\sqrt{3}$ B. π
C. $\frac{4}{0}$ D. $\frac{0}{4}$

10. The number 0.318564318564318564.... is:
A. a natural number
B. an integer
C. a rational number
D. an irrational number

11. If n is a natural number, then $\sqrt{n}$ is:
A. always a natural number
B. always an irrational number
C. always an irrational number
D. sometimes a natural number and sometimes an irrational number

12. Which of the following numbers can be represented as non-terminating, repeating decimals?
A. $\frac{39}{24}$ B. $\frac{3}{16}$
C. $\frac{3}{11}$ D. $\frac{137}{25}$

13. Every point on a number line represents:
A. a unique real number
B. a natural number
C. a rational number
D. an irrational number

14. An irrational number between 2 and 2.5 is:
A. $\sqrt{11}$ B. $\sqrt{5}$
C. $\sqrt{22.5}$ D. $\sqrt{12.5}$

15. Which of the following is irrational?
A. 0.15 B. 0.01516
C. $0.\overline{1516}$ D. 0.5015001500015

16. The number of consecutive zeros in $2^3 \times 3^4 \times 7$, is:
A. 3 B. 2
C. 4 D. 5

17. The number 1.27 in the form $\frac{p}{q}$, where p and q are integers and $q \neq 0$, is:
A. $\frac{14}{9}$ B. $\frac{14}{11}$
C. $\frac{14}{13}$ D. $\frac{14}{15}$

18. The number $0.\overline{3}$ in the form $\frac{p}{q}$, where p and q are integers and $q \neq 0$, is:
A. $\frac{33}{100}$ B. $\frac{3}{10}$
C. $\frac{1}{3}$ D. $\frac{3}{100}$

19. The smallest rational number by which $\frac{1}{3}$ should be multiplied so that its decimal expansion terminates after one place of decimal, is:
A. $\frac{1}{10}$ B. $\frac{3}{10}$
C. 3 D. 30

20. $0.3\overline{2}$ when expressed in the form $\frac{p}{q}$ (p, q are integers, $q \neq 0$), is:
A. $\frac{8}{25}$ B. $\frac{29}{90}$
C. $\frac{32}{99}$ D. $\frac{32}{199}$

21. $23.\overline{43}$ when expressed in the form $\frac{p}{q}$ (p, q are integers, $q \neq 0$), is:
A. $\frac{2320}{99}$ B. $\frac{2343}{100}$
C. $\frac{2343}{999}$ D. $\frac{2320}{199}$

22. $0.\overline{001}$ when expressed in the form $\frac{p}{q}$ (p, q are integers, $q \neq 0$), is:
A. $\frac{1}{1000}$ B. $\frac{1}{100}$
C. $\frac{1}{1999}$ D. $\frac{1}{999}$

23. The value of $0.\overline{23} + 0.\overline{22}$ is:
A. $0.\overline{45}$ B. $0.\overline{43}$
C. $0.\overline{42}$ D. 45

24. $5.\overline{23} + 6.\overline{33} - 3.\overline{11}$ = ?
A. 8.55 B. $7.\overline{45}$
C. $8.\overline{45}$ D. $9.\overline{25}$

25. If $\sqrt{12} = 3.464$, value of $\sqrt{\frac{3}{4}} + 2\sqrt{\frac{4}{3}}$ is:
A. 3.17
B. 3.464
C. 3.1753
D. None of these

ANSWERS

1	2	3	4	5	6	7	8	9	10
A	B	C	C	B	B	C	D	D	C
11	**12**	**13**	**14**	**15**	**16**	**17**	**18**	**19**	**20**
D	C	A	B	D	A	B	C	B	B
21	**22**	**23**	**24**	**25**					
A	D	A	C	C					

EXPLANATORY ANSWERS

7. $\sqrt{\frac{4}{9}} = \frac{2}{3}, \ \frac{p}{q}$ form $q \neq 0$ rational number

$\frac{4}{5}, \frac{p}{q}$ form, $q \neq 0$ rational number

$\sqrt{7}, \sqrt{7}$ is not an integer $\therefore$ Irrational number

$\sqrt{81} = \frac{9}{1}, \ \frac{p}{q}$ form, $q \neq 0$, rational number

10. 0.318564318564318 ....

$0.\overline{31854}$ (Recurring form)

$\therefore$ This is a rational number

14. An irrational number between 2 and 2.5 is

$= \sqrt{2 \times 2.5} = \sqrt{5}$

16. We get zero if 2 × 5 = 10

$\therefore \quad 2^3 \times 5^3 = 1000$

we get three zero.

17. $1.\overline{27} = 1 + 0.\overline{27} = 1 + \frac{27}{99} = 1 + \frac{3}{11} = \frac{14}{11}$

18. $0.\overline{3} = \frac{3}{9} = \frac{1}{3}$

20. $0.3\overline{2} = \frac{32-3}{90} = \frac{29}{90}$

21. $23.\overline{43} = 23 + 0.\overline{43} = 23 + \frac{43}{99}$

$= \frac{23 \times 99 + 43}{99} = \frac{2277 + 43}{99} = \frac{2320}{99}$

23. $0.\overline{23} + 0.\overline{22} = \frac{23}{99} + \frac{22}{99}$

$= \frac{23 + 22}{99} = \frac{45}{99} = 0.\overline{45}$

24. $5 + 0.\overline{23} + 6 + 0.\overline{33} - 3 - 0.\overline{11}$

$= 8 + 0.\overline{56} - 0.\overline{11} = 8 + 0.\overline{45} = 8.\overline{45}$

25. $\sqrt{\frac{3}{4}} + 2\sqrt{\frac{4}{3}} = \sqrt{\frac{9}{12}} + 2 \times \sqrt{\frac{12}{9}}$

$= \frac{3}{\sqrt{12}} + 2 \times \frac{\sqrt{12}}{3} = \frac{3}{3.464} + 2 \times \frac{3.464}{3}$

$= 0.8660 + 2.3093$

$= 3.1753$

□□□□□

2

Square and Square Root

☛ Points To Remember

- A number n is a perfect square number, if $n = m^2$
- A perfect square number is never negative.
- A square number never ends in 2, 3, 7 or 8.
- The number of zeros at the end of a perfect square is even.
- The square of an even number is even.
- The square of an odd number is odd.
- There are no natural number p and q such that $p^2 = 2q^2$.
- A number m is a square root of n, if $n = m \times m = m^2$. Positive square root of n is written as $\sqrt{n}$.
- If p and q are perfect squares ($q \neq 0$), then
  (i) $\sqrt{p \times q} = \sqrt{p} \times \sqrt{q}$
  (ii) $\sqrt{\dfrac{p}{q}} = \dfrac{\sqrt{p}}{\sqrt{q}}$
- A perfect squares leaves remainder 0 or 1 on division by 3.
  The following table gives the possible remainders for some other prime divisors.

Divisor	Possible Remainders
3	0, 1
5	0, 1, 4
7	0, 1, 2, 4
11	0, 1, 3, 4, 5, 9
13	0, 1, 3, 4, 9, 10, 12

- The unit's digit of the square of a natural number is the unit's digit of the square of the digit at unit's place of the given natural number.

Unit's digit of the number	Unit's digit of the square of the number
0	0
1 or 9	1
2 or 8	4
3 or 7	9
4 or 6	6
5	5

- For every natural number n,
  $(n + 1)^2 - n^2 = (n + 1) + n$
  e.g.; $9^2 - 8^2 = 9 + 8 = 17$
  $19^2 - 18^2 = 19 + 18 = 37$
- The square of a natural number n is equal to the sum of first n odd natural numbers.
  e.g.; $2^2 = 1 + 3$
  $4^2 = 1 + 3 + 5 + 7 = 16$
  n^2 = Sum of first n odd natural numbers.
- A triplet (m, n, p) of three natural numbers m, n and p is called a pythagorean triplet if $m^2 + n^2 = p^2$
- The square root of a perfect square number can be obtained by :
  (i) the prime factorization.
  (ii) the division method.
- If n is not a perfect square, then $\sqrt{n}$ is not a rational number.
- Squares of natural numbers having all digits 1 have a following pattern:

$$\begin{aligned}
1^2 &= 1\\
11^2 &= 1\,\mathbf{2}\,1\\
111^2 &= 1\,2\,\mathbf{3}\,2\,1\\
1111^2 &= 1\,2\,3\,\mathbf{4}\,3\,2\,1\\
11111^2 &= 1\,2\,3\,4\,\mathbf{5}\,4\,3\,2\,1\\
111111^2 &= 1\,2\,3\,4\,5\,\mathbf{6}\,5\,4\,3\,2\,1\\
&\vdots\\
111111111^2 &= 1\,2\,3\,4\,5\,6\,7\,8\,\mathbf{9}\,8\,7\,6\,5\,4\,3\,2\,1
\end{aligned}$$

In this pattern the sum of the digits of every number on the right hand side is a perfect square at given below:

$$\begin{aligned}
1 + 2 + 1 &= 4 = 2^2\\
1 + 2 + 3 + 2 + 1 &= 9 = 3^2\\
1 + 2 + 3 + 4 + 3 + 2 + 1 &= 16 = 4^2
\end{aligned}$$

....

$1 + 2 + 3 + 4 + 5 + 6 + 7 + 8 + 9 + 8 + 7 + 6 + 5 + 4 + 3 + 2 + 1 = 81 = 9^2$.

- Observe the following pattern

$$\begin{aligned}
11^2 &= 121\\
101^2 &= 10201\\
1001^2 &= 1002001\\
10001^2 &= 100020001
\end{aligned}$$

- Observe the following pattern

$$11^2 = 121$$
$$101^2 = 10201$$
$$10101^2 = 102030201$$
$$1010101^2 = 1020304030201$$
$$101010101^2 = 10203040504030201$$

- **Short Cut Method to find Squares Column Method**

Using $(a + b)^2 = a^2 + 2ab + b^2$.

Make three columns: What is square of 86

$a = 8, b = 6$

Step	Column I (a^2)	Column II $2ab$	Column III b^2
I	$(8)^2 = 64$	$2 \times 8 \times 6 = 96$	$(6)^2 = 36$
II	64	96 + 3 99	**6**
III	64 + 9 **73**	96 + 3 **9**9	3**6**

The bold digits give the required square $86^2 = 7396$.

Square Root

Square root of a given number is that number which is multiplied by itself is equal to the given number.

For example, square root of 81 is 9 because 92 = 9 × 9 = 81.

Methods of Finding the square root

(a) Prime Factorization Method

(i) Prime Factorization Method

(ii) Group the Factors in Paris

(iii) Take one number from each pair of factors and then multiply them together.

Example: Find the square root of 4761?

Solution: $4761 = \underbrace{23 \times 23} \times \underbrace{3 \times 3}$

$\therefore \sqrt{4761} = 23 \times 3 = 69.$

(b) Method of Division: This method is used when the number is large and the factors cannot be easily determined.

Example: Find the square root of 226576?

Solution:

	476
4	226516
	16
87	665
7	609
946	5676
6	5676
	×

$\sqrt[2]{226576} = 476.$

Multiple Choice Questions

1. $\sqrt{53824} = ?$

A. 202 B. 232
C. 242 D. 332

2. The value of $\sqrt{10+\sqrt{25+\sqrt{108+\sqrt{154+\sqrt{255}}}}}$ is:

A. 4 B. 6
C. 8 D. 10

3. Evaluate : $\sqrt{41-\sqrt{21+\sqrt{19-\sqrt{9}}}}$.

A. 3 B. 5
C. 6 D. 6.4

4. $\left(\frac{\sqrt{625}}{11} \times \frac{14}{\sqrt{25}} \times \frac{11}{\sqrt{196}}\right)$ is equal to:

A. 5 B. 6
C. 8 D. 11

5. If $x * y = x + y + \sqrt{xy}$, the value of 6*24 is:

A. 41 B. 42
C. 43 D. 44

6. $\sqrt{\frac{25}{81} - \frac{1}{9}} = ?$

A. $\frac{2}{3}$ B. $\frac{4}{9}$
C. $\frac{16}{81}$ D. $\frac{25}{81}$

7. The value of $\sqrt{0.01}+\sqrt{0.81}+\sqrt{1.21}+\sqrt{0.0009}$ is:

A. 2.03 B. 2.1
C. 2.11 D. 2.13

8. If $\sqrt{18225} = 135$, then the value of $\left(\sqrt{182.25}+\sqrt{1.8225}+\sqrt{0.018225}+\sqrt{0.00018225}\right)$ is:

A. 1.49985 B. 14.9985
C. 149.985 D. 1499.85

9. If $\sqrt{3^n} = 729$, then the value of n is:

A. 6 B. 8
C. 10 D. 12

10. If $\sqrt{1+\frac{x}{169}} = \frac{14}{13}$, then x is equal to:

A. 1 B. 13
C. 27 D. None of these

11. If $\sqrt{1+\frac{55}{729}} = 1+\frac{x}{27}$, then the value of x is:

A. 1 B. 3
C. 5 D. 7

12. The value of $\frac{\sqrt{80}-\sqrt{112}}{\sqrt{45}-\sqrt{63}}$ is:

A. $\frac{3}{4}$ B. $1\frac{1}{3}$
C. $1\frac{7}{9}$ D. $1\frac{3}{4}$

13. Given $\sqrt{2} = 1.414$. The value of $\sqrt{8}+2\sqrt{32}-3\sqrt{128}+4\sqrt{50}$ is:

A. 8.426 B. 8.484
C. 8.526 D. 8.876

14. $\sqrt{\frac{0.081\times0.324\times4.624}{1.5625\times0.0289\times72.9\times64}}$ is equal to:

A. 0.024 B. 0.24
C. 2.4 D. 24

15. The value of $\sqrt{\frac{(0.03)^2+(0.21)^2+(0.065)^2}{(0.003)^2+(0.021)^2+(0.0065)^2}}$ is:

A. 0.1 B. 10
C. 10^2 D. 10^3

16. The square root of $(7+3\sqrt{5})(7-3\sqrt{5})$ is:

A. $\sqrt{5}$ B. 2
C. 4 D. $3\sqrt{5}$

17. $\left(\sqrt{3}-\frac{1}{\sqrt{3}}\right)^2$ simplifies to:

A. $\frac{3}{4}$ B. $\frac{4}{\sqrt{3}}$
C. $\frac{4}{3}$ D. None of these

18. $\left(\sqrt{2}+\frac{1}{\sqrt{2}}\right)^2$ is equal to :

A. $2\frac{1}{2}$ B. $3\frac{1}{2}$
C. $4\frac{1}{2}$ D. $5\frac{1}{2}$

19. If $3a = 4b = 6c$ and $a + b + c = 27\sqrt{29}$, then $\sqrt{a^2+b^2+c^2}$ is:

A. $3\sqrt{29}$ B. 81
C. 87 D. None of these

20. The square root of $0.\bar{4}$ is:

A. $0.\bar{6}$ B. $0.\bar{7}$
C. $0.\bar{8}$ D. $0.\bar{9}$

21. Which one of the following numbers has rational square root?

A. 0.4 B. 0.09
C. 0.9 D. 0.025

22. The value of $\sqrt{0.4}$ is:

A. 0.02 B. 0.2
C. 0.51 D. 0.63

23. The greatest four-digit perfect square number is:

A. 9000 B. 9801
C. 9900 D. 9981

24. The least number of 4 digits which is a perfect square, is:

A. 1000 B. 1016
C. 1024 D. 1036

25. If $x = (7-4\sqrt{3})$, then the value of $\left(x+\frac{1}{x}\right)$ is:

A. $3\sqrt{3}$ B. $8\sqrt{3}$
C. 14 D. $14+8\sqrt{3}$

26. If $x = \frac{\sqrt{3}+1}{\sqrt{3}-1}$ and $y = \frac{\sqrt{3}-1}{\sqrt{3}+1}$, then the value of $(x^2 + y^2)$ is:

A. 10 B. 13
C. 14 D. 15

27. If $a = \frac{\sqrt{5}+1}{\sqrt{5}-1}$ and $b = \frac{\sqrt{5}-1}{\sqrt{5}+1}$, the value of $\left(\frac{a^2+ab+b^2}{a^2-ab+b^2}\right)$ is:

A. $\frac{3}{4}$ B. $\frac{4}{3}$
C. $\frac{3}{5}$ D. $\frac{5}{3}$

28. The least number by which 294 must be multiplied to make it a perfect square, is:

A. 2 B. 3
C. 6 D. 24

29. What is the smallest number by which 5808 should be multiplied so that the product becomes a perfect square?

A. 2 B. 3
C. 7 D. 11

30. The least number by which 1470 must be divided to get a number which is a perfect square, is:

A. 5 B. 6
C. 15 D. 30

31. What is the least number which should be subtracted from 549162 in order to make it a perfect square?

A. 28 B. 36
C. 62 D. 81

32. If $\sqrt{\left(1+\frac{27}{169}\right)}=1+\frac{x}{13}$, then x equals:

A. 1 B. 3
C. 5 D. 7

33. $\sqrt{3\sqrt{3\sqrt{3\sqrt{3\sqrt{3\sqrt{3}}}}}}=?$

A. $3^{\frac{31}{64}}$ B. $3^{\frac{31}{32}}$
C. $3^{\frac{1}{64}}$ D. None of these

34. $\sqrt{248+\sqrt{52+\sqrt{144}}}=?$

A. 14 B. 16
C. 16.6 D. 18.8

35. Given that $\sqrt{4096}=64$, the value of $\sqrt{4096}+\sqrt{40.96}+\sqrt{.004096}$ is:

A. 70.4 B. 70.464
C. 71.104 D. 71.4

36. If $\sqrt{0.03\times0.3\times a}=0.03\times0.3\times\sqrt{b}$, then the value of $\frac{a}{b}$ is:

A. 0.009 B. 0.03
C. 0.09 D. None of these

37. If $\sqrt{1+\sqrt{1-\frac{2176}{2401}}}=1+\frac{x}{7}$, then the value of x is:

A. 3 B. 1
C. 5 D. 7

38. If $a=\frac{\sqrt{5}+1}{\sqrt{5}-1}$ and $b=\frac{\sqrt{5}-1}{\sqrt{5}+1}$; then the value of $\frac{a^2+ab+b^2}{a^2-ab+b^2}$ is:

A. $\frac{3}{4}$ B. $\frac{4}{3}$
C. $\frac{3}{5}$ D. $\frac{5}{3}$

39. The smallest number by which 3600 must be multiplied to make if perfect cube, is:

A. 40 B. 60
C. 20 D. 15

40. If $\sqrt{12}=3.464$, then the value of $\sqrt{\frac{3}{4}}+2\sqrt{\frac{4}{3}}$ is:

A. 3.17 B. 3.464
C. 3.1753 D. None of these

ANSWERS

1	2	3	4	5	6	7	8	9	10
B	A	C	A	B	B	D	B	D	C
11	**12**	**13**	**14**	**15**	**16**	**17**	**18**	**19**	**20**
A	B	B	A	B	B	C	C	C	A
21	**22**	**23**	**24**	**25**	**26**	**27**	**28**	**29**	**30**
B	D	B	C	C	C	B	C	B	D
31	**32**	**33**	**34**	**35**	**36**	**37**	**38**	**39**	**40**
D	A	B	B	B	A	B	B	B	C

EXPLANATORY ANSWERS

1.

```
  2 | 53824 (232
    | 4
 43 | 138
    | 129
462 |  924
    |  924
    |   ×
```

$\therefore\ \sqrt{53824}=232.$

2. Given exp. $=\sqrt{10+\sqrt{25+\sqrt{108+\sqrt{154+15}}}}$

$=\sqrt{10+\sqrt{25+\sqrt{108+\sqrt{169}}}}$

$=\sqrt{10+\sqrt{25+\sqrt{108+13}}}=\sqrt{10+\sqrt{25+\sqrt{121}}}$

$=\sqrt{10+\sqrt{25+11}}=\sqrt{10+\sqrt{36}}$

$=\sqrt{10+6}=\sqrt{16}=4$

3. Given exp. = $\sqrt{41-\sqrt{21+\sqrt{19-3}}}$

$= \sqrt{41-\sqrt{21+\sqrt{16}}} = \sqrt{41-\sqrt{21+4}}$

$= \sqrt{41-\sqrt{25}} = \sqrt{41-5} = \sqrt{36} = 6$

4. Given exp. = $\frac{25}{11} \times \frac{14}{5} \times \frac{11}{14} = 5$

5. $6*24 = 6 + 24 + \sqrt{6 \times 24} = 30 + \sqrt{144} = 30 + 12 = 42$

6. $\sqrt{\frac{25}{81} - \frac{1}{9}} = \sqrt{\frac{25-9}{81}} = \sqrt{\frac{16}{81}} = \frac{\sqrt{16}}{\sqrt{81}} = \frac{4}{9}$

7. Given exp. = $\sqrt{\frac{1}{100}} + \sqrt{\frac{81}{100}} + \sqrt{\frac{121}{100}} + \sqrt{\frac{9}{10000}}$

$= \frac{1}{10} + \frac{9}{10} + \frac{11}{10} + \frac{3}{100}$

$= 0.1 + 0.9 + 1.1 + 0.03 = 2.13$

8. Given exp. = $\sqrt{\frac{18225}{10^2}} + \sqrt{\frac{18225}{10^4}} + \sqrt{\frac{18225}{10^6}} + \sqrt{\frac{18225}{10^8}}$

$= \sqrt{\frac{18225}{10}} + \sqrt{\frac{18225}{10^2}} + \sqrt{\frac{18225}{10^3}} + \sqrt{\frac{18225}{10^4}}$

$= \frac{135}{10} + \frac{135}{100} + \frac{135}{1000} + \frac{135}{10000}$

$= 13.5 + 1.35 - 0.135 + 0.0135 = 14.9985$

9. $\sqrt{3^n} = 729 = 3^6 \Leftrightarrow \left(\sqrt{3^n}\right)^2 = (3^6)^2$

$\Leftrightarrow 3^n = 3^{12} \Leftrightarrow n = 12$

10. $\sqrt{1+\frac{x}{169}} = \frac{14}{13} \Rightarrow 1 + \frac{x}{169} = \frac{196}{169}$

$\Rightarrow \frac{x}{169} = \left(\frac{196}{169} - 1\right) = \frac{27}{169} \Rightarrow x = 27.$

11. $\sqrt{1+\frac{55}{729}} = 1 + \frac{x}{27} \Rightarrow \sqrt{\frac{784}{729}} = \frac{27+x}{27}$

$\Rightarrow \frac{28}{27} = \frac{27+x}{27} \Rightarrow 27 + x = 28 \Rightarrow x = 1$

12. $\frac{\sqrt{80}-\sqrt{112}}{\sqrt{45}-\sqrt{63}} = \frac{\sqrt{16\times5}-\sqrt{16\times7}}{\sqrt{9\times5}-\sqrt{9\times7}}$

$= \frac{4\sqrt{5}-4\sqrt{7}}{3\sqrt{5}-3\sqrt{7}} = \frac{4\left(\sqrt{5}-\sqrt{7}\right)}{3\left(\sqrt{5}-\sqrt{7}\right)} = \frac{4}{3} = 1\frac{1}{3}$

13. Given exp. = $\sqrt{4\times2} + 2\sqrt{16\times2} - 3\sqrt{64\times2} + 4\sqrt{25\times2}$

$= 2\sqrt{2} + 8\sqrt{2} - 24\sqrt{2} + 20\sqrt{2}$

$= 6\sqrt{2} = 6 \times 1.414 = 8.484$

14. Given exp. = $\sqrt{\frac{81\times324\times4624}{15625\times289\times729\times64}}$

$= \frac{9\times18\times68}{125\times17\times27\times8} = \frac{3}{125} = 0.024$

15. Given exp. = $\sqrt{\frac{(0.03)^2+(0.21)^2+(0.065)^2}{\left(\frac{0.03}{10}\right)^2+\left(\frac{0.21}{10}\right)^2+\left(\frac{0.065}{10}\right)^2}}$

$= \sqrt{\frac{100\ [(0.03)^2+(0.21)^2+(0.065)^2}{(0.03)^2+(0.21)^2+(0.065)^2}}$

$= \sqrt{100} = 10$

16. $\sqrt{(7+3\sqrt{5})(7-3\sqrt{5})} = \sqrt{(7)^2-(3\sqrt{5})^2}$

$= \sqrt{49-45} = \sqrt{4} = 2$

17. $\left(\sqrt{3}-\frac{1}{\sqrt{3}}\right)^2 = \left(\sqrt{3}\right)^2 + \left(\frac{1}{\sqrt{3}}\right)^2 - 2\times\sqrt{3}\times\frac{1}{\sqrt{3}}$

$= 3 + \frac{1}{3} - 2 = 1 + \frac{1}{3} = \frac{4}{3}$

18. $\left(\sqrt{2}+\frac{1}{\sqrt{2}}\right)^2 = \left(\sqrt{2}\right)^2 + \left(\frac{1}{\sqrt{2}}\right)^2 + 2\times\sqrt{2}\times\frac{1}{\sqrt{2}}$

$= 2 + \frac{1}{2} + 2 = 4 + \frac{1}{2} = 4\frac{1}{2}$

19. $4b = 6c \Rightarrow b = \frac{3}{2}c$ and $3a = 4b$

$\Rightarrow \quad a = \frac{4}{3}b = \frac{4}{3}\left(\frac{3}{2}c\right) = 2c$

$a + b + c = 27\sqrt{29}$

$2c + \frac{3}{2}c + c = 27\sqrt{29}$

$\Rightarrow \quad \frac{9}{2}c = 27\sqrt{29} \Rightarrow c = 6\sqrt{29}$

$\therefore \sqrt{a^2+b^2+c^2} = \sqrt{(a+b+c)-2(ab+bc+ca)}$

$= \sqrt{\left(27\sqrt{29}\right)^2 - 2\left(2c\times\frac{3}{2}c + \frac{3}{2}c\times c + c\times2c\right)}$

$= \sqrt{(729\times29) - 2\left(3c^2 + \frac{3}{2}c^2 + 2c^2\right)}$

$= \sqrt{(729\times29) - 2\times\frac{13}{2}c^2}$

$= \sqrt{(729\times29) - 13\times\left(6\sqrt{29}\right)^2}$

$$= \sqrt{29(729-468)}$$
$$= \sqrt{29 \times 261} = \sqrt{29 \times 29 \times 9} = 29 \times 3 = 87$$

20. $\sqrt{0.\bar{4}} = \sqrt{\frac{4}{9}} = \frac{2}{3} = 0.666.... = 0.\bar{6}$.

21. $\sqrt{0.09} = \sqrt{\frac{9}{100}} = \frac{3}{10} = 0.3$, which is rational.

$\therefore$ 0.09 has rational square root.

22.

```
  6 | 0.400000 (0.63
    | 36
123 |  400
    |  369
```

23. Greatest number of four digits is 9999.

```
  9 | 9999 (99
    | 81
189 | 1899
    | 1701
    |  198
```

$\therefore$ Required number = (9999 − 198) = 9801.

24. Least number of 4 digits is 1000.

```
  3 | 1000 (31
    | 9
 61 | 100
    |  61
    |  39
```

$\therefore (31)^2 < 1000 < (32)^2$.

Hence, required number $= (32)^2 = 1024$.

25. $x + \frac{1}{x} = (7-4\sqrt{3}) + \frac{1}{(7-4\sqrt{3})} \times \frac{(7+4\sqrt{3})}{(7+4\sqrt{3})}$

$$= (7-4\sqrt{3}) + \frac{(7+4\sqrt{3})}{(49-48)}$$
$$= (7-4\sqrt{3}) + (7+4\sqrt{3}) = 14$$

26. $x = \frac{(\sqrt{3}+1)}{(\sqrt{3}-1)} \times \frac{(\sqrt{3}+1)}{(\sqrt{3}+1)} = \frac{(\sqrt{3}+1)^2}{(3-1)}$

$$= \frac{3+1+2\sqrt{3}}{2} = 2+\sqrt{3}$$

$$y = \frac{(\sqrt{3}-1)}{(\sqrt{3}+1)} \times \frac{(\sqrt{3}-1)}{(\sqrt{3}-1)} = \frac{(\sqrt{3}-1)^2}{(3-1)}$$

$$= \frac{3+1-2\sqrt{3}}{2} = 2-\sqrt{3}$$

$$\therefore x^2 + y^2 = (2+\sqrt{3})^2 + (2-\sqrt{3})^2$$
$$= 2(4+3) = 2 \times 7 = 14$$

27. $a = \frac{(\sqrt{5}+1)}{(\sqrt{5}-1)} \times \frac{(\sqrt{5}+1)}{(\sqrt{5}+1)} = \frac{(\sqrt{5}+1)^2}{(5-1)}$

$$= \frac{5+1+2\sqrt{5}}{4} = \left(\frac{3+\sqrt{5}}{2}\right)$$

$$b = \frac{(\sqrt{5}-1)}{(\sqrt{5}+1)} \times \frac{(\sqrt{5}-1)}{(\sqrt{5}-1)} = \frac{(\sqrt{5}-1)^2}{(5-1)}$$

$$= \frac{5+1-2\sqrt{5}}{4} = \left(\frac{3-\sqrt{5}}{2}\right)$$

$$\therefore a^2 + b^2 = \frac{(3+\sqrt{5})^2}{4} + \frac{(3-\sqrt{5})^2}{4}$$

$$= \frac{(3+\sqrt{5})^2 + (3-\sqrt{5})^2}{4}$$

$$= \frac{2(9+5)}{4} = 7$$

Also, $ab = \frac{(3+\sqrt{5})}{2} \cdot \frac{(3-\sqrt{5})}{2} = \frac{(9-5)}{4} = 1.$

$$\therefore \frac{a^2+ab+b^2}{a^2-ab+b^2} = \frac{(a^2+b^2)+ab}{(a^2+b^2)-ab}$$

$$= \frac{7+1}{7-1} = \frac{8}{6} = \frac{4}{3}$$

28. 294 = 7 × 7 × 2 × 3.

To make it a perfect square, it must be multiplied by 2 × 3 *i.e.*, 6.

$\therefore$ Required number = 6.

29. 5808 = 2 × 2 × 2 × 2 × 3 × 11 × 11

$= 2^2 \times 2^2 \times 3 \times 11^2$

To make it a perfect square, it must be multiplied by 3.

30. 1470 = 7 × 7 × 5 × 6. To make it a perfect square, it must be divided by 5 × 6, *i.e.*, 30.

31.

```
   7 | 549162 (741
     | 49
 144 |  591
     |  576
1481 |   1562
     |   1481
     |     81
```

$\therefore$ Required number to be subtracted = 81.

32. $\sqrt{1+\frac{27}{169}} = 1 + \frac{x}{13}$

$$\sqrt{\frac{196}{169}} = \frac{13+x}{13}$$

$$\frac{14}{13} = \frac{13+x}{13}$$
$$14 = 13 + x$$
$$\therefore \quad x = 1$$

33. $\sqrt{3\sqrt{3\sqrt{3\sqrt{3.3^{\frac{1}{2}}}}}} = \sqrt{3\sqrt{3\sqrt{3.3^{\frac{3}{4}}}}} = \sqrt{3\sqrt{3.3^{\frac{7}{8}}}}$

$$= \sqrt{3.3^{\frac{15}{16}}} = 3^{\frac{31}{32}}$$

34. $\sqrt{248+\sqrt{52+12}} = \sqrt{248+\sqrt{64}}$

$$= \sqrt{248+8} = \sqrt{256} = 16$$

35. $\sqrt{4096}+\sqrt{\frac{4096}{100}}+\sqrt{\frac{4096}{1000000}}$

$$= 64 = \frac{64}{10}+\frac{64}{1000}$$
$$= 64 + 6.4 + 0.064$$
$$= 70.464$$

36. $\sqrt{0.03\times 0.3\times a} = 0.03\times 0.3\times \sqrt{b}$

Taking square of both sides, we get

$0.03 \times 0.3 \times a = 0.03 \times 0.3 \times 0.03 \times 0.3 \times b$

$$\frac{a}{b} = \frac{0.03\times 0.3}{1} = 0.009$$

37. We have,

$$\sqrt{1+\sqrt{\frac{225}{2401}}} = 1+\frac{x}{7}$$
$$\sqrt{1+\frac{15}{49}} = 1+\frac{x}{7}$$
$$\sqrt{\frac{64}{49}} = 1+\frac{x}{7}$$
$$\frac{8}{7} = 1+\frac{x}{7}$$
$$1+\frac{1}{7} = 1+\frac{x}{7}$$
$$\therefore \quad x = 1$$

38. $a + b = \frac{\sqrt{5}+1}{\sqrt{5}-1}+\frac{\sqrt{5}-1}{\sqrt{5}+1}$

$$= \frac{(\sqrt{5}+1)^2+(\sqrt{5}-1)^2}{(\sqrt{5})^2-(1)^2}$$
$$\therefore \quad = \frac{2(\sqrt{5})^2+(1)^2}{5-1} = \frac{6}{2} = 3$$
$$ab = \frac{\sqrt{5}+1}{\sqrt{5}-1}\times\frac{\sqrt{5}-1}{\sqrt{5}+1} = 1$$
$$\frac{a^2+ab+b^2}{a^2-ab+b^2} = \frac{(a+b)^2-2ab+ab}{(a+b)^2-2ab-ab}$$
$$= \frac{(a+b)^2-ab}{(a+b)^2-3ab}$$
$$= \frac{(3)^2-1}{(3)^2-3\times 1} = \frac{9-1}{9-3} = \frac{8}{6} = \frac{4}{3}$$

39.

3	3600
3	1200
2	400
2	200
2	100
2	50
5	25
5	5
5	1

$$3600 = 3 \times 3 \times 2 \times 2 \times 2 \times 2 \times 5 \times 5$$
$$= 3 \times 2 \times 2 \times 5$$
$$= 60$$

40. $\sqrt{\frac{3}{4}}+2\sqrt{\frac{4}{3}} = \sqrt{\frac{12}{16}}+2\sqrt{\frac{12}{9}}$

$$= \frac{\sqrt{12}}{4}+2\times\frac{\sqrt{12}}{3}$$
$$= \frac{3.464}{4}+2\times\frac{3.464}{3}$$
$$= 0.866 + 2.3093$$
$$= 3.1753$$

□□□□□

3

Cubes and Cube Roots

☛ Points To Remember

- If n is a perfect cube and $n = m^3$, then m is a cube root of n. A cube root of n is written as $\sqrt[3]{n}$ or $(n)^{1/3}$.
- The cube root of a perfect cube can be obtained by prime factorization of the number.
- The cube root of a product of two perfect cubes is the product of the cube roots of the perfect cubes *i.e.,*

  $\sqrt[3]{ab} = \sqrt[3]{a} \cdot \sqrt[3]{b}$
- The cube root of a Quotient of two perfect cubes is the quotient of their cube roots *i.e.,*

  $\sqrt[3]{\frac{a}{b}} = \frac{\sqrt[3]{a}}{\sqrt[3]{b}}$, $b \neq 0$, where a and b are perfect cubes.
- The cube root of a negative perfect cube is negative.

Number m	Perfect cubes m^3	Cube roots $\sqrt[3]{m^3}$
1	1	1
2	8	2
3	27	3
4	64	4
5	125	5
6	216	6
7	343	7
8	512	8
9	729	9
10	1000	10

Cube Root

The cube root of a given number is that number which when raised to the third power produces the given number, that is the cube root of a number x is the number whose cube is x.

The cube root of x is written as $\sqrt[3]{x}$

For example, cube root of 64 is 4 as $4 \times 4 \times 4 = 64$.

Method to find Cube Root

Method of Factorisation

(1) Write a given number as product of prime factors.

(2) Take the product of prime numbers; choosing one out of three of each type.

This product gives the cube root of the given number.

Example: Find the cube root of 42875.

Solution: Resolving 42875 into prime factors, we get

$$42875 = \underbrace{5 \times 5 \times 5}\times\underbrace{7 \times 7 \times 7}$$

$$\therefore \quad \sqrt[3]{4287} = 5 \times 7 = 35.$$

Multiple Choice Questions

1. What is the cube root of 2197?

A. 13 B. 15
C. 17 D. 19

2. What is the cube root of 117649?

A. 39 B. 49
C. 59 D. 65

3. What is the cube root of $\frac{343}{125}$?

A. $\frac{5}{7}$ B. $\frac{9}{11}$
C. $\frac{7}{5}$ D. $\frac{9}{5}$

4. What is the cube root of $-\frac{2197}{1331}$?

A. $-\frac{13}{11}$ B. $-\frac{13}{9}$
C. $-\frac{11}{13}$ D. $-\frac{13}{17}$

5. What is the unit digits of the cube root of 226981?

A. 1 B. 9
C. 6 D. 8

6. What is the unit digits of the cube root of 175616?

A. 2 B. 4
C. 6 D. 8

7. What is the smallest number by which 392 must be multiplied so that the product is a perfect cube?

A. 2 B. 5
C. 7 D. 9

8. What is the smallest number by which 3087 must be divided so that the quotient is a perfect cube?

A. 7 B. 9
C. 11 D. 13

9. What is the value of following expression $= [(5^2 + 12^2)^{1/2}]^3$

A. 2197 B. 14615
C. 15620 D. 16625

10. $[(6^2 + 8^2)^{1/2}]^3$

A. 4812 B. 1000
C. 5913 D. 4313

11. $\sqrt[3]{0.1 \times 0.1 \times 0.1 \times 13 \times 13 \times 13}$

A. 1.4 B. 1.2
C. 1.3 D. 1.7

12. $\sqrt[3]{\frac{0.027}{0.008}} \sqrt[3]{\frac{0.09}{0.04}} - 1$

A. −1 B. −2
C. −3 D. 1

13. Three numbers are in the ratio 1 : 2 : 3. The sum of their cubes is 98784. What is the smallest number?

A. 12 B. 14
C. 16 D. 18

14. What is the volume of a cube whose surface area is 150 m^2?

A. 120 m^3 B. 122 m^3
C. 125 m^3 D. 135 m^3

15. The volume of a cube is 9261000 m^3. What is the side of the cube?

A. 210 m B. 220 m
C. 230 m D. 245 m

16. if $\sqrt[3]{3^n} = 729$, then value of n is:

A. 16 B. 18
C. 20 D. 22

17. The cube root of .000216 is:

A. .6 B. .06
C. .006 D. None of these

18. $\sqrt[3]{4\frac{12}{125}} = ?$

A. $1\frac{2}{5}$ B. $1\frac{3}{5}$
C. $1\frac{4}{5}$ D. $2\frac{2}{5}$

19. $\sqrt[3]{\sqrt{.000064}} = ?$

A. .02 B. .2
C. 2 D. None of these

20. The largest four-digit number which is a perfect cube, is:

A. 8000 B. 9261
C. 9999 D. None of these

21. By what least number 675 be multiplied to obtain a number which is a perfect cube?

A. 5 B. 6
C. 7 D. 8

22. What is the smallest number by which 3600 be divided to make it a perfect cube?

A. 9 B. 50
C. 300 D. 450

23. $\sqrt[3]{0.000216}$ is equal to:

A. 0.0006 B. 0.006
C. 0.06 D. 0.6

24. If $1^3 + 2^3 + 3^3 + ... + 10^3 = 3025$, then the value of $2^3 + 4^3 + 6^3 + ... + 20^3$ is equal to:

A. 6050 B. 9075
C. 12100 D. 24200

25. $\sqrt[3]{333 + \sqrt[3]{987 + \sqrt[3]{2197}}}$

A. 21 B. 18
C. 7 D. 3

ANSWERS

1	2	3	4	5	6	7	8	9	10
A	B	C	A	A	C	C	B	A	B
11	**12**	**13**	**14**	**15**	**16**	**17**	**18**	**19**	**20**
C	A	B	C	A	B	B	B	B	B
21	**22**	**23**	**24**	**25**					
A	D	C	A	C					

EXPLANATORY ANSWERS

1. $(2197)^{1/3} = (13 \times 13 \times 13)^{1/3}$

$= [(13)^3]^{1/3} = (13)^{3 \times 1/3}$

13	2197
13	169
13	13
	1

$= 13.$

Other Method: 2197, here unit digit is 7. Unit digit is cube root of 3, after striking out the last three digit from the right, the number is 2. 1 is the largest number whose cube is less than 2. The required cube root is 13.

2. $(117649)^{1/3} = 49$

3. $\sqrt[3]{\frac{343}{125}} = \sqrt[3]{\frac{7 \times 7 \times 7}{5 \times 5 \times 5}} = \frac{7}{5}$

4. $-\sqrt[3]{\frac{2197}{1331}} = -\sqrt[3]{\frac{13 \times 13 \times 13}{11 \times 11 \times 11}}$

13	2197
13	169
13	13
	1

$= -\frac{13}{11}$

5. Unit digit of 226981 is

$(1)^3 = 1$

6. Unit digit of 175616 is

$(6)^3 = 6$

7. Resolving 392 into prime factor.

$392 = 2 \times 2 \times 2 \times 7 \times 7$

2	392
2	196
2	98
7	49
7	7
	1

For perfect cube, given number must be multiplied by 7.

8. Resolving 3087 into prime factor

$3087 = 7 \times 7 \times 7 \times 3 \times 3$

3	3087
3	1029
7	343
7	49
7	7
	1

For perfect cube given number must divided by $3 \times 3 = 9$.

9. $\left[(5^2 + 12^2)^{1/2}\right]^3 = \left[(25 + 144)^{1/2}\right]^3$

$= \left[(169)^{1/2}\right]^3$

$= \left[(13)^{1/2}\right]^3$

$= (13)^3 = 2197$

10. $\left[(6^2 + 8^2)^{1/2}\right]^3 = \left[(36 + 64)^{1/2}\right]^3$

$= \left[(100)^{1/2}\right]^3 = (10)^3$

$= 1000.$

11. $\sqrt[3]{0.1 \times 0.1 \times 0.1 \times 13 \times 13 \times 13}$

$= 0.1 \times 13 = 1.3.$

12. $\sqrt[3]{\frac{0.027}{0.008}} = \sqrt[3]{\frac{27}{8}} = \sqrt[3]{\frac{3 \times 3 \times 3}{2 \times 2 \times 2}} = \frac{3}{2}$

$\sqrt{\frac{.09}{.04}} = \sqrt{\frac{9}{4}} = \frac{3}{2}.$

Required expression

$\frac{3}{2} - \frac{3}{2} - 1 = -1$

13. Let the number be

x^3, $2x^3$ and $3x^3$.

According to question

$x^3 + (2x)^3 + (3x)^3 = 98784$

$x^3 + 8x^3 + 27x^3 = 98784$

$36x^3 = 98784$

$x^3 = \frac{98784}{36} = 2744$

$x = (2744)^{1/3}$

$= (14^3)^{1/3} = 14.$

Smallest number = 14.

14. Surface area of cube $= 150\ m^2$.

$6l^2 = 150$

$$l^2 = \frac{150}{6} = 25$$

$$l = \sqrt{25} = 5.$$

Volume of cube $= l^3 = 5^3$

$= 125\ m^3$

15. Volume of a cube $= 9261000\ m^3$

$l^3 = 9261000$

$= 210^3$

$l = (210^3)^{1/3}$

$= 210\ m$

16. $(3)^{n/3} = (3)^6$

$\frac{n}{3} = 6$

$n = 18$

17. $(.000216)^{1/3} = \left(\frac{216}{10^6}\right)^{1/3} = \left(\frac{6 \times 6 \times 6}{10^2 \times 10^2 \times 10^2}\right)^{1/3}$

$= \frac{6}{10^2} = \frac{6}{100} = .06$

18. $\sqrt[3]{4\frac{12}{125}} = \sqrt[3]{\frac{512}{125}} = \left(\frac{8 \times 8 \times 8}{5 \times 5 \times 5}\right)^{1/3} = \frac{8}{5} = 1\frac{3}{5}$.

19. $\sqrt{.000064} = \sqrt{\frac{64}{10^6}} = \frac{8}{10^3} = \frac{8}{1000} = .008$

$\therefore \sqrt[3]{\sqrt{.000064}} = \sqrt[3]{.008} = \sqrt[3]{\frac{8}{1000}} = \frac{2}{10} = 0.2$

20. Clearly, 9261 is a perfect cube satisfying the given property.

21. $675 = 5 \times 5 \times 3 \times 3 \times 3$.

To make it a perfect cube, it must be multiplied by 5.

22. $3600 = 2^3 \times 5^2 \times 3^2 \times 2$.

To make it a perfect cube, it must be divided by $5^2 \times 3^2 \times 2$ *i.e.*, 450.

23. $\sqrt[3]{\frac{216}{1000000}} = \frac{6}{100} = 0.06$

24. $2^3 + 4^3 + 6^3 + ... + 20^3$

$= 2(1^3 + 2^3 + 3^3 + ... + 10^3$

$= 2 \times 3025 = 6050$

25. $\sqrt[3]{333 + \sqrt[3]{987 + \sqrt[3]{(13)^3}}}$

$= \sqrt[3]{333 + \sqrt[3]{987 + 13}} = \sqrt[3]{333 + \sqrt[3]{1000}}$

$= \sqrt[3]{333 + 10} = \sqrt[3]{343} = 7$

□□□□□

4

Exponents and Powers

☛ Points To Remember

- If n is a positive integer and a is a rational number, then $a^n = a \times a \times a \times ... \times a$ (n times)

  a^n is called the nth power of a. The rational number a is called **base** and n is called **Index** or **exponent** of the nth power of a.
- If $a^n = x$ then

  $a = (x)^{1/n}$.

  $(x)^{1/n}$ is also written in the form as $\sqrt[n]{x}$ and it is read as nth root of x. $\sqrt[n]{x}$ is called **Surd** and n is known as the **index of the Surd.**
- **Laws of indices :** If a and b be any two rational numbers and m, n are integer, then:

  (i) $a^m \times a^n = a^{m+n}$

  (ii) $a^m \div a^n = a^{m-n}$

  (iii) $a^m \div a^m = a^{m-m} = a^0 = 1$

  (iv) $(a \times b)^m = a^m \times b^m$

  (v) $(a^m)^n = a^{mn}$

  (vi) $(-a)^m = (-1)^m a^m$

  (vii) $\left(\frac{p}{q}\right)^m = \frac{p^m}{q^m}$, where p, q are integers and $q \neq 0$.

  (viii) $\left(\frac{p}{q}\right)^{-m} = \left(\frac{q}{p}\right)^m$

  (ix) $\left(\frac{p}{q}\right)^m \times \left(\frac{p}{q}\right)^n = \left(\frac{p}{q}\right)^{m+n}$

  (x) $\left(\frac{p}{q}\right)^m \div \left(\frac{p}{q}\right)^n = \left(\frac{p}{q}\right)^{m-n}$

  (xi) $\left[\left(\frac{p}{q}\right)^m\right]^n = \left(\frac{p}{q}\right)^{mn}$
- If a is a negative rational number and n is an odd positive integer, then the nth root of a is minus of the nth root of $|a|$.
- If a is a negative rational number and n is an even positive integer, then the nth root of a is not defined.
- Let a be any positive rational number and $\frac{m}{n}$ be a positive rational number in the lowest form. Then $a^{\frac{m}{n}}$ is defined as the nth root of a^m. *i.e.,* $a^{m/n} = (a^m)^{1/n}$.

  $$a^{-m/n} = \frac{1}{a^{m/n}}.$$
- If a is a rational number and n is a positive integer such that nth root of a *i.e.,* $(a)^{1/n}$ or $\sqrt[n]{a}$ is an irrational number, then $a^{1/n}$ is called a radical or a Surd of index n and a is called the radical.
- A radical that contains no rational factor other than 1, is called a pure radical.
- A radical which has a rational factor other than unity, the other factor being irrational, is called a mixed radical.
- A square root radical is said to be in simplest form, if
  (i) there is no fraction in the radicand
  (ii) no perfect square is a factor of radicand.
  (iii) there is no radical in the denominator.

Rationalisation

Some Identities : Let a and b be positive real numbers, then

(i) $\left(\sqrt{a}\right)^2 = a$

(ii) $\sqrt{a}\sqrt{b} = \sqrt{ab}$

(iii) $\frac{\sqrt{a}}{\sqrt{b}} = \sqrt{\frac{a}{b}}$

(iv) $\left(\sqrt{a}+\sqrt{b}\right)\left(\sqrt{a}-\sqrt{b}\right) = a - b$

(v) $\left(a+\sqrt{b}\right)\left(a-\sqrt{b}\right) = a^2 - b$

(vi) $\left(\sqrt{a}\pm\sqrt{b}\right)^2 = a \pm 2\sqrt{ab} + b$

(vii) $\left(\sqrt{a}+\sqrt{b}\right)\left(\sqrt{c}+\sqrt{d}\right) = \sqrt{ac}+\sqrt{ad}+\sqrt{bc}+\sqrt{bd}$

Rationalisation factor for $\frac{1}{\sqrt{a}}$ is $\sqrt{a}$ and for $\frac{1}{a\pm\sqrt{b}}$, the rationalisation factor is $a\mp\sqrt{b}$ [if $a^2 - b^2 = 1$]

Rationalisation factor for $\frac{1}{\sqrt{a}\pm\sqrt{b}}$ is $\sqrt{a}\mp\sqrt{b}$ [if $a^2 - b^2 = 1$)

Comparison of Surd

(*i*) If two surds are of the same order, then the one whose radicand is larger, is the larger of the two.

Ex: $\sqrt[3]{19} > \sqrt[3]{15}$, $\sqrt{7} > \sqrt{5}$ etc.

(*ii*) If two surds are distinct order, we change them into the surds of the same order.

This order is the L.C.M. of the orders of the given surds.

Ex. Which is the greatest out of $\sqrt[3]{5}, \sqrt[4]{3}, \sqrt[5]{4}$?

$\sqrt[3]{5} = (5)^{\frac{1}{3}}$

$\sqrt[4]{3} = (3)^{\frac{1}{4}}$

$\sqrt[5]{4} = (4)^{\frac{1}{5}}$

$\therefore$ LCM of (3, 4, 5) = 60

$\sqrt[3]{5} = (5)^{\frac{1}{3}} = (5)^{\frac{20}{60}} = \sqrt[60]{(5)^{20}}$

$\sqrt[4]{3} = (3)^{\frac{1}{4}} = (3)^{\frac{15}{60}} = \sqrt[60]{(3)^{15}}$

$\sqrt[5]{4} = (4)^{\frac{1}{5}} = (4)^{\frac{12}{60}} = \sqrt[60]{(4)^{12}}$

$\therefore$ $\sqrt[3]{5}$ is the greates.

Multiple Choice Questions

1. The value of $\{2 - 3(2 - 3)^3\}^3$ is:

A. 5 B. 125
C. 1/5 D. –125

2. $(256)^{0.16} \times (256)^{0.09}$:

A. 4 B. 16
C. 64 D. 256.25

3. If $10^{2y} = 25$, then 10^{-y} equals:

A. $-\frac{1}{5}$ B. $\frac{1}{50}$
C. $\frac{1}{625}$ D. $\frac{1}{5}$

4. The value of $x - y^{x-y}$ when $x = 2$ and $y = -2$ is:

A. 18 B. –18
C. 14 D. –14

5. If $9^{x+2} = 240 + 9^x$, then $x =$

A. 0.5 B. 0.2
C. 0.4 D. 0.1

6. If $8^{x+1} = 64$, what is the value of 3^{2x+1}?

A. 1 B. 3
C. 9 D. 27

7. If $4^x - 4^{x-1} = 24$, then $(2x)^x$ equals:

A. $5\sqrt{5}$ B. $\sqrt{5}$
C. $25\sqrt{5}$ D. 125

8. $\dfrac{5^{n+2} - 6 + 5^{n+1}}{13 \times 5^n - 2 \times 5^{n+1}}$ is equal to:

A. $\frac{5}{3}$ B. $-\frac{5}{3}$
C. $\frac{3}{5}$ D. $-\frac{3}{5}$

9. If $\left(\frac{2}{3}\right)^x \left(\frac{3}{2}\right)^{2x} = \frac{81}{16}$, then $x =$

A. 2 B. 3
C. 4 D. 1

10. If $(16)^{2x+3} = (64)^{x+3}$, then $4^{2x-2} =$

A. 64 B. 256
C. 32 D. 512

11. If $\dfrac{3^{5x} \times 81^2 \times 6561}{3^{2x}} = 3^7$, then $x =$

A. 3 B. –3
C. $\frac{1}{3}$ D. $-\frac{1}{3}$

12. If $x = \sqrt{5} + 2$, then $x - \frac{1}{x}$ equals:

A. $2\sqrt{5}$ B. 4
C. 2 D. $\sqrt{5}$

13. If $\dfrac{\sqrt{3} - 1}{\sqrt{3} + 1} = a - b\sqrt{3}$, then:

A. $a = 2, b = 1$ B. $a = 2, b = -1$
C. $a = -2, b = 1$ D. $a = b = 1$

14. If $x = \dfrac{2}{3 + \sqrt{7}}$, then $(x - 3)^2 =$

A. 1 B. 3
C. 6 D. 7

15. If $x = 7 + 4\sqrt{3}$ and $xy = 1$, then $\frac{1}{x^2} + \frac{1}{y^2} =$

A. 64 B. 134
C. 194 D. 1/49

16. If $x + \sqrt{15} = 4$, then $x + \frac{1}{x} =$

A. 2 B. 4
C. 8 D. 1

17. If $x=\sqrt[3]{2+\sqrt{3}}$, then $x^3+\frac{1}{x^3}=$

A. 2 B. 4
C. 8 D. 9

18. If $x=\frac{\sqrt{5}+\sqrt{3}}{\sqrt{5}-\sqrt{3}}$ and $y=\frac{\sqrt{5}-\sqrt{3}}{\sqrt{5}+\sqrt{3}}$, then $x + y + xy =$

A. 9 B. 5
C. 17 D. 7

19. If $x=\frac{\sqrt{3}-\sqrt{2}}{\sqrt{3}+\sqrt{2}}$ and $y=\frac{\sqrt{3}+\sqrt{2}}{\sqrt{3}-\sqrt{2}}$, then $x^2 + xy + y^2 =$

A. 101 B. 99
C. 98 D. 102

20. The value of $\sqrt{3-2\sqrt{2}}$ is:

A. $\sqrt{2}-1$ B. $\sqrt{2}+1$
C. $\sqrt{3}-\sqrt{2}$ D. $\sqrt{3}+\sqrt{2}$

21. The Value of $\sqrt{5+2\sqrt{6}}$ is:

A. $\sqrt{3}-\sqrt{2}$ B. $\sqrt{3}+\sqrt{2}$
C. $\sqrt{5}+\sqrt{6}$ D. None of these

22. If $x=\sqrt{6}+\sqrt{5}$, then $x^2+\frac{1}{x^2}-2=$

A. $2\sqrt{6}$ B. $2\sqrt{5}$
C. 24 D. 20

23. If $\sqrt{13-a\sqrt{10}}=\sqrt{8}+\sqrt{5}$, then $a =$

A. –5 B. –6
C. –4 D. –2

24. If $\frac{5-\sqrt{3}}{2+\sqrt{3}}=x+y\sqrt{3}$, then

A. $x = 13, y = -7$ B. $x = -13, y = 7$
C. $x = -13, y = -7$ D. $x = 13, y = 7$

25. Simplify : $18-\left[5-\left\{6+2\left(7-\overline{8-5}\right)\right\}\right]$

A. 13 B. 15
C. 27 D. 32

26. If $x * y = x^2 + y^2 - xy$, then the value of $9 * 11$ is:

A. 93 B. 103
C. 113 D. 121

27. $\dfrac{3\frac{1}{4}-\frac{4}{5}\text{ of }\frac{5}{6}}{4\frac{1}{3}\div\frac{1}{5}-\left(\frac{3}{10}+21\frac{1}{5}\right)}$ is equal to:

A. $\frac{1}{6}$ B. $2\frac{7}{12}$
C. $15\frac{1}{2}$ D. $21\frac{1}{2}$

28. If $\frac{x}{2y}=\frac{6}{7}$, then the value of $\frac{x-y}{x+y}+\frac{14}{19}$ is:

A. $\frac{13}{19}$ B. $\frac{15}{19}$
C. 1 D. $1\frac{1}{19}$

29. The value of $\dfrac{1}{2+\dfrac{1}{2+\dfrac{1}{2-\frac{1}{2}}}}$ is:

A. $\frac{3}{8}$ B. $\frac{19}{8}$
C. $\frac{8}{3}$ D. $\frac{8}{19}$

30. If $2=x+\dfrac{1}{1+\dfrac{1}{3+\frac{1}{4}}}$, then the value of x is:

A. $\frac{12}{17}$ B. $\frac{13}{17}$
C. $\frac{18}{17}$ D. $\frac{21}{17}$

31. If $\frac{37}{13}=2+\dfrac{1}{x+\dfrac{1}{y+\frac{1}{z}}}$, where x, y, z are natural numbers, then x, y, z are:

A. 1, 2, 5 B. 1, 5, 2
C. 5, 2, 11 D. 11, 2, 5

32. When simplified, the product $\left(1-\frac{1}{2}\right)\left(1-\frac{1}{3}\right)\left(1-\frac{1}{4}\right)....\left(1-\frac{1}{n}\right)$ gives:

A. $\frac{1}{n}$ B. $\frac{2}{n}$
C. $\frac{2(n-1)}{n}$ D. $\frac{2}{n(n+1)}$

33. The value of $\left(1+\frac{1}{2}\right)\left(1+\frac{1}{3}\right)\left(1+\frac{1}{4}\right)...\left(1+\frac{1}{120}\right)$ is:

A. 30 B. 40.5
C. 60.5 D. 121

34. What is the sum :

$$\frac{1}{2}+\frac{1}{6}+\frac{1}{12}+\frac{1}{20}+\frac{1}{30}+\frac{1}{42}+\frac{1}{56}+\frac{1}{72}+\frac{1}{90}+\frac{1}{110}+\frac{1}{132}$$

A. $\frac{7}{8}$ B. $-\frac{1}{4}$

C. $\frac{1}{4}$ D. None of these

35. The value of $999\frac{995}{999}\times 999$ is:

A. 990809 B. 998996

C. 998999 D. 999824

36. $\left(999\frac{1}{7}+999\frac{2}{7}+999\frac{3}{7}+999\frac{4}{7}+999+\frac{5}{7}+999\frac{6}{7}\right)$

is simplified to

A. 2997 B. 5979

C. 5994 D. 5997

37. The value of $1+\frac{1}{4\times 3}+\frac{1}{4\times 3^2}+\frac{1}{4\times 3^3}$ is:

A. $\frac{121}{108}$ B. $\frac{3}{2}$

C. $\frac{31}{2}$ D. None of these

38. $\left(\frac{785\times 785\times 785+435\times 435\times 435}{785\times 785+435\times 435-785\times 435}\right)$ simplifies to:

A. 350 B. 785

C. 1220 D. 1320

39. $\frac{1}{5}+999\frac{494}{495}\times 99=?$

A. 90000 B. 90900

C. 99000 D. 99990

40. $\left(1+\frac{1}{x+1}\right)\left(1+\frac{1}{x+2}\right)\left(1+\frac{1}{x+3}\right)\left(1+\frac{1}{x+4}\right)=?$

A. $\frac{x+5}{x+1}$ B. $\left(x+\frac{1}{x+5}\right)$

C. $\frac{1}{(x+5)}$ D. $\left(1+\frac{1}{x+5}\right)$

ANSWERS

1	2	3	4	5	6	7	8	9	10
B	A	D	D	A	D	C	B	C	B
11	**12**	**13**	**14**	**15**	**16**	**17**	**18**	**19**	**20**
B	B	A	D	C	C	B	A	B	A
21	**22**	**23**	**24**	**25**	**26**	**27**	**28**	**29**	**30**
B	D	C	A	C	B	C	C	D	D
31	**32**	**33**	**34**	**35**	**36**	**37**	**38**	**39**	**40**
B	A	C	B	B	D	A	C	C	A

EXPLANATORY ANSWERS

2. $(256)^{0.16+0.09} = (256)^{0.25} = (256)^{\frac{1}{4}} = 4$

3. We have, $10^{2y} = 25$

$$(10^y)^2 = 25$$

$$10^y = \sqrt{25} = 5$$

$$10^{-y} = \frac{1}{5}$$

4. $2-(-2)^{2-(-2)} = 2-(-2)^4$

$$= 2-16 = -14$$

5. $9^x \times 9^2 = 240 + 9^x$

$$81\times 9^x = 240 + 9^x$$

$$80\times 9^x = 240$$

$$9^x = 3$$

$$3^{2x} = 3^1$$

$$2x = 1$$

$$x = \frac{1}{2} = 0.5$$

6. $8^{x+1} = 8^2$

$$x + 1 = 2$$

$$x = 1$$

$$3^{2x+1} = 3^{2\times 1+1} = 3^3 = 27$$

7. $4^x - 4^{x-1} = 24$

$$4^x - \frac{4^x}{4} = 24$$

$$4\times 4^x - 4^x = 96$$

$$3\times 4^x = 96$$

$$4^x = 32$$

$$2^{2x} = 2^5$$

$$2x = 5$$

$$x = \frac{5}{2}$$

$$(2x)^x = \left(2\frac{5}{2}\right)^{5/2} = (5^5)^{\frac{1}{2}} = 25\sqrt{5}$$

8. $$\frac{5^{n+1}(5-6)}{5^{n+1}(13\times 5^{-1})-2} = \frac{-1}{\frac{13}{5}-2} = -\frac{5}{3}$$

9. $$\left(\frac{3}{2}\right)^{-x}\left(\frac{3}{2}\right)^{2x} = \left(\frac{3}{2}\right)^{4}$$

$$-x + 2x = 4$$
$$x = 4$$

10. $$(4)^{2\,(2x+3)} = (4)^{3(x+3)}$$
$$4x + 6 = 3x + 9$$
$$x = 3$$
$$4^{2x-2} = 4^{2\times 3-2}$$
$$= 4^4 = 256$$

11. $$\frac{3^{5x}\times 81^2\times 6561}{3^{2x}} = 3^7$$
$$\frac{3^{5x}\times 3^{4\times 2}\times 3^8}{3^{2x}} = 3^7$$
$$3^{5x+8+8-2x} = 3^7$$
$$3x + 16 = -7$$
$$3x = -9$$
$$x = -3$$

12. $$x = \sqrt{5}+2$$
$$\frac{1}{x} = \sqrt{5}-2$$
$$x-\frac{1}{x} = 4$$

13. After Rationalisation, we get

$$\frac{\sqrt{3}-1}{\sqrt{3}+1}\times\frac{\sqrt{3}-1}{\sqrt{3}-1} = \frac{\left(\sqrt{3}-1\right)^2}{\left(\sqrt{3}\right)^2-(1)^2} = \frac{3+1-2\sqrt{3}}{3-1}$$
$$= \frac{4-2\sqrt{3}}{2} = 2-\sqrt{3}$$

After comparison, $a = 2$, $b = 1$ with $a-b\sqrt{3}$

14. $$x = \frac{2}{3+\sqrt{7}}\times\frac{3-\sqrt{7}}{3-\sqrt{7}} = \frac{2\left(3-\sqrt{7}\right)}{(3)^2-\left(\sqrt{7}\right)^2}$$
$$x = 3-\sqrt{7}$$
$$(x-3)^2 = \left(3-\sqrt{7}-3\right)^2 = \left(-\sqrt{7}\right)^2 = 7$$

15. $$x = 7+4\sqrt{3}$$
$$\frac{1}{x} = 7-4\sqrt{3}$$
$$x+\frac{1}{x} = 14 \qquad ...(1)$$
$$\because \quad xy = 1 \quad \therefore \frac{1}{y} = x$$
$$\frac{1}{x^2}+\frac{1}{y^2} = x^2+\frac{1}{x^2}$$

Taking square of eq. (1), we get

$$x^2+\frac{1}{x^2}+2 = 196$$
$$x^2+\frac{1}{x^2} = 194$$

16. $$x+\sqrt{15} = 4$$
$$x = 4-\sqrt{15}$$
$$\frac{1}{x} = 4+\sqrt{15}$$
$$x+\frac{1}{x} = 8$$

17. We have,

$$x = \sqrt[3]{2+\sqrt{3}}$$
$$x^3 = 2+\sqrt{3}$$
$$\frac{1}{x^3} = 2-\sqrt{3}$$
$$x^3+\frac{1}{x^3} = 4$$

18. $$xy = 1$$
$$x + y = \frac{\sqrt{5}+\sqrt{3}}{\sqrt{5}-\sqrt{3}}+\frac{\sqrt{5}-\sqrt{3}}{\sqrt{5}+\sqrt{3}}$$
$$= \frac{\left(\sqrt{5}+\sqrt{3}\right)^2+\left(\sqrt{5}-\sqrt{3}\right)^2}{\left(\sqrt{5}\right)^2-\left(\sqrt{3}\right)^2}$$
$$= \frac{2(5+3)}{5-3} = 8$$
$$\therefore \quad x + y + xy = 8 + 1 = 9$$

19. $$x^2 + y^2 + xy = (x + y)^2 - xy$$
$$xy = 1$$
$$x + y = \frac{\sqrt{3}-\sqrt{2}}{\sqrt{3}+\sqrt{2}}+\frac{\sqrt{3}+\sqrt{2}}{\sqrt{3}-\sqrt{2}}$$

$$= \frac{(\sqrt{3}-\sqrt{2})^2+(\sqrt{3}+\sqrt{2})^2}{(\sqrt{3})^2-(\sqrt{2})^2}$$

$$= \frac{2(3+2)}{3-2} = 10$$

$$(x+y)^2 - xy = (10)^2 - 1 = 99$$

20. $\sqrt{3-2\sqrt{2}} = \sqrt{(\sqrt{2})^2+(1)^2-2\times\sqrt{2}\times 1}$

$a^2+b^2 \quad 2\times a\times b = \sqrt{(\sqrt{2}-1)^2} = \sqrt{2}-1$

22.
$$x = \sqrt{6}+\sqrt{5}$$
$$\frac{1}{x} = \sqrt{6}-\sqrt{5}$$
$$x+\frac{1}{x} = 2\sqrt{6}$$

Taking square of both sides, we get

$$x^2+\frac{1}{x^2}+2 = 24$$
$$x^2+\frac{1}{x^2} = 22$$
$$\therefore \quad x^2+\frac{1}{x^2}-2 = 22-2 = 20$$

23.
$$\sqrt{13-a\sqrt{10}} = \sqrt{8}+\sqrt{5}$$

Taking square of both sides, we get

$$13-a\sqrt{10} = 8+5+2\sqrt{40}$$
$$13-a\sqrt{10} = 13+4\sqrt{40}$$

After comparing both sides, we get

$$a = -4$$

24.
$$\frac{5-\sqrt{3}}{2+\sqrt{3}} = x+y\sqrt{3}$$

After Rationalisation, we get

$$\frac{5-\sqrt{3}}{2+\sqrt{3}}\times\frac{2-\sqrt{3}}{2-\sqrt{3}} = \frac{(5-\sqrt{3})(2-\sqrt{3})}{(2)^2-(\sqrt{3})^2}$$
$$= \frac{10-5\sqrt{3}-2\sqrt{3}+3}{1}$$
$$= 13-7\sqrt{3}$$

After comparing with $x+y\sqrt{3}$, we get

$$x = 13,\ y = -7$$

25. Given exp. = 18 – [5 – {6 + 2 (7 – 3)}]
= 18 – [5 – {6 + 2 × 4}]
= 18 – [5 – {6 + 8}]
= 18 – [5 – 14}] = 18 – [– 9]
= 18 + 9 = 27

26. $9 * 11 = 9^2 + (11)^2 - 9 \times 11$
$= 81 + 121 - 99 = 103.$

27. Given exp. $= \dfrac{\frac{13}{4}-\frac{1}{4}\text{ of }\frac{5}{6}}{\frac{13}{3}\div\frac{1}{5}-\left(\frac{3}{10}+\frac{106}{5}\right)}$

$$= \frac{\frac{13}{4}-\frac{2}{3}}{\frac{13}{3}\times 5-\frac{215}{10}} = \frac{\frac{31}{12}}{\frac{65}{3}-\frac{43}{2}}$$

$$= \left(\frac{31}{12}\times 6\right) = \frac{31}{2} = 15\frac{1}{2}$$

28.
$$\frac{x}{2y} = \frac{6}{7}$$
$$\Rightarrow \quad \frac{x}{y} = \left(2\times\frac{6}{7}\right) = \frac{12}{7}$$
$$\therefore \quad \frac{x-y}{x+y}+\frac{14}{19} = \frac{\frac{x}{y}-1}{\frac{x}{y}+1}+\frac{14}{19}$$
$$= \frac{\frac{12}{7}-1}{\frac{12}{7}+1}+\frac{14}{19} = \frac{(5/7)}{(19/7)}+\frac{14}{19}$$
$$\left(\frac{5}{7}\times\frac{7}{19}\right)+\frac{14}{19} = \frac{5}{19}+\frac{14}{19} = \frac{19}{19} = 1$$

29. Given exp. $= \dfrac{1}{2+\dfrac{1}{2+\dfrac{1}{(3/2)}}} = \dfrac{1}{2+\dfrac{1}{2+\dfrac{2}{3}}}$

$$= \frac{1}{2+\frac{1}{(8/3)}} = \frac{1}{2+\frac{3}{8}} = \frac{1}{(19/8)} = \frac{8}{19}$$

30.
$$x = 2-\frac{1}{1+\frac{1}{(13/4)}} = 2-\frac{1}{1+\frac{4}{13}}$$
$$= 2-\frac{1}{(17/13)} = 2-\frac{13}{17} = \frac{21}{17}$$

31. $$2+\cfrac{1}{x+\cfrac{1}{y+\cfrac{1}{z}}} = \frac{37}{13} = 2\frac{11}{13} + 2 + \frac{11}{13}$$

$$\Rightarrow \cfrac{1}{x+\cfrac{1}{y+\cfrac{1}{z}}} = \frac{11}{13}$$

$$\Rightarrow x+\cfrac{1}{y+\cfrac{1}{z}} = \frac{13}{11}$$

$$\Rightarrow x+\cfrac{1}{y+\cfrac{1}{z}} = 1+\frac{2}{11}$$

$$\Rightarrow x = 1,\ y+\frac{1}{z} = \frac{11}{2} = 5\frac{1}{2} = 5+\frac{1}{2}$$

$$\Rightarrow x = 1,\ y = 5,\ z = 2$$

32. Given exp. $= \frac{1}{2}\times\frac{2}{3}\times\frac{3}{4}\times\ldots\times\frac{(n-1)}{n} = \frac{1}{n}$

33. Given exp. $= \frac{3}{2}\times\frac{4}{3}\times\frac{5}{4}\times\ldots\times\frac{121}{120} = \frac{121}{2} = 60.5$

34. Given exp. $= \left(1-\frac{1}{2}\right)+\left(\frac{1}{2}-\frac{1}{3}\right)+\left(\frac{1}{3}-\frac{1}{4}\right)+\left(\frac{1}{4}-\frac{1}{5}\right)+\ldots$

$$+\left(\frac{1}{11}-\frac{1}{12}\right) = \left(1-\frac{1}{12}\right) = \frac{11}{12}$$

35. Given exp. $= \left(1000-\frac{4}{999}\right)\times 999$

$= 999000 - 4 = 998996$

36. Given exp. $= \left(1000-\frac{6}{7}\right)+\left(1000-\frac{5}{7}\right)+\left(1000-\frac{4}{7}\right)+$

$$\left(1000-\frac{3}{7}\right)+\left(1000-\frac{2}{7}\right)+\left(1000-\frac{1}{7}\right)$$

$$= 6000-\left(\frac{6}{7}+\frac{5}{7}+\frac{4}{7}+\frac{3}{7}+\frac{2}{7}+\frac{1}{7}\right)$$

$$= 6000-\frac{21}{7} = 6000-3 = 5997$$

37. Given exp. $= \frac{4\times 3^3+3^2+3+1}{4\times 3^3}$

$$= \frac{108+9+3+1}{108} = \frac{121}{108}$$

38. Given exp. $= \left(\frac{a^3+b^3}{a^2+b^2-ab}\right) = (a+b),$

where $a = 785,\ b = 435$

$= (785 + 435) = 1220$

39. $\frac{1}{5}+\left(999+\frac{494}{495}\right)\times 99$

$$= \frac{1}{5}+(999\times 99)+\frac{494}{495}\times 99$$

$$= \frac{1}{5}+\frac{494}{5}+999\times 99$$

$$= \frac{495}{5}+(1000-1)\times 99$$

$= 99 + 99000 - 99 = 99000$

40. $\left(\frac{x+2}{x+1}\right)\left(\frac{x+3}{x+2}\right)\left(\frac{x+4}{x+3}\right)\left(\frac{x+5}{x+4}\right) = \frac{x+5}{x+1}$

□□□□□

5

Direct and Inverse Proportions

Important Facts and Formulae

1. **Direct Proportion:** Two quantities are said to be directly proportional, if on the increase (or decrease) of the one, the other increases (or decreases) to the same extent

   Ex. 1. Cost is directly proportional to the number of articles.
   (*More Articles, More Cost*)

   Ex. 2. Work done is directly proportional to the number of men working on it.
   (*More Men, More Work*)

2. **Indirect Proportion :** Two quantities are said to be indirectly proportional, if on the increase of the one, the other decreases to the same extent and vice-versa.

   Ex. 1. The time taken by a car in covering a certain distance is inversely proportional to the speed of the car.
   (*More speed, Less is the time taken to cover a distance*)

   Ex. 2. Time taken to finish a work is inversely proportional to the number of persons working at it.
   (*More persons, Less is the time taken to finish a job.*)

   Remark : In solving questions by chain rule, we compare every item with the term to be found out.

Formulae:

(*i*) If $W_1 = W_2$

$$M_1 \times D_1 \times T_1 \times E_1 = M_2 \times D_2 \times T_2 \times E_2$$

(*ii*) If $W_1 \neq W_2$

$$\frac{M_1 \times D_1 \times T_1 \times E_1}{W_1} = \frac{M_2 \times D_2 \times T_2 \times E_2}{W_2}$$

where M → Number of Men
D → Number of Days
T → Time
E → Efficiency
W → Work

Multiple Choice Questions

1. If the cost of x metres of wire is d rupees, then what is the cost of y metres of wire at the same rate?

A. ₹ $\left(\frac{xy}{d}\right)$ B. ₹ (xd)
C. ₹ (yd) D. ₹ $\left(\frac{yd}{x}\right)$

2. If the price of 6 toys is ₹ 264.37, what will be the approximate price of 5 toys?

A. ₹ 140 B. ₹ 100
C. ₹ 200 D. ₹ 220

3. The price of 357 mangoes is ₹ 1517.25. What will be the approximate price of 9 dozens of such mangoes?

A. ₹ 3000 B. ₹ 3500
C. ₹ 4000 D. ₹ 2500

4. If a quarter kg of potato costs 60 paise, how many paise will 200 gm cost?

A. 48 paise B. 54 paise
C. 56 paise D. 72 paise

5. If 11.25 m of uniform iron rod weighs 42.75 kg, what will be the weight of 6 m of the same rod?

A. 22.8 kg B. 25.6 kg
C. 28 kg D. 26.5 kg

6. On a scale of map, 0.6 cm represents 6.6 km. If the distance between the points on the map is 80.5 cm, the actual distance between these points is:

A. 9 km B. 72.5 km
C. 190.75 km D. 885.5 km

7. An industrial loom weaves 0.128 metres of cloth every second. Approximately, how many seconds will it take for the loom to weave 25 metres of cloth?

A. 178 B. 195
C. 204 D. 488

8. A flagstaff 17.5 m high casts a shadow of length 40.25 m. The height of the building, which casts a shadow of length 28.75 m under similar conditions will be:

A. 10 m B. 12.5 m
C. 17.5 m D. 21.25 m

9. A man completes $\frac{5}{8}$ of a job in 10 days. At this rate, how many more days will it take him to finish the job?
A. 5 B. 6
C. 7 D. $7\frac{1}{2}$

10. 36 men can complete a piece of work in 18 days. In how many days will 27 men complete the same work?
A. 12 B. 18
C. 22 D. 24

11. A fort had provision of food for 150 men for 45 days. After 10 days, 25 men left the fort. The number of days for which the remaining food will last, is :
A. $29\frac{1}{5}$ B. $37\frac{1}{4}$
C. 42 D. 54

12. A wheel that has 6 cogs is meshed with a larger wheel of 14 cogs. When the smaller wheel has made 21 revolutions, then the number of revolutions made by the larger wheel is:
A. 4 B. 9
C. 12 D. 49

13. In a camp, there is a meal for 120 men or 200 children. If 150 children have taken the meal, how many men will be catered to with the remaining meal?
A. 20 B. 30
C. 40 D. 50

14. The cost of 16 packets of salt, each weighing 900 grams is ₹ 28. What will be the cost of 27 packets, if each packet weighs 1 kg?
A. ₹ 52.50 B. ₹ 56
C. ₹ 58.50 D. ₹ 64.75

15. 4 mat-weavers can weave 4 mats in 4 days. At the same rate, how many mats would be woven by 8 mat-weavers in 8 days?
A. 4 B. 8
C. 12 D. 16

16. Running at the same constant rate, 6 identical machines can produce a total of 270 bottles per minute. At this rate, how many bottles could 10 such machines produce in 4 minutes?
A. 648 B. 1800
C. 2700 D. 10800

17. In a dairy farm, 40 cows eat 40 bags of husk in 40 days. In how many days one cow will eat one bag of husk?
A. 1 B. $\frac{1}{40}$
C. 40 D. 80

18. 12 men working 8 hours per day complete a piece of work in 10 days. To complete the same work in 8 days, working 15 hours a day, the number of men required, is:
A. 4 B. 5
C. 6 D. 8

19. 10 men, working 6 hours a day can complete a work in 18 days. How many hours a day must 15 men work to complete the same work in 12 days?
A. 6 B. 10
C. 12 D. 15

20. 39 persons can repair a road in 12 days, working 5 hours a day. In how many days will 30 persons, working 6 hours a day, complete the work?
A. 10 B. 13
C. 14 D. 15

21. If 7 spiders make 7 webs in 7 days, then 1 spider will make 1 web in how many days?
A. 1 B. $\frac{7}{2}$
C. 7 D. 49

22. If 18 binders bind 900 books in 10 days, how many binders will be required to bind 660 books is 12 days?
A. 22 B. 14
C. 13 D. 11

23. If 18 pumps can raise 2170 tonnes of water in 10 days, working 7 hours a day, in how many days will 16 pumps raise 1736 tonnes, working 9 hours a day?
A. 9 days B. 8 days
C. 7 days D. 6 days

24. 120 men had provisions for 200 days. After 5 days, 30 men died due to an epidemic. The remaining food will last for:
A. 150 days B. $146\frac{1}{4}$ days
C. 245 days D. 260 days

25. A garrison of 500 men had provisions for 24 days. However, a reinforcement of 300 men arrived. The food will now last for:
A. 18 days B. $17\frac{1}{2}$ days
C. 16 days D. 15 days

26. A garrison had provisions for a certain number of days. After 10 days (1/5)th of the men desert and it is found that the provisions will now last just as long as before. How long was that?
A. 35 days B. 15 days
C. 25 days D. 50 days

27. 20 men complete one-third of a piece of work in 20 days. How many more men should be employed to finish the rest of the work in 25 more days?

A. 10 B. 12
C. 15 D. 20

28. If 17 labourers can dig a ditch 26 metres long in 18 days, working 8 hours a day, how many more labourers should be engaged to dig a similar ditch 39 metres long in 6 days, each labourer working 9 hours a day?

A. 51 B. 68
C: 85 D. 34

29. If x men working x hours per day can do x units of a work in x days, then y men working y yours per day would be able to complete in y days:

A. $\frac{x^2}{y^3}$ units of work B. $\frac{x^3}{y^2}$ units of work
C. $\frac{y^2}{x^3}$ units of work D. $\frac{y^3}{x^2}$ units of work

30. A contractor undertakes to do a piece of work in 40 days. He engages 100 men at the beginning and 100 more after 35 days and completes the work in stipulated time. If he had not engaged the additional men, how many days behind schedule would it be finished?

A. 5 B. 6
C. 3 D. 9

ANSWERS

1	2	3	4	5	6	7	8	9	10
D	D	D	A	A	D	B	B	B	D
11	12	13	14	15	16	17	18	19	20
C	B	B	A	D	B	C	D	A	B
21	22	23	24	25	26	27	28	29	30
C	D	C	D	D	D	B	A	D	A

EXPLANATORY ANSWERS

1. Cost of x metres = ₹ d. Cost of 1 metre

$$= ₹\left(\frac{d}{x}\right)$$

Cost of y meters $= ₹\left(\frac{d}{x} \times y\right) = ₹\left(\frac{dy}{x}\right)$.

2. Let the required price be ₹ x. Then,

Less toys, Less cost (Direct proportion)

$\therefore$ 6 : 5 : : 264.37 : $x \Leftrightarrow 6x = (5 \times 264.37)$

$\Leftrightarrow \quad x = \frac{(5 \times 264.37)}{6}$

$\Leftrightarrow \quad x = 220.308$

$\therefore$ Approximate price of 5 toys = ₹ 220.

3. Let the required price be ₹ x. Then, *More mangoes, More price (Direct Proportion)*

$\therefore$ 357 : (49 × 12) : : 1517.25 : x

$\Leftrightarrow \quad 357x = (49 \times 12 \times 1517.25)$

$\Leftrightarrow \quad x = \frac{(49 \times 12 \times 1517.25)}{357} \Leftrightarrow x = 2499.$

Hence, the approximate price is ₹ 2500.

4. Let the required cost be x paise. *Less weight, Less cost (Direct Proportion)*

$\therefore$ 250 : 200 : : 60 : x

$\Leftrightarrow \quad 250 \times x = (200 \times 60)$

$x = \frac{(200 \times 60)}{250} \Leftrightarrow x = 48.$

5. Let the required weight be x kg. Then, *Less length, Less weight (Direct Proportion)*

$\therefore$ 11.25 : 6 : : 42.75 : x

$\Leftrightarrow \quad 11.25 \times x = 6 \times 42.75$

$\Leftrightarrow \quad x = \frac{(6 \times 42.75)}{11.25}$

$\Leftrightarrow \quad x = 22.8.$

6. Let the actual distance be x km. Then,

More distance on the map. *More is the actual distance (Direct Proportion)*

$\therefore$ 0.6 : 80.5 : : 6.6 : x

$\Leftrightarrow \quad 0.6x = 80.5 \times 6.6$

$\Leftrightarrow \quad x = \frac{80.5 \times 6.6}{0.6}$

$\Leftrightarrow \quad x = 885.5.$

7. Let the required time be x seconds. *Then, More metres, more time (Direct Proportion)*

$\therefore$ 0.128 : 25 : : 1 : x

$\Leftrightarrow \quad 0.128 \times x = 25 \times 1$

$\Leftrightarrow \quad x = \frac{25}{0.128} = \frac{25 \times 1000}{128}$

$\Leftrightarrow \quad x = 195.31$

$\therefore$ Required time = 195 sec (approximately).

8. Let the height of the building be x metres.
Less lengthy shadow, *Less is the height (Direct Proportion)*

$\therefore$ 40.25 : 28.75 : : 17.5 : x

$\Leftrightarrow \quad 40.25 \times x = 28.75 \times 17.5$

$\Leftrightarrow \quad x = \frac{(28.75 \times 17.5)}{40.25} \Leftrightarrow x = 12.5$

9. Work done = $\frac{5}{8}$. Balance work = $\left(1 - \frac{5}{8}\right) = \frac{3}{8}$.
Less work, Less days (Direct Proportion)
Let the required number of days be x

Then $\frac{5}{8} : \frac{3}{8} :: 10 : x \Leftrightarrow \frac{5}{8} \times x = \frac{3}{8} \times 10$

$\Leftrightarrow \quad x = \left(\frac{3}{8} \times 10 \times \frac{8}{5}\right) = 6.$

10. Let the required number of days be x.
Then, *Less men, More days (Indirect Proportion)*

$\therefore$ 27 : 36 : : 18 : x

$\Leftrightarrow \quad 27 \times x = 36 \times 18$

$\Leftrightarrow \quad x = \frac{36 \times 18}{27} \Leftrightarrow x = 24.$

11. After 10 days : 150 men had food for 35 days.
Suppose 125 men had food for x days. Now, *Less men, more days (Indirect Proportion)*

$\therefore$ 125 : 150 : : 35 : x

$\Leftrightarrow \quad 125 \times x = 150 \times 35$

$\Leftrightarrow \quad x = \frac{150 \times 35}{125} \Leftrightarrow x = 42.$

Hence, the remaining food will last for 42 days.

12. Let the required number of revolutions made by larger wheel be x.
Then, *More cogs, Less revolutions (Indirect Proportion)*

$\therefore$ 14 : 6 : : 21 : x

$\Leftrightarrow \quad 14 \times x = 6 \times 21$

$\Leftrightarrow \quad x = \left(\frac{6 \times 21}{14}\right) = 9.$

13. There is a meal for 200 children. 150 children have taken the meal. Remaining meal is to be catered to 50 children.
Now, 200 children ≡ 120 men

50 children ≡ $\left(\frac{120}{200} \times 50\right)$ men = 30 men.

14. Let the required cost be ₹ x. Then,
More packets, More cost *(Direct Proportion)*
More weight, More cost *(Direct Proportion)*

$$\left.\begin{array}{ll}\text{Packets} & 16:27 \\ \text{Weight} & 900:1000\end{array}\right\} :: 28 : x$$

$\therefore \quad (16 \times 900 \times x) = (27 \times 1000 \times 28)$

$\Leftrightarrow \quad x = \frac{(27 \times 1000 \times 28)}{16 \times 900}$

$= \frac{105}{2} =$ ₹ 52.50

15. Let the required number of mats be x.
More weavers, More mats *(Direct Proportion)*
More days, More mats *(Direct Proportion)*

$$\left.\begin{array}{ll}\text{Weavers} & 4:8 \\ \text{Days} & 4:8\end{array}\right\} :: 4 : x$$

$\therefore \quad 4 \times 4 \times x = 8 \times 8 \times 4$

$\Leftrightarrow \quad x = \frac{(8 \times 8 \times 4)}{(4 \times 4)} = 16.$

16. Let the required number of bottles be x.
More machines, More bottles *(Direct Proportion)*
More minutes, More bottles *(Direct Proportion)*

$$\left.\begin{array}{ll}\text{Machines} & 6:10 \\ \text{Time (in Minutes)} & 1:4\end{array}\right\} :: 270 : x$$

$\therefore \quad 6 \times 1 \times x = 10 \times 4 \times 270$

$\Leftrightarrow \quad x = \frac{10 \times 4 \times 270}{6} \Leftrightarrow x = 1800.$

17. Let the required number of days be x.
Less cows, More days *(Indirect Proportion)*
Less bags, Less days *(Direct Proportion)*

$$\left.\begin{array}{ll}\text{Cows} & 1:40 \\ \text{Bags} & 40:1\end{array}\right\} :: 40 : x$$

$\therefore \quad 1 \times 40 \times x = 40 \times 1 \times 40 \Leftrightarrow x = 40.$

18. Let the requred number of men be x.
Less days, More men *(Indirect Proportion)*
More working hrs per day, Less men *(Indirect Proportion)*

$$\left.\begin{array}{ll}\text{Days} & 8:10 \\ \text{Working Hrs} & 15:8\end{array}\right\} :: 12 : x$$

$\therefore \quad 8 \times 15 \times x = 10 \times 8 \times 12$

$\Leftrightarrow \quad x = \frac{10 \times 8 \times 12}{8 \times 15} \Leftrightarrow x = 8.$

19. Let the required number of hours per day be x.
More men, Less hours per day *(Indirect Proportion)*
Less days, More hours per day *(Indirect Proportion)*

$$\left.\begin{array}{ll}\text{Men} & 15:10 \\ \text{Days} & 12:18\end{array}\right\} :: 6 : x$$

$\therefore \quad 15 \times 12 \times x = 10 \times 18 \times 6$

$\Leftrightarrow \quad x = \dfrac{10 \times 18 \times 6}{15 \times 12} \Leftrightarrow x = 6.$

20. Let the required number of days be x.

Less persons, More days (*Indirect Proportion*)

More working hrs per day, (*Indirect Proportion*)

Less days

$$\left.\begin{array}{ll}\text{Persons} & 30:39\\ \text{Working hrs/day} & 6:5\end{array}\right\} :: 12 : x$$

$\therefore \quad 30 \times 6 \times x = 39 \times 5 \times 12$

$\Leftrightarrow \quad x = \dfrac{39 \times 5 \times 12}{30 \times 6} \Leftrightarrow x = 13.$

21. Let the required number of days be x. Then,

Less spiders, More days (*Indirect Proportion*)

Less webs, Less days (*Direct Proportion*)

$$\therefore \left.\begin{array}{ll}\text{Spiders} & 1:7\\ \text{Webs} & 7:1\end{array}\right\} :: 7 : x$$

$\therefore \quad 1 \times 7 \times x = 7 \times 1 \times 7 \Leftrightarrow x = 7.$

22. Let the required number of binders be x.

Less books, Less binders (*Direct Proportion*)

More days, Less binders (*Indirect Proportion*)

$$\left.\begin{array}{ll}\text{Books} & 900:600\\ \text{Days} & 12:10\end{array}\right\} :: 18 : x$$

$\therefore \quad (900 \times 20 \times x) = (600 \times 10 \times 18)$

$\Leftrightarrow \quad x = \dfrac{600 \times 10 \times 18}{900 \times 12} = 11.$

23. *Less pumps, more days* (*Indirect*)

Less Water, less days (*Direct*)

More working hrs., less days (*Indirect*)

$$\left.\begin{array}{ll}\text{Pumps} & 16:18\\ \text{Water} & 2170:1736\\ \text{Working hours} & 9:7\end{array}\right\} :: 10 : x$$

$\therefore \quad x = \left(\dfrac{18 \times 1736 \times 7 \times 10}{16 \times 2170 \times 9}\right) = 7$ days.

24. The remaining food is sufficient for 120 men for 195 days.

But, now remaining men = 90.

Less men, more days (Indirect)

$\therefore$ 90 : 120 :: 195 : x

or $\quad x = \left(\dfrac{120 \times 195}{90}\right) = 260$ days.

25. More men, less number of days (Indirect)

800 : 500 : : 24 : x

or $\quad x = \left(\dfrac{500 \times 24}{800}\right) = 15$ days.

26. Let, initially there be x men having provisions for y days.

After 10 days, x men had provisions for $(y - 10)$ days.

These provisions were for $\left(x - \dfrac{x}{5}\right)$ *i.e.,* $\dfrac{4x}{5}$ men for y days.

$\therefore \quad x(y - 10) = \dfrac{4x}{5} y$ or $xy - 50x = 0$

or $\quad x(y - 50) = 0$ or $y - 50 = 0$ *i.e.* $y = 50$ days.

27. Work done $= \dfrac{1}{3}$, work to be done $= \dfrac{2}{3}$.

Now, more work, more men (*Direct*)

More days, less men (*Indirect*)

$$\left.\begin{array}{ll}\text{Work} & \dfrac{1}{3}:\dfrac{2}{3}\\ \text{Days} & 25:20\end{array}\right\} :: 20 : x$$

$\therefore \quad x = \left(\dfrac{2}{3} \times 20 \times 20 \times \dfrac{3}{25}\right) = 32$ men.

So, 12 more men should be employed.

28. More length, more labourers (*Direct*)

More daily hours, less labourers (*Indirect*)

Less days, more labourers (*Indirect*)

$$\left.\begin{array}{ll}\text{Length} & 26:39\\ \text{Daily hrs.} & 9:8\\ \text{Days} & 6:18\end{array}\right\} :: 17 : x$$

or $\quad x = \left(\dfrac{39 \times 8 \times 18 \times 17}{26 \times 9 \times 6}\right) = 68.$

So, more labourers to be engaged = (68 – 17) = 51.

29. More men, more work (*Direct*)

More working hrs., more work (*Direct*)

More days, more work (*Direct*)

$$\left.\begin{array}{ll}\text{Men} & x:y\\ \text{Working hrs.} & x:y\\ \text{Days} & x:y\end{array}\right\} :: x : z$$

$\therefore \quad z = \left(\dfrac{y \times y \times y \times x}{x \times x \times x}\right) = \dfrac{y^3}{x^2}$ units of work.

30. [(100 × 35) + (200 × 5)] working for 1 day can finish the work.

Thus, 4500 men can finish it in 1 day.

So, 100 men can finish it in $\left(\dfrac{4500}{100}\right) = 45$ days,

i.e., 5 days behind schedule.

□□□□□

6

Comparing Quantities

Percentage

I. Concept of Percentage : By a certain percent, we mean that many hundredths. Thus, x percent means x hundredths, written as $x\%$.

To express $x\%$ as a fraction : We have, $x\% = \frac{x}{100}$.

Thus, $20\% = \frac{20}{100} = \frac{1}{5}$; $48\% = \frac{48}{100} = \frac{12}{25}$, etc.

To express $\frac{a}{b}$ as a percent : We have, $\frac{a}{b} = \left(\frac{a}{b} \times 100\right)\%$.

Thus, $\frac{1}{4} = \left(\frac{1}{4} \times 100\right)\% = 25\%$;

$0.6 = \frac{6}{10} = \frac{3}{5} = \left(\frac{3}{5} \times 100\right)\% = 60\%$.

II. If the price of a commodity increases by R%, then the reduction in consumption so as not to increase the expenditure is

$$\left[\frac{R}{(100+R)} \times 100\right]\%$$

If the price of a commodity decreases by R%, then the increase in consumption so as not to decrease the expenditure is

$$\left[\frac{R}{(100-R)} \times 100\right]\%$$

III. Results on Population : Let the population of a town be P now and suppose it increases at the rate of R% per annum, then :

1. Population after n years $= P\left(1+\frac{R}{100}\right)^n$.

2. Population n years ago $= \dfrac{P}{\left(1+\frac{R}{100}\right)^n}$.

IV. Results on Depreciation : Let the present value of a machine be P. Suppose it depreciates at the rate of R% per annum. Then :

1. Value of the machine after n years $= P\left(1-\frac{R}{100}\right)^n$.

2. Value of the machine n years ago $= \dfrac{P}{\left(1-\frac{R}{100}\right)^n}$.

V. If A is R% more than B, then B is less than A by

$$\left[\frac{R}{(100+R)} \times 100\right]\%$$

If A is R% less than B, then B is more than A by

$$\left[\frac{R}{(100-R)} \times 100\right]\%.$$

Multiple Choice Questions

1. If the cost of a book worth ₹ 50 is increased by ₹ 25. What is the rate of increase?

A. 50% B. 60%
C. 70% D. 80%

2. A number decreases by $72\frac{1}{2}\%$ gives 87. What is the number?

A. 90 B. 100
C. 120 D. 140

3. 25% of a number is less than 18% of 650 by 19. What is the number?

A. 193 B. 392
C. 396 D. 492

4. Two candidates fought an election, one get 65% of the votes and won by 300 votes. What is the total number of votes polled?

A. 1000 B. 1200
C. 1400 D. 1500

5. 96% of the population of a town is 23040. What is the total number of population?
A. 21000 B. 24000
C. 26000 D. 24000

6. If 75% of students in a school are boys and the number of girls is 420. What is the number of boys?
A. 1160 B. 1170
C. 1260 D. 1420

7. The population of a village is 5000; and it increase at the rate of 2% every year. What will be the population after 2 years?
A. 5200 B. 5400
C. 5202 D. 6300

8. The population of a town increases by 5% annually. If it is 15435 now, what was the population 2 years ago?
A. 8400 B. 9300
C. 9700 D. 9850

9. The population of a town is 8000. It increases by 10% during first year and by 20% during second year. What will be the population after 2 years.
A. 10,120 B. 10,560
C. 11,420 D. 12,460

10. Kavita went to school for 216 days in a year. If her attendance was 90%, then find out the number of days the school was open in that year?
A. 100 days
B. 140 days
C. 240 days
D. 280 days

11. Dinesh spends 23% of his monthly income on his children's education and donates 2% of it to an organisation. If he spends ₹ 2500 in one month on these two, then find his monthly income?
A. ₹ 9000 B. ₹ 10,000
C. ₹ 11,000 D. ₹ 17,000

12. In a school the number of students increased by 6% of the number at the beginning. If this increases in the number of students is 150, then find the number of students in the school before the increase and after the increase?
A. 2500, 2650 B. 2450, 2730
C. 2400, 2750 D. 2600, 2710

13. There are 1500 trees in a garden, out of which 15% are mango trees, 18% are lemon trees and the remaining are orange trees. What is the number of orange trees?
A. 1005 B. 1102
C. 1010 D. 1002

14. In an examination 70% students were successful. What is the total number of students, if the number of successful students was 210.
A. 90 B. 150
C. 300 D. 350

15. A cricket team won 60% of the matches played in a year. What is the total number of matches played in the year if the team lost 10 matches and no match ended in a draw?
A. 22 B. 25
C. 27 D. 29

Profit & Loss

Cost Price : The price at which an article is purchased, is called its cost price, abbreviated as C.P.

Selling Price : The price at which an article is sold, is called its selling price, abbreviated as S.P.

Profit or Gain : If S.P. is greater than C.P., the seller is said to have a profit or gain.

Loss : If S.P. is less than C.P., the seller is said to have incurred a loss.

Formulae :

1. Gain = (S.P.) – (C.P.)
2. Loss = (C.P.) – (S.P.)
3. Loss or gain is always reckoned on C.P.
4. Gain % = $\left(\frac{\text{Gain} \times 100}{\text{C.P.}}\right)$
5. Loss % = $\left(\frac{\text{Loss} \times 100}{\text{C.P.}}\right)$
6. S.P. = $\frac{(100 + \text{Gain\%})}{100} \times \text{C.P.}$
7. S.P. = $\frac{(100 - \text{Loss\%})}{100} \times \text{C.P.}$
8. C.P. = $\frac{100}{(100 + \text{Gain\%})} \times \text{S.P.}$
9. C.P. = $\frac{100}{(100 - \text{Loss\%})} \times \text{S.P.}$
10. If an article is sold at a gain of say, 35%, then S.P. = 135% of C.P.

11. If an article is sold at a loss of say, 35%, then S.P. = 65% of C.P.

12. When a person sells two similar items, one at a gain of say, x%, and the other at a loss of x%, then the seller always incurs a loss given by:

$$\text{Loss \%} = \left(\frac{\text{Common Loss and Gain\%}}{10}\right)^2 = \left(\frac{x}{10}\right)^2.$$

13. If a trader professes to sell his goods at cost price, but uses false weights, then

$$\text{Gain\%} = \left[\frac{\text{Error}}{(\text{True Value}) - (\text{Error})} \times 100\right]\%.$$

Multiple Choice Questions

1. A former sold two bullocks for ₹ 18000 each. On one bullock he gained 20% and on the other he lost 20%. What is his total loss or gain?

A. ₹ 1500 B. ₹ 1600
C. ₹ 1750 D. ₹ 1520

2. By selling 144 hens, Mukesh lost the S.P. of 6 hens. What is the loss per cent?

A. 2% B. 4%
C. 6% D. 8%

3. A shopkeeper purchased 100 blankets at ₹ 2000 each. He found that 10 blankets were defective and he sold these at ₹ 1200 each. At what rate should he sell the remaining blankets so as to gain 14% on the whole?

A. ₹ 2400 B. ₹ 2600
C. ₹ 2800 D. ₹ 3200

Directions (4 and 5) : *A goldsmith bought 100g of gold for ₹ 54000 from a wholesaler. He then sold it at a gain of 10%.*

4. S.P. of 10g of gold for the goldsmith.

A. ₹ 5820 B. ₹ 5460
C. ₹ 5370 D. ₹ 5940

5. C.P. of 10g of gold for the wholesaler, if his profit is 8%.

A. ₹ 2000 B. ₹ 4000
C. ₹ 5000 D. ₹ 5500

Directions (6 to 8) : *William sells a quintal of wheat for ₹ 924 and earns a profit of 12%. By selling a quintal of rice for the same amount he loses 12%. Find,*

6. C.P. of wheat :

A. ₹ 825 B. ₹ 935
C. ₹ 945 D. ₹ 1025

7. C.P. of rice :

A. ₹ 920 B. ₹ 980
C. ₹ 1050 D. ₹ 1120

8. Gain or loss per cent on the whole transaction.

A. ₹ 23 B. ₹ 25
C. ₹ 27 D. ₹ 29

9. A tricycle is sold at a gain of 16%. Had it been sold for ₹ 100 more, the gain would have been 20%. What is the C.P. of the tricycle?

A. ₹ 2500 B. ₹ 2210
C. ₹ 2350 D. ₹ 2400

10. Manish bought 20 dining tables for ₹ 1,20,000 and sold these at a profit equal to the selling price of 4 dining tables. What is the S.P. of one dining table?

A. ₹ 5500 B. ₹ 7500
C. ₹ 8500 D. ₹ 9000

11. Yogita sold a plot of land at 20% gain to Dimpi. Dimpi sold it to Anjali at 10% profit. If Anjali had to pay ₹ 3,30,000 for the plot. What is the C.P. of the plot for Yogita?

A. ₹ 2,50,000 B. ₹ 2,45,000
C. ₹ 2,70,000 D. ₹ 2,90,500

12. A man buys a plot of agricultural land for ₹ 3,00,000. He sells one-third at a loss of 20% and two-fifths at a gain of 25%. At what price must he sell the remaining land so as to make an overall profit of 10%?

A. ₹ 75,000 B. ₹ 95,000
C. ₹ 1,00,000 D. ₹ 1,50,000

13. A dishonest dealer professes to sell his goods at cost price, but he uses a weight of 960 grams for 1 kg. What is the gain per cent?

A. $4\frac{1}{6}\%$ B. $5\frac{1}{7}\%$
C. $7\frac{1}{6}\%$ D. $9\frac{1}{3}\%$

14. A man purchase two fans for ₹ 2160. By selling one fan at a profit of 15% and the other at a loss of 9% he neither gains nor losses in the whole transaction. What is the cost price of fan which is sold at 9% less?

A. ₹ 1150 B. ₹ 1200
C. ₹ 1350 D. ₹ 1400

15. By reducing the selling price of an article by ₹ 50, a gain of 5% turns into a loss of 5%. What is the original selling price of the article?

A. ₹ 425 B. ₹ 525
C. ₹ 650 D. ₹ 720

16. If the selling price of 10 pens is equal to cost price of 14 pens. What is the gain per cent?
A. 40% B. 50%
C. 60% D. 70%

17. If selling price is doubled, the profit triples. What is the profit per cent?
A. $66\frac{2}{3}$ B. 100
C. $105\frac{1}{3}$ D. 120

18. If the cost price of 12 pens is equal to the selling price of 8 pens, the gain per cent is:
A. 25% B. $33\frac{1}{3}$%
C. 50% D. $66\frac{2}{3}$%

19. The cost price of 20 articles is the same as the selling price of x articles. If the profit is 25%, then the value of x is:
A. 15 B. 16
C. 18 D. 25

20. A man bought apples at the rate of 8 for ₹ 34 and sold them at the rate of 12 for ₹ 57. How many apples should be sold to earn a net profit of ₹ 45?
A. 90 B. 100
C. 135 D. 150

21. Some articles were bought at 6 for ₹ 5 and sold at 5 for ₹ 6. Gain per cent is:
A. 30% B. $33\frac{1}{3}$%
C. 35% D. 44%

22. A trader mixes 26 kg of rice at ₹ 20 per kg with 30 kg of rice of other variety at ₹ 36 per kg and sells the mixture at ₹ 30 per kg. His profit per cent is:
A. No profit, no loss B. 5%
C. 8% D. 10%

23. A dishonest dealer uses a scale of 90 cm instead of a metre scale and claims to sell at cost price. His profit is:
A. 9% B. 10%
C. 12% D. None of these

24. A sells a bicycle to B at a profit of 20%. B sells it to C at a profit of 25%. If C pays ₹ 225 for it, the cost price of the bicycle for A is:
A. ₹ 110 B. ₹ 120
C. ₹ 125 D. ₹ 150

25. A shopkeeper sells two watches for ₹ 308 each. On one he gets 12% profit and on the other 12% loss. His profit or loss in the entire transaction was:
A. Neither profit, nor loss B. $1\frac{11}{25}$% loss
C. $1\frac{11}{25}$% profit D. $3\frac{2}{25}$% loss

Discount

Market Price (M.P.)—The attached price is called the market price (M.P.) or list price (L.P.) of the article and the reduction allowed in the price is called the **discount**.

(i) Discount = M.P. – S.P.

(ii) $\text{Discount } \% = \frac{\text{Discount} \times 100}{\text{M.P.}}$

(iii) $\text{S.P.} = \text{M.P.} - \frac{\text{Discount\%} \times \text{M.P.}}{100}$

(iv) $\text{S.P.} = \text{M.P.} \times \left(1 - \frac{\text{Discount\%}}{100}\right)$

(v) $\text{M.P.} = \frac{100 \times \text{S.P.}}{100 - \text{Discount\%}}$

$\text{S.P.} = \text{M.P.}\left(\frac{100 - \text{Discount\%}}{100}\right)$

$\text{M.P.} - \text{S.P.} = \frac{\text{M.P.} \times \text{Discount\%}}{100}$

$\text{Discount\%} = \left(\frac{\text{M.P.} - \text{S.P.}}{\text{M.P.}}\right) \times 100$

Multiple Choice Questions

1. A cloth merchant offers 15% festival discount on every saree sold. If a certain saree is sold for ₹ 680, what is its marked price?
A. ₹ 800 B. ₹ 900
C. ₹ 1250 D. ₹ 1300

2. A shopkeeper offers 10% discount on an article and still makes a profit of 20%. What is the C.P. of the article if the marked price is ₹ 350?
A. ₹ 259.20 B. ₹ 262.50
C. ₹ 265.75 D. ₹ 272.5

3. A manufactures marks his goods in such a way that after allowing 20% discount, he makes a profit of 18%. What is the marked price of an item which costs him ₹ 200?

A. ₹ 295 B. ₹ 310
C. ₹ 315 D. ₹ 375

4. The marked price of a brand of coffee is ₹ 35 for 100g. But the shopkeeper gives a cup costing ₹ 7.50 free with it. Even then he gets a gain of 10%. What is the cost price of 100g of coffee?

A. ₹ 15 B. ₹ 25
C. ₹ 35 D. ₹ 65

5. A car is marked at ₹ 2,25,000. The manufacturer gives a discount of 10%. The dealer also gives a discount of 5%. What is the S.P. of the car?

A. ₹ 1,72,369 B. ₹ 1,64,370
C. ₹ 1,52,393 D. ₹ 1,92,375

6. A cycle merchant allows 25% commission on his advertised price and still makes a profit of 20%. If he gains ₹ 60 over the sale of one cycle. What is his advertised price?

A. ₹ 290 B. ₹ 310
C. ₹ 480 D. ₹ 520

7. The marked price of a shirt was ₹ 165 and it was at a discount of 12%. What the selling price of the shirt?

A. ₹ 145.20 B. ₹ 155.30
C. ₹ 165.20 D. ₹ 175.25

8. A trader marks his goods 40% above the cost price and gives a discount of 20% on the marked price. What is his gain per cent?

A. 8% B. 9%
C. 12% D. 15%

9. How much per cent more than the C.P. should a manufacturer mark his goods so that after allowing a discount of 20% on the marked price, he gains 10%.

A. 34.5% B. 27.5%
C. 37.5% D. 38.5%

10. A shopkeeper allows a discount of 10% to his customers and still gains 20%. What is the marked price of an article which costs ₹ 450 to the shopkeeper?

A. ₹ 600 B. ₹ 700
C. ₹ 800 D. ₹ 900

11. A dealer of scientific instruments allows 20% discount on the marked price of the instruments and still makes a profit of 25%. If his gain over the sale of an instrument is ₹ 150. What is the marked price of the instrument?

A. ₹ 917.25 B. ₹ 937.50
C. ₹ 945.75 D. ₹ 947.25

12. Jyoti and Meena run a ready-made garment shop. They mark the garments at such a price that even after allowing a discount of 12.5%, they make a profit of 10%. What is the marked price of a suit which costs them ₹ 1470?

A. ₹ 1820 B. ₹ 1848
C. ₹ 1868 D. ₹ 1948

Simple Interest

Important Facts and Formulae

1. **Principal** : The money borrowed or lent out for a certain period is called the **principal** or the sum.

2. **Interest :** Extra money paid for using other's money is called **interest**.

3. **Simple Interest (S.I.) :** If the interest on a sum borrowed for a certain period is reckoned uniformly, then it is called **simple interest**.

Let Principal = P, Rate = R% per annum (p.a.) and Time = T years. Then,

(*i*) $\text{S.I.} = \left(\frac{P \times R \times T}{100}\right)$

(*ii*) $P = \left(\frac{100 \times \text{S.I.}}{R \times T}\right)$; $R = \left(\frac{100 \times \text{S.I.}}{P \times T}\right)$ and $T = \left(\frac{100 \times \text{S.I.}}{P \times R}\right)$

Multiple Choice Questions

1. What is the interest on ₹ 2000 for 3 years at 8% per annum?

A. 480 B. 490
C. 510 D. 420

2. What is the simple interest on ₹ 4000 for 3 years at the rate of 10% p.a.?

A. ₹ 1200 B. ₹ 1300
C. ₹ 2200 D. ₹ 1424

3. What is the simple interest on ₹ 9280 at the rate of $4\frac{1}{2}$% per annum for 5 months?

A. ₹ 374 B. ₹ 174
C. ₹ 184 D. ₹ 192

4. Pawan borrowed ₹ 3000 from a friend at simple interest. After 5 years he paid ₹ 4500; and cleared his debt. What is the rate of interest?
A. 12% B. 15%
C. 10% D. 20%

5. In what time will a sum amount to 5 times of itself at the rate of $7\frac{1}{2}\%$ per annum?
A. 2 years B. $5\frac{1}{2}$ years
C. $13\frac{1}{3}$ years D. $53\frac{1}{3}$ years

6. A sum was put at simple interest at a certain rate for 2 years. Had it been put at 3% higher rate, it would have fetched ₹ 300 more. What is the sum?
A. ₹ 6000 B. ₹ 5000
C. ₹ 5500 D. ₹ 6500

7. What simple interest will discharge a debt of ₹ 2210 due in 4 years at 7% per annum?
A. ₹ 628.2 B. ₹ 638.4
C. ₹ 618.8 D. ₹ 698.2

8. ₹ 800 amount to ₹ 920 in 3 years at simple interest. If the interest rate is increased by 3%. What is the amount?
A. ₹ 892 B. ₹ 992
C. ₹ 1002 D. ₹ 782

9. Kamal lent ₹ 600 to Meena for 2 years and ₹ 150 to Anil for 4 years and received altogether from both ₹ 90 as simple interest. What is the rate of interest?
A. 6% p.a. B. 5% p.a.
C. $8\frac{1}{2}\%$ p.a. D. 10% p.a.

10. The difference between the interest received from two different banks on ₹ 500 for 2 years is ₹ 2.50. What is the difference between their rates?
A. 0.35% B. 0.55%
C. 0.25% D. 0.65%

11. A sum was put at simple interest at a certain rate for 2 years. Had it been put at 1% higher rate, it would have fetched ₹ 24 more. What is the sum?
A. ₹ 1200 B. ₹ 1400
C. ₹ 1500 D. ₹ 1600

12. In what time will the simple interest on ₹ 780 at 5% be equal to the simple interest on ₹ 600 at $6\frac{1}{2}\%$?
A. 2 years B. 5 years
C. 8 years D. All of these

13. In what time will a sum of money double itself at $6\frac{1}{4}\%$ p.a. simple interest?
A. 12 years B. 16 years
C. 18 years D. 22 years

14. A sum of money doubles itself in 10 years. In how many years would it treble itself?
A. 10 years B. 15 years
C. 20 years D. 25 years

15. The simple interest on a sum of money at 8% per annum for 6 years is half the sum. What is the sum?
A. ₹ 1000 B. ₹ 1200
C. ₹ 1500 D. Data in adequate

Compound Interest

Compound Interest : Sometimes it so happens that the borrower and the lender agree to fix up a certain unit of time, say yearly or half-yearly or quarterly to settle the previous account.

In such cases, the amount after first unit of time becomes the principal for the second unit, the amount after second unit becomes the principal for the third unit and so on.

After a specified period, the difference between the amount and the money borrowed is called the Compound Interest (*abbreviated* as C.I.) for that period.

Important Facts and Formulae

Let Principal = P, Rate = R% per annum, Time = n years.

I. When interest is compound Annually:

$$\text{Amount} = P\left(1+\frac{R}{100}\right)^n$$

II. When interest is compounded Half-yearly :

$$\text{Amount} = P\left[1+\frac{(R/2)}{100}\right]^{2n}$$

III. When interest is compounded Quarterly :

$$\text{Amount} = P\left[1+\frac{(R/4)}{100}\right]^{4n}$$

IV. When interest is compounded Annually but time is in fraction, say $3\frac{2}{5}$ years.

$$\text{Amount} = P\left(1+\frac{R}{100}\right)^3 \times \left(1+\frac{\frac{2}{5}R}{100}\right)$$

V. When Rates are different for different years, say $R_1\%$, $R_2\%$, $R_3\%$ for 1st, 2nd, 3rd year respectively.

Then, $\text{Amount} = P\left(1+\frac{R_1}{100}\right)\left(1+\frac{R_2}{100}\right)\left(1+\frac{R_3}{100}\right)$.

VI. Present worth of Rs. x due n years hence is given by :

$$\text{Present Worth} = \frac{x}{\left(1+\frac{R}{100}\right)^n}.$$

Multiple Choice Questions

1. What is the amount of ₹ 6000 lent at 5% per annum for 2 years if the interest is compounded annually?
   A. ₹ 6615 B. ₹ 6720
   C. ₹ 6625 D. ₹ 6612

2. What is the compound interest on ₹ 25600 for 2 years at 6.25% per annum?
   A. ₹ 3300 B. ₹ 3500
   C. ₹ 4000 D. ₹ 3350

3. What is the amount and compound interest on ₹ 16000 for 3 years, if the rate of interest is 2% per annum?
   A. ₹ 989.2 B. ₹ 987.43
   C. ₹ 979.33 D. ₹ 991.24

4. Simple interest on a sum of money for 3 years at $6\frac{1}{4}\%$ per annum is ₹ 2400. What will be the compound interest on that sum at the same rate for the same period?
   A. ₹ 2430.43 B. ₹ 2553.13
   C. ₹ 2522.17 D. ₹ 2532.19

5. The difference between the compound interest and the simple interest on a certain sum for 2 years at 10% per annum is ₹ 300. What is the sum?
   A. ₹ 20,000 B. ₹ 25,000
   C. ₹ 30,000 D. ₹ 35,000

6. A certain sum amounts to ₹ 5832 in 2 years at 8% compound interest. What is the sum?
   A. ₹ 4000 B. ₹ 5000
   C. ₹ 7000 D. ₹ 9000

7. At what rate per cent will a sum of ₹ 1000 amount to ₹ 1102.50 in 2 years at compound interest?
   A. 7% p.a. B. 8% p.a.
   C. 5% p.a. D. 10% p.a.

8. The difference between the compound interest and simple interest on a certain sum for 2 years at 7.5% per annum is ₹ 360. What is the sum?
   A. ₹ 54,000 B. ₹ 64,000
   C. ₹ 63,500 D. ₹ 62,500

9. The difference in simple interest and compound interest on a certain sum of money at $6\frac{2}{3}\%$ per annum for 3 years is ₹ 46. What is the sum?
   A. ₹ 3375 B. ₹ 3250
   C. ₹ 3340 D. ₹ 3450

10. A sum of money deposited at 2% per annum compounded annually becomes ₹ 10404 at the end of 2 years. What is the sum deposited?
    A. ₹ 11,000 B. ₹ 10,000
    C. ₹ 12,500 D. ₹ 13,600

11. A sum of money amounts to ₹ 4,53,690 in 2 years at 6.5% p.a. compounded annually. What is the sum?
    A. ₹ 3,50,000 B. ₹ 4,00,000
    C. ₹ 2,25,000 D. ₹ 5,50,000

12. What sum of money will amount to ₹ 45,582.25 at $6\frac{3}{4}\%$ p.a. in two years interest being compounded annually?
    A. ₹ 30,000 B. ₹ 35,000
    C. ₹ 40,000 D. ₹ 42,000

13. At what rate per cent per annum will a sum of ₹ 4000 yield compound interest of ₹ 410 in 2 years?
    A. 6% p.a. B. 5% p.a.
    C. 10% p.a. D. 12% p.a.

14. In how much time will a sum of ₹ 1600 amount to ₹ 1852.20 at 5% per annum compound interest?
    A. 2 years B. 3 years
    C. 4 years D. 5 years

15. Reena invested a sum of ₹ 12,000 at 5% per annum compound interest she received an amount of ₹ 13,230 after n years. What is the value of n?
    A. 2 years B. 3 years
    C. 5 years D. 9 years

16. What is the compound interest on ₹ 12000 for 3 years at 10% per annum compound annually?
    A. ₹ 3732 B. ₹ 3827
    C. ₹ 3972 D. ₹ 4000

17. Abhay lent ₹ 8000 to his friend for 3 years at the rate of 5% per annum compound interest. What amount does Abhay get after 3 years?
    A. ₹ 9241 B. ₹ 9261
    C. ₹ 9132 D. ₹ 9232

18. Vijay obtains a loan of ₹ 64,000 against his fixed deposits. If the rate of interest be 2.5 paise per rupee per annum, calculate the compound interest payable after 3 years.
    A. ₹ 68,421 B. ₹ 67,431
    C. ₹ 68,921 D. ₹ 66,921

19. What is the compound interest at the rate of 10% per annum for four years on the principal which in four years at the rate of 4% per annum gives ₹ 1600 as simple interest?
A. ₹ 1557.78
B. ₹ 1697.79
C. ₹ 1798.22
D. ₹ 1696.23

20. What is the compound interest of ₹ 12,000 for 2 years at 20% per annum when compounded half-yearly?
A. 5569.2
B. 5562.3
C. 5571.4
D. 5671.2

ANSWERS

Percentage

1	2	3	4	5	6	7	8	9	10
A	C	B	A	B	C	C	A	B	C
11	**12**	**13**	**14**	**15**					
B	A	A	C	B					

Profit & Loss

1	2	3	4	5	6	7	8	9	10
A	B	A	D	C	A	C	C	A	B
11	**12**	**13**	**14**	**15**	**16**	**17**	**18**	**19**	**20**
A	C	A	C	B	A	B	C	B	A
21	**22**	**23**	**24**	**25**					
D	B	D	D	B					

Discount

1	2	3	4	5	6	7	8	9	10
A	B	A	B	D	C	A	C	C	A
11	**12**								
B	B								

Simple Interest

1	2	3	4	5	6	7	8	9	10
A	A	B	C	D	B	C	B	B	C
11	**12**	**13**	**14**	**15**					
A	D	B	C	D					

Compound Interest

1	2	3	4	5	6	7	8	9	10
A	A	C	B	C	B	C	B	A	B
11	**12**	**13**	**14**	**15**	**16**	**17**	**18**	**19**	**20**
B	C	B	B	A	C	B	C	B	A

EXPLANATORY ANSWERS

Percentage

1. Cost price = ₹ 50

Increase = ₹ 25

$$\text{Rate of increase} = \frac{25\times100}{50} = 50\%$$

2. Let Number = x

$$72\frac{1}{2}\% \text{ of } x = 87$$

$$\frac{145}{2\times100}\times x = 87$$

$$x = \frac{87\times2\times100}{145} = 120$$

3. Let number = x

$$18\% \text{ of } 650 - x \times 25\% = 19$$

$$\frac{18}{100}\times650 - 19 = \frac{25x}{100}$$

$$117 - 19 = \frac{x}{4}$$

$$98 \times 4 = x$$

$$x = 392$$

4. Let total number of votes = x

$$65\% \text{ of } x - 35\% \text{ of } x = 300$$

$$30\%\ x = 300$$

$$\frac{30}{100}\times x = 300 \Rightarrow x = \frac{300\times100}{30}$$

$$x = 1000$$

5. Let total population = x

$$96\% \text{ of } x = 23040$$

$$\frac{96}{100}\times x = 23040$$

$$x = \frac{23040\times100}{96}$$

$$= 960 \times 25$$

$$= 24000$$

6. Per cent of girls = 25%

Let total number of students = x

$$25\% \text{ of } x = 420$$

$$\frac{25}{100}\times x = 420$$

$$x = 420 \times 4 = 1680$$

Total number of students = 1680.

No. of boys = 75% of 1680

$$= \frac{75}{100}\times1680$$

$$= 1260$$

7. Population = 5000

$$\text{Increase in 1st year} = 5000\times\frac{2}{100} = 100$$

Population after 1 year = 5000 + 100 = 5100

Increase in population in 2nd year

$$= 5100\times\frac{2}{100}$$

$$= 102$$

Population of 2 years

$$= 5100 + 102$$

$$= 5202$$

8. Population = 15435

Time = 2 yrs.

Rate = 5% p.a.

Population after 2 years

$$= \frac{P}{\left(1+\frac{r}{100}\right)^n} = \frac{15435}{\left(1+\frac{5}{100}\right)^2}$$

$$= \frac{15435}{\left(\frac{21}{20}\right)^2} = \frac{15435\times20\times20}{21\times21}$$

$$= 21 \times 400$$

$$= 8400$$

9. P = 8000

$r_1 = 10\%$

$r_2 = 20\%$

Time = 2 years

Population after two years

$$= P\left(1+\frac{r_1}{100}\right)\left(1+\frac{r_2}{100}\right)$$

$$= 8000\left(1+\frac{10}{100}\right)\left(1+\frac{20}{100}\right)$$

$$= 8000\times\frac{11}{10}\times\frac{6}{5}$$

$$= 10560$$

10. Let total no. of days = x

$$90\% \text{ of } x = 216$$

$$\frac{90}{100}\ x = 216$$

$$x = \frac{216\times10}{9} = 240 \text{ days}$$

11. Let total income = ₹ x

$$25\% \text{ of } x = 2500$$

$$\frac{25}{100}\times x = 2500$$

$$x = \frac{2500\times100}{25} = ₹\ 10000$$

12. Let number of student in beginning = x

6% of $x = 150$

$$\frac{6}{100}\times x = 150 \Rightarrow x = \frac{150\times100}{6}$$

$x = 2500$

Increased number of student

$= 2500 + 150 = 2650$

13. Total trees = 1500

Nos. of Mangoes $= 1500 \times 15\%$

$= 1500 \times \frac{15}{100} = 225.$

Nos. of Lemon trees $= 1500 \times 18\%$

$= 1500 \times \frac{18}{100}$

$= 15 \times 18 = 270.$

Nos. of Orange trees $= 1500 - (225 + 270)$

$= 1500 - 495 = 1005$

14. Let total nos. of students = x

70% of $x = 210$

$$\frac{70}{100}\times x = 210 \Rightarrow x = \frac{210\times100}{70}$$

$x = 300$

15. Let total number of matches = x

40% of $x = 10$

$\frac{40}{100}\times x = 10$

$x = \frac{10\times5}{2}$

$x = 25$

Total number of matches = 25

Profit & Loss

1. S.P. = 18000

Profit = 20%

Let C.P. = x

$x + x \times 20\% = 18000$

$\frac{120}{100}x = 18000$

$x = \frac{18000\times5}{6} = 15000$

C.P. of 1st bullock = 15000

Again,

S.P. = 18000

Loss = 20%

Let C.P. = x

$x - x\times\frac{20}{100} = 18000$

$\frac{80}{100}x = 18000$

$x = \frac{18000\times5}{4}$

$x = 22500$

Total C.P. $= 22500 + 15000$

$= 37500$

Total S.P. $= 18000 + 18000 = 36000$

Loss $= 37500 - 36000$

$=$ ₹ 1500

2. Let S.P. of 1 hen = ₹ 1

S.P. of 144 hens = ₹ 144

Loss = S.P. of 6 hens = 6×1 = ₹ 6

C.P. of 144 hens = 144 + 6 = ₹ 150

$$\text{Loss\%} = \frac{\text{loss}\times100}{\text{C.P}} = \frac{6\times100}{150}$$

$= 4\%$

3. C.P. of 100 blankets $= 100 \times 2000$

= ₹ 200000

Profit = 14%

S.P. $= 200000 + 200000 \times \frac{14}{100}$

$= 228000$

S.P. of 10 blankets $= 1200 \times 10$

$= 12000$

Remaining S.P. $= 228000 - 12000$

S.P. of 90 blankets $= 216000$

S.P. of 1 blanket $= \frac{216000}{90}$

= ₹ 2400

Direction (4 and 5): C.P. of 100g. gold = ₹ 54000

Profit = 10%

S.P. of 100g. gold $= 54000 + 54000 \times \frac{10}{100}$

$= 54000 + 5400$

$= 59400$

4. S.P. of 100g. gold $= \frac{59400}{100}\times10$

= ₹ 5940

5. S.P. of wholesaler (10 gm.) $= \frac{54000}{100}\times10$

$= 5400.$

C.P. of wholesaler for 10g. = x

$x + x \times 8\% = 5400$

$\frac{108}{100}\times x = 5400$

$x = \frac{5400\times100}{108}$

= ₹ 5000

Directions (6 to 8) : Let C.P. of Wheat = ₹ x

6. $x + x \times 12\% = 924$

$\frac{112}{100}x = 924$

$x = \frac{924 \times 100}{112}$

$x = ₹\ 825$

7. Let C.P. of Rice = ₹ x

$x - x \times \frac{12}{100} = 924$

$\frac{88}{100}x = 924$

$x = \frac{924 \times 100}{88} = ₹\ 1050$

8. Total S.P. = 924 + 924 = 1848

Total C.P. = 825 + 1050 = 1875

Profit = 1875 − 1848 = ₹ 27

9. Let C.P. of tricycle = ₹ x

$116\% \text{ of } x + 100 = 120\%\ x$

$\frac{116}{100} \times x + 100 = \frac{120}{100}x$

$\frac{6}{5}x - \frac{29}{25}x = 100$

$\frac{30x - 29x}{25} = 100 \Rightarrow x = 100 \times 25$

$\Rightarrow \quad x = ₹\ 2500$

10. C.P. of 20 dining tables = ₹ 120000

C.P. of 1 dining table $= \frac{120000}{20}$

= ₹ 6000.

Let his profit = ₹ x per dining table

S.P. of 1 dining table = $6000 + x$

Total profit = $4\,(6000 + x)$

$= 24000 + 4x$

S.P. price of 20 dining table

$= 120000 + 24000 + 4x$

$= 144000 + 4x.$

S.P. price of 1 dining table

$\frac{6000 + x}{1} = \frac{144000 + 4x}{20}$

$120000 + 20x = 144000 + 4x$

$16x = 144000 - 120000$

$16x = 24000$

$x = \frac{24000}{16}$

Profit = 1500

S.P. of 1 dining table

= 6000 + 1500 = ₹ 7500

11. Let C.P. of Dimpi = ₹ x

$x + x \times 10\% = 330000$

$\frac{110}{100}x = 330000$

$x = \frac{330000}{11} \times 10 = 300000$

Let C.P. of Yogita = ₹ y

$y + y \times 20\% = 300000$

$\frac{120}{100}y = 300000$

$y = \frac{300000}{12} \times 10$

$y = ₹\ 250000$

12. C.P. of entire land = ₹ 300000

Profit = 10%

S.P. $= 300000 + 300000 \times \frac{10}{100}$

= ₹ 330,000

C.P. of $\frac{1}{3}$rd land $= \frac{1}{3} \times 300000$

= 100000

Loss = 20%

S.P. $= 100000 - 100000 \times \frac{20}{100}$

= 80000

C.P. of 2/5rd land $= \frac{2}{5} \times 300000$

= ₹ 120000

Gain = 25%

S.P. $= 120000 + 120000 \times \frac{25}{100}$

= 150000

Remaining S.P. = 330000 − (150000 + 80000)

= 330000 − 230000

= ₹ 100000

13. Gain = 1000g − 960g = 40g.

Gain % $= \frac{40 \times 100}{960} = \frac{25}{6}$

$= 4\frac{1}{6}\%$

14. Let C.P. of 1st Fan = ₹ x

C.P. of other = $(2160 - x)$

$115\%\ x + 91\%\ (2160 - x) = 2160$

$\frac{115}{100} \times x + \frac{91}{100}(2160 - x) = 2160$

$\frac{23}{20}x - \frac{91}{100}x = 2160 - 2160 \times \frac{91}{100}$

$\frac{115x - 91x}{100} = 2160\left(\frac{100 - 91}{100}\right)$

$$\frac{24x}{100} = \frac{2160 \times 9}{100}$$

$$x = \frac{2160 \times 9}{24} = 810$$

C.P. of 1st fan = ₹ 810

C.P. of 2nd fan = 2160 – 810 = ₹ 1350

15. Let C.P. = ₹ x

105% of x – 50 = 95% x

105% of x – 95%x = 50

10% of x = 50

$$x = \frac{50 \times 100}{10} = ₹\ 500$$

$$\text{Original S.P.} = 105\%\ x = \frac{105}{100} \times 500 = ₹\ 525$$

16. Gain = 14 – 10 = 4

$$\text{Gain \%} = \frac{4 \times 100}{10} = 40\%$$

17. Let C.P. be ₹ x and S.P. be ₹ y.

Then, $3(y - x) = (2y - x) \Rightarrow y = 2x$

Profit = ₹ $(y - x)$ = ₹ $(2x - x)$ = ₹ x.

$$\therefore \quad \text{Profit\%} = \left(\frac{x}{y} \times 100\right)\% = 100\%$$

18. Let C.P. of each pen be ₹ 1. Then, C.P. of 8 pens = ₹ 8; S.P. of 8 pens = ₹ 12.

$$\therefore \quad \text{Gain\%} = \left(\frac{4}{8} \times 100\right)\% = 50\%.$$

19. Let C.P. of each article be ₹ 1. C.P. of x articles = ₹ x, S.P. of x articles = ₹ 20. Profits = ₹ = $(20 - x)$.

$$\therefore \quad \frac{20 - x}{x} \times 100 = 25 \Rightarrow 2000 - 100x = 25x$$

$$\Rightarrow \quad 125x = 2000 \Rightarrow x = 16.$$

20. C.P. of 1 apple = ₹ $\left(\frac{34}{8}\right)$ = ₹ 4.25. S.P. of 1 apple = ₹ $\left(\frac{57}{12}\right)$ = ₹ 4.75. Profit on each apple = ₹ 0.50

$\therefore$ Number of apples required = $\left(\frac{45}{0.50}\right) = 90.$

21. Suppose, number of articles bought = L.C.M. of 6 and 5 = 30.

C.P. of 30 articles = ₹ $\left(\frac{5}{6} \times 30\right)$ = ₹ 25. S.P. of 30 articles = ₹ $\left(\frac{6}{5} \times 30\right)$ = ₹ 36.

$$\therefore \text{ Gain \%} = \left(\frac{11}{25} \times 100\right)\% = 44\%.$$

22. C.P. of 56 kg rice = ₹ (26 × 20 + 30 × 36) = ₹ (520 + 1080) = ₹ 1600.

S.P. of 56 kg rice = ₹ (56 × 30) = ₹ 1680.

$$\therefore \text{ Gain} = \left(\frac{80}{1600} \times 100\right)\% = 5\%.$$

23. Gain % = $\left(\frac{10}{90} \times 100\right)\% = 11\frac{1}{9}\%$

24. 125% of 120% of A = 225

$$\Rightarrow \quad \frac{125}{100} \times \frac{120}{100} \times A = 225$$

$$\Rightarrow \quad A = \left(225 \times \frac{2}{5}\right) = ₹\ 150.$$

25.
$$\text{Loss\%} = \left(\frac{\text{Common Loss and Gain\%}}{10}\right)^2 \%$$

$$= \left(\frac{12}{10}\right)^2 \% = \frac{36}{25}\% = 1\frac{11}{25}\%.$$

Discount

1. S.P. = ₹ 680

Discount = 15%

$$\text{M.P.} = \frac{100 \times \text{S.P.}}{100 - \text{Discount\%}}$$

$$= \frac{100 \times 680}{100 - 15} = \frac{100 \times 680}{85} = ₹\ 800$$

2. C.P. = ₹ x

120% of x = 350 – 350 × 10%

$$\frac{120}{100} \times x = 350 - 35 = 315.$$

$$x = \frac{315 \times 5}{6} = \frac{525}{2}$$

C.P. = ₹ 262.50

3. Let M.P. = ₹ x

80% x = 118% of 200

$$\frac{80}{100} \times x = \frac{118}{100} \times 200$$

$$x = \frac{236 \times 5}{4} = ₹\ 295$$

4. Let C.P. of 100 gm coffee = ₹ x

110% of x = 35 − 7.50 = 27.50

$$\frac{110}{100}\times x = 27.50$$

$$x = \frac{27.50\times100}{110\times100}$$

C.P. = ₹ 25.

5. M.P. = ₹ 225000

$$\text{1st S.P.} = 225000 - 225000 \times \frac{10}{100}$$

= 225000 − 22500 = 202500

$$\text{2nd S.P.} = 202500 - 202500 \times \frac{5}{100}$$

= 202500 − 10125 = ₹ 192375

6. Let M.P. = 100

Commission = 25%

S.P. = 100 − 25 = 75

Profit = 20%

$$\text{C.P.} = \frac{100}{120}\times75 = \frac{375}{6} = 62.50$$

Gain = 75 − 62.50 = ₹ 12.50

$$\text{M.P.} = \frac{100}{12.50}\times60 = ₹\ 480$$

7.
$$\text{S.P.} = \frac{\text{M.P.}(100-\text{Discount})}{100}$$

$$= \frac{165\times(100-12)}{100} = \frac{165\times88}{100}$$

= 33 × 4.4 = ₹ 145.20

8. Let C.P. = 100

M.P. = 140

Discount = 20%

$$\text{S.P.} = 140 - 140\times\frac{20}{100}$$

= 140 − 28 = 112

Profit = 112 − 100 = 12

$$\text{Profit \%} = \frac{12\times100}{100} = 12\%$$

9. Let C.P. = ₹ x

$$\text{S.P.} = 110\% \text{ of } x = \frac{110}{100}\times x = \frac{11}{10}x.$$

Discount = 20%

$$\text{M.P.} = \frac{100\times\frac{11}{10}x}{100-20} = \frac{100\times\frac{11}{10}x}{80} = \frac{11}{8}x.$$

$$\text{Required \%} = \frac{\frac{11x}{8}-x}{x}\times100 = \frac{3x\times100}{8x} = 37.5\%$$

10. C.P. = 450

Gain = 20%

$$\text{S.P.} = 450 + 450\times\frac{20}{100}$$

= 450 + 90 = 540

Discount = 10%

$$\text{M.P.} = \frac{100\times\text{S.P.}}{100-\text{Discount}} = \frac{100\times540}{100-10}$$

$$= \frac{100\times540}{90} = ₹\ 600$$

11. Gain % = 25

Gain = ₹ 150

C.P. = x

25% of x = 150

$$x = \frac{150\times100}{25} = 600$$

C.P. = 600

S.P. = 600 + 150 = 750

$$\text{M.P.} = \frac{100\times750}{100-20} = \frac{100\times750}{80}$$

M.P. = 5 × 187.50 = ₹ 937.50

12. C.P. = 1470

Gain = 10%

$$\text{S.P.} = 1470 + 1470\times\frac{10}{100}$$

= 1470 + 147 = 1617

$$\text{M.P.} = \frac{100\times1617}{100-12.5} = \frac{100\times1617}{87.5}$$

M.P. = ₹ 1848

Simple Interest

1. P = ₹ 2000

T = 3 yrs

R = 8% p.a.

$$\text{Interest} = \frac{\text{PRT}}{100} = \frac{2000\times8\times3}{100} = ₹\ 480$$

2. P = ₹ 4000

T = 3 yrs.

R = 10% p.a.

$$\text{S.I.} = \frac{\text{PRT}}{100} = \frac{4000\times10\times3}{100}$$

= ₹ 1200

3. P = 9280

$$R = \frac{9}{2}\%\ \text{p.a.}$$

$T = \frac{5}{12}$ yr.

$S.I. = \frac{PRT}{100} = \frac{9280 \times 9 \times 5}{100 \times 2 \times 12}$

$= 58 \times 3 = ₹\ 174$

4. P = ₹ 3000
A = ₹ 4500
S.I. = A – P = 4500 – 3000 = 1500
T = 5 yrs.

$R = \frac{S.I. \times 100}{P \times T} = \frac{1500 \times 100}{3000 \times 5} = 10\%$

5. P = ₹ 100
A = ₹ 500
S.I. = 500 – 100 = ₹ 400

$R = \frac{15}{2}\%$ p.a.

$T = \frac{S.I. \times 100}{P \times R}$

$= \frac{400 \times 100 \times 2}{100 \times 15} = \frac{160}{3} = 53\frac{1}{3}$ yrs.

6. Let Rate = $x\%$

$\frac{P \times (x+3) \times 2}{100} - \frac{P \times x \times 2}{100} = 300$

$\frac{2P(x+3)}{100} - \frac{2Px}{100} = 300$

$2Px + 6P - 2Px = 30000$

$P = \frac{30000}{6}$

Principle = ₹ 5000

7. P = 2210
R = 7
T = 4

$S.I. = \frac{PRT}{100} = \frac{2210 \times 7 \times 4}{100} = ₹\ 618.80$

8. P = 800
A = 920
T = 3 yrs.
S.I. = 920 – 800 = 120

$R = \frac{S.I. \times 100}{P \times T} = \frac{120 \times 100}{800 \times 3} = 5\%$ p.a.

New rate = 5 + 3 = 8%

$S.I. = \frac{PRT}{100} = \frac{800 \times 8 \times 3}{100} = ₹\ 192$

A = P + S.I. = 800 + 192 = ₹ 992

9. $\frac{600 \times 2 \times R}{100} + \frac{2150 \times 4 \times R}{100} = 90$

12 R + 6 R = 90

18 R = 90

$R = \frac{90}{18}$

R = 5% p.a.

10. $\frac{500 \times r_1 \times 2}{100} - \frac{500 \times r_2 \times 2}{100} = 2.50$

$10(r_1 - r_2) = 2.50$

$r_1 - r_2 = \frac{2.50}{10}$

$r_1 - r_2 = 0.25\%$

11. $\frac{P \times (x+1) \times 2}{100} - \frac{P \times x \times 2}{100} = 24$

$2Px + 2P - 2Px = 2400$

P = ₹ 1200

12. T = ?

$P_1 = ₹\ 780$

$R_1 = ₹\ 5\%$

$P_2 = ₹\ 600$

$R_2 = \frac{13}{2}\%$

According to question

$\frac{P_1R_1T_1}{100} = \frac{P_2R_2T_2}{100}$

$\frac{780 \times 5 \times T_1}{100} = \frac{600 \times 13 \times T_2}{100 \times 2}$

$T_1 = T_2$

It is true for all values of T.

13. Let sum = 100
Amount = 200
S.I. = 200 – 100 = ₹ 100

$R = \frac{25}{4}\%$ p.a.

$T = \frac{S.I. \times 100}{P \times R} = \frac{100 \times 100 \times 4}{100 \times 25}$

= 16 yrs.

14. Let sum = ₹ 100
Amount = ₹ 200
S.I. = ₹ 100
T = 10 years

$R = \frac{S.I. \times 100}{P \times T} = \frac{100 \times 100}{100 \times 10}$

R = 10% p.a.

Again, P = ₹ 100
A = ₹ 300
S.I. = ₹ 200
R = 10% p.a.
T = ?

$T = \frac{S.I. \times 100}{P \times R} = \frac{200 \times 100}{100 \times 10}$

T = 20 years.

15. Let sum = ₹ x

S.I. = ₹ $x/2$

R = 8% p.a.

T = 6 years.

$$\text{S.I.} = \frac{\text{PRT}}{100}$$

$$x/2 = \frac{x\times8\times6}{100} = \frac{12x}{25}$$

$$\Rightarrow \frac{1}{2} = \frac{12}{25}, \text{ which is false.}$$

So, data is inadequate.

Compound Interest

1. P = ₹ 6000

R = 5% p.a.

T = 2 years

$$A = P\left(1+\frac{r}{100}\right)^n = 6000\left(1+\frac{5}{100}\right)^2$$

$$= 6000\times\frac{21}{20}\times\frac{21}{20}$$

$$= 15\times21\times21 = ₹\ 6615$$

2. P = ₹ 25600

R = 6.25 p.a.

T = 2 years

$$A = P\left(1+\frac{r}{100}\right)^n = 25600\left(1+\frac{6.25}{100}\right)^2$$

$$= 25600\left(\frac{17}{16}\right)^2$$

$$= 25600\,\frac{17}{16}\times\frac{17}{16}$$

$$= 28900$$

$$\text{C.I.} = A - P = 28900 - 25600$$

$$= ₹\ 3300$$

3. P = ₹ 16000

n = 3 years

R = 2% p.a.

$$A = P\left(1+\frac{R}{100}\right)^n = 16000\left(1+\frac{2}{100}\right)^3$$

$$= 16000\times\frac{51}{50}\times\frac{51}{50}\times\frac{51}{50}$$

$$= \frac{16\times51\times51\times51}{125} = \frac{2122416}{125}$$

$$= ₹\ 16979.\ 33$$

$$\text{C.I.} = A - P$$

$$= 16979.33 - 16000$$

$$= ₹\ 979.33$$

4. S.I. = ₹ 24000

$$R = \frac{25}{4}\%\ \text{p.a.}$$

T = 3 years

$$P = \frac{\text{S.I.}\times100}{R\times T} = \frac{2400\times100\times4}{25\times3}$$

$$= ₹\ 12800.$$

$$A = P\left(1+\frac{r}{100}\right)^n = 12800\left(1+\frac{25}{400}\right)^3$$

$$= ₹\ 12800\times\frac{17}{16}\times\frac{17}{16}\times\frac{17}{16} = \frac{245650}{16}$$

$$= 15353.13$$

$$\text{C.I.} = A - P$$

$$= 15353.13 - 12800 = ₹\ 2553.13$$

5. $$P\left[\left(1+\frac{r}{100}\right)^n - 1\right] - \frac{\text{PRT}}{100} = 300$$

$$P\left[\left(1+\frac{10}{100}\right)^2 - 1\right] - \frac{P\times10\times2}{100} = 300$$

$$P\left(\frac{121}{100}-1\right) - \frac{P}{5} = 300$$

$$P\times\frac{21}{100} - \frac{P}{5} = 300$$

$$\frac{21P-20P}{100} = 300$$

$$P = 300\times100$$

$$= ₹\ 30,000$$

6. $$A = P\left(1+\frac{r}{100}\right)^n$$

$$5832 = P\left(1+\frac{8}{100}\right)^2$$

$$= P\times\frac{108}{100}\times\frac{108}{100}$$

$$P = \frac{5832\times100\times100}{108\times108}$$

$$= ₹\ 5000$$

7. $$1102.50 = 1000\left(1+\frac{r}{100}\right)^2$$

$$\frac{1102.50}{1000} = \left(1+\frac{r}{100}\right)^2$$

$$\left(\frac{21}{20}\right)^2 = \left(1+\frac{r}{100}\right)^2$$

$$\frac{21}{20} = 1+\frac{r}{100}$$

$$\frac{1}{20} = \frac{r}{100}$$

$$r = \frac{100}{20} = 5\% \text{ p.a.}$$

8. $$P\left[\left(1+\frac{r}{100}\right)^n-1\right]-\frac{PRT}{100} = 360$$

$$P\left[\left(1+\frac{7.5}{100}\right)^2-1\right]-\frac{P\times 7.5\times 2}{100} = 360$$

$$P\left[\frac{43}{40}\times\frac{43}{40}-1\right]-\frac{6P}{40} = 360$$

$$P\times\frac{43\times 43-40\times 40}{40\times 40}-\frac{6P}{40} = 360$$

$$P\times\frac{1849-1600}{1600}-\frac{6P}{40} = 360$$

$$\frac{249}{1600}P-\frac{6P}{40} = 360$$

$$\frac{249\,P-240\,P}{1600} = 360$$

$$9P = 360\times 1600$$

$$P = \frac{360\times 1600}{9}$$

$$P = 40\times 1600$$

$$= ₹\ 64000$$

9. $$P\left[\left(1+\frac{r}{100}\right)^n-1\right]-\frac{PRT}{100} = 46$$

$$P\left[\left(1+\frac{20}{300}\right)^3-1\right]-\frac{P\times 20\times 3}{100\times 3} = 46$$

$$P\left(\frac{16}{15}\times\frac{16}{15}\times\frac{16}{15}-1\right)-\frac{P}{5} = 46$$

$$P\left(\frac{16\times 16\times 16-15\times 15\times 15}{15\times 15\times 15}\right)-\frac{P}{5} = 46$$

$$P\left(\frac{4096-3375}{3375}\right)-\frac{P}{5} = 46$$

$$P\times\frac{721}{3375}-\frac{P}{5} = 46$$

$$\frac{721\,P-675\,P}{3375} = 46$$

$$\frac{46P}{3375} = 46$$

$$P = \frac{46\times 3375}{46}$$

$$= ₹\ 3375$$

10. $$A = P\left(1+\frac{r}{100}\right)^n$$

$$10404 = P\left(1+\frac{2}{100}\right)^2 = P\times\frac{51}{50}\times\frac{51}{50}$$

$$P = \frac{10404\times 50\times 50}{51\times 51}$$

$$= 4\times 2500 = 10000$$

$$P = ₹\ 10000$$

11. $$A = P\left(1+\frac{r}{100}\right)^n$$

$$453690 = P\left(1+\frac{6.5}{100}\right)^2 = P\times\frac{1065\times 1065}{1000\times 1000}$$

$$P = \frac{453690\times 1000000}{1065\times 1065}$$

$$P = 400000$$

12. $$A = P\left(1+\frac{r}{100}\right)^n$$

$$45582.25 = P\left(1+\frac{27}{400}\right)^2 = P\times\frac{427}{400}\times\frac{427}{400}$$

$$P = \frac{45582.25\times 400\times 400}{427\times 427}$$

$$= 25\times 400\times 4$$

$$= ₹\ 40000$$

13. $$C.I. = P\left[\left(1+\frac{r}{100}\right)^n-1\right]$$

$$410 = P\left[\left(1+\frac{r}{100}\right)^2-1\right]$$

$$410 = 4000\left[\left(1+\frac{r}{100}\right)^2-1\right]$$

$$\frac{410}{4000} = \left(1+\frac{r}{100}\right)^2-1$$

$$\frac{41}{400}+1 = \left(1+\frac{r}{100}\right)^2$$

$$\frac{441}{400} = \left(1+\frac{r}{100}\right)^2$$

$$\left(\frac{21}{20}\right)^2 = \left(1+\frac{r}{100}\right)^2$$

$$1+\frac{r}{100} = \frac{21}{20} \Rightarrow \frac{r}{100} = \frac{21}{20}-1 = \frac{1}{20}$$

$$r = \frac{100}{20} = 5\% \text{ p.a.}$$

14. $$A = P\left(1+\frac{r}{100}\right)^n$$

$$1852.20 = 1600\left(1+\frac{5}{100}\right)^n$$

$$\frac{1852.20}{1600} = \left(1+\frac{1}{20}\right)^n = \left(\frac{21}{20}\right)^n$$

$$\frac{9261}{8000} = \left(\frac{21}{20}\right)^n$$

$$\left(\frac{21}{20}\right)^3 = \left(\frac{21}{20}\right)^n \Rightarrow n = 3 \text{ years}$$

15. $$13230 = 12000\left(1+\frac{5}{100}\right)^n$$

$$\frac{13230}{12000} = \left(\frac{21}{20}\right)^n$$

$$\left(\frac{21}{20}\right)^2 = \left(\frac{21}{20}\right)^n$$

$\Rightarrow$ $n = 2$ years

16. $$\text{C.I.} = P\left[\left(1+\frac{r}{100}\right)^n - 1\right]$$

$$= 12000\left[\left(1+\frac{10}{100}\right)^3 - 1\right]$$

$$= 12000\left(\frac{11\times11\times11}{1000} - 1\right)$$

$$= 12000\left(\frac{1331-1000}{1000}\right) = 12000 \times \frac{331}{1000}$$

$$= 12 \times 331 = ₹\ 3972$$

17. $$A = P\left(1+\frac{r}{100}\right)^n$$

$$= 8000\left(1+\frac{5}{100}\right)^3$$

$$= 8000 \times \frac{21\times21\times21}{20\times20\times20}$$

$$= ₹\ 9261$$

18. R = 2.5 paise per rupee per annum
= 2.5% per annum

$$A = P\left(1+\frac{r}{100}\right)^n = 64000\left(1+\frac{2.5}{100}\right)^3$$

$$= 64000 \times \frac{41}{40} \times \frac{41}{40} \times \frac{41}{40}$$

$$= 41 \times 41 \times 41 = ₹\ 68921$$

19. $$\text{S.I.} = \frac{PRT}{100}$$

$$P = \frac{\text{S.I.} \times 100}{R \times T} = \frac{1600\times100}{4\times4}$$

$$P = 10000$$

$$\text{C.I.} = P\left[\left(1+\frac{r}{100}\right)^n - 1\right]$$

$$= 10000\left[\left(1+\frac{4}{100}\right)^4 - 1\right]$$

$$= 10000\left(\frac{26}{25}\times\frac{26}{25}\times\frac{26}{25}\times\frac{26}{25} - 1\right)$$

$$= 10000\left(\frac{26\times26\times26\times26 - 25\times25\times25\times25}{25\times25\times25\times25}\right)$$

$$= 10000\left(\frac{456976-390625}{390625}\right)$$

$$= \frac{10000\times66351}{390625} = ₹\ 1697.79$$

20. $n = 4$

$$r = \frac{20}{2}\% = 10\%$$

$$P = 12000$$

$$A = P\left(1+\frac{r}{100}\right)^n = 12000\left(1+\frac{10}{100}\right)^4$$

$$= 12000 \times \frac{11}{10}\times\frac{11}{10}\times\frac{11}{10}\times\frac{11}{10}$$

$$= 1.2 \times 11 \times 11 \times 11 \times 11$$

$$= 17569.2$$

$$\text{C.I.} = A - P = 17569.2 - 12000$$

$$= ₹\ 5569.20$$

□□□□□

7

Algebraic Expressions and Identities Including Factorization

Algebric Identies

Some Important Formula

(i) $(a + b)^2 = a^2 + 2ab + b^2$

(ii) $(a - b)^2 = a^2 - 2ab + b^2$

(iii) $a^2 - b^2 = (a - b)(a + b)$

(iv) $(a + b + c)^2 = a^2 + b^2 + c^2 + 2ab + 2bc + 2ca$

(v) $(a + b - c)^2 = a^2 + b^2 + c^2 + 2ab - 2bc - 2ca$

(vi) $(a - b + c)^2 = a^2 + b^2 + c^2 - 2ab - 2bc + 2ca$

(vii) $(-a + b + c)^2 = a^2 + b^2 + c^2 - 2ab + 2bc - 2ca$

(viii) $(a + b)^3 = a^3 + b^3 + 3ab(a + b)$ or
$= a^3 + b^3 + 3a^2b + 3ab^2$

(ix) $(a - b)^3 = a^3 - b^3 - 3ab\,(a - b)$ or
$= a^3 - b^3 - 3a^2b + 3ab^2$

(x) $a^3 + b^3 = (a + b)\,(a^2 + b^2 - ab)$ or
$= (a + b)^3 - 3ab(a + b)$

(xi) $a^3 - b^3 = (a - b)\,(a^2 + b^2 + ab)$ or
$= (a - b)^3 + 3ab\,(a - b)$

(xii) $a^3 + b^3 + c^3 - 3abc = (a + b + c)(a^2 + b^2 + c^2 - ab - bc - ca)$
If $a + b + c = 0$
$a^3 + b^3 + c^3 = 3abc$

(xiii) $(x + a)\,(x + b) = x^2 + (a + b)x + ab$

(xiv) $(a + b)^2 + (a - b)^2 = 2(a^2 + b^2)$

(xv) $(a + b)^2 - (a - b)^2 = 4ab$

(xvi) $(a + b)^3 + (a - b)^3 = 2(a^3 + 3ab^2)$

(xvii) $(a + b)^3 - (a - b)^3 = (2(b^3 + 3a^2b)$

(xviii) If $x+\frac{1}{x}=t$
Then, $x^2+\frac{1}{x^2}=t^2-2$

(xix) If $x-\frac{1}{x}=t$
Then, $x^2+\frac{1}{x^2}=t^2+2$

(xx) $x^3+\frac{1}{x^3}=\left(x+\frac{1}{x}\right)^3-3\left(x+\frac{1}{x}\right)$

(xxi) $x^2-\frac{1}{x^3}=\left(x-\frac{1}{x}\right)^3+3\left(x-\frac{1}{x}\right)$

(xxii) $x+\frac{1}{x}=\sqrt{x^2+\frac{1}{x^2}+2}$

(xxiii) $x-\frac{1}{x}=\sqrt{x^2+\frac{1}{x^2}-2}$

Factorization of Algebraic Expressions

Factorization : The process of writing an algebraic expression as the product of two or more algebraic expressions is called factorization.

Factors : The algebraic expressions that may be multiplied to obtain the given algebraic expressions are called factors of the given expression.

Factor Theorem : If $f(x)$ is completely divisible by $(x - a)$ then $f(a) = 0$, $(x - a)$ is called factor of $f(x)$, if and only if $f(a) = 0$

Remainder Theorem : If an expression $f(x)$ is divided by $(x - a)$ then the remainder is $f(a)$.

e.g., $f(x) = ax^3 + bx + cx + d$

$f(a) = a\,.\,a^3 + b\,.\,a + c\,.\,a + d$ is known as remainder of the given polynomials.

Multiple Choice Questions

1. $(28)^3 + (-15)^3 + (-13)^3 = ?$

A. 16380 B. 16250
C. 16420 D. 16280

2. If $x+\frac{1}{x}$ = 5, What is the value of $x^3+\frac{1}{x^3}$:

A. 120 B. 210
C. 110 D. 105

3. If $x^2+\frac{1}{x^2}=83$, what is the value of $x^3-\frac{1}{x^3}=?$

A. 756 B. 754
C. 856 D. 932

4. $23^3 - 17^3 = ?$

A. 7254 B. 7153
C. 7271 D. 7154

5. If $x + \frac{1}{x} = 15$, then the value of $x^2 + \frac{1}{x^2}$ will be:

A. 228 B. 230
C. 323 D. 223

6. If $x = 12$ and $y = 4$, the value of $(x + y)^{x/y}$ will be:

A. 4096 B. 3896
C. 4196 D. 5086

7. If $x + y = 2z$, then the value of $\left(\frac{x}{x-z} + \frac{z}{y-z}\right)$ will be:

A. 1 B. 4
C. 3/2 D. 2

8. If $x + y + z = 0$, then the value of $\frac{(x+y)(y+z)(z+x)}{xyz}$ will be:

A. −3 B. −2
C. 0 D. −1

9. If $x + \frac{1}{x} = 3$, the value of $x^4 + \frac{1}{x^4}$ will be:

A. 49 B. 47
C. 37 D. 42

10. If $\left(x+\frac{1}{x}\right)^2 = 0$, then the value of $\left(x^2+\frac{1}{x^2}\right)$ will be:

A. 1 B. −1
C. 2 D. −2

11. If $\left(a+\frac{2}{a}\right) = 3$, then the value of $\left(a-\frac{2}{a}\right)$ will be:

A. ± 4 B. ± 5
C. ± 2 D. ± 1

12. If $\sqrt{a}+\frac{1}{\sqrt{a}} = 4$, then the value of $a^2 + \frac{1}{a^2}$ will be:

A. 194 B. 199
C. 178 D. 192

13. Factors of $x^2 - 25$ are:

A. $(x - 1)(x - 25)$ B. $(x + 25)(x - 1)$
C. $(x + 5)(x - 5)$ D. $(x - 5)(x - 5)$

14. Square of $\left(x-\frac{1}{x}\right)$ will be

A. $x^2 - 2 - \frac{1}{x^2}$ B. $x^2 - 2 + \frac{1}{x^2}$
C. $x^2 - 4 - \frac{1}{x^2}$ D. $x^2 - 2 + \frac{1}{x}$

15. Factors of $36 - 9x^2$ will be:

A. $(6 + 3x)(6 - 3x)$
B. $(3x - 6)(6 - 3x)$
C. $(3x + 6)(3x - 6)$
D. $(12x - 3x)(3 + 3x)$

16. Factors of $8x^3 + y^3$ are:

A. $(2x + y)(4x^2 - 2xy + y^2)$
B. $(2x + y)(4x^2 + 2xy + y^2)$
C. $(2x - y)(4x^2 - 2xy + y^2)$
D. $(2x + y)(4x^2 - 2xy - y^2)$

17. If the expression $x^3 + 5x^2 - 2 + k$ is completely divisible by $(x - 1)$, the value of k will be:

A. −3 B. −8
C. −3 D. −4

18. What is the factors of $x^2 + 3x - 10$

A. $(x - 1)(x - 10)$ B. $(x - 2)(x + 5)$
C. $(x + 2)(x - 5)$ D. $(x + 2)(x + 5)$

19. Factors of $(x + y)^3 - x - y$ are:

A. $(x - y)[(x - y)^2 - 1]$
B. $(x + y)[(x + y)^2 - 1]$
C. $(x + y)[(x + y)^2 + 1]$
D. $(x - y)[(x + y)^2 + 1]$

20. Factors of $x^3y^3z^3 - 27$ are:

A. $(xyz - 3)(x^2y^2z^2 + 3xyz + 9)$
B. $(xyz + 3)(x^2y^2z^2 + 3xyz + 9)$
C. $(3 - xyz)(x^2y^2z^2 - 3xyz + 9)$
D. $(xyz - 3)(x^2y^2 + y^2z^2 + z^2x^2)$

21. If $x = \sqrt{3}$, the value of $x^4 + 2 + \frac{1}{x^4}$ will be:

A. $\frac{9}{100}$ B. $\frac{81}{100}$
C. $\frac{101}{9}$ D. $\frac{100}{9}$

22. Factors of $4x^2 + 8x - 5$ will be:

A. $(2x - 1)(2x + 5)$ B. $(2x + 1)(2x + 5)$
C. $(2x - 5)(2x - 1)$ D. $(2x + 5)(1 - 2x)$

23. Factors of $a^2 + \frac{1}{4} + a$ will be:

A. $\left(a+\frac{1}{2}\right)\left(a-\frac{1}{2}\right)$ B. $\left(a+\frac{1}{2}\right)^2$
C. $\left(a+\frac{1}{2}\right)^3$ D. $\left(a+\frac{1}{2}\right).a$

24. If $(x - 2)$ is a factor of $x^2 + 2x - a$, the value of a will be:

A. 8 B. 6
C. 11 D. 3

25. Factors of $x^8 - x^4 - 30$ will be:

A. $(x^4 - 5)(x^4 + 6)$
B. $(x^4 + 5)(x^4 - 6)$
C. $(x^4 + 5)(x^4 + 6)$
D. $(x^4 - 10)(x^4 + 3)$

ANSWERS

1	2	3	4	5	6	7	8	9	10
A	C	A	A	D	A	A	D	B	D
11	**12**	**13**	**14**	**15**	**16**	**17**	**18**	**19**	**20**
D	A	C	B	A	A	D	B	B	A
21	**22**	**23**	**24**	**25**					
D	A	B	A	B					

EXPLANATORY ANSWERS

1. Let $a = 28$, $b = -15$ and $c = -13$. Then

$$a + b + c = 28 - 15 - 13 = 0$$
$$a^3 + b^3 + c^3 = 3abc$$
$$(28)^3 + (-15)^3 + (-13)^3 = 3 \times 28 \times (-15) \times (-13) = 16380$$

2. $$x^3 + \frac{1}{x^3} = \left(x+\frac{1}{x}\right)^3 - 3\left(x+\frac{1}{x}\right)$$
$$= (5)^3 - 3 \times 5 = 125 - 15 = 110$$

3. If $x^2 + \frac{1}{x^2} = 83$, what is the value of $x^3 - \frac{1}{x^3} = ?$

$$\left(x-\frac{1}{x}\right)^2 = x^2 + \frac{1}{x^2} - 2$$
$$x - \frac{1}{x} = \sqrt{83-2} = \sqrt{81}$$
$$x - \frac{1}{x} = 9$$
$$\therefore \left(x^3 - \frac{1}{x^3}\right) = \left(x-\frac{1}{x}\right)^3 + 3\left(x-\frac{1}{x}\right)$$
$$= (9)^3 + 3 \times 9 = 729 + 27 = 756$$

4. $$23^3 - 17^3 = (20+3)^3 - (20-3)^3$$
$$= 2(3^3 + 3 \times 20^2 \times 3) \quad [\because (a+b)^3 - (a-b)^3 = 2(b^3 + 3a^2b)]$$
$$= 2\,(27 + 3600) = 54 + 7200 = 7254$$

5. $\because x + \frac{1}{x} = 15$

$$\Rightarrow \left(x+\frac{1}{x}\right)^2 = (15)^2 \Rightarrow x^2 + \frac{1}{x^2} + 2.x\frac{1}{x} = 225$$
$$\therefore x^2 + \frac{1}{x^2} = 225 - 2 = 223.$$

6. $(x+y)^{x/y} = (12+4)^{12/4} = (16)^3 = 4096.$ $[\because x = 12, y = 4]$

7. $\because x + y = 2z \Rightarrow x - z = z - y = -(y - z)$

$$\therefore \frac{x}{x-z} + \frac{z}{y-z} = \frac{x}{-(y-z)} + \frac{z}{y-z} = \frac{z-x}{y-z} = 1.$$
$[\because x - z = z - y]$

8. $\because$ $x + y + z = 0 \Rightarrow x + y = -z$
$x + y + z = 0 \Rightarrow y + z = -x$
and $x + y + z = 0 \Rightarrow z + x = -y$

$$\therefore \frac{(x+y)(y+z)(z+x)}{xyz} = \frac{(-z)(-x)(-y)}{xyz} = -1.$$

9. $\because x + \frac{1}{x} = 3 \Rightarrow \left(x+\frac{1}{x}\right)^2 = (3)^2$

$$\Rightarrow x^2 + \frac{1}{x^2} + 2.x.\frac{1}{x} = 9 \Rightarrow x^2 + \frac{1}{x^2} = 9 - 2 = 7$$
$$\because x^2 + \frac{1}{x^2} = 7 \Rightarrow \left(x^2 + \frac{1}{x^2}\right)^2 = (7)^2$$
$$\Rightarrow x^4 + \frac{1}{x^4} + 2.x^2.\frac{1}{x^2} = 49$$
$$\therefore x^4 + \frac{1}{x^4} = 49 - 2 = 47.$$

10. $$\left(x+\frac{1}{x}\right)^2 = 0 \Rightarrow x^2 + \frac{1}{x^2} + 2x.\frac{1}{x} = 0$$
$$\Rightarrow x^2 + \frac{1}{x^2} = -2.$$

11. $\because$ $$\left(a-\frac{2}{a}\right)^2 = \left(a+\frac{2}{a}\right)^2 - 4.a.\frac{2}{a} = (3)^2 - 8 = 9 - 8 = 1$$
$$\therefore \left(a-\frac{2}{a}\right) = \pm\sqrt{1} = \pm 1.$$

12. $\because$ $$\sqrt{a} + \frac{1}{\sqrt{a}} = 4$$
$$\Rightarrow \left(\sqrt{a} + \frac{1}{\sqrt{a}}\right)^2 = (4)^2 \Rightarrow a + \frac{1}{a} + 2.\sqrt{a}.\frac{1}{\sqrt{a}} = 16$$
$$\because \left(a+\frac{1}{a}\right) = 14 \Rightarrow \left(a+\frac{1}{a}\right)^2 = (14)^2$$

$\Rightarrow \quad a^2 + \frac{1}{a^2} + 2.a.\frac{1}{a} = 196$

$\therefore \quad a^2 + \frac{1}{a^2} = 196 - 2 = 194.$

13. $x^2 - 25 = (x)^2 - (5)^2,$ [which is of the form $a^2 - b^2$]
$= (x + 5)(x - 5).$

14. According to question:

Square of $\left(x - \frac{1}{x}\right) = \left(x - \frac{1}{x}\right)^2$

$= x^2 - 2.x.\frac{1}{x} + \left(\frac{1}{x}\right)^2 = x^2 - 2 + \frac{1}{x^2}.$

15. $36 - 9x^2 = (6)^2 - (3x)^2$ [which is of the form $a^2 - b^2$]
$= (6 + 3x)(6 - 3x).$

16. $8x^3 + y^3 = (2x)^3 + (y)^3$ [which is of the form $a^3 + b^3$]
$= (2x + y)[(2x)^2 - 2x.y + (y)^2]$
$= (2x + y)(4x^2 - 2xy + y^2).$

17. Since the expression $x^3 + 5x^2 - 2 + k$ is completely divisible by $(x - 1)$

$\therefore$ on substituting $x = 1$ in the given expression, its value will be zero

i.e., $(1)^3 + 5(1)^2 - 2 + k = 0 \Rightarrow 1 + 5 - 2 + k = 0$

$\Rightarrow \quad 4 + k = 0 \Rightarrow k = -4$

Hence value of k is -4.

18. $\because x^2 + 3x - 10 = x^2 + 5x - 2x - 10$
$= x(x + 5) - 2(x + 5) = (x - 2)(x + 5)$

19. $\because (x + y)^3 - x - y = (x + y)^3 - (x + y) = (x + y)[(x + y)^2 - 1].$

20. $\because \; x^3y^3z^3 - 27 = (xyz)^3 - (3)^3$[which is of the form $a^3 - b^3$]
$= (xyz - 3)[(xyz)^2 + xyz.3 + (3)^2]$
$= (xyz - 3)(x^2y^2z^2 + 3xyz + 9).$

21. $\because x^4 + 2 + \frac{1}{x^4} = (x^2)^2 + 2.x^2.\frac{1}{x^2} + \left(\frac{1}{x^2}\right)^2 = \left(x^2 + \frac{1}{x^2}\right)^2$

$\therefore$ On substituting $x = \sqrt{3}$

$= \left((\sqrt{3})^2 + \frac{1}{(\sqrt{3})^2}\right)^2 = \left(3 + \frac{1}{3}\right)^2$

$= \left(\frac{10}{3}\right)^2 = \frac{100}{9}.$

22. $\because \; 4x^2 + 8x - 5 = 4x^2 + 10x - 2x - 5$
$= 2x(2x + 5) - 1(2x + 5)$
$= (2x - 1)(2x + 5).$

23. $\because \; a^2 + \frac{1}{4} + a = (a)^2 + 2.\frac{1}{2}.a + \left(\frac{1}{2}\right)^2 = \left(a + \frac{1}{2}\right)^2.$

24. Since $(x - 2)$ is a factor of $x^2 + 2x - a$

$\therefore$ On substituting $x = 2$ in the expression, the result obtained will be zero

$\therefore \quad (2)^2 + 2.2 - a = 0$

or $\quad 4 + 4 - a = 0$

or $\quad a = 8$

25. $\because \; x^8 - x^4 - 30 = x^8 - 6x^4 + 5x^4 - 30$
$= x^4(x^4 - 6) + 5(x^4 - 6)$
$= (x^4 + 5)(x^4 - 6).$

□□□□□

8

Linear Equations in One Variable

An equation is called linear equation in one variable or an equation of degree one in one variable, if only a single variable with degree one occurs in the equation. For example,

$x + 3 = 0$, $3x + 5 = 8$, $2t + 3 = t + 16$

Multiple Choice Questions

1. The difference between two numbers is 8. If 2 is added to the greater number, the result will be three times the smaller. What are the numbers?
A. 13, 5 B. 5, 13
C. 12, 6 D. 13, 6

2. Find three consecutive numbers such that if they are divided by 4, 7 and 11 respectively, the sum of the quotients will be 10.
A. 20, 21, 22 B. 22, 23, 24
C. 25, 26, 27 D. 28, 29, 30

3. In a bag one-fifth of the balls are black and one-third are red, there are 15 dozen green balls and 30 blue balls. What is the number of black balls and red balls in the bag?
A. 90, 110 B. 90, 150
C. 80, 150 D. 150, 110

4. The sum of the ages of A and B is 30 years. Five years hence, A will be three times as old as B. What is their present ages?
A. 25 years, 8 years B. 30 years, 9 years
C. 25 years, 5 years D. 30 years, 10 years

5. Two persons A and B start walking in opposite directions at 8 a.m. from two places which are 27 km. apart. Both of them meet at 11 a.m. If A's speed is 3 km/hr more than that of B, find their respective speeds?
A. 3 km/hr, 6 km/hr B. 4 km/hr, 6 km/h
C. 3 km/h, 5 km/hr D. 5 km/h, 7 km/h

6. The length of a room exceeds its breadth by 30 cm. If the length is increased by 30 cm and the breadth is decreased by 20 cm, the area remains the same. What is the length and breadth of the room?
A. 120 cm, 150 cm B. 140 cm, 160 cm
C. 130 cm, 150 cm D. 120 cm, 140 cm

7. One number exceeds another by 5. Their sum is 29. What are the numbers?
A. 13, 14 B. 14, 16
C. 12, 17 D. 15, 18

8. The sum of two number is 8, if 22 is added to the smaller number then it becomes five times the other. What are the numbers?
A. 4, 5 B. 3, 5
C. 3, 7 D. 5, 8

9. A motorboat goes downstream in a river and covers the distance between two coastal towns in five hours. It covers this distance upstream in six hours. If the speed of the stream is 2 km/hr., find the speed of the boat in still water.
A. 11 km/hr B. 20 km/hr
C. 22 km/hr D. 32 km/hr

10. A race-boat covers a distance of 66 km downstream in 110 minutes. It covers this distance upstream in 120 minutes. The speed of the boat in still water is 34.5 km/hr, find the speed of the stream.
A. 1.5 km/hr B. 2.5 km/hr
C. 3.0 km/hr D. 4.5 km/hr

11. A steamer, going down stream in a river, covers the distance between two towns in 20 hours. Coming back up stream, it covers this distance in 25 hours. The speed of water is 4 km/hr, find the distance between the two towns.
A. 600 km B. 700 km
C. 800 km D. 900 km

12. The sum of two numbers is 2490. If 6.5% of one number is equal to 8.5% of the other, find the numbers.
A. 1412, 1072 B. 1411, 1079
C. 1415, 1092 D. 1417, 1095

13. The distance between two stations A and B is 230 km. Two motor cyclists start simultaneously from A and B in the opposite directions and the distance between them after three hours is 20 km. If the speed of one motor cyclist is less than that of the other by 10 km/hr, find the speed of each motor cyclist.
A. 30 km/hr, 40 km/hr B. 30 km/hr, 50 km/hr
C. 40 km/hr, 60 km/hr D. 50 km/hr, 70 km/hr

14. Divide ₹ 1380 among Ahmed, John and Mamta so that the amount Ahmed receives is 5 times as much as Mamta's share and is 3 times as much as John's share. What is John's share?
A. ₹ 180 B. ₹ 300
C. ₹ 920 D. ₹ 900

15. The length of a rectangle is 15 cm. more than its width. The perimeter is 150 cm, find the dimensions of the rectangle.

A. 30 cm, 25 cm B. 20 cm, 25 cm
C. 30 cm, 45 cm D. 32 cm, 42 cm

16. An altitude of a triangle is five-thirds the length of its corresponding base. If the altitude were increased by 4 cm. and the base be decreased by 2 cm, the area of the triangle would remain the same. What is the base and the altitude of the triangle?

A. 12 cm, 16 cm B. 12 cm, 20 cm
C. 14 cm, 18 cm D. 12 cm, 24 cm

17. The perimeter of a triangle measuring 49 cm. The one side 7 cm. longer than the other and 5 cm. shorter than the third. What is the length of smaller side of the triangle?

A. 5 cm B. 17 cm
C. 22 cm D. 10 cm

18. If I add ten to four times a number, the result is five less than five times the number. What is my number?

A. 13 B. 14
C. 15 D. 21

19. The denominator of a rational number is greater than its numerator by 3. If 3 is subtracted from the numerator and 2 is added to its denominator, the new number becomes $\frac{1}{5}$. What is the original number?

A. $\frac{5}{8}$ B. $\frac{7}{8}$
C. $\frac{9}{11}$ D. $\frac{8}{13}$

20. The denominator of a rational number is greater than its numerator by 5. If the numerator is increased by 11 and the denominator decreased by 14, the new number becomes 5. What is the original number?

A. $\frac{14}{39}$ B. $\frac{12}{23}$
C. $\frac{14}{19}$ D. $\frac{14}{29}$

ANSWERS

1	2	3	4	5	6	7	8	9	10
A	A	B	C	A	A	C	B	C	A
11	**12**	**13**	**14**	**15**	**16**	**17**	**18**	**19**	**20**
C	B	A	B	C	B	D	C	A	C

EXPLANATORY ANSWERS

1. According to question.

$x - y = 8$ ...(*i*)

$x + 2 = 3y \Rightarrow x - 3y = -2$ ...(*ii*)

Eqn. (*i*) and (*ii*)

$$x - y = 8$$
$$x - 3y = -2$$
$$-\quad +\quad +$$
$$2y = 10 \Rightarrow y = 5$$

Eqn (i)

$\Rightarrow x - 5 = 8 \Rightarrow x = 13$ and $y = 5$

2. Let three consecutive numbers

$x, x + 1, x + 2$

$$\frac{x}{4}+\frac{x+1}{7}+\frac{x+2}{11} = 10$$

$$\frac{77x+44x+44+28x+56}{308} = 10$$

$$\frac{149x+100}{308} = \frac{10}{1}$$

$$149x + 100 = 3080$$

$$\Rightarrow 149x = 2980$$

$$\Rightarrow x = \frac{2980}{149} = 20$$

Required Numbers

$x = 20, x + 1 = 20 + 1 = 21$ and

$x + 2 = 20 + 2 = 22,$

i.e. 20, 21, 22

3. Let total number of balls be x

According to question,

$$\frac{x}{5}+\frac{x}{3}+15\times12+30 = x$$

$$\frac{x}{5}+\frac{x}{3}+210 = x$$

$$x-\frac{x}{5}-\frac{x}{3} = 210$$

$$\Rightarrow \frac{15x-3x-5x}{15} = 210$$

$$\Rightarrow \frac{7}{15}x = 210 \Rightarrow x = \frac{210\times15}{7}$$

$$x = 450$$

$$\text{Black balls} = \frac{x}{5} = \frac{450}{5} = 90$$

Red balls $= \frac{x}{3} = \frac{450}{3} = 150$

4. Let present age of A = x yrs.
then B = $30 - x$ yrs.
According to question,

$$x + 5 = 3\,(35 - x) = 105 - 3x$$
$$4x = 100 \Rightarrow x = 25$$

A's present age = 25 yrs.
B's present age = 30 – 25 = 5 yrs.

5. Let B's speed be x km/hr.
A's speed = $(x + 3)$ km/hr.
According to question,

$$3x + 9 + 3x = 27$$
$$6x = 18 \Rightarrow x = 3 \text{ km/hr}$$

B's speed = 3 km/hrs.
A's speed = 6 km/hr.

6. Let breadth = x cm.
length = $(x + 30)$ cm.
Area = $x\,(x + 30) = (x^2 + 30x)$ cm^2
New breadth = $x - 20$ and New length = $x + 60$ cm.
New Area = $(x - 20)\,(x + 60)$
$= x^2 + 40x - 1200$

According to question

$$x^2 + 40x - 1200 = x^2 + 30x$$
$$10x = 1200$$
$$x = 120 \text{ cm.}$$

Breadth = 120 cm.
Length = 120 + 30 = 150 cm.

7. Let another number = x
One number = $x + 5$

$$x + x + 5 = 29$$
$$2x + 5 = 29$$
$$2x = 24 \Rightarrow x = 12$$

Required Number,
12, 17

8. Let smaller number = x
Other number = $8 - x$

$$x + 22 = 5\,(8 - x) = 40 - 5x$$
$$6x = 40 - 22 = 18$$
$$x = 3$$

Required Numbers
3, 5

9. Let speed of still water = x km/hr.
Speed of stream = 2 km/hr.
Downstream = $(x + 2)$ km/hr.
Upstream = $(x - 2)$ km/hr.

According to question

$$5\,(x + 2) = 6\,(x - 2)$$
$$5x + 10 = 6x - 12$$
$$x = 22 \text{ km/hr.}$$

Speed in still water = 22 km/hr.

10. Let speed of stream = x km/hr.
Downstream = $(34.5 + x)$ km/hr.
Upstream = $(34.5 - x)$ km/hr.

$$\text{Downstream} = \frac{66}{\frac{110}{60}} = \frac{66 \times 6}{11}$$
$$= 36 \text{ km/hr.}$$
$$34.5 + x = 36$$
$$x = 36 - 34.5 = 1.5 \text{ km/hr.}$$

Speed of stream = 1.5 km/hr.

11. Let distance = x km.

$$\text{Downstream} = \frac{x}{20} \text{ km/hr.}$$
$$\text{Upstream} = \frac{x}{25} \text{ km/hr.}$$

Speed of water = 4 km/hr.

$$\text{Speed of water} = \frac{1}{2}\,(\text{down stream} - \text{up stream})$$
$$4 = \frac{1}{2}\left(\frac{x}{20} - \frac{x}{25}\right)$$
$$8 = \frac{5x - 4x}{100} = \frac{x}{100}$$
$$x = 8 \times 100 = 800 \text{ km.}$$

12. Let 1st number = x
Other number = $2490 - x$
According to question

$$6.5\%\,x = 8.5\%\,(2490 - x)$$
$$\frac{65}{1000}x = \frac{85}{1000}(2490 - x)$$
$$13x + 17x = 17 \times 2490$$
$$30x = 17 \times 2490$$
$$x = \frac{17 \times 2490}{30} = 17 \times 83$$
$$x = 1411$$

Other number = 2490 – 1411
= 1079

Required nos. 1411 and 1079

13.

x km/hr. (x+10) km/hr.
A ———————————— B
← 230 km. →

Relative speed = $x + x + 10 = (2x + 10)$ km/hr.
Distance after three hours = 230 – 20
= 210 km.

According to question,

$$3\,(2x + 10) = 210$$
$$2x + 10 = 70$$
$$2x = 60$$
$$\Rightarrow x = 30$$

Speed of each motorcyclist is 30 km/hr. and 40 km/hr.

14. Let Mamta's share = ₹ x
Then,

Ahmed's share = $5x$
John's share = $1380 - 6x$

Hence,

$$5x = 3(1380 - 6x) = 4140 - 18x$$
$$23x = 4140$$
$$x = \frac{4140}{23} = 180$$

Mamta's share = ₹ 180
Ahmed's share = 5×180 = ₹ 900
John's share = $1380 - 1080$ = ₹ 300

15. Let width = x cm.
Length = $x + 15$ cm.

$$2(x + x + 15) = 150$$
$$2x + 15 = 75$$
$$2x = 60$$
$$x = 30$$

width = 30 cm. and length = 45 cm.

16.

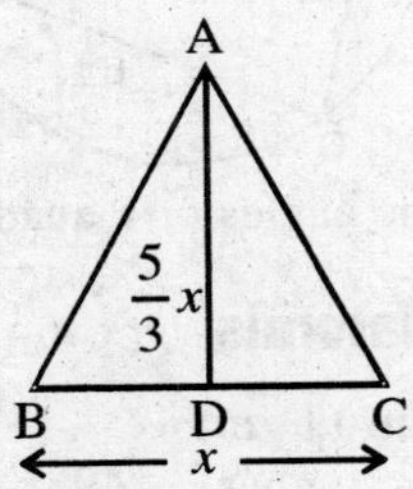

According to question

$$\frac{1}{2}x \times \frac{5}{3}x = \frac{1}{2}\left(\frac{5}{3}x + 4\right)(x-2)$$
$$2 \times \frac{5}{6}x^2 = \frac{5}{3}x^2 - \frac{10}{3}x + 4x - 8$$
$$\frac{5}{3}x^2 = \frac{5}{3}x^2 - \frac{10}{3}x + 4x - 8$$
$$4x - \frac{10}{3}x = 8 \Rightarrow \frac{2}{3}x = 8$$
$$\Rightarrow \quad 2x = 8 \times 3 \Rightarrow x = \frac{8 \times 3}{2} = 4 \times 3$$
$$x = 12 \text{ cm.}$$

Base = 12 cm.

Altitude = $\frac{5}{3} \times 12 = 20$ cm.

17. Let other side = x cm.
One side = $(x + 7)$ cm.
Third side = $x + 12$ cm.

According to question

$$x + x + 7 + x + 12 = 49$$
$$3x = 49 - 19 = 30$$
$$x = 10$$

Hence smaller side is 10 cm.

18. Let number be x
Then,

$$4x + 10 = 5x - 5$$
$$x = 10 + 5 = 15$$

19. Let numerator = x
Denominator = $x + 3$

$$\frac{x-3}{x+3+2} = \frac{1}{5} \Rightarrow \frac{x-3}{x+5} = \frac{1}{5}$$
$$\Rightarrow \quad 5x - 15 = x + 5$$
$$4x = 20 \Rightarrow x = 5$$

Required fraction = 5/8

20. Let Numerator = x
denominator = $x + 5$

Hence,

$$\frac{x+11}{x+5-14} = \frac{5}{1}$$
$$\Rightarrow \quad \frac{x+11}{x-9} = \frac{5}{1}$$
$$\Rightarrow \quad 5x - 45 = x + 11$$
$$4x = 56 \Rightarrow x = 14.$$

Required fraction = $\frac{x}{x+5} = \frac{14}{14+5} = \frac{14}{19}$

❒❒❒❒❒

9

Understanding Quadrilaterals
(Parallelogram, Rhombus, Rectangle, Square, Kite)

Area

(*a*) Area = $\frac{1}{2}$ (Product of diagonals) × (sine of the angle between them)

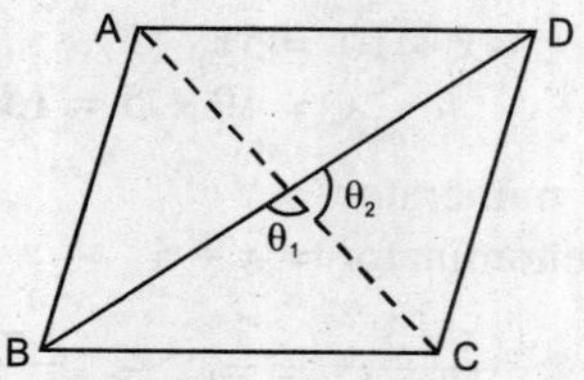

If θ_1 and θ_2 are the two angles made between themselves by the two diagonals, we have by the property of intersecting lines

$$\Rightarrow \quad \theta_1 + \theta_2 = 180°$$

Then, the area of quadrilateral

$$= \frac{1}{2} d_1 d_2 \sin\theta_1$$

$$= \frac{1}{2} d_1 d_2 \sin\theta_2$$

(*b*) Area = $\frac{1}{2}$ × diagonal × sum of the perpendiculars to it from opposite vertices = $\frac{d(h_1 + h_2)}{2}$

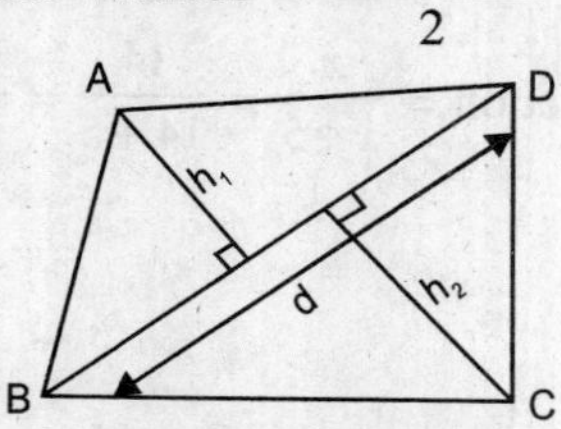

(*c*) Area of circumscribed quadrilateral

$$A = \sqrt{S(S-a)(S-b)(S-c)(S-d)}$$

Where $\quad S = \frac{a+b+c+d}{2}$

where, *a*, *b*, *c* and *d* are the length of the sides.

Properties

1. In a convex quadrilateral inscribed in a circle, the product of the diagonals is equal to the sum of the products of the opposite sides. For example, in the figure below:

   $(a \times c) + (b \times d) = AC \times BD$

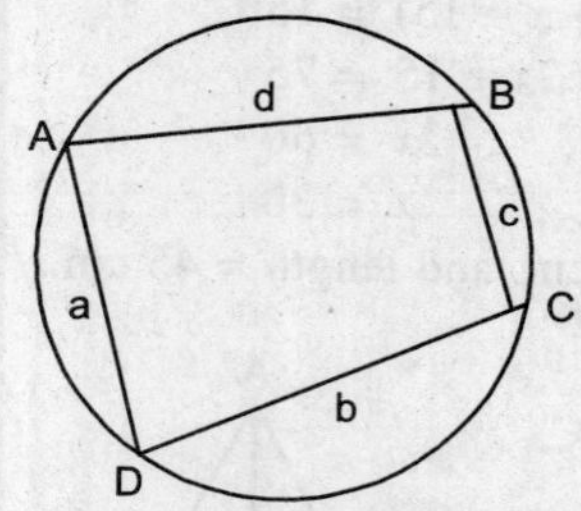

2. Sum of all the angles of a quadrilateral = 360°.

Types of Quadrilaterals

1. Parallelogram (|| gm)

A parallelogram is a quadrilateral with opposite sides parallel (as shown in figure below)

(*a*) Area = Base (*b*) × height (*h*) = *bh*

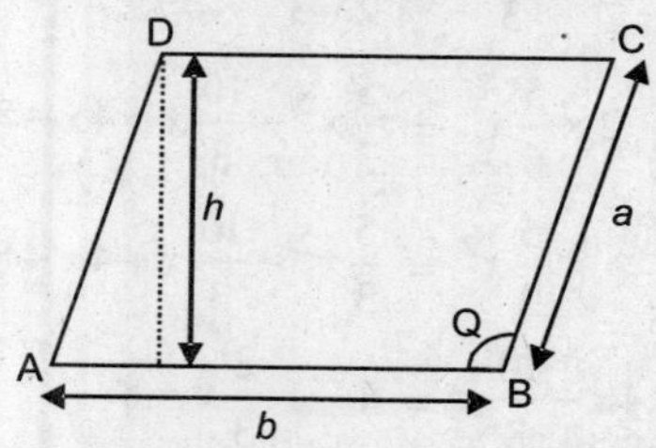

(*b*) Area = product of any two adjacent sides × sine of the included angle

$= ab \sin Q$

(*c*) Perimeter = $2(a + b)$

where *a* and *b* are any two adjacent sides.

Properties

1. Diagonals of a parallelogram bisect each other.
2. Bisectors of the angles of a parallelogram form a rectangle.
3. A parallelogram inscribed in a circle is a rectangle.
4. A parallelogram circumscribed about a circle is a rhombus.
5. The opposite angles in a parallelogram are equal.

6. The sum of the squares of the diagonals is equal to the sum of the squares of the four sides in the figure:
$AC^2 + BD^2 = AB^2 + BC^2 + CD^2 + AD^2$
$= 2(AB^2 + BC^2)$

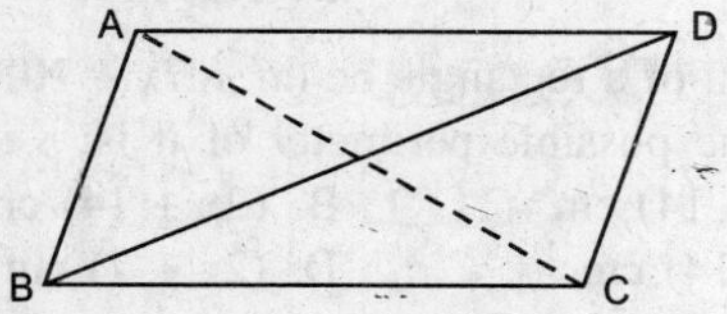

Rectangles

A rectangle is a parallelogram with all angles 90°

(*a*) Area = Base × Height = $b \times h$

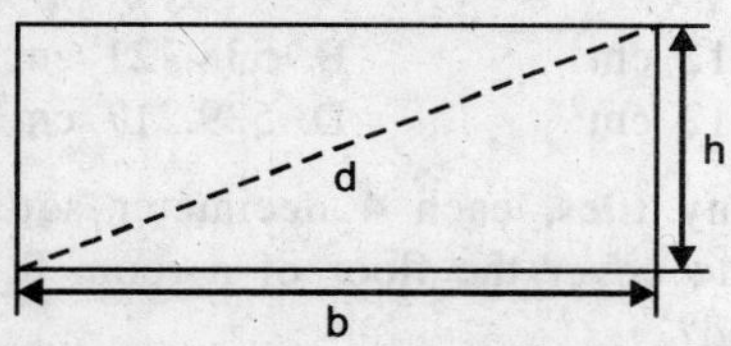

Note : Base and height are also referred to as the length and the breadth in a rectangle.

(*b*) Diagonal (*d*) = $\sqrt{b^2 + h^2}$ → by Pythagoras theorem

Properties

1. Diagonals are equal and bisect each other.
2. Bisectors of the angles of a rectangle (a parallelogram) form another rectangle.
3. All rectangles are parallelograms but the reverse is not true.

Rhombus

A parallelogram having all the sides equal is a rhombus.

(*a*) Area = $\frac{1}{2}$ × product of diagonals × sine of the angle between them.

$= \frac{1}{2} \times d_1 \times d_2 \sin 90°$

(Diagonals in a rhombus intersect at right angles) (since sin 90° = 1)

$= \frac{1}{2} \times d_1 d_2$

(*b*) Area = product of adjacent sides × sine of the angle between them.

Properties

1. Diagonals bisect each other at right angles.
2. All rhombuses are parallelograms but the reverse is not true.
3. A rhombus may or may not be a square but all squares are rhombuses.

Square

A square is a rectangle with adjacent sides equal or a rhombus with each angle 90°.

(*a*) Area = base × height = a^2

(*b*) Area = 1/2 (diagonal)^2 = 1/2 d^2 (square is a rhombus too).

(*c*) Perimeter = $4a$ (a = side of the square)

(*d*) Diagonal = $a\sqrt{2}$

(*e*) In radius = $\frac{a}{2}$

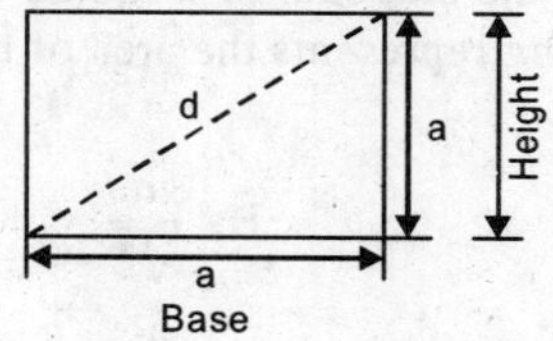

Properties

1. Diagonals are equal and bisect each other at right angles.
2. Side is the diameter of the inscribed circle.
3. Diagonal is the diameter of the circumscribing circle.

⇒ Diameter = $a\sqrt{2}$.

Circumradius = $\frac{a}{\sqrt{2}}$

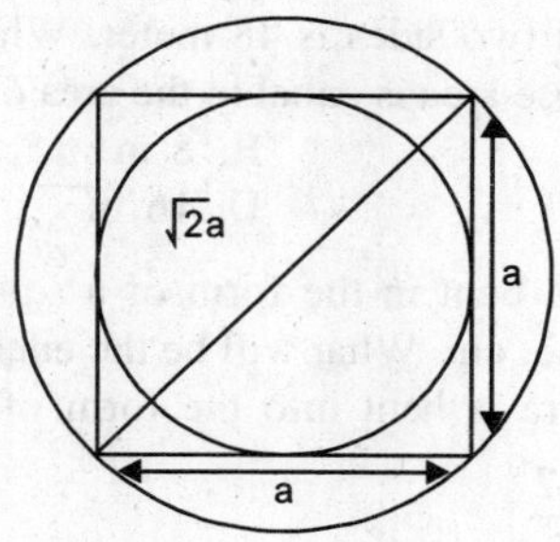

Trapezium

A trapezium is a quadrilateral with only two sides parallel to each other.

(*a*) Area = $\frac{1}{2}$ × sum of parallel sides × heights = $\frac{1}{2}$ (AB + DC) × h — For the figure below.

(*b*) Median = $\frac{1}{2}$ × sum of the parallel sides (median is the line equidistant from the parallel sides). For any line EF parallel to AB

$$EF = \frac{\{[P \times (AB)] + Q \times (DC)]\}}{AD}$$

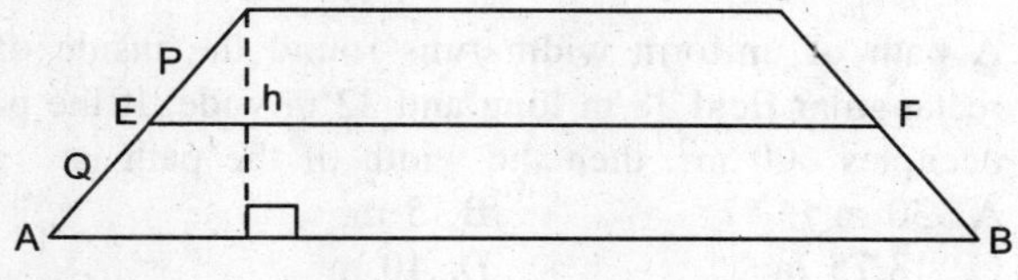

Properties

1. If the non-parallel sides are equal then diagonals will be equal too.

Multiple Choice Questions

1. If the length of the diagonal AC of a square ABCD is 5.2 cm, then the area of the square is:
A. 15.12 sq. cm B. 13.52 sq. cm
C. 12.62 sq. cm D. 10.00 sq. cm

2. The length of the diagonal of a square is 'a' cm. Which of the following represents the area of the square (in sq. cm)?
A. $2a$ B. $\frac{a}{\sqrt{2}}$
C. $\frac{a^2}{2}$ D. $\frac{a^2}{4}$

3. What is the length of the largest rod that can be placed in a room 16 m long, 12 m broad and $10\frac{2}{3}$ m high?
A. 123 m B. 68 m
C. $22\frac{2}{3}$ m D. $22\frac{1}{3}$ m

4. The perimeter of a rectangle is 160 meter and the difference of two sides is 48 meter. What is the side of a square whose area is equal to the area of this rectangle?
A. 32 m B. 8 m
C. 4 m D. 16 m

5. A wire when bent in the form of a square encloses an area of 484 sq. cm. What will be the enclosed area when the same wire is bent into the form of a circle?
$\left(\text{Take } \pi = \frac{22}{7}\right)$
A. 125 cm^2 B. 230 cm^2
C. 550 cm^2 D. 616 cm^2

6. A took 15 sec. to cross a rectangular field diagonally walking at the ratio of 52 m/min and B took the same time to cross the same field along its sides walking at the rate of 68 m/min. The area of the field is:
A. 30 m^2 B. 40 m^2
C. 50 m^2 D. 60 m^2

7. The difference between the length and breadth of a rectangle is 23 m. If its perimeter is 206 m, then its area is:
A. 1520 m^2 B. 2420 m^2
C. 2480 m^2 D. 2520 m^2

8. A path of uniform width runs round the inside of a rectangular field 38 m long and 32 m wide. If the path occupies 600 m^2, then the width of the path is:
A. 30 m B. 5 m
C. 18.75 m D. 10 m

9. The perimeter of the floor of a room is 18 m. What is the area of the walls of the room, if the height of the room is 3 m?
A. 21 m^2 B. 42 m^2
C. 54 m^2 D. 108 m^2

10. If the area of a rectangle be $(x^2 + 7x + 10)$ sq. cm, then one of the possible perimeter of it is:
A. $(4x + 14)$ cm B. $(2x + 14)$ cm
C. $(x + 14)$ cm D. $(2x + 7)$ cm

11. A kite in the shape of a square with a diagonal 32 cm attached to an equilateral triangle of the base 8 cm. Approximately how much paper has been used to make it? (Use $\sqrt{3}$ = 1.732)
A. 539.712 cm^2 B. 538.721 cm^2
C. 540.712 cm^2 D. 539.217 cm^2

12. How many tiles, each 4 decimeter square, will be required to cover the floor of a room 8 m long and 6 m broad?
A. 200 B. 260
C. 280 D. 300

13. If each edge of a square be doubled, then the increase percentage in its area is:
A. 200% B. 250%
C. 280% D. 300%

14. The length of a room is 3 m more than its breadth. If the area of a floor of the room is 70 m^2, then the perimeter of the floor will be:
A. 14 metres B. 28 metres
C. 34 metres D. 17 metres

15. The diagonals of a rhombus are 32 cm and 24 cm respectively. The perimeter of the rhombus is:
A. 80 cm B. 72 cm
C. 68 cm D. 64 cm

16. The perimeter of a rhombus is 40 cm. If one of the diagonals be 12 cm long, what is the length of the other diagonal?
A. 12 cm B. $\sqrt{136}$ cm
C. 16 cm D. $\sqrt{44}$ cm

17. A parallelogram ABCD has sides AB = 24 cm and AD = 16 cm. The distance between the sides AB and DC is 10 cm. What is the distance between the sides AD and BC?
A. 15 cm B. 18 cm
C. 16 cm D. 9 cm

18. The adjacent sides of a paralleogram are 36 cm and 27 cm in length. If the distance between the shorter sides is 12 cm, then the distance between the longer sides is:
A. 10 cm B. 12 cm
C. 16 cm D. 9 cm

19. ABCD is a trapezium in which AB || DC and AB = 2 CD. The diagonals AC and BD meet at O. The ratio of area of triangles AOB and COD is:

A. 1 : 1 B. 1 : $\sqrt{2}$

C. 4 : 1 D. 1 : 4

20. The length of each side of a rhombus is equal to the length of the side of a square whose diagonal is $40\sqrt{2}$ cm. If the length of the diagonals of the rhombus are in the ratio 3 : 4, then its area (in cm²) is:

A. 1550 B. 1600

C. 1535 D. 1536

21. The area of a rhombus is 216 cm² and the length of its one diagonal is 24 cm. The perimeter (in cm) of the rhombus is:

A. 52 B. 60

C. 120 D. 100

22. The area of a rhombus is 256 sq. cm. and one of its diagonal is twice the other in length. Then length of its larger diagonal is:

A. 32 cm B. 48 cm

C. 36 cm D. 24 cm

23. The floor of a corridor is 100 cm long and 3 m wide. Cost of covering the floor with carpet 50 cm wide at the ratio of ₹ 15 per m is:

A. ₹ 4500 B. ₹ 9000

C. ₹ 7500 D. ₹ 1900

24. The length and breadth of a rectangle are increased by 12% and 15% respectively. Its area will be increased by:

A. $27\frac{1}{5}\%$ B. $28\frac{4}{5}\%$

C. 27% D. 28%

25. The length of rectangle is increased by 60%. By what per cent would the breadth to be decreased to maintain the same area?

A. $37\frac{1}{2}\%$ B. 60%

C. 75% D. 120%

ANSWERS

1	2	3	4	5	6	7	8	9	10
B	C	C	A	D	D	D	B	C	A
11	**12**	**13**	**14**	**15**	**16**	**17**	**18**	**19**	**20**
A	D	D	C	A	C	A	D	C	D
21	**22**	**23**	**24**	**25**					
B	A	B	B	A					

EXPLANATORY ANSWERS

1. Side of a square = $\frac{\text{Diagonal}}{\sqrt{2}}$

Area of square = $\left(\frac{\text{Diagonal}}{\sqrt{2}}\right)^2$

$= \frac{(5.2)^2}{2} = \frac{5.2 \times 5.2}{2}$

= 2.6 × 5.2 = 13.52 cm².

2. Area of square = $\frac{\text{Diagonal}^2}{2} = \frac{a^2}{2}$

3. Since the room is in cuboid shape

Length of largest rod = Diagonal of cuboid

$= \sqrt{l^2 + b^2 + h^2}$

$= \sqrt{16^2 + 12^2 + \frac{32^2}{3^2}}$

$= \sqrt{256 + 144 + \frac{1024}{9}}$

$= \sqrt{\frac{2304 + 1296 + 1024}{9}}$

$= \sqrt{\frac{4624}{9}} = \frac{68}{3} = 22\frac{2}{3}$ m.

4. According to question,

$2(l + b) = 160$

$l + b = 80$ ...(*i*)

$l - b = 48$ ...(*ii*)

on solving (*i*) and (*ii*)

$l = 64, \quad b = 16$

area of square = area of rectangle

(side)² = 64 × 16

side = $\sqrt{64 \times 16}$

= 32 m.

5. $(\text{side})^2 = 484$ cm

side = 22 cm

perimeter of square = 4 × 22 = 88 cm

According to question,

$2\pi r = 88$ cm

$$r = \frac{88 \times 7}{2 \times 22} = 14 \text{ cm}$$

$$\text{area of circle} = \pi r^2 = \frac{22}{7} \times 14 \times 14 = 616 \text{ cm}^2.$$

6.

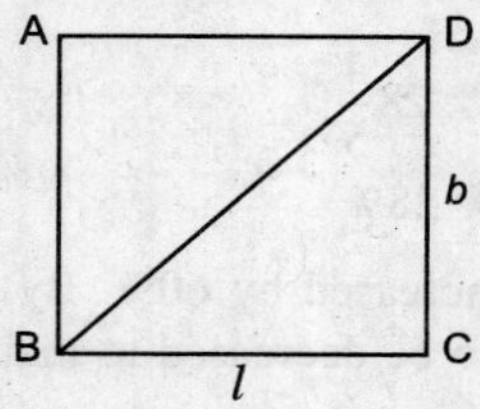

BD = length of diagonal = speed × time

$$= \frac{52}{60} \times 15 = 13 \text{ m}$$

$$BD = \sqrt{l^2 + b^2}$$

$$\Rightarrow \quad l^2 + b^2 = 13^2 = 169$$

$$\text{Again,} \quad l + b = \frac{68}{60} \times 15 = 17$$

$$(l + b)^2 = l^2 + b^2 + 2\,lb$$

$$17^2 = 169 + 2\,lb$$

$$lb = \frac{120}{2} = 60 \text{ m}^2.$$

7. Let the breadth be = x m

∴ length = $(23 + x)$ m

$\Rightarrow$ $2(x + 23 + x) = 206$

$4x = 206 - 46$

$$x = \frac{160}{4} = 40 \text{ m}$$

∴ length = 40 + 23 = 63 m

∴ Required area = 63 × 40 = 2520 m^2.

8.

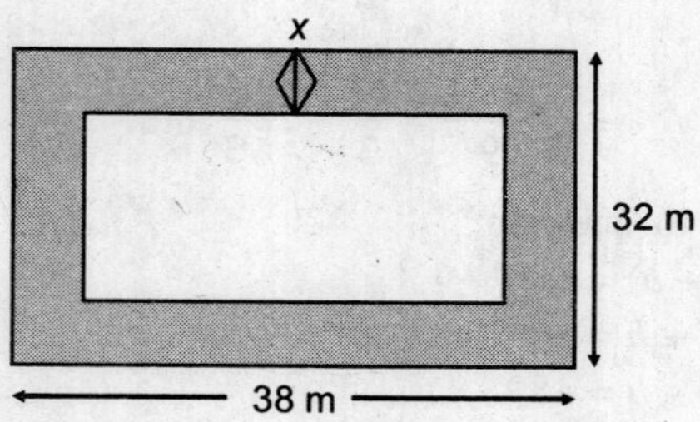

area of path = 600 m^2

$$(l + b - 2x)2x = 600$$

$$(38 + 32 - 2x)2x = 600$$

$$(70 - 2x)2x = 600$$

$$(70 - 2x)x = \frac{600}{2} = 300$$

$$70x - 2x^2 = 300$$

$$2x^2 - 70x + 300 = 0$$

$$x^2 - 35x + 150 = 0$$

$$x^2 - 30x - 5x + 150 = 0$$

$$x(x - 30) - 5(x - 30) = 0$$

$$(x - 30)(x - 5) = 0$$

$x = 30$ not possible

$x = 5$ (right).

9. Area of walls = Perimeter of base × heaght

= 18 × 3 = 54 m^2.

10. $x^2 + 7x + 10 = x^2 + 5x + 2x + 10$

$= x(x + 5) + 2(x + 5)$

$= (x + 2)(x + 5)$

∴ Two sides of rectangle

$= (x + 2)(x + 5)$

∴ Perimeter = $2(x + 2 + x + 5)$

$= 2(2x + 7) = (4x + 14)$ cm.

11.

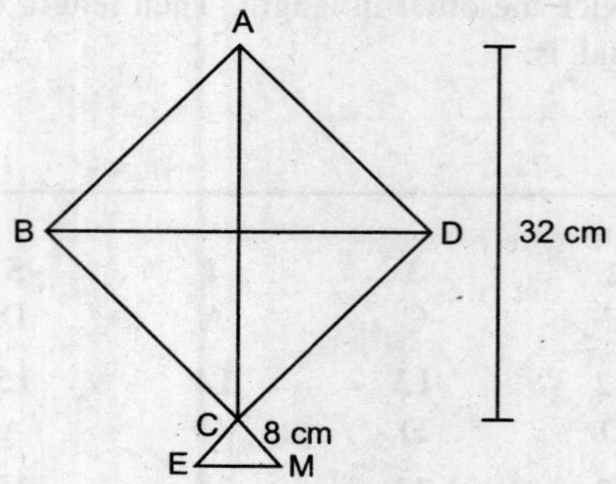

$$\text{area of square} = \frac{1}{2}\,(\text{Diagonal})^2$$

$$= \frac{1}{2}(32)^2 = \frac{1}{2} \times 32 \times 32 = 16 \times 32$$

$$= 512 \text{ cm}^2$$

$$\text{area of triangle} = \frac{\sqrt{3}}{4}8^2 = \frac{1.732 \times 8 \times 8}{4}$$

$$= 1.732 \times 2 \times 8 = 27.712 \text{ cm}^2$$

Required are = (512 + 27.712) cm^2

= 539.712 cm^2.

12. Area of the floor = 8 × 6 = 48 m^2

= 4800 dm^2 (1 m = 10 dm)

Area of square tile = 4 × 4 = 16 dm^2

$$\text{No. of tiles} = \frac{4800}{16} = 300.$$

13. Percentage increase in area

$$= \left(x + y + \frac{xy}{100}\right)\%$$

Here, $x = 100\%$, $y = 100\%$

$$= \left(100 + 100 + \frac{100 \times 100}{100}\right)\% = 300\%.$$

14. Let the breadth of floor = x m

Then the length of floor = $(x + 3)$ m

A.T.Q.

$$x \times (x + 3) = 70$$
$$x^2 + 3x - 70 = 0$$
$$x^2 + 10x - 7x - 70 = 0$$
$$(x + 10)(x - 7) = 0$$
$$x = 7, x = -10$$

Breadth = 7 m

Length = 10 m

Perimeter of floor = 2 (L + B)

= 2(10 + 7) = 34 m.

15. We know that rhombus is parallelogram whose all four sides are equal and its diagonals bisect each other at 90°.

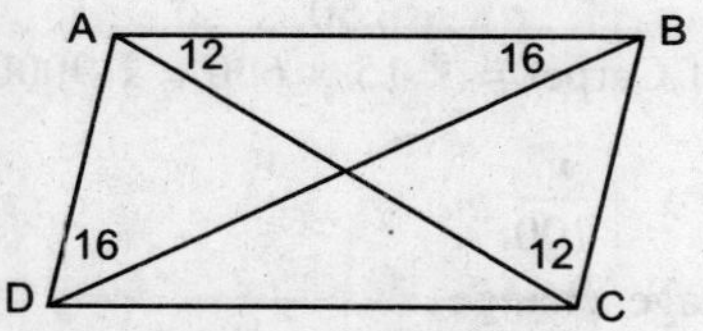

$\therefore$ AB = $\sqrt{16^2 + 12^2} = \sqrt{400}$ = 20 cm

= side of rhombus

$\therefore$ perimeter of the rhombus

= 20 × 4 = 80 cm.

16. 4 × side = 40 cm (given)

side = $\dfrac{40}{4} = 10$ cm

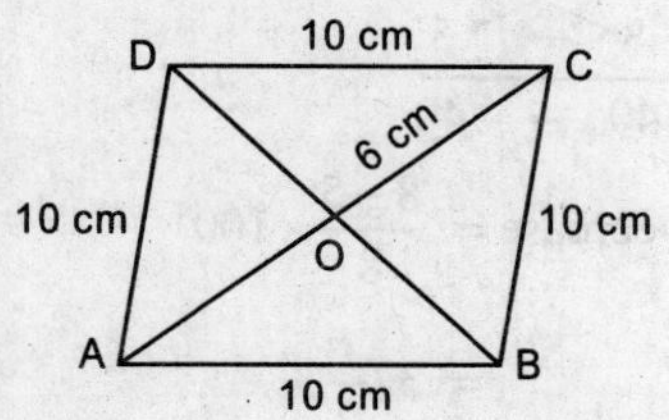

In Δ AOB,

OB = $\sqrt{10^2 - 6^2} = \sqrt{100 - 36}$

= $\sqrt{64}$ = 8 cm

Diagonal BD = 8 × 2 = 16 cm.

17.

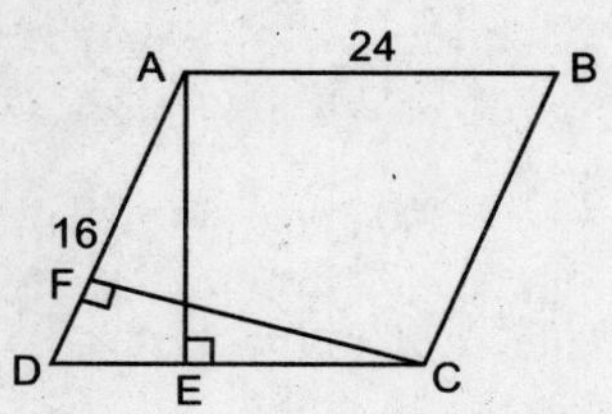

AB = 24 cm

AD = 16 cm

AE = 10 cm (Given)

Area of Parallelogram

= AE × DC = 10 × 24

= 240 cm^2

also, area of Parallelogram

= FC × AD = 240

FC × 16 = 240

FC = 15

$\therefore$ Distance between AD and BC = 15 cm.

18.

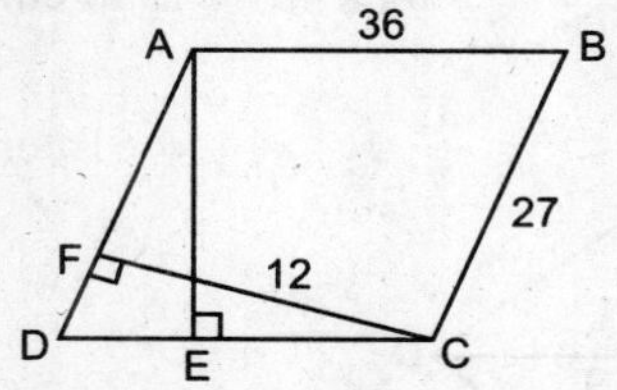

Area of parallelogram

= AE × DC = CF × AD

AE × 36 = 12 × 27

= AE = 9 cm

$\therefore$ Distance between bigger sides = 9 cm.

19.

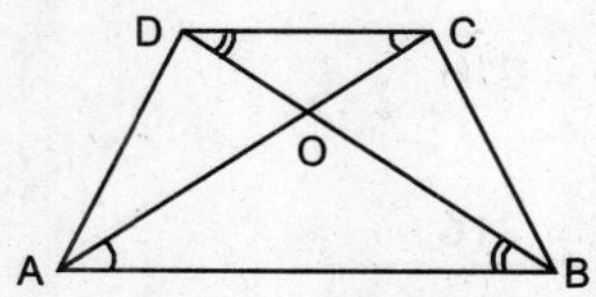

$\therefore$ AB = 2 CD

$$\frac{AB}{CD} = \frac{2}{1}$$

$$\frac{ar(\Delta AOB)}{ar(\Delta COD)} = \left(\frac{2}{1}\right)^2 = \frac{4}{1} = 4:1$$

(Δ AOB ~ Δ COD).

20.

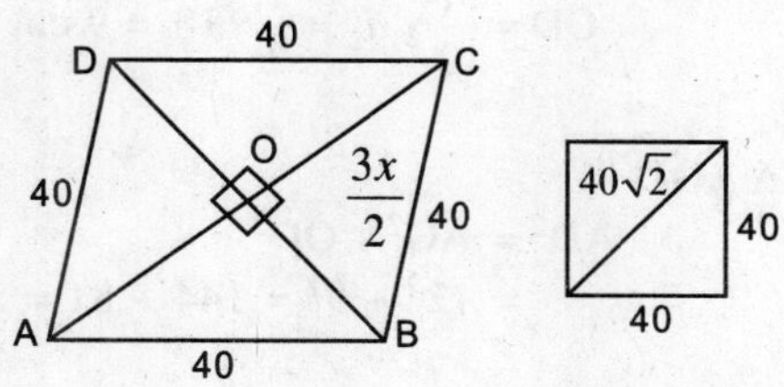

Let AC = $4x$ and BD = $3x$

$\therefore$ OA = $2x$ and OB = $\dfrac{3x}{2}$

In Right Δ OAB

$$\sqrt{(2x)^2 + \left(\frac{3x}{2}\right)^2} = 40$$

$$4x^2 + \frac{9x^2}{4} = 40^2 = 1600$$

$$16x^2 + 9x^2 = 1600 \times 4$$

$$25x^2 = 6400$$

$$x^2 = \frac{6400}{25}$$

$$x = \sqrt{\frac{6400}{25}} = \frac{80}{5} = 16$$

$\therefore$ AC = $4x = 4 \times 16 = 64$

BD = $3x = 3 \times 16 = 48$

$$\text{area} = \frac{1}{2} \times AC \times BD$$

$$= \frac{1}{2} \times 64 \times 48 = 1536 \text{ cm}^2.$$

21.

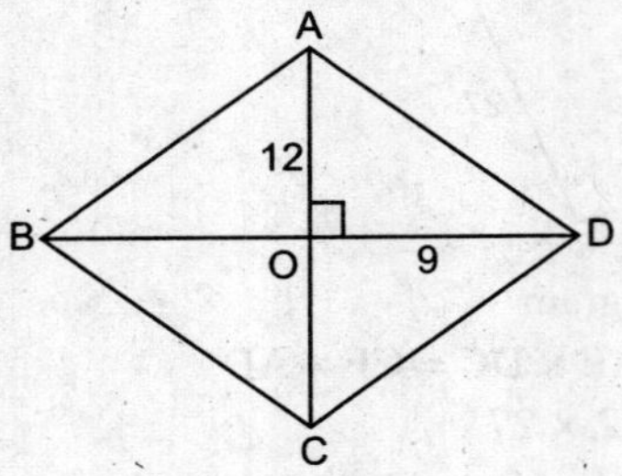

$d_1 = 24$ cm

area of Rhombus = 216

$$\frac{1}{2} \times d_1 \times d_2 = 216$$

$$\frac{1}{2} \times 24 \times d_2 = 216$$

$$d_2 = \frac{216 \times 2}{24} = 18 \text{ cm}$$

$$OA = \frac{1}{2} \times d_1 = \frac{1}{2} \times 24 = 12 \text{ cm}$$

$\therefore$ Diagonals of Rhombus bisect each other at right angle

$$OD = \frac{1}{2} \times d_2 = \frac{1}{2} \times 18 = 9 \text{ cm}$$

Now,

In Right Δ AOD

$$AD^2 = AO^2 + OD^2$$

$$= 12^2 + 9^2 = 144 + 81 = 225$$

$$AD = \sqrt{225} = 15 \text{ cm}$$

$\therefore$ Perimeter of Rhombus

$$= 4 \times AD = 4 \times 15 = 60 \text{ cm}.$$

22. Let the diagonal of rhombus

$$d_1 = x \ \& \ d_2 = 2x$$

$$\text{Area of rhombus} = \frac{1}{2} d_1 d_2$$

$$256 = \frac{1}{2}(x)(2x)$$

$$16 = x$$

Longer diagonal = $2x = 2(16) = 32$ cm.

23. Area of corridor = $100 \times 3 = 300$ m^2

$$\text{Carpet length} = \frac{300 \times 100}{50} = 600 \text{ cm}$$

Cost of Carpet = ₹ 15 × 600 = ₹ 9000.

24. Use $x + y + \frac{xy}{100}$

percentage change

$$= 12 + 15 + \frac{12 \times 15}{100}$$

$$= 27 + \frac{9}{5}$$

$$= 27 + 1 + \frac{4}{5} = 28\frac{4}{5}\%.$$

25.

Length	5	→	8
Breadth	8	→	5
Area	40	→	40

$$\Rightarrow \% \text{ Decrease} = \frac{8-5}{8} \times 100$$

$$= 37\frac{1}{2}\%.$$

□□□□□

10

Geometry

LINES AND ANGLES

A line is made up of an infinite number of points and it has only length. *i.e.*, A line has no end points on either side. A line segment has two end points. A ray has one end point.

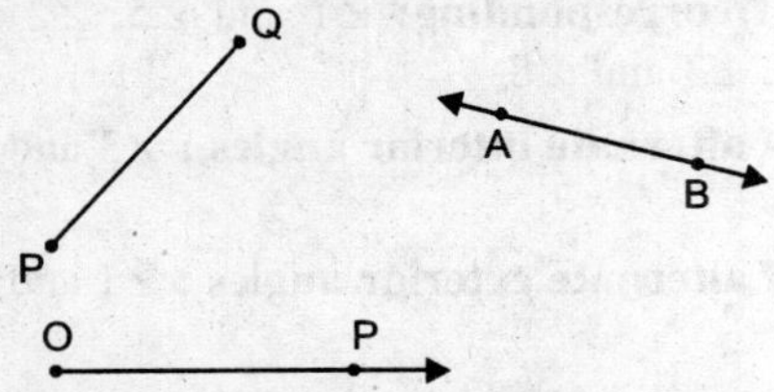

Line Segment Line Ray

- A line segment PQ is generally denoted by $\overline{PQ}$
- A line AB is denoted by $\overleftrightarrow{AB}$
- And the ray OP is denoted by $\overrightarrow{OP}$
- **Collinear points :** Three or more than three points are said to be collinear if there is a line which contains them all.

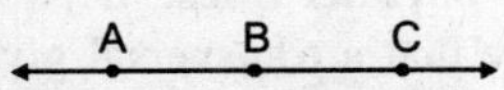

Here A, B and C are collinear points.

- **Concurrent lines :** Three or more than three lines are said to be concurrent if there is a point which lies on all of them.
AB, CD and EF are concurrent lines.

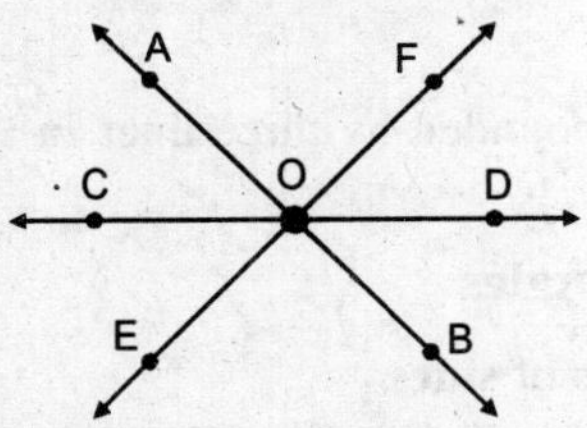

Recall that an "angle" is formed when lines or line segments meet.

E.g.

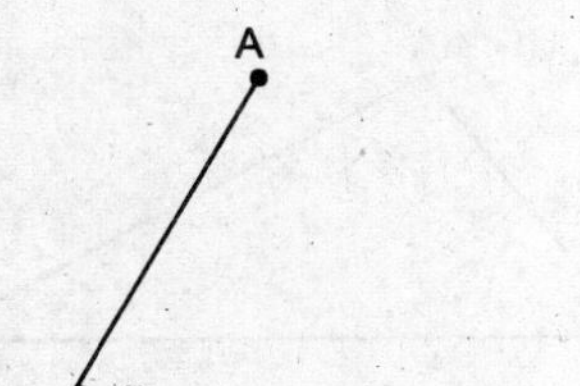

Fig. 1

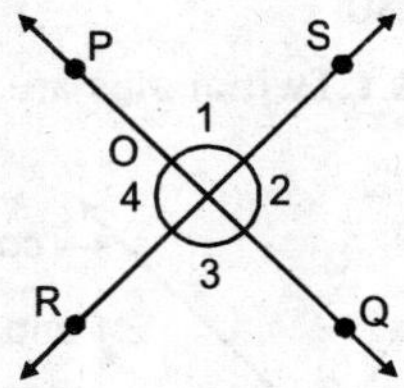

Fig. 2

in figure (1) ∠α fomed by AB and BC in figure (2) ∠1, ∠2, ∠3 and ∠4 are formed by PQ and RS.

Related Angles

- **Acute Angle :**

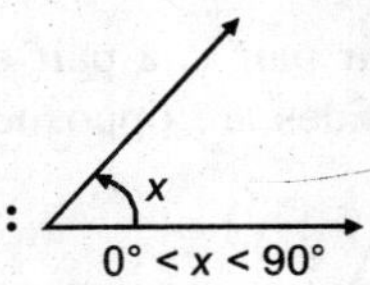

- **Right Angle :**

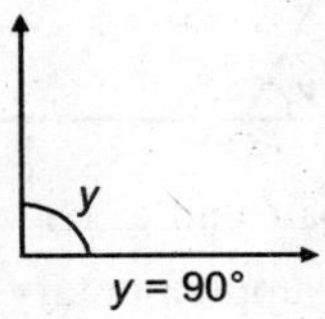

- **Obtuse Angle :**

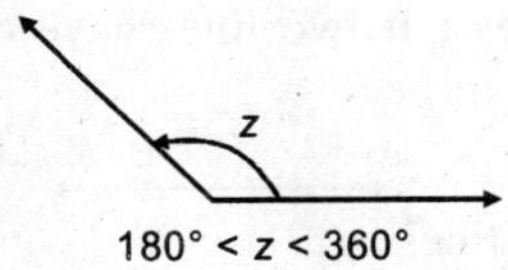

- **Straight Angle :**

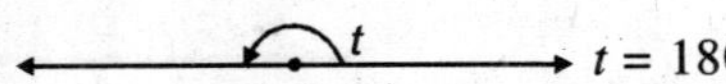

- **Reflex Angle :**

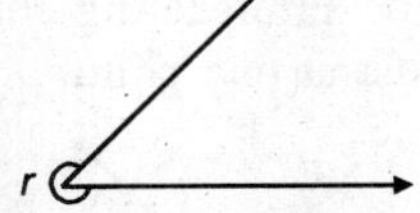

- **Complementary Angles :** When the sum of the measures of the two angles is 90°, the angles are called "Complementary Angles".

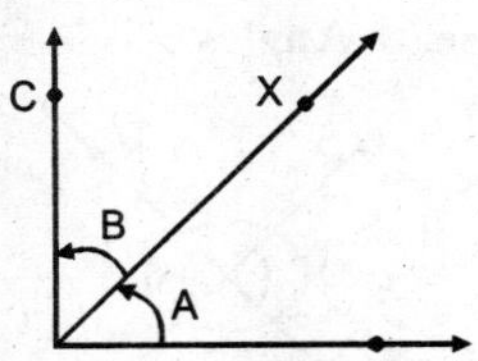

i.e. $\angle A + \angle B = 90^\circ$ or $\angle A = \angle 90^\circ - \angle B$

- **Supplementary Angles :** Sum of two angles which are supplementary is 180°.

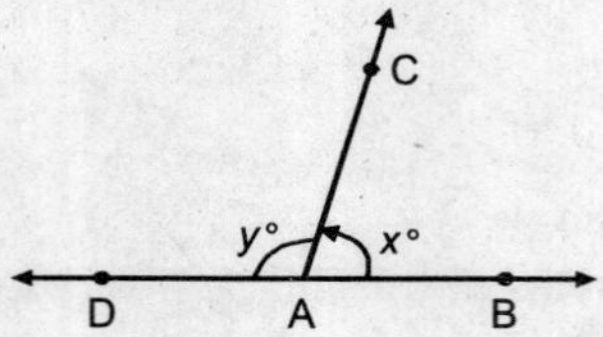

i.e. $\angle x + \angle y = 180^\circ$

- **Adjacent Angles :** Two angles are said to be adjacent if

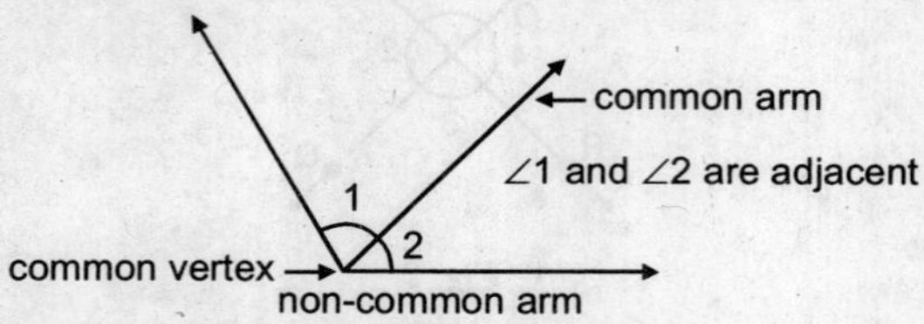

1. They have a common vertex;
2. They have a common arm; and
3. The non-common arms are on either side of the common arm.

- **Linear pair :** A linear pair is a pair of adjacent angles whose non-common sides are opposite rays.

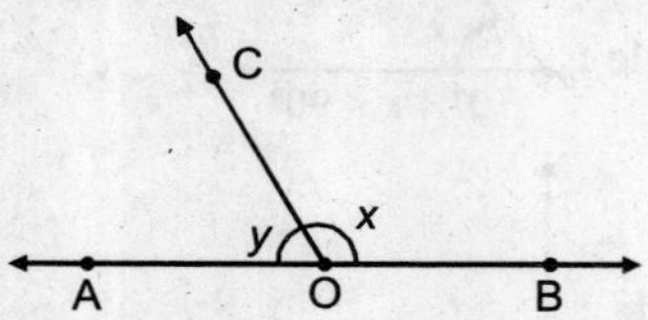

$\angle x$, $\angle y$ and A linear pair and $\angle x + \angle y = 180^\circ$

i.e. linear pair Angles are supplementary.

- **Parallel Lines :** If two lines have no point in common they are said to be

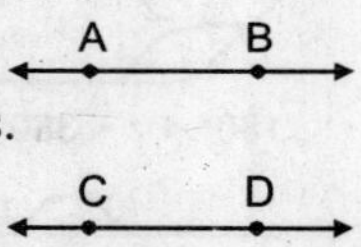

Parallel lines.

- **Intersecting Lines :** If two lines have a point in common, they are said to be intersecting lines. Two lines can intersect at the most at one point.

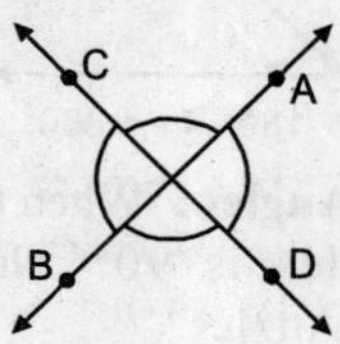

- **Vertically opposite Angles :**

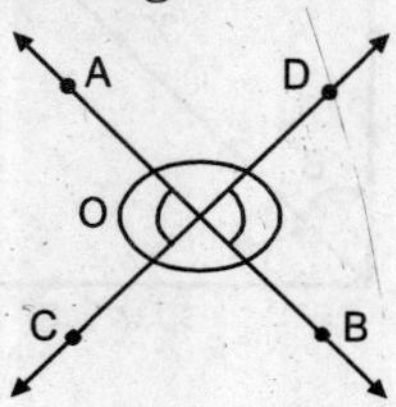

$\left.\begin{matrix}\angle AOD\ \angle BOC \\ \angle AOC\ \angle BOD\end{matrix}\right\}$ are vertically opposite angles

- **Angles made by a transversal line :**

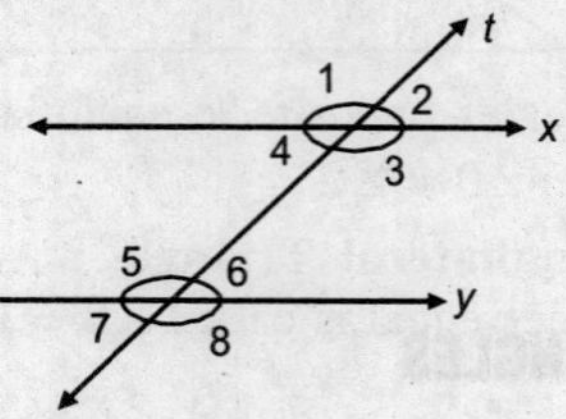

Interior Angles : $\angle 3, \angle 4, \angle 5, \angle 6$

Exterior Angles : $\angle 1, \angle 2, \angle 7, \angle 8$

Pairs of corresponding: $\angle 1$ and $\angle 5$, $\angle 2$ and $\angle 6$, $\angle 4$ and $\angle 7$, $\angle 3$ and $\angle 8$

Pairs of alternate interior angles : $\angle 3$ and $\angle 5$, $\angle 4$ and $\angle 6$

Pairs of alternate exterior angles : $\angle 1$ and $\angle 8$, $\angle 2$ and $\angle 7$

Pairs of interior angles on the same side of the transversal : $\angle 3$ and $\angle 6$, $\angle 4$ and $\angle 5$

→ If two parallel lines are interested by a transversal then:
1. Each pair of corresponding angles are eqal.
2. Each pair of alternate interior are equal.
3. Interior angles on the same side of the transversal are supplementary.

→ **Checking for parallel lines:** If two lines are parallel, then you know that a transversal gives rise to
- pairs of equal corresponding angles
- pairs of equal alternate interior angles and
- interior angles on the same side of the transversal being Supplementary.

TRIANGLES

A plane figure bounded by three lines in a plane is called a triangle.

Type of Triangles

1. On the basis of sides

(*i*) **Scalene Triangle :** All three sides are of different lengths is called a Scalene Triangle.

AB ≠ BC ≠ CA

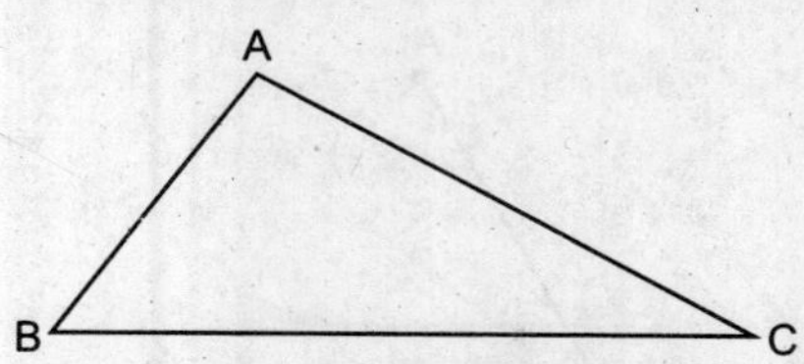

(*ii*) **Isosceles Triangle :** Two sides are of equal length, is called a Isosceles Triangle.

AB = AC

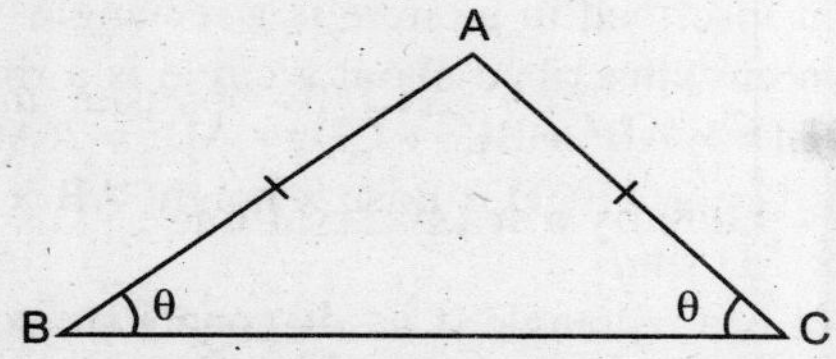

→ Angles opposite to equal sides are equal.
i.e. ∠B = ∠C

(iii) **Equilateral Triangle :** A triangle having all sides equal is called AB = BC = CA

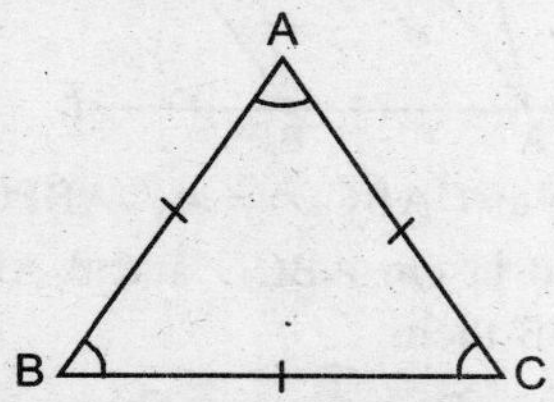

All angles are equal and is equal to 60°.

∠A = ∠B = ∠C = 60°

2. On the basis of Angles

(i) **Right-angled Triangle :** In a triangle, in which one of the angles measures 90° is called a right-angled triangle.

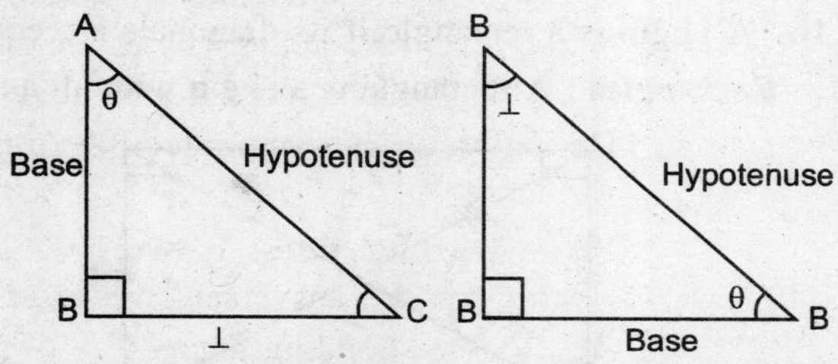

(ii) **Acute-angled Triangle :** A triangle in which every angle is more than 0° and less than 90° is called an acute-angle triangle.

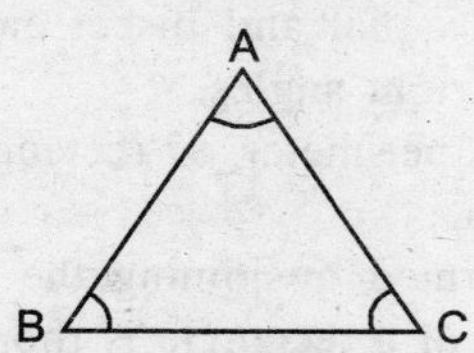

(iii) **Obtuse-angled Triangle :** A triangle in which one of the angles is more than 90° is called an obtuse-angle triangle.

Note : An equilateral triangle is an isosceles triangle but the converse is not true.

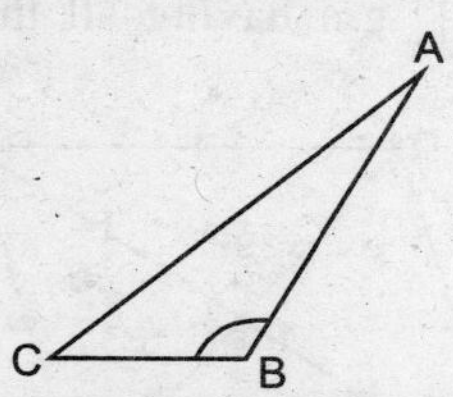

- **Perimeter of Triangle (2*s*) :** The sum of lengths of three sides of a triangle is called its perimeter.

$2s = a + b + c$

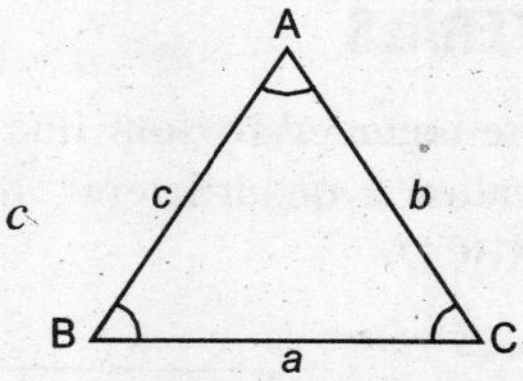

- **Types of Triangles:** Angle Sum property of a triangle:

Theorem 1: The sum of the angles of a Δ is 180°.

Theorem 2: (Exterior angle Theorem): If a side of a triangle is produced, the exterior angle so formed is equal to the sum of the two interior opposite angles.

∠ACD = ∠ABC + ∠BAC

⇒ ∠4 = ∠1 + ∠2

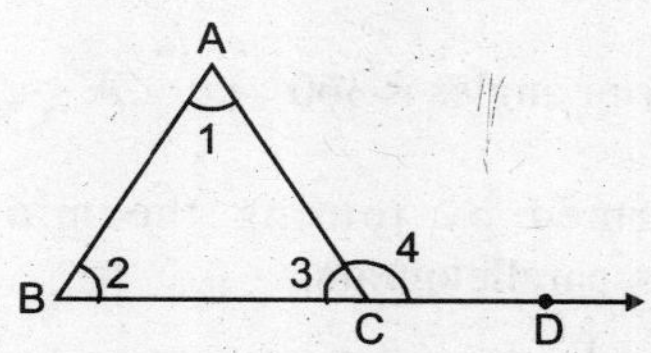

Note : An exterior angle of a triangle is greater than either of the interior opposite angles.
i.e. 4 > 1, and 4 > 2

If three sides of triangle be produced in order then sum of exterior angles so formed is 360°.

∠1 + ∠2 + ∠3 = 360°

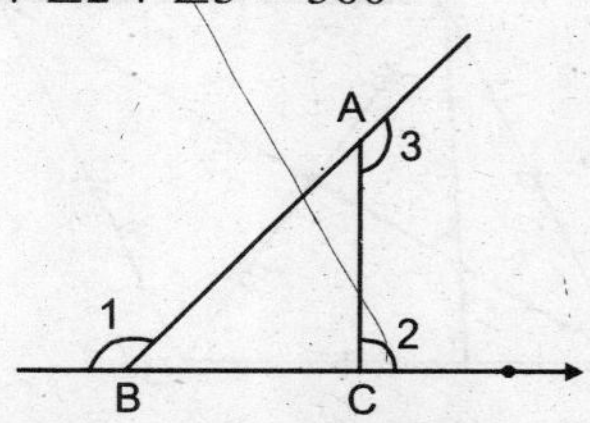

→ **Some properties of triangle:**

Theorem 3: Angles opposite to equal sides of an isosceles triangle are equal.

Here Δ ABC is an isosceles Δ *i.e.* AB = AC

∠ABC = ∠BCA

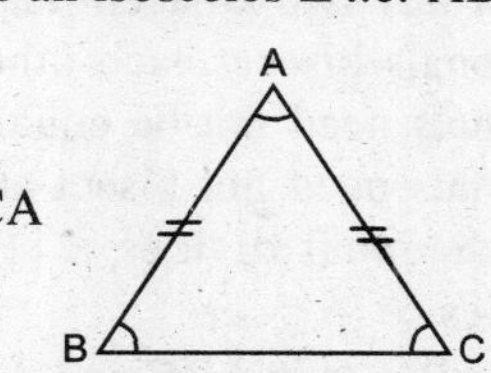

Theorem 4: The sides opposite to equal angles of a triangle are equal.

Here, ∠B = ∠C ⇒ ∠1 = ∠2

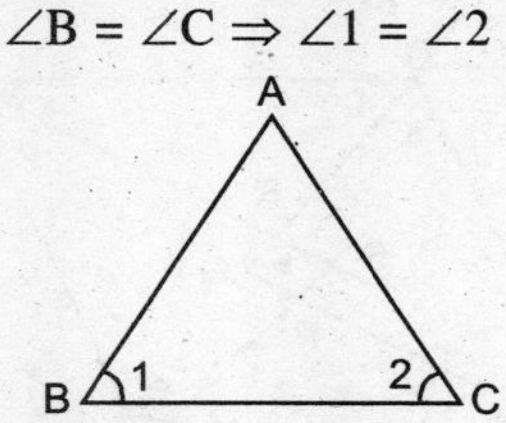

∴ AB = AC

QUADRILATERALS

A plane figure bounded by four line segments AB, BC, CD, and DA is called a quadrilateral. It is denoted by symbol '□' *i.e.* □ ABCD.

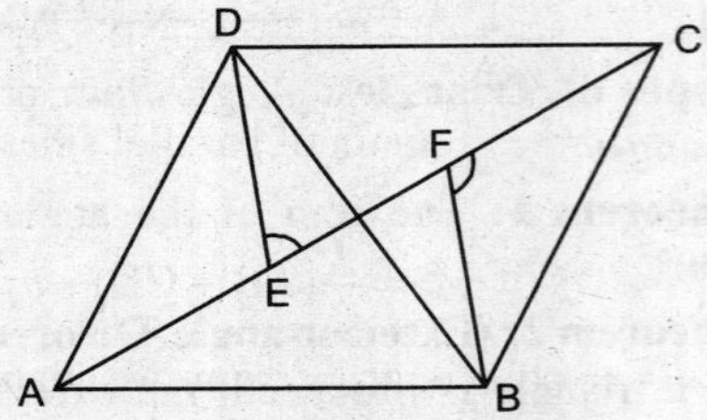

pairs of consecutive (adjacent) angles:
(∠A, ∠B), (∠B, ∠C), (∠C, ∠D), (∠D, ∠A)
(AB, BC), (BC, CD), (CD, DA) and (DA, AB)

Properties

Sum of four interior angles is 360°. *i.e.* ∠A + ∠B + ∠C + ∠D = 360°.

The figure formed by joining the mid-points of a quadrilateral is a parallelogram.

$$\text{Area of ABCD} = \frac{1}{2}\text{AC} \times (\text{DE} + \text{BF})$$

Types of Quadrilaterals

1. Parallelogram (|| gm) : A quadrilateral whose opposite sides are parallel.

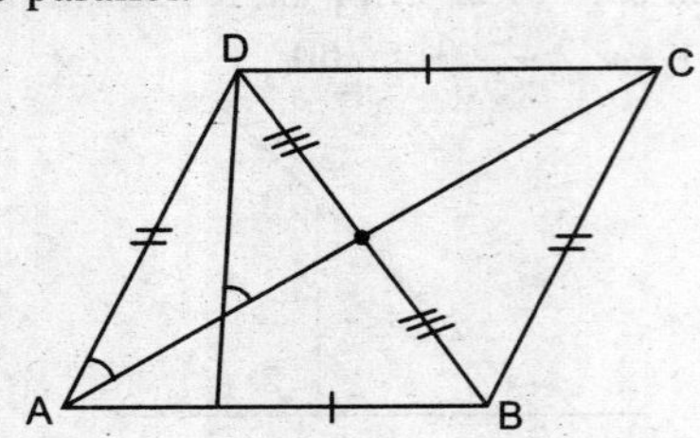

Properties

1. The opposite sides are equal and parallel.
2. Opposite angles are equal. (∠A = ∠C) and (∠B = ∠D)
3. Sum of any two adjacent angles is 180°.
4. Diagnonals bisecet each other.
5. Diagonals need not be equal in lengths.
6. Diagonals need not bisect at right angle.
7. Each diagonal divides a || gm into two congruent triangles.
   i.e., Δ ABC ≅ Δ ADC and Δ ABD ≅ Δ BCD
8. Bisectors of the angles of a || gm form a rectangle. *i.e.* PQRS is rectangle.

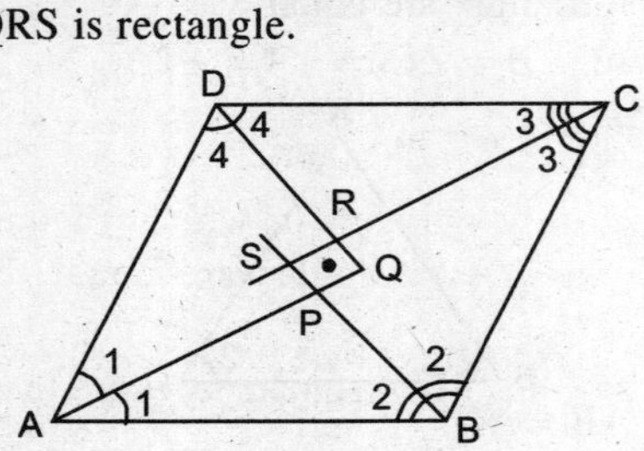

9. A || gm inscribed in a circle is a rectangle.
10. A || gm circumscribed about a circle is a rhombus.
11. $AC^2 + BD^2 = AB^2 + BC^2 + CD^2 + AD^2 = 2(AB^2 + BC^2)$
12. Area of || gm ABCD = Base × height AB × h
    = AB × AD sin$q$
13. A || gm is a rectangle if its diagonals are equal.
14. || gm that lie on the same base and between the same parallel lines are equal in area, *i.e.*

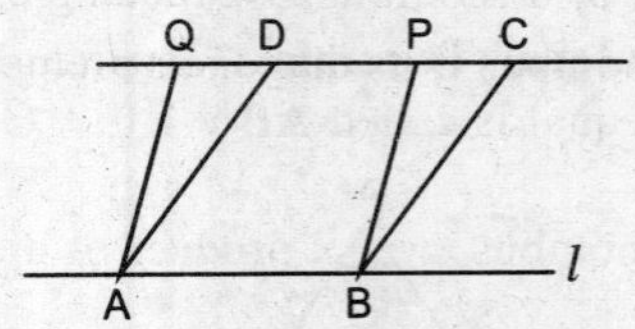

if l || m, then ar(□ABCD) = ar(□ABPQ)

15. If l || m, and || gm ABCD and Δ APB made on the same base AB then,

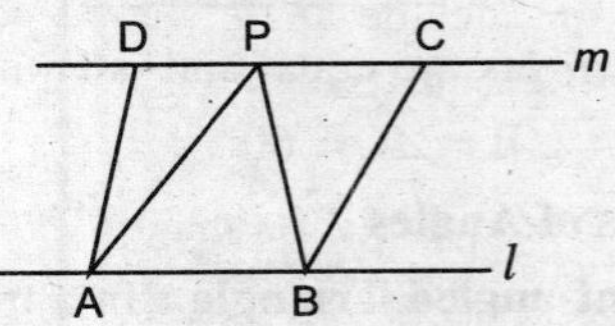

$$\text{ar}(\Delta\ \text{APB}) = \frac{1}{2} ar\ (\square\text{ABCD})$$

16. A || gm is a rectangle if its diagonals are equal.

2. Rectangles : A rectangle is a || gm with all angles 90°.

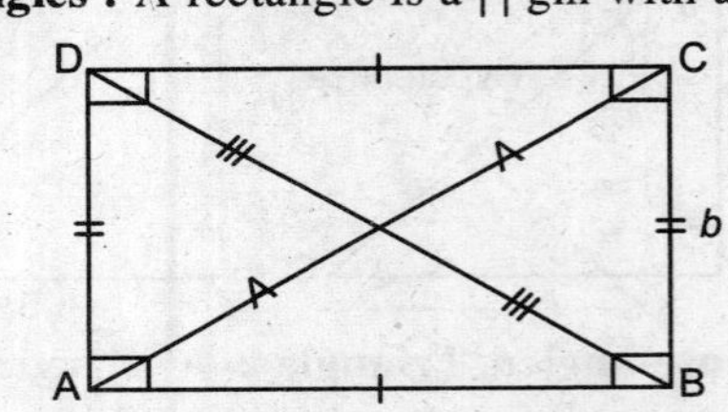

Properties

1. Diagonals are equal and bisect each other, but not necessarily at right angles.
2. For the given perimeter of rectangles, a square has maximum area.
3. The figure formed by joining the mid-points of the adjacent sides of a rectangle is rhombus.
4. Area of rectangles ABCD = length × breadth = $l \times b$
5. Diagonals of a rectangle = $\sqrt{l^2 + b^2}$
6. Bisectors of the angles of a rectangle (a || gm) form another rectangle.

3. Rhombus : A || gm having all the sides equal is a "rhombus".

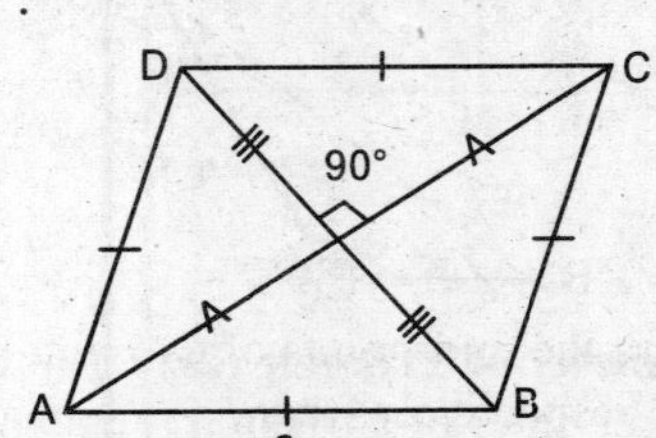

Properties

1. AB = BC = CD = DA = a (say)
2. Diagonals bisect each other at right angle, but they are not necessarily equal.
3. A rhombus may or may not be a square but all squares are rhombus.
4. The figure formed by joining the mid-points of the adjacent sides of a rhombus is a rectangle.
5. A || gm is a rhombus if its diagonals are perpendicular to each other.
6. (*a*) Area of rhombus = $\frac{1}{2}$ × product of diagonals

   $= \frac{1}{2} \times d_1 d_2$

   (*b*) Area of rhombus = product of adjacent sides × sine of the include angle.
7. AC = d_1 and BD = d_2 (say)

   then, $d_1^2 + d_2^2 = 4a^2$
8. A rhombus is a square if its diagonals are equal.

   i.e. if $d_1 = d_2 \Rightarrow$ ABCD is a square.

4. Square : A square is a rectangle with adjacent sides equal or a rhombus with each angle 90°.

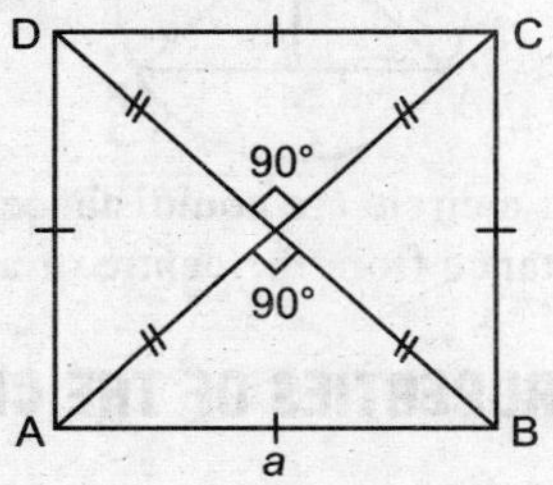

Properties

1. AB = BC = CD = AD = a (say)

   & ∠A = ∠B = ∠C = ∠D = 90°
2. Diagonals are equal and bisect each other at right angle.
3. The figure formed by joining the mid-points of the adjacent sides of a square is a square.
4. Area = (side)^2 = $a^2 = \frac{d^2}{2}$, and diagonal (*d*) = $a\sqrt{2}$.

5. Trapezium : A trapezium is a quadrilateral with only two sides parallel to each other.

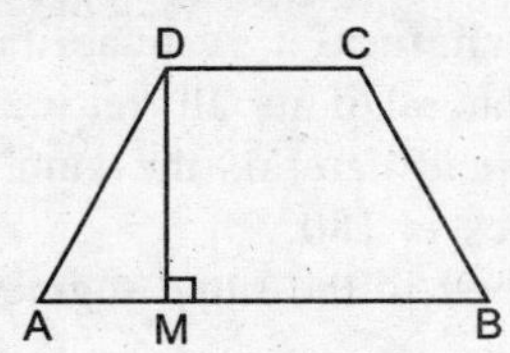

Properties

1. ∠A + ∠D = ∠B + ∠C = 180°
2. If E and F are the mid-points of two non-parallel sides AD and BC respectively, then,

   Median (EF) = $\frac{1}{2}$(AB + DC)

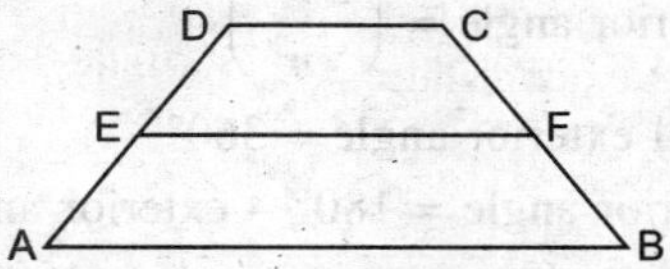

3. Area of trapezium = $\frac{1}{2}$ (sum of parallel sides) × height

   $= \frac{1}{2} \times (AB + CD) \times DM = \frac{1}{2}(AB + CD) \times h$
4. Sum of square of diagonals = (sum of squares of non-parallel side) + 2(product of || sides)

   i.e. $AC^2 + BD^2 = BC^2 + AD^2 + 2AB.CD$
5. By joining the mid-points of adjacent sides of a trapezium four similar triangles are obtained.

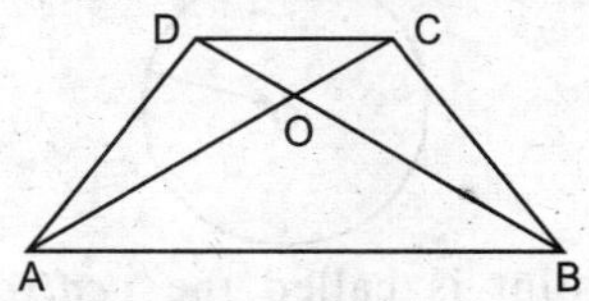

6. $\frac{AO}{OC} = \frac{BO}{OD}$

The mid-point Theorem:

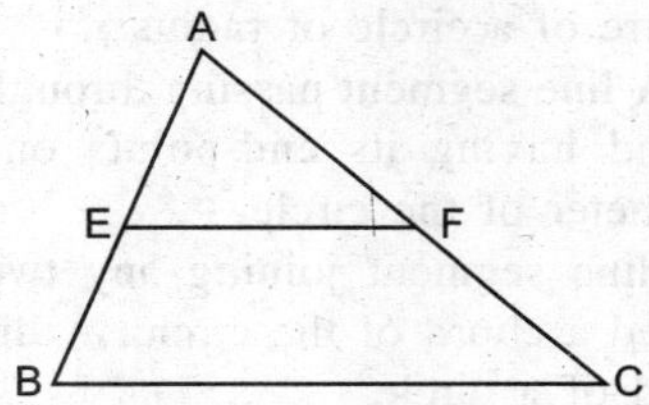

E and F are the mid-points of side AB and AC respectively then,

EF = $\frac{1}{2}$BC and EF || BC

Polygons : A closed-figure bounded by three or more than three straight lines.

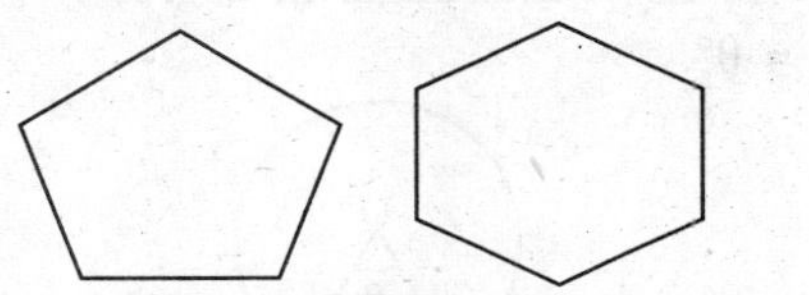

e.g. No. of sides	Name
3	Triangle
4	Quadrilateral
5	Pentagon
6	Hexagon
7	Heptagon
8	Octagon
9	Nonagon
10	Decagon

Regular Polygon : A polygon in which all the sides are equal and also the interor angles are equal, is called a 'Regular polygon'.

if *n* = total no. of sides of a regular polygon, then:

1. Sum of interor angles = $(n - 2) \times 180°$
2. Each exterior angle = $\left(\dfrac{360°}{n}\right)$
3. Sum of all exterior angle = 360°
4. Each interior angle = 180° – exterior angle
   ⇒ interior angle + exterior angle = 180°
5. Number of diagonals = $\dfrac{n(n-3)}{2}$

CHORDS OF A CIRCLE

Points To Remember

- **Circle :** A circle is a set of those points in a plane that are at a given constant distance from a given fixed point in the plane.

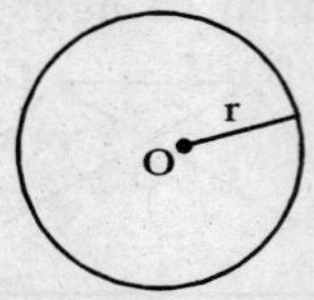

The fixed point is called the *centre* and the given constant distance is called the radius of the circle. O is the centre of a circle of radius *r*.

- **Diameter :** A line segment passing through the centre of the circle and having its end-points on the circle is called a diameter of the circle.
- **Chord :** A line segment joining any two points on a circle is called a chord of the circle. A diameter is the longest chord of a circle.
- **Secant :** A secant is a line segment that intersects a circle at two points.
- **Circumference of a circle :** The perimeter of a circle is called its circumference.
  Perimeter of a circle (C) = $2\pi r$.
- **Degree Measure of An Arc :** The degree of an arc is the measure of its central angle in degrees.
  $m\ \widehat{(AB)} = \theta°$.

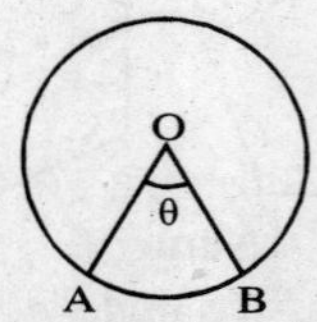

- **Sector of a Circle :** A sector of a circle is the region enclosed by an arc of the circle and the two radii of its end-point.

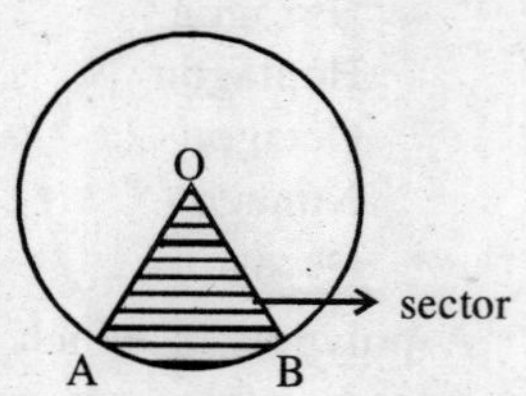

- **Segment of a Circle :** The segment of a circle is the region bounded by an arc of the circle and the chord joining the end-points of the arc.

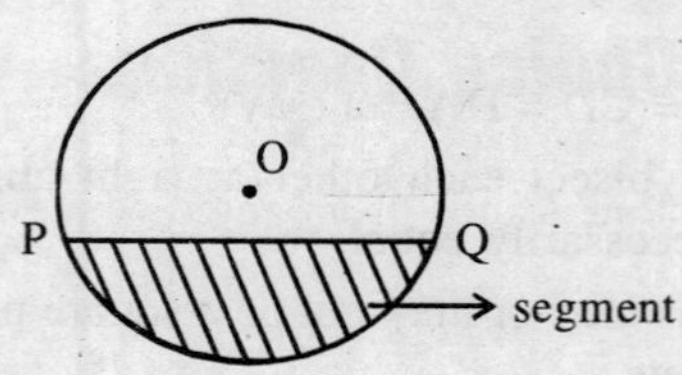

Properties of Chord of a Circle

- The perpendicular from the centre of a circle to a chord bisects the chord.
  i.e. AC = BC

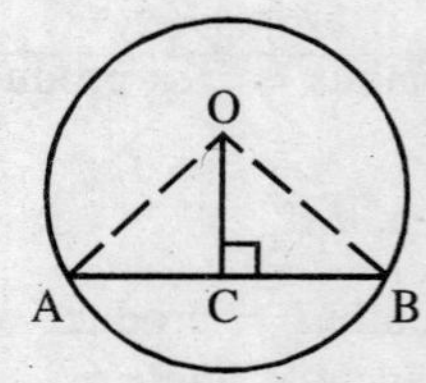

- The line joining the centre of a circle to the mid-point of a chord is perpendicular to the chord.
  i.e. AM = BM
  then OM ⊥ AB

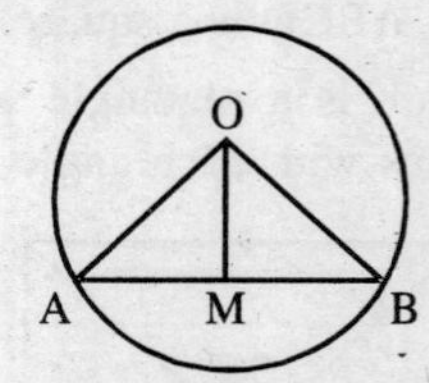

- Equal chords of a circle are equidistance from the centre.
- Chords equidistance from the centre of a circle are equal.

SOME ANGLE PROPERTIES OF THE CIRCLE

Points To Remember

- **Intercepted Arc :** An arc of a circle is said to be intercepted by a circle if,
  (*i*) the end-point of the arc lie on the arms of the circle.
  (*ii*) each arm of the angle contains at least one end-point of the arc.
  (*iii*) the arc lies in the interior of the angle, except for the end-point of the arc.
- The angle subtended by an arc of a circle at the centre of the circle is double the angle it subtends at any point on the remaining part of the circle.
- **Cyclic Quadrilateral :** A quadrilateral is called a cyclic quadrilateral if its all vertices lie on a circle.
- In a cyclic quadrilateral, the sum of each pair of opposite angles is 180°.
- Angles inscribed in the same segment of a circle are equal.
- Angle of a semi-circle is a right angle.
- Equal chords of a circle subtend equal angles at the centre.
- Chords of a circle which subtend equal angles at the centre are equal.

Multiple Choice Questions

1. What is the measures of an angle which is complement of itself?

A. 40° B. 30°
C. 45° D. 50°

2. Determine the value of *y*.

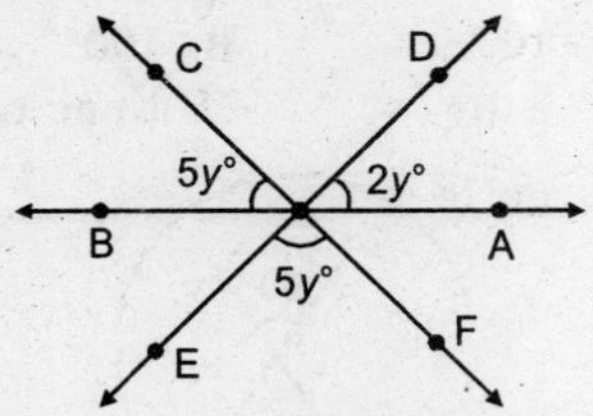

A. 17° B. 15°
C. 20° D. 25°

3. In the given figure, the arms of two angles are parallel. If ∠ABC = 70°, then find ∠DGC and ∠DEF :

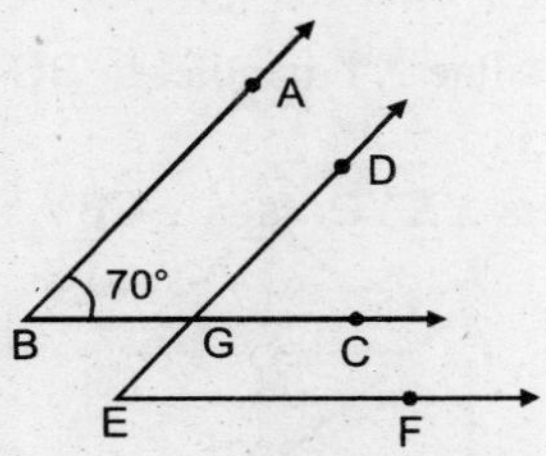

A. 70°, 60° B. 60°, 50°
C. 70°, 70° D. None of these

4. In the given figure, AB || CD, then X is equal to:

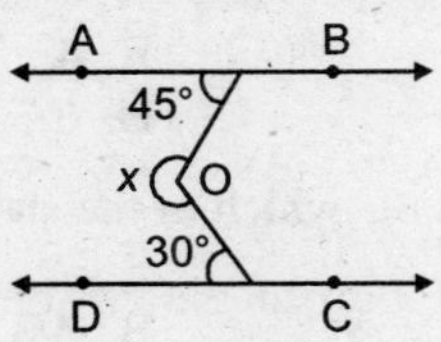

A. 290° B. 300°
C. 280° D. 285°

5. In the given two straight lines PQ and RS intersect each other at 'O'. If ∠SOT = 75°, find the value of *a*, *b* and *c*:

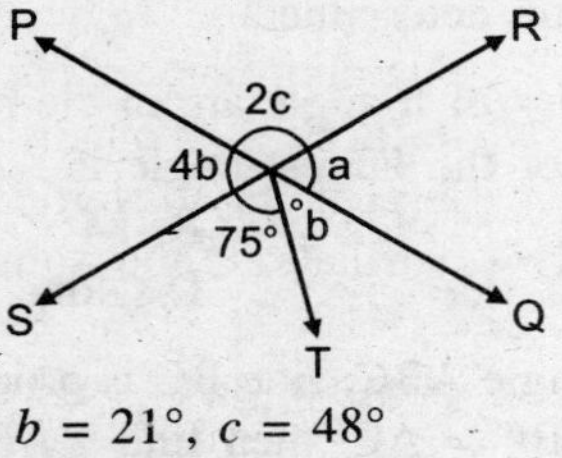

A. a = 84°, b = 21°, c = 48°
B. a = 48°, b = 20°, c = 50°
C. a = 72°, b = 24°, c = 54°
D. a = 64°, b = 28°, c = 45°

6. In the given figure XY and MN intersect at O. If POY = 90° and $a : b$ = 2 : 3, then find *c*:

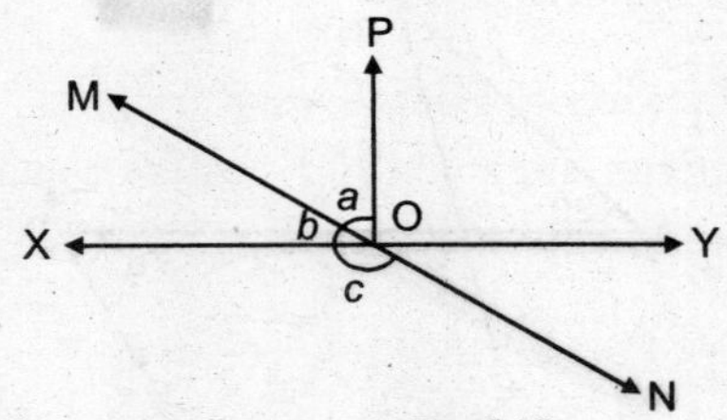

A. 113° B. 54°
C. 126° D. 48°

7. In the given diagram AB || GH || DE and GF || BD || HI, ∠FGC = 80°. What is the value of ∠CHI?

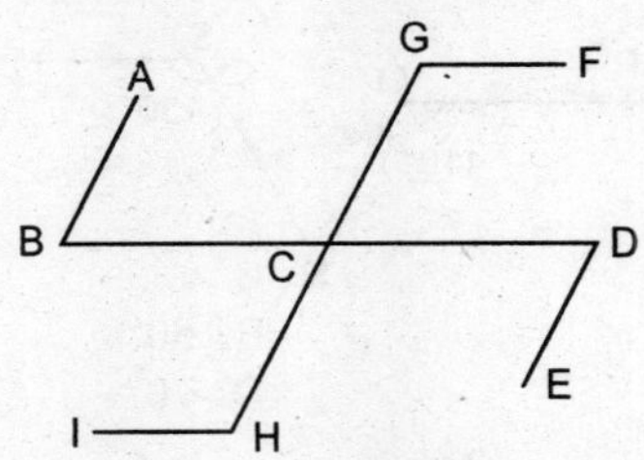

A. 80° B. 120°
C. 100° D. 160°

8. An Angle is equal to one-third of its supplement. What is its measure?

A. 45° B. 50°
C. 55° D. None of these

9. Lines 1 || *m*, *p* || *q*. What are *a*, *b*, *c*, *d*?

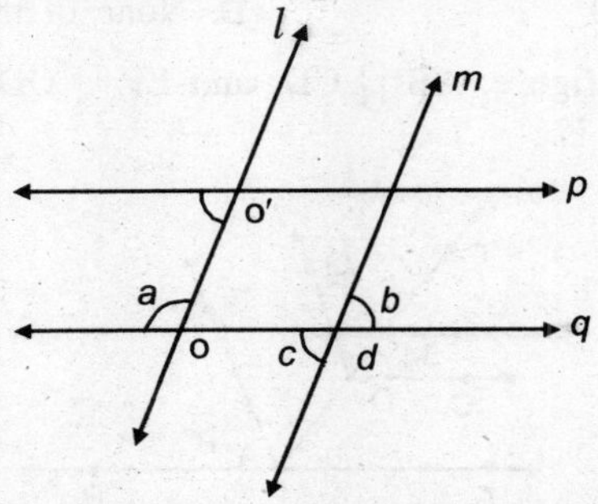

A. a = 120°, b = 60°, c = 60°, d = 120°
B. a = 120°, b = 120°, c = 60°, d = 120°
C. a = 120°, b = 60°, c = 120°, d = 60°
D. None of these

10. In figures, AB || CD. What is θ ?

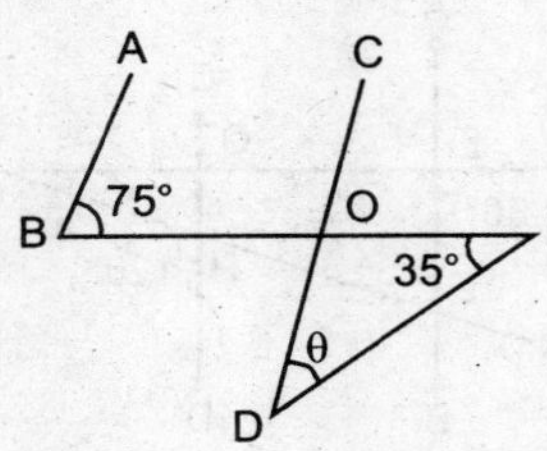

A. 30° B. 35°
C. 40° D. 45°

11. From the given figure, find $\angle ABC$, if BE || DE :

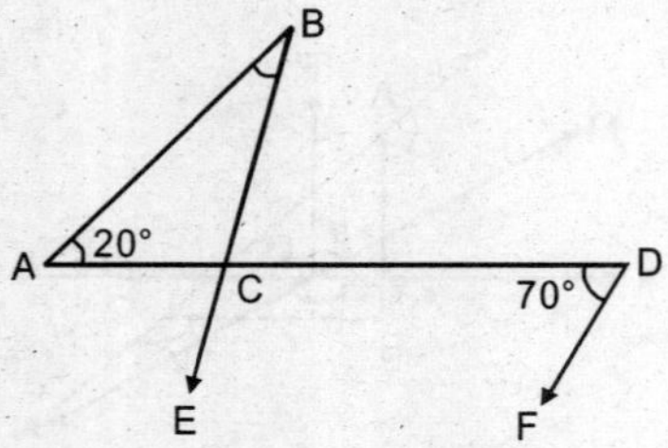

A. 50° B. 40°
C. 35° D. None of these

12. In the figure, if PQ || ST, $\angle PQR = 110°$ and $\angle RST = 130°$, find $\angle QRS$.

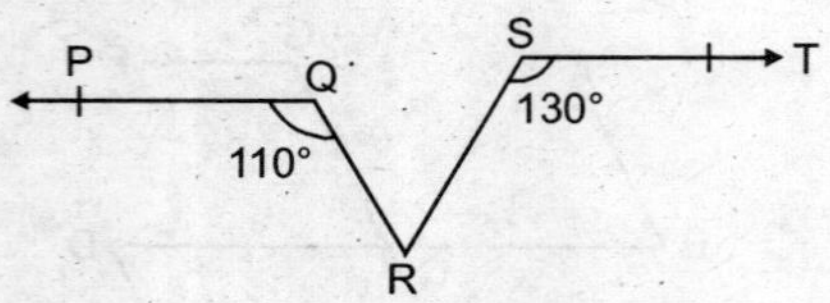

A. 40° B. 50°
C. 60° D. 70°

13. In the figure, AB || CD, the value of x is :

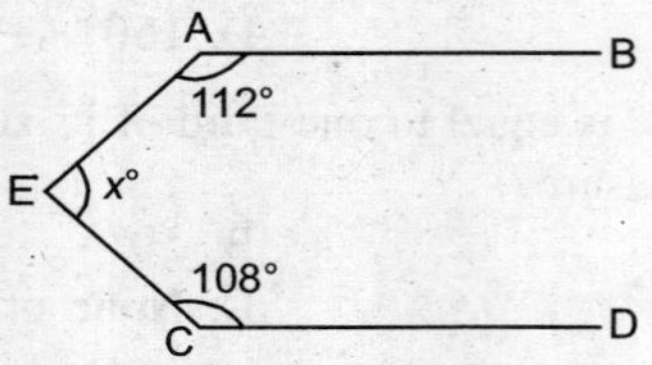

A. 220° B. 140°
C. 150° D. None of these

14. In the figure, AB || CD, and EF || QD, the value of $\angle PDQ$ is :

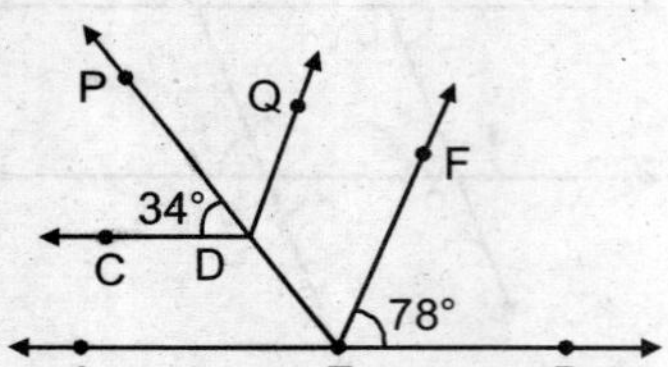

A. 68° B. 78°
C. 56° D. None of these

15. In the given figure AB || CD, given that $\angle PEB = 80°$, $\angle QHD = 120°$ and $\angle PQR = X°$, find the value of x:

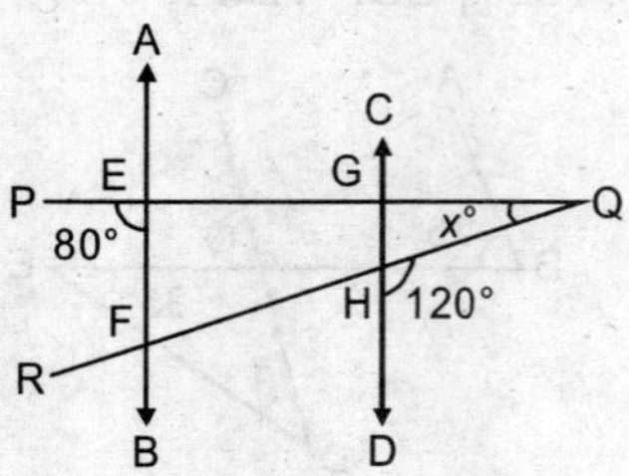

A. 40° B. 20°
C. 100° D. 30°

16. In the given figure, if $\angle ABC = 90°$, and $\angle A = 30°$, then $\angle ACD =$

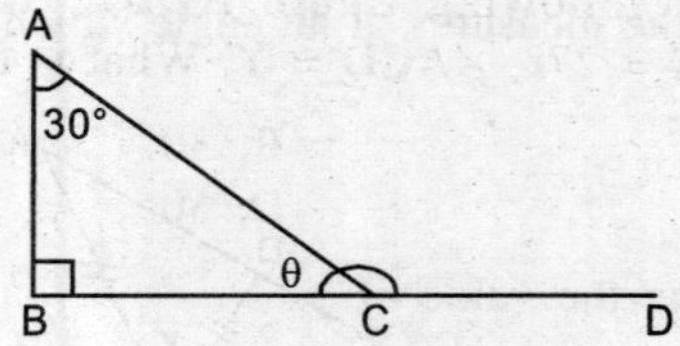

A. 120° B. 100°
C. 110° D. None of these

17. Value of x and y is :

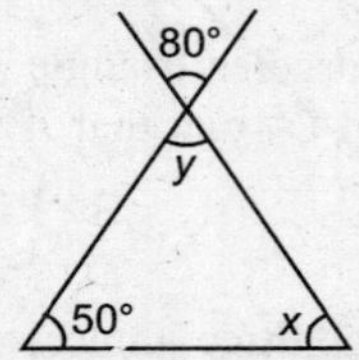

A. $x = 60°$, $y = 80°$ B. $x = 80°$, $y = 50°$
C. $x = 50°$, $y = 80°$ D. None of these

18. In Δ ABC, a line XY parallel to BC intersects AB at X and AC at Y:

If BY bisects $\angle XYC$, then $\angle CBY : \angle CYB$ is :

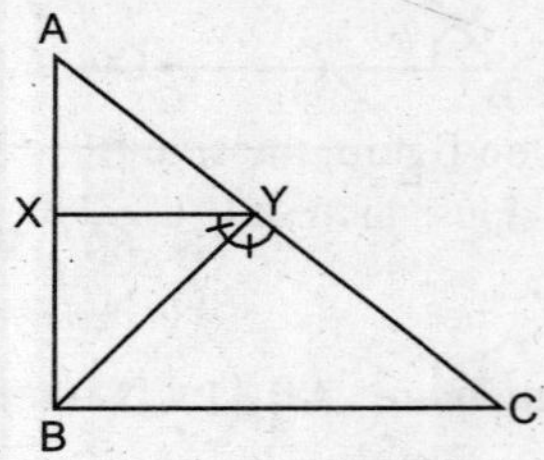

A. 5 : 4 B. 4 : 5
C. 1 : 1 D. 6 : 5

19. In a triangle ABC which of the statements is necessarily true?

A. AB + BC < AC B. AB + BC > AC
C. AB + BC = AC D. $AB^2 + BC^2 = AC^2$

20. In ΔABC, $\angle A > 90°$, then $\angle B$ and $\angle C$ must be :

A. acute
B. obtuse
C. one acute and one abtuse
D. Can't be determined

21. If the angles of triangle are in the ratio 1 : 4 : 7, then the value of the largest angle is :

A. 135° B. 84°
C. 105° D. None of these

22. In the triangle ABC, side BC is produced to D, $\angle ACD = 100°$ if BC = AC, then find $\angle ABC$ is :

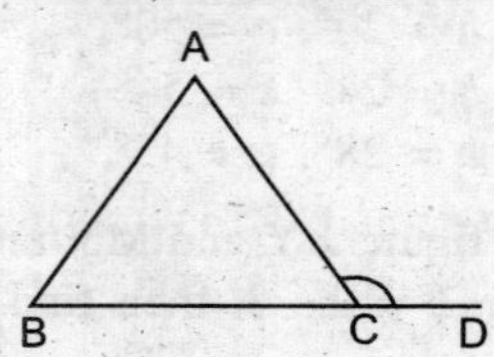

A. 40° B. 50°
C. 80° D. can't be determined

23. In the following figure ADBC, BD = CD = AC, $\angle ABC = 27°$, $\angle ACD = Y$. What is the value of y ?

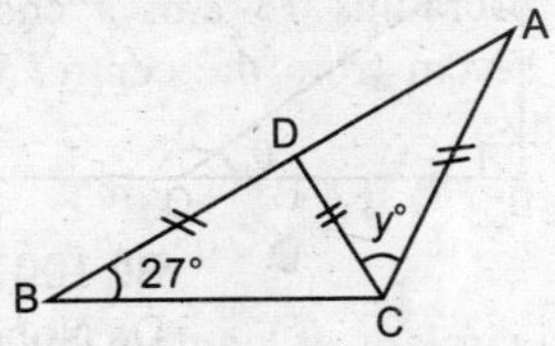

A. 27° B. 54°
C. 72° D. 58°

24. ABC is an isosceles triangle with AB = AC. Side BA is produced to D such that AB = AD. What is $\angle BCD$?
A. 60° B. 90°
C. 120° D. can't be determined

25. A, B, C are the three angles of a Δ. If A – B = 15° and B – C = 30°, then $\angle A$ is equal to :
A. 65° B. 80°
C. 75° D. 85°

26. In a Δ ABC, if $2\angle A = 3\angle B = 6\angle C$, then $\angle A$ is equal to :
A. 60° B. 30°
C. 90° D. 120°

27. In the given figure, the side BC of a Δ ABC is produced on both sides, then $\angle 1 + \angle 2$ is equal to :

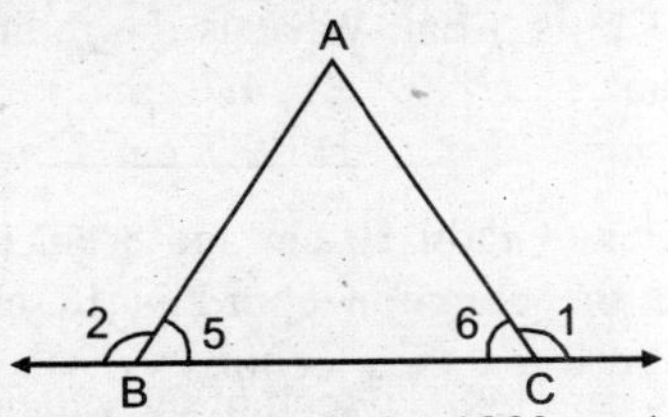

A. $\angle A + 180°$ B. $180° - \angle A$
C. $\frac{1}{2}(\angle A + 180°)$ D. $\angle A + 90°$

28. In a Δ ABC, $\angle A = x°$, $\angle B = y°$ and $\angle C = (y + 20)°$. If $4x - y = 10$, then the triangle is :
A. Right-angled B. Obtuse-angled
C. Equilateral-angled D. None of these

29. It is given that $d° = 70°$, $b° = 120°$, then :

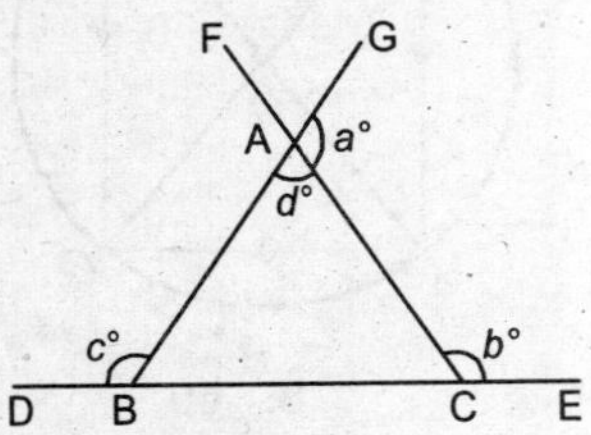

A. $c° = 130°$
B. $a° = 110°$
C. Both (A) and (B) are correct
D. Both (A) and (B) are wrong

30. It is given that AB ⊥ BC. Which one of the following is true?

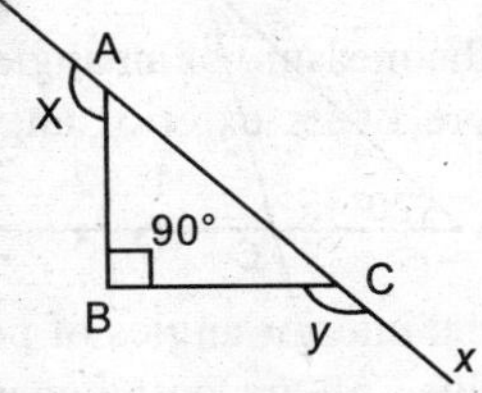

A. $x + y = 180°$ B. $x + y = 270°$
C. $x + y = 300°$ D. can not be said

31. In which of the following is the lengths of diagonals equal?
A. Rhombus B. Rectangle
C. Parallelogram D. Trapezium

32. How many diagonals are there in a octagon?
A. 10 B. 14
C. 18 D. 20

33. A polygons has 44 diagonals. The number of sides of the polygon is:
A. 11 B. 10
C. 13 D. 12

34. The angles of a quadrilateral are in the ratio 1 : 2: 3 : 4, the largest angle is:
A. 120° B. 134°
C. 144° D. 150°

35. The sides BA and DC of a quadrilateral ABCD are produced as shown in figure. Then the true statement is:

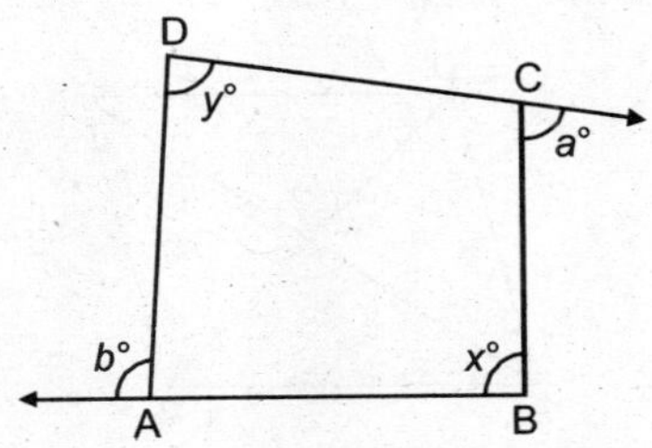

A. $x° + y° = a° + b°$ B. $x° + a° = y° + b°$
C. $2x° + y° = a° + b°$ D. $x + \frac{1}{2}y° = \frac{a° + b°}{2}$

36. Each interior angle of a regular polygon is 120°. The number of sides is:
A. 7 B. 6
C. 5 D. 8

37. Each interior angle of a regular octagon is:
A. 120° B. 90°
C. 135° D. None of these

38. □ABCD is a || gm, AB = 14 cm, BC = 18 cm and AC = 16 cm. What is the length of the other diagonal?
A. 30 cm B. 32 cm
C. 26 cm D. 28 cm

39. If ABCD is a rhombus, then:
A. $AC^2 + BD^2 = 4AB^2$ B. $AC^2 + BD^2 = AB^2$
C. $AC^2 + BD^2 = 2AB^2$ D. $2(AC^2 + BD^2) = 3AB^2$

40. The ratio of the measure of an angle of a regular octagon to the measure of its exterior angle is:
A. 1 : 3 B. 2 : 3
C. 3 : 1 D. 3 : 2

41. The sum of the interior angles of polygon is 1440°. The number of sides of the polygon is:
A. 9 B. 10
C. 8 D. 12

42. Two parallelograms stand on equal bases and between the same parallels. The ratio of their areas is:
A. 1 : 1 B. $\sqrt{2}:1$
C. 1 : 3 D. 1 : 2

43. The length of a side of a rhombus is 13 cm and one of its diagonal is 24 cm. The length of the other diagonal is:
A. 14 cm B. 12 cm
C. 20 cm D. 10 cm

44. The sum of all exterior angles of a convex polygon of *n* sides is:
A. 4 right angle B. $\frac{2}{n}$ right angle
C. $(2n - 4)$ right angle D. $\frac{n}{2}$ right angle

45. The diagonals AC and BD of a || gm ABCD intersect each other at the point O such that ∠DAC = 50° and ∠AOB = 80°. Then ∠DBC = ?

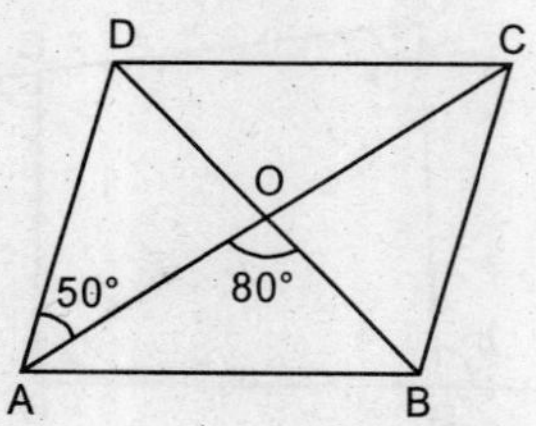

A. 50° B. 40°
C. 45° D. 30°

46. In a circle of radius 10 cm, a chord is at a distance 6 cm from the centre. What is the length of the chord?
A. 16 cm B. 12 cm
C. 9 cm D. 8 cm

47. AB is a chord of a circle of radius 5 cm with centre O. If OM ⊥ AB and AB = 8 cm. What is the length OM?
A. 4 cm B. 5 cm
C. 3 cm D. 2 cm

48. AB is a chord of the circle with centre O and radius 13 cm. If OM ⊥ AB and OM = 5 cm. What is the length of the chord AB?
A. 20 cm B. 24 cm
C. 15 cm D. 18 cm

49. A chord of a circle of radius 7.5 cm with centre O is of length 9 cm. What is its distance from the centre?
A. 3 cm B. 4 cm
C. 5 cm D. 6 cm

50. In a circle of radius 13 cm, a chord is drawn at a distance of 12 cm from the centre. What is the length of the chord?
A. 10 cm B. 8 cm
C. 11 cm D. 9 cm

51. A chord of a circle is of length 6 cm and is at a distance of 4 cm from the centre. What is the radius of the circle?
A. 3 cm B. 4 cm
C. 5 cm D. 2 cm

52. In a circle whose radius is 10 cm, a chord is at a distance of 6 cm from the centre. How long is the chord?
A. 12 cm B. 16 cm
C. 9 cm D. 20 cm

53. AB and CD are two parallel chords of a circle such that AB = 10 cm and CD = 24 cm. If the chords are on the opposite sides of the centre and the distance between them is 17 cm. What is the radius of the circle?
A. 9 cm B. 10 cm
C. 12 cm D. 13 cm

54. AB and CD are two chords of a circle such that AB = 6 cm, CD = 12 cm and AB || CD. If the distance between AB and CD is 3 cm. What is the radius of the circle?
A. 6.7 cm B. 4.7 cm
C. 5.7 cm D. 9.7 cm

55. Two circles of radii 10 cm and 8 cm intersect and the length of the common chord is 12 cm. What is the distance between their centres?
A. 10.25 cm B. 11.27 cm
C. 13.29 cm D. 12.24 cm

56. AB and CD are diameters of circle C (O, *r*) where AC || DB and DA || BC. If ∠OBD = 50°, the measure of ∠AOC is:

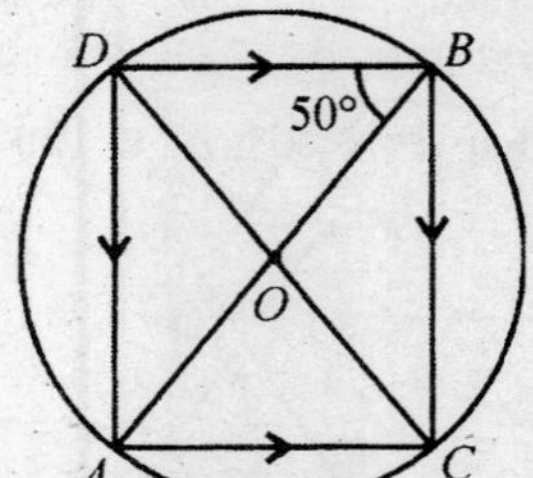

A. 50° B. 60°
C. 70° D. 80°

57. In two circles C(O, 5) and C(O′, 5), Chord PQ = Chord RS. If $m\left(\overset{\frown}{PQ}\right) = 80°$, then $m\left(\overset{\frown}{SR}\right)$ is:

A. 80° B. 180°
C. 280° D. 300°

58. In adjacent figure, measure of ∠AOB is:

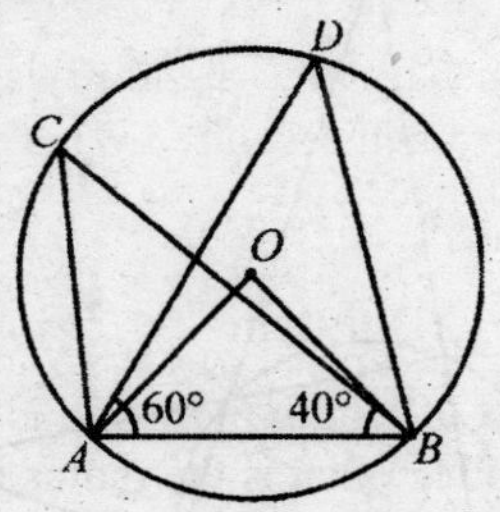

A. 110° B. 160°
C. 80° D. 90°

59. In the figure, the value of ∠PSY is:

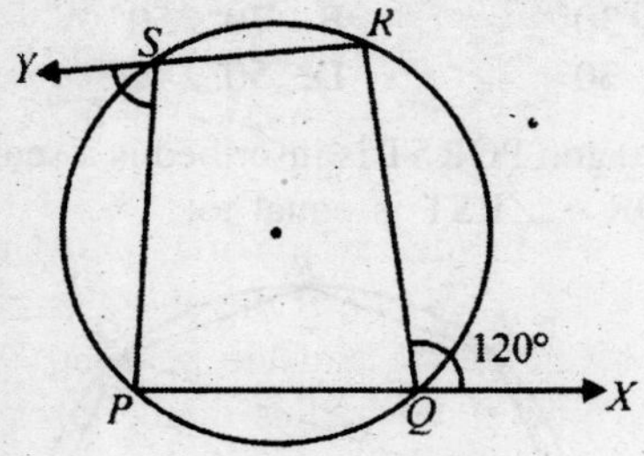

A. 45° B. 50°
C. 60° D. 80°

60. In adjoining figure, O is the centre of the circle, then measure of ∠x is:

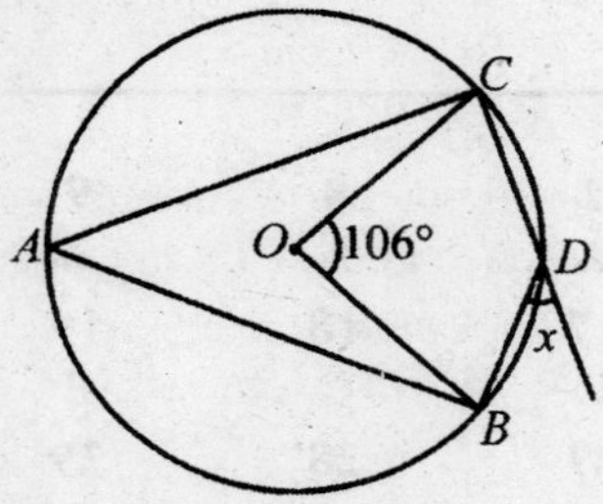

A. 106° B. 90°
C. 67° D. 53°

61. In adjacent figure, O is the centre of the circle ∠ABD = 28°, then measure of ∠y is:

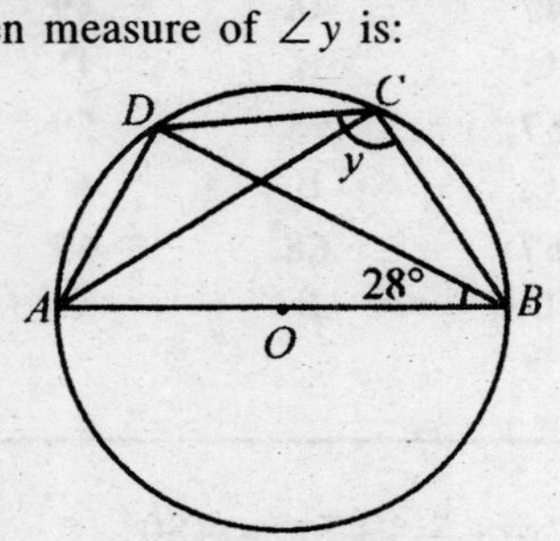

A. 106° B. 118°
C. 126° D. 132°

62. In the given figure, O is the centre of a circle and ABCO is a parallelogram, then values of x and y, respectively are:

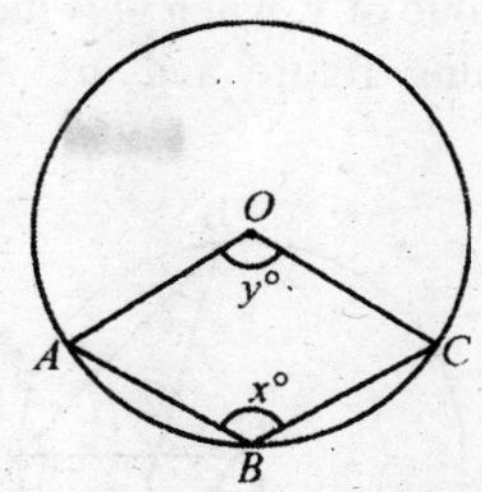

A. 80°, 100° B. 50°, 130°
C. 100°, 80° D. 120°, 120°

63. PQ is a diameter of a circle with centre O and radius OR is perpendicular on PQ. If S be any point in the arc QS, then ∠QPR and ∠PSR are:
A. 70°, 45° B. 60°, 50°
C. 50°, 70° D. 45°, 45°

64. If O is the centre of the circle, find the value of ∠ACB in the adjoining figure:

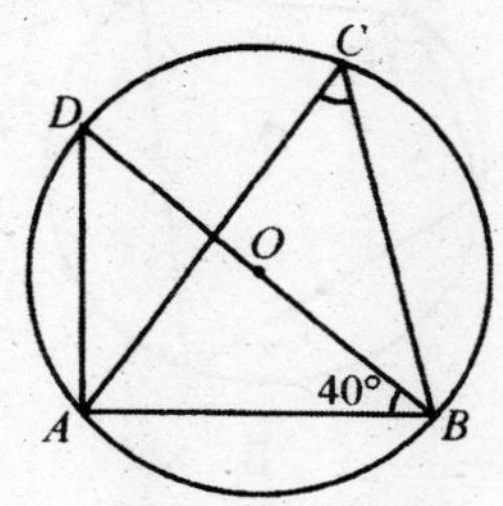

A. 40° B. 50°
C. 80° D. 160°

65. What is the value of x, O is the centre of the circle in the adjoining figure?

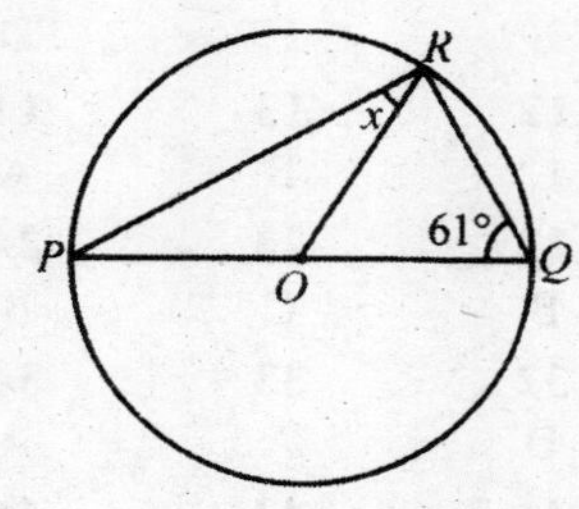

A. 16° B. 23°
C. 29° D. 30½°

66. What is the value of x, O is the centre of the circle?

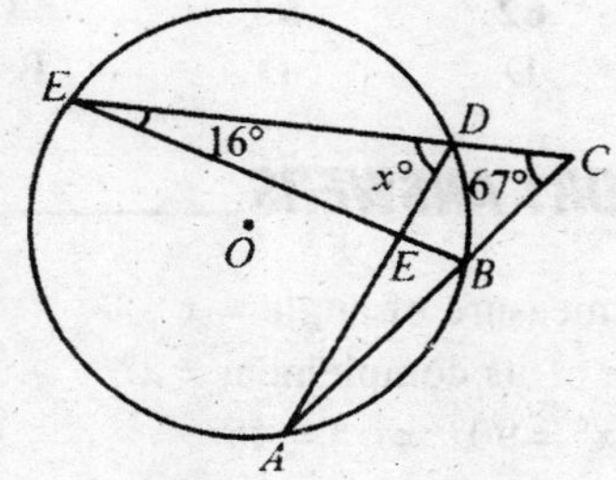

A. 36° B. 43°
C. 23° D. 83°

67. What is the value of x, when O is the centre of the circle in the adjoining figure and arc AB is equal to arc BC?

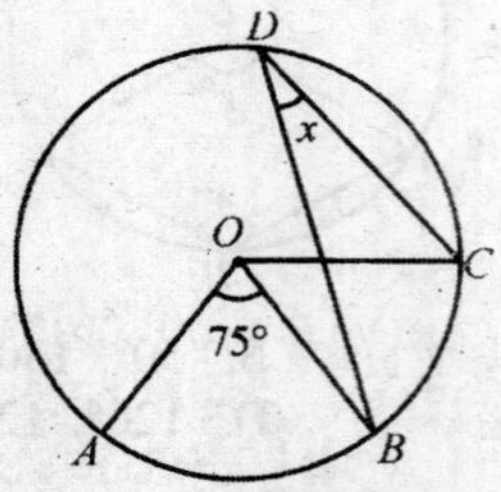

A. 15° B. 22½°
C. 28° D. 37½°

68. In the adjoining figure, ABCD is a cyclic quadrilateral. If CD || BE, ∠DAB = 115° and ∠EBF = 21°, then ∠ADC is equal to:

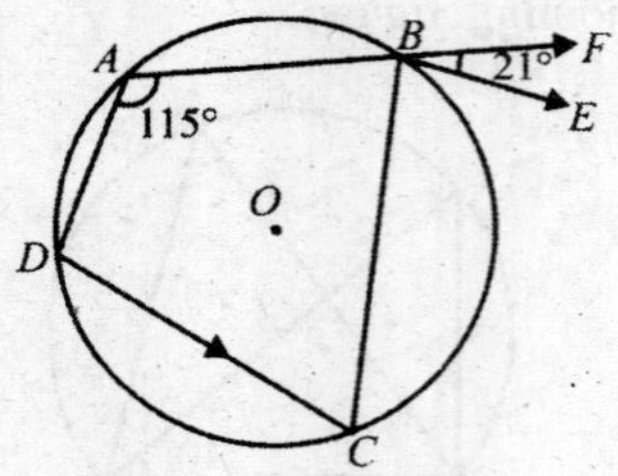

A. 73° B. 86°
C. 105° D. 110°

69. In the adjoining figure, the measure of ∠DPC an
∠BQC respectively is:

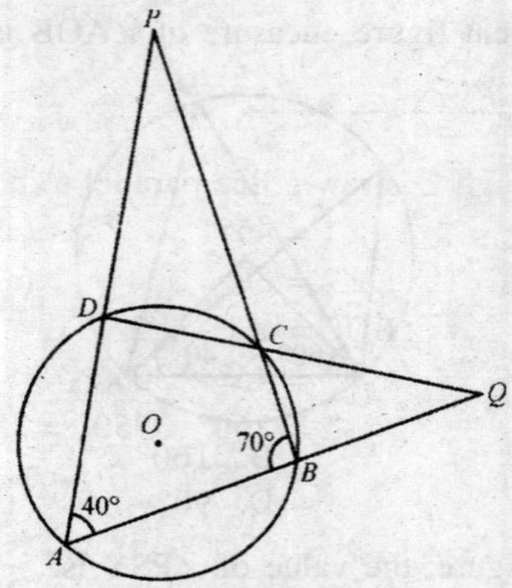

A. 50°, 30° B. 70°, 50°
C. 70°, 30° D. 50°, 70°

70. If a pentagon PQRST is inscribed is a semi-circle, valu
of ∠PQR + ∠RST is equal to:

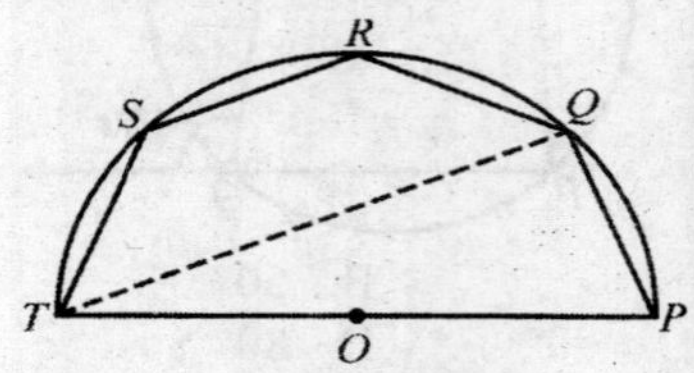

A. 180° B. 230°
C. 270° D. 360°

ANSWERS

1	2	3	4	5	6	7	8	9	10
C	B	C	D	A	C	A	A	A	C
11	**12**	**13**	**14**	**15**	**16**	**17**	**18**	**19**	**20**
A	C	B	A	B	A	C	C	B	A
21	**22**	**23**	**24**	**25**	**26**	**27**	**28**	**29**	**30**
C	B	C	B	B	C	A	A	C	B
31	**32**	**33**	**34**	**35**	**36**	**37**	**38**	**39**	**40**
B	D	A	A	A	B	C	D	A	C
41	**42**	**43**	**44**	**45**	**46**	**47**	**48**	**49**	**50**
B	A	D	A	D	A	C	B	D	A
51	**52**	**53**	**54**	**55**	**56**	**57**	**58**	**59**	**60**
C	B	D	A	C	D	C	B	C	D
61	**62**	**63**	**64**	**65**	**66**	**67**	**68**	**69**	**70**
B	D	D	B	C	D	D	B	C	C

EXPLANATORY ANSWERS

1. Let the measure of angle = $x°$
measure of its complement = $x°$
$\therefore x° + x° = 90° \Rightarrow x° = 45°$

2. ∠COD = ∠EOF = 5Y° (vertically opposite angle)
∴ ∠AOD + ∠DOC + ∠COB = 180°

$\Rightarrow \quad 2y° + 5y° + 5y° = 180°$

$\Rightarrow \quad 12y° = 180°$

$y = 15°$

3. ∠DGC = ∠DEF = ∠ABC = 70° (corresponding angles).

4. 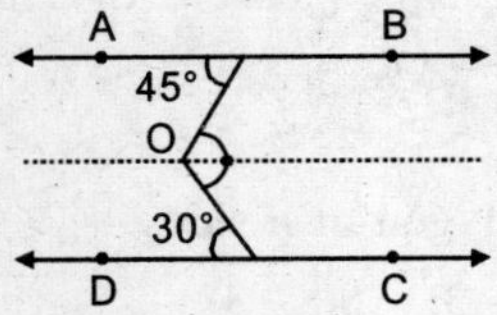

Through O, draw a line parallel to both AB & CD.

Then, $\angle 1 = 45°$ (alternative angle)

and $\angle 2 = 30°$ (alternative angle)

$\therefore$ $\angle BOC = \angle 1 + \angle 2$

$= 45° + 30° = 75°$

So, $x = 360° - 750° = 285°$

Hence, $x = 285°$

5. $\angle ROQ = \angle POS$ (vertically opposite angle)

$\therefore$ $a = 4b$

$75° + b + a = 180°$

$\Rightarrow$ $b + 4b = 180° - 75° = 105°$

$\Rightarrow$ $b = 21°$

$\therefore$ $a = 4b = 4 \times 21 = 84°$

$a + 2c = 180°$

$\Rightarrow$ $2c = 180° - 84° = 48°$

$\Rightarrow$ $c = 48°$

$\therefore$ $a = 84°, b = 21°, c = 48°$

6. $\angle POQ = 90°$

by line property – $\angle a + \angle b = 90°$

$a : b = 2 : 3$

So, $\angle a = 36°$ and $\angle b = 54°$

Here MN is a line so

$\Rightarrow$ $54° + \angle C = 180°$

$\Rightarrow$ $\angle C = 126°$

8. Let the measure of angle $= x°$

$\therefore$ its supplement $= (180 - x)°$

$x = \frac{1}{3}(180 - x) \Rightarrow x = 45°$

9. $60° + a = 180° \Rightarrow a = 120°$

$\therefore$ $\angle loq = 180° - a = 60°$

$\therefore$ $\angle c = \angle loq = 60°$ (Alternate angles)

and $\angle b = \angle c = 60°$

(Vertically opposite angles)

and $\angle d = 180° - \angle c = 120°$

$\therefore$ $a = 120°, b = 60°, c = 60°, d = 120°$

10. $\angle COE = \angle ABE = 75°$ (corresponding angles)

$\therefore$ $\angle DOE = 180° - \angle COE = 180° - 75°$

$= 105°$

in Δ DOE – $105° + 35° + \theta = 180°$

$\Rightarrow$ $\theta = 180° - 140° = 40°$

11. $\because$ BE || DF

$\therefore$ $\angle ACE = \angle CDF = 70°$

$\therefore$ $\angle ACB = 180° - \angle ACE = 110°$

$\therefore$ $\angle ABC = 180° - 20° - 110° = 50°$

12. 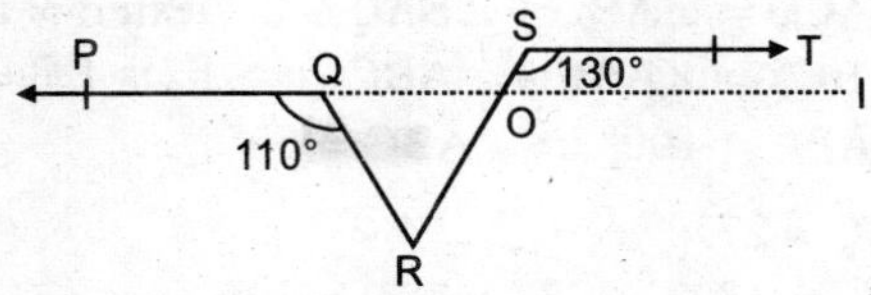

draw a line QI, then

$\angle RQO = 180° - 110° = 70°$

$\angle ROI = 130°$ (corresponding)

So, $\angle ROQ = 180° - 130° = 50°$

Now in Δ QRO

$\Rightarrow$ RQO + $\angle ROQ + \angle QRO = 180°$

$\Rightarrow$ $\angle QRO = 180° - (70° + 50°)$

$= 60° = \angle QRS$

13. 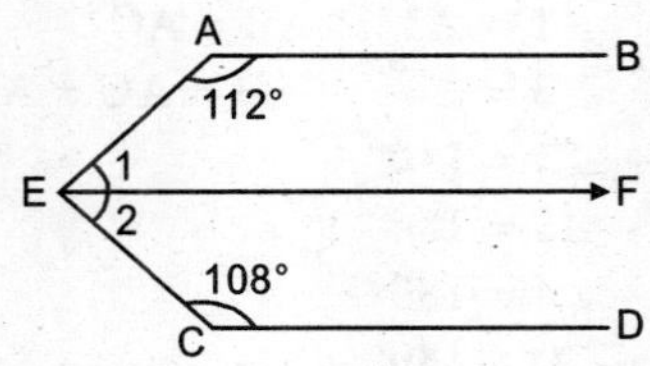

Draw EF parallel to both AB and CD

$\because$ AB || EF and AE transversal cuts them at A and E respectively.

$\therefore$ $\angle BAE + \angle FEA = 180°$

$\Rightarrow$ $112° + \angle 1 = 180°$

$\angle 1 = 68°$

again EF || CD and transversal cuts them at C and E.

$\therefore$ $\angle FEC + \angle ECD = 180°$

$\Rightarrow$ $\angle 2 + 108° = 180°$

$\Rightarrow$ $\angle 2 = 72°$

Now, $x = \angle 1 + \angle 2$

$\Rightarrow$ $x = 72° + 68° = 140°$

14. CD || AB $\therefore$ $\angle AED = \angle PDC = 34°$

$\therefore$ $\angle DEF = 180° - 78° - 34° = 68°$

$\because$ QD || EF

$\therefore$ $\angle PDQ = \angle DEF = 68°$ (corresponding)

15. $\angle PGH = 80° \Rightarrow \angle QGH = 100°$

$\angle QHD = 120° \Rightarrow \angle CHQ = 60°$

$\therefore$ $\angle x + 100° + 60° = 180° \Rightarrow x = 20°$

16. $\angle ACD = \angle B + \angle A = 90° + 30°$

$= 120°$ (exterior angle)

17. $y = 80°$ (vertically opposite angle)

$\therefore$ $x = 180° - 50° - 80° = 50°$

18. $\angle XYB = \angle YBC$ and $\angle XYB = \angle BYC$

$\Rightarrow \angle YBC = \angle BYC$

20. $\angle B + \angle C < 90°$

$\because \angle A + \angle B + \angle C = 180°$

21. $x + 4x + 7x = 180° \Rightarrow x = 15°$

$\therefore$ $7x = 105°$

22. $\angle ACD = \angle ABC + \angle BAC$ (exterior angle)

$\Rightarrow \quad 100° = \angle ABC + \angle ABC \quad (\because BC = AC)$

$\Rightarrow \quad 2\angle ABC = 100° \Rightarrow \angle ABC = 50°$

23. $\angle ABC = 27°$

$\angle BDC = 180° - (27° + 27°) = 126$

$\therefore \angle ACD = 180° - (54° + 54°) = 72°$

24.

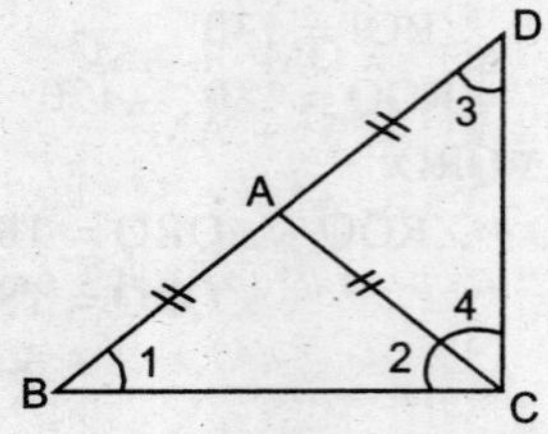

$\angle 1 = \angle 2 \quad \because AB = AC$

and $\angle 3 = \angle 4 \quad \because AB = AC = AD$

Now, $\angle B + \angle C + \angle D = 180°$

$\Rightarrow \angle 1 + \angle 2 + \angle 4 + \angle 3 = 180°$

$\Rightarrow \angle 2 + \angle 2 + \angle 4 + \angle 4 = 180°$

$\Rightarrow \quad 2(\angle 2 + \angle 4) = 180°$

$\Rightarrow \quad \angle 2 + \angle 4 = 90° \Rightarrow \angle C = 90°$

25. Since A, B and C are the angles of a Δ.

$\therefore \quad \angle A + B + C = 180°$

Now, $A - B = 15°, B - C = 30°,$

$\therefore \quad B = C + 30°$

$\therefore \quad \angle A = B + 15° = C + 30° + 15° = C + 45°$

$\therefore \quad A + B + C = (C + 45°) + (C + 30°) + C = 180°$

$3C = 180° - 75° = 105°$

$\Rightarrow \quad C = 35°$

$\therefore \quad \angle A = 35° + 45° = 80°$

26. Let $2\angle A = 3\angle B = 6\angle C = K$

$\therefore \quad \angle A = \frac{K}{2}, \angle B = \frac{K}{3}, \angle C = \frac{K}{6}$

But $\angle A + \angle B + \angle C = 180°$

$\frac{K}{2} + \frac{K}{3} + \frac{K}{6} = 180° \Rightarrow K = 180°$

$\therefore \quad \angle A = \frac{180°}{2} = 90°$

27. $\angle 1 = \angle A + \angle 5$

and $\angle 2 = \angle A + \angle 6$ (exterior angle)

$\angle 1 + \angle 2 = \angle A + (\angle A + \angle 5 + \angle 6)$

$= \angle A + 180°$

28. $x + y + (y + 20) = 180°$

$\Rightarrow \quad x + 2y = 160$

$4x - y = 10 \Rightarrow y = 70, x = 20$

$\therefore$ The angles of the triangle are 20°, 70°, 90°.

29. $a° = 180° - d° = 180° - 70° = 110°$

and $C° = d° + \angle ACB$

$= 70° + (180° - b°)$

$= 70° + 60° = 130°$

30. $\angle BCA = 180° - Y$

$\therefore \quad x = 90° + (180° - y)$

$\Rightarrow \quad x + y = 270°$

32. No. of diagonals of a polygon of n sides

$= \frac{n(n-3)}{2} = \frac{8(8-3)}{2} = 20$

33. $\frac{n(n-3)}{2} = 44 \Rightarrow n(n-3) = 88 = 11 \times 8$

$\therefore \quad n = 11$

34. Angles be x, $2x$, $3x$, $4x$

$\therefore \quad x + 2x + 3x + 4x = 360°$

$\Rightarrow \quad 10x = 360° \Rightarrow x = 36°$

$\therefore$ Largest angle $= 4x = 144°$

35. $\angle DAB = 180° - b$ and $\angle BCD = 180° - a$

But, $\angle A + \angle B + \angle C + \angle D = 360°$

$\Rightarrow (180° - b°) + x° + (180° - a°) + y = 360°$

$\Rightarrow x° + y° = a° + b°$

36. Each interior angle = 120°

$\therefore$ Exterior angle $= 180° - 120° = 60°$

$\therefore$ No. of sides $= \frac{360°}{\text{exterior angle}} = \frac{360}{60} = 6$

37. Exterior angle of a regular octagon $= \frac{360}{8} = 45°$

$\therefore$ Interior angle $= 180° - 45° = 135°$

38.

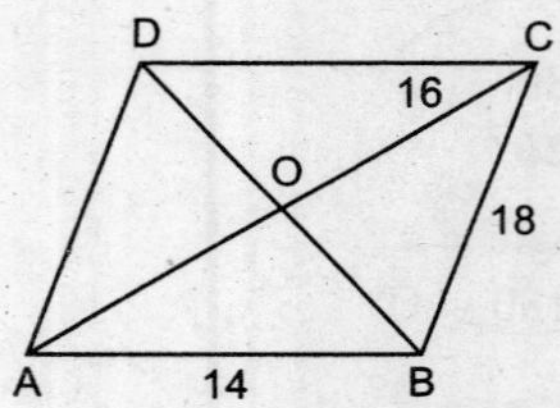

$2(AB^2 + BC^2) = AC^2 + BD^2$

$\Rightarrow \quad BD^2 = [2(196 + 324)] - 256$

$BD^2 = 784 \Rightarrow BD = 28$ cm

39. Since diagonals bisect each other at right angles and all sides are equal.

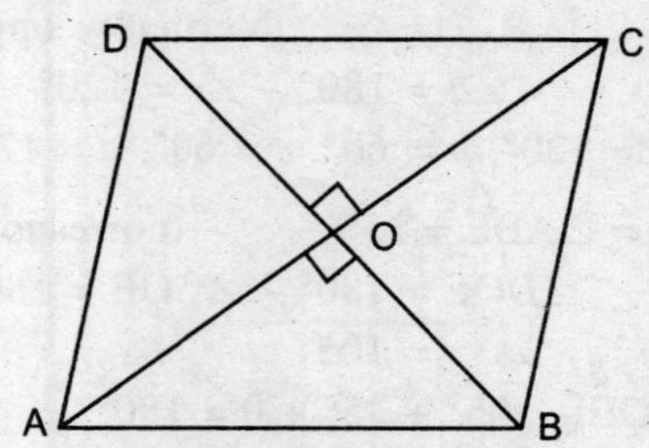

$AO^2 + BO^2 = AB^2$

$\left(\frac{1}{2}AC\right)^2 + \left(\frac{1}{2}BD\right)^2 = AB^2$

$AC^2 + BD^2 = 4AB^2$

40. Exterior angle = 360/8 = 45

Interior angle = 180 – 45 = 135

∴ Interior angle : exterior angle

= 135 : 45 = 3 : 1

41. Sum of all interior angles = $(n - 2) \times 180°$

$\Rightarrow \quad 1440 = (n - 2) \times 180$

$\Rightarrow \quad n = 10 (n \to \text{no. of sides})$

42. Since, their base and perpendicular heights are same.

43.

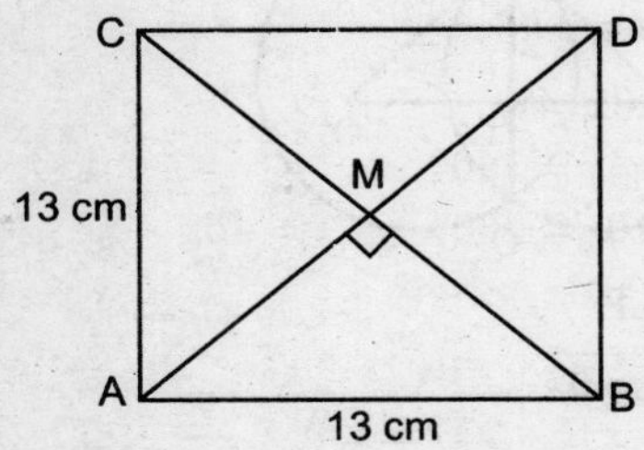

Let BD = 24 cm

∴ BM = 12 cm

$AM = \sqrt{13^2 - 12^2} = 5$ cm

∴ AD = 2AM = 10 cm

45. ∠ACB = ∠DAC = 50° (Alternate inerior ∠s)

∠BOC = 180° – 80° = 100°

∴ Now, in Δ BOC,

∠DBC = 180° – (100° + 50°) = 30°

46. In right angled Δ AOM

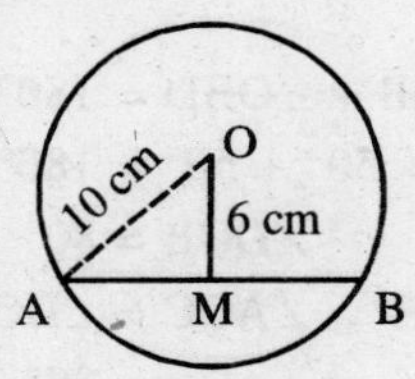

$AO^2 = OM^2 + AM^2$

$10^2 = 6^2 + AM^2$

$100 - 36 = AM^2$

$\Rightarrow AM^2 = 64$

$AM = \sqrt{64} = 8$ cm

AB = 2 AM = 2 × 8 = 16 cm.

47. In right angled Δ AOM.

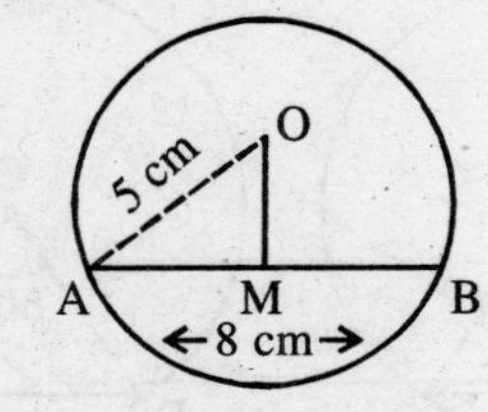

$AO^2 = OM^2 + AM^2$ AB = 8 cm

$5^2 = OM^2 + 4^2$ 2AM = 8

$25 - 16 = OM^2$ AM = 4 cm

$\Rightarrow OM = \sqrt{9} = 3$ cm.

48. In right angled Δ AOM.

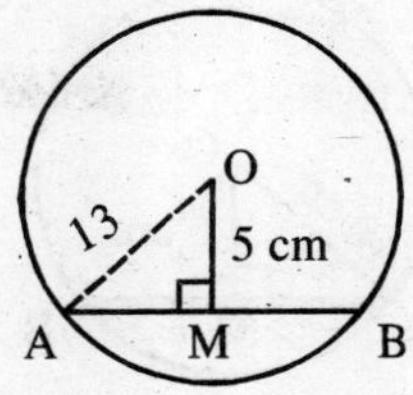

$AO^2 = OM^2 + AM^2$

$13^2 = 5^2 + AM^2$

$169 - 25 = AM^2$

$\Rightarrow AM = \sqrt{144} = 12$ cm.

AB = 2 AM = 2 × 12 = 24 cm.

49. In right angled Δ AOM.

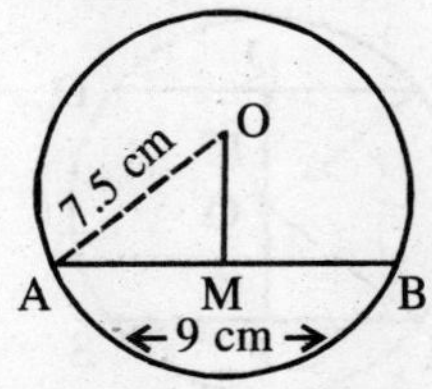

[AB = 9 cm
2AM = 9 cm
AM = 4.5 cm]

$AO^2 = AM^2 + OM^2$

$(7.5)^2 = (4.5)^2 + OM^2$

$56.25 = 20.25 + OM^2$

$56.25 - 20.25 = OM^2$

$36.00 = OM^2$

$\Rightarrow OM = \sqrt{36} = 6$ cm

50. In right angled Δ AOM

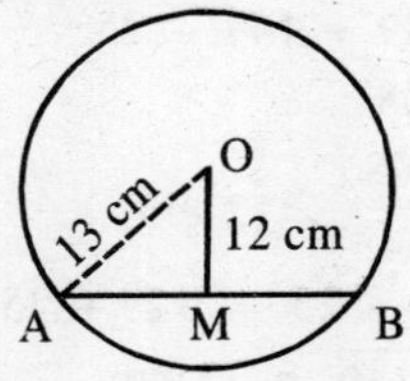

$AO^2 = AM^2 + OM^2$

$13^2 = AM^2 + 12^2$

$169 - 144 = AM^2$

$\Rightarrow AM = \sqrt{25} = 5$ cm

AB = 2AM = 5 × 2 = 10 cm.

51. In right angled Δ AOM

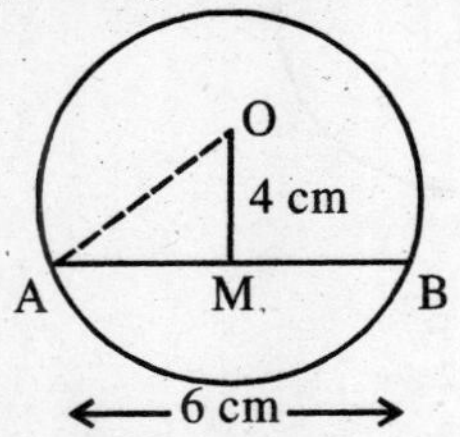

[∵ AB = 6 cm
∴ $AM = \frac{6}{2} = 3$ cm]

$OA^2 = OM^2 + AM^2$

$= 4^2 + 3^2 = 16 + 9 = 25$

$OA = \sqrt{25} = 5$ cm.

Radius of the circle = 5 cm.

52. In right angled Δ AOM.

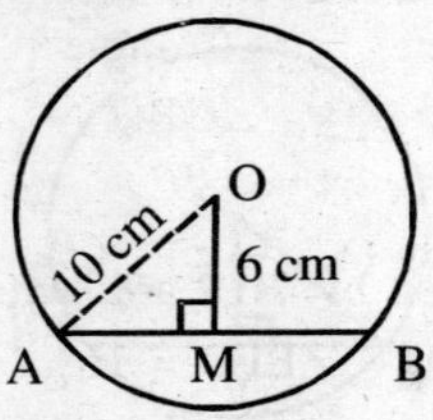

$$AO^2 = OM^2 + AM^2$$
$$10^2 = 6^2 + AM^2$$
$$100 - 36 = AM^2$$
$$\Rightarrow \quad AM = \sqrt{64} = 8 \text{ cm.}$$
$$AB = 2AM = 2 \times 8 = 16 \text{ cm.}$$

53. In right angle Δ OAP and OCQ.

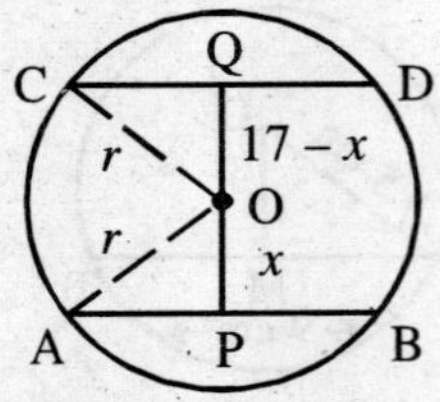

$$OA^2 = OP^2 + AP^2$$
$$r^2 = x^2 + 5^2 \quad \ldots (i)$$
$$OC^2 = OQ^2 + CQ^2$$
$$r^2 = (17 - x)^2 + 12^2 \quad \ldots (ii)$$

Eqn. (*i*) and (*ii*)

$$x^2 + 25 = (17 - x)^2 + 144$$
$$x^2 + 25 = 289 - 34x + x^2 + 144$$
$$34x = 289 + 144 - 25$$
$$34x = 408$$
$$x = \frac{408}{34} = 12 \text{ cm.}$$
$$r^2 = x^2 + 25 = 12^2 + 25 = 144 + 25.$$
$$r = \sqrt{169} = 13 \text{ cm.}$$

54. Let, $OQ = x.$

$$OP = 3 + x$$

In right angle Δ OAP and OCQ.

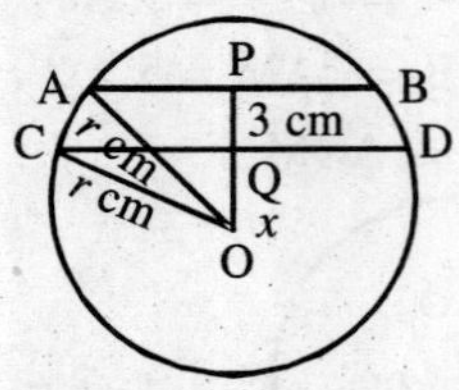

$$OA^2 = OP^2 + AP^2$$
$$r^2 = (x + 3)^2 + 3^2 \quad \ldots (i)$$
$$OC^2 = OQ^2 + CQ^2$$
$$r^2 = x^2 + 6^2 \quad \ldots (ii)$$

Eqn. (*i*) and (*ii*)

$$(x + 3)^2 + 3^2 = x^2 + 6^2$$
$$x^2 + 6x + 9 + 9 = x^2 + 36$$
$$6x = 18$$
$$x = 3 \text{ cm}$$
$$r^2 = x^2 + 6^2 = 9 + 36 = 45$$
$$r = \sqrt{45} = 6.7 \text{ cm.}$$

55. $PL = \frac{1}{2} PQ = \frac{1}{2} \times 12 = 6 \text{ cm.}$

In right triangle OLP.

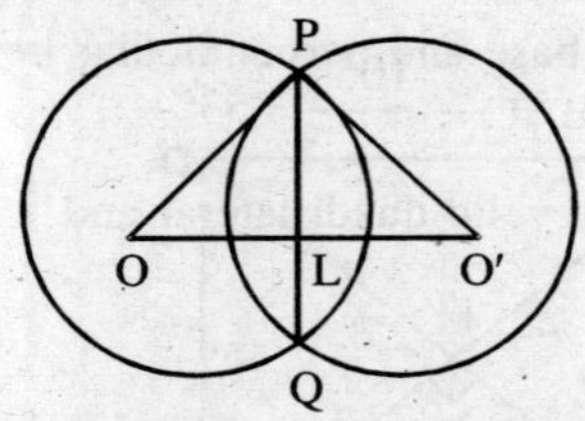

$$OP^2 = OL^2 + LP^2$$
$$OL = \sqrt{OP^2 - LP^2}$$
$$= \sqrt{10^2 - 6^2} = \sqrt{100 - 36} = \sqrt{64} = 8 \text{ cm.}$$

Again in right triangle O′LP

$$O'P^2 = O'L^2 + LP^2$$
$$O'L = \sqrt{O'P^2 - LP^2}$$
$$= \sqrt{8^2 - 6^2} = \sqrt{64 - 36} = \sqrt{28} = 5.29 \text{ cm}$$
$$OO' = OL + LO' = 8 + 5.29 = 13.29 \text{ cm.}$$

56. $OB = r \text{ (given)} = OD$

⇒ Δ OBD is an isosceles triangle

$$\Rightarrow \quad \angle ODB = 50°$$

From Δ ODB,

$$\angle DOB + \angle ODB + \angle OBD = 180°$$
$$\Rightarrow \quad \angle DOB + 50° + 50° = 180°$$
$$\Rightarrow \quad \angle DOB = 80°$$
$$\therefore \quad \angle AOC = \angle DOB = 80°$$

(Vertically opposite angles).

57. $m(\widehat{PQ}) = 80°$

$$\Rightarrow \quad m(\widehat{RS}) = 80°$$
$$\Rightarrow \quad m(\widehat{SR}) = 360° - 80° = 280°$$

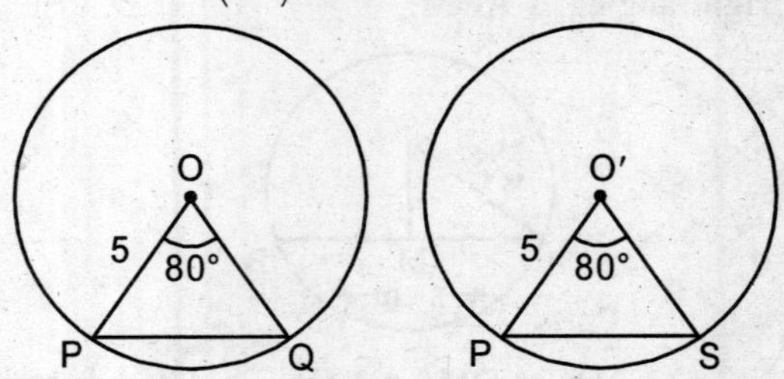

58. From Δ ABC,

$\angle ACB = 180° - (60° + 40°) = 80°$, which is the angle subtended by $\widehat{AB}$ on the circle.

$\therefore$ angle subtended by $\overset{\frown}{AB}$ at the centre of the circle
$= 2 \times \angle ACB = 2 \times 80° = 160°$.

59. $\angle PSR = \angle RQX = 120°$

($\because$ exterior angle of a cyclic quadrilateral is equal to its opposite angle)

But XSR is a straight line.

So, $\angle YSP = 180° - 120° = 60°$.

60. $\angle BAC = \frac{106°}{2} = 53°$

$\because$ ABDC is a cyclic quadrilateral and x is its exterior angle,

$x = \angle BAC = 53°$.

61. $\angle ADB = 90°$ (angle in the semi-circle)

In Δ ADB, $\angle DAB = 180° - (28° + 90°) = 62°$

$\because$ ABCD is a cyclic quadrilateral,

$\angle DAB + y = 180°$

$\Rightarrow$ $y = 180° - \angle DAB$

$= 180° - 62° = 118°$.

62. Angle subtended by $\overset{\frown}{CA}$ at centre $= 2x°$

Now, $2x° + y° = 360°$ and opposite angles of parallelogram are equal,

$\therefore$ $x° = y°$

Thus, $3x° = 360°$

$\Rightarrow$ $x° = 120°$

$\Rightarrow$ $x° = y° = 120°$.

63. $\angle ROQ$ = angle made by $\overset{\frown}{RQ}$ at centre

$= 90°$

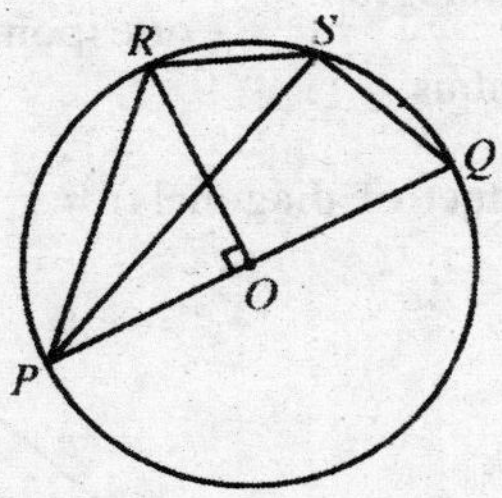

$\therefore \angle QPR = \frac{90°}{2} = 45°$

$\angle ROP$ = angle made by chord PR at the centre

$= 90°$

$\therefore \angle PSR = \frac{90°}{2} = 45°$.

64. $\angle BAD = 90°$

($\because$ angle in a semi-circle is a right angle)

In Δ ABD,

$\angle ABD = 180° - (40° + 90°) = 50°$

$\because$ angles in the same segment of a circle are equal,

$\therefore$ $\angle ACB = 50°$.

65. $\angle ORQ = \angle OQR$ (since Δ OQR is an isoceles Δ)

$\therefore$ $\angle PRQ = 90°$ (angle in the semi-circle)

$\therefore$ $\angle PRO = x° = 90° - \angle ORQ$

$= 90° - 61° = 29°$.

66. $\because$ Angle subtended by $\overset{\frown}{BD}$ are same,

$\angle BAD = \angle BFD = 16°$

$x°$ is exterior angle of Δ ADC,

$\therefore$ $x° = 67° + 16° = 83°$.

67. $\overset{\frown}{BC} = \overset{\frown}{AB}$

$\Rightarrow$ angle subtended by alternate segments by them are also equal.

$\therefore$ Angle subtended by $\overset{\frown}{BC}$ in the alternate segment

$x° = \frac{75°}{2} = 37½°$.

68. $\because$ Sum of the opposite angles of a cyclic quadrilateral is 180°.

$\therefore$ $\angle A + \angle C = 180°$

$\Rightarrow$ $\angle C = 180° - 115° = 65°$

DC $\parallel$ BE

$\Rightarrow$ $\angle DCB = \angle CBE = 65°$

$\therefore$ $\angle CBF = 65° + 21° = 86°$

Since exterior angle of a cyclic quadrilateral is equal to the interior opposite angle,

$\angle ADC = 86°$

69. ABCD is a cyclic quadrilateral,

$\angle B + \angle D = 180°$

$\Rightarrow$ $\angle D = 110°$

and $\angle A + \angle C = 180°$

$\Rightarrow$ $\angle C = 140°$

In Δ PDC, $\angle PDC = 180° - \angle D$

$= 180° - 110° = 70°$

and $\angle PCD = 180° - \angle C$

$= 180° - 140° = 40°$

$\therefore$ $\angle DPC = 180° - (70° + 40°) = 70°$

Similarly, in Δ QBC,

$\angle QBC = 180° - 70° = 110°$

and $\angle QCB = 180° - \angle C$

$= 180° - 140° = 40°$

$\therefore$ $\angle CQB = 180° - (110° + 40°) = 30°$

70. QRST is a cyclic quadrilateral,

$\angle TSR + \angle RQT = 180°$

$\angle TQP = 90°$

(since it is the angle in a semi-circle)

$\therefore \angle TSR + \angle RQT + \angle TQP$

$= 180° + 90° = 270°$

$\Rightarrow \angle RST + \angle PQR = 270°$.

□□□□□

11

Mensuration

PART–A
AREA OF PLANE FIGURES

AREA OF RECTILINEAR FIGURES

Points to Remember

Rectilinear Figure : A figure made up of some line segment is called a rectilinear figure and the line segments forming the figure are known as its sides.

Closed Rectilinear Figure : A rectilinear figure is said to be a closed rectilinear figure if it has no free ends.

Simple Rectilinear Figure : A rectilinear figure is said to be simple if no two sides of it intersect except at a common end-point.

Region : The part of the plane enclosed by a simple closed rectilinear figure is called the region enclosed by it.

Area : The magnitude of the plane region enclosed by a simple closed figure is called its area.

Various units of Measurement of Area

1 dm^2	=	$10 \times 10\ cm^2$	=	$100\ cm^2$
1 m^2	=	$10 \times 10\ dm^2$	=	$100\ dm^2$
1 m^2	=	$100 \times 100\ cm^2$	=	$10000\ cm^2$
1 dam^2	=	$10 \times 10\ m^2$	=	$100\ m^2$
1 arc	=	1 dam^2	=	$100\ m^2$
1 hm^2	=	$100 \times 100\ m^2$	=	$10000\ m^2$
1 hectare	=	$10000\ m^2$		
1 hectare	=	100 acres		
1 km^2	=	$(1000 \times 1000) m^2$	=	$10^6 m^2$
1 km^2	=	100 hectares.		

Some Important Formula

(*i*) Area of rectangle = $l \times b$

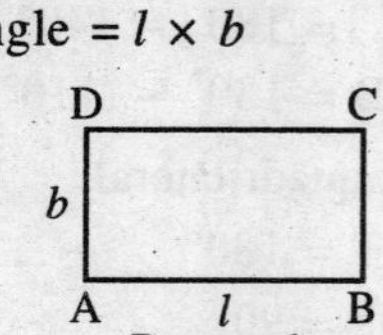

Rectangle

(*ii*) Length = $\dfrac{\text{Area}}{\text{Breadth}}$ (*iii*) Diagonal = $\sqrt{l^2 + b^2}$

(*iv*) Perimeter = $2(l + b)$

(*v*) Area of the square = a^2 sq units

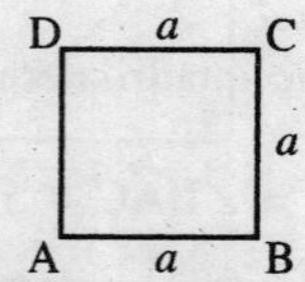

(*vi*) Diagonal of the square = $\sqrt{2}\,a$ units

(*vii*) Perimeter of the square = $4a$ units

(*viii*) Side of the square = $\dfrac{1}{\sqrt{2}}$ (diagonal)

(*ix*) Side of the square = $\sqrt{\text{Area}}$ units

(*x*) Area of parallelogram = Base × height = $a \times h$

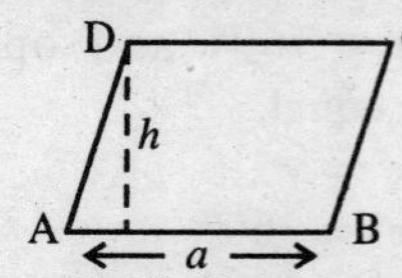

Parallelogram

(*xi*) Base of a parallelogram = $\dfrac{\text{Area}}{\text{Height}}$

(*xii*) Side of parallelogram = $\dfrac{\text{Area}}{\text{Corresponding altitude}}$

(*xiii*) Area of rhombus

$$= \frac{1}{2}\text{(product of diagonals)} = \frac{1}{2}(d_1 \times d_2)$$

(*xiv*) $d_1{}^2 + d_2{}^2 = 4a^2$

or $a = \dfrac{1}{2}\sqrt{d_1^2 + d_2^2}$

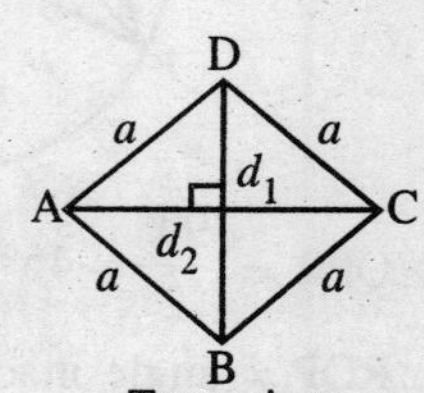

Trapeziun

(*xv*) Area of Trapezium

$$= \frac{1}{2} \times \text{(Sum of parallel sides)} \times \text{height}$$

(*xvi*) Area of quadrilateral

$$\text{ABCD} = \frac{1}{2} \times d\,(h_1 + h_2)$$

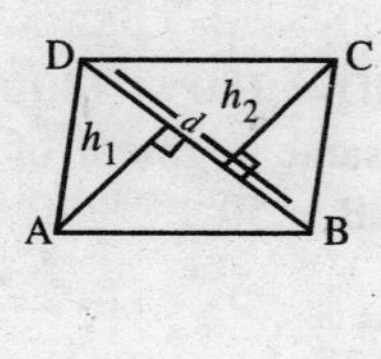

(*xvii*) Area of four walls = 2 (Length + Breadth) × Height

Triangle

(*i*) Area of right angle triangle.

$= \frac{1}{2} \times \text{base} \times \text{height} = \frac{1}{2} \times a \times h$

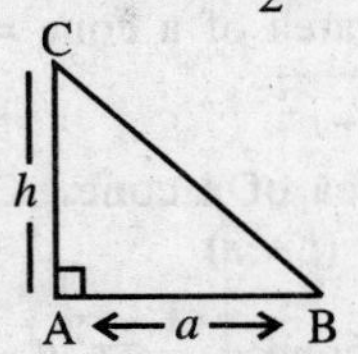

inradius, $r = \frac{\text{Height + Base – Hypotenuse}}{2}$

Circum radius, $R = \frac{\text{Hypotenuse}}{2}$

(*ii*) Area of triangle whose three sides are given.

$s = \frac{a+b+c}{2}$

Area of Δ ABC $= \sqrt{s(s-a)(s-b)(s-c)}$

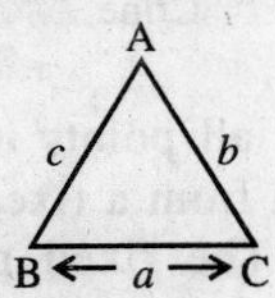

$r = \frac{\Delta}{s}$, $R = \frac{abc}{4\Delta}$

(*iii*) Area of an equilateral triangle

ABC $= \frac{\sqrt{3}}{4}(\text{side})^2 = \frac{\sqrt{3}}{4}(a)^2$

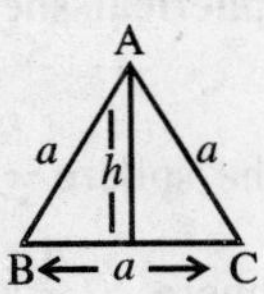

$r = \frac{a}{2\sqrt{3}}$, $R = \frac{a}{\sqrt{3}}$, $R : r = 2 : 1$

(*iv*) Height of equilateral triangle

$= \frac{\sqrt{3}}{2} \times \text{side} = \frac{\sqrt{3}}{2} \times a$

(*v*) Area of an isosceles triangle

ABC $= \frac{1}{2} \times \text{base} \times \sqrt{(\text{equal side})^2 - \frac{1}{4}(\text{base})^2}$

$= \frac{1}{2} a \times \sqrt{b^2 - \frac{1}{4}a^2}$

(OR)

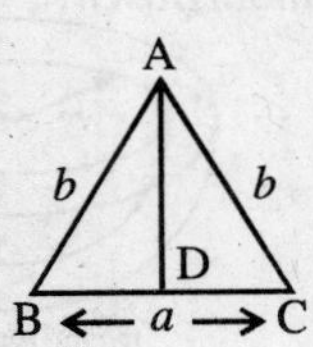

$= (s - b)\sqrt{s(s-a)}$

where s is semi-perimeter

$s = \frac{b+b+a}{2} = \frac{2b+a}{2}$

Circumference and Area of A Circle

Points To Remember:

- The perimeter of a circle is called its circumference.
- The ratio of the circumference of a circle to its diameter is the same for all circles. The constant ratio is denoted by π.

$\pi = \frac{22}{7}$ or 3.14 $\qquad \frac{\text{Circumference}}{\text{Diameter}} = \pi$

- Circumference of a circle $= 2\pi r$
- Area of a circle of radius r is given by $A = \pi r^2$
- Radius of a circle $= \frac{\sqrt{A}}{\pi}$
- Length of arc $\overset{\frown}{AB}$
- $(l) = \frac{\pi r\theta}{180°}$

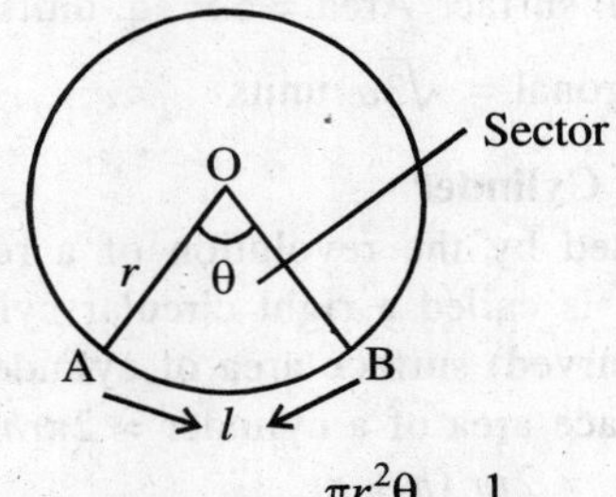

- Area of Sector AOB $= \frac{\pi r^2\theta}{360°} = \frac{1}{2}rl.$
- Area of segment $= \frac{\pi r^2\theta}{360°} - \frac{1}{2}r^2 \sin\theta$

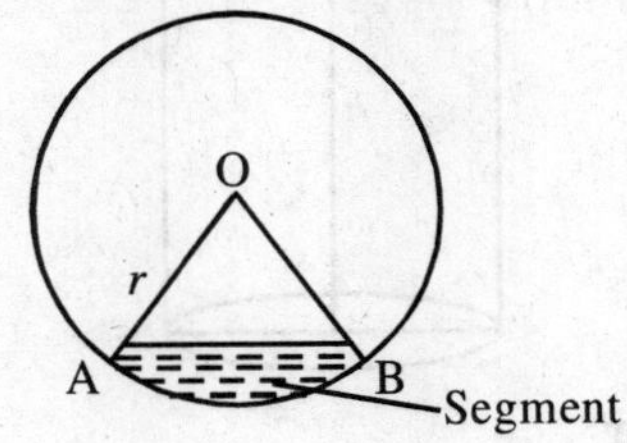

PART–B
SURFACE AREA AND VOLUME OF CUBE, CUBOIDS AND CYLINDER

Surface Area and Volume

(A) Cube and Cuboid

1. Cuboid : Let length = l, breadth = b and height = h units. Then,

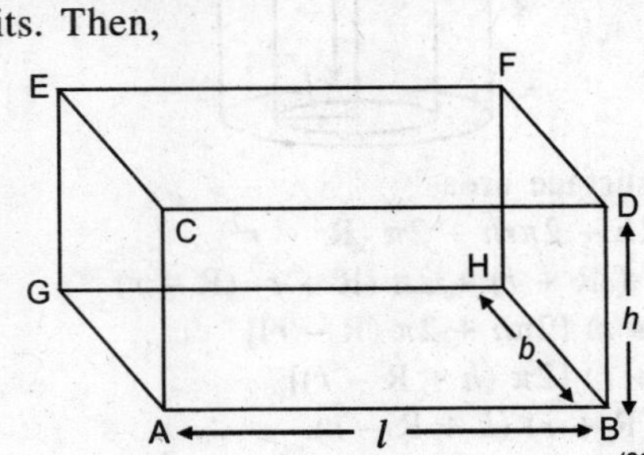

(1) Volume = $(l \times b \times h)$ cubic units

(2) Curved surface area = $2(l + b)h$ sq. units (area of four walls of a room)

(3) Total surface area = $2(lb + bh + hl)$ sq. units

(4) Diagonal = $\sqrt{l^2 + b^2 + h^2}$ units.

2. Cube : Let each edge of a cube be of length a. Then,

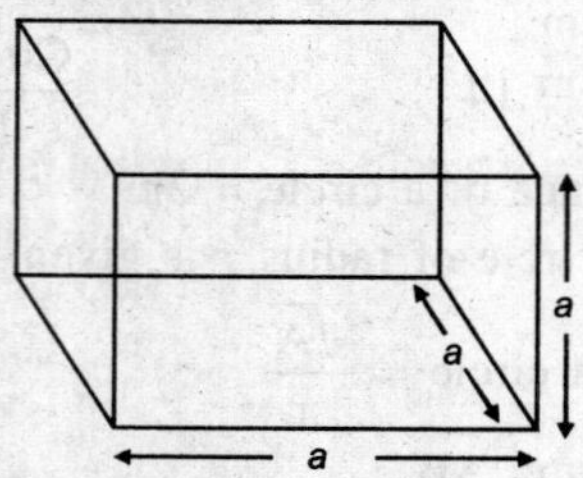

(1) Volume = a^3 cubic units

(2) Curved surface Area = $4a^2$ sq. units

(3) Total surface Area = $6a^2$ sq. units

(4) Diagonal = $\sqrt{3}a$ units

Right Circular Cylinder

A solid generated by the revolution of a rectangle about one of its sides is called a right circular cylinder.

(*i*) Lateral (curved) surface area of cylinder = $2\pi rh$

(*ii*) Total surface area of a cylinder = $2\pi rh + 2\pi r^2$
$= 2\pi r\,(h + r)$

(*iii*) Volume of a cylinder = $\pi r^2 h$

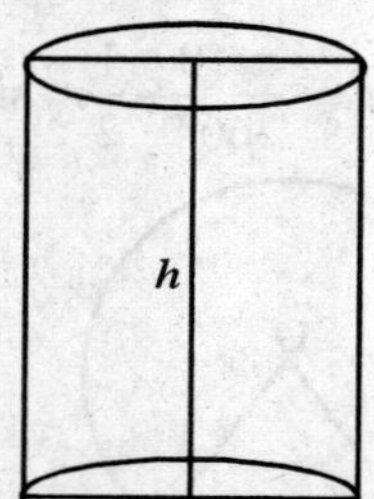

Hallow Cylinder

(*i*) Each base surface area = $\pi\,(R^2 - r^2)$

(*ii*) Curved surface area = External surface area + Internal surface area = $2\pi Rh + 2\pi rh = 2\pi h\,(R + r)$

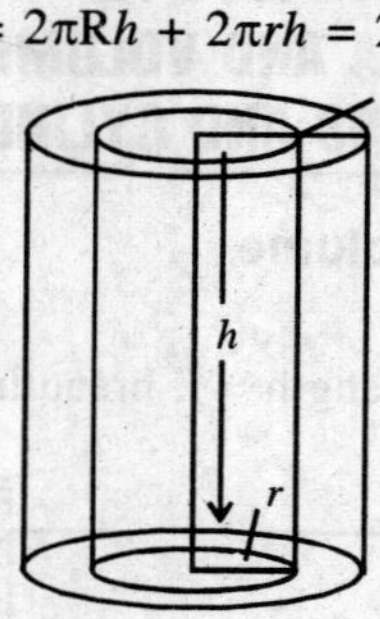

(*iii*) Total surface area

$= 2\pi Rh + 2\pi rh + 2\pi\,(R^2 - r^2)$

$= 2\pi h\,(R + r) + 2\pi\,(R + r)\,(R - r)$

$= (R + r)\,[2\pi h + 2\pi\,(R - r)]$

$= (R + r)\,[2\pi\,(h + R - r)]$

$= 2\pi\,(R + r)\,(h + R - r).$

(*iv*) Volume of the material

= Exterior volume – Interior volume

$= \pi R^2 h - \pi r^2 h = \pi h(R^2 - r^2)$

Right Circular Cone

A right circular cone is a solid generated by revolving a line segment which passes through a fixed point and which makes a constant angle with a fixed line.

(*i*) Curved surface area of a cone = πrl

Where $l = \sqrt{h^2 + r^2}$

(*ii*) Total surface area of a cone
$= \pi rl + \pi r^2 = \pi r\,(l + r)$

(*iii*) Volume of the cone = $\frac{1}{3}\pi r^2 h$

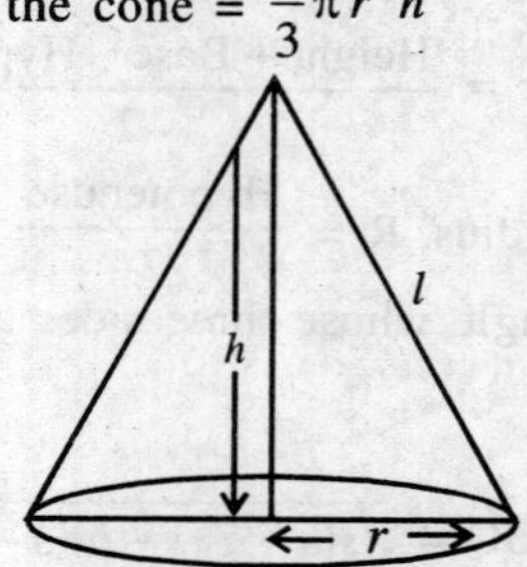

Cone

Sphere/Hemisphere

- **Sphere:** The set of all points in space which are equidistant from a fixed point, is called a *sphere*. The fixed point is called the *centre* of the sphere and constant distance is called its *radius*.

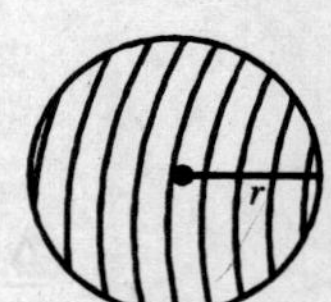

Sphere

- **Hemisphere :** A plane through the centre of a sphere divides the sphere into two equal parts, each of which is called a hemisphere.
- **Spherical shell :** The difference of two solid concentric spheres is called a spherical shell.

Important formula

(*i*) Surface area of the sphere = $4\pi r^2$

(*ii*) Volume of the sphere = $\frac{4}{3}\pi r^3$

(*iii*) Curved surface area of a hemisphere = $2\pi r^2$

(*iv*) Total surface area of a hemisphere = $3\pi r^2$

(*v*) Volume of a hemisphere = $\frac{2}{3}\pi r^3$

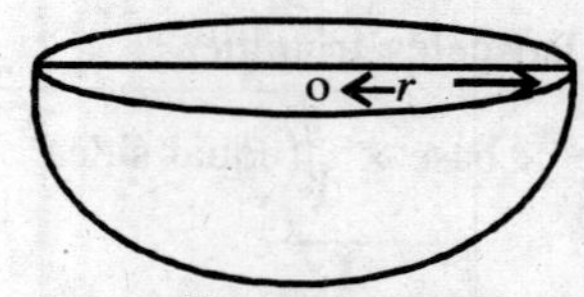

Hemisphere

(*vi*) Volume of a hemispherical Shell/Bowl

Volume = $\frac{2}{3}\pi(r_1^3 - r_2^3)$

Curved surface area
$= 3\pi r_1^2 + 3\pi r_2^2 = 3\pi(r_1^2 + r_2^2)$

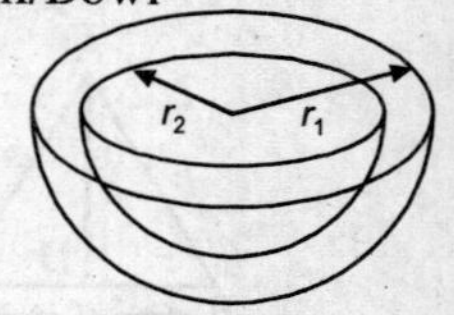

Multiple Choice Questions

1. The length of a rectangle is twice its breadth. What is the dimensions of the rectangle if its area is 288 cm^2?
A. 24 cm, 12 cm B. 16 cm, 10 cm
C. 20 cm, 16 cm D. 28 cm, 10 cm

2. The length and breadth of a rectangular field are in the ratio 3 : 2. If the area of the field is 3456 m^2. What is its dimensions?
A. 48 m, 60 m B. 72 m, 48 m
C. 40 m, 70 m D. 64 m, 52 m

3. What is the area of a rectangular plot if one side of it is 48 cm and its diagonal is 50 cm?
A. 560 cm^2 B. 620 cm^2
C. 672 cm^2 D. 682 cm^2

4. The area of square ABCD is 16 cm^2. What is the area of the square joining the mid-points of the sides?
A. 4 cm^2 B. 6 cm^2
C. 10 cm^2 D. 8 cm^2

5. The area of 4 walls of a room is 375 m^2. The breadth and height of the room are 10 m and 7.5 m respectively. What is the length of the room?
A. 15 m B. 16 m
C. 17 m D. 18 m

6. A room 5 m long and 4 m wide is surrounded by a verandah. What is the width of the verandah, if it occupies 22 m^2?
A. 1.5 m B. 1 m
C. 2.5 m D. 2 m

7. The cost of fencing a square field at 60 paise per metre is ₹ 1200. What is the cost of reaping the field at the rate of 50 paise per 100 sq metres?
A. ₹ 8 B. ₹ 12
C. ₹ 10 D. ₹ 9

8. What is the altitude of a rhombus whose area is 420 cm^2 and perimeter is 140 cm?
A. 12 cm B. 10 cm
C. 11 cm D. 13 cm

9. Two sides of a parallelogram are 20 cm. and 25 cm. If the altitude corresponding to the sides of length 25 cm. is 10 cm. What is the altitude corresponding to the other pair of sides?
A. 10.5 cm B. 12.5 cm
C. 11.5 cm D. 9.5 cm

10. The area of trapezium is 105 cm^2 and its height is 7 cm. If one of the parallel sides is longer than the other by 6 cm. What are the two parallel sides?
A. 12 cm, 18 cm B. 16 cm, 20 cm
C. 10 cm, 15 cm D. 11 cm, 20 cm

11. What is the circumference of a circle whose diameter is 35 cm?
A. 110 cm B. 112 cm
C. 115 cm D. 120 cm

12. What is the circumference of a cycle wheel whose radius is 3.7 dm?
A. 20.35 cm B. 23.24 cm
C. 22.34 cm D. 24.24 cm

13. The diameter of a coin is 2 cm. What is its circumference?
A. 5.28 cm B. 6.28 cm
C. 7.28 cm D. 5.25 cm

14. Two circles having the same centre have radii 350 m and 490 m. What is the difference in their circumferences?
A. 820 m B. 840 m
C. 880 m D. 860 m

15. The diameter of a cycle wheel is 70 cm. How many times the wheel will revolve in order to cover a distance of 110 m?
A. 50 B. 60
C. 40 D. 45

16. A water sprinkler in a lawn sprays water as far as 7 m in all directions. What is the length of the outer edge of wet grass?
A. 40 m B. 42 m
C. 48 m D. 44 m

17. An ox in a kolhu is tethered to a rope 3 m long. How much distance does it cover in 14 rounds?
A. 264 m B. 260 m
C. 262 m D. 268 m

18. A circular piece of thin wire is converted into a square of side 6.25 cm. If there is no loss or gain in its length, find the radius of the circular wire.
A. 3.75 cm B. 3.98 cm
C. 3.25 cm D. 4.25 cm

19. The ratio of the radii of two wheels is 3 : 4. What is the ratio of their circumferences?
A. 2 : 3 B. 2 : 5
C. 3 : 4 D. 4 : 5

20. A piece of thin wire in the form of an equilateral triangle of side 31.4 dm is bent into a ring with no loss in wire. What is the diameter of the ring?
A. 15 dm B. 10 dm
C. 12 dm D. 14 dm

21. What is the surface area of a 10 cm × 4 cm × 3 cm brick?
A. 84 sq. cm B. 124 sq. cm
C. 164 sq. cm D. 180 sq. cm

22. A cistern 6 m long and 4 m wide contains water up to a depth of 1 m 25 cm. The total area of the wet surface is:
A. 49 m^2 B. 50 m^2
C. 53.5 m^2 D. 55 m^2

23. The area of the base of a rectangular tank is 6500 cm^2 and the volume of water contained in it is 2.6 cubic metres. The depth of water in the tank is:
A. 3.5 m B. 4 m
C. 5 m D. 6 m

24. Half cubic metre of gold sheet is extended by hammering so as to cover an area of 1 hectare. The thickness of the sheet is:
A. 0.0005 cm B. 0.005 cm
C. 0.05 cm D. 0.5 cm

25. In a shower, 5 cm of rain falls. The volume of water that falls on 1.5 hectares of ground is:
A. 75 cu. m B. 750 cu. m
C. 7500 cu. m D. 75000 cu. m

26. The volume of a rectangular block of stone is 10368 dm^3. Its dimensions are in the ratio of 3 : 2 : 1. If its entire surface is polished at 2 paise per dm^2, then the total cost will be:
A. ₹ 31.50 B. ₹ 31.68
C. ₹ 63 D. ₹ 63.36

27. The edges of a cuboid are in the ratio 1 : 2 : 3 and its surface area is 88 cm^2. The volume of the cuboid is:
A. 24 cm^3 B. 48 cm^3
C. 64 cm^3 D. 12 cm^3

28. What is the length of the longest rod that can be placed in a room 16 m long, 12 m broad and $10\frac{2}{3}$ m high?
A. $22\frac{1}{3}$ m B. $22\frac{2}{3}$ m
C. 23 m D. 68 m

29. How many bricks, each measuring 25 cm × 11.25 cm × 6 cm, will be needed to build a wall 8 m × 6 m × 22.5 cm?
A. 5600 B. 6000
C. 6400 D. 7200

30. 50 men took a dip in a water tank 40 m long and 20 m broad on a religious day. If the average displacement of water by a man is 4 m^3, then the rise in the water level in the tank will be?
A. 20 cm B. 25 cm
C. 35 cm D. 50 cm

31. The curved surface area of a right circular cylinder of height 14 cm is 88 cm^2. What is the radius of the base of the cylinder?
A. 2 cm B. 3 cm
C. 1 cm D. 4 cm

32. It is required to make a closed cylinderical tank of height 1 m and base diameter 140 cm from a metal sheet. How many square metres of the metal sheet are required for the same?
A. 3.4 m^2 B. 4.4 m^2
C. 2.4 m^2 D. 5.4 m^2

33. Inner and outer radii of a metallic pipe are 3 cm and 3.5 cm respectively if the length of the pipe is 56 cm. What is its total surface area?
A. 2225 cm^2 B. 2244 cm^2
C. 2264 cm^2 D. 2288 cm^2

34. A right circular cylinder has base radius 8 cm and height 35 cm. What is the curved surface area of the cylinder?
A. 1760 cm^2 B. 1780 cm^2
C. 1750 cm^2 D. 1770 cm^2

35. The circumference of the base of a right circular cylinder is 176 cm. If the height of the cylinder is 1 m, what is the lateral surface area of the cylinder?
A. 17500 cm^2 B. 17400 cm^2
C. 17600 cm^2 D. 17800 cm^2

36. A closed circular cylinder has diameter 10 cm and height 15 cm. What is the total surface area of the cylinder?
A. 620 cm^2 B. 625 cm^2
C. 628 cm^2 D. 630 cm^2

37. The radius of the base of a closed right circular cylinder is 21 cm and its height is 1 m. What is the total surface area of the cylinder?
A. 15972 cm^2 B. 15827 cm^2
C. 15944 cm^2 D. 15895 cm^2

38. The diameter of a roller is 84 cm and its length is 120 cm. It takes 500 complete revolutions to move once over to level a playground. What is the area of the playground in m^2.
A. 1275 m^2 B. 1584 m^2
C. 1484 m^2 D. 1348 m^2

39. A cylindrical pillar is 50 cm in radius and 3.5 m in height. What is the cost of white washing the curved surface of the pillar at the rate of ₹ 12.50 per m^2?
A. ₹ 127.50 B. ₹ 227.50
C. ₹ 132.50 D. ₹ 137.50

40. Curved surface area of a right circular cylinder of height 35 cm is 121 cm^2. What is the radius of its base?
A. 0.25 cm B. 0.35 cm
C. 0.55 cm D. 0.45 cm

41. Diameter of the base of a cone is 10.5 cm and its slant height is 10 cm. What is the curved surface area of the cone?
A. 154 cm^2 B. 165 cm^2
C. 175 cm^2 D. 185 cm^2

42. The height of a cone is 16 cm and the radius of its base is 12 cm. What is the curved surface area and the total surface area of the cone?
A. 753.6 cm^2, 1205.76 cm^2
B. 853.6 cm^2, 1208.76 cm^2
C. 953.5 cm^2, 1212.76 cm^2
D. 764.6 cm^2, 1185.76 cm^2

43. Curved surface area of a cone is 308 cm^2 and its slant height is 14 cm. What is the radius of the base and total surface area of the cone?
A. 7 cm, 462 cm B. 5 cm, 460 cm^2
C. 6 cm, 452 cm^2 D. 4 cm, 475 cm^2

44. The radius of the base of a conical tent is 12 m. The tent is 9 m high. What is the cost of the canvas required to make the tent, if one square metre of canvas costs ₹ 120?
A. ₹ 67885.20 B. ₹ 68885.20
C. ₹ 66985.20 D. ₹ 68675.20

45. What is the curved surface area of a right circular cone whose slant height is 10 cm and base radius is 7 cm?
A. 210 cm^2 B. 220 cm^2
C. 230 cm^2 D. .215 cm^2

46. The diameter of a right circular cone is 14 cm and its slant height is 9 cm. What is its curved surface area and total surface area?
A. 190 cm^2, 341 cm^2 B. 195 cm^2, 348 cm^2
C. 198 cm^2, 352 cm^2 D. 196 cm^2, 350 cm^2

47. What is the curved surface area of a cone if its slant height is 60 cm and the radius of its base is 25 cm?
A. 4710 cm^2 B. 4690 cm^2
C. 4720 cm^2 D. 4725 cm^2

48. What is the total surface of a cone, if its slant height is 9 dm and diameter of its base is 24 dm?
A. 692 dm^2 B. 792 dm^2
C. 892 dm^2 D. 698 dm^2

49. The radius of the base of a cone is 9 cm and its height is 12 cm. What is the curved surface area of the cone?
A. 410.42 cm^2 B. 375.42 cm^2
C. 339.42 cm^2 D. 336.42 cm^2

50. A conical tent is 10 m high and the radius of its base is 24 m. What is slant height of the tent and cost of the canvas required to make the tent, if the cost of 1 m^2 canvas is ₹ 90?
A. 26 m, ₹ 176502.60
B. 24 m, ₹ 182408.60
C. 25 m, ₹ 196232.60
D. 10 m, ₹ 188402.60

51. Diameter of a sphere is 10 cm. What is its surface area?
A. 314.28 cm^2 B. 318.24 cm^2
C. 312.28 cm^2 D. 310.28 cm^2

52. The surface of a solid hemisphere with its circular base is to be painted. If the radius of the hemisphere is 28 cm, find the cost of painting the surface at the rate of ₹ 3 per 100 cm^2.
A. ₹ 220.76 B. ₹ 218.76
C. ₹ 221.76 D. ₹ 230.5

53. Assuming the earth to be a sphere of radius 6370 km. What is surface area of the earth?
A. 510109600 km^2 B. 410109600 km^2
C. 520109600 km^2 D. 490109600 km^2

54. What is the surface area of a sphere whose diameter is 14 cm?
A. 616 cm^2 B. 612 cm^2
C. 624 cm^2 D. 620 cm^2

55. The radius of a spherical balloon increases from 7 cm to 14 cm as air is being pumped into it. What is the ratio of surface areas of the balloon in the two cases?
A. 2 : 3 B. 1 : 4
C. 3 : 4 D. 4 : 5

56. A hemispherical bowl made of brass has inner diameter 10.5 cm. What is the cost of tin plating it on the inside at the rate of ₹ 16 per 100 cm^2?
A. ₹ 25.72 B. ₹ 28.72
C. ₹ 27.72 D. ₹ 26.72

57. The dome of a building is in the form of a hemisphere. Its radius is 6.3 m. What is the cost of painting it at the rate of ₹ 12 per m^2?
A. ₹ 2993.76 B. ₹ 2996.76
C. ₹ 2988.76 D. ₹ 2991.76

58. A solid sphere of radius 3 cm is melted and then cast into small spherical balls each of radius 0.6 cm. What is the number of balls?
A. 115 B. 118
C. 120 D. 125

59. How many spherical bullets can be made out of a solid cube of lead whose edge measures 44 cm, each bullet being 4 cm in diameter?
A. 2496 B. 2525
C. 2541 D. 2552

60. How many spherical lead shots each 4.2 cm in diameter can be obtained from a rectangular solid of lead with dimensions 66 cm, 42 cm, 21 cm?
A. 1200 B. 1500
C. 1400 D. 1300

ANSWERS

1	2	3	4	5	6	7	8	9	10
A	B	C	D	A	B	C	A	B	A
11	**12**	**13**	**14**	**15**	**16**	**17**	**18**	**19**	**20**
A	B	B	C	A	D	A	B	C	A
21	**22**	**23**	**24**	**25**	**26**	**27**	**28**	**29**	**30**
C	A	B	B	B	D	B	B	C	B

31	32	33	34	35	36	37	38	39	40
C	B	D	A	C	C	A	B	D	C
41	**42**	**43**	**44**	**45**	**46**	**47**	**48**	**49**	**50**
B	A	A	A	B	C	A	B	C	A
51	**52**	**53**	**54**	**55**	**56**	**57**	**58**	**59**	**60**
A	C	A	A	B	C	A	D	C	B

EXPLANATORY ANSWERS

1. Let length of rectangle = x cm.

$$\text{Breadth} = \frac{x}{2} \text{ cm.}$$

$$\text{Area of rectangle} = 288$$
$$l \times b = 288$$
$$x \times \frac{x}{2} = 288$$
$$x^2 = 288 \times 2 = 576$$
$$x = \sqrt{576} = \sqrt{24 \times 24} = 24 \text{ cm.}$$
$$\text{Length} = 24 \text{ cm.}$$
$$\text{Breadth} = \frac{24}{2} = 12 \text{ cm.}$$

2. Let length = $3x$ and breadth = $2x$

$$\text{Area of rectangular field} = 3456\ m^2$$
$$l \times b = 3456$$
$$3x \times 2x = 3456$$
$$x^2 = \frac{3456}{6}$$
$$x = \sqrt{576} = 24.$$
$$\text{Length} = 3x = 3 \times 24 = 72 \text{ m.}$$
$$\text{Breadth} = 2x = 2 \times 24 = 48 \text{ m.}$$

3. Area of rectangular plot = length × breadth

$$AD^2 = BD^2 - AB^2 = 50^2 - 48^2$$
$$= (50 + 48)(50 - 48)$$
$$= 98 \times 2 = 14 \times 7 \times 2$$
$$= 7 \times 2 \times 7 \times 2$$
$$AD = \sqrt{7 \times 2 \times 7 \times 2} = 7 \times 2 = 14 \text{ cm.}$$
$$\text{Area} = 48 \times 14 = 672 \text{ cm}^2.$$

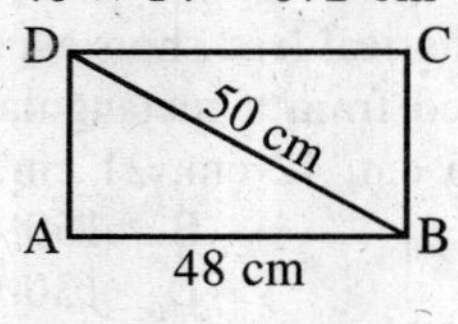

4. Area of square = 16

$$\text{side}^2 = 16$$
$$\text{side} = \sqrt{16}$$
$$AB = 4$$

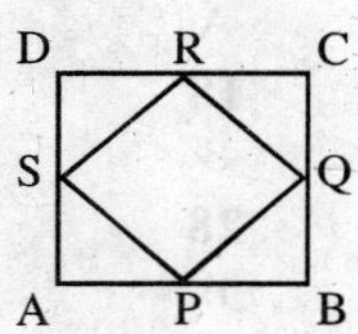

Diagonal of PQRS = 4 cm.

$$\sqrt{2}\ \text{side} = 4$$
$$2\ \text{side}^2 = 16$$
$$\text{Area} = \text{side}^2 = \frac{16}{2} = 8 \text{ cm}^2.$$

5. Area of four walls = $2(l + b) \times h$

$$2(l + b) \times h = 375$$
$$2(l + 10) \times 7.5 = 375$$
$$l + 10 = \frac{375}{15}$$
$$l = 25 - 10 = 15 \text{ m.}$$

6. Area of room = $5 \times 4 = 20 \text{ m}^2$

$$(l + 2x)(b + 2x) = 20 + 22$$
$$(5 + 2x)(4 + 2x) = 42$$
$$20 + 10x + 8x + 4x^2 = 42$$

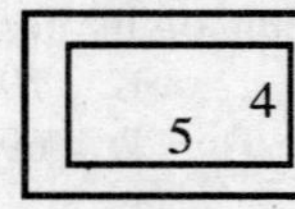

$$4x^2 + 18x - 22 = 0$$
$$2x^2 + 9x - 11 = 0$$
$$2x^2 + 11x - 2x - 11 = 0$$
$$x(2x + 11) - 1(2x + 11) = 0$$
$$\Rightarrow (x - 1)(2x + 11) = 0$$
$$x - 1 = 0,\ 2x + 11 = 0$$
$$x = 1,\ x = -11/2$$

Not possible

∴ Width of varandah = 1 m.

7. Area of square field = $\dfrac{\text{Total cost}}{\text{Per sq. m. cost}}$

$$= \frac{1200}{\frac{60}{100}} = \frac{1200 \times 100}{60} = 2000 \text{ m}^2.$$

$$\text{The cost of reaping} = \frac{\frac{50}{100} \times 2000}{100} = ₹\ 10.$$

8. $4a = 140,\ a = \dfrac{140}{4} = 35$

Side of rhombus = 35 cm.

$$\text{Altitude of rhombus} = \frac{\text{Area}}{\text{Side}} = \frac{420}{35} = 12 \text{ cm.}$$

9.

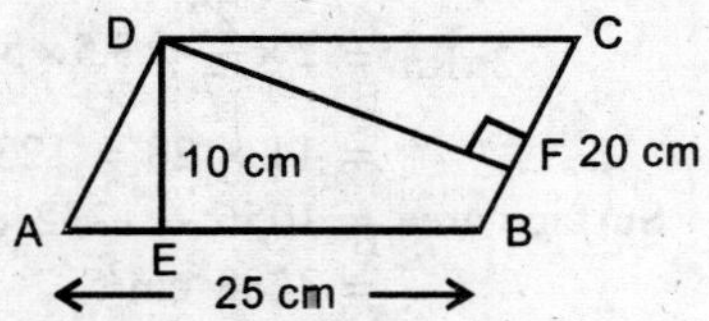

Area of parallelogram = base × height

$$BC \times DF = AB \times DE$$

$$20 \times DF = 25 \times 10$$

$$DF = \frac{25 \times 10}{20} = 12.5 \text{ cm.}$$

10. Let other side = x cm.

One side = $(x + 6)$ cm.

$$\frac{1}{2}(x + x + 6) \times 7 = 105$$

$$2x + 6 = \frac{105 \times 2}{7} = 30$$

$$2x = 24 \Rightarrow x = 12$$

Sides = 12 cm, 18 cm.

11. $d = 35$ cm.,

$$r = \frac{d}{2} = \frac{35}{2} \text{ cm.}$$

$$\text{Circumference} = 2\pi r = 2 \times \frac{22}{7} \times \frac{35}{2}$$

$$= 22 \times 5 = 110 \text{ cm.}$$

12. $r = 3.7$ dm

Circumference $= 2\pi r$

$$= 2 \times \frac{22}{7} \times 3.7 = 2 \times 3.14 \times 3.7$$

$$= 23.236 \text{ cm} = 23.24 \text{ cm.}$$

13. $d = 2$ cm.

$$r = \frac{2}{2} = 1 \text{ cm}$$

$$\text{Circumference} = 2\pi r = 2 \times \frac{22}{7} \times 1$$

$$= 2 \times 3.14 = 6.28 \text{ cm.}$$

14. Difference in circumference $= 2\pi R - 2\pi r$

$= 2\pi (R - r)$ R = 490 m

$= 2 \times \frac{22}{7}(490 - 350)$ r = 350 m

$= 2 \times \frac{22}{7} \times 140 = 44 \times 20 = 880$ m.

15. Nos. of revolution

$$= \frac{110}{2 \times \pi \times \frac{70}{2} \times \frac{1}{100}} = \frac{110 \times 100 \times 2 \times 7}{2 \times 22 \times 70} = 50.$$

16. Circumference $= 2\pi r = 2 \times \frac{22}{7} \times 7 = 44$ m.

17. Distance covered $= 14 \times 2 \times \frac{22}{7} \times 3$

$= 12 \times 22 = 264$ m.

18. Circumference of wire = Perimeter of square

$$2\pi r = 4 \times 6.25$$

$$2 \times \frac{22}{7} \times r = 25$$

$$r = \frac{25 \times 7}{44} = \frac{175}{44}$$

$$= 3.977 \text{ cm} = 3.98 \text{ cm.}$$

19. The ratio of circumference

$$= \frac{2\pi 3x}{2\pi 4x} = \frac{3}{4} = 3 : 4.$$

20. Circumference of circle

= Perimeter of Equilateral triangle = 3 × 31.4

$$2\pi r = 3 \times 31.4$$

$$2 \times 3.14 \times r = 3 \times 31.4$$

$$r = \frac{3 \times 31.4}{3.14 \times 2} = 15 \text{ dm.}$$

21. Surface area $= [2(10 \times 4 + 4 \times 3 + 10 \times 3)] \text{ cm}^2$

$= (2 \times 82) \text{ cm}^2 = 164 \text{ cm}^2.$

22. Area of the wet surface $= [2(lb + bh + lh) - lb]$

$= 2(bh + lh) + lb$

$= [2(4 \times 1.25 + 6 \times 1.25) + 6 \times 4] \text{ m}^2$

$= 49 \text{ m}^2.$

23. Volume = (2.6 × 100 × 100 × 100) cu. cm.

$$\text{Depth} = \frac{\text{Volume}}{\text{Area of the base}} = \left(\frac{2.6 \times 100 \times 100 \times 100}{6500}\right) \text{cm}$$

$= 400$ cm $= 4$ m.

24. Volume of gold $= \left(\frac{1}{2} \times 100 \times 100 \times 100\right) \text{cm}^3.$

Area of sheet $= 10000 \text{ m}^2 = (10000 \times 100 \times 100) \text{ cm}^2$

$$\therefore \text{Thickness of the sheet} = \left(\frac{1 \times 100 \times 100 \times 100}{2 \times 10000 \times 100 \times 100}\right) \text{cm}$$

$= 0.005$ cm.

25. Area $= (1.5 \times 10000) \text{ m}^2 = 15000 \text{ m}^2.$

$$\text{Depth} = \frac{5}{100} \text{m} = \frac{1}{20} \text{m}.$$

$\therefore$ Volume = (Area × Depth)

$$= \left(15000 \times \frac{1}{20}\right) \text{m}^3 = 750 \text{ m}^3.$$

26. Let the dimensions be $3x$, $2x$ and x respectively. Then,

$$3x \times 2x \times x = 10368 \Leftrightarrow x^3 = \left(\frac{10368}{6}\right) = 1728 \Leftrightarrow x = 12.$$

So, the dimensions of the block are 36 dm, 24 dm and 12 dm.

Surface area $= [2(36 \times 24 + 24 \times 12 + 36 \times 12)] \text{ dm}^2$

$= [2 \times 144 (6 + 2 + 3)] \text{ dm}^2$

$= 3168 \text{ dm}^2$

$\therefore$ Cost of polishing = ₹ $\left(\frac{2 \times 3168}{100}\right)$ = ₹ 63.36.

27. Let the dimensions of the cuboid be x, $2x$ and $3x$.
Then, $2(x \times 2x + 2x \times 3x + x \times 3x) = 88$
$\Leftrightarrow 2x^2 + 6x^2 + 3x^2 = 44 \Leftrightarrow 11x^2 = 44$
$\Leftrightarrow x^2 = 4 \Leftrightarrow x = 2.$
$\therefore$ Volume of the cuboid = $(2 \times 4 \times 6)$ cm^3 = 48 cm^3.

28. Required length $= \sqrt{(16)^2 + (12)^2 + \left(\frac{32}{3}\right)^2}$ m

$= \sqrt{256 + 144 + \frac{1024}{9}}$ m

$= \sqrt{\frac{4624}{9}}$ m $= \frac{68}{3}$ m $= 22\frac{2}{3}$ m.

29. Number of bricks $= \frac{\text{Volume of the wall}}{\text{Volume of 1 brick}}$

$= \left(\frac{800 \times 600 \times 22.5}{25 \times 11.25 \times 6}\right) = 6400.$

30. Total volume of water displaced = (4×50) m^3 = 200 m^3.

$\therefore$ Rise in water level $= \left(\frac{200}{40 \times 20}\right)$ m

$= 0.25$ m $= 25$ cm.

31. Curved surface of right circular cylinder = 88 cm^2

$2\pi rh = 88$

$2 \times \frac{22}{7} \times r \times 14 = 88$

$r = \frac{88}{88} = 1$ cm.

32. Area of cylinder $= 2\pi rh$

$= 2 \times \frac{22}{7} \times 100 \times 70$

$= \frac{44 \times 1000}{100 \times 100}$ m^2 $= 4.4$ m^2.

33. $h = 56$ cm

$r = 3$ cm

R = 3.5 cm

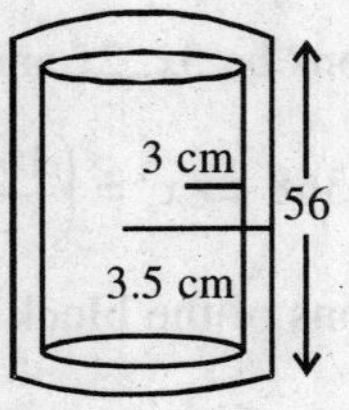

$2\pi rh = 2 \times \frac{22}{7} \times 3 \times 56$

$= 44 \times 24 = 1056$ cm^2

$2\pi Rh = 2 \times \frac{22}{7} \times 3.5 \times 56$

$= 44 \times 28 = 1232$ cm^2

Surface area = 1056 + 1232 cm^2

= 2288 cm^2.

34. Curved surface of the cylinder

$= 2\pi rh$

$= 2 \times \frac{22}{7} \times 8 \times 35$

$= 44 \times 40 = 1760$ cm^2.

35. $2\pi r = 176 = 2 \times \frac{22}{7} \times r = 176$

$\Rightarrow \quad r = \frac{176 \times 7}{2 \times 22} = 28$ cm

$h = 1$ m $= 100$ cm

Lateral surface of the cylinder

$= 2\pi rh$

$= 2 \times \frac{22}{7} \times 28 \times 100$

$= 17600$ cm^2.

36. $r = 5$ cm, $h = 15$ cm

Total surface area of the cylinder

$= 2\pi r\,(h + r)$

$= 2 \times \frac{22}{7} \times 5(15+5)$

$= 2 \times \frac{22}{7} \times 5 \times 20$

$= 2 \times 3.14 \times 100 = 628$ cm^2.

37. $h = 1$ m $= 100$ cm, $r = 21$

Total surface area $= 2\pi r\,(r + h)$

$= 2 \times \frac{22}{7} \times 21(21+100)$

$= 2 \times \frac{22}{7} \times 21 \times 121$

$= 132 \times 121 = 15972$ cm^2.

38. $r = \frac{84}{2} = 42\,\text{cm} = \frac{42}{100} = .42\,\text{m}$

$h = 120\text{ cm} = \frac{120}{100} = 1.2\,\text{m}$

Area of playground $= 500 \times 2\pi rh$

$= 500 \times 2 \times \frac{22}{7} \times .42 \times 1.2$

$= 30 \times 44 \times 1.2 = 1584$ m^2.

39. Curved surface of the pillar

$= 2\pi rh$

$= 2 \times \frac{22}{7} \times \frac{50}{100} \times 3.5 = 11$ m^2

The cost of white washing

$= 11\ m^2 \times 12.50 = ₹\ 137.50.$

40. Curved surface of the cylinder = 121 cm^2

$$2\pi rh = 121\ cm^2$$

$$2 \times \frac{22}{7} \times r \times 35 = 121$$

$$r = \frac{121}{2 \times 22 \times 5} = \frac{121}{220} cm$$

$$r = \frac{121}{220}\ cm = 0.55\ cm.$$

41. Curved surface of the cone = πrl

$$= \frac{22}{7} \times \frac{10.5}{2} \times 10$$

$$= 22 \times 7.5 = 165\ cm^2.$$

42. Curved surface of the cone

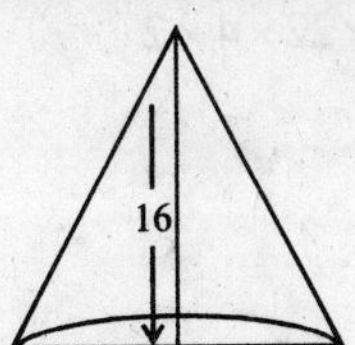

$$l^2 = 16^2 + 12^2$$
$$= 256 + 144$$
$$= 400$$
$$l = \sqrt{400}$$
$$= 20$$

$$= \pi rl$$

$$= \frac{22}{7} \times 12 \times 20$$

$$= 3.14 \times 240 = 753.6\ cm^2.$$

Total surface area

$$= \pi rl + \pi r^2$$

$$= 753.6 + \frac{22}{7} \times 12 \times 12$$

$$= 753.6 + 3.14 \times 144$$

$$= 753.6 + 452.16 = 1205.76\ cm^2.$$

43. Curved surface area of cone, $\pi rl = 308$

$$\frac{22}{7} \times r \times 14 = 308 \Rightarrow r = \frac{308 \times 7}{22 \times 14}$$

$$r = 7\ cm.$$

Total surface area of the cone = $\pi rl + \pi r^2$

$$= 308 + \frac{22}{7} \times 7 \times 7$$

$$= 308 + 154 = 462\ cm^2.$$

44. Curved surface area of the tent = πrl

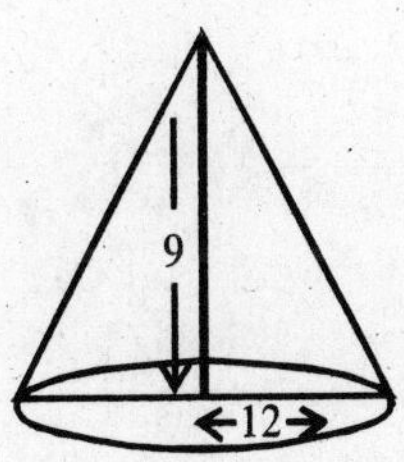

$$l^2 = 12^2 + 9^2$$
$$= 144 + 81$$
$$= 225$$
$$l = \sqrt{225} = 15$$

$$= \frac{22}{7} \times 12 \times 15 = \frac{3960}{7}$$

$$= 565.71\ m^2$$

The cost of canvas = 565.71 × 120

$= ₹\ 67885.20.$

45. Curved surface of the cone = πrl

$$= \frac{22}{7} \times 7 \times 10 = 220\ cm^2.$$

46. Curved surface = πrl

$$= \frac{22}{7} \times 7 \times 9 = 198\ cm^2$$

Total surface = $\pi rl + \pi r^2$

$$= 198 + \frac{22}{7} \times 7 \times 7$$

$$= 198 + 154 = 352\ cm^2.$$

47. Curved surface = πrl

$$= \frac{22}{7} \times 25 \times 60$$

$$= 3.14 \times 1500 = 4710\ cm^2.$$

48. Total surface area of the cone

$$= \pi rl + \pi r^2 = \pi r\,(l + r)$$

$$= \frac{22}{7} \times 12 \times (9 + 12) = \frac{22}{7} \times 12 \times 21$$

$$= 22 \times 36 = 792\ dm^2.$$

49. Curved surface = πrl

$$= \frac{22}{7} \times 9 \times 12 = \frac{2376}{7}$$

$$= 339.42\ cm^2.$$

50. $l^2 = 10^2 + 24^2$

$$= 100 + 576 = 676$$

$$l = \sqrt{676} = 26\,m.$$

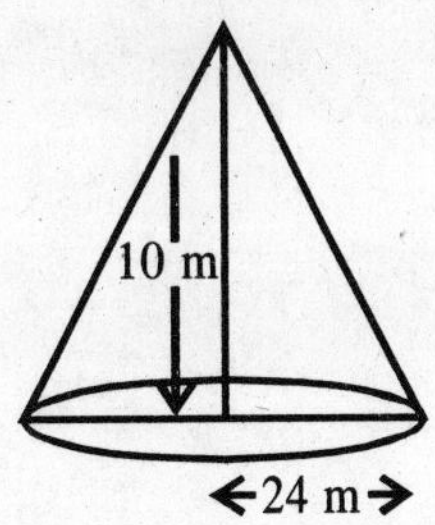

Curved surface = πrl

$$= \frac{22}{7} \times 24 \times 26 = \frac{13728}{7}$$

$$= 1961.14\,m^2$$

The cost of canvas

$= 1961.14 \times 90 = ₹\ 176502.60.$

51. $r = \frac{10}{2} = 5$ cm

Surface area of the sphere = $4\pi r^2$

$$= 4 \times \frac{22}{7} \times 5 \times 5 = \frac{88 \times 25}{7} = \frac{2200}{7}$$

$$= 314.28\ cm^2.$$

52. The cost of painting

$= 3\pi r^2 \times \frac{3}{100}$

$= 3\times\frac{22}{7}\times 28\times 28\times\frac{3}{100}$

$= \frac{66\times 84}{25} = \frac{5544}{25}$

$=$ ₹ 221.76.

53. Surface area of the earth $= 4\pi r^2$

$= 4\times\frac{22}{7}\times 6370\times 6370$

$= 88 \times 910 \times 6370$ km^2

$= 510109600$ km^2.

54. Surface area of sphere $= 4\pi r^2$

$= 4\pi \times 7 \times 7$

$= 4\times\frac{22}{7}\times 7\times 7 = 4\times 154 = 616$ cm^2.

55. The ratio of Areas

$= \frac{4\pi\times 7\times 7}{4\pi\times 14\times 14} = \frac{1}{4} = 1 : 4.$

56. The cost of tin plating

$= 2\times\frac{22}{7}\times\frac{10.5}{2}\times\frac{10.5}{2}\times\frac{16}{100}$

$= 1.76 \times 1.5 \times 10.5 =$ ₹ 27.72.

57. Area of hemisphere

$= 2\times\frac{22}{7}\times 6.3\times 6.3$

$= 44 \times 0.9 \times 6.3$

The cost of painting

$= 12 \times 44 \times 0.9 \times 6.3$

$=$ ₹ 2993.76.

58. The number of balls

$= \frac{\frac{4}{3}\pi\times 3\times 3\times 3}{\frac{4}{3}\pi\times .6\times .6\times .6} = \frac{1}{.008} = \frac{1000}{8} = 125.$

59. Nos. of bullets

$= \frac{44\times 44\times 44}{\frac{4}{3}\times\frac{22}{7}\times\frac{4}{2}\times\frac{4}{2}\times\frac{4}{2}} = \frac{44\times 44\times 44\times 21}{4\times 22\times 4\times 2}$

$= 11 \times 11 \times 21 = 2541.$

60. Nos. of spherical lead shots

$= \frac{66\times 42\times 21}{\frac{4}{3}\times\frac{22}{7}\times 2.1\times 2.1\times 2.1}$

$= \frac{66\times 42\times 21}{4\times 22\times 2.1\times .7\times .3} = 1500.$

❑❑❑❑❑

12

Data Handling

Graphical Representation of Statistical Data

One of the most convincing and appearing ways in which statistical result may be presented is through diagrams and graphs. The impressions created by diagrams last much longer than those created by the figures presented in a tabular form.

> *Rather than present data numerically in the form of a table it can sometimes be better to illustrate the information through the use of graphs, charts, diagrams and so on.*

The frequency distribution of a discrete value is best represented by a bar diagram. The height of the bars is proportional to the frequency of each variate-value. The bars must be kept distinct to show that the variate-values are distinct.

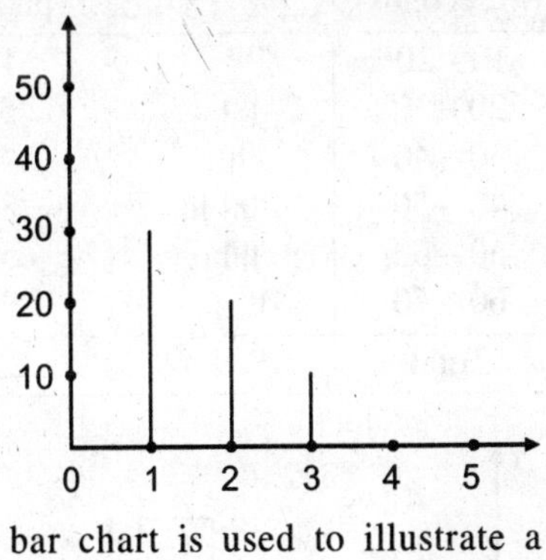

A simple bar chart is used to illustrate a frequency distribution. The lengths of the bars are proportional to the frequency and the bars are of equal width.

Some Important Types of Diagrams and Graphs

The different types of Diagrams and Graphs

(1) Bar diagram
(2) Histogram
(3) Frequency circle
(4) Cumulative frequency curve of the ogive
(5) Pie diagram.

Bar Diagram

Bar diagram is the easiest and most adaptable general purpose chart. In this, bars or rectangles of uniform width are drawn with equal spaces in between on the axis. Along the y-axis is shown, the scale of the height of the rectangles. Thickness of bars is not taken into account, they should be so constructed that they look attractive and beautiful. This can be done by colouring them or by preparing designs in them. However, the colour or designs of all bars representing one type of data should be identical. The bars may be vertical or horizontal. Some of the main bar diagrams are:

(*i*) Simple Bar-Diagram
(*ii*) Sub-divided Bar-Diagram
(*iii*) Multiple Bar-Diagram

The following Examples of Illustrate :

Example: The following table gives the population of India (in millions). Draw a bar diagram of the data:

Population (in million) of India 1931-1971

Year	Population (*in millions*)
1931	275.5
1941	312.1
1951	356.9
1961	439.9
1971	546.9

Solution: The above data is represented by a simple bar diagram as follows :

Simple Bar Diagram Showing Population (in Millions)

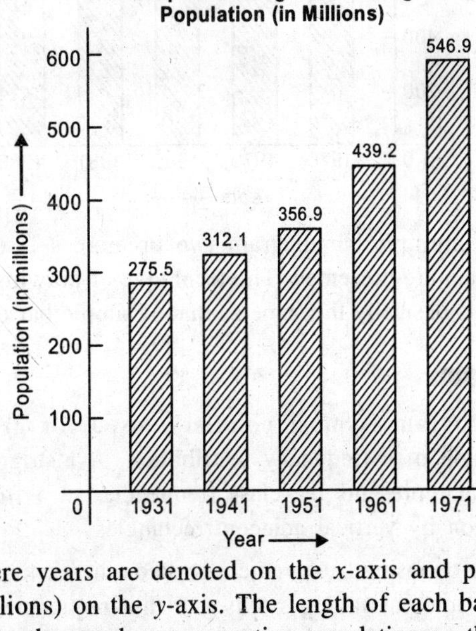

Here years are denoted on the x-axis and population (in millions) on the y-axis. The length of each bar corresponds to the number representing population on the y-axis.

Sub-Divided or Component Bar Diagram

The sub-divided bar diagram is used where the total magnitude of the given variable is to be divided into various parts or sub-classes. The bars are drawn proportional in length to the total and divided in the ratios of their components. Different colours, shades, designs, etc. are used to distinguish the various components.

Example: Represent the following data of sex-wise distribution of students in a school by a bar diagram.

Year	No. of Students		Total
	Male	*Female*	
1978	800	250	1050
1979	900	300	1200
1980	950	375	1325
1981	1000	400	1400
1982	1150	450	1600

Solution: The above data, are represented by a sub-divided bar diagram, as follows.

Sub-Divided Bar Diagram showing Sex-wise Distribution of Students

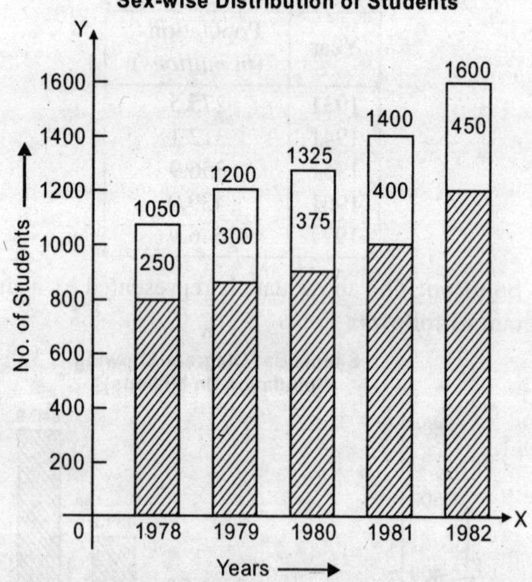

In a multiple bar diagram two or more sets of inter-related data are presented. The technique of drawing such a diagram is basically the same as that of simple bar diagram.

Histograms

The histogram is most popularly used for graphical presentation of a frequency distribution. A histogram is a graph that represents the class frequencies in a frequency distribution by vertical adjacent rectangles.

After choosing a convenient scale on the axes, mark off the class intervals along x-axis and the frequencies of the respective class intervals along y-axis. Then construct rectangles with each class intervals as breadth and the respective frequency of the class interval as height. The set of the all adjacent rectangles so constructed form a histogram.

Note : A histogram is a development of the bar chart but remember when drawing a histogram it is the Area of each bar which is proportional to the frequency and there are no gaps between the bars because the classes are usually arranged so that there are no gaps.

The following Examples of Illustrates:

Example: The time taken, in seconds, to solve a problem by each of 25 pupils is as follows:

16, 20, 26, 27, 28, 30, 33, 37, 38, 40, 42, 42, 43, 46, 46, 48, 49, 50, 53, 58, 59, 60, 64, 52, 20.

(*a*) Construct a frequency distribution for these data, using a class interval of 10 seconds.

(*b*) Draw a histogram to represent the frequency distribution.

Solution:

(*a*) Lowest observation = 10

Highest observation = 64

Range = 64 – 10 = 54

We can have six classes, each of width 10.

Frequency Distribution Table

Time (in seconds)	Tally marks	Number of pupils
10 – 20	|	1
20 – 30	卌	5
30 – 40	||||	4
40 – 50	卌 |||	8
50 – 60	卌	5
60 – 70	||	2
Total		25

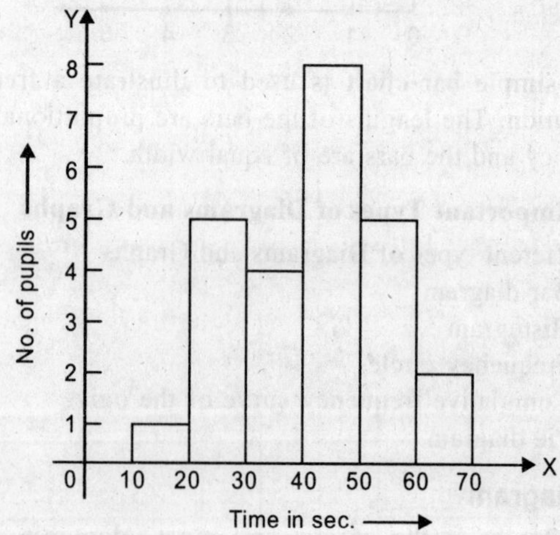

Frequency Polygon

A frequency polygon is a graph of frequency distribution. The steps constructing a frequency polygonal are:

1. Draw a suitable histogram keeping in view all the basic principles.
2. Get the mid-points of the upper horizontal side of each rectangle.
3. Join these mid-points of the adjacent rectangles of the histogram by straight lines taken in order, they form a polygon called frequency polygon.
4. End of frequency polygon preferably extended to the base line.

In a frequency polygon the variables or individuals of each class are assumed to be concentrated at the class-intervals.

Note: If only frequency polygon is to be drawn, first represent the class-marks (x_i) on the x-axis and corresponding frequencies (f_i) on y-axis. Plot all the points (x_i, f_i). Then join these points by line segments. The figure so obtained is known as the frequency polygon. The polygon should be brought down at the ends to the x-axis at each and of the drawn.

The following Examples of Illustrate:

Example: In a city the following weekly observations were made in a study on cost of Living Index for the year 1970–71.

Cost of Living Index	No. of weeks
140 – 150	5
150 – 160	10
160 – 170	20
170 – 180	9
180 – 190	6
190 – 200	2

Draw a histogram and frequency polygon on the same scale.

Solution:

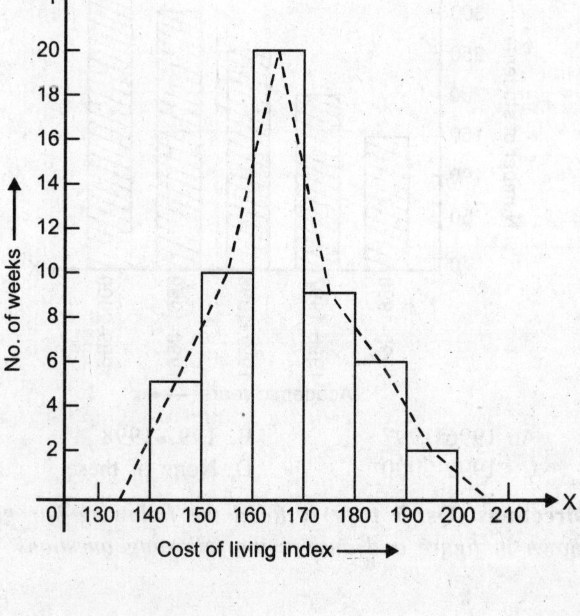

Pie Diagram

Pie-diagrams are used to represent a relative frequency distribution. A pie diagram consists of a circle divided into as many sectors as there are classes in a frequency distribution. The area of each sector is proportional to the relative frequency of the class.

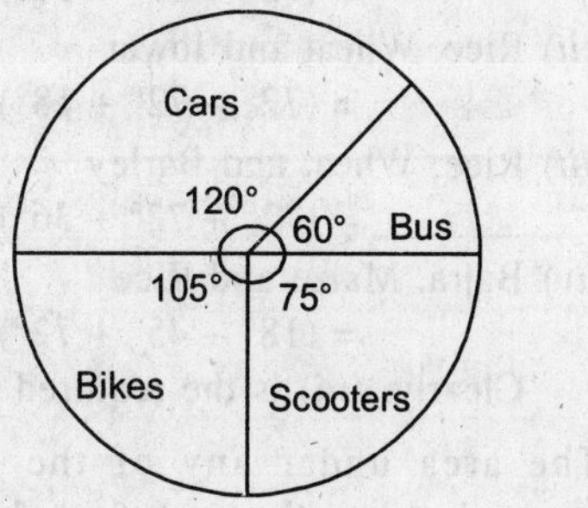

Now we make angles at the centre proportional to the relative frequencies. And in order to get the angles of the disired sectors, we divide 360° in the proportion of the various relative frequencies, *i.e.*,

$$\text{Central angle} = \left[\frac{\text{Frequency} \times 360°}{\text{Total frequency}}\right]$$

Example : The pie-chart provided below gives the distribution of land (in a village) under various food crops. Study the pie-chart carefully and answer the questions that follow.

Distribution of Areas (in Acre) Under various Food Crops

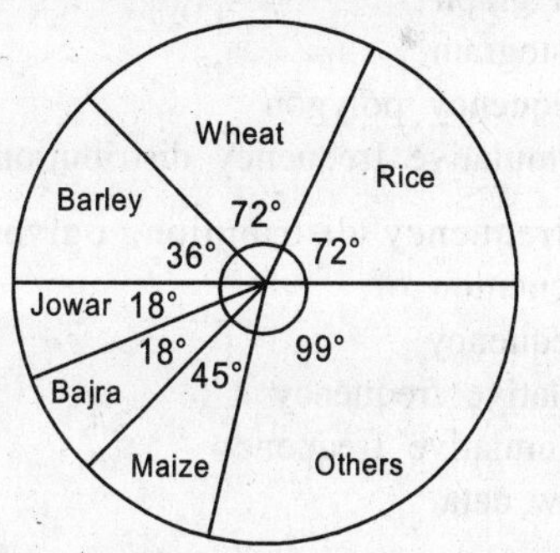

1. Which combination of three crops contribute to 50% of the total area under the food crops?
(*a*) Wheat, Barley and Jowar
(*b*) Rice, Wheat and Jowar
(*c*) Rice, Wheat and Barley
(*d*) Bajra, Maize and Rice

2. If the total area under jowar was 1.5 million acres, then what was the area (in million acres) under rice?
(*a*) 6 (*b*) 7.5
(*c*) 9 (*d*) 4.5

3. If the production of wheat is 6 times that of barley, then what is the ratio between the yield per acre of wheat and barley?
(*a*) 3 : 2 (*b*) 3 : 1
(*c*) 12 : 1 (*d*) 2 : 3

Solution:

1 (*c*): The total of the central angles corresponding to the three crops which cover 50% of the total area, should be 180°. Now, the total of the central angles for the given combinations are:

(*i*) Wheat, Barley and Jowar
$= (72° + 36° + 18°) = 126°$

(*ii*) Rice, Wheat and Jowar
$= (72° + 72° + 18°) = 162°$

(*iii*) Rice, Wheat and Barley
$= (72° + 72° + 36°) = 180°$

(*iv*) Bajra, Maize and Rice
$= (18° + 45° + 72°) = 135°$

Clearly, (*iii*) is the required combination.

2 (*a*): The area under any of the food crops is proportional to the central angle corresponding to that crop.
Let, the area under rice production be *x* million acres.

Then, $18 : 72 = 1.5 : x \Rightarrow x = \left(\frac{72 \times 1.5}{18}\right) = 6.$

Thus, the area under rice production = 6 million acress

3 (*b*): Let, the total production of barley be T tonnes and let Z acres of land be put under barley production.
Then, the total production of wheat = (6T) tonnes.
Also, area under wheat production = (2Z) areas.

$$\left[\because \frac{\text{Area under Wheat production}}{\text{Area under Barley production}} = \frac{72°}{36°} = 2 \text{ and therefore, Area under wheat} = 2 \times \text{Area under barley} = (2Z) \text{ acres}\right]$$

Now, yield per acre for wheat = $\left(\frac{6T}{2Z}\right)$ tonnes/acre = $\left(\frac{3T}{Z}\right)$ tonnes/acre and yield per acre for barley = $\left(\frac{T}{Z}\right)$ tonnes/acre.

$\therefore$ Required Ratio = $\left(\frac{3T/Z}{T/Z}\right) = 3:1.$

Multiple Choice Questions

1. Which one of the following is not the graphical representation of statistical data?
A. Bar graph
B. Histogram
C. Frequency polygon
D. Cumulative frequency distribution

2. In a frequency distribution, ogives are graphical representation of:
A. Frequency
B. Relative frequency
C. Cumulative frequency
D. Raw data

3. A frequency polygon is constructed by plotting frequency of the class interval and the:
A. upper limit of the class
B. lower limit of the class
C. mid value of the class
D. any values of the class

4. In a histogram the area of each rectangle is proportional to:
A. the class mark of the corresponding class interval
B. the class size of the corresponding class interval
C. frequency of the corresponding class interval
D. cumulative frequency of the corresponding class interval

5. In a histogram, each class rectangle is constructed with base as:
A. frequency
B. class-intervals
C. range
D. size of the class

6. Read the bar graph shown in figure and answer the following question:
In which year is the increase of students maximum?

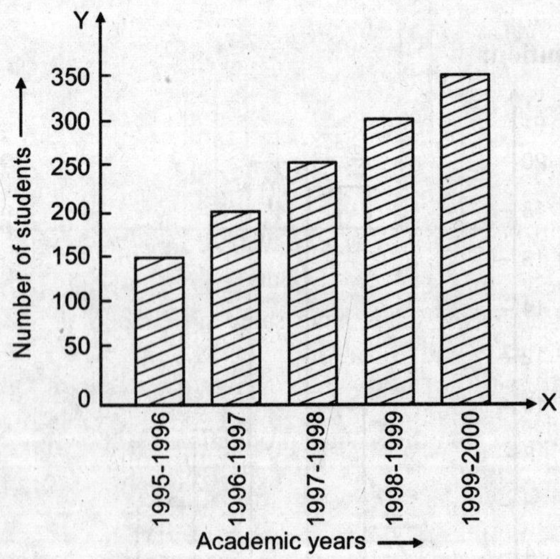

A. 1996-1997
B. 1997-1998
C. 1999-2000
D. None of these

Directions (Qs. 7 to 9) : *Read the following bar graph shown in figure and answer the following questions:*

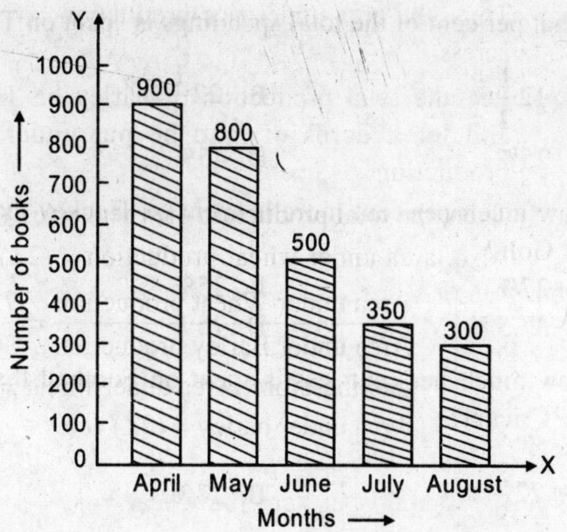

7. In which month was the sale of the books maximum?
A. April B. May
C. June D. August

8. In which month was the sale of the books minimum?
A. April B. May
C. July D. August

9. What is the total sale during these five months?
A. 3800 copies B. 2850 copies
C. 2800 copies D. 2950 copies

Directions (Qs. 10 to 12) : *Read the following bar graph given in figure and answer the following questions:*

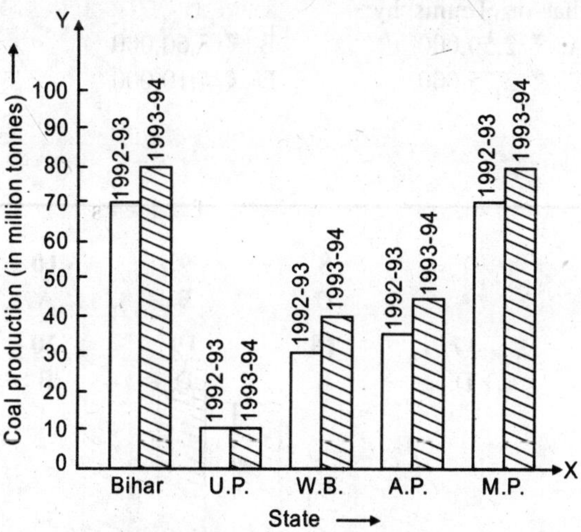

10. Which two states have same production in 1993-94?
A. M.P. and Bihar B. M.P. and U.P.
C. U.P. and Bihar D. W.B. and U.P.

11. Which state has same production in both the years?
A. M.P. B. Bihar
C. U.P. D. W.B.

12. Which state has minimum production?
A. M.P. B. A.P.
C. W.B D. U.P.

Directions (Qs. 13 to 15) : *The following bar graph shows the results of an annual examination in a secondary school.*

Read the bar graph and choose the correct alternative in each of the following.

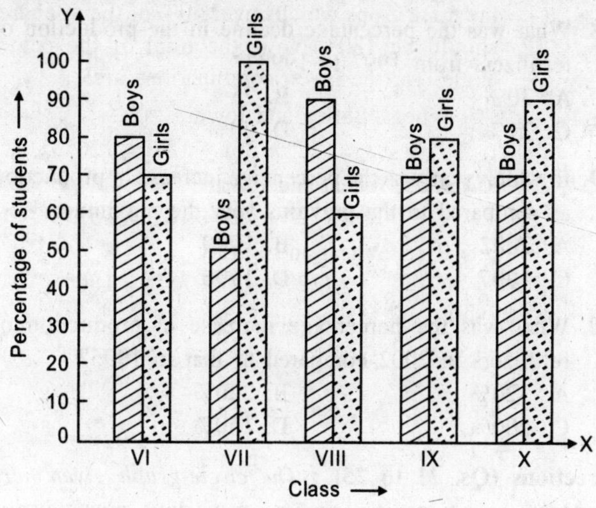

13. The pair of classes in which the results of boys and girls are inversely proportional are:
A. VI, VIII B. VI, IX
C. VIII, IX D. VIII, X

14. The class having the lowest failure rate of girls is:
A. VII B. X
C. IX D. VIII

15. The class having the lowest pass rate of boys is:
A. VI B. VII
C. VIII D. IX

Directions (Qs. 16 to 20) : *Study the following bar-graph and answer the questions given below.*

Production of Fertilizers by a Company (in 10000 tonnes) over the Years

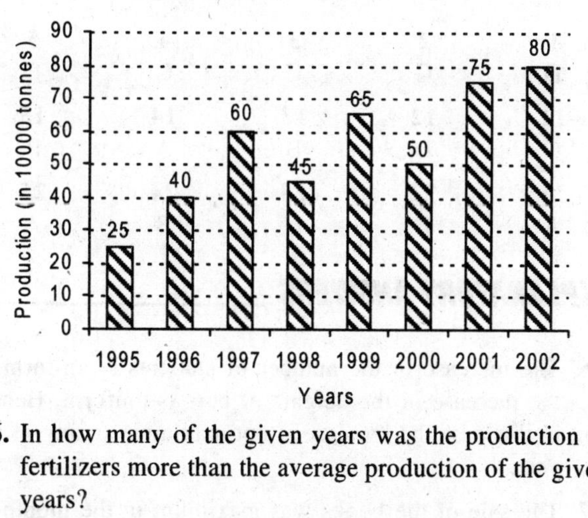

16. In how many of the given years was the production of fertilizers more than the average production of the given years?
A. 1 B. 2
C. 3 D. 4

17. The average production of 1996 and 1997 was exactly equal to the average production of which of the following pairs of years?

A. 2000 and 2001 B. 1999 and 2000
C. 1995 and 1999 D. 1995 and 2001

18. What was the percentage decline in the production of fertilizers from 1997 to 1998?
A. 30% B. 25%
C. 21% D. 20%

19. In which year was the percentage increase in production as compared to the previous year the maximum?
A. 2002 B. 1999
C. 1997 D. 1996

20. What was the percentage increase in production of fertilizers in 2002 compared to that in 1995?
A. 320% B. 220%
C. 200% D. 150%

Directions (Qs. 21 to 25) : *The circle-graph given here shows the spendings of a country on various sports during a particular year. Study the graph carefully and answer the questions given below it.*

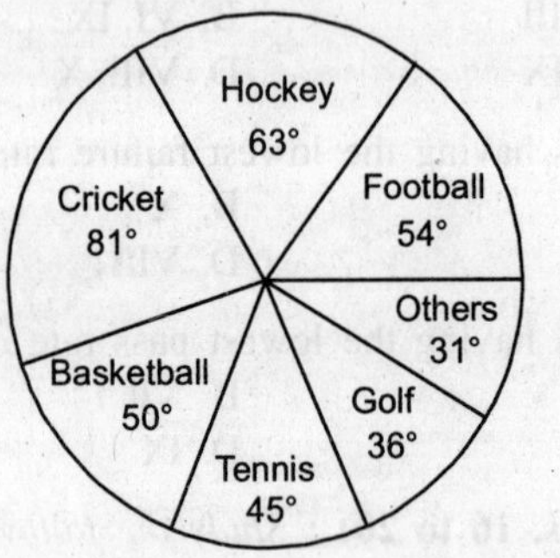

21. What per cent of the total spendings is spent on Tennis?
A. $12\frac{1}{2}\%$ B. $22\frac{1}{2}\%$
C. 25% D. 45%

22. How much per cent more is spent on Hockey than that on Golf?
A. 27% B. 35%
C. 37.5% D. 75%

23. How much per cent less is spent on Football than that on Cricket?
A. $22\frac{2}{9}\%$ B. 27%
C. $33\frac{1}{3}\%$ D. $37\frac{1}{2}\%$

24. If the total amount spent on sports during the year was ₹ 2 crores, the amount spent on Cricket and Hockey together was:
A. ₹ 8,00,000
B. ₹ 80,00,000
C. ₹ 1,20,00,000
D. ₹ 1,60,00,000

25. If the total amount spent on sports during the years be ₹ 1,80,00,000, the amount spent on Basketball exceeds that on Tennis by:
A. ₹ 2,50,000 B. ₹ 3,60,000
C. ₹ 3,75,000 D. ₹ 4,10,000

ANSWERS

1	2	3	4	5	6	7	8	9	10
D	C	C	C	B	D	A	D	B	A
11	**12**	**13**	**14**	**15**	**16**	**17**	**18**	**19**	**20**
C	D	B	A	B	D	D	B	D	B
21	**22**	**23**	**24**	**25**					
A	D	C	B	A					

EXPLANATORY ANSWERS

6. The increase in the number of students is uniform as the increase in the heights of bars is uniform. Hence, in this case the increase is not maximum in any of the year.

7. The sale of the books was maximum in the month of April as the height of the rectangle corresponding to April month is maximum.

8. The sale of the books was minimum in the month of August as the height of the corresponding rectangle is minimum.

9. Total sale of the books during 5 months.
(900 + 800 + 500 + 350 + 300) = 2850 copies.

10. M.P. and Bihar have same production in 1993-1994.

11. U.P. has the same production in both the years.

12. U.P.

16. Average production (in 10000 tonnes) over the given years

$$= \frac{1}{8} \times (25 + 40 + 60 + 45 + 65 + 50 + 75 + 80) = 55$$

$\therefore$ The productions during the years 1997, 1999, 2001 and 2002 are more than the average production.

17. Average production (in 10000 tonnes) of 1996 and 1997 = $\frac{40+60}{2} = 50.$

We shall find the average production (in 10000 tonnes) for each of the given alternative

(*a*) 2000 and 2001 = $\frac{50+75}{2} = 62.5$

(*b*) 1999 and 2000 = $\frac{65+50}{2} = 57.5$

(*c*) 1995 and 1999 = $\frac{25+65}{2} = 45$

(*d*) 1995 and 2001 = $\frac{25+75}{2} = 50$

$\therefore$ The average production of 1996 and 1997 is equal to the average production of 1995 and 2001.

18. Required percentage = $\left[\frac{(45-60)}{60}\times 100\right]\% = -25\%.$

$\therefore$ There is a decline of 25% in production from 1997 to 1998.

19. The percentage increase in production compared to previous year for different years are :

In 1996 = $\left[\frac{(40-25)}{25}\times 100\right]\% = 60\%$

In 1997 = $\left[\frac{(60-40)}{40}\times 100\right]\% = 50\%$

In 1999 = $\left[\frac{(65-45)}{45}\times 100\right]\% = 44.44\%$

In 2002 = $\left[\frac{(80-75)}{75}\times 100\right]\% = 6.67\%$

Clearly, there is maximum percentage increase in production in 1996.

20. Required percentage = $\left[\frac{(80-25)}{25}\times 100\right]\% = 220\%.$

21. Percentage of money spent on Tennis

$$= \left(\frac{45}{360}\times 100\right)\% = 12\frac{1}{2}\%$$

22. Let the total spendings on sports be ₹ x. Then,

Amount spent on Golf = ₹ $\left(\frac{36}{360}\times x\right) = ₹\frac{x}{10}$

Amount spent on Hockey = ₹ $\left(\frac{63}{360}\times x\right) = ₹\frac{7}{40}x.$

Difference = ₹ $\left(\frac{7}{40}x - \frac{x}{10}\right) = ₹\frac{3x}{40}$

$\therefore$ Required Percentage = $\left[\left(\frac{3x/40}{x/10}\right)\times 100\right]\% = 75\%$

23. Let the total spendings on sports be ₹ x. Then,

Amount spent on Cricket = ₹ $\left(\frac{81}{360}\times x\right) = ₹\left(\frac{9}{40}x\right)$

Amount spent on Football = ₹ $\left(\frac{54}{360}\times x\right) = ₹\left(\frac{3}{20}x\right)$

Difference = ₹ $\left(\frac{9}{40}x - \frac{3}{20}x\right) = ₹\frac{3}{40}x$

$\therefore$ Required Percentage = $\left[\left(\frac{3x/40}{9x/40}\right)\times 100\right]\% = 33\frac{1}{3}\%$

24. Amount spent on Cricket and Hockey together

= ₹ $\left[\frac{(81+63)}{360}\times 2\right]$ crores = ₹ 0.8 crores = ₹ 8000000.

25. Amount spent on Basketball exceeds that on Tennis by :

₹ $\left[\frac{(50-45)}{360}\times 18000000\right]$ = ₹ 250000.

□□□□□

13

Statistics

Statistics is defined as the mathematics of the collection, organisation and interpretation of numerical data, especially the analysis of population characteristics by inference from the sampling.

Points To Remember

- Observations gathered initially are called **Raw data**.
- The difference between the highest and the lowest values of the observations in given data is called the range.
- Mean of given data

$$= \frac{\text{Sum of all observations}}{\text{Total number of observation}}$$

- In given data, the number of times a particular observation occurs is called its **frequency**.
- A table showing the frequencies of various observations of data is called a frequency distribution table or simply a frequency table.
- When the number of observations is large, we make use of tally marks to count the frequencies.
- Tallies are usually marked in bunches of five for ease of counting.
- When the list of observations is very large, we organise the data into groups called classes or class interval. The data so obtained is called grouped data or a grouped frequency distribution.
- The lower value of a class interval called its lower class limit and the upper value of a class interval is called its upper class limit.
- The difference between the upper and lower values of a class interval is called its **width** or **size**.
- The mid-value of a class interval is called its class mark.
- The frequency of a class interval is called its class frequency.
- A histogram is a graphical representation of grouped data in which class intervals are taken along the horizontal axis and frequencies along the vertical axis.

Measures of Central Tendency

Generally, average value of a distribution in the middle part of the distribution, such type of values are known as measures of central tendency.

The following are the five measures of central tendency:

1. Arithmetic Mean
2. Geometric Mean
3. Harmonic Mean
4. Median
5. Mode

1. Arithmetic Mean : The arithmetic (or simple mean) of a set of observations is obtained by dividing the sum of the value of observations by the number of observations.

***(i)* Arithmetic Mean for Unclassified (Ungrouped) Data:** If n observations, $x_1, x_2, x_3, ..., x_n$, then their arithmetic mean

$$\text{A or } \bar{x} = \frac{x_1 + x_2 + ... + x_n}{n} = \frac{\sum_{i=1}^{n} x_i}{n}$$

***(ii)* Arithmetic Mean for Frequency Distribution :** Let $f_1, f_2, ... f_n$ be corresponding frequencies of $x_1, x_2, ..., x_n$. Then, arithmetic mean

$$A = \frac{x_1 f_1 + x_2 f_2 + ... + x_n f_n}{f_1 + f_2 + ... + f_n} = \frac{\sum_{i=1}^{n} x_i f_i}{\sum_{i=1}^{n} f_i}$$

***(iii)* Arithmetic Mean for Classified (Grouped) Data :** For a classified data, we take the class marks $x_1, x_2, ..., x_n$ of the classes as variables, then arithmetic mean by

$$\text{Direct method is } A = \frac{\sum_{i=1}^{n} x_i f_i}{\sum_{i=1}^{n} f_i}$$

***(iv)* Combined Mean :** If $A_1, A_2, ..., A_n$ are the n arithmetic mean having number of corresponding observations $n_1, n_2, ..., n_r$, then arithmetic mean of the combined group x is called the combined mean of the observation

$$A = \frac{n_1 A_1 + n_2 A_2 + ... + n_r A_r}{n_1 + n_2 + .. + n_r} = \frac{\sum_{i=1}^{r} n_i A_i}{\sum_{i=1}^{r} n_i}$$

***(v)* Weighted Arithmetic Mean :** If $w_1, w_2, ..., w_n$ are the weights assigned to the values $x_1, x_2, ...,$

x_n respectively, then the weighted arithmetic mean is:

$$A_w = \frac{\sum_{i=1}^{n} w_i x_i}{\sum_{i=1}^{n} w_i}$$

Properties of Arithmetic Mean

(*i*) Mean is dependent of change of origin and change of scale.

(*ii*) Algebraic sum of the deviations of a set of values from their arithmetic mean is zero.

(*iii*) The sum of the squares of the deviations of a set of values is minimum when taken about mean.

2. Geometric Mean

(*i*) If $x_1, x_2, ..., x_n$ be n non-zero observations, then their geometric mean is defined as:

$$G = \sqrt[n]{x_1 x_2 ,... x_n}$$

3. Harmonic Mean : The harmonic mean of n non-zero observations $x_1, x_2,..., x_n$ is defined as

$$HM = \frac{n}{\frac{1}{x_1}+\frac{1}{x_2}+...+\frac{1}{x_n}} = \frac{n}{\sum_{i=1}^{n}\frac{1}{x_i}}$$

4. Median : The median of a distribution is the value of the middle variable, when the variables are arranged in ascending or descending order.

Median (M_d) is an average of position of the numbes.

(*i*) **Median for Simple Distribution :** Firstly, arrange the data in ascending or descending order and then find the number of observations n.

(*a*) If n is odd, then $\left(\frac{n+1}{2}\right)$ th term is the median.

(*b*) If n is even, then there are two middle terms namely $\left(\frac{n}{2}\right)$ th and $\left(\frac{n}{2}+1\right)$ th terms. Hence,

Median = Mean of $\left(\frac{n}{2}\right)$ th and $\left(\frac{n}{2}+1\right)$ th observations

$$= \frac{1}{2}\left[\left(\frac{n}{2}\right)\text{th} + \left(\frac{n}{2}+1\right)\text{th}\right] \text{ of observations}$$

Properties

(*i*) The median can be calculated graphically, while mean cannot be.

(*ii*) The sum of the absolute deviations taken from the median is less than the sum of the absolute deviations taken from any other observation in the data.

(*iii*) Median is not affected by extreme values.

5. Mode : The mode (M_o) of a distribution is the value at the point about which the observations tend to be most heavily concentrated. It is generally the value of the variable which appears to occur most frequently in the distribution.

The value which is repeated maximum number of times, is the required mode.

e.g. Mode of the data 70, 80, 90, 96, 70, 96, 90 is 96 as 96 occurs maximum number of times.

Propperties

(*i*) It can be calculated graphically.

(*ii*) It is not affected by extreme values.

(*iii*) It can be used for open-ended distribution and qualitative data.

In a moderately symmetric distribution mean, median and mode are connected by the following formula

Mode = 3 Median – 2 Mean

Relation between Mean, Median and Mode

(*i*) Mean – Mode = 3(Mean – Median)

(*i*) Mode = 3 Median – 2 Mean

Effects of Average and Dispersion on Change of Origin and Scale

	Change of Origin	Change of Scale
Mean	Dependent	Dependent
Median	Not Dependent	Dependent
Mode	Not Dependent	Dependent

Note : (*i*) Change of origin means either subtract of add in observation

(*ii*) Change of scale means either multiply or divide in observations.

Multiple Choice Questions

1. The mean of n observations is $\bar{X}$. If k is added to each observation, then the new mean is:

A. $\bar{X}$ B. $\bar{X}+k$

C. $\bar{X}-k$ D. $k\bar{X}$

2. The mean of n observations is $\bar{X}$. If each observation is multiplied by k, the mean of new observations is:

A. $k\bar{X}$ B. $\frac{\bar{X}}{k}$

C. $\bar{X}+k$ D. $\bar{X}-k$

3. The mean of a set of seven numbers is 81. If one of the numbers is discarded, the mean of the remaining numbers is 78. The value of discarded number is:

A. 98 B. 99
C. 100 D. 101

4. For which set of numbers do the mean, median and mode all have the same value?
A. 2, 2, 2, 2, 4 B. 1, 3, 3, 3, 5
C. 1, 1, 2, 5, 6 D. 1, 1, 1, 2, 5

5. For the set of numbers 2, 2, 4, 5 and 12, which of the following statements is true?
A. Mean = Median B. Mean > Mode
C. Mean < Mode D. Mode = Median

6. The empirical relation between mean, mode and median is:
A. Mode = 3 Median – 2 Mean
B. Mode = 2 Median – 3 Mean
C. Median = 3 Mode – 2 Mean
D. Mean = 3 Median – 2 Mode

7. The mean of a, b, c, d and e is 28. If the mean of a, c, and e is 24, what is the mean of b and d?
A. 31 B. 32
C. 33 D. 34

8. Which of the following is dependent of the change of origin?
A. Mean B. Median
C. Mode D. Variance

9. What is the mean of first nine even natural numbers?
A. 10 B. 12
C. 11 D. 13

10. What is the median of first 15 odd numbers?
A. 15 B. 17
C. 19 D. 21

11. If the mean of a given data is 51 kg and its median is 50 kg. What is the mode of that data?
A. 52 kg B. 51 kg
C. 53 kg D. 54 kg

12. What is the mean of first 12 multiple of 7?
A. 45 B. 46
C. 45.5 D. 46.5

13. What is the mode of the given data :
16, 20, 8, 17, 27 34, 28, 32, 27, 15, 27, 54, 42.
A. 8 B. 27
C. 54 D. None of these

14. What is the mean of the following data?

Marks obtained	45	27	20	56	82	75	17
No. of students	5	3	8	7	2	4	12

A. 34.22 B. 36.22
C. 37.22 D. None of these

15. What is the median of the following data?

Marks obtained	72	47	62	57	42	52	67
No. of students	9	8	11	8	3	6	5

A. 56.5 B. 57.5
C. 58.5 D. 59.5

16. The ages in years of 15 teachers of a school are 41, 32, 51, 43, 24, 38, 49, 56, 42, 28, 37, 48, 45, 47, 50. What is the range of ages of teachers?
A. 32 years B. 30 years
C. 28 years D. None of these

17. Following are the margins of victory in the football matches of a league.
1, 3, 2, 5, 1, 4, 6, 2, 5, 2, 2, 2, 4, 1, 2, 3, 1, 1, 2, 3, 2, 6, 4, 3, 2, 1, 1, 4, 2, 1, 5, 3, 3, 2, 3, 2, 4, 2, 1, 2.
What is the mode of this data?
A. 1 B. 2
C. 3 D. 4

18. If the mean and mode of a given data is 51 and 48 respectively, what is the median?
A. 48 B. 49
C. 50 D. 52

19. What is mean of first 10-prime numbers?
A. 12.9 B. 12.7
C. 11.3 D. None of these

20. The mean of 6 observations was found to be 40. Later on, it was detected that one observation 82 was misread as 28. What is the correct mean?
A. 45 B. 46
C. 47 D. 49

21. The rainfall (in mm) in a city on 7 days of a certain week were recorded as follows?

Day	Mon	Tue	Wed	Thur	Fri	Sat	Sun
Rainfall (in mm)	2.2	21.3	25.6	0.0	4.9	0.0	5.5

What is the range of the rainfall in the above data?
A. 25.6 B. 24.4
C. 20.7 D. 20.1

22. The mean of marks scored by 100 students was found to be 40. Later on it was discovered that a score of 53 was misread as 83. What is the correct mean?
A. 39.7 B. 38.9
C. 39.4 D. 38.7

23. The median of the observations 11, 12, 14, 18, $x + 2$, $x + 4$, 30, 32, 35, 41 arranged in ascending order is 24. What is the value of x?
A. 18 B. 19
C. 20 D. 21

24. Calculate the median of the following data:
83, 37, 70, 29, 45, 63, 41, 70, 30, 54.
A. 46.5 B. 49.5
C. 47.5 D. 48.5

25. The median of the following observations, arranged in ascending order is 30. What is the x?
11, 12, 14, 18, $x + 2$, $x + 4$, 30, 32, 35, 41, 45.
A. 24 B. 25
C. 26 D. 28

26. Mean temperature of a certain week was 25°C. If mean temperature of Monday, Tuesday, Wednesday and Thursday was 23°C and that of Thursday, Friday, Saturday and Sunday was 28°C. What is the temperature of Thursday?

A. 25°C B. 27°C
C. 29°C D. 31°C

27. What is the arithmetic mean of the scores 8, 6, 10, 12, 1, 3, 4, 4 and what is the range of the data?

A. 5, 8 B. 6, 11
C. 7, 10 D. 8, 9

28. Determine the median of the following data 24, 23, *a*, *a* – 1, 12, 16, where *a* is the mean of 10, 20, 30, 40, 50.

A. 23.5 B. 24.5
C. 22.5 D. 22.8

29. If the mean of the following distribution is 6. What is the value of P?

x	2	4	6	10	P + 5
f	3	2	3	1	2

A. 4 B. 5
C. 6 D. 7

30. Following are the ages (in years) of 10 teachers in a school:
32, 41, 28, 54, 35, 26, 23, 33, 38, 40.
What is the range of the age of the teachers?

A. 28 years B. 29 years
C. 30 years D. 31 years

ANSWERS

1	2	3	4	5	6	7	8	9	10
B	A	B	B	B	A	D	A	A	B
11	**12**	**13**	**14**	**15**	**16**	**17**	**18**	**19**	**20**
C	C	B	C	D	A	B	C	A	D
21	**22**	**23**	**24**	**25**	**26**	**27**	**28**	**29**	**30**
A	A	D	B	C	C	B	A	D	D

EXPLANATORY ANSWERS

9. Mean $= \dfrac{2+4+6+8+10+12+14+16+18}{9} = \dfrac{90}{9} = 10$

10. First 15 odd numbers are 3, 5, 7, 9, 11, 13, 15, 17, 19, 21, 23, 25, 27, 29, 31

n = 15, which is odd

Median $= \left(\dfrac{15+1}{2}\right)$th term = 8th term = 17

11. Mode = 3 × median – 2 × Mean
= 3(51) – 2(50) = 153 – 100 = 53 kg

12. Mean $= \dfrac{7+14+21+28+35+42+49+56+63+70+77+84}{12} = \dfrac{546}{12} = 45.5$

13. Mode = 27, as it occurs 3 times.

14.

Marks obtained (x_i)	No. of Students (f_i)	$x_i f_i$
45	5	225
27	3	81
20	8	160
56	7	392
82	2	164
75	4	300
17	12	204
	$\Sigma f_i = 41$	$\Sigma f_i x_i = 1526$

Mean $= \dfrac{\Sigma f_i x_i}{\Sigma f_i} = \dfrac{1526}{41} = 37.219 \approx 37.22$

15.

Marks obtained	No. of Students	Cumulative frequency
42	3	3
47	8	3 + 8 = 11
52	6	11 + 6 = 17
57	8	17 + 8 = 25
62	11	25 + 11 = 36
67	5	36 + 5 = 41
72	9	41 + 9 = 50

N = 50 (even)

$$\text{Median} = \frac{\left(\frac{50}{2}\right)\text{th term} + \left(\frac{50}{2}+1\right)\text{th term}}{2}$$

$$= \frac{\text{25th term} + \text{26th term}}{2}$$

$$= \frac{57+62}{2} = \frac{119}{2} = 59.5$$

16. The age in the ascending order are
24, 28, 32, 37, 38, 41, 42, 43, 45, 47, 48, 49, 50, 51, 56
Range = 56 – 24 = 32
Maximum value – Minimum value

17. The frequency of 2 is highest

So, Mode = 2

18. Mode = 3 Median − 2 Mean

48 = 3 Median − 2 × 51

⇒ 3 Median = 102 + 48

⇒ 3 Median = 150

⇒ $\text{Median} = \frac{150}{3} = 50$

19. $\text{Mean} = \frac{2+3+5+7+11+13+17+19+23+29}{10}$

$= \frac{129}{10} = 12.9$

20. $\text{Correct Mean} = \frac{40\times 6+(82-28)}{6}$

$= \frac{240+54}{6} = \frac{294}{6} = 49.$

21. Range = 25.6 − 0 = 25.6 mm.

22. Total Marks by 100 students

= 100 × 40 = 4000

$\text{Correct Mean} = \frac{4000-(83-53)}{100} = \frac{3970}{100}$

= 39.7.

23. n = 10 (even)

$$\text{Median} = \frac{\frac{n}{2}\text{th term} + \left(\frac{n}{2}+1\text{th term}\right)}{2}$$

$$24 = \frac{\text{5th term} + \text{6th term}}{2}$$

$$24 = \frac{x+2+x+4}{2} = \frac{2x+6}{2}$$

$2x + 6 = 48$

$2x = 42$

$x = \frac{42}{2} = 21.$

24. Data in ascending order.

29, 30, 37, 41, 45, 54, 63, 70, 70, 83

n = 10 (even)

$$\text{Median} = \frac{\frac{n}{2}\text{th term} + \left(\frac{n}{2}+1\text{th}\right)\text{ term}}{2}$$

$$= \frac{\text{5th term} + \text{6th term}}{2}$$

$$= \frac{45+54}{2} = \frac{99}{2} = 49.5.$$

25. n = 11 (odd)

$\text{Median} = \frac{n+1}{2}\text{th term} = \text{6th term}$

$30 = x + 4$

$x = 30 - 4 = 26.$

26. Total temp. of a week = 7 × 25 = 175°

Total temp. of Mon, Tues, Wed, Thurs.

= 23 × 4 = 92°C

Total temp. of Thurs, Fri, Sat and Sunday

= 28 × 4 = 112°C

Temp. of Thursday = (112 + 92) − 175

= 204 − 175 = 29°C.

27. $\text{Mean} = \frac{8+6+10+12+1+3+4+4}{8}$

$= \frac{48}{8} = 6.$

Range = Maximum value − Minimum value

= 12 − 1 = 11.

28. $a = \frac{10+20+30+40+50}{5} = \frac{150}{5}$

= 30

The given data in ascending order

12, 16, 23, 24, 29, 30

n = 6 (even)

$$\text{Median} = \frac{\frac{n}{2}\text{th term} + \left(\frac{n}{2}+1\right)\text{th term}}{2}$$

$$= \frac{\text{3rd term} + \text{4th term}}{2}$$

$$= \frac{23+24}{2} = \frac{47}{2} = 23.5.$$

29.

x	f	fx
2	3	6
4	2	8
6	3	18
10	1	10
P + 5	2	2 (P + 5)
Total	11	42 + 2P + 10

= 2P + 52

$$\text{Mean} = \frac{\Sigma fx}{\Sigma f} = \frac{2P+52}{11}$$

$$6 = \frac{2P+52}{11}$$

2P = 66 − 52 = 14 ⇒ P = 7.

30. 54 − 23 = 31 years.

14

Probability

Important Facts and Formulae

1. Experiment : An operation which can produce some well-defined outcomes is called an experiment.

2. Random Experiment : An experiment in which all possible outcomes are known and the exact output cannot be predicted in advance, is called a random experiment.

Examples of Performing a Random Experiment:

(*i*) Rolling an unbiased dice.

(*ii*) Tossing a fair coin.

(*iii*) Drawing a card from a pack of well-suffled cards.

(*iv*) Picking up a ball of certain colour from a bag containing balls of different colours.

Details:

(*i*) When we throw a coin. Then either a Head (H) or a Tail (T) appears

(*ii*) A dice is a solid cube, having 6 faces, marked, 1, 2, 3, 4, 5, 6 respectively. When we throw a die, the outcome is the number that appears on its upper face.

(*iii*) A pack of cards has 52 cards.
It has 13 cards of each suit, namely Spades, Clubs, Hearts and Diamonds.
Cards of spades and clubs are black cards.
Cards of hearts and diamonds are red cards.
There are 4 honours of each suit.
These are Aces, Kings, Queens and Jacks.
These are called face cards.

3. Sample Space : When we perform an experiment, then the set S of all possible outcomes is called the sample space.

Examples of Sample Spaces:

(*i*) In tossing a coin, S = {H, T}.

(*ii*) If two coins are tossed, then S = {HH, HT, TH, TT}.

(*iii*) In rolling a dice, we have, S = {1, 2, 3, 4, 5, 6}.

4. Event : Any subset of a sample space is called an event.

5. Probability of Occurrence of an Event:
Let S be the sample space and let E be an event. Then, $E \subseteq S$.

$$\therefore \quad P(E) = \frac{n(E)}{n(S)}$$

6. Results on Probability:

(*i*) $P(S) = 1$

(*ii*) $0 \le P(E) \le 1$

(*iii*) $P(\phi) = 0$

(*iv*) For any events A and B, we have:
$P(A \cup B) = P(A) + P(B) - P(A \cap B)$

(*v*) If $\bar{A}$ denotes (not-A), then $P(\bar{A}) = 1 - P(A)$.

Example 1 : Two unbiased coins are tossed. What is the probability of getting at most one head?

Solution: Here S = {HH, HT, TH, TT}.

Let E = event of getting at most one head.

$\therefore$ E = {TT, HT, TH}

$$\therefore \quad P(E) = \frac{n(E)}{n(S)} = \frac{3}{4}.$$

Example 2 : An unbiased die is tossed. Find the probability of getting a multiple of 3.

Solution : Here S = {1, 2, 3, 4, 5, 6}

Let E be the event of getting a multiple of 3.

Then, E = {3, 6}

$$\therefore \quad P(E) = \frac{n(E)}{n(S)} = \frac{2}{6} = \frac{1}{3}$$

Example 3 : A bag contains 6 white and 4 black balls. Two balls are drawn at random. Find the probability that they are of the same colour.

Solution : Let S be the sample space. Then,

$n(S)$ = Number of ways of drawing 2 balls out of (6 + 4)

$$= {}^{10}C_2 = \frac{(10 \times 9)}{(2 \times 1)} = 45.$$

Let E = Event of getting both balls of the same colur. Then,

$n(E)$ = Number of ways of drawing (2 balls out of 6) or (2 balls out of 4)

$$= ({}^6C_2 + {}^4C_2) = \frac{(6\times5)}{(2\times1)} + \frac{(4\times3)}{(2\times1)} = (15+6) = 21$$

$$\therefore\ P(E) = \frac{n(E)}{n(S)} = \frac{21}{45} = \frac{7}{15}.$$

Example 4 : Two dice are thrown together. What is the probability that the sum of the numbers on the two faces is divisible by 4 or 6?

Solution : Clearly, $n(S) = 6 \times 6 = 36$.

Let E be the event that the sum of the numbers on the two faces is divisible by 4 or 6. Then

$$E = \{(1, 3), (1, 5), (2, 2), (2, 4), (2, 6), (3, 1), (3, 3), (3, 5), (4, 2), (4, 4), (5, 1), (5, 3), (6, 2), (6, 6)\}$$

$\therefore\ n(E) = 14.$

Hence, $P(E) = \frac{n(E)}{n(S)} = \frac{14}{36} = \frac{7}{18}.$

Multiple Choice Questions

1. Following table shows the marks scored by a group of 90 students in a mathematics test of 100 marks.

Marks	0-20	20-30	30-40	40-50	50-60	60-70	70-100
No. of students	7	10	10	20	20	15	8

What is the probability that a student obtained less then 20% marks?

A. $\frac{5}{90}$ B. $\frac{7}{90}$

C. $\frac{1}{10}$ D. None of these

2. A dice is rolled 600 times and the occurrence of the outcomes 1, 2, 3, 4, 5 and 6 are given below:

Outcome	1	2	3	4	5	6
Frequency	200	30	120	100	50	100

The probability of getting a prime numbers is:

A. $\frac{1}{3}$ B. $\frac{2}{3}$

C. $\frac{49}{60}$ D. $\frac{39}{125}$

3. A bag contains 50 coins and each coin is marked from 51 to 100. One coin is picked at random. The probability that the number on the coin is not a prime number, is

A. $\frac{1}{5}$ B. $\frac{3}{5}$

C. $\frac{2}{5}$ D. $\frac{4}{5}$

4. In a football match, a player makes 4 goals from 10 penalty kicks. The probability of converting a penalty kick into a goal by the player, is:

A. $\frac{1}{4}$ B. $\frac{1}{6}$

C. $\frac{1}{3}$ D. $\frac{2}{5}$

5. Three coins are tossed simultaneously 200 times with the following frequencies of different outcomes:

Outcome	3 heads	2 heads	1 head	No head
Frequency	23	72	77	28

What is the probability of getting at most two heads?

A. $\frac{177}{200}$ B. $\frac{172}{200}$

C. $\frac{19}{40}$ D. None of these

6. In Q. No. 5, what is the probability of getting at least two heads?

A. $\frac{13}{40}$ B. $\frac{19}{40}$

C. $\frac{23}{40}$ D. None of these

Directions (Qs. 7 to 10) : *1000 families with 2 children were selected randomly, and the following data were recorded:*

Number of boys in a family:	0	1	2
Number of families :	140	560	300

If a family is chosen at random, find the probability that it has:

7. No boy

A. 0.14 B. 0.56

C. 0.3 D. None of these

8. One boy

A. 0.56 B. 0.3

C. 0.14 D. None of these

9. At least one boy

A. 0.14 B. 0.56

C. 0.86 D. 0.7

10. At most one boy

A. 0.7 B. 0.56

C. 0.14 D. 0.86

11. In a simultaneous throw of two coins, the probability of getting at least one head is:

A. $\frac{1}{2}$ B. $\frac{1}{3}$

C. $\frac{2}{3}$ D. $\frac{3}{4}$

12. Three unbiased coins are tossed. What is the probability of getting at least 2 heads?

A. $\frac{3}{4}$ B. $\frac{1}{4}$

C. $\frac{3}{8}$ D. $\frac{7}{8}$

13. In a single throw of a die, what is the probability of getting a number greater than 4?

A. $\frac{1}{2}$ B. $\frac{1}{3}$

C. $\frac{2}{3}$ D. $\frac{1}{4}$

14. In a simultaneous throw of two dice, what is the probability of getting a total of 7?

A. $\frac{1}{6}$ B. $\frac{1}{4}$

C. $\frac{2}{3}$ D. $\frac{3}{4}$

15. What is the probability of getting a sum 9 from two throws of a dice?

A. $\frac{1}{6}$ B. $\frac{1}{8}$

C. $\frac{1}{9}$ D. $\frac{1}{12}$

16. In a simultaneous throw of two dice, what is the probability of getting a total of 10 or 11?

A. $\frac{1}{4}$ B. $\frac{1}{6}$

C. $\frac{7}{12}$ D. $\frac{5}{36}$

17. Two dice are thrown simultaneously. What is the probability of getting two numbers whose product is even?

A. $\frac{1}{2}$ B. $\frac{3}{4}$

C. $\frac{3}{8}$ D. $\frac{5}{16}$

18. Tickets numbered 1 to 20 are mixed up and then a ticket is drawn at random. What is the probability that the ticket drawn bears a number which is a multiple of 3?

A. $\frac{3}{10}$ B. $\frac{3}{20}$

C. $\frac{2}{5}$ D. $\frac{1}{2}$

19. From a pack of 52 cards, one card is drawn at random. What is the probability that the card drawn is a ten or a spade?

A. $\frac{4}{13}$ B. $\frac{1}{4}$

C. $\frac{1}{13}$ D. $\frac{1}{26}$

20. The probability that a card drawn from a pack of 52 cards will be a diamond or a king, is:

A. $\frac{2}{13}$ B. $\frac{4}{13}$

C. $\frac{1}{13}$ D. $\frac{1}{52}$

21. A bag contains 6 black and 8 white balls. One ball is drawn at random. What is the probability that the ball drawn is white?

A. $\frac{3}{4}$ B. $\frac{4}{7}$

C. $\frac{1}{8}$ D. $\frac{3}{7}$

22. A box contains 5 green, 4 yellow and 3 white marbles. Three marbles are drawn at random. What is the probability that they are not of the same colour?

A. $\frac{3}{44}$ B. $\frac{3}{55}$

C. $\frac{52}{55}$ D. $\frac{41}{44}$

23. A bag contains 4 white, 5 red and 6 blue balls. Three balls are drawn at random from the bag. The probability that all of them are red, is:

A. $\frac{1}{22}$ B. $\frac{3}{22}$

C. $\frac{2}{91}$ D. $\frac{2}{77}$

24. A box contains 10 black and 10 white balls. The probability of drawing two balls of the same colour, is:

A. $\frac{9}{19}$ B. $\frac{9}{38}$

C. $\frac{10}{19}$ D. $\frac{5}{19}$

25. Two dice are tossed. The probability that the total score is a prime number is:

A. $\frac{1}{6}$ B. $\frac{5}{12}$

C. $\frac{1}{2}$ D. $\frac{7}{9}$

ANSWERS

1	2	3	4	5	6	7	8	9	10
B	A	D	D	A	B	A	A	C	A
11	**12**	**13**	**14**	**15**	**16**	**17**	**18**	**19**	**20**
D	D	B	A	C	D	B	A	A	B
21	**22**	**23**	**24**	**25**					
B	D	C	A	B					

EXPLANATORY ANSWERS

1. Total No. of students = 90
No. of students scoring less than 20 marks = 7

Required probability = $\frac{7}{90}$

2. Total outcomes = 600
Total outcomes of getting prime numbers,
(2, 3, 5) = 30 + 120 + 50 = 200

$\therefore$ Required probability = $\frac{200}{600} = \frac{1}{3}$

3. Total prime no. between 51 to 100 (53, 59, 61, 67, 71, 73, 79, 83. 89, 97) = 10
$\therefore$ Total Non-prime No = 50 – 10 = 40

$\therefore$ Required probability = $\frac{40}{50} = \frac{4}{5}$

4. Required probability = $\frac{4}{10} = \frac{2}{5}$

5. No. of coins getting at most two heads
= 28 + 77 + 72 = 177

Required probability = $\frac{177}{200}$

6. No. of coins getting at least two heads = 23 + 72 = 95

Required probability = $\frac{95}{200} = \frac{19}{40}$

7. Total number of families = 1000
Number of families having no boy child = 140.

$\therefore$ Probability that a family chosen at random does not have a boy child

$= \frac{140}{1000} = 0.14$

8. Total number of families = 1000
Number of families having one boy child = 560
$\therefore$ Probability that a family chosen at random has one boy child

$= \frac{560}{1000} = 0.56$

9. Total number of families = 1000
Number of families having at least one boy child
= 560 + 300 = 860

$= \frac{860}{1000} = 0.86$

10. Total number of families = 1000
Number of families having at most one boy child
= 140 + 560 = 700

$\therefore$ Probability that a family chosen at random has at most one boy child

$= \frac{700}{1000} = 0.7$

11. Here S = {HH, HT, TH, TT},
Let E = event of getting at least one head
= {HT, TH, HH}

$\therefore$ $P(E) = \frac{n(E)}{n(S)} = \frac{3}{4}.$

12. Here $S = \{TTT, TTH, THT, HTT, THH, HTH, HHT, HHH\}$.

Let E = event of getting at most two heads

Then, $E = \{TTT, TTH, THT, HTT, THH, HTH, HHT\}$

$$\therefore \quad P(E) = \frac{n(E)}{n(S)} = \frac{7}{8}.$$

13. When a die is thrown, we have $S = \{1, 2, 3, 4, 5, 6\}$

Let E = event of getting a number greater than 4 $= \{5, 6\}$

$$\therefore \quad P(E) = \frac{n(E)}{n(S)} = \frac{2}{6} = \frac{1}{3}.$$

14. We know that in a simultaneous throw of two dice,

$n(S) = 6 \times 6 = 36$.

Let E = event of getting a total of $7 = \{(1, 6), (2, 5), (3, 4), (4, 3), (5, 2), (6, 1)\}$

$$\therefore \quad P(E) = \frac{n(E)}{n(S)} = \frac{6}{36} = \frac{1}{6}.$$

15. In two throws of a die, $n(S) = (6 \times 6) = 36$.

Let E = event of getting a sum 9 $= \{(3, 6), (4, 5) (5, 4), (6, 3)\}$

$$\therefore \quad P(E) = \frac{n(E)}{n(S)} = \frac{4}{36} = \frac{1}{9}.$$

16. In a simultaneous throw of two dice, we have

$n(S) = (6 \times 6) = 36$

Let E = event of getting a total of 10 or 11 $= \{(4, 6), (5, 5), (6, 4), (5, 6), (6, 5)\}$

$$\therefore \quad P(E) = \frac{n(E)}{n(S)} = \frac{5}{36}.$$

17. In a simultaneous throw of two dice, we have

$n(S) = (6 \times 6) = 36$

Let E = event of getting two numbers whose product is even.

Then, $E = \{(1, 2), (1, 4), (1, 6), (2, 1), (2, 2), (2, 3), (2, 4), (2, 5), (2, 6), (3, 2), (3, 4), (3, 6), (4, 1), (4, 2), (4, 3), (4, 4), (4, 5), (4, 6), (5, 2), (5, 4), (5, 6), (6, 1), (6, 2), (6, 3), (6, 4), (6, 5), (6, 6)\}$.

$\therefore \quad n(E) = 27$.

$$\therefore \quad P(E) = \frac{n(E)}{n(S)} = \frac{27}{36} = \frac{3}{4}$$

18. Here, $S = \{1, 2, 3, 4, ..., 19, 20\}$

Let E = event of getting a multiple of 3 $= \{3, 6, 9, 12, 15, 18\}$

$$\therefore \quad P(E) = \frac{n(E)}{n(S)} = \frac{6}{20} = \frac{3}{10}.$$

19. Here, $n(S) = 52$

There are 13 spades (including one ten) and there are 3 more tens.

Let E = event of getting a ten or a spade.

Then, $n(E) = (13 + 3) = 16$

$$\therefore \quad P(E) = \frac{n(E)}{n(S)} = \frac{16}{52} = \frac{4}{13}.$$

20. Here, $n(S) = 52$

There are 13 cards of diamond (including one king) and there are 3 more kings.

Let E = event of getting a diamond or a king.

Then $n(E) = (13 + 3) = 16$

$$\therefore \quad P(E) = \frac{n(E)}{n(S)} = \frac{16}{52} = \frac{4}{13}.$$

21. Total number of balls $= (6 + 8) = 14$.

Number of white balls $= 8$.

$$P \text{ (drawing a white ball)} = \frac{8}{14} = \frac{4}{7}.$$

22. Let S be the sample space. Then,

$n(S)$ = number of ways of drawing 3 marbels out of 12

$$= {}^{12}C_3 = \frac{(12 \times 11 \times 10)}{(3 \times 2 \times 1)} = 220$$

Let E be the event of drawing 3 balls of the same colour.

Then, E = event of drawing (3 balls out of 5) or (3 balls out of 4) or (3 balls out of 3)

$$\Rightarrow \quad n(E) = ({}^5C_3 + {}^4C_3 + {}^3C_3) = ({}^5C_2 + {}^4C_1 + 1)$$

$$= \frac{(5 \times 4)}{(2 \times 1)} + 4 + 1 = 15$$

$$\Rightarrow \quad P(E) = \frac{n(E)}{n(S)} = \frac{15}{220} = \frac{3}{44}$$

$$\therefore \text{ Required probability} = \left(1 - \frac{3}{44}\right) = \frac{41}{44}.$$

23. Let S be the sample space. Then,

$n(S)$ = number of ways of drawing 3 balls out of 15

$$= {}^{15}C_3 = \frac{(15 \times 14 \times 13)}{(3 \times 2 \times 1)} = 455$$

Let E = event of getting all the 3 red balls.

$\therefore \quad n(E) = {}^5C_3 = {}^5C_2 = \dfrac{(5 \times 4)}{(2 \times 1)} = 10$

$\therefore \quad P(E) = \dfrac{n(E)}{n(S)} = \dfrac{10}{455} = \dfrac{2}{91}.$

24. Total number of balls = 20

Let S be the sample space. Then,

$n(S) =$ Number of ways of drawing 2 balls out of 20

$= {}^{20}C_2 = \dfrac{(20 \times 19)}{(2 \times 1)} = 190$

Let E = event of drawing 2 balls of the same colour

$n(E) = ({}^{10}C_2 + {}^{10}C_2)$

$= 2 \times \dfrac{(10 \times 9)}{(2 \times 1)} = 90$

$\therefore \quad P(E) = \dfrac{n(E)}{n(S)} = \dfrac{90}{190} = \dfrac{9}{19}.$

25. Clearly, $n(S) = (6 \times 6) = 36$.

Let E = Event that the sum is a prime number.

Then, E = {(1, 1), (1, 2), (1, 4), (1, 6), (2, 1), (2, 3), (2, 5), (3, 2), (3, 4), (4, 1), (4, 3), (5, 2), (5, 6), (6, 1), (6, 5)}

$\therefore \quad n(E) = 15$

$\therefore \quad P(E) = \dfrac{n(E)}{n(S)} = \dfrac{15}{36} = \dfrac{5}{12}.$

□□□□□

GENERAL SCIENCE

1

Food-Crop Production and Management; Microorganism; Food Preservation

CROP PRODUCTION AND MANAGEMENT

We all know that every living organism needs food to survive. Plants can synthesise their own food but, animals including human beings are dependent on others for food. So for providing food for large number of people we need proper management. So for this large scale demand of food for humans, they started agriculture practises.

AGRICULTURE: It is a human activity of cultivating crops and plantations for the large scale production of food and goods such as bio fuels, fibres, animal feed etc.

CROPS: When the plants of same types are cultivated at a place on a very large scale are known as crop.

Types of Crops in India

India is a vast country where diverse practices of farming are seen in different parts. But crops in India can be divided into two main types, which are basically:

Kharif (monsoon crops): These are sown in the beginning of rainy season. Ex-paddy, maize, cotton etc.

Rabi (winter crops): These are sown in the beginning of winter season. Ex—wheat, gram, pea etc.

Basic Practices of Crop Production

Cultivation of crop involves various activities and steps which are referred as agriculture practices. There are seven agriculture practices.

These activities are:

1. Preparation of soil
2. Sowing
3. Adding manure and fertilisers
4. Irrigation
5. Protection from weeds
6. Harvesting
7. Storage

Preparation of Soil

One of the most important steps in preparation of soil is to loosen it, which allows the microorganism and earthworm to enrich the soil. This helps the root to penetrate deep into the soil and also bring the nutrient rich soil on the top layer. The process of loosening or turning of soil is called tilling or ploughing.

Ploughing

- This is done with the help of plough.
- Ploughed field contains big pieces of soil called crumbs.
- Further it is levelled using a wooden or an iron leveller to prevent the soil from being eroded by wind or water.
- Next manure or fertilizer is added to increase the soil fertility.

Plough

- It is tool for ploughing in olden days.
- Made up of wood or iron.
- It contains triangular iron strip called as the plough-share.
- The main part is a rod of wood known as plough shaft.
- The last end is attached to the beam which is attached to the bull.

Hoe

- It helps in removing the weeds.
- It has long rod made up of wood or iron.
- A strong bent plate made up of iron is present at one end.
- This is pulled generally by ox.

Sowing

Seeds which are used for sowing should be of good quality, healthy and free from infections.

- Seeds must be planted at correct depth in the soil.
- Proper amount of water is needed for the seeds to germinate.

The gap between the seeds should be proper and at the right distance.

Traditional tool

- It is shaped like a funnel.
- Funnel's end is pierces into the soil.
- Funnel is passes through the funnel.

Seed drill

- Now days drills are used present in the tractors.
- It sows the seeds uniformly at proper distance and depth.
- It ensures that seeds are properly covered by the soil.

Adding Manure and Fertilizers

- Soil itself supplies necessary minerals and nutrients to the plant.
- In certain areas when farmer grows crops after crops it decrease the fertility of the soil.

Difference between Manure and Fertilizers

S.N.	Manure Fertilizers	Fertilizers
1.	Made up of animal and plants waste	Made up of chemicals in factories
2.	Provides mainly organic matter	Provides mainly nutrients
3.	No side effects as it is natural	Gives side effects
4.	Provides long term soil fertility	Not good for long term soil fertility
5.	It is cheaper	It is costlier than manures
6.	It gives slow result	Provides fast and effective result

Irrigation

- Supply of water to crops at different interval of time is known as IRRIGATION.
- Water is the basic and important requirement for growth and development of plants.
- Germination of seeds doesn't take place under dry conditions.
- Proper irrigation system will ensure the timely and adequate required water to crops. This will lead to more yield.

Sources of irrigation: wells, tube wells, ponds, lakes, rivers, dams and canals.

1. **Traditional method of irrigation:** The water available in wells, lakes and canals is lifted up by different regions, for taking it to the fields.
2. **Modern methods of irrigation:**

   (*a*) Sprinkler system:
   - Used where uneven land is present.
   - Perpendicular pipes, having rotating nozzles on top.
   - Joined to the main pipeline at regular intervals.

   (*b*) Drip System:
   - Water Falls drop by drop at the position of the roots.
   - Best technique for watering fruit plants, garden and trees.
   - Very less water wastage.

Protection from Weed

- Weeds are the undesirable plants which grow naturally along with the crops.
- Removal of weeds is called weeding.
- Weeding is important as they effect the growth of crop by compete with the crop plants.

Weed Control

- Tilling before sowing of crops helps in uprooting and killing of weeds.
- Manual removal includes physical removal of weeds by cutting them.
- Weeds are control by spraying weedicides.
- Weedicides are the chemical to kill the weed.

Harvesting

Cutting of crops after it is mature is called harvesting.

- Crops are pulled out or cut close to the ground.
- It can be done manually by sickle or by machine.
- The grain seed need to be separated from the chaff with the help of machine called "combined".

Storage

- Grains are kept for the longer time without getting spoiled is known as storage.
- Should be kept safe from moisture, insect, rats and microorganism.
- If grains are stored without drying they may get spoilt and lose their germination capacity.
- Small scale storage in jute bags and metallic bins.
- Large scale storage in silos and granaries.

Food from Animals

- Like plants, animals also provide us with different kinds of foods.
- People living in coastal areas consume fish as a major part of their diet.
- Just like crop production involve number of steps, similarly animals reared at home or in farm.
- When this is done on large scale it is known as animal husbandry.

MICROORGANISMS : AN INTRODUCTION

Microscopic organisms, commonly known as microorganisms or microbes, are found all around us and even inside our bodies. The category 'Microbes' includes a massive range of organisms including bacteria, fungi, viruses, algae, archaea and protozoa. Some of these, such as bacteria and fungi, are well known, but others such as archaea much less so.

Microorganisms, as their name implies, are so small that they usually require a microscope to see. The vast majority of microbes on the earth pose no real threat to humans, plants or animals; in fact they actually work alongside humans to make world go round, aiding decomposition, decay and even helping us to digest our food. However, there are some microorganisms which negatively impact our lives, causing illness, bad odours and damaging products and surfaces. Some of the names we regularly hear in the media are Salmonella, E.Coli, MRSA, Malaria and Bird flu.

We will briefly explore some major divisions within microorganisms, and hopefully highlight some interesting facts and differences within each group.

Bacteria

Bacteria, perhaps the most well-known microorganism, are a member of the prokaryotes; they have no nucleus within the cell and contain no organelles (specialised cellular 'organs'). Within bacteria there are two classes, Gram positive bacteria which have thicker cell wall and Gram negatives which have a thinner layer sandwiched between an inner and outer membrane.

Bacteria are extremely diverse and in terms of number are by far the most successful organism on Earth. Bacteria are the only microorganisms which can live harmlessly within the human body, often aiding bodily functions such as digestion. In fact there are more bacterial cells within the human body than humans cells, albeit much smaller in size.

Bacteria, of all the 'living' microorganisms, cause the most problems in terms of disease in humans, despite only relatively few bacteria being dangerous.

Fungi

Fungi are eukaryotes which means they have a defined nucleus and organelles. The cells are larger than prokaryotes such as bacteria. Fungal colonies can be visible to the human eye once they have achieved a certain level of growth, for example mould on bread. Fungi can be split into three main groups, 1) moulds which display thread-like (filamentous) growth and multicellular structures, 2) yeasts which are typically non-filamentous and can be single celled and 3) mushrooms which possess a fruiting body for production of spores.

Fungi can be problematic for the immuno compromised and contain significant pathogens which can cause disease in plants. However, we also recognise organisms from this group from widespread use in the food industry, for production of beer and other foodstuffs.

Viruses

Viruses are considered by many experts to not be living organisms. They essentially consist of nucleic acid (DNA or RNA,) and a protein coat. A virion (a virus particle) requires a host cell in order to replicate. Within the human anatomy a virus enters a human cell and hijacks the it, using the cell to replicate.

In many cases the immune system detects the presence of the virus and takes action leaving us with the symptoms of a common cold or influenza. Some viruses can cause permanent and irreversible damage to cells, for example HIV.

Algae

Algae are a more difficult to define group of organisms, containing both prokaryotes and eukaryotes by some definitions. Unlike other micro-organisms algae are typically photosynthesisers and are typically found in marine environments. Prokaryotic algae, or Cyanobacteria, are often called blue-green algae although some definition or opinions will state that algae are eukaryotes only (that they are essentially small aquatic plants). There are other groups such as **Archaea** and **Protozoa** which are generally less well known.

FOOD PRESERVATION

The term food preservation refers to any one of a number of techniques used to prevent food from spoiling. It includes methods such as canning, pickling, drying and freeze-drying, irradiation, pasteurization, smoking, and the addition of chemical additives. Food preservation has become an increasingly important component of the food industry as fewer people eat foods produced on their own lands, and as consumers expect to be able to purchase and consume foods that are out of season.

The vast majority of instances of food spoilage can be attributed to one of two major causes:

- The attack by pathogens (disease-causing micro-organisms) such as bacteria and molds, or
- Oxidation that causes the destruction of essential biochemical compounds and/or the destruction of plant and animal cells. The various methods that have been devised for preserving foods are all designed to reduce or eliminate one or the other (or both) of these causative agents.

Traditional techniques

Drying

Drying is one of the oldest techniques used to hamper the decomposition of food products.

Vegetables and fruits are naturally dried by the sun and wind, but "still houses" were built in areas that did not have enough sunlight to dry things. A fire would be built inside the building to provide the heat to dry the various fruits, vegetables, and herbs.

Cooling

Cooling preserves food by slowing down the growth and reproduction of microorganisms and the action of enzymes that cause food to rot.

Freezing

Freezing is also one of the most commonly used processes, both commercially and domestically, for preserving a very wide range of foods, including prepared foods that would not have required freezing in their unprepared state.

Boiling

Boiling liquid food items can kill any existing microbes. Milk and water are often boiled to kill any harmful microbes that may be present in them.

Heating

Heating to temperatures which are sufficient to kill microorganisms inside the food is a method used with perpetual stews. Milk is also boiled before storing to kill many microorganisms.

Salting

Salting or curing draws moisture from a substance through a process of osmosis. Substances are cured with salt or sugar, or a combination of the two. Nitrates and nitrites are also often used to cure meat and contribute the characteristic pink colour.

Sugaring

The earliest cultures have used sugar as a preservative, and it was commonplace to store fruit in honey. Similar to pickled foods, sugar cane was brought to Europe through the trade routes. In northern climates without sufficient sun to dry foods, preserves are made by heating the fruit with sugar.

Pickling

Pickling is a method of preserving food in an edible anti-microbial liquid. Pickling can be broadly classified into two categories: chemical pickling and fermentation pickling. In chemical pickling, the food is placed in an edible liquid that inhibits or kills bacteria and other micro-organisms. Typical pickling agents include brine (high in salt), vinegar, alcohol, and vegetable oil, especially olive oil but also many other oils.

Lye

Sodium hydroxide (lye) makes food too alkaline for bacterial growth. Lye will saponify fats in the food, which will change its flavour and texture. Lutefisk uses lye in its preparation, as do some olive recipes. Modern recipes for century eggs also call for lye.

Canning

Canning involves cooking food, sealing it in sterile cans or jars, and boiling the containers to kill or weaken any remaining bacteria as a form of sterilization. Foods have varying degrees of natural protection against spoilage and may require that the final step occur in a pressure cooker. High-acid fruits like strawberries require no preservatives to can and only a short boiling cycle, whereas marginal vegetables such as carrots require longer boiling and addition of other acidic elements. Low-acid foods, such as vegetables and meats, require pressure canning. Food preserved by canning or bottling is at immediate risk of spoilage once the can or bottle has been opened.

Jellying

Food may be preserved by cooking in a material that solidifies to form a gel. Such materials include gelatin, agar, maize flour, and arrow root flour. Some foods naturally form a protein gel, when cooked, such as eels and elvers, and sipunculid worms, which are a delicacy in Xiamen, in the Fujian province of the People's Republic of China.

Jugging

Meat can be preserved by jugging. Jugging is the process of stewing the meat (commonly game or fish) in a covered earthenware jug or casserole. The animal to be jugged is usually cut into pieces, placed into a tightly-sealed jug with brine or gravy, and stewed. Red wineand/or the animal's own blood is sometimes added to the cooking liquid. Jugging was a popular method of preserving meat up until the middle of the 20th century.

Modern industrial techniques

Pasteurization

Pasteurization is a process for preservation of liquid food. It was originally applied to combat the souring of young local wines. Today, the process is mainly applied to dairy products. In this method, milk is heated at about 70 °C (158 °F) for 15–30 seconds to kill the bacteria present in it and cooling it quickly to 10 °C (50 °F) to prevent the remaining bacteria from growing. The milk is then stored in sterilized bottles or pouches in cold places. This method was invented by Louis Pasteur, a French chemist, in 1862.

Vacuum packing

Vacuum packing stores food in a vacuum environment, usually in an air-tight bag or bottle. The vacuum environment strips bacteria of oxygen needed for survival. Vacuum packing is commonly used for storing nuts to reduce loss of flavour from oxidization. A major drawback to vacuum packaging, at the consumer level, is that vacuum sealing can deform contents and rob certain foods, such as cheese, of its flavour.

Freeze drying

Freeze drying, also known as lyophilisation, is a low temperature dehydration process which involves freezing the product, lowering pressure, then removing the ice by sublimation. This is in contrast to dehydration by most conventional methods that evaporate water using heat. Freeze drying results in a high quality product because of the low temperature used in processing.

Food irradiation

Food irradiation is the process of exposing food and food packaging to ionizing radiation. Ionizing radiation, such as from gamma rays, x-rays or electron beams, is energy that can be transmitted without direct contact to the source of the energy (radiation) capable of freeing electrons from their atomic bonds (ionization) in the targeted food.

Hurdle technology

Hurdle technology is a method of ensuring that pathogens in food products can be eliminated or controlled. This means the food products will be safe for consumption, and their shelf life will be extended.

MULTIPLE CHOICE QUESTIONS

1. Which one of the following condition is not essential to grow maize?
A. High temperature B. Humidity
C. Low temperature D. Rainfall

2. Propagation of ginger is generally done using
A. seed B. stem (rhizome)
C. root D. leaf

3. Which of the following statement is not true for organic manure?
A. It enhances water holding capacity of soil.
B. It has a balance of all plant nutrients.
C. It provides humus to soil.
D. It improves texture of soil.

4. The term used for the process of separation of grains from chaff is:
A. sieving B. threshing
C. winnowing D. hand picking

5. Read the statements given below.
(*i*) Seeds require moisture for germination.
(*ii*) Plants can absorb nutrients mostly in dissolved form.
(*iii*) Irrigation protects crops from both frost and hot air currents.
(*iv*) Irrigation improves soil texture.
Choose the combination of statements which indicate the need to irrigate crops.
A. (*i*) and (*ii*)
B. (*i*), (*ii*), (*iii*)
C. (*i*), (*ii*), (*iii*), (*iv*)
D. (*i*) and (*iii*)

6. Which of the following tools would a farmer use to remove weeds from the field?
A. Hoe B. Plough
C. Axe D. Cultivato

7. Which of the following is not true for fertilisers?
A. They increase the yield.
B. Their excessive use disturbs the balance of nutrients in soil.
C. They are generally used in small quantity.
D. They are environment friendly.

8. Given below are statements about the harmful effects of weeds on crop plants.
(*i*) They interfere in harvesting.
(*ii*) They help crop plants to grow healthily.
(*iii*) They compete with crop plants for water, nutrients, space and light.
(*iv*) They affect plant growth.

Choose the correct combination of statements.
A. (*i*), (*iii*), (*iv*) B. (*iii*) only
C. (*iii*), (*iv*) D. (*i*), (*ii*), (*iii*), (*iv*)

9. The process of loosening and turning of soil is called:
A. irrigation and manuring
B. digging and winnowing
C. tilling and ploughing
D. harvesting and storage

10. The monsoon season in our country is during the months:
A. April to December B. June to September
C. November to March D. January to May

11. The system of irrigation where in water is supplied drop by drop near the roots of plants, is called:
A. pulley system B. drip system
C. sprinkler system D. lever system

12. The process of loosening and turning the soil is called:
A. Broadcasting B. Irrigation
C. Ploughing D. Levelling

13. The organic substance obtained from dead plants and animal wastes is:
A. Manure B. Fertilizer
C. Irrigation D. Agriculture

14. In which of the following methods of irrigation rotating nozzles are used?
A. Moat B. Drip system
C. Chain Pump D. Sprinkler system

15. The management and care of farm animals by humans for profit is known as:
A. Granary B. Animal Husbandry
C. Poultry farm D. Warehouse

16. The process of separating grain from chaff is called:
A. Threshing B. Weeding
C. Sowing D. Winnowing

17. Weeds can be removed by using:
A. Pesticides B. Fungicides
C. Weedicides D. Bactericides

18. The conversion of nitrogen into nitrates is known as:
A. Nitrogen fixation B. Ammonification
C. Nitrate Assimilation D. Nitrogen cycle

19. Animals like horse, donkey that carries load are called:
A. Drought species B. Load carrying Animals
C. Dairy Animals D. Draught Animal

20. Raising of fish in inland waters and coastal waters are called:
A. Pisciculture B. Fishery
C. Fish culture D. Harvesting

21. The process of loosening and turning the soil is called ______.
A. broadcasting B. irrigation
C. tilling D. levelling

22. Which of the following is not a rabi crop?
A. Rice B. Mustard
C. Wheat D. Barley

23. In which of the following method of irrigation rotating nozzles are use:
A. Moat B. Drip System
C. Chain pump D. Sprinkler System

24. Which of the following nutrient replenish the soil after growing legum plants?
A. Nitrogen B. Oxygen
C. Phosphorus D. Potassium

25. The management of rearing animals for food and other products is *k* ______.
A. Granaries B. Animal husbandry
C. Poultry D. Warehouse

26. The process of separating the grain from the chaff is:
A. Threshing B. Weeding
C. Sowing D. Tilling

27. Weeds can be removed by using?
A. Pesticides B. Fungicides
C. Weedicides D. Bactericides

28. Which leaves are used by farmers to protect their crops from weeds insects?
A. Peepal leaves B. Basil leaves
C. Neem leaves D. Mango leaves

29. Who discovered the fungus called Pencillium from which Pencillin is produced?
A. James D. Watson B. Louis Pasteur
C. Alexander Flemming D. Sir Ronald Ross

30. Fermentation is carried out by the yeast cells in the absence of:
A. Nitrogen B. Carbondioxide
C. Hydrogen D. Oxygen

31. Bacteria in the root nodules of the plant and the plant help each other for mutual benefit. This is called:
A. Combination B. Symbiosis
C. Adoption D. Amalgamation

32. Which of the following bacteria live in the root nodules of plants?
A. Azotobacter
B. Pencillium
C. Rhizobium legumino sarum
D. Mycobacterium leprae

33. Which of the following are damaged by the growth of Fungus?
A. Wood B. Clothes
C. Paper D. All the above

34. Antibiotic called penicillin is produced from fungus called:
A. Entamoeba B. Penicillium
C. Plasmodium D. Aspergillus

35. The fungi look like a group of fine threads called:
A. Flagella B. Fronds
C. Hyphae D. Calyx

36. The microorganism Fungi are found in:
A. Water
B. Decaying bodies of plants and animals
C. Rotting fruits, bread, pickles
D. All the above

37. Which of the following is true about Protozoans?
A. Some of the protozoans move with Pseudopodium
B. Some of the protozoans move with Cilia
C. Some of the protozoans do not move
D. All the above

38. The green Algae swims in water with the help of hair like projections called:
A. Diatoms B. Fronds
C. Flagella D. Corolla

39. Genera Science Which of the following are the kinds of the Algae?
A. Brown Algae B. Blue Green Algae
C. Green Algae D. All the above

40. The green Algae in oceans is called:
A. Flagella B. Diatoms
C. Fronds D. Stigma

41. Which of the following are formed by Bacteria when conditions are not suitable?
A. Fronds B. Corolla
C. Spores D. Flagella

42. In which of the following places Bacteria are found?
A. Air B. Water
C. Soil D. All the above

43. Which of the following is true about the bacteria?
A. They do not have nucleus
B. They are unicellular organisms
C. Some bacteria live in group
D. All the above

44. What is the shape of the Bacteria?
A. Rod shape B. Comma shape
C. Round shape D. All the above

45. The thread like structures of the bacteria are called:
A. Fronds B. Flagella
C. Spores D. Ranvier

46. Bacteria were first discovered by Leeuwenhoek in:
A. 1721 B. 1725
C. 1674 D. 1689

47. Which of the following diseases are caused by Viruses?
A. AIDS and Polio
B. Mumps, Common cold
C. Measles and Chicken pox
D. All the above

48. Viruses are transmitted from one organism to another through:
A. Insects
B. Dust particles in air
C. Body fluids of infected person
D. All the above

49. The virus which lives inside the cell is called:
A. Parasite B. Host Cell
C. Host D. Leucocyte

50. The cell in which viruses live is called:
A. Host cell B. Leucocyte
C. Erythrocyte D. Parasite

51. Viruses live inside the living cells of:
A. Animals B. Plants
C. Bacterium D. All the above

52. The study of disease condition is called:
A. Microbiology B. Bacteriology
C. Pathology D. Virology

53. The study of microorganisms is called:
A. Microbiology B. Bacteriology
C. Pathology D. Virology

54. The study of Bacteria is called:
A. Microbiology B. Bacteriology
C. Pathology D. Virology

55. The study of viruses is called:
A. Microbiology B. Bacteriology
C. Pathology D. Virology

56. The microorganisms which can prepare their food are called:
A. Eukaryotes
B. Prokaryotes
C. Autotrophic organisms
D. Heterotrophic organisms

57. The microorganisms that depend on other organisms for food are called
A. Heterotrophic organisms
B. Autotrophic organisms
C. Eukaryotes
D. Prokaryotes

58. The microorganisms which have a nucleus are called:
A. Autotrophic organisms
B. Heterotrophic organisms
C. Eukaryotes
D. Prokaryotes

59. Microorganisms which do not have a nucleus are called:
A. Prokaryotes
B. Eukaryotes
C. Heterotrophic organisms
D. Autotrophic organisms

60. Which of the following is true about microorganisms?
A. The cells contain small amount of protoplasm
B. They have either DNA or RNA
C. They are usually single celled organisms
D. All the above

61. Which of the following are the different types of microorganisms?
A. Viruses and Bacteria B. Protozoans
C. Algae and Fungi D. All the above

62. Antony Van Leeuwenhoek first discovered microorganisms in the year:
A. 1612 B. 1674
C. 1690 D. 1698

63. Amoeba belongs to:
A. Algae B. Fungi
C. Protozoa D. Virus

64. Pasteurization is the process of heating milk:
A. above 121 °C
B. above boiling point
C. below boiling point
D. above 150 °C

65. The process of preserving food by rapid freezing followed by dehydration under vacuum is called
A. Lyophilisation B. Sterilization
C. Cold Dehydration D. Cryopreservation

66. 'Cold sterilization' refers to the preservation of food by:
A. Refrigeration B. Radiation
C. Dehydration D. Lyophilisation

67. All the following techniques are household preservation technique except:
A. Smoking
B. Lyophilisation
C. Dehydration
D. Salting

68. What is the purpose for blanching (immersing food in hot water) vegetables during canning?
A. to soften products to fill better
B. to denature enzymes that change colour, texture
C. to reduce microbial population
D. All of the above

69. Who is regarded as the father of canning?
A. Nicolas Appert
B. Louis Pasteur
C. John Hall
D. Bryan Dokin

70. The method of preventing or reducing pathogens in food products by combining many methods like high temperature during processing, low temperature during storage, increasing the acidity etc is called:
A. Mixed preservation approach
B. High pressure food preservation
C. Hurdle technology
D. Stumbling technology

71. Which of the following methods dehydrates microbial cells by plasmolysis thereby killing them?
A. Sugaring
B. Smoking
C. Heating
D. Pasteurization

72. The reason for food spoilage is:
A. Growth of microorganisms like bacteria, fungus etc or insects
B. Autolysis
C. Oxidation by air that causes rancidity or colour changes
D. All of the above

73. The process of preserving meat by stewing in a covered earthenware jug:
A. burial
B. curing
C. jugging
D. all of these

ANSWERS

1	2	3	4	5	6	7	8	9	10
C	B	B	C	A	A	D	A	C	B
11	**12**	**13**	**14**	**15**	**16**	**17**	**18**	**19**	**20**
B	C	A	D	B	A	C	A	B	A
21	**22**	**23**	**24**	**25**	**26**	**27**	**28**	**29**	**30**
C	A	D	A	B	A	C	C	C	D
31	**32**	**33**	**34**	**35**	**36**	**37**	**38**	**39**	**40**
B	C	D	B	C	D	D	C	D	B
41	**42**	**43**	**44**	**45**	**46**	**47**	**48**	**49**	**50**
C	D	D	D	B	C	D	D	A	A
51	**52**	**53**	**54**	**55**	**56**	**57**	**58**	**59**	**60**
D	C	A	B	D	C	A	C	A	D
61	**62**	**63**	**64**	**65**	**66**	**67**	**68**	**69**	**70**
D	B	C	B	A	B	B	D	A	C
71	**72**	**73**							
A	D	C							

★ ★ ★

2

Synthetic Fibres; Metals and Non-Metals; Coal and Petroleum; Fossil Fuels

CARBON AND ITS COMPOUNDS

Some Important Facts

- Carbon is a non-metallic element, represented by the symbol C.
- All living things contain carbon. All the things that support life, such as proteins, fats, carbohydrates and vitamins contain carbon.
- Carbon had a unique property that it can join with other carbon atoms to form carbon—carbon bonds.
- This can result in the formation of compounds with long chains. This property is called Catenation.
- The name carbon is derived from the Latin word *carbo,* which means *charcoal.*
- Carbon constitutes only 0.03% of the earth crust.
- Carbon is present in coal and petroleum wood, coke, charcoal, saw dust, kerosene, alcohol, petrol, Liquefied Petroleum Gas (LPG), Compressed Natural Gas (CNG) and Gobbar Gas (Biogas).
- Carbon is present in the form of calcium carbonate ($CaCO_3$) in minerals like chalk, marble and limestone.
- Carbon also occurs in the form of CO_2 (0.03%) in the atmosphere.
- The exchange of carbon between the living and the non-living things by the processes of respiration and photosynthesis.
- The process of heating wood or coal in the absence of air is known as **destructive distillation**.
- When an element can exist in more than one structural form in the same physical state is called **allotropy**.
- The different forms of the same element are known as **allotropes.**
- Allotropes of the same element possess the same chemical properties. Carbon, phosphorus, sulphur and oxygen shows the property of allotropy.
- Carbon exists mainly in two allotropic forms:
  — Crystalline form
  — Non-crystalline or amorphous form

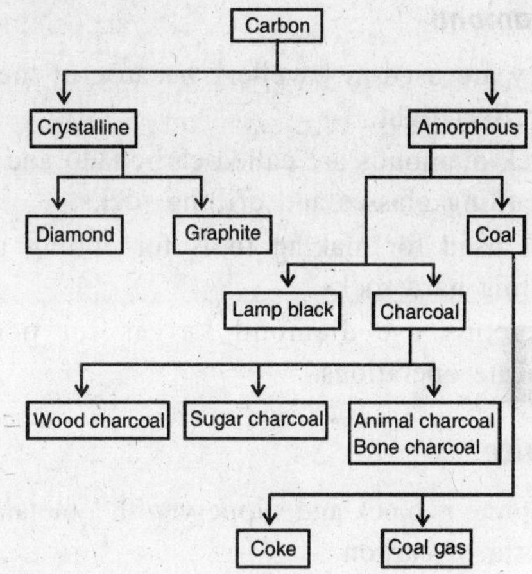

Crystalline forms of Carbon

Diamond and graphite are the two crystalline forms of carbon.

Diamond

It is one of the purest forms of carbon. Diamond crystals found in nature are generally **octahedral** (eight faced). In diamond, each carbon atom is attached to four other carbon atoms by strong forces. This results in a three-dimensional rigid structure which makes the **hardest substance**.

- The density of diamond is 3.5 gm per cubic centimetre (g/cm^3).
- The weight of diamond is expressed in **Carats.**
  1 Carat = 200 mg
- Melting and Boiling point of Diamond are 3550°C & 4827°C respectively.
- It does not conduct electricity.
- Diamonds are found in South Africa, Brazil, Congo, Angola, Tanzania and the USA.
- In India diamonds are found in **Panna** mines of Madhya Pradesh and Wajrakarur in Andhra Pradesh.
- The largest producer of diamonds in the world is South Africa.
- The famous diamonds in the world are **the Kohinoor**, **the Pitt** and **the Hope**.

Properties of Diamond

(i) It occurs naturally in free state and has octahedral shape.
(ii) It is the hardest known substances.
(iii) It has high specific gravity (3.5 g/cm^3)
(iv) It is transparent and has high refractive index (about 2.4).
(v) On heating of 800°C in the presence of oxygen it gives carbon dioxide.

$$\underset{\text{Diamond}}{C + O_2} \xrightarrow{800°C} CO_2$$

Uses of Diamond

(i) They are used in jewellery because of their ability to reflect light.
(ii) Black diamonds are called carbonado and are used in cutting glasses and drilling rocks.
(iii) It is used for making tools for cutting glass and drilling hard rocks.
(iv) Surgeons use diamond knives for performing delicate operations.

Graphite

- Graphite is black and slippery with a metallic lustre, a form of carbon.
- In graphite, each carbon is bonded to only three neighbouring carbon atoms in the same plane forming layers of hexagonal networks separated by larger distances.
- The different layers are held together by weak forces, called Vanderwaals forces.
- The layers can easily slide over one another. This makes graphite lubricating soft and greasy to touch.
- Graphite conducts electricity.
- The density of graphite ranges from 1.9 to 2.3 gram per cubic centimetre (g/cm^3).
- The melting and boiling point of graphite are 3697 °C and 4827 °C respectively.
- It is found in Sri Lanka, Mexico, Austria, North Korea, China and India.

In India, graphite is found in Andhra Pradesh, Bihar, Jammu and Kashmir, Odisha, Rajasthan, Tamil Nadu and Uttar Pradesh.

(i) It is soft and greasy to touch.
(ii) Its specific gravity is 2.3 g/cm^3.
(iii) It is greyish black and opaque.
(iv) It is a good conductor of heat and electricity.
(v) It occurs in hexagonal layers.
(vi) When heated at 700 °C in presence of oxygen it gives CO_2.

$$\underset{\text{graphite}}{C + O_2} \xrightarrow{700°C} CO_2$$

Uses of Graphite

(i) It is used for making pencil lead printer's ink, black point and artificial diamond.
(ii) It is used as dry lubricant for heavy machinery.
(iii) It is used in making crucibles for melting substances.
(iv) It is used as an electrode in batteries and electric furnaces.
(v) It is used in nuclear reactors as moderator to regulate nuclear reactions.
(vi) It is used in making pencil leads.

The graphite can transform into diamond by applying extremely high pressure more than 1 lakh times the atmospheric pressure at the sea level and temperature about 3700°C. High temperature and pressure make the carbon atoms in graphite to rearrange themselves into a diamond structure. About 90% of diamonds used in making tools are made from graphite.

Differences between properties of Diamond and Graphite

Property	*Diamond*	*Graphite*
Hardness	The hardest natural Substance	Very soft
Density	3.5 g/cm^3	2.4 g/cm^3
Tendency to conduct electric current	Bad conductor	Good conductor
Colour	Pure diamond is colourless	Black
Transparency	Transparent	Opaque
Occurrence	Rare	Abundant

Fullerenes

Fullerene is a naturally occurring allotrope of carbon in which 60 carbon atoms are linked to form a stable structure, called fullerenes.

American architect Buekminister Fuller, who designed such domes that had hexagons and pentagons to provide rigid structures with a three dimensional geometry. Fullerenes having C_{70}, C_{90} and C_{120} also have now been discovered. It forms compounds such as $Rb_3\ C_{60}$ are superconductors i.e. they can conduct electricity with no resistance. Fullerenes are the materials of the future.

Amorphous Carbon

Amorphous carbon has physical and chemical properties that may vary depending on its method of manufacture and conditions to which it is later subjected. Amorphous carbon burns relatively easily in air.

The important varieties of amorphous carbon are:

(i) Charcoal
(ii) Coke
(iii) Carbon Black

(i) Charcoal

Wood charcoal is obtained from wood by a process known as **destructive distillation** or **pyrolysis**, by heating it in the absence of air.

The various varieties of charcoal are: wood charcoal, animal charcoal and sugar charcoal.

Wood charcoal is a black porous solid and contains 35% carbon, density 1.5 g/cm^3. It floats over water and is a bad conductor of electricity.

It is used in gas masks. It is used as a fuel and also for filtration of water. It is also used in the manufacture of gun powder.

Animal charcoal or Bone charcoal: Contains about 10% carbon. It is obtained from the bones of animals. It absorbs coloured impurities mixed with water and some other liquids, such as cane sugar syrup. Bone charcoal is extensively used in the manufacturing of sugar to produce the **white crystals**.

Sugar charcoal: The sugar charcoal is obtained from sugar, is a pure form of carbon. It is obtained destructive distillation of sugar.

The following chemical reaction takes place in this process:

$$\text{Sugar} \xrightarrow[-\text{ Water}]{\text{Conc. } H_2SO_4} \text{Carbon.}$$

Sugar charcoal is used as reducing agent in metallurgy.

$ZnO + C \rightarrow Zn + CO$

Zinc oxide Zinc Carbon monoxide

Lampblack

Carbon black is obtained by burning mustard oil, turpentine oil, petroleum and its several products form lampblack, also known as **carbon black**. Carbon black contains about 99% carbon. It is the purest form of carbon.

Uses of Carbon Black

(*i*) In making black printing ink.
(*ii*) As a filler in tyres to increase their durability.
(*iii*) In shoc polish and kajal.

(ii) Coke

Coke is obtained from coal by heating it in the absence of air. This process is called destructive distillation of coal.

Uses of Coke

(*i*) As a fuel
(*ii*) For making gaseous fuels
(*iii*) For reducing iron ore to iron in blast furnace
(*iv*) For making electrodes

Coal

Coal is a mixture of compounds of carbon, hydrogen, oxygen and some free carbon.

Coal is formed at the result of high temperature and pressure on the logs of wood and the remains of animals which got buried under the earth due to earthquakes and volcanoes millions of years ago. The different varieties of coal are obtained as a result of slow chemical conversion of wood into coal called carbonization.

Type of Coal	*% of Carbon*
Peat	11%
Lignite (Soft Coal)	38%
Bituminous Coal	65%
Anthrasite Coal	96%

The Unique Properties of Carbon

Carbon is a non-metal in Group IV of the Periodic Table. It forms covalent compounds. The uniqueness of carbon lies in the versatility of that bonding.

- The carbon atoms can join to each-other to form long chains.
- The carbon atoms in a chain can be linked by single, double or triple covalent bonds.
- Carbon atoms can also arrange themselves in rings.

Compounds of Carbon and Hydrogen

Hydrocarbons are compounds that contain only the elements of hydrogen and carbon.

There are two basic groups of hydrocarbon:

— Aliphatics &
— Aromatics

In aliphatics hydrocarbons, the carbon atoms are usually linked in chains.

Methane is an example of an aliphatic hydrocarbon. Its chemical formula is **CH_4**.

Aromatic hydrocarbons are made up of rings. Toluene is an example of an aromatic hydrocarbon. Its chemical formula is $C_6H_5CH_3$.

Structure formula —

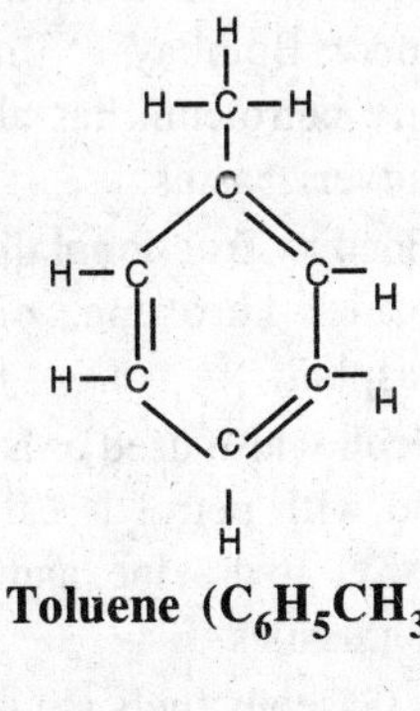

Toluene ($C_6H_5CH_3$)

Methane

Chemical formula: CH_4

Structure formula:

The first and the simplest hydrocarbon is methane. Saturated hydrocarbon, such as methane, ethane, propane, butane etc., are known as **Alkane**.

General formula of Alkane: $\mathbf{C_n H_{2n+2}}$.

n = 1, CH_4 — (Methane)
n = 2, C_2H_6 — (Ethane)
n = 3, C_3H_8 — (Propane)
n = 4, C_4H_{10} — (Butane)
n = 5, C_5H_{12} — (Pentane)
n = 6, C_6H_{14} — (Hexane)
n = 7, C_7H_{16} — (Heptane)

Fuels: A fuel is a substance which burns in air to produce heat energy. The burning of fuel is an exothermic reaction. Carbon and compounds of carbon are used as domestic fuels. The chief property of a fuel is its **Calorific value**—is the amount of heat produced by complete combustion of a unit mass or volume of fuel.

There are three types of fuels:

(*i*) **Solid fuels:** Wood, charcoal, coal and coke are common example of solid fuels.

(*ii*) **Liquid Fuels:** The common liquid fuels are kerosene oil, petrol and diesel. They are all hydrocarbon and are obtained by **fractional distillation of Petroleum.**

Heat Value of Liquid Fuels

Name of Fuel	*Heat value Kj/Kg*
Petrol	47000
Kerosene	45000
Diesel	45000
Spirit (ethanol)	28000

The petroleum is dark oily liquid with unpleasant odour. It is insoluble in water and floats on it. Petroleum is usually formed in sedimentary rocks.

In India, petroleum is found in the states of Assam, Gujarat, and also near Bombay— Bombay High in the Arabian sea. Recently petroleum has also been discovered in Godavari and Cauveri basins.

Petroleum is refined by **fractional distillation** producing the fractions gasoline, kerosene, diesel oil, fuel oil, lubricating oil and asphalt.

Ethanol is an alcohol also used as a fuel in Spirit lamps. Alcohol when mixed with petrol is called **power alcohol**. A mixture of dimethyl hydrazine and nitric acid is now used in rockets and missiles.

Gaseous Fuels: Gaseous fuels are used for domestic as well as industrial heating. Natural gas, LPG, producer gas, water gas and coal gas.

The calorific value of a fuel is measured in a **Calorimeter**.

- **Biogas** is the mixture of CH_4, H_2, CO and H_2S.
- **Natural gas** mainly contains methane (CH_4) and small proportion of ethane (C_2H_6).
- The main components of **producer gas** are carbon monoxide (CO), hydrogen (H_2), nitrogen (N_2) and carbon dioxide (CO_2).
- The main components of **coal gas** are hydrogen (H_2), methane (CH_4), carbon monoxide (CO).
- The main components of **water gas** are carbon monoxide (CO), Hydrogen (H_2), carbon dioxide (CO_2) and Nitrogen (N_2).
- The main components of LPG (Liquified Petroleum Gas) are ethane (C_2H_6), propane (C_3H_8) and butane (C_4H_{10}). It has no own odour, a very small quantity of strong smelling ethyl mercaptan (C_2H_5SH) is added to it.
- The fuels which are used in rockets are called **propellants.** They are:

— Liquid hydrogen	— Synthetic rubber
— Liquid Ammonia	— Alcohol
— Hydrazine	— Kerosene oil
— Paraffin wax and	— Cellulose.

Points to Remember

- Carbon forms the largest number of compounds and about 85% of known compounds contain carbon.
- Carbon has a unique property that it can join with other carbon atoms to form carbon—carbon bonds. This property is called **Catenation.**
- Coal is a mixture of compounds of carbon hydrogen, oxygen and some free carbon.
- Allotropy is the property by virtue of which an element exists in more than one form and each form has different physical properties but identical chemical properties.
- Carbon occurs naturally in the form of graphite and diamond. Graphite and diamond are allotropes of carbon.
- Charcoal, coke and carbon black are amorphous forms of carbon.
- Carbon on burning in an insufficient supply of oxygen, forms carbon monoxide which is a poisonous gas.
- Carbon dioxide is an important constituent of air (0.03%). Carbon dioxide reacts with metal oxide to form metal carbonates.
- Diamond is very hard solid at room temperature with a melting point of 3550°C and boiling point of 4827°C.
- Diamond has a rigid structure. In graphite the carbon atoms are arranged in layers. These layers are loosely joined to each other i.e. the layer of carbon atoms in graphite can slip over each other.
- Graphite is soft, slippery solid at room temperature with a melting point of 3697°C and boiling point 4827°C.

- **Fullerenes** are one of the allotropic forms of carbon. They may have 60, 70, 90, or 120 carbon atoms in their molecules. Fullerenes are the materials of the future.
- In the laboratory, carbon dioxide is prepared by the action of dilute HCl on lime stone or marble chips.
- Hydrocarbon are the organic compounds which are made up of only two elements—hydrogen and carbon.
- There are two basic groups of hydrocarbons—aliphatics and aromatics.
- Carbon dioxide is an important greenhouse gas. It is useful for us in many ways.
- Carbon dioxide turns freshly prepared lime water into milky.
- Methane (CH_4) is the simplest hydrocarbon in which each carbon atom is attached to four hydrogen atoms.
- Methane is found inside coal mine and in marshy lands.
- Methane is a very useful gas. It is used as a clean fuel for heating. Compressed Natural Gas (CNG) consists mainly of methane. It is an important domestic and industrial fuel.
- **Propane** and **Butane** can be liquified under pressure, hence they are supplied in cylinder (LPG — Liquid Petroleum Gas) for domestic use.
- Petroleum and coal are fossil fuels.
- Anthracite is the oldest form of fossil coal having 95% carbon.
- The main solid fuels are wood, charcoal and coal.
- The main liquid fuels are kerosene, petrol and diesel.
- The main gaseous fuels are natural gas, biogas and bottled gas (LPG).
- Biogas is produce by animal faces and contains mainly methane.
- Combustion is a process of oxidation.
- Very rapid combustion occurs in an explosion.
- Charcoal is obtained by heating wood in the absence of air.
- Coke is obtained by the destructive distillation of coal.
- Bituminous coal is a solid fossil fuel of plant origin.
- Distillation is the process of converting liquid into vapour and then changing again to liquid.
- C^{12} (Carbon - 12) is used as a standard for atomic weights.
- C^{14} shows radioactive characters.
- Carbon shows a covalency of four.
- Coke and Coaltar are products of destructive distillation of coal.
- Fractional distillation of Coaltar produces Asphalt (Pitch) and **Creosote** a wood preservative.
- Synthetic graphite is produced by heating anthracite to 2500°C in an electrical furnance in the absence of air.
- Dry ice (Solid Carbon dioxide) is often used to create **artificial rain** and used for **refrigeration**. On warming Dry ice vaporises directly into a gas. It passes from the solid state straight to gaseous state without going through liquid state, hence it is called **Dry ice**.

METALS AND NON-METALS

Some Important Facts

Elements are pure form of substances. Chemical elements can be classified into: • metals, • metalloids and • non-metal

On the basis of their physical and chemical properties.

Out of the 92 naturally occurring elements, about 70 are metals and 22 are non-metals. Some example of metals are — iron, copper, aluminium, zinc, sodium, gold, sulphur, tungsten, cadmium, nickel, uranium and mercury etc.

Examples of non-metals are — sulphur, iodine, bromine, chlorine, helium, oxygen, carbon, fluorine etc. Metalloids have some chemical and physical properties of metals and other properties of non-metals.

Example of metalloids are — silicon, germanium, arsenic which are also semiconductors.

Semiconductor: is an element that does not conduct electricity as efficiently as metal, but does conduct slightly better than a non-metal.

Ore: An ore is a naturally occuring mineral from which one or more metals can be profitably extracted.

Metallurgy: is the science of extracting metals from their ores and purifying them. Metallurgical processes may contain three main operations:

Concentration of Ore: It is the primary treatment of the ore in which impurities are removed. The ore gets concentrated in this process.

Reduction: The metal compound is reduced to get free metal.

Refining of metal: The metal is purified. After refining, some substances are added to give the desired properties to the final product.

Physical Properties of Metals

- Metals have a shiny appearance.
- Metals are generally hard.
- Metals are malleable.
- Metals are ductile.
- Metals are good conductors of heat.
- Metals are good conductors of electricity.

- Metals in general have high melting points.
- Metals are sonorous.
- Metals have high densities.

Classification of Metals

Metals

Ferrous | Non-Ferrous

(*i*) Ferrous metals — Iron.

(*ii*) Non-ferrous metals are further divided into:

(*i*) Heavy metals — Pb, Hg, Cu, Ag, Au, Pt.

(*ii*) Light metals — Na, K, Mg, Al.

(*iii*) Noble metals — Au, Ag, Pt.

(*iv*) Rare metals — Li, Be, Sr.

(*v*) Radioactive metals — Ra, U, Th.

(*vi*) Protective metals — Cr, Ni, Zn, Sn.

Chemical Properties of Metals

(1) Reaction of metals with oxygen

Metals combine with oxygen to form basic oxides:

$2\,Mg + O_2 \rightarrow 2\,MgO$

$MgO + H_2O \rightarrow Mg(OH)_2$ (Basic oxide)

$Mg(OH)_2$ turns red litmus blue *i.e.*, $Mg(OH)_2$ is basic oxide.

$Zn + O_2 \rightarrow 2\,ZnO$

Zinc oxide (Basic oxide)

$4\,Na + O_2 \rightarrow 2\,Na_2O$ (burn with yellow light)

$2\,Cu + O_2 \rightarrow 2\,CuO$ (copper gets blackened but does not burn)

$S + O_2 \rightarrow SO_2$

Sulphur dioxide (Acidic oxide)

$SO_2 + H_2O \rightarrow H_2SO_3$ (Sulphurous acid)

(2) Reaction of metals with water

Metals react with water to form metal hdyroxide and evolve hydrogen gas:

$2\,Na + 2H_2O \rightarrow 2\,NaOH + H_2\uparrow$

This reaction takes places very vigorously so, sodium metal is stored in kerosene oil.

$Mg + H_2O \rightarrow MgO + H_2\uparrow$

$MgO + H_2O \rightarrow Mg(OH)_2$

Magnesium hydroxide

Magnesium oxide when dissolved in water forms a base.

$Zn + H_2O \rightarrow ZnO + H_2\uparrow$

$3\,Fe + 4\,H_2O \rightarrow Fe_3O_4 + 4\,H_2\uparrow$

Ag (silver), Au (Gold), Cu (Copper) do not react even with stream.

(3) Reaction of metals with dilute acids

Metals react with dilute acids to form metal salt and liberate hydrogen gas.

$Na + 2HCl \rightarrow 2NaCl + H_2\uparrow$

dilute Sodium chloride

$Mg + 2HCl \rightarrow MgCl_2 + H_2\uparrow$

dilute Magnesium chloride

$Zn + 2HCl \rightarrow ZnCl_2 + H_2\uparrow$

dilute Hydrogen gas

$Fe + 2HCl \rightarrow FeCl_2 + H_2\uparrow$

dilute Ferrous chloride

(4) Reaction of metals with Salt solutions

More reactive metal displaces a less reactive metal from its salt solution.

$Zn + CuSO_4 \rightarrow Cu + ZnSO_4$

Copper Sulphate Zinc Sulphate

Zinc displaces copper from copper sulphate solution.

$Fe + CuSO_4 \rightarrow Cu + FeSO_4$

Ferrous Sulphate

Iron metal displaces copper from copper sulphate solution.

$Mg + CuSO_4 \rightarrow Cu + MgSO_4$

Magnesium Sulphate

$2\,AgNO_3 + Cu \rightarrow Cu(NO_3)_2 + 2\,Ag$

(Silver nitrate) Copper nitrate Silver metal

Reactivity Series: The arrangement of metals in the order of decreasing reactivities is called reactivity series of metals. The most reactive metal is at the top and the least reactive metal is at the bottom of the series.

Reactivity Series of Metals

Metals		*Reactivity*
K	Potassium	Most reactive metal
Na	Sodium	
Ba	Barium	
Ca	Calcium	
Mg	Magnesium	
Al	Aluminium	
Zn	Zinc	
Cr	Chromium	
Fe	Iron	
Cd	Cadmium	
Co	Cobalt	
Ni	Nickel	
Sn	Tin	Least reactive metals
Pb	Lead	
H	Hydrogen —	[Hydrogen is a non metal although placed in the reactivity series of metal due to its nature of loses electron and form positive (H^+) ions.]
Cu	Copper	
Hg	Mercury	
Ag	Silver	
Au	Gold	
Pt	Platinum	Least reactive metal.

Physical Properties of Non-Metals

(*i*) Non-metals are brittle in nature, e.g. sulphur and phosphorus.
(*ii*) Non-metals are non-ductile.
(*iii*) Non-metals are bad conductor of heat and electricity except Graphite.
(*iv*) Non-metals are non-lustrous and cannot be polished.
(*v*) Non-metals are not strong and have low tensile strength.
(*vi*) Non-metals may be solid, liquid or gases at the room temperature.
Solid non-metals: Carbon, Sulphur, Phosphorus
Liquid non-metals: Bromine
Gaseous non-metals: hydrogen, nitrogen, oxygen, fluorine, chlorine, helium, argon, neon, xenon, krypton and radon.
(*vii*) Non-metals are soft *e.g.*, sulphur and phosphorus. Except Diamond.
(*viii*) Non-metals have low densities.
(*ix*) Non-metals are non-sonorous.

Chemical Properties of Non-Metals

(1) **Non-metals are electronegative in nature.**
(2) **Reaction of non-metals with oxygen.**
Non-metals form active or neutral oxides.

$$C + O_2 \rightarrow CO_2$$
$$S + O_2 \rightarrow SO_2$$
$$4P + 5O_2 \rightarrow 2P_2O_5$$
$$2H_2 + O_2 \rightarrow 2H_2O$$
$$N_2 + 2O_2 \rightarrow 2NO_2$$
$$2C + O_2 \rightarrow 2CO$$

(3) **Reaction of non-metals with water**
Non-metals do not react with water or steam to evolve hydrogen gas. It is due to the reason that non-metals cannot give electrons to hydrogen ions of water.
(4) Non-metals do not react with dilute acids.
(5) A more reactive non-metal displaces a less reactive non-metal from its salt solution.

$$2NaBr(aq) + Cl_2(g) \rightarrow 2\ NaCl(aq) + \underset{\text{Bromine}}{Br_2(l)}$$

Occurrence of Metals

Metals occur either in the native or free state or in the combined state. This is mainly due to the reason that different metals posses different chemical reactivities.

(*i*) **Free or nature state:** Metals which do not react with moisture, oxygen and CO_2 of air occur in the nature state. e.g. gold, platinum, copper, silver and mercury can occur in free as well as or combined states.

(*ii*) **Combined state:** These metals react with moisture, oxygen and CO_2 of the air and occur in the combined state in the form of compounds known as minerals.

Important Compounds of Metals (Ores)

Ore	*Formula*	*Ore of Metal*
1. Oxides Ore		
Zincite	ZnO	Zinc
Haematite	Fe_2O_3	Iron
Magnetite	Fe_3O_4	Iron
Corundum	Al_2O_3	Aluminium
Cuprite	Cu_2O	Copper
Calcia	CaO	Calcium
Cassiterite	SnO_2	Tin
Pyrolusite	MnO_2	Manganese
2. Hydrated oxides		
Bauxite	$Al_2O_3.\ 2H_2O$	Aluminium
Limonite	$2\ Fe_2O_3.\ 3H_2O$	Iron
3. Carbonates		
Calamine	$ZnCO_3$	Zinc
Siderite	$FeCO_3$	Iron
Malachite	$CuCO_3.\ Cu(OH)_2$	Copper
Marble or Lime Stone	$CaCO_3.$	Calcium
Azurite	$2\ CuCO_3.\ Cu(OH)_2$	Copper
Dolomite	$CaCO_3.\ MgCO_3$	Calcium, Magnesium
Magnesite	$MgCO_3$	Magnesium
Trona, Natron	$NaCO_3$	Sodium
4. Sulphides		
Zinc blends	ZnS	Zinc
Iron Pyrites	FeS_2	Iron
Copper Pyrites	$Cu_2S,\ Fe_2S$	Copper
Galena	PbS	Lead
Connabar	HgS	Mercury
Argentite	Ag_2S	Silver
Copper glance	Cu_2S	Copper
Greenockite	CdS	Cadmium
Pyragyrite	Ag_3SbS_3	Silver
5. Sulphates		
Gypsum	$CaSO_4.\ 2H_2O$	Calcium
Epsom salt	$MgSO_4.\ 7H_2O$	Magnesium
Anglesite	$PbSO_4$	Lead
Barytes	$BaSO_4$	Barium
Alunite	$K_2SO_4\ Al_2(SO_4)_3\ 4Al\ (OH)_3.$	Aluminium
Schonite	$K_2SO_4.\ MgSO_4.6H_2O$	Potassium

Ore	Formula	Ore of Metal
6. Chlorides/Fluorides		
Cryolite	AlF_3. 3NaF	Aluminium
Common Salt or Rock Salt	NaCl	
Fluorspar	CaF_2	Calcium
Carnallite	KCl $MgCl_2$. $6H_2O$	Potassium and magnesium
Horn Silver	AgCl	Silver
Sylvine	KCl	Potassium
7. Nitrates		
Chili Saltpetre	Na NO_3	Sodium
Nitre	KNO_3	Potassium
Borax	Na_2 B_4O_7 $10H_2O$	Boron.

Occurrence of Inert gas

Helium, Neon, Argon, Krypton, Radon and Xenon are found in the atmosphere. Helium is the second lightest gas after hydrogen and is found with natural gas deposits. All stars contain Helium. During the nuclear reaction hydrogen in stars are changed into helium and give enormous amount of energy. About 1 per cent air is Argon. Radon is found in associated radium bearing minerals, while Neon occurs in small amounts in the air. All of these inert gases are colourless and odourless.

Occurrence of the Halogens

The elements like fluorine, chlorine, bromine and iodine are commonly known as halogens. The halogens are so active, none of then is found free in Nature.

Element	Occurrence
Fluorine	The mineral fluorspar CaF_2 The mineral cryolite Na_3AlF_6
Chloride	In Sea water Rock Salt (NaCl), Salt beds of KCl, $MgCl_2$ and $CaCl_2$. In the human gastric juices as HCl (0.05%).
Bromine	As bromide ion (Br^-) in sea water (0.008%). As NaBr in salt beds.
Iodine	As iodine ion (I^-) in sea water (0.000004%). As sodium iodate $NaIO_3$

Fluorosis

If the concentration of fluorine increases to 3 parts per million in the drinking water than it leads to a diseases called **fluorosis** in which teeth became mottled with brown spots.

Noble Metals

The group is made up of the metals like gold, silver, platinum, iridium, rhodium, osmium, ruthenium and palladium. They are called noble because they are very unreactive.

Carats

The proportion of gold in an alloy is measured in carats. Pure gold is 24 carat gold. *e.g.* 20 carat gold contain 83.33 per cent of pure gold.

The weight of the diamond is measured in carats. One carat weight is 200 mg. This is not the same carat that is used in purity of gold.

Alloys

An alloy is generally a homogenous mixture of two or more metals prepared by mixing the components in the molten state. When one of the metals is mercury the alloy is called as **amalgam**.

Properties of Alloys

—Alloys are harder than the metals from which they are made.

—They are also more resistance to corrosion.

—Their melting point usually lower than those of the constituent metals.

Some important Alloys

Name of Alloys	Composition
Amalgam	Hg + any other metal
Alpax	Al + Si
Alnico	12% Al, 20% Ni and 5% Co
Bell metal	80% Cu, 20% Sn
Brass	Cu — 60 - 80% Zn — 40 - 20%
Bronze	Cu — 75% to 90% Sn — 25% to 10%
Constantan	60% Cu, 40% Ni
Common Solder	50% Pb, 50% Sn
Coinage Alloy	75% Cu and 25% Ni
Delto metal	Cu + Zn + Fe
Duralumin	Al — 94.4% Cu — 4% Mg — 1.6%
Dutch metal	Cu — 80% Zn — 20%
Fine Solder	Sn — 67% Pb — 33%
German Silver	Cu — 60% Zn — 25% Ni — 15%

Name of Alloys	Composition
Gun metal	Cu — 86%
	Sn — 10%
	Zn — 4%
Invar	Fe — 63%
	Ni — 36%
	C — 1%
Maganin	Cu — 84%
	Mn — 12%
	Ni — 4%
Magnelium	Al — 85% to 99%
	Mg — 15% to 1%
Monel metal	Cu — 30%
	Ni — 70%
Munz metal	Cu — 60%
	Zn — 40%
Newtons metal	Sn + Pb + Bi
Nichrome	Cr (15%) + Ni (60%) + Fe (25%)
Pewter	Sn — 75%
	Pb — 25%
Phosphor Bronze	Cu — 85%
	Sn — 13%
	P — 2%
Plumber's Solder	Pb — 70%
	Sn — 30%
Rolled Gold	Cu — 90%
	Al — 10%
Stainless Steel	Fe — 73%
	Cr — 18%
	Ni — 8%
	C — 1%

Corrosion and its prevention

Corrosion is the action of atmospheric oxygen, also of other gas, on metals to form a layer of oxides or other compounds. Dry corrosion involves atmospheric gases only. Wet corrosion involves water in addition to atmospheric gases. It results in loss of metals and the metal cannot be used further as it loses its strength.

The presence of air and water are necessary for corrosion to occur. Corrosion in case of iron is called **rusting**. Rusting is a slow oxidation process. The formula of rust is Fe_2O_3.

$2Fe(OH)_2$. (hydrated ferric oxide).

$$4Fe + 3O_2 + 3H_2O \rightarrow Fe_2O_3 + 2\,Fe(OH)_3$$

Iron ↑Moist air↑ ↑ Rust ↑

Aluminium is more reactive than iron and starts corroding immediately as it comes in contact with moist air.

$$4Al + 3O_2 \rightarrow 2Al_2O_3$$

Aluminium oxide (protective coating)

A thin layer of aluminium oxide is deposited on aluminium articles by passing electric current. This method is called *anodising* and it protects aluminium from corrosion.

- Copper domes deposit a green coating on their surfaces when copper combines with water and carbon dioxide and makes coating of basic copper carbonate.
  $$2Cu + CO_2 + H_2O + O_2 \rightarrow CuCO_3.\,Cu(OH)_2$$
  green mass of basic copper carbonate.
- Silver farnishes because it readily combines with hydrogen sulphide present in air. It forms a black coating of silver sulphide.
  $$2Ag + H_2S \rightarrow Ag_2S + H_2\uparrow$$
  Silver sulphide
  Titanium metal is highly resistant to corrosion.

Method of Preventing Corrosion

- By using oil and grease.
- By using paints.
- **Galvanisation:** It is a process of coating iron with zinc to prevent rusting. Zinc forms a protective layer of zinc oxide on exposure to air. A thin layer of zinc on the surface of iron protects iron from rusting. This process is called **galvanisation**.
- **Electroplating:** Iron and steel are protected from corrosion by coating them with a layer of tin or chromium metals which are resistant to corrosion.

Alloying: Some metals when alloyed with other metals become more resistant to corrosion. e.g. Alloy of Iron with chromium and nickel forms stainless steel, which is resistant to corrosion and does not rust at all.

Points to Remember

- Elements can be classified into metals and non-metals on the basis of their physical and chemical properties.
- Metals are generally hard, malleable ductile, lustrous and sonorous.
- Metals are good conductors of heat and electricity.
- Some metals as well as non-metals occur in a free state.
- Metals on combustion produce basic oxides.
- Non-metals on combustion produce acidic oxides.
- Non-metals exhibit a dull lustre. They are poor conductors of heat and electricity and are brittle.
- A semiconductor is an element that does not conduct electricity as efficiently as metal, but does conduct slightly better than a non-metal.
- Some metals react with acids and replace the hydrogen gas from the acids. Gold, copper and silver are not affected by dilute acids like HCl.
- Metals occur either in the native or free state or in the combined state. This is mainly due to the reason that different metals posses different chemical reactivities.

- The noble metals are a group of metallic elements. The group is made up of the metal like gold, silver, platinum, iridium, rhodium, osmium, ruthenium and palladium.
- The weight of the diamond is measured in carats. One carat weight is 200 mg.
- An alloy is generally a homogenous mixture of two or more metals prepared by mixing the components in the molten state.
- Eating away of metals by oxygen, water, acids or other chemicals is called corrosion.
- Corrosion can be prevented by oiling, painting, galvanizing, electroplating and anodizing.
- Some active metals like sodium react with water.
- Metals like aluminium, magnesium react with acids.
- Non-metals like sulphur reacts with concentrated acids.
- A metal higher in the activity series replaces metals that are lower in the activity series.
- Alloys are the homogenous mixtures of metals and non-metals.
- Rocks contain minerals.
- The average thickness of earth's crust is about 35 Km.
- The most common sedimentary rock is sandstone.
- Fossils are mostly formed in sedimentary rocks.
- Minerals show colour due to the presence of impurities.
- The red colour of ruby is due to the presence of chromium oxide.
- German Scientist Mohs devised the scale of hardness.
- Talc is softest mineral with hardness of 1, and diamond is hardest mineral with hardness of 10.
- Specific gravity of gold is 19.3 and of copper is 8.9.
- Ruby is also known as **red corrundum.**
- Titanium is said to be metal of future.
- Uraninite (pitch blende) is the ore of Uranium and found in Jaduguda (Jharkhand).
- Iron is mainly extracted from haematite.
- Copper is mainly extracted from copper pyrite.
- All metals are solid except mercury, which is **liquid**.
- Metals have mostly high melting point.
- Iodine is denser than many metals.
- Sodium is very soft and can be cut by a knife.
- Copper is non-magnetic while iron is magnetic.
- Most metals react with acids to form salts and hydrogen.
- Iron, magnesium and zinc are more reactive than copper.
- Air and water are necessary for corrosion to take place.

CHEMICAL REACTIONS AND EQUATIONS

Some Important Facts

Chemical Reaction is a process in which some known substances are changed into new substance or new substances. The starting substances are called **reactants**. The new substances formed are called products.

e.g.

Hydrogen +	Oxygen →	Water	
(reactant)	(reactant)	(product)	
Zinc +	sulphuric →	Zinc	+ Hydrogen
(reactant)	acid (reactant)	sulphate (product)	(product)

Chemical Equation: A shorthand notation of describing an actual chemical reaction in terms of the symbols and formula along with the number of atoms and molecules of the reactant and products is called **chemical equation.**

e.g., $CH_4(g) + 2O_2(g) \rightarrow CO_2(g) + 2H_2O\ (l)$ + Heat

Balanced chemical equation: A chemical equation is said to be balanced when the number of atoms of each element on the reactant side is equal to the number of atoms of corresponding element on the product side,

e.g.,

$$CH_4(g) + 2O_2(g) \rightarrow CO_2(g) + 2H_2O(l) + \text{Heat}$$

Reactant Side		*Product Side*	
Element	***No. of atoms***	***Element***	***No. of atoms***
C	1	C	1
H	4	H	4
O	4	O	4

It is clear that the number of each element on the reactant side is equal to the number of atoms of the corresponding element on the product side. Therefore the chemical equation is balanced.

Rules to write a balanced chemical equation for a reaction

- It should represent an actual chemical change.
- The correct symbols and formula of reactants are written on left hand side. If there are two or more reactants then plus (+) sign is written between them.
- An arrow directing toward right (→) is written after the formulae of reactants.
- The number of atoms of different elements on the two sides of the equation must be equal.
- All the substances concerned could be expressed as molecules.

Information conveyed by chemical equation

- The formulae, symbol, names and physical states of the reactants and products.
- The relative number of atoms and molecules of the reactants that take part in the reaction.
- The relative number of atoms and molecules of the products formed in the reaction.
- The ratio of the moles of the reactants and products.
- The ratio of the masses of the reactants and product.
- The ratio of the volumes of the gaseous reactants and products.
- The energy change in the reaction.

Limitations of a chemical equations

It gives us no information about the followings:

- The physical state of the reactants
- The concentration of the reactants
- The time taken for the reaction to complete
- The rate at which the reaction proceeds
- The conditions necessary to start and carry on the reaction. What is the temperature needed to start and continue the reaction?
- Is the reaction exothermic or endothermic?

Some Chemical reactions and balanced chemical equations

(*i*) Phosphorous burns in oxygen to give phosphorus pentoxide.

$P_4(s) + 5O_2(g) \rightarrow 2P_2O_5$
Phosphorus pentoxide

(*ii*) Barium chloride reacts with zinc sulphate to give zinc chloride and barium sulphate.

$BaCl_2(aq) + ZnSO_4(aq) \rightarrow BaSO_4(s) + ZnCl_2(aq)$

(*iii*) Zinc metal reacts with hydrochloric acid to give hydrogen gas and an aqueous solution of zinc chloride:

$Zn(s) + 2HCl(aq) \rightarrow H_2(g) + ZnCl_2(aq)$
Zinc Hydrochloric acid Hydrogen Zinc chloride

(*iv*) Solid mercury (II) oxide is heated to give liquid mercury and oxygen gas.

$2HgO(s) \rightarrow 2Hg(l) + O_2(g)$

(*v*) Carbon disulphide burns in air to give carbon dioxide and sulphur dioxide

$CS_2(l) + 3O_2(g) \rightarrow CO_2(g) + 2SO_2(g)$

(*vi*) Hydrogen gas combines with nitrogen gas to give ammonia gas.

$3H_2(g) + N_2(g) \rightarrow 2NH_3(g)$
Ammonia

(*vii*) Sodium metal reacts with water to give sodium hydroxide and hydrogen gas.

$2Na(s) + 2H_2O(l) \rightarrow 2NaOH(aq) + H_2(g)$

(*viii*) Hydrogen sulphide gas burns in air to give water and sulphur dioxide

$2H_2S(g) + 3O_2(g) \rightarrow 2H_2O(l) + 2SO_2(g)$

(*ix*) Phosphorus burns in chlorine to give phosphorus pentachloride.

$P_4(s) + 10Cl_2(g) \rightarrow 4PCl_5(g)$

(*x*) Aluminium metal replaces iron from oxide (Fe_2O_3) giving aluminium hydroxide and iron.

$Fe_2O_3 + 2Al \rightarrow Al_2O_3 + 2Fe$

(*xi*) Aqueous solutions of sulphuric acid and sodium hydroxide react to give sodium sulphate and water.

$H_2SO_4\ (aq) + 2NaOH(aq) \rightarrow Na_2SO_4(aq) + H_2O$

Types of Chemical Equations

Based on the change the chemical reactions can be categorised as shown in the following chart:

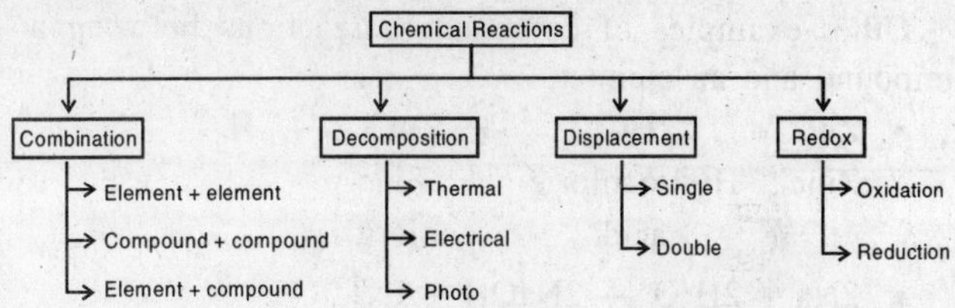

Combination Reactions

Combination reactions are those reactions in which two types of pure substances react and form a new single substances.

$$A + B \rightarrow AB.$$

Types of combination reactions

There are three types of combination reactions:

(*i*) Both A and B are two elements.
(*ii*) Both A and B are two compounds.
(*iii*) A is an element and B is a compound.

(I) Combination reaction between two elements

When hydrogen and oxygen combine water is formed.

$$2H_2(g) + O_2(g) \rightarrow 2H_2O(l)$$

Mercury and oxygen together form oxide of mercury.

$$2Hg + O_2 \rightarrow 2HgO$$

Mercury oxide

When magnesium is burnt it combines directly with the oxygen of the air to form magnesium oxide.

$$2Mg(s) + O_2(g) \rightarrow 2MgO(s)$$

(II) Combination reaction between two Compounds

The reaction between two compounds to form a third compound is also combination reaction.

When ammonia gas and hydrogen chloride gas combine to form solid ammonium chloride is an example of combination reaction between two compounds.

$$NH_3(g) + HCl(g) \rightarrow NH_4Cl(s).$$

Some other examples of combination reaction between two compounds as below:

$$CaCO_3(s) + 2HCl \rightarrow CaCl_2 + H_2O + CO_2\uparrow$$
Calcium chloride

$$MgO(s) + H_2O(l) \rightarrow Mg(OH_2)$$
Magnesium hydroxide

$$CO_2(g) + H_2O(l) \rightarrow H_2CO_3$$
Carbonic acid

(III) Combination reactions between a Compound and an element

Burning of carbon monoxide gas (CO) in oxygen gas (O_2) to form carbon dioxide gas (CO_2) is an example of combination reaction between a compound (CO) and an element (O_2).

$$2CO(g) + O_2(g) \rightarrow 2CO_2(g)$$

Other examples of combination reactions between a compound and an element

- $Zn + 2HCl \rightarrow ZnCl_2 + H_2\uparrow$
  Zinc, Hydrochloric acid, Zinc chloride
- $2Na + 2H_2O \rightarrow 2NaOH + H_2\uparrow$
- $Fe + H_2SO_4 \rightarrow FeSO_4 + H_2\uparrow$
- $Zn + 2NaOH \rightarrow Na_2ZNO_2 + H_2\uparrow$

Decomposition Reactions

Such reactions where two or more products are obtained from a single reactant are decomposition reactions.

e.g. In presence of manganese dioxide, hydrogen peroxide decomposes into water and oxygen

$$2H_2O_2 \rightarrow 2H_2O + O_2$$

$$NH_4\,NO_3(s) \rightarrow N_2O(g) + 2H_2O$$
Ammonium nitrate → Nitrous oxide + Water

$$CaCO_3 \xrightarrow{heat} CaO + CO_2\uparrow$$
Calcium carbonate → Calcium oxide + Carbon dioxide

Decomposition reactions are classified as follows:

— Thermal decomposition (caused by heat)
— Electric decomposition (caused by electricity)
— Photo decomposition (caused by light)

Examples of thermal decompositions

Mercury (II) oxide decomposes on heating to form mercury and oxygen.

$$2HgO(s) \xrightarrow{heat} 2Hg(l) + O_2(g)$$

- When potassium chlorate is heated it gives potassium chloride and oxygen gas.

$$2KClO_3 \xrightarrow{Heat} 2KCl(s) + 3O_2(g)$$

- $CaCO_3 \xrightarrow{Heat} CaO(s) + CO_2(g)$
  Calcium carbonate → Calcium oxide + Carbon oxide

Electric decomposition reaction

On passing electricity through acidified water it decomposed into hydrogen and oxygen.

$$2H_2O \xrightarrow[Current]{Electric} 2H_2(g) + O_2(g)$$
Water → Hydrogen + Oxygen

Photo decomposition reaction

In the presence of sunlight hypochlorous acid decomposes to give back oxygen and hydrochloric acid.

$$2HClO(aq) \xrightarrow{Sunlight} 2HCl(aq) + O_2(g)$$
Hypochlorous acid → Hydrochloric acid + Oxygen

Displacement Reactions

In this reaction one substance has replaced the other substance in a compound is called displacement reactions.

Displacement reactions are of two types:

(*i*) Single displacement reactions
(*ii*) Double displacement reactions

Single Displacement Reactions: When an iron nail is dipped in a copper sulphate solution, it is coated with copper.

$$Fe + CuSO_4 \rightarrow FeSO_4 + Cu.$$

Fe is more reactive metal than Cu.

When a piece of zinc metal is immersed in mercury II nitrate solution it coated with mercury.

$$Zn + Hg(NO_3)_2 \rightarrow Zn(NO_3)_2 + Hg$$

When zinc metal is dipped in a solution of copper sulphate, zinc reduces copper from copper sulphate.

$$Zn + CuSO_4 \rightarrow ZnSO_4 + Cu$$

When zinc reacts with sulphuric acid, hydrogen gas is liberated and zinc sulphate is formed.

$$Zn(s) + H_2SO_4(aq) \rightarrow ZnSO_4 + H_2(g)$$
Zinc sulphate

Zn is more reactive than hydrogen.

Double Displacement Reactions

Double displacement reactions are those reactions in which two compounds exchange ions to form two new compounds.

$$AB + CD \rightarrow AD + CB.$$

Here, A and C are cations of the two compounds, while B and D are their anions. The new compounds are AD and CB.

Types of double displacement reactions

— formation of precipitate
— evolution of gas
— change of colour

Double Displacement reaction with the formation of precipitate

When a solution of sodium chloride is mixed with a solution of silver nitrate a white precipitate of silver chloride is formed.

$NaCl$	+ $AgNO_3$	→ $AgCl$	+ $NaNO_3$
Sodium Chloride	Silver Nitrate	Silver chloride	Sodium Nitrate

$BaCl_2(aq)$	+ $Na_2SO_4(aq)$	→ $BaSO_4$	+ $2NaCl$
Barium Chloride	Sodium Sulphate	Barium Sulphate	

Double displacement with the evolution of gas

When Iron sulphide reacts with sulphuric acid the double displacement reaction takes place resulting into the formation of hydrogen sulphide gas and iron sulphate solution.

FeS	+ H_2SO_4	→ $FeSO_4$	+ $H_2S(g)$
Iron sulphide	Sulphuric acid	Iron sulphate	Hydrogen sulphide

Double displacement with the change of Colour

When hydrogen sulphide gas is passed through the blue solution of copper sulphate, a black precipitate of copper sulphide is formed.

$CuSO_4$	+ $H_2S(g)$	→ CuS	+ H_2SO_4
Copper sulphate (Blue)	Hydrogen sulphide	Copper sulphide (Black)	

Double decomposition and neutralization reaction

A reaction between an acid and a base is called neutralization reaction salt and water are formed and heat is liberated.

HCl	+ $NaOH$	→ $NaCl$	+ H_2O + Heat
Hydrochloric acid	Sodium hydroxide	Sodium chloride	

Oxidation and Reduction Reactions

Oxidation-reduction reactions are called **redox reactions.** In redox reaction one substance is reduced while other is oxidised.

Oxidation Reaction

(*i*) Oxidation is a process in which oxygen combines with a substance, e.g.,

$4Na$	+ O_2	→ $2Na_2O$
Sodium	Oxygen	Sodium Oxide
Mg	+ O_2	→ $2MgO$
Magnesium	Oxygen	Magnesium oxide
S	+ O_2	→ SO_2
Sulphur	Oxygen	Sulphur dioxide
C	+ O_2	→ CO_2
Carbon	Oxygen	Carbon dioxide

In these reactions Na, Mg, S and C are oxidised.

(*ii*) Oxidation is a process in which hydrogen is removed, e.g.,

$4\,HCl + MnO_2 \rightarrow MnCl_2 + 2H_2O + Cl_2$

$H_2S + Cl_2 \rightarrow 2HCl + S$

$8\,HCl + Pb_3O_4 \rightarrow 3\,PbCl_2 + 4H_2O + Cl_2$

(*iii*) Oxidation is the process of loss of electrons. It is represented by

Atom → Cations + Electrons

$A \rightarrow A^{n+} + ne^-$

Atom A loses n electrons to become a positively charged ion A^{n+}. The positively charged ion is called **cation.**

Reduction Reaction

(*i*) Reduction is a process of combination of hydrogen.

$2H_2(g) + O_2(g) \rightarrow 2H_2O(l)$

Reduction of oxygen.

$H_2(g) + Cl_2(g) \rightarrow 2HCl$ (Hydrogen chloride)

Reduction of chlorine

(*ii*) Reduction is a process of removal of oxygen.

$CuO(s) + H_2(g) \rightarrow Cu(s) + H_2O(l)$

$CuO(s) + CO(g) \rightarrow Cu(s) + CO_2(g)$

In this reaction CuO reduces to Cu.

(*iii*) The gain of electrons by an atom or ion is called reduction. It is represented as

$B + ne^- \rightarrow B^{n-}$

The atom B gain n electrons to become negatively charged ion B^{n-}. The negatively charged ion is called **anion.**

Redox Reaction: Oxidation and reduction occur simultaneously, is called redox reaction. Only oxidation or only reduction is called half reaction.

Thus

$A \rightarrow A^{n+} + ne^-$ oxidation

$B + ne^- \rightarrow B^{n-}$ Reduction on Adding

$A + B \rightarrow A^{n+} + B^{n-} \rightarrow AB$ Redox

e.g. gain of electron is reduction

$Na + Cl \rightarrow \overset{+}{Na}\overset{-}{Cl} \rightarrow NaCl$

2,8,1 2,8,7 2,8 2,8,8

loss of electron is oxidation

$Zn + CuSO_4 \rightarrow ZnSO_4 + Cu$

is example of redox reaction

$Zn + Zn^{2+} + 2e^-$ loss of electron is oxidation

$Cu^{2+} + 2e^- \rightarrow Cu$ gain of electron is reduction

gain of $2e^-$ electron

$Zn + Cu^{2+} \rightarrow Zn^{2+} + Cu$

loss of $2e^-$ (electron)

The redox reaction is called displacement reaction also.

Oxidising agent: The atom which oxidises another atom or ion is called **oxidising agent**. An oxidising agent itself is reduced.

$Na + \frac{1}{2}\,Cl_2 \rightarrow Na^+\,Cl^-$

Here Cl_2 is an oxidising agent. It oxidies Na into Na^+ and Cl_2 is reduced to Cl^-.

Reducing agent: Reducing agent is that which oxidises itself and reduces others. *e.g.* Na reduces Cl_2 but Na itself is oxidised. So Na is reducing agent.

The oxidation number is defined as the charge which an atom appears to have when electrons are counted in ion, molecules or compounds.

For counting the oxidation number some points are more useful to you.

These are:

(*i*) In the elementary or uncombined state, the atoms having **zero** oxidation number.

(*ii*) In compounds the oxidation number of fluorine is always –1.

(*iii*) In compounds, the group IA elements having oxidation number +1 and the group IIA element having an oxidation number +2.

(*iv*) Oxidation number of hydrogen in compounds is generally +1 except in metalic hydrides wherein its oxidation number is –1.

(*v*) In compounds, the oxidation number of oxygen is generally –2 except in F_2O wherein oxidation number of fluorine is –1 and that of oxygen is +2.

(*vi*) In neutral molecules, the sum of the oxidation numbers of all the atoms is zero.

(*vii*) The sum of the oxidation numbers of all the atoms is equal to the net charge on the ion.

e.g., What is the oxidation number of S in

(*a*) H_2SO_4 (*b*) H_2S

(*c*) $H_2S_2O_7$ (*d*) $Na_2S_2O_3$.

Sol.: Let oxidation number of S be *x*.

(*a*) $2 \times (+1) + x + 4 \times (-2) = 0 \Rightarrow x = +6$

(*b*) Let oxidation number of S be *x*

$$2 \times (+1) + x = 0$$
$$x = -2$$

Oxidation of S = –2.

(*c*) Let oxidation number of S be *x*

$$2 \times (+1) + 2x + 7 \times (-2) = 0$$
$$2 + 2x - 14 = 0$$
$$2x = +12$$
$$x = +6.$$

Oxidation number of S = +6.

(*d*) Let oxidation number of S be *x*

$$2 \times (+1) + 2x + 3(-2) = 0$$
$$2 + 2x - 6 = 0$$
$$2x = 4$$
$$x = 2$$

Oxidation number of S in $Na_2S_2O_3$ = +2.

Oxidation and Reduction in Terms of Oxidation Numbers

Oxidation refers to any chemical change involving **increase** in oxidation number where as the **reduction** refers to any chemical change involving **decrease** in oxidation number, e.g.,

$$\overset{0}{2H_2} + \overset{0}{O_2} \Rightarrow 2\overset{+4}{H_2}\overset{-4}{O}$$

Here, oxidation number of hydrogen changes from zero to +1 i.e. oxidation of hydrogen.

Oxidation number of oxygen changes from zero to –2 i.e. reduction of oxygen.

Points to Remember

- Atoms are the building blocks of matter.
- Atom is composed of subatomic particles **electron, proton** and **neutron**.
- Mass of the entire atom is concentrated in its centre known as **nucleus**.
- Loss or gains of electron from or to an atom leads to the formation of ions.
- Atomic number is the characteristic property of an element. It gives the number of protons, which is also equal to the number of electrons in the neutral atom. (Z = P).
- The number of protons together with the number of neutrons give us the mass number of that atom. *i.e.* mass number, A = *n* + *p*.
- Atoms of an element having the same atomic number but different mass number are called isotopes.
- Each element has a specific combining capacity is called its **valence**.
- Formula of a compound can be obtained using the valence of combining elements.
- Chemical equation is a symbolic representation of a chemical reaction.
- Removal of unwanted components leads to the purification of the substances.
- Purity of a given sample of a substances can be tested by determining its melting point or boiling point or both.
- Chemical reactions are characterised by the evolution of a gas, change of colour, formation of precipitate, change of energy or change of state.
- Chemical reactions are different types. They can be classified as .... combination, decomposition, displacement, neutralisation and redox reactions.
- Matter exists in three states .... solid, liquid and gas.
- All matter is made up of tiny particles. These tiny particles are known as atoms or molecules.
- In solid, state, atoms or molecules are fixed in their positions.
- The liquid state is not rigid because atoms or molecules can move around.
- In gaseous state, atoms or molecules can move freely and randomly.
- Solid substances are hard because the atoms or molecules in them are held very close to one another

by strong attractive forces. That is why solids have definite shape and volume.

- Liquids take the shape of the container in which they are kept. The liquids can be compressed slightly because molecules in them are held together less firmly.
- In gases, the force of attraction between molecules is negligible as compared to solids or even liquids. They therefore assume the shape and even volume of the container and can be compressed easily.
- Irregular or haphazard movement of solid particles in a gas or a liquid is called **Brownian movement**.
- The process by which different substances mix also a result of the haphazard or random motions of their particles is called **diffusion**.
- The substances, which contain only one kind of atoms having same atomic number is called **element**.
- A compound is a substance composed of two or more elements that are chemically combined in definite proportions.
- A mixture could contain several elements or compounds or both in any proportions.
- The components of a mixture can be separated easily by applying appropriate physical methods.
- The components of a compound can be separated only by applying chemical methods.
- Symbols and groups of symbol are used to represent elements and compounds.
- Symbol of a chemical element denotes one atom of that element.
- Molecules of mono atomic elements contain only one atom.
- Molecules of diatomic elements contain two atoms.
- Some elements exist in the form of aggregates of their atoms.
- The chemical formula of a substance represents its one molecule.
- In a molecule of a compound, the atoms are present in whole numbers.
- A balanced chemical equation shows the fact that atoms are neither created nor destroyed during a chemical reaction.
- A chemical equation provides us the following information:
  — Substances that take part in the chemical reaction and those that are produced.
  — Number of atoms or molecules of different reactants taking part in a chemical reaction and the number of atoms or molecules of the products formed.
- Major component of the solution is called **Solvent** while its other components are called **Solute**.
- The concentration of a solution is expressed as mass per cent, mole per cent molarity or normality.
- Mass per cent of a component is equal to its mass in 100 mass units of solution.
- **Suspension** is a heterogeneous mixture in which the suspended particles are visible.
- **Atomic mass unit (amu)**: $\frac{1}{12}$th of mass of an atom of ^{12}C is called atomic mass unit. Its value is 1.6603×10^{-24} grams.
- **Relative atomic mass:** The mass of an atom of a substances relative to $\frac{1}{12}$th of the mass of a ^{12}C atom whose atomic mass is exactly 12 amu.

  Mole: Collection of 6.023×10^{23} particles of definite formula/symbol is called **mole**. It is the unit to represent the amount of a substance.

  Molar mass: The mass of 6.023×10^{23} particles of a substance is called molar mass.

  Empirical formula: The simplest ratio of the atoms of the constituent elements of a compound is called its empirical formula.

  Molecular formula: Actual number of all types of atoms of the constituent elements of a molecule is called its molecular formula.

  Molecular formula = (Empirical formula) × n
- Characteristics of a chemical reaction are:
  — Evolution of gas
  — Change of colour
  — Formation of precipitate
  — Energy change
  — Change of state
- The process of converting a liquid into its vapours by heating and then condensing the vapours back into original liquid is called **distillation**.
- There are two methods which can be used to check the purity of a substance. These methods are:
  — Chromatography method
  — Measuring melting and boiling point of a substance.
- Temperature does not rise while a substance is melting or boiling.
- The fixed temperature at which solid starts melting is called its **melting point**.
- The constant temperature at which the pressure of the vapours leaving the surface of the liquid equals the atmospheric pressure is called boiling point of the liquid.
- Some materials may change directly form a solid to a gas. This is called sublimation.
- Condensation is the reverse of evaporation.
- A reaction in which an atom loses electrons is called an **oxidation reaction**.
- A reaction in which an atom gains one or more electrons is called **reduction reaction**.
- The reactions in which both oxidation and reduction takes place together are called as **redox reactions**.

- Oxidizing agent is that which reduces itself and oxidizes others while reducing agent oxidises itself and reduces others.
- John Dalton's invented symbols for the atoms of the elements. He also made first table of atomic weights.
- J.J. Thomson discovered negatively charged particles *i.e.,* electrons which is a fundamental part of an atom.
- Goldstein discovered positively charged rays, known as **Canal rays** which later, known as **protons**.
- **Chadwick** discovered the presence of neutral particles inside the atoms and called them as **neutrons**.
- Ernest Rutherford preformed gold foil experiment for the discovery of **nucleus**.
- An ion is a particle with an electric charge on it. Metals form positive ions and non-metals form negative ions.
- Atoms of an element that have the same numbers of protons but different numbers of neutrons are called **isotopes**.
- A group of atoms may also have a valency. Such a group is called a **ralical**.
- Chemical reactions are described as interactions between particles (Atoms molecules or ions) which involved the breaking and making of chemical bonds.

Acids, Bases and Salts

Acid: According to Arrhenius's theory an acid was a compound which dissolved in water to give hydrogen ions (H^+).

All Acids contain Hydrogen.

The oxides of non-metals, when dissolved in water form acids, *e.g.,*

$CO_2 + H_2O \rightarrow H_2CO_3$

Carbon dioxide — Carbonic acid

$SO_2 + H_2O \rightarrow H_2SO_3$

Sulphur dioxide — Sulphurous acid

The formation of acids in these reactions can be tested by dipping **blue** litmus paper in these solutions. It turns **red**.

Uses of Acids

— Hydrochloric acid (HCl) is used in cleaning kitchen sink and sanitarywares.

— Nitric acid (HNO_3) is used by goldsmiths for cleaning gold and silver ornaments.

— Sulphuric acid (H_2SO_4) is used in batteries for cars, buses, trucks, tractors and inverters. These acids are called mineral acids.

Some acids are found in animals and plants are called organic acids.

Example of organic acids are:

Lactic acid	(in soured milk)
Citric acid	(in citrus fruits)
Tartaric acid	(Tamarind)
Acetic acid	(Vinegar)
Formic acid	(Ants)
Ascorbic acid	(Vitamin C).

The Chemical formulas of some important Acids

Name of the Acid	*Chemical Formula*
Hydrochloric acid	HCl
Nitric acid	HNO_3
Sulphuric acid	H_2SO_4
Carbonic acid	H_2CO_3
Acetic acid	CH_3COOH
Formic acid	$HCOOH$
Sulphurous acid	H_2SO_3
Nitrous acid	HNO_2
Phosphoric acid	H_2PO_4
Boric acid	H_3BO_3
Hydrobromic acid	HBr
Hydroiodic acid	HI
Chloric acid	$HClO_3$
Tetraboric acid	$H_2B_4O_7$
Hydrocyanic acid	HCN
Oxalic acid	$H_2C_2O_4$
Chromic acid	H_2CrO_4
Dichromic acid	$H_2Cr_2O_7$
Thiosulfuric acid	$H_2S_2O_3$
Pyro-sulphuric acid	$H_2S_2O_7$
Per sulphuric	$H_2S_2O_8$

Base: A base is a compound which dissolved in water to give hydroxide ions (OH^-).

Some metal oxides on reacting with water is formed hydroxides of that metal oxide.

Some metal oxides on reacting with water to form hydroxides.

$MgO + H_2O \rightarrow Mg(OH)_2$

Magnesium oxide + water → Magnesium hydroxide

$Na_2O + H_2O \rightarrow 2\,NaOH$

Sodium oxide + water → Sodium hydroxide

$K_2O + H_2O \rightarrow 2KOH$

Potassium oxide + water → Potassium hydroxide

$CaO + H_2O \rightarrow Ca(OH)_2$

Calcium oxide + water → Calcium hydroxide

The hydroxides of metals which dissolve in water are known as **alkalies.** Thus all soluble hydroxides are **alkalies.**

Neutralisation reactions: Acid and base react with one another neutralising each other's characteristic properties.

Salt and water are formed as products in the neutralisation reactions. e.g.,

HCl	+	NaOH →	NaCl	+ H_2O
Hydrochloric acid		Sodium hydroxide	Sodium chloride (Salt)	
HNO_3	+	NaOH →	$NaNO_3$	+ H_2O
Nitric acid		Sodium hydroxide	Sodium nitrate (Salt)	
H_2SO_4	+	2NaOH →	Na_2SO_4	+ H_2O
Sulphuric acid		Sodium hydroxide	Sodium sulphate (Salt)	

Indicators of Testing Acids and Bases

Indications	*Acid*	*Base*
Litmus paper	turns blue to red	turns red to blue
Methyl orange	pinkish red	yellow
Phenolphthalein	Colourless	Pink

Salts: A salt is a compound made from an acid when a metal takes the place of the hydrogen in the acid. e.g.,

HCl	+	NaOH →	NaCl	+ H_2O
Hydrochloric acid		Sodium hydroxide	Sodium chloride (Salt)	
HNO_3	+	NH_4OH →	NH_4NO_3	+ H_2O
		Ammonium hydroxide	Ammonium nitrate	
H_2SO_4	+	$Ca(OH)_2$ →	$CaSO_4$	+ $2H_2O$
Sulphuric acid		Calcium hydroxide	Calcium Sulphate	

In these reactions, the hydrogen atom of the acid has been replaced by a sodium/calcium atom or a group of atoms (NH_4).

Some Salts in Common Use

Name of Salt	*Chemical Formula*	*Uses*
Calcium carbonate (marble, chalk, lime)	$CaCO_3$	Building materials, lime, cement, iron.
Calcium Sulphate gypsum, plaster of Paris	$CaSO_4$	Wall plaster Statue, Surgery
Sodium Carbonate Washing soda	Na_2CO_3	Water softening making glass
Magnesium Sulphate' (epsom salt)	$MgSO_4$	Health salts laxative
Copper Sulphate (Blue Vitriol)	$CuSO_4$	Fungicides
Calcium phosphate	$Ca_3(PO_4)_2$	Fertilizers
Ammonium chloride	NH_4Cl	Fertilizer, dry cell
Ammonium nitrate	NH_4NO_3	Fertilizers explosives
Ammonium sulphate	$(NH_4)_2SO_4$	Fertilizers

Some Hydrated Salts

Name of Hydrated Salt	*Chemical Formula*	*Colour*
Copper Sulphate	$CuSO_4 \cdot 5H_2O$	Blue
Iron sulphate	$FeSO_4 \cdot 6H_2O$	Green
Magnesium sulphate	$MgSO_4 \cdot 7H_2O$	White
Sodium carbonate	$Na_2CO_3 \cdot 10H_2O$	White
Barium chloride	$BaCl_2 \cdot 2H_2O$	White

Uses of Salts

Some of its important uses are given below:

- As table Salt.
- In the manufacture of butter and cheese.
- In leather industry for taming of leather.
- For manufacturing washing soda and baking soda.
- For preparing sodium hydroxide by electrolysis of brine.
- Rock salt is spread on ice roads to melt ice in cold countries.

Points to Remember

- The oxides of non-metals mainly form acidic solutions and the oxides of metals if soluble, mainly form alkaline solutions.
- All bases are not alkalies. Some bases are soluble in water. They are called alkalies.
- Acid and alkali solutions conduct electricity.
- All acids contain hydrogen and dissolve in water.
- Acids turn blue litmus into red. Whereas alkalies turn red litmus into blue.
- Acids neutralise bases and bases neutralise acids. Salt and water are formed in these neutralisation reactions. Acids also react with metals to form salt and hydrogen gas. They also react with metal carbonates to give salt, water and carbon dioxide gas.
- Acids and alkalies can be weak or strong.
- Salts are substances, which are produced from acids by reactions in which the hydrogen in the acid is replaced by a metal.
- Some salts have the tendency to absorb water from air and turn into a solution. Such substances are called **deliquescent**.
- The crystals, which have lost their water of crystallisation, are called **anhydrous**.
- The crystals of some salts have some water molecules associated with them. These water molecules are known as **water of crystallisation**.
- **Neutral salts** are formed by the neutralisation of a strong acid with a strong base.
  $HCl + NaOH \rightarrow NaCl + H_2O$
- **Acidic Salts** are formed when a strong acid is neutralised by a weak base.
  $HCl + NH_4OH \rightarrow NH_4Cl + H_2O$
- **Basic Salts** are formed by the neutralisation of a weak acid by a strong base.
  $CH_3COOH + NaOH \rightarrow CH_3COONa + H_2O$.

MULTIPLE CHOICE QUESTIONS

1. The isomeric pair is:
A. ethane and propane
B. propane and butane
C. ethane and ethane
D. butane and 2-methyl propane

2. Which of the following is used to oxidise ethanol to ethanoic acid?
A. Alkaline $KMnO_4$ B. Conc. H_2SO_4
C. Acidified $K_2Cr_2O_7$ D. All of above

3. Which is denatured spirit?
A. ethanol only
B. ethanol and methanol (50%)
C. ethanol and methanol (5%)
D. methanol only

4. Tertiary butane gets oxidised with oxidising agents like alkaline $KMNO_4$ to:
A. Isobutane
B. Ter-butyl alcohol
C. Seconadary-propyl alcohol
D. All of above

5. The substance not responsible for the hardness of water is:
A. Sodium nitrate
B. Calcium hydrogen carbonate
C. Calcium carbonate
D. Magnesium carbonate

6. The by product of soap is:
A. isoprene B. glycerol
C. butene D. ethylene glycol

7. Covalent compounds:
A. (a) have high melting and boiling point
B. are mostly soluble in water
C. are formed between atoms of metals and non-metals
D. are formed by the sharing of electrons in the bonding atoms.

8. Which of the following can be used for the denaturation of ethyl alcohol?
A. Methyl alcohol B. Pyridines
C. Copper sulphate D. All of above

9. Soaps are formed by saponification of:
A. alcohols B. glycosides
C. simple esters D. carboxylic acids

10. What is the common name of ethanoic acid?
A. Acetic acid B. Formic acid
C. Propionic acid D. Butanoic acid

11. What type of flame is produced when the oxygen supply is sufficient?
A. Yellow flame B. Blue flame
C. Orange flame D. None of the above

12. Which of the following is the chemical property of carbon compounds?
A. Combustion reactions B. Substitution reactions
C. Addition reactions D. All of the above

13. The cooking gas (LPG) mainly consists of:
A. Butane B. Ethene
C. Ethyne D. Propene

14. The reaction in which an unsaturated hydrocarbon combines with another substance to give a single product is called:
A. Addition reaction B. Combustion reaction
C. Combination reaction D. Substitution reaction

15. What is the boiling point of ethanol?
A. 100 °C B. 50 °C
C. 88 °C D. 78 °C

16. Which of the following is used as a fuel in cars along with petrol?
A. Methane B. Ethane
C. Butane D. Ethanol

17. What is formed when ethanol reacts with ethanoic acid on warming in the presence of a few drops of concentrated sulphuric acid?
A. Ester B. Ethene
C. Sodium Ethoxide D. Ethane

18. Which of the following is a use of ethanol?
A. Manufacturing paints
B. In cough syrups
C. In alcoholic drinks
D. All of the above

19. What is used as an antiseptic to sterilise wounds and syringes in hospitals?
A. Propanol B. Ethyl alcohol
C. Butanol D. Methanol

20. Carbon exists in the atmosphere in the form of
A. Only carbon monoxide
B. Carbon monoxide in traces and carbon dioxide
C. Only carbon dioxide
D. Coal

21. Which of the following statements are usually correct for carbon compounds? These
(*i*) Are good conductors of electricity.
(*ii*) Are poor conductors of electricity.
(*iii*) Have strong forces of attraction between their molecules.
(*iv*) Do not have strong forces of attraction between their molecules.
A. (*i*) and (*iii*) B. (*ii*) and (*iii*)
C. (*i*) and (*iv*) D. (*ii*) and (*iv*)

22. A molecule of ammonia (NH_3) has:
A. Only single bonds
B. Only double bonds
C. Only triple bonds
D. Two double bonds and one single bond

23. Buckminsterfullerene is an allotropic form of:
A. Phosphorus B. Sulphur
C. Carbon D. Tin

24. Oils on treating with hydrogen in the presence of palladium or nickel catalyst form fats. This is an example of:
A. Addition reaction
B. Substitution reaction
C. Displacement reaction
D. Oxidation reaction

25. In which of the following compounds -OH is the functional group?
A. Butanone B. Butanol
C. Butanoic D. Butanal

26. The soap molecule has a:
A. Hydrophilic head and a hydrophobic tail
B. Hydrophobic head and a hydrophilic tail
C. Hydrophobic head and a hydrophobic tail
D. Hydrophilic head and a hydrophilic tail

27. Chlorine reacts with saturated hydrocarbons at room temperature in the:
A. absence of sunlight
B. presence of sunlight
C. presence of water
D. presence of hydrochloric acid

28. Ethanol reacts with sodium and forms two products. These are:
A. Sodium ethanoate and hydrogen
B. Sodium ethanoate and oxygen
C. Sodium ethoxide and hydrogen
D. Sodium ethoxide and oxygen

29. Which of the following is a noble gas?
A. Carbon B. Argon
C. Nitrogen D. Hydrogen

30. How many electrons are there in the outermost shell of carbon?
A. 1 B. 2
C. 3 D. 4

31. Which allotrope of carbon is in the form of the geodesic globe?
A. Graphite B. Diamond
C. Fullerene D. Carbon nanotube

32. Which of the following has a triple bond?
A. Hydrogen molecule B. Oxygen molecule
C. Nitrogen molecule D. Ammonia molecule

33. Which of the following has a double bond?
A. Hydrogen molecule B. Oxygen molecule
C. Nitrogen molecule D. Methane molecule

34. Which of the following is not a saturated hydrocarbon?
A. cyclohexane B. benzene
C. butane D. isobutene

35. The bond between two identical non metallic atom has a pair of electron?
A. un equally shared between two atoms.
B. transferd completely from one atom to another.
C. with identical spins
D. equally shared between them.

36. Covalent compounds are generally:
A. soluble in water B. insoluble in water
C. ionize in water D. hydrolyse in water

37. Propane with the molecular formula C_3H_8 has
A. 7 covalent bonds B. 8 covalent bonds
C. 9 covalent bonds D. 10 covalent bonds

38. A hydrocarbon reacts with ammonical cuprous chloride solution to form a red precipitate. The hydrocarbon is:
A. ethane B. ethene
C. butane D. 1-propyne

39. Which of the following substance is added to denature Ethanol?
A. methanol B. pyridine
C. copper sulphate D. all of them

40. Which of the following is not an allotropic form of carbon?
A. fluorine B. fullerene
C. diamond D. graphite

41. Which of the following represents the correct decreasing order of hydrogen atoms?
A. alkanes, alkenes, alkynes
B. alkanes, alkaynes, alkenes
C. alkenes, alkynes, alkanes
D. alkynes, alkanes, alkenes

42. Detergents are sodium or potassium salts of long chain of:
A. aldehydes B. ketones
C. carboxylic acid D. sulphonic acid

43. Which of the following represents the structure of N_2 molecule?
A. $N \equiv N$ B. $N = N$
C. $N - N$ D. None of the above

44. In double covalent bond there is sharing of:
A. 2 electrons B. 4 electrons
C. 6 electrons D. 3 electrons

45. Cation is formed when:
A. atom gains electrons
B. atom loses electrons
C. proton is lost by the atom
D. atom shared by electrons

46. The total no. of electrons that take part in forming a bond in N_2 is:
A. 2 B. 4
C. 6 D. 10

47. Which of the following has the weakest carbon-carbon strength?
A. C_2H_2
B. C_2H_4
C. C_2H_6
D. all have the same bond strength

48. Which of the following salt when dissolved in water produces hard water.
A. Calcium sulphate
B. Magnesium bicarbonate
C. Calcium chloride
D. Any of the above

49. The most reactive metal is:
A. Iron B. Gold
C. Zinc D. Potassium.

50. The liquid metal at room temperature
A. Mercury B. Bromine
C. Sodium D. Gold

51. Non-metals are:
A. generally liquids
B. generally gases
C. generally solids and gases
D. generally gases and liquids.

52. The metal which is stored in kerosene:
A. Phosphorus B. Magnesium
C. Sodium D. None of these

53. The non-metal which is liquid at room temperature is:
A. Carbon B. Iodine
C. Bromine D. Chlorine.

54. Materials around us can be classified into:
A. Elements and compounds
B. Metals and non-metals
C. Acids and bases
D. None of these.

55. All metals are solids except:
A. Sodium B. Calcium
C. Mercury D. Hydrogen.

56. Metal oxides are of nature:
A. Acidic B. Basic
C. Neutral D. All of these

57. The metal which can be cut with a knife:
A. Sodium and potassium
B. Barium and calcium
C. Sodium and mercury
D. Potassium and calcium

58. When non-metals react with water then:
A. Hydrogen gas is formed
B. Carbon dioxide gas is formed
C. Non-metals do not react with water
D. None of these

59. The property of metals by which they can be beaten in to thin sheets is called:
A. Malleability B. Ductility
C. Conduction D. Expansion

60. Which one of the following is metal?
A. C B. N
C. Na D. O

61. Which one of the following is non metal?
A. Zn B. Al
C. Fe D. N

62. All materials shown property of malleability expect:
A. Iron B. Graphite
C. Aluminium D. Silver

63. Which one of the following is a good conductor of electricity?
A. Iron B. Plastic
C. Wood D. Glass

64. The property of metal by which it can be drawn into wires is called:
A. Conductivity B. malleability
C. Ductility D. Decorating

65. The metals that produce ringing sounds, are said to be:
A. malleable B. sonorous
C. Lustrous D. hard

66. Which metal is found in liquid state at room temperature?
A. Fe B. Zn
C. Hg D. Al

67. The solution of ash of magnesium ribbon is:
A. Acidic B. Basic
C. Neutral D. All of these

68. What is the product when sulphur reacts with oxygen?
A. Sulphuric acid B. Sulphur trioxide
C. Sulphurous acid D. Sulphur dioxide

69. When sulphur dioxide is dissolve in water then:
A. Sulphur is formed
B. Sulphur trioxide is formed
C. Sulphuric acid is formed
D. Sulphurous acid is formed

70. What is the chemical formula of sulphurous acid?
A. H_2SO_4 B. SO_2
C. SO_3 D. H_2SO_3

71. The sulphuric acid turns blue litmus paper into:
A. Red B. Green
C. Yellow D. Dark blue

72. Oxides of non metals are _______ in nature.
A. Basic B. Acidic
C. Neutral D. All of these

73. Sodium metal is stored in:
A. Water B. Alcohol
C. Kerosene D. Ether

74. Which one of the following metal reacts vigorously with oxygen and water?
A. Sodium B. Potassium
C. Calcium D. Magnesium

75. Which metal is present in Calcium Hydroxide?
A. C B. O
C. Ca D. H

76. Which non-metal catches fire if the exposed to air?
A. Sodium B. Phosphorous
C. Calcium D. Uranium

77. What is the chemical formula of copper sulphate?
A. $CuSO_4$ B. $CuCO_3$
C. $CuCl_2$ D. CuO

78. Which gas are produced when metal react with acids?
A. Oxygen B. Nitrogen
C. Hydrogen D. Carbon dioxide

79. Which one of the following does not react with acids?
A. Cu B. Ni
C. Cr D. O

80. Which one of the following gas burns with the "pop" sound?
A. Oxygen B. Hydrogen
C. Chlorine D. Hydrogen sulphide

81. Which of the following can be beaten in to thin sheets?
A. Zinc B. Phosphorus
C. Sulphur D. Oxygen

82. Which of the following statements are correct?
A. All metals are ductile
B. All non metals are ductile
C. Generally metals are ductile
D. some metals are ductile

83. What happens when dilute sulphuric acid is poured on a copper plate?
A. Copper sulphate formed
B. Zinc sulphate formed
C. Copper chloride formed
D. Zinc sulphate formed.

84. On burning metals react with oxygen to produce:
A. Metal hydroxide B. Metal chloride
C. Metal oxide D. Metal sulphate

85. Which gas produced by piece of burning charcoal?
A. CO_2 B. CO
C. H_2S D. O_2

86. Which non metal is essential for our life and inhale during breathing?
A. H B. O
C. C D. N

87. Non metals used in:
A. Aeroplanes B. making machinery
C. Water boilers D. Fertilisers

88. Which one of the following is applied on wounds as an antiseptic?
A. Metals B. Non metals
C. Metalloids D. All of these

89. Which metal is found in plants?
A. Fe B. Cr
C. Mg D. CO

90. Copper sulphate ($CuSO_4$) possesses:
A. Red colour B. Blue colour
C. Green colour D. Yellow colour

91. Which one of the following are very reactive non metals?
A. Sodium B. Potassium
C. Carbon D. Phosphorous

92. Which one of the following is the good conducter of electricity?
A. Iron rod B. Sulphur
C. Coal piece D. Wood

93. Which material show shiny appearance?
A. Coal B. Sulphur
C. Aluminium D. Carbon

94. Which material is hard in nature?
A. Iron B. Coal
C. Oxygen D. Wood

95. Gold is used in:
A. Thermometers B. Fuel
C. Jewellery D. Machinery

96. Which one of the following metal is used thermometers?
A. Copper B. Mercury
C. Aluminium D. Iron

97. Which one of the following can't be drawn into wires?
A. Fe B. Al
C. Cu D. Coal

98. Which substance is present in fuel?
A. Copper B. Iron
C. Gold D. Carbon

99. Zinc replaces copper from:
A. Zinc sulphate B. Copper sulphate
C. Sulphuric acid D. Copper oxide

100. Metallic oxides are:
A. Acidic is nature B. Neutral
C. Basic in nature D. Either acidic or basic

101. Aluminium foil used for wrapping:
A. Food B. Clothes
C. Plastic D. Wires

102. Which one of the following is used for decorating sweets?
A. Aluminium foil B. Copper foil
C. Silver foil D. All of these

103. Which one of the following enhances the growth of plants?
A. Industrial gadgets B. Fertilisers
C. Automobiles D. Water boilers

104. Which one of the following is in crackers?
A. metals B. Semi metals
C. Non-metal D. All of these

105. Hydrogen gas produce when metal react with:
A. Acid B. Base
C. Salt D. Both acid & base

106. Which of the following can't be beaten into sheets?
A. Zinc B. Iron
C. Aluminium D. Sulphur

107. Heat conduction is the property of:
A. Non-metal B. Metal
C. Metalloids D. All of these

108. Moist air is the combination of:
A. $H_2O + CO_2 + O_2$ B. $H_2O + CO + O_2$
C. $H_2O + CO_2 + H_2$ D. $H_2O + O_2 + H_2$

109. Which of the following product is formed when calcium oxide reacts with water?
A. Slaked lime B. Carbon dioxide
C. Calcium oxide D. Oxygen gas

110. What is the another name of quick lime?
A. Calcium hydroxide B. Calcium oxide
C. Carbon dioxide D. Sodium oxide

111. What is the chemical name for slaked lime?
A. Calcium carbonate B. Calcium oxide
C. Calcium hydroxide D. Carbon monoxide

112. Heating of ferrous sulphate gives which of the following product?
A. Ferric oxide B. Sulphur dioxide
C. Sulphur trioxide D. All of the above

113. In which of the following category will you put the reaction of heating of ferrous sulphate?
A. Decomposition reaction
B. Combination Reaction
C. Displacement reaction
D. All of the above

114. In which of the following category will you put the reaction of heating of calcium carbonate?
A. Decomposition reaction
B. Thermal decomposition reaction
C. Endothermic reaction
D. All of the above

115. Which of the following product is formed after heating of limestone?
A. Calcium oxide
B. Calcium carbonate
C. Hydrogen gas
D. All of the above

116. What happens when silver chloride is put under sunlight?
A. Silver metal and chlorine gas are formed
B. Silver metal and hydrogen gas are formed
C. Only silver metal is formed
D. Only hydrogen gas is formed

117. Which of the following is formed when lead nitrate is put under thermal decomposition?
A. Lead oxide B. Nitrogen dioxide
C. Oxygen gas D. All of the above

118. What happens when carbon dioxide is passed in lime water?
A. Lime water turns milky because of formation of calcium carbonate
B. Lime water turns milky because of formation of water
C. Lime water turns red because of formation permanganate
D. Lime water turns red because of formation of copper sulphate

119. What happens when silver bromide is exposed to sunlight?
A. Hydrogen gas is formed
B. Bromine gas is formed
C. Chlorine gas is formed
D. Iodine gas is formed

120. Which metal is displaced when lead is put in the solution of copper chloride?
A. Lead B. Copper
C. Chlorine D. All of the above.

121. Which of the following is formed when lead metal reacts with the solution of copper chloride?
A. No reaction takes place
B. Copper chlorine
C. Lead chloride
D. Copper-lead chloride

122. Which metal is displaced when zinc metal is put in the solution of copper sulphate?
A. Copper B. Zinc
C. Sulphate D. All of the above

123. What happens when sodium sulphate solution is mixed with the solution of barium chloride?
A. Barium sulphate is formed
B. Sodium sulphate is formed
C. Sulphur dioxide gas is formed
D. No reaction takes place

24. What happens when Copper metal is dipped in the solution of zinc sulphate?
A. Copper sulphate is formed
B. Oxygen gas is formed
C. Zinc metal is separated
D. No reaction takes place

25. What happens when zinc metal is dipped in the solution of copper sulphate?
A. Zinc sulphate is formed
B. Zinc oxide is formed
C. Zinc sulphide is formed
D. No reaction takes place

26. Why are articles made of iron painted to prevent rust?
A. Paint makes articles made of iron beautiful
B. Paint prevents iron articles to come in contact with moisture present in air.
C. Paint prevents iron articles to getting sticky
D. All of the above

27. Which of the following is termed as rancidity?
A. Reduction of oxygen present in food
B. Oxidation of oil present in food
C. Oxidation of sugar present in food
D. All of the above

28. How rancidity can be prevented?
A. By adding antioxidants in food
B. By adding more oxygen to food
C. By keeping food items in open
D. All of the above

29. Which of the following product is formed when calcium oxide reacts with water?
A. Slaked lime B. Carbon dioxide
C. Calcium oxide D. Oxygen gas

30. What is the another name of quick lime?
A. Calcium hydroxide B. Calcium oxide
C. Carbon dioxide D. Sodium oxide

31. What is the chemical name for slaked lime?
A. Calcium carbonate
B. Calcium oxide
C. Calcium hydroxide
D. Carbon monoxide

32. Heating of ferrous sulphate gives which of the following product?
A. Ferric oxide
B. Sulphur dioxide
C. Sulphur trioxide
D. All of the above

33. In which of the following category will you put the reaction of heating of ferrous sulphate?
A. Decomposition reaction
B. Combination Reaction
C. Displacement reaction
D. All of the above

134. In which of the following category will you put the reaction of heating of calcium carbonate?
A. Decomposition reaction
B. Thermal decomposition reaction
C. Endothermic reaction
D. All of the above.

135. Which of the following product is formed after heating of limestone?
A. Calcium oxide B. Calcium carbonate
C. Hydrogen gas D. All of the above

136. What happens when silver chloride is put under sunlight?
A. Silver metal and chlorine gas are formed
B. Silver metal and hydrogen gas are formed
C. Only silver metal is formed
D. Only hydrogen gas is formed

137. Which of the following is formed when lead nitrate is put under thermal decomposition?
A. Lead oxide B. Nitrogen dioxide
C. Oxygen gas D. All of the above

138. What happens when carbon dioxide is passed in lime water?
A. Lime water turns milky because of formation of calcium carbonate
B. Lime water turns milky because of formation of water
C. Lime water turns red because of formation permanganate
D. Lime water turns red because of formation of copper sulphate

139. Which of the following is termed as exothermic reaction?
A. Reaction in which heat is evolved
B. Reaction in which heat is absorbed
C. Reaction in which there is loss of oxygen
D. Reaction in which there is gain of hydrogen

140. Which of the following is termed as endothermic reaction?
A. Reaction in which heat is evolved
B. Reaction in which heat is absorbed
C. Reaction in which there is loss of oxygen
D. Reaction in which there is gain of hydrogen

141. What is the name of reaction which decomposes after supply of heat?
A. Combination reaction
B. Thermal decomposition
C. Displacement reaction
D. Redox reaction

142. What is the name of reaction in which both oxidation and reduction takes place?
A. Combination reaction
B. Thermal decomposition
C. Displacement reaction
D. Redox reaction

143. What is the name of substance which does get deposited over iron because of moisture present in air?
A. Sulphide B. Rust
C. Carbonate D. Oxygen

144. Why magnesium ribbon is cleaned before burning?
A. To remove dust
B. To remove magnesium oxide
C. To remove ribbon oxide
D. All of the above

145. On the basis of evolution or absorption of heat, chemical reactions can be divided in how many types?
A. Two B. Three
C. Four D. One

146. Which of the following gas is produced when carbon is burnt in air?
A. Carbon dioxide B. Sulphur dioxide
C. Oxygen D. Hydrogen

147. Which of the following gives energy while respiration?
A. Burning of coal B. Burning of natural gas
C. Burning of oxygen D. Burning of glucose

148. What happens when hydrogen reacts with oxygen?
A. Carbon dioxide is formed
B. Water is formed
C. Hydrogen carbonate is formed
D. All of the above

149. The chemical formula of lead sulphate is:
A. Pb_2SO_4 B. $Pb(SO_4)_2$
C. $PbSO_4$ D. $Pb_2(SO_4)_3$

150. Which information is not conveyed by a balanced chemical equation?
A. Physical states of reactants and products
B. Symbols and formulae of all the substances involved in a particular reaction
C. Number of atoms/molecules of the reactants and products formed
D. Whether a particular reaction is actually feasible or not

151. Chemically rust is:
A. hydrated ferrous oxide
B. only ferric oxide
C. hydrated ferric oxide
D. none of these

152. Both CO_2 and H_2 gases are:
A. heavier than air B. colourless
C. acidic in nature D. soluble in water

153. Which of the following gases can be used for storage of fresh sampel of an oil for a long time?
A. Carbon dioxide or oxygen
B. Nitrogen or helium
C. Helium or oxygen
D. Nitrogen or oxygen

154. The electrolytic decomposition of water gives H_2 and O_2 in the ratio of:
A. 1: 2 by volume B. 2: 1 by volume
C. 8: 1 by mass D. 1: 2 by mass

155. In the decomposition of lead (II) nitrate to give lead (II) oxide, nitrogen dioxide and oxygen gas, the coefficient of nitrogen dioxide (in the balanced equation) is:
A. 1 B. 2
C. 3 D. 4

156. Fatty foods become rancid due to the process of:
A. oxidation B. corrosion
C. reduction D. hydrogenation

157. We store silver chloride in a dark coloured bottle because it is:
A. a white solid
B. undergoes redoc reaction
C. to avoid action by sunlight
D. none of the above

158. Silver article turns black when kept in the open for a few days due to formation of
A. H_2S B. AgS
C. $AgSO_4$ D. Ag_2S

159. When crystals of lead nitrate are heated strongly in a dry test tube
A. crystals immediately melt
B. a brown residue is left
C. white fumes appear in the tube
D. a yellow residue is left

160. Dilute hydrochloric acid is added to granulated zinc taken in a test tube. The following observations are recorded. Point out the correct observation.
A. The surface of metal becomes shining
B. The reaction mixture turns milky
C. Odour of a pungent smelling gas is recorded
D. A colourless and odourless gas is evolved

161. When carbon dioxide is passed through lime water,
A. calcium hydroxide is formed
B. white precipitate of CaO is formed
C. lime water turns milky
D. colour of lime water disappears.

162. When a magnesium ribbon is burnt in air, the ash formed is:
A. black B. white
C. yellow D. pink

163. In which of the following, heat energy will be evolved?
A. Electrolysis of water
B. Dissolution of NH_4Cl in water
C. Burning of LPG
D. Decomposition of AgBr in the presence of sunlight

164. Rancidity can be prevented by:
A. adding antioxidants
B. storing food away from light
C. keeping food in refrigerator
D. all of these

165. The reaction of H_2 gas with oxygen gas to form water is an example of
A. combination reaction
B. redox reaction
C. exothermic reaction
D. all of these reactions

166. The reaction in which two compound exchange their ions to form two new compounds is called:
A. displacement reaction
B. combination reaction
C. double displacement reaction
D. redox reaction

167. On immersing an iron nail in $CuSO_4$ solution for few minutes, you will observe
A. no reaction takes place
B. the colour of solution fades away
C. the surface of iron nails acquire a black coating
D. the colour of solution changes to green

168. An element X on exposure to moist air turns reddish-brown and a new compound Y is formed. The substance X and Y are:
A. X = Fe, Y = Fe_2O_3
B. X = Ag, Y = Ag_2S
C. X = Cu, Y = CuO
D. X = Al, Y = Al_2O_3

169. A chain of small chemical units combined to form a large single units is called _______.
A. Polymer B. Poly
C. Polythene D. None of the above

170. Polythene and PVC are examples of:
A. Bio degradable substance
B. Thermosetting plastics
C. Thermoplastics
D. Rayon

171. Plastics which when moulded once, cannot be softened by heating. Such plastics are called ______.
A. Polythene B. Thermoplastics
C. Polyster D. Thermosetting plastics

172. Polycot is made by mixing two types of fibres namely:
A. Silk + Cotton B. Polythene + Cotton
C. Silk + Polyester D. Polyester + Cotton

173. The 4R Principle is:
A. Reduce, Reuse, Recycle, Recover
B. Remember, Reduce, Recycle, Rejoice
C. Repeat, Rejoice, Recycle, Reduce
D. None of the above

174. ______ is an example of natural polymer.
A. Rayon B. Cellulose
C. Nylon D. All of the above

175. Which of the following is Non-biodegradable?
A. Woolen clothes B. Plastic bag
C. Cotton cloth D. Wood

176. Bakelite and Melamine are examples of:
A. Thermosetting plastics
B. Silk
C. Nylon
D. Rayon

177. Fire proof plastic uniform worn by fire fighters has a coating of ______ to make it fire resistant.
A. Nylon B. Rayon
C. Melamine Plastic D. Silk

178. The coating on modern non-stick cookware and electric iron is of:
A. Terrycot B. Rayon
C. Polyester D. Teflon

179. The property of metals by which they can be beaten into thin sheets is called ______.
A. Ductility B. Sheetability
C. Metallic D. Malleability

180. The property of metal by which it can be drawn into wires is called ______.
A. Ductility B. Sheetability
C. Metallic D. Malleability

181. The metal found in liquid state is:
A. Iron B. Aluminium
C. Mercury D. Gold

182. When a copper vessel is exposed to moist air for long, it acquires a dull green coating. The green material is a mixture of:
A. Copper oxide and Copper Nitrate
B. Copper hydroxide and Copper Carbonate
C. Copper carbonate and Copper sulfate
D. Copper hydroxide and Copper Nitrate

183. When sulphur dioxide is dissolved in water ______ is formed.
A. Sulphuric acid
B. Sulphoxy acid
C. Sulphurous acid
D. Sulphur trioxide

184. Sodium metal is stored in:
A. Water
B. Kept under open air
C. Alcohol
D. Kerosene

185. Phosphorus is stored in:
A. Water B. Kept under open air
C. Alcohol D. Kerosene

ANSWERS

1	2	3	4	5	6	7	8	9	10
D	D	C	B	A	B	D	D	C	A
11	**12**	**13**	**14**	**15**	**16**	**17**	**18**	**19**	**20**
B	D	A	A	D	D	A	D	B	C
21	**22**	**23**	**24**	**25**	**26**	**27**	**28**	**29**	**30**
D	A	C	A	B	A	B	C	B	D
31	**32**	**33**	**34**	**35**	**36**	**37**	**38**	**39**	**40**
C	C	B	B	D	B	D	D	D	A
41	**42**	**43**	**44**	**45**	**46**	**47**	**48**	**49**	**50**
A	D	A	B	B	C	A	D	D	A
51	**52**	**53**	**54**	**55**	**56**	**57**	**58**	**59**	**60**
C	C	C	B	C	B	A	C	A	C
61	**62**	**63**	**64**	**65**	**66**	**67**	**68**	**69**	**70**
D	B	A	C	B	C	B	D	C	D
71	**72**	**73**	**74**	**75**	**76**	**77**	**78**	**79**	**80**
A	B	C	A	C	B	B	C	D	B
81	**82**	**83**	**84**	**85**	**86**	**87**	**88**	**89**	**90**
A	C	A	C	B	B	D	B	C	B
91	**92**	**93**	**94**	**95**	**96**	**97**	**98**	**99**	**100**
D	A	C	A	C	B	D	D	B	C
101	**102**	**103**	**104**	**105**	**106**	**107**	**108**	**109**	**110**
A	C	B	C	B	D	B	A	A	B
111	**112**	**113**	**114**	**115**	**116**	**117**	**118**	**119**	**120**
C	D	A	D	A	A	D	A	B	B
121	**122**	**123**	**124**	**125**	**126**	**127**	**128**	**129**	**130**
C	A	A	D	A	B	B	A	A	B
131	**132**	**133**	**134**	**135**	**136**	**137**	**138**	**139**	**140**
C	D	A	D	A	A	D	A	A	B
141	**142**	**143**	**144**	**145**	**146**	**147**	**148**	**149**	**150**
B	D	B	B	A	A	D	B	C	D
151	**152**	**153**	**154**	**155**	**156**	**157**	**158**	**159**	**160**
C	B	B	B	D	A	C	D	B	D
161	**162**	**163**	**164**	**165**	**166**	**167**	**168**	**169**	**170**
C	B	C	D	A	C	D	A	A	C
171	**172**	**173**	**174**	**175**	**176**	**177**	**178**	**179**	**180**
B	D	A	B	B	A	C	D	D	A
181	**182**	**183**	**184**	**185**					
C	B	C	D	A					

★ ★ ★

3

Living/Non-Living; Cell Structure and Function; Conservation of Plants and Animals

FUNDAMENTAL UNITS OF LIFE

Some Important Facts

- The cell is the basic structural and functional unit of living organisms.
- A cell is made of life giving substance called **protoplasm**.
- A single cell may constitute a whole organism. Such organisms are called unicellular organisms and include bacteria, Amoeba, Euglena, Paramecium, Yeast.
- Non-cellular organisms which do not contain any cell in their body organisation, e.g., Viruses.
- Cellular organisms which contain either one or many cells in their bodies e.g. bacteria, plants and animals.
- All the living beings are made up of cells.
- The structure of plants and animals is different, they perform basic functions of life.
- In spite of variations in structure, shape and the size, all organisms are made up of basic units called cells. These were first observed by **Robert Hooke**.
- The smallest cell observed is that of a bacteria. Ostrich egg represents the largest cell visible to unaided eye.
- Each cell has smaller components called cell organelles. These are common to all cells. Each organelles performs a specific function.
- There are some differences between plant and animal cells.
- The word **cell** is derived from the Latin word **cellula** which means **"a little room"**. An English botanist **Robert Hooke** (1635-1703) who in 1665 discovered and named the **cells**.
- **Adenosine triphosphate (ATP):** An energy rich compound that is found in all cells and serves as an energy source for various cellular functions.
- **Amino Acid:** The basic building block of protein.
- **Bacterium:** An unicellular organisms which lacks an organised nucleus.
- **Carbohydrates:** Organic molecules containing carbon, hydrogen and oxygen in the ratio of CH_2O, e.g., glucose, starch, glycogen, sugar, cellulose.
- **Centromere:** It is the point of attachment of sister chromatids and site of chromosomes attachment to the spindle fibres.
- **Chlorophyll:** Green photosynthetic, light capturing pigment of plant cells, typically located in the grana of chloroplasts.
- **Chromosomes:** Thread-like stainable condensed chromatin, visible at cell division and containing hereditary information in the form of genes.
- **Cytology:** The study of cells and their parts using microscope.
- **Cytoplasm:** The living matter in a cell, outside the nucleus.
- **Deoxyribonucleic acid (DNA):** Genetic material deoxyribose containing nucleic acid that stores hereditary informations in the form of code words and makes chromosomes and genes.
- **Differentiation:** Specialisation of cells to perform different specific functions in the organism.
- **Diploid:** An individual or cell with two complete sets of chromosomes symbolised as 2n characteristic of somatic cells.
- **Enzymes:** An organic catalyst, usually a protein which modifies the rate of chemical reaction without being consumed or permanently modified in the process.
- **Genes:** Hereditary units, specific functional units along chromosomes responsible for given traits of an organism.
- **Homologous chromosomes:** A pair of chromosomes of the same size and shape bearing corresponding genes governing the same set of traits. One member of such a pair is derived from each of two parents.
- **Leucoplast:** A colourless plastid which stores proteins, lipids and starch.
- **Lipid:** A type of a fatty organic compound, e.g. fats, oils and steriods.
- **Lysosome:** A membrane-bounded cytoplasmic organelle having various hydrolytic enzymes.

- **Matrix:** The essentially unstructured colloidal ground substance of a cell or organelle consisting of a suspension of particles and molecules in a watery medium.
- **Osmosis:** The tendency of water to move across a differentially permeable membrane from a dilute to a concentrated solution.
- **Plasma Membrane:** Membrane surrounding the cell.
- **Prokaryote:** Organisms lacking nucleus and membrane-bounded organelles in their cells.
- **Protein:** A specific chain of amino acids. Essential in producing cell structure and a variety of enzymes.
- **Ribonucleic acid (RNA):** A nucleic acid containing phosphate, ribose sugar and the nitrogen base, uracil besides adenine, guanine and cytosine. Functions in protein synthesis.
- **Ribosome:** A grainy structure having RNA and proteins and acts as the site of protein synthesis.
- **Stroma:** The granular matrix of the chloroplast.
- **Virus:** An infections, submicroscopic cellular parasite that consists of a RNA or DNA core with a protein coat.
- **Xanthophyll:** The yellow, red or orange pigments of green plants.

Prokaryotic and Eukaryotic Cells

- **Prokaryotic Cell:** These have primitive and incomplete cells. It has all three basic structures of a typical cell but lack nuclear membranes around their genetic substances (DNA). *e.g.* bacteria, blue-green algae.
- **Eukaryotic Cell:** These cells contain membrane bound cellular organelles and are called eukaryotic cells. e.g. plants and animals cells.

Differences between Prokaryotic Cells and Eukaryotic Cells

Prokaryotic Cell	*Eukaryotic Cell*
(*i*) Size of the cell is generally small.	(*i*) Size of cell is generally large.
(*ii*) Nucleus is absent.	(*ii*) Nucleus is present.
(*iii*) It contains single chromosomes.	(*iii*) It contains more than one chromosomes.
(*iv*) Membrane bound cell organelles are absent.	(*iv*) Cell organelles are present.
(*v*) Cell division takes place by fission or budding.	(*v*) Cell division occurs by miotic and miosis.

- Cells were discovered in 1665 by **Robert Hooke**.
- **Anton Von Leeuwenhoek** discovered in 1674 the free cells in the form of bacteria. He also discovered sperm in 1678 and discovered the sperm cells of human, dogs, frogs and insects.
- **Robert Brown** discovered and named the **nucleus** in plant cells.
- **J.E. Purkinje** gave the term **protoplasm** for the living fluid substance present inside the cell.
- In 1883, **Jakob Matthias Schleiden** a German botanist and **Theodor Schwann**, a German zoologist gave the **cell theory**.

The basis of the cell theory are given below:

(*i*) All organisms are composed of cells and cell products.

(*ii*) All metabolic reactions take place in cells. Thus, cells are structured and functional units of life.

(*iii*) All cells arise from pre-existing cells only.

(*iv*) Every organism starts its life as a single cell.

Characteristics of Cells

(*i*) All cells are covered by a cell membrane.

(*ii*) Cell membrane encloses a jelly like substance—the cytoplasm.

(*iii*) A round ball—like nucleus is present in the centre of the cell which controls all the activities of the cell.

(*iv*) Mitochondria helps in respiration.

(*v*) Chloroplasts help in photosynthesis.

(*vi*) Endoplasmic Reticulum helps in transport of substances within the cell.

(*vii*) Plant cells posses an outer cell wall surrounding the cell membrane. It provides rigid shape to the cell and prevents it from bursting.

Structure of Cell

Cell Shape: Cells may have diverse shapes such as polyhedral, spherical, spindle shaped, elongated, branched, discoidal.

Cell Size: The size of different cells ranges between broad limits. Some plant and animals cells are visible to the naked eye.

Most cells, however, are visible only with a microscope.

Average Size of Different Cells in the Living Organisms

S.No.	Type of Cell	Size 1μ = 10^{-6} m
1.	Living red blood cell	9μm [9 × 10^{-6} m]
2.	Nerve cell	more than a metre long
3.	Green algae	10 cm
4.	Ostrich egg	170 mm in diameter

- **Cell organelles, their location and shape and their main functions:** Plant and animal cells have the same basic structure, sharing many features. Cell contain smaller units called **organelles**.

Cell organelle	Location and shape	Main Function
1. Plasma Membrane	Outermost covering of each cells that provides and maintains shape of the cell. It is a living, thin, delicate, elastic, selectively, permeable membrane. It encloses a liquid substance known as protoplasm.	• Provides and maintains shape of the cell. Regulates the transportation of materials in and out of the cell.
2. Cell Wall	Present in plant cell only. It is present outer to the cell membrane. It is made up of non-living cellulose.	• Provides mechanical support, protection and rigidity to the plant cells. • Helps the plant cells to bear unfavourable conditions. • Provides shape. • Prevent osmotic bursting of the cell.
3. Cytoplasm	The part of the cell which occurs between the plasma membrane and nuclear envelop is called the cytoplasm. It is an aggregation of carbohydrates, proteins, fats, vitamin and minerals dissolved in water.	• Physical basis of all metabolic activities. • It acts as a store of vital chemicals such as amino acids, glucose vitamins, irons etc. • Living cytoplasm is always in a stable of movement.
4. Endoplasmic Reticulum (ER)	Irregular, interconnected network of flattened sacs made up of double membrane. It is connected with cell membrane nuclear membrane golgi bodies. ER is of two types: (*i*) Rough endoplasmic reticulum (RER) (*ii*) Smooth endoplasmic reticulum (SER). The ER is absent in the red blood cells of mammals.	• It forms cytoskeleton. • It forms intracellular transporting system. • It provides space for cellular secretions, storage and helps in transportation. • It forms many cell organelles. • It is site of lipid and steroid synthesis.
5. Ribosomes	Ribosomes are dense, spherical and grannular particles which occur freely in the matrix, Ribosomes are made up of RNA and proteins.	• Ribosomes play an important part in the synthesis of protein.
6. Golgi Apparatus	It consists of a set of membrane-bounded, fluid filled vesicles, vacuoles and flattened sacs. Golgi apparatus is absent in bacteria, blue green algae, nature sperm and red blood cells of mammals and other animals.	• Its main function is secretory. • It forms internal processing and transport system. • It helps in the formation of lysosomes and cell wall. • It acts as a way-station of assembly area for the storage, packaging of various cellular secretions.
7. Lysosomes	Lysosomes are simple tiny spherical Sac—like structures evenly distributed in the cytoplasm. It contain powerful enzymes.	• Intracellular digestion. • Digestion of worn-out cell organelles. • Destroy foreign substances.
8. Mitochondria	Double membrane bag like structure whose outer membrane is smooth whereas inner membrane is thrown into finger like structure, called **cristae**. Contain enzymes needed for aerobic oxidation of glucose.	• Sites of cellular respiration. • The energy released is stored in the form of ATP and is used by the cell. They are known as power house of the cell.
9. Plastids	Present in plant cells and absent in animal cells. They have the green pigment called chlorophyll. Trap solar energy for the process of photo-synthesis. So chloroplasts are known as **kitchens of the cells**.	• Chloroplasts trap solar energy and utilise it to manufacture food for the plant. • Provide bright colours to fruits and flowers. • Leucoplasts store food in the from of carbo.

Cell organelle	Location and shape	Main Function
10. Centrosome	Centrosome is found only in animal cells. It is present near the nucleus.	• Initiates and regulates cell division. • Produces basal bodies from which cilia and flagella.
11. Vacuoles	Vacuoles are fluid filled and membrane bounded spaces. The vacuole is covered from outside by a covering called tonoplast. In plant cells, the vacuoles are large and permanent.	• To maintain the osmotic pressure in a cell. • They store toxic metabolic by products.
12. Granules	These are also nonliving cytoplasmic inclusions. These are small particles crystals or droplets.	• Starch grains, fat droplets, help in the storage of food in cells.
13. Nucleus	The nucleus is a major, centrally located spherical cellular component. It is bounded by two nuclear membranes both forming a nuclear envelops. Nucleus contain chromosomes. It contain many segments called genes.	• Controls all the functions of a cell directly or indirectly. • Helps in the transmission of characters from parents to offspring. • Control cell division. • Variations help in evolution.

Chromosome Number of Some Organisms

Organism	*Chromosome number in each body cell*
Round Worm	2
Mosquito	6
Frog	26
Rat	42
Human beings	46
Guinea pig	64
Gold fish	100
Sunflower	34
Garden pea	14
Maize	20
Rice	24
Onion	16

Differences between Animal and Plant Cells

Animal Cell	*Plant Cell*
(*i*) Animal cells are generally small in size.	(*i*) Plant cells are larger than animal cells.
(*ii*) Cell wall is absent.	(*ii*) Cell wall made up of cellulose is present around the cell membrane. It is non living.
(*iii*) Chloroplasts are absent.	(*iii*) Chloroplasts are present.
(*iv*) Vacuoles are many but small in size.	(*iv*) Vacuoles are fewer but large in size.
(*v*) Animal cells have centrosome and centrioles.	(*v*) Plant cells lack centrosome and centrioles.

Chemical Constituents of the Cytoplasm

S.No.	*Chemical*	*Percentage*
1.	Oxygen	64.00
2.	Carbon	18.00
3.	Hydrogen	10.00
4.	Nitrogen	03.00
5.	Trace elements (Ca, P, Cl, S, K, Na, Mg, I, Fe)	05.00

Comparison of Plant and Animal Cells

S.No.	*Component organelle*	*Planet cell*	*Animal cell*
1.	Cell wall	Present	Absent
2.	Plasma Membrane	Present	Present
3.	Plastids	Present	Absent
4.	Vacuoles	Large size	Small size
5.	Nucleus	Present	Present
6.	Mitochondria	Present	Present

Cell Division

The process through which multiplication is achieved is called cell division. Cells multiplies by dividing itself again and again. Cells divide in two different ways:

— Mitosis and

— Meiosis.

- **Mitosis** is the kind of cell division that occurs in the somatic (body) cells of all plants and animals during growth and asexual reproduction.
- **Meiosis** takes place in the germinal cells of organisms during gametogenesis or formation of gametes—eggs and sperms.

NATURAL RESOURCES, AGRICULTURE AND ENVIRONMENT

The Natural Resources

The assets of nature, which are useful to mankind, are called natural resources.

Natural resources are two types:

(*i*) **Inexhaustible natural resources:** These resources are present in unlimited quantity in the nature and they are not likely to be exhausted by human activities. *e.g.* Solar radiation, air, water, precipitation and atomic power.

(*ii*) **Exhaustible natural resources:** These natural resources are liable to be degraded in quantity and quality by the human activities. *e.g.* Soil, minerals, fossil fuels etc.

Management and Replacement of Natural Resources

Management and conservation means scientific utilisation of resources while maintaining their sustained yield and quality.

Conservation of forests

Afforestation of deforested areas becomes necessary to get sufficient rainfall for the conservation of soil, for the conservation of rare forest plants and for conservation of unique wild life of the area.

The conservation of forest includes the following methods: (*i*) Afforestation (*ii*) Ex-situ conservation.

Afforestation

Afforestation is the process of transforming an area into forest.

(*i*) **Conservation of reserve forests:** Reserve forests are areas where water regimes are located. *e.g.* Himalayas and Western and Eastern Ghats. In reserve forests no commercial exploitation is allowed.

(*ii*) **Commercial forestry:** The basic aim of commercial forestry is to supply goods and services to meet the needs of local people for firewood, fodder, food fertiliser etc. It includes two main types of forestry:

- **Social forestry:** In social forestry those forest trees are planted on community lands, individuals holdings and other public lands which are needed by local rural and tribal populations.

  Social forestry has the following objectives:

  (*i*) To use public and common land to produce fire wood, fodder and timber.

  (*ii*) To manage soil and water conservation.

  (*iii*) To relieve pressure from conservation forests.

  (*iv*) To improve the environment of denuded or degraded wasteland by social forestry.

- **Ex-situ Conservation:** It involves plantation of trees of aesthetic value and ornamental trees in the botanical gardens.

Conservation of wildlife

The International Union for Conservation of Nature (IUCN) and Natural Resources, has made five main conservation categories of wild animals and plants.

(*i*) **Extinct species:** A species is considered extinct when there is no reasonable doubt that its last individual has died. *e.g.* Mountain quail, pink headed duck, Lesser one horned rhino, cheetah. Extinct plant species—Sarpgandha, Brahmkamal etc.

(*ii*) **Endangered species:** It is the species which is in danger of extinction and whose survival is causal factor continue to operate. *e.g.* Brow antlered deer, Hispid hare, Lion-tailed macaque, Asiatic lion, Great Indian bustard, Crocodile, Musk deer, Blue whale etc.

(*iii*) **Vulnerable species:** Such a species contains sufficient number of individuals in its habitat, but in near future, it may represent the category of endangered species. *e.g.* Crab-eating macaque, Golden langur, Chinkara deer etc.

(*iv*) **Rare species:** Such a species contains small world population that are not presently endangered or vulnerable, but are at risk. *e.g.* Indian egg-eating snake, Olive Ridley turtle, Golden cat etc.

(*v*) **Insufficiently known species:** Such a species requires more information for its conservation.

Some of the important measures for the conservation of Indian wildlife are following:

The protection of natural habitat and maintenance of endangered and other important species by certain protected areas such as national parks, wildlife or bird sanctuaries. In India, there are 104 national parks 544 sanctuaries and 18 biosphere reserves.

Biosphere Reserves: Biosphere reserves are multi-purpose protected areas with following major objectives:

(*i*) to conserve diversity and integrity of plants, animals and micro-organisms.

(*ii*) to promote ecological conservation.

(*iii*) to educate, train and create awareness about environmental aspects and eco-friendly living.

In India, 18 biospheres have been set up to year 2018.

1. Nilgiri (1986)
2. Nandadevi (1988)
3. Nokrok (1988)
4. Great Nicobar (1989)
5. Gulf of Mannar (1989)
6. Manas (1989)
7. Sunderbans (1989)
8. Simplipal (1994)
9. Dibrusaikhowa (1997)
10. Debong-Debang (1998)
11. Panchmarhi (1999)
12. Kanchanjangha (2000)
13. Agasthyamalai (2001)
14. Achanakmar–Amarkantak (2005)
15. Kachchh (2008)
16. Cold Desert (2009)
17. Seshachalom (2010)
18. Panna (2011)

MULTIPLE CHOICE QUESTIONS

1. The largest cell in the human body is:
A. Nerve cell B. Muscle cell
C. Liver cell D. Kidney cell

2. The barrier between the protoplasm and the other environment in an animal cells:
A. Cell wall B. Nuclear membrane
C. Tonoplast D. Plasma membrane

3. The term 'Cell' was given by:
A. Leeuwenhoek B. Robert hooke
C. Flemming D. Robert Brown

4. Who proposed the cell theory?
A. Schleiden and Schwann
B. Watson and Crick
C. Darwin and Wallace
D. Mendel and Morgan

5. A plant cell differs from an animal cell in the absence of:
A. Endoplasmic Reticulum
B. Mitochondria
C. Ribosome
D. Centriole

6. Centrosome is found in:
A. Cytoplasm B. Nucleus
C. Chromosomes D. Nucleolus

7. The power house of a cell is:
A. Chloroplast B. Mitochondrion
C. Golgi apparatus D. Nucleolus

8. Within a cell the site of respiration (oxidation) is the:
A. Ribosome
B. Golgi apparatus
C. Mitochondrion
D. Endoplasmic Reticulum

9. Which is called 'Suicidal Bag'?
A. Centrosome B. Lysosome
C. Mesosome D. Chromosome

10. Ribosomes are the center for:
A. Respiration B. Photosynthesis
C. Protein synthesis D. Fat synthesis

11. Double membrane is absent in:
A. Mitochondrion B. Chloroplast
C. Nucleus D. Lysosome

12. Cell organelle found only in Plant is:
A. Golgi apparatus B. Mitochondria
C. Plastids D. Ribosomes

13. Organisms lacking nucleus and membrane bound organelle are:
A. Diploids B. Prokaryotes
C. Haploids D. Eukaryotes

14. Animal cell is limited by:
A. Plasma membrane B. Shell membrane
C. Cell wall D. Basement membrane

15. The network of Endoplasmic Reticulum is present in the:
A. Nucleus B. Nucleolus
C. Cytoplasm D. Chromosomes

16. Lysosome are reservoirs of:
A. Fat
B. RNA
C. Secretary Glycoprotein
D. Hydrolytic Enzymes

17. The membrane surrounding the vacuole of a plant cell is called:
A. Tonoplast B. Plasma membrane
C. Nuclear membrane D. Cell wall

18. Cell secretion is done by:
A. Plastids B. ER
C. Golgi apparatus D. Nucleolus

19. Centrioles are associated with:
A. DNA synthesis B. Reproduction
C. Spindle formation D. Respiration

20. Main difference between animal cell and plant cell is:
A. Chromosome
B. Ribosome
C. Lysosome
D. Endoplasmic Reticulum

21. Animal cell lacking nuclei would also lack in:
A. Chromosome B. Ribosome
C. Lysosome D. Endoplasmic Reticulum

22. Plasmolysis occurs due to:
A. Absorption B. Endosmosis
C. Osmosis D. Exosmosis

23. A plant cell becomes turgid due to:
A. Plasmolysis B. Exosmosis
C. Endosmosis D. Electrolysis

24. Solute concentration is higher in the external solution:
A. Hypotonic B. Isotonic
C. Hypertonic D. None of the above

25. A cell placed in hypertonic solution will:
A. Shrink
B. Show Plasmolysis
C. Swell up
D. No change in shape or size

26. The radiant energy of sunlight is converted to chemical energy and is stored as:
A. AMP B. ADP
C. ATP D. APP

27. Which of the following organelle does not have membrane?
A. Ribosome B. Nucleus
C. Chloroplast D. Mitochondria

28. Root hair absorbs water from soil through:
A. Osmosis B. Active transport
C. Diffusion D. Endocytosis

29. The number of lenses in compound light microscope is:
A. 2 B. 3
C. 4 D. 1

30. The history of the cell began in 1665 with the publication of Micrographia in London by:
A. Robert Hooke B. Robert Brown
C. Strasburger D. Dujardin

31. Cell inclusions are:
A. Non-living materials present in the cytoplasm
B. Another name of cell organelle
C. Cytoskeletal framework of cell
D. Combined name for cell wall and plasma membrane

32. Which cell organelle is not bounded by a membrane?
A. Ribosome B. Lysosome
C. ER D. Nucleus

33. Which of the following cellular part possess a double membrane?
A. Nucleus B. Chloroplast
C. Mitochondrion D. All of the above

34. Cristae and Oxysomes are associated with:
A. Mitochondria B. Plastids
C. Golgi apparatus D. Plasma membrane

35. Karyotheca is another name of:
A. Nuclear envelope B. Nucleus
C. Nuclear pores D. Nucleolus

36. Cell organelle that acts as supporting skeletal framework of the cell is:
A. Golgi apparatus B. Nucleus
C. Mitochondria D. ER

37. Plastids are present in:
A. Animal cell only
B. Plant cells only
C. Both animal cells and Plant cells
D. Neither animal nor plant cells

38. Cell wall of plant is chiefly composed of:
A. Hemicellulose B. Cellulose
C. Phospholipids D. Proteins

39. Intercellular connections of plant cells are called:
A. Middle lamella B. Micro fibrils
C. Matrix D. Plasmodesmata

40. Genes are located on the:
A. Chromosomes B. Nucleolus
C. Nuclear membrane D. Plasma membrane

41. Chromatin consists of:
A. RNA
B. DNA
C. RNA and histones (proteins)
D. DNA and histones (proteins)

42. Different types of chromosomes can be recognized by the positions of the following separating the two arms:
A. Centromere B. Genes
C. Spindle D. Nucleus

43. Name of the process that requires energy provided by ATP:
A. Diffusion B. Osmosis
C. Active transport D. Plasmolysis

44. Mitochondria are found:
A. in all type of living cells
B. only in animal cells
C. only in plant cells
D. in eukaryote cells only

45. Who discovered the first living cell?
A. Robert Hooke B. Leeuwenhoek
C. Purkinje D. Robert Brown

46. Which of the following can be made into crystal?
A. A bacterium B. An Amoeba
C. A virus D. A sperm

47. Who used the word 'protoplasm first time for living cells?
A. Robert Hooke B. Leeuwenhoek
C. Purkinje D. Robert Brow

48. The main constituent of cell-wall is:
A. Starch B. cellulose
C. protein D. none of these

49. Function of centriole is:
A. formation of spindle fibre
B. nucleolus formationation
C. cell wall formation
D. cell division initiation

50. Which organelle is the power house of the cells?
A. Plastids B. Mitochondria
C. Golgi D. Nucleus

51. Chromosomes are made up of nucleic acid and ________.
A. Phosphorus B. Protein
C. Sugar D. Calcium

52. Which organelle is considered as a suicide bag?
A. Centrosome B. Mesosomes
C. Lysosomes D. Chromosome

53. Plastids which are responsible for giving colors to fruits and flowers are:

A. chloroplasts B. leucoplasts
C. protoplasts D. chromoplasts

54. Which of the following organelle is present onion cells but not in human cheek cells?

A. cell wall B. cytoplasm
C. nucleus D. plasma membrane

55. Which cell organelle plays a crucial role in detoxifying many poisons and drugs?

A. Golgi Apparatus
B. Lysosomes
C. Smooth Endoplasmic Reticulum
D. Vacuoles

56. Projections of different lengths protruding out of the body of Amoeba is called:

A. Walking legs B. Legs
C. Pseudopodia D. Needle

57. Which of the following cells can change its shape?

A. White blood cell B. Egg cell
C. Red blood cell D. All of the above

58. One millionth of a metre is:

A. Millimetre B. Micrometre
C. Nanometre D. Centimetre

59. Which of the following combinations are present in plant cell but not in animal cell?

A. Cell Wall & Plastid
B. Cell wall and Cell membrane
C. Plastid and Nucleus
D. Cell Membrane and Cytoplasm

60. Nucleus is separated from cytoplasm by:

A. Protoplasm
B. Cell membrane
C. Cell Wall
D. Nuclear membrane

61. Deforestation means:

A. Planting more trees
B. Designing a forest
C. Demanding a forest
D. Clearing of forests and using that land for c purposes

62. Species of plants and animals which are fc exclusively in a particular area are called:

A. Exotic species B. Local species
C. Specific species D. Endemic species

63. Increased level of carbon dioxide in the atmosp traps the heat rays reflected by the earth causing increase in the temperature on the earth. This is:

A. Local warming B. House warming
C. Global warming D. Country warming

64. Part of the earth which supports life where living bei exists is called ______.

A. Atmosphere B. Biosphere
C. Biology D. Biodiversity

65. Variety of organisms existing on the earth, their ir relationships and their relationship with the environn is called:

A. Diversity B. Biosphere
C. Biology D. Biodiversity

ANSWERS

1	2	3	4	5	6	7	8	9	10
A	D	B	A	D	A	B	C	B	C
11	**12**	**13**	**14**	**15**	**16**	**17**	**18**	**19**	**20**
D	C	B	A	C	D	A	C	C	A
21	**22**	**23**	**24**	**25**	**26**	**27**	**28**	**29**	**30**
A	D	C	C	C	C	A	A	A	A
31	**32**	**33**	**34**	**35**	**36**	**37**	**38**	**39**	**40**
A	A	D	A	A	D	B	B	D	A
41	**42**	**43**	**44**	**45**	**46**	**47**	**48**	**49**	**50**
D	A	C	D	B	C	C	B	A	B
51	**52**	**53**	**54**	**55**	**56**	**57**	**58**	**59**	**60**
B	C	D	A	C	C	A	B	A	D
61	**62**	**63**	**64**	**65**					
D	D	C	B	D					

★ ★ ★

4

Reproduction–Asexual and Sexual Reproduction, Reaching the Age of Adolescence

Some Important Facts

- The production of new organisms from the existing organisms of the same species is known as reproduction.
- Reproduction is essential for the survival of a species on this earth.
- The process of reproduction ensures continuity of life on earth.
- Reproduction by human beings ensures that the human species will continue to exist on this earth for all the time to come.
- Reproduction gives rise to more organisms with the same basic characteristics as their parents.
- Reproduction multiplies organisms while development builds up the body structures.
- The methods of reproduction show much diversity offspring may arise
  (*i*) from a single individual or
  (*ii*) by the participation of two individuals.
- There are two main methods of reproduction in living organisms:
  (*i*) Asexual reproduction and
  (*ii*) Sexual reproduction.
- **Asexual Reproduction:** The production of a new organism from a single parent without the involvement of sex cells is called asexual reproduction.

Some of the examples of asexual reproduction are: ry fission in Amoeba, budding in hydra, spore formation hizopus fungus, regeneration in Spirogyra and Planaria vegetative propagation in flowering plants.

Asexual reproduction takes place by five different ods. These are:

i) Fission
'i) Budding
'i) Spore formation
v) Regeneration and
v) Vegetative propagation.

ission

n the individual cell is fully mature, it divides into two. is called fission.

Fission are two types: (*i*) Binary fission and (*ii*) Multiple on.

(*i*) **Binary Fission:** When two individuals are formed during fission, the process is called **binary fission**. *e.g.,* The unicellular organisms like Amoeba, Paramecium, bacteria etc. reproduce by binary fission.

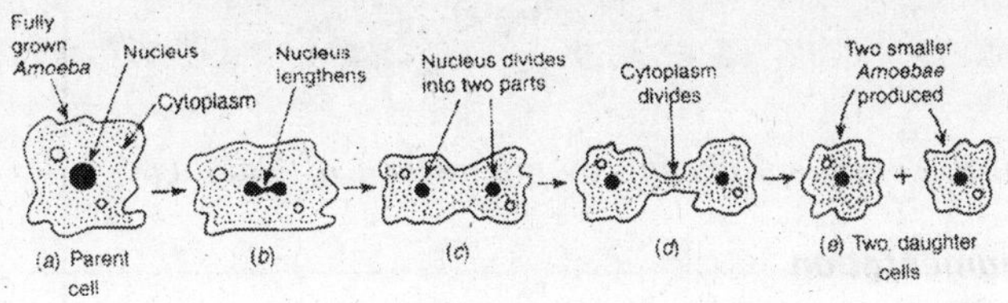

Fig. 1. *Amoeba reproducing by binary fission*

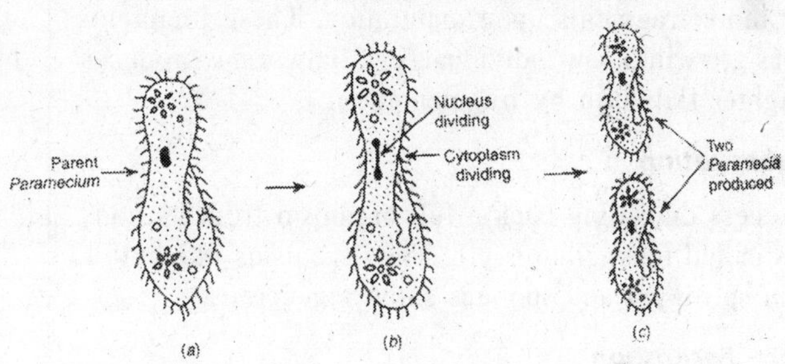

Fig. 2. *Paramecium reproducing by binary fission*

(*ii*) **Multiple Fission:** The cell divides many times within the cyst to produce many daughter cells. This is called **multiple fission**. *e.g.* Plasmodium is a protozoan which reproduces by the asexual method of multiple fission. About 1000 daughter cells are produced by the multiple fission of one plasmodium cell.

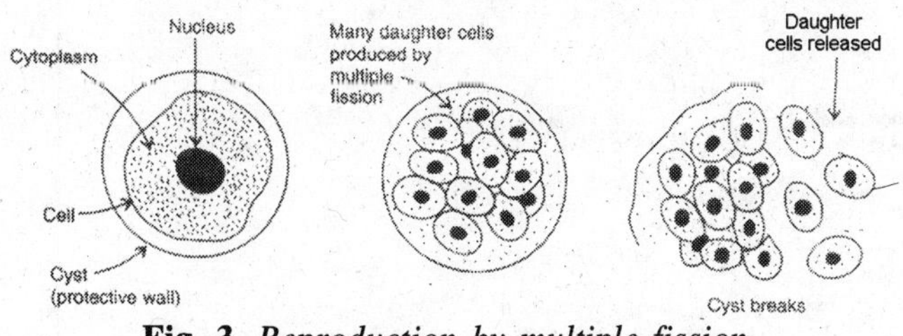

Fig. 3. *Reproduction by multiple fission*

2. Budding

A bulb—like projection formed on the body is known as the **bud**. The nucleus of the body divides into two and one of the nuclei passes into the bud. The bud detaches itself from the parent body, grows to full size and becomes a new individual. e.g. Yeast and Hydra.

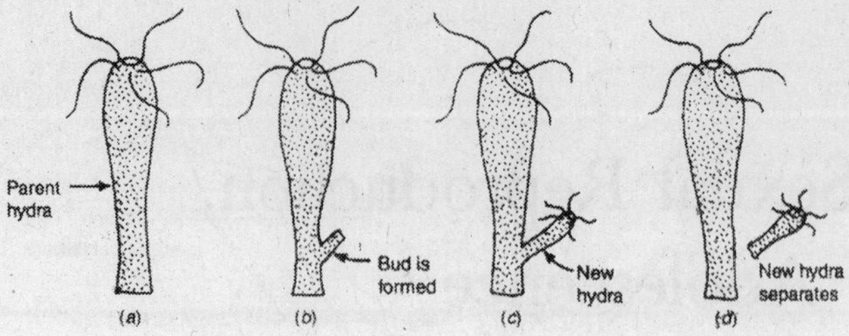

Fig. 4. *Hydra reproducing by the method of budding*

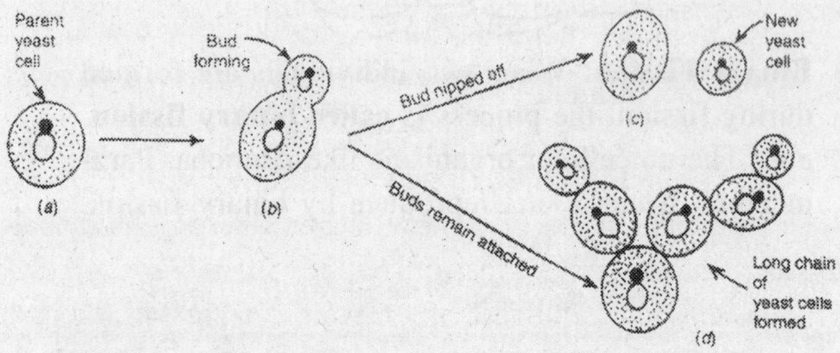

Fig. 5. *Yeast reproducing by the method of budding*

3. Fragmentation

Some organisms such as spirogyra (algae) break up into two or more fragments upon maturation. These fragments or pieces grow into new individuals e.g. flatworm reproduces its daughter flatworm by fragmentation.

4. Regeneration

The process of getting back a full organism from its body parts is called regeneration. e.g. The organisms like hydra, planaria spirogyra and sponges show regeneration.

5. Spore Formation

Some bacteria and lower forms of life form spores. It is a resting state in which the cell is protected by a thick wall during unfavourable conditions of heat or dryness. On return of favourable conditions, the thick wall breaks open and the bacteria reproduce and grow. e.g. Most of the fungi and bacteria reproduce by the method of spore formation.

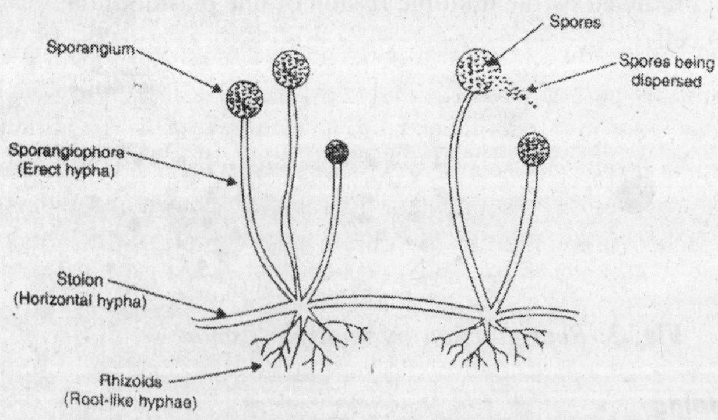

Fig. 6. *Rhizopus fungus plant (or bread mould) reproduces by forming spores.*

Vegetative Propagation

- Vegetative propagation is an asexual method of propagation in some higher plants.
- In vegetative propagation some plants can reproduced by growing new plants from the single parent plant are obtained from the parts of old plants (like stems, roots and leaves) without the help of any reproductive organs. *e.g.* Strawberry, iris, potato and rose plants can reproduce by this method.

There are many other plants which can grow by vegetative propagation.

(*i*) **Strawberry runners:** Shoots have buds which grow into new plants.

(*ii*) **Potato tubers:** A potato is an underground stem of a potato plant. The eyes on the potato sprout into new plants.

(*iii*) **Rhizomes (ginger):** Rhizomes are stems that grow and produce new plants.

(*iv*) **Gladiolus corms:** A corm is a short stem and form new plants.

(*v*) **Leaves:** The leaves of some plants. *e.g.* Bryophyllum.

A number of methods of artificial propagation of plants are used in agriculture and horticulture.

The common methods for the artificial vegetative propagation are:

(*i*) Grafting (*ii*) Cutting (*iii*) Layering.

(*i*) **Grafting:** Grafting is a method in which the cut stems of two different plants (one with roots and the other without roots) are joined together in such a way that the two plant stems join and grow as a single plant. The cut stem of a plant having roots is called **stock**. The cut stem of another plant without root is called **scion**. Using their practice plants of desired quality and fruits are obtained. Many varieties.

(*ii*) **Cutting:** A part of the plant which is a removed by cutting it, is called a cutting. A cutting may be a piece of stem, root or leaf. The cutting mode of propagation can be used to grow bougainvillea, sugarcane and cactus. Cutting allows to produce many new plants from one plant, without waiting for flowers and seeds.

(*iii*) **Layering:** In this method, a branch of the plant bends towards the ground and gets covered with moist soil. After some time, new roots emerge from the branch and produce new plantlets. These plantlets can be separated from the parent plant and made to grow as new individual plants.

e.g. Jasmine, roses and bougainvillea.

Advantages of Artificial Vegetative Propagation

The artificial vegetative propagation has the following advantages:

(*i*) The new plants produced by artificial vegetative propagation will be exactly like the parent plants.

(*ii*) Fruit trees grown from seeds may take many years before they start to bear fruits. Fruit trees grown from cutting or by grafting start to bear fruits after only a few growing seasons.

(*iii*) The plants grown by vegetative propagation usually need less attention in their early years than the plants grown for seeds.

Tissue Culture

The production of new plants from isolated plant cells or small pieces of plant tissue in a synthetic medium is called micropropagation or tissue culture.

The plant material is grown in special synthetic medium called culture solution it contains various plant nutrients and plant hormones. Which are necessary for plant growth.

Tissue culture for producing new plants is as follows:

(*i*) Some plant cells is taken from the tip of the plant and put into a suitable synthetic medium under sterile conditions.

(*ii*) The callus is then transferred to another medium containing suitable plant hormones which stimulus the callus to develop roots.

(*iii*) The callus with developed roots is then put into a yet another medium containing a different set of hormones which stimulate the development of shoots.

(*iv*) The callus having roots and shoots separate into tiny plantlets.

(*v*) The plantlets thus produced are transplanted into pots or soil where they can grow to form mature plants. Orchids, chrysanthemums, asparagus and many other plants are now grown using plant tissue culture.

Sexual Reproduction in Plants

The function of a flower is to make male and female gametes and to ensure that fertilisation will take place to make new seeds for the reproduction of plants.

Sexual reproduction is the most common method of reproduction in flowering plants.

The sexual reproduction in plants takes place in the following steps:

(*i*) The male organ of flower called **Stamen** makes the male gametes of the plant. These male sex cells are present in pollen grains.

(*ii*) The female organ of a flower called carpel or pistil makes the female gametes of the plant. These female sex cells are presented in ovules.

(*iii*) The male gametes present in pollen grains fertilise the female gametes present in ovules.

(*iv*) The fertilised ovules grow and become seeds.

(*v*) The seeds produce new plants.

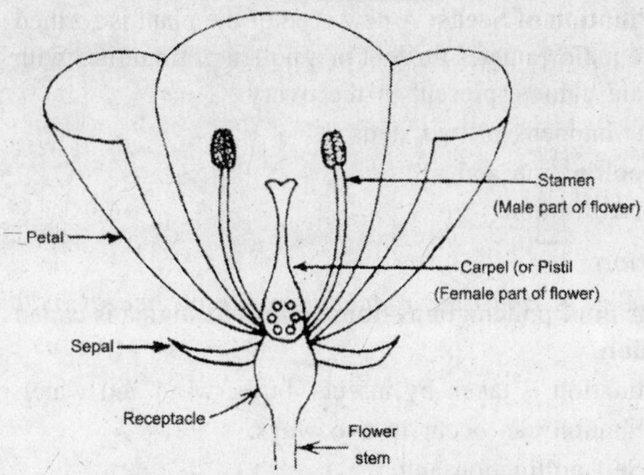

Fig. 7. *The parts of a flower.*

The main parts of a flower are: Receptacle, Sepals, Petals, Stamen and Carpel or Pistil.

Receptacle: The base of a flower to which all the parts of a flower are attached is called receptacle.

Sepals: The green, leaf-like parts in the outermost circle of a flower are called sepals. All the sepals taken together are called calyx.

Petals: The colourful parts of a flower are called **petals**. The petals lie inside the sepals. All the petals taken together are called corolla. The petals are usually scented. The function of petals is to attract insect for pollination.

Stamen: Stamen is the male reproduction organ of the plant. The stamen is made of two parts:

(*i*) a filament and

(*ii*) an anther

The Stalk of Stamen is called filament and the swollen top of stamen is called anther. Anther makes the pollen grains and stores them. Pollen grains contain the male gametes of the plant. Each pollen grain contains two male gametes of the plant.

Carpel or pistil: Carpel is the female reproductive organ of the plant. A carpel is made of three parts:

(*i*) Stigma (*ii*) Style and (*iii*) Ovary.

The top part of carpel is called **stigma**. Stigma is for receiving the pollen grains from the anther of stamen. The middle part of carpel is called **style**. Style is a tube which connects stigma to the ovary. The swollen part at the bottom of a carpel is called **ovary**. The ovary makes ovules and stores them. Ovules contain the female gametes of the plant. Each ovule contains only one female gametes of the plant.

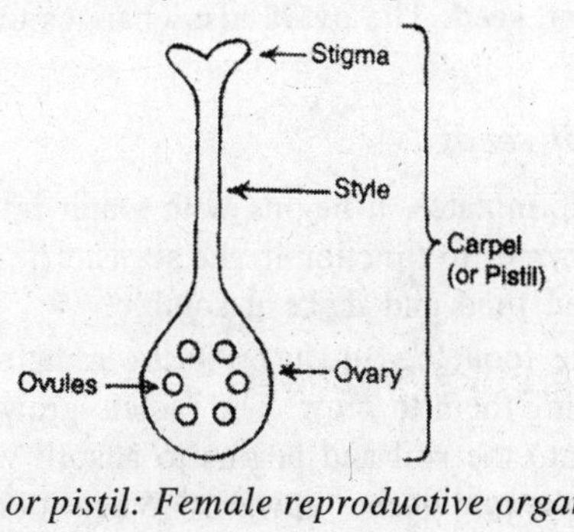

Fig. 8. *Carpel or pistil: Female reproductive organ of plant*

Formation of Seeds: A new seed of the plant is formed when the male gametes present in a pollen grain unites with the female gamete present in the ovary.

Thus happens in two steps:

(*i*) pollination and
(*ii*) fertilisation.

Pollination

The transfer of pollen grains from anthers to stigma is called **pollination**.

Pollination is taken by insects, birds, wind and water. Pollination can occur in two ways:

(*i*) Self-pollination and
(*ii*) Cross-pollination.

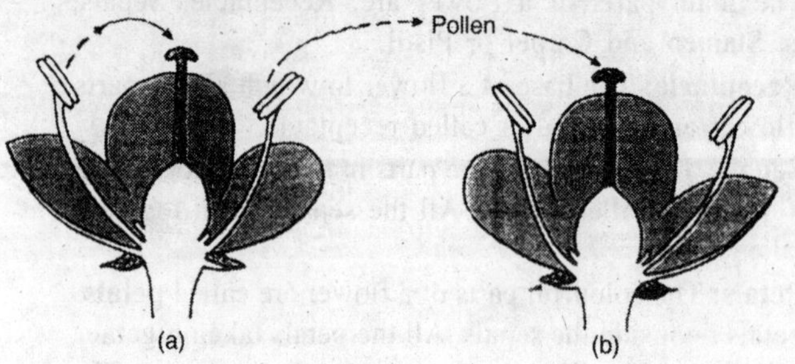

Fig. 9. *(a) Self-pollination and (b) cross-pollination*

Self-pollination: When the pollen grains from the anther of a flower are transferred to the stigma of the same flower is called self-pollination.

Cross-pollination: When the pollen grains from the anther of a flower on one plant are transferred to the stigma of a flower on another plant, it is called cross pollination.

Fertilisation

During pollination, pollen grains are carried from the anther to the stigma. The stigma secretes a liquid, containing sugar. If the stigma belongs to the right species of flower, the pollen grain responds to this liquid by beginning to form a tube. The tube grows out of the pollen grain and reaches one of the ovules.

The male gamete leaves the pollen grain and makes its way along the tube. When it reaches the ovule, it goes inside and fuses with the female gamete. Fertilisation has taken place. The fertilised egg cell is known as a **zygote**.

The fertilised and developed ovule, which contain embryo, is called **seed**. The ovary also changes to become a **fruit**.

Germination of seeds

When a seed germinates, it begins with water intake. The water helps enzymes to function in the seeds. The enzymes digest the stored food and make it soluble.

The soluble food then diffuses to the radicle and the plumule, allowing them to grow. The radicle grows first. It pushes down into the soil and begins to absorb water and minerals. The plumule pushes upwards. When it breaks out above the soil into the light, it becomes green and begins to photosynthesis.

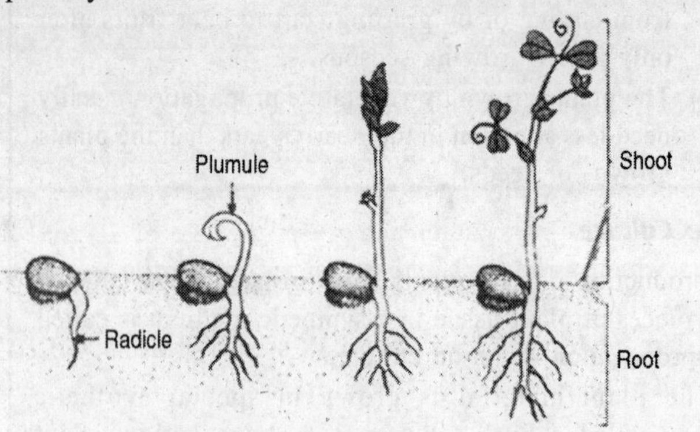

Fig. 10. *Germination of seed*

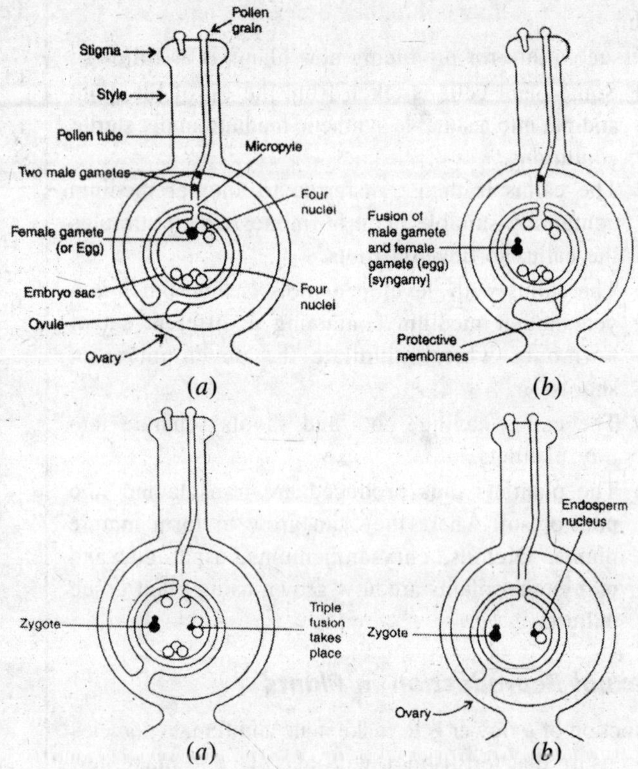

Fig. 11. *Explanation of the fertilisation in plants (including syngamy and triple fussion).*

Reproduction in Animals

Reproduction takes place in animal in two ways:

(*i*) Asexual and
(*ii*) Sexual.

Sexual Reproduction in Animals: The fusion of a male gamete with a female gamete to form a zygote during the sexual reproduction, is called **fertilisation.**

The stage of development between the zygote and the newly formed body is called **embryo.**

The fertilisation which occurs inside the female body is called **internal fertilisation.**

e.g., In mammals, birds and reptiles the fertilisation occurs inside the female body.

The fertilisation which occurs outside the female body is called **external fertilisation.**

e.g., Frogs, toads and fishes the fertilisation of eggs occurs outside the female body.

Sexual Reproduction in Humans: The age at which the sex hormones begin to be produced and the boy and girl become sexually mature is called **puberty**.

Generally boys attain puberty at the age of 13 to 14 years which girls reach puberty at a comparatively lower age of 10 to 12 years.

The testes produce the male sex hormone called testosterone and the ovaries produce two female sex hormones estrogen and progesterone. The sex hormons play an important role in the process of reproduction.

The various function of sex hormone are given below:

(*i*) The sex hormones control the process of gametogenesis.

(*ii*) The sex hormones maintain the structure and functions of accessory sex organs.

(*iii*) The sex hormones develop the secondary sex characteristics.

The Male Reproductive System

The human male reproductive system consists of the following organs:

(*i*) Testes

(*ii*) Scrotum and

(*iii*) Epididymis.

Testes are the primary reproductive organs in man. The function of testes is to make the male sex cells called sperms and also to make the male sex hormone called testosterone.

The sperms formed in testes come out and go into a coiled tube called epididymis. The sperms get stored temporarily in epididymics.

The Female Reproductive System

The human female reproductive system consists of the following organs:

(*i*) Ovaries

(*ii*) Fallopian tubes

(*iii*) Uterus

(*iv*) Vagina.

Ovaries are the oval shaped organs which are inside the abdominal cavity of a woman near the kidneys. The function of ovaries is to make the female sex cells called ova or eggs and also make the female sex hormones called estrogen and progesterone.

The fallopian tubes are not directly connected to ovaries but have funnel shaped openings which almost cover the ovaries. The fertilisation of egg by a sperm takes place in the fallopian tube.

The two fallopian tubes connect to a bag like organ called uterus. The growth and development of a fertilised ovum into a body takes place in the uterus. The embedding of embryo in the thick lining of the uterus is called implantation. The exchange of nutrients, oxygen and waste products between the embryo and the mother takes place through the placenta.

The time period from the fertilisation upto the birth of the body is called **gestation**. The average gestation period in humans is about 40 weeks or 280 days. The average weight of a new born baby is about 3.5 kilograms.

MULTIPLE CHOICE QUESTIONS

1. The two oviducts in a human female unite into an elastic bag like is known as:
A. Vagina B. Uterus
C. Fallopian tube D. Cervix

2. Which of the following disease is transmitted sexually?
A. Kala azar B. Jaundice
C. Cholera D. Syphilis

3. Which of the following is a contraceptive?
A. Copper-T B. Condom
C. Diaphragm D. All of these

4. When a animal is cut into pieces and each piece grows into a complex organism. What is the process?
A. Budding B. Fragmentation
C. Spore formation D. Regeneration

5. Which is the portion on which grafting is done it provides the roots?
A. Stock B. Scion
C. Both A and B D. None of these

6. Where does fertilization occur in human females?
A. Uterus B. Cervix
C. Oviduct D. None of these

7. Growing foetus derive nutrition from mother's blood through:
A. Uterus B. Fallopian tube
C. Placenta D. Cervix

8. What is the puberty age in human males?
A. 8-10 B. 10-12
C. 12-14 D. 14-16

9. Fruits are formed from:
A. Stamen B. Stigma
C. Ovary D. Ovule

10. IUCD is for:
A. Vegetative propagation
B. Contraception
C. Increasing fertility
D. Avoiding miscarriage

11. The male hormone testesterone is produced by ________.
A. Leydig cells B. Seminiferous tubules
C. Epididymis D. Vas deferens

12. Male gonads are called ________.
A. testes B. ovaries
C. scrotal sacs D. sperm duct

13. The fertilized egg is called ________.
A. ovum B. blastocyst
C. diploid cell D. zygote

14. The ultimate stoppage of menstrual cycle is called ________.
A. puberty B. menarche
C. menopause D. old age

15. The process by which the sperms are produced is known as ________.
A. ovulation B. spermatogenesis
C. oogenesis D. gestation

16. The tube that carries the sperms out of the testes is the ________.
A. vasa efferentia B. vas deferens
C. oviduct D. epididymis

17. The process by which the sperms are released is called ________.
A. spermatogenesis B. oogenesis
C. ovulation D. ejaculation

18. The external genitalia in females is called ________.
A. pubis B. vagina
C. vulva D. clitoris

19. Sterilisation in males is called as ________.
A. tubectomy B. vasectomy
C. IVF D. GIFT

20. Binary fission is seen in ________.
A. plasmodium B. hydra
C. amoeba D. mucor

21. The endosperm nucleus is ________.
A. haploid B. diploid
C. triploid D. tetraploid

22. The fertilization of human egg by the sperms takes place in ________.
A. ovary B. oviduct
C. vagina D. uterus

23. Pollen tube contains ________.
A. one male nucleus B. two male nuclei
C. three male nuclei D. four male nuclei

24. If the pollen is transferred to the stigma of the same flower, it is called ________.
A. allogamy B. autogamy
C. cross pollination D. double fertilization

25. Pollen grains are produced by ________.
A. ovary B. filament
C. stigma D. anther

26. The collective name for sepals is ________.
A. androecium B. gynoecium
C. corolla D. calyx

27. The individual units of corolla are called ________.
A. petals B. sepals
C. stamens D. pistils

28. The attachment of the embryo to the uterus is called ________.
A. gestation B. fertilisation
C. implantation D. menstruation

29. The onset of the reproductive age is called ________.
A. menstruation B. menarche
C. menopause D. puberty

30. The first time that the monthly bleeding occurs is called ________.
A. maturity B. menarche
C. menopause D. puberty

31. The most important part of the plant for continuation of the life of the species is________.
A. stem B. root
C. flower D. leaf

32. The type of vegetative propagation seen in chrysanthemum is ________.
A. runner B. sucker
C. stolon D. offset

33. Successfully grafted plants bear the flowers and fruits characteristic of the ________.
A. scion
B. stock
C. either scion or stock
D. a mixture of scion and stock

34. Sugarcane is normally grown by ________.
A. cutting B. grafting
C. layering D. seeds

35. Unequal daughter cells are produced in ________.
A. fragmentation B. sporulation
C. fission D. budding

36. Vegetative propogation in sweet potato is by ________.
A. stem B. root
C. leaf D. none of the above

37. Vegetative propogation in *Bryophyllum* is by ________.
A. stem B. root
C. leaf D. none of the above

38. An example of a hermaphrodite is ________.
A. frog B. fish
C. earthworm D. hydra

39. Multiple fission is seen in ___________.
A. yeast B. paramoecium
C. plasmodium D. rhizopus

40. Progesterone is secreted by ___________.
A. Ovarian follicle B. Graffian follicle
C. Corpus luteum D. Corpus albicans

41. The hormone secreted by the pituitary to start the ovulation process is ___________.
A. FSH B. Luteinizing hormone
C. Oestrogen D. Progesterone

42. Sperms are produced at a temperature that is ______ the body temperature.
A. same as B. lower than
C. higher than D. immaterial to

43. The part of the sperm that contains the lytic enzymes is ___________.
A. acrosome B. nucleus
C. mid-piece D. tail

44. The life span of the sperm is ___________.
A. 2 days B. 1-3 days
C. 1-3 weeks D. 7 days

45. The sperms are temporarily stored in ___________.
A. vas deferens B. vas efferens
C. epididymis D. bladder

46. Identical gametes are also known as:
A. heterogametes
B. isogametes
C. anisogamete
D. hypogametes

47. Placenta passes out through vagina:
A. 10-20 minutes after birth
B. 10-15 minutes after birth
C. 10-30 minutes after birth
D. 10-45 minutes after birth

48. Germinating pollen grain is a rich source of:
A. cytokinin B. gibberellin
C. auxin D. rennin

49. Secondary spermatocytes and spermatids are formed by meiotic division in:
A. primary spermatocytes
B. spermatogonia
C. primary oocytes
D. polar body

50. Multiple fission is a characteristic reproduction mechanism in:
A. plant like protoctists
B. animal like protoctists
C. hydra
D. earthworm

ANSWERS

1	2	3	4	5	6	7	8	9	10
B	D	D	D	A	D	C	C	C	B
11	**12**	**13**	**14**	**15**	**16**	**17**	**18**	**19**	**20**
A	A	D	C	B	B	D	C	B	C
21	**22**	**23**	**24**	**25**	**26**	**27**	**28**	**29**	**30**
C	B	B	B	D	D	A	C	D	B
31	**32**	**33**	**34**	**35**	**36**	**37**	**38**	**39**	**40**
C	B	A	A	D	B	C	C	C	C
41	**42**	**43**	**44**	**45**	**46**	**47**	**48**	**49**	**50**
B	B	A	B	C	B	D	C	A	B

★ ★ ★

5

Force–Frictional Force; Gravitational Force; Thrust and Pressure

Physical Quantities

- Physical quantities may be divided in two classes:
  (*i*) Scalar Quantities
  (*ii*) Vector Quantities
- A scalar quantity is one which has only magnitude.
- A vector quantity has both magnitude and direction.
- Force, Velocity, Momentum, Acceleration are examples of vector quantities.
- Mass, length, time, volume, speed, energy, work are examples of scalar quantities.

Units

- All measurements in physics require standard units.
- In 1960, the General Conference of Weights and Measures recommended that a metric system of measurements called the International System of Units, abbreviated as SI units, be used.

Some Important Units

S. No.	Units	Quantity
1.	Metre	Length
2.	Kilogram	Mass
3.	Second	Time
4.	Ampere	Electric Current
5.	Candela	Luminous Intensity
6.	Newton	Force
7.	Joule	Workdone
8.	Watt	Power
9.	Coulomb	Quantity of Electricity
10.	Volt	Potential Difference
11.	Ohm	Electrical Resistance
12.	Farad	Capacitance
13.	Henry	Inductance
14.	Lumen	Luminous Flux

- Very small distances are measured in micrometers or (microns) (μm), angstroms (Å), nanometers (nm) and femtometers (fm).
- 1 m = 10^6 μm = 10^9 nm = 10^{10} Å = 10^{15} fm
- 1 micron (1μ) = 10^{-4} cm = 10^{-6} m
- 1 Angstrom (1 Å) = 10^{-8} cm = 10^{-10} m
- 1 Fermi (1F) = 10^{-13} cm = 10^{-15} m

Motion

- When a body changes its position with respect to something else as time goes on, we say the body is in motion.
- There are two types of motion— translational (linear) and rotational (spin).
- The motion of a car on a road is translational whereas the motion of a top, spinning on its axis is rotational.

Speed

- It is a scalar form of velocity and is defined as the distance travelled irrespective of direction in one second.
- $\text{Speed} = \dfrac{\text{distance travelled}}{\text{time required}}$
- SI unit of speed is meters per second (m/s).

Velocity

- The distance covered by an object in a specified direction in unit time interval is called velocity.
- The SI unit of velocity is m/s.
- Velocity is a vector quantity.

Acceleration

- The velocity of a body changes due to change in its speed or direction or both. The rate of change of the velocity of a body is called its acceleration.
- $\text{Acceleration} = \dfrac{\text{change in velocity}}{\text{time}}$
- Negative acceleration is known as retardation. It indicates that the velocity of the object is decreasing with respect to time.
- Acceleration is uniform when neither its direction nor magnitude changes with respect to time.

Acceleration Due to Gravity

- When a body falls freely, then the increase in velocity per second is called acceleration due to gravity. It is represented by '*g*'.

$$g = \frac{GMe}{Re^2}$$

where G = Universal Gravitational Constant
Me = Mass of Earth
Re = Radius of the Earth

- Value of 'g' depends upon the radius of the earth as $g \propto \frac{1}{R}$.
- Value of 'g' is maximum at poles and minimum at equator.

Equations of Motion

1. $V = u + at$
2. $S = ut + \frac{1}{2}at^2$
3. $V^2 = u^2 + 2as$

where u is initial velocity; V is final velocity; t is time; a is acceleration; s is distance

Force

Gravitational Force

- It is the force of attraction between two masses.
- The gravitational force exists between all bodies, even between two apples lying on a table.
- It is gravitational force that holds the moon in its orbit round the earth and the earth in its orbit round the sun.
- **Newton's Law of Universal Gravitation** states that every particle in the universe attracts every other particle with a force that is directly proportional to the product of their masses and inversely proportional to the square of the distance between them.
- In equation form, the gravitational force

$$F = G\frac{m_1 m_2}{r^2}$$

where r is the distance between two particles of masses m_1 and m_2 and G the universal gravitational constant.

- The value of G is 6.67×10^{-11} SI units.

Centripetal Force

- The force acting towards the centre on a particle executing uniform circular motion is called centripetal force and is given by

$$F = \frac{mv^2}{r}$$

where m = Mass of the object
v = Speed
r = Radius of the Circular Path

- In case of the moon, gravitational force between the earth and the moon acts as the centripetal force.
- When a stone tied at one end of a string is whirled in a circle, the pull in the string provides the centripetal force.
- Without centripetal force there can be no circular motion.
- Centripetal force always acts on the particle performing circular motion.

Centrifugal Force

- The pseudo force that balances the centripetal force in uniform circular motion is called centrifugal force.
- Centrifugal force is directed away from the centre along the radius.
- The centrifugal force is zero exactly at the poles and maximum at the equator.

Weight

- The weight of a body is the force with which the earth attracts the body towards its centre.
- The weight of a body should not be confused with its mass, which is a measure of the quantity of matter contained in it. When we say that a person weighs 60 kg, we are actually describing his mass and not weight.
- The mass of a body is a constant quantity whereas its weight varies slightly from place-to-place on the earth.
- The weight of a body is maximum at the poles and minimum at the equator. This variation in weight is due to:
  1. The shape of the earth.
  2. The rotation of the earth about its axis.
- The weight of an object is less at high elevations them at sea level.
- At the centre of the earth, the weight of a body would be zero.
- The weight of a body can also be expressed in terms of the acceleration due to gravity (g). The weight (w) of a body of mass m is given by the product of m and g, *i.e.*, $w = mg$
- On the surface of the moon the value of the acceleration due to gravity is nearly one-sixth of that on earth and, therefore, an object on the moon would weigh only one-sixth its weight on the earth. The mass of an object on the moon would be the same as on earth.
- The weight of a body would be more if the earth stopped rotating. Conversely, if the speed of rotation were higher, the weight would be lesser.
- A person weighs more in a lift, which is accelerating upward.
- An astronaut feels weightlessness in a spaceship because he is not pushing against anything.

Friction

- Friction is the force which opposes the relative motion of two surfaces in contact.
- It is friction between the ground and the soles of our shoes that makes walking possible and it is lack of friction that makes our feet slip on highly polished surfaces.

- The force of friction that acts when a body is moving (sliding) on a surface is called sliding friction.
- When a cylindrical or spherical body rolls over a surface, the force opposing the motion is called rolling friction. For the same pair of materials rolling friction is much smaller than sliding friction.
- Friction in machines wastes energy and also causes wear and tear. This friction is reduced by using (1) lubricants, and (2) ball bearings.
- Rolling friction is always lesser than the sliding friction and hence it is easier to move a heavy object on rollers rather than to slide it. This property can be attributed to the fact that in case of rolling friction, the area of contact between the two surfaces is far less.

Newton's Laws of Motion

First Law

- Every object continues in its state of rest or of uniform motion in a straight line if no net force acts upon it. It is also known as **law of inertia.**
- **Examples:**
  1. An unwary passenger in a fast-moving bus falls forward when it stops suddenly. This happens because the feet of the passenger come to rest suddenly whereas his body continues to be in motion.
  2. A person getting down from a moving bus has to run some distance, in the direction of the bus, before stopping. If he does not run he is bound to fall because his feet come to rest whereas his body continues to be in motion.

Momentum

- The momentum of a body is defined as the product of its mass and velocity.

Second Law

- This law states that "the rate of change of momentum of a body is proportional to the applied force and takes place in the direction of the force".
- If we express force (F) in Newtons, mass (m) in kilograms and acceleration (a) in metres per second squared, we can write the second law as

$$F = ma$$

- In travelling the same distance, a car consumes more fuel on a crowded road than on a free road. This happens because the car has to stop and start quite often on a crowded road. The repeated acceleration requires a force (second law), which ultimately comes from the fuel. On a free road the car runs at almost uniform speed requiring fewer accelerations and hence less fuel consumption.

Third Law

- This law states that "to every action there is an equal and opposite reaction". The statement means that if body A exerts a force on body B, then B exerts an equal and opposite force on A along the same line of action.
- When a bullet is fired from a gun, equal and opposite forces are exerted on the bullet and the gun.
- A rocket contains solid chemicals which burn to produce a high velocity blast of hot gases. Space rockets have liquid fuel together with a supply of liquid oxygen to enable the fuel to burn. In either case, the large force created by chemical reaction propels out hot gases through the tail nozzle with a very high velocity. The reaction to this force propels the rocket forward.
- The engine in a jet aeroplane works on the same principle as a rocket but there is a difference in the method of obtaining the high velocity gas jet.
- The fuel used in a jet engine in Kerosene (paraffin).

Impulse

- If a force acts on a body for a very short time, then the product of force and time is called the impulse.

  Impulse = Change in momentum

  = Force × Time

Application of Impulse

1. A cricket player draws his hand back while catching.
2. A person jumping on hard cement floor receives more injuries than a person jumping on muddy or sandy floor.

Work, Power and Energy

Work

- Whenever a force acting on a body displaces it, work is said to be done.

  Work = Force × Distance moved in the direction of force.
- Work is a scalar quantity and its SI unit is Joule (J).

Power

- Power is defined as the rate of doing work.

$$\text{Power} = \frac{\text{Work done}}{\text{Time taken}}$$

- The SI unit of power is Watt (W) and is also measured in horse power.

  1 HP = 746 W

Energy

- Energy is defined as the capacity to do work.
- The SI unit of energy is Joule (J).
- There are two forms of mechanical energy—Kinetic and Potential.

Kinetic Energy

- The energy possessed by an object due to its motion is called kinetic energy and is described by the expression

$$KE = \frac{1}{2}mv^2$$

where m = mass of the object
v = speed

Potential Energy

- Potential energy is the energy possessed by the body by virtue of its position, configuration or any condition of stress or strain.
- One of the commonest forms of potential energy is that possessed by an object when it is above the level of the earth's surface. This is called gravitational potential energy and is described by the expression

$$PE = mgh$$

where m is the mass of the object, g the acceleration due to gravity and h the height of the object above the earth's surface.
- There are many examples of potential energy. A stone held at some height above the ground has potential energy. Water in an elevated reservoir possesses potential energy.

Conservation of Energy

- Energy can neither be created nor destroyed; it can only be transformed from one form into another, but the total amount of energy remains constant.

Transformation of Energy

S.No.	Equipment	Transformation
1.	Dynamo	Mechanical energy into electrical energy
2.	Microphone	Sound energy into electrical energy
3.	Loud Speaker	Electrical energy into sound energy
4.	Electric Bulb	Electrical energy into light and heat energy
5.	Battery	Chemical energy into electrical energy
6.	Electrical Motor	Electrical energy into mechanical energy

Einstein Relation

- According to Einstein, mass can be converted into energy and energy can be converted into mass. One can be obtained at the cost of the other. The equivalence between mass and energy is expressed in terms of Einstein Relations:

$$E = mc^2$$

where m is the mass that disappears, E is the energy that appears and c is the velocity of light in vacuum ($c = 3 \times 10^8$ m/s)

Centre of Gravity

- The centre of gravity of a body is the point where the whole weight of the body can be considered to act.
- The centre of gravity of a body may even lie outside the actual material of the body. For example, the centre of gravity of a ring lies at its centre, which is outside its material.
- The stability of an object is connected with the position of its centre of gravity (CG).
- If the vertical through the CG passes through the base of an object, then it is stable, otherwise it is unstable and topples down.
- Racing cars are built low and with wide wheel bases to reduce the risk of overturning at sharp bends.
- While crossing a river in a boat, passengers are not allowed to stand. This keeps the CG of the system (boat and passengers) low and ensures stability.
- A porter carrying a load on his back leans forward to keep the vertical line passing through the CG of the system between his feet.

Artificial Satellites

- In the case of a satellite, the centripetal force is provided by the gravitational pull of the earth.
- The speed of the satellite does not depend on its mass. It means that at a particular distance from the earth, all objects would have the same speed of revolution. If a satellite moves from a higher orbit to a lower orbit, its speed increases.
- If the speed of a satellite is more than 11.2 km/s or 25,000 miles/hour, the satellite would escape the earth entirely and would never come back. This is called escape velocity.
- The existence of gaseous atmosphere on the earth is due to the high value of its escape velocity.
- On the moon the value of the escape velocity is 1.9 km/s (nearly one-sixth of that on earth). If any gases are formed on the moon, the molecules would have velocities greater than 1.9 km/s and would therefore escape, leaving the moon bare.
- The value of escape velocity does not depend upon the mass of the projected body, instead it depends on the mass and radius of the planet from which it is being projected.
- The value of escape velocity does not depend on the angle and direction of projection.
- The root mean square velocity of hydrogen is more than that of the escape velocity of earth, therefore, hydrogen is not found in earth's lower atmosphere.

Geostationary Satellites

- Geostationary satellites are stationary with respect to an observer on the earth. Their time period is 24-hour. There height above the surface of earth is 36,000 km. They are always in equatorial plane and their orbits are circular. They are also called parking orbits.

Density and Relative Density

- The mass per unit volume of a substance is called its density.

$$\text{Density} = \frac{\text{Mass}}{\text{Volume}}$$

- The SI unit of density is kilogram per metre cubed (kg/m^3).

Densities of Some Common Substances

Sr. No.	*Substance*	*Density in kg/m^3*
1.	Alcohol	790
2.	Water	1,000
3.	Aluminium	2,700
4.	Steel (vories)	7,800
5.	Copper	8,900
6.	Lead	11,300
7.	Mercury	13,600
8.	Gold	19,300
9.	Platinum	21,500

- The relative density of a substance is the ratio of the density of the substance to the density of water.
- Relative density has no unit.

Pressure

- Pressure is defined as force acting per unit area.

$$\text{Pressure} = \frac{\text{Force}}{\text{Area}}$$

- The SI unit of pressure is newton per metre square or pascal.
- There is a inverse relationship between magnitude of pressure and area of contact.
- It is much easier to cut fruit with a sharp knife than with a blunt one. In the case of a sharp knife the blade makes such a small area of contact with the fruit that the pressure below it, is very high and easily cuts the fruit.
- Broad wooden sleepers are placed below the rails to reduce the pressure exerted by the weight of a train.
- The pressure of water increases with depth, therefore bottom of a dam is made much thicken than the top.
- The pressure exerted on an enclosed liquid at one place is transmitted equally throughout the liquid. This is called Pascal's Principle.
- Hydraulic presses, hydraulic brakes, hydraulic door closers, etc. are applications of the Pascal's Principle.
- At high attitudes where atmosphere pressure is less nose bleeding may occur due to the greater pressure of blood.
- It is due to the pressure of the atmosphere that ink rises in the tube of a fountain pen or liquid rises in a syringe when the piston is pulled.
- In an aircraft flying at high altitude, normal atmospheric pressure is maintained by the use of air pumps. If this were not done, the crew and passengers would experience difficulty in breathing and consequently face dangers.
- Atmospheric pressure is measured with an instrument called the **Barometer.**
- Aneroid barometer does not use any liquid.
- If the barometric height falls suddenly, it indicates the coming of a storm. A gradual fall in the barometric height indicates the possibility of rain. A gradual increase in the barometric height indicates fair weather.

Archimede's Principle

- This principle states that when a body is wholly or partially immersed in a fluid, it experiences an upthrust (upward force) equal to the weight of the fluid displaced.
- When an object is immersed in a fluid, two forces act on it: (*i*) the weight of the object acting downward, and (*ii*) upthrust acting upward.
- It is due to upthrust that objects apparently weightless when immersed in fluids.

Law of Floatation

- When a body is immersed in a fluid then if—
  1. The weight of body is equal to upthrust, the body floats with whole of its volume inside the liquid.
  2. The weight of body is more than the upthrust, the body will sink.
  3. The weight of body is less than the upthrust, the body will float with some of its part outside the liquid.
- An iron nail sinks in water whereas a ship made of iron and steel floats. This is due to the fact that a ship is hollow and contains air and, therefore, its density is less than that of water.
- The density of sea water is more than that of river water, due to this a ship sinks less in sea water. It is for this reason that a ship rises a little when it enters a sea from a river.
- It is because of the higher density of sea water that it is easier to swim in the sea.
- A solid chunk of iron will sink in the water but float in mercury because the density of iron is more than that of water but less than that of mercury.
- A balloon filled with a light gas, such as hydrogen, rises because the average density of the balloon and the gas is less than that of air. The balloon cannot rise indefinitely because the density of the air decreases with increasing altitude. At a certain height, where the density of air is equal to the average density of the balloon, it ceases to rise and drifts sideways with the wind.

- When an ice block floats in water the water level will remain the same when all the ice melts into water.
- A **hydrometer** is an instrument used for measuring the relative density of liquids.
- A special type of a hydrometer called **Lactometer** is used for testing milk by measuring its density.

Surface Tension

- Surface tension is that property of liquids owing to which they tend to acquire minimum surface area.
- Surface tension is caused by molecular attractions.
- When a paint brush is dipped in water all its hair spread out but when it is taken out it is covered with a thin film of water which contracts due to surface tension and pulls the hair together.
- Liquid drops, such as raindrops, oildrops, drops of molten metals, dewdrops etc. are all spherical because their surface tend to contract in order to have minimum surface area. For a given volume, a sphere has the minimum surface area.
- Soaps and detergents lower the surface tension of water. This increases the wetting power of water or its ability to detach dirt particles from clothes and untensils.
- Cohesive forces are the forces of attraction acting between molecules of same substance. The liquids for which cohesive forces are large do not wet the walls of the vessel, *e.g.*, mercury. Surface tension forces arise due to cohesive forces.
- Adhesive forces are the forces of attraction acting between the molecules of different substances. If adhesive forces are greater than cohesive force then the liquid wets the walls of the vessel, *e.g.*, water wets the walls of a glass-capillary.
- The force of attraction between unlike molecules is called **adhesion** and that between like molecules **cohesion.**
- The melted wax of a candle is drawn up into the wick by capillary action. Oil rises up a lamp wick for the same reason.
- If one end of a sugar cube is dipped into tea, the entire cube is quickly wet on account of capillary action.
- The fine pores of a blotting paper act as tiny capillary tubes. The ink rises into the blotting paper through these pores.

Viscosity

- The force which opposes the relative motion between different layers of liquid or gases is called viscous force.
- Viscosity is the property of liquids and gases both.
- The viscosity of a liquid is due to cohesive force between its molecules.
- The viscosity of a gas is due to diffusion of its molecules from one layer to other layer.

Bernoulli's Theorem

- According to Bernoulli's theorem, in case of streamline flow of incompressible and non-viscous fluid (ideal fluid) through a tube, total energy (sum of pressure energy, potential energy and kinetic energy) per unit volume of fluid is same at all points.
- An important corollary of this theorem is: pressure in a fluid decreases with increased velocity of the fluid. Examples:
  1. When a bowler spins a ball, it changes its direction (swings) in the air due to unequal pressure acting on it.
  2. The shape of the wings of an aeroplane is such that wind velocity above the wings is higher than that below them. Consequently, there is higher pressure below the wings and this lifts the aeroplane.
  3. When the piston of a sprayer is pushed, air is forced past the upper end of a tube, whose lower end dips in the liquid to be sprayed. Due to the increased velocity of air, the pressure near the upper end of the tube is reduced. The atmospheric pressure in the container, therefore, pushes the liquid to the top, from where it is carried away by the stream of air.

Heat

- Heat is that form of energy which flows from one body to other body due to difference in temperature between the bodies. The amount of heat contained in a body depends upon the mass of the body.

Temperature and Heat

- The temperature of a body is the quantity that tells how hot or cold it is with respect to some standard body.
- Heat is the internal energy transferred from one body to another due to temperature difference.

Measurement of Temperature

- Temperature is measured by a thermometer.
- To measure temperature two fixed points are taken on each thermometer. One of the fixed points is the freezing point of water or ice point as lower fixed point (LFP). The other fixed point is the boiling point of water or steam point as upper fixed point.
- A thermometer may be graduated in following scales—
  1. The upper and lower points of centigrade scale are 100°C and 0°C.

2. The upper and lower points of Fahrenheit scale are 212°F and 32°F.
3. The upper and lower points of Reaumur scale are 80°R and 0°R.
4. The upper and lower points of Kelvin scale are 373K and 273K.
5. The upper and lower points of Rankine scale are 672° Ra and 460° Ra.

- Relation between different temperature scales

$$\frac{C}{100} = \frac{F-32}{180} = \frac{R}{80} = \frac{K-273}{100} = \frac{Ra-460}{212}.$$

- At – 40 degrees both celsius and Fahrenheit scales will show identical readings.
- **Pyrometer** is a instrument for measuring high temperatures.
- Weather reports in newspapers carry the maximum and the minimum temperatures recorded during the last 24 hours.
- Mercury is used in thermometers because—
  1. It is opaque and shining and, therefore, temperature can be read conveniently.
  2. It is a good conductor of heat, and, therefore, records temperatures rapidly.
  3. It does not stick to glass and also does not vapourise much and therefore yields correct readings.
- Water cannot be used in a thermometer because it freezes at 0°C and also because of its irregular expansion.
- In cold countries where winter temperatures of –40°C are not uncommon, mercury thermometers cannot be used because mercury freezes at –39°C. In such countries, alcohol thermometers are useful, since alcohol freezes at –115°C.

Thermal Expansion

- Solids, liquids and gases generally expand when heated and contract when cooled.
- Gaps have to be left in railway tracks to make allowance for expansion, otherwise the rails will buckle. Allowance is made for the expansion of long steel bridges. One end of such bridge is fixed while the other rests on rollers.
- Telephone wires sag more in summer than in winter due to thermal expansion.

Expansion of Water

- Water has its minimum volume and maximum density at 4°C.
- Water shows unusual expansion. If we take a cube of ice at –5°C and heat it, it expands till ice starts melting. During melting its temperature remains 0°C but its volume decreases. If heat is continuously supplied to water at 0°C, it further contracts up to 4°C and then it starts expanding.
- Anomalous expansion of water helps preserve aquatic life during very cold weather. When temperature falls, the top layer of water in a pond contracts, becomes denser and sinks to the bottom. A circulation is thus set up until the entire water in the pond reaches maximum density at 4°C. If the temperature falls further, the top layer expands and remains on top till it freezes. Thus, even though the upper layers are frozen the water near the bottom is at 4°C and the fishes etc., can survive in it easily.

Transmission of Heat

- There are three ways of heat transmission:
  1. Conduction
  2. Convection
  3. Radiation

Conduction

- In this process, heat is transferred from one place to other place by the successive vibration of the particles of the medium without bodily movement of the particles of the medium.
- Conduction takes place mainly in solids.
- Air is a very bad conductor of heat. The good insulating properties of wool, cotton, etc. are mainly due to the air spaces they contain.
- Sawdust is a bad conductor of heat. Therefore, ice slabs are covered with sawdust to minimise melting.
- On a cold night two thin blankets are preferred to a single thick blanket because the layer of air between the two blankets serves as a better insulator.

Convection

- In this process, heat is transferred by the actual movement of particles of the medium from one place to other place.
- In liquids and gases heat is transmitted by convection.

Radiation

- It is the fastest means of heat transfer.
- In this mode of heat transmission heat is transferred from one place to another without effecting the intervening medium.
- Both conduction and convection require a material medium for conveying heat from one part to another. Radiation, on the other hand, does not require any medium.

Newton's Law of Cooling

- This law states that the rate of which a hot body loses heat is directly proportional to the difference between its temperature and the surrounding temperature.
- **Example:** Hot water takes much less time in cooling from 90°C to 80°C than in cooling from 40°C to 30°C.

Kirchhoff's Law

- According to Kirchhoff's law, the ratio of emissive power to absorptive power is same for all surfaces at the same temperature and is equal to emissive power of black body at that temperature.

Greenhouse Effect

- A greenhouse acts like a radiation trap.
- In a greenhouse, heat radiation from the sun passes through the glass and keeps the plants and the air inside warm. The glass prevents warm air from escaping.
- A car parked in the sun with its windows closed gets terribly warm due to the greenhouse effect.

Heat Capacity

- The heat capacity of a body is defined as the heat required to raise the temperature of the body by 1 K. Its SI unit is J/K.

Specific Heat Capacity

- The specific heat capacity of a substance is the heat required to raise the temperature of a unit mass of the substance by 1 K.
- Its SI unit is J/kg K.
- Water has a very high specific heat capacity.
- It is because of its high specific heat capacity that water is used as a cooling liquid in car engine.

Latent Heat

- It is defined as the amount of heat absorbed or given out by a body during the change of state.
- The latent heat of fusion of a substance is defined as the heat required to convert a unit mass of the substance from the solid to the liquid state without change of temperature.
- The latent heat of vapourization of a substance is the heat required to change a unit mass of the substance from liquid to the vapour state without change of temperature.
- The latent heat of steam is 2260000 J/kg or 2260 J/g.
- Each gram of ice that melts absorbs 336 J of heat.
- Scalding (burning) with steam is more severe than that caused by boiling water because steam contains more energy than boiling water at the same temperature.
- Latent heat of vapourisation is maximum at 0°C and decreases on increasing temperature.
- Melting point decreases on adding impurity.
- Boiling point increases on adding impurity.
- Boiling point increases on increasing pressure.
- Bottled drinks are cooled more effectively when surrounded with lumps of ice than with iced water because ice absorbs more heat than does the same amount of iced water.

Evaporation

- Water can change into the vapour state either by boiling or by evaporation at lower temperatures.
- When evaporation takes place at room temperature, the energy required for evaporation is taken from the liquid itself, which cools as a consequence.
- When sweat evaporates from the skin it draws much heat from the body and produces a cooling sensation.
- In summer, water is stored in pitchers for cooling. Water oozes out of the pores of the pitchers and cools on evaporation.
- The rate of evaporation increases with increase in temperature.
- Evaporation increases with increase in surface area.

Refrigerator

- In a refrigerator, cooling is produced by the evaporation of a volatile liquid, freon, inside a copper coil (evaporator), which surrounds the freezer.
- The cooling unit (freezer) in a refrigerator is fitted near the top to cool the whole of the interior.
- A thermostat switch regulates the temperature inside the refrigerator by switching the pump on and off at intervals.

Relative Humidity

- Relative humidity is defined as the ratio of the mass of water vapour in a given volume of air to the mass required for saturating the same volume of air at the same temperature.
- The weather report in newspapers expresses relative humidity as percentage.
- Relative humidity is measured with an instrument called the hygrometer.

Pressure Cooker

- The boiling point of a liquid depends on external pressure.
- When the atmospheric pressure is 76 cm of mercury, water boils at 100°C. But when the pressure is increased, the boiling point of water is raised.
- In a pressure cooker, water boils at temperatures higher than 100°C due to increased pressure. The increased boiling temperature allows water to hold more heat which cooks food faster.
- At higher altitudes, atmospheric pressure is reduced. This lowers the boiling point of water and food takes much longer to cook.

MULTIPLE CHOICE QUESTIONS

1. What is force?
   A. pull B. push
   C. push and push both D. none of these
2. What is state of motion?
   A. position of rest
   B. position of motion
   C. both by the state of rest or motion
   D. none of these
3. The strength of force is expressed by:
   A. weight B. mass
   C. magnitude D. longitudinal force
4. The force between two charged bodies is called:
   A. muscular force B. gravitational force
   C. magnetic force D. electrostatic force
5. When two forces act in opposite directions, then net force acting two forces:
   A. sum of two factors
   B. difference bwteen two factors
   C. both of these
   D. none of these
6. Magnetic force is:
   A. contact force B. non-contact force
   C. both A and B D. none of these
7. Force acts on an object may change:
   A. direction B. shape
   C. speed D. all of above
8. Leaves or fruits fall on the ground due to:
   A. magnetic force B. gravitational force
   C. electrostatic force D. muscular force
9. Displacement is a:
   A. Scalar quantity B. Vector quantity
   C. Base quantity D. Derived quantity
10. SI unit for force is:
    A. Kilograms B. Newton
    C. Joules D. Acceleration
11. Adding of two vectors to get a single vector is termed as:
    A. Final vector B. Resultant vector
    C. Dominant vector D. Recessive vector
12. The ___________ forces are used are used in the method of sections for the calculation of the internal forces.
    A. Internal rotational B. Couple rotational
    C. Translational D. External
13. Twisting moment is also called as _________.
    A. Moment of line B. Moment of section
    C. Moment of plane D. Torsional moment
14. The loading generally act upon the _________ of the body.
    A. Centroid B. Symmetrical centre
    C. Rotational centre D. Chiral centre
15. Torsional moment is applied at the__________ part of the beam.
    A. The centroid
    B. The left end
    C. The right end
    D. The axis beyond the body of the beam
16. If the normal force creates a tension then the force is said to be __________.
    A. Positive B. Negative
    C. Rotational D. Collinear
17. If the bending of the beam is concave upwards then the bending moment developed is called ________ moment.
    A. Positive B. Negative
    C. Rotational D. Collinear
18. The force of friction acts in a direction _____ to the direction of motion of object.
    A. Same B. Opposite
    C. Perpendicular D. Downwards
19. The force of friction depends upon:
    A. Nature of surface of contact
    B. Material of objects in contact
    C. Both 'A' and 'B'
    D. None of the above
20. The body will move only when:
    A. Force of friction = applied force
    B. Force of friction < applied force
    C. Force of friction > applied force
    D. All of the above
21. The ratio of the limiting force of friction (F) to the normal reaction (R) is known as:
    A. Coefficient of friction B. Force of friction
    C. Angle of friction D. None of the above
22. When the two surfaces in contact have a thick layer of lubricant in between them, it is known as:
    A. Solid friction B. Rolling friction
    C. Greasy friction D. Film friction
23. Which motion has magnitude of static frictional force directly proportional to normal reaction?
    A. Actual motion B. Impending motion
    C. Both A and B D. None of the above
24. Frictional force depends on _______.
    A. surface area in contact B. roughness of surface
    C. both A and B D. none of the above

25. Which of the following statements is true for flat belts?
A. They are used for short distances between the pulleys
B. They have high efficiency
C. They are used in lathe machines
D. All of the above

26. There will be a great distance in stopping a vehicle which is moving?
A. slowly B. steady
C. fast D. continuously

27. A bowling ball on a bowling lane is an example of what type of friction?
A. Dry friction B. Rolling friction
C. Fluid friction D. Static Friction

28. Whenever the surfaces in contact tend to move or move with respect to each other, the force of friction comes into play:
A. only if the objects are solid.
B. only if one of the two objects is liquid.
C. only if one of the two objects is gaseous.
D. irrespective of whether the objects are solid, liquid or gaseous

29. To sharpen the blade of a knife by rubbing it against a surface, which of the following will be most suitable?
A. stone B. plastic block
C. wooden block D. glass block

30. A toy car released with the same initial speed will travel farthest on:
A. muddy surface B. polished marble surface
C. cemented surface D. brick surface

31. If we apply oil on door hinges, the friction will:
A. increase
B. decrease
C. disappear altogether
D. will remain unchanged

32. Which of the following statements is incorrect?
A. Friction acts on a ball rolling along the ground.
B. Friction acts on a boat moving on water.
C. Friction acts on a bicycle moving on a smooth road.
D. Friction does not act on a ball moving through air

33. A boy rolls a rubber ball on a wooden surface. The ball travels a short distance before coming to rest. To make the same ball travel longer distance before coming to rest, he may
A. spread a carpet on the wooden surface.
B. cover the ball with a piece of cloth.
C. sprinkle talcum powder on the wooden surface.
D. sprinkle sand on the wooden surface.

34. Complete the sentence. Friction always ___________
A. helps the motion B. opposes the motion
C. both of these D. none of these

35. Which one of these characteristics does a smooth surface has?
A. Less frictional force
B. More frictional force
C. Sometimes less and sometimes more force
D. All of above

36. Friction is a __________.
A. Contact force B. Non-contact force
C. Magnetic force D. None of these

37. What kind of substances are known as lubricants?
A. Increase friction
B. Decrease friction
C. Increase or decrease friction
D. None of these

38. Fluid are ____.
A. Gases B. Liquids
C. Gases and liquids both D. None of these

39. On what force of friction depends?
A. Smoothness of surface
B. Roughness of surface
C. Inclination of surface
D. All of above

40. Friction is a /an______.
A. Evil B. Foe
C. Both A and B D. None

41. Lubricants ________.
A. Increase friction B. Reduce friction
C. Both A and B D. None

42. Rolling friction is smaller than?
A. Sliding friction B. Static friction
C. Fluid friction D. All of the above

43. The shape of the airplane is like a:
A. Bird B. Car
C. Dog D. All

44. If the displacement is measured with strain gauge then the number of strain gauge normally required are:
A. One B. Two
C. Three D. Four

45. The instruments used for the measurement of pressure is/are:
A. Bellows
B. Diaphragms
C. Fiber optic pressure sensors
D. All of these

46. Bourdon tube is used for the measurement of gauge pressure of:
A. Gas B. Liquid fluid
C. Solid D. Both A and B

47. The ionization gauge an instrument used for the measurement of:
A. Very low pressure B. Medium pressure
C. High pressure D. Very high pressure

48. When visual indication of pressure level is required then the instrument generally used is:
A. Monometers B. Diaphragm sensors
C. Bourdon tube D. Resonant wire device

49. Advantage of passive instrument is:
A. It does not need power supply
B. Cheap
C. Sensitive
D. Accurate

50. Which of the following statements is false? The pressure at a given depth in a fluid:
A. is equal in all directions
B. is independent of the shape of the container
C. acts at right angles to the surface containing the fluid
D. depends on the area of the surface

51. Which of the following devices does not measure pressure?
A. barometer B. McLeod gauge
C. thermocouple D. manometer

52. The universal law of gravitation was propounded by:
A. Kepler B. Galileo
C. Newton D. Copernicus

53. The gravitational force with which the sun attracts the earth:
A. is less than the force with which the earth attracts the sun
B. is the same as the force with which earth attracts the sun
C. is more than the force with which the earth attracts the sun
D. is constant throughout the year

54. The mass of a body is different from its weight because:
A. mass is a variable quantity whereas weight is constant
B. mass varies very little at different places whereas weight varies a lot
C. mass is constant but weight increases as the body moves from the poles to the equator
D. mass is a measure of the quantity of matter whereas weight is a force

55. The weight of a body is:
A. the same everywhere on the surface of the earth
B. maximum at the poles
C. maximum at the equator
D. more on the hills than in the plains

56. A person weighs more in a lift, which is:
A. moving up with a constant velocity
B. moving down with a constant velocity
C. accelerating upward
D. accelerating downward

57. Atmospheric pressure is measured with a:
A. hydrometer B. barometer
C. hygrometer D. altimeter

58. The atmosphere exerts enormous pressure on us. But we do not feel it because:
A. we are used to it
B. our bones are very strong and can withstand this pressure
C. the surface area of our head is very small
D. our blood exerts a pressure slightly more than that of the atmosphere

59. In a barometer, mercury is preferred over water because:
A. mercury is a good conductor of heat
B. mercury is shining and therefore its level can be read easily
C. mercury is available in pure form
D. mercury has high density and low vapour pressure

60. Raindrops are spherical due to:
A. viscosity of water
B. surface tension
C. continuous evaporation
D. air friction

ANSWERS

1	2	3	4	5	6	7	8	9	10
C	C	C	D	B	B	D	B	B	B
11	12	13	14	15	16	17	18	19	20
B	D	D	A	A	A	A	B	C	B
21	22	23	24	25	26	27	28	29	30
A	D	B	B	A	C	B	D	A	C
31	32	33	34	35	36	37	38	39	40
B	D	C	B	A	A	B	C	D	C
41	42	43	44	45	46	47	48	49	50
B	D	A	D	D	D	A	A	A	D
51	52	53	54	55	56	57	58	59	60
C	C	B	D	B	C	B	D	D	B

★ ★ ★

6

Light and Sound

LIGHT

- **Source of light:** An object, which emits light, is called a source of light.
- **Scattering of light:** The process in which objects spreads the light in all directions is called scattering of light.
- **Rectilinear propagation of light:** Light travels in a straight line. This property of light is called rectilinear propagation of light.
- **Speed of light** is 3,00,000 km per second. Light takes about 8 mintues to travel from the sun to the earth.
- When light or a ray of light falls on an object, three things can happen:
  (*i*) It may be transmitted through the object almost completely.
  (*ii*) Only part of it may be transmitted and the rest absorbed or spread out.
  (*iii*) It may not be allowed to pass through at all.
- **Transparent:** Such materials absorb or spread out only a small part of light falling on them and transmit the remaining of it. Which completely transmit light rays through them are called transparent, e.g., air, pure water, glass, some plastics.
- **Translucent:** Materials which transmit only a small part of the light rays are called translucent. Translucent materials absorb and scatter the remaining light. e.g. butter paper, gelatin sheet, smoked glass, muddy water.
- **Opaque:** Such materials which allow very little or no light to pass through them. These materials are called Opaque. e.g. wood, coaltar, paints, metal sheets.
- Object Scatter the light falling on than from the source and make then visible to our eyes.
- Rectilinear propogation of light explains the formation of the image of an object in a pin hole camera.
- The materials through which we are able to see clearly because light passes through them almost completely are called transparent.
- The materials which do not allow light to pass through them at all are called opaque.
- The materials which allow only part of the incident light to pass through them are called translucent.
- In the presence of a source of light, opaque objects act as obstacles to propagation of light and form shadows beyond them in the form of Umbra and Penumbra.
- The region of the space where the light from the source does not reach and hence is the darkest, is called Umbra.
- The region where the light does not reach from all parts of the source is called Penumbra.
- Eclipses of the Moon and the Sun occur due to the shadows cast by the Earth and the Moon respectively.
- When light rays fall on polished surface they change their direction in a well-defined manner. This is called regular reflection.
- Light falling on non-polished surfaces does not change the direction in a well-defined manner. This is called diffuse reflection.
- There are two laws of reflection:
  (*i*) The incident ray, the normal at the point of incidence and the reflected rays are in the same plane.
  (*ii*) The angle of incidence and the angle of reflection are equal.
- In a plane mirror, the reflected rays appear to come from some object kept behind the mirror. This is called a virtual image of the object.
- Laws of reflection are also applicable to polished curved surfaces.
- In case of curved reflecting surfaces the normal at different points of incidence have different directions.
- Part of a spherical surface, when polished, gives rise to spherical mirrors.
- Spherical mirrors are two types:
  (*i*) Concave mirror
  (*ii*) Convex mirror
  depanding upon the surface that us polished/silvered to allow regular reflection.
- The centre of the sphere of which the spherical mirror is a part, is called the centre of curvature of the mirror.

- Any straight line joining the centre of curvature with any point on the spherical mirror is normal to the mirror at that point.
- The point through which the incident rays parallel to the principal axis, after reflection from the mirror, pass through or appers to pass through is called focus of the spherical mirror.
- When the reflected rays meet in front of the mirror, they are supposed to form a real image.
- A real image can be obtained on a screen.
- Any ray passing through the focus or appearing to pass through the focus becomes parallel to the principal axis after reflection.
- Any ray passing through or appearing to pass through the centre of curvature is reflected back along the same path.
- Concave mirrors are used by dentists and in optical instruments.
- Concave mirror forms a real and inverted image of the object when it is kept beyond the focus and a virtual, erect but magnified image is formed when an object us kept in between the mirror and the focus.
- Convex mirrors are used as rear view mirrors in cars and for viewing images of larger areas.
- Convex mirror always forms a smaller and virtual image.
- Light affects plants and animals.
- **Incident ray:** The light ray striking a surface is called the incident ray.
- **Point of incidence:** The point at which the incident ray strikes the surface is called the point of incidence.
- **Reflected ray:** The light ray obtained after reflection from the surface, in the medium in which the incident ray is coming, is called the reflected ray.
- **Normal:** The perpandicular drawn to the surface at the point of incidence is called the normal.
- **Angle of incidence:** The angle which the incident ray makes with the normal at the point of incidence, is called angle of incidence.
- **Angle of reflection:** The angle which the reflected ray makes with the normal at the point of incidence, is called angle of refleciton.
- **Plane of incidence:** The plane containing the incident ray and the normal is called the plane of incidence.
- **Plane of refleciton:** The plane containing the reflected ray and the normal is called the plane of refleciton.
- **Real and Virtual image:** An image which can be obtained on a screen is called a real image. It is formed when the light rays after reflection actually intersect.
- The image which can not be obtained on a screen is called a *virtual image.* It is formed when the light rays after reflection do not actually intersect but appear to diverge from it.
- Light is a form of radiant energy.
- Light may be regarded as a form of electromagnetic radiation.
- Light can travel without a medium.
- In a homogeneous medium light travels in a straight line.
- The velocity of light is different in different medium.
- A ray of light bends towards the normal as it passes from a rarer medium to denser medium and bends away from the normal when it travels from a denser medium to a rarer medium.
- A convex lens converges a parallel beam of light as its focal point and a concave lens diverges a parallel beam of light.
- The distance between the lens and its focal point is called the *focal length* of the lens.
- The image of an object formed by a convex lens when the object is placed beyond the focal length is real and inverted.
- The image of an object formed by a convex lens when the object is placed between the lens and the focal point is virtual and magnified.
- The term eclipse literally means the act of disappearing or becoming invisible.
- An object can become invisible to an observer under the following conditions:
  (*i*) Objects itself is not a source of light and light from any other source is not falling on it.
  (*ii*) View of the object is blocked completely by an obstacle started between the object and the observer.
- The lunar eclipse occurs due to the first of the above conditions. The solar eclipse occurs due to the second condition.

The Lunar Eclipse

On a certain full-moon night, the shadow of the Earth falls on the moon's surface. When this happens a part or whole of the Moon is not visible to us for some time from some parts on the Earth. This phenomena is known as *Lunar Eclipse*. A lunar eclipse does not occur on every full moon day. Thus happens because the centres of the Sun, the Earth and the Moon do not lie on a straight line on every full-moon day.

This diagram shows the various positions of the Moon as it passes through the penumbra and the Umbra of the earth during a lunar eclipse. At position A, the Moon is yet to enter the penumbro and it looks bright as usual. At position B, it has entered the penumbro. At this position, the Moon looks pale, as if it has gone behind the clouds. After some time, a part of the Moon enters the Umbro. This part is then not visible from the Earth, but the remaining part of the Moon is still visible. This is called a *partial lunar eclipse.* At positon C, the Moon has completely enterd the Umbra and is not visible from the Earth. This is called total lunar eclipse. During the total lunar eclipse, the Moon completely disappears from the sight. The Moón than moves again to position D, the perumbra and finally emerges out of the shadow of the Earth, position E. Thus a total lunar eclipse is again followed by a partial lunar eclipse. Finally, the Moon becomes as bright as before the beginning of the eclipse.

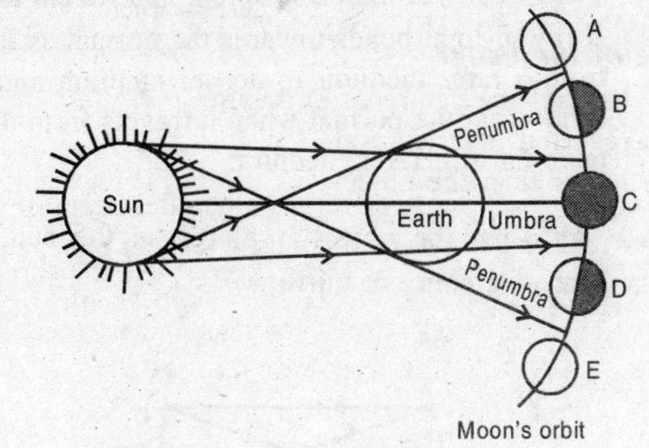

Fig. *Occurence of Lunar Eclipse*

The Solar Eclipse

On a new-moon day, the Moon lies in between the Earth and the Sun. Sometimes, their centres may lie on the same straight line. When this happens, the moon's shadow may fall on the Earth. This event occurs only on certain new-moon days and not on all new-moon days. Thus event is known as *solar eclipse.*

Occurrence of the solar eclipse can be explained with the help of figures given below:

A Solar eclipse may be partial or total. The type of Solar eclipse that would be visible from a given place on the earth depends whether it lies in the Umbro or the Penumbro of the moon. The sun cannot be seen from that region on the earth where the Umbra of the moon falls. This is because the Moon blocks the view of the Sun.

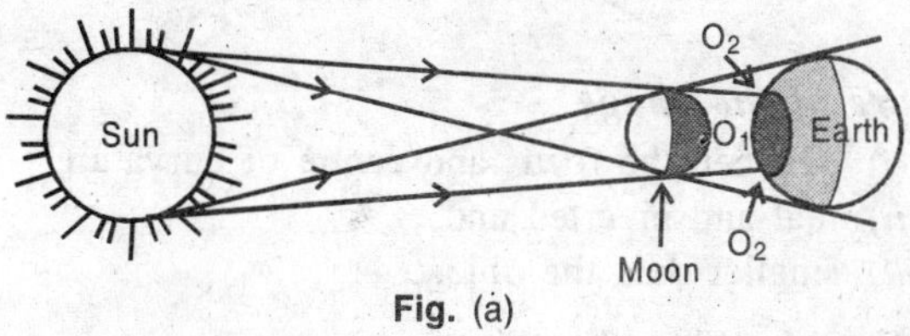

Fig. (a)

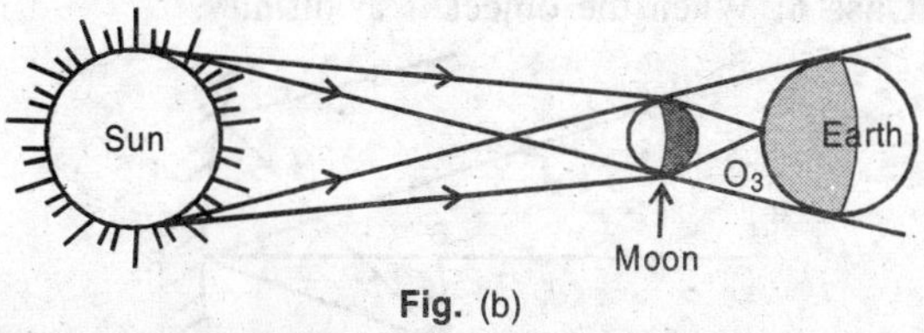

Fig. (b)

Fig. *(a, b) Occurence of different types of solar eclipse*

From the given Fig.(a), point O_1 on the earth, the Sun is completely blocked by the Moon. This is called a total Solar eclipse. The point O_2 in the penumbro the Sun is only partly visible, a *partial Solar eclipse* occurs when this happens. As *annular solar eclipse* occurs when only the tip of the Umbra of the Moon falls on the earth, the point O_3 lies the view of the Sun would be completely blocked by the Moon. The outer rim of the Sun is known as *Corona* is visible for a very short period, a very bright ring, known as *diamond ring*, appears in the sky. A total Solar eclipse is a rare event.

Lateral inversion: The image in a plane mirror formed the left side appears on the right and the right side appears on the left in the mirror. This phenomenon is called *Lateral inversion.*

Kaleidoscope: Is an device fased on the principle of multiple reflections in inclined mirrors. It is called *Kaleidoscope.* It consists of three plane mirrors inclined at an angle of 60° to each other.

Periscope: Is a device, used to see objects which are not in the direct line of sight. e.g. it is used to see ships on the surface of water from a submarine.

Spherical mirror: Is a part of a sphere. It has two surfaces or faces. The inner face is called *Concave* and outer face is known as *Convex.*

There are two type of spherical mirrors:

(*i*) Concave mirror and

(*ii*) Convex mirror.

Concave mirror: The central point (P) is called the pole of the mirror, which is denoted by P.

Centre of curvature: The centre of the sphere, of which the given spherical mirror is a part is called its centre of Curvature. It is denoted by C. The centre of Curvature of a Concave mirror is in front of the mirror where as that of a Convex mirror is behind the mirror.

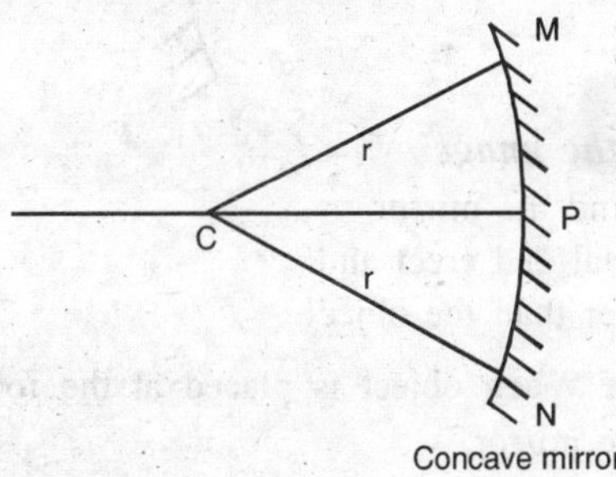

Concave mirror

Principal axis: The straight line, joining the points C and P, is called the principal axis of the mirror. The steps to draw a ray diagram for the formation of image by a spherical mirror as follows:

- A ray of light parallel to the principal axis passes through the focus of the mirror after reflection.

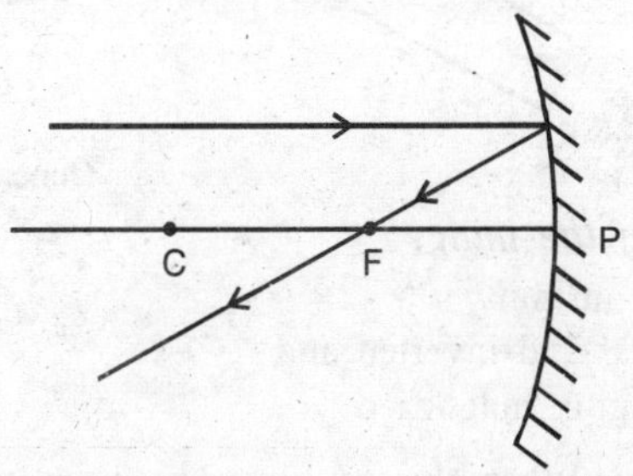

Concave mirror

- A ray of light that passes through the focus of the mirror becomes parallel to its principal axis after reflection.
- A ray of light passing through the centre of curvature of the mirror returns along the same path after reflection from the mirror.

The images formed by a Concave mirror

The type of image formed by a Concave mirror depends on the position of object in front of the mirror.

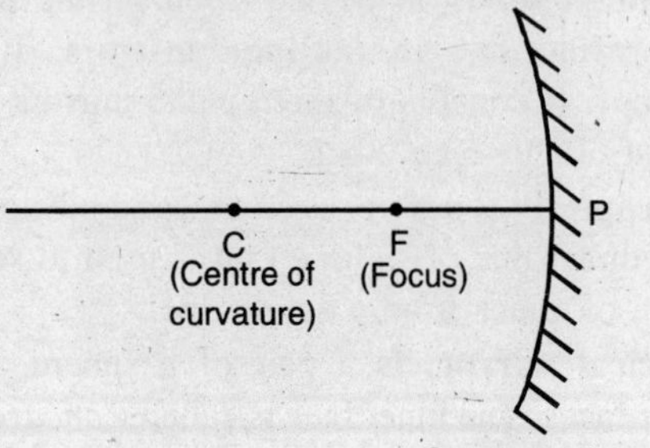

Concave mirror

☛ **Case 1:** Image formed by a Concave mirror when the object is placed between pole and focus of the mirror.

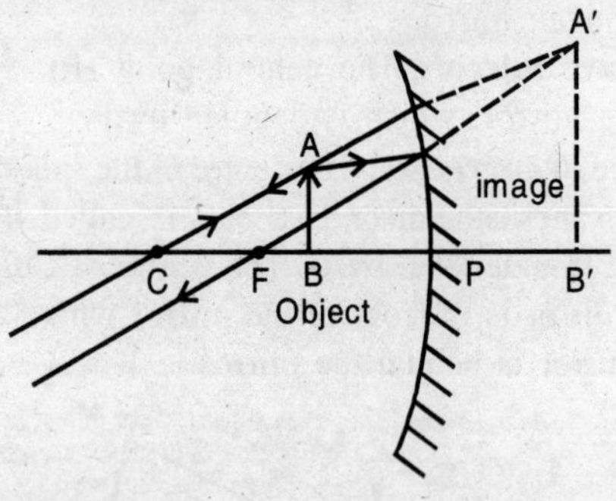

Nature of the image

(*i*) behind the mirror
(*ii*) virtual and erect and
(*iii*) larger than the object.

☛ **Case 2:** When object is placed at the focus (f) of a Concave mirror.

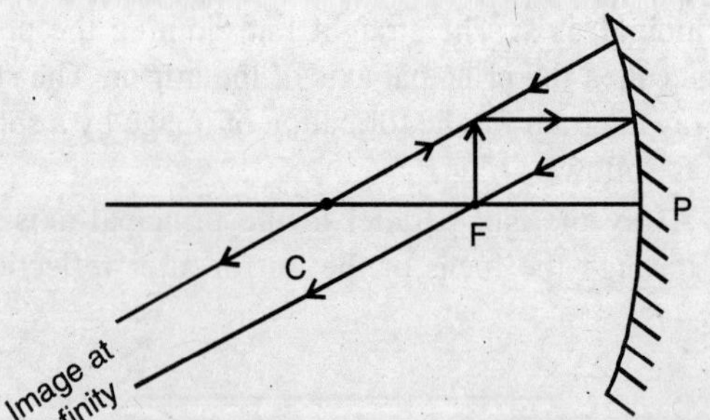

Concave mirror

Nature of the image

(*i*) at infininty
(*ii*) real and inverted and
(*iii*) highly magnified.

☛ **Case 3:** When object is placed between focus and centre of Curvature (F & C).

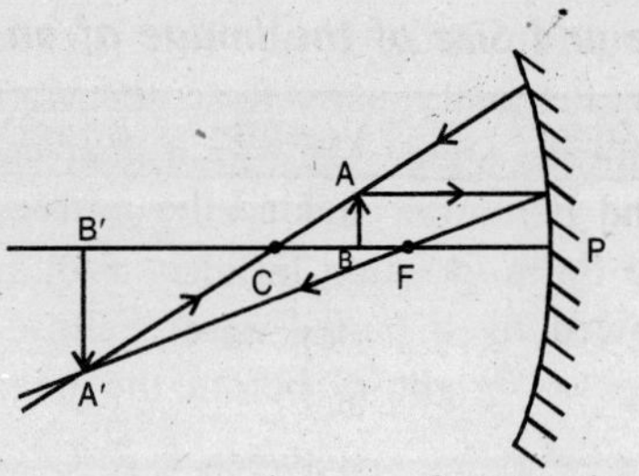

Concave mirror

Nature of the image

(*i*) beyond the centre of curvature
(*ii*) real and inverted and
(*iii*) larger than the object.

☛ **Case 4:** When the object is placed at the centre of curvature of a concave mirror.

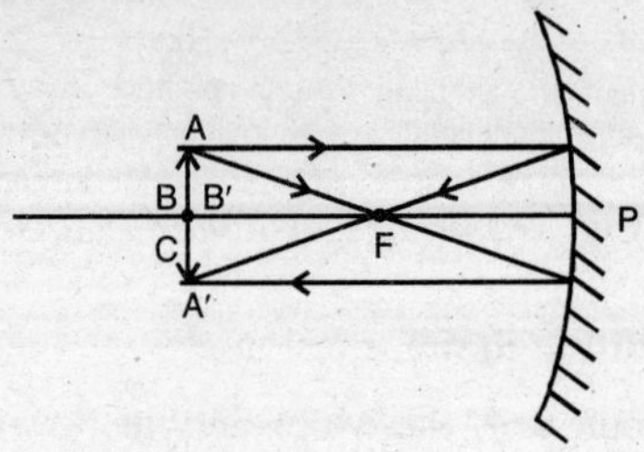

Nature of the image

(*i*) at the centre of curvature C
(*ii*) real and inverted, and
(*iii*) same size as the object.

☛ **Case 5:** When the object is beyond the centre of curvature of the concave mirror.

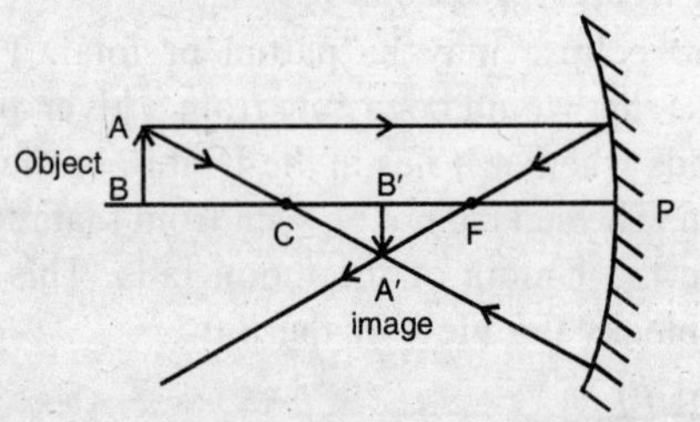

Nature of the image

(*i*) between the focus and centre of curvature
(*ii*) real and inverted and
(*iii*) smaller than the object.

☛ **Case 6:** When the object is at infinity.

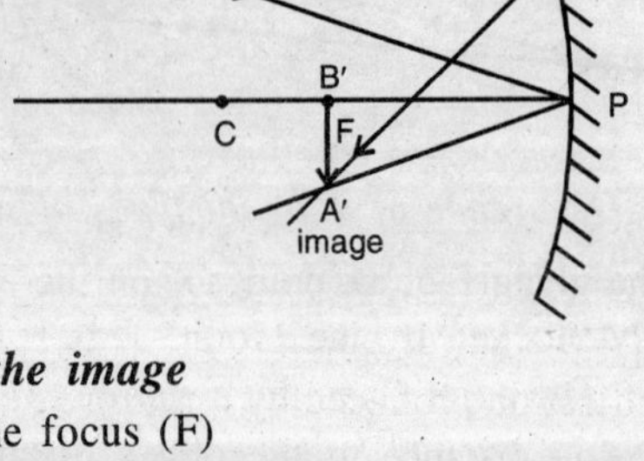

Nature of the image

(*i*) at the focus (F)
(*ii*) real and inverted and
(*iii*) highly diminished.

Position, Nature and Size of the image of an object formed by Concave mirror.

Position of object	Position of image	Size of image	Nature of image
Between P and F	Behind the mirror	Enlarged	Vital and erect
At focus (F)	At infinity	Highly enlarged	Real and inverted
Between F & C	Beyond C	Enlarged	Real and inverted
At C	at C	Equal to object	Real and inverted
Beyond C	Between F & C	Diminished	Real and inverted
At infinity	At focus (F)	Highly diminished	Real and inverted

Sign Convention for Spherical Mirrors

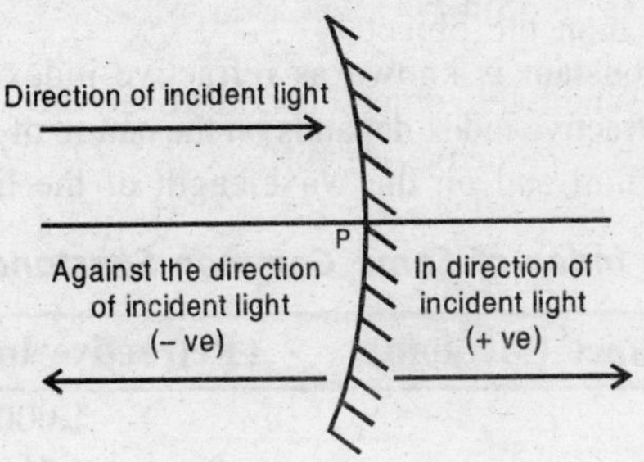

According to the new Cartesion Sign Convention:

(*i*) All the distances are measured from pole of the mirror as origin.

(*ii*) Distance measured in the same direction as that of incident light are taken as positive (+ve).

(*iii*) Distances measured against the direction of incident light are taken as negative.

(*iv*) Distances measured upward and perpendicular to the principal axis are taken as positive.

(*v*) Distances measured downward and perpendicular to the principal axis are taken as negative.

Mirror Formula

A formula which gives the relationship between image distance (*v*), object distance (*u*) and focal length (*f*) of a mirrror is known as the mirror formula as given below.

$$\frac{1}{v}+\frac{1}{u}=\frac{1}{f}$$

where v = distance of image from mirror.

u = distance of object from mirror.

f = focal length of the mirror.

Magnification Produced by Mirrors

The ratio of the height of image to the height of object is known as magnification.

i.e. $$m=\frac{h_2}{h_1}$$

where h_2 = height of image.

h_1 = height of object.

The magnification produced by a mirror is equal to the ratio of the image distance to the object distance with a minus sign.

i.e. $$m=-\frac{v}{u}$$

where v = image distance

u = object distance.

$$m=\frac{h_2}{h_1}=-\frac{v}{u}$$

Formation of image by a Convex Mirror

☛ **Case 1:** When object is placed any where between pole P and infinity.

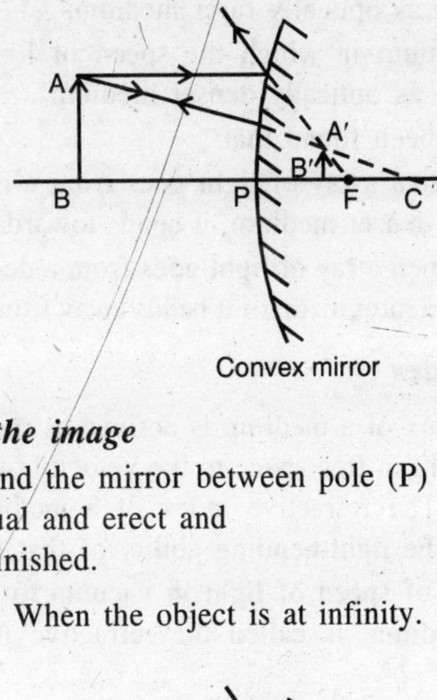

Convex mirror

Nature of the image

(*i*) behind the mirror between pole (P) and focus (F)

(*ii*) virtual and erect and

(*iii*) diminished.

☛ **Case 2:** When the object is at infinity.

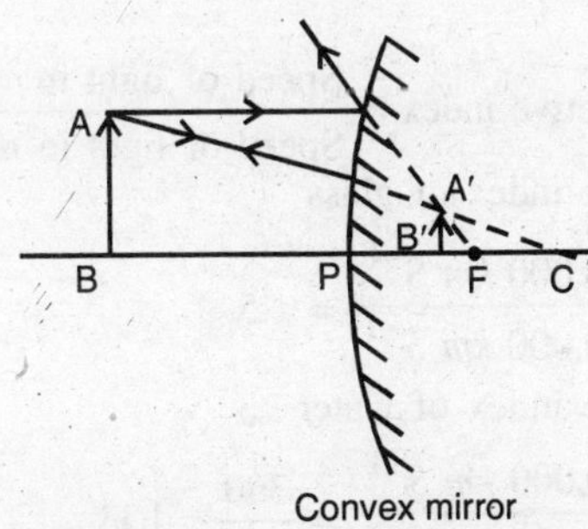

Convex mirror

Nature of the image

(*i*) behind the mirror at focus (F)

(*ii*) virtual and erect and

(*iii*) highly diminished.

Refraction of Light

The change in direction of light when it passes from one medium to another, is called refraction of light.

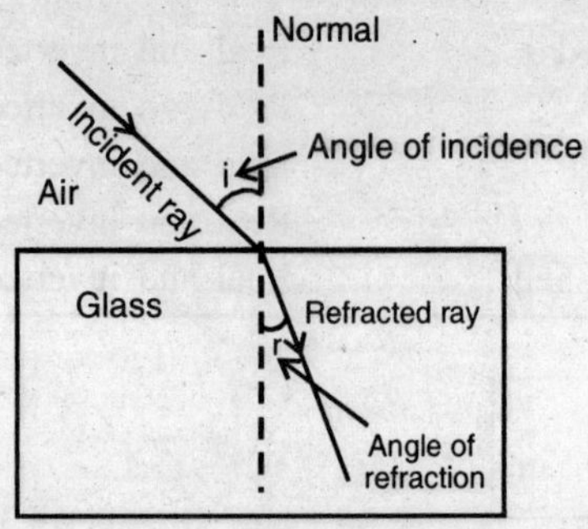

The angle between incident ray and normal is called the *angle of incidence.*

The angle between the refracted ray and the normal is called the *angle of refraction.*

Case of Refraction

The refraction of light takes place on going from one medium to another because the speed of light is different in the two media.

- A medium in which the speed of light is more is known as optically rarer medium.
- A medium in which the speed of light is less, is known as optically denser medium

  It has been found that:

  (*i*) When a ray of light goes from a rarer medium to denser medium, it bends towards the normal.

  (*ii*) When a ray of light goes from a denser medium to a rarer medium it bends away from the normal.

Refractive Index

Refractive Index of a medium is defined as the ratio of the velocity of light in free space to the velocity of light in that medium. i.e. The refractive index of a medium gives an indication of the light-bending ability of that medium.

The ratio of speed of light in vacuum to the speed of light in a medium, is called the refractive index of that medium.

i.e. Refractive index $= \dfrac{\text{Speed of light in vacuum}}{\text{Speed of light in medium}}$

Refractive index of glass

$$= \frac{3{,}00{,}000\ km\ S^{-1}}{2{,}00{,}000\ km\ S^{-1}} = 1.5.$$

Refractive index of water

$$= \frac{3{,}00{,}000\ km\ S^{-1}}{2{,}25{,}000\ km\ S^{-1}} = \frac{300}{225} = 1.33.$$

Laws of Refraction of Light

There are two laws of refraction of light. These are:

(*i*) The incident ray, the refracted ray and the normal at the point of incidence, all lie in the same plane.

(*ii*) The ratio of sine of the angle of incidence to the sine of angle of refraction is a constant for the two given media.

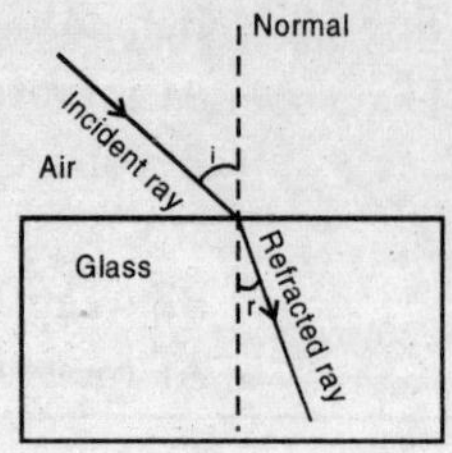

i..e $\dfrac{\text{Sin } i}{\text{Sin } r}$ = Constant.

This constant is known as refractive index.

The refractive index depands on the nature of the material of the medium and on the wavelength of the light used.

Refractive Index of Some Common Substances

Substance (Medium)	Refractive Index (n)
Air	1.0003
Ice	1.31
Water	1.33
Alcohal	1.36
Sulphuric Acid	1.43
Kerosene	1.44
Turpentine Oil	1.47
Benzene	1.50
Crown Glass	1.52
Carbon Disulphide	1.63
Dense Flint Glass	1.65
Ruby	1.71
Sappire	1.77
Diamond	2.42
Glycerine	1.47

Dispersion of Light

The phenomenon of splitting of light into its constituent colours is known as *dispersion of light.* The band of seven colours formed on a white screen, when a beam of white light is passed through a glass prism, is called spectrum of white light.

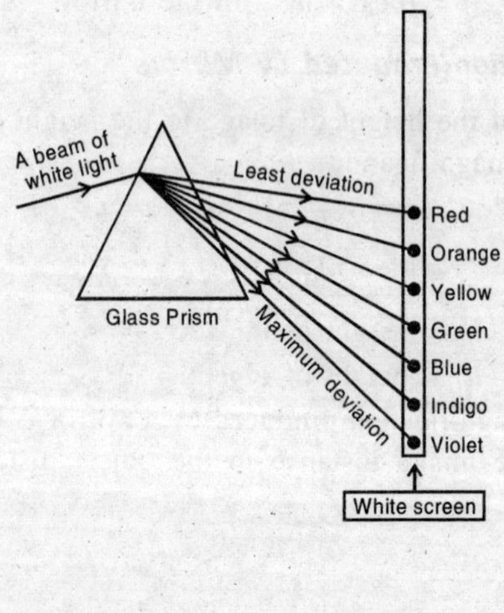

White light is made from seven colours: red, orange, yellow, green, blue, indigo and violet.

The dispersion of white light occurs because the angle of refraction of different colours is different when passing through the glass prism.

Primary Colours of Light

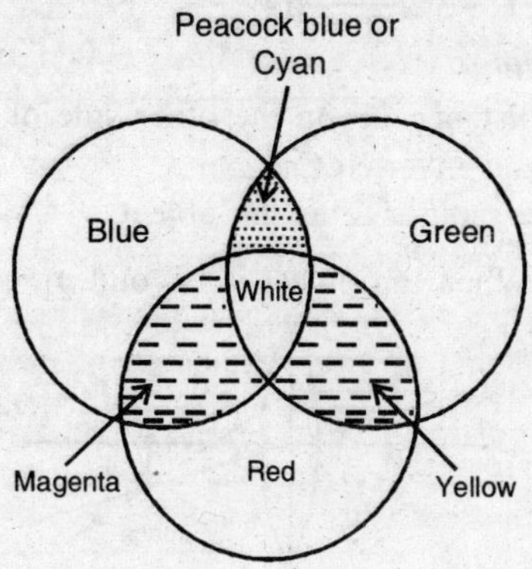

Red, Green and Blue are called primary colours of light, because all the other colours can be obtained by mixing these three colours in suitable proportions.

These results can be written as:

(*i*) Red + Blue = Magenta.
(*ii*) Blue + Green = Pecock Blue.
(*iii*) Red + Green = Yellow.

Refraction of Light by Spherical Lenses

Any transparent material bound with two surface of different curvature form a lens. There are two type of lenses:

- Convex lens and
- Concave lens.

Convex Lens: A convex lens is thick at the centre but thinner at the edges.

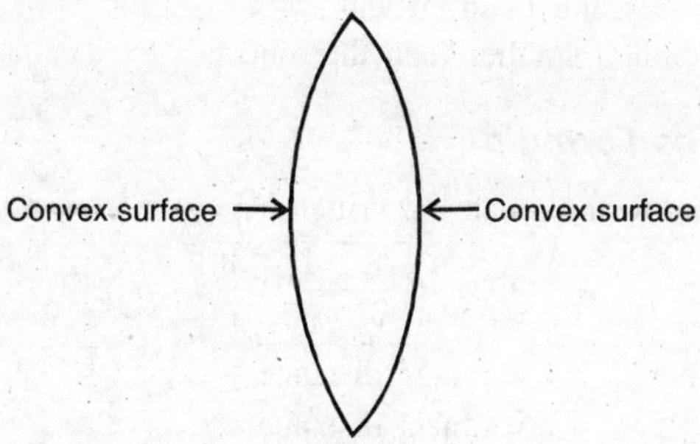

Convex lens

Concave Lens: A concave lens is thin in the middle but thicker at the edges.

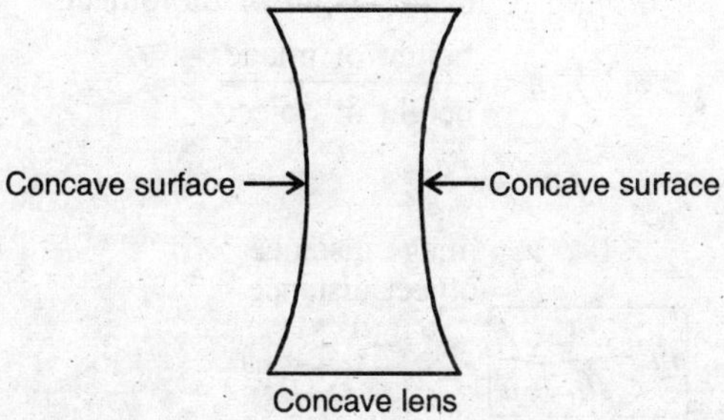

Concave lens

Principal Focus and Focal length of a Convex Lens

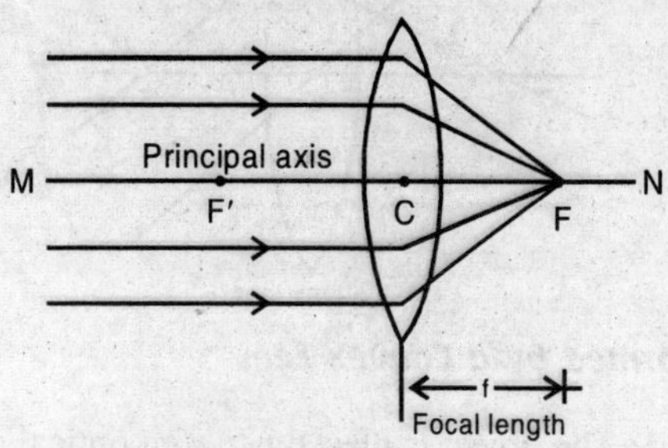

The principal focus of a convex lens is a point on its principal axis to which light rays parallel to the principal axis converge after passing through the lens. MN is called principal axis of the lens. The point C is called the centre or the optical centre of the lens.

The point F is called principal focus or the foucs of the lens.

The distance between the centre of the lens and its focus is known as the *focal length* of the lens.

A convex lens is also known as a *converging lens* because it converges a parallel beam of light rays.

Principal Focus and Focal length of the Concave Lens

The point F is the principal focus of the concave lens. A concave lens is also known as a diverging lens because it diverges a parallel beam of light rays. A concave lens has a virtual focus.

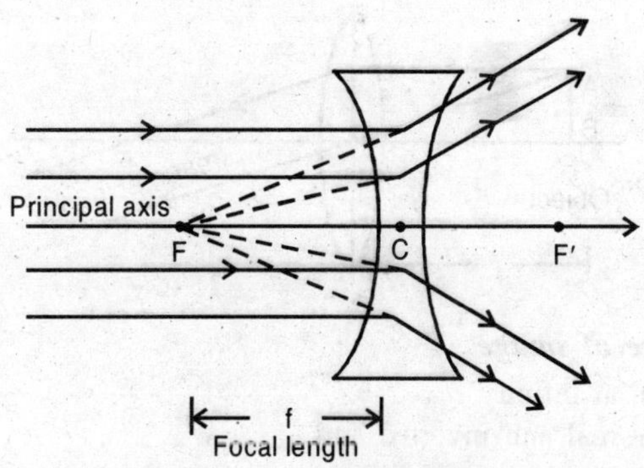

Concave lens

Rules for obtaining images Formed by Convex Lenses

There are three rules for obtaining images by convex lenses. These are:

(*i*) An incident ray parallel to the principal axis of a convex lens passes through the focus of the lens after refraction.

(*ii*) An incident ray passing through the optical centre of a convex lens goes straight after refraction through the lens. It does not get deviated.

(*iii*) An incident ray passing through the foucs of a convex lens, becomes parallel to the principal axis after refraction through the lens.

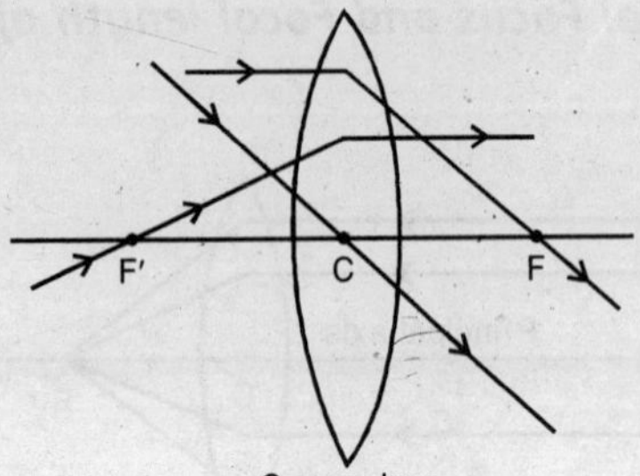

Convex lens

Image Formed by a Convex Lens

☛ **Case 1:** The object is placed between optical centre and focus.

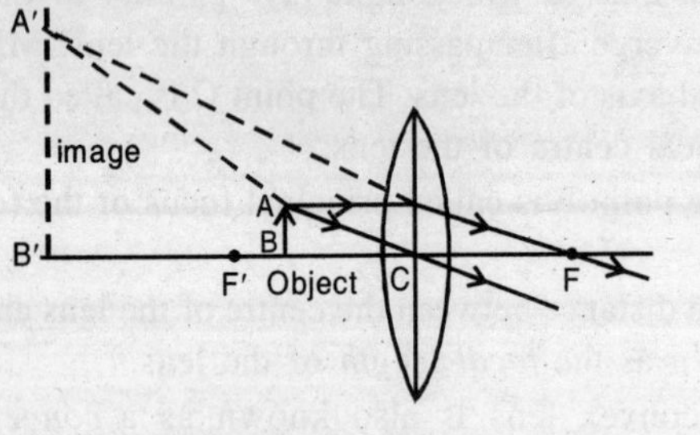

Nature of image

(*i*) behind the object
(*ii*) virtual and erect and
(*iii*) larger than the object.

☛ **Case 2:** When the object is placed at the focus of a convex lens.

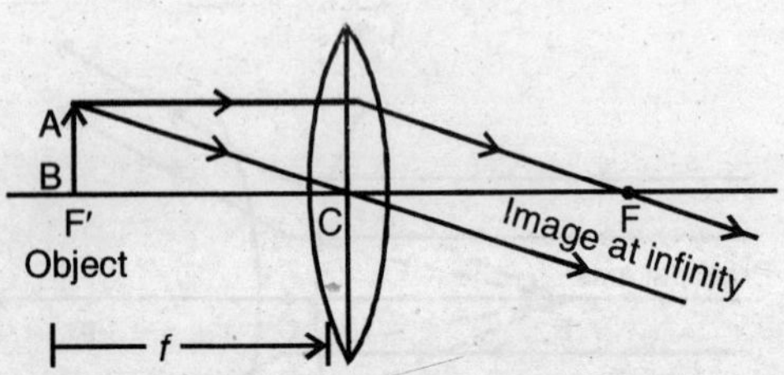

Nature of image

(*i*) at infinity
(*ii*) real and inverted and
(*iii*) highly enlarged.

☛ **Case 3:** When the object is between F′ & 2F′.

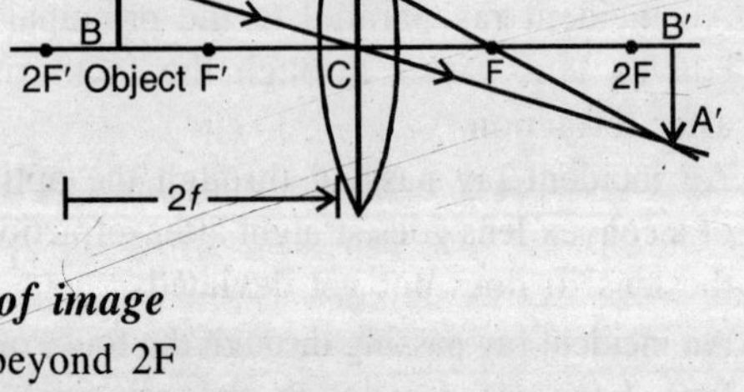

Nature of image

(*i*) beyond 2F
(*ii*) real and inverted and
(*iii*) larger than the object.

☛ **Case 4:** When the object is at 2F′.

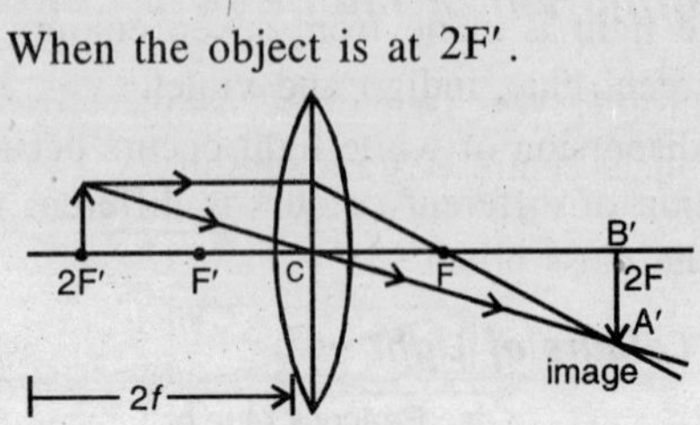

Nature of image

(*i*) at a distance 2F on the other side of the lens.
(*ii*) real and inverted and
(*iii*) of the same size as the object.

☛ **Case 5:** When the object is beyond 2F′.

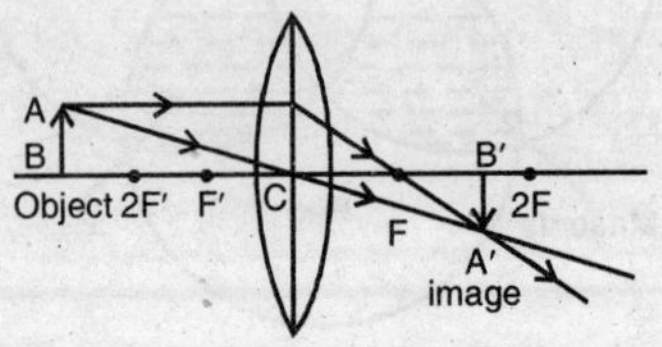

Nature of image

(*i*) between F and 2F on the other side of the lens.
(*ii*) real and inverted and
(*iii*) smaller than the object.

☛ **Case 6:** When the object is at infinity.

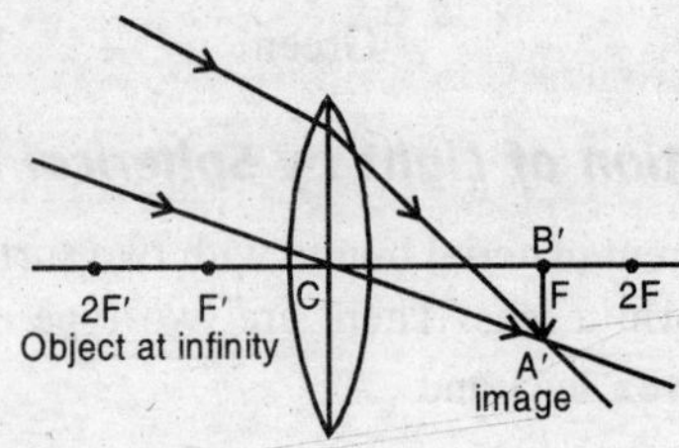

Nature of image

(*i*) at the focus
(*ii*) real and inverted and
(*iii*) much smaller than the object.

Lens Formula

The lens formula can be written as:

$$\boxed{\frac{1}{v} - \frac{1}{u} = \frac{1}{f}}$$

Where v = image distance
u = object distance
f = focal length.

Magnification: The magnification is the ratio of the height of the image to the height of the object.

i.e. $$m = \frac{\text{height of image}}{\text{height of object}}$$

$$m = \frac{h_2}{h_1}$$

If v = image distance
u = object distance

$$\boxed{m = \frac{h_2}{h_1} = \frac{v}{u}}$$

Formation of Image by a Concave Lens

☛ **Case 1:** When an object is placed anywhere between optical centre (C) and infinity.

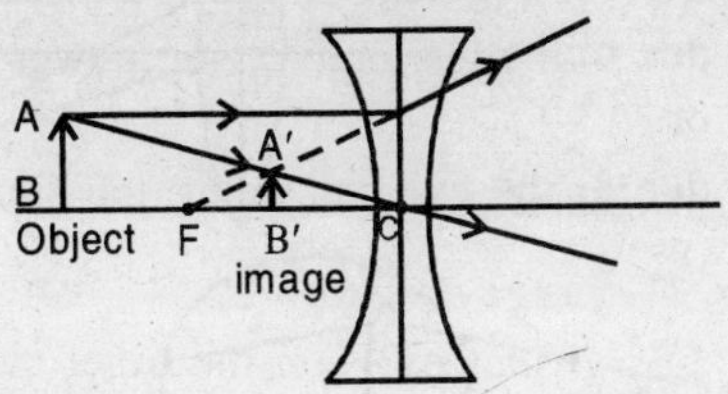

Nature of image

(*i*) between optical centre (C) and focus (F)

(*ii*) virtual and erect and

(*iii*) smaller than the object.

☛ **Case 2:** When an object is at infinity.

Nature of image

(*i*) at focus F

(*ii*) virtual and erect

(*iii*) highly diminished.

Power of a Lens

The power of a lens is a measure of the degree of convergence or divergence of light rays falling on it. The power of a lens is defined as the reciprocal of its focal length in metres.

$$\text{Power of lens} = \frac{1}{\text{focal length of the lens in (metres)}}$$

$$\boxed{P = \frac{1}{f}}$$

where P = power of the lens.

f = focal length of the lens.

The S.I. unit of the power of a lens is **dioptre**. Which is denoted by the letter D. One dioptre is the power of a lens whose focal length is 1 metre.

Total Internal Reflection

The critical angle for a medium is the angle of incidence in the medium for which the angle of refraction in air is 90°. When the angle of incidence of a beam of light travelling in a denser medium is greater than the critical angle of the medium, then, there is no refraction of light into the rarer medium, all the light is reflected back into the denser medium. This phenomenon is called total internal reflection of light.

Condition for Total Internal Reflection

(*i*) The incident light must pass from a denser medium into a rarer medium.

(*ii*) The angle of incidence in denser medium must be greater than the critical angle of the medium.

The Human Eye: A Living Lens

The main parts of human eye are: Cornea (C), iris (I), pupil (P), ciliary muscles (M), convex lens (called eye lens) (L), retina (R) and optic nerve (N).

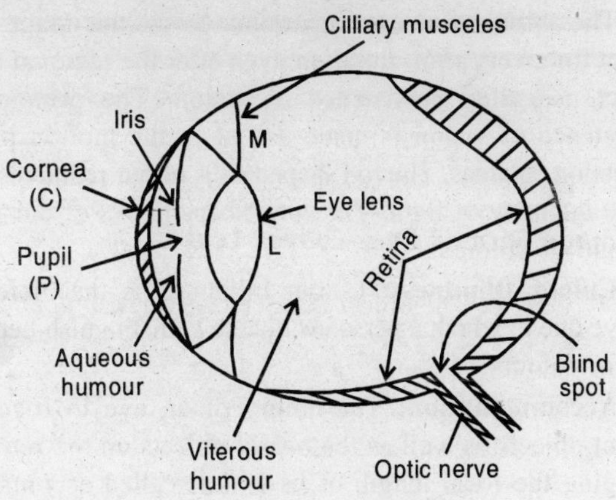

Fig. Structure of human eye

Construction of Eye: The front part of the eye is called cornea. It is made of a transparent substance and it is bulging outwards. The light coming from objects enters the eye through cornea. Just behind the cornea is the **iris**. There is a hole in the middle of the iris which is called pupil of the eye. The pupil appears black because no light is reflected from it.

The eye-lens is a convex lens made of a transparent and flexible material like jelly made of proteins. The eye-lens is held in position by ciliary muscles. The focal length of eye-lens can be changed by the action of ciliary muscles. The screen on which the image is formed in the eye is called **retina**. The retina is behind the eye-lens and at the back part of the eye. The retina of an eye is just like the film in a camera. The retina has a large number of light sensitive cells called rods and cones. Which respond to the intensity of light and colour of objects respectively, by generating electrical signals. The space between cornea and eye-lens is filled with a viscous liquid called **aqueous humour** and the space between eye-lens and retina is filled with another liquid called **vitreous humour**.

Working: The eye-lens in the front of the eyeball makes a real and inverted image of the objects on the retina, which is located behind it. The retina is a thin tissue that has many layers of cells. The most important layer of the retina consists of nerve cells that are sensitive to the brightness as well as to the colours of light. The nerve cells carry the message about the image from the retina to the brain in the form of special signals. The brain then interprets these signals and enables us to see the objects we are looking at. The ciliary muscles contract or tighten up when looking at close things. The eye-lens because thicker and shortens its focal length. This enables eyes to form image on the retina of the objects close to you. The relaxing of muscles makes the eye-lens thinner and increases its focal length to focus the image of distant objects on the retina.

Persistence of Vision: The image of an object seen by our eyes persists. On the retina for about $\frac{1}{16}$th of a second even after we have stopped seeing the object.

The ability of an eye to continue to see the image of an object for a very short duration even after the removal of the object, is called persistence of vision. The principle of persistence of vision is made use of in the motion picture projection cinemas. The rod shaped cells of our retina respond to the intensity of light. The cone shaped cells of our retina respond of colours.

Colour Blindness: Colour blindness is that defect of the eye due to which a person is unable to distinguish between certain colours.

Accommodation: The ability of an eye to focus the distant objects as well as the nearly objects on the retina by changing the focal length of its lens is called accommodation.

A normal eye has a power of accommodation which enables objects as far as infinity and as close as 25 cm to be focused on the retina.

Least Distance of Distinct Vision: The minimum distance at which a object must be placed so that a normal eye may see it clearly, is called the least distance of distinct vision. The least distance of distinct vision for a normal human eye is about 25 cm.

Defects of Vision

There are four defects of vision which can be corrected by using suitable eye glasses or spectacles. These are:

I. Myopia (Short-Sightedness or Near-Sightedness)
II. Hypermetropia (Long-Sightedness or Far-Sightedness)
III. Presbyopia and
IV. Astigmatism

I. Myopia or Short-Sightedness: Myopia is that defect of the eye due to which an eye cannot see the distant objects clearly. This defect of eye is caused;
— due to the high converging power of the eye-lens
or
— due to the eye-ball being too long.

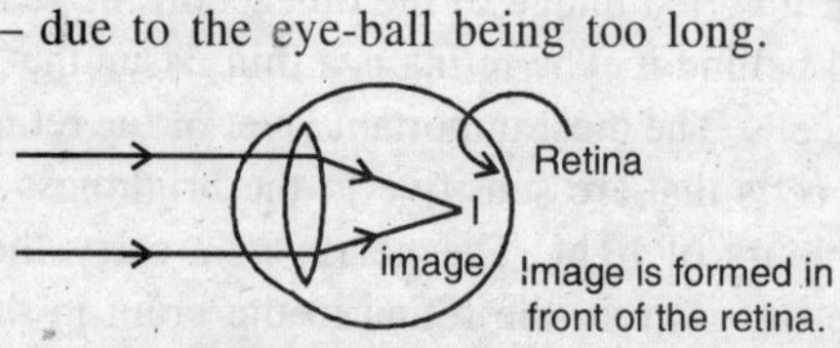

Fig. An eye suffering from myopia.

Myopia or short-sightedness is corrected by using concave lenses.

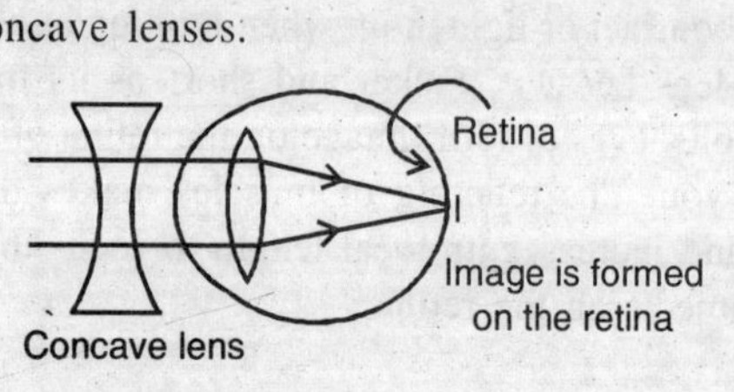

II. Hypermetropia or Long-Sightedness: Hypermetropia or long-sightedness is that defect of the eye due to which an eye cannot see the nearby objects clearly. This defect of eye is caused:
— due to the low converging power of the eye-lens
or
— due to the eye-ball being too short.

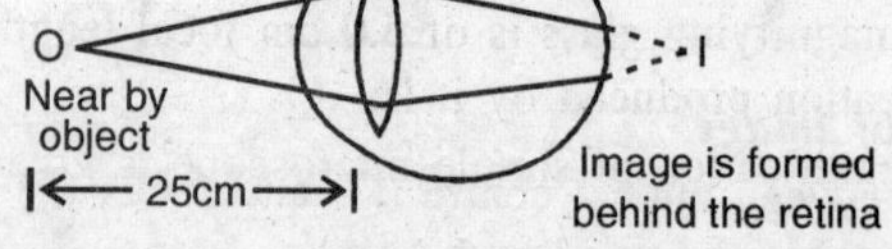

Fig. An eye suffering from hypermetropia.

Hypermetropia or long-sightedness is corrected by using spectacles containing **convex lenses.**

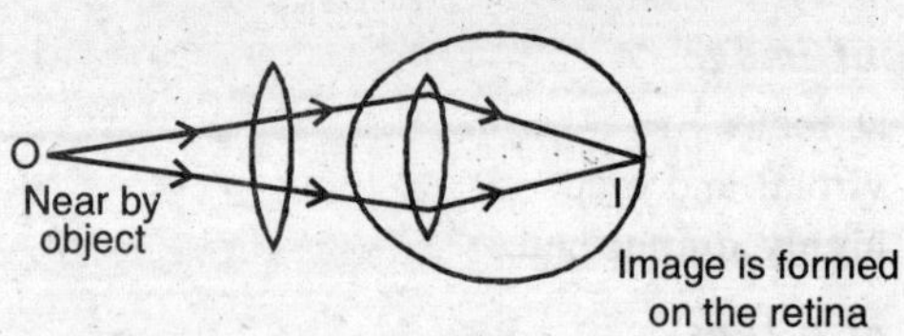

III. Presbyopia: Presbyopia is that defect of the eye due to which an old person cannot read comfortably and clearly without spectacles.

Presbyopia occurs in old age due to the gradual weakening of the ciliary muscles and diminishing flexibility of the eye-lens.

Presbyopia defect is corrected by using spectacles having **bifocal lenses.**

IV. Astigmatism is that defect of the eye due to which a person cannot focus on both horizontal and vertical lines simultaneously. This defect arises due to the irregularities in the surface of **cornea.**

Astigmatism can be corrected by superimposing cylindrical lenses upon the spherical shape of spectacle lenses. **Contract** develops when the eye-lens of a person becomes opaque due to the formation of a membrane over it.

Applications of Lenses

Magnifying Glass or Simple Microscope: The simple microscope is a convex lens of short focal length. It is also called magnifying glass. It is used to get magnified and erect image of small objects. A watchmaker's glass is also a magnifying lens.

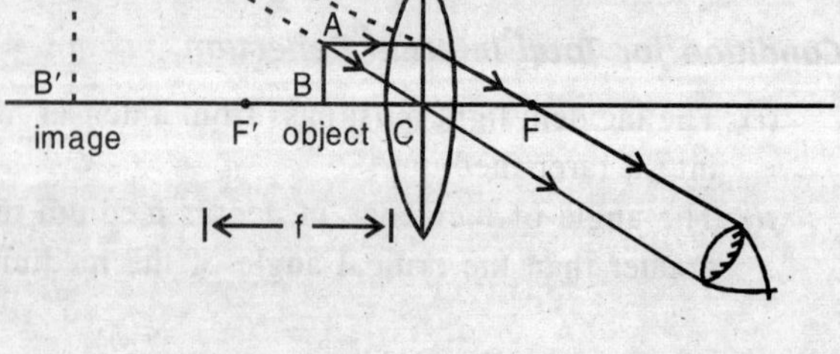

Magnification produced by a Simple Microscope

Magnification, $m = \dfrac{\text{size of image}}{\text{size of object}}$

The magnification of a simple microscope is given by

$$m = 1 + \frac{D}{f}$$

where D = Least distance of distinct vision (25 cm.)

f = Focal length of the convex lens.

e.g. A magnifying glass is of 5.0 cm focal length then the magnification produced by it is:

Sol. Magnification of simple microscope is given by

$$m = 1 + \frac{D}{f}$$

$$D = 25 \text{ cm.}$$

$$f = 5.0 \text{ cm.}$$

$$m = 1 + \frac{25}{5} = 1 + 5 = 6.$$

This means that the object will appear 6 times larger with this magnifying glass.

Compound Microscope

The most commonly used microscope has two convex lenses fixed at two ends of a small cylindrical tube. Such a microscope is known as a compound microscope.

Anton Van Leeuwenhoek (1632-1723) invented the compound microscope. The lens fixed at viewing or the upper end of the microscope, which is used to took at enlarged image of the object, is known as its **eye-piece lens**. The object is kept in front of the lens at the other end, which is known as the **objective lens** of the microscope. The objective and eye-piece of a compound microscope are convex lenses of very short focal lengths.

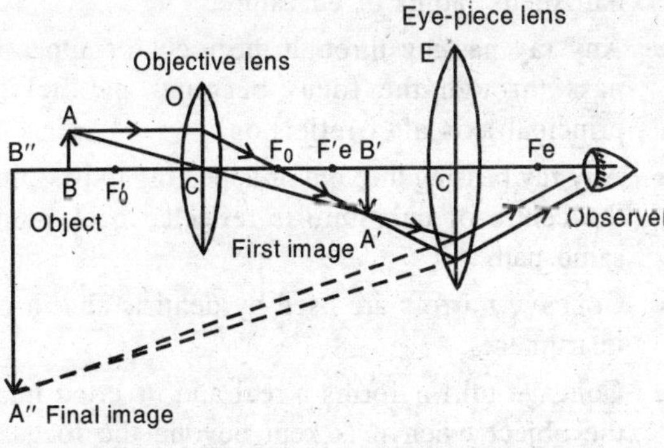

Fig. Ray-diagram of a compound microscope.

Working of a Compound Microscope: The distance of the object from the objective lens is kept slightly more than its focal length. This lens forms a real, inverted and enlarge image of the object. This acts as an object for the eye-piece lens. The distance between the two lenses of micro-scope is so adjusted that the image formed by the objective falls between the eye-piece and its focus. The eye-piece, formed a further enlarged but virtual image of the object.

Magnification Produced by a Compound Microscope is given by

$$m = \frac{v_o}{u_o}\left(1 + \frac{D}{f_e}\right)$$

where, D = Least distance of distinct vision (25 cm)

v_o = Image distance for the objective lens (in cm.)

u_o = Object distance for the objective lens (in cm.)

f_e = Focal length of eye-piece lens (in cm.)

Telescope

A telescope is an optical instrument which is used for viewing distant objective such as the moon, stars, planets etc.

There are two types of telescope:

— Astronomical telescope and

— Terrestrial telescope.

Astronomical Telescope: An astronomical telescope is used to see the details of celestial bodies like stars, planets and satellite. This telescope produces a virtual, inverted and magnified image of the distance object. It was invented by **Kepler in 1611**.

Construction: This telescope consists of two convex lenses.

— Objective, which is towards the object and

— Eye-piece, which is towards the eye.

The objective is of larger focal length (50-100 cm.), while the eye-piece is of shorter focal length (2-5 cm.).

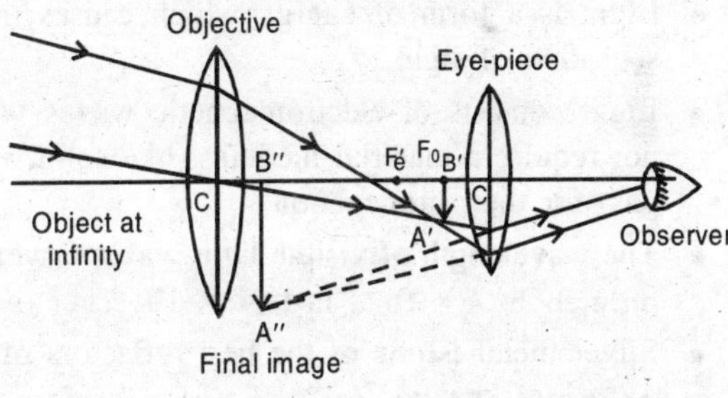

Fig. Ray-diagram for an astronomical telescope.

Working: The objective forms a real and very small image of the distant object near its focus. The real image formed by the objective is inverted and acts as an object for the eye-piece. The distance between the objective and the eye-piece in a telescope is so adjusted that the image formed by the objective lies between the eye-piece and its focus. Therefore the final image formed by the eye-piece is enlarged and virtual. The final image of the object seen through the telescope is inverted with respect to the object.

Magnification: The magnification of a telescope is given by

$$m = \frac{f_o}{f_e}$$

where f_o = focal length of objective of the telescope

f_e = focal length of eye-piece of the telescope

Points to Remember

- An object, which has its own light is called a source of light.
- Source of light are natural as well as man-made.
- Objects scatter the light falling on them from the source and make them visible to our eyes.
- Light travels in straight line. It is called rectilinear propagation of light.
- Rectilinear propagation of light explains the formation of the image of an object in a pinhole camera.
- The materials through which we are able to see clearly because light passes through them almost completely are called **transparent**.
- The materials which do not allow light to pass through them at all are called **opaque**.
- The materials which allow only part of the incident light to pass through them are called **translucent**.
- In the presence of a source of light, opaque objects act as obstacles to propagation of light and form shadows beyond them in the form of Umbra and Penumbra.
- The region of the space where the light from the source does not reach and hence is the darkest, is called **Umbra**.
- The region where the light does not reach from all parts of the source is called penumbra.
- Eclipses of the Moon and the Sun occur due to the shadows cast by the Earth and the Moon respectively.
- Light is a form of energy which causes in us the sensation of sight.
- Light consists of electromagnetic waves which do not require a material medium (like solid, liquid or gas) for their propagation.
- The wavelength of visible light waves is very small only about 4×10^{-7} m to 8×10^{-7} m.
- Silver metal is one of the best reflectors of light.
- A bundle of light rays is called a beam of light.
- When light rays fall on polished surfaces, they change their direction in a well-defined manner. This is called regular reflection.
- Light falling on non-polished surfaces does not change the direction in a well-defined manner. This is called **diffuse reflection**.
- There are two laws of reflection:
  (*i*) The incident ray, the normal at the point of incidence and the reflected rays are in the same plane.
  (*ii*) The angle of incidence and the angle of reflection are equal.
- In a plane mirror, the reflected rays appear to come from some object kept behind the mirror. This is called a **virtual image** of the object.
- The image which can be obtained on a screen is called a **real image**.
- The image which cannot be obtained on a screen is called a virtual image. A virtual image can be seen only by looking into a mirror or a lens.
- Laws of reflection are also applicable to polished curved surfaces.
- In case of curved reflecting surfaces the normal at different points of incidence have different directions.
- The image formed in a plane mirror is laterally inverted with respect to the object.
- A spherical mirror is that mirror whose reflecting surface is the part of a hollow sphere of glass.
- Spherical mirrors are two types:
  — concave mirror and
  — convex mirror.
- The centre of curvature of a concave mirror is in front of it but the centre of curvature of a concave mirror is behind it.
- The centre of the sphere of which the spherical mirror is a part, is called the centre of curvature of the mirror.
- Any straight line joining the centre of curvature with any point of the spherical mirror is normal to the mirror at that point.
- The centre of a spherical mirror is called its pole.
- The point through which the incident rays parallel to the principal axis, after reflection from the mirror, pass through or appear to pass through, is called focus of the spherical mirror.
- When the reflection rays meet in front of the mirror, they are to form a **real image**.
- The focal length of a spherical mirror is equal to half of its radius of curvature.
- Any ray passing through the focus or appearing to pass through the focus becomes parallel to the principal axis after reflection.
- Any ray passing through or appearing to pass through the centre of curvature is reflected back along the same path.
- Concave mirrors are used by dentists and in optical instruments.
- Concave mirror forms a real and inverted image of the object when it is kept beyond the focus and a virtual, erect but magnified image is formed when the object is kept in between the mirror and the focus.
- Convex mirrors are used as rear view mirrors in care and for viewing images of larger areas.
- Convex mirror always forms a smaller and virtual image.
- Refraction takes place when light enters from one transparent medium to another.

- Objects kept partly in a transparent liquid, like water, appear to bend at the surface.
- The speed of light is different in different transparent media. Light travels with maximum speed in vacuum.
- The ratio of speed of light in two media is expressed as refractive index of one medium with respect to the other.
- The angle of incidence is larger than the angle of refraction, when light travels from an optically rarer to an optically denser medium.
- A ray incident obliquely on a rectangular glass slab and the emergent ray corresponding to it are parallel but laterally displaced with respect to each other.
- Refraction of Sunlight through a glass prism splits in into a band of seven colours.
- The seven colours in the spectrum of white light are Violet, Indigo, Blue, Green, Yellow, Orange and Red. These are often represented by the acronym **"VIBGYOR"**.
- Lenses could be divergent or convergent depending on the nature of the curvature of their surfaces.
- A convex lens is a converging lens, which can produce a real or virtual image of an object depending on its position with respect to it.
- A concave lens is a divergent lens, which always produces a virtual image of the object irrespective of where it is placed.
- Convex lenses are used as a magnifying glass and also in making telescope and microscopes.
- The most important component of a photographic camera is its lens, which forms a real image of the objects on the film.
- Our eyes have a convex lens whose focal length can be changed at will with the action of **ciliary muscles**.
- The reciprocal of the focal length expressed in metres is called the power of lens.
- The phenomenon of splitting of white light into its constituent seven colours is called dispersion and the coloured band obtained on a screen is called a **spectrum**.
- The magnifying glass is also called a **simple microscope**.
- The magnification of an object can be described as the increase in apparent area of the object.
- A microscope that has more than one lens is called a compound microscope.
- The focal length of the objective lens is short and that of eye-piece is comparatively more in a compound microscope.
- A telescope is an optical instrument which is used for viewing distance object such as the moon, stars, planets etc.
- Astronomical telescope forms inverted image while terrestrial telescope form erect images.
- In a telescope the objective lens is larger focal length, while the eye-peace lens is of shorter focal length.
- A camera is an optical instrument based on the principal of formation of a real, inverted and usually diminished image of the object by a **convex lens**.
- A person suffering from myopia can see near objects distinctly. It can be corrected with diverging lenses.
- A person suffering from hypermetropia can see distant objects clearly but cannot see near objects distinctly. It can be corrected with converging lens.

SOUND

Sound Waves

It emerges from a source—a voice, an instrument or an engine which gives the sensation of hearing. It begins with vibration. Everything which is in the state of vibration must produce a sound and it travels in a medium as a wave motion.

In solid and liquid sound travels as a transverse wave motion and in a gas sound travels as a longitudinal wave motion.

Transmission of Sound

Sounds are always transmitted through a definite medium. The speed of sound depends upon the medium through which it travels.

Mathematically, $v = n\lambda$

where v is the frequency, λ is the wavelength.

Wavelength

It is defined as the distance transversed by a wave during the time a particle of the medium vibrating about its mean position, completes one vibration.

Frequency

It is defined as the number of vibration made per second.

Phase

It is defined as the fraction of time period or the angle 2π which has elapsed since the particle last passed through the mean position in the +ve direction.

Newton's Formula

The velocity of sound in air is given by $v = \sqrt{\frac{P}{d}}$

where P is the pressure, d is the density of the medium.

Laplace's Correction

$v = \sqrt{\lambda p / d}$

where γ is the ratio of two specific heats of a gas.

Speed of Sound

The speed of sound depends on the following factors:

(*a*) **Effect of temperature:** It increases with the increase in temperature as $v \propto \sqrt{t}$

(*b*) **Effect of pressure:** It is independent of the pressure at the same temperature.

(c) **Effect of humidity:** It decreases with increase in density $v \propto \frac{1}{\sqrt{d}}$.

Characteristics of Sound

There are three characteristics of sound

(*a*) **Loudness or intensity of sound:** It depends on the amplitude of vibration of the sound-walling object and on the distance from the object to the ear.

(*b*) **Pitch or Frequency:** It is the highness or loudness of sound. It depends upon the speed vibration of the sounding object.

(*c*) **Quality of Timbre:** It makes sound distinctive.

Reflection of Sound

- **Echo:** When the reflected sound is heard separately it is called an echo.
- **Refraction of sound:** When waves pass through a different medium they are refracted.
- **Resonance of sound:** It is a phenomenon of forced vibration due to which sound waves can be produced with a large amplitude or intensity.
- **Musical sound:** The sound which produces pleasing effect upon the ear is called a musical sound and which produces displeasing effect upon the ear is called noise.
- **Beats:** When two notes of nearly the same frequency are produced together, alternate loud and low sounds are heard.

  This phenomenon is called beats.

  No. of beats = difference in their frequency

  $= (n_1 - n_2)$
- **Melody and Harmony:** It is important to establish a relationship between tones of different pitch. This holds true for the tones that follow each other in a melody as well as for those which are sounded together in a chord. When two combined tones have a whole number ratio, they are called consonant. If they do not, they are called dissonant.

Sonar

- Sonar stands for Sound Navigation and Ranging.
- The SONAR technique is used to determine the depth of sea and to locate under water hills, valleys, icebergs, submarines, sunken ships etc.
- A beam of ultrasonic sound is produced and transmitted by the transducer (it is a device that produces ultrasonic sound) of the SONAR, which travels through sea water. Ultrasound is reflected by seawater. The echo produced by the reflection of this ultrasonic sound is detected and recorded by the detector, which is converted into electrical signals. Using the time taken for echo to come back, we can find the depth of sea.
- The distance (*d*) of the under-water object is calculated from the time (*t*) taken by the echo to return with speed (*v*) is given by $2d = v \times t$. This method of measuring distance is also known as 'echo-ranging'.
- Echo ranging is the process of finding distances using process of ultrasound.

Human Ear

Structure of Human Ear

- The human ear can be divided into three main parts, viz. outer ear, middle ear and internal ear.
- **Outer Ear:** The outer ear is outside the body and is also called pinna. It extends into the ear canal. Ear canal is filled with air.
- **Middle Ear:** The middle ear is composed of the ear drum or tympanum (it is an elastic membrane, circular in shape) and the bone ossicles. There are three bone ossicles, namely, the hammer, the anvil and the strirrup.
- **Internal/inner Ear:** The internal ear is composed of a cochlea and three semi-circular canals. The cochlea is filled with liquid. The cochlea makes the hearing apparatus and the auditory nerve from it goes to the brain.
- Eardrum is the intersection of the outer and middle ear.
- Oval Window is the intersection of middle and inner ear.

Working of Human Ear

The outer ear called pinna collects the sound waves. The sound waves passes through the ear canal to a thin membrane called eardrum. The eardrum vibrates. The vibrations are amplified by the three bones of the middle ear called hammer, anvil and stirrup. The middle ear then transmits the sound waves to the inner ear. In the inner ear the sound waves are converted into electrical signals by the cochlea and sent to the brain through the auditory nerves. The brain then interprets the signals as sound.

MULTIPLE CHOICE QUESTIONS

1. Focal length of plane mirror is.................. .
A. Infinity B. Zero
C. Negative D. None of these

2. Image formed by plane mirror is:
A. Real and erect B. Real and inverted
C. Virtual and erect D. Virtual and inverted

3. A concave mirror gives real, inverted and same size image if the object is placed:
A. At F B. At infinity
C. At C D. Beyond C

4. Power of the lens is –40, its focal length is:
A. 4 m B. –40 m
C. –0.25 m D. –25 m

5. A concave mirror gives virtual, refract and enlarged image of the object but image of smaller size than the size of the object is:
A. At infinity B. Between F and C
C. Between P and F D. At E

6. In optics an object which has higher refractive index is called:
A. Optically rarer B. Optically denser
C. Optical density D. Refractive index

7. The optical phenomena, twinkling of stars, is due to:
A. Atmospheric reflection
B. Total reflection
C. Atmospheric refraction
D. Total refraction

8. Convex lens focus a real, point sized image at focus, the object is placed:
A. At focus B. Between F and 2F
C. At infinity D. At 2F

9. The unit of power of lens is:
A. Metre B. Centimeter
C. Diopter D. None of these

10. The radius of curvature of a mirror is 20 cm the focal length is:
A. 20 cm B. 10 cm
C. 40 cm D. 5 cm

11. The end product of alcoholic fermentation is:
A. pyruvic acid B. acetaldehyde
C. ethyl alcohol D. formic acid

12. Light wave is a:
A. Transverse wave B. Longitudinal wave
C. Any of both D. None of these

13. Protons and neutrons are bound in a nucleus by the:
A. short range 'weak interaction'
B. short range 'strong interaction'
C. long range 'electromagnetic interaction'
D. long range 'gravitational interaction'

14. To an astronaut in space, the sky will appear to be:
A. violet B. red
C. blue D. black

15. On a rainy day, small oily films on water show brilliant colours. This is due to:
A. scattering B. interference
C. polarisation D. none of these

16. Rainbow formation is due to:
A. absorption of sunlight by water droplets
B. diffusion of sunlight through water droplets
C. ionisation of water droplets
D. refraction and reflection of sunlight by water droplets

17. Golden view of sea shell is due to:
A. diffraction B. dispersion
C. polarisation D. reflection

18. A star appears twinkling in the sky because of:
A. scattering of light by atmosphere
B. reflection of light by atmosphere
C. refraction of light by atmosphere
D. diffraction of light by atmosphere

19. When a strong beam of light is passed through a colloidal solution, the light will:
A. be scattered B. pass unchanged
C. be absorbed D. be reflected

20. Persons suffering from myopia are advised to use:
A. convex lens B. concave lens
C. plano-convex lens D. plano-concave lens

21. The primary colours in photography are:
A. red, blue, yellow B. red, yellow, green
C. red, blue, green D. blue, yellow, green

22. Mirage is an example:
A. refraction of light only
B. total internal, reflection of light only
C. refraction and total internal reflection of light
D. dispersion of light only

23. Optical fibres are based on the phenomenon of:
A. interference B. dispersion
C. diffraction D. total internal reflection

24. The phenomenon of light associated with the appearance of blue colour of the sky is:
A. interference B. reflection
C. refraction D. scattering

25. Lens in made up of:
A. pyrex glass B. flint glass
C. ordinary glass D. cobalt glass

26. Lambert's law is related to:
A. reflection B. refraction
C. interference D. illumination

27. A water tank appears shallower when it is viewed from top due to:
A. rectilinear propagation of light
B. reflection
C. total internal reflection
D. refraction

28. To draw maximum current from a combination of cells, how should the cells be grouped?
A. Series
B. Parallel
C. Mixed
D. Depends upon the relative values of external and internal resistance

29. The image formed by retina of human eye is:
A. Virtual and erect B. Real and inverted
C. Virtual and inverted D. Real and erect

30. The change in the focal length of human eye is caused due to:
A. Ciliary muscles B. Pupil
C. Cornea D. Iris

31. The least distance of distinct vision for a young adult with normal vision is:
A. 25 m B. 20 m
C. 25 cm D. 20 cm

32. The persistence of vision for human eye is:
A. 1/10th of a second B. 1/16th of a second
C. 1/6th of the second D. 1/18th of a second

33. The light sensitive cell present on retina and is sensitive to the intensity of light is:
A. Cones B. Rods
C. Both rods and cones D. None of these

34. The phenomena of light responsible for the working of the human eye is:
A. Reflection
B. Refraction
C. Power of accommodation
D. Persistence of vision

35. Which of the following colors is least scattered by fog, dust of smoke?
A. Violet B. Blue
C. Red D. Yellow

36. The colored light that refracts most while passing through a prism is:
A. Yellow B. Violet
C. Blue D. Red

37. The amount of light entering the human eye is controlled by:
A. Ciliary muscles B. Pupil
C. Cornea D. Iris

38. The part of the eyes refracts light entering the eye from external objects?
A. Lens B. Cornea
C. Iris D. Pupil

39. Variation of focal length to form a sharp image on retina is called:
A. accommodation B. aperture
C. retina control D. sutter

40. In human eye, image is formed:
A. behind retina
B. in front of retina
C. on retina
D. in between lens and retina

41. Eardrum is a part of:
A. Sound producing organ
B. Skeletal system
C. Hearing organ
D. Reproductive organ

42. The hearing range of human ear is:
A. 20 Hz to 20,000 Hz B. Less than 20 Hz
C. More than 20,000 Hz D. 20 Hz to 25,000 Hz

43. The voice box is called:
A. Stomach B. Heart
C. Larynx D. Mouth

44. Large amplitude of sound vibrations will produce:
A. Loud sound B. Meak sound
C. Slow sound D. Shreak

45. The pitch of sound depends on:
A. frequency B. amplitude
C. both of these D. none of these

46. Sound is kind of:
A. Work B. Energy
C. Force D. None

47. To an fro motion of an object is called:
A. Waves B. Amplitude
C. Vibration D. All of the above

48. Voice box or larynx of human process:
A. Sound B. Wind
C. Loudness D. None

49. Sound propagates maximum in:
A. Gas B. Liquid
C. Solid D. All

50. Noise pollution is harmful for:
A. Human B. Cat
C. Bird D. All

51. Which of the following connects the external ear with the inner structures?
A. Cornea
B. Iris
C. External Auditory Meatus
D. Cornea

52. Which of the following bones contain in the Middle Ear?
A. Malleus B. Incus
C. Stapes D. All the above

53. Old people cannot hear sounds even above:
A. 5,000 Hz B. 15,000 Hz
C. 10,000 Hz D. 8,000 Hz

54. A normal human ear can hear a sound only if its frequency lies between:
A. 30 Hz to 30,000 Hz B. 50 Hz to 50,000 Hz
C. 20 Hz to 20,000 Hz D. 10 Hz to 10,000 Hz

55. When frequency of sound increases, wavelength and period:
A. becomes negative B. remains constant
C. also increases D. decreases

56. Middle ear consists of:
A. Malleus, incus and stapes
B. Vestibule, semicircular canals and cochlea
C. Pinna, auditory canal and ear drum
D. None of these

57. External ear consists of:
A. Malleus, incus and stapes
B. Vestibule, semicircular canals and cochlea
C. Pinna, auditory canal and ear drum
D. Eustachian tube and oval window

58. Ear drum is also called:
A. Tympanum B. Pinna
C. Auditory canal D. Vestibule

59. Characteristic of sound by which we can distinguish between two sounds of same loudness and pitch is known as:
A. loudness B. pitch
C. quality D. intensity

60. Range of frequencies which a human ear can hear is called:
A. pitch of sound
B. loudness of sound
C. audible frequency range
D. quality of sound

61. Decibel scale is a logarithm measure of amplitude of:
A. sound waves B. light waves
C. heat waves D. electric current

62. Soft materials absorb large amount of:
A. heat energy
B. light energy
C. electromagnetic waves
D. sound energy

63. Louder sound can cause damage to:
A. hearing B. sight
C. skin D. brain

64. Sound having frequencies above 20000 Hz are called:
A. infrasound B. ultrasound
C. mega sound D. micro sound

65. If we tighten strings of instrument pitch will be:
A. higher B. lower
C. constant D. no pitch

ANSWERS

1	2	3	4	5	6	7	8	9	10
A	C	C	C	C	B	C	C	C	B
11	**12**	**13**	**14**	**15**	**16**	**17**	**18**	**19**	**20**
C	A	B	D	B	D	A	C	A	B
21	**22**	**23**	**24**	**25**	**26**	**27**	**28**	**29**	**30**
C	C	D	D	B	D	D	D	B	A
31	**32**	**33**	**34**	**35**	**36**	**37**	**38**	**39**	**40**
C	B	B	B	C	B	B	B	A	C
41	**42**	**43**	**44**	**45**	**46**	**47**	**48**	**49**	**50**
C	A	C	A	A	B	C	A	C	D
51	**52**	**53**	**54**	**55**	**56**	**57**	**58**	**59**	**60**
C	D	B	C	D	A	C	A	C	C
61	**62**	**63**	**64**	**65**					
A	D	A	B	A					

★ ★ ★

7

Chemical Effects of Electric Current; Electroplating

Electrolysis

Electrolysis is the process by which ionic substances are decomposed into simpler substances when an electric current is passed through them.

Electrolysis Process

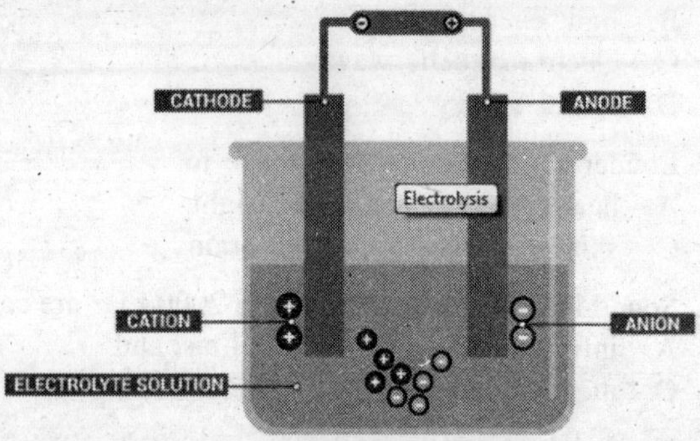

ELECTROLYSIS

- Ionic compounds contain charged particles called ions. For example, Sodium Chloride contains positively charged Sodium ions and negatively charged Chlorine ions.
- The ions must be free to move in order to start the electrolysis process. When an ionic substance is dissolved in water or melted then the ions are free to move. During electrolysis, positively charged ions move to the negative electrode and negatively charged ions move to the positive electrode. Then positively charged ions receive electrons and negatively charged ions lose electrons. Both the products of the dissociation get collected at the electrodes.
- For instance, if electricity is passed through molten sodium chloride, the sodium chloride is broken into sodium and chlorine and they collect at their respective electrodes. The metals get precipitated and the gases escape. This ability to break down substance with current is used in many ways.
- Electrolysis is widely used for Electroplating.

Implementation of Electrolysis

In the medieval times, aluminium was almost as precious as silver. Its extraction was not known and pure aluminium was extremely hard to come by. The application of electrolysis turned aluminium from a precious metal to one of the most largely used metals by humans. Aluminium is extracted from its ore by the process of electrolytic decomposition and deposition.

Uses of Electrolysis

- Electrolysis is done for coating one metal on another.
- The industrial use includes various metals such as aluminium, magnesium, chlorine, and fluorine.

Electroplating

Electroplating is basically the process of plating a metal onto the other by hydrolysis mostly to prevent corrosion of metal or for decorative purposes. The process uses an electric current to reduce dissolved metal cations to develop a lean coherent metal coating on the electrode. Electroplating is often applied in the electrical oxidation of anions on a solid substrate like the formation of silver chloride on a silver wire to form silver chloride electrodes.

Electroplating is majorly applied to modify the surface features of an object (e.g corrosion protection, lubricity, abrasion), but the process can also be used to build thickness or make objects by electroforming.

To understand the concept further, let's take an example of gold coating. In this instance, a layer of gold is to be electrodeposited on a metallic jewellery to enhance its appearance.

Usually, the gold plating is connected to the anode (+ve charged electrode) of the circuit and the jewellery is kept at the cathode (–ve charged electrode). Both are kept immersed in a highly developed electrolytic bat (solution). At this stage, a DC current is supplied to the anode that oxidizes the gold atoms and dissolves them into the solution.

The dissolved ions of gold are reduced at the cathode and plated on the jewellery. However, there are major factors that influence the last plating. These include:

- The voltage level of current.
- The temperature and chemical composition of the bath.
- The current length of time.
- The distance between the cathode and the anode.

Uses of Electroplating

Talking about the uses of electroplating, apart from enhancing the appearance of the substrate it is used in various other purposes as well. The major application is to optimize a material's resistance towards corrosion. The plated layer often serves as a sacrificial coating which reveals that it dissolves before the base substance. Some of the other common applications of electroplating involve:

- Improving wear resistance.
- Improving the thickness of metal surface.
- Enhancing the electrical conductivity like plating a copper layer on an electrical component.
- Minimizing Friction.
- Improving surface uniformity.

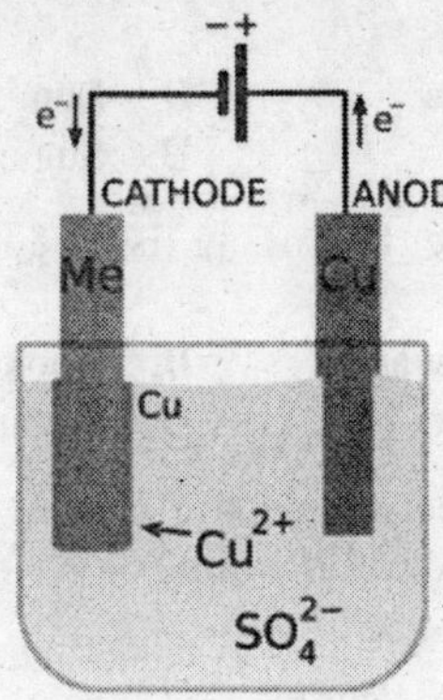

How does Electroplating work?

The positive electrode should be the metal that you want to coat the object with. The negative electrode will be the object that should receive the deposit of the electroplating metal. The electrolyte should be a solution of the coating metal, as it is a metal nitrate or sulphate. We can examine this better with few examples;

Silver Plating

The object that is to be plated is connected to the negative terminal of the power supply. A piece of silver is connected to the positive terminal. The electrolyte is a silver nitrate solution. This process can also be used to purify silver. We can take an impure block at the positive terminal and a strip of pure silver to the negative. The pure silver is deposited via electrolysis at the negative terminal leaving behind the impurities.

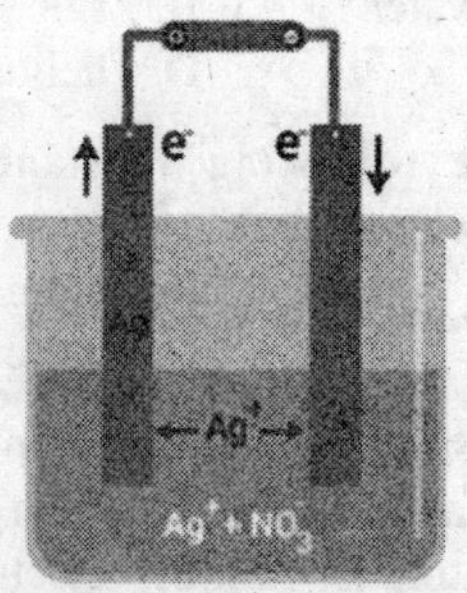

$Ag(s) \rightarrow Ag(s)^+ + e^-$ $Ag^+ + e^- \rightarrow Ag(s)$

Copper Plating

The object that is to be plated is connected to the negative terminal of the power supply. A piece of copper is connected to the positive terminal. The electrolyte is copper Sulphate solution.

Like with silver plating, copper deposition can be used to purify copper. In this case, both the electrodes are made from copper. As the impure positive electrode gradually disappears leaving the impurities behind the negative electrode gradually gets coated with pure copper.

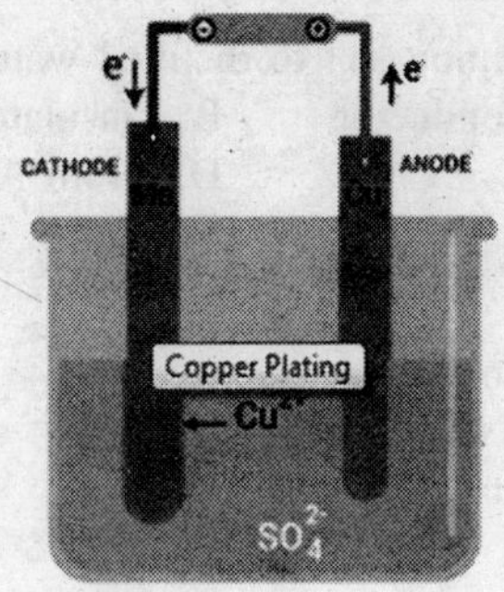

Some Important Facts:

- The materials which allow electric current to pass through are called good conductors of electricity. For example, metals like copper and aluminium.
- The materials which do not allow electric current to pass through them easily are called poor conductor of electricity. For example, rubber, plastic and wood.
- Due to the heating effect of current, the filament of the bulb of the tester gets heated to a high temperature and it starts glowing.
- If the current through a circuit is too weak, the filament does not get heated sufficiently and it does not glow.
- LED (Light Emitting Diodes) can be used in place of the electric bulb in the tester, LED glows even when a weak electric current flows through it.
- Electric current produces magnetic current, a tester can be prepared by using a compass needle. The deflection of the magnetic needle can be seen, even when current is small.
- Distilled water is poor conductor of electricity. Water collected from taps, hand pumps, wells and ponds is not pure contain dissolved salts so it is good conductor of electricity.
- Most liquids that conduct electricity are solutions of acids, bases and salts.
- Chromium has a shiny appearance, does not corrode and is resistant to scratches. But, chromium is expensive and it is not economical to make the whole object out of chromium. So, the objects, such as taps, car parts, wheel rims etc. made from a cheaper metal and electroplated with chromium.

MULTIPLE CHOICE QUESTIONS

1. Plastic wire is:
A. An insulator B. A conductor
C. Both of these D. None of these

2. Electroplating is based on:
A. Magnetic effect of electricity
B. Chemical effect of electricity
C. Heating effect of electricity
D. Physical effect of electricity

3. Adding common salt to distilled water makes it:
A. Good conductor B. Insulator
C. No D. Both A and B

4. An electrolyte is:
A. a metal
B. a solution
C. a liquid that conducts current
D. all of above

5. Copper wire is a:
A. Good conductor B. Poor conductor
C. Both A and B D. None of these

6. Poor conductors are:
A. Plastics B. Clothes
C. Wood D. All of these

7. Distilled water is:
A. Poor conductor B. Good conductor
C. Both A and B D. None

8. Flow of electron is called:
A. Electroplating B. Electric current
C. Electrodes D. Electrolyte

9. Electroplating prevents:
A. Current B. Chemical effect
C. Rusting D. All

10. An electric lamp glows due to:
A. Chemical effect B. Magnetic effect
C. Heating effect D. None

11. Steel cans are made of:
A. lead B. tinplate
C. tungsten D. cobalt

12. Pure piece of metal which is used to be plated, is made the:
A. anode B. cathode
C. nematode D. posit rode

13. Shiny objects are often made by electroplating steel with:
A. nickel B. titanium
C. chromium D. zinc

14. In our daily life, we find most of compounds contain:
A. sodium B. chlorine
C. oxygen D. hydrogen

15. A sheet of pure copper is used as:
A. cathode B. anode
C. positrode D. negatrode

16. Electric poles are coated with a layer of which metal?
A. Chromium B. Zinc
C. Silver D. Aluminium

17. Sanitary fittings are generally coated with a layer of which metal?
A. Chromium B. Zinc
C. Silver D. Aluminium

18. Which of the following is a bad conductor of electricity?
A. Tap water B. Lemon juice
C. Vinegar D. Sugar solution

19. Which of the following is a good conductor of electricity?
A. Distilled water B. Cooking oil
C. Tap water D. Sugar solution

20. Chemical effect of electric current is primarily used for which of the following?
A. Electroplating
B. Separating oxygen
C. Separating hydrogen
D. Separating gold

21. Which of the following will work best as a tester for electric current?
A. Bulb B. LED
C. CFL D. Magnetic compass

22. Which material is used for making the central rod in an electric cell?
A. Copper B. Carbon
C. Aluminium D. Iron

23. Which scientist was the first to show electrolysis of water?
A. Oersted B. William Nicholson
C. Michael Faraday D. Galileo

24. The liquid will conduct electric current in a circuit when the vessel is with _________.
A. distilled water B. salt solution
C. air D. helium

25. Which of the following substance is not a good conductor of electricity?
A. copper B. aluminium
C. rubber D. mercury

26. The decomposition of liquid compound on passing an electric current though it is known as ______ .
A. electroplating B. electrolysis
C. magnetic effect D. electro-resistivity

27. The glowing of filament bulb is due to:
A. heating effect of electric current
B. physical effect of electric current
C. magnetic effect of electric current
D. chemical effect of electric current

28. In a LED, the longer lead/leg is connected to _______.
A. positive terminal of the battery
B. negative terminal of the battery
C. either positive of negative terminal of the battery
D. none of these

29. Most liquids that conduct electricity are solutions of _______.
A. acids B. bases
C. salts D. all of these

30. Name the chemist who showed bubbles of oxygen and hydrogen are when electric current passes through water.
A. William Nicholson B. William Harvey
C. Luigi Galvani D. Alessandro Volt

31. To prevent iron from corrosion it is electroplated with _______.
A. aluminium B. copper
C. oxygen D. zinc

32. The whole apparatus of electrodes, electrolytes and vessel container is called _____.
A. thermometer B. electrometer
C. voltameter D. ammeter

33. What is current?
A. The flow of matter B. The flow of electrons
C. The flow of protons D. The flow of charge

34. In electrolytic solutions, which of the following acts as carrier of charge?
A. Protons B. Electrons
C. Neutrons D. Ions

35. What are insulators?
A. Materials that conduct electricity
B. Materials that do not conduct electricity
C. Materials that conduct electricity only at low temperatures
D. Materials that conduct electricity at room temperature

36. Which of the following is an insulator?
A. Wood B. Iron
C. Graphite D. Silver

37. Which of the following energy conversions takes place in a cell?
A. Electrical energy into chemical energy
B. Chemical energy into electrical energy
C. Magnetic energy into electrical energy
D. Electrical energy into mechanical energy

38. Which of the following are the characteristics of an electrolyte?
A. It has a positive charge.
B. It has a negative charge.
C. It conducts charge without dissociating.
D. It forms positive and negative ions.

39. Which acid is present in lemon juice that acts as an electrolyte?
A. Sulphuric acid B. Nitric acid
C. Hydrochloric acid D. Citric acid

40. Which of the following is the electrolyte in a dry cell?
A. Copper sulphate B. Zinc sulphate
C. Sulphuric acid D. Ammonium chloride

41. In a dry cell, which of the following acts as the positive terminal?
A. Carbon rod
B. Manganese dioxide
C. Manganese dioxide and powdered carbon
D. A metal cap on the carbon rod

42. What is the common voltage produced by a dry cell?
A. 1.5 V B. 30 V
C. 60 V D. 3 V

43. What happens when electric current is made to flow through a conductor?
A. Some amount of electrical energy is converted into heat energy.
B. Some amount of electrical energy is converted into mechanical energy.
C. Some amount of mechanical energy is converted into electrical energy.
D. Some amount of heat energy is converted into electrical energy.

44. Nichrome is an alloy. Which of the following metals make up this alloy?
A. Nickel and chromium
B. Nitrogen and chromium
C. Nitrogen, chlorine and chromium
D. Nickel, chromium and manganese

45. What is the splitting of a compound using electricity called?
A. Electrolysis B. Electrolyte
C. Electrokinesis D. Electrochemistry

46. What is the principle involved in the glowing of an electric bulb?
A. Magnetic effect of current
B. Heating effect of current
C. Chemical effect
D. Conduction of current

47. Which of the following is the best conductor of electricity?
A. Tap water B. Distilled water
C. Sea water D. Rain water

48. Which of the following effects of current is responsible for the deflection of a compass needle in an electric field?
A. Heating effect of current
B. Magnetic effect of current
C. Conducting effect of heat
D. Chemical effect of current

49. Which of these is the industrial applications of the chemical effects of electric current?
A. Electroplating B. Galvanizing
C. Anodizing D. All of the above

50. Which of the following liquids is a bad conductor of electricity?
A. Lemon juice B. Vinegar
C. Sea water D. Distilled water

51. A positively charged ion is called:
A. Atom B. Anion
C. Cation D. Neutral Ion

52. The instrument needed to measure the current flowing through a circuit is:
A. voltmeter B. voltameter
C. galvanometer D. ammeter

53. The process in which any electrolyte gets decomposed when electricity is passed through it, is called
A. electrolysis B. decomposition
C. dissociation D. splitting

54. The process of depositing a thin layer of any superior metal over an object of a cheaper metal with the help of electricity is called
A. electrorefining B. electrometallurgy
C. electroplating D. electrowinning

55. Which of the following is the most essential for an electric circuit to work?
A. A switch B. An electric current
C. A switch board D. None of these

56. In LEDs, the longer lead (wire) is always connected to the ______ terminal:
A. negative B. neutral
C. positive D. Any terminal

57. Tap water is a good conductor of electricity while distilled water is not because:
A. Tap water contain salts
B. Distilled water do not contain salt
C. Only A is correct
D. Both A and B is correct

58. When electrodes are immersed in water and electricity passed, the bubbles formed on the positive terminal is actually ______ gas.
A. Hydrogen B. Carbon dioxide
C. Oxygen D. Nitrogen

59. Some liquids are good conductors of electricity and some are poor conductors. Which one is a poor conductor?
A. Distilled water
B. Alkaline solution
C. Common salt solution
D. Acidic solution

60. Why do we add little dilute sulphuric acid to copper sulphate solution during electroplating?
A. To increase acidity
B. To increase conductivity
C. So that the colour becomes more prominent
D. To burn copper sulphate

ANSWERS

1	2	3	4	5	6	7	8	9	10
A	B	A	C	A	D	A	B	C	C
11	**12**	**13**	**14**	**15**	**16**	**17**	**18**	**19**	**20**
B	A	C	A	A	B	A	D	C	A
21	**22**	**23**	**24**	**25**	**26**	**27**	**28**	**29**	**30**
D	B	B	B	C	B	A	A	D	A
31	**32**	**33**	**34**	**35**	**36**	**37**	**38**	**39**	**40**
D	C	D	D	B	A	B	B	D	D
41	**42**	**43**	**44**	**45**	**46**	**47**	**48**	**49**	**50**
D	A	A	A	A	B	C	B	D	D
51	**52**	**53**	**54**	**55**	**56**	**57**	**58**	**59**	**60**
C	D	A	C	B	C	D	C	A	B

★ ★ ★

8

Natural Phenomena–Lightning; Earthquakes, Pollution of Air and Water

Lightning

Lightning, the visible discharge of electricity that occurs when a region of a cloud acquires an excess electrical charge, either positive or negative, that is sufficient to break down the resistance of air.

Lightning is a sudden electrostatic discharge that occurs typically during a thunderstorm. This discharge occurs between electrically charged regions of a cloud (called intra-cloud lightning or IC), between two clouds (CC lightning), or between a cloud and the ground (CG lightning).

The charged regions in the atmosphere temporarily equalize themselves through this discharge referred to as a flash. A lightning flash can also be a strike if it involves an object on the ground. Lightning creates light in the form of black body radiation from the very hot plasma created by the electron flow, and sound in the form of thunder. Lightning may be seen and not heard when it occurs at a distance too great for the sound to carry as far as the light from the strike or flash.

Causes of Lightning

Lightning is an electric current. Within a thundercloud many small bits of ice (frozen raindrops) bump into each other or collide as they move around in the air. Those collisions create an electric charge.

After a period of time, the whole cloud fills up with electrical charges. The positive charges, or protons, form at the top of the cloud and the negative charges, or electrons, form at the bottom of the cloud. Since opposites attract, that causes a positive charge to build up on the ground beneath the cloud. The ground's electrical charge concentrates around anything that sticks up, such as mountains, people, or single trees. The charge coming up from these points eventually connects with a charge reaching down from the thundercloud and lightning strikes!

As storms develop, clouds become charged with electricity. Scientists are still not sure exactly what causes this, but they do know that when the voltage becomes high enough for the electricity to leap across the air from one place to another, lightning flashes!

Lightning can strike within a cloud, from one cloud to another, from a cloud to the ground, or from the ground to a cloud.

Lightning protection systems

Hundreds of devices, including lightning rods and charge transfer systems, are used to mitigate lightning damage and influence the path of a lightning flash.

A lightning rod (or lightning protector) is a metal strip or rod connected to earth through conductors and a grounding system, used to provide a preferred pathway to ground if lightning terminates on a structure. The class of these products are often called a 'finial' or 'air terminal'. A lightning rod or 'Franklin rod' in honor of its famous inventor, Benjamin Franklin, is simply a metal rod, and without being connected to the lightning protection system, as was sometimes the case in the old days, will provide no added protection to a structure. Other names include 'lightning conductor', 'arrester', and 'discharger'; however, over the years these names have been incorporated into other products or industries with a stake in lightning protection. Lightning arrester, for example, often refers to fused links that explode when a strike occurs to a high voltage overhead power line to protect the more expensive transformers down the line by opening the circuit. In reality, it was an early form of a heavy duty surge protection device (SPD). Modern arresters, constructed with metal oxides, are capable of safely shunting abnormally high voltage surges to ground while preventing normal system voltages from being shorted to ground.

Earthquake

An earthquake is a natural occurrence, like rain. Earthquakes affect almost every part of the Earth and like rain they can be either mild or catastrophic. Over the course of geological time, earthquakes, floods, and other natural events have helped to shape the surface of our planet. An earthquake may last only a few seconds, but the processes that cause earthquakes have operated within the Earth for millions and millions of years.

Why does the earth shake?

The release of energy occurs along a fault. A fault is a sharp break in the crustal rocks. Rocks along a fault tend to move in opposite directions. As the overlying rock strata press them, the friction locks them together. However, their tendency to move apart at some point of time overcomes the friction. As a result, the blocks get deformed and eventually, they slide past one another abruptly. This causes a release of energy, and the energy waves travel in all directions. The point where the energy is released is called the focus of an earthquake, alternatively, it is called the hypocentre. The energy waves travelling in different directions reach the surface. The point on the surface, nearest to the focus, is called epicentre. It is the first one to experience the waves. It is a point directly above the focus.

Earthquake Waves

All natural earthquakes take place in the lithosphere. An instrument called 'seismograph' records the waves reaching the surface. A curve of earthquake waves recorded on the seismograph is given in figure. Note that the curve shows three distinct sections each representing different types of wave patterns. Earthquake waves are basically of two types - body waves and surface waves. Body waves are generated due to the release of energy at the focus and move in all directions travelling through the body of the earth. Hence, the name body waves. The body waves interact with the surface rocks and generate new set of waves called surface waves. These waves move along the surface. The velocity of waves changes as they travel through materials with different densities. The denser the material, the higher is the velocity. Their direction also changes as they reflect or refract when coming across materials with different densities.

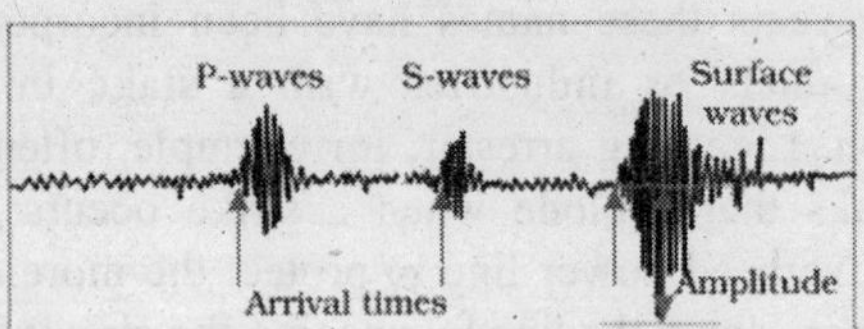

Figure: *Earthquake wave*

There are two types of body waves. They are called P and S-waves. P-waves move faster and are the first to arrive at the surface. These are also called 'primary waves'. The P-waves are similar to sound waves. They travel through gaseous, liquid and solid materials. S-waves arrive at the surface with some time lag. These are called secondary waves. An important fact about S-waves is that they can travel only through solid materials. This characteristic of the S-waves is quite important. It has helped scientists to understand the structure of the interior of the earth.

Types of Earthquakes

- The most common ones are the tectonic earthquakes. These are generated due to sliding of rocks along a fault plane.
- A special class of tectonic earthquake is sometimes recognised as volcanic earthquake. However, these are confined to areas of active volcanoes.
- In the areas of intense mining activity, sometimes the roofs of underground mines collapse causing minor tremors. These are called collapse earthquakes.
- Ground shaking may also occur due to the explosion of chemical or nuclear devices. Such tremors are called explosion earthquakes.
- The earthquakes that occur in the areas of large reservoirs are referred to as reservoir induced earthquakes.

Measuring Earthquakes

The earthquake events are scaled either according to the magnitude or intensity of the shock. The magnitude scale is known as the Richter scale. The magnitude relates to the energy released during the quake. The magnitude is expressed in numbers, 0-10. The intensity scale is named after Mercalli, an Italian seismologist. The intensity scale takes into account the visible damage caused by the event. The range of intensity scale is from 1-12.

Effects of Earthquake

Earthquake is a natural hazard. The following are the immediate hazardous effects of earthquake:

(*i*) Ground Shaking
(*ii*) Differential ground settlement
(*iii*) Land and mud slides
(*iv*) Soil liquefaction
(*v*) Ground lurching
(*vi*) Avalanches
(*vii*) Ground displacement
(*viii*) Floods from dam and levee failures
(*ix*) Fires
(*x*) Structural collapse
(*xi*) Falling objects
(*xii*) Tsunami

MULTIPLE CHOICE QUESTIONS

1. Name the resin which produces spark is:
A. Gum B. Amber
C. Both A and B D. None of these

2. The like charges:
A. Repel each other
B. Attract each other
C. No interaction takes place
D. All of these

3. The shaking of earth is called:
A. Tsunami B. Volcano
C. Earthquake D. All of these

4. Lightening occurs due to:
A. Electric discharge
B. Rain
C. Wind
D. None of these

5. Interaction of charges is called:
A. Lightening B. Electrical discharge
C. Earthing D. Electricity

6. Sparkers can be seen on electric pole. Which wires become?
A. Loose B. Tight
C. Wrinkle D. None

7. Benjamen Franklin showed lightening in:
A. 1725 B. 1527
C. 1752 D. 1572

8. The charge acquired by a glass rod when it is rubbed with silk is:
A. Negative B. Positive
C. Both D. None

9. As per convention, what is the charge on a glass rod when it is rubbed with silk cloth?
A. Positive B. Negative
C. Either 'A' or 'B' D. No charge

10. As per convention, what is the charge on silk cloth when a glass rod is rubbed with silk cloth?
A. Positive B. Negative
C. Either 'A' or 'B' D. No charge

11. Transfer of which atomic particle produces charge in a body?
A. Neutron B. Proton
C. Electron D. All of the above

12. A place where an earthquake originates is called the __________.
A. Focus B. Tsunami
C. Fault Line D. Epicenter

13. As the magnitude of natural disasters increases their frequency of occurrence ________.
A. increases B. decreases
C. remains the same D. varies over time

14. Which natural hazard has resulted in the greatest monetary losses in a single even for the period of time listed?
A. earthquake B. hurricane
C. fire D. flood

15. The largest wave during a tsunami event is ______.
A. the first
B. the third
C. the fifth
D. unpredictable, it could be any of them

16. The destructive powers of tsunami result mainly from their ________________.
A. incredible height
B. unpredictability
C. cold water
D. momentum and long wavelength

17. Which event produces the biggest tsunami?
A. Earthquake
B. Underwater landslides
C. Hurricanes
D. Impacts of asteroids and comets

18. Powerful tsunami are most frequently produced by ________.
A. volcanoes B. underwater landslides
C. earthquakes D. impacts of asteroids

19. Which device is used to protect building from lightning conductor?
A. Seismograph B. Lightning Conductor
C. Barometer D. Thermal Conductor

20. Name the scientist who showed that lightning and the spark from your clothes are essentially the same phenomena?
A. Thomas Alva Edison
B. Benjamin Franklin
C. Franklin D. Roosevelt
D. Isaac Newton

21. Two objects with like charges will ______.
A. attract each other
B. repel each other
C. either attract or repel
D. neither attract nor repel

22. Two objects with unlike charges will ______.
A. attract each other
B. repel each other
C. either attract or repel
D. neither attract nor rep

23. The charge acquired by a glass rod when it is rubbed with silk is considered as ______.
A. neutral
B. either positive or negative
C. positive
D. negative

24. When charges move, they constitute an ________ .
A. electric current B. magnetic effect
C. heating effect D. all of the above

25. Device can which be used to test whether an object is carrying charge or not is known as ______
A. Electroscope B. Microscope
C. Periscope D. Telescope

26. In thunderstorm, the charges accumulate near the upper edges of clouds are ________ .
A. negatively charged B. positively charged
C. neutral D. none of these

27. Which scale is used to measure the magnitude of earth quake?
A. Celsius B. Kelvin
C. Richter D. Pascal

28. During lightning which of the following is a NOT a safe place?
A. Open field B. Inside a house
C. Bus Stop D. Elevated Ridge

29. Using science and technology damaged caused by natural disasters like hurricane, earthquakes can be:
A. prevented B. 'reduced
C. enhanced D. raised

30. Catastrophic natural disaster losses in developed countries involve which of the following?
A. large numbers of deaths
B. large financial costs to individuals and companies
C. primarily losses borne by insurance companies
D. large numbers of deaths and large financial costs

31. Areas of cities that are subjected to significant natural hazards should be used for which of the following?
A. office buildings because they can withstand the effects of the hazard
B. inexpensive single-family houses
C. parks and golf courses
D. shopping malls

32. What kind of natural hazards are not normally insurable?
A. earthquakes B. volcanoes
C. landslides D. floods

33. Which of the following is not part of geological disaster?
A. Volcanoes B. Earthquakes
C. Tsunami D. Sea Surge

34. What is the rank of India in the world for natural disasters after China as per UNISDR?
A. Third B. Second
C. Seventh D. Eighth

35. Which of the following types of volcanic eruptions associated with Lacroix?
A. Hawaii Eruption
B. Strombolian Eruption
C. Vulcanian
D. All of the above

36. The volcanic eruption in Iceland falls under which volcanic belt in the World?
A. Belts of Convergent boundaries
B. Divergent Plate Boundaries
C. Hot Spots
D. None of the above

37. A geophysicist who studies earthquakes and the mechanical characteristics of the Earth is called ____________.
A. Seismologist B. Geologist
C. Geographer D. Archaeologist

38. What causes Tsunami?
A. Sudden vertical movement of the Earth
B. Convergence of destructive plates in the ocean floor
C. Explosive volcanic eruptions in the seas/oceans.
D. All of the above

39. An earthquake of magnitude 8-9 is:
A. strong B. very strong
C. mild D. not felt

40. Which of the following is the leading cause of death and diseases worldwide?
A. water pollution B. radioactive pollution
C. air pollution D. soil pollution

41. All the following are notorious oil spills except:
A. Deepwater Horizon, 2010
B. Love canal disaster
C. Exxon Valdes, 1991
D. Gulf War, 1991

42. Eutrophication by sewage pollution refers to the:
A. nutrient enrichment of freshwater bodies
B. nutrient depletion of freshwater bodies
C. toxic chemical accumulation in freshwater bodies
D. Heavy metal accumulation in freshwater bodies

43. Which of the following is the major reason for algal bloom?
A. Presence of heavy metals
B. Contamination by pathogens
C. Eutrophication
D. Soil erosion

44. Which of the following is the major cause of biomagnifications?
A. Eutrophication B. Detergent pollution
C. Pesticide pollution D. Industrial pollution

45. Which of the following is an indicator of organic water pollution?
A. BOD B. pH
C. Salinity D. Eutrophication

46. Blue baby syndrome is due to the presence of:
A. excess sulphate in drinking water
B. excess chlorine in drinking water
C. excess heavy metals in drinking water
D. excess nitrates in drinking water

47. Mercury poisoning in water is the reason for:
A. Pellegra B. Minimata disease
C. Itai-Itai disease D. Scurvy

48. Itai-itai disease is caused by:
A. Pb poisoning B. Cd poisoning
C. Hg poisoning D. Cu poisoning

49. Which of the following is not a green house gas?
A. carbon dioxide B. nitrous oxide
C. methane D. nitrogen

50. Which of the following air pollutant reduces the oxygen-carrying capacity of a blood to a large extent?
A. carbon dioxide B. nitrogen monoxide
C. carbon monoxide D. sulphur dioxide

51. The constituent of polluted air which contributes in producing acid rain is:
A. nitrogen B. sulphur dioxide
C. oxygen D. argon

52. Which of the following will be reduced in air in a city forest where lot of dust and fly ash is emitted by a coal based factory in the vicinity?
A. nitrogen B. carbon dioxide
C. oxygen D. water vapour

53. Which of the following disease cannot be caused by drinking of river water contaminated with untreated sewage?
A. cholera B. typhoid
C. tuberculosis D. diarrhoea

54. Drinking water can be made absolutely safe by adding some:
A. aspirin tablets B. iodine tablets
C. chlorine tablets D. cholorophyll tablets

55. Which of the following are used in electric water filters to kill all the harmful microrganisms present in tap water and make it absolutely safe for drinking?
A. infrared radiation B. gamma radiation
C. visible radiation D. ultraviolet radiation

56. Which of the following will reach the earth in greater amounts, if the amount of chlorofluorocarbons released into the air increases?
A. infrared rays B. X-rays
C. gamma rays D. ultraviolet rays

57. Highest percentage of air consists of:
A. Oxygen B. Carbon dioxide
C. Nitrogen D. Argon

58. The Taj Mahal is being affected by:
A. Noise pollution B. Air pollution
C. Water pollution D. None of these

59. Most polluted river in the world is:
A. Yamuna B. Cavery
C. Chenab D. Ganga

60. Air pollution causes:
A. Global warming B. Respiratory problems
C. Soil erosion D. None of these

61. Green House gas is:
A. Nitrogen B. Oxygen
C. Methane D. Carbon dioxide

62. The percentage of nitrogen is:
A. 21% B. 78%
C. 12% D. 87%

63. What causes pollution?
A. Human activities B. Trees
C. Both of these D. None of these

64. CNG is a:
A. Polluted fuel B. Clean fuel
C. Harmful fuel D. None

65. Pollution of water is responsible for:
A. Oil refineries B. Paper factories
C. Sugar mills D. All

66. Chlorofluorocarbon is used in:
A. Refrigerators B. Air conditioners
C. Perfumes D. All

ANSWERS

1	2	3	4	5	6	7	8	9	10
B	A	C	A	A	A	C	B	A	B
11	**12**	**13**	**14**	**15**	**16**	**17**	**18**	**19**	**20**
C	A	B	B	D	D	D	C	B	B
21	**22**	**23**	**24**	**25**	**26**	**27**	**28**	**29**	**30**
B	A	C	D	A	B	C	D	B	B
31	**32**	**33**	**34**	**35**	**36**	**37**	**38**	**39**	**40**
C	C	D	B	D	B	A	D	B	A
41	**42**	**43**	**44**	**45**	**46**	**47**	**48**	**49**	**50**
B	A	C	C	A	D	B	B	D	C
51	**52**	**53**	**54**	**55**	**56**	**57**	**58**	**59**	**60**
B	B	C	C	D	D	C	B	D	B
61	**62**	**63**	**64**	**65**	**66**				
D	B	A	B	D	D				

★ ★ ★

9

Solar System; Stars and Constellations

OUR SOLAR SYSTEM

For thousands of years, from our small world, we have looked upon the cosmic ocean. Early star watchers thought that the Earth was in the middle of the solar system and that the sun and all the other stars spun around the Earth. Copernicus showed that Earth and the other planets in our solar system revolved around our sun. Early astronomers perceived dots of light that seemed to move in the midst of the stars. They called these objects "planets," meaning nomads, and titled them after Ancient Roman holy beings Jupiter, ruler of the divinities; Mercury, an emissary of the gods; Venus, the deity of love and beauty, Mars, the god of war and Saturn, dad of Jupiter and god of cultivation. The astronomers also detected Comets with twinkling tails, and meteors or shooting stars seemingly falling from the heavens.

Subsequently, the telescope was invented, and three more planets were revealed in our solar system: Uranus in 1781, Neptune in 1846, and now demoted to a dwarf planet, Pluto was discovered in 1930. Moreover, there are thousands of smaller bodies such as comets and asteroids. Almost all asteroids orbit in a section sandwiched between the orbits of Mars and Jupiter while the comets lie in the Oort Cloud, outside the orbit of Pluto.

Mercury, Venus, Earth and Mars are closest to the sun and are termed as the terrestrial planets because they have compact stony surfaces. Saturn, Jupiter, Neptune and Uranus are the four huge planets (Jovian Planets) past the trajectory of Mars and are called gas giants. Petite, distant, Pluto has a hard but frostier surface than the other planets.

Just about every planet and even some of the moons have an atmosphere. Our world's atmosphere is mainly made up of oxygen and nitrogen. Venus has a thick atmosphere of carbon dioxide, with hints of poisonous gases, for instance, sulphur dioxide. Mars has a carbon dioxide atmosphere which is very thin. Jupiter, Saturn, Uranus, and Neptune are mainly helium and hydrogen.

Let us know about some members of the solar family:

The Sun

The Sun is the nearest star from us. It is continuously emitting huge amounts of heat and light. The Sun is the source of almost all energy on the Earth. In fact, the Sun is the main source of heat and light for all the planets.

The Planets

The planets look like stars, but they do not have light of their own. They merely reflect the sunlight that falls on them. Can you distinguish between planets and stars? The simplest method of identifying planets from stars is that stars twinkle, whereas planets do not. Also the planets keep changing their positions with respect to the stars. A planet has a definite path in which it revolves around the Sun. This path is called an orbit. The time taken by a planet to complete one revolution is called its period of revolution.

The period of revolution increases as the distance of the planet increases from the sun. Besides revolving around the Sun, a planet also rotates on its own axis like a top. The time taken by a planet to complete one rotation is called its period of rotation.

Some planets are known to have moons/satellites revolving round them. Any celestial body revolving around another celestial body is called its satellite.

The Earth can be said to be a satellite of the Sun, though generally we call it a planet of the Sun. We use the term satellite for the bodies revolving around planets. Moon is a satellite of the Earth. There are many man-made satellites revolving round the Earth. These are called artificial satellites.

Mercury

The planet mercury is nearest to the Sun. It is the smallest planet of our solar system. Because Mercury is very close to the Sun, it is very difficult to observe it, as most of the time it is hidden in the glare of the Sun. However, it can be observed just before sunrise or just after sunset, near the horizon. So it is visible only at places where trees or buildings do not obstruct the view of the horizon. Mercury has no satellite of its own.

Venus

Venus is earth's nearest planetary neighbour. It is the brightest planet in the night sky.

Sometimes Venus appears in the eastern sky before sunrise. Sometimes it appears in the western sky just after sunset. Therefore it is often called a morning or an evening star, although it is not a star. Try to locate Venus in the night sky. Venus has no moon or satellite of its own. Rotation of Venus on its axis is somewhat unusual. It rotates from east to west while the Earth rotates from west to east.

The Earth

The Earth is the only planet in the solar system on which life is known to exist. Some special environmental conditions are responsible for the existence and continuation of life on the Earth. These include just the right distance from the Sun, so that it has the right temperature range, the presence of water and suitable atmosphere and a blanket of ozone. From space, the Earth appears blue-green due to the reflection of light from water and landmass on its surface. The axis of rotation of the Earth is not perpendicular to the plane of its orbit. The tilt is responsible for the change of seasons on the Earth. The Earth has only one moon.

Moon

The moon that we see almost every night is a natural satellite of the Earth. This means that the moon revolves around the earth in a regular path. The gravitational attraction between the earth and the natural satellite holds it in its orbit even as the earth revolves around the earth. We all know that, Neil Armstrong was the first person to land on this celestial body in 1969.

Phases of the Moon

If you look up at the moon at night, you would have noticed that it changes its shape every day. This is because, the heavenly body has no light of its own; it can only reflect light from the sun. Only the side of the moon which faces the sun can reflect this light and can appear bright; the other side appears dark. As this celestial bod revolves around the earth we can see different amounts of the region illuminated by the sun. Thus it appears to change its shape.

When this heavenly body is behind the earth and sun, we can see the entire illuminated portion - this is a full-moon (Paurnami). When it is between the sun and earth we can only see the dark portion and a new moon (Amavasya) occurs. Between these two extremes we see intermediate phases such as a half moon and crescent.

This Planetoid takes almost 27 days to revolve around the earth. But between two full moons there are 29.5 days. This is because the earth also travels a distance through space during that time around the sun. It has to cover an extra distance (which takes 2 more days) if it has to be exactly behind the earth and sun again.

The celestial body only shows us only one side of itself. One side of it called dark side or far side never faces the earth. This is because the moon takes the same amount of time to rotate about its axis as it does to revolve around the earth. This is not a coincidence and occurs due to a phenomenon known as Tidal Locking.

Mars

The next planet, the first outside the orbit of the Earth is Mars. It appears slightly reddish and, therefore, it is also called the red planet. Mars has two small natural satellites.

Mangalyan

The Mars Orbiter Mission (MOM), also called Mangalyaan is a space probe orbiting Mars since 24 September 2014. It was launched on 5 November 2013 by the Indian Space Research Organisation (ISRO). It is India's first interplanetary mission and it made it the fourth space agency to reach Mars, after Roscosmos, NASA, and the European Space Agency. It is the first Asian nation to reach Mars orbit, and the first nation in the world to do so in its first attempt.

Jupiter

Jupiter is the largest planet of the solar system. It is so large that about 1300 earths can be placed inside this giant planet. However, the mass of Jupiter is about 318 times that of our Earth. It rotates very rapidly on its axis. Jupiter has a large number of satellites. It also has faint rings around it. You can easily recognise Jupiter as it appears quite bright in the sky. Jupiter has 79 known moons, including the four large Galilean moons discovered by Galileo Galilei in 1610. Ganymede, the largest of these, has a diameter greater than that of the planet Mercury.

Saturn

Beyond Jupiter is Saturn which appears yellowish in colour. What makes it unique in the solar system is its beautiful rings. These rings are not visible with the naked eye.

You can observe them with a small telescope. Saturn also has a large number of satellites.

One interesting thing about Saturn is that it is the least dense among all the planets. Its density is less than that of water.

Uranus and Neptune

These are the outermost planets of the solar system. They can be seen only with the help of large telescopes. Like Venus, Uranus also rotates from east to west. The most remarkable feature of Uranus is that it has highly tilted rotational axis (Fig. 1) As a result, in its orbital motion it appears to roll on its side.

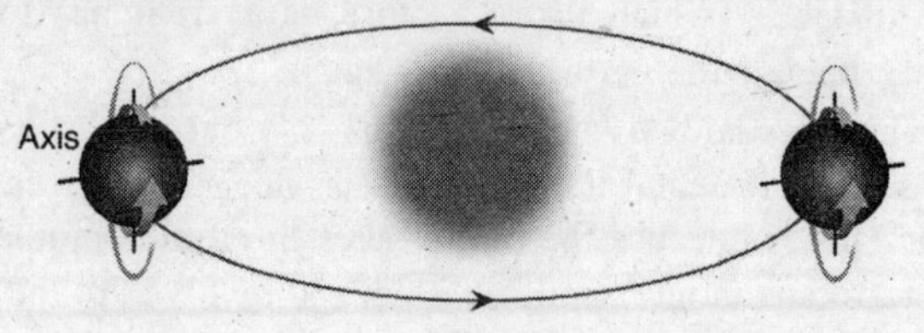

Fig. 1: *Uranus in its Orbital Path*

Inner Planets

- These planets are very close to the sun.
- They are made up of rocks.
- Inner Planets are:
  - Mercury- One orbit around sun - 88 days, One spin on axis - 59 days.
  - Venus - One orbit around sun - 255 days. One spin on axis - 243 days.
  - Earth - One orbit around sun - 365 days. One spin on axis - 1 day Number of moons - 1.
  - Mars - One orbit around sun - 687 days One spin on axis - 1 day, number of moons - 02.

Outer Planets

- Very-very far from the sun and are huge planets made up of gases and liquids:
  - Jupiter - One orbit around sun - 11 years, 11 months about 12 years. One spin on axis - 9 hours, 56 minutes, number of moons - 16.
  - Saturn - One orbit around sun - 29 years, 5 months. One spin on axis - 10 hours 40 minutes, number of moons - about 18.
  - Uranus - One orbit around sun - 84 years. One spin around axis - 17 hours 14 minutes, number of moons - about 17.
  - Neptune - One orbit around sun - 164 years. One spin on axis-16 hours 7 minutes, number of moons - 8.

SOME OTHER MEMBERS OF THE SOLAR SYSTEM

The Asteroid

The asteroid belt lies between Mars and Jupiter (Fig. 2). It contains lumps of rock much smaller than planets. These lumps are called asteroids or minor planets. They are not visible from Earth with the naked eye, but many may be seen through binoculars or small telescopes.

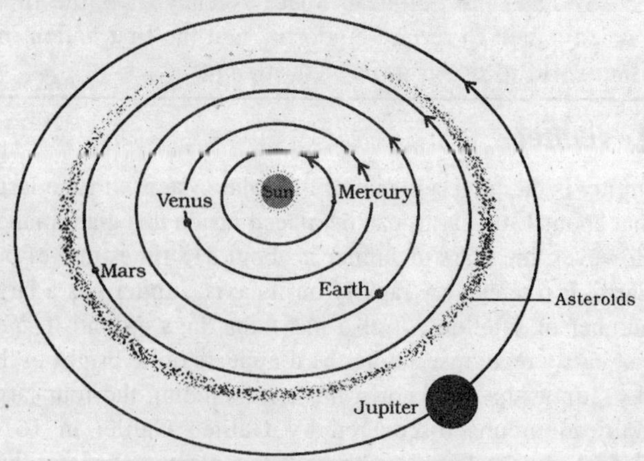

Fig. 2: *The Asteroid belt*

How big are the asteroids?

The largest asteroid is Ceres, which is 1032 km across. The next largest, which is called Pallas, is 588 km across. Asteroids less than a kilometer across have also been seen. Unofficially the limit has been set at 50 m, and anything smaller than that is going to be simply called a meteoroid. With advances in telescopes and particularly for objects that travel close to the Earth, some objects have been seen that are indeed smaller than 50 meters that merely pass nearby the Earth.

How many are there?

There are probably several million asteroids in the solar system. Over 96,000 asteroids have been given numbers. Almost 12,000 of them have names. But even though there are a lot of asteroids, the asteroid belt is mostly empty space. Traveling through the asteroid belt in a space ship would not be very much like what you see in a science fiction film.

Comets

Comets are also members of our solar system. They revolve around the Sun in highly elliptical orbits. However, their period of revolution round the Sun is usually very long. A Comet appears generally as a bright head with a long tail. The length of the tail grows in size as it approaches the sun. The tail of a comet is always directed away from the sun (Fig. 3).

Many comets are known to appear periodically. One such comet is Halley's comet, which appears after nearly every 76 years.

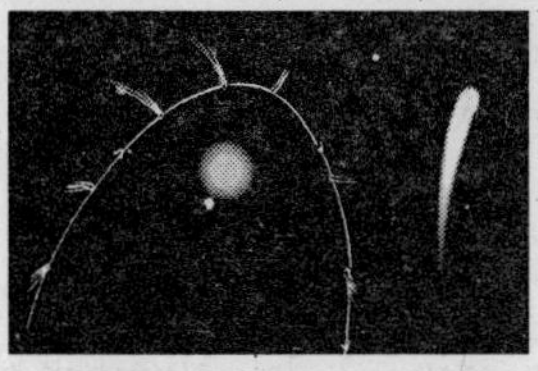

Fig. 3: *Different position of a Comet*

Meteors and Meteorites

At night, when the sky is clear and the moon is not there, you may sometimes see bright streaks of light in the sky (Fig. 4). These are commonly known as shooting stars, although they are not stars. They are called meteors. A meteor is usually a small object that occasionally enters the earth's atmosphere. At that time it has a very high speed. The friction due to the atmosphere heats it up. It glows and evaporates quickly. That is why the bright steak lasts for a very short time. Some meteors are large and so they can reach the Earth before they evaporate completely. The body that reaches the Earth is called a meteorite.

Fig. 4: *Streak of a Meteor*

Artificial Satellites

You must have heard that there are a number of artificial satellites which are orbiting the Earth. You might wonder how artificial satellites are different from natural satellites. Artificial satellites are man-made. They are launched from the Earth. They revolve around the Earth much closer than earth's natural satellite, the moon. India has built and launched several artificial satellites. Aryabhata was the first Indian satellite. Some other Indian satellites are INSAT, IRS, Kalpana-1, EDUSAT, etc.

Constellations and Constellations of Stars

On a clear moonless night we can see thousands upon thousands of stars dotting the night sky. If we are a little creative, we can imagine shapes and patterns these stars can make. Some of these patterns made up of groups of bright stars are easy to recognize and we call such groups as a constellations.

The ancients named many of these recognizable constellation after the objects or animals they resembled. They built stories around them too. For example, the constellation Perseus, Andromeda, Cetus, Cassiopeia and Pegasus are all linked to the mythology of the Greeks. Common constellation names are similar across cultures such as Pisces - the fish in Greek is also called Meena (also meaning fish) in Sanskrit.

All the constellations appear to move in the sky from west to east because the earth rotates from west to east. Moreover, all constellations in the southern hemisphere are not visible in the northern hemisphere and vice versa. This is because the earth is round and some constellations do not fall in the line of sight. A person in the equator can see almost all the constellations.

Zodiac constellations

There are 12 major constellations that line up along the sun's path along the sky (called the ecliptic). These are the Zodiac constellations: Aries (Mesha), Taurus (Vrushabha), Gemini (Mithuna), Crab/Cancer (Karka), Leo (Simha), Virgo (Kanya), Libra (Tula), Scorpion (Vruschika), Saggitarius (Dhanusha), Capricorn (Makara), Aquarius (Kumbha), Pisces (Meena). These constellations were used to track the movement of the sun and track time in ancient times.

Big Dipper

The big dipper also called as Saptarishi in India is a group of seven stars visible in the northern hemisphere. The constellation looks like a big ladle or like a wheel barrow and is part of a bigger constellation called Ursa Major (The great Bear). Two of the stars on this constellation appear to point to the pole star (Polaris/Dhruva). The pole star is the only star in the night sky that does not appear to move east to west but appears fixed. This is because it is directly above the earth's axis.

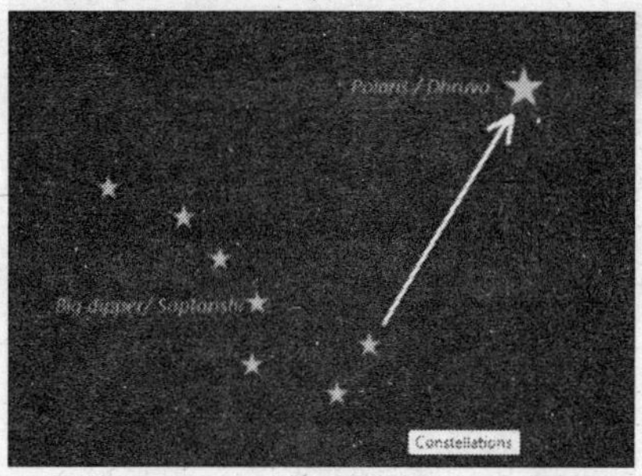

Orion

This is a constellation known as 'the hunter' or Mriga in India. It has a large number of bright stars in it. Three bright stars that are in line make up the 'belt' of the hunter. These three stars point to the brightest star in the night sky —Sirius.

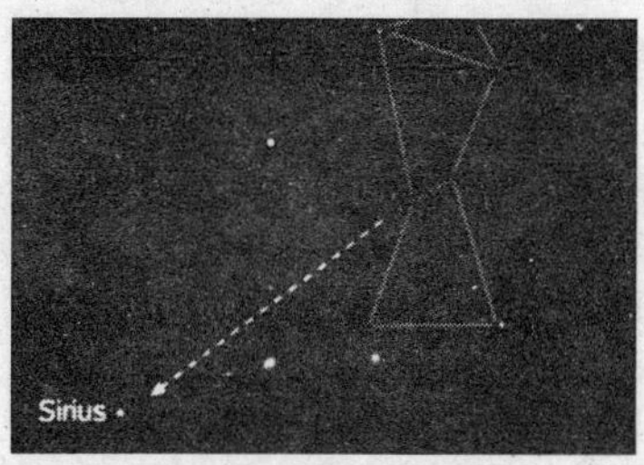

MULTIPLE CHOICE QUESTIONS

1. Which is the brightest planet in the universe?
A. Mercury B. Venus
C. Earth D. Saturn

2. Which is the nearest planet to the sun?
A. Neptune B. Mars
C. Mercury D. Earth

3. On which planet the life exists?
A. Earth B. Moon
C. Jupiter D. None

4. Which planet appears to be yellowish?
A. Asteroids B. Mars
C. Uranus D. Saturn

5. Which is the farthest planet of solar system?
A. Neptune B. Jupiter
C. Mercury D. Earth

6. The first outside orbit of the earth planet is:
A. Jupiter B. Mars
C. Saturn D. Uranus

7. Which is the largest planet in solar system?
A. Mercury B. Mars
C. Jupiter D. Saturn

8. What is the gap between the orbit of mars and Jupiter called?
A. Asteroids B. Comets
C. Meteor D. Meteorite

9. Stars appear to move from:
A. West to east
B. East to west
C. North to south
D. South to west

10. The tilting of the earth is responsible for:
A. Change of days
B. Change of the sun's rays
C. Change of the season
D. None

11. Largest Planet of the Inner Planets of Solar system is:
A. Mercury B. Venus
C. Earth D. Mars

12. Galileo discovered 4 moons in 1660 of which planet?
A. Earth B. Venus
C. Saturn D. Jupiter

13. The exact time taken by the earth to rotate one of its own axis is:
A. 24 hours
B. 23 hours 51 minutes
C. 23 hours 48 minutes 46 seconds
D. 23 hours 56 minutes 4 seconds

14. What is the black hole?
A. Star that has no atmosphere
B. Star with high temperature
C. Contracted Star that has high gravitational pull.
D. Pulsating star

15. What is great bear?
A. Constellation B. planet
C. Neutron Star D. Sun

16. What type of orbit planets have while revolving around the sun?
A. Parabolic and Hyperbolic
B. Circular and Parabolic
C. Elliptical and circular
D. Elliptical and Hyperbolic

17. What is the colour of lunar sky during day time from moon?
A. Blue B. Black
C. Red D. White

18. What is the distance between Earth and Sun?
A. 149 million B. 136 million
C. 159 million D. 196 million

19. The Brightest star in the sky observed from earth is:
A. Sun B. Alfa Centauri
C. Proxima Centauri D. Sirius

20. Sun Spots are:
A. The opposite surface of moon where no light reaches.
B. Dark patches of sun surface where temperature fall below 4050 K.
C. Black spot on moon
D. Polar region of Sun

21. Why pole star always seen at the one point in the sky?
A. pole star rotate with the same period of the Earth
B. pole star has opposite to the sun from earth
C. This is one another star from our galaxy.
D. pole star lies in the axis of spin of the earth

22. Parsec is a unit of:
A. Measurement of density of star
B. Astronomical unit of Distance
C. Brightness of Star
D. Unit of magnetic moment

23. What idea we get from the light coming from stars?
A. Density of Stars B. Temperature of Stars
C. Mass of the Stars D. Size of the stars

24. The time period of sun revolve around the galaxy is known as:
A. light years B. Astronomical year
C. Cosmic Year D. Parsec

25. What is supernova?
A. A dying star
B. A worm hole
C. A special type of comet
D. A bright asteroid of size equal to sun

26. Laws of planetary motion discovered by:
A. Galileo B. Copernicus
C. Kepler D. Newton

27. Twelve constellations or Zodiac are referred to which of the following?
A. A group of stars
B. All planet of solar system
C. It is the symbol of Roman God
D. None of these

28. What is the evidence that comets are the member of our solar system?
A. Their properties of compositions
B. Their Shape and size
C. Their shape of the orbit
D. Their structure of tails

29. We can see Full moon once a month and that night is called as _______.
A. Half Poornima B. Amavasya
C. Poornima D. Half Amavasya

30. Poornima is also called as _______.
A. Half Moon Night B. New Moon Night
C. Full Moon Night D. Old Moon Light

31. The sun, the moon and all those objects shining in the night sky are called _________.
A. Shining Satellites
B. Shining Earth
C. Astrological Satellites
D. Celestial Bodies

32. Celestial Bodies that have their own heat and which emit light in large amounts is called as _______.
A. Android B. Planets
C. Constellations D. Stars

33. Which of the following is considered as Star?
A. Earth B. Sun
C. Moon D. Galaxy

34. While watching the night sky, various patterns formed by different groups of stars are called as _______.
A. Star Patterns B. Pole Star
C. Android D. Constellations

35. Most easily recognisable Constellation is _________.
A. Capricornus B. Saptarshi
C. Norma D. Chamaeleon

36. Saptarishi is a group of ______ stars.
A. 8 B. 10
C. 9 D. 7

37. In ancient times, people used to determine directions during the night with the help of ______.
A. Pole B. Stars
C. Planets D. Constellations

38. The North Star which indicates the north direction is also called the _______.
A. Constellations B. Pole Star
C. Asteroids D. Androids

39. Which of the star remains in the same position in the sky?
A. Vega B. Sirius
C. Pole Star D. Aldebaran

40. Position of the Pole Star with can be easily find with the help of the _________.
A. Norma B. Saptarishi
C. Reticulum D. Phoenix

41. Some celestial bodies do not have their own heat and light are called as _______.
A. Planets B. Galaxy
C. Universe D. Stars

42. The word planet came from _______ language.
A. English B. Greek
C. Sanskrit D. Roman

43. Planets are depends on __________ for getting light and heat.
A. Constellations B. Stars
C. Galaxy D. Satellite

44. Planet on which we are living is called as _________.
A. Pluto B. Mars
C. Jupitor D. Earth

45. Which is nearest star of the Earth?
A. Spica B. Sirius
C. Sun D. Deneb

46. Asteroids and Meteoroids consists of ____.
A. Satellites B. Nine planets
C. All of these D. The sun

47. How many days it takes to complete one revolution around sun for Planet Mercury?
A. 88 days B. 255 days
C. 155 days D. 365 days

48. How many days Mercury took to complete one spin around own axis?
A. 12 days B. 59 days
C. 365 days D. 1 day

49. Venus took ____ days to spin around sun and ______ days to spin around own axis.
A. 255 and 243
B. 255 and 1
C. 687 and 243
D. 365 and 1

50. To complete one revolution around sun, Mars took ________ days.
A. 155 B. 365
C. 687 D. 255

51. Arrange the following planets in increase order of time require to complete one rotation around sun:
(*a*) Earth (*b*) Uranus
(*c*) Mars (*d*) Jupiter
A. (*a*) (*c*) (*b*) (*d*) B. (*c*) (*a*) (*d*) (*b*)
C. (*c*) (*a*) (*b*) (*d*) D. (*a*) (*c*) (*d*) (*b*)

52. Arrange following planets in the increasing order of number of moons:
(*a*) Uranus (*b*) Jupiter
(*c*) Earth (*d*) Saturn
A. (*c*) (*d*) (*a*) (*b*) B. (*c*) (*a*) (*b*) (*d*)
C. (*c*) (*a*) (*d*) (*b*) D. (*c*) (*b*) (*a*) (*d*)

53. Which is nearest known planet to Sun?
A. Saturn B. Mars
C. Mercury D. Earth

54. Which is farthest planet to a sun?
A. Pluto B. Uranus
C. Mercury D. Neptune

55. Sun provides pulling force to a solar system that binds complete solar system in one unit:
A. True B. False
C. Cant Say D. None of these

56. Which of the following is ultimate source of light and heat on earth?
A. Satellite B. Constellations
C. Sun D. Moon

57. Planets revolves around the sun in __________ path.
A. Elongated B. Circular
C. Rectangular D. Semi Circular

58. Earth is the _______ nearest planet to the Sun.
A. Second B. Fourth
C. First D. Third

59. Earth is slightly flattened at the poles and so its shape is described as _______.
A. Diamond B. Ellipsoid
C. Asteroid D. Geoid

60. Conditions favourable to support life are probably found on __________ planet.
A. Mars B. Jupiter
C. Earth D. Pluto

ANSWERS

1	2	3	4	5	6	7	8	9	10
B	C	A	D	A	B	C	A	B	C
11	**12**	**13**	**14**	**15**	**16**	**17**	**18**	**19**	**20**
C	D	D	C	A	C	B	A	D	B
21	**22**	**23**	**24**	**25**	**26**	**27**	**28**	**29**	**30**
D	B	B	C	A	B	A	C	C	C
31	**32**	**33**	**34**	**35**	**36**	**37**	**38**	**39**	**40**
D	D	B	D	B	D	B	B	C	B
41	**42**	**43**	**44**	**45**	**46**	**47**	**48**	**49**	**50**
A	B	B	D	C	C	A	B	A	C
51	**52**	**53**	**54**	**55**	**56**	**57**	**58**	**59**	**60**
D	D	C	A	A	C	A	D	D	C

★ ★ ★

SOCIAL SCIENCE

- History
- Democratic Politics
- Geography
- Economics

HISTORY

Ancient India

INDUS VALLEY CIVILIZATION

The Indus Valley Civilization or The Harappan culture was the most extensive of the ancient civilizations in area, including not only the Indus plain (the Punjab and Sind), but also northern Rajasthan and the region of Kathiawar in western India. It was essentially a city culture.

Common Characteristic Features

The most important feature is the systematic town planning on the lines of the 'grid system', that is streets and lanes cutting across one another almost at right angles, thus dividing the city into several rectangular blocks. At Harappa, Mahan-jo-daro and Kalibangan, this consists of two distinct elements: on the west a 'citadel' mound built on a high podium of mud brick, with a long axis running north to south, and to the east a lower town consisting of the main residential areas.

Another important feature is the large scale use of standardised burnt bricks in almost all kinds of constructions and total absence of stone buildings. The width of each brick was twice its height, and its length twice as large as its width ($7.5 \times 15 \times 30$ cm or $10 \times 20 \times 40$ cm). The bricks were mainly made in an open mould, but for special purposes, such as bathroom, sawn bricks were used, and wells constructed with wedge-shaped moulded bricks. Hammer dressed limestone slabs are occasionally found covering bricks drains. Timber was used for the flat roofs.

Another unique feature was the underground drainage system connecting all houses to the street drains which were covered with either bricks or stone slabs and equipped with manholes.

The citadel was defined by wall and on it were constructed the public buildings such as religious buildings, granaries, residences of the ruling class etc. Below this citadel was the town proper, consisting of the houses of the commoners. Houses stood on both sides of the streets. Houses generally had side entrances and there were no windows facing the main streets.

An average house had besides kitchen and baths, four to six living rooms, large houses with thirty rooms and staircases suggest that there were large two or three storeyed buildings. Most of the houses had wells within them. There were also arrangement for street lighting.

Town Planning

The first thing that strikes us with regard to Harappan culture is the town planning and urbanisation. Mohenjo-daro, Harappa, Lothal or Sutkagendor were built on similar plan. To the west of each was a citadel built on a high platform. It was defended by wall and on it were constructed the public buildings. Below this citadel was the town proper. Everywhere, the main streets ran from north to south and other streets ran at right angles to the main streets. Houses, residential or others, stood on both sides of the streets. Both at Harappa and Mohenjo-daro, houses were built of kiln-burnt bricks. At Lothal and Kalibangan, residential houses were made of sun-dried bricks. The drains, wells and bathing platforms were made of kiln-burnt bricks. An average house had, besides kitchen and bath, four to six living rooms. Large houses with thirty rooms and staircases suggest that there were large two or three storyed buildings. Most of the houses had wells within them and a drainage system carried the waste water to the main underground drain of the street. There were also public baths with wells. The covered drains of the streets had soak-pits and manholes for clearing. There were also arrangements for street lighting.

VEDIC CULTURE

With the arrival of Aryans, a new era began in India. That is called Vedic Age. The Vedic Age has been divided into two parts-The Early Vedic Age or Rigvedic Age and the Later Vedic Age. The Rigvedic era belongs from (1500-1000 B.C.). Historians and scholars have expressed different opinions regarding the original home land of the Aryans. They did not live in cities. Different scholars have different opinion regarding the home land of Aryans. India, Central Asia, South Russia, Plateau of Pamir, Scandinavia, Germany, Austria, Hungary etc., have been alternatively suggested as the original home of the Aryans by scholars who have tried to justify their respective contentions on the basis of history, philology, archaeological discoveries. But the majority of scholars have thought that the original home land of Aryans was from Poland and South Russia to Central Asia.

RIGVEDIC PERIOD

The only source of the Early Vedic Age is the Rigveda. Most of the hymns of the Rigveda were composed between the period 1500-1000 B.C.

The Aryans called their state as the Rashtra. Political organisation was based on patriarchal family. The State was divided into *Grama, Vis* and *Jana.* The relationship between all three divisions was not stated clearly. Grama was the smallest unit and gramani was the Lord of Grama. The lord of Vis was called Vispati and Gopa was the protector of Jana. The prevailing form of government among the Rig-Vedic tribes was monarchical.

Kingship was usually hereditary. The foremost duty of the king was the protection of the tribe and the tribal territory. He fought against external enemies. The king had no right over the land but he had the right to disown anybody from it. The plough land and the domestic animals were regarded the personal property of the farmer and the pasture-land was the property of the village.

Bhag, Sulk and Bali were the taxes collected by the king. The land revenue was 1/10 to 1/6 of the production. The king was assisted by a number of functional areas like purohit, senani etc. Senani was the leader of army. The army was divided into two parts. One part included foot soldiers later called patti and the other part were called Rathis who fought from chariots. The main weapons were bow, arrows, spears, lancess and strings.

There was no regular court for Justice. Justice was provided by the king and assisted by purohits. Punishment were also given. It may be turned out of the state, fined, put to physical torture or put to death. There were two popular assemblies to assist the king in administration. Majority of historians believe that one assembly is known as *Samiti* and the other was *Sabha.* Samiti was the assembly of larger group of people while Sabha was the council of elders. The powers of these assemblies were not defined but these were quite influential during the early Vedic Age.

LATER VEDIC PERIOD

The period between B.C. 1000 and B.C. 600 is generally known as Later Vedic period. This age is also called as the Epic Age because the two great epics Ramayana and Mahabharata were written during this period. The Aryans during this period moved to the Gangetic Valley.

The Gangetic Valley or Aryavartha became the centre of political activity. Kingdoms like Kosala, Videha, Kuru,Magadha, Kasi, Avanti and Panchala came into existence. The position of the king was considerably high. Sabha and Samiti did not stand in his way. Kingship became hereditary. The kings were in charge of defense and maintaining law and order of their kingdoms. They built vast empires. They tried to extend their territories. Therefore frequent wars were fought. Rituals and sacrifices such as Rajasuya, Ashvamedha, Vajapeya and Yagas were performed by the kings.

Kings assumed titles like Ekrat, Samrat and Sariahaurna. Village administration was looked after by the village councils. Taxes like Sulk and Bhaga were collected from the people. The revenue was spent for the benefit of the subjects.

EARLY STATES

MAHAJANPADAS

In the later Vedic period, the tribal organisations changed its identity and gradually shifted to the territorial identity, and the area of settlement were now regarded as *janapadas* or states. In transition from tribe to monarchy, they lost the essential democratic pattern of the tribe but retained the idea of government through an assembly representing the tribes. These states consisted of either a single tribe such as the *Shakyas*, *Kolias*, *Mallas* etc. or a confederacy of tribes such as the *Vrijis*, *Yadavas*, *Parchala* etc.

The people in the lower Ganges Valley and Delta, which were outside the Aryan pale, were regarded as M*lecchas*. There was, therefore, a strong consciousness of the pure land of the Aryans called *Aryavarta*. Each *janapada* tried to dominate and subjugate other *janapadas* to become *Mahajanapadas*.

According to *Anguttara Nikaya,* there were about sixteen *Mahajanapadas* in the sixth century BC. Their capitals and locations are given in a table on the 16 *Mahajanapadas*.

Important Republics

The kings in these states had the supreme authority. The *Mahajanapadas* of Vrijji, Malla, Kuru, Panchal and Kamboj were republican states and so were other smaller states like Lichhavi, Shakya, Koliya, Bhagga, and Moriya. These republican states had a *Gana-parishad* or an Assembly of senior and responsible citizens. This *Gana-Parishad* had the supreme authority in the state. All the administrative decisions were taken by this *Parishad*. Again, the republics were basically of two types: (*a*) the republics comprising a single tribe like those of the Sakyas, the Kolias and the Mallas, and (*b*) the republics comprising a number of tribes or the republics of confederacy like the Vrijjis.

RISE OF MAGADH

The Haryankas : Magadha came into prominence under the leadership of **Bimbisara** (542-493 BC), who belonged to the ***Haryanka dynasty.*** He strengthened his position by marriage alliances. He took three wives. His first wife was the daughter of the king of Kosala and the sister of Prasenajit. His second wife Chellana was a *Lichchhavi* Princess from Vaishali, and his third wife was the daughter of the chief of the Madra clan of Punjab. Marriage relations with the different princely families gave enormous diplomatic prestige and paved the way the expansion of Magadha westward and northward.

The earliest capital of Magadha was at Rajgir, which was called Girivraja at that time. It was surrounded by five hills, the openings in which were closed by stone walls on all sides. This made Rajgir impregnable.

Bimbisar was succeeded by his son **Ajatasatru** (492-460 BC). Ajatasatru killed his father and seized the throne for himself. Throughout his reign, he pursued an aggressive policy of expansion.

Ajatasatru was succeeded by **Udayin** (460-444 BC). His reign is important because he built the fort upon the confluence of the Ganga and Son at Patna. This was done because Patna lay in the centre of the Magadhan kingdom.

The Sisunagas : Udayin was succeeded by the dynasty of ***Sisunagas***, who temporarily shifted the capital to Vaishali. Their greatest achievement was the destruction of the power of Avanti with its capital at Ujjain. This brought to an end the 100 years old rivalry between Magadha and Avanti.

The Nandas : The *Sisunagas* were succeeded by the *Nandas*, who proved to be the most powerful rulers of Magadha. So great was their power that Alexander, who invaded Punjab at that time, did not dare to move towards the east. The Nandas added to the Magadhan power by conquering Kalinga from where they brought an image of the Jina as a victory trophy. All this took place in the reign of **Mahapadma Nanda**. He claimed to be *ekarat,* the sole sovereign who destroyed all the other ruling princes.

The Nandas were the first non-kshatriya rulers. The last Nanda ruler was defeated by Chandragupta Maurya who founded the Maurya Empire.

ALEXANDER'S INVASION

- Alexander marched to India through the Khyber Pass in 326 B.C.
- He was bravely checked by the local chieftains despite the fact that they had no chance of success.
- He was even checked by the queens of the vanquished and dead chiefs.
- His advance was checked on the bank of the Beas because of the mutiny of his soldiers.
- In 325 B.C., he began his homeward journey.
- In 324 B.C., he reached Susa in Persia and died the next year.
- The Greek invasion of India opened the trade route between north-west India and Western Asia.
- Eastwards trade went through the Ganga delta to the coast of Northern Burma and south along the east coast.
- Guilds (*Shreni*) came into existence.
- Money was introduced. Punch-marked coins in gold and silver and of copper cast have been discovered.
- Introduction of money facilitated the trade.

JAINISM AND BUDDHISM

JAINISM

The Founder : Rishabha, who was the father of king Bharata, the first *chakravarti* king of India, founded Jainism. The *Vishnu Purana* and *Bhagavat Purana* describe Rishabha as an incarnation of Narayana.

Risabha was succeeded by 23 other *Tirthankaras*. Parsvanatha (850 BC) was the 23rd *Tirthankara*. Jainism became a major religion under Vardhamana Mahavira, the 24th Tirthankara.

According to Jainism, the Tirthankaras descended on earth from time to time to guide the masses.

Vardhamana Mahavira : Vardhamana Mahavira was born in 540 BC in a village (Kundagrama) near Vaishali. His father was the head of a famous kshatriya clan (Inatrika), and his mother a Lichachhavi princess. They were also connected with the royal family of Magadha. In the beginning Mahavira led the life of a householder, but in the search for truth, he abandoned the world at the age of thirty and became an ascetic. He kept on wandering for twelve years from place to place. During the course of his long journey, it is said, he never changed his clothes for twelve years, and abandoned them altogether when he attained perfect knowledge or *kaivalya* at the age of 42. Through *kaivalya,* he conquered misery and happiness. Because of this conquest, he is known as Mahavira or the great hero or *jina,* i.e., the conqueror, and his followers are known as *Jainas*. He propagated his religion for thirty years, and his mission took him to Kosala, Magadha, Mithila, Champa, etc. He passed away at the age of 72 in 468 BC at a place called Pavapuri near modern Rajgir in Bihar.

Teachings : Jainism taught five doctrines: (i) do not commit violence, (ii) do not speak a lie, (iii) do not steal, (iv) do not acquire property, and (v) observe continence (*brahmacharya*). It is said that only the fifth doctrine was added by Mahavira, the other four being taken over by him from Prasavanath.

Jainism recognized the existence of the gods but placed them lower than the *jina.* It did not condemn the varna system. According to Mahavira, a person is born in a high or in a lower varna in consequence of the sins or the virtues acquired by him in the previous birth. In his opinion, through pure and meritorious life, members of the lower castes can attain liberation.

Jainism rejected the authority of the *Vedas* and *Vedic* retrials. It did not believe in the existence of God, but it believed in *Karma* and the transmigration of soul (Nirvana).

BUDDHISM

Gautama Buddha : Gautama Buddha or Siddhartha was a contemporary of Mahavira. He was born in 563 BC in a Shakya (kshatriya) family in Lumbini near Kapilavastu, which is situated on the foothills of Nepal. Gautama's father (Shudhodana) seems to have been the elected ruler of Kapilavastu, and headed the republican clan of the Shakyas. His mother (Mahamaya) was a princess from the Kosalan dynasty. From his early childhood, Gautama showed a meditative bent of mind. **Alara Kama** was his teacher of meditation. His charioteer was **Channa**, while his horse's name was **Kanthaks**. He was married early, but married life did not interest him. At the age of 29, he left home. He kept on, wandering for about seven years and then attained knowledge at the age of 35 at Bodh Gaya under a *pipal* tree, From this time onwards, he began to be called the Buddha or **The Enlightened.**

Gautama Buddha delivered his first sermons at Sarnath in Banaras. Gautama Buddha passed away at the age of 80 in 483 BC at a place called Kusinagar, identical with the village called Kasia in the district of Deoria in eastern Uttar Pradesh.

Teachings : Buddha said that the world is full of sorrows and people suffer on account of desires. If desires are conquered, *nirvana* will be attained. He recommended an **eight-fold path** (*astangika marga*) for the elimination of human misery. It comprised : Right Observation, Right Determination, Right Speech, Right Action, Right Livelihood, Right Exercise, Right Memory and Right Meditation. Buddha also laid down a code of conduct for his followers. The main items in this social conduct are: (i) do not covet the property of others, (ii) do not commit violence, (iii) do not use intoxicants, (iv) do not tell a lie, and (v) do not indulge in corrupt practices.

Buddha (The Entightened), ***Dhamma*** (The Doctrine) and ***Sangha*** (The order) are **three jewels of Buddhism**.

Buddhism does not recognize the existence of god and soul (*atman*). It particularly won the support of the lower orders as it attacked the varna system. Women also were admitted to the *sangha* and thus, brought at a par with men.

MAURYA AGE

The Maurya Empire was the first and one of the greatest empires that were established on Indian soil. Chandra Gupta Maurya was the first ruler who unified enitre Indian under one political unit. About Mauryan rulers we have epigraphical sources, literary sources, foreign accounts and materials obtained from archaelogical excavations. The Arthasashtra of Kautilya gives its detailed information about the administrative system of the Mauryan Empire.

Chandragupta Maurya (321-293 BC)

The Maurya dynasty was founded by Chandragupta

Maurya. He took advantage of the growing weakness and unpopularity of the Nandas in the last days of their rule. With the help of Chanakya, who is known as Kautilya, he overthrew the Nandas and established the rule of the Maurya dynasty.

Chandragupta built up a vast empire which included not only Bihar and good portions of Bengal, but also western and north-western India, and the Deccan. Leaving Kerala, Tamil Nadu and parts of north-eastern India, the Mauryas ruled over the whole of the subcontinent. In the north-west, they held sway over certain areas which were not included even in the British empire.

Bindusara (293-273 BC)

He was son of Chandragupta and was known as *Amitraghta* (slayer of foes) by the Greek writers. He continued his friendly links with the Syrian King Antiochus I and is stated to have requested him for a present of figs and wine together with a sophist. Antiochus sent figs and wine but replied that Greek philosophers were not for export. He received a Greek ambassador, Daimachos, from Antiochus I. Pliny tells that Ptolemy II Philadelphus of Egypt sent an envoy, Dionysios, to Bindusara's court.

Ashoka (273-232 BC)

Ashoka was the third and the greatest of the Mauryan rulers. He occupies a high position not only in the history of India but in the world history also. He was coronated four years after the death of his father, Bindusara (273BC). The gap is interpreted differently by different historians.

Ashoka's Dhamma: There was a great difference between Ashoka's personal religion and the religion he preached. His personal religion was, of course, Buddhism as he frankly admitted in the *Bhabru Edict* that he believed in the principles of Buddhism. In several of his edicts, in the capacity of the defender of the faith, he prescribed rules of punishment for those *Bhikshus* (monks) who violated the principles of Buddhism. He undertook journeys to the holy places of Buddhism and also called a Buddhist Council to meet in his time. However, the greatness of the Ashoka lies in the fact that he never thrusted his own religion upon anyone else. The *Dhamma* he placed before the world to follow was not pure Buddhism but it was the essence of all religions.

He appointed a new class of officers called *dharmayuktas, dharma-mahamatras* and *stri-adhyaksha* for the moral and spiritual uplift of the subjects.

KANVA DYNASTY

The last Sunga ruler was put to death by Vasudev Kanva, who ruled for about nine years. The dynasty lasted for about 45 years. The other rulers of the dynasty were Bhumiputra, Narayana and Susharma.

SATAVAHANAS

King Simuka established Satavahana dynasty in the Andhra region. Their empire, at one time, was expanded in a large Deccan area. Paithan, Vaijayanti and Amaravati were famous towns of that time.

1. The Satavahana kings being Brahmans felt strongly to revive Brahmanism. They were also zealous to revive the Varna Ashrama system.
2. The religious notions, during the Satavahana period were quite considerate and tolerant.
3. During Satavahana period Buddhism flourished. The Buddhist religion contributed significantly in the domain of art.

LATER MAURYAN AGE

BACTRIANS

- Demetrius, the Greek ruler of Bactria invaded Afghanistan and Punjab and occupied them. From Taxila, he sent two of his Commanders, Appolodotus and Menander for further conquests.
- Menander extended his rule up to Mathura and from there he made attempts to capture Pataliputra. But he was stopped by the army of Vasumitra, the grandson of Pushyamitra Sunga.
- Menander was also known as Milinda and the capital of his kingdom was Sakala (Sialcot). He evinced much interest in Buddhism and his dialogues with the Buddhist monk Nagasena was compiled in the Pali work, Milindapanho (Questions of Milinda).
- A Greek ambassador Heliodorus became a Vaishnavite and erected the Garuda Pillar at Besnagar(Vidisha).

SAKAS

- The Sakas or the Scythians attacked Bactria and Parthia and captured them from the Greek rulers.
- The founder the Saka rule in India in the first century B.C. was Maues.
- The most famous Saka ruler in India was Rudradaman I. His achievements are highlighted in his Junagarh inscription.

KUSHANAS

- The Kushanas were a branch of Yuchi tribe, whose original home was central Asia.
- The founder of the Kushana dynasty was Kujula Kadphises or Kadphises I.
- Wima Kadphises or Kadphises II conquered the whole of northwestern India as far as Mathura. He issued gold coins with high-sounding titles like the 'Lord of the Whole World'.

Kanishka (78–120 A.D.)

- Kanishka was the most important ruler of the Kushana dynasty. His capital was **Purushapura** or **Peshawar**. He constructed a city called **Kanishkapuram**.
- He was the founder of the Saka era which starts from 78 A.D.
- According to Kalhana, Kanishka invaded Kashmir and occupied it.
- Kanishka had convened the **Fourth** Buddhist Council at **Kundalvana** in Kashmir. Many Buddhist monks like **Vasumitra, Nagarjuna** and **Parsva** attended it. **Ashwagosha** presided over the council. He wrote **Buddha Charita**.
- **Vasumitra** wrote the great **Mahavibhasha**. **Nagarjuna** wrote the book titled, **Madhyamika Sutra**.
- Kanishka patronised **Charaka**.
- **Charaka** wrote the **Charaka Samhita**. It deals with medicine. Another medical scholar **Susruta** also belonged to Kanishka's time. He has written the **Susruta Samhita**. It is devoted to surgery.
- In the age of Kanishka the Mahayana Buddhism came into vogue.
- A new school of sculpture developed during Kanishka's time. It is called **Gandhara Sculpture**.

GUPTA AGE

The Early Guptas

Srigupta and his son Ghatotkachagupta were non-entities assuming the simple title of maharaja. As it is not known definitely where these Gupta kings ruled and whether they owed allegiance to any paramount soverign, it is better to leave undecided the status of the first two Gupta kings.

Chandragupta-I (320-335 AD)

The third ruler Chandragupta-I, the son and successor at Ghatotkacha, was definitely a strong ruler whose hands were sought by the Lichchhavis who gave their princess Kumardevi in marriage to him. This matrimonial alliance with this ancient historic family no doubt enhanced the status of the obscure Guptas. The Lichchhavi territory of north Bihar and the adjoining principality over which the Guptas ruled were united under Chandragupta and the latter was able to extend his dominion over Avadh as well as Magadha, and along the Ganges as far as Prayaga or Allahabad. Chandragupta-I is usually regarded as the founder of the Gupta era, which commenced on 26 February, A.D. 320 to commemorate his accession or coronation–an era which continued in parts of India for several centuries.

Samudragupta (335-375 AD)

Chandragupta-I was succeeded by his son Samudragupta, who became the ruler after subduing his rival, Kacha, an obscure prince of the dynasty. The Allahabad Pillar Inscription, written by Harisena, gives a detailed account of the conquests of his royal master. This account contains a long list of states, kings and tribes which were conquered and brought under various degrees of subjugation.

Chandragupta-II (380-415 AD)

Samdura Gupta was succeeded by his son Chandra-gupta-II, surnamed Vikramaditya. But according to some scholars, the immediate successor of Samudra Gupta was his son Ramagupta, the elder brother of Chandragupta-II. A drama Chandraguptam, by Visakhadatta, mentions that Ramagupta agreed to surrender his queen Dhruvadevi to the infatuation of a Saka Chief (Basana) who had invaded his kingdom. The honour of the queen was saved by Chandragupta, younger brother of Ramagupta, who killed the Saka chief, usurped the throne and married the widow. This story with slight variations is referred to in Bana's Harshacharita, Rajasekhara's Kavyamimamsa and some Rashtrakuta inscriptions of the 9th and 10th centuries. However, the historicity of Ramagupta is a matter of great doubt as neither the contemporary inscriptions nor the coins mention any king of this name.

LATER GUPTAS

EMERGENCE OF REGIONAL STATES (NORTH AND SOUTH INDIA)

North India

Prathiharas

- **Nagabhatta** I founded this dynasty. **Kanuaj** was their capital.
- The most famous king of the Prathiharas was king **Mihira Bhoja**. He ruled from 836 A.D. to 885 A.D.
- **Mihira Bhoja's son Mahendrapal** was also equally great and powerful. Under his rule, the Prathihara empire reached its zenith. His court poet and dramatist **Rajashekara** wrote **Bala Ramayana, Bala Bharatha** and a few more works in Sanskrit.

Chauhans

- Another branch of the Rajputs was the **Chauhans of Ajmer**.
- This kingdom was founded at the end of the 8th century A.D. The famous king of this dynasty was **Visaldeva**. He captured Delhi from the **Tomaras**.
- The last and the most powerful king of this dynasty was **Prithviraj Chauhan**. He defeated Muhammad of Ghor in the **First Battle of Tarain** in 1191 A.D. But in the next year Prithviraj was defeated and killed by Muhammed of Ghor in the Second **Battle of Tarain**.

Chandelas

- The **Chandelas** had ruled the region called **Bundelkhand**.
- The important rulers of this dynasty were **Dhanga** and **Kirtivarman**.
- The famous **Vishnu Temple** was built by **Yashovarman** at **Khajuraho** in 955 A.D. He made **Mahoba** his capital. Two other temples of this period are the **Parshwanath Jain** temple and the **Kandariya Mahadeva** temple at **Khajuraho**.
- The last ruler of this dynasty was defeated by **Qutb-ud-din Aibak**. And thus came the end of the Chandella rule in Bundelkhand.

Paramaras

- **Upendra** was the **founder** of this dynasty.
- The most important king of this dynasty was **Bhoja** (1010 A.D.- 1055 A.D.). He dug a very big lake (more than 250 square miles). It is situated to the South East of Bhopal.

Palas of Bengal

- **Gopala** (A.D. 765-A.D.769) was the first ruler of the Pala Dynasty of Bengal.
- **Gopala** was succeeded by **Dharmapala** (A.D.769-A.D.815). He ruled Bengal for nearly four decades. He was a follower of Buddhism. He founded the **University of Vikramasila**.

South India

Pallavas

- The Pallavas established their kingdom in Tondaimandalam with its capital at Kanchipuram. Their rule continued till Tondaimandalam was captured and annexed by the Imperial Cholas in the beginning of the 10th century A.D.
- The early Pallava rulers from 250 A.D. to 350 A.D. issued their charters in Prakrit. Important among them were Sivaskandavarman and Vijayaskandavarman.
- Other great Pallava rulers were Mahendravarman I, Narasimhavarman I, and Narasimhavarman II.
- The Pallavas introduced the art of excavating temples from the rock. In fact, the Dravidian style of temple architecture began with the Pallava rule.
- Mahendravarman I introduced the rock-cut temples. This style of Pallava temples are seen at places like Mandagappattu, Mahendravadi, Mamandur, Dalavanur, Tiruchirappalli, Vallam, Siyamangalam and Tirukalukkunram.

Chalukyas (543 – 755 A.D.)

- Pulakesin I was the founder of the Chalukya dynasty. He established a small kingdom with Vatapi or Badami as its capital.
- **Pulakesin II** was the contemporary of Harsha Vardhana.
- There was a battle between Harsha and Pulakesin II on the banks of the river **Narmadha**. Pulakesin II defeated Harsha.
- The Chalukyas were great patrons of art. They developed the vesara style in the building of structural temples.
- The structural temples of the Chalukyas exist at Aihole, Badami and Pattadakal (**Virupaksha temple**). Cave temple architecture was also famous under the Chalukyas. Their cave temples are found in Ajanta, Ellora and Nasik.

Rashtrakutas (755 – 975 A.D.)

- Dantidurga was the founder of the Rashtrakuta dynasty. He defeated the Gurjaras and captured Malwa from them. Then, he annexed the Chalukya kingdom by defeating Kirtivarman II. Thus, the Rashtrakutas became a paramount power in the Deccan.
- Dantidurga was succeeded by Krishna I.
- Krishna I built the magnificent rock-cut monolithic Kailasa temple at Ellora.
- The art and architecture of the Rashtrakutas were found at Ellora and Elephanta.

Cholas

- Cholas became prominent in the ninth century and established an empire comprising the major portion of South India. Their capital was Tanjore.
- The founder of the Chola kingdom was Vijayalaya.
- The most powerful Chola kings were Rajaraja I and his son Rajendra I. Rajaraja ruled from A.D. 985 to A.D 1012. He had conquered the neighbouring Pandya kingdoms and extended his conquest upto to the Northern part of Ceylon.
- Rajendra I assumed a number of titles, the most famous being Mudikondan, Gangaikondan, Kadaram Kondan and Pandita Cholan.
- Rajendra III was the last Chola king who was defeated by Jatavarman Sundarapandya II. The Chola country was absorbed into the Pandya Empire.
- The Dravidian style of art and architecture reached its perfection under the Cholas.
- The chief feature of the Chola temple is the vimana.
- Raja Raja Chola built the famous **Brahadeeswara temple** at **Tanjore**. It is also known as the **Big temple**.
- **Rajendra I** founded a new capital at **Gangaikonda Cholapuram** in 1025 A.D . He also built a temple at this place.
- The bronzes of the Chola period are world-famous. The bronze statues of Nataraja or dancing Siva are master pieces.

Medieval India

SULTANS OF DELHI

- The Muslim invasions into India had ultimately resulted in the establishment of Delhi Sultanate which existed from A.D. 1206 to 1526.
- The five dynasties which ruled Delhi were :
  1. The Slave dynasty 1206-1290
  2. The Khilji dynasty 1290-1320
  3. The Tughlaq dynasty 1320-1414
  4. The Sayyid dynasty 1414-1451
  5. The Lodi dynasty 1451-1526

SLAVE DYNASTY

- The Slave dynasty was also called Mamluk dynasty. Mamluk was the Quranic term for slave.
- The Slave dynasty ruled Delhi from A.D. 1206 to 1290. In fact, three dynasties were established during this period. They were-
  1. Qutbi dynasty (1206-1211) founded by Qutbuddin Aibak.
  2. First Ilbari dynasty (1211- 1266) founded by Iltutmish.
  3. Second Ilbari dynasty (1266-1290) founded by Balban.

Qutb-ud-din Aibak

- **Qutb-ud-din Aibak** was the first Sultan of Delhi.
- Qutbuddin Aibak was a slave of Muhammad Ghori, who made him the Governor of his Indian possessions.
- After the death of Ghori in 1206, Aibak declared his independence. He assumed the title Sultan and made Lahore his capital.
- Muslim writers call Aibak *Lakh Baksh* or giver of lakhs because he gave liberal donations to them.
- Aibak died of injuries received in a fall from his horse while playing **chaugan** (Polo) in 1210.

Iltutmish

- Iltutmish belonged to the Ilbari tribe and hence his dynasty was named as Ilbari dynasty.
- He shifted his capital from Lahore to Delhi.
- He received the mansur, the letter of recognition, from the Abbasid Caliph in 1229 by which he became the legal sovereign ruler of India.
- He patronized many scholars and a number Sufi saints came to India during his reign. Minhaj-us-Siraj, Taj-ud-din., Nizam-ul-mulk Muhammad Janaidi, Malik Qutb-ud-din Hasan and Fakhrul-Mulk Isami were his contemporary scholars who added grandeur to his court.

Raziya

- She was the first and last Muslim lady who sat on the throne of Delhi.
- She appointed an Abyssinian slave Yakuth as Master of the Royal Horses.
- In 1240, Altunia, the governor of Bhatinda revolted against her. She went in person to suppress the revolt but Altunia killed Yakuth and took Raziya prisoner.

Ghiyas-ud-din Balban

- Ghiyas-ud-din Balban, who was also known as Ulugh Khan, served as Naib or regent to Sultan Nasiruddin Mahmud.

- Balban introduced rigorous court discipline and new customs such as prostration and kissing the Sultan's feet to prove his superiority over the nobles.
- He also introduced the Persian festival of *Nauroz* to impress the nobles and people with his wealth and power.
- He established a separate military department - *diwan-i-arz* – and reorganized the army.

KHILJI DYNASTY

Jalaluddin Khilji

- The founder of the Khilji dynasty was Jalaluddin Khilji.
- The important event of Jalaluddin's reign was the attack on Devagiri in the Deccan. His nephew and son-in-law **Ala-ud-din Khilji** plundered **Devagiri** and defeated its ruler **Ramachandra Deva** and returned to Kara. During the reception there, Alauddin Khilji treacherously murdered his father-in-law Jalaluddin Khilji and usurped the throne of Delhi.

Alauddin Khilji

- **Ala-ud-din Khilji** was the greatest ruler of the Khilji Dynasty.
- He was the first Muslim ruler to extend his empire right upto Rameshwaram in the South.
- The Sultan had built a new city called **Siri** near Delhi.
- **Amir Khusrau** the great Persian poet, patronised by Balban, continued to live in Alauddin Khilji's court also.
- He introduced the system of *dagh* (branding of horses) and prepared *huliya* (descriptive list of soldiers).
- Alauddin Khilji maintained a large permanent standing army and paid them in cash from the royal treasury.
- The introduction of paying salaries in cash to the soldiers led to price regulations popularly called as Market Reforms.

TUGHLAQ DYNASTY

Ghiyas-ud-din Tughlaq

- Ghiyas-ud-din Tughlaq was the founder of the Tughlaq dynasty.
- Ghiyas-ud-din laid the foundation for Tughlaqabad near Delhi.
- Ghiyas-ud-din Tughlaq's son Ulugh Khan killed his father and ascended the throne with the title Muhammad bin Tughlaq in 1325.

Muhammad bin Tughlaq

- Muhammad bin Tughlaq was the only Delhi Sultan who had received a comprehensive literary, religious and philosophical education.
- To have the capital at the centre of the empire and safe from the Mongol raids, Tughlaq chose Devagiri as his new capital in A.D. 1327.The Sultan renamed the new capital **Daulatabad.**
- In 1329-30, Muhammad bin Tughlaq introduced a token currency.
- A separate department for agriculture, *Diwan-i- Kohi* was established.
- Muhammad bin Tughlaq died in 1351.

Firoz Shah Tughlaq

- **Firuz Shah Tughlaq** became Sultan after the death of Muhammad-bin-Tughlaq in A.D. 1351.
- He appointed *Khan-i-Jahan* Maqbal, a Telugu Brahmin convert as wazir (prime minister).
- He was the first Sultan to impose irrigation tax.
- **Firuz Shah Tughlaq** constructed many canals for irrigation. The longest canal was about 200 kilometres from Sutlej to Hansi. Another canal was between Yamuna and Hissar.
- A new department called *Diwan-i-Khairat* was created to take care of orphans and widows.
- He had built new towns of **Firozabad, Jaunpur, Hissar** and **Firozpur**.

Invasion of Timur

- **Timur,** the Turkish chief of Central Asia, was a great conqueror. Taking advantage of India's weakness, he had entered India in A.D. 1398. At that time, Nasiruddin Mahmud was the ruler.
- When Timur entered Delhi there was no opposition and he sacked Delhi for three days murdering thousands of people and looting enormous wealth.
- **Timur** withdrew from India in 1399 and his invasion in fact delivered a death blow to the Tughlaq dynasty.

SAYYID DYNASTY

- Before his departure from India, Timur appointed Khizr Khan as governor of Multan. He captured Delhi and founded the Sayyid dynasty in 1414.
- **Mubarak Shah, Mohammed Shah** and **Alam Shah** were some of the other important noteworthy rulers of Sayyid Dynasty.
- Muhammad Shah died in 1445 and was succeeded by his son Alam Shah (1445-1451)

the weakest of the Sayyid princes. He handed over the throne to Bahlol Lodi and retired to Badaun.

LODIS

- The Lodis, who succeeded Sayyids, were Afghans.
- Bahlol Lodi was the first Afghan ruler while his predecessors were all Turks. He died in 1489 and was succeeded by his son, Sikandar Lodi.
- In 1504, Sikandar Lodi founded the city of Agra and transferred his capital from **Delhi** to **Agra**.
- Sikander was the greatest of the Lodi Kings.
- On Sikandar Lodi's death in A.D. 1517, his son **Ibrahim Lodi** unanimously became the Sultan of Delhi.
- Ibrahim Lodi failed to get the support of Afghan nobles.
- A powerful Afghan noble, **Daulatkhan Lodi**, invited **Babar**, the ruler of Afghanistan, to invade India and overthrow Ibrahim Lodi.
- Babar marched against Delhi and defeated and killed Ibrahim Lodi in the first battle of Panipat (1526).

VIJAYANAGAR AND BAHMANI KINGDOM

THE VIJAYANAGAR KINGDOM (1350-1564 A.D.)

The origin of the kingdom of Vijayanagar is still a matter of controversy. According to tradition, the kingdom was founded by the five sons of Sangama of whom the two most prominent were Harihara and Bukka who reverted to Hinduism after having been converted to Islam. They were encouraged in their enterprise by two scholars, Madhava Vidyaratna and his brother Sayana. According to Father Heras, this kingdom was founded by the Hoysala King, Vira Bailala III. However, it seems certain that the kingdom owed its origin to a reaction to the devastating Muslim raids which threatened to overwhelm the Hindu civilisation in southern India. The capital of the kingdom was Hastinavati (Hampi).

Reasons for Growth of Vijayanagar Empire

- Growth in agriculture and trade in the territories of Karnataka.
- Chola state was finished. The re-emergence of powerful chieftainships over portions of Tamil country outside of Cholamandalam firmly established independent bases of competitive power.
- Early Vijayanagar expansion came at the expense of great Hindu kingdoms such as the Hoysala states of Karnataka and the Reddi kingdom of Kondavidu in Andhra.
- These northern warriors drew resources from the newly overrun areas by way of tributes.
- Small warriors of *nayakas* were the leading political figures in the Vijayanagar states and European sources refer to the acquisition and shifting of some part of the resources commanded by them to the capital city in the form of tribute.

Vijayanagar Dynasties

Dynasty	Founder	Period
Sangama	Harihara and Bukka	1336-1485
Saluva	Saluva Narsimha	1485-1505
Tuluva	Veer Narsimha	1505-1570
Aravidu	Trumala	1570-mid 17th Century

THE BAHMANI KINGDOM (1347-1526 A.D.)

The Bahmani kingdom was founded in 1347 by Hasan Gangu who revolted and proclaimed his independence, from the Sultanate. He assumed the title of *Alauddin Bahmani* (Also Bahman Shah). Gulbarga was his capital. He divided his kingdom into four *Tarafs* (provinces) and placed each one under a Tarafdar (Governor). He was succeeded by Muhammad Shah I (1358-73) whose reign was chiefly occupied in waging savage wars against Vijayanagar and Warangal. Some of the other notable rulers of the dynasty were Firoz Shah (1397-1422) who twice defeated Vijayanagar but was ultimately defeated at Pangul; Ahmad Shah (1422-33) who conquered warangal and shifted the capital to Bidar and who was also known as Wali on account of his association with a sufi, Gesu Daraz; Humayun (1451-61) famous for his minister, Khwaja Mahmud Gawan; Muhammad Shah III (1463-82) whose reign saw Mahmud Gawan expand the Kingdom as never before. In his campaign against Vijaynagar in 1481, he even reached and plundered Kanchi. He overran Dabhol and Goa on the western coast. However, Gawan was a Persian by birth and hence disliked by the 'Deccani' chiefs who were native. The Deccani party conspired against him and got him executed in 1481.

Gradually, the Bahmani Kingdom declined in power till in 1526, Amir Barid usurped the throne. Thus the dynasty came to end. Five independent kingdoms rose on the ruins of the Bahmani kingdom, namely Berar, Bidar, Ahmednagar, Golconda and Bijapur.

Berar

It was the first province to break loose from the Bahmani Kingdom when in 1484, Fathulla, the governor of Gowilgarh, revolted against Mahmud Bahmani. The dynasty he founded was called the Imad Shahi dynasty because he borne the title of Imadoul-Mulk. His capital was at Elichpur. The dynasty lasted for about 90 years until 1574 when it was annexed by Ahmednagar.

Bidar

The kingdom comprised the territory around the Bahmani capital. Qasim Barid, a former minister of Mahmud Gawan, had become its de facto ruler as early as 1492. But he and his successor hesitated from assuming formal ranks until 1527. The dynasty lasted till 1619 when, it was annexed by Bijapur.

Ahmednagar

In 1490, Malik Ahmad, the governor of Junmar, successfully revolted and established himself as an independent sovereign. He founded the city of Ahmednagar and along with, the Nizam Shahi dynasty. Frequently embroiled in wars with Bijapur and Golkonda, it formed a Subha of Akbar's Empire and was finally annexed to the Mughal in 1637 under Shahjahan.

Golkonda

Founded the last of all (1518), the Golkonda kingdom comprised the ruins of the Kakatiya principality of Warangal and was extensive, fertile and rich in territory. It was founded in 1518 by a Turkish officer, Sultan Quli Qutub Shah, who was appointed the Governor of Golkonda by Mahmud Gawan. He moved the capital from Warangal to Golkonda. Initially, in spite of the incessant warfare that waged between Bijapur and Ahmednagar, it enjoyed a comparative seclusion. Gradually, however, Golkonda too got embroiled in the Deccan politics, fought serious war against Bijapur and in 1565 joined the Muslim confederacy against the Vijayanagar kingdom.

Like Bijapur, Golkonda too became a famous centre of art and architecture and is famous for its tombs which were made of granite. Golkonda fort and Charminar are its famous examples of architecture. The state was finally annexed to the Mughal Empire by Aurangzeb in 1687.

Bijapur

Out of the five kingdoms of the Deccan Sultanate, Bijapur was the most important. It was founded by Yusuf Adil Shah, who waged wars against Vijayanagar and his neighbours but his great achievement was the recovery of Goa from the Portuguese commander, Albuquerque, though the Portuguese retook it in 1510. He was succeeded by his minor son, Ismail Shah, who recovered Raichur Doab from Vijayanagar. During the reign of Ibrahim Adil Shah, the kingdoms of Golkonda, Bidar and Ahmednagar attacked Bijapur but it was well defended by its able minister Asad Khan. Ibrahim died in 1557 and was succeeded by his son, Ali Adil Shah. Ibrahim Adil Shah II (1579-1626) was perhaps the greatest of the Adil Shah kings. He was a good administrator and introduced a very efficient system of revenue settlement. He was tolerant of all creeds and faiths. He kept friendly relations with the Portugese and allowed them to preach Christianity in his dominions.

Bahmani Kingdoms

Kingdom	Year	Founder	Dynasty	Annexation
Berar	1484	Fataullah Imad	Imad Shahi Shah	1574 (Ahmednagar)
Bijapur	1489	Yusuf Adil Khan	Adil Shahi	1686 (Aurangzeb)
Ahmednagar	1490	Malik Ahmad	Nizam Shahi	1633 (Shahjahan)
Golkonda	1512-1581	Quli Shah	Qutab Shahi	1687 (Aurangzeb)
Bidar	1526-1527	Amir Ali Barid	Barid Shahi	1618 (Bijapur)

RELIGIOUS MOVEMENT

The exchange of ideas between Hindus and Muslims resulted in the development of two popular movements. *The Bhakti movement in the Hindus* and *the sufi movement/sufism in the Islam.*

BHAKTI MOVEMENT

The term Bhakti means single minded devotion to one god. *The god may have a form (Saguna)* or *may be even formless (Nirguna)*. The Saguna Bhakti worshipped their gods in the various incarnations of god. The followers of *Nirguna* Bhakti do not believe in idol worship. To them god is omnipresent. Yet, both believed in the Upanishadic philosophy of *Advaita* (Non-duality of god).

Nirguna Bhakti and their Exponents

(i) **Kabir:** Kabir, a Muslim weaver, was one of the greatest pupils of Ramananda. According to tradition, he was the abandoned child of a Brahmin widow. He grew up as the foster-child of the weaver Niru and his wife. He flourished, most probably, in the end of the fourteenth and early fifteenth century. He composed beautiful verses in Hindi which are still familiar in Northern India. His followers are called *Kabirpanthis* meaning, 'the travellers in the path of Kabir' and Kabir himself was claimed to be '*at once the child of Allah and of Ram'*. When he died both Muslims and Hindus claimed his corpse. The story goes that when they raised the shroud covering the corpse, they found nothing but a heap of flowers. The Hindus took half and cremated it at Varanasi; the Muslim buried the other half near Gorkhpur.

***(ii)* Guru Nanak:** Nanak was born in a Khatri family on 1469 at Talwandi in the Lahore district. He spent his life preaching the gospel of tolerance. In order to put an end to the religious conflicts he laid stress on moral virtues. " Religious consistent not in mere words" said Nanak; he who looks on all men as equal is religious. Religion consistent not in wandering to tombs or places of cremation, or sitting in attitudes of contemplation. Religion consistent not in wandering in foreign countries, or in bathing at places of pilgrimage. Abide pure amidst the impurities of the world, thus shall they find the way to religion."

***(iii)* Namadeva:** Namdeva was born in 1270, he was a *Nirguna Upasaka*. Some of his abhangas are included in Guru Granth Sahib.

***(iv)* Ramananda:** Ramananda was a Bhakti saint in the North, who was a great devotee of Sri Rama. He opened his doors to all-upper castes, untouchables, Muslims etc. Kabir thereby, come across him and was greatly influenced.

Ten Sikh Gurus
(i) Guru Nanak (1496-1539)
(ii) Guru Angad (1539-1552)
(iii) Guru Amardas (1552-1574)
(iv) Guru Ram Das (1574-1581)
(v) Guru Arjun Dev (1581-1606)
(vi) Guru Har Gobind (1606-1644)
(vii) Guru Har Rai (1645-1661)
(viii) Guru Har Kishan (1661-1664)
(ix) Guru Tegh Bahadur (1664-1675)
(x) Guru Gobind Singh (1675-1708)

SUFI MOVEMENT

Sufism represents the spiritual and mystical dimensions of Islam. The term *Sufi* probably came from the Arabic word Sof (wool). This was perhaps due to the result of the old ascetic practice of wearing only a coarse woollen garment.

This movement was first born in Iran when some of the religious scholars and liberal thinkers in that country realised that there was little difference among the various beliefs like the Shia and the Sunni sects. In the realm of ideas, it marks the end of the domination of the Mutazila or rationalist philosophy, and the rise of orthodox schools base on the *Quran* and *Hadis (Traditions* of the Prophet and his companions) and of the *Sufi* mystic orders.

The Sufi silsilas were named after the name or surname of the founder of the particular order. Such as Chishti, Suhrawardi, Naqshbandi etc.

Chishti Silsila: The Chishti order was founded by *Khwaja Abdal Chisti* in Herat, it was brought to India by *Khwaja Moin-ud-din Chisti* (1142-1236). He arrived at Lahore in 1161 AD and settled at Ajmer in about 1206. However, the most famous of Chishti saints were *Nizamuddin Auliya* and *Nasiruddin Chirag-i-Delhi*. Auliya was generally known as *Mahbub-i-Ilahi* (beloved of God). They made themselves popular by adopting musical recitation called *Saint* to create mood of nearness to god.

Suhrawardi Silsila: It was founded by *Sheikh Shihabuddin Suhrawardi*. The credit of organising it goes to *Shaikh Bahauddin Zakariya*. Its main centre was Multan. Saints of this order had big jagirs and had closed contact with the state.

Firdausi Silsila: *Sheikh Badruddin of Samark* first moved to Bihar and became the most influential mystic order. Its most distinguished saints was *Sheikh Shamasuddin Yahya Munair* who believed in pantheistic monoism.

Shattari Silsila: It was founded in India by *Shah Abdullah Shattan*. However, it gained in popularity under *Sheikh Muhammad Ghauth* of Gwalior. Among his disciples were the famous musician *Tansen*. The shattari saints sought to synthesize Hindu and mystical Muslim thoughts to practice.

Qadiri Silsila: *Shah Niamatullah Qadri* was probably the first notable saint of this order to enter India but it was *Syed Muhammad Jilani* who organised it on effective basis. *Dara Shikoh*, the eldest son of Shahjahan was follower of this order.

Naqshbandi Silsila: This Silsila was introduced in India by *Khwaja Baqi Billah* during the later years, of Akbar's reign. It attained a position of great importance in India under the leadership of *Sheikh Ahmad Sirhindi*. He was opposed to pantheistic philosophy *Wahadat-ul-Wajud* and propounded the theory of *wahadat-ul-shudud.*

Mahadawi Movement: It was initiated by *Syed Muhammad Mahadi* of Jaunpur. He concentrated his energies on regeneration of people.

Raushaniyah Movement: The movement owed its origin to *Miyan Bayazid Ansari*, a native of Jalandhar. He emphasised inter-organisation of religious rites and inspired his followers with the ideal of ascetic self-denial.

MUGHAL EMPIRE

Babar

- Babar was the founder of the Mughal Empire in India. His original name was Zahiruddin Muhammad. He was related to Timur from his father's side and to Chengaz Khan through his mother.
- **Daulat Khan Lodi,** the Governor of Lahore, openly invited Babar to invade India.
- On 21st April 1526 the first Battle of Panipat took place between Babar and Ibrahim Lodi, who was killed in the battle. Babar's success was due his cavalry and artillery.
- Artillery was used for the first time in the battle of Panipat.
- Babar defeated **Rana Sanga** of **Mewar** in the battle of **Kanwah** in A.D. 1527. Babur assumed the title Ghazi.
- Babar died at Agra in 1530 at the age of forty seven.

Humayun

- Humayun succeeded to the throne of Delhi in A.D. 1530.
- **Sher Shah** defeated Humayun at **Chausa** in A.D. 1539 and again at **Kanauj** in A.D. 1540.
- After losing his kingdom, Humayun became an exile for the next fifteen years.
- He married **Hamida Banu Begam** who gave birth to Akbar at **Amarkot** in A.D.1542.
- In 1555, Humayun defeated the Afghans and recovered the Mughal throne. After six months, he died in 1556 due to his fall from the staircase of his library.

Sher Shah Suri

- The founder of the Sur dynasty was Sher Shah, whose original name was Farid.
- Sher Shah became the ruler of Delhi in 1540.
- Sher Shah introduced new silver coins called "Dam" and they were in circulation till 1835.
- He built a new city on the banks of the river Yamuna near Delhi. Now the old fort called Purana Quila and its mosque is alone surviving.
- He built a Mausoleum at Sasaram, which is considered as one of the master pieces of Indian architecture.

Akbar

- When Akbar ascended the throne in A.D. 1556 he was only 14 years old. His guardian **Bairam Khan** served him as a faithful minister and tutor.
- Bairam Khan, along with Akbar met Hemu in the second Battle of Panipat in 1556. Hemu was initially successful, but lost his consciousness after an arrow hit him. Akbar killed him.
- Akbar abolished the pilgrim tax and in 1564, he abolished jiziya.
- Akbar evolved a new faith called **Din-i-Illahi** or **Divine Faith**. However, his new faith proved to be a failure.
- The land revenue system of Akbar was called Zabti or Bandobast system. It was further improved by Raja Todar Mal. It was known as Dahsala System.

Jahangir

- Jahangir's **'Memoirs'** or **Tuzuk-i-Jahangiri** - (an autobiography of Jahangir) gives an account of his reign.
- He enjoyed a reputation for Justice. He had fixed a big bell with a golden chain. It was hung at the gates of his royal palace. Anyone could pull the chain and ask for justice.
- Jahangir's eldest son, **Khusrau**, rebelled against him. He was arrested and put into prison. **Guru Arjun Dev,** the **fifth Sikh Guru,** who assisted him was killed for refusal to pay a fine.

- During Jahangir's reign **Captain William Hawkins** and **Sir Thomas Roe** visited his court.
- Sir Thomas Roe secured permission from Jahangir in A.D. 1615 to trade at Surat.
- Jahangir died in A.D. 1627.

Shahjahan

- The reign of Shah Jahan is generally considered as the Golden Age of the Mughal period.
- Shah Jahan is called as the Prince of Builders. He had built the Jama Masjid & Red Fort in Delhi and Taj Mahal in Agra.
- The Taj Mahal is the most famous building of Shahjahan. It is located at Agra on the banks of the river Yamuna. Shahjahan built it in memory of his beloved wife Mumtaj Mahal.

Aurangazeb

- Aurangazeb was the last great Mughal ruler. He ascended the throne after killing his three brothers Dara, Shuja and Murad in a fratricidal war.
- Aurangazeb defeated Sikandar Shah of Bijapur and annexed his kingdom. Then, he proceeded against Golkonda and eliminated the Kutb Shahi dynasty. It was also annexed by him.
- Aurangazeb forbade music in the Mughal court. He discontinued the practice of Jarokhadarshan. He also discontinued the celebration of Dasarah and royal astronomers and astrologers were also dismissed from service.
- In 1679, he reimposed jiziya and pilgrim tax.
- Aurangazeb was also against the Sikhs and he executed the ninth Sikh Guru Tegh Bahadur. This had resulted in the transformation of Sikhs into a warring community. The tenth Sikh Guru, Guru Govind Singh, built up a powerful army called the Khalsa to drive the Mughals out of India.
- Aurangazeb died in A.D.1707.

Mughal Administration

- Akbar borrowed Sher Shah's administrative features. So, Sher Shah is regarded as the forerunner of Akbar's administration.
- The empire was divided into 15 provinces during Akbar's rule. They were called Subas.
- The head of a Suba was called Subedar. He was responsible for the civil and military duties.
- The Diwan was in charge of Subas' finance.
- The provinces were divided into Sarkars or districts. Faujdar was the civil and military head of the district. Each Sarkar was administered by a number of officers.
- The Sarkar was further divided into Parganas. Shiqdar, Amil and Fotadar were the officers who were in-charge of the Parganas.
- The lowest unit in Mughal administration was the village.
- The Mughal army consisted of infantry, artillery and elephantry, but no navy.
- Akbar introduced the Mansabdari system, and it was followed by his successors.
- Mansab means Rank or place. There was a grade of Mansabdars. It ranged from owners of 10 to 10,000 horses. Besides the horses, they had to maintain foot soldiers also.
- Raja Todar Mal, the famous revenue minister, worked under Akbar. He also worked under Sher Shah, the forerunner of Akbar.
- Akbar introduced the Zabti system.

SOCIAL SCIENCE

Modern India

THE ESTABLISHMENT OF COMPANY POWER

The Portuguese

On his arrival at Calicut, Vasco-da-Gama was received by its Hindu ruler, known by the title of Zamorin. The arrival of Vasco da Gama led to the establishment of trading stations at Calicut.

Vasco-da-Gama established a factory at Cochin in 1502. He was followed by Alfonso de Albuquerque in 1503. In 1505, the Portuguese decided to appoint a governor to look after their Indian affairs. Francisco de Almeida became the first governor. Albuquerque succeeded him in 1509. Albuquerque was the real founder of the Portuguese empire in the east.

After Albuquerque, the Portuguese began to decline and in the end, they were left only with Goa, Diu and Daman, which they retained till 1961.

The Dutch

The lucrative trade which prospered the Portuguese merchants compelled the jealous Dutch to get direct access to the spice markets in South-East Asia. After undertaking a series of voyages since 1596, they set up a small commercial organisation, named the **United East India Company** in 1602.

- **Formation of the Company :** The Dutch East India Company was formed in March, 1602, by a Charter of the Dutch Parliament,
- **Establishment of Factories:** The Dutch set up factories at Masulipatam (1605), Pulicat (1610), Surat (1616), Bimilipatam (1641), K.Arikal (1645), Chinsura (1653), Kasimbazar, Barangore, Patna, Balasore, Negapatam (all in 1658) and Cochin (1663).
- Pulicat was their main centre in India till 1690, after which Negapatam replaced it.

The French

In the middle of the seventeenth century Louis XIV's finance minister Colbert formed a **French East India Company** named **Compagnie des Indes Orientales** in 1664. Louis XIV provided the Company with an interest-free loan of 3 million livre. The Company was thus, created and financed by the State. After initial attempts made to colonise Madagascar had proved a failure, the Company undertook a fresh expedition in 1667 under the command of Francis Caron accompanied by Marcara, a native of Ispahan reached India and set up the first French factory at Surat in 1668. The second factory was set up at Masulipatnam in 1669. A factory was also developed at Chandernagar (Bengal) between 1690 and 1692. Two major French trading posts in India were Pondicherry, established in 1674 by Francis Martin, and Chandernagar.

In 1693, the newly built French factory at Pondicherry was captured by the Dutch but by the Treaty of Ryswick between the European powers, there was restoration of mutual conquests and the Dutch returned Pondicherry to the French in 1697.

When Dupleix become Governor of Pondicherry, there was a change in the character and objective of the French Company motive of imperial expansion replaced their former commercial motive. This naturally opened a new chapter in the Anglo-French conflict in India.

The English

On 31st December, 1600, Queen Elizabeth granted a Charter to the Company named 'The Governor and Company of Merchants of London Trading in the East Indies' the rights to carry on trade with all countries of the East. This company is commonly known as the English East India Company.

For a few years, the English East India Company confined its activities to the spice trade with Java, Sumatra and the Moluccas. But in 1608 **Captain William Hawkins** came to the court of Jehangir with a letter from James I, king of England, requesting permission for the English merchants to establish in India. But due to vehement opposition of the Portuguese and the Surat merchants, Emperor Jehangir had to change his mind and Hawkin's mission failed. Next year, Jehangir issued a *farman* permitting the English to establish a factory permanently at Surat. In 1615, a British mission under Sir Thomas Roe succeeded in obtaining *firmans* from the Mughal court confirming free trade without liability to pay inland toll. In 1632, the English obtained from the Sultan of Golconda the *Golden farman* granting them the right to trade throughout the kingdom of Golconda on payment of a fixed customs duty of 500 *pagodas* per year. This *farman* was renewed in 1634.

The Company obtained from the Nawab Shuja-ud-din a *farman* in 1651 granting the English the right to carry on their trade on payment of a fixed duty of Rs. 3,000 per year.

British Success in Bengal

The Nawab of Bengal, during the middle of 18th century, was, for all practical purposes, an independent ruler though he nominally acknowledged the supremacy of Mughal king. However, Bengal lacked any political strength or stability. Utilising the opportunity, the English Company not only strengthened themselves but also interfered in Bengal politics. Nawab Sirajud-dulah, realising the danger of English power, captured their Calcutta Fort. English got reinforcement from Madras and regained Calcutta Fort. In the Battle of Plassey in 1757, Englishmen, getting the support from Siraj-ud-dullah's commander-in-chief Mir Jafar, defeated Bengal's army. This battle marked the beginning of the establishment of British power in India. Subsequently, the English Company became all powerful, with Nawab Mir Jafar being a puppet only. The Company made unreasonable demands, leaving Nawab's treasury empty. Mir Qasim, the successor of Mir Jafar, realised the desperate position and took steps to strengthen his position. English angered at it, defeated him in a battle, forcing him to take refuge in Awadh. The combined forces of Nawabs of Awadh and Bengal and Mughal Emperor Shah Alam fought war against British forces in Buxar but were defeated. The Battle of Buxar in 1764 proved to be a turning point in Indian history as Britishers got right to collect revenue in Bengal, Bihar and Orissa and. were left with no potential enemy in the Gangetic plains of India.

THE REVOLT OF 1857

The Revolt of 1857, a watershed in the history of British rule in India, shook the very foundation of the British empire in India. It changed the character of British rule, marking the end of the rule of the East India Company and bringing British India directly under the British Crown.

Causes of the Revolt

As about the nature of the rebellion, there is also considerable controversy regarding its actual causes. Historians, both British and Indian, have over emphasised the importance of military grievances and the greased cartridges affair. But recent research has established beyond doubt that the "greased cartridge" was not the only cause nor even the most important. On the contrary, there were a variety of causes—political, social, religious and economic—which combined to produce the rebellion.

Political Causes: The British policy of annexations had disturbed the political equilibrium in the country. The indiscriminate application of the "Doctrine of Lapse" by Lord Dalhousie had caused widespread discontent. The overthrow of Nawab Wajid Ali Shah of Awadh, annexation of several Hindu principalities and forfeiture on the ex-Peshwa's pension had alarmed the Princely States. The annexation of Princely States was not a blow to the princely families alone, but to their dependent subjects as well.

Administrative and Economic Causes: The annexation of Indian states produced startling economic and social consequences under the British rule. Not only was the Indian aristocracy deprived of power and position, but all high posts, civil and military, were reserved for the Europeans. Racial discrimination was evident everywhere.

The administrative machinery of the East India Company was inefficient and inadequate. The land revenue policy was most unpopular. Many districts in the newly annexed states were in permanent revolt. Many taluqdars (hereditary landlords) were deprived of their position and resources. Large estates were confiscated and auctioned off. Thus the new land revenue settlements made by the East India Company in the newly annexed states, made the aristocracy poor without benefiting the peasantry, who fell into the clutches of unprincipled money-lenders and groaned under the weight of heavy assessments and excessive duties. The judicial system that the Company introduced in India became an instrument of oppression.

Social and Religious Causes: The Traditional Indian social system and culture appeared to be in danger under the reformist zeal of the British administrators. The sway of leaders of orthodoxy both maulvis and pandits regarding common law in matters of succession, inheritance, etc. was challenged. The missionaries were given ample facilities for the propagation of Christianity. The Religious Disabilities Act of 1856 modified Hindu customs; a change in religion did not debar a son from inheriting the property of his heathen father. The Indian mind was getting increasingly convinced that the English were conspiring to convert them into Christianity.

Military Causes: There was widespread discontent amongst the Indian soldiers serving in the British army, in which the majority of the soldiers and junior officers were Indians. The Indian soldiers resented their low pay and poor prospects of promotion. Campaigns in strange lands outside the boundaries of India were unpopular with them, on account of the great hardships involved. Indian soldiers serving overseas were either not given overseas allowances (bhatta) at all or paid much lower than the European soldiers serving in the British army, which was one of the major causes of discontent among Indian soldiers.

Suppression of the Revolt

The rebel leaders could not consolidate their initial gains, while the Governor General, Lord Canning took all possible steps to gather the forces from Bombay, Madras, Calcutta and Punjab to quell the rebellion. On July 16, 1857 Bithur and Kanpur were captured from Nana Saheb, who probably escaped to Nepal. Nana Saheb's Prime Minister Tantia Tope with his soldiers then joined Rani Lakshmibai at Jhansi. On September 20, 1857, the British troops captured Delhi. Bahadur Shah II surrendered to the English on the sole condition that his life should be spared. Thereupon he, along with his favourite Queen Begum Zinnat Mahal and her son, were made captives in the palace of the fort. On September 2, three young sons of Bahadur Shah II were shot dead publicly. Emperor Bahadur Shah was tried by a court martial, found guilty and sentenced to imprisonment for life. He was exiled to Rangoon with his queen Zinnat Mahal, and died after four years, on November 7, 1862.

By the end of 1859 all the great leaders of the Revolt, such as Kunwar Singh, the Ruhela leader Khan Bahadur Khan of Bareilly, Maulvi Ahmadullah of Awadh, Tantia Tope etc. were dead and Begum Hazrat Mahal and Nana Saheb had escaped to Nepal leading to the restoration of the British authority in India fully and firmly.

SOCIAL AND RELIGIOUS MOVEMENT

In the 19th century the emancipation of women and dalit became a matter of prime concern for the socio-religious reformers. Women then were shamelessly exploited, kept backward and were victims of many degrading customs like Sati, female infanticide, purdah, child marriage, polygamy, etc.

In the view of the reformers, as long as women, constituting roughly one-half of the population, remained exploited and backward, society could not advance. Women's status was, therefore, the most important symbol of social change. By the second half of the 19th century British India was bristling with the activity of reform groups which focused attention on women-related issues. Their activities provided a stimulus and the atmosphere to improve the lot of the Indian women. Name of the some pioneers who contributed for the emancipation of women are as follow :

Raja Rammohan Roy : Raja Rammohan Roy was a man of extraordinary intellect. He fought vehemently against the custom of *sati* prevalent in the contemporary society. In 1815, Rammohan founded the *Atmiya Sabha.* On 20th August 1828, he founded the *Brahmo Samaj.*

The *Brahmo Samaj* led a crusade against *sati*, polygamy, child-marriage, caste-system, *purdah* system, untouchability, use of intoxicants etc. The leaders of Brahmo Samaj also worked for the welfare of peasants, liberty of press, social legislation. The *Brahmo Samaj* participated in building up national sentiment by glorifying the Indian culture.

Ishwar Chandra Vidyasagar : Ishwar Chandra Vidyasagar (1820-91) was another reformer in Bengal who championed female education. He was an impassioned supporter of widow remarriage and vehement opponent of polygamy. He urged the British to pass legislation enabling Hindu widows to remarry and prohibiting polygamy. He submitted petitions to this effect to the Indian Legislative Council and to the British Government. Vidyasagar's effort led to the passing of the Hindu Widow Remarriage Act in 1856. To promote female education, Vidyasagar opened a number of schools for girls in Bengal and was closely associated with the Hindu Kanya Vidyalaya founded by J.E.D. Bethune.

Kandukuri Virasalingam Pantulu : Kandukuri Virasalingam Pantulu (1848-1919), a Telugu Brahmin of Madras Presidency, was the earliest champion in South India of women's emancipation. He published

Viveka Vardhani (Journal to Promote Enlightenment), opened his first girls' school in 1874 and made widow remarriage and female education the key points of his programme for social reform.

Mahadev Govind Ranade : Mahadev Govind Ranade (1842-1901) and his wife Ramabai also contributed greatly to the cause of women. In 1869, Ranade joined the Widow Remarriage Association and encouraged widow remarriage and female education and opposed child marriage. He founded the National Social Conference, which became a pre-eminent institution for social reform. The role of Pandita Ramabai (1858-1922) was remarkable as a pioneer in women's education and a rebel champion of women's rights. She founded the ***Sharda Sadan***, a school for widows, in Bombay and at Mukti, near Pune. Her greatest legacy was her effort, the first in India, to educate widows.

Swami Vivekananda : At the turn of the century, Swami Vivekananda argued that women could become a powerful regenerative force.

Swami Dayanand Saraswati : Swami Dayanand Saraswati, the founder of the Arya Samaj, encouraged female education and widow remarriage and condemned the customs he regarded as degrading to women, such as child marriage, dowry and polygamy.

Behramji Malabari : The Parsi social reformer, Behramji Malabari, captured the attention of the British people with his articles in ***The Times*** (of London) on the evils of child marriage and the tragedy of enforced widowhood for young women.

Dhondo Keshav Karve : The greatest champion of the cause of women's emancipation was Dhondo Keshav Karve (1858-1962), who worked the longest for this cause. Karve encouraged widow remarriage. He founded the female school and widow homes in Pune. The curriculum in his schools was designed to make young widows employable and self-sufficient. Karve believed that "widows needed an education that would make them economically independent and enable them to think for themselves". He also founded the first Indian women's university in 1916.

Some Associations for Women

Movements for the emancipation of women and spread of education among women led to the establishment of a number of associations formed for women, which became the medium for the expression of women's opinion. Some of these important associations were as under:

The Bharat Mahila Parishad: was a part of the National Social Conference to provide a forum for the discussion of social issues.

The Arya Mahila Samaj: was founded by Ramabai, wife of Justice Ranade, to provide a support network for newly educated women.

The Bharat Stree Mahamandal: was founded by Sarladevi Chaudhurani at Allahabad in 1910. It was the first permanent association of Indian women to promote their common interests. The Mahamandal's leaders regarded purdah as the main stumbling-block to female education and defined women's issues such as female education, child marriage and women's status in the family.

The Women's Indian Association: was founded by an Irish feminist and theosophist. Dorothy Jinarajadasa, in 1915, with its membership open to both Indians and Europeans. Annie Besant became its first President. The principal work of the WIA was educational and its branches were encouraged to set up adult classes for literacy, sewing and first aid. The WIA was politically active from the beginning and in 1917, it sent a delegation to the Secretary of State, Montagu, to grant franchise for women. The WIA also set up widow homes. Its journal, ***Stri Dharma***, carried news of events of interest to women, reports from its branches, and articles on women's condition.

The National Council of Women for India: was an all-India organisation established in 1925, which was affiliated to the International Council of Women. Mehribai Tata (wife of Dorab Tata) played a key role in its advancement. But on account of its elitist nature, the Council failed to grow and became a vital national organisation.

THE NATIONALIST MOVEMENT

Allan Octavian Hume (A.O. Hume), a retired British member of the Indian Civil Service who had settled at Simla, founded the Indian National Union the fore runner of the Indian National Congress, in 1884. After touring Calcutta, Bombay and Madras (Kolkata, Mumbai and Chennai), Hume announced that a conference of the Indian National Union would be held at Pune in December, which would be composed of educated delegates from all parts of the three presidencies. But cholera having broken out at Pune, the venue of the conference was shifted to Tejpal Sanskrit Pathsala, Bombay. The first session of the Indian National Union was held on December 28, 1885. At the suggestion of Dadabhai Naoroji the name of the organisation was changed to Indian National Congress (INC). Womesh Chandra Banerjee, a leading lawyer of Calcutta (Kolkata), was elected its president.

Early Political Associations

- The British Indian Association — 1851, Bengal
- The Bombay Association — 1852
- East India Association — 1856, London
- Madras Native Association 1852
- Poona Sarvojanik Sabha — 1870
- The Madras Mahajana Sabha — 1884

Indian National Movement (1905-1916)

- The period from 1905 was known as the era of extremism in the Indian National Movement.
- The important extremist leaders were Lala Lajpat Rai, Bal Gangadhar Tilak, Bipin Chandra Pal and Aurobindo Ghosh.

Causes for the Rise of Extremism

1. The failure of the Moderates to win any notable success other than the expansion of the legislative councils by the Indian Councils Act (1892).
2. The economic conditions of the people became worse.
3. The Russo-Japanese war of 1904-05 in which Japan defeated the European power Russia. This encouraged Indians to fight against the European nation, Britain.
4. The immediate cause for the rise of extremism was the reactionary rule of Lord Curzon:
   - He passed the Calcutta Corporation Act, (1899) reducing the Indian control of this local body.
   - The Universities Act (1904) reduced the elected members in the University bodies. It also reduced the autonomy of the universities and made them government departments.
   - The Sedition Act and the Official Secrets Act reduced the freedoms of all people.
   - His worst measure was the Partition of Bengal (1905).

- Bal Gangadhar Tilak is regarded as the real founder of the popular anti-British movement in India. He was known as **'Lokamanya'**. He attacked the British through his weeklies *The Mahratta* and the *Kesari*.
- Tilak set up the Home Rule League in 1916 at Poona and declared "Swaraj is my birth-right and I will have it."

Partition of Bengal and the Rise of Extremism

- The partition of Bengal in 1905 provided a spark for the rise of extremism in the Indian National Movement.
- Curzon's real motives behind this partition were:
  - To break the growing strength of Bengali nationalism since Bengal was the base of Indian nationalism.
  - To divide the Hindus and Muslims in Bengal.
  - To show the enormous power of the British Government in doing whatever it liked.
- The anti-partition movement culminated into the Swadeshi Movement and spread to other parts of India.

Swadeshi Movement

- The Swadeshi Movement involved programmes like the boycott of government service, courts, schools and colleges and of foreign goods, promotion of Swadeshi goods, Promotion of National Education through the establishment of national schools and colleges. It was both a political and economic movement.

Formation of the Muslim League (1906)

- In December 1906, Muslim delegates from all over India met at Dacca for the Muslim Educational Conference.
- Taking advantage of this occasion, Nawab Salimullah of Dacca proposed the setting up of an organisation to look after the Muslim interests. The proposal was accepted.
- The All-India Muslim League was finally set up on December 30, 1906.

Minto-Morley Reforms – 1909

- Minto, the Viceroy and Morley, the Secretary of State for India jointly proposed reforms to the Indian Councils. An Act, called the **Indian Councils Act or the Minto-Morley Reforms Act** was passed in 1909.
- It introduced reforms in the functioning of the Indian Councils. It increased the number of elected members in the Councils.
- A separate communal electorate was introduced for the Muslims.

The Lucknow Pact (1916)

- During the 1916 Congress session at Lucknow two major events occurred. The divided Congress became united. An understanding for joint action against the British was reached between the Congress and the Muslim League and it was called the Lucknow Pact.
- It was at this session Jawaharlal Nehru met Gandhiji for the first time.
- The signing of the Lucknow Pact by the Congress and the Muslim League in 1916

marked an important step in the Hindu-Muslim unity.

The Home Rule Movement (1916)

- Two Home Rule Leagues were established, one by B.G. Tilak at Poona in April 1916 and the other by Mrs. Annie Besant at Madras in September 1916.
- The aim of the Movement was to get self-government for India within the British Empire. It believed freedom was the natural right of all nations.
- While Tilak's Movement concentrated on Maharashtra, Annie Besant's Movement covered the rest of the country.

Montague – Chelmsford Reforms Act, 1919

- **Montague,** the Secretary of State for India and **Chelmsford,** the Viceroy of India were jointly responsible for passing of this Act in the British Parliament.
- By this Act separate electorates were given to three other communities – **Christians, Anglo Indians** and **the Sikhs.**
- It introduced Dyarchy in the Province. More Indians entered the Legislative bodies.
- Mrs. Annie Besant described this Act as ungenerous for England to offer and unworthy for India to accept.

Revolutionary Movements

- The revolutionaries were not satisfied with the methods of both the moderates and extremists. Hence, they started many revolutionary secret organizations.
- In Bengal, Anusilan Samiti and Jugantar were established. In Maharashtra Savarkar brothers had set up Abhinava Bharat. In the Madras Presidency, Bharathmatha Association was started by Nilakanta Bramachari.
- In Punjab, Ajit Singh set up a secret society to spread revolutionary ideas among the youth.
- In London, at India House, Shyamji Krishna Verma gathered young Indian nationalists like Madan Lal Dhingra, Savarkar, V.V.S. Iyer and T.S.S. Rajan.
- Lala Hardyal set up the 'Ghadar Party' in USA to organise revolutionary activities from outside India.

Rowlatt Act (1919)

- In 1917, a committee was set up under the presidentship of Sir Sydney Rowlatt to look into the militant Nationalist activities. On the basis of its report the Rowlatt Act was passed in March 1919 by the Central Legislative Council. As per this Act, any person could be arrested on the basis of suspicion. No appeal or petition could be filed against such arrests.
- This Act was called the Black Act and it was widely opposed. An all-India hartal was organized on 6 April 1919. Meetings were held all over the country. Mahatma Gandhi was arrested near Delhi. Two prominent leaders of Punjab, Dr. Satya Pal and Dr. Saifuddin Kitchlew, were arrested in Amritsar.

Jallianwala Bagh Massacre (13 April, 1919)

- The Jallianwala Bagh Massacre took place on 13 April 1919 and it remained a turning point in the history of India's freedom movement.
- On 13th April, the Baisakhi day (harvest festival), a public meeting was organized at the Jallianwala Bagh (garden). Gen. Dyer marched in and without any warning opened fire on the crowd. The firing continued for about 10 to 15 minutes and it stopped only after the ammunition exhausted.

Khilafat Movement

- The chief cause of the Khilafat Movement was the defeat of Turkey in the First World War.The harsh terms of the Treaty of Sevres (1920) was felt by the Muslims as a great insult to them.
- The whole movement was based on the Muslim belief that the Caliph (the Sultan of Turkey) was the religious head of the Muslims all over the world. The Muslims in India were upset over the British attitude against Turkey and launched the Khilafat Movement.
- Maulana Abul Kalam Azad, M.A. Ansari, Saifuddin Kitchlew and the Ali brothers were the prominent leaders of this movement.
- A Khilafat Committee had been formed and on 19th October 1919, the whole country had observed the Khilafat day. On 23 November, a joint conference of the Hindus and the Muslims had also been held under the chairmanship of Mahatma Gandhi.

Non-Co-operation Movement (1920-1922)

- Mahatma Gandhi announced his plan to begin Non-Cooperation with the government as a sequel to the Rowlatt Act, Jallianwala Bagh massacre and the Khilafat Movement. It was approved by the Indian National Congress at the Nagpur session in December, 1920.
- The Congress observed the Non-Co-operation movement in 1920. The main aim of this movement was to attain Swaraj through non–violent and peaceful means.

- The programmes of the Non-Co-operation Movement were:
  - Surrender of titles and honorary positions.
  - Resignation of membership from the local bodies.
  - Boycott of elections held under the provisions of the 1919 Act.
  - Boycott of government functions.
  - Boycott of courts, government schools and colleges.
  - Boycott of foreign goods.
  - Establishment of national schools, colleges and private panchayat courts.
  - Popularizing swadeshi goods and khadi.
- National schools such as the Kashi Vidyapeeth, the Bihar Vidyapeeth and the Jamia Millia Islamia were set up.
- On 5th February an angry mob set fire to the police station at Chauri Chaura and twenty two police men were burnt to death.

Swaraj Party

- Leaders like Motilal Nehru and Chittranjan Das formed a separate group within the Congress known as the Swaraj Party on 1 January 1923.
- The Swarajists wanted to contest the council elections and wreck the government from within. Elections to Legislative Councils were held in November 1923. In this, the **Swaraj Party** gained impressive successes. In the Central Legislative Council Motilal Nehru became the leader of the party whereas in Bengal the party was headed by C.R. Das.

Simon Commission (1927)

- The Act of 1919 included a provision for its review after a lapse of ten years. However, the review commission was appointed by the British Government two years earlier of its schedule in 1927. It came to be known as Simon Commission after the name of its chairman, Sir John Simon.
- All its seven members were Englishmen. As there was no Indian member in it, the Commission faced a lot of criticism even before its landing in India. Almost all the political parties including the Congress decided to oppose the Commission.
- The report of the Simon Commission was published in May 1930.

Nehru Report (1928)

- The Secretary of State, Lord Birkenhead, challenged the Indians to produce a Constitution that would be acceptable to all. The challenge was accepted by the Congress, which convened an all party meeting on 28 February 1928.
- A committee consisting of eight was constituted to draw up a blueprint for the future Constitution of India. It was headed by Motilal Nehru. The Report published by this Committee came to be known as the **Nehru Report**.

Lahore Session (1929)

- On Dec. 19, 1929, under the Presidentship of J.L. Nehru, the INC, as its Lahore session, declared *Poorna Swaraj* (Complete Independence) as its ultimate goal.
- On Dec. 31, 1929, the newly adopted tricolour flag was unfurled and Jan. 26. 26, 1930 was fixed as the First Independence Day, which was to be celebrated every year.

Civil Disobedience Movement (1930-1934)

- In December 1929,the annual session of the Congress was held at Lahore. During this session presided over by Jawaharlal Nehru the Congress passed the **Poorna Swaraj** resolution.
- The Congress had observed January 26, 1930 as the Day of Independence. Since then January 26th had been observed as a day of independence every year. The same date later became the Republic Day when the Indian Constitution was enforced in 1950.
- On 12th March 1930, Gandhi began his famous March to Dandi with his chosen 79 followers to break the salt laws. He reached the coast of Dandi on 5 April 1930 after marching a distance of 200 miles and on 6 April formally launched the Civil Disobedience Movement by breaking the salt laws.

Round Table Conference

- The first Round Table Conference was held in November 1930 at London and it was boycotted it by the Congress.
- On 8 March 1931 the **Gandhi-Irwin Pact** was signed. As per this pact, Mahatma Gandhi agreed to suspend the Civil-Disobedience Movement and participate in the Second-Round Table Conference.
- In September 1931, the Second Round Table Conference was held at London. Mahatma Gandhi participated in the Conference but returned to India disappointed as no agreement could be reached on the demand of complete independence and on the communal question.
- In January 1932, the Civil-Disobedience Movement was resumed. The government responded to it by arresting Mahatma Gandhi

and Sardar Patel and by reimposing the ban on the Congress party.

Poona Pact (1932)

- On 16 August 1932 the British Prime Minister Ramsay MacDonald made an announcement, which came to be as the **Communal Award**. According to this award, the depressed classes were considered as a separate community and as such provisions were made for separate electorates for them.
- Mahatma Gandhi protested against the Communal Award and went on a fast unto death in the Yeravada jail on 20 September 1932. Finally, an agreement was reached between Dr. Ambedkar and Gandhi. This agreement came to be called as the **Poona Pact**. The British Government also approved of it. Accordingly, 148 seats in different Provincial Legislatures were reserved for the Depressed Classes in place of 71 as provided in the Communal Award.

The Government of India Act 1935

- The Government of India Act was passed in 1935. It was based on the **Simon Commission** report and the proposals of the three Round Table Conferences.
- It introduced the following changes. This act(1) Introduced provincial autonomy, (2) Abolished dyarchy in the provinces, (3) Established federal Government at the Centre, (4) Provided for the establishment of a federal court to decide the conflicts between the provinces and the centre and (5) Provided for the establishment of a Federal Reserve Bank.

Cripps Mission (1942)

- The British Government in its effort to secure Indian co-operation in the Second World War sent Sir Stafford Cripps to India on 23 March 1942. This is known as **Cripps Mission**.
- The main recommendations of Cripps were:
  - The promise of Dominion Status to India,
  - Protection of minorities,
  - Setting up of a Constituent Assembly in which there would be representatives from the Princely States along with those of the British Provinces,
  - There would be provision for any Province of British India not prepared to accept this Constitution, either to retain its present constitutional position or frame a constitution of its own.
- Gandhi called Cripp's proposals as a **"Post-dated Cheque"**.

Quit India Movement (1942-1944)

- The All India Congress Committee met at Bombay on 8 August 1942 and passed the famous **Quit India Resolution**. On the same day, Gandhi gave his call of **'do or die'.**
- On 8th and 9th August 1942, the government arrested all the prominent leaders of the Congress. Mahatma Gandhi was kept in prison at Poona. Pandit Jawaharlal Nehru, Abul Kalam Azad, and other leaders were imprisoned in the Ahamednagar Fort.
- Quit India Movement was the final attempt for country's freedom.

Naval Mutiny (1945)

- A revolt took place in *HMS Talwar* on Feb. 18, 1945 in Bombay due to racial discrimination, unpalatable food and abuse after the rarrest of B.C. Dutta who had written 'British Quit India' on the wall.
- Next day, *HMS Hindustan* in Karachi also revolted.
- Soon the revolt spread to other places also. Im Bombay, the mutineers hoisted the tricolour on their ship masts together with a portrait of S.C. Bose and shouted Jai Hind those belonging to the Inidna National Army.
- It was suppressed after persuasion by the Indian leaders.

Indian National Army

- On 2 July 1943, Subhash Chandra Bose reached Singapore and gave the rousing war cry of **'Dilli Chalo'**. He was made the President of Indian Independence League and soon became the supreme commander of the **Indian National Army**.He gave the country the slogan of **Jai Hind**.
- The Indian National Army marched towards Imphal after registering its victory over Kohima. After Japan's surrender in 1945, the INA failed in its efforts.
- The trial of the soldiers of INA was held at Red Fort in Delhi. Pandit Jawaharlal Nehru, Bhulabhai Desai and Tej Bahadur Sapru fought the case on behalf of the soldiers.

Cabinet Mission (1946)

- After the Second World War, Lord Atlee became the Prime Minister of England.
- On 15 March, 1946 Lord Atlee made a historic announcement in which the right to self-determination and the framing of a Constitution for India were conceded. Consequently, three members of the British Cabinet - Pathick Lawrence, Sir Stafford Cripps and A. V. Alexander - were sent to India. This is known as the **Cabinet Mission**.

- The Cabinet Mission put forward a plan for solution of the constitutional problem. Provision was made for three groups of provinces to possess their separate constitutions. The Cabinet Mission also proposed the formation of a Union of India, comprising both the British India and the Princely States. The Union would remain in charge of only foreign affairs, defence and communications leaving the residuary powers to be vested in the provinces. A proposal was envisaged for setting up an Interim Government, which would remain in office till a new government was elected on the basis of the new Constitution framed by the Constituent Assembly. Both the Muslim League and the Congress accepted the plan.

Mountbatten Plan (1947)

- On 20 February 1947, Prime Minister Atlee announced in the House of Commons the definite intention of the British Government to transfer power to responsible Indian hands by a date not later than June 1948.
- Lord Mountbatten armed with vast powers became India's Viceroy on 24 March 1947. The partition of India and the creation of Pakistan appeared inevitable to him.
- After extensive consultation Lord Mountbatten put forth the plan of partition of India on **3 June 1947.** The Congress and the Muslim League ultimately approved the **Mountbatten Plan.**

Indian Independence Act 1947

- The salient features of this Act were:
  - The partition of the country into India and Pakistan would come into effect from 15 August 1947.
  - The British Government would transfer all powers to these two Dominions.
  - A Boundary Commission would demarcate the boundaries of the provinces of the Punjab and Bengal.
  - The Act provided for the transfer of power to the Constituent Assemblies of the two Dominions, which will have full authority to frame their respective Constitutions.
- **C. Rajagopalachari** became the first and last Indian Governor-General of India. When India became a Republic on 26 January 1950 **Dr. Rajendra Prasad** became the first President of our country.

World History

RENAISSANCE

Renaissance means rebirth. It was initially used to describe revival of interest in the learning of older civilizations of Greece and Rome. Knowledge of their achievements led to a series of new developments in the field of art, literature, religion, science and politics. Renaissance began in Italy in the 16th century. Its main emphasis was on freedom of the individual, inalienable rights of the individual and respecting the dignity of man. It stressed on the limitless potentialities of man rejected religious asceticism and withdrawal from the world. It aimed at providing happiness to man. The emphasis shifted from divinity to humanity, i.e., human being. The Renaissance era gave rise to quest for knowledge, especially history and literature. The effects of Renaissance were development of humanism, nationalism, spread of education, growth in trade and commerce, exposure of myths and establishment of reasoning. Some of the greatest achievements were made in painting, sculpture and architecture. Leonardo da Vinci, Michael Angelo and Raphael were famous artists of that time. Dante was a great poet of that time while Machiavelli, a diplomat, historian and political philosopher wrote about sta:tecraft. As the Renaissance spread throughout Europe, it took on a more religious character, paving the way for Reformation. Moreover, during the period, Europeans began to look for sea route to Asia, with Columbus reaching Central America in 1492 and Vasco-da-Gama in India in 1498.

REFORMATION

The key event of the 16th century in Europe was the Reformation, a movement to reform the Catholic church. It began in Germany and then spread throughout northern Europe. Martin Luther, a German theologian and religious transformer set alight widespread discontent against the Church. New Protestant Church belonging to reformers sprang up, with the aim of following only the teachings of the Bible, and getting rid of church traditions. Several powerful kings and princes supported the reformers like John Calvin, Olrich Zwingli and others. Although the Catholic church responded by introducing reforms from within, violent conflicts between Catholics and Protestants erupted. In 1534, King Henry VIII took the help of the English church because the Pope would not let him divorce his first wife. Though Queen Mary tried to restore Church's authority in England, getting the nickname "Bloody Mary" due to execution of Protestants, the Catholics were reduced to minority in England.

ENGLISH REVOLUTION OF 1688

England was ruled by despotic rulers in the first half of 17th century — James I and Charles I. They believed that they were appointed by God, not answerable to Parliament or people. The dispute ,between the King and Parliament led to civil war in England in 1642. James I was defeated and executed. In 1660, Charles II was appointed king on the condition that he will not interfere in religious affairs of the people and rule with consultation with Parliament. However, James II followed his father's footsteps and tried to breakaway from Parliament's supervision and gave more powers to Catholics in the Protestant dominated country. This led to revolt by the people who invited the Dutch Protestant King William to come to England. James II fled to France. Williams and daughters of James II, Mary were declared joint Monarchs. The revolution has been described as glorious due to lack of bloodshed. The revolution led to end of divine rights of Kings, acceptance of the authority of the Parliament, independent judiciary, freedom of Press and supremacy of Protestants in England.

AMERICAN WAR OF INDEPENDENCE

With the rise of Capitalism and industrial revolution in Europe, the demand for raw materials, cheap labour and markets grew. European kings encouraged exploration of new areas which were subsequently colonized. In 1492, Columbus had discovered West Indies and later America was found. By the middle of 18th century, a large part of North America had come under England's occupation. Landless peasants, Protestants and others started living in this area. English Parliament put severe restrictions on the American colonies, politically as well as economically. Colonies were forbidden to start certain industries and heavy duties were imposed. The imposition of stamp duty in 1765 aroused violent resentment among Americans and there were uprisings, besides boycott of English goods. Though English Parliament agreed to revoke stamp duty, it later imposed tax on tea to assert their right to levy taxes. Several colonies refused to unload the tea and in 1773, a group of people boarded a ship in Boston and threw tea into water. The incident is called "Boston Tea Party". Subsequently, in 1775, English troops fought with local troops. On July 4, 1776, the Declaration of Independence was adopted by American leaders. It said all men are created equal; People have a right to set up their own government and the colonies have right to be free and independent states. The war between English and American forces intensified with other European countries favouring the colonial forces. The English forces surrendered in 1781 and in 1783, England recognized the independence of its 13 former colonies.

England, despite being a powerful nation, lost against the local troops due to distance constraints, help by other European nations to American leaders, good leadership of the war of Americans and lack of coordination among English Generals.

The independence of America was an important event in the world history. For the first time, a federal Government, democratic in character, was sworn in under the written constitution. The event was a great setback to England. It served as an example to other revolutionaries of the world and the French Revolution followed a few years later.

FRENCH REVOLUTION

France was a strong and powerful state in the 18th century. However, internally there were problems. A small section of people owned most of the land and occupied all senior administrative and army positions. There was a large number of peasants who lived under miserable conditions. In between was the middle class, which was educated and sometimes rich, yet did not have social status or political rights. There were a large number of thinkers in France who advocated rationalism, democracy and attacked clergy. Moreover, the wars abroad and large patronage brought the King to the point of bankruptcy. A stand off between the royal forces and protestors led to the fall of Bastille prison on July 14, 1789. A new constitution was adopted, declaring equality, liberty and fraternity for everyone. The privileged class people tied to other countries to sought their help and France was involved in wars with its neighbouring countries. However, a new order had been established in France and it reached new heights under the leadership of Napolean Bonaparte.

INDUSTRIAL REVOLUTION

In middle ages, the occupation of majority of the population in Europe was Agriculture and whatever trade was undertaken, was done on barter system: However, discoveries and new inventions, spread of education and new ideas led to development of methods and machineries that could produce faster, better and cheaper goods. The industrial revolution began in England because of availability of coal and iron, availability of labour, peaceful atmosphere and availability of good Navy to carry new methods to England and finished goods to the markets. However, it spread to other European nations as well because colonies were being established in Asia and Africa and cheap raw material and labour was easily available. These were good markets for ready material and the businessmen supported the scientists and engineers to do more research. The profits made from selling goods were ploughed back into the industry, leading to more development. The development of mechanical and electrical energy and establishment of big industries also helped the revolution. It led to large scale changes in textiles, iron extraction, mining, transportation, communication, agriculture and energy. The industrial revolution also had some adverse impacts as small farmers and industries were wiped off. It led to exploitation of poor, ladies, children and people of colonies; unemployment, wars for colonies, urbanization and increase in crimes. The positive impact was improvement in life-styles, increase in national income, increase in agricultural output and enactment of legislations for workers' welfare.

COLONIALISM

To sustain the growth of their industries, European nations needed raw material, cheep labour and ready markets. Asian and African nations were their easy targets. Moreover, for strategic, religious and military reasons, it was found useful by Europeans to have as many colonies as possible. However, these European nations fought among themselves several times to take control over colonies. The colonies were economically exploited by the Europeans and their social and political setup demolished. Their cultures were spoiled -and their inhabitants were tortured. The positive aspect of colonialism was spread of education, scientific temperament, nationalism, good administration and development of infrastructure in these colonies. Some of the colonies and colonisers were as follows:

- **Colonies of Belgium:** Congo
- **Colonies of England:** Cape Colony, Bechuanaland, Rhodesia, Natal, Transvaal, Orange Free State, Gold Coast, Nigeria, Egypt, Sudan, India, Canada, New Zealand, Australia
- **Colonies of France:** Algeria, Tunisia, Senegal, Moracco, Somaliland, Mada gascar, Cambodia, Parts of India, Laos
- **Colonies of Holland:** Malaya Islands, Indonesia
- **Colonies of Germany:** Tanganika, Cameroon
- **Colonies of Portugal:** Angola, Goa in India
- **Colonies of Italy:** Eriterea, Syria, parts of Somaliland, Libya
- **Colonies of Russia:** Afghanistan, Persia, Manchuria, Korea

NATIONALISM

The spirit of love for the nation got prominent in the 18th century. It began in Europe and then spread to Asia and Africa. Several countries became independent consequently:

(a) **Spain:** Democratic government established in 1870

(b) **Greece:** Got independence from Turkey in 1829

(c) **Belgium:** Got independence from Holland in 1930

(d) **Poland:** People of Warsaw revolted against Russian rule in 1848

(e) **Australia:** Democratic Constitution accepted in 1867

(f) **Balkon States:** Serbia, Romania and Montanegro got liberated from Turkey in 1855

(g) **Italy:** Unification of Italy completed in 1871 with the efforts of Mazzini and Garibaldi

(h) **Germany:** Unification of Germany completed in 1870 with the efforts of Bismarck

(i) **China:** Dr Sun-Yat-Sen led a successful movement in establishing a democracy in 1911 but in 1949, a Communist government was set up under Mao-Tse-Tung

(j) **Turkey:** Mustafa Kamal Pasha established democracy in 1923, after ousting the forces of Italy, France and Greece

(k) **Iran:** Feudalism ended in 1925 and Sardar Raza Khan became King

(l) **Syria:** Syrians opposed French forces and became independent in 1936

(m) **Palestine:** After England's departure, Jews declared an independent nation by name 'Israel'

(n) **Afghanistan:** Rebellion in 1926 forced the British to free it

(o) **Egypt:** Movement under the leadership of Jagalul Pasha led to independence in 1936; Suez Canal nationalised in 1956 leading to end of European interference

(p) **Indonesia:** It was a colony of Holland but went under Japan's control during Second World War. However, after the end of war, Indonesia became independent in 1949

(q) **Malaysia:** People there opposed the British rule and it got independence in 1957

(r) **Ghana:** Got independence in 1957

(s) **Algeria:** National Movement got momentum during Second World War and independence came in 1963

(t) **Kenya:** "Mao-Mao" movement led to its independence in 1965

In 1960, Congo and Mali became independent while in 1961, Sierre Lone, Somalia, in 1962 Jamaica, Rwanda, Trinidad, Tobago, Uganda and in 1965, Zanzibar became independent. East Timor(2002) is the latest country to join the independent nations.

RUSSIAN REVOLUTION

In 1917, the monarchs of Russia Czars were overthrown and the world's first communist state was set up by Bolshaviks under the leadership of Lenin. The revolution was sparked by Russia's crippling defeat in the first world war, the resultant hardship at home and the inability of the king to cope up with this. Riots and strikes spread throughout the country. The removal of the Czar was an easy job but Bolsheviks were opposed by nationalists, non-Russians, democrats and military dictators but by 1920, the Communist government was firmly in the seat.

FIRST-WORLD WAR

Rivalry between European nations over the issue of colonies and political dominations led to tension that had been building up since late 19th century. Germany was a late entrant into the race for colonies and hence resented the expansion of French and British empire. France had been defeated completely by Germans in 1870. In Balkan area, Russia and Austria-Hungary had deep suspicion about each other. Britain had been traditional rival of France but fearing the might of German navy, both the countries agreed to cooperate in case of an attack. Moreover, German economy had made tremendous progress, leaving Britain and France far behind. The Ottoman Empire, comprising Turkey had occupied areas in Balkan but in 1912 they became independent after fighting a war. The precipitating matter for the first world war was the assassination of Archduke Francis Ferdinand, heir to the throne of Austria-Hungary in Sarajevo. Austria, suspecting Serb hand, declared war on Serbia. Russia declared support for Serbia. Germany declared war on Russia and France while Britain declared war on Germany. A large number of new weapons, like aircrafts, tanks, submarines and poison gas were used in the war. America entered into the war in 1917, siding with France and Britain. Russia withdrew from the war in 1918, after the revolution at home. All the colonies in the world took part in the war as per their ruler's intention. The war ended in 1918 with Bulgaria, Germany, Turkey and Austria-Hungary surrendering.

SECOND WORLD WAR

The Second World War, like the first, started in Europe and assumed the character of a world war. In Germany, the Nazi forces under the leadership of Adolf Hitler, had come into power, exploiting Germany's humiliation at defeat in the first world war and signing of an unjust treaty after the war. The League of Nations set up after the first world war did not prove effective in dealing with the problems of that period. Fascist forces had taken over in Italy while Japan was pursuing policies of expansion and militarism. Britain, France, USA initially overlooked the German invasion and avoided Russia's call to form alliance to check the aggression, but finally they had to come under an umbrella of Allied Power to check the advance of Axis powers which included Germany, Italy, Japan and their satellites. Allied powers included Britain, France, Russia, USA, China, Australia, Belgium etc. The war started on September 1, 1939 when Germany attacked Poland. This was followed by attacks on Norway, Denmark, Belgium and Holland. France surrendered in June, 1940. A year later, Germany attacked Soviet Union, Japan attacked American naval base of Pearl Harbour in Hawai in December, 1941 bringing in USA into war. By the middle of 1942, Axis forces had reached their peak but then their decline began. In all fronts, Germany and Italy suffered setbacks and they surrendered in May 1945. But Japan had to be attacked by nuclear bombs twice before being subjected to surrender.

REUNIFICATION OF GERMANY

Mikhail Gorbachev's tenure as the President of Soviet Union was period of weakening of Communist forces all over the world. The East Germany Communist regime collapsed in late 1989, as waves of East Germans took advantage of ending of travel restrictions between Hungary and Austria to leave their country. About 2 lakh East Germans left for the West and on November 9, 1989, the Berlin Wall was breached and within a weak, 3 million East Germans crossed over. The Politburo and Central Committee of Communist Party resigned within weeks. In 1990, the action of reunification got unprecedented momentum and on October 3, 1990, the two states became one country. Two months later, a united Germany voted in the first nationwide elections since 1932.

Multiple Choice Questions

1. Indus Valley Civilisation people did not probably know about the use of:
   A. cow B. bull
   C. horse D. dog
2. Among the four Vedas, the first one was:
   A. Rig Veda B. Sama Veda
   C. Yajur Veda D. Atharva Veda
3. The Ramayana was written by:
   A. Ved Vyas B. Tulsidas
   C. Dronacharya D. Valmiki
4. Vardhman Mahavir was the .... Tirthankar of Jainism.
   A. first B. second
   C. third D. twenty fourth
5. The forces of Alexander and Porus fought on the banks of river:
   A. Ravi B. Jhelum
   C. Sutlej D. Indus
6. At the time of Alexander's invasion, Magadha was being ruled by:
   A. Nanda Kings B. Gupta Kings
   C. Maurya Kings D. Vardhana King
7. The Satavahans ruled mostly in:
   A. Avadh B. Andhra
   C. Central India D. Magadh
8. Ashoka belonged to:
   A. Gupta dynasty B. Maurya dynasty
   C. Kushan dynasty D. Saka dynasty
9. Vikramaditya was the name given to:
   A. Chandragupta Maurya
   B. Bindusar
   C. Chandragupta II
   D. Samudragupta
10. Harshavardhana, the last great Hindu King of Northem India ruled in the:
    A. 2nd century AD B. 4th century AD
    C. 7th century AD D. 10th century AD
11. The slave dynasty was established by:
    A. Balban B. lltutmish
    C. Razia Begum D. Outb-ud-din Aibak
12. Razia Begum was the daughter of:
    A. Iltutmish
    B. Balban
    C. Alauddin Khilji
    D. Ghayasuddin Tughlak
13. Tughlaq dynasty occupied Delhi throne after decline of:
    A. Lodhi dynasty B. Khilji dynasty
    C. Slave dynasty D. Suri dynasty
14. The King, known for transferring the capital from Delhi to Daulatabad was:
    A. Firoz Tughlaq
    B. Ghyasuddin Tughlaq
    C. Muhammad Tughlaq
    D. Muhammad Bin Oasim
15. In the first battle of Panipat, Babar fought against:
    A. Sher Shah Suri B. Firoz Tughlaq
    C. Humayun D. Ibrahim Lodhi
16. Fatehpur Sikri has been built by:
    A. Babur B. Aurangzeb
    C. Akbar D. Jahangir
17. Khurram was the original name of:
    A. Akbar B. Jahangir
    C. Shahjahan D. Shah Alam
18. Din-i-Ilahi was launched by:
    A. Akbar B. Humayun
    C. Babur D. Jahangir
19. Sher Shah defeated which Mughal King:
    A. Babur B. Humayun
    C. Akbar D. Aurangzeb
20. The last Mughal King was:
    A. Shah Alam
    B. Muhammad Shah Rangeela
    C. Bahadur Shah Zafar
    D. Dost Muhammad
21. Which battle proved crucial in giving foothold to the British in India?
    A. Battle of Plassey
    B. Battle of Buxar

C. Third Battle of Panipat
D. Battle of Mysore

22. Sati was abolished by:
A. Lord Comwallis B. Lord Clive
C. Lord Wellesley D. Lord Bentinck

23. The partition of Bengal was carried out by:
A. Lord Minto B. Lord Curzon
C. Lord Canning D. Lord Ripon

24. At the time of independence, the Governor General of India was:
A. Lord Mountbatten
B. Lord Wavell
C. Rajgopalachari
D. Lord Linlithgow

25. Krishnadeva Rai was the great:
A. Chola King
B. Pallava King
C. Rashtrakuta King
D. King of Vijayanagar empire

26. The Sikh guru to be beheaded by Mughal King was:
A. Guru Gobind Singh
B. Guru Tegh Bahadur
C. Guru Angad Dev
D. Guru Arjan

27. Who was not involved in 1857 rebellion:
A. Nana Saheb B. Kunwar Singh
C. Ranjit Singh D. Rani Jhansi

28. People of Ongese tribe live in:
A. Andaman Islands B. Bihar
C. Nilgiri hills D. Meghalaya

29. Rajput King Rana Pratap fought the Mughal forces in the:
A. Battle of Khanwah
B. Battle of Haldighati
C. Battle of Thanesar
D. Battle of Wandiwash

30. Chand Bibi is known for:
A. Participating in 1857 revolt
B. Social religious reforms process
C. Valiantly fighting the Mughal forces
D. None of the above

31. Simon Commission came to India in:
A. 1927 B. 1928
C. 1929 D. 1930

32. The Congress split among the extremists and the moderates in:
A. 1906 B. 1915
C. 1907 D. 1927

33. Chauri-Chaura incident led to the suspension of:
A. Civil Disobedience Movement
B. Quit India Movement
C. Khilafat Agitation
D. Non-Cooperation Movement

34. The Congress participated in which Round Table Conference:
A. First only B. Second only
C. First and Third D. All three

35. At the time of Indian independence, Britain was being ruled by:
A. Labour party B. Conservative party
C. Liberal party D. National government

36. Delhi was made capital by the British govemment in:
A. 1892 B. 1905.
C. 1911 D. 1927

37. Permanent settlement of Bengal was introduced in:
A. 1757 B. 1763
C. 1793 D. 1858

38. The first President of the Congress was:
A. A.O. Hume B. S.N. Banerjee
C. D.B. Naoroji D. W.C. Banerjee

39. The Grand Trunk Road was built by:
A. Chandragupta B. Sher Shah Suri
C. Jahangir D. Lord Bentinck

40. Balban belonged to:
A. Khilji dynasty B. Tughlaq dynasty
C. Slave dynasty D. Suri-dynasty

41. Which among the following was not a Rajput dynasty?
A. Solankis B. Rashtrakutas
C. Chauhans D. Chandelas

42. Aryabhatta was the famous:
A. Gupta King
B. astronomer and mathematician
C. poet
D. spy

43. Hieun Tsang came to India during the reign of:
A. Ashok B. Chandragupta
C. Skandagupta D. Harshavardhana

44. Who among the following was an expert in medicine?
A. Banabhatta B. Ashvaghosha
C. Charaka D. Satkarni

45. The favourite pastime of the early Aryans was:
A. chariot racing B. playing dice
C. painting D. dancing and music

46. Poet Amir Khusro lived during the reign of:
A. Balban B. Qutub-ud-din Aibak
B. Iltutmish D. Alau-din Khilji

47. Chinese pilgrim Fa-hien visited India during:
A. 3rd century BC B. 4th century BC
C. 5th century AD D. 4th century AD

48. Sufi saints mostly belonged to:
A. Islam B. Hinduism
C. Christianity D. Buddhism

49. Who among the following is known as the Indian Napoleon?
A. Chandragupta Maurya
B. Samudragupta
C. Chandragupta Vikramaditya
D. Bindusar

50. The Bahmani Kingdom existed in the:
A. 13th century B. 14th century
C. 15th century D. 16th century

51. English was made medium of higher education in India by:
A. Lord Mayo B. Lord Chelmsford
C. Lord Rippon D. Lord Bentinck

52. First Indian to be Governor-General was:
A. C. Rajagopalachari
B. Pt. Nehru
C. Sardar Patel
D. Rajendra Prasad

53. Nadir Shah invaded and sacked Delhi in the year:
A. 1645 B. 1695
C. 1739 D. 1752

54. Brahmo Samaj was founded by:
A. Devendranath Tagore
B. A.O. Hume
C. Dayanand Saraswati
D. Raja Ram Mohan Roy

55. The battle of Wandiwash was fought between:
A. the English and the French
B. the English and Tipu Sultan
C. the English and the Dutch
D. the English and the Mughal emperor

56. The reign of which Mugal emperor is called the golden age of the Mughal dynasty?
A. Humayun B. Akbar
C. Shahjahan D. Aurangzeb

57. Banaras Hindu University was founded by:
A. C.R. Das
B. Pt. J.L. Nehru
C. Madan Mohan Malviya
D. Vivekananda

58. Gandhara School of Art flourished during:
A. Ashoka
B. Kanishka
C. Chandragupta Maurya
D. Samudragupta

59. Treaty of Seringapatam was signed between:
A. Tipu Sultan and Nawab of Hyderabad
B. Tipu Sultan and the French
C. Tipu Sultan and the English
D. Tipu Sultan and Hyder Ali

60. Which of the following happened first?
A. Simon Commission
B. Jallianwala Bagh tragedy
C. Resolution of Purna Swaraj
D. Non-Cooperation Movement

61. The first woman President of the Congress was:
A. Annie Besant
B. Sarojini Naidu
C. Indira Gandhi
D. Vijaya Lakshmi Pandit

62. Who among the following was an extremist leader in the early phase of the Congress?
A. Dadabhai Naoroji
B. Gopal Krishna Gokhale
C. C. Rajgopalachari
D. Bal Gangadhar Tilak

63. The main aim of the Swaraj party was:
A. to launch Non-Cooperation Movement
B. to support the extremist
C. to take part in the legislative council meetings and voice the problems of India and the Indians
D. Boycott the foreign goods

64. "Delhi Chalo" was the slogan of:
A. Bhagat Singh
B. Subhash Chandra Bose
C. Mahatma Gandhi
D. Lala Lajpat Rai

65. 'Sardar' was the title given to Vallabh Bhai Patel by:
A. Mahatma Gandhi
B. the British government
C. M.L. Nehru
D. G.K. Gokhale

66. Annual festivals in memory of Shivaji and Lord Ganesha were started by:
A. G.K. Gokhale B. A.A. Pandurang
C. B.R. Ambedkar D. B.G. Tilak

67. 'Champaran Movement' was meant for:
A. securing rights of lower castes
B. separate electorate of Muslims
C. solving problems of Indian farmers
D. protest against the government's education policy

68. Who among the following died due to hunger strike in prison?
A. Lala Lajpat Rai B. Sukhdev
C. Jatin Das D. Mangal Pandey

69. The Non-Cooperation Movement was suspended in:
A. 1921 B. 1922
C. 1929 D. 1930

70. Lala Lajpat Rai suffered fatal injuries while protesting against:
A. Cripps Mission
B. Simon Commission
C. Cabinet Commission
D. Bengal Partition

71. The Quit India Movement was launched in:
A. 1939 B. 1941
C. 1942 D. 1945

72. Muslim League for the first time gave a call for a separate state in:
A. 1916 B. 1929
C. 1937 D. 1940

73. Gandhiji launched his first mass movement in India in:
A. Champaran B. Wardha
C. Sabarmati D. Bardoli

SOCIAL SCIENCE

74. Kuka Movement was started by:
A. the Congress B. the Muslim League
C. the Army D. the Sikhs

75. The Home Rule Movement was started by:
A. Mrs Annie Besant
B. Mahatma Gandhi
C. G.K. Gokhale
D. MA Jinnah

76. The first use to which wheel was put appears to be:
A. chariot B. pottery
C. ornament D. none of the above

77. Which metal was found first?
A. Bronze B. Brass
C. Iron D. Copper

78. Which city does not belong to Harappa Civilization?
A. Lothal B. Mohan-jo-daro
C. Memphis D. Banavali

79. Pharaohs belonged to which civilization?
A. Egypt B. Mesopotamian
C. Chinese D. Harappan

80. Chinese calendar was based on:
A. Solar
B. Lunar
C. Solar and Lunar both
D. Movement of stars

81. Shvetamber sect belongs to:
A. Jainism B. Buddhism
C. Islam D. Hinduism

82. Napolean was finally arrested after the battle of:
A. Borodino B. Leipzig
C. Waterloo D. Austerlitz

83. Which country was not among the Allied powers in World War I?
A. Belgium B. Bulgaria
C. Britain D. France

84. Rasputin was a:
A. Spanish explorer
B. French King
C. British General
D. Russian monk

85. 'Adi Granth' the sacred book of Sikhism was compiled by:
A. Guru Arjun
B. Guru Hargovind
C. Guru Tegh Bahadur
D. Guru Ramdas

86. The Iran-Iraq war ended in:
A. 1984 B. 1987
C. 1991 D. 1992

87. Zulus are natives of:
A. North Pole B. South Pole
C. South Africa D. Persia

88. Who is described as a man of blood and iron?
A. Bismark
B. Woodrow Wilson
C. Louis XIV
D. Garibaldi

89. The turning point in American Independence War was:
A. Boston tea party
B. Battle of Gettysberg
C. Battle of Trafalgar
D. Battle of Verdum

90. Shintoism is popular in:
A. China B. India
C. America D. Japan

91. Protestant movement was started by:
A. St. Augustine
B. Martin Luther
C. Martin Luther King
D. Pope John V

92. The "Fall of Bastille" is linked to:
A. American War of Independence
B. Russian Revolution
C. French Revolution
D. Chinese Revolution

93. United States of America at the time of independence had:
A. 13 colonies
B. 26 colonies
C. 50 colonies
D. 52 colonies

94. The writer of Declaration of American Independence was:
A. Milton B. Harrington
C. Locke D. Jefferson

95. Which great artist does not belong to renaissance age?
A. Raphael
B. Piccaso
C. Leonardo da Vinci
D. Michaelangelo

96. The Incas civilization existed in:
A. Africa B. South America
C. Central America D. North America

97. Jerusalem is not a sacred place for the followers of:
A. Christianity
B. Islam
C. Zoroastrianism
D. Judaism

98. Saxon dynasty ruled in:
A. Germany B. France
C. England D. Italy

99. Germany's attack on which country sparked the second world war?
A. Poland B. Austria
C. Czechoslovakia D. Russia

100. Gunpowder was discovered by:
A. Egyptians B. Indians
C. Chinse D. Assyrians

ANSWERS

1	2	3	4	5	6	7	8	9	10
A	A	D	D	B	A	B	B	C	C
11	**12**	**13**	**14**	**15**	**16**	**17**	**18**	**19**	**20**
D	A	B	C	D	C	C	A	B	C
21	**22**	**23**	**24**	**25**	**26**	**27**	**28**	**29**	**30**
A	D	B	A	D	B	C	A	B	C
31	**32**	**33**	**34**	**35**	**36**	**37**	**38**	**39**	**40**
B	C	D	B	A	C	C	D	B	C
41	**42**	**43**	**44**	**45**	**46**	**47**	**48**	**49**	**50**
B	B	D	C	A	D	C	A	B	B
51	**52**	**53**	**54**	**55**	**56**	**57**	**58**	**59**	**60**
D	A	C	D	A	C	C	B	C	B
61	**62**	**63**	**64**	**65**	**66**	**67**	**68**	**69**	**70**
A	D	C	B	A	D	C	C	B	B
71	**72**	**73**	**74**	**75**	**76**	**77**	**78**	**79**	**80**
C	D	A	D	A	B	D	C	A	C
81	**82**	**83**	**84**	**85**	**86**	**87**	**88**	**89**	**90**
A	C	B	D	A	B	C	A	B	D
91	**92**	**93**	**94**	**95**	**96**	**97**	**98**	**99**	**100**
B	C	A	D	B	B	C	C	A	C

DEMOCRATIC POLITICS

DIVERSITY AND DEMOCRACY

DIVERSITY

Diversity, one of the buzzwords of the early twenty-first century, has become a concept that has multiple meanings to different groups of people. Although dictionaries usually define diversity by using terms like "variety," "difference," or "dissimilarity." Social scientists usually talk about diversity in at least four different ways.

1. Counting diversity refers to empirically enumerating differences within a given population. Using this definition, social scientists take a particular population and simply count the members according to specific criteria, often including race, gender, and ethnicity. In addition, it is possible to take a particular unit within a society like a school, workplace, or government and compare its race, ethnic, or gender distribution to that of the general population. Often, suspicious questions are raised the farther the diversity of a subunit differs from that of the larger population.
2. Culture diversity refers to the importance of understanding and appreciating the cultural differences between race, ethnic, and gender groups. Since members of one culture often view others in relationship to their own standards, social scientists using the culture diversity definition would argue that it is important to show that differences do not have to be evaluated along a good-bad or moral-immoral scale. With greater tolerance and understanding, the argument goes, different cultural groups can coexist with one another in the same society.
3. Good-for-business diversity refers to the belief that businesses will be more profitable and government agencies and not-for-profit corporations will be more efficient with diverse labour forces. According to this approach, members of particular cultural groups are more effective than non-group members in dealing with their own groups so it is in the interests of organizations to diversify workers and managers.
4. Conflict diversity refers to understanding how different groups exist in a hierarchy of inequality in terms of power, privilege, and wealth. According to this definition,dominant groups oppress subordinate groups in many societies and it is important for social scientists to understand the nature of this oppression in order to help attain a more egalitarian society.

In the real world, above mentioned approaches often overlap. However, people using different approaches often ask different types of questions.

A social scientist with a counting diversity perspective might compare the black and Hispanic distribution in the police department with the distribution in the city. Typically, blacks and Hispanics would be underrepresented in the police department and even more highly underrepresented at the upper levels of the department.

A culture diversity scholar, on the other hand, would be more concerned with how the police understand the black and Hispanic communities since this also affects their actions. Do the predominantly white police interpret certain types of speech and clothing as threatening when it is simply part of the black and Hispanic subculture? Do they act in ways that inadvertently disrespect members of the community, thus causing even more tension? Being more sensitive to black and Hispanic cultural values might make the job of the police easier.

The good-for-business perspective would argue that the police would be more effective if they had more black and Hispanic officers who would be more likely to be familiar with the culture of those communities. In addition, members of the community might not be so hostile if the police were seen as some of their own.

Finally, culture conflict social scientists would argue that the police represent the interests of the dominant group: wealthy, white men in business and politics. The police represent the property rights of the dominant group and enforce the laws that they have enacted. Black and Hispanic police officers enforce the same unfair laws as their white colleagues, although they may do it more humanely. The goal is not just to have a more representative and culturally sensitive police force. The goal is to change the laws in order to have a more equitable society.

Concerns about diversity, however it is defined, also intersect with policies like affirmative action. Employment-based affirmative action is based on comparing the racial distribution of employees in a given workplace with the racial distribution of the pool of workers who are qualified for a specific job. This is counting diversity. In the United States, employers with $50,000 in federal contracts and fifty or more employees are required to make a "good faith effort" to achieve a representative labour force; that is, they must try. Formal hiring quotas, where employers are legally obligated to hire a certain percentage of underrepresented workers, are more difficult to justify. In India, on the other hand, these hiring quotas are used much more extensively.

In higher education, both counting diversity and a version of culture diversity are involved. According to the 2003 Grutter and Gratz decisions of the U.S. Supreme Court, affirmative action in college admissions is constitutional because it is in the educational interests of all students to be exposed to a diversity of views on campus. Racial diversity is one way to enhance the diversity of views. However, strict numerical comparisons and formulas cannot be used. Instead, "holistic" assessments of each candidate must take place in order to achieve an undefined "critical mass" of each student group. Since white and Asian students are overrepresented in American higher education, these critical mass guidelines refer mainly to underrepresented minorities like blacks, Hispanics, and Native Americans. A good-for-business perspective is also involved since the court noted that law schools and, to a lesser extent, all of higher education train future leaders who should be selected from all racial groups.

Neither affirmative action in employment nor in higher education reflects the conflict diversity perspective since the role and structure of higher education and the economy is not questioned. The relative power of workers and their bosses/managers is not addressed. The purpose of higher education is not addressed. All that is addressed is the racial characteristics of those who occupy various positions. When reading an article about diversity, it is critical to understand which approach the author is using.

DEMOCRACY

Meaning and Definition

In the dictionary definition, democracy "is government by the people in which the supreme power is vested in the people and exercised directly by them or by their elected agents under a free electoral system." In the words of Abraham Lincoln, democracy is a government "of the people, by the people, and for the people." There is no clear – cut, universal definition of democracy. Most definitions of democracy focus on qualities, procedures, and institutions. There are many types of democracy and their varied practices produce similarly varied effects.

The word 'democracy' itself means 'rule by the people. "A democracy is a system where people can change their rulers in a peaceful manner and the government is given the right to rule because the people say it may.

Types of Democracy

Democracies fall into two categories: Direct and Indirect.

Direct Democracy

In a direct democracy, all citizens, without the intermediary of elected or appointed officials, can participate in making public decisions. Such a system is clearly only practical with relatively small numbers of people in a community organization to tribal council, for example, or the local unit of a labor union, where members can meet in a single room to discuss issues and arrive at decisions by consensus or majority vote.

Ancient Athens, the world's first democracy, managed to practice direct democracy with an assembly of as many as 5,000 to 6,000 persons. In Switzerland direct democracy is followed even at the national level.

Indirect Democracy

Everyone has the right to take part in the government of his country, directly or though freely chosen representatives. The will of the people shall be the basis of the authority of government; this shall be expressed in periodic and genuine election that shall be held by universal and equal suffrage and shall be held by secret vote or the equivalent free voting procedures.

India is the best example of a representative democracy. Voting is one of the mechanisms that guides a democratic state and keeps its leaders on track, and it serves to let the leadership know how they have performed.

During elections, citizens vote for the candidate for their choice. Elected leader represent "the people" and govern for a set period of office. Representatives are chosen through elections based on the constituency or proportional representation system, or on a combination of the two.

Merits of Democracy

1. The participation of the individual members in the government facilitates to enlist their sympathy and co-operation to the success of the government.
2. It is an effective form to educate the public about political, economic and social affairs.
3. It is helpful to promote patriotism among the people and prevents occurrence of violent revolutions.
4. It helps to make progress and development and enables changes to take place in a peaceful manner.
5. It ensures to the people freedom of speech, conscience, assembly and action.
6. It guarantees liberty and equality, which are necessary for human development.

Demerits of Democracy

1. It sometimes leads to establish the majority view over the minority view.
2. Party leaders and political office holders in government control the citizens and the members of the party.
3. It does not encourage individuals to give their opinions.
4. It is a very expensive form of government because elections have to be conducted periodically to various office.
5. It is difficult to prevent corruption and malpractices.
6. It is also known as government by amateurs and lead to domination of masses.

THE CONSTITUTION

The Indian Constitution is a systematic outgrowth of following factors.

1. India's subjection to colonial rule and struggle for independence.
2. The ideological and intellectual inputs provided by stalwarts like Gandhi, Nehru, Ambedkar, Rajendra Prasad and others.
3. Socio-economic milieu of Indian society.
4. Liberal democratic ideas of representative government, adult franchise, elected institutions etc. which was more pragmatic and commensurate with Indian ethos.

Apart from the above cited factors many factors have contributed to affect the constitutional provisions and it would be far from truth to accept that Indian Constitution is still in the process of evolution.

SOURCES OF CONSTITUTIONAL PROVISIONS

Great Britain	: Parliamentary form of Government, process of law making, institution of speaker, writ jurisdiction.
America	: Federal structure, supremacy of the constitution, independent judiciary, Judicial review, impeachment, process of ratification of Constitutional amendments by state Legislatures, Fundamental Rights.
Ireland	: Directive Principles, Method of the election of President, nomination of members in the Rajya Sabha.
Canada	: Definition of Indian Federation as an Union of State and giving residuary power to the Union.
Australia	: Concurrent List Article 245-258.
Japan	: Article-21 Procedure established by law.
Germany	: Emergency provisions.
USSR	: Fundamental Duties
South Africa	: Constitutional Amendments

BASIC FEATURES OF THE CONSTITUTION

The Constitution of a country is the legal document with the help of which a country's affairs are managed. It is a combination of many factors, viz., history, values, traditions, ethos, socio-political milieu and alike. It is a document which establishes the doctrine of limited government and promotes democratic rule. Indian constitution drafted and enacted after a period of struggle and deliberation is among the longest in the world. Though most of it is taken from the Government of India Act 1935, the Indian framers gave it a twist so as to be an instrument of socio-economic justice without compromising the aspect of security, good governance and other aspects.

The following are the basic features of Indian Constitution.

1. One of the longest document in the world. Originally it contained 395 Articles and 8 schedule.
2. Indian Constitution is a written Constitution like American, Canadian and French Constitution.
3. India has a federal system with unitary bias. The desire and commitment to preserve the unity without compromising the issue of development of different regions, made this choice inevitable.
4. Independent and impartial judiciary is hallmark of Indian Constitution.
5. Novel features like fundamental rights, fundamental duties and directive principles of state policy in a single document.
6. Parliamentary system of government.
7. Compromise between Parliamentary supremacy and Judicial Review.
8. A democratic Republic, head of the state is elected indirectly. He/she is not hereditary.
9. A mix of rigid and flexible elements the constitution amendment procedure as moderate enough to address the needs of change. But, is also strict in the sense that crucial provisions need special majority.
10. Citizenship is single, everybody fulfilling certain qualification is entitled for citizenship of the country, not of a particular state.

FUNDAMENTAL RIGHTS

The Constitution of India is committed to a fundamental change in the social order so as to ensure more human life of people. Fundamental Rights are classified as:

1. Right to Equality
2. Right to Freedom
3. Right against Exploitation
4. Right to freedom of Religion
5. Cultural and cducational rights
6. Right to Constitutional Remedies

The Original Constitution provided for the Right to property but it has been abolished by the 44th Amendment.

Recently, Right to primary education has been included in Part three under Article 21 A.

1. **Right to Equality :** Article 14 to 18 deals with the Right to Equality.
   Article 14, says that "the state shall not deny to any person equality before the law or the equal protection of the laws within the territory of India.
   - **Equality Before Law :** It is an expression of English common law and is somewhat negative concept implying absence of special privilege on grounds of birth, caste, creed, colour or sex.
     Equality before law is second corrollary from Dicey's concept of the "rule of law." It implies that no one is above the law of land. It is the law no one is supreme. However, exceptions are granted to the office of President and Governor.
   - **Equal Protection of the Law :** It is of American origin and is a more positive concept implying equality of treatment in equal circumstances.

   It provides for protective discrimination.
2. **Right to Freedom :** Article 19 to 22 deals with the Right to Freedom.
   Article 19(1) includes six freedoms.
   (*a*) Freedom of Speech and Expression.
   (*b*) Freedom of Assembly.
   (*c*) Freedom of Association.
   (*d*) Freedom of Movement.
   (*e*) Freedom of Residence and settlement.
   (*f*) Freedom of profession, occupation, trade and business.
   (*g*) included freedom 'to acquire hold and dispose of property' which has been abolished by the 44th Amendment.

   Freedom of the Press is included under Article 19(1)(a).
   Article 20 provides protection against arbitrary and excessive punishment to any person who commits an offence. It can not be suspended during the period of emergency.
   Article 21 guarantees right to life and personal liberty. It says that "No person shall be deprived of his life or personal liberty except according to the procedure established by law."
   It is the most important Article which has been hailed as backbone of Part III and Part IV of the Constitution by the Supreme Court. It can never be suspended.
   Article 21 is the bedrock from which many rights have been inferred by the Supreme Court.
   Article 22 provides protection against arbitrary arrest and detention. It includes
   - informing the detainee of the cause of his arrest.
   - allowing him to consult and be defended by a legal practitioner of his choice.
   - producing him before a nearest magistrate within the period of 24 hours.
3. **Right against Exploitation :** There are two Articles : 23 and 24 under it.
   Article 23 : it seeks to ban traffic in human beings, begar or any form of forced Labour.

Article 24 it prohibits employment of children below the age of 14 years in any factory or mine or any hazardous condition.

4. **Right to Freedom of Religion :** it includes four rights under Article 25, 26, 27, 28.
   Article 25 entitles everyone the freedom of conscience and the right to process, practice and propagate a religion of one's choice.
   Article 26 grants right to religious denominations to
   - establish institutions for practice or propagating their religion.
   - manage its own affairs in matters of religion.
   - passes and dispose of their immovable property.

   Article 27 provides for exempting religious institutions from paying taxes to state for religious purposes.
   Article 28 deals with religious instruction to be imparted in educational institutions.
   - No religious instruction can be provided in institutions owned and administered by the state.
   - Religious instruction may be imparted but pupil may not be compelled to attend them in institutions recognized by the state and receiving aid out of state funds.
   - Religious instructions can be imparted and people can be compelled to attend them in educational institutions administered by state established by a religious endowment or religious trust.
5. **Cultural and Educational Rights :** It includes Articles 29 and 30.
   Article 29 provides for criteria for determination of minority.
   Article 30 provides that all minorities shall have the right to establish and administer educational institution of their choice.
6. **Right to Constitutional Remedies :** It has only one Article 32. In the words of Dr. Ambedkar Article 32 is fundamental of all Fundamental Rights. This right makes it constitutionally obligatory on the part of the Supreme Court to enforce the Fundamental Rights.
   It includes five kinds of writ jurisdiction adopted from England.

- Habeas Corpus
- Mandamus
- Certeorari
- Prohibition
- Quo Warranto

''Habeas Corpus'' is in the nature of an order calling upon the person who has detained another to produce the latter before the court. It literally means 'to have a body.' In addition to aggrieved person; other individual or organization can head for its enforcement.

''Mandamus'' means command. It is issued to command a person or a body to do what is his or its duty to do. It is a discretionary remedy at the hands of HC and an aggrieved person can approach the court. It can be issued against public offices as well as inferior courts and judicial bodies.

''Prohibition'' issued to an inferior court to keep within limits of their jurisdiction. It is a matter of right for which only aggrieved person can approach the Court.

''Quo Warranto'' issued to enquire into the legality of the claim of a public office. It asks 'What is your authority.' Its intention is to see that unlawful claimant does not usurp a public office.

''Certeorari'' issued to quash orders passed in excess of jurisdiction of a court.

FUNDAMENTAL DUTIES

In ancient times, it was felt that if everyone performs his duties, then the rights would automatically be safeguarded.

There was no provision of Fundamental Duties in the original Constitution. The Constitution (Forty Second Amendment) Act, 1976 added part IVA and a new Article 51A to the Constitution. It gives a list of 11 Fundamental Duties. They are as follows :

1. To abide by the Constitution and respect its ideals and institutions, the National flag and the National Anthem.
2. To cherish and follow the noble ideals which inspired our national struggle for freedom.
3. To uphold and proved the sovereignty, unity and integrity of India.
4. To defend the country and render national service when called upon to do so.
5. To promote harmony and spirit of common brotherhood amongst all the people of India transcending religious, linguistic and regional or sectional diversities, to renounce practices derogatory to the dignity of women.
6. To value and preserve the rich heritage of our composite culture.
7. To protect and improve the natural environment including forests, lakes, rivers and wild life and to have compassion for living creatures.
8. To develop the scientific temper, humanism and the spirit of inquiry and reform.
9. To safeguard public property and to abjure violence.
10. To strive towards excellence in all spheres of individual and collective activity so that the nation constantly rises to higher levels of endeavour of achievement.
11. Every citizen to offer opportunities for education to his child the age of 6-14 years.

DIRECTIVE PRINCIPLES OF STATE POLICY

The Directive Principles of State Policy mentioned in Part IV of the Constitution contain 15 Articles (36-51). They are one of the many novel elements of the Constitution which have been adopted from the Irish Constitution. They are in the nature of certain ideals the state should strive for. They give certain directions to executive and the legislature. They give certain unforcible rights which the state shall aim at securing by its various policies. These features have undergone evolution and represent context and experience of India. They are a combination of socialist ideals, Gandhian perception, Western liberalism and the ideals of India's freedom struggle.

Provisions

The various articles on Directive Principles are as follows.

Article 38 instructs the state to promote the welfare of people by securing and protecting a social order in which justice (socio-economic and political) shall inform all the institutions of national life.

Article 39(a) it talks about state's role in providing adequate means of livelihood to all its citizens.

Article 39(b) provides for state's direction for equitable distribution of resources.

Article 39(c) provides for prevention of concentration of wealth in fewer hands.

Artcile 39(d) provides for equal pay for equal work, for both; men and women.

Article 39(a) provides for equal justice and free legal Aid.

Article 40 says that the state shall organize village Panchayats as units of self-government.

Article 41 provides for right to work, public assistance in case of unemployment, old age, sickness and disablement keeping in view the limitations of economic resources.

Article 43 provides for living wages for worker and a decent standard of life, leisure and social and cultural opportunities for people.

Article 43(a) provides for participation of workers in the management of industry and other undertakings. It has been added by 42nd Amendment.

Article 44 provides for a Uniform Civil Code applicable to the entire country.

Article 45 provides free and compulsory education to children till 14 years of age. It has now been made a fundamental right under Article 21A.

Article 46 provides for protection of educational and economic interests of weaker sections of the society and in particular, of the scheduled castes and scheduled tribes.

Article 47 provides for prohibition of consumption of intoxicating liquor and to raise the level of nutrition and five improvement of public health.

Article 48 provides for preserving and improving the breeds and prohibiting the slaughter of cows, calves and other milks and draught cattles.

Article 48A added by 42nd Amendment, provides for protection and improvement of the environment and to safeguard the forests and wild life of the country.

Article 49 provides for protection of monuments of historical and national importance.

Article 50 provides for separation of judiciary from executive.

Article 51 provides for promotion of international peace and security.

Significance of Directive Principles of State Policy

Firstly, they are intended to usher an egalitarian order, once the limitations or resources is overcome and state is competent enough to fulfil them. For, most of the directives are resource consuming.

Secondly, they have exercised an important check on the government. Rightly remarked by Ambedkar that the directives 'can be the best election manifesto.'

Thirdly, they guide both, the government and the people in the realm of politics and society. They have significant educative value.

Fourthly, they emphasize the goal of welfare state and social justice that are warranted in Indian polity and keep check on elitist or populist measures.

PARLIAMENT AND UNION GOVERNMENT

The Constitution of India adopts a Parliamentary form of government like the British Westminster model. However, it is not sovereign in the British sense. Instead, it was expected to suit the requirements of federal polity and acts as an instrument of governance, change and social transformation. It is specifically outlined in Part V of the Constitution from Article 79-123.

The Indian Parliament or the Union Legislature in India consists of the President and the two houses viz, the Lok Sabha and the Rajya Sabha. Unlike the Presidential system that is promised on the principle of separation of powers, the Parliamentary system envisage a scheme of interrelationship between executive and legislative branch of government.

Composition

1. The President.
2. The Lok Sabha or the Lower House or the House of People.
3. The Rajya Sabha or the upper house or council of state.

Functions

1. To enact laws for the administration of the country.
2. To reflect federal sentiment of the Indian polity.
3. To exercise control over the government and ensure limited government.
4. To provide forum for deliberation on issues concerning affairs of the polity.
5. To integrate the polity by providing membership to the representatives.

THE LOK SABHA

Composition : The members of Lok Sabha are elected directly by people from their respective constituencies. Under the provision of the constitution.

- Lok Sabha at present consists of 543 members elected from States and Union Territories.
- 2 members were nominated from the Anglo-Indian community by the President, but by the 104th amendment of the constitution this provision have been abolished.

Term : The term of Lok Sabha is of 5 years from the date appointed for its first meeting. It may be dissolved before the expiration of its full term by the President if the government loses the confidence of the Lower House and there are no other alternative to form the government.

The term of Lok Sabha can be extended (not necessarily).

When a proclamation of emergency is in force, for a period not exceeding one year at a time and not exceeding a period of six months after the proclamation of Emergency cease to operate.

Qualifications : To be a member of the Lok Sabha a person should be

- an Indian Citizen
- Completed 25 years of age

Disqualifications : A member of the Lok Sabha can be disqualified if the person

- holds any office of profit under the Govern-men of India or the State.
- is of unsound mind and stands so declared by competent court.
- is an undischarged insolvent
- is not a citizen of India, or has voluntaril acquired the citizenship of a foreign state.
- is to be disqualified by or under any law mad by Parliament.

Sessions : The Lok Sabha is to meet at leas twice a year and the interval between two consecutiv sessions shall be less than 6 months.

A special session of the Lok Sabha can be calle if a notice in writing signed by not less than one tenth of members of the Lok Sabha is given to th Speaker.

When such a notice is given to the President h must summon the session within 14 days.

Speaker

The Speaker is the presiding officer of the Lok Sabh who is elected from amongst the members by a simpl majority. His office is an office of much dignit honour and prestige.

Election : Governed by Article 93. Under th influence of convention that has developed in Indi a candidate of the ruling party is elected unoppose to the post of speaker of Lok Sabha.

Removal : Article 94. A speaker can be remove only by a resolution passed by effective majori after 14 days notice of moving of such a resolutic has been given.

Powers and Functions of Speaker

The speaker is endowed with a wide range of power His powers are

1. To see that there is decorum and discipline the House.
2. To decide who shall hold the floor and spea in deliberations of the House.
3. To safeguard the rights and privileges of th members of the House.
4. To put the motion of the vote to announce th result. He does not vote but in case of a tie, casts his vote.
5. To act as administrative head of the Lok Sab Secretariat.
6. To accept resignations sent by members of L Sabha.
7. To protect the House from unnecessa executive intrusion.
8. To allot time for each item on the agenda the House.

Some of his special powers are:

9. To certify whether a particular Bill is a money Bill or not (Article 110).
10. To preside over joint sitting of both the houses of the Parliament.
11. To admit a vote of no-confidence against the Government.

Parliamentary Privileges

Certain privileges and immunities are granted to members of the Parliament to enable them to work freely and efficiently. They are as follows :

1. Freedom of speech.
2. Freedom from arrest in civil cases for duration of session of Parliament and 40 days before and after.
3. To summon any person to produce documents or to answer charges for contempt of the house.
4. Right to exclude outsiders from the proceedings of the house.
5. Power to punish for breach of privileges committed, mode or outside the Parliament.
6. Right to regulate its own internal proceedings without interference from any executive or judicial authority.

THE RAJYA SABHA

Also called Upper House or Council of States.

Composition : Article 80 of the Constitution outlines that

- Not more than 238 representatives to be sent from States and Union Territories.
- Twelve members to be nominated by the President having special knowledge or practical experience in the field of science, art, literature and social service.

However, the Parliament by law has fixed the total strength of Rajya Sabha to be not more than 245 (233 elected + 12 nominated).

Term : The Rajya Sabha is a permanent body, not subject to dissolution. The term of the members of the house is six years. Nearly one-third of the members of the Rajya Sabha retire after every two years.

Method of Election : Except for a few members (twelve) who are nominated by the President, the members are elected indirectly by proportional representation by means of single transferrable vote. They are elected by an electoral college consisting of elected members of the state Legislative Assemblies. Union Territories elect through the same method by special electoral college.

Qualification : A person seeking membership of Rajya Sabha must be 30 years of age.

THE PRESIDENT

The Constitution makers of India adopted a Parliamentary form of Government based on British westminster model. But, unlike the British model, they opted for a chosen head of state elected indirectly for five years. He occupies a position of pre-eminence in the institutional set of the country and regarded as first citizen of the country.

Qualification : A person should be

1. a citizen of India.
2. must not be less than 35 years.
3. must be qualified to be elected as member of Lok Sabha.
4. must not hold any office of profit under the state.

Election : According to Article 54, the President shall be elected by a electoral college. The election of President is held in accordance with system of proportional representation by means of single transferable vote.

Term : The term of President's office is five years from the date on which he enters upon his office. However, he is eligible for re-election.

Resignation : President may resign his office by writing under his hand addressed to the Vice-President.

Impeachment : The President may be impeached for 'violation of the Constitution' in accordance with the provisions in Article 61 of the Constitution.

Procedure for Impeachments : A motion seeking removal of the President can be introduced in either house of the Parliament by giving a notice signed by not less than 1/4 of the total strength of the house. The resolution can be moved after a fourteen days notice is served on him.

If the house passes the resolution by not less than 2/3rd of the total strength of the house, the matter is to be referred to the other house which will investigate the charges.

The President however, has the right to defend himself in the other house either by himself or through an attorney. If the second house also passes the resolution by majority of not less than 2/3rd of the total strength of the house, the President is considered removed from his office from the date of passing of such resolution.

Powers and Functions of the President

The Parliamentary form of government depends on principles and practices wherein the President is the formal executive and council of minister headed by the Prime Minister is the real executive. All the actions of government are undertaken in the name of President but only on the advice of ministers chosen by him. According to Article 53 of the Constitution "executive powers of the Union shall be vested in the hands of the President who shall exercise it either directly or through officers subordinate to him in accordance with the provisions of the Constitution.''

The powers of the President can be broadly categorized as :

1. **Executive Power :** All executive actions are taken in his name. He has power to appoint the Prime Minister, other ministers of the Government of India, Attorney General for India, the Comptroller and Auditor General of India, the Judges of the Supreme Court, the Judges of High Court of States, the Governors of State, Members of Union and Joint Public Service Commission, the members of Finance Commission, the Chief Election Commissioner and members of election commission.
   The President shall also have the power to remove ministers, Attorney General, judge of Supreme Court or High Court or Election Commissioner on the advice of Parliament, Chairman and member of Public Service Commission on the report of Supreme Court.
2. **Legislative Power :** President is an integral part of Indian Parliament. In this respect
   - he can prorogue or summon the houses of Parliament, dissolve the Lok Sabha and summon the Joint session of the two houses of Parliament in case of a deadlock.
   - he gives his assent to all bills passed by the Parliament to become a law.
   - he addresses either or both houses of Parliament, at the first session of the lower house after each general election and at the commencement of first session each year.
   - he has power to send messages to either house of Parliament which the House must consider.
   - he has power to nominate not more than 12 members to the Rajya Sabha.
   - he has power to promulgate an ordinance when the Parliament is not in the session (Article 123). Presidential ordinance has the same force and effect as an Act of Parliament.
   - he has power to declare his assent to a bill declare that he withholds his assent return the bill for reconsideration (not money bill)
   - The Governor of a state may reserve a bill for President assent, but it is obligatory when the Bill derogates the power of High Court. In cases where a state bill is reserved for Presidential assent, he can declare that he withhold his assent or can give assent.
3. **Military Power :** The President is the Commander-in-Chief of the Defence forces. However, the exercise of his power is to be regulated by law of the Parliament.
4. **Judicial Power :** The President is accorded the power to grant pardon, reprieve, respite, remission of punishment in cases of (a) Court Martial (b) offences against laws made under the Union and Concurrent lists (c) death sentences. He also appoints judges of the Supreme Court and High Courts through an integrated consultative process.
5. **Diplomatic Power :** As the highest constitutional dignitary, the President appoints ambassadors to foreign countries and receives diplomatic delegates of foreign countries.
6. **Financial Power :** It is President who causes to laid before the Parliament, the annual budget. Money Bill can be introduced only with his prior recommendation.
7. **Emergency Power :** President is assigned three kinds of emergency powers under Article 352, 356 and 360.

THE JUDICIARY

Article 233-237: provides for a single, unified, hierarchically organised judiciary.

One court exercises administrative control over court below and judges of one hierarchy getting elevated and appointed as judges of courts above.

SUPREME COURT

The Constitution makers of India adopted the concept of Supreme Court from the United States of America. However, unlike the U.S.A., the Supreme Court in India is not the sovereign body. It is endowed with vast powers and functions including the power of judicial review. In the last 75 years of its working, the court has helped in strengthening democracy, protecting people's right and checked authoritarianism. It is vested with administrative powers over courts lying below it. Indian constitution provides for a single integrated judiciary with the Supreme Court, at the top of hierarchy.

Composition

The Supreme Court at present consists of Chief Justice and 33 other Judges. In 1950, it had only eight Judges. Parliament was, however, authorised to change the number of its Judges. On account of the increase in its work load, the strength of the Supreme Court judges has been raised from time to time. In 1956, the Parliament passed the Supreme Court

Number of Judges Act, which raised the total strength to 11. In 1960, the Supreme Court number of Judges Amendment Act was passed further raising the strength of the Court Judges to 14 including the Chief Justice. Its strength was further increased to 18 in 1977, 26 in 1986 and 31 in 2008. In 2019 it was increased from 31 to 34.

Appointment : Article 124 a judge of the Supreme Court is appointed by the President in consultation with such of the judges of the Supreme Court and of the High Court in the States as the President may deem necessary for the purpose. In the Case of appointment of a Judge other than the Chief Justice, the Chief Justice of India must be consulted. In practice, the appointment of the Chief Justice of India as well as of the other judges of the Supreme Court is recommended by the Home Ministry and after the matter has been examined by the Appointments Committee of the Indian Cabinet and the decision receives the blessings of the Prime Ministers, it is formalised by the Indian President.

Salary : Provided in Second Schedule

Chief Justice	:	2,80,000
Other Judges	:	2,50,000 (same of CAG)

Qualifications : A person shall not be qualified for appointment as a Judge of the Supreme Court unless he is a citizen of India and :

(a) has been for at least five years a Judge of a High Court or of two or more such courts in succession; or

(b) has been worked for at least ten years as an advocate of a High Court or of two or more such courts in succession; or

(c) is, in the opinion of the President, a distinguished jurist.

The inclusion of the last provision which would enable the President to appoint a distinguished jurist on the Supreme Court, even if he did not qualify by a specified number of years of practices at the Bar, was intended to open a wider field of choice.

Tenure

No minimum age is prescribed for appointment as a Judge of the Supreme Court, nor any fixed period office. Once appointed, a Judge of the Supreme Court may cease to be so, on any one of the following grounds (other than death); (a) on attaining the age of 65 years; (b) on resigning his office by writing addressed to the President; (c) on being removed by the President upon an address to that effect being passed by a special majority of each House of Parliament.

Independence of Supreme Court

To ensure the independence of Supreme Court following steps have been undertaken

- Appointment of judges by the President in consultation with CJI and such other judges as he may deem fit.
- Fixed tenure and removal only on ground of proved misbehaviour or incapacity and address by both houses of Parliament by special majority.
- The terms and conditions of Service of a judge can be varied to his disadvantage after his appointment (Article 125).
- The Salaries and allowances of the judges as well as of the staff are charged on the consolidated fund of India and not subjected to vote in Parliament (Art 146).
- No discussion can take place in the Parliament, with respect to conduct of any judge in the discharge of his duties except when a resolution for his removal is under consideration (Article 121).
- No person who has held office as a judge of the Supreme Court can plead or act in any court or before any authority within the territory of India.

Court of Record : Article 129 provides The Supreme Court shall be a Court of record and shall have all powers of such a Court, including the power to punish for contempt itself. A Court of record obviously is one where the acts and Judicial proceedings are kept for memory and testimony. As a court of record the Supreme Court has power to punish those who are adjudged as guilty of contempt of court. The Court has taken up the cases for their contempt.

Jurisdiction of the Supreme Court

Indian Supreme Court enjoys a number of powers evident in its jurisdiction. They are of following kinds

1. Original
2. Writ
3. Appellate
4. Advisory
5. Revisory

1. **Original Jurisdiction :** Article 131 of Indian Constitution provides for original jurisdiction that deals with disputes (i) between the Government of India and one or more States, (ii) between the Government of India and any State or States on the one side and one or more other States on the other, or (iii) between two or more states. However, disputes arising out of the provisions of treaties with the former Indian States or to which any such State is a party are excluded from the Original Jurisdiction of the Supreme Court.
2. **Writ Jurisdiction :** Supreme Court enjoys powers under Article 32 for the enforcement of Fundamental Rights. It is exercised in the nature of writs, viz; Habeas Corpus, Mandamas, Certeorari, Quo Warranto and Prohibition.

3. **Appellate Jurisdiction :** The Supreme Court is the highest court of appeal in all Civil, Criminal and Constitutional cases. Moreover, under "special leave to Appeal" provided in Article 136; the Supreme Court has discretionary powers to take cases from High Courts.
Article 134 of the Constitution for the first time provides for an appeal to the Supreme Court from any judgement, final order or sentence in a criminal proceeding of a High Court, as of right, in two specified classes of cases—(a) where the High Court has on an appeal reversed an order of acquital of an accused person and sentenced him to death; (b) where the High Court has withdrawn for trial before itself any case from any Court subordinate to its authority and has in such trial convicted the accused and sentenced him to death. In these two classes of cases relating to a sentence of death by the High Court, appeal lies to the Supreme Court as of right.
Moreover, an appeal may lie to the Supreme Court in any criminal case if the High Court certifies that the case is a fit one for appeal to the Supreme Court.
4. **Advisory Jurisdiction :** Under Article 143 of the Constitution, President can seek advisory opinion of the Supreme Court when it appeals to him that a question of law or fact has arisen, or is likely to arise, which is of such a nature and of such public importance that it is expedient to obtain the opinion of the Supreme Court upon it. The President is not bound to accept the opinion of the Supreme Court. The Court is not bound to give its advice.
5. **Revisory Jurisdiction :** Under Article 137 the Supreme Court can revise its own judgement, order or direction. Besides, Article 138 and Article 139 provides that Parliament by law can extend the jurisdiction of the Supreme Court.

Judicial Review

Judicial review is the power of Supreme Court and High Court to declare a law as unconstitutional and void if it is inconsistent with one or more provisions of the constitution to the extent of such inconsistency.

Under this it can examine legislature enactments and their constitutionality.

It can examine the validity of any order of the executive or any law of the legislature.

It is the Supreme Court to declare what the provisions of the Constitution mean.

The Supreme Court has power to review any judgement or order made by it earlier.

The power of judicial review is more implicit and traceable to Article 82, 226 and also under Article 13.

HIGH COURTS

The Constitution provides for a High Court for every State. However, the Parliament can provide for one High Court for two or more States. The Parliament can provide for a separate High Court for a Union Territory or include a Union Territory in the jurisdiction of a High Court of a State.

Each High Court has a Chief Justice and several judges whose number is decided by the President. The State Governor is consulted in their appointment. In the appointment of other judges, Chief Justice of the High Court is also consulted. The judges hold office upto the age of 62. The salaries and allowances of the judges once fixed cannot be changed to their disadvantage except in financial emergency. Their salaries are charged to the consolidated fund of India.

The Government can appoint additional and acting judges, if required. The President has the powers to transfer a judge from one High Court to the other. This provision in the Constitution was made to ensure impartiality and unbiasedness by the judges. However, these transfers cannot be used as punishments. Effective consultation with the Chief Justice of Supreme Court is essential before ordering the transfer.

Qualification

The qualifications required for judges of a High Court are: (*i*) He must be a citizen of India; (*ii*) He must have held a judicial office in India, or must have practised as an advocate of a High Court for at least 10 years. A High Court judge can resign before the retirement age of 62 years or can be promoted to Supreme Court. He can also be removed from his office by the President on an address presented to him by the Parliament after having passed it in each house by a majority of its total membership as well as by two-thirds of those present and voting. The only ground on which such an address can be passed by the Parliament is either proven misbehaviour or incapacity.

Jurisdiction

Ordinarily, the jurisdiction of a High Court of a State or of a Union Territory is coterminus with the territorial limits of that State or Union Territory. However, the Parliament has powers to extend the jurisdiction of one High Court to an adjoining State or Union Territory. Usually, High Courts are courts of appeal and their area of original jurisdiction is limited. In the presidency towns of Kolkata, Mumbai and Chennai, High Courts had some original jurisdiction, *e.g.,* they could hear the cases, involving Christians and Parsis. After the independence also, these High Courts have retained these powers. Cases, involving marriage laws, divorce, inheritance or contempt of

High Court can be directly taken to the High Court.

Otherwise, High Courts have wide powers in appeal cases. In the criminal cases, an appeal against the Session Court judgement can be made in a High Court. In civil cases, an appeal can go to the High Court if the amount involved in the case exceeds the limits. In the economic offences, appeals against tribunal can be made in the High Courts. High Courts have power to issue writs, for the enforcement of fundamental rights and other purposes. High Courts have the power to transfer cases either to themselves or from one court to another. If a case involves interpretation of Constitution, High Court can transfer the case to itself. High Court acts as a court of record. Its decisions are published and can be referred to. It can sentence anyone for the contempt of Court.

High Courts have superintendence over all courts and tribunals throughout the territories in relation to which it exercises jurisdiction except military courts. This is a wide power because it includes all courts or tribunals whether an appeal against its decision lies to the High Court or not. High Courts can intervene and revise the decisions where it feels gross injustice or non-exercise or abuse of jurisdiction. High Courts have administrative control over the subordinate judiciary in the State which includes district judges, judges of city civil courts as well as Metropolitan magistrates and members of the judicial service of the State. This control is exercised in the manner of appointments, posting, promotion and administrative controls. They can make and issue general rules and prescribe forms for regulating the practice and proceedings of lower courts. They can transfer case from the court to the other.

STATE GOVERNMENT

THE GOVERNOR

The Constitution provides for a Governor as the **head of the executive** at the state level. But, for a long time the institutional functioning was determined by one party dominant system. A major change occurred after the **fourth General Elections in 1967**. In a number of States, the party in power was different from that of the Union. There occurred fragmentation of political parties and emergence of new regional parties. Unpredictable realignments of political parties and groups took place for the purpose of forming Government. The Governors were called upon to exercise their discretionary powers more frequently. The manner in which they exercised those functions direct affect impact on Union-State relations.

The state executive consists of a Governor with a council of ministers with Chief Minister at its head.

Powers of The Governor

1. **Executive :** All the executive functions in the state are carried on in the name of the Governor. He appoints the Chief Minister and on his advice appoints other Ministers and distribute portfolios among them.
   He also appoints Advocate-General, Chairman and members of State public service commission. Members of the state public service commission cannot be removed by him, they can be removed only by the President on the report of the Supreme Court on reference made by the President.
   He is entitled to be consulted by the President in the matter of appointment of Judges of State High Court. He can nominate 1/6 part of the total members of the Legislative Council.
   In the states of **Jharkhand, Chattisgarh, Madhya Pradesh and Odisha, it is the special responsibility** of the Governor to see that a Minister is placed in charge of tribal welfare. **In Assam**, the Governor is given certain **special powers** with respect to the administration of the tribal areas provided in the sixth schedule of the Constitution. In fact, all executive actions of the government are taken in his name.
2. **Legislative :** Governor is an integral part of the state legislature. Governor of state enjoys extensive legislative powers. He summons either or both Houses of the State Legislature to meet at a time and at a place as he thinks fit. The only condition is that six months shall not intervene between its last sitting in one session and the date appointed for its first sitting in the next session. He may prorogue either House or dissolve the Legislative Assembly. He may address either House and may send messages to it. It is provided that the Houses to which he send message will consider any matter required by the message to be taken into consideration. The Governor addresses the House or the Houses on the commencement of the first session after general election and at the commencement of the first session on each year. When a bill has been passed by a House or Houses, it must be presented to the Governor. The Governor shall declare that he assents to it or that he withholds his assent or that he reserves the bill for the consideration of the

DEMOCRATIC POLITICS

President. The Governor may return a Non-Money bill with a message for reconsideration. He may suggest amendments. The House or Houses must consider his suggestions without delay. If the bill is passed again by the House or Houses without amendment, he cannot with hold his assent.

3. **Judicial : Article 161** empowers Governor to grant pardons, reprieves, respites or remission of punishment or to suspend or commute the sentence of death to any person convicted of any offence against which executive power of state extends. He has **no power to pardon in case of defence of death**. But has the power to suspend, remit a sentence of death. He is entitled to be consulted by the president in appointment of Judges of State High Court.
4. **Emergency :** Governor has the power to make a report to the President whenever he is satisfied that a situation has arisen in which Government of the state cannot be carried on in accordance with the provisions of the constitution [Article 356]. But this power has often been misused as Rajiv Dhawan has indicated.
5. **Financial :** He causes the annual financial statement to be laid before state legislature and recommmends for introducing money Bill. No demand for grants can be made except on the recommendation of the Governor.

Ordinance Making Power

The Governor can promulgate ordinance only when houses are not in the session. It is not a discretionary power. Ordinance cease to have effect at the expiry of six weeks from the date of reassembly, unless disapproved earlier. He himself is competent to withdraw the ordinance at any time.

Ordinance making power is co-extensive with legislative power of State Legislature. If the provisions of ordinance are repugnant with a union law relating a concurrent subject, the Governor's ordinance will prevail notwithstanding repugnancy, if the ordinance had been made in pursuance of the instructions of the President.

STATE LEGISLATURE

Every state has a legislature consisting of the Governor and the Legislative Assembly. Some states have the second chamber, called Legislativ Council.

Legislative Assembly

- It consists of not more than 500 or less than 60
- Assembly of Mizoram and Goa have 40 member each, while Puduherry has 30 and Sikkim has 3 only.
- The member must be 25 years of age.
- Term of the Assembly is 5 year.
- To be elected to Legislative Council o Legislative Assembly, a person must be a electo for any seat in Legislative Assembly in the stat

As regards disqualifications of members, th decision of Governor in consultation with th election commission shall be final.

Constitution provides for joint sitting for onl one purpose at the state level : When the Govern adresses the legislature at the beginning of Budg session or immediately after the general election.

Legislative Council

- It exists in six states, viz; Bihar, Karnatak Andhra Pradesh, Telangana, Maharashtra ar U.P.
- Under **Article 169**, the Parliament by law, ca provide for the creation of Legislative Counc in a state or abolition if it exists, provided t Legislative Assembly of the state passes resolution to that effect (by a majority of t total membership of the Assembly and by majority of not less than two-thirds of t members present and voting).
- Its total members not to exceed 1/3 of Legislati Assembly.
- The total membership in no case be less than 4
- Composition

  1/3 elected by Vidhan Sabha

  1/3 elected by Local bodies

  1/12 elected by graduates of three years standi

  1/12 elected by teachers school & colleges

  1/6 elected by Governor (also from co-operati

  Thus 5/6 elected indirectly elected 1 nominated.
- To become, a member a person must be 30 ye age.

LOCAL GOVERNMENT

The term 'Panchayati Raj' in India signifies the system of rural local self-government. It is created in all the states in India by the acts of the state legislatures to establish democracy at the grass roots level. It entrusted with the duties and responsibilities in field of rural development. It was constitutionali through the 73rd Constitutional Amendment Act of 1992. At the central level, the Ministry_of Rural Development looks after the matters relating to the Panchayati Raj bodies.

In the scheme of division of powers between the centre and the states in the Indian federal system, the item of *'Local Government'* is given to the states. Thus the fifth entry of the State List of the seventh schedule to the constitution of India deals with 'local government'.

Balwantray Mehta Committee

In January 1957, the Government of India appointed a committee to examine the working of the Community Development Programme (1952) and the National Extension Service (1953) and to suggest measures for their better working. The chairman of this committee was Balwantray G. Mehta. The committee submitted its report in November 1957 and recommended the establishment of the scheme of 'democratic decentralisation' which ultimately came to the known as panchayati raj. The specific recommendations made by it are:

1. Establishment of three-tier Panchayati Raj System—Gram Panchayat at the village level, Panchayat Samiti at the block level, and Zila Parishad at the district level. These tiers should be organically linked through a device of indirect elections.
2. The village Panchayat should be constituted with directly elected representatives, whereas the Panchayat Samiti and Zila Parishad should be constituted with indirectly elected members.
3. All planning and developmental activities should be entrusted to these bodies.
4. The Panchayat Samiti should be the executive body while the Zila Parishad should be the advisory, coordinating and supervisory body.
5. The District Collector should be the chairman of the Zila Parishad.
6. There should be a genuine transfer of power and responsibility to these democratic bodies.
7. Adequate resources should be transferred to these bodies to enable them to discharge their functions and fulfil their responsibilities.

RURAL LOCAL GOVERNMENT

73rd Amendment Act of 1992

This act has added Part-IX to the Constitution of India. It is entitled as 'The Panchayats' and consists of provisions from articles 243 to 243-O. In addition, the Act has also added Eleventh schedule to the Constitution. It contains 29 functional items of the Panchayats and deals wih Article 243-G.

The salient features of the Act are:

1. **Gram Sabha:** The Act provides for a Gram Sabha as the foundation of the Panchayati Raj system. It is a body consisting of persons registered in the electoral rolls of a village comprised within the area of Panchayat at the village level.
2. **Three-Tier System:** The Act provides for a three-tier system of Panchayati Raj in every state, that is Panchayats at the village, intermediate, and district levels. The Act defines all these terms in the following manner.
   (*i*) Panchayat means an institution (by whatever name called) of self-government for rural areas.
   (*ii*) Village means, a village specified by the Governor by public notification to be a village for this purpose, and includes a group of villages so specified.
   (*iii*) Intermediate level means a level between the village and district levels specified by the Governor by public notification for this purpose.
   (*iv*) District means a district in a state.

   Thus, the Act brings about uniformity in the structure of Panchayati Raj throughout the country. However a state having a population not exceeding 20 lakhs may not constitute panchayats at the intermediate level.
3. **Election of Members and Chairpersons:** All the members of Panchayats at the village, intermediate and district levels shall be elected directly by the people. Further, the chairperson of Panchayats at the intermediate and district levels shall be elected indirectly—by and from amongst the elected members of. However, the chairperson of a Panchayat at the village level shall be elected in such manner as the state legislature determines.
4. **Reservation of seats:** The Act provides for the reservation of seats for scheduled castes and scheduled tribes in every Panchayat in proportion of their population to the total population in the Panchayat area. Further, the state legislature shall provide for the reservation of offices of chairpersons in the Panchayat at the village or any other level for the SC and ST. The Act provides for the reservation of not less than one-third of the total number of seats for women. Further, not less than one-third of the total number of offices of chairpersons in the Panchayat at each level shall be reserved for women.

   The Act also authorises the legislature of a state to make any provision for reservation of seats in any Panchayat or offices of chairperson in the Panchayat at any level in favour of backward classes.

5. **Duration of Panchayats:** The Act provides for a five-year term of office to the Panchayat at every level. However, it can be dissolved before the completion of its term. Further, fresh election to constitute a Panchayat shall be completed *(i)* before the expiry of its duration of five years; or *(ii)* in case of dissolution, before the expiry of a period of six months from the date of its dissolution.
6. **Disqualifications:** A person shall be disqualified for being chosen as or for being a member of Panchayat if he is so disqualified *(i)* under any law for the time being in force for the purposes of elections to the legislature of the state concerned, or *(ii)* under any law made by the state legislature. However, no person shall be disqualified on the ground that he is less than 25 years of age if he has attained the age of 21 years. Further, all questions of disqualifications shall be referred to such authority as the state legislature determines.
7. **Powers and Functions:** The state legislature may endow the Panchayats, with such powers and authority as may be necessary to enable them to function as institutions of self-government. Such a scheme may contain provisions for the devolution of powers and responsibilities upon Panchayats at the appropriate level with respect to *(i)* the preparation of plans for economic development and social justice; *(ii)* the implementation of schemes for economic development and social justice as may be entrusted to them, including those in relation to the 29 matters listed in the Eleventh Schedule.
8. **Finances:** The state legislature may *(i)* authorise a Panchayat to levy, collect and appropriate taxes, duties, tolls and fees; *(ii)* assign to a Panchayat taxes, duties, tolls end fees levied and collected by the state government; *(iii)* provide for making grants-in-aid to the Panchayats from the Consolidated Fund of the state; and *(iv)* provide for constitution of funds crediting all moneys of the panchayats.

URBAN LOCAL GOVERNMENT

The term *'Urban Local Government'* in India signifies the governance of an urban area by the people through their elected representatives. The jurisdiction of an urban local government is limited to a specific urban area which is demarcated for this purpose by the state government.

There are eight types of urban local governments in India-Municipal Corporation, Municipality, Notified Area Committee, Town Area Committee, Cantonment Board, Township, Port Trust and Special Purpose Agency. The system of urban government was constitutionalised through the 74th constitutional Amendment Act of 1992. At the central level, the subject of 'urban local government' is dealt with by the following three ministries.

1. Ministry of Urban Development created as a separate ministry in 1985.
2. Ministry of Defence in the case of cantonment boards.
3. Ministry of Home Affairs in the case of Union Territories.

Historical Perspective

The institutions of urban local government originated and developed in modern India during the period of British rule. The major events in this context are:

(i) In 1687, the first municipal corporation in India was set up at Madras.

(ii) In 1726, the municipal corporations were set up in Bombay and Calcutta.

(iii) Lord Mayo's Resolution of 1870 on financial decentralisation visualised the development of local self-government institutions.

(iv) Lord Ripon's Resolution of 1882 has been hailed as the 'Magna carta' of local self-government. He is called as the father of local-self government in India.

(v) The Royal Commission on decentralisation was appointed in 1907 and it submitted its report in 1909. Its chairman was Hobhouse.

(vi) Under the dyarchical scheme introduced in Provinces by the Government of India Act of 1919, local self-government became a transferred subject under the charge of a responsible Indian minister.

(vii) In 1924, the Cantonments Act was passed by the Central legislature.

(viii) Under the provincial autonomy scheme introduced by the Government of India Act of 1935, local self-government was declared a provincial subject.

74th Amendment Act of 1992

This Act has added Part IX-A to the Constitution of India. It is entitled as "The Municipalities' and consists of provisions from articles 243-P to 243-ZG. In addition, the Act has also added Twelfth Schedule to the Constitution. It contains 18 functional items of municipalities and deals with Article 243-W.

The Act gave constitutional status to the municipalities. It has brought them under the purview of justiciable part of the constitution. In other words, state governments are under constitutional obligation to adopt the new system of municipalities in accordance with the provisions of the Act.

The Act aims at revitalising and strengthening the urban governments so that they function effectively as units of local government.

The salient features of the Act are:

1. **Three Types of Municipalities:** The Act provides for the constitution of the following three types of municipalities in every state.
   (*a*) A Nagar Panchayat (by whatever name called) for a transitional area, that is, an area in transition from a rural area to an urban area.
   (*b*) A Municipality for a smaller urban area.
   (*c*) A Municipal Corporation for a larger urban area.

A transitional area, a smaller urban area or a larger urban area means such area as the Governor may specify by public notification for this purpose with regard to the following factors.

(*a*) Population of the area
(*b*) Density of population
(*c*) Revenue generated for local administration
(*d*) Percentage of employment in non-agricultural activities
(*e*) Economic importance or such other factors as the Governor may deem fit.

2. **Composition:** All the members of a municipality shall be elected directly by the people of the municipal area. For this purpose, each municipal area shall be divided int territorial constituencies to be known as wards. The state legislature may provide the manner of election of the chairperson of a municipality. It may also provide for the representation of the following persons in a municipality.
   (*i*) Persons having special knowledge or experience in municipal administration without the right to vote in the meetings of municipality.
   (*ii*) The members of the Lok Sabha and the state legislative Assembly representing constituencies which comprise wholly or partly the municipal area.
   (*iii*) The members of the Rajya Sabha and the state legislative council registered as electors with the municipal area.
   (*iv*) The chairpersons of committees (other than wards committees).
3. **Wards Committees:** There shall be constituted a wards committee, consisting of one or more wards, within the territorial area of a municipality having population of three lakhs or more. The state legislature may make provision with respect to the composition and the territorial area of a wards committee and the manner in which the seats in a wards committee shall be filled. It may also make any provision for the constitution of committees in addition to the wards committees.
4. **Reservation of Seats:** The Act provides for the reservation of seats for the scheduled castes and the scheduled tribes in every municipality in propor-tion of their population to the total population in the municipal area. Further, it provides for the reservation of not less than one-third of the total number of seats for women (including the number of seats reserved for women belonging to the SCs and the STs). The state legislature may provide for the manner of reservation of offices of chairpersons in the municipalities for the SCs, the STs and the women. It may also make any provision for the reservation of seats in any municipality or offices of chairpersons in municipalities in favour of backward classes.
5. **Duration of Municipalities:** The Act provides for a five-year term of office for every municipality. However, it can be dissolved before the completion of its term. Further, the fresh election to constitute a municipality shall be completed (*i*) before the expiry of its duration of five years; or (*ii*) in case of dissolution, before the expiry of a period of six months from the date of its dissolution.
6. **Disqualifications:** A person shall be disqualified for being chosen as or for being a member of a municipality if he is so disqualified
   (*i*) under any law for the time being in force for the purposes of elections to the legislature of the state concerned; or
   (*ii*) under any law made by the state legislature.

   However, no person shall be disqualified on the ground that he is less than 25 years of age if he has attained the age of 21 years. Further, all questions of disqualifications shall be referred to such authority as the state legislature determines.
7. **State Election Commission:** The superintendence, direction and control of the preparation of electoral rolls and the conduct of all elections of the municipalities shall be vested in the State Election Commission.
8. **Powers and Functions:** The state legislature may endow the municipalities with such powers and authority as may be necessary to enable them to function as institutions of self-government. Such a scheme may contain provisions for the devolution of powers and responsibilities upon municipalities at the appropriate level with respect to (*i*) the preparation of plans for economic development and social justice; (*ii*) the implementation of schemes for economic development and social justice as may be entrusted to them including

those in relation to the 18 matters listed in the Twelfth Schedule.

9. **Finances:** The state legislature may (*i*) authorise a municipality to levy, collect and appropriate taxes, duties, tolls and fees; (*ii*) assign to a muicipality taxes, duties, tolls and fees levied and collected by state government; (*iii*) provide for making grants-in-aid to the municipalities from the Consolidated Found of the state; and (*iv*) provide for constitution of funds for crediting all moneys of the municipalities.

SOCIAL JUSTICE AND THE MARGINALISED

WOMEN

After a brief spell of equality of sexes in the vedic period, there began deterioration in status of women. During the medieval age purdah became a custom among muslim and sati became prevalent among Hindus. Patriarchal norms were expressed through cultural metaphors. British system of education together with liberal sentiments led to reformist movement. Organization and persons took cognizance of injustices meted out to women. Social legislation, viz. Abolition of Sati (1829) Widow Remarriage Act (1856), Civil Marriage Act (1872) were important steps in this regard. The Nationalist Movement and Gandhiji's call dragged women into the mainstream of Indian politics. **All India Women's Conference** was organized in 1927.

After independence a number of steps were taken to ensure equality and dignity of women and free them from the clutches of unjustified subjugation. These include :

Constitutional Provisions

Article 14 : provides that the state shall not delay to any person equality before the law or equal protection of law.

Article 15 : prohibits discrimination on grounds such as caste, religion and sex.

Article 16 : provides for equality of opportunity in matters relating to public employment.

Article 16(4) : empowers the state to make special provisions for women and children.

These provisions are justifiable.

Article 39(a) : equal right to and adequate means of livelihood.

Article 39(c) : equal pay for equal work for both; men and women.

Article 42 : make provisions for just and human conditions of work and maternity relief.

42 Amendment Part IV A Article 51A imposes a **fundamental duty to renounce practices derogatory to the dignity of women.**

The 73rd and 74th Amendment Act heralded a new era by reserving 1/3 seats at all levels of rural and urban local self government for women.

Enactments

Special Marriage Act 1954

Hindu Marriage Act 1955

Hindu Maintenance and Adoption Act 1956

Dowry Prohibition Act 1961

Equal Remuneration Act 1976

Child Marriage Restraint (Amendment) Act 1978

Dowry Prohibition (Amendment) Act 1984.

Judiciary has also been active as shown in the Shah Bano case (1982)

The Protection of Women from Domestic Violence Act, 2005 came into force on October 26, 2006.

Other Measures

Social Welfare Board was constituted in 1953 to grant aid, promote welfare and development services for women.

In 1985 a separate department of women and child development was set up at the centre.

In 1986 National Policy on Education outlined several features for women's education.

In 1987 programme of support to training cum employment for women was started.

In 1990 Parliament enacted a law to create National Commission for women. It came into existence in 1992.

In 1995 Indira Mahila Yojna was started with the aim of organizing women at grassroots level.

In 2001 National Policy for Empowerment of women was launched.

National Commission for Women

- Statutory body created in 1992
- Consists of a Chairman nominated by the Government.
- There are 5 other members and a member secretary.
- It is vested with power of civil court.

Functions

1. To investigate and examine all matters relating to safeguards for women.

2. Make recommendation for effective implementation of safeguards.
3. Review the existing provision of the Constitution.
4. Call for special studies or investigations into specific problems.

How to Empower

- Widening the ambit of women's participation in public institutions and bringing them directly into the mainstream to enjoy the benefits of society.
- Universalizing existing developmental programmes to include women.
- To promote gender sensitiveness by proactive measures like one child norm (providing free education to the lone girl child).
- To invest in sectors where women could be a better performer.
- Skilling women through training and workshops.
- Insuring credit facilities.
- Creating legal awareness through producing book, pamphlets and media campaign.
- Ensure equal access to quality education for girls.
- Provide scholarships, mentorship, and support for women in higher education.
- Promote literacy and vocational training in rural or marginalised communities.
- Ensure equal pay for equal work.
- Support women entrepreneurs with credit, training and markets.
- Provide maternity benefits and safe working environments.
- Encourage workplace leadership and representation.
- Enforce laws against gender-based violence, harassment and discrimination.
- Encourage women's participation in politics and governance.
- Reform property, inheritance and family laws that disadvantage women.
- Promote women's leadership in community, business and government roles.
- Support women's organisations, media platforms and advocacy groups.
- Challenge stereotypes that silence or belittle women's contributions.
- Challenge gender stereotypes in media and education.
- Engage men and boys as allies in promoting gender equality.
- Celebrate women's achievements in history, art, science and leadership.
- Ensure access to quality healthcare, including reproductive rights.
- Provide safe spaces and support systems for survivors of violence.

DALITS

The category 'Dalits' includes the castes who fall outside the Varna system. They are also called by various names; such as outcastes, untouchables or achhuts. They are marginalised sections whose major source of frustration relates to individual behaviour, norms of the society and state apparatus. Though their position has improved due to constitutional provisions, welfare policies and positive discrimination measures, a firm commitment is required to hinder the hindrances in ensuring equality.

Constitutional Provisions

1. **Article 341** deals with the criteria for identification of scheduled castes.
2. **Article 342** deals with Scheduled Tribes.
3. **Article 17** abolished practice of untouchability in any form.
4. **Articles 14, 15 ,16 and 16(4)** place them in equal position with other members and entrust state to make special provisions.
5. **Article 38** enjoins the state to promote the welfare of people by ensuring justice in society.
6. **Article 46** entrusts the state to promote the educational and economic interests of scheduled caste.
7. 65th Amendment Act, 1990 provided for **National Commission** for SCs and STs. But, recently there has been bifurcation of the commission to deal exclusively with one category.

Legal Enactments

1. Untouchability offences Act 1995.
2. Protection of Civil Rights Act 1975.
3. SC and ST (Prevention of Atrocities) Act 1989.

Development Measures

1. Book Bank Scheme
2. Girls Hostel and Boys Hostel Schemes
3. Coaching
4. Scheduled Caste Development Corporation
5. Separate plan of Action for Primitive Tribe
6. Tribal sub plan strategy to provide legal and administrative support and promote their development.

SOCIAL SCIENCE

Multiple Choice Questions

1. The Constitution of India was adopted on:
   A. 15 August, 1947
   B. 26 January, 1950
   C. 26 November, 1949
   D. 15 August, 1950
2. Who administers the oaths of office to the Vice-President?
   A. Chief Justice of India
   B. President of India
   C. Speaker of the Lok Sabha
   D. Attorney-General of India
3. Who among the following is not appointed by the President?
   A. Chairman of UPSC
   B. Governor of State
   C. Judge of a High Court
   D. Vice-President
4. The President can dissolve the Lok Sabha before expiry of its term, on the advice of:
   A. Prime Minister
   B. Speaker
   C. Vice-President
   D. Election Commissioner
5. A presidential ordinance remains in force for:
   A. three months B. one month
   C. six months D. till it is revoked
6. The idea of Fundamental Duties is derived from:
   A. Russian Constitution
   B. British Constitution
   C. American Constitution
   D. German Constitution
7. The Fundamental Right, which cannot be suspended even during an emergency is:
   A. Right to equality
   B. Right to freedom of expression
   C. Right to movement
   D. Right to life
8. Whether the bill in the Parliament, is a money bill or not, is decided by:
   A. Prime Minister
   B. Speaker
   C. President
   D. Comptroller and Auditor General
9. Which of the following is presided over by a non-member:
   A. Lok Sabha
   B. Rajya Sabha
   C. Vidhan Sabha
   D. Joint sitting of Lok Sabha and Rajya Sabha
10. For the Union Territories, not having legislatures of their own, laws are enacted by:
    A. Parliament B. President
    C. Administrators D. Union Law Ministry
11. Arunachal Pradesh was granted statehood in:
    A. 1972 B. 1984
    C. 1985 D. 1987
12. The official language of Jammu and Kashmir is:
    A. Dogri B. Kashmiri
    C. Urdu D. Hindustani
13. The minimum age to qualify for the membership of Rajya Sabha is:
    A. 18 years B. 21 years
    C. 25 years D. 30 years
14. A minister, who is not a member of either house of the Parliament must get himself elected within:
    A. a year B. six months
    C. three months D. two months
15. By convention, the Governor of a state generally belongs to:
    A. ruling party in the state
    B. opposition party of the state
    C. IAS cadre of the state
    D. some other state
16. The world 'secular' in the Preamble of the Indian Constitution was incorporated by the:
    A. 42nd amendment
    B. 62nd amendment

C. 44th amendment
D. 41st amendment

17. Constitution describes India as a:
A. Federation of states
B. Quasi-federation
C. Union of states
D. Dominion of free states

18. Which of the following article cannot be amended by simple majority?
A. Creation of new states
B. Procedure of election of the President
C. Official language of the Union
D. Quorum in the Parliament

19. Constitution provides residual powers to the:
A. Union Government
B. State Government
C. President
D. Supreme Court

20. President of India has immunity from:
A. Civil proceedings during the term of office
B. Criminal proceedings during the term of office
C. Civil and criminal proceedings during the term of office
D. Civil and criminal proceedings after the retirement

21. Minimum age to qualify for the President's post is:
A. 21 years B. 25 years
C. 30 years D. 35 years

22. The constitutional amendment which made Sikkim a state of India was:
A. 34th B. 35th
C. 36th D. 37th

23. State legislatures are not allowed to discuss:
A. conduct of speaker
B. conduct of any High Court judge
C. autonomy issue
D. taxation

24. Reservation of seats for Scheduled Castes/Tribes was initially provided till:
A. 1955 B. 1960
C. 1970 D. 1980

25. In case of unavailability of the President and Vice-President, the duties of the President are discharged by:
A. Prime Minister
B. Speaker of the Lok Sabha
C. Senior-most Cabinet Minister
D. Chief Justice of India

26. Which Fundamental Right can be described as the soul and heart of the Constitution:
A. Right to equality
B. Right to prosperity
C. Right to constitutional remedies
D. Right to freedom of speech

27. Ordinances are promulgated by:
A. Prime Minister
B. Lok Sabha Speaker
C. President
D. Rajya Sabha Chairman

28. Indian states have been constituted on the basis of:
A. geographical continuity
B. language
C. administrative convenience
D. economic conditions

29. The Chief Election Commissioner can be removed by:
A. Prime Minister
B. President
C. Supreme Court's Chief Justice
D. Parliament

30. Speaker of the Lok Sabha can only:
A. adjourn the house
B. prorogue the house
C. summon the house
D. dissolve the house

31. Membership of state assembly range from:
A. 30 to 300 B. 40 to 400
C. 50 to 600 D. 60 to 500

32. Salaries of Supreme Court judges are drawn from:
A. Law Ministry Grants
B. Consolidated Fund of India
C. Home Ministry Grants
D. Parliamentary Grants

33. The need of establish Panchayati Raj institutions is prescribed in:
A. Directive Principles
B. Fundamental Rights
C. Preamble
D. Seventh Schedule

34. Which Constitutional amendment curtailed the power of judicial review by the Supreme Court?
A. 24th amendment
B. 42nd amendment
C. 43rd amendment
D. 44th amendment

35. The quorum in Lok Sabha is:
A. 50
B. 55
C. one-fourth of the strength
D. one-tenth of the strength

36. The disagreement between Lok Sabha and Rajya Sabha is solved by:
A. setting up Joint Select Committee
B. dissolving Lok Sabha
C. setting up adjudication committee
D. calling a joint session

37. The seventh schedule consists of:
A. List of national languages
B. List of oaths and affirmations
C. List of subjects
D. List of States and Union Territories

SOCIAL SCIENCE

38. Provisions of disqualification on ground of defection are listed in:
A. second schedule B. fourth schedule
C. eighth schedule D. tenth schedule
39. The Union Territories get representation in:
A. only Lok Sabha
B. only Rajya Sabha
C. both Lok Sabha and Rajya Sabha
D. neither Lok Sabha nor Rajya Sabha
40. If Lok Sabha and Rajya Sabha disagree on a constitutional amendment bill:
A. the bill lapses
B. a joint sitting is called
C. Lok Sabha's decision prevails
D. Rajya Sabha's decision prevails
41. The Preamble of the Constitution was amended by:
A. 1st amendment B. 26th amendment
C. 42nd amendment D. 44th amendment
42. Eighth General Elections were held in:
A. 1980 B. 1985
C. 1989 D. 1991
43. The retirement age for Supreme Court judges is:
A. 58 years B. 60 years
C. 62 years D. 65 years
44. One can be disqualified from voting, only on the grounds of:
A. Age B. Sex
C. Religion D. Education
45. Governors of states are:
A. appointed by Chief Ministers
B. appointed by the President
C. elected by members of Legislative Assembly
D. elected by people
46. First General elections in the country were held in:
A. 1948 B. 1950
C. 1949 D. 1952
47. A total of ...... members can be nominated by the President of Rajya Sabha.
A. 6 B. 12
C. 15 D. 18
48. The Union executive is responsible to:
A. Lok Sabha B. Rajya Sabha
C. President D. Supreme Court
49. Attorney-General of India is appointed by:
A. UPSC B. President
C. Prime Minister D. Lok Sabha Speaker
50. Time gap between two sessions of Parliament cannot exceed:
A. 3 months B. 6 months
C. 1 year D. no fixed gap
51. Supreme Commander of defence forces is:
A. Army Chief B. Defence Minister
C. Prime Minister D. President
52. Which of the following is not a state?
A. Mizoram B. Manipur
C. Puducherry D. Arunachal Pradesh
53. India is a republic because:
A. every adult can take part in elections
B. executive is responsible to legislature
C. elected representatives can be recalled
D. President is elected for a fixed term
54. Article 356 deals with:
A. National emergency
B. Constitutional emergency
C. Financial emergency
D. Fundamental Rights during emergency
55. The only President to be elected twice is:
A. Rajendra Prasad
B. Radhakrishnan
C. V.V. Giri
D. Neelam Sanjeeva Reddy
56. Vice-President can submit his resignation to:
A. President
B. Prime Minister
C. Chief Justice of India
D. Deputy Chairman of Rajya Sabha
57. Which two words were added to Preamble of Constitution by amendment?
A. Secular democratic
B. Democratic republic
C. Secular socialist
D. Republic socialist
58. The Chairman of the drafting committee of the Constitution was:
A. Rajendra Prasad B. Jawaharlal Nehru
C. B.R. Ambedkar D. Sardar Patel
59. The Fundamental Rights are:
A. only available to citizens
B. only a few are available to citizens
C. none is available to non-citizens
D. only a few are available to non-citizens
60. Which one is not a national duty?
A. Respect the Constitution
B. Respect the President
C. Defend the country
D. Protect natural environment
61. Which one of the following is not a writ, issued by Supreme Court?
A. Prohibition B. Habeas Corpus
C. Certiorari D. Suo-Moto
62. Which one is not a Directive Principle?
A. Equal pay for equal work
B. Prevention of cow slaughter
C. Pollution control
D. Promotion of international peace
63. Governments try to follow Directive Principles because:
A. Legislatures can pass no-confidence motion on the issue

B. they represent the demands and aspirations of people
C. courts can pass injunctions, if not accepted
D. President can dismiss Government

64. Which Directive Principle has been fully implemented in the country?
A. Setting up village Panchayats as the unit of self-Government
B. Securing the Uniform Civil Code throughout the country
C. Prohibition of the use of intoxicants
D. Providing adequate means of livelihood for all citizens

65. Which house of Parliament can create All-India Services?
A. Lok Sabha
B. Rajya Sabha
C. Either house
D. Joint sitting of both houses

66. Two houses of the Parliament enjoy equal powers with regard to:
A. Money Bill
B. Election of President
C. Removal of Government
D. Creation of All India Services

67. The Committee which looks after the financial matters of the Government is:
A. Business Advisory Committee
B. Committee on Government Assurances
C. Privilege Committee
D. Public Accounts Committee

68. Lok Sabha cannot be addressed by:
A. Vice-President
B. Attorney-General
C. Minister, not a member of Lok Sabha
D. Speaker

69. President does not appoint:
A. Prime Minister
B. Lok Sabha Speaker
C. Election Commissioner
D. Comptroller and Auditor-General

70. Prime Minister of India, at the time of appointment, need not be:
A. citizen of India
B. above 25 years of age
C. Member of Parliament
D. of sound mind

71. The Prime Minister, who could not face the Parliament even once, was:
A. V.P. Singh B. Charan Singh
C. Morarji Desai D. Deve Gowda

72. Among the judicial powers, the President can not:
A. grant pardon B. grant reprieve
C. grant amnesty D. grant change of court

73. National emergency can not be imposed in case of:
A. Armed rebellion
B. Political crisis
C. Internal aggression
D. War

74. Constitutional emergency can be renewed upto:
A. six months B. two years
C. three years D. indefinitely

75. Vice-President is ex-officio:
A. Member of Rajya Sabha
B. Chairman of Rajya Sabha
C. Member of Lok Sabha
D. Speaker of Lok Sabha

76. Governor can consult the President, in regard to:
A. Appointment of Chief Minister
B. Money bill
C. Non-money bill
D. Dissolving assembly

77. The resolution to abolish or create legislative council should be:
A. approved by two-third of majority of assembly members voting
B. approved by two-third majority of total strength of assembly
C. approved by a simple majority of assembly members voting
D. approved by a simple majority and forwarded by the Governor

78. Which of the following High Court has jurisdiction over a Union Territory?
A. Calcutta B. Patna
C. Karnataka D. Allahabad

79. Which state does not have its High Court at the Capital?
A. Andhra Pradesh B. Kerala
C. Bihar D. Maharashtra

80. Tax not imposed by the Central Government is:
A. Income tax B. Corporation tax
C. Professional tax D. Capital gains tax

81. Official language of the Union is:
A. Hindi in Devanagri script
B. Hindi in Roman script
C. English in Roman script
D. Hindi and English

82. The first constitutional amendment related to:
A. Preamble
B. Directive Principles
C. Fundamental Duties
D. Ninth Schedule

83. The number of schedules in the Constitution is:
A. 395 B. 100
C. 12 D. 8

84. Indian citizenship cannot be terminated by:
A. Renunciation B. Termination
C. Deprivation D. Imprisonment

85. Supreme Court comes to the rescue of Fundamental Rights, if:
A. Executive violates
B. Legislature violates
C. An individual violates
D. either of the above

86. The residuary power of making law vests with:
A. Centre
B. State
C. Both of them
D. Supreme Court decides

87. Finance Commission is constituted by:
A. Parliament B. President
C. Prime Minister D. Lok Sabha Speaker

88. Which of the following is not a state subject?
A. Administration of justice
B. Agriculture
C. Audit and Accounts
D. Public health

89. The dispute relating to the election of the President is referred to:
A. Election Commissioner
B. Supreme Court
C. Parliament
D. Parliament and State assemblies

90. In the absence of the Prime Minister, cabinet meetings are presided over by:
A. Defence Minister
B. Home Minister
C. Finance Minister
D. Prime Minister decides

ANSWERS

1	**2**	**3**	**4**	**5**	**6**	**7**	**8**	**9**	**10**
C	B	D	A	C	A	D	B	B	A
11	**12**	**13**	**14**	**15**	**16**	**17**	**18**	**19**	**20**
D	C	D	B	D	A	C	B	A	B
21	**22**	**23**	**24**	**25**	**26**	**27**	**28**	**29**	**30**
D	C	B	B	D	C	C	B	D	A
31	**32**	**33**	**34**	**35**	**36**	**37**	**38**	**39**	**40**
D	B	A	B	D	D	C	D	C	A
41	**42**	**43**	**44**	**45**	**46**	**47**	**48**	**49**	**50**
C	B	D	A	B	D	B	A	B	B
51	**52**	**53**	**54**	**55**	**56**	**57**	**58**	**59**	**60**
D	C	D	B	A	A	C	C	D	B
61	**62**	**63**	**64**	**65**	**66**	**67**	**68**	**69**	**70**
D	C	B	A	B	B	D	A	B	C
71	**72**	**73**	**74**	**75**	**76**	**77**	**78**	**79**	**80**
B	D	B	C	B	C	A	A	B	C
81	**82**	**83**	**84**	**85**	**86**	**87**	**88**	**89**	**90**
A	D	C	D	D	A	B	C	B	D

World Geography

THE SOLAR SYSTEM

The solar system is a group of celestial bodies comprising the sun and the large number of bodies that are bound gravitationally to the sun and revolve around it.

THE SUN

The sun is the star at the centre of the solar system. It is the nearest star to the earth. The next nearest star, Alpha Centauri, is more than 4.0×10^{13} km away. The general statistics of the sun is as:

Diameter	1.392×10^6 km
Volume	1.304×10^6 times the volume of earth
Temperature	6000ºC at surface and 15 million degree C at the centre
Relative Density	1.4
Gravitational Pull	28 times the gravitational pull of the earth

The outermost part of sun's atmosphere is called corona. The visible surface of the sun and source of the adsorption spectrum is called *Photosphere* which is characteristic of the most stars. The stratum of sun's atmosphere immediately above the photosphere and below is *Chromosphere*. The whole body of the sun is gaseous in form. The gas is mostly hydrogen, which accounts 70% of its mass. The remainder is made up of 28% helium and 2% all other heavier elements from lithium to uranium. The generation of solar energy comes from thermo-nuclear reactions.

The dark spot in the Sun is called sunspot which appears dark by contrast with the solar surface, because they have a somewhat lower temperature of about 4500º K. The number of sunspot are found to vary from year to year with a period of about 11 years. This periodicity is known as Sunspot-cycle.

THE EARTH

The earth is a member of a group of celestial bodies which comprises the sun and Eight planets, Mercury, Venus, Earth, Mars, Jupiter, Saturn, Uranus and Neptune. Planets have no light of their own and all of them, except Venus and Uranus rotate upon their axis from west to east. Venus and Uranus rotate upon their axis from east to west. Many satellites are revolving around their respective planets. Thousands of comets and billions of meteoroids are there in the space. The Earth has only one satellite the moon while Mercury and Venus have none. The average distance of the earth from the sun is 1.496×10^8 km. The earth is the third nearest planet to the sun and is the fifth largest planet.

The Earth: Facts and Figures	
Mass of Earth	5.880×10^{21} tons
Density of Earth	5.517 times that of water
Volume of Earth	1.083×10^{11} cubic km
Equatorial Circumference	4.007×10^4 km
Polar Diameter	12, 714 km
Equatorial Diameter	12756 km
Polar or Meridional Circumference	4.0×10^4 km

Estimated Age	At least 4600 million years
Land Surface	148,951,000 sq km
Water Surface	361,150,000 sq km (71 per cent of total area
Highest Point of the land surface	Mt. Everest (8,848 metres)
Lowest point of the land surface	Shores of the Dead Sea (396 metres below the sea level)
Greatest Ocean Depth	Mariana Trench, East of Philippines (11,033 metres below the sea level)

Shape of the Earth

The earth is an oblate spheroid and not a true sphere because it is flattened at the poles and bulges out at the equator. The polar diameter of the earth is 42 km shorter than the equatorial diameter, therefore the earth oblate.

Motion of the Earth

The earth spins like a top on its axis completing one rotation every 24 hours and revolves around the sun once in 365.25 days. While the daily rotation, *i.e.*, spin of the earth causes day and night, the revolution is responsible for the change of the seasons. The earth is a non-luminous sphere, emitting no light of its own. The part of the earth's surface which is towards the sun at any time is lit, while the remaining past, on the other side of the earth, is dark. The earth rotates from west to east. That is why the sun, the moon and the stars appears to us to be moving in the opposite direction.

Effect of Rotation

The daily axial rotation of the earth causes:

(i) Formation of day and night
(ii) Difference in Longitude and Time
(iii) Change in direction of winds and currents
(iv) Tides occur twice a day

Effect of Revolution

The earth revolves around the sun in a vast elliptical orbit. One such revolution takes about 365.25 days. One ordinary year contains 365 days, and to make up for the difference, every fourth year which is called a Leap Year, is calculated as 366 days. The change of seasons is mainly due to the revolution.

- **21st June:** At this time it is summer in the Northern Hemisphere and winter in the Southern Hemisphere. The midday sun shines vertically over the Tropic of Cancer.
- **22nd December:** At this time it is winter in the Northern Hemisphere and summer in the Southern Hemisphere. The midday sun shines vertically over the Tropic of Capricorn.

Equinoxes

On 21st March and 23rd September the season is either spring or Autumn. These days, days and nights are equal everywhere. Sun's rays fall vertically on the equator. These two position of the earth are called Equinoxes due to the equal length of the days and nights.

Inclination of the Earth's Axis

The earth's polar axis is not vertical but inclined and it make an angle of 66½° with the plane of the elliptic and is tilted 33½° from a line perpendicular to the plane in which the earth's orbit and the sun lie. The plane is imagined to be horizontal and to pass through the centre of globe. As a result of the inclination of the axis of the earth and its elliptical orbit around the sun, the earth attains four critical position in respect of the sun. On 21st June, the earth is so located in its orbit that the north polar end of its axis leans at the maximum angle of 23½° towards the sun, *i.e.*, the Tropic of Cancer receives the vertical rays of the sun. This condition is known as summer solstice, the longest day in the norther hemisphere. On 22nd December the earth is in an equivalent but opposite position in its orbit, *i.e.*, the Tropic of Capricorn receives the vertical rays of the sun. This condition is the winter solstice, the longest day in the southern hemisphere. Equinoxes occur when the earth's axis makes 90° angle with a line drawn to the sun, *i.e.*, the equator receives the vertical rays of the sun and day and night are equal. The vernal equinox occurs on 21st March and autumnal equinox on 23rd September. At the time of winter solstice the sun is not visible to a person on the north pole and during the summer solstice, the sun is not visible to a person on the south pole.

Latitude and Longitude

Lines of latitude and longitude are drawn on a map to locate position of the place on the surface of the earth. The latitude of place is defined as its distance north or south of the equator, measured as an angle. Latitudes are thus lines drawn parallel to the equator which is at 0° and they are counted up to 90° north and south, the two poles. The longitudes show the distance of a point east or west of the Prime Meridian which is at 0° and passes through Greenwich village near London in U.K. There are 360° Longitude and all the longitudinal lines join the poles. The longitude of a place can be defined as its distance east or west the meridian of Greenwich, measured as an angle.

Tropics

Tropics are literally the turning points. They refer to those parallels where the sun is imagined to stop its movement and turn about northward or southward, as the case may be. They are the 23° North parallel or Tropic of Cancer and 23½° South parallel or Tropic of Capricorn. Both are imaginary lines.

- **Local Time:** The system in which we measure time is based on the concept of the solar day. The time when the sun's altitude is the highest at that place, the shadow of a vertical rod fixed in the ground is the shortest. If at this time we set our watch at 12 O'clock. It will indicate local time.
- **Standard Time:** If every place were to are its own local time that would cause confusion in administration and other activities. So the local time of a place generally in the middle of the country, is used everywhere in that country as the Standard Time of that country and is taken in to be uniform throughout Standard Time of India is the local time of a place near Allahabad situated at 82½° E longitude.

  However, in bigger countries like Russia, America etc, it is not possible to have a single standard time for the whole country. Therefore, a number of standard times are chosen which are applicable for a limited region.

THE MOON

Moon is the only natural satellite of the earth. It has diameter of about 3,480 km and has a mass of 1/81 that of the earth. The moon's period of revolution with reference to the sun is about 29.53 days. This period is called a synodic month. Moon also rotates on its own axis. The time taken by the moon to complete one rotation on its axis in 27.32 days. This fact has an important bearing upon the earth-moon relationship. Consequent to this relationship, we always see the same face of the moon from the earth. Only 59% of the moon's surface is directly visible from earth.

- **Eclipses:** Eclipses are caused by the fact that light travels in a straight line, producing clearly well defined shadows of objects in its path. When the earth comes between the moon and the sun, and it shuts off the light of the sun from falling upon the moon and this is called *Lunar Eclipse*. When the moon comes directly between the sun and the earth it obstructs light of the sun from falling upon the earth and this is called Solar Eclipse. Solar and Lunar eclipses do not occur every month because the moon's path around the earth is at an angle to the path of the earth around the sun. Sometimes only, the bodies fall in a line, producing an eclipse.

ATMOSPHERE

Atmosphere is the thin gaseous envelope surrounding and protecting the earth. It contains about 5.0×10^2 tonnes of gases a small amount of water vapour and some dust particle. The dry air of the atmosphere comprises of nitrogen 78.09%, oxygen 20.95%, and argon 0.93%. Besides, there are minute proportions of other gases, including carbon dioxide, helium, methane, hydrogen, ozone, neon, xenon, etc. The amount of carbon dioxide varies from place to place being greatest around the cities and smallest in the countryside.

The atmosphere is essential for life on earth. Oxygen and carbon dioxide in the atmosphere are necessary for animal and plant life. The ozone layer in the stratosphere protects life on earth by absorbing most of the sun's harmful radiation.

ATMOSPHERIC LAYERS

The atmosphere has been divided into subspheres according to the general characteristics of temperature variations. The different atmospheric layers are:

(i) **Troposphere:** It is the nearest to the earth's surface and extends to a distance of about 13 km. In Troposphere, generally, the temperature decreases as height increases. It is the densest of all layers and contains water vapours, moistures and dust. It also profoundly influences earth's climate since 80% of the mass of air comprising the entire atmosphere is concentrated in this zone.

(ii) **Tropopause:** It refers to the boundary region which separates troposphere from the adjoining atmospheric layer known as stratosphere.

(iii) **Stratosphere:** It is a region of uniform temperature extending from an altitude of about 11 km above the earth to a height of nearly 30 km. It is free from water vapour, clouds and dust. The upper part of stratosphere has plenty of ozone which affords protection to human beings on the earth against the fatal effects of solar ultraviolet radiations.

(iv) **Mesosphere:** It is a very cold region above the ozone rich layer of stratosphere.

(v) **Ionosphere:** It comes immediately above mesosphere, extends from about 50 km to 500 km above the earth. It includes the thermosphere and exosphere. The region contains ionised or electrically charged air and reflects radio waves facilitating wireless communication between distant places. The ionised air also protect those on earth from the falling meteorites, most of which are made to burn out at this region.

(vi) **Thermosphere:** It constitutes the middle layer of ionosphere and has a temperature of 100° C.

(vii) **Exosphere:** It is the uppermost region of the atmosphere, where the air density is so low that an air molecule moving rapidly straight upward is more than 50% likely to escape from the atmosphere instead of hitting other molecules.

Weather: It refers to conditions of temperature wind, humidity, rainfall at a given time and place.

Climate: It refers to the average weather conditions of a region as a whole over a comparatively long period of time.

PRECIPITATION

The term precipitation refers to falling of water snow or hail from the clouds and results when condensation is occurring rapidly with in a cloud. The most common form of precipitation is rain and is formed when many cloud droplets coalesce into drops too large to remain suspended in the air. Sometimes the raindrops freeze before reaching the ground, then the precipitation occurs in form of pellets, called sleet. Precipitation can be orographic, conventional or cyclonic in nature. When the air is caused to rise upwards due to cyclonic circulation. The resulting precipitation is said to be of the cyclonic type.

- **Clouds:** Clouds are huge collection of water-vapours. They are formed by very minute suspended water particles present in the air. When there is very low temperature, they are formed by huge collection of very small crystal like structure of snow.

  Clouds are of different type and they can be classified on the basis of their form and altitude. On the basis of form clouds are known as stratiform or layered types, and cumuliform or massive type. According to the altitudes, clouds are called cirrus and the combination of these two lead to the cirrocumulus, cirrostratus.
- **Fog:** When moist air meets cold surface of earth, some of the water vapours condense on the particles of dust in air. This cloud of condensed vapour is called fog.
- **Mist:** Like fog, it is also formed on account of the fall of temperature of air. Here the droplet of water formed on account of condensation are heavier than those of the fog, therefore, mist is always seen close to the earth and does not rise up so high as the fog.
- **Dew:** At night, the earth may frequently become cooler than the air above it. This causes water vapour contained in the air to get condensed and deposited on the cooled surface. This is known as dew. Dew is more likely to occur on clear and calm nights.
- **Rainfall:** When the rain-laden clouds rise up, they expand and become cooler. They also become cooler because they are moving away from hotter region. The cooling of the air resulting in the precipitation of rain etc. It may be due to relief, convention and cyclone.

  As we ascend a hill or a mountain temperature decreases. If, then, a wind blowing from the sea and saturated with water vapour comes to a mountain, it is forced to rise. On rising the clouds reach thinner layers of air and consequently it expands. Expansion produces cooling. The moisture in the clouds is then condensed and falls as rain. Such rains are called the relief rains. When air is heated, it tends to rise up. As it rises, it is cooled and rain falls even though there are no mountains nearby. The air at the Equator is intensely heated almost each day and hence it rises each day, causing rain each afternoon. This rising of the wind when heated is called convection, and the rain that is so caused is called the convectional rain.

  A cyclones has a low pressure at the centre, and it brings rainy or stormy weather. The rain brought about by a cyclone is called the cyclonic rain.

WINDS

Air moving from one direction to another horizontally is known as winds. It is air in motion and is caused by difference in pressure. Wind blows from region of high pressure to a region of low pressure. Due to earth's rotation on its axis from west to east, all winds are deflected to the right in the northern hemisphere and to the left in the southern hemisphere. There are certain identifiable wind systems in the world:

1. The low pressure region round the equator, is calm usually and is called doldrum. Although there are no regular winds there, violent squalls and thunderstorms are frequent which come from high pressure areas north and south of the equator.
2. **Trade Winds:** As the temperature at equators is high, the air becomes hot and rises up. The air moves northwards and southwards and descends near 30°N and 30°S, causing high pressure. The wind then blows from here towards the equator and this is called trade wind. They are named so because trading ships take advantage of the direction of these winds.
3. **Westerlies:** These are also called anti-trade wind as they blow from about 40°N to the Arctic circle and from about 35°S to the Antarctic circle

throughout the year. They derive their name from the direction in which they blow. In the northern hemisphere, they blow in the south-westerly direction and in the north-westerly direction in the southern hemisphere.

4. **Polar winds:** They blow from the high pressure area around the poles towards the temperate regions. Since they rise from the colder regions, they are extremely cold.
5. **Periodical Winds:** They blow in one direction at a particular time or during a particular season. Monsoons and land and sea breezes belong to this category. In India, South-west monsoon blow in summer and North-east in winter.
6. **Variable winds:** They are irregular winds like cyclones and anti-cyclones which originate due to local factors.

Cyclones and Anticyclones

Cyclones is wind rotating round the centre of minimum of low barometric pressure. The wind rush inwards from all direction. Due to the inclination of earth's axis and the rotation of the earth, in northern hemisphere the winds circulates in an anticlockwise direction and in the southern hemisphere in clockwise direction.

Anticyclone refers to the region in which the atmospheric is high, with the highest point at the centre. In this situation the winds blow spirally outwards from the centre, clockwise in northern hemisphere and anticlockwise in southern hemisphere. In summer anti-cyclones are associated with warm and sunny conditions, in winter they imply frost and fog as well as sunshine.

HYDROSPHERE

Hydrosphere is the name given to the masses of water that cover about 70.8% of the surface of the earth. The great stretches of salt water called oceans and seas. Pacific ocean, which is the largest among the ocean sprawls over an area of about 1.65×10^8 sq. km an area which is more than total combined area of all the continents. The average depth of oceans is about 4 km.

The water in the oceans totals over 1,300 million cubic km which is more than 97% of world's total water. The balance of water resources are contributed by glaciers, ice and snow, fresh water lakes, rivers and the underground water.

The oceans occupy the deep hollows of the earth's crust. The floor of the ocean beds are covered with ridges and valleys. The raised parts of the ocean floor are called ridges. The valley are called deeps or trenches. The most famous ridge is the Mid Atlantic Ridge and the most famous trenches include the Tuscarora Deep and Mariana Trench.

All the oceans of the world are interconnected. Antarctica is entirely surrounded by a great stretch of water called the southern ocean. From there stretch northwards, the three most oceans — the Indian, Pacific and Atlantic Oceans. The fifth ocean is the Arctic ocean which surrounds the North pole.

The Ocean Floor

The bottom of oceans is not as smooth as it is presented to be. It can categorised into four parts:

1. **Continental Shelf:** It is the seaward extension of the continent and is a shallows platform with a variable width of a few miles in the north-west pacific coast to over 100 miles near north-west Europe. They are of great significance because shallow water enables sunlight to penetrate and help growth of planktons. This helps in large growth of fishes in the area near the banks.
2. **Continental Slope:** The continental shelf abruptly starts declining and showing large slopes.
3. **Ocean Trough:** They are deep sea plains which are undulating with an average depth of 3000 organic deposits. They have extensive submerged plateaus, ridges, trenches, basins and oceanic islands.
4. **Ocean Deeps:** They are long, narrow and deep trenches, often plunging upto 30,000 feet.

Salinity

A number of minerals which are held in solution in the sea water have great importance. As a result of large concentration of minerals, like sodium sulphate, sodium chloride, magnesium chloride and calcium chloride etc., sea water is salty to taste. The proportion of dissolved salts to pure water is called Salinity. It varies from place to place in the oceans. The average figure being 35 gm per 1000 cc. Usually salinity is higher where the addition of fresh water is less and evaporation is high and vice-versa. Chlorine is the most abundant element causing salinity in sea water.

Waves and Current

Wave is a disturbance on the surface of a liquid body e.g. a sea or a lake. Wave is mainly caused by the wind which heaps up the water. Along coasts, waves are destructive agents of erosion.

Currents are those powerful movements of the ocean that proceed regularly, constantly and in definite direction. The movement of these current is clearly visible on the surface of the water and may be called gushing streams of water over the otherwise calm surface of the ocean. Hence streams of water move with a greater velocity than their counterparts do on the surface of the earth. They modify the climate of a coastal region. The warm Gulf stream brings in ice-free winter conditions along the south eastern coast of USA. Winds passing over warm current pick up moisture and bring rain. Japan, British Isles etc. receive rainfall in this manner. Kalahari and Atacama deserts are drier than they would be because of cold Peruvian current. The meeting of cold and warm current causes dense fog which is dangerous for navigation. However, at the meeting place, growth of the fishes gets enhanced due to abundance of nutrients.

LITHOSPHERE

The Lithosphere refers to the top crust of the earth on which our continents countries and the ocean basins rest. The lithosphere has a thickness between 38 to 52 km in the continental regions, but becomes thin between 7 to 13 km under the ocean beds. In the high mountain regions, its thickness is estimated at about 65 km. It includes both the land mass as well as the ocean floors, generally it is used to denote only the land surface which occupies a little less than 30% of total area of the earth.

INTERIOR STRUCTURE OF THE EARTH

The interior structure of the earth is based on the seismic waves, as they travel through the earth. The centre of the earth is occupied by the core, about 3500 km in radius. The outer part of the core is believed to have the properties of a liquid and the innermost part of the core may be called solid. The core is the densest part of the earth and is known as nife. Outside the core lies the mantle, a layer about 2925 km thick, composed of minerals in a solid state. The rocks in this layer may be in glassy state. The topmost portion of earth, the crust is the land mass comprising soil, sand and rock. In fact all the sand and much of the soil that we have has come to us from ancient rocks that crumbled down under the impact of heat of the sun and the cool of the rain, a process that has gone on for thousands years.

PLAIN

A plain is defined as an area with gently sloping land and very low local relief. It can be classified as peneplain, flood plain, delta plain, alluvial plain, coastal plain, lacustrine plain, karst plain and glacial plain etc.

The combined action of weathering and streams on land makes peneplain. The deposition of material by rivers makes flood plains, delta plains and alluvial plains. Coastal plains are those parts of the continental shelf which have been uplifted. Lacustrine plains are old lake beds and are made up of sediments deposited by rivers. Karst plains are formed in limestone areas mainly by the agency of underground water. Glacial plains are formed through glacial erosion and deposition.

PLATEAUS

It can be classified as intermontane, piedmont and continental. Intermontane plateaus are formed in association with mountains and are enclosed by them *e.g.* the Tibetan plateau. Piedmont plateaus lie between mountains on one side and the sea on the other *e.g.* the Patagonian plateau in South America. Continental plateau rise abruptly from the seas or low lands and are extensive e.g. the Indian plateau and Greenland.

MOUNTAINS

Mountains are masses of land considerably higher than the surrounding areas, higher than a hill, and with fairly steep slopes. They are classified as fold mountain, block mountains, volcanic mountains, and residual mountains.

As the molten centrosphere cooled and contracted, the crust at several places became crumpled, *i.e.*, full of wrinkles or folds. The elevated parts became mountains termed as fold mountains and the intervening depressions are known as valleys. The great mountain chains of the world like, the Himalayas, the Alps, Andes and the Rockies have been formed by this process.

If there are two parallel vertical faults in the earth's crust, the contraction of the inner molten rock to matter causes the parts on either side of the middle block of the rock to subside. This process causes the formation of a Block Mountain.

Volcanic mountains results from volcanic eruptions and the outflow of lava. The Fujiyama of Japan is an example of volcanic mountains. Sometimes, the mountains are carved out as a result of erosion of plateaus and high plains by various agents of erosion. These are known as residual mountains *e.g.* the Highlands of Scotland and the Sieroas of Central Spain.

The sinking down of the part of the earth's crust between two parallel vertical faults forms a Rift Valley. It is U-shaped, whereas a Fold Valley is V-shaped. The Red Sea, Dead Sea and Narmada Valley in India are example of rift valleys.

ROCKS

Rocks are the main materials composing the earth's crust. Rocks are composed of minerals. Minerals are natural inorganic substance each with a fairly definite chemical composition and recognisable crystal form, colour, hardness, lustre, texture and other physical characteristics. Rocks of the earth are grouped in three principal classes — Igneous, Sedimentary and Metamorphic.

Rocks which are solidified directly from molten materials are called igneous rocks. These rocks are crystalline in nature and make up nearly 85 per cent of the earth's crust. Granites, Basalt are examples of Igneous rocks. Sedimentary rocks are formed in layers on beds of rivers, lakes and seas. They are formed over a long period of time and natural factors like Streams, Rivers, Glaciers or Wind etc. play an important role in their formation. They often contain fossils of plants, animals and other micro-organisms. Sandstone, Shale, Clay, Rock salts, Gypsum, Potash and Nitrates are examples of Sedimentary rocks. Metamorphic rocks are literally rocks which have changed their form. In course of time, the original form of these rock is changed owing to excessive heat and great pressure, like clay changing into slate. Granite changes into gneiss, limestone into marble, sandstone into quartzite and coal into graphite.

VOLCANO

It is an opening in the earth's crust through which lava is ejected. The thrown up lava forms a conical hill with a funnel-shaped hollow called Crater at its top. Crater is the mouth of a volcano. It is usually cup-shaped and serves as the vent for the lava to erupt. Volcanoes which are no longer active are called extinct volcanoes. A volcano which is only sleeping and may become active is called a dormat volcano. The volcanoes which erupt frequently are called active volcanoes. Mt Etna in Italy is an example of active volcano while Fujiyama in Japan and Chimborazo in Andes are examples of dormant and extinct volcanoes respectively. The eruption of lava from a volcano can be of explosive type or quiet type.

There are several thousands volcanoes in the world. They are distributed in several belts across the continents. The most important belt runs right round the Pacific ocean. Another, rather less important, runs from Iceland just touching the British Isles, through the Azones across the Atlantic to the West-Indies with a branch running through the Mediterranean sea.

EARTHQUAKES

It is the shaking of the earth's crust sometimes accompanied by a permanent elevation or depression, but often no lasting effect is visible on the surface except the damage done by shaking. The main cause of earthquakes are due to sudden cooling and contraction of the earth's surface, coming into activity of some dormant volcanos, and due to internal heat, sometimes water changes into steam, expands and this causes an earthquake. Earthquakes occur in almost every part of the world. They are very common in volcanic districts, and where the earth's crust is weak. The most active region is a belt surrounding the Pacific ocean which includes western coasts of North and South America, the eastern coast of Asia, New Zealand and the islands of the South-east Pacific. In India, the North-East region and Shivalik range of Himalayas are more susceptible of earthquakes though Plateau has also experienced it sometimes. The intensity of an earthquake is measured on Richter-Scale by an instrument seismograph. An earthquake that originates in or near the sea, causing gigantic waves, is called Tsunami.

MAIN NATURAL REGIONS OF THE WORLD

A natural region is a geographical unit which contains countries or parts of countries, where the condition of temperature, rainfall and cultivated vegetation and consequently human activity are almost uniform.

(i) **Hot Deserts:** They are situated near the tropics between 20° and 30° in the West of the land masses. These occupy about one-fourth of the land surface of the earth. The climate of the region is mostly hot and dry. The Sahara, Arabia, West Rajasthan and Sindh deserts are included in this region. Gold, silver, copper and diamonds are available in these deserts.

(ii) **Tropical Grasslands:** Agriculture and cattle-rearing are the chief occupations, and wool, skins and hides the chief commercial products of this region.

(iii) **Monsoon Region:** It lies mostly in the south-east of Asia and includes portions of Australia, Africa and America. Hence the climate is hot and moist in summer and warm and dry in winter. Natural vegetation is forests.

(iv) **Equatorial Region:** These regions have dense forests of evergreen trees but they are not suitable for human habitation. Some medicinal forest products are gathered.

(v) **Mediterranean Region:** This region lies around the Mediterranean sea and on both sides of the equator, in the west of the land masses and between 30° and 45° north and south of equator. The climate is hot in summer and wet in winter. It is famous for fruit trees like olive, vine, lemon almonds, etc.

(vi) **Cool Temperate Region:** On the western margins of continents. In these regions cereals are grown, cattle are raised for dairy product and fishing is also important. In the eastern margins coniferous forests provide soft wood. Lumbering, fishing and farming are important.

(vii) **Polar Tundra Regions:** Too cold for most human activity. Only mineral extraction can attract a large concentration of people in the future. Gold and oil are found in Alaska, and nickel in Siberia.

(viii) **Siberian Type Region:** It includes Siberia, north Europe, specially north Russia, Finland, Scandinavian countries, etc. Here winters are very severe. Natural vegetation is coniferous forests. Wheat, potatoes, etc are grown in summer.

(ix) **China Type Region:** It lies in the east of land masses between 30° and 45° degree. Here summers are warm and moist and winters are very cold. Natural vegetation is forests.

(x) **British Type:** It includes the area of British Columbia, North-West Europe including British Isles, South Chile, Tasmania and South Islands of New Zealand. The countries in this region are industrially advanced, and agriculture is carried on by scientific method. People on the whole are engaged in different industries.

PATTERN OF CLIMATE

Different regions of the world have different climates and the factor for this variation is presence of different temperature, winds, precipitation and their interaction with the surface of the earth. The hottest and wettest regions of the world are found along the equators. The areas located near Tropic of Capricorn usually have dry climates, except for small area of Australia, Africa and South America. There is more climate variation along the Tropic of Cancer. The climate of a region is an important factor in the lifestyle of people, crop pattern, housing pattern and economic pattern. The main types of climates are as follows:

(a) **Equatorial Climate:** This type of climate is found in the area lying in a belt stretching about 5° on both sides of the equator. The temperature is high all round the year and does not vary much. Rainfall is large and continues for the whole year, making the climate sultry. The Amazon and Congo basins, East and West Indies, the Malay Peninsula and Andaman and Nicobar show this type of climate.

(b) **Desert Climate:** As the sand heats up quickly and losses heat also fast, the highest temperatures in the world are found in the regions affected by desert climate. The nights are very cold. The hot deserts, occupy lowlands along the Tropics of Cancer and Capricorn. Sahara, Thar and deserts of Arabia, Australia, South Africa (Kalahari) and South America (Atacama) are examples of such deserts. However, cold deserts are also found in plateaus outside the tropics. They show very low temperatures, particularly during winter. Gobi (Central Asia), Colorado (North America) and deserts of Iran belong to this climate.

(c) **Mediterranean Climate:** The climate in areas around the Mediterranean sea is known by the sea. The region lies between latitudes 30° and 45°. The area is hot and dry in summer but moist and mild weather is observed during winter. This type of climate is also prevalent on western sides of North and South America South Africa and South of Australia.

(d) **Temperate Maritime Climate:** This type of climate is prevalent in North-West Europe, West Canada, South Chile and New Zealand. The area gets rain throughout the year but compared to tropical regions, the quantum is usually less.

(e) **Continental Climate:** This type of climate is found in regions far away from the oceans. Due to lack of moderating influence of seas, the summers are very hot and winters are very cold. Rains fall mostly in spring and early summer but quantity is not much. The grasslands where this climate occurs are the Prairies of Canada and USA, the Steppes of Russia, Pampas of South America, Downs of Australia and Veldt of South Africa.

(f) **Monsoon Climate:** The areas which receives rain in summer due to monsoon, show this type of climate. It is characterised by three seasons — the cold season with a little rain from November to February, the summer from March to June and finally rainy season from late June to October. The summers are hot. The climate is prevalent in northern hemisphere around the Indian ocean area like India, Myanmar etc. North-West Australia and parts of the Africa also show the climate.

(g) **Cold Forest Climate:** The summers are cool and winter are colder with moisture coming down as snow and not as rain. The area is known for coniferous trees, and occurs in Northern parts of America, Europe and Asia.

(h) **Tropical Climate:** This climate is found on either side of the equatorial belt and is well developed in Africa. Rainfall is heavier during summer and winter remains dry.

(i) **Alpine Climate:** The climate has been named after the mountain chain of Europe, the Alps. The climate changes as the height of mountain increases and becomes colder. Due to low density of air, the climate is different from other snow bound areas of Arctic or Antarctica.

(j) **Arctic Climate:** The winters here are very long and very cold. The summers are very short. The climate is prevalent in the Arctic and Antarctica circles.

On the South and North poles, permanent ice and snow exists and these are called Polar Caps. They receive very little sunlight. During winter, no sunlight touches either pole while in summer, much of the light reaching the poles is reflected into space by the glare of the snow. The North Pole lies on a frozen sea, the Arctic Ocean while the South Pole sits upon the continent of Antarctica, covered by a layer of ice and snow at least a mile deep.

Indian Geography

India, the largest country in the Indian sub-continent, lies in South Asia between latitude 8°4' north and 37°6' north and from longitude 68°7' east to 97°25' east. The Tropic of Cancer passes right through the centre cutting the country into two halves. The territories of India's mainland extend for 3,214 km between the extremes of north and south and 2,933 km in east-west extreme point. The total length of the mainland coastline is nearly 6,100 km and the land frontier about 15,200 km. With an area of about 32,87,263 sq. km, India is the seventh largest country in the world accounting for about 2.4% of total world area.

India's neighbours in the north are China, Nepal and Bhutan, in the East are Myanmar, Bangladesh, in the West is Pakistan and in the South is Sri Lanka. Indian states bordering with Pakistan are Jammu and Kashmir, Punjab, Rajasthan and Gujarat and with Bangladesh are West Bengal, Assam, Meghalaya and Tripura.

PHYSICAL FEATURES

The Himalayas form India's northern boundary beyond which lie China, Nepal and Bhutan, which also border India in the north and north-east covering a portion of Himalayan region. A series of mountain ranges in the east separates India from Myanmar. In the East, lies Bangladesh bounded by the Indian States of West Bengal, Assam, Meghalaya, Tripura and Mizoram. In the north-west, Pakistan and Afghanistan border on India. In the South, the Gulf of Mannar and the Palk Strait separate India from Sri Lanka. The Andaman and Nicobar Islands in the Bay of Bengal and the Lakshadweep Islands in the Arabian Sea are parts of the territory of India. India can be divided into three natural region:

The Himalayas

The Himalayas are one of the youngest mountain ranges in the world. They form the northern boundary of India, extending from Jammu and Kashmir in the west to Assam, Manipur and Mizoram in the east. The total length of this chain is about 5000 km of which about 2500 km stretches in the form of an arc along the border. The Himalayas comprise a number of almost parallel ranges. The main range rises to an average elevation of 6000 meter above mean sea level. This is the birth place of multitude of glaciers some of which are among the longest in the world. These are called Himadri or Greater Himalayas. The average height is 6,100 metres above mean sea level. It is snow-bound throughout the year. It contains the world's highest peaks, e.g., Mt Everest (8,848 m), Kanchenjunga (8,598 m), Dhaulagiri (8,166 m) and Nanga Parbat (8,126 m).

These ranges have passes through them which are sometimes blocked by ice. Some important passes are Zojila in Ladakh, Bara Lacha La and Shipki La in Himachal Pradesh, Thag La and Lipu Lekh pass in Uttarakhand and Jelep La in Sikkim. The lesser Himalaya lying south of the main range is the middle range with an average height between 2600 and 4600 m. The lesser Himalaya does not support any glaciers, as its altitude is below the snowline. They have a width of 60 to 80 km. They are known as the Himachal range and have numerous hill stations like Nainital, Mussoorie, Ranikhet etc. Pir Panjal is the most important range of lesser Himalayas. The outer Himalaya comprises the mountain range that lies between the lesser Himalaya and the plain of India. It has an average elevation of 1000-1300 meters. These are also called Siwaliks, with width varying from 50 km in the west and 15 km in the east. They are made up mostly of tertiary sediments brought by various rivers.

North of the main range lies the Trans-Himalayas or Tibet-Himalayas. This range acts as a watershed between rivers flowing to the north and those flowing to the south. There are also some minor ranges in the

Himalayan System. They include the Karakoram (highest Peak — K2) and Zanskar ranges in the west and the Pathkoi, Lushai and Garo ranges in the east.

Aravalli range in the north-western India is one of the oldest mountain system in the world. The present Aravalli range is only a remnant of the gigantic system that existed in prehistoric times with several of its summits rising above the snowline and nourishing glaciers of stupendous magnitude which in turn fed many great rivers.

The Punjab Himalayas extended over 562 km between rivers Indus and Sutlej. The Kumaun Himalayas extend further east for 320 km from the Sutlej to river Kali. The Nepal Himalayas cover a distance of about 800 km from the river Kali to river Teesta. The highest peaks of the Himalayas extend east of the Teesta up to the Brahmaputra over about 750 km.

The Plain of Ganga

This plain is about 2400 km in length and 240 to 320 km broad and formed by the basin of three distinct river systems the Indus, the Ganga and the Brahmaputra. These rivers have deposited soil which originates due to friction with the mountains. They include an area of 7 lakh square km, one of the largest among the plains of the world. They are widest in Punjab-Haryana and narrowest in Bihar. The older alluvium deposited higher than the level of flood plain is called bhangar whereas the newer alluvium forming the flood plain is called Khadar. It extends from West-Bengal to Punjab. They are one of the most *densely* populated area on the earth. Soil is very fertile and climate very healthy. This plain is very productive.

The Peninsular Plateau

The peninsular plateau is the name given to the area spreading south of the Indo-Gangetic plain and flanked by sea on three sides. The Deccan plateau is shaped like a triangle with its base in the north. The River Narmada, which flows through a rift valley, divides the region into two parts: the Malva plateau in the north and the Deccan Trap in the south. Most of the rock in the plateau region are very old and are of igneous type.

The Peninsular Deccan Plateau from the Vindhya mountain to Cape Comorin, is a table land 300 to 1000 meters above sea level. It resembles a triangle in shape with the Eastern Ghat and the Western Ghats as the two sides of the triangle. It is uneven and rocky. The Mahanadi, Godavari, Krishna, Narmada and Tapti are the chief rivers.

The western ghats or Sahyadris are a continuous chain of range that commence in Maharashtra and run parallel to the west coast upto Kanyakumari. The continuity is disturbed by a few gaps. Dodabetta peak (2,637 m) in Tamil Nadu is the largest in western ghats. The eastern ghats form a chain of a discontinuous range broken up by numerous river valleys and called by different names in different area. They are Nallamalla hills and Palkonda hills in Andhra Pradesh; Javadi hills, Pachimalai, Gondumalai and Bilgiri range hills in Tamil Nadu.

The Western Ghats are connected to the Eastern Ghats by the Nilgiri Hills. South of these are the Annamalai which are separated from the former by the Palghat Pass. Two branches of the Annamalai Hills are known as the Palani Hills and the Yelagiri Hills. Many rivers of the Western Ghats make waterfalls. The Sivasamudram Fall, the Gokak Fall and the Mahatma Gandhi Fall are important waterfalls in this area.

Coastal Plains

In between the ghats and coasts on eastern as well as western side, there exists plains. The western plains are narrower than the eastern plains. The eastern coastal plain consists of river deltas formed by Mahanadi, Godavari, Krishna and Cauvery interspersed with the lakes, namely Chilka (between Godavari and Mahanadi), Kolleru (Godavari and Krishna) and Pulicat (North of Chennai). The western plains are formed by alluvial plains in Gujarat which continues as Konkan plains in the south. The comparatively narrow plains in Kerala has numerous lagoons and splits along it. A lagoon is a shallow stretch of water which is partly or completely separated from the sea by a narrow strip of land and a split is a narrow low lying area of sand.

Besides, there are 247 Indian islands of which 204 lie in the Bay of Bengal and remaining in the Arabian sea. The western islands are called Lakshdweeps and eastern ones are Andamans and Nicobars.

RIVER SYSTEMS

The Himalayan Rivers

The great river water system of Northern India are Indus, Ganga and Brahmputra. The most important river system is the Indus system. The Rivers Indus dominates this system and is joined by the rivers Shyoke, Shigar and Gilgit in Jammu and Kashmir. The important tributaries, including the Jhelum, Chenab, Ravi, Beas and Sutlej join it after entering Pakistan. The second major system is of the Ganga river. The Ganga, the head stream is constituted of two major rivers — Bhagirathi and Alaknanda, which combine at Dev Prayag to form the Ganga. The Yamuna which joins the Ganga at Allahabad, is the major tributary. Other tributaries of Ganga include Ghaghara, Sone, Gandak, Kosi and Damodar. The important tributaries of the Yamuna include the

Chambal, Betwa and Ken. The Brahmaputra is the third major system in the north. The head stream of the Brahmaputra rises in Tibet, where it is called Tsangpo, and enters Indian territory under the name of Dihang. The Subansiri, Kameng, Dharsiri, Manas and Teesta are the major rivers, joining it from the north and Bushi, Dihing, Disang and Kopoli join it from the south. The Lohit is also an important tributary of the Brahmaputra.

The Deccan Rivers

The rivers of the Deccan are different from those of Northern India. They rise in the hills of the plateau and are fed only by monsoon rains. The most important of these rivers are Mahanadi, Godawari, Krishna and Cauvery. They become dry when there are no monsoon rain. Mahanadi, Godavari, Krishna and Cauvery are east flowing rivers and form large deltas before getting merged in the sea. On the other hand, the west flowing rivers — Narmada, Tapti and Sarasvati run through valleys and form estuaries instead of deltas.

CLIMATE

India is nearer to the Equator and its position at the head of the Indian Ocean are two main factors that influence the climate. On the whole, the Climate of India is of the monsoon type and India is termed as a monsoon country, the climate is far from uniform, with variations being spatial as well as temporal. At one extreme are the highly humid areas in the north-east, where total amount of rainfall exceeds 1000 cm. At the other extreme are areas like the Thar Desert and the cold desert area in the Laddakh region which receive less than 10 cm of precipitation most years. Likewise, the higher reaches of the Himalayas are characterised by very low temperatures while areas in central and southern India touch very high temperature in summer. The climate is also determined by latitude of place. The tropic of cancer divides the country into two, the temperate half in the north and tropical half in the south. Himalayas play an important role in climate determination by acting as meteorological barrier. They give the country tropical character by maintaining high temperature uniformly throughout the year. They block the South-West monsoon and bring about rainfall.

An important feature of the monsoon is the complete reversal of winds which leads to the alternation of seasons. On the basis of monsoon variations, the year is divided into four seasons which are more observable in northern parts of the country.

(*i*) Winter season — December to February
(*ii*) Summer season — March to May
(*iii*) Rainy season — June to September
(*iv*) Autumn season — October to November

The Winter season, starts in December and the cold weather season becomes fully established in January and the temperature distribution over India shows a marked decline as one moves from south to north. The days are bright and sunny, however occasionally disturbed by the western disturbances which bring light rainfall and severe cold waves.

The Summer season comes between March and May with rising temperatures and decreasing air pressure as the belt of intense heat shift from south to north. By the end of May, low pressure trough is developed which occasionally attracts the moisture laden winds, while coming into contact with the hot dryland winds which cause pre-monsoon rains.

The Rainy season comes by early June. The low pressure area over north-western plains becomes highly intense to attract the south-west rain bearing winds which approach suddenly with thunder and lightning. Within almost one month time, these winds over-run almost the entire country. The south-west monsoons originate from the Indian ocean and blow over the land mass of India from June to September. Due to the intense summer heat a low pressure area is formed the northern plains of India. But the oceanic region has a low temperature and a high pressure centre. Consequently, air starts moving from the high pressure area of the Indian ocean towards the low pressure area over the land mass of India in the form of rain bearing monsoon winds.

The Autumn season starts by mid September leaving the land moist and the atmosphere humid. The weather during this season is characterised by the high day temperature, clear sky and pleasant nights.

Climatic Regions of India

India has several climatic regions:

(*a*) ***Tropical rain forest:*** This type of climate is found in the West Coastal Plains, on western ghats and in Assam. The temperatures are high throughout the year. South-West monsoon bring heavy rains and squally winds. Dense forests, tea and coffee plantations and spices are grown in the region.

(*b*) ***Tropical Savanna:*** This type of climate is found in Peninsula except in the leeside of the Sahyadris. It is marked by long dry weather in winter and early summer. The temperature is high even during winter and goes up in summer. The rainfall varies from 75 to 160 cm, mostly received from south-west monsoon except in Tamil Nadu. A variety of crops are raised.

(*c*) ***Tropical Semi-arid Steppe:*** This type of climate is found in the rain shadow belt from Maharashtra to Tamil Nadu on the leeside of the western ghats and Cardamom hills. The rainfall is scanty, usually less than 75 cm. High average temperatures are recorded. The region is suitable only for dry farming and livestock rearing though it also suffers from recurring droughts.

(d) ***Tropical and Sub-tropical Steppe:*** This type of climate is found in area stretching from Punjab to Kutch, forming the transition from the humid Ganga plains in the east and Thar desert in the west. The rainfall varies from 30 to 63 cm. The temperature varies from about 10°C in winter to around 40°C in summer. Scanty and low rainfall in the region permits only dry farming besides cattle and sheep rearing.

(e) ***Tropical desert:*** Western part of Rajasthan and a large region of Kutch in Gujarat form Thar desert which experiences tropical desert climate. The average rainfall is about 30 cm which occurs in the form of cloud bursts between July and September. High temperatures are recorded during summers with hot, dry winds blowing throughout the day. Winters are cold with temperatures going below freezing point. Dry farming and cattle rearing are common in the area.

(f) ***Humid Sub-tropical with dry weather:*** This type of climate is found in areas south of Himalayas from Punjab to Assam and in east of Aravalli ranges. The annual rainfall in the area varies from 60 cm in the west to more than 250 cm in the east. Rainfall is received during south-west monsoon season. Winters are cold and dry while summers are hot. As the temperature and rainfall changes, the crop variation is large.

(g) ***Mountain climate:*** The mountains, at 6,000 m above sea level, expe-rience this type of climate. The climate is dry and cold. As we go eastwards, the rainfall increases. On the southern slopes, there is heavy rainfall and temperature here is comparatively large due to protection from chilly winds coming north. In places like Laddakh, where south-west monsoon winds fail to reach, vegetation is sparse and stunted. Dense forests exist in lower slopes of the Himachal and Siwaliks range.

Monsoon in India

Monsoons are periodic winds which blow from sea to land for six months in summer and from land to sea for six months in winter. Monsoon winds prevail over India at different seasons.

(a) ***South-West Monsoon:*** These are rain-bearing winds prevailing from end-May to the end of September. During summer, the sun's rays fall vertically on the Tropic of Cancer making the Indian Plains intensely hot but the rays fall obliquely over the Indian Ocean during the period. The land is hotter than the sea, and it causes building up of low pressure on the land and high pressure on the sea. The winds blow from high to low pressure, *i.e.*, from sea to the land. Thus, the wind is moist and when they hit a mountain the rainfall is observed. Due to rotation of the earth, the monsoon winds blowing over India deflect to the right after crossing the equator and become south-west winds. India depends on these winds mostly for rainfall. From June to September, India gets 90% of its rainfall.

(b) ***North-East Monsoon:*** As the sun moves southwards, its rays start falling vertically on Tropic of Capricorn. The air over the Indian Ocean becomes hot and light, causing low pressure zone. As the sun's rays are falling obliquely on the plains of India during the months of October to January, the air over the plains becomes cold and heavy and there is a high pressure zone. The winds blow from plains to the sea while crossing the equator, they deflect to the left and are known as north-east monsoons. They bring about 10% of total rain in India, particularly in Tamil Nadu.

SOILS

The soils of India can be classified on the basis of several criteria. Indian Agricultural Research Institute (IARI) Delhi divides soils into eight groups.

(i) **Alluvial Soil:** The largest and the most important group is alluvial soil, which cover about 24% of India's land surface. This type of soil is composed of sediments deposited by the mighty rivers in the interior parts of India and by the sea wave in the coastal areas of the country. The Great Plains of India running from Punjab to Assam possess rich alluvial soil. It is also found in Narmada and Tapti valleys in Madhya Pradesh and Orissa, Godavari valley in Andhra Pradesh and Cauvery valley in Tamil Nadu. It also occurs in the deltas of Mahanadi, Godavari, Krishna and Cauvery rivers. Alluvial soils are generally deficient in nitrogen and humus and thus need repeated use of fertilizers. Such soils are suitable for growing all types of cereals, pulses, sugarcane, vegetables, oilseeds etc.

(ii) **Black Soil:** The second major group is black soil. Ideal for the cultivation of cotton crop, it is frequently referred to as black cotton soil and covers large tracts of the Deccan plateau. This soil is also classified as Chernozem though locally known as regur soil. It covers large areas in Maharashtra, Gujarat, Madhya Pradesh, Karnataka, Andhra Pradesh and in Tamil Nadu. The black colour is due to the presence of compounds of iron and aluminium. The soil is sticky when wet and its level of fertility is well known. Possessing high moisture retention capacity, black soil does not require much irrigation.

(iii) **Red Soil:** The red soil, the third major group occurs mostly in the southern peninsula and extends up to Jhansi in the north, Kutch in the west and Rajmahal Hills in the east. This soil is made up of crystalline and metamorphic rocks and is rich in ferromagnese minerals and soluble salts but is deficient in nitrogen and humus and thus needs fertilisers. It has a light texture and a porous structure. Red soil is most suited to growth of rice, ragi, tobacco and vegetables.

(iv) **Laterite Soil:** Laterites and lateritic soil are the fourth group formed through the process of laterisation. They contain iron oxides which import a red to the soil. The soil occurs in the higher reaches of the Sahyadris, Eastern Ghats, Rajmahal Hills and other higher areas in the peninsular region. It can also be found on the lower lands in parts of Maharashtra, Karnataka and in many parts of Kerala, as well as pockets of Orissa, West Bengal and Assam Generally poor in nitrogen and mineral salts due to heavy leaching, it is suitable for rice and ragi cultivation if manured.

(v) **Forest Soil:** Forest soil is rich in organic matter and humus. It is found in the Himalayas and other mountain regions of the north, higher summit of the Sahyadris, Eastern Ghats, Karnataka, Tamil Nadu, Kerala, Manipur, Jammu and Kashmir and Himachal Pradesh. Crops like tea, coffee, spices and tropical fruits are grown on this type of soil.

(vi) **Arid and Desert Soil:** It is found in north western India. It covers the entire area west of the Aravalli's in Rajasthan and parts of Haryana, Punjab and Gujarat. It is rich in phosphates but poor in nitrogen and proves quite fertile if irrigated.

(vii) **Saline and Alkaline Soil:** Soils in many parts of the arid and semi-arid areas of Rajasthan, Punjab, Haryana and Uttar Pradesh. Bihar have saline and alkaline effervescences mainly of sodium, calcium and magnesium. These soil are called reh or kallar or usar and are infertile. The salts are usually confined to the upper layers and soil can be reclaimed by improving drainage.

(viii) **Peaty and other Organic Soils:** Peaty soils contain large accumulations of humus, organic matter and soluble salts. These soils are highly saline and are deficient phosphorus and potash. Marshy soil occurs in regions of Orissa, West-Bengal and Tamil Nadu. They are also found in central and north Bihar and in Almora district of U.P.

NATURAL VEGETATION IN INDIA

The natural vegetation in India is largely of tropical type but there is a variation with respect to species and growth of plants, due to changes in temperature and rainfall condition. Variation in soil gives rise to variation in forests. The forest cover in India has been on decline because of clearing for the purpose of cultivation and industrialisation. Forests are unequally distributed in the country, with Punjab, Haryana, Rajasthan and Gujarat having less than 10 per cent of forest coverage. The low coverage here is primarily due to scanty rainfall. The natural vegetation is of following types:

1. ***Tropical Wet Evergreen and Semi-Evergreen Forests:*** They are found where the rainfall is more than 250 cm. Such forests exist in Assam, North-Eastern States, Andaman and Nicobar Islands and the West Coast. These forests provide timber, firewood and bamboo. The products of tropical evergreen forests are used in paper and match factories, plywood and tea processing industries. Due to dense nature of these forests, transport facility is problem, thereby protecting the wealth from exploitation. Timber varieties are Ebony, Paan, Ironwood, and Rosewood.

2. ***Tropical Moist and Dry Deciduous Forests:*** The deciduous forests are also called monsoon forests. They are found between the Himalayas, the Thar and the Western Ghats. They grow in areas with a rainfall of 100 to 200 cm annually. They are economically most important as commercially valuable species are grown here in large number. They can be exploited easily. The important trees are Sal, Teak, Sandalwood, Shisham, Mahua, Khair. The moist deciduous forests grow in Orissa, eastern Madhya Pradesh, Chhota Nagpur plateau and a strip along the Siwaliks where rainfall is large. The trees are large sized with a denser undergrowth than in wet evergreen forests. They shed their leaves during spring and early summer. Dry deciduous forests occur in area with rainfall 100 to 150 cm. The variety of trees is almost the same as the moist one but the growth is stunted and trees are widely spaced.

SOCIAL SCIENCE

3. ***Tidal Forests:*** They occur along the seaward fringes, channels and islands of the deltas of Ganga, Mahanadi, Godavari and Krishna. The Sunderbans delta is known for tidal forests. The trees are used to growth in mud and silt. The water may be fresh or brackish. Mangrove, Sundari, Pines, Cane and Palms are the common varieties of tidal forests.
4. ***Tropical Dry Evergreen Forests:*** They are found in coastal Tamil Nadu where retreating monsoon gives about 100 cm of rainfall.
5. ***Tropical Thorn Forests:*** They are found in the north and north-western parts of the country and on the beside of the Sahyadris. The rainfall is about 75 cm. The vegetation is of open stunted nature degenerating into desert type in the Thar desert. Khair, Babul, Neem, Pipal and Khardhari are some important trees.
6. ***Montane Sub-tropical and Temperate Types:*** They occur mostly on the hills of South India. Wet hill forests are found in Nilgiri and Palani hills at a height of 1000 to 1500 metres while wet temperature forests are found above 1500 m on these hills. Magnolia, Laurel, Elm, Cinchona, Wattle and Eucalyptus are common trees.
7. ***Vegetation in the Himalayan Region:*** The vegetation on the Himalayas vary with the altitude and temperature. Wet hill forests comprise dense and high trees and are found in the eastern Himalayas at a height of 1000 to 2000 metre. Evergreen oak, Chestnut, and beech grow in these forests. Sub-tropical pine forests grow in western Himalayas at a height of 1000 to 2000 metre. Chir, a variety of pine is common here which is used for making railway sleepers and construction work. Sub-tropical dry evergreen forests appear in the Himalayan foothills of Kashmir where the rainfall is between 50 and 100 cm. Wild olives and acacia are important species of the region. Moist temperate forests cover the range where the rainfall is 100 to 250 cm and altitude 1500 to 3700 metre. Oak, Laurel, Chestnut, Pine, Cedar, Silverfir, Spruce and Deodar are common trees. In the dry temperate forests, the rainfall is less than 100 cm and trees commonly grown are Deodar, Birch, Oak, and Elm. In the Himalayas between 2800 and 3600 m, a dense and stunted growth of Silver fir, Juniper, Pine and Birch is found. The dwarfish growth gives the trees a shrubby appearance. They are called Alpine forests.

WILDLIFE SANCTUARIES AND NATIONAL PARKS

India is rich in flora and fauna. However, due to increasing population and industrial and commercial activities, there has been acute pressure on forests. The Government has taken several steps to check the sharp fall in the number of these species. Among the measures are declaration of certain habitats as national parks and sanctuaries. 106 national parks and 573 sanctuaries have been established till June 2025, important ones being given below:

Assam: Kaziranga National Park (know for one-horn Rhinoceroses); Manas Sanctuary.

Jharkhand: Hazaribagh National Park; Palamau Reserve.

Gujarat: Valvadar National Park, Bhavnagar; Marine National Park, Gulf of Kutch; Gir Forests.

Himachal Pradesh: Rohla National Park; Motichur Sanctuary.

Jammu & Kashmir: Dachigam Sanctuary.

Karnataka: Bandipur National Park; Bannargheta National Park, Bangalore; Nagorhole National Park, Coorg; Ranganthitto Bird Sanctuary.

Kerala: Eravikulam Rajmallay National Park, Idduki; Periyar Game Sanc-tuary.

Madhya Pradesh: Kanha National Park; Bandhavgarh National Park, Shahdol; Shivpuri National Park.

Maharashtra: Taloba National Park, Chandrapur; Panch National Park, Nagpur; Borivali National Park, Mumbai; Nawagaon National Park, Bandara; Melghat National Park.

Manipur: Reibul Lamjao National Park.

Odisha: Simlipal.

Rajasthan: Sarsika Sanctuary; Ghana Bird Sanctuary, Bharatpur.

Sikkim: Khangchandzenda National Park, Gangtok.

Tamil Nadu: Vedanthangal Bird Sanctuary; Guindy National Park, Chennai; Mudumalai Sanctuary; Kalakad-Munden Thurai Reserve.

Uttar Pradesh: Chandraprabha Sanctuary; Dudhwa National Park, Lakhimpur.

West Bengal: Jaldapara Sanctuary; Sunderbans.

Uttarakhand: Corbett National Park; Nainital

A 'National Park' is a relatively large area o land kept by the national government for its peopl to enjoy, because of its natural beauty. They ar given the status by their law making bodies. Forestry settlement or trespassing are not allowed. They protec the entire ecosystem.

A 'Wild Life Sanctuary' is a place for preservatio and protection of animals and plants in the natura state. Forestry activities are permitted and huma settlements for original inhabitants or tribal people i allowed.

A 'Game Sanctuary' is a place for protecting wild animals and birds that are hunted or caught for sport or for food. These resorts are developed to prevent poaching; stealing and hunting without permission.

Biosphere reserves

They are multi-purpose protected areas to preserve the genetic diversity in representative eco-systems. The major objectives of setting up these reserves are to conserve diversity and integrity of plants, animals and micro-organisms; to promote research on ecological conservation and other environmental aspects; and to provide facilities for education, awareness and training. So far, 18 biosphere reserves have been set up, Important are—(1) Nilgiri; (2) Nanda Devi; (3) Nokrek; (4) Great Nicobar; (5) Gulf of Mannar; (6) Manas; (7) Sunderbans; and (8) Similipal.

Project Tiger

This is one of the premier conservation efforts of the country that was taken up in 1973 to protect one of the magnificient species of the land. Under the scheme, 58 Tiger Reserves are notified all over the country to provide natural environment to the animal and rule out poaching. A Global Tiger Forum has been set up for Tiger range countries and India playing a lead role has hosted its interim secretariat.

After success of Project Tiger, Project Elephant was taken up to ensure long-term survival of identified viable populations of elephants in their natural habitats.

AGRICULTURE IN INDIA

"Agriculture is the art or technique of raising plant life from the soil for the use of mankind. The object of agriculture is to raise and fruitful crops and plants".

Agriculture is the mainstay of the people of India; about 49 per cent of the people of India are dependent upon it

Agricultural crops of India may be divided into food crops and non-food crops.

Food Crops

- **Rice:** It is the chief food crop of India. The chief rice-growing states are West-Bengal, U.P., Punjab, Andhra Pradesh, Tamil Nadu and Bihar. It is also grown in several other parts of India. Due to Japanese method of rice cultivation the production of rice has increased, but even then India is not anywhere near the world productivity. Rice is grown in areas where abundant water is available. Northern states of Punjab and Haryana took up rice cultivation after the establishment of irrigation facilities.
- **Wheat:** It is second in importance to rice in India. It is the staple food of the people of Punjab, Haryana and U.P. It is largely grown in U.P., M.P., Punjab, Haryana and Rajasthan. Total area under wheat in the Indian Union is over 10 million hectares. A new type of Mexican wheat has been introduced and this has led to increased yield (four to five times) per acre. Punjab and Haryana have increased their wheat production considerably on account of better seeds what is grown during the winter season.
- **Millets (Jowar and Bajra):** It is largely grown in Tamil Nadu, Maharashtra, Gujarat, M.P., U.P., Haryana and the dry areas of Andhra Pradesh. It forms the staple food of the poor. It thrives best in hot and dry climate with moderate rainfall at intervals.
- **Barley:** It is used as food grain and also for preparing beer. The main barley growing states are U.P., Punjab and Haryana.
- **Maize:** It grows more or less all over India but chiefly in Karnataka, Madhya Pradesh, Andhra Pradesh, Bihar, U.P., Punjab, Rajasthan, Maharashtra and Gujarat.
- **Pulses:** They are grown in different parts of India, especially in M.P., Maharashtra, Punjab, U.P., West Bengal, and Gujarat. At present over 30 million hectares are used for growing pulses and gram in the Indian Union, and the total yield is about 26.06 million tons. The per capita availability of pulses has been gradually declining on account of the serious shortfalls in production.
- **Sugarcane:** India is one of the biggest cane producing country in the world. It is grown nearly in all the states of the Indian Union, but mostly in U.P., Maharashtra, Karnataka, Bihar and A.P. Production of sugar in India has been fluctuating very widely from year to year. As on 31st August, 2024 there were more than 700 installed sugar factories in the country against 138 during 1950-51. In 2023-24 the sugarcane production was 453.2 million tonnes. India has to import sugar in some years on account of a shortfall in production, while in some years, we are in search of export markets, when the production suddenly jumps to dizzy heights. Sugar industry is the second important industry of India, textile being the first.

Non-Food Crops or Cash Crops

- **Tea:** India is the second largest tea producing country in the world. It is mainly grown in

Assam, West Bengal, the Nilgiris, Kerala, Dehra Dun (Uttarakhand) and Kangra Valley. At present, India supplies more than 40 per cent of the world's trade in tea.

- **Coffee:** It requires a warm moist climate, and height of 1500 ft. to 2500 ft. It is largely grown in Karnataka, Kerala and Tamil Nadu. Half the annual production of coffee is consumed in India and the other half is exported to U.K., Germany, Holland, Belgium, Australia and Iraq. Coffee is gradually emerging as one of our major exchange earners.
- **Tobacco:** India occupies a dominant place as a tobacco producing country in the world; U.S.A. comes first. It is mainly produced in A.P., Bihar, U.P., Tamil Nadu, Karnataka, Maharashtra, Gujarat and in some parts of Punjab.
- **Oilseeds:** India is one of the biggest oilseed producing countries. They are grown chiefly in Rajasthan, M.P., Gujarat, Bihar, Odisha, U.P., Maharashtra, Andhra Pradesh and Punjab. There is an acute shortage of edible oils in India.
- **Cotton:** Maharashtra, Gujarat, M.P., Tamil Nadu and Andhra Pradesh are the chief producers. Before the partition, India was self-sufficient in cotton and exported a part of it. But after the partition, it had to import cotton to meet the growing requirements of the textiles mills.
- **Jute:** It is chiefly grown in West Bengal, Assam, Bihar, Odisha and some parts of U.P., India is almost self-sufficient in the production of raw jute; Bangladesh is the largest exporter of raw jute. The jute mills are mostly situated near Kolkata.
- **Rubber:** It is mainly grown in Tamil Nadu, Karnataka and Kerala. Indian Union produces nearly 7,00,000 tons annualy. Rubber industry is fast developing in this country. Kerala produces 95% of rubber in India. Production of rubber has been undertaken in Tripura and the results have been encouraging.
- **Silk:** In India, silk is produced in Karnataka, West Bengal, Bihar, Assam and Kashmir. The silkworm is fed on mulberry leaves, or on the leaves of castor plant and it produces cocoons which, when boiled, give us the silk thread.
- **Hemp:** Russia is the largest producer of hemp (a type of fibre); Italy, the U.S.A., India and China come next.
- **Wool:** It is obtained from the hilly tracts of Punjab, U.P., and Kashmir and also from Tamil Nadu and Rajasthan; Kalimpong (Bengal) is a main wool collecting centre.
- **Coconut:** Production of coconut in India comes from Karnataka, Kerala, Maharashtra, Gujarat and Tamil Nadu.

MINERALS

Nature has been very kind to India in term of endowment of mineral resources. Of the various minerals found in India, the most important are coal, manganese, ilmenite, mica, iron ore and salt. India is the world's main source of supply of manganese, mica, monazite and zircon.

- **Coal & Lignites:** Coal is our largest available mineral resource and presently India ranks third in the world after China and USA in the realm of coal production. The main centres of coal in India are the West Bengal-Jharkhand region, Madhya Pradesh, Maharashtra, Odisha and Andhra regions. Bulk of the coal production comes from Bengal-Jharkhand coal fields. They contribute 60 to 65% of the total production. The total known geological reserves of all types of coal in gondwana and tertiary coal-fields stands estimated at 378.21 billion tonnes as on April 1, 2023. The reserves of lignite has been estimated at around 47.37 billion tonnes April 2023 out of which the major contributor is the lignite basins of Tamil Nadu.
- **Fluorspar:** The total resources of fluorite in the country is estimated at 18.2 million tonnes. This mineral is mainly available in Gujarat, Chhattisgarh, Rajasthan and Maharashtra. The total resources of fluorspar is about 18.2 million tonnes.
- **Manganese:** Its maximum deposit is found in Karnataka. Besides, Odisha, Maharastra and Goa also possess relatively larger deposits of manganese. Some deposits are also found in Andhra Pradesh, Jharkhand, Rajasthan, Gujarat and West Bengal.
- **Copper:** Singhbhum Copper Belt (Jharkhand); Darjeeling (West Bengal), Agnigundla (Andhra Pradesh) and Khetri (Rajasthan) and Malanjkhand (M.P.) are known for copper deposits.
- **Gold:** Kolar goldfields are in the state of Karnataka. These mines were nationalised in 1956. Gold deposits have been located in Chittoor and Anantapur districts of Andhra Pradesh.
- **Mica:** The important mica bearing pegmatite occurs in Andhra Pradesh, Jharkhand, Bihar, Rajasthan. The total reserves of the mica in the country are placed at 5,32,237 tonnes.

Its maximum deposit is found in Andhra Pradesh, Rajasthan and Jharkhand.

- **Ilmenite:** India is its largest producer. It is the whitest of all substances; it is found in the 'black sand' on the beaches near Cape Comorin, the southernmost point of India.
- **Petroleum:** Digboi, Badarpur, Masimpur and Palhara fields of Assam, Ankleshwar, Moran, Mumbai High and Palanpur (Gujarat).
- Drilling was carried on in Jawalamukhi (Punjab) but only natural gas deposits were found. It was also carried on in Jaisalmer (Rajasthan) for the exploration of oil and natural gas. Oil has been struck at Cambay, Ankaleshwar and Kalol (Gujarat), Naharkatiya, Rudrasagar, Sibsagar and Moran (Assam). Efforts are being made to locate oil in the offshore region of the Gulf of Cambay. Sagar Samrat, a big ship equipped with drilling machinery, has been purchased from Japan for this purpose. In February, 1974, vast deposits of oil and natural gas were located at Mumbai High. Oil is likely to be found in Bakultala in West Bengal, Tripura and Arunachal Pradesh.
- **Refining:** The present refining capacity in the country as on 1st April, 2024 was 256.8 Million Metric Tonnes Per Annum (MMTPA). Out of 22 refineries operating in the country, 18 are in public sector, 3 are in private sector and one is in JV (Joint venture) of Public Sector. Out of 18 Public Sector refineries, 9 are owned by Indian Oil Corporation Ltd. (IOCL), 2 each by Chennai Petroleum Corporation Limited (a subsidiary of IOCL), Hindustan Petroleum Corporation Limited (HPCL), Bharat Petroleum Corporation Limited (BPCL) and Oil & Natural Gas Corporation Limited (ONGC). Numaligarh Refinery Limited (a subsidiary of BPCL) and Mangalore Refinery & Petrochemicals Limited have one each.
- **Iron:** India has a very high grade iron ore. These ores are available in Odisha (Keonjhar, Talcher, Bonai and Mayurbhanj), Jharkhand (Singbhum district), Chhattisgarh, Madhya Pradesh, Karnataka and Maharashtra. India is the second largest producer of crude steel only after China. India is also the second largest consumer of steel. However, its per capita total finished steel consumption was around 74.7 kg during FY20 as against the global average of 229 kg. Further, the capacity utilization in crude steel plants continues to be low. Kudremukh iron ore deposits were developed primarily for export to Iron.
- **Salt:** It is obtained from the Sambhar Lake (Rajasthan). It is also obtained by the evaporation of sea water, especially near Kutch, Tamil Nadu, Mumbai, Kathiawar Coasts of India. Rock Salt is found in Mandi (Himachal Pradesh). India is self-sufficient in salt; rather it export, this commodity.
- **Monazite:** Found in sandy beaches of Kerala. India supplies 88% of world needs. Due to its thorium content, it is used for the generation of nuclear energy.
- **Bauxite:** Bauxite is a main source of metal like aluminium. India stands fifth in the world in having deposits of bauxite resources. The areas of bauxite deposits in India are : Andhra Pradesh, Jharkhand, Goa, Gujarat, J&K, Karnataka, Kerala, Madhya Pradesh, Maharashtra, Odisha, Rajasthan, Tamil Nadu and Uttar Pradesh. Major reserves are concentrated in the East Coast bauxite deposits of Odisha and Andhra Pradesh.
- **Silver:** A small quantity of silver is obtained from Kolar mines (Karnataka) and also from Manbhum (Jharkhand).
- **Gypsum:** Most of its deposits are found in Rajasthan, Tamil Nadu, Jammu & Kashmir, Himachal Pradesh and Uttar Pradesh. Some deposits are also found in Gujarat. Rajasthan is the main producer of Gypsum followed by Jammu & Kashmir.
- **Graphite:** Jammu & Kashmir, Jharkhand, Madhya Pradesh and Tamil Nadu. Odisha is the main producing state of graphite.
- **Magnesite:** Uttarakhand, Tamil Nadu, Karnataka and Rajasthan.
- **Zinc:** It is obtained from Zawar mines near Udaipur (Rajasthan), Maharashtra
- **Asbestos:** It is extensively used in the manufacture of special type of cement, for lining in the automobile industry and for heat insulation. Deposits occur in Andhra Pradesh, Jharkhand and Karnataka.
- **Minerals for Atomic Energy — Uranium:** At present the minerals containing uranium are used for the generation of atomic energy. Uranium is chiefly mined in Zaire. In India Uranium is found in Jharkhand (Jaduguda mines).
- **Thorium:** It is the potential atomic fuel of the future. The chief ore of thorium is the mineral monazite, which occurs in the sands on Kerala and Tamil Nadu coast.
- **Beryllium:** Though not radioactive, it is of great importance in the atomic energy development because of its property of slowing down neutrons without absorbing them. It is thus extensively used as a moderator in atomic piles. The deposits in India are in Rajasthan, Jharkhand and Andhra Pradesh.
- **Kyanite:** It is used in ceramic industries. The deposits are found in Singbhum district (Jharkhand), Mayurbhanj district (Odisha) and Nellore district (Andhra).

- **Zircon:** The rare metal is used in atomic energy and in alloy metallurgy. It is found in the beach sands on Malabar and Coromandel coasts.
- **White Marble:** Obtained from Makrana mines (Rajasthan) and from Jabalpur (M.P.).
- **Diamonds:** Available in Kimberley mines (South Africa), Ghana and Congo. In India, diamonds are available in Panna mines (M.P.). India has produced some famous historical diamonds like the Kohinoor.

INDUSTRIES

- **Cotton Textile Industry:** The origin of the cotton textile industry, the largest single industry in the country, dates back to 1818 when the first cotton mill was established at Fort Gloster near Kolkata. There are now over 800 mills in the country — and over 24 lakh looms. Maharashtra, Gujarat, Tamil Nadu, U.P., West Bengal, M.P., Karnataka, Kerala and Delhi are the chief centres of this industry.

  Mumbai is especially suited for this industry because of: (1) Abundant supply of raw materials. (2) Black soil of Mumbai is good for cotton. (3) A large supply of cheap labour. (4) Cheap electric power is available. (5) There is a good harbour to export the textiles. (6) Climate is moist.

  South India (Coimbatore, Madurai and Chennai); Madhya Pradesh (Akola has a number of cotton mills) and Delhi specialise in the production of coarse cloth.
- **Jute Industry:** Raw Jute was almost the monopoly of Bangladesh for few years, but now, India is providing raw jute from West Bengal, Bihar, Assam, Orissa and U.P. Most of the requirements of jute mills are met by local production.

  Almost all the jute mills are concentrated in Calcutta. The reasons are that (i) the soil of Bengal is suitable for jute; (ii) availability of coal; (iii) a large supply of cheap labour and water required for the Industry; (iv) the port of Calcutta can easily export all the jute goods.
- **Sugar Industry:** The sugar industry ranks second amongst the major agro-industries in India. Dual pricing has been introduced for sugar. Under this policy, 65 per cent of the total production of the factories is procured by government as levy sugar at controlled prices and the balance 35 per cent is allowed to be sold in the open market without any price control. U.P., and Bihar are regarded as sugar belts — Kanpur, Gorakhpur, Lucknow, Bareilly (U.P.), Champaran, Muzaffarpur, Bhagalpur and Dalmianagar (Bihar). Other sugar centres are Coimbatore in Tamil Nadu and Amritsar and Phagwara in the Punjab. Sugar mills have been set up in Maharashtra also.
- **Silk Industry:** Mysore, Murshidabad and Srinagar produce raw silk. This industry is mainly confined to these area.
- **Woollen Industry:** Kanpur, Dhariwal, Mumbai, Panipat, Ludhiana.
- **Blankets:** Amritsar, Srinagar, Bangalore, Agra, Mirzapur and Kanpur.
- **Shawls:** Kashmir.
- **Iron and Steel:** Jameshdpur (Jharkhand); Burnpur (W. Bengal); Bhadrawati (Karnataka); Bhilai (Chhatisgarh); Rourkela (Orissa); Durgapur (West Bengal), Bokaro (Jharkhand); and Vishakhapatnam (A.P.). The earliest successful attempt to manufacture iron and steel by modern methods was made in the country in 1874. But the first efforts at large-scale production got underway when Tata Iron and Steel Company (TISCO) was set up at Jamshedpur in 1907. This was followed by the establishment of the Indian Iron and Steel Company (IISCO) at Burnpur in 1919. The first unit in the public sector, now known as the Visvesvaraya Iron and Steel Works Ltd., started functioning at Bhadravati in 1923.

TRANSPORTATION

Railways

The first train in India was started on a small rail route of 34 kilometres between Bombay and Thane on April 16, 1,853. Indian Railways is one of the world's largest rail networks with 69,181 Route kilometres of route lengths as on March 31, 2024. Out of this Broad Gauge (BG) constitutes 66,820 route kilometres (96.58%), Metre Gauge (MG) 1,159 route kilometres (1.67%) and Narrow Gauge (NG) 1,202 route kilometres (1.73%). Indian Railways' network is the second railways in Asia and the fourth biggest railways in the world. [US (25,0000 km); China (1,00,000 km); Russia (85,500 kms)]. About 90% (62,253 km) of the route kilometres, has been electrified. Indian railways is the world's eighth largest employer, with more than 1.190 million employees as of March 2024.

First Double-decker Train Runs on Wheel in India

India's first double-decker fully air-conditioned train has been put on the wheels. The them Railway Minister Mr. Dinesh Trivedi started it with green flag between Howrah and Dhanbad on Oct. 1, 2011. This train, having 9 coaches, consists seven double decker coaches. These coaches has been made in Kapurthala

Coach Factory. The maximum speed of this train between Howarah and Dhanbad has been fixed at 110 km per hour.

Konkan Railway Project

The Konkan Railway project consisting of the 760 km long broad gauge line from Roha (150 km south of Mumbai) to Mangalore has been completed. The construction of this line is a big technical feat as it has 1,998 bridges and 73 tunnels, with the longest tunnel and the tallest viaduct in Asia. This new line has substantially reduced the journey time between Mumbai and Mangalore, Mumbai and Cochin and Mumbai and Goa. This line will largely benefit the Konkan Region.

Uni-Gauge Project

In a bid to get rid of a multi-gauge system in favour of uniform gauge systems, Indian Railway in 1992, had decided to get rid of multi-gauge system in favour of uniform gauge systems. This is being done by gradually converting railway lines of other gauges to broad gauge in a planned manner. It has already converted more than 10,000 km of track to broad gauge in the last 10 years and work is still in progress.

Railway Zones

The network of railways is divided into zones. These zones are headed by a General Manager, who is responsible to the Railway Board for operation, maintenance and financial matters. The zones with their headquarters are as follows :

Name of the Zones		Headquarters
1. Northern Railway	–	New Delhi
2. Western Railway	–	Church gate Mumbai
3. South Central Railway	–	Secunderabad
4. South Eastern Railway	–	Kolkata
5. Central Railway	–	Mumbai CST
6. Southern Railway	–	Chennai
7. North-Eastern Railway	–	Gorakhpur
8. Eastern Railway	–	Kotkata
9. North-East Frontier Railway	–	Maligaon (Guwahati)
10. East-Central Railway	–	Hajipur
11. North Western Railway	–	Jaipur
12. East-Coast Railway	–	Bhubaneshwar
13. North-Central Railway	–	Prayagraj
14. South-Western Railway	–	Hubli
15. Western-Central Railway	–	Jabalpur
16. South-East Central Railway	–	Bilaspur
7. Kolkata Metro	–	Kolkata
8. South Coast Railway	–	Vishakhapatnam (Proposed)

Roads

The Indian road network, the largest in the world aggregating 63.45 lakh km consists of 1,46,195 km of National Highways, 1,79,535 km of State Highways and about 60,19,723 km of Other District and Rural Roads. The National Highways account for about 2.08% of the total road network but carry as much as 40% of the total road traffic in the country.

Roads are classified into six classes according to their importance : 1. Golden Quadrilateral Super Highways, 2. National Highways, 3. State Highways, 4. Border Roads, 5. Major District Roads, and 6. Rural Roads including other district roads.

1. Golden Quadrilateral Super Highways

The government has launched a major road development project linking Delhi-Kolkata-Chennai-Mumbai and Delhi by six-lane Super Highways. The North-South corridors linking Srinagar (Jammu & Kashmir) and Kanyakumari (Tamil Nadu), and East-West Corridor connecting Silcher (Assam) and Porbander (Gujarat) are part of this project. The major objective of these Super Highways is to reduce the time and distance between the mega cities of India. These highway projects are being implemented by the National Highway Authority of India (NHAI).

2. National Highways

National Highways link extreme parts of the country. These are the primary road systems and are laid and maintained by the Central Public Works Department (CPWD). A number of major National Highways run in North-South and East-West directions. The historical Sher-Shah Suri Marg is between Delhi and Amritsar. National Highway 44 (NH44) is the longest-running major North-South National Highway in India. It starts from Srinagar and terminates in Kanyakumari.

3. State Highways

Roads linking a state capital with different district headquarters are known as State Highways. These roads are constructed and maintained by the State Public Works Department (PWD) in State and Union Territories.

Air Transport

The scheduled civil air transport in India commenced during 1929-30 when the British, French and the Dutch extended their services to and beyond India. The first internal air service was established between Karachi and Chennai via Mumbai in 1922. By the beginning of the Second World War, major cities like Karachi, Lahore, Delhi, Mumbai, Kolkata and Chennai had scheduled air services operated by private companies. At the time of independence, there were four companies. By 1951, from more private companies were operating air services. The Air Transport Enquiry Committee setup in 1950 recommended the merger of these eight companies into a corporation. Under the Air Corporation Act 1953, the Indian Airlines Corporation was set up to operate all internal civil air services and Air India International was constituted for managing international air transport.

SOCIAL SCIENCE

The Governement ended the monopoly of Indian Airlines and Air India on the scheduled operations by repealing the Air Corporation Act, 1953. There are at present ten scheduled airlines operating on the domestic network rendering the passengers a wide choice of flights.

Apart from this, more than 40 companies are holding non-scheduled operators permit. The policy on domestic air transport service was approved in April 1997 according to which barriers to entry and exit from this sector have been removed.

The main trunk routes having high density of traffic are operated by Air Bus and Boeing aircraft. The remote areas are served by smaller aircraft. A third airline—Vayudoot—was incorporated as private limited company in January 1981. The Pawan Hans Limited was set up in October 1985 to provide transport services for short distances.

Airport Authority of India (AAI) provides for safe efficient air traffic and aeronautical communication services in the India Air Space.

Privatization of Air India

On January 27, 2022 the Government of India successfully handed over Air India to the Tata Group, nearly 69 years after it was taken from TATAs. The Tata Group, as part of the deal are also handed over the Air India express and a 50% stake in the ground handling arm of Air India SATS. Air India will be the third airline brand in Tata's stable as the conglomerate holds a majority interest in Air Asia India and Vistara. Tata Group chairman N. Chandrashekhar witnessed the formal transfer of the Air India to Tata Group. The Government of India on October 8, 2021 had announced the sale of the national carrier to its original developer–the salt-to-software conglomerate Tata Group at an enterprise value of ₹ 18,000 crore. This is the first major privatisation step in about two decades.

Some Important International Airports are :

Mumbai (Chhatrapati Shivaji International Airport). **Delhi** (Indira Gandhi International Airport). **Kolkata** (Subhash Chandra Bose I.A.), **Chennai** (Meenambakkam I.A.), **Trivendrum** (Thiruvananthpuram) **Ahmedabad** (Sardar Vallabh Bhai Patel Airport), **Cochin** (Needumbassery I.A.), **Goa** (Dabolim I.A.), **Guwahati** (Lokpriya Gopinath Bardoloi I.A.), **Hyderabad** (Rajiv Gandhi I.A.), **Amritsar** (Sri Guru Ram Dass Jee International Airport) **Bengaluru** (Kempegowda International Airport). Civeli Aviation Training College (Prayagraj) provides training on various operational areas.

National Institute of Aviation Management and Research (NIAMAR) at Delhi is managed by AAI.

Indira Gandhi Rastriya Udan Academy at Fursat Ganj in U.P is an autonomous body under Ministry of Civil Aviation. It imparts training.

Water Transport

India has a vast coastline of about 7,515 km and over two million sq. km of Exclusive Economic Zone (EEZ). The entire coastline is studded with 13 major ports handle about 15,000 Cargo vessels per annum. In terms of cargo handling, Mumbai is the biggest port in India.

Major Ports

There are 12 major ports and 200 minor working ports in the country. Major ports are the direct responsibility of the Central Government while minor ports including intermediate ports fall in the concurrent list of the Constitution and are managed and administered by the respective maritime state government.

Marmagaon, Kandla, Bombay, New Manglore and Cochin are the major ports on the west coast. A new major port at Nhava Sheva off Bombay is highly developed. On the east coast, Tuticorin, Chennai, Vishakhapatnam, Paradip, Ennore, and Kolkata-Haldia are the major ports.

1. **Mumbai :** It is the biggest port in the country. It is a natural harbour and handles more than one-fifth of the total traffic of the ports. The bulk of the total traffic consists of petroleum products and dry cargo.
2. **Shyama Prasad Mukherjee (Kolkata) :** It is a riverine port handling diversified commodities. It is the largest terminal port in South Asia. Haldia dock-system is a fully equipped containerised berth. Its mechanised dock system with provision for deep draft vessels downstream of Kolkata supplement the facilities already available at Kolkata port. It mainly handles coal, petroleum products and dry cargo.
3. **Kochi :** It is a natural harbour on the west coast. It largely handles petroleum products, fertilisers, raw materials and general cargo.
4. **Deendayal (Kandla) :** It is a tidal port having a free trade zone. It largely handles petroleum products and fertilizers. Foodgrains, cotton, cement and edible oils are also handled.
5. **Chennai :** It is one of the oldest ports on the east coast and caters to traffic in iron ore, petroleum products and dry cargo.
6. **New Mangaluru :** On the west coast, it was declared a major port in 1947. Facilities have been developed at this port for the export of Kudremukh iron granite stone. dry cargo is also handled at this port.

7. **Mormugao (Goa) :** It enjoys the second position in total traffic tonnage, bulk of which is iron ore for export.
8. **Paradip :** In Odisha, it mainly handles iron ore, coal and general cargo.
9. **V.O. Chidambaranar (Tuticorin) :** On the east coast, it was declared a major port in 1947. It handles mainly salt, coal, edible oils, foodgrains, fertilizers, petroleum products and dry cargo.
10. **Vishakhapatnam :** It is the deepest landlocked and protected port where an outer harbour has been developed for exporting mainly iron ore to Japan. Crude oil, petroleum products, coal and dry cargo are also handled.
11. **Jawaharlal Nehru Port (Nhava Sheva) :** Jawaharlal Nehru Port is India's biggest and most modern seaport near Mumbai. This port has large berthing facilities, latest traffic and cargo handling equipment and most modern operational techniques.
12. **Kamarajar Port Limited (Ennore) :** Kamarajar Port Limited (KPL), the 12th major port under the Ministry of Shipping was commissioned in 2001, primarily as a coal port dedicated to handling thermal coal requirements of Tamil Nadu Electricity Board (TNEB). KPL has the distinction of being the only corporate port amongst the major ports administered by the central government.

Inland Waterways

India has over 14,500 km of navigable waterways. Considering the inherent advantages of Inland Water Transport (IWT) mode namely; fuel efficiency, environment friendlines, cost effectiveness and decongestion of road and rail networks, particularly for movement to bulk goods, hazardous good and over dimensional approach. Inland Waterways Authority of India (IWAI) was set up in 1986 for regulation and development of inland waterways for the purpose of shipping and navigation. IWAI is primarily responsible for development, maintenance and regulation of national waterways.

Following five waterways have so far been declared as national waterways:

- Allahabad-Haldia stretch (1620 km) of the Ganga-Bhagirathi-Hooghly river system (NW-1) in 1986.
- Sadiya-Dhubri stretch (891 km) of Brahmaputra river (NW-2) in 1988).
- Kottapuram-Kollam stretch of West Coast Canal along with Champakara Canal and Udyogmandal Canal (205 km) (NW-3) in 1993.
- Kakinada-Puducherry stretch of Canal and Kalurelly Tank, stretches of river Godavari and Krishna (1928 km) in 2008.
- Talcher-Dhamra stretch of river Brahmani, Geonkhali Charbatia stretch of East Coast Canel, Charbatia-Dhamra stretch of Matai river along with Mahanadi delta river system (585 km) in 2008. (NW-5)
- Lakhipur to Bhanga of River Barak, NW-6, proposed in 2013, total length 121 km.

Pipelines

Pipelines transport network is a new arrival on the transportation map of India. In the past, these were used to transport water to cities and industries. Now, these are used for transporting crude oil, petroleum products and natural gas from oil and natural gas fields to refineries, fertilizer factories and big thermal power plants.

Solids can also be transported through a pipeline when converted into slurry. The far inland locations of refineries like Barauni, Mathura, Panipat and gas based fertilizer plants could be thought of only because of pipelines.

Initial cost of laying pipelines is high but subsequent running costs are minimal. It rules out trans-shipment losses or delays. There are three important network of pipeline transportation in the country.

- From oil field in upper Assam to Kanpur (Uttar Pradesh), via Guwahati, Barauni and Prayagraj. It has branches from Barauni to Haldia, via Rajbandh to Maurigram and Guwahati to Siliguri. From Salaya in Gujarat to Jalandhar in Punjab, via Viramgam, Mathura, Delhi and Sonipat. It has branches to connect Koyali (near Vododara in Gujarat) Chakshu and other places.
- **Gas pipeline** from Hazira in Gujarat connects Jagdishpur in Uttar Pradesh, via Vijaipur in Madhya Pradesh. It has branch to Kota in Rajasthan, Shahjahanpur, Babrala and other places in Uttar Pradesh.

SOCIAL SCIENCE

Multiple Choice Questions

1. Which is the biggest planet?
A. Venus B. Mars
C. Mercury D. Jupiter

2. Which is the smallest continent in the world?
A. Australia B. Africa
C. South America D. Europe

3. Which is the lowest body of water in the world?
A. Black Sea B. Dead Sea
C. Adriatic Sea D. Red Sea

4. In which state the famous Kamakhya Temple is situated?
A. West Bengal B. Gujarat
C. Uttar Pradesh D. Assam

5. Which is the largest island sea in the world?
A. Caribbean Sea B. Mediterranean Sea
C. Red Sea D. Beaufort Sea

6. Which is the largest continent of the world?
A. Asia B. Africa
C. Australia D. North America

7. Name the highest peak in the Indian sub-continent:
A. Nanda Devi B. Everest
C. Trishul D. Kanchanjunga

8. Which is the largest island in the world?
A. New Guinea B. Brneo
C. Madagascar D. Greenland

9. Which of the following is not a peak of the Himalayas?
A. Mount Koyo B. Kanchenjunga
C. Dhaulagiri D. Makalu

10. Which is the biggest ocean?
A. Pacific Ocean B. Atlantic Ocean
C. Antarctic Ocean D. Indian Ocean

11. Which is the largest peninsula in the world?
A. Pacific B. Arabia
C. Bangladesh D. Africa

12. Which is the largest Archipelago in the world?
A. Indonesia B. Malaysia
C. New Zealand D. Malta

13. Which is the deepest ocean in the world?
A. Arctic B. Atlantic
C. Pacific D. Indian

14. The State producing maximum vegetables in India is:
A. West Bengal B. Uttar Pradesh
C. Punjab D. Maharashtra

15. What does the 17th Parallel line separate?
A. South and North America
B. North and South Korea
C. South and North Yemen
D. South and North Vietnam

16. Which continent/portion of the world is uninhabited?
A. Antarctica B. Rajasthan
C. Australia D. Gobi

17. Land of the Golden Fleece is:
A. Bhutan B. Japan
C. Canada D. Australia

18. Which mountains are called the Blue Mountains?
A. Nilgiri Mountains B. The Alps
C. Mount Everest D. The Himalayas

19. Name the countries which lie on either side of Durand Line?
A. India and Pakistan
B. Indian and Bangladesh
C. Afghanistan and Pakistan
D. Iran and Iraq

20. Which is the largest lake in the world?
A. Caspian (C.I.S., Iran)
B. Lake Huron (Canada, U.S.)
C. Nyanza (Tanzania-Kenya)
D. Lake Superior (U.S.A. Canada)

21. Name the countries which lie on either side of MacMohan Line?
A. South Vietnam and North Vietnam
B. India and China
C. India and Ceylon
D. France and Germany

22. Which is the largest Gulf in the world?
A. Gulf of Aqaba B. Gulf of Bengal
C. Gulf of Mexico D. Gulf of Aden

23. Which country is called the "Land of Morning Calm"?
A. Sweden B. Netherlands
C. Norway D. Korea

24. Which is called the Dark Continent?
A. Africa B. Australia
C. Greenland D. South America

25. What does the 38th Parallel Line separate?
A. India from Bangladesh
B. India from China
C. North Korea from South Korea
D. India from Pakistan

26. The Panama Canal connects:
A. The Pacific and Atlantic Oceans
B. The Pacific and Arctic Oceans
C. The Atlantic and Arctic Oceans
D. The Atlantic and Indian Oceans

27. What is the habitable portion of the world land area?
A. Less than 35%
B. Less than half of it
C. 50%
D. About 75%

28. Which one of the following ocean current is not a cold ocean current?
A. Canary Current
B. California Current
C. Kuroshio Current
D. Oyashio Current

29. The Regur soil is also known as:
A. Red soil B. Black soil
C. Yellow soil D. Alluvial soil

30. Rome is the:
A. Eternal city B. Forbidden city
C. City of palaces D. Cleanest city

31. The capital of Israel is:
A. Palestine B. Tel Aviv
C. Vatican D. Jerusalem

32. The City of Seven Hills is:
A. Rome B. Athens
C. Cairo D. Tokyo

33. Laplands is a group of countries located in:
A. Europe B. Australia
C. Asia D. America

34. Zanzibar is called:
A. Island of cloves B. Eternal city
C. Holy land D. Land of spices

35. The Himalayas constitute the natural boundary between :
A. China and India
B. China and Afghanistan
C. India and Nepal
D. India and Myanmar

36. Hermit Kingdom is:
A. Korea B. Palestine
C. Rome D. Haridwar

37. The highest of all the plateaus in the world is the:
A. Deccan Plateau B. Bolivian Plateau
C. Tibetan Plateau D. Colombian Plateau

38. Eternal City is:
A. Kolkata B. Rome
C. Athens D. Bangkok

39. The city of Khartoum is situated on the banks of:
A. Hudson B. Nile
C. Tiber D. Seine

40. In which continent some of its parts are over 1500 miles from the sea and in which the hottest as well as the coldest climates of the world are to be found:
A. America B. Asia
C. Europe D. Australia

41. Paris is situated on the river:
A. Tibea B. Seine
C. Danube D. None of the above

42. Name the place where Blue and White Nile Rivers effect a confluence:
A. Cairo
B. Constantinople (except Greenland)
C. Khartoum
D. Teheran

43. The basin of Godavari River does not lie in which of the following states?
A. Odisha B. Chhattisgarh
C. Gujarat D. Madhya Pradesh

44. Australia is the:
A. only continent in the Southern Hemisphere
B. island continent
C. smallest continent
D. all the above points are true

45. Name the place where Rhine and Spree rivers meet in Europe:
A. Lyons B. Paris
C. Hamburg D. Berlin

46. Moscow is situated on the bank of:
A. Moskva B. Spree
C. Volga D. Tagus

47. The country Congo is in the ..... continent:
A. European B. Australian
C. Asian D. African

48. China's Sorrow is:
A. Lin Piao B. Sinkiang
C. Hwang-ho D. I'sang Ho

49. Sugar Bowl of the world is:
A. Manila B. Japan
C. Cuba D. Havana

50. The City of Palaces is:
A. Peru B. Rome
C. Kolkata D. Bangkok

SOCIAL SCIENCE

51. The highest peak in Europe is:
A. Mont Blanc B. Andes
C. Monte Rosa D. Elburz

52. Land of the Rising Sun is:
A. Japan B. Norway
C. Assam D.Myanmar

53. Where was electricity supply first introduced in India?
A. Darjeeling B. Kolkata
C. Mumbai D. Delhi

54. Name the largest island in the world:
A. New Guinea B. Greenland
C. Madagascar D. Great Britain

55. Land of the Midnight Sun is:
A. Japan B. Myanmar
C. Norway D. Manipur

56. The longest river in the world is:
A. Nile B. Amazon
C. Yangtze D. Missouri-Mississippi

57. The Island Continent is:
A. Asia B. America
C. Africa D. Australia

58. Suez Canal joins:
A. London to Paris
B. Tokyo to Osaka
C. Mediterranean to the Red Sea
D. Rangoon to Philippines

59. The Radcliffe Line was drawn on 15th August, 1947 between:
A. India and Myanmar (Burma)
B. Pakistan and China
C. Pakistan and India
D. Pakistan and Nepal

60. New York is situated on the river bank of:
A. Rhine B. Thames
C. Hudson D. Amazon

61. Which place is called the land of Golden Fleece?
A. Australia B. Cuba
C. Austria D. Myanmar

62. Kiel is a:
A renowned explorer
B. American antelope
C. big American sea bird
D. shipping canal between London and Baltic Sea

63. USA consists of so many States:
A. 30 B. 50
C. 20 D. 40

64. The Turan Type of Regions have the climate of extremes because:
A. These lie in the interior ports of the continent
B. These have either too much or too less rain
C. These are either on hills or near the deserts
D. None of the above

65. Which country tops in the mining of gold:
A. U.S.A. B. Canada
C. China D. India

66. The largest Fresh water lake is:
A. Lake Superior B. Caspian Sea
C. Lake Baikal D. Hind Sea

67. ..... is the most important occupation of the people in the Monsoon Lands:
A. Forestry B. Agriculture
C. Industry D. Mining

68. There is the great variations of vegetation in the Monsoon Region because of:
A. It depends on nearness to forests, oceans, mountains
B. Variation in the amount of rainfall in different places
C. The effect of rainfall is different in different regions.
D. None of the above

69. In the Amur Valley of the Russia ..... is the most important economic activity:
A. agriculture B. animal rearing
C. mining D. industry

70. Which is the Land of White Elephants?
A. Korea B. Japan
C. Thailand D. Tanzania

71. The most important occupation of the people in the Turan Type of Regions is .....
A. agriculture
B. cattle and animal rearing
C. mountaineering
D. industry

72. Which is the City of Magnificent Buildings?
A. Tokyo B. New York
C. Washington D. Rome

73. In the West European Type of Regions, the summer temperature hardly exceeds ..... °C.
A. 10°C B. 16°C
C. 7°C D. 8°C

74. The extensive treeless tracts of North America, which are covered with tall coarse grass, are called:
A. Savanna B. Tundras
C. Pampas D. Prairies

75. ....., ... and ..... are the important animal products of the Iran Type of Regions.
A. Skins and hides
B. Meat canning and export
C. Wool, meat and skins
D. Wool and hides

76. Which is the largest country of the world (in area)?
A. U.S.A. B. Russia
C. China D. Canada

77. The main natural regions of the world are:
A. Hot, Polar, Arctic and Antarctic
B. Forests, deserts, sea, ocean
C. Tropical Regions, Warm Temperate Region, Cool Temperate Regions, Polar Regions
D. None of these

78. The second highest peak in the world is:

A. Kanchanjunga B. K-2
C. Himalayas D. Andes

79. Which state in the world occupies the smallest area:

A. Bermuda B. Peru
C. Monaco D. Vatican

80. The source of the origin of river Narmada is:

A. Amarkantak B. Bhedaghat
C. Brahmagiri D. Mahabaleshwar

81. The Toda tribes are the original inhabitants of:

A. Aravali Hills B. Satpura Hills
C. Nilgiri Hills D. Guru Shikhar

82. Korba is famous for

I. Thermal power plant
II. Aluminium plant
III. Hydroelectric power plant

The correct answer out of these is

A. I only B. II only
C. I and II only D. I, II and III

83. India's biggest multi-purpose river valley scheme is

A. Kosi B. Hirakud
C. Bhakra Nangal D. Nagarjunasagar

84. Match the following columns:

(*a*) Spain 1. Madrid
(*b*) Finland 2. Oslo
(*c*) Lebanon 3. Helsinki
(*d*) Norway 4. Beirut

	(*a*)	(*b*)	(*c*)	(*d*)
A.	1	3	4	2
B.	1	4	3	2
C.	4	1	2	3
D.	2	1	4	3

85. Arrange the following states in the descending order of their respective population?

1. West Bengal
2. Uttarakhand
3. Maharashtra

A. 1, 2, 3 B. 3, 1, 2
C. 2, 3, 1 D. 1, 3, 2

86. From which of the following places is Kathmandu nearest by air route?

A. Patna B. Gorakhpur
C. Varansi D. Kolkata

87. Chota Nagpur region in Jharkhand is famous for:

A. oil refinery B. fertile soil
C. lac industry D. textiles

88. Which of the following pairs is correct?

A. Bhilai—Bihar
B. Bokaro—Madhya Pradesh
C. Durgapur—Karnataka
D. Rourkela—Orissa

89. The state where Shipki-la pass is located:

A. Sikkim
B. Arunachal Pradesh
C. Himachal Pradesh
D. Meghalaya

90. Khetri is famous for

A. copper complex
B. gold fields
C. aluminium complex
D. fertilisers

91. Savana grasslands are found in—

A. Australia
B. East Asia
C. South America
D. Africa

92. Which of the following ports is not a major port in India?

A. Marmugao
B. Cochin
C. Kozhikode
D. Kandla

93. Which of the following is associated with the creation of a Third World news agency?

A. NAMEDIA
B. CHOGM
C. COMECON
D. NAM

94. Which of the following ports has a free trade zone?

A. Kandla B. Cochin
C. Chennai D. Tuticorin

95. Approximately how many kilometres are represented by 1° of latitude?

A. 421 km B. 111 km
C. 91 km D. 211 km

96. Which state in India has the largest area?

A. Assam B. Uttar Pradesh
C. West Bengal D. Rajasthan

97. Which of the following winds cause rainfall in Tamil Nadu?

A. Cyclonic winds in the Bay of Bengal
B. South-West monsoons
C. North-East monsoons
D. North-West monsoons

98. 'Aeroflot' is the name of the airline of:

A. Germany B. Thailand
C. Indonesia D. Russia

99. The water of which of the following seas is most saline?

A. Black Sea B. Dead Sea
C. Baltic Sea D. Red Sea

100. Beirut is the capital of:

A. Libya B. Lebanon
C. Jordan D. Syria

ANSWERS

1	2	3	4	5	6	7	8	9	10
D	A	B	D	B	A	B	D	A	A
11	**12**	**13**	**14**	**15**	**16**	**17**	**18**	**19**	**20**
B	A	C	A	D	A	D	A	C	A
21	**22**	**23**	**24**	**25**	**26**	**27**	**28**	**29**	**30**
B	C	D	A	C	A	B	C	B	A
31	**32**	**33**	**34**	**35**	**36**	**37**	**38**	**39**	**40**
D	A	A	A	A	A	C	B	B	B
41	**42**	**43**	**44**	**45**	**46**	**47**	**48**	**49**	**50**
B	B	C	D	A	A	D	C	C	C
51	**52**	**53**	**54**	**55**	**56**	**57**	**58**	**59**	**60**
D	A	A	B	C	A	D	C	C	C
61	**62**	**63**	**64**	**65**	**66**	**67**	**68**	**69**	**70**
A	D	B	A	C	A	B	B	A	C
71	**72**	**73**	**74**	**75**	**76**	**77**	**78**	**79**	**80**
B	C	B	D	C	B	C	B	D	A
81	**82**	**83**	**84**	**85**	**86**	**87**	**88**	**89**	**90**
C	A	C	A	B	A	C	D	C	A
91	**92**	**93**	**94**	**95**	**96**	**97**	**98**	**99**	**100**
D	C	A	A	B	D	D	D	B	B

ECONOMICS

MICRO AND MACRO ECONOMICS

The Subject-matter of economics has been divided into two Parts—**Microeconomics** and **Macroeconomics. Ragner Frisch** was the first to use the terms "micro" and "macro" in economics in **1933.** The term microeconomics is derived from the Greek word **mikros,** meaning **"small"** and the term macroeconomics is derived from the Greek word **makros,** meaning **"large"**. Thus micro economics related to the study of individual economic units while the latter is a study of the economy as a whole.

Micro Economics

Microeconomics is the study of economic actions and behaviour of individual units and small groups. In the other words, in microeconomics we make a microscopic study of the economy. The determination of equilibrium output of the firm or industry, the wage of a particular type of labour, the price of a particular commodity are some of the fields of microeconomics theory. Thus the theory of product pricing and the theory of factor pricing (or the theory of distribution) fall within the domain of microeconomics. The whole content of microeconomic theory is presented in the following chart :

MICRO ECONOMIC THEORY

- *Product Pricing*
  - Theory of Demand
  - Theory of Production and Cost
- *Factor Pricing* (Theory of Distribution)
  - Wages
  - Rent
  - Interest
  - Profits
- *Theory of* Economic Welfare

Macro Economics

Macroeconomics is the study of aggregates or averages covering the entire economy, such as total employment, the national product or income, the general price level of the economy. Therefore, macroeconomics is also known as **aggregative economics.** Macroeconomics analyses and establishes the functional relationship between these large aggregates. Thus **Professor Boulding** says, "Macroeconomics deals not with individuals quantities as such but with the aggregates of these quantities; not with individual incomes but with the national income; not with individual prices but with the price level; not with individual outputs but with the national output."

Macroeconomics is also known as the theory of income and employment, or simply income analysis. It is concerned with the problems of unemployment, economic fluctuations, inflation or deflation, international trade and economic growth.

We have now stated, in brief, all aspects of macroeconomic theory. These various aspects of macroeconomic theory are shown, in the following chart :

MACRO ECONOMIC THEORY

- Theory of Income and Employment
  - Theory of Consumption Functions
  - Theory of Investment
- Theory of General Price Level and Inflation
- The Theory of Economic Growth
- Macro Theory of Distribution (Relative Shares of Wages and Profits)

CONSUMER DEMAND THEORY

There are two basic approaches to the study of consumer demand theory. The first, or **classical approach,** involves the use of measurable marginal utility (satisfaction). It is generally called the **Cardinal utility approach.** The second, or indifference curve approach, is generally called the **ordinal approach.**

MARGINAL UTILITY ANALYSIS

Marginal utility analysis is the oldest theory of demand which provides an explanation of Consumer's demand for a product and it derives the law of demand which establishes an inverse relationship between price and quantity demanded of the product. Though marginal utility approach to the theory of demand is very old, its final shape emerged at the hands of **Marshall.** Marginal utility analysis is based on the concept of **Cardinal approach** which assumes that utility is measurable and additive. It is expressed as a quantity measured in hypothetical units which are called **'utils'.** If a consumer imagines that one mango has 8 utils and an apple 4 utils, it implies that the utility of one mango is twice that of an apple.

Basic Assumptions of Marginal Utility Analysis

Marginal utility analysis of demand is based upon certain important assumptions. Before explaining how utility analysis explains consumer's equilibrium in regard to the demand for goods, it is essential to describe those basic assumptions on which the whole utility analysis rests. The following are the main assumptions.

1. **Rationality :** The consumer is rational. He aims at the maximisation of his utility subject to the constraint imposed by his given income.
2. **Cardinal Utility :** The utility of each commodity is measurable. Utility is a Cardinal concept. The most convenient measure is money. The utility is measured by the monetary units that the consumer is prepared to pay for another unit of the commodity.
3. **Constant Marginal Utility of Money :** Another important assumption of the marginal utility analysis is that the marginal utility of money remains constant even though the quantity of money with consumer is diminished by the successive purchases made by him. It is assumed that while marginal utility of a commodity varies with the quantity of the commodity purchased, the marginal utility of money remains throughout the same as the quantity of the good purchased varies. This assumption becomes necessary because the marginal utility of a commodity is measured in terms of money.
4. **Diminishing Marginal Utility :** The utility gained from successive units of a commodity diminishes. In other words, the marginal utility of a commodity diminishes as the consumer acquires large quantities of it. This is the axion of **diminishing marginal utility.**
5. **Utilities are Independent :** Marginal utility analysis assumes that the utilities of different commodities are independent of one another. That is, the utility of one commodity does not in any way affect that of another. In other words, the satisfaction derived from the consumption of one good is the function of that good alone and is not affected by the consumption of another. On this assumption, the total utility of all goods consumed by a consumer is simply the sum of total of the separate utilities of all the goods consumed by a consumer.
6. **Introspective Method :** Another important hypothesis of the marginal utility analysis is the use of introspective method in judging the behaviour of marginal utility. "Introspection is the ability of the observer to reconstruct events which go on in the mind of another person with the help of self-observation. This form of comprehension may be just guess work or intuition or the result of long-lasting experience."

TOTAL UTILITY AND MARGINAL UTILITY

When a consumer purchases a good, he obtains satisfaction from the possession of that good. That is, he derives utility from the possession of the good. When the consumer buys apples he receives them in units, 1, 2, 3, 4, etc. 2 apples have more utility than 1, 3 more utility than 2, and 4 more than 3. The units of apple's which the consumer chooses are in a descending order of their utilities. In his estimation, the first apple is the best out of the lot available to him and thus gives him the highest satisfaction, measured as 20 utils. The second apple will naturally be the second best with lesser amount of utility than the first, and has 15 utils. The third apple has 10 utils and the fourth 5 utils. In our illustration, the total utility of two apples is 35 = 20 + 15 utils, of three apples is 45 = 20 + 15 + 10 utils, and of four apples is 50 = 20 + 15 + 10 + 5. **Marginal utility is the addition made to total utility by having an additional unit of the commodity.** The total utility of the two apples is 35 utils. When the consumer consumes the third apple, the total utility becomes 45 utils. Thus, marginal utility of the third apple is 10 utils (45 – 35). In other words, marginal utility is defined as the change in total utility resulting from a unit change in the consumption of the good in question per unit of time.

Algebraically, the marginal utility (MU) of n units of a commodity is the total utility (TU) of n units minus the total utility of $(n - 1)$. Thus,

$$MU_n = TU_n - TU_{n-1}$$

The relation between the total and marginal utility is explained with the help of following table.

TABLE

Units of Apple	TU in Utils	MU in Utils
0	0	0
1	20	20
2	35	15
3	45	10
4	50	5
5	50	0
6	45	– 5
7	35	– 10

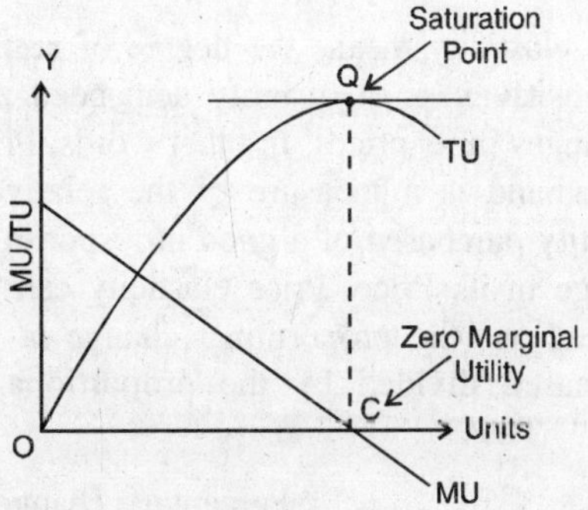

Fig.

So long as total utility is increasing, marginal utility is decreasing upto the 4th unit. When total utility is maximum (at the fifth unit), marginal utility is zero. It is the point of **Satiety (Saturation)** for the consumer. When total utility is decreasing, marginal utility is negative.

LAW OF DIMINISHING MARGINAL UTILITY

Satisfaction of human wants follows some very importants laws and one of them is the Law of Diminishing Marginal utility. **Hermann Heinrich Gossen** was the first to formulate this law in 1854 though the name was given by Marshall. **Javons** called it **Gossen's First Law.** Gossen stated it thus. "The magnitude of one and the same satisfaction, when we continue to enjoy it without interruption, continually decreases until satisfaction is reached." According to this law the marginal utility of a good diminishes as an individual consumes more units of a good. In other words, as a consumer takes more units of a good, the extra utility or satisfaction that he derives from an extra unit of the good goes on falling. It should be carefully noted that it is the marginal utility and not the total utility that declines with the increase in the consumption of a good. The law of diminishing marginal utility means that the total utility increases but at a decreasing rate.

Marshall states the Law thus : "The additional benefits which a person derives from a given increase of his stock of a thing diminishes with every increase in the stock that he already has."

This Law is based upon two important facts. **Firstly,** while the total wants of a man are virtually unlimited, each single want is satiable. Therefore, as an individual consumes more and more units of a good, intensity of his want for the good goes on falling and a point is reached where the individual no longer wants any more units of the good. That is **when Saturation Point is reached marginal utility of a good becomes zero.** The second fact on which the law of diminishing marginal utility is based is that the different goods are not perfect substitutes for each other in the satisfaction of various particular wants. When an individual consumes more and more units of a good, the intensity of his particular want for the good diminishes but if the units of that good could be devoted to the satisfaction of other wants and yielded as much satisfaction as they did initially in the satisfaction of the first want, marginal utility of the good would not have diminished.

The significance of the diminishing marginal utility of a good for the theory of demand is that the quantity demanded of a good rises as the price falls and **vice-versa.** Thus it is because of the diminishing marginal utility that the demand curve slopes downward.

Law of diminishing marginal utility is a universal law and applies to all objects of desire including money. But, it is worth mentioning that marginal utility of money is generally never zero or negative. Money represents purchasing power over all other goods, that is, a man can satisfy all his material wants if he possesses enough money. Since man's total wants are practically unlimited, therefore the marginal utility of money to him never falls to zero.

DEMAND

Demand is a function of price, income, price of related goods and tastes and is expressed as

$$D = f(p, y, pr, t).$$

When income, prices of related goods and tastes are given, the demand function is

$$D = f(p).$$

It shows quantities of a commodity purchased at given prices. Demand is also related to a period of time. In the **Marshallian analysis,** the other determinants of demand are taken as given and constant.

Types of Demand

Three kinds of demands may be distinguished :

(*a*) Price Demand

(*b*) Income Demand

(*c*) Cross Demand

Price Demand : Price demand refers to the various quantities of a commodity or service that a consumer or service that a consumer would purchase at a given time in a market at various hypothetical prices. It is assumed that other things, such as consumer's income, his tastes and prices of inter-related goods, remain unchanged.

The demand of the individual consumer is called **Individual Demand** and the total demand of all the consumers combined for the commodity or service is called **Industry Demand.** The total demand for the product of an individual firm at various prices is known as firm's demand or **Individual Seller's Demand.**

Income Demand : The income demand refers to the various qualities of goods and services which would be purchased by the consumers at various levels of incomes. Here we assume that the price of the commodity or service as well as the prices of inter-related goods and the tastes and desires of consumers do not change.

Cross Demand : The cross demand means the quantities of a good or service which will be purchase with reference to change in price not of this good but of other inter-related goods. These goods are either substitutes or complementary goods. A change in the price of tea, for instance, will affect the demand fo[r] coffee.

Law of Demand

This law expresses a relationship between the quantity demanded and its price. It may be defined i[n] Marshall's words as "the amount demanded increase[s] with a fall in price, and diminishes with a rise i[n] price." Thus it expresses an inverse relation betwee[n] price and demand. The inverse price-deman[d] relationship is based on **other things remaining equal**. This phrase points towards certain importan[t] assumption on which this law is based.

These assumptions are :

(*i*) There is no change in the tastes an[d] preferences of the consumer;

(*ii*) The income of the consumer remains constant

(*iii*) There is no change in customs;

(*iv*) There should not be any change in the price of other products;

(*v*) There should not be any change in the qualit[y] of the product;

(*vi*) The habits of the consumers should remai[n] unchanged.

Given these conditions, the law of deman[d] operates. If there is change even in one of thes[e] conditions, it will stop operating.

Elasticity of Demand

It is price elasticity of demand which is usuall[y] referred to as elasticity of demand. But, besides pric[e] elasticity of demand, there are various other concept[s] of demand elasticity. Demand for a good is determine[d] by its price, incomes of the people, prices of relate[d] goods etc. Quantity demanded of a good will chang[e] as a result of a change in the size of any of thes[e] determinants of demand. The concept of elasticity o[f] demand therefore refers to the **degree of responsiveness** of quantity demanded of a good to a change i[n] its price, income or prices of related goods. Accor[d]ingly, there are three kinds of demand elasticity-

1. Price Elasticity
2. Income Elasticity
3. Cross Elasticity

Price Elasticity of Demand

Price elasticity means the degree of **responsive-nes[s]** or **sensitiveness** of quantity demanded of a good t[o] a changes in its prices. In other words, Price elasticit[y] of demand is a measure of the relative change i[n] quantity purchased of a good in response to a relativ[e] change in its Price. Price elasticity can be precisel[y] defined as "the proportional change in the quantit[y] purchased divided by the proportional change i[n] price." Thus

$$\text{Price Elasticity} = -\frac{\text{Percentage change in quantity}}{\text{Percentage change in price}}$$

Cross Elasticity of Demand

The change in the demand for one good in response to the change in price of the other good represents the cross elasticity of demand of one good for the other. In other words, the cross elasticity of demand is the relation between percentage change in the quantity demanded of a good to the percentage in the price of a related good.

Income Elasticity

The responsiveness of demand to changes in income is termed **income elasticity of demand.** It shows how the quantity demanded will change when the income of the purchaser changes, the price of the commodity remaining the same, it may be defined thus : The Income Elasticity of demand for a good is the ratio of the percentage change in the amount spent on the commodity to a percentage change in the consumer's income price of commodity remaining constant. Thus,

$$\text{Income Elasticity} = \frac{\text{Percentage change in quantity demanded}}{\text{Percentage change in income}}$$

CONSUMER'S SURPLUS

Concept of consumer's surplus is a very important concept in economic theory especially in welfare economics. The concept of consumer's surplus was first of all evolved by **Dr. Alfred Marshall,** who maintained that it can be measured in monetary units, and is equal to the difference between the amount of money that a consumer actually pays to buy a certain quantity of a commodity X, and the amount that he would be willing to pay for this quantity rather than do without it.

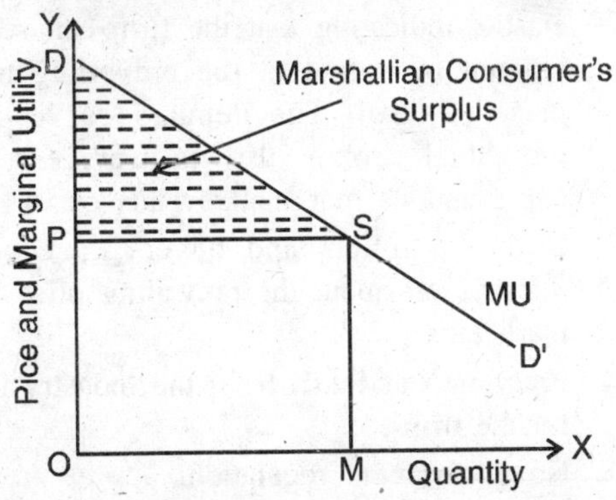

Fig.: *Marshall's Measure of Consumer's Surplus*

The concept of consumer surplus is important not only in economic theory but also in economic policies, such as taxation by the Government and price policy pursued by the monopolistic seller of a product. The essence of the concept of consumer's surplus is that a consumer derives extra satisfaction from the purchases he daily makes over the price he actually pays for them. **Marshall** defines the consumer's surplus in the following words :-

"Excess of the price which a consumer would be willing to pay, rather than go without a thing over that which he actually does pay, is the economic measure of this surplus satisfaction ... it may be called consumer's surplus."

The amount of money which a person is prepared to pay for a good indicates the amount of utility he derives from that good, the greater the amount of money he is willing to pay, the greater the satisfaction or utility he will obtain from it. Therefore, the marginal utility of a unit of a good determines the price a consumer will be prepared to pay for that unit. The total utility which a person will get from a good will be given by sum of marginal utilities (ΣMU) of the units of the good purchased and the total price which he will actually pay is equal to the price per unit multiplied by the number of units purchased. Thus,

Consumer's Surplus = What a consumer is prepared to pay minus what he actually pays.

$= \Sigma\,MU - (\text{Price} \times \text{Number of units purchased})$

CONSUMER'S EQUILIBRIUM

A consumer is in equilibrium when given his tastes, and prices of the two goods, he spends a given money income on the purchase of two goods in such a way as to get the maximum satisfaction. In the indifference curve technique the consumer's equilibrium is discussed in respect of the purchases of two goods by the consumer.

The indifference curve analysis of consumer's equilibrium is based on the following assumptions :

1. The consumer has a given indifference map exhibiting his scale of preferences for various combinations of two goods, X and Y.
2. He has a fixed amount of money to spend on the two goods. He has to spend whole of his given money on the two goods.
3. Prices of the goods are given and constant for him. He cannot influence the prices of the goods by buying more or less of them.
4. Goods are homogeneous and divisible.

LAWS OF PRODUCTION

The laws of production describe the technically possible ways of increasing the level of production. Output may increase in various ways.

Output can be increased by changing all factors or production. Clearly this is possible only in the long-run. Thus **the laws of returns to scale** refer to the long-run analysis of production.

In the short run output may be increased by using more of the variable factor, while capital (and possibly other factors as well) are kept constant. The marginal product of the variable factor will decline eventually as more and more quantities of this factor are combined with the other constant factors. The expansion of output with one factor constant is described by the **law of diminishing returns** of the variable factor, which is often referred to as the **law of variable proportions.**

Laws of Returns to Scale

In the long run expansion of output may be achieved by varying all factors. In the long run all factors are variable. The laws of returns to scale refer to the effects of scale relationships.

In the long run output may be increased by changing **all factors by the same proportion,** or by different proportions. Traditional theory of production concentrates on the first case, that is, the study of output as all inputs change by the **same proportion. The term 'return to scale' refers to the changes in output as all factors change by the same proportion.**

THE CONCEPT OF REVENUE

The term 'revenue' refers to the receipts obtained by a firm from the sale of certain quantities of a commodity at various prices. The revenue concept relates to total revenue, average revenue and marginal revenue.

Total Revenue : Total revenue refers to the total amount of money that the firm receives from the sale of its products. Thus, the total revenue is obviously equal to the quantity sold multiplied by the selling price of the commodity, *i.e.,*

$$TR = P.Q.$$

where

TR = total revenue

P = price per unit

Q = quantity

Average Revenue : Average revenue can be obtained by dividing by the total revenue by the number of units sold. Thus,

$$\text{average revenue} = \frac{\text{total revenue}}{\text{total output sold}}$$

$$\text{or,} \quad AR = \frac{TR}{Q} = \frac{P.Q}{Q} = P$$

Thus, average revenue is the price of commodity. It follows from this that the curve which relates average revenue to output is identical with the demand curve that relates price to output.

Marginal Revenue : Marginal revenue is the net revenue earned by selling on additional unit of the product. In other words, marginal revenue is the addition made to the total revenue by selling one more unit of the good. Putting it in algebraic expression marginal revenue is the addition made to total revenue by selling n units of a product instead of $(n - 1)$ where n is any given number. Therefore,

Marginal Revenue = difference in total revenue in increasing sales from $(n - 1)$ units to n units

$$MR_n = TR_n - TR_{n-1}$$

If TR stands for total revenue and Q stands for output, then marginal revenue (MR) can be expressed as follows :

$$MR = \frac{d(TR)}{dQ}$$

$\frac{d(TR)}{dQ}$ indicates the slope of the total revenue curve. Thus if the total revenue curve is given to us, we can find out marginal revenue at various levels of output by measuring the slopes at the corresponding points on the total revenue curve.

PERFECT COMPETITION

Perfect competition is a market structure characterised by a complete absence of rivalry among the individual firms. In other words, perfect competition implies no rivalry among firms.

Assumptions

The model of perfect competition is based on the following assumptions.

1. There are a large number of firms producing and selling a product.
2. The product of all firms is homogeneous. The assumptions of large numbers of sellers and of product homogeneity imply that the individual firm in perfect competition is a **price-taker :** Its demand curve is infinitely elastic, indicating that the firm can sell any amount of output at the prevailing market price (figure). The demand curve of the individual firm is also its average revenue curve and its marginal revenue curve.
3. Both the sellers and buyers have perfect information about the prevailing price in the market.
4. Entry into and exit from the industry is free for the firms.
5. No government regulation.
6. Perfect mobility of factors of production.

Equilibrium of the Firm in the Short Run

The firm is in equilibrium when it maximises its profits (π), defined as the difference between the total cost and total revenue.

$$\pi = TR - TC$$

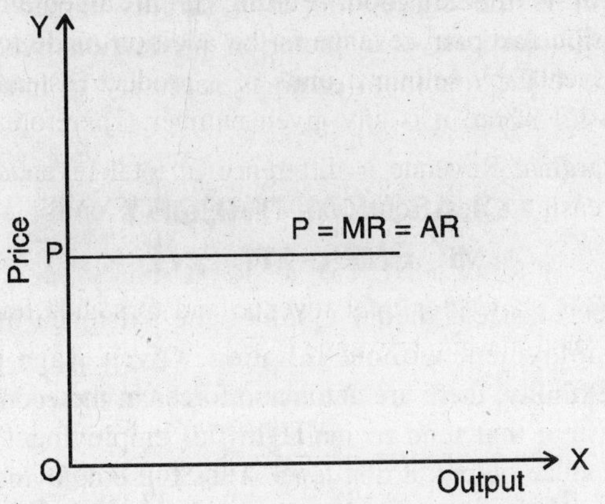

Fig.: *Perfect Competition'*

Given that the normal rate of profit is included in the cost items of the firm, π is the profit above the normal rate of return on capital and the remuneration for the risk-bearing function of the entrepreneur. The firm is in equilibrium when it produces the output that maximises that difference between total receipt and total costs. The equilibrium of the firm may be shown graphically in two ways. Either by using the TR and TC curves, or the MR and MC curves.

MONOPOLY

Monopoly is a market structure in which there is a single seller, there are no close substitutes for the commodity it produces and there are barriers to entry. Two points are worth noting in this definition. *Firstly,* there must be a single producer or seller of a product if there is to be monopoly. A *second condition* which is essential for a firm to be called monopolist is that no *close substitutes* for the product of that firm should be available.

We can express the second condtion of monopoly in terms of *cross elasticity of demand* also. Cross elsticity of demand shows a change in the demand for a good as a result of change in the price of another good. Therefore, if there is to be monopoly *the cross elasticity of demand between the product of the monopolist and the product of any other producer must be very small.*

The above two conditions ensure that the monopolist can set the price of his product and can pursue an independent price policy. Power to influence price is very essence of monopoly. From this it must not be gathered that the monopolist is so powerful that he can dictate the price as wel as the amount sold. Monopolist can do one of these things only; either he can fix the price leaving the amount sold to the consumers, or he can fix the quantity he wants to produce and sell and leave the price to be determined by the demand of the consumers.

UTILITY MAXIMISATION

Williamson has developed the utility maximisation hypothesis as against profit maximisation. Like Baumol's sales maximisation theory, it is one of the managerial theories. It is also known as the **'managerial discretion theory.'**

In large modern firms, shareholders and managers are two separate groups. The former want the maximum return on their investment and hence the maximisation of profits. The managers, on the other hand, have consideration other than profit maximisation in their utility functions. Thus the managers are interested not only in their own emoluments but also in the size of their staff and expenditure on them. Thus Williamson's theory is related to the maximisation of the manager's utility which is a function of the expenditure on staff and emoluments and discretionary funds.

To pursue his goal of utility maximisation, the manager directs the firms's resources in three ways:

First, the manager desires to expand his staff and to increase their salaries. "More staff are valued because they lead to the manager getting more salary, more prestige and more security." **Second,** to maximise his utility, the manager indulges in "feather bedding" such as pretty secretaries, company cars, too many company phones, 'perks' for employees etc. Such expenditures are characterised as **'management slack'** by Williamson. **Third,** the manager likes to set up "discretionary funds" for making investments to advance or promote company projects that are close to his heart Discretionary funds (or profits or investments) are what remains with the manager after paying taxes, and dividends to shareholders in order to retain effective control of the firm.

CONCEPTS OF PRODUCTIVITY

Average Physical Productivity is the total production divided by the number of units of a factor employed.

Average Productivity of a factor

$$= \frac{\text{Total Output}}{\text{Total Number of units of a factor}}$$

Marginal physical productivity of a factor is the increase in total output caused by employing an additional unit of the factor, quantity of other factors remaining fixed.

$$MP_L = \frac{dX}{dL} \text{ and } MP_K = \frac{dX}{dK}$$

Where

MP_L = marginal productivity of labour

MP_K = marginal productivity of capital

dX = change in output

ECONOMICS

dL = change in labour

dK = change in capital.

Marginal Revenue Product (MRP)

Marginal Revenue Product is the increment in the total value product caused by employing an additional unit of a factor, the expenditure on other factors remaining unchanged. In other words, marginal revenue product is the marginal physical product of the factor multiplied by the marginal revenue.

$$MRP = MPP \times MR$$

THE THEORY OF RENT

Rent as an economic surplus, as used by modern economists means the earning of a factor of production in excess of the minimum amount necessary to keep it in its present use. It is not a differential surplus, the difference between the superior and the inferior grades of lands as **Ricardo** meant by rent. Moreover, it accrues not to land alone, but to all other factor services.

Ricardian Theory of Rent

David Ricardo was a brilliant 19th century economist of England who propounded a systematic theory of rent which is in many ways the basis of the modern concept of rent.

Ricardo defined rent as follows: **"Rent is that portion of the produce of earth which is paid to the land lord for the use of the original and indestructible powers of the soil."** It should be noticed that land rent, according to Ricardian definition, is a payment for the use of only land and is different from contractual rent which includes.

- According to Ricardo, marginal land earns no rent.
- In Ricardian Theory, rent is not price determining. In fact, in this theory rent is price determined, that is, it is price which determines rent. To quote Ricardo, **"Corn is not high because a rent is paid, but a rent is paid because corn is high."**

Modern Theory of Rent

Modern theory of rent does not confine itself to the determination of the reward of only land as a factor of production. Rent according to the modern sense can arise in respect of any factor of product ion. It is a surplus payment in excess of transfer earnings of that factor. **Transfer earnings means the amount of money which any particular unit of a factor could earn in its next best alternative use.** In other words, economic rent in such a case is the difference between the present earnings and transfer earnings. **In Joan Robinson's words,** "The essence of the conception of rent is the conception of a surplus earned by a particular part of a factor of production over and above the minimum earnings necessary to induce it to its work."

CLASSICAL THEORY OF EMPLOYMENT

The classical theory assumes the existence of full employment without inflation. Given wage-price flexibility, there are automatic forces in the economic system that tend to maintain full employment, and produce output at that level. Thus full employment is ragarded as a normal situation and any deviation from this level is something abnormal which automatically tends towards full employment. The classical theory of output and employment is based on the following assumptions:

1. There is the existence of full employment without inflation.
2. There is perfect competition in labour and product markets.
3. There is a closed *laissez faire* capitalist economy without foreign trade.
4. Labour is homogenous.
5. Total output of the economy is divided between consumption and investment expenditures.
6. The quantity of money is given.
7. Wages and prices are flexible.
8. Money wages and real wages are directly related and proportional.
9. Capital stock and technological knowledge are given in the short run.

DETERMINATION OF NATIONAL INCOME : KEYNESIAN THEORY

The Keynesian theory is relevant in the context of the **short run** only since the stock of capital, techniques of production, efficiency of labour, the size of population, forms of business organisation have been assumed to remain constant in this theory. Therefore, in the Keynesian theory which deals with the short run, the level of income of the country will change as a result of changes in the level of labour employment. Thus, in an advanced capitalist economy in the short-run, income is a function of employment. Infact, both income and employment go together. The higher the level of employment; the higher the level of income. As level of employment is determined by aggregate demand and aggregate supply, the level of income is also determined by aggregate demand and aggregate supply.

Aggregate Supply

Equilibrium level of national income in the short run depends upon aggregate demand and aggregate supply. The aggregate supply depends on physical or technical conditions of production which do not change in the short-run. Since Keynes assumes the aggregate supply to be stable, he concentrates his entire attention upon the aggregate demand to fight depression and unemployment.

Aggregate Demand

Aggregate demand is determined by consump-tion demand and investment demand. Therefore,

Aggregate Demand = Consumption Demand + Investment Demand

$$AD = C + I$$

Where AD = aggregate demand

C = consumption demand

I = investment demand

Equilibrium Level of Income

The equilibrium level of national income is determined at a point where the aggregate demand function intersects the aggregate supply function.

NATIONAL INCOME ANALYSIS

There are various concepts of national income which we shall study one by one.

1. Gross National product (GNP)

Gross National product is defined as the total market value of all final goods and services produced in a year. Two things must be noted in regard to gross national product. *First,* it measures the market value of annual output. In other words, GNP is a *monetary measure.*

Secondly, for calculating gross national product accurately, all goods and services produced in any given year must be counted once, and not more than once.

2. GNP at Factor Cost

GNP at factor cost is the sum of the money value of the income produced by and accruing to the various factors of production in one year in a country.

GNP at market prices, always includes indirect taxes levied by the government on goods which raise their prices. But GNP at factor cost is the income which the factors of production receive in return for their services alone. It is the cost of production. Thus GNP at market prices is always higher than GNP at factor cost.

3. Gross Domestic Product (GDP)

GDP = GNP – Net Foreign Investment

Net Foreign Investment = Export – Import (X – M)

∴ GDP = GNP – (X– M)

4. Net National Product (NNP)

GNP includes the value of total output of consumption goods and investment goods. But the process of production uses up a certain amount of fixed capital. Some fixed equipment wears out, its other components are damaged or destroyed, and still other some rendered obsolete through technological changes. All this process is termed depreciation or capital consumption allowance. In order to arrive at NNP, we deduct depreciation from GNP. The word 'net' refers to the exclusion of that part of total output which represents depreciation.

NNP = GNP – Depreciation

5. NNP at Market Prices

Net National Product at Market prices is the net value of final goods and services evaluated at market prices in the course of one year in a country. If we deduct depreciation from GNP at market prices, we get NNP at market prices. Thus NNP at Market Prices = GNP at Market Prices – Depreciation.

6. NNP at Factor Cost

Net National Product at factor cost is the net output evaluated at factor prices. It includes income earned by factors of production through participation in the production process such as wages and salaries, rates, profits, etc. It is also called *National Income.* This measure differs from NNP at market prices in that indirect taxes are deducted and subsidies are added to NNP at market prices in order to arrive at NNP at factor cost. Thus

NNP ar factor cost = NNP at Market Prices – Indirect Taxes + Subsidies.

= GNP at Market Prices – Depreciation – Indirect Taxes + Subsidies.

7. NDP at Factor Cost

Net Domestic Product at factor cost is arrived by making adjustments for net indirect taxes *i.e.* indirect taxes and subsidies in the Net Domestic Product at market prices. The market prices contain an element of indirect taxes which though paid out by the buyers in the form of Product Prices, do not accrue to the production units.

Hence to find out factor incomes, we deduct the indirect taxes from the Net Domestic Product at market prices. Like wise, we add subsidies to the Net Domestic Product at market prices because these subsidies form the factor incomes though they are not a part of the market prices. Thus,

Net Domestic Product at Factor Cost = Net Domestic Product at Market Prices – Indirect Taxes + Subsidies.

8. Per Capita Income

The average income of the people of a country in a particular year is called Per Capital Income for that year. This concept also refers to the measurement of income at current prices and at constant prices. For instance, in order to find out the per capital income for 2001, at current prices, the national income of a country is divided by the population of the country in that year

Per Capita Income for 2001

$$= \frac{\text{National income for 2001}}{\text{population in 2001}}$$

CHARACTERISTICS OF INDIAN ECONOMY

India's economy is in the stage of developing, *i.e.*, in transition from under-developed to developed. Each person in India was earning on income of just $2182.18 per year in 2023-24. This compares poorly with rich countries (Germany: $49,530, Japan: $42,870, USA: $58,030 France: $42,380, and China: $15,500) or even the low income countries (Egypt: $11,110). Even in terms of Gross National Product, our share in the world economy was only 1.1 % in 2016 though the population's share was 17.7%. Indian economy is characterised by:

1. **Low Per Capita Income:** India's per capita income is very low.
2. **High Population Growth:** India is passing through the phase of large birth rate and low death rate. Population is increasing at nearly 1.64% per annum. In Japan, the growth rate is 0.4%, 0% in Switzerland, 0% in Germany, - 0.1 % in Denmark, 0.8% in Australia and 0% in South Korea.
3. **Widespread Unemployment:** Under employment, Unemployment and disguised unemployment is widespread in India.
4. **Predominance of Agriculture:** About 14.4% of the national income comes from the primary sector. However, 49% of the population is employed in the sector.
5. **Inequalities in Income Distribution:** Richest 8% in rural India take away 46% of the total income while poorest 39% get only 5%.
6. **Poor Quality of Human Capital:** India fares poorly in terms of the Human Development Index. Poor quality of human capital manifests itself from low life expectancy at birth (68.45 years), population with access to safe water (75%), women literacy rate (64.6%) and mean years of schooling (2.4).
7. **Inadequate Capital Formation:** Rate of investment in India is only 28 to 34% of the GDP, as compared to more in developed countries. This rate is insufficient for India as a large investment is needed to offset the population growth itself.
8. **Technical Backwardness:** India spends only a small amount on research and development activities. The expenditure in the private sector also is very meagre.
9. **Infrastructural Inadequacies:** Transport, power, communication network, financial system are not sufficiently developed.
10. **Dualistic Economy:** Coexistence of a traditional low-productivity sector with a modern high-productivity sector.
11. **Lack of Foreign Trade Orientation:** Since Indian population is large, a large produce is consumed at the domestic markets itself. Moreover, due to poor quality consciousness, India is a small player in foreign trade.
12. **Unfavourable Social Value Structure:** Indians are divided on the basis of language, caste, religion and region, thus fragmenting the social structure of the country.
13. **Market Imperfections:** Indian market is imperfect, based towards the rich and prosperous. Limited market information availability, formation of pressure groups and use of strong arm tactics creates imperfections.
14. **Vicious Circles:** People are poor because they are unemployed. They are unemployed because they are illiterate, ill-trained and ill-equipped This is a vicious circle which seems to have no end.

PLANNING IN INDIA

Leaders of Indian National Movement were greatly impressed by the planned economic growth of the Soviet Union. In the 1931 Karachi session of the Indian National Congress, a resolution was passed stressing the nationalisation of key and basic industries. In 1937, the Congress appointed a National Planning Committee with Mr Jawaharlal Nehru as its chairman. At the Government level, a planning department was set up by the British Viceroy in 1945 However, after the independence, the need for planned development was acutely felt. An executive resolution was passed in March, 1950 to set up the Planning Commission. The directive principles of state policy of the Constitution also emphasise the need of planning.

NITI AAYOG

65-year-old Planning Commission has been dissolved and a new institution named NITI Aayog has been constituted by the National Democratic Alliance (NDA) government. Like Planning Commission the newly established NITI Aayog is also be chaired by the Prime Minister. NITI Aayog or National Institution for Transforming India serves as a government think tank and is meant to reflect changes required in India's governance structures and provide a more active role for the state governments in achieving national objectives. The newly constituted institution provides governments at the central and state levels with strategic and technical advice across the spectrum of policy making. As per official declaration, this institution includes matters of national and international import on the economic front, dissemination of best practices from within the country as well as from the nations, the infusion of new policy ideas and specific issue-based support. NITI Aayog is headed by the Prime Minister, who is its chairperson. The Prime Minister appoints a vice-chairperson and a chief executive officer (CEO). The CEO is appointed for a fixed tenure; who has a secretary-level position. The organization have full-time members and up to two part-time members from leading universities, research organizations and other relevant institutions. It also has up to four ex-officio members from the Union council of ministers who are nominated by the Prime Minister. While this is the full-time organizational structure, the new institution comprises a governing council which includes state chief ministers and lieutenant governors of Union Territories.

The NITI Aayog works towards the following main objectives :

(*i*) To evolve a shared vision of national development priorities, sectors and strategies with the active involvement of States in the light of national objectives.

(ii) To foster cooperative federalism through structured support initiatives and mechanisms with the States on a continuous basis, recognizing that strong States make a strong nation.

(iii) To develop mechanisms to formulate credible plans at the village level and aggregate these progressively at higher levels of government.

(iv) To ensure, on areas that are specifically referred to it, that the interests of national security are incorporated in economic strategy and policy.

(v) To offer a platform for resolution of inter-sectoral and inter-departmental issues in order to accelerate the implementation of the development agenda.

(vi) To focus on technology upgradation and capacity building for implementation of programmes and initiatives.

INDIAN AGRICULTURE

Role of Agriculture in Indian Economy

1. **Share of Agriculture in National Income :** Agriculture is an important sector of the economy. Though the share of agriculture in national income has come down since the inception of planning era in the economy but still it has substantial share in GDP. The share of agriculture and allied sectors in Gross Value Added (GVA) of the country at current prices was 18.4 per cent for the year 2022-23.
2. **Important Contribution to Employment :** Due to lack of industrialisation and no significant development in service sector, these sectors have contributed very less in employment generation. So, agriculture is the largest employment providing sector in the economy. Agriculture sector, provides employment to 49% of country's work force.
3. **Important Source of Industrial Development:** It provides raw materials to various industries and other agro-based industries. Cotton and Jute textile indus-tries, sugar, vanaspati industry etc. are directly depen-dent on agriculture. This highlights the importance of agriculture in industrial development of the nation.
4. **Importance in International Trade :** India's foreign trade is deeply associated with agriculture sector. Value of agriculture exports to total exports of the country was 10.32 per cent in 2023-24.

LAND REFORMS

Land reforms are institutional changes that make the tenurial system more favourable to the actual tillers and attempt to adjust the size of farms at the operationally viable level. The scope of land reforms includes abolition of intermediaries, tenancy reforms and ceiling on land holdings; consolidation of subdivided and fragmented land holdings; and cooperative farming.

Land reforms are important as they provide incentives and encouragement to the actual tillers by providing a congenial climate and hence act as a costless method of increasing production.

Abolition of Intermediaries

The actual abolition of intermediaries started in 1948 with the enactment of legislation in Madras (Chennai). Intermediary tenural systems like Zamindari, Jagirdari, Inamdari etc, which prevailed over 40% of the country were abolished. Waste and fallow land distributed to the landless.

Tenancy Reforms

Measures of tenancy reforms pertain to—

1. regulation of rent
2. security of tenure
3. conferment of ownership on tenants

Various states have passed necessary legislation for the regulation of rent, but owing to the weak position of the tenants and prevalence of wide spread hunger for land, the rent-regulating law is more breached than complied with. Experience of the implementation of Zamindari abolition showed that, on the plea of resumption for personal cultivation, evictions of tenants took place on a massive scale. During the second plan, the states framed provisions for resumption broadly on the following three different patterns:

(i) All tenants have been given full security of tenure, without giving owners the right of personal cultivation.

(ii) Owners have been given the right to retain a limited area, however, subject to the condition that a minimum area is left with the tenant.

(iii) A limit has been placed on the extent of land, which a land owner may retain, but the tenant is not entitled to retain minimum area for cultivation in all cases.

Ceiling on Land Holding

Land ceiling laws were first enacted in the 50s and 60s. It was further revised in 1972. Family ceilings were lowered to 5 hectares for irrigated land with two crops, 7.5 hectares for irrigated land with one crop and 12 hectares for other lands. The Benami Transactions ordinance, 1988 also makes "benami" transaction illegal. It is an important step towards land reform.

The land reforms policies have been formulated in the right direction but the basic purpose of introducing land reforms has been adversely affected because of various shortcomings in the legislation, lack of political will for implementation of various laws and programmes, absence of pressure from below because the poor agricultural workers and peasants are passive, unorganised and inarticulate, luke- warm and often apathetic attitude of bureaucracy, absence of upto-date land records and legal hurdles in the way of implementation of land reforms.

NEW INDUSTRIAL POLICY (1991)

The Congress Government led by Mr. Narasimha Rao announced the new industrial policy in July 1991. The main aim of the new industrial policy was:

(*i*) to unshackle the Indian industrial economy from the cobwebs of unnecessary bureaucratic control,

(*ii*) to introduce liberalisation with a view to integrate the Indian economy with the world economy,

(*iii*) to remove restrictions on direct foreign investment as also to free the domestic entrepreneur from the restrictions of MRTP Act, and

(*iv*) the policy aimed to shed the load of the public enterprises which have shown a very low rate of return or were incurring losses over the years.

All these reforms of industrial policy led the government to take a series of initiatives in respect of policies in the following areas:

(*a*) Industrial Licensing
(*b*) Foreign Investment
(*c*) Foreign Technology Policy
(*d*) Public Sector Policy
(*e*) MRTP Act.

Abolition of Industrial Licensing

Industrial licensing policy in India has been governed by the Industries (Development and Regulation) Act, 1951. Industrial licensing policy and procedures have been liberalised considerably from time to time. Yet, the industrial licensing policy has all along been resented to by the entrepreneurs as it led to unnecessary governmental interference, delays in investment decisions and bureaucratic red-tapism, curruption etc. Not only this, the industrial licensing policy was also unable to achieve the objectives laid down for it by the government. On account of these considerations, and in order to liberalise the economy and to enable the entrepreneurs to make investment decisions on the basis of their own commercial judgement, the 1991 industrial policy abolished industrial licensing for all but 18 industries. The 18 industries for which licensing was kept necessary were—coal and lignite; petroleum (other than crude) and its distillation products; distillation and brewing of alcoholic drinks; sugar; animal fats and oils; cigars and cigarettes; asbestos and asbestos based products; plywood and other wood based products; raw hides and skins and leathers; tanned or dressed furskins;

motor cars; paper and news print; electronic aero-space and defence equipment; industrial explosives; hazardous chemicals; drugs and pharmaceuticals; entertainment electronics; and white goods (domestic refrigerators, washing machines, air conditioners, etc.). With the passage of time, most of these industries have also been delicensed. As of now, licensing is compulsory for only 5 industries. These are alcohol, cigarettes, hazardous chemicals, defence equipment and industrial explosives.

Public Sector's Role Diluted

The 1956 Resolution had reserved 17 industries for the public sector. The 1991 industrial policy reduced this number to 8 :

1. arms and ammunition,
2. atomic energy,
3. coal and lignite,
4. mineral oils,
5. mining of iron ore, manganese ore, chrome ore, gypsum, sulphur, gold and diamond,
6. mining of copper, lead, zinc, tin, molybdenum and wolfarm
7. minerals specified in the schedule to the atomic energy (control of production and order), 1953 and
8. rail transport.

In 1993, items (5) and (6) were deleted from the reserved list. In 1998-99, items (3) and (4) were also taken out from the reserved list. On May 9, 2001, the government opened up arms and ammunition sector also to the private sector. This now leaves only 3 industries reserved exclusively for the public sector.

The new industrial policy also states that the government will undertake review of the existing public enterprises in low technology, small scale and non-strategic areas as also when there is low or nil social consideration or public purpose. Sick units will be referred to the Board for Industrial and Financial Reconstruction (or a similar body) for advice about rehabilitation and reconstruction. For enterprises remaining in the public sector, it is stated that they will be provided a much greater degree of management autonomy through the system of MOU (memorandum of understanding).

The government has also announced its intention to offer a part of government share holding in the public sector enterprises to mutual funds, financial institutions, the general public and the workers. A beginning in this direction was made in 1991-92 itself by divesting part of the equities of selected public sector enterprises. The new industrial policy indicates the government's intention to invite a greater degree of participation by the private sector in important areas of the economy.

POVERTY AND UNEMPLOYMENT IN INDIA

Poverty is a social phenomenon in which a section of society is unable to fulfil even its basic necessities of life. The term 'Poverty' has been defined in different societies in a different way but all of them are conditioned by the version of minimum or good life to be obtained in society. For instance, the concept of poverty in USA would be significantly different from that in India because the ability to afford a higher living standard is much higher in the United States.

Several economists and organisations have given different estimates of poverty. Most of them estimated the number of persons below the poverty line on the basis of an average calorie intake of 2250 per capita per day. According to the report of 'Task Force on Minimum Needs and Effective Consumption Demand'— an expert group of planning commission, defined poverty line on a nutritional norm of per capita daily intake of 2400 calories in rural areas and 2100 calories for urban areas. A person who fails to obtain this minimum level of calories is treated as being below the poverty line.

The expert committee set up by the Planning Commission under C. Rangarajan former chairperson of Prime Minister's Economic Advisory Council, has redefined the poverty line. According to the report of the committee, the new poverty line should be ₹ 32 in rural areas and ₹ 47 in urban areas. The earlier poverty line figure was ₹ 27 for rural India and ₹ 33 for Urban India.

	No. of Rural poor	No. of Urban poor	Total	Percent of poor
Rangarajan Committee	260.5 million	102.5 million	363 million	29.5
Tendulkar Committee	216.5 million	52.8 million	269 million	21.9%
Difference	44 million	49.7 million	93.7 million	

The Rangarajan report has added 93.7 million more to the list of the poor assessed as per the Suresh Tendulkar Committee formula. Now the total number of poor has reached 363 million from 269 million in 2011-12.

This raise in the poverty line income bar means 93.7 million more people are now below poverty line (BPL).

Various Employment Programmes in India

S. N.	Programmes	Year of beginning	Objectives
1.	Community Development Programme (CDP)	1952	Overall development of rural areas with people's participation
2.	Food for Work Programme	1977-78	Providing foodgrains to labour for the works of development
3.	Antyodaya Yojana	1977-78	To make the poorest families of the village economically independent (only in Rajasthan State)
4.	Training Rural Youth for Self-Employment (TRYSEM)	Aug., 15, 1979	Programme of training rural youth for self-employment
5.	Integrated Rural Development Programme (IRDP)	Oct., 2, 1980	All-round development of the rural poor through a programme of asset endowment for self-employment
6.	National Rural Employment Programme (NREP)	1980	To provide profitable employment opportunities to the rural poor
7.	Development of Women and Children in Rural Areas (DWCRA)	Sept., 1982	To provide suitable opportunities of self-employment to the women belonging to the rural families who are living below the poverty line
8.	Rural Landless Employment Guarantee Programme (RLEGP)	Aug., 15, 1983	For providing employment to landless farmers and labourers
9.	Self-Employment to the Educated Unemployed Youth (SEEUY)	1983-84	To provide financial and technical assistance for self-employment
10.	Self-Employment Programme for the Urban Poor (SEPUP)	Sept., 1986	To provide self-employment to urban poor through provision of subsidy and bank credit
11.	Swarna Jayanti Shahari Rozgar Yojana (SJSRY)	Dec., 1997	To provide gainful employment to urban unemployed and under employed poor through self-employment or wage employment
12.	Pradhan Mantri Gramodaya Yojana	2000	To fulfil basic requirements in rural areas
13.	Antyodaya Anna Yojana	Dec., 25, 2000	To provide food security to poor
14.	Pradhan Mantri Gram Sadak Yojana (PMGSY)	Dec., 25, 2000	To line all villages with pucca road
15.	Mahatama Gandhi National Rural Employment Guarantee Act	Feb., 2, 2006	To Provide at least 100 days wage employment in rural areas
16.	Atal Pension Yojana	1 June 2015	To provide old age income security to workers in unorganised sector.
17.	Pradhan Mantri Suraksha Bima Yojana	1 June 2015	To provide insurance in case of death or accident.
18.	Pradhan Mantri Jeevan Jyoti Yojana	1 June 2015	To provide life insurance cover for death due to any reason.
19.	Pradhan Mantri Garib Kalyan Yojanaye (PMGKY)	April 2015	Implement the pro-poor welfare schemes in more effective way and reaches out to more poor population across the country.
20.	Startup India, Standup India	16 Jan. 2016	To provide support to all start-up businesses in all aspects of doing business in India.
21.	Pradhan Mantri Jan Aushadhi Yojana (PMJAY)	March 2016	Provides Drugs/Medicines at affordable cost across the country.
22.	Atmanirbhar Bharat Abhiyan	May, 2020	Economic Stimulus relief package announced for the poor to overcome difficulties caused by Coronavirus.
23.	SMILE	2022	Support for Marginalised Individuals for Livelihood and Enterprises.
24.	PM Vishwakarma Scheme	Sep. 17, 2023	This scheme supports artisans and Craftsmen engaged in 18 traditional crafts.
25.	Pradhan Mantri Vidyalakshmi Yojana	2024	A new Central Sector scheme that seeks to provide financial support to meritorious students.
26.	Prime Minister Dhan Dhaanya Krishi Yojana	2025	It aims to enhance agricultural productivity.

POPULATION IN INDIA

India and many other Third World countries are now passing through the phase of population explosion. It is being argued that this situation has arisen because economic development in these countries has failed to maintain pace with population growth. The thrust of this argument is that since rapid growth of population causes poverty and proves to be a barrier to development, these countries should take care of their population growth if they seriously wish to solve their poverty problem and put their economy on the path of economic development.

Size and Growth

India's population as on 1 March 2011 stood at 121.08 million (623 million males and 587 million females). India accounts for a meagre 2.4 per cent of the world surface area of 135.79 million sq km. Yet, it supports and sustains a whopping 17.5 per cent of the world population.

The population of India, which at the turn of the twentieth century was around 238.4 million, increased to reach 1028 million at the dawn of the twenty-first century. The population of India as recorded at each decennial census from 1901 has grown steadily except for a decrease during 1911-21.

The per cent decadal growth of population in the inter-censal period 2001-11 varies from a low of –0.6 in Nagaland to a very high 27.9 in Meghalaya.

Population Density

It is defined as the number of persons per sq km. The population density of India in 2011 was 382 per sq km. The density of population was increased in all States and Union Territories between 2001 and 2011. Among major states, Bihar is the most thickly populated state with a population density of 1106 in 2011. West Bangal is now the second highest densely populated state pushing Kerala to the third place.

Sex Ratio

Sex ratio, defined as the number of females per thousand males. The sex ratio in the country had always remained unfavourable to females. It was 72 at the beginning of the 20th century and thereafter showed continuous decline until 1941.

Literacy

For the purpose of census 2011, a person aged seven and above, who can both read and write with understanding in any language, is treated as literate. A person, who can only read but cannot write, is not literate. In the censuses prior to 1991, children below five years of age were necessarily treated as illiterates.

The results of 2011 census reveal that there has been an increase in literacy in the country. The literacy rate in the country is 73.0 per cent, 80.9 for males and 64.6 for females.

Kerala retained its position by being on top with a 94.0 per cent literacy rate, closely followed by Mizoram (91.3 per cent) and Tripura (87.2 per cent). Bihar with a literacy rate of 61.8 per cent ranks last in the country preceded by Arunachal Pradesh (65.4 per cent) and Rajasthan (66.1 per cent). Kerala also occupies the top spot in the country both in male literacy with 96.1 per cent and female literacy with 92.1 per cent. On the contrary, Bihar has recorded the lowest literacy rates in case of males (71.2 per cent) and Rajasthan in females (52.1 per cent).

Multiple Choice Questions

1. The law of Demand refers to
   A. Price-supply relationship
   B. Price-cost relationship
   C. Price-demand relationship
   D. Price-income relationship
2. In a typical demand schedule, quantity demanded
   A. Varies directly with price
   B. Varies proportionately with price
   C. Varies inversely with price
   D. Is independent of price
3. Normally when price per unit of a good falls, its
   A. Quantity demanded increases
   B. Quantity demanded decreases
   C. Quantity demanded remains constant
   D. None of these happens
4. A fall in the price of a commodity leads to
   A. A shift in demand
   B. A fall in demand
   C. A rise in consumers real income
   D. A fall in the consumers real income
5. Market demand for any good is a function of the
   A. Price per unit of the good
   B. Price per unit of other goods
   C. Income of consumers
   D. All of the above
6. A typical demand curve cannot be
   A. Convex to the origin
   B. A straight line parallel to y-axis
   C. A straight line parallel to x-axis
   D. Rising upwards to the right
7. When the law of demand operates the demand curve
   A. Slopes downward from left to right
   B. Slopes upward from left to right
   C. Slopes upward from right to left
   D. Parallel to horizontal axis
8. Which one of the following is true increase of normal goods?
   A. When Price increases, demand decreases
   B. When Price increases, demand also increases
   C. When Price remains constant, demand falls down
   D. When Price falls down, demand remains constant
9. An exceptional demand curve is one that slopes:
   A. Upwards to the right
   B. Down wards to the right
   C. Upwards to the left
   D. Horizontally
10. When there is decrease in demand the demand curve–
    A. Moves downwards towards the axis
    B. Moves upwards away from the axis
    C. Remains unchanged
    D. None of the above
11. Two goods have to be consumed simultaneously are
    A. Identical B. Complementary
    C. Substitutes D. None of these
12. Which of the following pairs of commodities is an example of substitutes
    A. Coffee and milk
    B. Diamond and Cow
    C. Pen and ink
    D. Mustard oil and coconut oil
13. Bread and butter, lamb and mint sauce, illustrate the type of inter related demand known as
    A. Rival demand
    B. Composite demand
    C. Competitive demand
    D. Joint demand
14. 'Change in quantity demanded' refers to
    A. Upward shift of the demand curve
    B. Downward shift of the demand curve
    C. Movement on the same demand curve
    D. None of these
15. An increase in demand can result from
    A. A decline in market price
    B. An increase in income

C. A reduction in the price of substitutes
D. An increase in the price of complements

16. If the price of coffee suddenly shoots up, ceteris paribus, the demand for Tea is expected to—
A. Move rightward along the original demand curve
B. Increase
C. Remain unaffected
D. Decrease

17. In the case of Giffen good like bajra, a fall in its price tends to—
A. Make the demand remain constant
B. Reduce the demand
C. Increase the demand
D. Change demand in an abnormal way

18. Market demand is
A. The sum of all individual demands
B. Demand at prevailing average prices
C. Ability to pay the price asked
D. Demand in a perfectly free market

19. A negative income elasticity of demand for a commodity indicates that as income falls the amount of the commodity purchased
A. Rises
B. Falls
C. Remains unchanged
D. Any of the above

20. When with a change in price the total outlay on a commodity remains constant, it is a case of
A. Perfect elasticity B. Perfect inelasticity
C. Unit elasticity D. Zero elasticity

21. Cross elasticity of complementary goods is
A. Negative B. Zero
C. High D. Infinite

22. Elasticity of demand is equal to unity while marginal revenue is
A. Positive B. Zero
C. Negative D. Indeterminate

23. When the income elasticity of demand is greater than unity, the commodity is
A. A necessity
B. A luxury
C. An inferior good
D. A non-related good

24. Marginal utility (MU) curve is always
A. Rising
B. Falling
C. Parallel to x-axis
D. Parallel to y-axis

25. The total utility is maximum when
A. M.U. is zero
B. A.U. is the highest
C. M.U. is the highest
D. M.U. is equal to A.U.

26. The price which a consumer would be willing to pay for a commodity equals to his
A. Total utility
B. Marginal utility
C. Average utility
D. Does not have any relation to any one of these

27. Consumer's surplus is the highest in the case of
A. Necessities
B. Comforts
C. Luxuries
D. Conventional necessities

28. The market period supply curve for perishable commodities is—
A. Relatively inelastic
B. Perfectly inelastic
C. Relatively elastic
D. Perfectly elastic

29. Supply of a commodity is a
A. Stock concept
B. A flow concept
C. Both stock and flow concept
D. None of these

30. "Production" may be defined as an act of—
A. Creating utility
B. Earning profit
C. Destroying utility
D. Providing services

31. All money costs can be regarded as:
A. Social costs B. Opportunity costs
C. Explicit costs D. Real costs

32. The real aim of production is
A. To create material goods
B. To eliminate poverty
C. To satisfy peoples wants
D. To provide basic necessities

33. In perfect competition, there is a process of
A. Free entry but restricted exit of the firms
B. Free entry and free exit of the firms
C. Restricted entry and exit of the firms
D. Semi-free exit but absolute free entry

34. The difference between gross domestic product and net domestic product equals
A. Transfer payments
B. Depreciation cost
C. Indirect taxes
D. Subsidies

35. The best method of computing national income is
A. Product Method
B. Income Method
C. Expenditure Method
D. Combination of income and production method

36. The National income is equal to
A. GNP – Subsides – Taxes
B. NNP – Indirect Taxes + Subsidies
C. NNP – Direct Taxes + Subsides
D. GNP – Subsidies + Taxes

37. Which state has maximum branches of public sector commercial banks?
A. U.P. B. Maharashtra
C. Karnataka D. Gujarat

38. In which plan phase of industrialisation was initiated?
A. Fourth B. Third
C. Second D. First

39. Which is the first Export Processing Zone declared as Free Trade Zone in India?
A. Santacruz B. Kandla
C. Falta D. Noida

40. Which institution is known as 'soft loan window' of World Bank?
A. IFC
B. IDA
C. IMF
D. Indian Development Forum

41. 'Backwash Effect' was firstly introduced by—
A. Gunnar Myrdal B. Peter Suderland
C. Arthur Dunkel D. Kindelberger

42. Meera Seth Committee was related to—
A. Development of Handlooms
B. Sex-differentiation in employment
C. Abolition of Child Labour
D. Welfare of working women

43. 'SAPTA' is related to—
A. Education B. Trade
C. Security D. Environment

44. National Income estimates in India is prepared by—
A. NITI Aayog
B. RBI
C. Finance Ministry
D. C.S.O.

45. Scheduled bank is that bank which is—
A. Nationalised
B. Not–nationalised
C. Based at foreign country
D. Included in the second schedule of R.B.F

46. The definition of small scale industry in India is based an—
A. Sales of a unit
B. Investment in machines and equipments
C. Market coverage
D. Export capacity

47. Which one of the following committees was set up to review the concept of poverty line?
A. S. Chakravarty Committee
B. K.N. Wanchoo Committee
C. D.T. Lakdawala Committee
D. R.C. Dutt Committee

48. The book 'Politics with Charkha' is written by—
A. Ashok Mehta
B. J.B. Kriplani
C. K.G. Mashruwala
D. Morarji Desai

49. CAPART is related with—
A. Assisting and evaluating rural welfare programmes
B. Computer hardware
C. Consultant service of export promotion
D. Controlling pollution in big industries

50. White revolution refers to:
A. Cement industry B. Dairying
C. Cotton industry D. None of these

51. Which of the following does not grant any tax rebate?
A. National Saving Certificate
B. Indira Vikas Patra
C. National Saving Scheme
D. Public Provident Fund

52. Who is the Chairman of 16th Finance Commission?
A. C. Rangrajan B. Arvind Pangariya
C. L.K. Jha D. None of these

53. SEBI was established in—
A. 1993 B. 1992
C. 1988 D. 1990

54. Asian Development Bank has opened its Residential Office in—
A. New Delhi B. Kolkata
C. Mumbai D. Bangalore

55. Chairman of Tax Reform Committee was—
A. Pranab Mukherjee B. K.P. Narsimham
C. S. Janakiraman D. Raja Chelliah

56. SAIL was established in—
A. 1974 B. 1984
C. 1990 D. 1964

57. Rural women can avail the benefit of Mahila Samriddhi Yojana if they open their account in–
A. Rural Post Offices
B. Commercial Banks
C. Rural Development Bank
D. Any of the above

58. Pradhan Mantri Gram Sadak Yojana (PMGSY) was launched in—
A. 2000 B. 1999
C. 2001 D. 2004

59. The Headquarter of CAPART is situated at—
A. Mumbai B. Kolkata
C. New Delhi D. Bangalore

60. The main security guard of International Trade is–
A. IMF B. World Bank
C. WTO D. IFC

61. 'Closed Economy' is that economy in which—
A. Only export takes place
B. Money supply is fully controlled
C. Deficit financing takes place
D. Neither export nor import takes place

62. National Rural Development Institute is situated at—
A. Shimla B. Hyderabad
C. Patna D. New Delhi

63. The Headquarter of World Bank is situated at—
A. Manila B. Washington D.C.
C. New York D. Geneva

64. Which of the rate is not determined of RBI?
A. Bank Rate B. CRR
C. SLR D. PLR

65. The main foodgrains of India is—
A. Rice B. Wheat
C. Sugarcane D. Maize

66. Which district of Hindi speaking belt has firstly been declared as fully literate?
A. Narsinghpur (M.P.)
B. Palampur (H.P.)
C. Jhunjhanu (Rajasthan)
D. Palamu (Jharkhand)

67. Which sector has the maximum quantum of disguised unemployment in India?
A. Agriculture B. Industry
C. Trade D. Transport

68. 'Food for work programme' was renamed as—
A. RLEGP B. IRDP
C. NREP D. MNP

69. India has emerged in the world as the
A. Second Largest Steel Producer
B. Third Largest Steel Producer
C. Fourth Largest Steel Producer
D. None of these

70. The goods can be taxed heavily to earn additional revenue if they are—
A. Highly elastic B. Unit elastic
C. Perfectly elastic D. Inelastic

71. Scheduled Bank is that bank which is—
A. Nationalised
B. Not nationalised
C. Based at foreign country
D. Included in the second schedule of RBI

72. Which fertilizer is mostly consumed in India?
A. N
B. P
C. K
D. All are used in equal ratio

73. Who is the Chairman of NDC?
A. Finance Minister B. Prime Minister
C. Planning Minister D. Lok Sabha Speaker

74. The field given to Rangarajan Committee was—
A. Modernisation of Cloth Industry
B. To probe Share scam
C. To probe Sugar scam
D. To suggest measures for controlling BOP deficit

75. VAT is imposed—
A. Directly on consumer
B. On final stage of production
C. On first stage of production
D. On all stages between production and final sale

76. Kutir Jyoti scheme is associated with—
A. Promoting cottage industry in villages
B. Promoting employment among rural unemployed youth
C. Providing electricity to rural families living below the poverty line
D. All of these

77. OTCEI is—
A. Atomic submarine of China
B. Economic policy of USA
C. A Indian Share Market
D. A defence research organisation

78. Which is the most liquid measure of money supply?
A. M_1 B. M_2
C. M_3 D. M_4

79. M_3 measure of money supply does not include—
A. Cash with public
B. Demand deposits with Post offices
C. Demand deposits with Banks
D. Time deposits with Banks

80. NITI Aayog was constituted in–
A. 2013 B. 2014
C. 2015 D. 2016

81. Gresham's Law is related to—
A. Consumption and Demand
B. Supply and Demand
C. Circulation of Money
D. Deficit Financing

82. Kelkar Committee report is related to—
A. Tax Reforms
B. Financial Sector Reforms
C. Trade Reforms
D. Administrative Reforms

83. What is 'Super 301'?
A. A name of modern computer
B. A new variety of Rice
C. American trade law
D. American treatment name for Aids

84. When development in economy takes place the share of tertiary sector in National Income?
A. Declines
B. Increases
C. Remains constant
D. First rises and then falls

85. Plan expenditure in India is met by—
A. Internal debt and other resources
B. Assistance from Aid India Club
C. Assistance from IMF
D. Assistance from OECD countries

86. Population Density means—
A. No. of persons living per sq. km.
B. No. of persons living per kilometre
C. Ratio of population living below poverty line to total population
D. No. of persons in a village

87. Which tax is collected by Panchayat?
A. Sales Tax B. Custom Duty
C. Land Revenue D. Tax on local fairs

SOCIAL SCIENCE

88. Centralised planning was first adopted in the economy of—
A. Russia B. Poland
C. China D. India

89. Which among the following states is a leading industrialised state?
A. West Bengal B. Odisha
C. Maharashtra D. Madhya Pradesh

90. Which of the following state has been announced as 'a state of total organic farming'?
A. Sikkim B. Karnataka
C. Kerala D. Punjab

91. Indian Green Revolution is the most successful in—
A. Wheat and Potato B. Jwar and Oil Seeds
C. Wheat and Rice D. Tea and Coffee

92. Economic Planning is in—
A. Union list B. State list
C. Concurrent list D. Not any specified list

93. Which types of tax helps in reducing disparities of income?
A. Proportionate tax B. Progressive tax
C. Regressive tax D. All of these

94. 'Golden Handshake Scheme' is associated with—
A. Inviting foreign companies
B. Private investment in public enterprises
C. Establishing joint enterprises
D. Voluntary retirement

95. Which is not a part of new economic reforms in India?
A. Globalisation B. Centralisation
C. Privatisation D. Liberalisation

96. The official exchange rate of Indian rupee i associated with
A. Pound Sterling
B. Dollar
C. SDR
D. A basket of selected currencies

97. As a result of Green Revolution which foodgrain had a reduced percentage in total foodgrair production?
A. Wheat B. Rice
C. Cereals and Pulses D. None of these

98. Corporate Tax is imposed by—
A. State Government
B. Local Government
C. Central Government
D. Both Centre and State Government

99. MRTP is related to—
A. Monopoly and trade restrictions
B. Inflation control
C. Transport control
D. Foreign Exchange Regulations

100. The basis of determining dearness allowance to employee in India is—
A. National Income
B. Consumer Price Index
C. Standard of Living
D. Per Capita Income

ANSWERS

1	2	3	4	5	6	7	8	9	10
C	C	A	B	D	D	A	A	A	A
11	12	13	14	15	16	17	18	19	20
B	D	D	C	B	B	B	A	A	C
21	22	23	24	25	26	27	28	29	30
A	B	B	B	A	D	A	B	B	A
31	32	33	34	35	36	37	38	39	40
C	C	B	B	D	B	A	C	A	B
41	42	43	44	45	46	47	48	49	50
A	A	B	D	D	B	C	B	A	B
51	52	53	54	55	56	57	58	59	60
B	B	C	A	D	A	A	A	C	C
61	62	63	64	65	66	67	68	69	70
D	B	B	D	A	A	A	C	B	D
71	72	73	74	75	76	77	78	79	80
D	A	B	D	D	C	C	A	B	C
81	82	83	84	85	86	87	88	89	90
C	A	C	B	A	A	D	A	C	A
91	92	93	94	95	96	97	98	99	100
C	C	B	D	B	D	C	C	A	B

CURRENT AFFAIRS

1. 25th Shanghai Cooperation Organisation (SCO) summit 2025 was held in:
A. Wuhan B. Shanghai
C. Tianjin D. Beijing

2. In which state Indiramma Atmiya Bharosa Scheme was recently launched?
A. Andhra Pradesh B. Telangana
C. Karnataka D. Tamil Nadu

3. Which state's tableau won the first prize in the states/ UTs category at the Republic Day Parade 2025?
A. Madhya Pradesh B. Maharashtra
C. Uttar Pradesh D. Rajasthan

4. Who inaugurated the Handloom conclave Manthan?
A. Narendra Modi B. Giriraj Singh
C. Piyush Goyal D. Smriti Irani

5. How many children were awarded the Pradhan Mantri Rashtriya Bal Puraskar 2025 by President Droupadi Murmu?
A. 15 B. 17
C. 18 D. 20

6. Which city hosted the AI Action Summit 2025?
A. New York B. Paris
C. Geneva D. Tokyo

7. How many individuals were honoured with the Padma Vibhushan Award in 2025?
A. 4 B. 5
C. 7 D. 6

8. Jitendra Pal Singh has been appointed as India's new Ambassador to which country?
A. United States of America
B. Israel
C. France
D. Germany

9. Where was the UTT 86th Senior National and Inter-state Table Championship 2024 held?
A. Bhopal B. Surat
C. Mumbai D. New Delhi

10. When was World Leprosy Day celebrated?
A. 23 Jan B. 24 Jan
C. 25 Jan D. 26 Jan

11. Who has been elected as the President of Belarus?
A. Michel Martin
B. Francois Barua
C. Alexander Lukashenko
D. NOT

12. Which organization has launched the enhanced Certificate of Origin (eCoO) 2.0 system?
A. Reserve Bank of India (RBI)
B. Export Promotion Council (EPC)
C. Directorate General of Foreign Trade (DGFT)
D. Federation of Indian Export Organisations (FIEO)

13. Which is the first Indian organisation received the Ramon Magsaysay Award 2025?
A. Pratham Education Foundation
B. The Foundation to Educate Girls Globally
C. The Akshaya Patra Foundation
D. Help Age India

14. In which of the following states the World's largest data centre will be built?
A. Gujarat B. Odisha
C. Maharashtra D. Uttar Pradesh

15. Who among the following has been appointed as the Director of the Liquid Propulsion Systems Centre of ISRO?
A. M. Mohan B. S. Somnath
C. V. Narayanan D. K. Sivan

16. Who has been awarded the ICC Men's Test Cricket of the Year 2024?
A. Azmatullah Omarzai B. Arshdeep Singh
C. Jasprit Bumrah D. Travis Head

17. Who among the following has won the Men's singles title in the recently held Australian Open 2025?
A. Jannik Sinner B. Alexander Zverev
C. Novac Djokovic D. Carlos Alkraz

18. How many people have been announced to be given the Padma Award by the government of India in 2025?
A. 121 B. 139
C. 140 D. 155

19. Which bank becomes the first Indian bank to implement Clari5's NCRP Integration Solution?
A. Punjab National Bank B. Bank of Baroda
C. Bank of India D. Canara Bank

20. Polavaram Multipurpose Project, which was seen in the news, is located in which state?
A. Kerala B. Karnataka
C. Andhra Pradesh D. Maharashtra

21. Rani Durgavati Tiger Reserve is located in which state?
A. Odisha B. Madhya Pradesh
C. Rajasthan D. Gujarat

22. Pangsau Pass, which was seen in the news, lies between which two countries?
A. India and Bhutan B. China and Nepal
C. India and Myanmar D. India and Bangladesh

23. India hosted the Second BIMSTEC Expert Group Meeting on Cyber Security Cooperation in which city?
A. Hyderabad B. Chennai
C. New Delhi D. Bengaluru

24. Who was appointed as the brand ambassador of FICCI FRAMES?
A. Sachin Tendulkar B. Akshay Kumar
C. Virat Kohli D. Ayushmann Khurrana

25. Which country hosted the Chess World Cup 2025?
A. India B. Germany
C. USA D. Norway

26. Which Ministry of the Government of India is responsible for the Kalagram for Mahakumbh 2025?
A. Ministry of Culture, Government of India
B. Ministry of Tourism, Government of India
C. Indian Council for Cultural Relations
D. Ministry of External Affairs, Government of India

27. The 14th edition of the India - Thailand joint military Exercise MAITREE-XIV was organised at:
A. Fort Vachiraprakan, Thailand
B. Umroi, Meghalaya
C. Mhow, Madhya Pradesh
D. Jodhpur, Rajasthan

28. Which day is observed as the International Day of Education every year?
A. 24 January B. 25 January
C. 26 January D. 27 January

29. Which Indian Navy ship conducted the hydrographic survey of Mauritius recently?
A. INS Viraat B. INS Sarvekshak
C. INS Kalvari D. INS Saryu

30. The United States jointly develops National Advanced Surface-to-Air Missile Systems (NASAMS) with which country?
A. France B. Norway
C. Greece D. Australia

31. What is "Australopithecus" that was recently seen in the news?
A. A genus of extinct Primates
B. A prehistoric species of Fish
C. Traditional irrigation technique
D. Newly discovered species of Frog

32. With which of the following, the First EAN Rupay Credit Card is seamlessly integrated?
A. BHIM B. Rupay Card
C. UPI D. None of these

33. IDFC First Bank has partnered with whom to launch the First EA₹N Credit Card?
A. VISA Card B. Rupay Card
C. Master Card D. None of these

34. What is SANJAY, recently seen in the news?
A. Battlefield Surveillance System
B. Light Weight Battle Tank
C. Drone
D. None of these

35. The Dhanauri wetland, recently which is seen in the news, is located in?
A. Maharashtra B. Uttarakhand
C. Uttar Pradesh D. Bihar

36. Which state is at the top of the Fiscal Health Index Report 2025, recently released by NITI Aayog?
A. Karnataka B. Tamil Nadu
C. Kerala D. Odisha

37. Typhoon Missile System was developed by which country?
A. Russia B. France
C. United States D. Japan

38. Who inaugurated the All India Campaign 'Our Constitution, Our Respect'?
A. J.P. Nadda B. PM Narendra Modi
C. Mr. Rajnath Singh D. Om Birla

39. Which player won the ICC Men's T20I Cricketer of the Year Award?
A. Kuldeep Yadav B. Rishabh Pant
C. Suryakumar Yadav D. None of these

40. Recently, Russian President Putin signed a new comprehensive strategic partnership agreement with which country after bilateral talks?
A. Brazil B. Ukraine
C. Iran D. None of these

41. Karpoori Thakur will be honoured with Bharat Ratna (posthumously), he was the former Chief Minister of which state?
A. Karnataka B. Jharkhand
C. Uttar Pradesh D. Bihar

42. Mount Ibu, which was seen in the news, is located in which country?
A. Indonesia B. America
C. Latvia D. Egypt

43. Which German company, along with its Indian partner, cleared field trials for submarines for the Indian Navy?
A. ThyssenKrupp B. BAE Systems
C. Siemens D. Rheinmetall

44. In which state the army launched two new Bailey bridges on the Shyok River?
A. Jammu and Kashmir B. Arunachal Pradesh
C. Ladakh D. Mizoram

45. What is the name of India's first indigenous micro-missile system designed to counter swarm drones?
A. Bhargavastra B. Agni
C. Vayu D. Saryu

46. Which day is observed as Kokborok Day in Tripura?
A. 18 January B. 19 January
C. 20 January D. 21 January

47. What is the theme of the Tri-services tableau being showcased during the 76th Republic Day Parade in 2025?
A. United India, Strong India
B. Shashakt aur Surakshit Bharat
C. India's Defence Heritage
D. Bharat's Joint Defence Vision

48. M JANMAN scheme, which was seen in the news, is associated with which category of people?
A. MSME Owners
B. Farmers
C. Particularly Vulnerable Tribal Groups
D. Non-Resident Indians

49. Recently, which country has pulled out of the Paris Climate Agreement?
A. France B. Germany
C. America D. None of these

50. Which three states were granted full statehood on January 21, 1972?
A. Nagaland, Manipur and Tripura
B. Tripura, Manipur and Meghalaya
C. Assam, Manipur and Mizoram
D. Sikkim, Meghalaya and Tripura

51. Who is the author of the recently launched book 'The World after Gaza'?
A. Arundhati Roy B. Pankaj Mishra
C. Chetan Bhagat D. Shashi Jharool

52. Which country recently became a partner state of the BRICS group?
A. Nigeria B. Saudi Arabia
C. Iran D. Argentina

53. When was the recently discussed Beti Bachao Beti Padhao (BBBP) Scheme launched?
A. 2014 B. 2015
C. 2016 D. 2017

54. In the Vijay Hazare Trophy 2024-25 final, which team defeated Vidarbha to win the title?
A. Tamil Nadu B. Karnataka
C. Maharashtra D. Uttar Pradesh

55. Which organization has launched the quantum processor 'Willow'?
A. Amazon B. Meta
C. Google D. Microsoft

56. When does the National Disaster Response Force (NDRF) celebrate its foundation day every year?
A. 18th January B. 20th January
C. 19th January D. 21st January

57. In which state is Kokborak Day celebrated?
A. Tripura B. Ladakh
C. Arunachal Pradesh D. Rajasthan

58. Donald Trump is which number president of the United States?
A. 46th B. 47th
C. 45th D. 44th

59. Who recently won the India Open 2025 men's singles title?
A. Kidambi Srikanth B. H.S. Prannoy
C. Viktor Axelsen D. Anthony Ginting

60. Which heritage site from India has been recently included in the World Monuments Watch List 2025?
A. Kaziranga National Park
B. Taj Mahal
C. Ajanta - Ellora Caves
D. Historic Building along the Musi River

61. Abdal-Kuri Island, which was seen in the news, is located in which ocean?
A. Pacific Ocean B. Indian Ocean
C. Atlantic Ocean D. Arctic Ocean

62. Which organisation released the Global Risks Report 2025?
A. International Monetary Fund
B. United Nations Development Programme
C. World Economic Forum
D. United Nations Environment Programme

63. The Nord Stream pipeline is constructed under which sea?
A. Red Sea B. Arabian Sea
C. Black Sea D. Baltic Sea

64. The Trajan 155 mm towed artillery gun system was developed by India and which country?
A. Russia B. Australia
C. Japan D. France

65. Which Indian Naval Ship (INS) participated in the fourth edition of the multinational exercise LA PEROUSE?
A. INS Surat B. INS Kolkata
C. INS Mumbai D. INS Vikrant

66. Project Veer Gatha 4.0 is a joint initiative of which ministries?
A. Ministry of Home Affairs and Ministry of Youth Affairs
B. Ministry of Defence and Ministry of Education
C. Ministry of Culture and Ministry of Defence
D. Ministry of Education and Ministry of Sports

67. Which ministry has launched the National River Traffic and Navigation System (NRT & NS)?
A. Ministry of Road Transport and Highways
B. Ministry of Ports, Shipping & Waterways
C. Ministry of Jal Shakti
D. Ministry of Defence

68. Cyber-Security Grand Challenge (CSGC 2.0) has been launched by whom?
A. Ministry of Defence and the Indian Army
B. Ministry of Science and Technology and ISRO
C. Ministry of Home Affairs and NITI Aayog
D. Ministry of Technology and Data Security Council of India

69. Who has been sworn in as the new Chief Justice of the Supreme Court?
A. Justice Ashok Ganguly B. Justice Surya Kant
C. Justice Vinod Kumar D. Justice Deepak Mishra

70. The falcated duck was recently spotted at which protected area in Haryana?
A. Nahar Wildlife Sanctuary
B. Bhindawas Wildlife Sanctuary
C. Sultanpur National Park
D. Kalesar National Park

71. Which institution developed the Central Suspect Registry?
A. Reserve Bank of India (RBI)
B. Indian Cyber Crime Coordination Centre (I4C)
C. Central Bureau of Investigation (CBI)
D. National Investigation Agency (NIA)

72. With which country has India signed a deal for the export of BrahMos supersonic cruise missiles?
A. Indonesia B. Bangladesh
C. Ukraine D. India

73. Which state government has launched the SHE COHORT 3.0 initiative to empower women-led startups?
A. Odisha B. Haryana
C. Punjab D. Gujarat

74. Which of the following is the best description of 'Nag Mk 2 Missile'?
A. It is a land variant of short-range submarine-launched Ballistic Missile (SLBM).
B. It is the third-generation Anti-Tank Fire-and-Forget Guided Missile.
C. It is India's first indigenously produced medium-range Surface to Air missile.
D. None of the above

75. What is the main objective of Exercise Devil Strike conducted by the Indian Army?
A. Testing new technologies
B. Expanding international military alliances
C. Enhancing combat preparedness and operational capabilities
D. Conducting humanitarian assistance missions

76. Which player of the Indian women's cricket team was appointed as DSP in UP Police?
A. Harmanpreet Kaur B. Smriti Mandhana
C. Deepti Sharma D. Richa Ghosh

77. Which State has inaugurated the International Saraswati Mahotsav?
A. Andhra Pradesh B. Haryana
C. Karnataka D. Uttar Pradesh

78. Recently, which scheme was launched by the government to provide loan guarantees for MSMEs?
A. Mutual Credit Guarantee Scheme for MSMEs (MCGS-MSMEs)
B. Credit-Linked Capital Subsidy Scheme
C. Stand-Up India Scheme
D. Pradhan Mantri Mudra Yojana

79. Who was named ICC Women's Cricketer of the Year 2024?
A. Smriti Mandhana B. Ellyse Perry
C. Amelia Kerr D. Alyssa Healy

80. In which of the following cities did the Inland Waterways Authority of India (IWAI) establish a new regional office?
A. Haridwar B. Varanasi
C. Kashi D. Ujjain

81. Which of the following is NOT a member of the Selection Committee for appointing the CEC and ECs?
A. The Prime Minister
B. The Chief Justice of India
C. The Leader of the Opposition in the Lok Sabha
D. A Cabinet Minister nominated by the Prime Minister

82. What is the limit of non-taxable income as per the new regime 2025?
A. 10 lakhs B. 12 lakhs
C. 11 lakhs D. 13 lakhs

83. When Indian Coast Guard Raising Day is celebrated every year?
A. 1st Feb B. 31st Jan
C. 30th Jan D. 2nd Feb

84. From which Udyan Utsav 2025 at Rashtrapati Bhavan will start?
A. 2nd Feb B. 3rd Feb
C. 1st Feb D. 4th Feb

85. Which country recently became the first in Africa to be acknowledged by the WHO for interrupting the transmission of Onchocerca volvulus?
A. Kenya B. Egypt
C. Nigeria D. Niger

86. Who was the pilot of the Axiom-4 mission to the International Space Station (ISS)?
A. Stawosz Uznanski-Wisniewski
B. Peggy Whitson
C. Group Captain Shubhanshu Shukla
D. Tibor Kapu

87. Which state recently approved a pilot study for regulated cannabis cultivation?
A. Himachal Pradesh B. Uttar Pradesh
C. Andhra Pradesh D. Haryana

88. Which board was established to promote Makhana cultivation in Bihar as part of the budget initiatives?
A. Fisheries and Aquaculture Board
B. Bihar Crop Improvement Board
C. Makhana Board
D. Agricultural Development Board

89. Greg Bell, who recently passed away, was a famous long jumper from which country?
A. Australia B. Germany
C. USA D. Canada

90. Point Nemo, which was seen in the news, is located in which ocean?
A. Atlantic Ocean B. Indian Ocean
C. Arctic Ocean D. Pacific Ocean

91. Which institution recently extracted silicon carbide from simulated moon soil?
A. IIT Bombay B. IIT Kanpur
C. IIT Delhi D. IIT Madras

92. Which city is the host of the first Raisina Middle East Conference?
A. Riyadh B. Abu Dhabi
C. Cairo D. Beirut

93. Ramappa Temple is located in which state?
A. Telangana B. Gujarat
C. Tamil Nadu D. Maharashtra

94. What is the name of the indigenous dog breed recently recognized by ICAR-NBAGR from the Himalayas?
A. Damchi B. Gaddi
C. Bakharwal D. Bangara

95. Who has taken oath as the New Governor of Bihar?
A. Sanjay Malhotra B. Sushil Kumar
C. Junaid Ahmad D. Arif Mohammad

96. India has recently rolled out Digital pilot licenses (Electronic Personnel License – EPL). What position does India hold globally in implementing this initiative?
A. 1st B. 2nd
C. 3rd D. 4th

97. Which state has Recently Launched the N proud (New Programme for Removal of Unused) initiative?
A. Tamil Nadu B. Maharashtra
C. Karnataka D. Kerala

98. Recently launched NAKSHA campaign is associated with which Ministry?
A. Ministry of Housing and Urban Affairs
B. Ministry of Rural Development and Agriculture Farmer's welfare
C. Ministry of Environment, forest and climate change
D. Ministry of Home Affairs

99. India and Qatar have set a target to double their bilateral trade to show much by 2030.
A. $20 Billion B. $35 Billion
C. $28 Billion D. $40 Billion

100. Recently, which organization developed the 10-tonne vertical planetary Mixer, the world's largest for solid propellants?
A. DRDO B. HAL
C. IISC D. ISRO

101. What is unique about the NISAR satellite, launched on 30 July 2025?
A. It is India's first satellite
B. It is the first to carry humans
C. It uses dual-frequency radar (L-band & S-band)
D. It is designed for lunar missions

102. Gen Z protests on mass scale erupted in which country?
A. Bangladesh B. Pakistan
C. Nepal D. Sri Lanka

103. When is International Tiger Day celebrated every year?
A. 28 July B. 15 August
C. 29 July D. 30 June

104. What is the full form of NISAR, the satellite launched by ISRO on July 30, 2025?
A. National Indian Satellite for Agricultural Research
B. NASA-ISRO Synthetic Aperture Radar
C. New Indian Satellite for Aerial Reconnaissance
D. None of the above

105. Which country's Prime Minister mediated and announced the ceasefire to resolve the Thailand-Cambodia border clashes in July 2025?
A. Thailand B. Cambodia
C. Vietnam D. Malaysia

106. Who won the FIDE Women's World Cup 2025?
A. Koneru Humpy B. Harika Dronavalli
C. Divya Deshmukh D. Tania Sachdev

107. Central Reserve Police Force (CRPF) Raising Day is observed on 27 July every year, What was the original name of the Central Reserve Police Force (CRPF) established in 1939?
A. British Reserve Police
B. Crown Representative's Police
C. Indian Territorial Force
D. Royal Indian Constabulary

108. Which historical site is at the center of the territorial dispute between Thailand and Cambodia that led to clashes in July 2025?
A. Angkor Wat B. Preah Vihear Temple
C. Golden Pagoda D. Phnom Penh Palace

109. What is the name of the joint military exercise between India and Singapore held in July–August 2025?
A. SIMBEX B. Garuda Shakti
C. Bold Kurukshetra D. Mitra Shakti

110. Where was the first hydrogen-powered train coach tested in July 2025?
A. Bhopal Rail Coach Factory
B. RCF Kapurthala
C. Integral Coach Factory, Chennai
D. Lucknow Workshop

111. Whose record did Narendra Modi surpass to become the second-longest-serving PM in consecutive terms in July 2025?
A. Atal Bihari Vajpayee B. Jawaharlal Nehru
C. Indira Gandhi D. Lal Bahadur Shastri

112. Kargil Vijay Diwas is observed on which date every year?
A. 15 August B. 3 December
C. 26 July D. 26 June

113. Which military operation was launched by India during the Kargil War?
A. Operation Blue Star B. Operation Meghdoot
C. Operation Vijay D. Operation Shakti

114. When was the National Cooperative Policy 2025 launched by Amit Shah, Union Minister of Home and Cooperation?
A. 15 August 2025 B. 24 July 2025
C. 1 January 2025 D. 30 June 2025

115. Under which constitutional amendment were cooperative societies recognized as a fundamental right?
A. 74th Amendment B. 86th Amendment
C. 97th Amendment D. 102nd Amendment

116. Which two leaders signed the India–UK Free Trade Agreement (FTA) in July 2025?
A. Narendra Modi and Rishi Sunak
B. Amit Shah and Keir Starmer
C. Narendra Modi and Keir Starmer
D. Rishi Sunak and Nirmala Sitharaman

117. India has achieved how much percentage ethanol blending in petrol in 2025, five years ahead of its original 2030 target?
A. 15% B. 20%
C. 18% D. 10%

118. Which two countries is PM Narendra Modi visited from July 23 to 26, 2025?
A. UK and Sri Lanka B. UK and Maldives
C. France and Maldives D. UAE and UK

119. What is the primary objective of the Indian Government's "World's Largest Grain Storage Plan in the Cooperative Sector"?
A. To increase grain exports
B. To promote organic farming
C. To centralize food procurement
D. To improve rural grain storage infrastructure and strengthen PACS

120. Who resigned as the Vice President of India in July 2025?
A. M. Venkaiah Naidu B. Jagdeep Dhankhar
C. Ram Nath Kovind D. Om Birla

121. When did FIDE Chess World Cup 2025 held in India?
A. August 10 – September 5
B. September 15 – October 12
C. October 30 – November 27
D. November 10 – December 5

122. How many gold medals did India win at the 66th International Mathematical Olympiad (IMO) 2025 held in Sunshine Coast, Australia in July 2025?
A. Two B. Three
C. Four D. One

123. When is International Moon Day observed?
A. July 16 B. July 20
C. August 5 D. June 21

124. Purple Fest 2025, organised on 10-11th September, 2025 in New Delhi is related to:
A. Deserted women B. Transgenders
C. LGBTQIA+ D. Divangjan

125. Which organization was designated as a Foreign Terrorist Organization (FTO) by the United States in July 2025 for its involvement in the deadly April 22 Pahalgam attack?
A. Jaish-e-Mohammed
B. The Resistance Front (TRF)
C. Hizbul Mujahideen
D. Indian Mujahideen

126. What is the name of the annual maritime bilateral exercise between India and Singapore, conducted in July 2025?
A. MILAN B. SIMBEX
C. VARUNA D. INDRA

127. Where did the 56th International Film Festival of India (IFFI) held in November 2025?
A. Mumbai B. New Delhi
C. Goa D. Hyderabad

128. Which city was declared India's cleanest city for the 8th consecutive year in the Swachh Survekshan 2024–25?
A. Ahmedabad B. Surat
C. Indore D. Navi Mumbai

129. What is the range of the Agni-I missile, which is capable of carrying both nuclear and conventional warheads?
A. 150 – 300 km B. 350 – 500 km
C. 700 – 900 km D. 1,000 – 1,500 km

130. What is the name of the government scheme launched in July 2025 to improve agriculture in low-productivity districts?
A. Pradhan Mantri Krishi Samriddhi Yojana
B. Dhan-Vikas Gramin Krishi Yojana
C. Prime Minister Dhan-Dhaanya Krishi Yojana
D. Kisan Utthan Abhiyan

131. What age group of children is required to complete the Mandatory Biometric Update (MBU) as per UIDAI guidelines?
A. Below 5 years B. 5 to 7 years
C. 7 years and above D. 10 years and above

132. Which government agency is responsible for issuing, updating, and managing Aadhaar in India?
A. National Informatics Centre (NIC)
B. Ministry of Home Affairs (MHA)
C. Unique Identification Authority of India (UIDAI)
D. Central Bureau of Investigation (CBI)

133. Ancy Sojan secured third place in the Lignano Meeting – World Athletics Continental Tour Bronze in July 2025 in which event?
A. 100m Sprint B. High Jump
C. Long Jump D. Triple Jump

134. What is the name of the mission that carried Shubhanshu Shukla to the International Space Station (ISS) in July 2025?
A. Chandrayaan-3
B. Gaganyaan-1
C. Axiom-4 (Akash Ganga)
D. Mission Prithvi

135. When is the 10th Anniversary of the Skill India Mission observed?
A. 12 July 2025 B. 15 July 2025
C. 1 August 2025 D. 5 June 2025

136. Which football club won the first-ever FIFA Club World Cup in 2025?
A. Paris Saint-Germain B. Bayern Munich
C. Manchester City D. Chelsea

137. Who has been appointed as the new Governor of Haryana in July 2025?
A. Prof. Ashim Kumar Ghosh
B. B.D. Mishra
C. Pusapati Ashok Gajapathi Raju
D. Kavinder Gupta

138. Who has been appointed as the new Governor of Goa in July 2025?
A. Prof. Ashim Kumar Ghosh
B. B.D. Mishra
C. Pusapati Ashok Gajapathi Raju
D. Kavinder Gupta

139. What is the name of India's second-longest cable-stayed bridge inaugurated in July 2025?
A. Bandra-Worli Sea Link B. Sharavathi Bridge
C. Sigandur Bridge D. Kalasavalli Bridge

140. What is India's longest cable-stayed bridge overall?
A. Pamban Bridge B. Bandra-Worli Sea Link
C. Sigandur Bridge D. Bogibeel Bridge

141. Under which Article of the Indian Constitution does the President nominate members to the Rajya Sabha?
A. Article 78 B. Article 370
C. Article 80(1)(a) D. Article 356

142. Who won the Wimbledon 2025 Men's Singles title?
A. Novak Djokovic B. Carlos Alcaraz
C. Jannik Sinner D. Daniil Medvedev

143. Who won the Wimbledon 2025 Women's Singles title?
A. Aryna Sabalenka B. Amanda Anisimova
C. Iga Swiatek D. Elena Rybakina

144. Which Indian heritage site was inscribed as the 44th UNESCO World Heritage Site in July 2025?
A. Hill Forts of Rajasthan
B. Maratha Military Landscapes of India
C. Ajanta Caves
D. Chola Temples

145. What is the primary objective of Operation SHIVA 2025, launched by the Indian Army in July 2025?
A. Border surveillance in Ladakh
B. Rescue operations in flood-hit areas
C. Ensuring safe conduct of the Shri Amarnath Yatra
D. Conducting joint military drills with foreign forces

146. According to the Aircraft Accident Investigation Bureau (AAIB) report, what caused the crash of the Air India flight AI 171?
A. Bird strike
B. Weather turbulence
C. Fuel supply to engines was cut off
D. Engine fire

147. Who recently (in July 2025) became the fastest Indian sprinter in the 100 meters?
A. Gurindervir Singh B. Neeraj Chopra
C. Animesh Kujur D. Amlan Borgohain

148. What is the name of the revolution that helped India's fish production double in 11 years (2013–14) to (2024–25)?
A. Green Revolution B. White Revolution
C. Blue Revolution D. Yellow Revolution

149. What is the name of the Indian Navy's first indigenously designed and built Diving Support Vessel (DSV)?
A. Samarth B. Nistar
C. Varun D. Rakshak

150. Dr. Syama Prasad Mookerjee was the founder of which political party?
A. Indian National Congress
B. Bharatiya Jana Sangh
C. Hindu Mahasabha
D. Swatantra Party

151. Who was appointed as the new CEO of the International Cricket Council (ICC) in July 2025?
A. Jay Shah B. Manu Sawhney
C. Sanjog Gupta D. Anurag Thakur

152. In July 2025, Prime Minister Narendra Modi was conferred which civilian honour by Brazil?
A. Order of the Star of Africa
B. Grand Collar of the National Order of the Southern Cross
C. Order of the Condor of the Andes
D. Order of Rio Branco

153. Who scored 430 runs across both innings and was named Player of the Match in the second Test of the Anderson-Tendulkar Trophy at Edgbaston, Birmingham?
A. Virat Kohli B. Shubman Gill
C. Rohit Sharma D. Rishabh Pant

154. Indonesia was formally inducted as a full member of BRICS during which summit?
A. 16th BRICS Summit, South Africa
B. 17th BRICS Summit, Brazil
C. 18th BRICS Summit, India
D. 15th BRICS Summit, China

155. Who will chair the BRICS Summit in 2026?
A. Brazil B. China
C. India D. Russia

156. Which of the following is not accepted as valid proof of citizenship during Special Intensive Revision (SIR) of electoral rolls in Bihar?
A. Passport B. Birth Certificate
C. School Certificate D. Aadhaar Card

157. Where was the 17th BRICS Summit held in 2025?
A. New Delhi, India
B. Beijing, China
C. Rio de Janeiro, Brazil
D. Cape Town, South Africa

158. Who among the following Indian boxers won gold medals at the World Boxing Cup 2025 held in Astana in July 2025?
A. Meenakshi, Sanju, Jaismine
B. Sakshi, Jaismine, Nupur
C. Jaismine, Pooja Rani, Hitesh Gulia
D. Nupur, Narender, Abhinash Jamwal

159. India recently qualified for the AFC Women's Asian Cup 2026 after how many years?
A. 18 years B. 20 years
C. 22 years D. 25 years

160. India ranks _______ in terms of income equality globally, based on the Gini Index of World Bank.
A. First B. Fourth
C. Tenth D. Fifteenth

161. Who won the Rapid section of the Grand Chess Tour 2025 in Zagreb?
A. Magnus Carlsen
B. Jan-Krzyszt of Duda
C. Gukesh Dommaraju
D. Praggnanandhaa Rameshbabu

162. Where has India set up its first Equine Disease-Free Compartment (EDFC) in July 2025?
A. Pune
B. Bikaner
C. Meerut Cantonment
D. Chennai

163. What is the name of the award PM Modi received from Trinidad and Tobago in July 2025?
A. Order of the Caribbean
B. National Hero Award
C. Order of the Republic of Trinidad and Tobago
D. West Indies Medal of Honour

164. Where did the first Khelo India Water Sports Festival held in August 2025?
A. Goa B. Chilika Lake
C. Dal Lake, Srinagar D. Naini Lake

165. What is the name of the sweeping legislation passed by the US House on July 3, 2025?
A. The Liberty Act B. Build Back Better Bill
C. One Big Beautiful Bill D. Freedom Finance Act

166. Which honour was conferred upon PM Modi during his visit to Ghana in July 2025?
A. Order of Africa
B. Commander of the Golden Star
C. Officer of the Order of the Star of Ghana
D. Star of Africa

167. Who is the current and 14th Dalai Lama?
A. Lobsang Sangay B. Tenzin Gyatso
C. Gyalwa Rinpoche D. Penpa Tsering

168. Who won the gold medal in U-15 Girls' Singles at the 29th Asian Youth Table Tennis Championships 2025?
A. Liu Ziling B. Zhu Qihi
C. Divyanshi Bhowmick D. P.B. Abhinand

169. What is the total outlay of the Employment-Linked Incentive (ELI) Scheme approved by the Union Cabinet on 1 July 2025?
A. ₹ 50,000 crore B. ₹ 1 lakh crore
C. ₹ 2 lakh crore D. ₹ 75,000 crore

170. What is the name of the new Indian Railways app launched on 1 July 2025?
A. RailConnect B. RailOne
C. RailMate D. UTSonMobile

171. What is the name of the advanced stealth frigate that was commissioned on 1 July 2025 at Yantar Shipyard, Kaliningrad, Russia?
A. INS Vikrant B. INS Talwar
C. INS Tamal D. INS Shivalik

172. Who became the first Indian to win a BWF World Tour title in 2025?
A. Lakshya Sen B. Kidambi Srikanth
C. Ayush Shetty D. Prannoy H.S.

173. Who has been appointed as the Secretary of RAW from July 1, 2025?
A. Ravi Sinha B. Rakesh Asthana
C. Parag Jain D. Samant Goel

174. Which two hydroelectric projects are at the center of the Indus Waters Treaty dispute?
A. Baglihar and Uri
B. Kishenganga and Ratle
C. Sardar Sarovar and Tehri
D. Dulhasti and Salal

175. Which was the NATO Summit 2025 held?
A. Brussels, Belgium
B. The Hague, Netherlands
C. Berlin, Germany
D. Paris, France

176. Samvidhaan Hatya Diwas is observed annually in remembrance of the Emergency, which was declared in India on which date?
A. 15 August 1975 B. 26 January 1975
C. 25 June 1975 D. 25 July 1975

177. Which major Government scheme for urban infrastructure development completed 10 years on 25 June 2025?
A. Smart Cities Mission
B. AMRUT (Atal Mission for Rejuvenation and Urban Transformation)
C. PM Awas Yojana – Urban
D. Swachh Bharat Mission – Urban

178. What is the name of the evacuation mission launched by India from Iran amid the conflict in June 2025?
A. Operation Vande Bharat
B. Operation Samudra Setu
C. Operation Sindhu
D. Operation Suraksha

179. Neeraj Chopra won the men's javelin throw at which Diamond League event in June 2025?
A. Doha Diamond League
B. Zurich Diamond League
C. Paris Diamond League
D. Rome Diamond League

180. Where did Prime Minister Narendra Modi lead the International Yoga Day 2025 celebrations?
A. Rishikesh B. Varanasi
C. Visakhapatnam D. New Delhi

181. Which university topped the QS World University Rankings 2026?
A. Stanford University
B. University of Oxford
C. Massachusetts Institute of Technology (MIT)
D. Harvard University

182. Which Indian institute ranked highest among Indian University in the QS World University Rankings 2026?
A. IIT Kanpur B. IIT Madras
C. IIT Bombay D. IIT Delhi

183. What is the theme for the 11th International Day of Yoga (IDY) 2025?
A. Yoga for Global Peace
B. Yoga for Wellness and Harmony
C. Yoga for One Earth, One Health
D. Yoga for Climate and Community

184. Which judge is facing possible impeachment over allegations of misconduct related to half-burnt cash found at his residence in March 2025?
A. Justice G.S. Sandhawalia
B. Justice Anu Sivaraman
C. Justice Yashwant Varma
D. Justice Sheel Nagu

185. What is the name of India's first Anti-Submarine Warfare Shallow Water Craft (ASW-SWC)?
A. INS Vikrant B. INS Kalvari
C. INS Arnala D. INS Vagir

186. Where was the G7 Summit 2025 held from 16 to 17 June 2025?
A. Paris B. Kananaskis
C. Berlin D. Tokyo

187. What is the name of the Indo-French joint military exercise held in June 2025?
A. Varuna B. Shakti
C. Indra D. Surya Kiran

188. Which is the number of the national Census to be conducted in 2026–2027?
A. 14th B. 15th
C. 16th D. 17th

189. A major armed conflict broke out between which two countries in June 2025?
A. Russia and Ukraine
B. Iran and Israel
C. China and Taiwan
D. North Korea and South Korea

190. Which team won the ICC World Test Championship Final 2025?
A. Australia B. England
C. India D. South Africa

191. What type of aircraft was involved in the Air India London Flight Crash on June, 12 2025?
A. Airbus A320 B. Boeing 777
C. Boeing 737 Max D. Boeing 787-8 Dreamliner

192. What is the name of the new postal service launched by the Department of Posts in June 2025 for affordable delivery of books?
A. Book Post B. Gyan Setu
C. Gyan Post D. Shiksha Mail

193. What is the name of Israel's military operation targeting Iran's nuclear and military sites in June 2025?
A. Desert Thunder B. Iron Shield
C. Rising Lion D. Storm Falcon

194. What are the two main routes for the Shri Amarnath Ji Yatra?
A. Jammu and Leh B. Pahalgam and Baltal
C. Gulmarg and Sonmarg D. Kargil and Pulwama

195. In terms of social protection beneficiaries, what is India's global rank, as per ILO's ILOSTAT data released in June 2025?
A. First B. Second
C. Third D. Fourth

196. Which Indian cricketer was included in the ICC Hall of Fame in June 2025?
A. Virat Kohli B. Rahul Dravid
C. MS Dhoni D. Sachin Tendulkar

197. Who won the Women's Singles title at French Open 2025?
A. Aryna Sabalenka B. Serena Williams
C. Coco Gauff D. Iga Swiatek

198. What is the revised policy repo rate after the June 2025 MPC meeting?
A. 5.0% B. 5.25%
C. 5.5% D. 6.0%

199. Which of the following bridges is the world's highest railway arch bridge inaugurated by PM Modi in June 2025?
A. Howrah Bridge B. Anji Khad Bridge
C. Pamban Bridge D. Chenab Bridge

200. Which of the following is India's first cable-stayed rail bridge?
A. Chenab Bridge B. Pamban Bridge
C. Anji Khad Bridge D. Godavari Arch Bridge

201. The PM Modi-led NDA government completed how many years at the Centre in June 2025?
A. 10 years B. 11 years
C. 12 years D. 9 years

202. When will the reference date for the Population Census 2027 be, for most parts of India?
A. January 1, 2027 B. March 1, 2027
C. April 1, 2027 D. February 28, 2027

203. What significant new feature is included in Census 2027?
A. Online data collection
B. Biometric verification
C. Caste enumeration
D. Use of Aadhaar-linked data only

204. What is the main theme of World Environment Day 2025, observed on June 5?
A. Climate Action
B. Clean Energy
C. Ending Plastic Pollution
D. Reforestation

205. Who won the Indian Premier League (IPL) 2025 title?
A. Punjab Kings
B. Chennai Super Kings
C. Royal Challengers Bengaluru
D. Gujarat Titans

206. Who won the 2025 presidential runoff election in Poland?
A. Rafal Trzaskowski B. Andrzcj Duda
C. Karol Nawrocki D. Helga Schmid

207. Who was crowned Miss World 2025?
A. Hasset (Ethiopia)
B. Krystyna Pyszková
C. Opal Suchata Chuangsri
D. Nandini Gupta

208. What is the name of the joint military exercise between India and Mongolia?
A. Desert Eagle B. Nomadic Elephant
C. Mountain Tiger D. Steppe Warrior

209. What is the purpose of next-generation defence technologies trials conducted by the Indian Army in June 2025?
A. Training cadets for disaster response

B. Enhancing public awareness
C. Evaluating advanced systems under near-combat conditions
D. Demonstrating systems to foreign allies

210. What award is conferred to recognize exceptional nursing professionals for outstanding contributions to India's healthcare system?
A. Padma Shri Award
B. Bharat Ratna Award
C. National Florence Nightingale Award
D. National Health Excellence Award

211. What historic first took place during the 148th Passing Out Parade of NDA in May 2025?
A. First foreign cadet graduated
B. First women cadets were commissioned into the Indian Armed Forces
C. President attended the ceremony for the first time
D. First drone display at NDA parade

212. Who won two gold medals at the Asian Athletics Championships 2025 for India?
A. Avinash Sable B. Gulveer Singh
C. Tejas Bhat D. Animesh Kujur

213. Which Indian state became the second to cross the nationally prescribed 95% benchmark for full literacy?
A. Kerala B. Goa
C. Tamil Nadu D. Himachal Pradesh

214. Which event did Avinash Sable win gold in 26th Asian Athletics Championships in Gumi, South Korea, on 29 May 2025?
A. 1500 m B. 10,000 m
C. 3000 m steeplechase D. 5000 m

215. AdFalciVax is being used in India against:
A. Malaria B. Filaria
C. Influenza D. Diphtheria

216. Chandrapuram Ponnusami Radhakrishnan took oath as the .... Vice President of India.
A. 14th B. 15th
C. 16th D. 17th

217. Which ministry released the industrial production data?
A. Ministry of Finance
B. Ministry of Commerce and Industry
C. Ministry of Statistics and Programme Imple-mentation
D. Ministry of Labour and Employment

218. Who won the gold medal in the Men's 10,000-metre race at the Asian Athletics Championships 2025?
A. Servin Sebasthiyan B. Wang Zhaozhao
C. Gulveer Singh D. Amit

219. Which of the following received the Padma Vibhushan posthumously in 2025 for his contribution in Folk Music?
A. Bibek Debroy B. Sharda Sinha
C. Colleen Gantzer D. Ajay Bhatt

220. Kunjiparamba caves were in the news recently. They are in which state?
A. Kerala B. Odisha
C. Madhya Pradesh D. Tamil Nadu

221. According to World Economic Forum's 'The Future of Jobs Report 2025' unemployment rate in India is:
A. 2% B. 3%
C. 4% D. 5%

222. Who set a new world record in the F42 javelin category in May 2025?
A. Sumit Antil
B. Roberto Floriani Edenilson
C. Mahendra Gurjar
D. Neeraj Chopra

223. Where did Prime Minister Narendra Modi inaugurate the new Locomotive Manufacturing Plant in May 2025?
A. Vadodara, Gujarat B. Surat, Gujarat
C. Dahod, Gujarat D. Rajkot, Gujarat

224. Who won the Palme d'Or at the 78th Cannes Film Festival?
A. Hayakawa Chie B. Suzuki Yui
C. Jafar Panahi D. Asghar Farhadi

225. Which country did India surpass to become the world's fourth-largest economy?
A. Germany B. China
C. Japan D. United Kingdom

226. Who is the current CEO of NITI Aayog (as of December 2025)?
A. Amitabh Kant B. Parameswaran Iyer
C. B.V.R. Subrahmanyam D. Rajiv Kumar

227. Who is the current Prime Minister of Singapore as of December 2025?
A. Lee Hsien Loong B. K. Shanmugam
C. Lawrence Wong D. Vivian Balakrishnan

228. Which forces are included in the cadre review order issued by the Supreme Court in May 2025?
A. ITBP and Indian Army
B. BSF, CISF, and Indian Navy
C. ITBP, BSF, CRPF, CISF, and SSB
D. Police and Coast Guard

229. Who among the following has been appointed as an Executive Director of International Monetary Fund?
A. Dr. Raghuram Rajan
B. Dr. Urjit Patel
C. Arvind Subramanian
D. Dr. Rajiv Kumar

230. What is the name of the islands that the UK returned to Mauritius in an agreement in May 2025?
A. Maldives B. Lakshadweep
C. Chagos Islands D. Seychelles

231. Where did the Rising North East Investors Summit 2025 held in May 2025?
A. Mumbai B. Guwahati
C. New Delhi D. Kolkata

232. Which state became the first in India to achieve full functional literacy in May 2025?
A. Kerala B. Tamil Nadu
C. Mizoram D. Himachal Pradesh

233. What is the name of the national literacy program that helped Mizoram achieve full literacy?
A. Sarva Shiksha Abhiyan
B. Digital India Literacy Mission
C. ULLAS – Nav Bharat Saaksharta Karyakram
D. Shiksha Setu Abhiyan

234. What is the primary purpose of the Golden Dome shield, announced by US President in May 2025?
A. To launch satellites for GPS
B. To detect and intercept long-range missile threats
C. To replace the U.S. Navy defense systems
D. To prevent cyber attacks

235. How many Asiatic lions were recorded in Gujarat's 16th lion census in 2025?
A. 721 B. 817
C. 891 D. 956

236. How many public EV charging stations are planned to be established under the PM E-Drive scheme?
A. 50,000 B. 60,000
C. 72,000 D. 75,000

237. What was the theme of the 78th World Health Assembly addressed by PM Modi on May 20, 2025?
A. Health for All
B. One Earth, One Health
C. Universal Health Coverage
D. One World for Health

238. Which core industry carries the highest individual weight in the Index of Eight Core Industries?
A. Coal
B. Steel
C. Electricity
D. Petroleum Refinery Products

239. Indian Navy inducted an Ancient Stitched Ship in May 2025. This recreation of a 5th-century CE ship was inspired by which of the following?
A. Ancient Sanskrit manuscripts
B. A painting from the Ajanta Caves
C. Shipwrecks found along the western coast of India
D. Ancient texts from the Vedic period

240. Which country is known for its traditional tea ceremony called 'Chanoyu'?
A. India B. China
C. Japan D. Sri Lanka

241. Where was the first edition of the Khelo India Beach Games (KIBG) held in May 2025?
A. Marina Beach, Chennai
B. Baga Beach, Goa
C. Ghoghla Beach, Diu
D. Juhu Beach, Mumbai

242. What caused the failure of ISRO's PSLV-C61 mission to place the EOS-09 satellite in orbit on May 18, 2025?
A. An issue with the rocket's first stage
B. Launch pad malfunction
C. An anomaly in the rocket's third stage
D. None of these

243. Who won the South Asian Football Federation (SAFF) Under-19 Football Championship 2025?
A. Nepal B. Bangladesh
C. India D. Sri Lanka

244. India has signed Bilateral Investment Agreement (BIA) with which country?
A. UK B. Italy
C. Israel D. Germany

245. What milestone did Neeraj Chopra achieve at 2025 Doha Diamond League?
A. First Diamond League win
B. First throw over 85 meters
C. First time crossing the 90-meter mark
D. First time beating Julian Weber

246. Who won the Superbet Chess Classic 2025 held in Bucharest, Romania in May 2025?
A. Alireza Firouzja
B. Maxime Vachier-Lagrave
C. D Gukesh
D. R Praggnanandhaa

247. Jagadguru Rambhadracharya was awarded the 58th Jnanpith Award for his contribution to the literature of which language?
A. Hindi B. Urdu
C. Sanskrit D. Tamil

248. According to United Nations' mid-year World Economic Situation and Prospects (WESP) report, which economy is expected to grow faster than China, the US, and the EU in 2025?
A. United States B. European Union
C. India D. Japan

249. Which state emerged as the overall champion in the Khelo India Youth Games 2025?
A. Haryana B. Rajasthan
C. Uttar Pradesh D. Maharashtra

250. Why did the government revoke the security clearance of Celebi Airport Services India Pvt. Ltd., a Turkish ground handling firm, in May 2025?
A. The Turkish support to Pakistan during Operation Sindoor
B. Poor financial performance of the company in India
C. Celebi's failure to comply with aviation safety standards
D. Allegations of employee exploitation and labour violations

251. Under which platform were the new India-EU research initiatives launched in May 2025 to address marine pollution and develop green hydrogen from waste?
A. India-EU Environmental Pact
B. India-EU Green Alliance
C. India-EU Trade and Technology Council (TTC)
D. India-EU Sustainable Development Forum

252. One of the seven PM MITRA park is being developed in which district of Madhya Pradesh?
A. Dhar B. Gwalior
C. Ujjain D. Dewas

253. Who received the honorary Palme d'Or at the opening of the 78th Cannes Film Festival in 2025?
A. Leonardo DiCaprio B. Juliette Binoche
C. Robert De Niro D. Anupam Kher

254. Where was BSF Jawan Purnam Kumar Shaw handed over by Pakistan Rangers to Indian authorities on May 14, 2025?
A. Wagah Border B. Ferozepur Post
C. Attari Joint Check Post D. Kartarpur Corridor

255. Who has been appointed as the new Chairman of the Union Public Service Commission (UPS C). in May 2025?
A. Rajiv Gauba B. Dr. Ajay Kumar
C. Sanjay Mitra D. Anil Baijal

256. The Promotion and Regulation of Online Gaming Act that bans all forms of online money games has been implemented from:
A. October 1, 2025 B. September 17, 2025
C. September 15, 2025 D. September 22, 2025

257. Who was appointed as the Foreign Minister of Canada in May 2025?
A. Ruby Sahota B. Randeep Sarai
C. Maninder Sidhu D. Anita Anand

258. Why was IPL 2025 temporarily suspended in June 2025?
A. Due to weather conditions
B. Due to player protests
C. Due to rising tensions between India and Pakistan
D. Due to scheduling conflicts with international cricket

259. Where were India's first design centres working on 3-nanometer chip design inaugurated?
A. Mumbai and Pune
B. Hyderabad and Chennai
C. Noida and Bengaluru
D. Delhi and Ahmedabad

260. Why were 32 airports in India temporarily shut down between May 9 and May 12, 2025?
A. Due to a nationwide airline strike
B. For routine maintenance and upgrades
C. Following cross-border drone and missile attacks after the Pahalgam massacre
D. Because of severe weather conditions across North India

261. Who are the only three Indian cricketers with more Test runs than Virat Kohli?
A. MS Dhoni, Rahul Dravid, Sunil Gavaskar
B. Sourav Ganguly, Sachin Tendulkar, Rahul Dravid
C. Sachin Tendulkar, Rahul Dravid, Sunil Gavaskar
D. VVS Laxman, Sunil Gavaskar, MS Dhoni

262. What was the main focus of the Directors General of Military Operations (DGMO)-level talks between India and Pakistan on 12 May 2025?
A. Trade agreements
B. Cultural exchange programs
C. Maintaining ceasefire and avoiding aggressive actions
D. Water-sharing agreements

263. Where was the Miss World 2025 pageant organized in May 2025?
A. Mumbai B. Bengaluru
C. New Delhi D. Hyderabad

264. Who won the final of the Tri-Nation Women's ODI Series 2025 held in Colombo in May 2025?
A. Sri Lanka B. Bangladesh
C. India D. Pakistan

265. National Technology Day (May 11) commemorates which major event in Indian history?
A. Launch of India's first satellite
B. Inauguration of ISRO
C. Successful Pokhran-II nuclear tests
D. Founding of DRDO

266. Who has been empowered to call out Territorial Army personnel as per the new government order in May 2025?
A. Defence Minister
B. Chief of Defence Staff
C. Chief of the Army Staff
D. President of India

267. Which Indian cricketer announced his retirement from Test cricket in May 2025?
A. Virat Kohli B. Ajinkya Rahane
C. Rohit Sharma D. Cheteshwar Pujara

268. What was the codename for the nationwide Civil Defence Mock Drill conducted on May 7, 2025?
A. Operation Raksha B. Operation Abhyas
C. Operation Suraksha D. Operation Agni

269. Where was International Maritime Defence Exhibition (IMDEX) Asia 2025 held from May 6 to May 8, 2025?
A. Kuala Lumpur, Malaysia
B. Jakarta, Indonesia
C. Changi Exhibition Centre, Singapore
D. Bangkok, Thailand

270. Who has been elected as the new Chancellor of Germany in May 2025?
A. Olaf Scholz B. Armin Laschet
C. Friedrich Merz D. Angela Merkel

271. During NEET (UG) 2025, which biometric method did UIDAI test for verifying candidate identity?
A. Iris scan
B. Fingerprint authentication
C. Aadhaar-based face authentication
D. Voice recognition

272. Why did the United Nations Security Council (UNSC) hold closed-door consultations on May 5, 2025?
A. To discuss climate change impacts in South Asia
B. At Pakistan's request, to discuss tensions with India
C. To issue sanctions against India
D. To approve a peacekeeping mission in Kashmir

273. Which of the following feature films was chosen as India's official entry for the 2026 Academy Awards (Oscars) in the Best International Feature category?
A. *'Pushpa 2'* B. *'The Bengal Files'*
C. *'Homebound'* D. *'Superboys of Malegaon'*

274. Who won a historic second term as Prime Minister of Australia in May 2025?
A. Peter Dutton B. Scott Morrison
C. Anthony Albanese D. Kevin Rudd

275. Where did DRDO conduct the maiden flight trial of the Stratospheric Airship Platform on May 3, 2025?
A. Agra, Uttar Pradesh
B. Pokhran, Rajasthan
C. Sheopur, Madhya Pradesh
D. Bengaluru, Karnataka

276. Where is the 7th edition of the Khelo India Youth Games held in 2025?
A. Maharashtra B. Haryana
C. Bihar D. Karnataka

277. Which country became the first to release genome-edited rice varieties?
A. China B. Japan
C. India D. USA

278. What was the total value of India's exports in FY 2024–25?
A. $778.1 billion B. $820.93 billion
C. $824.9 billion D. $387.5 billion

279. Who among the following has been honoured with the prestigious Dadasaheb Phalke Award for 2023?
A. Koduri Srisaila Sri Rajamouli
B. Mohanlal
C. Sanjay Leela Bhansali
D. Dr. Vishnuvardhan

280. Who among the following won the 2025 Nobel Peace Prize?
A. Donald Trump B. Johann Wadephul
C. Maria Corina Machado D. Lawrence Wong

281. Who was awarded the 2025 Nobel Peace Prize for her courage in leading the democratic movement in Venezuela?
A. Maria Ressa
B. Narges Mohammadi
C. María Corina Machado
D. Malala Yousafzai

282. Which author received the 2025 Nobel Prize in Literature for his visionary Central European prose?
A. Jon Fosse B. László Krasznahorkai
C. Haruki Murakami D. Salman Rushdie

283. In December 2025, who became the youngest and first Asian to receive the Global Humanitarian Award for Animal Welfare?
A. Ratan Tata B. Anant Ambani
C. Sundar Pichai D. Dr. Jane Goodall

284. The 2025 Nobel Prize in Chemistry was awarded to Susumu Kitagawa, Richard Robson, and Omar M. Yaghi for the development of:
A. Quantum dots
B. Metal-organic frameworks (MOFs)
C. Click chemistry
D. Lithium-ion batteries

285. Who won the 2025 Nobel Prize in Physics for discoveries concerning "macroscopic quantum mechanical tunnelling"?
A. John M. Martinis, Michel H. Devoret, and John Clarke
B. Alain Aspect and John Clauser
C. Pierre Agostini and Ferenc Krausz
D. Moungi Bawendi and Louis Brus

286. The 2025 Nobel Prize in Physiology or Medicine was awarded for discoveries concerning:
A. mRNA vaccines
B. MicroRNA
C. Peripheral immune tolerance
D. Hepatitis C virus

287. Who were the laureates of the 2025 Sveriges Riksbank Prize in Economic Sciences?
A. Claudia Goldin and Joshua Angrist
B. Joel Mokyr, Philippe Aghion, and Peter Howitt
C. Ben Bernanke and Douglas Diamond
D. Abhijit Banerjee and Esther Duflo

288. Which Indian personality was honored with the 2025 United Nations "Champions of the Earth" award in the Inspiration and Action category?
A. Supriya Sahu B. Afroz Shah
C. Narendra Modi D. Sunita Narain

289. Which team won the 2025 ICC Women's Cricket ODI World Cup held in India?
A. Australia B. England
C. India D. South Africa

290. Who was named the 'Player of the Tournament' in the 2025 Women's Cricket World Cup?
A. Smriti Mandhana B. Deepti Sharma
C. Laura Wolvaardt D. Shafali Verma

291. In December 2025, which Indian cricketer became the first Indian woman to cross 4,000 runs in T20 Internationals?
A. Harmanpreet Kaur
B. Shafali Verma
C. Smriti Mandhana
D. Jemimah Rodrigues

292. Which state won its maiden Syed Mushtaq Ali Trophy (SMAT) title in December 2025?
A. Maharashtra B. Haryana
C. Jharkhand D. Tamil Nadu

293. Who won the 2025 F1 World Drivers' Championship, securing his fifth consecutive title?
A. Lewis Hamilton B. Max Verstappen
C. Lando Norris D. Charles Leclerc

294. Who is the current President of the World Bank?
A. Ajay Banga
B. David Malpass
C. Kristalina Georgieva
D. Janet Yellen

295. Who was appointed as the new Comptroller and Auditor General (CAG) of India in November 2025?
A. Girish Chandra Murmu
B. K. Sanjay Murthy
C. T.V. Somanathan
D. Shaktikanta Das

296. Who took oath as the 51st Chief Justice of India (CJI) in late 2024/early 2025, continuing his term through late 2025?
A. Justice D.Y. Chandrachud
B. Justice Sanjiv Khanna
C. Justice B.R. Gavai
D. Justice Surya Kant

297. Who was appointed as the MD & CEO of Airtel India in May 2025?
A. Gopal Vittal B. Shashwat Sharma
C. Sunil Mittal D. Anant Goenka

298. Which Indian Justice was elected as the Chairperson of the WIPO (World Intellectual Property Organization) Advisory Board of Judges?
A. Justice Prathiba M. Singh
B. Justice Indu Malhotra
C. Justice Hima Kohli
D. Justice Nagarathna

299. Who was appointed as the 29th Controller General of Accounts (CGA) of India?
A. S.S. Dubey B. T.C.A. Kalyani
C. Bharati Das D. Sonali Singh

300. Which Indian star athlete was conferred with the rank of 'Honorary Lieutenant Colonel' in the Territorial Army in October 2025?
A. MS Dhoni B. Neeraj Chopra
C. Abhinav Bindra D. Sachin Tendulkar

301. In December 2025, ISRO used its LVM3 rocket to launch which next-generation commercial satellite for direct-to-smartphone connectivity?
A. GSAT-24 B. BlueBird Block-2
C. OneWeb Gen-2 D. Starlink-V3

302. What is the name of India's first space docking mission successfully demonstrated in early 2025, which paved the way for the late 2025 space station modules?
A. Gaganyaan-2 B. SpaDeX
C. Chandrayaan-4 D. AstroDock

303. Which company launched the largest commercial communication satellite ever deployed in LEO in December 2025?
A. SpaceX B. Blue Origin
C. AST SpaceMobile D. OneWeb

304. In November 2025, which country became the first to appoint an "AI Cabinet Minister"?
A. Estonia B. Albania
C. UAE D. South Korea

305. What is the theme of the Union Budget 2025, which significantly impacted the economy in late 2025?
A. Atmanirbhar Bharat
B. Sabka Vikas
C. Viksit Bharat 2047
D. Digital India

306. Which Indian city hosted the 11th India International Science Festival (IISF) in December 2025?
A. Bengaluru B. Pune
C. Panchkula D. Lucknow

307. The "Waqf (Amendment) Act 2025" was renamed as:
A. Waqf Reforms Act
B. UMEED Act
C. Unified Trust Act
D. Waqf Transparency Act

308. In May 2025, India carried out "Operation Sindoor." What was its primary objective?
A. Evacuation of Indians from Sudan
B. Precision strikes on terror camps
C. Humanitarian aid to Gaza
D. Earthquake relief in Nepal

309. Which state government passed the first-of-its-kind "Gig Workers Welfare Act" in December 2025?
A. Rajasthan B. Karnataka
C. Jharkhand D. Telangana

310. Who was sworn in as the 11th Chief Minister of Haryana in October 2024?
A. Bhupinder Singh Hooda
B. Nayab Singh Saini
C. Anil Vij
D. Dushyant Chautala

311. In October 2024, which global leader won the US Presidential Election (returning to power for a second term)?
A. Joe Biden B. Kamala Harris
C. Donald Trump D. Ron DeSantis

312. Which country hosted the G20 Summit in late 2025 (Nov/Dec)?
A. Brazil B. South Africa
C. India D. USA

313. In November 2025, which nation's leader, Viktor Orban, mediated a high-stakes peace dialogue between Russia and the US?
A. Poland B. Hungary
C. Austria D. Turkiye

314. The COP30 Climate Summit (November 2025) was hosted by which country?
A. UAE B. Azerbaijan
C. Brazil D. Australia

315. Which veteran Indian actor, known as the "He-Man of Bollywood," passed away in November 2025?
A. Kadar Khan B. Dharmendra
C. Mahendra Nath D. Rishi Kapoor

316. What is the rank of India in the "Global Innovation Index 2025" released in late 2025?
A. 35th B. 38th
C. 40th D. 42nd

317. Which day is observed as "World Soil Day"?
A. December 1 B. December 5
C. December 10 D. October 16

318. The "Statue of Unity" celebrated its anniversary in October. It is located in which district of Gujarat?
A. Narmada B. Ahmedabad
C. Surat D. Vadodara

319. Which international organization celebrated its 80th anniversary on October 24, 2025?
A. World Bank
B. IMF
C. United Nations (UN)
D. WHO

320. According to reports in late 2025, India has become the world's ___ largest economy.
A. 3rd B. 4th
C. 5th D. 6th

321. The "Securities Markets Code Bill 2025" aims to consolidate laws governing which body?
A. RBI B. SEBI
C. IRDAI D. PFRDA

322. Which bank launched the "Avni" savings account specifically for women?
A. HDFC Bank B. ICICI Bank
C. Bandhan Bank D. SBI

323. Which organization launched 'Tax Pragya', an AI-powered tax research platform, in December 2025?
A. KPMG B. Deloitte India
C. EY D. PWC

324. "Cyclone Dana," which hit the eastern coast of India in late 2025, was named by which country?
A. Oman B. Qatar
C. Saudi Arabia D. UAE

325. Which national park in India was in the news for the successful birth of five Cheetah cubs in November 2025?
A. Jim Corbett B. Kuno National Park
C. Kaziranga D. Gir National Park

326. Which state government launched the 'Mukhya Mantri Maiya Samman Yojana' in late 2025?
A. West Bengal B. Odisha
C. Jharkhand D. Bihar

327. The "Global Biodiversity Framework" meeting (COP16) took place in late 2024/2025 in which city?
A. Cali, Colombia B. Montreal, Canada
C. Kunming, China D. Paris, France

328. Which Indian city was recognized as a 'City of Literature' by UNESCO in late 2025?
A. Gwalior B. Kozhikode
C. Jaipur D. Varanasi

329. The 2025 Commonwealth Heads of Government Meeting (CHOGM) was hosted by:
A. Rwanda B. Samoa
C. India D. UK

330. The "Vibrant Gujarat Global Summit" 2025 was themed:
A. Gateway to the Future
B. Atmanirbhar Gujarat
C. Investing in Tomorrow
D. Green Growth

ANSWERS

1	2	3	4	5	6	7	8	9	10
C	B	C	B	B	B	C	B	B	D
11	**12**	**13**	**14**	**15**	**16**	**17**	**18**	**19**	**20**
C	C	B	A	A	C	A	B	A	C
21	**22**	**23**	**24**	**25**	**26**	**27**	**28**	**29**	**30**
B	C	C	D	A	A	B	A	B	B
31	**32**	**33**	**34**	**35**	**36**	**37**	**38**	**39**	**40**
A	C	B	A	C	D	C	A	C	C
41	**42**	**43**	**44**	**45**	**46**	**47**	**48**	**49**	**50**
D	A	A	C	B	B	B	D	C	B
51	**52**	**53**	**54**	**55**	**56**	**57**	**58**	**59**	**60**
B	A	B	B	C	C	A	B	C	B
61	**62**	**63**	**64**	**65**	**66**	**67**	**68**	**69**	**70**
B	C	D	D	C	B	B	D	B	C
71	**72**	**73**	**74**	**75**	**76**	**77**	**78**	**79**	**80**
B	A	C	B	C	C	B	A	C	B
81	**82**	**83**	**84**	**85**	**86**	**87**	**88**	**89**	**90**
B	B	A	A	D	C	A	C	C	D
91	**92**	**93**	**94**	**95**	**96**	**97**	**98**	**99**	**100**
D	B	A	B	D	B	D	B	C	D
101	**102**	**103**	**104**	**105**	**106**	**107**	**108**	**109**	**110**
C	C	C	B	D	C	B	B	C	C

111	112	113	114	115	116	117	118	119	120
C	C	C	B	C	C	B	B	D	B
121	**122**	**123**	**124**	**125**	**126**	**127**	**128**	**129**	**130**
C	B	B	D	B	B	C	C	C	C
131	**132**	**133**	**134**	**135**	**136**	**137**	**138**	**139**	**140**
C	C	C	C	B	D	A	C	C	B
141	**142**	**143**	**144**	**145**	**146**	**147**	**148**	**149**	**150**
C	C	C	B	C	C	C	C	B	B
151	**152**	**153**	**154**	**155**	**156**	**157**	**158**	**159**	**160**
C	B	B	B	C	D	C	B	C	B
161	**162**	**163**	**164**	**165**	**166**	**167**	**168**	**169**	**170**
C	C	C	C	C	C	B	C	B	B
171	**172**	**173**	**174**	**175**	**176**	**177**	**178**	**179**	**180**
C	C	C	B	B	C	B	C	C	C
181	**182**	**183**	**184**	**185**	**186**	**187**	**188**	**189**	**190**
C	D	C	C	C	B	B	C	C	D
191	**192**	**193**	**194**	**195**	**196**	**197**	**198**	**199**	**200**
D	C	C	B	B	C	C	C	D	C
201	**202**	**203**	**204**	**205**	**206**	**207**	**208**	**209**	**210**
B	B	C	C	C	C	C	B	C	C
211	**212**	**213**	**214**	**215**	**216**	**217**	**218**	**219**	**220**
B	B	B	C	A	B	C	C	B	A
221	**222**	**223**	**224**	**225**	**226**	**227**	**228**	**229**	**230**
A	C	C	C	C	C	C	C	B	C
231	**232**	**233**	**234**	**235**	**236**	**237**	**238**	**239**	**240**
C	C	C	B	C	C	D	D	B	C
241	**242**	**243**	**244**	**245**	**246**	**247**	**248**	**249**	**250**
C	C	C	C	C	D	C	C	D	A
251	**252**	**253**	**254**	**255**	**256**	**257**	**258**	**259**	**260**
C	A	C	C	B	A	D	C	C	C
261	**262**	**263**	**264**	**265**	**266**	**267**	**268**	**269**	**270**
C	C	D	C	C	C	C	B	C	C
271	**272**	**273**	**274**	**275**	**276**	**277**	**278**	**279**	**280**
C	B	C	C	C	C	C	C	B	C
281	**282**	**283**	**284**	**285**	**286**	**287**	**288**	**289**	**290**
C	B	B	B	A	C	B	A	C	B
291	**292**	**293**	**294**	**295**	**296**	**297**	**298**	**299**	**300**
C	C	C	A	B	B	B	A	B	B
301	**302**	**303**	**304**	**305**	**306**	**307**	**308**	**309**	**310**
B	B	C	B	B	C	B	B	C	B
311	**312**	**313**	**314**	**315**	**316**	**317**	**318**	**319**	**320**
C	B	B	C	B	B	B	A	C	B
321	**322**	**323**	**324**	**325**	**326**	**327**	**328**	**329**	**330**
B	C	B	B	B	C	A	B	B	A

●●●